W9-CFI-385

The Chicago
of Fiction

A Resource Guide

James A. Kaser

The Scarecrow Press, Inc.
Lanham, Maryland • Toronto • Plymouth, UK
2011

SCARECROW PRESS, INC.

Published in the United States of America
by Scarecrow Press, Inc.
A wholly owned subsidary of
The Rowman & Littlefield Publishing Group, Inc.
4501 Forbes Boulevard, Suite 200, Lanham, Maryland 20706
www.scarecrowpress.com

Estover Road
Plymouth PL6 7PY
United Kingdom

British Library Cataloguing in Publication Information Available

Library of Congress Cataloging-in-Publication Data

Kaser, James A., 1960-
  The Chicago of fiction : a resource guide / James A. Kaser.
    p. cm.
  Includes bibliographical references and index.
  ISBN 978-0-8108-7724-5 (cloth : alk. paper)
  1. Chicago (Ill.)—In literature—Bio-bibliography. 2. American fiction—Illinois—
Chicago—Bio-bibliography. 3. American fiction—20th century—Bio-bibliography. 4.
American fiction—19th century—Bio-bibliography 5. Authors, American—20th century—
Biography—Dictionaries. 6. Authors, American—19th century—Biography—
Dictionaries. I. Title.
  Z1278.C5K37 2011
  [PS374.C44]
  016.813009'35877311—dc22
  [B]   2010032540

♾™ The paper used in this publication meets the minimum requirements of
American National Standard for Information Sciences—Permanence of
Paper for Printed Library Materials, ANSI/NISO Z39.48-1992.
Manufactured in the United States of America.

To Michael for his support during the writing of this book and, as always, to my family.

Contents

Preface

Prior to the 1980s, catalogers rarely gave subject designations for works of fiction. Increasing researcher interest did not lead to the issuance of official cataloging guidelines by the American Library Association until 2000. So, although very complete databases of bibliographic information are available to scholars, these tools are of little use in locating works of fiction set in Chicago published before the 1970s. This work guides scholars to novels and short story collections with Chicago settings and was created by consulting libraries with collections of Chicago fiction, as well as online and published bibliographies that offered a subject approach to fiction.

Acknowledgments

Research for this work was funded in part by grants from the Professional Staff Congress of the City University of New York. Further support was obtained from the College of Staten Island/CUNY in the form of reassignment leave used for extended periods of research.

I am also grateful for the encouragement and assistance I received from a number of people. The enthusiasm and advice of my department chair, Prof. Wilma Jones, Chief Librarian, College of Staten Island, kept me focused and productive over four years of research and writing. In addition, she proofread manuscript pages, as did my friends Ted Cornwell and Sally Milner, to whom I am grateful for helping me see all to which I was blinded by authorial propinquity. For aiding me with bibliographical and biographical research, I thank the research assistants who worked with me at various times, most prominently Antonio Golán and Jeffrey Coogan. Finally, I thank the staff of the Manuscripts and Rare Books Department of the Richard J. Daley Library at the University of Chicago at Illinois, the Interlibrary Loan Office at the College of Staten Island, and the staff of the Library of Congress for aiding me in accessing information and many of the books annotated in this volume.

Introduction

This book includes works of fiction set in Chicago; specifically, novels and collections of short stories for juveniles and adults (dramatic works are not included). Only short story collections whose works are wholly or mostly set in Chicago are included. Annotations are provided for works dating from 1852 to 1980; bibliographic information for works dating from 1981 to 2008 is included in an appendix. While attempting to be as inclusive as possible, some works have been excluded. Such books might have only a few pages, or even a chapter, or more, set in Chicago, but few references to the city. On the other hand, works that are mostly or wholly set in the city, but have little overt Chicago content, are included. Furthermore, works that have as little as a chapter set in Chicago were sometimes included if the use of the city was significant. In these works, Chicago usually has a strong symbolic role throughout the book. For instance, through the majority of a book a man might live in a small town in the Midwest, but dream of becoming a successful artist, businessman, or writer in Chicago, the cultural and financial capital of the region. Although, as a reader, I was fascinated by what the novels revealed about changing understandings of Chicago and what the city symbolizes, my role in this book is merely to identify the materials that future researchers will use to analyze the novels and their interrelationships.

Several lists of Chicago fiction predated this work and although the supplemental material and extent of the annotations in the current work distinguish it from all other efforts, I take this opportunity to acknowledge these other works and identify distinctions that make the present work unique. Several literary histories have been written: Kenny J. Williams, *Prairie Voices: A Literary History of Chicago from the Prairie to 1893*, Nashville, Tenn.: Townsend, 1980; Clarence A. Andrews, *Chicago in Story: A Literary History*, Iowa City, Iowa: Midwest Heritage, 1982; Carl S. Smith, *Chicago and the American Literary Imagination*, Chicago: Chicago University, 1984. However, these books use evaluative criteria that exclude the bulk of Chicago fiction. One of the most complete overviews of the Chicago novel is Lennox Bouton Grey's *Chicago and The Great American Novel: A Critical Approach to the American Epic* (dissertation, University of Chicago, 1935), but the work only includes titles through 1935. The annotated bibliography written by Kenny Jackson as his dissertation was completed in 1950 and is limited to works published from 1900 to 1948 (*A Critical Bibliography of Novels Written about Chicago: 1900-1948*, De Paul University, 1950).

An effort by Clarence Andrews in *The Great Lakes Review* was puzzling upon closer examination. Andrews published his bibliography in two articles, *Literature of Place: Chicago: Part I* [5, no. 1 (1978), 67-92] and *Literature of Place: Chicago: Part II* [5, no. 2 (1979), 36-67]. Although he quite honestly admitted that he could only strive for completeness and welcomed information on additional titles, his list has only 875 entries, even though he included plays, poetry anthologies, and films. Furthermore, in addition to leaving out a large number of titles included in the volume in hand, the articles included titles that, when read by this author, proved to have no Chicago content. (He does retract one title as an addenda to his second article, but there are many others that were mistakenly included). Perhaps, Andrews drew upon secondary sources that were misleading. He also wrote one or two sentence annotations without indicating if they were drawn from his own reading.

A more recent effort, the Web site *Illinois, Illinois!: An Annotated Bibliography of Fiction* by Thomas L. Kilpatrick and Patsy-Rose Hoshiko, includes a large number of works set in Chicago. However, the work in hand is more comprehensive, including books published through 2007 and totaling over 2,240 entries. *Illinois, Illinois!* ends with works published through 1997 and has only 2,233 entries, even though it covers the entire state of Illinois, not just Chicago. Furthermore, the annotations in the work in hand are based on reading the works annotated, rather than relying on review sources.

Because of the obscurity of so many authors of pre-1980s books, biographical information is provided in a section that also serves as an author index. The reader who wishes to browse this section will discover the wide range of people who were motivated to write about Chicago, including journalists, politicians, society women, and freelance writers of genre fiction. As in any group of people randomly gathered, there are also some remarkable lives worthy of further exploration.

The decision not to annotate works published after 1980 responds to book cataloging and marketing phenomena. As library catalogs became electronic and publishers began providing information electronically, more information about fiction, including geographic designators, became easily available and was incorporated into catalog records. More recently as catalogs have become Web based, images of book jackets, jacket text, and review excerpts can be found in catalogs. This cataloging trend is one factor that led to the creation of an official geographic descriptor for fiction works in cataloging rules published in 2000. In addition, Web-based book marketers, such as Amazon, provide researchers the opportunity of keyword searching an extensive bibliographic database and increasingly provide the option of full-text searching for phrases or words (such as Chicago). In such an environment, researchers have many ways of identifying recent Chicago fiction and reviewing abstracts of book contents.

Appendix A provides a bibliography of works published from 1981 to 2008; Appendix B presents citations for the pre-1980s fiction in a chronological arrangement so that themes common to a specific era can be easily discovered. By 2007 the amount of information incorporated directly into bibliographic databases was so pronounced that it seemed unnecessary to make an already lengthy work almost one hundred pages longer by including citations for these works. Researchers can easily discover the titles on their own.

Annotated Bibliography, 1852–1980

1. Abson, Ben J. *On to the White House*. Chicago: True Truth, 1931. 188pp.

   This satirical novel treats Chicago as the locus of vices that have swept over and threaten to destroy the country. Most of the characters are members of the Teufel family. Herr Louie Teufel, is a corrupt lawyer who has made a large fortune from his improprieties. He specializes in divorces from his offices in the Blackstone Building in the heart of the Loop. At the beginning of the novel, his daughter Lesbia is just sixteen years old; however she has already begun frequenting the Hotel Villa Roma on Lake Shore Drive, an opulent structure owned by Signor Alberto Capra, a bootlegger who controls a number of other vice operations that spread, web-like, across the country. At the Villa Roma, wealthy young men gamble and Lesbia is by their sides until the early morning hours, distressing her married sisters, Belinda and Miranda. The scanty plot concerns Lesbia's marriages and divorces until she tires of such formal alliances and merely becomes the belle of the Villa Roma. Along the way the author finds opportunities to decry the power of Sicilian gangsters, the use of cosmetics by women, Prohibition, divorce, football, the collapse of the American educational system, smoking by women, sexual immorality, and gambling. In an afterward, Abson attacks a long list of actual senators and projects a 1940 presidential race that includes Alberto Capra, whose mistress, Lesbia, stands a good chance of becoming the mistress of the White House.

2. Adams, Frederick Upham. *President John Smith: The Story of a Peaceful Revolution*. Chicago: Charles H. Kerr, 1897. 290pp.

   Published by The Majority Rule Club (an organization formed to advocate government reform proposals), this futurist novel envisions a country led by John Smith, who had grown up during the period that Chicago was becoming a major city, transformed by industrial growth, the commodities exchange, and the skyscrapers on its skyline. However, the city is not used as a realistic setting but as a symbol for the abuses of capitalism and for the birth of trade unionism. In this work, the Chicago World's Fair is blamed for the nation-wide economic depression of 1893-1894 and much analysis is given to support this claim. In the reformed political and economic system created by Smith and his Cabinet, Chicago takes an important lead in transforming municipal government that is followed by other cities. Throughout, however, Chicago has a minimal presence in the novel as a physical place.

3. Ade, George. *Artie. A Story of the Streets and Town*. Chicago: Herbert S. Stone, 1896. 192pp.

   In this novel that depicts male friendship between office workers, Artie Blanchard's activities and observations are documented through first-person narrator and office mate, Miller (he is never given a first name). Artie, a native Chicagoan, speaks in dialect and uses slang for almost every other word. He has interactions with people up and down the social ladder. Miller has a genteel background, came to Chicago from the East, and moves in upper-middle-class society. Although a great friend of Artie, he also serves as a foil for many of his opinions. Throughout the novel, Artie's courtship of Mamie Carroll, who works in a printing office, plays a major role. Artie is very sociable and he describes at great length to Miller: poker parties, dances, church charitable events, conversations in cigar store hangouts, shopping on State Street, a wedding (for which he is best man), walks along the lake, a trip to the country, and nights at the theater. He has very strong opinions about "appropriate" male behavior and critiques a wide range of individuals, often to their faces, including the effete "Percival, the perfect lady;" Bancroft Walters, a young man living off his father's income; and Jim Landon, a powerful, but corrupt politician. A number of lengthy descriptions capture some of the material culture of the period, including the furnishings of Carroll's parlor, the bicycle craze and its special clothing, and women's fashion, particularly bloomers (that receive unfavorable reviews). The physical descriptions, and Artie's stories about social interactions, combine to evoke middle-class, turn-of-the-century Chicago.

4. Ade, George. *Bang! Bang!* New York: Sears, 1928. 147pp.
    These stories for boys were originally published in the 1890s as part of the Nickel Library. The heroes include Eddie Parks, the Newsboy Detective; Cyril Smith, the Handsome Messenger Boy; Clarence Allen, the Hypnotic Boy Journalist; and Rollo Johnson, the Boy Inventor. Aged from nine to thirteen, each protagonist is fairly similar—they succeed due to cleverness or special skills. Each is contented with his job and gives away the reward he earns to charity or to a family member. If they are helping a beautiful woman, she often turns out to be a lost sister or mother. The young heroes solve bank robberies, the theft of important documents and jewels, kidnappings, and train and streetcar robberies. Two of the stories revolve, in part, around athletic competitions (a bicycle race and a boxing match). The villains are often wealthy men. One of the stories reveals the strong anti-British sentiment of the 1890s and several of the stories include patriotic interludes.

5. Ade, George. *Breaking into Society*. New York: Harper and Brothers, 1904. 208pp.
    Written in fable format, the short works in this volume concern social advancement, variously conceived. Although rarely explicit in their physical setting, Ade wrote the fables while living in Chicago and based his characters on the people moving to the city and attempting to establish themselves in urban society. The fables capture the concerns of this group of strivers.

6. Ade, George. *Chicago Stories*. Illustrated by John T. McCutcheon. Chicago: Henry Regnery, 1963. 278pp.
    This is a republication of *Stories of the Streets and of the Town* (entry 12).

7. Ade, George. *Doc' Horne: A Story of the Streets and Town*. Illustrated by John T. McCutcheon. Chicago: Herbert S. Stone, 1899. 292pp.
    Set in the Alfalfa Hotel, where most guests are long-term residents and all are men, this novel records the social interactions of the men and the stories they tell each other. The biggest story-teller is Doc Horne, whose title is honorific, partly stemming from respect accorded him because of his age and partly from his wide range of life experiences, which involve heroic work in the Civil War, the 1857 Mississippi flood, thwarting counterfeiters, etc., that some of the inmates consider fabulist. When a resident questions one of Doc's stories, a tense period follows as Doc withdraws to his room and contemplates moving. However, the main theme of the book is that in the little community of the hotel the men accept each other as they wish others to see them. When Doc gets sick, all of his acquaintances look after him and he finds it easy to accept the apology of his questioner. Other characters in the book, for whom personal names are rarely assigned, include a

racetrack tout, an actor, a book agent, a bicycle salesman, a dentist, and "a lush." Each of them, except for Doc, is from somewhere outside Chicago—such places as an Ohio farm, a New York village, Indiana, and Kentucky. In one section of general description, the author describes Chicago as suburbs interspersed with farms, with the Loop area, where the hotel is located, the only really urban section and observes that its rapid population growth stems from immigration from all over the country and the world. Through the personal situations and stories of the characters the author addresses attitudes towards courtship and marriage, alcohol use, patent medicine, and what makes for appropriate social discourse. In addition to descriptions of the hotel and its operations, Ade describes Chicago street scenes, a lunch counter, clothing, and a beer garden. The great crisis in the novel stems from the activities of a con man and huckster who gets Doc wrongly accused of being his accomplice. Fortunately, the accusation does not hold up in court. Soon afterwards, Doc unexpectedly inherits money from his sister. He travels to Europe on a long-desired trip and upon his return finds a perfect illustration of the rapid changes occurring in Chicago—the hotel, along with the other buildings on the block, has been torn down to make way for an office tower and all the residents are irrecoverably scattered.

8. Ade, George. *In Babel; Stories of Chicago.* New York: McClure, Phillips, 1903. 357pp.
    These rewritten versions of stories published in the *Chicago Record* are more concerned with evoking settings than Ade's other short stories and fables. Some of the venues presented are: a lunch counter, residence hotels and boarding houses, a courtroom, private residences in the city and the suburbs, a law office, and a private club. Some of the themes presented concern Christmas gift-giving, servant/employer relationships, books as status symbols, masquerade balls in commercial venues, and door-to-door salesmen.

9. Ade, George. *More Fables.* Illustrated by Clyde J. Newman. Chicago: Herbert S. Stone, 1900. 218pp.
    Written in fable format and intended to present themes prevalent in the culture of the period, physical setting is rarely important in these short works, most of which are presumed to be set in Chicago where Ade was living and publishing such work in the *Chicago Record.* The fables capture the speech patterns of the general population and present such elements of popular culture as betting on horse races, married life, political culture, musical culture, club life for men and women, single women looking for husbands, reformers, and settings such as haberdasheries, millinery shops, and hotel dining rooms.

10. Ade, George. *People You Know.* Illustrated by John T. McCutcheon and others. New York: Russell, 1903. 224pp.
    In these twenty-six stories, Ade captures the concerns and speech patterns of Chicago's typical citizens. Among the themes are bar culture, courtship, high culture as an expression of social status, college life, vaudeville, the Arts and Crafts movement, leisure travel, and domestic life.

11. Ade, George. *Pink Marsh: A Story of the Streets and Town.* Chicago: Herbert S. Stone, 1897. 197pp.
    In this novel, that unselfconsciously illustrates race relations in late-nineteenth-century Chicago, the narrator, self-denominated as "the morning customer," is a businessman who becomes fascinated with the freely expressed opinions and stories of African-American William Pinkney Marsh, a shoe shine boy. He starts getting a daily shine although he makes his social superiority

clear to Pink does not tolerate any illusion of friendship. Pink's adventures mostly center on gambling and courting young women. He tries to mimic his customers' eloquence and employ multi-syllable words, but never does so successfully. After his malapropisms get him into trouble with his employer and his lady friends, he gets "the morning customer" to produce grammatically accurate letters, dictated and typewritten by the customer's secretary with space left for Pink's signature. Pink's opinions are usually based on some misapprehension, but he holds forth volubly and with confidence on what he would do with a million dollars, the United States' conflict with Britain over Venezuela, the office of President of the United States (held in this case by William McKinley), the literal truth of the Bible, the efficacy of dreams, and the powers of conjuration. Pink is willing to have his beliefs shaped by his socially superior "morning customer" on matters such as the theory of evolution and the value of education over wealth, but he does not have the self-discipline to follow the advice to save money. After Pink is fired, He becomes a Pullman porter and marries a widow who owns a boarding house and manages his finances giving him only small amounts of money, which he continues to squander on gambling. Some readers will find disturbing the racism, including the internalized racism expressed by Pink; however, the book is useful as a social document particularly as it relates to the social status and material welfare of African-Americans in turn-of-the-century Chicago.

12. Ade, George. *Stories of the Streets and of the Town: From "The Chicago Record" 1893-1900*. Illustrated by John T. McCutcheon. Chicago: Caxton Club, 1941. 274pp.

This book of short sketches, each several pages in length, includes descriptive pieces about places (Green Tree Inn, small shops, The Art Institute), types of employment (sidewalk merchants, coachmen, and Chinese immigrants), and other aspects of Chicago life. However, a number of the sketches are actually short stories, possibly featuring actual characters and conversations that the author overheard. Several settings are popular for these stories: barber shops, taverns, and boarding houses. However, one story is set in a French table d'hôte restaurant that captures the reactions of the diners to this new form of dining in what is normally a meat and potatoes town. There are also stories set in a hobo camp, a restaurant that specializes in "chidluns" (chitterlings), and a lunch counter. In all of these pieces the author fulfills his intention of capturing a wide range of Chicagoans, although the emphasis is on working and lower-middle-class people, their pastimes and social interactions.

13. Adler, Katherine Keith. *The Crystal Icicle*. New York: Harcourt Brace, 1930. 287pp.

Nancy and Harold "Hal" Muir live forty miles from downtown Chicago in a large house with gardens maintained by servants who include a cook, lady's maid (Nancy's former governess), butler, gardener, and a nanny for their little boy, Peter. Harold commutes each day by train to his job as a cartoonist for what appears to be the *Chicago Tribune* from the description of the building and its location. The plot centers on Hal's affair with Mrs. Joan Peal, the wife of a university professor of classics twice her age who lives in a Near North Side Victorian townhouse. Joan works as a commercial artist (which is how she met Hal) and trained as a painter in Paris. Her artistic interests and emotional availability attract Hal (she has an open marriage) and distinguish her from his wife who, embracing her Roman Catholic faith, believes that sexual intercourse should only be for the purpose of procreation. When Hal confesses his desires to Nancy she employs hysterical scenes and threats to hold on to him. By the time the ardor of the affair begins to wane, Nancy is pregnant and Hal settles back into the role of paterfamilias. The descriptions of Chicago focus on the Loop and office life, although there are descriptions of restaurants and observations on the development of Chicago prompted by the neighborhood in which Joan lives. Through the novel's characters, several positions are articulated on the nature of marriage, sexual relations, and gender roles.

14. Adler, Katherine Keith. *The Girl*. New York: Henry Holt, 1917. 251pp.

Although this first-person account of Marian Crosby's life from childhood, around the time of the death of her paternal grandfather, to her first love affair is, according to contemporary reviews, set in Chicago, there is little internal evidence of the fact. The granddaughter of a wealthy and socially prominent man, Marian's family disapproves of her high-spiritedness and dreamy nature which leads her to make up imaginary playmates and adventures. When she continues her childishness beyond the age for governesses (who have been responsible for her since her infancy), she is sent to boarding school. She returns to continue to disappoint her family by choosing to go to college, undertaking charity among poor immigrants, and becoming the assistant editor of a literary journal. Although she initially rejects becoming a debutante, she eventually cedes to her grandmother's wishes, yet she continues to defy social conventions. Her first romantic friendship is with the son of a respected German artist, but in the end she accepts the middle-aged artist's attentions and eventually marries him. Even though concrete details (including street names) are disguised in this work, the book does capture a great deal of social detail, particularly in regard to gender roles and expectations in early-twentieth-century Chicago.

15. Albert, Marvin H. *Party Girl*. Greenwich, Conn.: Gold Medal Books / Fawcett Publications, 1958. 128pp.

This novelization of a movie released by Metro-Goldwin Mayer the same year as the book and with the same title concerns Thomas Farrell, an attorney who represents gangster Rico Angelo in 1930s Chicago. When Farrell becomes smitten with showgirl Vicki Gayle he is inspired to become respectable before proposing marriage. He braves dire repercussions (legal prosecution and a gangland execution) and survives to enjoy the prospect of married life with Vicki. The portrayal of Chicago is filled with all of the stereotypes of earlier gangster novels.

16. Alcock, Gudrun. *Turn the Next Corner*. New York: Lothrop, Lee, and Shepard, 1969. 160pp.

This work for children gives a sense of life on the Near North Side in the 1960s and deals with racial tensions that occasionally erupt in violence. Protagonist John Ritchie Osborne is a twelve-year-old Caucasian who has moved into the city from the suburbs with his mother to live in an apartment building on State Street. His lawyer father is in jail for embezzlement and his mother works as a proofreader. Ritchie's new life is dramatically different from his suburban existence and he comments on his new neighborhood, the nearby business district on Wells Street, and the African-American neighborhood west of Wells. Ritchie thinks a good deal about racial issues since among his diverse classmates he is in the racial minority. He befriends an African-American boy who lives in his building and is courageously recovering, through exercise and operations, from partial paralysis after a bicycle accident. Ritchie's rehearsal of cover stories for why his father does not live with them and, later, when Mr. Osborne is paroled, his explanations for visits by a parole officer demonstrates, and implicitly stresses, the boy's intense desire to conform to social norms. A good deal is made of the implications of social status, as well, when Ritchie makes friends with a boy whose affluent family lives on Lake Shore Drive.

17. Aldis, Dorothy. *All the Year Round*. Boston: Houghton Mifflin Company, Riverside Press, 1938. 245pp.

Chicago in this novel is a place of unhealthy influences and unexpected dangers. Mrs. Myrvin Conover would much prefer to live in the suburban childhood home of her husband Robert, which he recently inherited after the death of his mother. The Conovers and their three children summer there, but Robert will not commute to work from the unnamed suburb. Instead, they live in an elegant apartment in a neighborhood that has become less than respectable, with its corner drugstores and neon bedecked nightclubs. The action of the novel, which takes place over the course of a few days, centers on how Myrvin copes with her awkward, adolescent, rebellious daughter, Susan; her eighteen-year-old daughter Ann's romance with a wealthy young man who has no occupation but his own pleasure; her son Peter's announcement that he is dropping out of Harvard; and her husband's quiet alcoholism. After attending the wedding of her husband's second cousin to a very wealthy young woman, Myrvin decides to open the family's summer house since Susan has made a trip to the Dunes and Robert has left to try to convince Peter to stay enrolled at Harvard. While she is there she learns that Ann has the mumps and may have meningitis (she does not) and then hears that a fire broke out in her apartment building and her husband was badly burned. As it turns out, her husband had not traveled to Cambridge, but was found in the basement of the apartment building, where he had accidentally started the fire with a cigarette. When she reaches Peter to tell him the news he explains that his father's increasingly erratic behavior is the reason he will return to Chicago (not the romance with a young woman that Myrvin had suspected). Although the novel is focused on human interactions, upper-middle-class life is detailed, including household furnishings, clothing, dining, and relations with domestic staff (the Conovers have an African-American cook).

18. Aldis, Dorothy. *The Magic City: John & Jane at the World's Fair*. New York: Minton, Balch and Company, 1933. 95pp.

In this work for children, Dick, Jane, and John, accompanied by their maternal uncle, visit the 1933 World's Fair being held to commemorate the one hundredth anniversary of their city, Chicago. During their visit, they learn about dinosaurs, oil, gasoline, electricity, the solar system, and the explorations of Admiral Byrd. In addition to verbal descriptions of world's fair exhibits and buildings, the book includes illustrations and maps.

19. Aldis, Dorothy. *Their Own Apartment*. New York: G.P. Putnam's Sons, 1935. 240pp.

This novel about upper-class family life is mostly set in the Chicago neighborhood of Lakeview in 1931. Twenty-three-year-old Ann Emmett was raised in San Francisco by parents who came from Portland, Maine. Her fiancé, Clifford McLevaine, is a Chicagoan who differs in every way from members of her family. He is tall and exuberant in manner whereas she and her parents are short and reserved. Her father, a surgeon, is as precise in his personal as in his professional life and her New England mother prides herself on her family heritage and good taste. Ann's new in-laws are all like Clifford. Mrs. McLevaine, who is called "Pussy," bellows out direct comments in her deep voice, while her husband, always called "Father," (the shortest in the family) is retiring and in poor health. Their two sons, Bill and Steve, laugh uproariously at jokes and are given to roughhousing. Pussy finds her daughter Rosemary, an architecture student, to be too serious. Although she is somewhat alarmed at her new family, Ann agrees to move to Chicago thinking she will be living in a six-room apartment in Lincoln Park and taking classes at the Art Institute. However, Pussy installs the couple at Windy Cliff for the summer, the family's house off Sheridan

Road on the lakefront. Ann finds Windy Cliff, a sprawling, cluttered house filled by all the McLe-vaines along with their servants (a chauffeur, cook, laundress, maid, and the mischievous, pre-school son of the unwed maid), an alien world. The experiences Ann has during her first year of marriage include: learning of her father-in-law's alcoholism, discovering that a next door neighbor is her husband's old girlfriend and that the two still have feelings for each other, and getting the news that her father has died in the apartment of his long-time mistress. On top of all this, she dis-covers that she is pregnant. Although her social life includes dinners and parties in the city, her daily life consists of swimming, horseback riding, tennis, and gardening, following the enthu-siasms of the household and not her own interest in art. Near the end of the novel, Ann realizes that she has adapted herself to her new environment and been accepted as part of the family, but still longs to move into her Lincoln Park apartment. Then, she learns that she is pregnant again and must resign herself to a Lakeview house with apple trees in the backyard. Despite, or perhaps because the book was written during the Depression, food, clothing, houses, furnishings, and so-cial events are described in great detail. Dorr Martin is an architect and works on the 1933 World's Fair which opens in the course of the novel and is also described. The rich level of detail makes the book a useful record of upper-middle-class life in the Chicago metropolitan area during the early 1930s. The reader can also learn about cultural attitudes toward women, servants, married life, and sexual relations.

20. Aldis, Dorothy. *Time at Her Heels*. Boston: Houghton Mifflin, 1937. 236pp.

Although contemporary reviews of this novel reveal the work to be set in Chicago, there is no internal evidence of the fact since the novel is tightly focused on the domestic life of Mary Strong, as revealed during the course of a single day. While physical description of the city is lacking, the book presents rich social details as Mary deals with the absent-minded romance languages profes-sor who is her husband, three children, a spinster aunt who lives with them, and a demanding, eld-erly invalid uncle who maintains a separate residence but is always getting into conflicts with the service providers upon whom he depends. While the demands of these family members are a con-stant, on this particular day, Mary must also deal with the funeral of a friend from childhood, the importuning of the young doctor who desires to be her lover, the haughty woman who has commissioned her to design a fountain for her garden, and the serious illness of her laundress. Although Mary is meant to represent a modern, young, middle-class, suburban housewife, her standard of living, particularly as the Depression is just beginning to ease, may surprise the twenty-first century reader. Paid domestic staff, ranging from gardeners, to nurses and nannies is taken for granted in her household and those of her friends and relatives. In addition, although some of the extras for her children are paid for out of her earnings from design projects, nonetheless her offspring have music lessons, dancing lessons, and orthodontia. The novel presents Mary as a woman to be admired for her level-headedness, vigor, people skills, and devotion to homemaking and one of the major themes of the novel is a woman's role in married life and in the community. In the final scene, as her family gathers around a candle-lit cake created for her own birthday, that she had forgotten, the reader is left with the image of Mary enjoying the glow that keeps out the darkness beyond her dining room windows, a light that symbolizes her own effective struggles to keep her family safe and happy.

21. Alger, Horatio. *Adrift in the City; or, Oliver Conrad's Plucky Fight*. Philadelphia: John C. Winston, 1895. 325pp.

Only part of this novel for children is set in Chicago and the setting is not notably different from that of New York City, where most of the work is set. The story tells how Oliver Conrad, who has been disinherited by his stepfather after the supposed death of his mother, recovers the family fortune. He finds that his mother is not really dead, but is being held in an insane asylum by his stepfather and he subsequently rescues her.

22. Alger, Horatio. *Luke Walton; or, the Chicago Newsboy*. Way to Success Series. Philadelphia: Coates, 1889. 346pp.

Alger uses Chicago as a backdrop in this story for children that extols the material rewards to be earned by hard work and honesty. Luke Walton, the exemplary hero, works long hours selling newspapers at the corner of Clark and Randolph Streets to support his mother and seven-year-old brother, Bennie. An evil man, Thomas Butler, cheated them out of a fortune in gold left by Luke's deceased father, Frederick Walton. Although Luke improves the family's lot step by step, his goal is to find Butler and get back the fortune. The respect he earns from his affluent customers translates into the support he needs to successfully accomplish his goal. Although Alger is more concerned with behavior than physical setting, he does mention real addresses and businesses, like restaurants and hotels. Clear distinctions are made between respectable, affluent areas of the city and those like that in which the Waltons are forced to live (on Green Street near Milwaukee Avenue).

23. Alger, Horatio Jr. *The Train Boy*. New York: Carleton, 1883. 298pp.

In this work for young adults, sixteen-year-old Paul Palmer lives in a modest, two-story house on Lake Street with his mother, who works at home as a seamstress, and his younger sister Susan. Paul, who sells reading materials to train passengers on a daily round trip route between Chicago and Milwaukee is the primary financial supporter of the family. When he thwarts a pickpocket, he earns the attention of Grace Dearborn, the criminal's intended victim. Grace lives with her wealthy aunt, Caroline Sheldon, on Ashland Avenue and her recognition of Mrs. Palmer's skill as a seamstress leads to new business from Grace's affluent friends that aids the Palmers. The real break for the family comes, however, as the result of a train wreck. Paul intervenes when a thief is in the process of stealing the billfold of an unconscious man who turns out to be a successful manufacturer. Paul's reward is a job as an office boy at a slightly higher wage than he earned on the train. However, after he proves himself, he leaps ahead, and within a short time has advanced in the firm and more than doubled his income. Alger's settings, in addition to the houses of the Palmers and Sheldons include an artist's studio on State Street, and downtown offices. Enough social details are provided to give some sense of life at different social levels in 1880s Chicago.

24. Alger, Horatio and A. M. Winfield. *Out for Business; or, Robert Frost's Strange Career*. Philadelphia: John Wanamaker, 1900. 287pp.

Running away from an abusive stepfather, young Robert Frost takes a job in a Chicago hotel where he recovers a stolen map showing valuable land grants. Intended to inspire an audience of young readers, the book stresses the importance of persistence and the financial rewards to be won by those who work hard.

25. Algren, Nelson. *The Last Carousel*. New York: Putnam's Sons, 1973. 435pp.

Most of the short stories in this collection are set in 1920s and 1930s Chicago and offer a nostalgic view of the city based on Algren's fictionalized memories of his boyhood and youth. Socioeconomically the people in the stories are at the lower end of the working class, a locus of both status insecurity and racism against Mexicans and African-Americans. Although Algren makes no excuses for his characters, he does emphasize their challenging social context. He tells the stories of a punch-drunk, Jewish heavy-weight, so confused that he has difficulty caring for himself; a prostitute from Texarkana whose only option seems to be trading on her looks before they fade; an underage, Polish gang member accused of murder; and pre-adolescents in reform school learning from each other about the life of crime. While Algren introduces little physical description of the city, his stories present a sociologically detailed depiction of Chicago's underclass. The usual settings are the racecourse, baseball field, bar, whorehouse, and police station and the neighborhoods of Garfield Park, Jackson Park, the Loop, and the West Side.

26. Algren, Nelson. *The Man with the Golden Arm*. Garden City, N.Y.: Doubleday, 1949. 343pp.

At age twenty-nine, Frankie Majcinek is a veteran and recipient of the Good Conduct Medal and Purple Heart. In the West Division Street neighborhood in which he lives, however, he is known for his skill as a gambling-house card dealer. Frankie's life is shaped by obsessions: his wife Zosh's psychotic need to hold onto him, his inability to find absolution from his guilt over causing the automobile accident that crippled her, and his own addiction to morphine. Frankie's only happiness comes from his sexual relationship with Molly Novotny. Frankie's fragile world collapses when he is pursued for the murder of drug-pusher Nifty Louie and, overcome by despair, commits suicide. The novel was adapted as a motion picture starring Frank Sinatra and directed by Otto Preminger (Otto Preminger Films, 1956). In this novel Algren captures Chicago's economically disadvantaged with compassion.

27. Algren, Nelson. *The Neon Wilderness*. Garden City, N.Y.: Doubleday, 1947. 286pp.

Although not all of the short stories in this collection are set in Chicago, those that are document life in the city's slums in the 1940s. The action takes place on the streets and in back alleys, bars, gambling parlors, police stations, boxing clubs, and jail and includes gang violence and drug use. The ethnicity of the characters is predominantly Polish; however there are also Mexicans and Indians. A number of the characters are veterans of the Second World War.

28. Algren, Nelson. *Never Come Morning*. New York: Avon Publications, 1942. 191pp.

This novel's realism won Algren his reputation as a Chicago novelist. Set in the 1930s, in a West Side slum inhabited by Poles, the grim plot focuses on the experiences of Bruno Bicek and Steffi Rostenkowski as their lives become irrevocably shaped by their desires—Bruno for power and conquest and Steffi for money. Bruno, a freight handler and boxer is also a member of his neighborhood gang, the members of which he permits to rape Steffi, who is forced into prostitution as a result. On the night of the rape, Bruno breaks the neck of a Greek whom he considers an interloper in the neighborhood and kills him. This act eventually destroys any hope he has for a future when he is arrested months later just as his boxing skill has made him a championship contender. Algren's physical descriptions of warehouses, barrooms, boxing rings, and gang hangouts underneath El tracks, viscerally convey life in the Chicago slums of the 1930s.

29. Algren, Nelson. *Somebody in Boots*. New York: Vanguard Press, 1935. 326pp.

Against the backdrop of social unrest produced by the Depression, this novel tells the story of Cass McKay, a disenfranchised, illiterate southerner who, at the beginning of the novel, is living with his family in a shack in West Texas, among impoverished Mexican immigrants. Born in 1901, by the time Cass is sixteen his father has been out of work for a year and the family is dependent on Cass's older brother Bryan, who, gassed in the World War has been disillusioned ever since and has become an alcoholic. Cass leaves home twice in his youth, once after seeing his father beat his mother and again when his father kills a man. After living in hobo camps and shuttling among Shreveport, New Orleans, San Antonio, and Fort Worth, he is imprisoned in a harsh El Paso jail. Upon his release he heads north to Chicago. For brief periods he can wear clean clothes and go to sleep with a full stomach on the proceeds of petty crime. He also has his first relationship with Norah Egan, who becomes his accomplice in hold-ups. However, when an undercover policeman appears as Cass is robbing a drugstore, Norah speeds away leaving him stranded. After serving jail time, Cass tries to find Norah, and gets his first job as a barker for a burlesque show, just as the World's Fair is beginning. When he finally meets Norah, she rejects his marriage proposal out of the belief that he is trying to get her alone and revenge himself on her. Shortly after his failed proposal, he loses his job. The Chicago section of the novel describes the despair of brothels, burlesque houses, and tenements and points out the cruel irony of the shining face the city is given during the boosterism of the Fair when so many lived in desperation and the streets around the fairgrounds are filled with the vice inspired by that desperation.

30. Allee, Marjorie Hill. *The Great Tradition*. Boston: Houghton Mifflin, 1937. 205pp.

This novel for girls is set at the University of Chicago and addresses issues of race and gender. Indiana farm girl, Merritt Lane, although committed to the scientific study of biology, was earlier forced to quit college for financial reasons. Her friend Jenny Wilson, saddened by Merritt's plight, invites her to come to Chicago, work as a lab assistant, and live in a shared apartment rent-free in a shared apartment, in exchange for managing the housekeeping. The apartment mates include: a Quaker, a bohemian international student, and a southerner, Charlotte White from Mississippi. Esther, an African-American housekeeper, cooks under Merritt's direction. The novel illustrates how shared living fosters personal growth. Although the girls each exemplify some good quality, Charlotte also has many flaws she must overcome: she is not systematic, is not good at concentrating, and is outspoken about her prejudices. Esther quits because of her and Charlotte objects to the replacement, an African-American, graduate biology student, Delinea Johnson. Charlotte claims Delinea is unprepared for graduate work and giving her a job is just patronizing her. All of the girls and Delinea must come to accept the fact that Delinea is unprepared due to the poor educational opportunities while they develop appreciation for her ambition, personal dignity, and capacity for hard work. The problem of how to help Delinea is discussed by the novel's characters, revealing cultural attitudes towards race. Attitudes toward gender roles are also revealed when the girls are considered ideal biologists since they are good at cleaning lab equipment, can operate heating units similar to ovens, and love plants and animals. Chicago plays only a slight role in the novel (the girls attend public concerts and eat at Chinese restaurants). The backyards, alleys, and parks of the city are only of interest to the girls as environments in which to find biological specimens. The only non-academics in the novel are the immigrant Gustafson family who live in the basement of the girls' apartment building since the father is the janitor. This family is out of place in the city and Merritt arranges for them to work as tenant farmers for her father.

31. Allee, Marjorie Hill. *The House*. Illustrated by Helen Blair. Boston: Houghton Mifflin, Riverside Press, 1944. 181pp.

This continuation of Merritt Lane's story, begun in *The Great Tradition*, is set in 1941 and 1942. Merritt, a budding zoologist, returns from fieldwork in the Caribbean, and joins a mixed gender, cooperative house on Woodlawn Avenue. The house is large and on a block filled with grand houses, but only a few are owner-occupied. Located near the University of Chicago, some have been turned into dormitory housing and others into fraternity houses. The Johnsons, a wealthy elderly brother and sister from a distinguished family, live in the house next to the cooperative. Arthur Johnson worries about people of color moving in next to him and threatens that, should this happen, he will influence the owner to evict the cooperative. When a Chinese woman applies to the cooperative, consideration of her application is deferred, but their lease is cancelled anyway. The cooperative is able to move to a more racially and socioeconomically integrated area. However, new individual and collective challenges emerge as they deal with illness, death, and the outbreak of World War II. Allee explores racial prejudice, socioeconomic disparities, and gender relations (through several romances). Although she is more concerned with social interactions than physical description, in several sections she details socioeconomic change in residential neighborhoods. She also includes information about health care delivery, the treatment of the developmentally disabled, and rental libraries (where several of the characters work).

32. Allen, James and Geneva Allen. *God Bless This Child, A Novel*. Hicksville, N.Y.: Exposition Press, 1975. 180pp.

Set in the impoverished, 1970s African-American community around Chicago's West Madison Street, this novel depicts the economic hardship and police oppression that destroy the lives of residents. The story is told through the brief life of Nicholas Pierce who goes from being an obedient thirteen-year-old in the household of a single mother with four siblings, to a criminal, drug dealer, and heroin addict. He dies of an overdose at the age of twenty-one. The authors' didactic intent to show how ghetto residents have no control over their lives, because of the lack of opportunities, is heavy-handed. However, through dialogue, and descriptions of social networks, businesses, and buildings, they also capture what it may have been like to live in a Chicago African-American ghetto in the 1970s.

33. Allen, Steve. *The Wake*. Garden City, N.Y.: Doubleday, 1972. 177pp.

Through the experiences of the Scanlan family, recounted during the days leading up to the funeral of their mother Bridget, who died in her sleep of cancer at the age of eighty-six, Irish immigrant and lower-class experience in Chicago is captured. Set in 1931, the book also gives some sense of the anxiety and displacement caused by the Depression. Bridget, an immigrant, began married life in the 1860s on Cottage Grove Avenue near Forty-seventh Street, an area that was farmland at the time. She had twelve children, only six of whom survived childbirth, and her husband died when he was forty-five. The Scanlans who gather in the two-bedroom apartment where Bridget lived her final decades with her unmarried daughter Margaret, have mostly left Chicago. Among them are an actress on the vaudeville circuit who has had several children out of wedlock, a jobless, alcoholic World War I veteran, and a journalist and published author who lives in Boston. Although the physical setting is claustrophobically confined to the Scanlan apartment, the book includes mentions of Chicago places, celebrities, food, and social realities, such as the difficulty of finding a job. Details of Bridget's wake and funeral and information concerning tradition in the Chicago Irish community connected with such events could be considered a form of social history.

34. Altrocchi, Julia Cooley. *Wolves Against the Moon*. New York: Macmillan, 1940. 572pp.

While most of this novel is not set near Chicago or even in Illinois, sections deal with the massacre at Fort Dearborn and the Indian treaty signed at "Chicagou." The novel tells the story of Joseph Bailly de Messein, a French-Canadian fur trader, during the time period 1794 to 1835, and imparts a great deal of regional history and information about the fur trade and Indian life.

35. Anderson, Sherwood. *Marching Men*. New York: John Lane, 1917. 314pp.

In his novel about wage laborers in the early twentieth century, Anderson uses Chicago to epitomize the plight of the disenfranchised. His protagonist, Beaut McGregor, abandons his life in Coal Creek, Pennsylvania to pursue Chicago's promise of material well-being. However, he arrives in a city oversupplied with laborers. Although Beaut secures a warehouse job, where his hard work leads to a foreman's position, he also studies at night to become a lawyer. After his admission to the bar, his defense strategy in a criminal trial wins attention that translates into a lucrative practice and he begins to use his new affluence to organize Chicago's laborers. In addition to describing conditions in a variety of work places typical of Chicago in the period, Anderson limns the home life, neighborhoods, pastimes, and emotional and physical health of working-class Chicagoans. He pays particular attention to issues of gender, ethnicity, and the tension between urban and rural culture.

36. Anderson, Sherwood. *Windy McPherson's Son*. New York: John Lane, 1916. 347pp.

Growing up in an impoverished household in Caxton, Iowa, Sam McPherson decides early that affluence will free him from want and bring meaning to his life. He is outraged that his father, Windy, has no ambition and tries to rest on the laurels he supposedly earned in the Civil War. Time after time, however, Windy is proven to be a liar and, eventually, Sam is so angered that he tries to strangle his father on the night of his mother's death. Sam leaves soon afterward for Chicago where he works in the produce market as a buyer. Through clever practice he begins to build his fortune, and starts to make money in earnest after accepting a job with the Rainey Arms Company, a manufacturer of guns. Although his advance in the company stems from his business skills, the firm's owner, Colonel Rainey, also becomes his mentor. Eventually, Sam marries the Colonel's daughter, Sue. Sam believes he can devote himself to Sue and is thrilled by the prospect, but a stillbirth changes their relationship. Afterwards, Sam finds an opportunity for a brilliant consolidation of Rainey Arms with an eastern firm. The Colonel opposes the merger and when Sam successfully pursues it Sue leaves him, taking the Colonel with her. Sam wins a five-million-dollar profit in the deal and lives the life of a wealthy man in Chicago with a vacation house in Wisconsin and a hunting preserve in Texas. However, he cannot find meaning in wealth alone and begins searching for truth again, a search that may lead him back to Sue. Throughout the novel the proper role of sex, women, and family in the life of men is debated. A number of Chicago's commercial neighborhoods are described, including the red-light district, but the novel is more concerned with Sam's inner life than making observations about the city.

37. Andrews, Robert Hardy [Shang Andrews, pseud.]. *Cranky Ann, the Street-Walker: A Story of Chicago in Chunks*. Chicago, 1878. 80pp.

In August 1876, on the day he is celebrating his sixty-fifth birthday and the day after he has announced his retirement from business, wealthy Alanson Baldwin is remorsefully considering his past. All his life he has worked hard, but he rebukes himself for not having done enough good in the world—for his sins of omission. By a coincidence, he finds a former employee, Harry Harper, has become a criminal and decides to use Harper as his entrée to Chicago's underworld in the hope of redeeming one of the fallen. On his first foray he meets a streetwalker named "Cranky Ann." She is the daughter of a wealthy Chicago merchant, but was forced to leave home after a libertine forced himself on her and she became pregnant at fifteen. A fallen woman, she turned to a life of prostitution. Later, by a strange coincidence, Jack Dunning hires Ann to impersonate a wealthy woman and school friend of the deceased Mrs. Baldwin, so that Dunning can be introduced to Baldwin's daughter, Josephine, who he wishes to court. Baldwin's son, Jeremiah, is present at the early meetings and he falls in love with Ann. Dunning invites Josephine to meet his mother, although he hires the madam of a whorehouse to play this role. When Dunning realizes that Josephine is too much of a lady to ever be his, he pays the madam to give Josephine drugged wine, so that he can force himself on her. Ann thwarts his plan and the grateful Baldwins accept her into their family. Baldwin decides he has seen enough of Chicago's underbelly. The trips Baldwin and Harper make provide a guide to vice in the city and include descriptions of the behavior and dress of men and women, as well as a sense of the buildings and streets.

38. Andrews, Robert Hardy [Shang Andrews, pseud.]. *Irish Mollie, Or a Gambler's Fate, a True Story of a Famous Chicago Tragedy*. Chicago: Garden City Books, 1882. 98pp.
    See, Andrews, *Queen of the Demi-Monde*, (entry 41).

39. Andrews, (Charles) Robert Douglas (Hardy). *Legend of a Lady: The Story of Rita Martin*. New York: Coward-McCann, 1949. 342pp.

Set inside the world of advertising at a time when sponsoring a radio show was the premier method of promoting a company, roughly the first half of this novel is set in Chicago; however the work contains almost no description of the city. When Rita Martin returns to the United States after divorcing her journalist husband while he was on assignment in Rome, she travels to Chicago as a place of opportunity for an ambitious young woman with some college education who needs to support herself and her six-year-old boy. Taking a studio apartment in a large old house that has been sub-divided; she places her son in a military school and begins a relentless work schedule that leads to rapid promotions when she finds ways to appeal to the psychology of women in advertising products. She also makes certain to align herself with the most creative partner of the advertising firm of Franklin-Hosmer-Denby, Carter Franklin. When Franklin's wife, ill from cancer for years, poisons herself, Rita assists him in opening a New York branch of the firm and eventually marries him. Rita shows no remorse for developing a plotline in the soap opera for which she is responsible in which a physically infirm character kills himself in an act of self sacrifice in the interests of his lover. Chicago in this novel is an urban center preoccupied with merchandising. Even the artists in the novel, no matter how bohemian their personal lives, work in the service of commerce, writing and creating artwork for advertising firms. The portrayal of Rita and other women in the novel illustrates attitudes toward women and gender roles current in the 1940, and Rita's treatment of her son presents one view of the working-woman's abandonment of maternal responsibilities.

40. Andrews, (Charles) Robert Douglas (Hardy). *One Girl Found: A Sequel to "Three Girls Lost."* New York: Grosset and Dunlap, 1930. 246pp.

Marcia Talent, Oregon beauty queen, moved to Chicago to start a modeling school. However, her goal is pushed even farther out of reach when a swindler manages to get her savings. She manages to get by on the gifts she receives from the men who date her. However, her life reaches a crisis when she unwittingly gets involved with bootleggers and when two men decide that she would be the ideal wife. In addition to physical descriptions of the city, Andrews illustrates the financial insecurity and limited options of women in the society of the time period.

41. Andrews, Robert Hardy. *The Queen of the Demi Monde: Gay Life in Chicago.* Chicago: Garden City Books, 1880. 98pp.

This book was also published by Andrews under the title *Irish Mollie; or A Gambler's Fate, the True Story of a Famous Chicago Tragedy,* and under the author name, Shang Andrews, as *A Gay Girl of the Town.* A novel of scandal, the book is a fictional account of a murder case of 1866 in which a gambler is murdered by a young woman he had corrupted. One fateful night in 1855 Irish Mollie (Mary Grossgrove), a waitress at the Matteson House hotel at the corner of Madison and Dearborn, is the center of attention for George Trussell, a Chicago gambler; James Parker, a newly arrived businessman; and a group of New York City gamblers. Trussell flirts with her and when he is called away, the New York City men abduct Mollie. Trussell and Parker give chase and rescue Mollie. She is overcome from the excitement and Trussell assures Parker he will see her home. He takes her to his hotel room and takes advantage of her, promising that they will marry. When Mollie realizes she has been ruined, she acknowledges that she has no choice but to live as Trussell's common law wife and eventually has his son, after which he forces her into prostitution. For years, James Parker watches the two and tries to get Trussell to act honorably. He follows Trussell on the gambling circuit and gathers proof that Trussell is cheating on Mollie. Once she confirms what Parker has told her, Mollie shoots Trussell to death and is tried and convicted, but the court is sensitive to the injustice done to her and she gets a one-year sentence. Upon her release Parker offers marriage, but she rejects him, claiming she has been too far corrupted. Parker then devises a plot involving a disguise and assumed name to get Mollie to become his wife. The novel includes little physical description of Chicago, but touches on a range of issues related to the role of women in society. Although presented as a sympathetic account of a wronged woman, the tone and illustrations make it clear that the story is presented to titillate.

42. Andrews, (Charles) Robert Douglas (Hardy). *The Stolen Husband, a Chicago Novel.* New York: Grosset and Dunlap, 1931. 238pp.

In this romance novel, female protagonist Nancy has bad experiences with men that convince her they are all evil. After only a year of marriage, her husband, Terry Wayne, admits to a workplace affair. Then, Nancy discovers that the kindly, aging Mrs. Dotson, who lives next door, has also been betrayed. Mr. Dotson has declared his love for his much younger secretary. Not only does he want a divorce, but he wants half of Mrs. Dotson's inherited money. Nancy and Mrs. Dotson flee; change their names, establish a household together; and enlist an old boyfriend of Nancy's, Eddie Mayhew, to help them transfer Mrs. Dotson's money into an account protected from Mr. Dotson. However, like the other men in their lives, Eddie betrays them and disappears with eighty thousand dollars. Then, while Nancy is at work, some police detectives frighten Mrs. Dotson. Thinking that she is going to be returned to Mr. Dotson, she flees, once again changing her name. With no resources of her own, Nancy eventually seeks assistance from her employer,

Hobart Drury, one of the city's most prominent lawyers. He uses his connections with the police to find Mrs. Dotson and Eddie Mayhew. To Nancy's surprise, Mr. and Mrs. Dotson reconcile. Hobart also secretly investigates Terry Wayne after discovering he works for a company which sells dubious stock. Satisfied as to Terry's reprobate character and his lack of any continuing affection for Nancy, Hobart is free to pursue Nancy, who has been won over by his demonstrations of trustworthiness. The novel presents convincing details of daily life in 1930s Chicago, including the material culture of domestic furnishings and apparel. Typical restaurant menus are also presented. Chicago is presented as a place where one may win wealth and power and enjoy sophisticated products and pleasures. However, the city is also a dangerous place filled with gangsters and grifters (both male and female).

43. Andrews, (Charles) Robert Douglas (Hardy). *Three Girls Lost*. New York: Grosset and Dunlap, 1930. 284pp.

Economic necessity, lack of opportunities in their hometowns, and dreams for the future all motivate three girls from the rural areas to relocate to Chicago, a place of opportunity. Traveling independently, Edna Best from South Dakota, Norene McCann from Nebraska, and Marcia Talent from Oregon meet en route and decide to band together. Although they aid each other, they make little progress and each of them get involved in unforeseen difficulties. Edna is subjected to the vengeance of an angry wife. Marcia gets caught up in a murder, and Norene struggles to help her beau, who is falsely accused of murder. Andrews gives some sense of the motivations that bring people to Chicago, reveals some of the struggles faced by newcomers, and touches on issues faced by the single woman of the 1920s.

44. Andrews, (Charles) Robert Douglas (Hardy). *Windfall: A Novel about Ten Million Dollars*. New York: John Day, 1931. 280pp.

Aware that he is about to die, John Gould suddenly decides to leave half of his twenty million dollar fortune to ten people chosen randomly from a Chicago city directory. This novel describes the meetings between Gould's lawyer Mark David (or his representative) and the recipients, as well as the mandatory meetings two years later in which each millionaire reports back to David. The lawyer had feared that the checks would destroy lives. Although that did not happen, still the money did not bring much good. In aggregate the stories constitute an extended reflection on money and they detail the very real impact of straight-forward financial considerations on peoples' lives. The author clearly attempted to present a cross-section of Chicagoans, including an upper-middle-class factory owner, a prostitute, a child, a poet, a housewife, a shoe manufacturer, a convict, a blinded former prizefighter, a secretary, an Irish man, a Jewish woman, and an immigrant. In addition to speculation on the meaning of wealth, gender issues are explored. Little of the content is specific to Chicago, although specific addresses and neighborhoods are mentioned.

45. Andrews, Robert Hardy [Shang Andrews, pseud.]. *Wicked Nell, a Gay Girl of the Town*. Chicago: Comet, 1878. 73pp.

Even as a ten-year-old, Nellie, the daughter of the widowed Mrs. O'Brien, spent her time on the streets and befriended prostitutes. When Nellie disappears for a week as a thirteen-year-old, the widow gets the assistance of the police and learns the truth. When she is discovered, Nell shows no remorse for being a "lost girl," curses her mother, and ignores her when she collapses. Arrested and taken to the Armory, Nell is bailed out by a real estate merchant who later pays her fines and establishes her in a rooming house operated by Mrs. Dodge and used as a place of assignation. Mrs. Dodge gets Nell to aid her in procuring a young girl for a respected businessman named Mr. Brown, something Dodge does all the time for men, by tricking innocent young girls into her house, then drugging them. When they awaken defiled, they are unable to return home and forced into prostitution. Nell pretends to become Dodge's accomplice, but tricks her with the help of "Red-haired Jennie," who poses as an innocent girl, but actually drugs Dodge and Brown and takes the money Brown paid Dodge. Brown, enamored by Nell's beauty and boldness, proposes to her and offers to send her away to a ladies' seminary. Moved by Brown's willingness to overlook her past and his respectful treatment, Nell agrees. She returns to Chicago three years later, a poised young woman, and marries Brown to become a respectable lady. Although this book contains no physical description of the city, besides specifying the streets where prostitution and vice are openly pursued, the author claims to be describing actual social conditions in the city.

46. Andrus, Louise. *Though Time Be Fleet*. Boston: Lothrop, Lee and Shepard, 1937. 328pp.

   In the early 1900s, actress Marcia Ellsworth is just about to get her big break, a part in a New York City production, when she is forced to return to her hometown outside of Chicago (the imaginary Pottawattamie) to care for her ailing, elderly parents. After their deaths, she becomes a journalist on a Chicago newspaper in 1916 and makes a niche for herself by covering women's issues, including women on the home-front during World War I (bond rallies, Red Cross training) and woman's suffragists. She later gets important assignments to interview Madame Breshkovskaya (now known as the grandmother of the Russian revolution) and cover the Republican National Convention of 1920. After the armistice, she resigns her job to marry a beau from her acting days, Eliphalet ("Trude") Jeremiah Truesdale, a returning veteran who is immediately successful in the oil prospecting business. She establishes a household on Sheridan Road near the lake, has a son, and becomes a clubwoman. Their affluence is short-lived. In the aftermath of the 1929 stock market crash, Trude loses his fortune and Marcia's inheritance and suffers a nervous breakdown (a relapse of shell shock). Marcia works as a public relations and membership officer for a large women's organization, the Columbian Club. Her success earns her a job offer from a Madison Avenue firm, but she decides to stick by Trude, just as she does when she rejects the advances of a famous author, who she had known before his fame and whom she loves more than her husband. Through her efforts she recovers some lost assets and engineers Trude's recovery by moving him to Pottawattamie. By the end of the novel, Trude has started a corruption-fighting tabloid and Marcia is proud of him and feels justified in her decisions. The novel provides rich documentation of social life in Chicago and changing roles for women from 1900 to 1935.

47. Anonymous. *The Beginning; A Romance of Chicago As It Might Be. With Introductory Letters by Hon. Hempstead Washburne, Dr. H. W. Thomas, Judge Tuthill, Judge Tuley, Judge Kohlsaat, and Professor Swing*. Chicago: Charles H. Kerr, 1893. 126pp.

   This utopian novel is primarily a discourse on the advantages of socialism presented in the form of a novel through which the author hopes to convert the reader in the same way the main character, Frank Wentworth, is converted. Wentworth, a shipping clerk for a Chicago wholesale house, has been given an ultimatum by his fiancée, Edith Gray. He has one year to reform and give up drinking, gambling, and the ill-behaved associates who encourage him in these vices. When he attends one of Dr. Plaintruth's inspirational sermons, he is immediately converted and begins dreaming of a Chicago perfected by socialism. Although the novel contains little description of the city, the work presents elements of late-nineteenth-century working-class life and a perspective on some of the challenges faced by the city.

48. Anonymous. *The Broken Pitcher; or, The Ways of Providence*. Chicago: Tomlinson, 1866. 282pp.

By the same author who penned *Luke Darrell, Chicago Newsboy*, the setting for this morality tale for children is assumed to be Chicago. The Halsted family, the widowed Caspar and his children, thirteen-year-old Frank and eight-year-old Hattie, are forced to leave their farm and move to the city after Caspar falls behind on the mortgage he took to get cash to buy the quantities of alcohol he has been drinking since his wife's death. Initially, the family has respectable quarters in an unappealing neighborhood named Harmony Court. However, Caspar only works enough to get money to support his drinking and they must move to cheaper and cheaper lodgings. Frank's modest income from factory work is their only support and in his desperation, Caspar has begun selling the children's clothing for alcohol. When the exhausted Hattie drops a milk pitcher she is carrying home, passerby Mr. Selby comforts her and buys her a new pitcher and a refill. Over time he makes certain that Frank and Harriet have clothes to wear to Sunday school, where they meet polite young children, like Selby's niece, Harriet Levers. All goes well as Frank and Hattie faithfully attend the school. Then, crisis strikes when Frank gets a fever and Hattie, rushing through the streets for help, is run down by a carriage, and suffers a broken arm. Fortunately, Dr. Thornhill is the carriage driver. He mends Hattie's arm, cures Frank, and begins to take an interest in the Halsteds. After Thornhill meets Selby who vouches for the children, he and Selby decide to watch the family to see if they are worthy of aid. Eventually, all of them, including the reformed Caspar, prove themselves and Thornhill reveals he holds the Halsted farm mortgage. He allows them to return to the country and work together to pay the farm debt. The novel captures the attitudes of the era of the middle-class toward the urban poor and their understanding that poverty signals a moral failing. Living conditions for the poor and the barrier presented by not owning middle-class status signifiers, in this case appropriate clothing, is also revealingly presented. No specific physical description is included although there is general description of the mud, dwellings, and roving bands of children in Harmony Court.

49. Anonymous. *The Great Cronin Mystery, or, the Irish Patriot's Fate*. Chicago: Laird and Lee, 1889. 199pp.

Published contemporaneously with investigations of a Chicago murder case, this work is written in journalistic style as the firsthand account of an anonymous private detective. The detective believes a case on which he was engaged the night of the murder may be connected to the crime, although by the end of the novel he concludes that he was wrong and the murder case goes unsolved. Although there are few descriptions of the city, many actual addresses in Chicago and in the suburb of Lakeview, where much of the action transpires, are included. The victim of the crime is Dr. P. H. Cronin, a physician who had been involved in the Irish Nationalist movement and the book touches on the Irish community in Chicago and aspects of the political movement, including the presence of British spies.

50. Anonymous. *Grey Towers, A Campus Novel*. Chicago: Covici-McGee, 1923. 287pp.

In this novel about academic life, Joan Burroughs escapes from teaching high school English in Michigan to return to Chicago and her alma mater (named Grey Towers, but clearly the University of Chicago) to work as an instructor of freshman English. Joan is quickly disenchanted when she realizes that bureaucratic practices have been instituted to the detriment of students. When Joan begins a reform crusade, her colleagues turn against her, and she eventually resigns, although the romance that has been developing throughout the story softens the blow. The novel describes the social life of young faculty members, much of it dependent on wealthy patrons of culture and the arts; however, most of the focus is on describing campus settings to expose the evils of modern academic administration (grading curves, reading only every third student essay, puerile research topics, and not getting to know anything about the personal circumstances of the students). The novel includes no significant physical descriptions of Chicago.

51. Anonymous. *Luke Darrell, the Chicago Newsboy*. Chicago: Tomlinson Brothers, 1865. 377pp.

In this work for children, nine-year-old Luke Darrell knows nothing about his parents and lives with the widowed Rachel Hilder who had adopted him, working on her farm. When Hilder's eighteen-year-old nephew, Dennis Bamsford, arrives, he tries to displace Luke, and eventually gives Hilder the ultimatum that either the nine-year-old must go, or he, a useful man will leave. Rachel pleads Luke's case, but Dennis will not listen. Although Luke is frightened to go out on his own, he does not want to be a burden to Hilder. So, he convinces her that he has come up with a plan to go to Chicago and seek his fortune and she reluctantly consents. Although Luke experiences hardship, he maintains the Christian morality Rachel taught him, never swearing, drinking, or wasting his money. He falls in with a group of newsboys, and through the influence of Philip Burgess, nicknamed "Red-Top," he is made one of them and begins earning his living selling newspapers. Unfortunately for him, he looks like a bad boy nicknamed "Droppy" who is in prison for theft. Several times he is accosted and punished for Droppy's crimes before a police officer clears up the case of mistaken identity. As a hard-working newsboy Luke becomes acquainted with several men who aid him. One, Alpheus Bridgewater, a printer, is a Sunday school teacher and Luke begins attending his classes. Bradford introduces Luke to Mr. Miles, an elderly, retired schoolteacher who has pledged his time to teaching newsboys. Bridgewater helps Luke open a bank account and relays information about Hilder to him, since he has family near the farm. Several boys of Luke's acquaintance volunteer to fight in the Civil War and Bridgewater dies a hero in the conflict. By the end of the novel, Dennis is dead after a long, painful illness and Luke has returned to pay off the mortgage on the farm and help Rachel once again with the farm work. Hilder eventually reveals that Luke's parents had been strangers visiting the area when they both died and he is given the option of seeking out his relatives, people of some affluence. He chooses, however, to remain loyal to Rachel and work on the farm. The novel's perspective of Chicago is from the 1860s streets, as experienced by homeless people and those who have made personal commitments to aiding them. Unlike later reform novels, no criticism of endemic social conditions is presented. Each individual must take responsibility for his fate and, through hard work and clean living, establish material comfort.

52. Anonymous. *Mabel Ross, the Sewing-Girl*. Illustrated by J. Hyde. Chicago: Tomlinson Brothers, 1866. 432pp.

Written by the same author who wrote *Luke Darrell*, this reform novel presents conditions in the garment industry with the intent of reforming social wrongs. The Dickensian tale focuses on the girls and women who labored sewing twelve hours or more per day, six days a week earning barely enough to support themselves, even though they were often responsible for whole families of siblings. The eponymous Mabel helps support three sisters (three-year-old Lilly, eleven-year-old Minnie, and fourteen-year-old Hilda) after the death of their mother less than a year after their father died, leaving no money, due to an unscrupulous business partner. As a sewing girl, Mabel witnesses many forms of mistreatment, both emotional and physical, including death, from exhaustion and illness. The sewing work is carried out on machines in their modest dwellings and in department stores, as a part of large sewing teams. Near the end of the novel a concealed will is recovered that accords the Ross girls half of a relative's estate; however the wealth comes too late to reverse the mortal illness of one of the sisters. The novel records many details of life in Chicago in the 1860s, including domestic arrangements, the threat of freezing to death in cold weather in unheated rooms, the irony of the sewers having difficulties clothing themselves, labor activism, and neighborhoods on Clark Street and Polk Street.

53. Anonymous. *The Walder Family: A Story for Families and Sabbath Schools, Written in Chicago*. Chicago: Griggs, 1864. 211pp.
    This work for children is assumed to have Chicago content, but no additional information is available.

54. Archer, Jeffrey. *Kane & Abel*. New York: Simon and Schuster, 1980. 540pp.
    This saga traces the lives of two successful businessmen from their births in 1906 to their deaths in 1967. One, Abel Rosnovski, is born in a field in Poland and saved by a passing hunter who comes upon the newborn still attached by umbilical cord to his dead mother. The other, William Kane, is born to a wealthy Boston banker. Abel's horrific struggles in his youth include detention by Germans and then Russians in concentration camps. He eventually arrives in New York City and works his way up to a position as waiter at the Plaza Hotel and comes to the attention of a Texas hotelier who hires him as assistant manager of the Chicago property in his hotel chain. Kane experiences struggles as well (the death of his father, the remarriage of his mother to a con man, and his mother's death during a miscarriage), but his inherited wealth, social prominence, and exceptional intelligence buoy him. The two men meet after the 1929 stock market crash when Abel appears before Kane to beg for time to save the hotel chain he now owns. Kane earns Abel's lifelong enmity for refusing. The Chicago content of the book is fairly shallow, although the city is clearly presented as a place of greater opportunity for an immigrant than the more settled cities in the East and Abel is known as the "Chicago Baron" even when his chain includes hotels around the world.

55. Ardizzone, Tony. *In the Name of the Father*. Garden City, N.Y.: Doubleday, 1978. 208pp.
    In this coming of age novel, Tonto Schwartz matures from his first day of parochial school in the 1950s, to his decision to become a writer when he is in his twenties. Schwartz lives in a working-class, immigrant neighborhood on Chicago's North Side, near the intersection of Fullerton and Southport Avenues. Tonto's name evinces the dislocation that shapes his experience and increases his self-awareness as he matures and enters adulthood. The product of a mixed marriage (a Catholic mother and Jewish father), Tonto's father died of an illness when he was an infant and his mother works as a waitress and struggles as a single parent. In the conservative society of the 1950s his name, his parentage, and his household all contribute to a marginal social status that inspire him to question religious and social convention. He begins college and his first serious relationship is with a suburban WASP. However, she is engaged to a man of her social class who is an officer in Vietnam. Then, one of Tonto's close school friends is killed in the war. Unable to embrace the social values that made such a war possible, Tonto stops going to his college classes and, when his money runs out, gets a factory job where he refuses promotions in order to work on the line and read philosophy while spending as little attention as possible on his meaningless tasks. He stands out in the factory where his youth and intelligence is distrusted and his appearance is scrutinized for signs that he is part of the despised counter culture. His inattention leads to an acci-

dent in which he loses two fingers and is jolted into an act of self-determination...he decides to become a writer. The novel describes social contexts in Chicago in the period 1950 though the 1960s (working-class home life, parochial school, public higher education, and work culture). Little physical description of the city is included, although Wrigley Field ball games and the 1968 Democratic Convention (during which Tonto scuffles with policemen) are depicted.

56. Armstrong, Dwight Leroy. *Byrd Flam in Town, Being a Collection of that Rising Young Author's Letters, Written at Chicago, and Published in The Trumpet, A Paper of General Circulation, at True's Mills, Indiana—Being Furthermore Shrewdly Construed as a Gentle Roast of Certain Business, Social, Political, Religious and Military Flams of a Great City.* Shadows Library, vol. 1, no. 1. Chicago: John Bearhope, 1894. 139pp.

The "letters" in this work were originally published in the *Chicago Herald* and use the device of a rube, J. Byrd Flam of True's Mills, Indiana, sending letters to his hometown newspaper, to satirize aspects of Chicago. Although the expected confidence men, prostitutes, and gamblers, appear, Flam also experiences an opium den and has several occasions to comment on the bicycle craze.

57. Armstrong, Dwight Leroy. *Dan Gunn; The Man From Mauston; A Countryman Who Did Up the Town.* Chicago: Rand, McNally, 1898. 235pp.

In the form of a romance, Armstrong presents another view of Chicago through the eyes of a naïf, pointing out as he did in the letters of *Byrd Flam in Town* the corruption of late nineteenth-century Chicago. The naïf, Dan Gunn, travels from his hometown of Mauston, Iowa to rescue his fellow townswoman, Alice Morrison, who has been lured to the city by a traveling photographer. In addition to the criminals he encounters, Gunn witnesses the poverty of Chicago's underclass. After helping the police capture the photographer, who, it turns out is also a counterfeiter, Dan marries Alice and returns with her to Mauston with the dream of living out the rest of their lives far away from the corrupt city.

58. Aschmann, Helen Tann. *Connie Bell, M.D.* New York: Dodd, Mead, 1963. 301pp.

Aschmann drew upon historical accounts and the testimony of an elderly female physician in writing her young adult novel about the early days of female medical students in Chicago (circa 1869-1871). Connie Bell's experiences of illness and death within her family and community were typical of her era, but her response—deciding to become a physician—was extraordinary. Bell was aided by her physician grandfather, but opposed by her parents. After her father's death and her mother's tubercular infection, she becomes even more determined and eventually Connie is one of the first students of a medical college operated by Dr. Mary Thompson, who arrives from Boston to open a hospital for women and children. Aschmann's account dramatizes the impediments, including physical violence, that women medical students faced, as well as presenting the challenges male physicians confronted introducing general anesthesia and germ theory. Near the end of the novel, Connie helps evacuate Dr. Thompson's hospital during the Chicago fire. Perhaps echoing the issues in the time period in which she wrote, Aschmann raises issues of the equality of women in society in general.

59. Ashenhurst, John M. *The World's Fair Murders.* Boston: Houghton Mifflin, 1933. 256pp.

While reporter Al Bennett is in the audience of a program at Chicago's 1933 World's Fair, he witnesses the murder of a foreign scientist in mid-speech. Bennett thinks that he is certain to be the first to cover the story. However, before he can solve the mystery and file his story, two more murders are committed. This rather formulaic murder mystery is mostly set in the world's fair grounds and makes shallow use of the rest of the city as a setting.

60. Athens, Christopher. *The Big Squeeze*. Chicago: Chicago Paperback House, 1962. 190pp.

Brod Rossett, a disc jockey who moved from Denver to look for a job in Chicago, quickly finds one at WCHI, a radio station with offices in the Merchandise Mart. To get the job, Rossett agrees to give program director Sammy Sparks fifteen percent of his salary. To prevent hard feelings, Sparks offers Rossett a date with his own secretary, Corlette, that turns out to include dinner, a performance of Rachmaninoff at Orchestra Hall and a visit to Corlette's apartment that ends in the bedroom. Although Rossett gets a high salary and "payola" on the side, a long line of characters, including shady union operatives, line up for their cut. The descriptions of the many women he beds, the steaks, scotches, and brandies he drinks, the beat lingo he uses, and the downtown restaurants and buildings he frequents evoke an early 1960 swingers' image of the city. In the end, after hospitalization for injuries received in a vengeful beating, Rossett leaves Chicago for a job in Springfield.

61. Atkinson, Eleanor. *Hearts Undaunted: A Romance of Four Frontiers*. New York: Harper, 1917. 354pp.

This fictionalized biography tells the story of Eleanor Lytle Kinzie, whose husband was the first permanent white settler of Chicago. Most of the book relates the details of Eleanor's life before she married Kinzie. An Indian captive among the Senecas from the age of five until she was a young woman, she was eventually returned to her family. However, she did not then find unalloyed happiness; she was forced to marry Daniel McKillip, instead of John Kinzie, whom she loved, and she was only united with Kinzie after McKillip's death. Approximately the last fifty pages of the book are set in what would become Chicago, and most of them have to do with the Fort Dearborn massacre.

62. Babcock, Bernie. *The Daughter of a Republican*. Chicago: New Voice Press, 1900. 115pp.

In this short temperance novel, Jean Thorn's charitable work brings her into contact with the Crowley family, whose poverty is caused by the drunkard, Damon Crowley. The impassioned Jean uses the influence and wealth of her father, the prominent Judge Thorn in her campaign against alcohol. Judge Thorn is non-committal at first, following the Republican Party line. However, when Republican government officials ignore the laws that are passed banning the sale of liquor in army canteens and exchanges, he begins actively supporting his daughter's campaign. The novel has little description specific to Chicago, but does capture some of the political climate in the city between 1898 and 1900.

63. Babcock, Bernie. *With Claw and Fang; A Fact Story in a Chicago Setting*. Indianapolis: Clean Politics, 1911. 112pp.

In this temperance novel, Babcock uses Russian immigrants to illustrate the evils of alcohol and the dangers it poses to society. Babcock's character, Ulig Golzosch, a heavy drinker and one of the Haymarket rioters, dies during the riot, but not before he offends against the Church during this action against the state by spitting on a crucifix. His son Nikola narrowly finds redemption just before his death by renouncing alcohol. Babcock identifies Chicago as "the Sodom of America."

64. Bailey, Bernadine. *José*. Boston: Houghton Mifflin, 1969. 141pp.

In this novel for children, twelve-year-old José Garcia lives with his family in Chicago. Eight months after they immigrate to Chicago from Puerto Rico, Mr. Garcia, who does not speak English well, is laid off from the small furniture factory where he works. As a result, everyone in the family gets part-time jobs, including José who helps with yard work. Other small crises follow (José is arrested at the site of a riot, although he is released without charge since he had not really been involved). Despite the Garcias' difficulties, the book emphasizes the importance of assimilation (learning English, voting, respecting and not fearing the police, and participating in national holidays), while at the same time being proud of one's origins. José is finally accepted by his classmates when he wins a swimming contest, demonstrating a skill he had learned on his native island.

65. Bailey, Bernadine. *Puckered Moccasins; a Tale of Old Fort Dearborn*. Chicago: Whitman, 1937. 293pp.

This novel for children presents elements of the history of the Northwest Territory through the character of Dave Rogers, a fifteen-year-old boy dispatched to Fort Dearborn with an important letter during the War of 1812. The fort and life there is described in some detail as well as the story of the massacre. A number of historical characters and their actions are dramatized in the book.

66. Baird, Edwin. *The City of Purple Dreams*. Illustrated by Craig M. Wilson. Chicago: Browne, 1913. 411pp.

Twenty-four-year-old Daniel Randolph Fitzhugh is living the life of a vagabond in Chicago until chance encounters with two very different women inspire love and ambition. Kathleen Otis, niece of the wealthy and powerful Symmington Otis, intervenes with the police to keep him out of jail when he is confronted by an undercover policeman and the next day, Fitzhugh saves Esther Strom from being trampled to death in a demonstration that is to culminate in a speech by Emma Goldman. Strom, the widow of a "nihilist" killed by Czarist forces in Russia, lives in a South Side basement. She wants Fitzhugh to aid the communist movement with his skilled oratory. Instead, he decides he must acquire the wealth and power of a Symington Otis so that he can marry Kathleen. Over many years, Fitzhugh builds a fortune through speculation, becoming the "King of Wheat." He acquires all the trappings of a society figure—the clothes, the house, and a "social valet," a well-connected young man, who introduces him into the right circles. Along the way he crushes Symington Otis and gloats in his death. However, he still does not win Kathleen's hand. Then he undertakes numerous public projects to lay the groundwork for running for mayor. When he loses the race, he gets new insight on the meaning of his life and decides to use his entire fortune to create shelters for the homeless across the country. Only then does Kathleen agree to marry him.

67. Baker, Elizabeth Gillette. *Fire in the Wind*. Boston: Houghton Mifflin, 1961. 244pp.

In this work for children about the Chicago fire, eleven-year-old Jeff Bellinger is the son of Richard Bellinger, a Civil War veteran who is a detective with the Chicago police department. The Bellingers are acquainted with Gurdon Hubbard, one of the most important businessmen in the city, and they live in Lincoln Park. In school, Jeff befriends Newman Higginbotham, a less fortunate boy whose father was killed in the Battle of Chickamauga. Jeff helps Newman get a job as a stable boy, but when a famous horse disappears at the same time as Newman, everyone assumes the boy is the culprit. Jeff goes undercover to investigate and experiences some of the hardships and lack of respect that working boys suffer on a daily basis. He clears his friend and helps the police capture the real culprit. In the dramatic conclusion of the novel, the Chicago fire breaks out and the Bellingers save their house when they act on Jeff's idea of using cider from their basement to keep their roof wet after they have run out of water. The book ends on an optimistic note with the assertion that the city will rebuild.

68. Baker, Frederick Sherman. *Bradford Masters*. New York: Dutton, 1949. 254pp.

Most of this book is set near Greenberg, Wisconsin and in Milwaukee. However the main character, James Bradford Masters, lives in Chicago for extended periods of time. Masters is a disaffected twenty-seven-year-old man who married a cultivated young woman (the daughter of an English professor) and traveled to Paris and other European capitals with her before trying to settle down into the life of suburban respectability that she desired. He found her life stifling, and divorced her, returning to the rural house his entrepreneur grandfather built in 1867. There, he supports himself by trapping fur-bearing animals and selling off family heirlooms (first editions of American renaissance writers, Audubon prints, and antiques). His life becomes complicated when he agrees to help his father in a failing family publishing business in Chicago and he has an affair with Jean Marsh, a woman who is separated from her husband. The novel establishes the Chicago locale by referencing the lakefront, Belmont Harbor, a German restaurant named Schermer's on Wells Street, and Edgewater Beach Hotel. Chicago, in this novel, epitomizes the larger world of twentieth-century responsibilities that Masters attempts to avoid by retreating to life in rural Wisconsin.

69. Baker, Frederick Sherman. *Hidden Fire*. Boston: Little, Brown, 1955. 308pp.

In this history of an affair between Max Ferguson and Martha Brown, sex serves as an anodyne to the disappointments of middle age and, in the end, prompts life changes. Max attended the Chicago Art Institute in his youth and when his sweetheart Nancy married him they both thought he was on the threshold of a career as a significant sculptor. An unplanned birth, financial necessity, and World War II intervened. Now, Max works as a partner in an industrial engineering firm creating charts and diagrams to present information in ways that are compelling for managers and stockholders and he earns a salary just adequate to support his family in suburban comfort in Winnetka. He does not get much satisfaction from his job and has no time for making art. Martha has a materially comfortable life with her husband Gene, an advertising executive, but no children and little emotional support from Gene. Although Max never really falls in love with Martha, he also does not know how to break off the affair with her and never stops her from planning that they will divorce their respective spouses. By the end of the novel, Max has resigned himself to performing poorly at work, realizing that he will be able to get rid of Martha if he loses his job, since she would never choose to live in reduced circumstances. When he finally confesses to Nancy, she forgives him, and the two become more passionate toward each other. In the aftermath, Max finishes some sculptures and begins considering jobs outside the city in communities without the competitiveness for social status typical of his Chicago life. Although there is little physical description of Chicago in this novel, the life of affluent suburban commuters is captured in some detail, especially through descriptions of dress and social conversation over endless cocktails.

70. Baker, North and William Bolton. *Dead to the World*. Garden City, N.Y.: Crime Club / Doubleday, Doran, 1944. 246pp.

This murder mystery, set in World War II Chicago, uses details about interiors, clothing, and objects to delay the action and increase suspense and in doing so creates a vivid record for the cultural historian. The protagonist, Danny Michaels is a medical student working as an intern. His life in a dormitory room that he shares with a football player is presented, and his workday is outlined. To further his training, he visits the city morgue and the mystery centers on what happens when he recognizes one of the corpses as the father of a woman he dated years before. The affluent man was made to look as though he died the death of a derelict (by consuming grain alcohol). The mystery deepens when the police learn that the man was already declared dead three years earlier via charred remains recovered from a fiery automobile crash. Michaels interacts with thickwitted policemen that fit mystery stereotypes. He also deals with wealthy men and women, visiting their dwellings that include private houses and apartments on the Gold Coast. Other settings are the elegant apartment of a Chicago gangster and opulent nightclubs.

71. Ball, Jane Mary Eklund. *The Only Gift*. Boston: Houghton Mifflin, Riverside Press, 1949. 278pp.

This novel, concerned with domestic life, tells the story of an affluent North Shore family, the Lemmings of Lemming Iron and Steel. The story is related mostly through the interior monologue of the mother of the family, Gertrude, as she watches each of her five children, who range in age from ten-years-old to mid-twenties, leave home. At the beginning of the novel the family is under the strict control of father, Jason, who, despite his wealth, still works long hours and expects each member of his family to do likewise. Although no extreme acts of rebellion occur, by the end of the novel several of the children have found ways to evade their father's wishes and Gertrude has begun to question Jason's mandate that a woman's sole purpose in life is to establish a family and create a suitable home life. The novel presents issues of gender roles and social expectations for vocational choice. In addition, upper-class domestic life is richly detailed, including relationships with servants, material culture, and social activities. The novel spans one year and the novel makes clear how markedly the course of Gertrude's life is shaped by holiday celebrations and social events associated with each season. Because of the novel's domestic focus, there is little physical description of Chicago. Social historians may be interested in the lingering impact of World War II on the lives of some of the characters.

72. Ballinger, Bill Sanborn. *The Body Beautiful*. New York: Harper and Brothers, 1949. 244pp.

Barr Breed, the principal in a Chicago private investigation firm, would have devoted himself to finding the murderer of Coffee Stearns, the beautiful showgirl he was dating, even if he had not been hired to investigate by a mysterious, anonymous client offering a high fee. The murder was discovered onstage, with Breed in the audience, when Stearns fell from her trapeze swing with a knife in her back. His investigation is mostly conducted in his typical haunts in and around the Loop and the Near North Side, including bars, residence hotels, and theaters featuring productions that highlight beautiful women barely concealing their genitals. In addition to bank accounts and correspondence linking Stearns to California, another important clue to solving her murder is the fact that she injected paraffin into her breasts to make them look youthful. Although the novel relies on stereotypical characters and devices, the author's descriptions of clothing, food, businesses, and locales convey a sense of 1940s Chicago and the plot and dialogue touch on issues of gender roles and sexual conventions.

73. Ballinger, Bill Sanborn. *The Body in the Bed*. New York: Harper and Brothers, 1948. 242pp.

When Chicago businessman Paul Wendell Gibbs gets out of the shower at the apartment of his girlfriend, Caroline MacCormack, he finds her strangled to death on the bed. Frightened that he will be accused of the crime, he quickly leaves and telephones private detective Barr Breed. The married Gibbs wants Breed to find the murderer, but also conceal the connection between MacCormack and himself, since his wife has been trying to find grounds for a divorce. Shortly afterwards, Gibbs is shot to death, but Breed continues the case because he had been beaten up in the process of the investigation and wants revenge. Breed spends a good deal of time questioning strippers and visiting strip clubs, since Caroline MacCormack was a professional escort. When the widowed Mrs. Gibbs is found shot to death in Breed's apartment after he has had sex with her, Breed becomes the police's prime suspect in her death and those of Paul Gibbs and Caroline MacCormack, driving him into hiding and heightening the stakes for him to find the real killer. The novel is filled with detailed descriptions of material culture, including clothing, the furnishings of nightclubs and apartments, and food and restaurants. At the center of the plot is a million dollars' worth of jewels that had been stolen near the end of World War II from a chateau in France by a Chicago criminal. The plot is complicated by the double-crosses and cover-ups for the robbery that lead to the murders.

74. Ballinger, Bill Sanborn. *Portrait in Smoke*. New York: Harper and Brothers, 1950. 213pp.

While telling the story of Krassy Almauniski's career of deception that takes her from poverty near Chicago's stockyards to the French Riviera, the author provides rich descriptions of workplaces, housing, and neighborhoods in 1940s and 1950s Chicago. The story is told through the voice of Dan April, who becomes increasingly infatuated with Krassy even though the two only met once, in 1940, and April would never have thought of her again had he not found a file on her in the collection agency he purchased in 1950. The folder documents the impressive amount of debt Krassy ran up as a seventeen-year-old, soon after winning a beauty contest. Even though the debts were cancelled, when April sees Krassy's picture he begins an absorbing investigation in the hope of initiating a romance with her. In addition to describing collection agency techniques as he applies them to his search, April also describes the secretarial schools, model and international advertising agencies, boarding houses, and apartment buildings with which Krassy was associated over the previous decade. With beauty as her only asset to free herself from degrading poverty, she takes a series of aliases and finds increasingly wealthy men to manipulate until she marries a multi-millionaire who becomes a burden. A sixty-year-old when Krassy marries him in her mid-twenties, he shows little sign of expiring once he reaches his seventies and neither does his libido. Her final accomplishment is to murder him in a foolproof manner. Throughout the novel, the descriptions of Chicago are evocative and the plot raises issues of gender and socio-economic inequality.

75. Balmer, Edwin. *Dangerous Business*. New York: Burt, 1927. 279pp.

In this novel about business culture in the 1920s, Jay Rountree [*sic*] leaves Harvard in his sophomore year to protect the reputation of Lida Haige, the girl he had been dating. Jay had taken Lida to a party and left her in the company of a friend of a friend when he had to depart the event. The acquaintance took advantage of Lida and Jay felt compelled to marry her. Jay's father, who has been antipathetic toward him since Jay's difficult birth damaged his mother's health in a way that led to her death a few months afterwards, sees the marriage as both a necessity and another reason to despise his son. However, he gives Jay a job in the vaguely described manufacturing company he owns. Jay's work experience is complicated not only by his relationship with his father, but by his daily contact with Ellen Powell, a senior private secretary to whom Jay has been attracted for several years. Despite the temptation presented by Ellen and his father's expectation that he will be a failure, Jay is successful in business. The novel describes how sociability and the ability to build friendships and establish loyalties lead to his success. In an era in which women are usually restricted to the domestic realm, Ellen plays a surprisingly important role in office operations, even though, as a woman, she has no real status or power. Characters in the novel make frequent trips to New York City on The Century express train and spend summers outside the city on the lake and winters in the Bahamas or North Carolina. Physical descriptions of Chicago are limited to scenes in expensive houses, apartments, and clubs. The novel gives a very thorough description of aspects of the Chicago business world in the boom years of the 1920s.

76. Balmer, Edwin. *Dragons Drive You*. New York: Dodd, Mead, 1934. 289pp.

This romance novel set in the 1920s focuses on twenty-three-year-old Agnes Gleneith's decision about who to marry and is set in the upper echelons of Chicago society. Gleneith, who grew up on Chicago's North Shore on a lakefront estate, has been pursued by two brothers for several years. The Braddon siblings are similar in appearance and have equal incomes from a sizeable trust fund, but have very different characters. Twenty-eight-year-old Judson attended Yale University and then went directly into business selling securities, and now has his own firm with impressive offices. Twenty-nine-year-old Rodney studied at Johns Hopkins University and is a medical researcher. Initially, Agnes thinks she may marry Judson, but does not directly respond to his proposal and becomes preoccupied with the idea of not marrying at all. Judson, however, believes she has tacitly agreed and begins taking her to look at apartments. On one of these trips they come upon a murder scene, at which a hysterical young bride, Myrtle Lorrie, seems to have killed her husband, Charles. When Lorrie begs Agnes for help, Agnes secures her father's acquaintance, Martin O'Mara, as Lorrie's attorney. Subpoenaed as a material witness, Agnes hears testimony about the troubled Lorries' marriage that influences her thinking about matrimony, then the stock market crashes, banks begin to fail, and all the affluence that had seemed a certainty disappears. Love and devotion to the civic good now seem to be the only verities and Agnes marries O'Mara, whom she has come to love and who is devoted to the civic good. The newlyweds set up a household together that soon includes a baby. In part a murder mystery, this novel includes extended reflections on the unique qualities of Chicago, gender relations, and human values.

77. Balmer, Edwin. *Fidelia*. New York: Dodd, Mead, 1924. 368pp.

This romance novel has an omniscient narrator who captures the thoughts of Fidelia Netley, a femme fatale from the West, who wins the hand of David Herrick, a minister's son, and defeats the wealthy Anne Southron. When Fidelia appears at Northwestern University, she immediately attracts men with her clear complexion, luxurious red hair, and full figure. However, the women on campus distrust her and question her past that includes study at the University of Minnesota and Stanford University and an eighteen-month gap. Fidelia's attentions focus on David Herrick the male half of the campus' ideal couple. He is attractive, considerate, upright, hard-working and his fiancée, Anne Southron, is the wealthiest woman on campus and also beautiful. Fidelia's hearty appreciation of nature, including Lake Michigan in zero degree weather, make her seem united to elemental forces, giving her an immediate hold over men, including David. Anne knows that there is some mystery in Fidelia's past, but is too nice have her investigated. She hopes Fidelia will be discredited by her own free-spirited behavior and lets David know how hurt she is by his increasing regard for the red-head. Then, a night-time walk on the lake leaves David and Fidelia stranded on an ice floe overnight. After their dramatic rescue, Anne breaks off the engagement and David impulsively marries Fidelia. He goes into partnership in an automobile dealership, becomes a success, and lives with Fidelia in an expensive residence hotel near the lake in Lincoln Park. His minister father is horrified that David is living only for the pleasure of Fidelia and not having children and cuts off relations with them. David is undeterred in his love until Fidelia's mysterious past breaks into their life. She gets news that her first husband is not dead. They were married for only a few days before a natural disaster separated them and Fidelia had been told by his family that he was dead. As World War I breaks out David enlists and Fidelia goes to France to be reunited with her first husband. By the end of the story David and Anne have been reconciled and Anne has been able to begin forgetting about Fidelia until word is received that Fidelia's husband, and later Fidelia, have died leaving an orphaned girl who looks just like Fidelia. The child will be a constant reminder to Anne of Fidelia since she will be raised as David's daughter. Although Fidelia's journals reveal that she stayed in love with David even after she reunited with her husband, the reader is left to wonder whether this woman of the West is to be admired or condemned for her free spirit. Although the book primarily deals with gender roles, the work is very descriptive and provides convincing settings for David, Fidelia, and Anne's lives in Chicago, that include descriptions of leisure activities, restaurants, and domestic interiors.

78. Balmer, Edwin. *Flying Death*. New York: Dodd, Mead, 1927. 198pp.
Roughly twenty pages of this novel are physically set in Chicago. Two men, Cawder and Bane, create an elaborate plot to dominate society through terror from the skies as they threaten to bomb ships and introduce a new age of feudalism. Their headquarters is in Chicago in a sky scraper with a landing strip that is described in some detail.

79. Balmer, Edwin. *Keeban*. Boston: Little, Brown, 1923. 295pp.
In this murder mystery that revolves around mistaken identity, Steve Fanneal must vindicate his adopted brother, Jerry. The Fanneals are affluent, but live together in a large house on Astor Street. Steve has already entered the family food-wholesale business and Jerry, recently graduated from Princeton is about also join the business, when he is accused of accosting and robbing Dorothy Crewe, the girl he had been dating, of a sapphire and diamond necklace. Jerry claims he has a doppelganger, Keeban, who is the culprit and goes into hiding. Jerry, who was discovered in Lincoln Park by the Fanneals' nanny and later adopted by them, was always thought to have mysterious origins, despite his charming disposition, because of his dark complexion. Could the accusations mean some evil aspect of his character is emerging, or is his bizarre story true? Steve is skeptical until he encounters Keeban. Soon afterwards, Jerry is accused of a new crime, a murder. In Steve's attempts to capture Keeban and vindicate his brother, he visits the Halsted Street area, a slum that he describes in detail; spends time in warehouse areas along the Chicago River; and attends a masquerade party held in a dance hall and attended by criminals. After thwarting a counterfeiting ring and nearly perishing when an evil gang tries to poison him with a peculiarly effective lethal gas they have invented, Steve is reunited with Jerry in the presence of Keeban's corpse and the two are finally able to convince the police of Jerry's innocence. The author attempts to portray the dark criminal underworld of Chicago by describing areas of the city frequented by gangsters. These attempts are much more convincing than his presentation of upper-class settings and can be assumed to benefit from the authenticity lent by direct observation.

80. Balmer, Edwin. *Resurrection Rock*. New York: Grosset and Dunlap, 1920. 383pp.

This gothic romance includes two mysterious households, a mansion constructed at great expense on an island, Resurrection Rock, off the Northern Peninsula of Michigan, and a Chicago mansion on Scott Street, being kept in readiness for the return of its chatelaine by a staff of servants. In January 1919, Ethel Carew is on her way to beg her lumber baron grandfather, who lives across from Resurrection Rock, for enough money to hold onto her deceased father's Western land holdings. During her visit she meets Barney Loutrelle, who was raised by Chippewa Indians in Northern Michigan, and was recovering from injuries World War I injuries when he received a spirit communication instructing him to travel to Resurrection Rock. Ethel fails with her grandfather and falls in love with Loutrelle. She flees back to Chicago when a murder, for which she blames her grandfather, takes place at Resurrection Rock. Almost penniless, she lives in the house of her Aunt Agnes, whose servants maintain her Scott Street mansion in readiness for her return. Agnes' ship to England was torpedoed during the war, but not enough time has passed for her to be declared dead. Loutrelle arrives in Chicago and the two begin exploring the murder, that is connected to old family secrets and could explain long held animosities dividing Ethel's extended family. Since additional spirit communications aid them, the novel includes several digressions on the nature of mediums and the spirit world. By the end of the novel, wrongs from long ago are redressed, Barney's true identity is revealed, and he and Ethel marry. While cultural historians may be interested in the respectability of séances and mediums in the work, the strong and independent female characters in the novel, and the way American Indians are described, the Chicago setting is fairly shallow. However, streets and neighborhoods are named and there are several lengthy paeans to areas along the lakefront, Lincoln Park, and the view of the city from the municipal pier.

81. Balmer, Edwin. *Ruth of the U.S.A.* Illustrated by Harold H. Betts. Chicago: McClurg, 1919. 361pp.

In this novel about Chicago during World War I that touches on gender issues, Ruth Alden has been forced into office work after the unexpected death of her father to help support her mother and three younger sisters. Ruth works for a real estate attorney, but longs to play some role in World War I and she is stymied by her responsibilities to her mother and sisters. Then, mistaken for another girl who had agreed to work as a spy, Ruth is handed instructions, a passport, and enough money to support her family while she is in abroad in the employ of the United States government. Only approximately the first sixty pages of the novel are set in Chicago; descriptions of the city focus on war rallies and society fundraisers, and there is some discussion of the allegiances of ethnic German Chicagoans.

82. Balmer, Edwin. *That Breath of Scandal*. Boston: Little, Brown. 1922. 360pp.

This novel is set in upper-class Chicago society in the 1920s and deals with the plight of young women who are forced to choose a husband for life based on scanty information. Marjorie Hale, a university college student, is the daughter of Mr. and Mrs. Charles Hale, Evanston residents and Chicago society figures, and her fiancé Bill Whittaker, is a successful young lawyer. Whittaker lives in a Chicago flat with Gregg Mowbry, a friend from student days at the University of Michigan, who is also in love with Marjorie, but must deny his feelings. As they gather for a dinner party, a telephone call is received that eventually changes the lives of every guest. The enigmatic call takes Whittaker, Mowbry, and Marjorie to the apartment Mr. Hale keeps for his mistress, Mrs. Sybill Russell, where he has been wounded by her gun-toting, estranged husband.

Marjorie impresses the men by her unemotional reaction and quick thinking to avoid a scandal in the newspapers. Some attempt is made to conceal the facts from Mrs. Hale, but she does find out and the Hales divorce. Marjorie is unsettled by the experience and then learns that Whittaker has been seeing other women while he was engaged to her. She strikes out on her own, supporting herself by selling cosmetics door to door and living with another young woman on Clearedge Street, until, in the aftermath of the accidental death of Whittaker, she returns to her father's house and is united with Gregg, to whom she becomes engaged. The novel deals with gender relations and social status in the setting of 1920s Chicago and includes strong descriptions of domestic arrangements, public entertainments, and nightclubs. The contrasts between the Hale household and the lower-middle-class characters are particularly well laid out.

83. Balmer, Edwin. *That Royle Girl*. New York: Dodd, Mead, 1925. 358pp.
    In this romance/murder mystery, issues of xenophobia and status anxiety are openly raised. Joan Daisy Royle, in her twenties, is still living with her mother and stepfather in a residence hotel in "Little Paris," near the intersection of Wilson Avenue and Sheridan Boulevard. Her natural father died when she was two and the peripatetic nature of her life has been determined by the fact that her mother is a veronal addict and her stepfather an alcoholic. The Royles typically move from one hotel room to another in the middle of the night, the bill for their stay unpaid, and Joan has been unable to attend school, though she educated herself and learned stenography. Pursued in an unwelcome way by the owner of the contracting company where she is a secretary, her unrequited love is for twenty-four-year-old Fred Ketlar, the musician who lives downstairs. Ketlar, with his own dance band, is a glamorous figure for Joan. However, he is only separated from his wife, an older woman he confusedly married as a nineteen-year-old. When Mrs. Ketlar is murdered on an evening Ketlar spent with Joan, she becomes a suspect along with him. The prosecuting attorney for the case, Calvin Clarke, is obsessed by the way immigrants and "mixed bloods" are destroying America and bringing a new lawlessness to the country. He is from Massachusetts and can trace his heritage back to before Queen Anne's War. When he meets Joan and decides she is a loose woman, he wishes to prosecute her, but realizes that no jury would convict on such scanty evidence. Dismissing outright the alibi Joan presents for Ketlar, Clarke indicts the musician and it seems likely that he will be convicted. However, new evidence emerges that reveals that an Italian gangster romanced Mrs. Ketlar and murdered her. This is consistent with Joan seeing a man in the murdered woman's apartment. Through most of the novel, Clarke finds evidence of the "downfall" of American civilization in Chicago, focusing on such establishments as automats, and the "mixed bloods" he sees on the streets. However, when he realizes that he was wrong about Joan and Ketlar, he somewhat unconvincingly changes his view of American society. By the end of the novel Clarke is engaged to be married to Joan (Ketlar having rushed off to marry another woman as soon as he was acquitted). Descriptions include Chicago nightlife, gangsters, and immigrant districts.

84. Balmer, Edwin and William Briggs MacHarg. *The Achievements of Luther Trant*. Illustrated by William Oberhardt. Boston: Small, Maynard, 1910. 365pp.
    Young Chicagoan Luther Trant, recently an undergraduate university student in experimental psychology, zealously applies scientific discoveries about human emotions to solve crimes in these short stories. His techniques include word association and physiological measurements that detect increases in sweating and breathing, as well as textual analysis, and basic forensic analysis of footprints and ballistics. The crime victims and most of the suspects are from the upper classes

and the settings are domestic. However, elements of exoticism stem from the foreign travels and collecting interests of some of the characters. Ethnic and racial distinctions are made with reference to science, and the Chinese exclusion act is crucial to one of the stories.

85. Balmer, Edwin and Philip Wylie. *The Shield of Silence*. New York: Frederick A. Stokes, 1936. 310pp.

In this mystery novel, set in upper-class Chicago social circles, Lucian Myrand is imprisoned in the state penitentiary in Joliet, the confessed murderer of his friend Serge Ralten. Inexplicably, he will not tell anyone why he committed the crime, even though any mitigating factors might result in a lesser sentence than life in prison. His daughter Alice and a young attorney, Ethan West, get drawn into solving the mystery when they find a murdered man in exactly the same room and position on the sixth anniversary of the original crime. An important key to the solution is the revelation of Myrand's war service as a fighter pilot and German prisoner during World War I. As Ethan and Alice pursue leads, they are taken to social events and restaurants in Chicago and Lake Forest (the Myrands have a house there, as well as on Astor Street in the city). However, the novel includes little physical description.

86. Banks, Charles Eugene. *John Dorn, Promoter*. Chicago: Monarch Books, 1906. 361pp.

This romance novel attributes spiritual insight and cultural sensitivity to a female character whose personality is associated with her family origins. Helen Chadbourne combines modern business sense with the nobility of spirit and noblesse oblige that the author identifies with the plantation owners of the antebellum South. Her father, heir to a Virginia plantation, was a Yale student during the war and married northerner, Mollie Whittleson. After failing to revive his plantation, he was persuaded by his brother-in-law to open a law office in Chicago. However, Chadbourne's southern gentility was a disadvantage in the brusque city and he died in debt leaving his oldest daughter, Helen, to try to find a way to support her mother and a younger sister. A Vassar graduate, Helen found work with John Dorn, an acquaintance of her father, who, though young, was a great success on the Board of Trade. Adept at business, Helen finds few opportunities for women and wants to dedicate her life to others. Two men are in love with her, Dorn and Ned Danvers, the adopted son of her uncle. She inspires each of them to have chthonic spiritual experiences. Her uncle is negotiating for the lumber rights to Indian lands on Michigan's Upper Peninsula, using Dorn to devise a financing plan and Danvers to meet with Eagle Wing, chief of the Winnebagos. Helen identifies with the chief's plight of wanting to aid his impoverished tribe, while not wanting to destroy their land. Her uncle believes only clear-cutting timber will be financially viable and Helen convinces Danvers and Dorn not only to aid the Indians with money, but ensure they are still able to live in a forest. Dorn comes up with a plan to build the Lumber Securities Company, a syndicate of the leaders in the timber industry, who would agree to a renewable forestry plan. Helen inspires Dorn to help impoverished Jewish immigrants by starting a lending library and a savings bank. She also encourages Danvers in his dream of becoming a writer. With the aid of Eagle Wing, he is able to reveal his deepest thoughts telepathically to Helen. Despite her feelings for Danvers, Helen realizes that he will always be slightly removed from the world, and good works require an engaged man like Dorn. A subplot traces the evil forces that seek to destroy the Lumber Securities Company through stock manipulation. At a crucial moment spiritual adepts Eagle Wing and a rabbi, whom Helen had aided, combine forces to defeat the evil men. The forces of spiritual enlightenment win, Danvers writes a play with a spiritual theme that is a great success,

Dorn wins Helen for his bride, and everyone involved with the Lumber Securities Company stands to make a fortune.

87. Banning, Margaret Culkin. *Give Us Our Years*. New York: Harper and Brothers, 1950. 274pp.

In this novel about Chicago family life in the 1940s, Alec and Eve Starr confront life-cycle issues as they enter middle age. They have lived an enviable life. Alec grew up in poverty in Hibbing, Minnesota, served overseas in World War I, and met Eve, one of Chicago's most brilliant and wealthy debutantes immediately upon his return at the demobilization center where she volunteered. Their love continued strong as Alec climbed the corporate ladder of the steel industry through his own skill and hard work, supported by his wife's charm and social rank. She raised their two children Charles and Belinda, skillfully, as well as taking on the burden of organizing social entertainments and undertaking the philanthropic activities important to her husband's career and her family's social position. Now, in the late 1940s, as recent grandparents, age is bringing them challenges. Forty-eight-year-old Eve wants to insure that her children are happily settled in life, while not being meddlesome. Alec must begin to withdraw from his active life as the president of a major steel corporation and prepare for his final years, instead of pursuing the romance he wants to initiate with a much younger woman. In addition to issues of social status, the novel deals with changing gender roles, particularly in married couples and questions of whether a woman will mostly support her husband, in the ways Eve did, or have their own careers, as one of Eve's daughters wants. The novel describes social events, clothing, and households (including details about income and expenses, listing, for instance, the costs of a party for two hundred guests and the costs of appropriate Christmas gifts).

88. Barnes, Margaret Ayer. *Edna, His Wife: An American Idyll*. Boston: Houghton Mifflin, Riverside Press, 1935. 628pp.

Approximately three hundred pages of this novel dealing with married life are set in Chicago and trace the rise of a couple from the modest household and social life of newlyweds through middle-age affluence. Edna Losser, the daughter of a railroad station agent in Blue Island, Illinois, meets Paul Jones in 1900. Jones, a lawyer at the very outset of his career is determined to become a wealthy man and marriage is not in his immediate plans. However, he and Edna's attraction carries him away and when Edna's family refuses his marriage proposal he arranges an elopement. In great detail Barnes describes the household furnishings, personal possessions, and acquaintances that Edna and Paul acquire and exchange as Paul climbs ever higher on the ladder of economic and social success, eventually moving to Washington, D. C. and, later, New York City. The couple's first apartment is on LaSalle near Oak Street, from there they move to a house in Oakwood, and then to the Near North Side to a house on Bank Street with a view of the grounds of the Potter Palmer Estate. Barnes' descriptions of households, clothing, and activities capture the social history in Chicago from 1900 to 1917. Although her focus is domestic, some historical events are detailed, including Chicago Street Railway litigation, the sinking of the excursion boat, *Eastland* (Edna's parents are killed in the disaster), and the violent consequences of anti-German sentiment during World War I.

89. Barnes, Margaret Ayer. *Prevailing Winds*. Boston: Houghton Mifflin, Riverside Press, 1928. 298pp.

Many of the eight short stories in this volume are set in Chicago and most have Chicago characters. One story in particular, "Shirtsleeves to Shirtsleeves" (pp. 93-128), encapsulates aspects of upper-class social life from the 1870s to World War I and mentions key events in Chicago history. The stories as a whole mostly center on female characters who have reached middle age and reflect on the course of their lives and the choices they have made. Although there is no physical description of Chicago, the upper-class households in which the stories are set get full descriptions, including the number of servants, the food served at meals, and the clothing and jewels of family members and guests.

90. Barnes, Margaret Ayer. *Wisdom's Gate*. Boston: Houghton Mifflin, 1938. 370pp.

Here Barnes continues the story begun in her novel *Years of Grace*. Unlike her mother, Jane, Cicily [*sic*] divorced and married for love, a decision enabled by inherited investments with a handsome income, allowing her to support her new husband, Albert, a cousin by marriage, in a career in the diplomatic corps. Posted in China for five years, Cicily and Albert are forced to return to the Chicago metropolitan area where they spent their childhoods and each began married life with other spouses. They deal with the attitudes of friends and family toward their divorces and marriage and later cope with financial disaster after the stock market crashes and Cicily's income disappears. Lecturing to Cicily and Albert of the positive effects of financial struggle, their wealthy relatives provide little assistance, and Albert accepts a mid-level position in his stepfather's advertising firm, a painful demotion for a man who expected to be an ambassador. Both Cicily and Albert chafe at life in "Suburbia." Albert is soon having an affair with a model, "Miss Wisconsin," from the advertising office. When her husband threatens to sue for alienation of affection, Albert's lawyer advises a settlement and Cicily decides to stand by her husband and sell some of her inherited investments at their reduced value, to give to the woman. Soon Albert begins an affair with another woman from the couple's social circle and Cicily seeks consolation from a male mutual friend. Just as Cicily is about to seek a divorce, having learned that her remaining stocks will begin paying a dividend again, Albert announces that his stepfather has decided to support his diplomatic career and Cicily decides she must stand by the man she really does love. In addition to her depiction of upper-class social events, food, and fashion, Barnes captures an array of social attitudes concerning gender roles and distinctions made on the basis of ethnicity and social rank.

91. Barnes, Margaret Ayer. *Within This Present*. Boston: Houghton Mifflin, 1933. 611pp.

In 1914 the Sewall family gathers in their mansion in Lakewood to celebrate the seventieth birthday of "Granny" Sewall and is surprised when she gives a lengthy speech, rehearsing the family history and expressing her observations on the negative impact that wealth has had on her children's lives. She describes the hardships of frontier life, the 1849 flood, the Civil War, the 1866 cholera epidemic, and the 1871 fire. Her deceased husband had founded a bank and her four children have known only luxury and acceptance from their birth into Chicago society. Granddaughter Sally, the novel's protagonist, listens to the speech and thinks about how different the life of her generation will be from that of her grandparents and parents. The novel traces that life up to 1933 when this third generation of Sewalls has entered middle age, presenting the impact of World War I, the 1920s, and the stock market crash on upper-class Chicagoans. By the end of the novel the family bank has failed, but Sally and Granny cannot help thinking that hardships will push family members to greater achievements. In the novel's final scene the Sewalls gather to listen to Franklin Roosevelt's inspiring 1933 inaugural address. Descriptions of interiors, clothing, architecture, changing attitudes toward social drinking, non-WASPs, and divorce blend together to present a rich evocation of upper-class social life in the first decades of the twentieth century.

92. Barnes, Margaret Ayer. *Years of Grace*. Boston: Houghton Mifflin, 1930. 581pp.

This novel, mostly set in Chicago, covers the events in Jane Ward's life from the time she is fourteen until she is fifty-one-years-old (1887-1938). Jane's childhood home is on Pine Street, near the intersection with Rush Street (at the time it was one of Chicago's most respectable neighborhoods), in a substantial Victorian house. Her childhood friends, who will remain with her in some way through the rest of her life, include two of whom her mother approves and two of whom she does not. Agnes Johnson is the daughter of a newspaper editor and has a mother who works as a secretary and is disqualified socially because of her middle-class parents and residence west of Clark Street. André Duroy's father is a French consul, but he is a foreigner with no connections in Chicago society and he is also Roman Catholic. Jane's two acceptable friends, Flora Furness and Muriel Lester, live only houses away from the Wards and because of their social standing in Chicago and their wealth, Mrs. Ward overlooks certain irregularities in the Furness and Lester households. Flora's mother Lily is too often in the company of thirty-five-year-old roué Bert Lancaster, and the Lesters are Jews, newly converted to the Episcopal Church. Three times Jane has an opportunity to transform her life by rejecting her mother's Victorian values. When she is seventeen, nineteen-year-old André proposes before leaving to study at the Sorbonne and Jane does not have the strength to fight her parents' opposition. When, after she turns twenty-one, André tries to renew their romance, she is upset that he has decided to accept the Prix de Rome and remain out of the country. Frustrated by the situation, she precludes any renewed romance by marrying Stephen Carver, scion of a socially prominent Boston banking family and a match her mother endorses. After Jane has been married for fifteen years, and has three children (Cicily, Jenny, and Steve), she is courted by Agnes' husband, Jimmy, while he is working in Chicago and Agnes remains in New York. Although Jane believes she is more deeply in love than she has ever been before, she rejects divorce and ends the affair. At the end of the book, fifty-one-year-old Jane realizes that each of her children have acted independently in a way that neither she nor her husband ever have. Cicily divorced and remarried for love; Jenny pursued a close personal friendship with another woman and lives with her in a Manhattan penthouse; Steve left his father's bank and the assurance of its presidency upon his father's retirement in order to move to Boston and take a job in his uncle's banking firm. However, Jane believes that she was right to sacrifice her personal interests to promote traditional family life, the bedrock of civilized society. While presenting Jane's story the novel describes social events, attire, domestic structures and furnishings, modes of travel, and changing social attitudes over a fifty-year period, presenting many details relevant to Chicago social history.

93. Barr, Robert. *The Speculations of John Steele*. New York: Frederick A. Stokes, 1905. 308pp.

The story of John Steele's life can mostly be summed up through his business transactions. His first successes are achieved through quick thinking when he averts a train wreck while a low-level railroad employee. Brought to the attention of his superiors, he continues to impress them with innovative thinking and promotions follow, although a jealous former supervisor makes difficulties for him. Then he inherits $300,000 worth of securities, mostly railroad stocks, from a miserly uncle, and his nemesis engineers a plot through which he loses most of it. He eventually recovers the money and invests in fixed-rate mortgages, until he takes a chance to purchase a railroad right of way and re-sells it at a great profit; afterward he uses inside information to make money in wheat futures. As his financial transactions become more complicated (creating a beet sugar syndicate, for instance) he becomes a speculator, getting further away from what he understands. His downfall is implemented by beautiful women and brought about by powerful men who dislike him. Although Chicago and its financial markets serve as a setting for a good deal of this novel decrying the dangers of speculation, little effort is made to describe the city.

94. Barrett, Mary Ellin. *American Beauty*. New York: Dutton, 1980. 310pp.

Only the first seventy-eight pages of this romance novel are set in Chicago where Mary Gay grows up, the impoverished daughter of a piano accompanist for opera singers. At nineteen, she moves to New York City to take a role in a Broadway musical, soon marrying the impresario who chose her for the role. By twenty she is a great success on the musical theater stage. The descriptions of Chicago focus on the world of singers, musicians, and their patrons, as well as holiday celebrations and winter landscapes. The novel's story is told through extended flashbacks on the night that Mary is about to be honored at a seventy-fifth birthday gala which she is delayed in attending by a jewel thief who breaks into her Central Park West townhouse.

95. Barton, William Eleazar. *The Prairie Schooner; A Story of the Black Hawk War*. Illustrated by H. Burgess. Boston and Chicago: Wilde, 1900. 382pp.

This work of historical fiction is based in part on the stories the author heard as a boy, the son of early Illinois settlers. The work's primary concern is with the Black Hawk War on the Illinois frontier, but includes eighty pages set in Chicago. The main character, Ned Putnam, arrives in the town in the spring of 1831 with a pair of oxen pulling a prairie schooner filled with homesteading supplies and the most lucrative of the goods that his father, recently dead of disease on the trip from Massachusetts, had sold as an itinerant peddler. His mother had died years before. Alone in the world, Ned is happy to befriend another teenage boy, Sam Leslie. The two agree to homestead on the Rock River Valley on land that Ned's father had earlier surveyed. During their stay in Chicago, they meet several historical figures including Mark Beaubien, and the Indian Sauganash and Shabonna, as well as gamblers and outlaws who will try to steal the Rock River land. The author summarizes the history of Chicago up to 1831 and evokes the rough settlement of the day as a location where people speculated on the future of the place. The population includes Indians, trappers, and settlers headed for land further west.

96. Bates, Elizabeth *Love is Like Peanuts*. New York: Holiday House, 1980. 125pp.

Fourteen-year-old Marianne Mandic needs a summer job to help pay for ballet lessons and freshman-year high school expenses. Through an introduction from her father, a doorman at an expensive lakefront building, she gets a sitter's job that exposes her to people, activities, and social situations that foster personal growth and broaden the perceptions of the book's young adult readers for whom the book was written. Marianne is hired as a companion for Catherine "Catsy" Kranz, who was born with brain damage. She must learn to deal with both Catsy's behavior and the attitudes people in public have toward Catsy. Catsy's father, an intimidating businessman, and the Kranz's unpleasant housekeeper present further social challenges. However, Marianne also interacts with Catsy's eighteen-year-old brother Toby. The two start dating and Toby takes Marianne out in his sailboat and to dinners and dances at the Chicago Yacht Club (there is an extended description of the annual Venetian Night party). Most of the physical descriptions in the book are of areas along the lakefront and include the Navy Pier, Belmont Harbor, and Buckingham Park. In addition to raising issues of social attitudes toward the developmentally disabled, the novel raises issues of gender roles and sexuality as the romance between Marianne and Toby advances.

97. Beach, Edgar Rice. *Hands of Clay: A Great City's Half—And the Other Half.* St. Louis: Edward R. Eddins, 1904. 348pp.

Originally published in 1890 as *Stranded* (*see* entry 98)

98. Beach, Edgar Rice. *Stranded, a Story of the Garden City.* Chicago: Donohue, Henneberry, 1890. 348pp.

In the author's preface he claims that the novel's action is based on real-life incidents, involving Chicagoans living between 1855 and 1865. This morality tale involves greed and jealous rivalry for the hands of beautiful women. Now a seventy-year-old, as a youth Ralph Skinner was in love with a woman who married another man, Duane Worsham. Skinner became preoccupied with getting revenge and money. A miser, he built a real estate fortune, mostly by taking advantage of others. After years of plotting, Skinnner finally bankrupts Worsham, who subsequently dies, and Skinner gets the pleasure of seeing Mrs. Worsham and her daughter Grace living penuriously. Fate throws Skinner an opportunity to continue his life's work when property deeds intended for to ease the widow's poverty fall into his hands. Skinner uses a cast of Dickensian co-conspirators to claim the properties. In the meantime, Mark Barry, who arranged the murder of the man who was carrying the deeds to Mrs. Worsham, to acquire the properties for himself, is trying to find out what happened to the documents and uses Michael Snoozer as his accomplice. The Snoozer character, described as a Spanish-Indian-"Negro"-Chinaman, who had become rich through political graft by employing all of the evil tendencies considered peculiar to each of his bloodlines illustrates the author's racism. After chases through darkened, snow-covered streets and alliances and counter-plots between villains, the efforts of honest citizens and power of the law bring horrible ends to the villains (e.g., suicide and being devoured by rats). There are also some spectacular redemptions as evil men convert to Christianity and begin preaching the gospel. The book ends with a series of weddings after which worthy impoverished people get the riches they deserve. The descriptions of Chicago are notable for limning what it was like to traverse the streets in winter in the mid nineteenth century.

99. Bech-Meyer, Nico, Mrs. *A Story from Pullmantown.* Chicago: Charles H. Kerr, 1894. 110pp.

Inspired by their visit to the Columbian Exposition, the Wright family, (mother, father, and young son), decide to exchange their store in South Dakota for one in Pullmantown and become part of the great success of American labor as illustrated at the fair. The Wrights' experiences turn into an extended exposé of Pullmantown as they try to alleviate the suffering of the town residents (many of whom have not had work for months and can barely feed themselves), and assist in the formation of labor unions. As a strike begins at the end of the novel (April 1894), the Wrights pledge to stay and help the workers even if it means bankruptcy. The novel contrasts dramatically with others written at the same time celebrating Chicago and the fair. However, as in other labor novels, the middle-class is encouraged to take responsibility for the living and working conditions of factory workers, even if it entails personal sacrifice. Although the novel provides little physical description of Chicago beyond the fairgrounds, the issues it raises attack the very heart of the city as a symbol for the virtues of American capitalism.

100. Bein, Albert [Charles Walt, pseud.]. *Love in Chicago.* New York: Harcourt, Brace, 1929. 254pp.

In the guise of a diary, this novel details the life of a hit man in Chicago and the types of intimidation he is hired to practice, including damaging property and delivering beatings. Ironically, the hit man's employer is A. A. Carmody, president of the Citizens Improvement Association. When he is not paid by Carmody, the writer convinces Carmody's other hired muscle to join him to form a gang. He meets with some success until he becomes obsessed with Lila Leonard, daughter of bakery owner and crooked politician, Henry Leonard. Readers will be interested in the descriptions of 1920s Chicago, including restaurants and popular forms of entertainment, gangsters, and political corruption. The book also reveals the open sexism and ethnic and racial hatred typical of the period.

101. Bellow, Saul. *The Adventures of Augie March*. New York: Viking Press, 1953. 536pp.
    Augie, born into an immigrant Chicago slum in the 1920s, grew up in a household his father had abandoned. His mother, left with three children to feed and clothe, works incessantly as a seamstress. Augie's brother Simon is motivated to live the American dream and through a combination of work and luck is wealthy while still a young man. Fiercely independent, Augie rejects his brother's assistance and the adoption offer of a sporting goods store owner, to find his own way in the world. His adventurous life includes a liaison with an eccentric wealthy woman, marriage to a woman who becomes a film actress, surviving a torpedoed ship, and working for a Parisian black marketer. Much of the book is set in Chicago and depicts immigrant and Jewish life.

102. Bellow, Saul. *Dangling Man*. New York: Vanguard Press, 1944. 191pp.
    Joseph, the twenty-seven-year-old narrator of this novel written in the form of journal entries is waiting to be inducted into the U.S. Army. He has already resigned his job at the Inter-American Travel Bureau and, when he finds he will be awaiting induction longer than expected, cannot get his job back because of the decline in leisure travel. He is forced to let his wife Iva, the daughter of German immigrants, support him. A graduate of the University of Wisconsin he devises reading programs to occupy his time and examines his life through his journal writing. Joseph had been involved in leftist political organizations and discusses these and the war's impact upon them. The novel provides skilled descriptions of boarding house life, the social aspects of public transportation, and World War II Chicago in general.

103. Bellow, Saul. *Herzog*. New York: Viking Press, 1964. 341pp.
    Jewish intellectual Professor Moses Herzog rehearses events in his past life and writes unmailed letters, instead of working on his second book on Romanticism. Divorced for the second time and feeling betrayed by his former wife, Madeleine, and his best friend, Valentine Gersbach, he is close to a mental breakdown as he alternately holes up in his kitchenette apartment in New York City's Chelsea and his house in the Berkshires. Herzog grew up in Chicago and reminisces about the city. His most recent job was also there, teaching at "Downtown College" in the Loop, and living in a leased house in Hyde Park. He returns to Chicago seeking revenge against Madeleine who is still living there, but is thwarted by her kindness and ends up spending time with his mistress Romona, occasionally overwhelmed by memories of his boyhood and youth in the city. The present of the novel is the 1950s, with flashbacks to the previous three decades.

104. Bellow, Saul. *Humboldt's Gift*. New York: Viking Press, 1975. 487pp.
    Much of this book is set in 1970s Chicago. During his travels around the city Charles Citrine, a money-making writer, remembers the Chicago of his youth and visits contemporary landmarks such as the Downtown Club, the Playboy Club, various restaurants, and an old-fashioned Russian steam bath, which had been in operation since before his birth. He also interacts with a number of

Chicago characters, most memorably Rinaldo Cantabile who affects the behavior of a 1920s style Chicago gangster. Citrine becomes inextricably bound to Cantabile when he loses to the gangster in a poker game and Cantabile insists he pays his debt. However, Citrine is haunted in a more inescapable way by the memory of a deceased friend, Von Humboldt Fleisher, a sometime intellectual and poet, who had achieved early fame in the 1930s for a book of poetry, then published nothing for years while Citrine's own books established him in literary circles. Fleisher's resentment soured their friendship, even though Citrine continued to admire Fleisher. When Fleisher dies, Citrine receives as a bequest a movie scenario that he had written with Fleisher years as a lark. When he is able to sell the work, Citrine's bank account and career are reinvigorated.

105. Benchly, Alexandra Jane. *If the Heart Be Hasty.* Berwyn, Ill.: Chekhov Publications, 1969. 280pp.

Over the years 1924 to 1944, this romance novel traces the life of Jennie Logan as she matures from childhood to adulthood in a working-class social setting. She is adopted by Kate Bundy, a fiercely protective neighbor on Fifty-second Place on the South Side, after Jennie's parents are killed in a car accident. The area is still middle-class and filled with free-standing houses, but it is rapidly changing as recent immigrants arrive. Jennie has playmates who are Italian, Irish, and Swedish. While Bundy appreciates the serious, responsible influence of Mike Nielsen on the young girl, she is concerned about the influence of Chuck Cassidy, whose father runs a neighborhood saloon where she finds Jennie dancing on a table for tips. Soon afterwards, Bundy sells her house to a Greek-immigrant family and moves Jennie to a better neighborhood near the intersection of Fifty-seventh Street and Western Avenue. When she finishes high school she gets a job with a Michigan Avenue art dealer, whose son she has been dating, and, as World War II begins, she volunteers in the Fort Nader canteen, and, later, at a U.S.O. near the Loop. Nielson enlists in the Merchant Marine, and Cassidy is drafted. While her childhood friends are away, Jennie marries Victor Franz, a second generation German who is 4-F and works in a defense plant stockroom. Before she is twenty-one, Jennie has her first baby and Victor dies from a job-related injury. She quickly goes on to have affairs and marry a truck driver, Kenneth Calhoun. She does not learn until after she is carrying his child that he is a deserter with wives in other cities. Jennie finally marries Neilson near the end of the novel. From the perspective of the book, he is the man she was meant to be with, but not until she had been "tamed" by her other experiences. The book presents scenes of working-class socializing and leisure, including trips to the Indiana Dunes, bowling, and drag car racing. Businesses and families in the neighborhoods in which Jennie resides are fully treated, especially their changing characters. The book also presents issues of ethnicity, gender roles, and a view of female sexuality.

106. Bigot, Marie Healy. *Lakeville; or, Substance and Shadow.* New York: David Appleton, 1873. 238pp.

In this young adult novel about 1860s social mores and women's position in society, the main character is Valerie Turner, the orphaned heiress to a fortune who has been educated at the St. Mary's Convent School boarding school. Her guardians, Mr. and Mrs. West, bring her back to Chicago (renamed Lakeville here) at the age of eighteen for her debutante year. Unfortunately, the West's daughters, Helen, Clare, and Jane provide little support for Valerie in her new social context. Although Jane is good-hearted and pleasant, she does not go into society because she is invalided by illness (she later dies). Helen and Clare, like their mother, are materialistic, socially ambitious, and self-centered. Valerie is soon a social success, liked for her innocence, beauty, and wealth. Without any guidance, however, Valerie's first suitors are inappropriate: the roué Bill Sherwood and the young flirt Edward Elliot. Fortunately, Mrs. Graham decides to take Valerie in hand. The older woman represents the best American society can offer in terms of comportment and principled behavior. Her son Alick has similar qualities. Under their guidance, Valerie learns how to protect herself from the wrong men and accurately assess her marriage prospects. Roughly half of the novel is set in European destinations popular at the time with upper-class Americans. In addition to presenting women's social position, scholars may be interested in the book's treatment of the Civil War. Although set in the 1860s, the conflict is barely mentioned and then only in connection with the dearth of suitably marriageable young men.

107. Bisno, Beatrice. *Tomorrow's Bread*. Philadelphia: Jewish Publication Society of America, 1938. 328pp.

In this fictionalized biography of labor organizer Abraham Bisno (here named Sam Karenski), most of the action is set in 1880s and 1890s Chicago. Karenski, with his immediate family, arrives in the United States from Russia at the age of fourteen and they settle in Chattanooga, Tennessee where Karenski works as a tailor's apprentice. He learns quickly and relocates to Chicago, opening his own shop at age fifteen, employing his entire family. Instead of focusing all of his energies on personal success, Karenski works at improving working conditions for garment industry workers in the Jewish ghetto through unionization. In fact, his labor organizing becomes a preoccupation, leading him to neglect everyone in his life, including his family, and to ignore his business. In addition to an account of the early days of labor organizing in Chicago, the book provides information about Jewish life, the settlement house movement, and, of course, the garment industry in the late nineteenth century.

108. Blake, Emily Calvin. *The Third Weaver*. Chicago: Willett, Clark and Colby, 1929. 252pp.

This novel set in bohemian and socialist circles in the World War I era is set in New York City and Portland, Oregon, as well as Chicago. Thaisa Worthington comes from an aristocratic English family, but her father, Richard, rejects the life of inherited ease to live as a socialist worker and theorist. Active as a writer and editor of socialist publications in the United States, he moves his family to Chicago, where they live in an apartment at Thirty-ninth Street and Ellis Avenue and later in a flat on Dearborn Avenue. However, Richard's chronic unemployment begins to force them from one wretched accommodation to another. Fortunately, Anglophile Chicagoans, appreciative of Richard's tailored clothing, speech, and manners, who are committed to art, culture, and socialism, provide modest financial support. After deciding socialism is best practiced in the country, Richard eventually buys a hop farm in a remote area of Oregon and moves his family there. One of their few visitors is Peter Dagmar, who met the Worthingtons soon after they arrived in the United States. A socialist, he felt an immediate connection with Richard and was smitten with Thaisa, pledging to marry her once she was of age (he is twelve years her senior). With the support of Thaisa's mother, Dagmar proposes and Thaisa returns to Chicago to be his wife. The bulk of the novel describes Thaisa's Chicago life, filled with acting in the little theater movement, attending lectures, and following Dagmar's enthusiasms for psychoanalysis and the quest for spiritual enlightenment. Since Dagmar is too preoccupied to work, Thaisa supports the household and pays the rent on a studio apartment on the North Side. Through her acting group, Thaisa makes friends with wealthy, artistic dilettante, Reba Van Valkenberg, bringing a crisis and separation for the couple who reunite in Oregon. In addition to its description of bohemian Chicago, the novel presents ideas about companionate marriage and contrasts working-class prejudices with upper-class perspectives.

109. Bland, Alden. *Behold a Cry*. New York: Charles Scribner, 1947. 229pp.

From an African-American perspective, Bland captures the excitement of people who moved from the Deep South to Chicago during World War I, experienced new economic and social opportunities and freedoms, and suffered from the speed with which the war's end dashed their hopes of equality. Ed Tyler has been in Chicago for some time as the story begins and is facing the unwelcome prospect of bringing his wife, Phom, and sons, Son and Dan, to the city. Tyler's job in a meatpacking plant enables him to buy fashionable clothes and he has begun living with a mistress who pampers him. However, the draft board has begun to question whether he really has a family to support. Even before they arrive, he regrets sending for them because the war ends and the only place he can find for them to live is with him and his mistress Mamie. Phom soon suspects the nature of Ed and Mamie's friendship, but feels powerless to object until Tyler is badly beaten in the aftermath of racial violence that starts when African-Americans try to swim on a beach unofficially reserved for whites, and Tyler crosses the color line demarcating the city to go to work. Mamie's reaction to Tyler's beating is too revealing for Phom to ignore and his weakened state allows her to insist on a housing change. He moves his family to a frame, tarpaper-roofed, alley house on the South Side. Then, within a few months he has designs on the wife of a friend and orchestrates the other couples' move into the upstairs rooms in the alley house. After a few more months he has run off with the woman. The novel illustrates the pressures of gender roles and poverty, presents arguments for and against unionism, and touches on the human costs of alcoholism and domestic violence. Through the character of Son, who loves reading and learning, and the varying reactions he gets from family and community members to his interests (Ed considers him "uppity"), the novel also deals with internalized racism and the costs of identifying with "white" culture. The action of the novel ends in 1919.

110. Bloch, Robert. *American Gothic*. New York: Simon and Schuster, 1974. 222pp.

Set in Chicago at the time of the 1893 Columbian Exposition, this fictionalized account of mass murderer Herman W. Mudgett, provides many historical details, although some of the facts of the Mudgett case are altered. The Mudgett character, here named G. Gordon Gregg, constructs a commercial building on the South Side within walking distance to the fairgrounds. Castle-like in its architectural elements, the structure includes a pharmacy on the first floor that stocks an elixir created by Gregg, rooms for rent on several floors, and Gregg's private apartment at the top. However, the building also conceals secret stairways and passages, a trap door and slide, and a basement gas chamber, all constructed to aid Gregg in the murder of people to whom he owes money, and others whom he has duped into giving him control of their assets. Although Mudgett was found out and tried for his crimes, Gregg is undone by the persistence of female reporter Crystal (never given a last name), who cannot get the police or her fiancé, insurance investigator Jim Frazer, to believe the evidence she unearths during her investigations. Finally, as Gregg is pursuing her through the house, her editor, Charlie Hogan, convinced by her story, arrives. The two narrowly escape Gregg, who is killed in his struggle with Hogan, and the castle catches fire. In addition to visits to the fairgrounds, the novel includes descriptions of saloons, barbershops, and opulent Clark Street bordellos.

111. Bloch, Robert. *The Scarf.* New York: Dial Press, 1947. 247pp.

Daniel Morley's life was shaped by the fact that his high school English teacher, Miss Frazer, was infatuated with him and that she attempted to murder him and kill herself. He goes on to a career as a mystery writer, drawing his plots from his real-life experiences as a murderer of women, usually in a way that involves the carefully preserved relic of Miss Frazer's scarf. Roughly fifty pages of the novel are set in Chicago (Morley's career includes stays in Minneapolis, New York City, and Hollywood). In the Chicago section, Morley writes his first novel after finding a victim in his work as a cab driver. He later works in an advertising agency, a position through which he secures a literary agent. The novel provides a graphic description of a Chicago dive bar, and describes some of the places in which Morley lives, including a residence hotel, a rented room in Garfield Park, and an apartment on North Clark Street.

112. Blossom, Henry Martyn, Jr. *Checkers; A Hard-Luck Story.* Chicago: Herbert S. Stone, 1896. 239pp.

During the Columbian Exposition, businessman Jack Preston meets twenty-three-year-old Edward "Checkers" Campbell, a racing tout and gambler, and after hearing Checkers hard-luck story, tries to mentor and reform him. They meet through mutual friend, Murray Jameson at the American Derby at Chicago's Washington Park. Checkers' melodramatic story involves inheriting thirty thousand dollars in gold, marrying an Arkansas beauty (the state where most of the action transpires), being widowed, and losing his personal property to his father-in-law. Most of the Chicago settings are bar-rooms, gambling parlors, restaurants, and the racetrack. The 1893 World's Fair is alluded to but not described in much detail.

113. Bodenheim, Maxwell. *Blackguard.* Chicago: Covici-McGee, 1923. 215pp.

In this story of cultural alienation set in the nineteen-teens and 'twenties, Carl Felman, the product of a middle-class Jewish family, defies his parents' expectations and social conventions to become a poet. Seeking independence from his parents, he joins the army, but soon returns to his parents. He moves into his own apartment after getting work as a telephone lineman's helper and later a plumber's assistant, boosting his income with occasional petty theft. In this first-person narrative, the reader sees the people Felman meets and the street scenes he encounters, through his misanthropic eyes. When he meets Clara Messenger, the editor of a poetry magazine, she points out that his art suffers from the way he cuts himself off from others. She helps him meet people for whom art and literature are important. Her attempts at getting him to stop deliberately antagonizing people are less successful. Carl finally meets Olga, a young actress, and begins to care about her because she shares his dark view of existence. After she dies suddenly in an accident, he sinks into a period of inconsolable grief that makes him unable to cope with daily life. His recovery is only partial and he begins to prowl the city in a predatory fashion, forcing himself on prostitutes and loose women and seeking out the company of violent thieves in the hope of an experience that will jolt him out of his numbed stupor and reunite him with other humans, even if a physical pain is required. He finally meets a prostitute who is entirely withdrawn from the world and who believes that she was born to be a nun. She is so absorbed in her interior life that she believes the physical acts she is forced into by men have never touched her true self. Carl joins her in a monastic order of two, letting himself be absorbed in self-reflection in a celibate union. The novel ends as this spiritual experiment begins in the midst of apparent degradation. Although the novel is primarily psychological, the work presents strong descriptions of Chicago street life.

114. Bodenheim, Maxwell. *Duke Herring*. New York: Horace Liveright, 1931. 242pp.

More about a personality than a place, this novel is a satirical attack on Bodenheim's former friend and fellow Chicago writer, Ben Hecht. Hecht had outraged Bodenheim by his caricature of him in the book *Count Bruga*. This work is set in the 1920s Chicago in which Hecht and Bodenheim were important members of the literati.

115. Bodenheim, Maxwell. *Sixty Seconds*. New York: Horace Liveright, 1929. 280pp.

Framed by the conceit that one's life passes before one's eyes in the final moments of mortality, Bodenheim presents the life story of convicted murderer John Musselman in the sixty seconds he has before the arrival of his executioner. Bodenheim conveys thirty-two-year-old Musselman's experiences as an example of the deleterious effects of prudery on society, claiming that in a society where sexuality is freely expressed Musselman would never have developed into a sociopath. The culprits in Bodenheim's account are sexually withholding women. With the exception of a few Texas and New York City scenes, the novel is set in impoverished Chicago neighborhoods, including Burnside and Roseland. Bodenheim traces Musselman's sexual history from his first experiences with a high school classmate, to visits within a few years to Chicago's red-light district, while continuing to have sex-free dates with girls of his social class. He falls in love with Elizabeth Harrison, a girl he saves from a mad dog. The two soon enroll in a Loop-based dancing and singing school with the hope of becoming vaudevillians. Only much later does Elizabeth reveal that she is one-eighth African-American. Although John eventually decides to ignore this aspect of her identity, when the Harrison family's neighbors discover Elizabeth has been dating a Caucasian, their threats drive the Harrisons out of town. Estranged from his family over his relationship with Elizabeth, John leaves Chicago to live as a hobo until he is picked up as a vagrant and forced to pick cotton. He later serves in the U.S. Army in World War I, works as a clerk, and then as a bouncer in New York City, where he violently kills a woman who had deceived him. In addition to sexuality, family dynamics, marriage, and gender roles, the novel presents the limitations of lower-class life.

116. Bodenheim, Maxwell. *A Virtuous Girl*. New York: Horace Liveright, 1930. 260pp.

Bodenheim uses his protagonist, Emmy Lou Filkins, to present his view of a virtuous girl, one who defies social convention to express her love sexually. As a seventeen-year-old, Emmy Lou Filkins is dating a nineteen-year-old Jewish boy, Dick Rosenstein, who she intends to marry. Her father owns a drug store near Fifty-fifth Street and Prairie Avenue and her mother aspires to upper-class gentility through adhering to high standards for social conduct. Free-spirited Emmy rejects her mother's code and is literally caught in the bushes with Rosenstein. In the aftermath, she is sent to an aunt in South Haven, Michigan. Then, disappointed in a flirtation with a popular music lyricist from Chicago, she flees to Kalamazoo and gets a job as a hotel chambermaid. She is soon infatuated with unemployed Elmer Reising who is seeking work at the hotel. Marginalized by Depression-era unemployment, they reject convention and only pretend to get married before living together. Later, still unemployed, they move to Chicago, and Emmy eventually visits her parents. She discovers that Dick Rosenstein had died, and in a *cri de coeur* response to her mother's assessment that he died a broken heart over Emmy, the girl defiantly asserts that she will henceforth love men as she chooses, without adhering to social convention. Except for a description of Derby Day in Washington Park in 1900, of the Refectory restaurant, and of the furnishings of the Filkins' apartment, the novel includes little physical description. However, the book does present the accepted sexual morality and gender roles of the first decades of the twentieth century.

117. Booth, Christopher Belvard. *Mr. Clackworthy*. New York: Chelsea House, 1926. 255pp.

Originally published in *Detective Story Magazine*, the main characters in these eight short stories are Amos Clackworthy and "The Early Bird," two Chicago grifters. Although the main focus is on the means by which they manipulate money out of people, 1920s Chicago is presented in enough detail to provide a backdrop.

118. Booth, Emma Scarr. *A Willful Heiress*. Buffalo, N.Y.: Charles Wells Moulton, 1892. 230pp.

Chicagoan Mercie Freeman is an affluent heiress who is preyed upon by Adolphus Pericles Montague, with the help of his sister Angelina Victoria Muggs. Deceived by the siblings' misrepresentation of themselves, Freeman marries Adolphus who gets control of all her assets. After the wedding, Freeman realizes that Montague is neither affluent, nor a gentleman; however, she is bound to him by their marriage vows. Montague eventually dies in a brawl, but not before spending all of Freeman's money. Emancipated from her marriage vows, and with no social expectations to meet, Freeman is able to marry for love. She chooses Sebastian Burness, a gardener, who has a lowly, but honorable, social status. Given the theme, the book is less concerned with physical description than in setting out the financial, legal, and social oppression of women in the late-nineteenth century.

119. Borden, Mary. *The Romantic Woman*. New York: Alfred A. Knopf, 1920. 347pp.

The unnamed protagonist of this first-person account reflects on the ways in which events and social attitudes from her youth in 1890s Chicago shaped her life. Now in her thirties, she lives in London during World War I, the wife of Captain Gilbert "Binky" Humphrey Fitzgerald Dawkins, the heir to a dukedom. In long flashbacks, she reflects on her childhood and youth in Chicago (renamed Iroquois here) where, from her parents and girlhood friends, Louise Bowers and Phyllis Day, she was introduced to social mores. The daughter of a wealthy industrialist and a mother committed to evangelical American Protestantism as presented by a charismatic minister, she observed the scandal that followed the divorce of Day's parents. The bulk of the novel deals with her relationship with Binky and how their marriage has been tested twice, once by the disclosure of his affair with an older woman before marriage (an affair that produced a child), and then by his renewed dalliance with Phyllis some years after their marriage. However, there is a lengthy description of Chicago in the 1890s that includes physical settings and presents values concerning social rank and gender roles. The protagonist and Binky return to Chicago for most of the last hundred pages of the novel. This is during the year 1909 and the city of that time is contrasted with the one the protagonist knew in her youth.

120. Borland, Kathryn Kilby and Helen Ross Speicher. *Good-by to Stony Crick*. Illustrated by Deanne Hollinger. New York: McGraw-Hill, 1974. 138pp.

In this book for children about the migration of Appalachian people to Chicago in the 1960s and 1970s, the Weatherhead family is forced to leave rural Kentucky after their house burns down and they realize that Appalachia can only offer continued poverty. The seven-member family (the five children are between six and nine-years-old, including a set of twins) find themselves sharing the upstairs of a small house with another Appalachian family of eight, with only one bathroom. Although Pa's difficulty in finding a job is an important plot element, most of the book is concerned with Jeremy Weatherhead's difficulties in school as he gets bullied by children expressing their parents' and schoolteachers' prejudices against the flood of Appalachian immigrants. Jeremy's only friend is a blind schoolteacher who lives by himself in one of the downstairs apartments. Later, he gets a new, tolerant schoolteacher who accepts diversity and even appreciates Ma's quilting, organizing a way for Ma to earn money through her sewing. In addition to regional prejudice toward Appalachian people, the book deals with racial prejudice.

121. Bowman, Heath. *All Your Born Days*. Indianapolis: Bobbs-Merrill, 1939. 348pp.

In this Depression-era novel, Allan Reed's life has been shaped by attitudes toward wealth. The son of the most prominent man in the fictional Midwestern town of Lawsonville, his mother had inherited money at the beginning of the 1920s boom years. She invested it with ease and watched it increase dramatically until she decides to live with her son, independently from her husband, in European cultural capitals. Reed was able to finish his studies at Princeton before his mother lost everything in the stock market crash and his social connections allow him to end his dangerous job of trucking bootleg liquor. After a South American venture that never materializes, he goes to Chicago in time for the 1933 World's Fair as the guest of his now wealthy Princeton roommate, George Andersen of a Chicago steel family. Reed is soon selling shares in one of George's companies that manufactures pre-fabricated steel houses and socializing with his wealthy friends. He even dates and marries an affluent society woman, Pat Ramsay. However, he never really feels rooted or entirely satisfied with his work until he returns to Lawsonville to visit his father, reconcile and feel re-connected to his hometown. Although the novel is set in Chicago and the city is used as a cultural symbol, physical setting is not emphasized and most scenes take place at social events, some of which are competitive bicycle races in which Allan participates.

122. Boyce, Neith. *Proud Lady*. New York: Alfred A. Knopf, 1923. 316pp.

This extended reflection on romantic love, gender roles, inherited ethnic traits, and social responsibility is set in a small town in Cooke County, outside Chicago. The city plays an important role as a center for entertainment and commerce for town residents. The "proud lady" of the title is Mary Lavinia Lowell who honors her promise to marry first-generation, Irish immigrant, Laurence Carlin, when he returns from the Civil War, even though, by that point, she is in love with minister Hilary Robertson. Even if she were not to honor her promise, however, she cannot imagine having the physical relationship with Robertson that married life would entail. Laurence studies law with the wealthy town judge, who takes him into his law office, goes with Mary and Laurence to Chicago when they marry, and establishes a suite of rooms for them in his opulent bachelor household. Throughout the novel Laurence makes trips to Chicago to conduct business, check on his real estate investments, and have liaisons with his mistress, whom he has established in a house. Mary makes allowances for many aspects of her husband's character, due to his Irish ancestry. One of the historical events that intrude on the plot is the 1871 Chicago fire. The townspeople see the red glow in the sky, cough on the smoke, and take in the refugees who have been burnt out of their homes. By the time of the novel's final dramatic scene Chicago has been rebuilt and developed into a city whose streets Mary is quickly driven through to get to the sickbed of her husband, ill with typhoid fever, in the house of his mistress. The novel introduces cultural values toward marriage, a woman's place in society, and ethnic traits, as well as presenting the dynamic between Chicago and its suburbs.

123. Boylan, Malcolm Stuart. *Tin Sword*. Boston: Little, Brown, 1950. 312pp.

In this humorous coming of age novel, Joshua Doty's military ancestry and physical characteristics enable a series of adventures that begin when he is a thirteen-year-old. Up to that time, son to a widowed mother, Victoria, who works as a Chicago journalist, Doty had been parked with his grandmother in Battle Creek, Michigan. At thirteen his mother brings him back into her life. She is a noted beauty and reporter with a wide acquaintanceship that includes such distinguished men as actor Otis Skinner, author Booth Tarkington, and publisher Edward Bok. On assignment in Bermuda, Victoria is embarrassed when he arrives, for her thirteen-year-old is six-feet tall with the broad-shouldered body of a twenty-one-year-old. Hoping to avoid gossip about her age, when the commander of a British navy steamship invites Doty to sail to New York, she eagerly grants permission. So begin Doty's adventures in New York, Battle Creek, and Chicago in which his demeanor, modeled on the military bearing of the general he wishes to become, eases his way to jobs, money, and respect from powerful individuals including generals, congressmen, and the president of the United States. Over the course of the one hundred pages of the novel that are set in Chicago, without his mother's help, Doty becomes a military authority for the *Chicago Morning Courier*, based on his representing himself as a lieutenant. He does become a lieutenant shortly after being drafted as an eighteen-year-old, at America's entrance into World War I. The early-twentieth-century Chicago of the book is a place of residence hotels and newsrooms and is filled with Irish and German immigrants who are frequently at odds with each other. A wealthy meat packer and an anarchist artist are two of the prominent Chicago characters.

124. Bradley, Mary Hastings. *Nice People Poison*. New York, London [and] Toronto: Longmans, Green, 1952. 216pp.
    In this murder mystery a lawyer is exposed to upper-class, suburban Chicagoans. As the youngest partner in his law firm, Nicholas Parr has never had to deal with members of the wealthy King family, the special clients of a senior partner. However, on a summer day when all the senior partners are out of town, Veronica King shows up late one afternoon demanding to change her will. Parr thinks King seems distressed and her decision to disinherit her seems husband odd, but he is under legal obligation to make the requested change. Only a few days later, King is dead and Parr is drawn into the mystery surrounding her death. The novel is mostly set in suburban Chicago and gives some indication of social life there, as well as describing upper-class households.

125. Bradley, Mary Hastings. *Old Chicago*. Illustrated by Edward C. Caswell. 4 vols. New York: David Appleton, 1933.
    The four volumes of this set, intended to teach young people the history of Chicago, consistently have romantic plotlines. Volume one, *The Fort*, dramatizes the 1812 fall of Fort Dearborn and the massacre of most of its inhabitants (the romance is between a British mercenary and an Indian woman). In *The Duel*, the second volume, Robert Heywood, a businessman, arrives in 1835 Chicago with his new bride, Barbara. Chicago is just beginning to resemble a town, even though there are still Indian cabins, a stockade, and mud everywhere. At a celebration, French trapper Pierre LeBrun flirts with Harriet and Robert's objections lead to plans for a duel. Trying to avoid bloodshed, Barbara speaks in private to LeBrun who agrees to leave town and never return. The story symbolizes the departure of the free-spirited French and Indians for the mercantile classes that would take their place and establish Chicago's more staid middle-class morality. In the third volume, *Debt of Honor*, Chicago in 1858 is a well-established city. The rivalry between two sisters, Judith and Jewel, serves as a metaphor for the crisis that would soon lead to the Civil War. In the final volume, *Metropolis*, the action covers the rapid changes from the opening of Crosby's Opera House in April 1865 to the 1893 World's Fair, as shown through the lives of Lockwood family members. Early in the novel William and Adeline Lockwood end their daughter Fanny's engagement to Walter Fielding because he was drunk during an afternoon of New Year's open

houses, attended a burlesque show, and may have had an overnight liaison with a showgirl. Romance never comes again to Fanny and in the 1890s, when the engagement of her niece is endangered by her fiancé's indiscretions, Fanny successfully helps the couple, revealing the social changes that have occurred since her youth.

126. Bradley, Mary Hastings. *Pattern of Three*. New York: David Appleton-Century, 1937. 305pp.

This romance novel is set in upper-class Chicago society. Middle-aged Richard Kendall falls in love with his twenty-four-year-old secretary Kay Hardy (a debutante fallen on hard times), divorces Eve, his wife of fifteen years, and marries Kay. Before the divorce, Eve schemes to remain in control by asserting the emotional needs of Richard's son Johnny. However, Johnny is killed in a boating accident. Then, Eve pretends to Kay that she is pregnant, and before the truth comes out, Kay decides to break-off contact with Richard and take a job in Manhattan. Supported by her husband's wealth and social codes, Eve is in a position of strength compared with Kay. However, her social status is clouded by her father's suicide and her family's slide into middle-class status. She tries to interest herself in the attractive, wealthy bachelor in pursuit of her, but she is truly in love with Richard. When Eve finally accedes to a divorce, she moves to Paris and as the Depression worsens, Richard must use most of his income to support her, although by this time he and Kay have two children. Then, Eve returns from abroad with terminal cancer and Kay must live in the Lake Forest house Richard gave Eve as part of the divorce to care for Eve in her final days. The novel details socializing at private clubs and expensive restaurants and interactions through which social status is conveyed. Although upper-class Chicago is affected by the Depression, as investment income falls, most changes are confined to giving up a second gardener, or one of several maids. As a social document, the book is of most interest for the attitudes toward romantic love and gender roles it conveys.

127. Bradley, Mary Hastings. *The Wine of Astonishment*. New York: David Appleton, 1919. 312pp.

In this romance novel a young couple's life is nearly destroyed by a mild indiscretion. Seventeen-year-old Jim Clarke is in love with Evelyn, a girl from his West Side neighborhood. He agrees to join his friends going to Chicago's red-light light district, thinking he will just be an observer at the scandalous sites. However, out of chivalry, Jim ends up escorting a girl to her residence and flees when he realizes she is a prostitute. Unfortunately, a young West Side reformer saw him and gossips to others about the incident. As a result Evelyn marries Christopher Stanley, even though she does not love him. In fact, although the marriage last six years, it is never consummated. Just as Evelyn is finally about to give herself to Christopher, he dies. A volunteer nurse, Evelyn meets Jim again while he is serving in World War I France. This time the two pledge their love for each other and their intent to marry. The novel describes the West Side at a time when the neighborhood's respectability slipped as residents moved to the suburbs. In addition to the physical setting, the novel presents the social networks based on neighborhood and church that would be less typical of a later urban society.

128. Brande, Dorothea Thompson. *My Invincible Aunt*. New York: Farrar and Rinehart, 1938. 376pp.

This mild satire of beauty culture and the American dream begins in 1930s Chicago. The story is told from the perspective of orphaned Stella Williams who has lived with her aunt, Kit

Willow, since her parents died. Kit, who was abandoned by her husband, has a modest apartment on the fifth-floor of a ten-unit, walk-up building eight minutes northeast of the Loop, and their apartment windows look directly onto the elevated train. After years of filling their days with rental library books, Kit decides they need a change. With the help of next-door neighbor, Dwyer Scatcherd, a college-educated chemist, she turns a family face cream recipe into a commercial product. Step by step, the product goes from a kitchen compound packaged in the parlor, to a factory-produced, commercially-packaged product. Kit's youthful appearance endorses the cream and she lectures nationwide, becoming the center of a movement. Kit, Stella, and Dwyer Scatcherd (with his maiden aunts) move into a furnished mansion on Ashland Boulevard and later to a grander one on Drexel Boulevard. Realizing that the cream's identification with Chicago will always hold back East Coast sales, the factory and the household later move to New York City. The Chicago neighborhoods described reflect Kit's increasing affluence and the accompanying changes in domestic life and possessions. Once Stella graduates from high school and begins dating she discovers Chicago's parks and restaurants. She later graduates from a finishing school, whose curriculum is detailed, and studies at the Art Institute. The novel also describes Chicago's commercial culture, detailing the way products are manufactured, promoted, and sold.

129. Brashler, William. *City Dogs*. New York: Harper and Row, 1976. 277pp.

Set in the 1970s in Uptown neighborhoods near Wrigley Field, many characters are involved in drug dealing and prostitution. Harry Lum, a man of Polish ethnicity who supports his meager, alcoholic existence with petty crime, gets recruited by pimp Jimmy del Corso and his pal, drug addict Ray Burl, to play a minor role in a store break-in. The break-in goes wrong and Lum is pursued by the police and by Corso and Burl since they think Lum has implicated them. In addition to Polish-Americans and Italian-Americans, the novel includes a number of Appalachian immigrants and Chicago policemen. The novel reveals contemporary attitudes toward women, various ethnic and economic minorities, and the general cultural importance of baseball, as well as the importance of the Chicago elevated train as a means of transportation and as a social space (particularly in the world beneath the tracks).

130. Brinig, Myron. *May Flavin*. New York: Farrar and Rinehart, 1938. 406pp.

The Chicago section of this novel (the first one hundred pages) is set in the Irish-American community of the 1880s (the entire novel spans the 1880s through World War I). May Flavin's mother, Nora, died when May was only a few years old and her older sister Madge has kept house ever since, supported by their father, Sean, a policeman. They live on Kiltie Street, the center of the Irish immigrant neighborhood in the 1880s, and the novel provides a rich description of the neighborhood, domestic furnishings, and food. Social relationships with neighbors and local business people play a large role in sixteen-year-old May's life. When Sean is shot in the line of duty the delivery of the body to the house, interactions with the undertaker, the wake, funeral, and burial are all described in detail. Two years later when eighteen-year-old May marries, the wedding preparations, the ceremony, and the party afterwards are all detailed. The novel gives a good indication of life in the Chicago Irish immigrant community in the 1880s, the limited employment opportunities, and the confines of gender roles for lower-class women.

131. Brooks, Gwendolyn. *Maud Martha*. New York: Harper, 1953. 180pp.

Through Maud Martha's experiences, Brooks captures what it was like to grow up as an African-American girl in 1940s Chicago. Maud copes with the death of family members, attends public entertainments, finishes school, gets a job, marries, and has a baby. A social club for African-Americans, houses, and apartments are all described, and characters include the people who inhabit each of the apartments in the building where Maud and her husband Paul live. The book openly presents the subtle expressions and effects of racial prejudice.

132. Brooks, Jerome. *The Big Dipper Marathon*. New York: Dutton, 1979. 134pp.

In this novel for children about the acceptance of physical disabilities, Horace Zweig has worn leg-braces since contracting polio as a seven-year-old. His family moved from Chicago to California when he was a toddler and he has always gone to special schools until very recently, when he started high school through a "main-streaming" program. Zweig has begun to chafe at his parents' protectiveness and when his aunt and uncle, Clara and Sol Cohen, invite him to visit them in Chicago, he swallows his anxiety and accepts. In Chicago, he spends most of his time with his cousin Bertram. The two visit the Museum of Science and Industry and, most importantly an amusement park where Zweig insists on riding a high-speed roller coaster only to get stuck in the car because of his leg braces. His visit to the city helps him understand the importance of accepting his limitations while realizing that he and his parents have developed emotional strengths that his relatives have not. The Chicago setting in the book includes little physical description.

133. Brooks, Jerome. *Make Me a Hero*. New York: Dutton, 1980. 152pp.

Roughly covering the years 1937 to 1944 in the life of Jacob Ackerman, who ages from seven to fourteen, this novel for children illustrates the effects of wartime fears, and exemplifies ways of coping. Ackerman lives with his family near Division Street and San Francisco Avenue. His three older brothers have been drafted and he is sick with worry that they will be killed. A witness to the violent, accidental death of one of his school friends, he can too easily visualize the deaths of his brothers. As a twelve-year-old, he seeks out adult responsibilities and gets a job embossing leather desk pads. He thinks the frightening open flames, the heat, and other physical discomforts will prepare him for the more intense discomforts of joining the army when he is older. On the job he meets Harry Katz, a boy his age who talks about preparing for his Bar Mitzvah. After losing faith through experiencing Russian pogroms, Ackerman's family has stopped practicing their religion, so Katz's religious life is new to Ackerman. Through the friendship, Ackermann decides to attend Hebrew school and use the Bar Mitzvah experience as another way to prepare for adulthood. In addition to depicting wartime Chicago, this book touches on male gender roles and Jewish religious life and culture.

134. Brooks, Jerome. *The Testing of Charlie Hammelman*. New York: Dutton, 1977. 129pp.

For high school junior Charlie Hammelman two events, the sudden death of his favorite teacher and a new requirement that all students must pass a swimming test before graduating, become the focus of fears and anxieties related to sex, death, and his self-image. Hammelman, who is overweight, cannot bring himself to be naked in the presence of other people. Through the course of this young adult novel, however, he devises various methods to help him overcome his anxieties. Charlie lives with his parents in an apartment and attends a public high school and his activities (ROTC, attending baseball games, having sodas at the neighborhood drugstore) reflect youth culture in early 1970s Chicago.

135. Brower, James Hattan. *The Mills of Mammon*. Illustrated by F. L. Weitzel and Henderson Howk. Joliet, Ill.: Murray, 1909. 491pp.

In this social reform novel, the author uses the family of Horace Holden, a Chicago industrialist who has accumulated a fortune through the sharp business practices he employs operating his steel mill, to attack a wide range of corruption and social evils including, white slavery, the hypocrisy of organized religion, and the vices of fraternal organizations. Horace, a widower, has two children, twenty-one-year-old Beatrice and twenty-five-year-old Joel. Growing up they were protected from the world outside the grounds of the Holden estate, and now, each of them engages with the world in very different ways. Beatrice, following in the steps of her deceased mother, is devoted to charity. Joel lives for pleasure, engaging in casual sexual relationships with chorus girls, while also enjoying the life of a society club man accepted at the best houses and invited to society social events. He disdains Beatrice's activities and convinces his father to stop funding them, which he does since he thinks she should concentrate on finding a husband. One of the households Beatrice frequents is that of John Bulman, a worker her father fired for promoting Socialism. Bulman claims Beatrice' charitable activity is worthless, for the root of poverty is the capitalist system. In addition to the Holden and Bulman households, Brower uses the story of the Jed Holcomb family to explore organized religion, and that of Estella Davis to illustrate the corruption of an innocent country girl through white slavery (one of the beneficiaries of her enslavement is Joel). Although when her father dies, Beatrice is primary legatee of her father's estate, the reader is left with the realization that it is unlikely that money alone will lead to social change in a corrupt political and economic system.

136. Brown, Frank London. *The Myth Maker*. Chicago: Path Press, 1969. 179pp.

This attempt to present the insidious racism of the 1950s is set on the South Side of Chicago. Ernest Day, an African-American absorbed by the life of the mind, took advantage of his modest opportunities and became a postal worker, married, and had a daughter. Unable to reconcile himself to the failures of a society where racial prejudice is openly tolerated, and feeling betrayed by the Western intellectual tradition, he left his job and family to work as a manual laborer and, later, to write liner notes for a jazz record label. Finding no alternative to the dominant white culture, he finally strangles a man as a way to vent his frustration and make a statement (a scholarly, gentle, man can be so deeply damaged by a racist society that he can perform such an act). Day performs the act ineptly and quickly realizes the wrong-headedness of his "statement." He is soon pursued both by a blackmailer and a corrupt policeman who wants him to deal drugs for a small percentage of the take. The novel, set in the impoverished areas along Fifty-eighth Street in Chicago is a powerful statement of the human cost of racial prejudice. A few area businesses are mentioned, including Dakota's Bar and Morrie's Record Mart.

137. Brown, Frank London. *Trumbull Park; a Novel*. Chicago: Henry Regnery, 1959. 432pp.

This novel addresses racial prejudice and violence in 1950s Chicago. When the Chicago Housing Authority finally helps Buggy and Helen Martin move from their tenement apartment, it is only because they have agreed to live in the formerly all-white neighborhood of Trumbull Park. The reaction of their new neighbors is swift, unpleasant, and prolonged, and includes a brick through their window and a snake in their mailbox. The novel is particularly strong in presenting the emotions of the Martins and their sense of helplessness in the face of unreasoning hatred.

138. Brown, Fred H. *For One Dollar's Worth*. Chicago, 1893. 177pp.

One of the longest works in this book of short stories, entitled "Listen to my Tale of Whoa" deals with the results of an experiment to hypnotize Chicagoans, those "denizens of the 'Wile and Wooly West,'" by using a chair to administer magnetism (pp. 45-86). Among the citizens are a retired sewing machine salesman, a beautiful girl from the South Side, and a professor of music.

139. Brown, Fredric. *Compliments of a Fiend*. A Guilt Edged Mystery. New York: Dutton, 1950. 256pp.

When his Uncle Ambrose, a fellow employee of the Starlock Detective Agency, does not show up at the rooming house where they live, Ed Hunter becomes worried. As time passes, strange comments made by other acquaintances at the rooming house begin to trouble him, and then another resident who worked for an insurance company and was an amateur astrologer, is found murdered. The culprits are involved in the numbers racket and the way the racket works is explained. Settings include restaurants and nightclubs and rooming house life is presented in detail.

140. Brown, Fredric. *Death Has Many Doors*. New York: Dutton, 1951. 215pp.

The uncle and nephew detective team, Ed and Am Hunter, characters used by Brown in a number of mysteries, refuse to accept twenty-two-year-old Sally Doerr as a client, because she seems to be psychotic when she wants to hire them to protect her from Martians. However, twelve hours later Sally is dead and the two receive a telephone call from someone who identifies himself as a Martian. Then, Sally's sister Dorothy is also found dead. Although the deaths could be natural, the circumstances are mysterious. Electrical engineering, uranium, and "mentalism" are all important to the plot. In addition to the Near North Side, the Rogers Park neighborhood serves as a setting and there are descriptions of apartment furnishings and restaurants.

141. Brown, Fredric. *The Fabulous Clipjoint*. New York: Dutton, 1947. 224pp.

The first in a series of murder mysteries featuring investigators Ed Hunter and his Uncle Ambrose, here eighteen-year-old Ed gets Ambrose's help in solving the murder of his own father, Wally. After pursuing leads that point alternately to Ed's stepmother, Madge, and his stepsister, Gardie, the two uncover a connection between Wally and a gang of bank robbers. In the course of the novel, worldly Ambrose, most recently employed by a traveling circus, details the adventurous life of Ed's father before he settled down to become a lithographer. Ambrose quickly becomes Ed's mentor, teaching him to read human nature to get information and to consider what you might want from others. Under his tutelage, Ed becomes more confident, has sex with a glamorous "gun moll," and gives up his printer's apprenticeship for a life on the road with Ambrose, hoping to follow his true ambition of becoming a big band trombonist. Ed and Ambrose pursue leads through a working-class Chicago filled with apartment hotels and saloons. As he introduces Ed to the world, Ambrose also provides a good deal of information to the reader about 1940s Chicago.

142. Brown, Fredric. *The Late Lamented*. New York: Dutton, 1959. 192pp.

Ben Starlock, the owner of the private detective firm where Ed and Ambrose Hunter got their start, refers a case to them. One of Starlock's employees, Wanda Rogers, is the daughter of the deceased Jason Rogers, former seven-term treasurer of Freeland, Illinois. After Jason was run down by a car, an audit found forty six thousand dollars missing. Jason's bonding agency believes Wanda knows the whereabouts of the missing money and Starlock hires the Hunters to investigate.

During the course of the novel, visits to restaurants, nightclubs, and a gambling parlor are described as well as the inmates of the boarding house where Ed rents a room. All of the settings are on Chicago's Near North Side.

143. Brown, Fredric. *Mrs. Murphy's Underpants*. New York: Dutton, 1963. 185pp.

In this detective novel, Ed Hunter, and his uncle, Ambrose Hunter, are hired by Vincent Dolan to protect his family. Vincent lives only a few blocks from the office of the detective agency owned and operated by the Hunters on the Near North Side. The Dolans live in a house with a modest exterior that is luxurious on the inside, with furnishings paid for by Vincent's clandestine income from operating a gambling syndicate. Although the Hunters make it clear that they believe that compulsive gambling is just as destructive as alcoholism; they take the attitude that nothing is innately wrong with making a bet now and then, just as nothing is innately wrong with drinking. So they have no compunctions about taking the case, particularly since Ed is interested in Dolan's beautiful daughter, Angela. The novel describes Chicago neighborhoods, restaurants, apartments, and gambling parlors.

144. Brown, Helen Dawes. *Two College Girls*. Boston: Houghton Mifflin, 1886. 325pp.

The women's college, in which almost this entire novel for young adults is set, is not located in Chicago. However, the city is a frequent reference point and two chapters are set there. Edna Howe defies the claims of her family that college is a waste of money for girls with the help of her mother, who aids her with funds from a modest inheritance. A serious student, Edna initially finds her roommate, Rosamond Mills, the daughter of a Chicago lumber tycoon, frivolous. When Edna's father dies unexpectedly, her school career is threatened. It is then that Rosamond's complexity emerges as she gets her father's permission to secretly use part of her allowance to pay Edna's fees (the school will present the money to Edna as a scholarship). Although Edna never learns the secret, she discovers Rosamond's admirable character and by their senior year the two are best friends. Rosamond invites Edna to the Mills' Chicago residence for Christmas, where she meets and falls in love with Rosamond's brother Jack. Uninterested in sight-seeing and dancing Edna is interested in the family lumber mill, which she tours with Jack. After Jack's leg is broken at the mill, Edna reads aloud to him and listens to his stories about college and the Chicago fire. By the end of the novel, the two are engaged, although Edna will first teach for a few years before getting married. Throughout the novel conversations reference membership and social precedence in Chicago society. The girls in Edna's graduating class have a wide range of career goals: chemist in an uncle's dye factory, journalist, novelist, and physician, as well as teacher, rounding out the novel's implicit argument for college attendance for girls.

145. Browne, Howard. [John Evans, pseud.]. *Halo in Blood: A Paul Pine Mystery*. Indianapolis: Bobbs-Merrill, 1946. 245pp.

In this hard-boiled detective novel of the 1940s, Chicago investigator Paul Pine happens upon a funeral attended by only twelve clergymen. The event is odd, but seemingly innocuous, until people, including a police officer, begin asking Pine questions. Gambling rings and murder become the focus once Pine is hired by a rich man to find damaging information about his daughter's thuggish boyfriend.

146. Browne, Howard [John Evans, pseud.]. *Halo in Brass: A Paul Pine Mystery.* Indianapolis: Bobbs-Merrill, 1949. 222pp.

Another in a series of books featuring Chicago detective Paul Pine, in this work Pine has been hired by anxious Lincoln, Nebraska, parents to find their daughter, Laura Fremont, who they suspect is somewhere in the city. The case develops into something more than tracing a missing person as Pine uncovers bribery, gambling, prostitution, and, most surprisingly, lesbianism. Although the book includes descriptions of 1940s Chicago, it is, perhaps, most notable for revealing attitudes toward homosexuality that were current at that time.

147. Browne, Howard [John Evans, pseud.]. *Halo for Satan.* Indianapolis: Bobbs-Merrill, 1948. 214pp.

Even though this novel is another in the author's series featuring Paul Pine, in this case the hard-boiled detective has a much more genteel assignment and a more refined client than usual. Pine is hired by Chicago's Bishop McManus to prove that a manuscript offered for sale to him for $25,000,000 and supposedly written by Jesus of Nazareth is a fraud. The story is very firmly set in 1940s Chicago.

148. Browne, Howard. *The Taste of Ashes.* New York: Simon, 1957. 282pp.

Paul Pine, a former investigator for the Illinois state attorney's Chicago office turned private detective, is featured in a series of Browne's detective mysteries. When socialite Serena Delastone wants to hire him to protect her daughter from a blackmailer, Pine finds her dictatorial attitude impossible and refuses the job. Pine is drawn into the case nonetheless when the detective Delastone hires, an old acquaintance named Sam Jellco, disappears and he is hired by Mrs. Jellco to investigate. He finds Sam dead and his murder investigation soon leads him back to the Delastones and Olympic Heights. He discovers that the police department there is controlled by Serena's husband, the Colonel, who is chairman of the board of commissioners. Pine's investigation takes him to offices and restaurants in Chicago and there are descriptions of furnishings and food, however the novel primarily focuses on Pine making snappy comebacks to those in authority and flirting with beautiful women.

149. Browne, Howard and Boris O'Hara. *The St. Valentine's Day Massacre.* New York: Dell, 1967. 158pp.

The novelization of a work that was originally a play and later a movie of the same name (Twentieth Century-Fox, 1967), the book is tightly focused on a few famous gangsters (including Al Capone) and the events surrounding the notorious 1929 shootout.

150. Brunner, Bernard. *The Face of Night.* New York: Frederick Fell, 1967. 235pp.

The 1960s Chicago of this novel is plagued by illegal drugs. Two police detectives, one African-American and the other Caucasian, must penetrate the world of drug lords, informants, and junkies as they investigate the drug overdose death of a young African-American woman. The drug world proves too dangerous even for these representatives of law and order and one meets with a violent death and the other resigns from the police force. The lawless Chicago described in this novel is primarily that of ghettos controlled by violent drug sellers and filled with derelicts, enslaved by their drug addiction. In addition to the social toll of illegal drug use, the novel deals with issues of race.

151. Brunner, Bernard. *The Golden Children*. New York: Frederick Fell, 1970. 350pp.

This novel about racial prejudice and hypocrisy is primarily set in an imaginary, all-white, Chicago suburb, Elm Village, however significant portions of the book are set in Chicago's South Side and the relationship between the city and its suburbs is a major theme. At the center of the story is the affair between white Clare Simmons and black Marcus Coleman. Clare's father, the Reverend John Simmons, has been a minister in Elm Village for forty years and has preached tolerance. Coleman lives in the South Side and works in an African-American boys' club. He meets Clare after he is injured thwarting an arson attempt at the boys' club and gets treatment at the hospital at which Clare volunteers. As Clare and Coleman's romance develops, Elm Village experiences a crisis when an African-American purchases a house and the town believes desegregation has begun. Many residents have already fled from urban racial unrest and most of the town's leaders have tried to keep Elm Village white. One leader is Clare's employer, the owner of a real estate firm, who believes property values will disintegrate. The town's newspaper publisher starts a lonely fight for racial tolerance Clare's father abandons his stance when he is told of Clare and Coleman's relationship. Through the young couple's story, a sophisticated take on racial hatred develops by the end of the book. Chicago is a major presence in the novel. Many of Elm Village's residents are commuters who are exposed on a daily basis to urban problems they thought they were escaping by moving to the suburbs. Furthermore, Clare's explorations of the South Side with Coleman, document social activities, cultural attitudes, and physical settings.

152. Brunner, Bernard. *Six Days to Sunday*. New York: McGraw-Hill, 1975. 307pp.

This novel about the culture of professional sports and the dynamics of male friendship is set in Chicago. The quarterback of the fictional Chicago Stags football team, Chip Hughes, had been the team's star player for years. However, even he realizes that he is aging and his arm is weakening. Then, the coaching staff and team management decide to replace him with a rookie. The inexperience of the replacement and Hughes' efforts to regain his star role divide the team and Hughes old friends (including some of the women with whom he has slept) find ways to sap the vitality of the new quarterback and he loses game after game. Finally, when Hughes is given a starting lineup chance, he intentionally plays poorly. Although most of this novel is set inside locker rooms and stadiums, the sporting culture is firmly rooted in Chicago. The novel includes homophobic and racist situations and language that reveals a good deal about the culture of the time.

153. Bryant, James McKinley. *Sporting Youth*. New York: Alfred H. King, 1931. 287pp.

In this novel about professional boxing in Chicago, the sport is intimately linked with organized crime. When college athlete Jimmy Burton gets into a speakeasy fight he catches gang boss, Giorgio Fabrizzi's attention. Enthused about a boxer who is "a nice clean-cut American" rather than the typical immigrant, Fabrizzi convinces Burton to turn professional. The gangster secures a trainer and supports Burton until his first fight. When Burton starts boxing, Chicago's 1920s gang wars are at their height, here involving recognizable figures with altered names, and Burton rationalizes his involvement with Fabrizzi. The woman he begins dating, Eleanor Rice, becomes part of his rationale, as he sets the goal of winning enough prize money to settle down with her. However, she becomes frustrated with his career choice and breaks off the relationship. Despite all of Fabrizzi's help, Burton never makes it as a prize-fighter and by the end of the novel he realizes his mistake in not giving up boxing for Eleanor. Only partially set in Chicago, the novel details the cars, food, women, and socializing of 1920s sporting circuit figures.

154. Buck, Pearl S. *Command the Morning*. New York: John Day, 1959. 317pp.

In this work of historical fiction, Buck tells the story of the Manhattan Project, utilizing historical figures like Burton Hall, Enrico Fermi, and Ernst Weiner. She also includes characters that are composites, like Jane Earl, and changes names (Leo Szilard becomes Professor Szigny) to present feminist themes and anti-nuclear sentiments. One of the main characters is a young scientist named Stephen Coast who is from Chicago. Although the novel is set in Oak Ridge and Los Alamos, Chicago plays an important role as the setting for early chain reaction tests conducted by Coast. Buck is most concerned with presenting personalities, scientific theories, politics, and historical information and physical settings are of little interest.

155. Budd, Lillian. *April Harvest*. New York: Duell, Sloan and Pearce, 1959. 309pp.

In this third volume of Budd's story of Swedish immigrants, Sigrid, the seventeen-year-old daughter of Karl and Elin, has been orphaned since her father was killed saving a boy from runaway horses. The boy's family wants to pay for high-school valedictorian Sigrid's university education, but she will not place such a burden on the struggling family and the book describes her economic and emotional struggles to support herself. Her deceased parents' friends and neighbors in West Chicago (in an area called "Calico Row") provide advice and practical assistance. She begins a correspondence with her grandmother in Sweden and takes Swedish language classes to learn what her parents did not teach their American daughter. As with earlier books in the trilogy, local and national events have a major impact on Sigrid's life. She is touched most immediately by the sinking of the excursion ship, *Eastland*, in the Chicago River when a fellow passenger who does not survive, places an infant into Sigrid's arms. Sigrid takes responsibility for the baby boy, Michael, and her friends help her care for the boy and follow her dreams as she works as a stenographer. When her father's writings, tracing the history of Chicago, are published as a book they win a prize and Sigrid uses the money to travel to Sweden. She learns from her grandmother about her heritage, but when an affluent nobleman proposes marriage, she realizes her true love is in Chicago where she will create a life that blends her Swedish heritage and her identity as an American. The book, roughly covering the years from 1915 to 1926, is filled with details that convey working-class life in Chicago.

156. Budd, Lillian. *Land of Strangers*. Philadelphia: Lippincott, 1953. 369pp.

The second in a trilogy of books about Swedish immigration, Karl Christianson and Elin Eklund meet in Sweden and separately leave for the United States. Arriving in New York City, Karl rejects the place as unrepresentative of the United States and heads for the Midwest. He settles in Chicago, works on the construction site of the Columbian Exposition and becomes a thorough enthusiast of the city. Elin also arrives in New York City but stays when she finds a job. When she gets to Chicago to bury her brother she finds Karl mourning the corpse. She gives up her plan of returning to New York and Karl convinces her to marry him. The last half of the book recounts their life in Chicago's immigrant community as they struggle financially but win friends among their neighbors who make their burdens manageable. Karl dreams of securing his family's financial future and he tries one unprofitable scheme after another, including investing in gold stocks and trying to grow ginseng. Elin is patient with his failures, loving him for his charitableness and his concern for his family's well-being. As the couple moves around in the Chicago metropolitan area, each neighborhood is described. Local and national news events (the Iroquois Theatre fire and the assassination of President McKinley) are included as well as discussions of political and economic matters that affect them. The family's greatest crisis arrives when they have a son who eventually dies of illness (they already have a daughter, Sigrid). At the end of the novel Karl too dies, heroically saving a boy from a runaway team of horses. The novel makes constructs the reality of immigrants, including their negotiation over recasting their identities, the physical aspects of economic hardship, and the painful constraints of ethnic stereotypes. It also touches on gender roles and presents a wide range of male characters who favor the enfranchisement of women.

157. Burgoyne, Leon E. *Ensign Ronan, a Story of Fort Dearborn*. Philadelphia: Winston, 1955. 184pp.
        This work of historical fiction focuses on Ensign George Ronan, a real-life, minor character who arrived at Fort Dearborn in 1811, fleshing out his story beyond the very basic historical record. Many other better-known historical personages are included in the story that focuses on the siege and final massacre that occurred at the fort. Ronan, though wounded, survives.

158. Burnett, Frances (Eliza) Hodgson. *Two Little Pilgrims' Progress: A Story of the City Beautiful*. New York: Charles Scribner's Sons, 1895. 191pp.
        In this children's book celebrating the virtues of hard work combined with spiritual awareness, the lives of two orphaned children are transformed by a visit to the Columbian Exposition. Margaret "Meg" Macleod and Robin "Rob" Macleod are twelve-year-old twins whose parents died when they were nine-year-olds. Their schoolteacher father had taught them to love reading and the life of the mind. Living with their only surviving relative, Mrs. Matilda Jennings, a widow with a large Illinois farm, is very different. Mrs. Jennings says she has no time for anything beyond caring for their physical needs; she does not even send them to school. The children work hard without complaining, but they also read and tell each other stories. One of the few books in the house is Paul Bunyan's *Pilgrim's Progress* and Meg begins to identify the Columbian Exposition with the book's "Celestial City." With savings earned in small-change from extra chores, they plan a trip to the fair within their means that includes sleeping outdoors and eating only hard-boiled eggs collected from their chickens. They interpret their adventure aloud through the lens of *Pilgrim's Progress* and are overheard by John Holt, a wealthy landowner whose young wife died in childbirth. He befriends them and when Aunt Matilda turns up to view the agricultural implements display, Holt easily persuades her to let him adopt the children. Many aspects of the exposition are described, including the event's importance in the history of Chicago.

159. Burnett, W. R. (William Riley). *Dark Hazard*. New York: Harper and Brothers, 1933. 295pp.
        In this Depression-era novel, the main character tries to overcome a gambling problem. Jim Turner had owned six racehorses before losing them in a faro game. Marg [*sic*] Mayhew met him while we worked and lived at the Bellport Racetrack in Barrowville, Ohio. Pledging to go straight, he married Marg and the couple moved to Chicago where they live in the Northland apartment hotel near the intersection of Lawrence and Kenmore Streets where Turner works as a night desk clerk. They are barely getting by and his wife's parents in Barrowville need help with medical expenses. When Jim gets fired after an altercation with one of the hotel's guests, things begin to look desperate, but only for a few hours. Turner meets an old acquaintance and is offered a job at a California dog track. Probably through the influence of his mob-connected friends, he also wins three thousand dollars at a gambling parlor and his days of going straight are over. More than eighty pages of the book are set in Chicago and they provide rich detail of the intimacy of life in an apartment hotel with its inventory of characters that includes a hypnotist, several barbers, and

some professional gamblers. There are also extended and offensive descriptions of the African-American man who takes care of the hotel boiler.

160. Burnett, W. R. (William Riley). *Iron Man*. New York: Lincoln MacVeagh, Dial Press, 1930. 312pp.

Professional boxing, racism, and gambling are at the center of this Depression-era novel. "Iron Man" Coke Mason, a prizefighter, abandoned by his chorus girl wife when he cannot afford to buy her an automobile, lives in a rooming house on Sheridan Road with his sparring partner George Regan, across the street from the Olympic Athletic Club. Desperate to attract attention and get a break in his career, Mason agrees to fight Prince Pearl, an African-American, when no other white man will. Mason is outraged when two gambling touts who offer him five thousand dollars and a match with the reigning middleweight champion if he will let Prince Pearl throw the fight. Mason wins the Pearl fight with a knockout and goes on to win several more Chicago fights before advancing to New York City where he wins the middleweight title. Most of the book is set in New York City, but the Chicago sections give some sense of the boxing scene there.

161. Burnett, W. R. (William Riley). *Little Caesar*. New York: Dial Press, 1929. 308pp.

Set in a 1920s Chicago plagued by corruption and crime, this innovative narrative is told from the perspective of a gangster and uses the patois of his world, instead of being told from the standpoint of police detectives or private investigators. Rico Bandellow rises, step-by-step, to become the most powerful of Chicago gang leaders. Bandellow is unusual in that he engages only in crime that increases his power; he does not engage in random violence. A worldwide best-seller, the book was made into a motion picture of the same name in 1931 (Warner Bros. Pictures) that made Edward G. Robinson famous and established his niche for portraying gangsters. The Chicago setting is mostly that of Little Italy around Halsted Street and includes Prohibition-era speakeasies and describes subterfuges used to preserve their secrecy. The novel touches on ethnic prejudices, particularly between Irish-Americans and Italian-Americans.

162. Burnett, W. R. (William Riley). *Little Men, Big World*. New York: Alfred A. Knopf, 1951. 308pp.

Chicago in the 1950s is filled with corrupt policemen and city officials who protect the gambling syndicates. Only investigative journalists are still battling organized crime. Ben Reisman, a senior reporter, has become a syndicated columnist and moved his family to the suburbs, but he still longs for his edgier days reporting on gangsters. He eagerly follows a lead concerning corruption in high office, even though he suspects the information is intentionally misleading. As he investigates the gambling syndicate run by "Ark," he gets support from maverick city commissioner, Thomas Stark, and follows a trail that leads to corrupt Judge Greet. Burnett details newsroom activities, reportorial methods, and the activities of gambling bosses and their foot soldiers. Interestingly, in this book, the recent immigrants involved in crime are from Syria and rural areas of the United States, like Arkansas.

163. Burnett, W. R. (William Riley). *The Silver Eagle*. New York: Lincoln MacVeagh, Dial Press, 1931. 310pp.

Meat packers of an earlier period were able to transcend their impoverished origins and crude manners to become members of Chicago's high society. However, Frank Harworth, a 1920s nouveau riche, who made his money by providing, alcohol and low entertainment in his nightclubs, cannot rise above his origins. In fact, his mansion, luxury automobile, and tailored clothes make him somewhat ridiculous. However, he keeps struggling to make ever more money, thinking that he will be able to buy his way into society. When he forms an alliance with a gangster, to make even more money, his downfall is guaranteed. In addition to the gangster culture that is at the center of his other books, here Burnett tries to portray aspects of Chicago's high society. Incidentally, he presents crude racial and ethnic stereotypes, particularly concerning Jewish people.

164. Burnham, Clara Louise. *Instead of the Thorn.* Boston: Houghton Mifflin, Riverside Press Cambridge, 1916. 390pp.

Most of this society novel is physically set near Portland, Maine, however the main characters are all Chicagoans and Chicago plays an important role in the novel. Linda Barry, a recent college graduate is being seriously courted by two young men while living in the family mansion on Michigan Avenue. Her father, Lambert Barry, is the founder and president of Barry and Company, a banking and investment firm. One of her courtiers is wealthy but fatuous and the other is Bertram King, a serious and clever young man whose intimacy and influence with her father, Linda resents. When Lambert dies of a heart attack after a firm in which he had heavily invested company money fails, Linda assumes that King had promoted the investment. While the rest of the Barry family appreciates King's efforts to save the company and preserve Lambert Barry's reputation, Linda bears her grudge. Her paternal aunt, Belinda Barry, gets her to the family home in seaside Maine and the setting, weather, and people relieve Linda's grief and bitterness. After learning that King had advised against the bad investment, he arrives in Maine, suffering from nervous exhaustion over having to manage company matters. Linda welcomes him and, by the end of the book, it is clear they will marry. In the Chicago sections of the novel, the characters socialize at the University Club, the South Side Club, have tea in private houses, and stroll around the lagoons in Lincoln Park. Although Chicago's location on Lake Michigan is celebrated by some characters, the city's upper-classes escape when the season is hot and when suffering from ill health, repair to rural settings like Maine and Colorado.

165. Burnham, Clara Louise. *Sweet Clover: A Romance of the White City.* Boston: Houghton Mifflin, 1894. 411pp.

In this work of romantic fiction, the women are long-suffering, but have affluent men to protect them. Clover Bryant faces many challenges. Her mother, for nine years a widow, is losing her health and income. Clover protects Mrs. Bryant from worrying and maintains a pleasant household for her slightly younger sister, Mildred, and much younger siblings, Frank and Elsie. She also tries to ensure that her sisters and brother will finish school. The only support she and her family get is the friendship of Mr. Van Tassel, who had known Clover's father and mother when they were all living in Hyde Park years ago. A widower, Van Tassel is now wealthy. However, he has not dropped the Bryants and has even thought his son Jack, just graduated from Harvard, might marry Clover or Mildred. When Jack begs off, Mr. Van Tassel proposes to Clover. She accepts since she knows he is good and realizes the marriage is the only solution to her family's financial woes. Jack is incensed by the engagement, believing Clover to be the instigator. In response, he leaves for Europe. He returns to learn that tragedy has pursued Clover. First, Frank and Elsie died of scarlet fever, then her mother died, and Mr. Van Tassel, a tireless promoter of Chicago's selection to be host of the World's Fair, who made stressful trips to Washington, is gravely ill. He dies before Jack can get back to Chicago and Jack blames Clover for his father's death. Over time Jack's relatives convince him of Clover's goodness and he follows her to California where she is recovering her health. As the World's Fair begins, Clover returns to Chicago, and amid descriptions that convey the excitement and romance of the fairgrounds, Jack and Clover fall in love and Mildred becomes engaged to Jack's cousin Paige. In addition to the descriptions of the fair, the novel presents upper-middle-class concerns about proper sentiment, filial devotion, and material well-being, as well as revealing the narrow choices available to women of the time.

166. Burnham, David. *This Our Exile*. New York: Charles Scribner's Sons, 1931. 423pp.

In this family novel, the Eatons deal with the serious illness and death of the forty-six-year-old patriarch, Ralph Eaton, who has built a banking fortune. The story is told from the perspective of son James, who has been studying architecture at Princeton for two years and decided to give it up in favor of music. Eaton's other son, Fred, has married Peter, the daughter of Eaton's best friend, Roy Grayson, and, having studied at Cambridge, is now living in Paris. Everyone had expected Peter to marry James and why she did not is one of the major plot elements, as is the relationship between James and his brother. While James is in Chicago he comes close to marrying Grayson's other daughter, Ruth, while hoping that he will still win the hand of Peter, who has left Fred. These troubled romantic relationships prompt digressions on the nature of love, and the obligations of marriage. However, consideration of what should be the true occupation of the "leisure" class is another major theme. Despite the importance of Chicago in their family history, Fred and his mother Mrs. Eaton depart for Paris after Ralph's death and James returns to Princeton, and will probably continue to live on the East Coast.

167. Burroughs, Edgar Rice. *The Efficiency Expert*. Originally published in *Argosy All-Story Weekly*, October 8 through October 29, 1921. Kansas City, Mo.: House of Greystoke, 1966. 84pp.

In this coming of age story, Chicago is the place where a young man can get a start in life. Although Jimmy Torrance is the son of the owner and proprietor of Beatrice Corn Mills in Beatrice, Nebraska, his father shames him when he is graduating from an East Coast college. He is the most popular man in his class with honors for baseball and boxing, yet he has a barely passable scholastic record and seems ill-prepared for adult life. Torrance decides to prove himself in Chicago. Although he has great difficulties getting even a modest job, his good character, pleasing manner, and attractive appearance win him friends and respect. Over time he works in a large store's hosiery department, as a waiter in a cabaret, and as a milkman. Finally, through the suggestion of his acquaintance, Edith Hudson, he gets a job as an efficiency expert at the International Machine Company on the strength of reading a second-hand book on industrial operations. He discovers that the assistant general manager, the future son-in-law of the company's owner, is defrauding the firm, sees evil-doers brought to justice, is cleared of a false murder charge, and wins the affections of an attractive young woman. Burroughs references specific areas of the city, but the novel is of most interest for portraying Chicago as a place for a young man of strong character to get a start in the world.

168. Burroughs, Edgar Rice. *The Girl from Farris's*. Originally published in *All-Story Magazine* (Frank A. Munsey, 1916). Kansas City, Mo.: House of Greystoke, 1965. 160pp.

In this novel about Chicago's white slave trade, Maggie Lynch (her name is later changed to June Lathrop), is found climbing down a fire escape outside Abe Farris's saloon by a police detective. Although she claims that she has been held at the saloon against her will, the police are only interested in her as a witness to a murder. She narrowly avoids being implicated in the murder when the grand jury foreman believes her account of being held against her will. He subsequently offers to help her and she is inspired to reform her life. However, because of her past, she has great difficulty finding work, changes her name, and by a coincidence, ends up working in the firm of the jury foreman, although he is abroad and unaware of this fact. When a crime is committed in the office and her true identity is revealed she is considered a collaborator and is once again narrowly vindicated. Although the melodramatic work references aspects of Chicago social problems and political corruption, it conveys little in the way of physical setting.

169. Butterworth, Hezekiah. *In the Boyhood of Lincoln*. New York: David Appleton, 1892. 266pp.

Butterworth presents factual information about Illinois history in this work of historical fiction that focuses on the experiences of itinerant minister, Jaspar the Parable, during the period when Illinois is seeking statehood. In addition to meeting the Lincoln family in Pigeon Creek, he stays long enough near Fort Dearborn to meet the son of John Kinzie, founder of Chicago.

170. Butterworth, Hezekiah. *Zigzag Journeys in the White City; With Visits to the Neighboring Metropolis*. Boston: Estes and Lauriat, 1894. 320pp.

Ephraim Marlowe and his son Manton travel to the 1893 Columbian Exposition and explore the fair, as well as Chicago. Ephraim makes the trip to attend the Peace Conference held in conjunction with the fair and Manton, an amateur folklorist, attends the folklore congress held in the Palace of Art. In addition to descriptions of the fairgrounds and the city, the book includes detailed accounts of the meetings in which Ephraim and Manton participate.

171. Butterworth, Hezekiah. *Zigzag Journeys on the Mississippi from Chicago to the Islands of the Discovery*. Boston: Estes and Lauriat, 1892. 319pp.

A study trip of an advanced Spanish class is the excuse for much expository writing on the history of the United States, the Mississippi River Valley, the history of Chicago and background on the planning of the Columbian Exposition.

172. Butterworth, W. E. (William Edmund). *Leroy and the Old Man*. New York: Four Winds Press, 1980. 154pp.

Although much of this young adult novel is set in Pass Christian, Mississippi, near New Orleans, Chicago is a major presence throughout. Seventeen-year-old LeRoy works in a Chicago restaurant, and lives with his mother in a housing project. After he witnesses Wolfs' [*sic*] gang members attack Mrs. Casson at the housing project, the police want him to testify. When the gang threatens him and destroys his mother's apartment, she sends him to live with his grandfather, Aaron Chambers, in Pass Christian. His grandfather thinks he must testify, but also wants him to permanently relocate and become his partner in his shrimping business. LeRoy, Sr., who had abandoned his family and dodged child support payments, appears in New Orleans, alerted by his underworld connections (he is a numbers runner). Since Mrs. Casson has died, charges against the Wolfs are much more serious. Fearing that his son will be killed, LeRoy, Sr. wants to take him to New York City to hide. LeRoy must decide between his father's worldview in which criminals are in control and his grandfather's moral universe in which one must behave honorably and fight criminality. In the end, LeRoy returns to testify. The novel contrasts the social networks that aid LeRoy's grandfather in his business and his life, and Chicago where one is left to fend for him or herself.

173. Cahill, Holger. *Profane Earth*. New York: Macaulay, 1927. 383pp.

Partly set in 1920s Chicago, in this coming of age story, a boy from the country moves to Chicago and commits himself to life there, no matter the difficulties. Initially, Ivor must choose between a small-town life, working in a store with no prospects, or leaving for the uncertainty of life he will make for himself elsewhere. Living in rural poverty, he witnessed the bankruptcy sale of his father's farm and the futility of his life, as well as the deaths of friends and family members (including his mother) from poor medical care. He leaves home, works as a steamboat cook, and then sells books door-to-door with a team. Reading the books becomes his college education and he is particularly inspired by *The Communist Manifesto*. Inspired to move to Chicago, Ivor stows away on freight trains, journeying through a small-town America in which people are feverish to seek Chicago's opportunities. He lives in a hobo camp in Chicago, until he connects with a socialist, attends lectures at Socialist Hall, and is guided to a white-collar job as a low-paid, railroad clerk. He then moves into a South Side boarding house and, through classes at the Chicago (State) University extension program, his life is transformed by Wilkes, a painter, who introduces him into artistic and intellectual circles and to Ann Wilson (one of the few characters given a surname), an artist's model. Eventually Ivor and Ann marry, despite their poverty, and move into a cold-water flat. When Ann reveals her pregnancy, Ivor persuades Ann to have an abortion because of their poverty. After an extended illness, she finally leaves for Springfield, Illinois, her hometown, defeated by Chicago and Ivor's absorption with it (he has begun working as a journalist). In the final scenes of the novel an influenza epidemic rages and unemployed men are taking over churches for shelter from the cold. After Ivor falls ill and is nursed to health by Wilkes over a period of months, the artist reveals his plans to move to the south of France, offering Ivor work as his studio assistant. Ivor decides he is committed to Chicago and will not abandon his life as his father and so many others abandoned their farms. The novel's descriptions of life on the margins of Chicago society are highly detailed and the tenuous neighborhoods in which Ivor lives (streets of abandoned mansions converted into boarding houses and the condemned buildings of Custom House Place) are highly evocative.

174. Caldwell, Lewis A. H. *The Policy King*. Illustrated by Frederick S. Banks. Chicago: New Vistas Publishing House, 1945. 303pp.

Through the story of the African-American Marshall family, Caldwell dramatizes the history of "policy" in Chicago, a form of lottery. A preface outlines the development of policy from prior to 1930 when rivals offered games and violence was frequent, to the syndicate period when the games were coordinated and organized by better-educated men and generated revenues of over one-million dollars per month. Joe, Jerry, and Helen Marshall are the children of an African-American minister from Paducah, Kentucky, who migrated to a Chicago suburb as he became a successful preacher. Joe, the oldest son, decides to run his own policy game. Allying himself with Pop Tyler, a policy kingpin, he models himself on Tyler and is soon wealthy. When his father dies, Joe supports the Marshall family. Jerry, who works as a bootblack to study law at Northwestern University is drawn into policy when Joe is gunned down and Jerry is forced to deal with Pop Tyler to get Joe a decent funeral (churches refused to hold a criminal's funeral). When Pop offers him a job, Jerry thinks he can end violence by creating a syndicate of game operators. The profits are so great that he begins living in a mansion with servants. His younger sister, Helen, earns her own way through college and becomes a social worker. A witness to lives destroyed by policy, she joins a campaign against the lotteries, allying herself with community leaders and African-American preachers. As the campaign grows, the "policy" syndicate responds violently and even bombs a church in 1940. By the end of the novel Helen has been appointed advisor to a legislative committee introducing legislation to license lotteries and impose rules. Jerry is convicted for his role in the policy syndicate, accepting a plea bargain agreement for five years in prison. Although focused on policy, the book describes the African-American community, including church services, restaurants, prayer meetings, and Depression-era hardships.

175. Calmer, Ned. *Late Show*. Garden City, N.Y.: Doubleday, 1974. 335pp.

Roughly one-third of this novel tracing the career of ambitious media star, Bud Butler, is set in Chicago. Butler, who got his start playing trumpet with dance bands became Chicago's biggest radio personality, but was always aiming for national fame. He leaves Chicago to become an emcee on a nationwide television program. Most of the narrative focuses on Butler's machinations to get what he wants and is set in hotel rooms, apartments, radio studios, and offices. Butler lives at the Ambassador East and socializes at the Pump Room, Fitzl's [*sic*], and Cliff Dwellers. In addition to analyzing the character of a striving media personality, the novel touches on gender issues by presenting stories of some of the women Butler uses and discards.

176. Capwell, Irene Stoddard. *Mrs. Alderman Casey*. New York: Fenno, 1905. 175pp.

The chapters of this novel primarily consist of a series of extended anecdotes told by Mrs. Bridget Casey in Irish dialect. Bridget emigrated from Ireland with her husband, Michael Casey, arriving in Chicago not long after the 1871 fire. Michael, a hard-working stone mason, soon became a contractor's foreman, and, after some profitable land investments, became a partner in his employer's firm. The Caseys begin their life in Chicago in a tenement, where Bridget helps her neighbors and gossips with them. As their family grows to include six children, the Caseys move to an apartment and later a two-story house in an Irish neighborhood. Their former neighbors are proud of the Caseys' increasing affluence and the couples' friendships and charitableness makes it easy for Michael to get elected alderman. The only real plot of the novel centers on the courting of their daughter Mary Anne, who by the end of the book is engaged to marry policeman Tom Donovan. Bridget's lengthiest anecdotes are about hired girls, lawn tennis, a euchre party, the bloomer fashion, and a women's club meeting.

177. Carroll, Charles. *Chicago*. New York: Pocket Books, 1976. 265pp.

In this political scandal novel, the Democratic Party machine is confronted with major challenges just one week prior to a city election. An investigative reporter discovers that city officials have been bribed in connection with favorable zoning legislation and fourteen city aldermen are subpoenaed for income tax evasion. Then John O'Reilly, Illinois Secretary of State, dies and shoeboxes containing over a million dollars are discovered in his closet. The novel recounts the criminality employed to make certain that the Democrats suffer as little as possible in the election. Published in the year of Chicago Mayor Richard Daley's death, fictional mayor Ed Denehy is clearly supposed to be Daley's counterpart, just as O'Reilly is meant to be Secretary of State Paul Powell's.

178. Carroll, Loren. *Wild Onion*. New York: Grosset and Dunlap, 1930. 312pp.

When Joe Dulac loses his job as a telephone linesman, he works unsuccessfully at a series of manual labor positions until he is recruited to become a bootleg runner, delivering bottles of alcohol directly to customers. Soon he runs his own operation and is on his way to being a powerful Chicago gangster. The novel outlines the history of bootlegging in 1920s Chicago and uses fictional wars between rival gangs to demonstrate the actual infighting that occurred and why it was dangerous to Chicagoans. The generally corrupt police force has no control and lawlessness is prevalent. The physical setting is apartment hotels and speakeasies and the most colorful events are shootouts and gangland funerals. Some neighborhoods and streets are described and there are several extended, lyrical descriptions of Chicago and its symbolic meaning. By the end of the novel it seems clear that Dulac's double-crosses and violence are about to catch up with him. Although his fate is not yet sealed, his cowardice at its approach is telling. Throughout the novel ethnic prejudice is clearly stated, particularly against Eastern European immigrants.

179. Carruth, Hayden. *Appendix A*. New York: Macmillan, 1963. 302pp.

Although the plot focuses on a love triangle between two men and a woman, the most vivid presence in the novel is the city of Chicago, which is lyrically described and analyzed. Through descriptions of social events and conversational exchanges, Chicago social life is also presented. The novel's narrator is a poet and works for a famous, old-fashioned Chicago literary magazine named *Pegasus*. The main characters—the married couple Alex (a woman) and Charley, and the narrator who is in love with Alex—are all still affected by events during World War II, even though the novel is set in 1961. They are also unshakably conscious of the threat of atomic warfare and of the Berlin Wall. They are all upper-middle-class, live near Lake Shore Drive and Forty-Seventh Street, and weekend out of the city at Lake Jones. Issues of Jewish identity, immigrant identity, and the eroticization of people from outside one's ethnic group are all themes.

180. Carter, John Stewart. *Full Fathom Five*. Boston: Houghton Mifflin, Riverside Press, 1965. 246pp.

Narrator Tom Scott conveys emotionally-charged memories of his family and their houses in Chicago before World War II. A grandson of Frederick Harrison Scott, who founded a Chicago bank, Scott describes the life of very affluent Chicagoans. Of the thirty-five rooms in the Frederick Harrison Scott house ten were bedrooms, one for each of his sons. Ruled over in the narrator's time by his grandmother, it was not torn down to make way for an apartment building until the 1940s, when, as in other Chicago mansions, staffing had become too difficult (there had originally been twelve indoor servants). By this time, too, the Scott family wealth had been considerably reduced after the failure of their bank during the Depression. Family life in the Scott mansion and elsewhere in the United States and in Europe is the primary focus, but the novel also presents cultural and social details that capture upper-class society life in Chicago in the first decades of the twentieth century. One main theme is the nature of privilege in a culture that prides itself on egalitarianism. The narrative is divided into three sections, one for each of the men who have played a significant role in Tom Scott's life (his namesake uncle; the opera singer Edward Sciarrha, who had been his grandmother's lover; and his father, a physician at Chicago's County Hospital).

181. Cary, Lucian. *The Duke Steps Out*. Garden City, N.Y.: Doubleday, Doran, 1929. 288pp.

This romance novel of the 1920s tells of lightweight prizefighter Duke Wellington's efforts to win the heart of Susan Corbin, a woman with whom he is immediately smitten, upon seeing her in a Chicago hotel lobby. Wellington, who was born poor in New York City, is famous and rich, but feels imprisoned by the social status accorded boxers. When he discovers that Corbin is a student at the University of Minnewaska, he suspends his life as a boxer to become a college student and gain legitimacy in Corbin's eyes. Eventually, he must go back to his life in professional sports, but only long enough to win one big fight that will make him truly rich. Corbin, whose father is a well-known lawyer, grew up in a Lake Forest mansion. Her father uses private detectives to keep Wellington from his daughter, but love is victorious in the end. Most of the Chicago scenes are set in hotels, boxing rings, and gymnasiums. In addition to social class, the novel touches on gender roles.

182. Casey, John. *An American Romance*. New York: Atheneum, 1977. 321pp.

Approximately one-third of this romance novel is set in Chicago where "Mac" MacKenzie, a naturalized Canadian from Schenectady, New York, and Anya Janek from Boston meet as graduate students. Anya, who attended the best East Coast prep schools and graduated from Radcliffe College, studies English at the University of Chicago and Mac, who graduated from Cornell University on a hockey scholarship, studies civil engineering at the Illinois Institute of Technology. In addition to their mutual romantic attraction, Anya and Mac are united in questioning social values and reconnecting with their origins. Although Anya was raised an affluent WASP, her mother was Jewish and she begins to explore her Jewish identity as Mac tries to reestablish his French-Canadian identity. Through Anya they have many affluent acquaintances whose values they question. Eventually, they become involved in a bohemian theater collective in Iowa (Anya as an actress and dramatist and Mac as a set builder). The novel portrays upper-class, intellectual circles in Chicago in the early years of the 1970s counter culture as the use of illegal drugs and fluid sexual mores are becoming common.

183. Casey, Robert J. (Robert Joseph). *Hot Ice*. Indianapolis: Bobbs-Merrill, 1933. 309pp.

Much of this 1920s detective novel takes place on Goose Island, a warehouse district at this point, near the intersection of West Division and Halsted Streets, as well North Side locales. Set during the Depression, the mystery concerns the death of Peter Bailey, a neighborhood philanthropist who provided children with milk and helped families living on or near Goose Island. Bailey died in an automobile crash, but as police detective Joseph Crewe and amateur sleuth Jim Sands investigate, they are surprised to realize that a number of unsolved jewelry thefts and a recent murder seem connected to Bailey's death. Sands, a former reporter who made a fortune in the stock market through skill (observation and memory) and got out before the crash is crucial to the investigation. As the work of detection proceeds, many details about daily life in 1920s Chicago are revealed, including such matters as milk deliveries by horse-drawn wagons, all night barber shops, and the operations of the Chicago river docks.

184. Casey, Robert J. (Robert Joseph). *The Secret of the Bungalow*. Indianapolis: Bobbs-Merrill, 1930. 304pp.

This book, another in the series of detective novels featuring Chicago police detective Joseph Crewe and the amateur investigator, Jim Sands, focuses on organized crime, unlike most of Casey's novels that feature individual criminals. Crewe and Sands are drawn into the case when they investigate the death of a mobster by arson.

185. Casey, Robert J. (Robert Joseph). *The Secret of 37 Hardy Street*. Indianapolis: Bobbs-Merrill, 1929. 322pp.

Although physically set in Chicago, the city plays only a limited role in this murder mystery. Cyrus Bradley, a retired playwright, is found tied to a chair in his dining room, dead of nicotine poisoning. Four places are set at the table, each with toast and coffee as though for breakfast, even though Bradley lived alone. Reporter and adjunct police detective, Jim Sands, is suspicious, even though the death was declared a suicide (an explanation was even given in court for the possibility that Bradley could have tied himself up). Sands believes the table setting is a crucial detail and when he questions Bradley's daughter, Esther, who had rushed to Chicago from New York City, she claims that soon before Bradley moved to Chicago after a break-in at the Bradley residence, the table had been set in the same way. In the end, the case proves to be an instance of mistaken identity and stems from a bank robbery that had taken place twenty years before. The murderer thought Bradley was involved in the crime and that he knew the location of the loot because of a scene in a play he had written. However, Bradley had co-written the play with Fred Carbine and it was actually Carbine who had provided the scene involving the set table, based on events connected to the robbery in which Carbine had participated.

186. Casey, Robert J. (Robert Joseph). *The Voice of the Lobster*. Indianapolis: Bobbs-Merrill, 1930. 306pp.

Opposing militants from an imaginary South American country named Pandorra arrive in Chicago and the result is bloodshed and confusion. One man, General Gonzalez has smuggled valuable ore molded into sash weights out of Pandorra that he plans to sell to fund arms purchases. General Copal from the opposite side of the conflict pursues him. Each man has supporters in the Chicago area and each side, using mobsters, makes assassination attempts on the leaders. The unfortunate Fred Patter gets embroiled in the conflict. Patter is a theater usher at the Super-Babylon, a movie palace with five acres of seats and dozens of ushers, all of them wearing a uniform. As an usher captain, Patter's uniform is elaborate and on the street he is mistaken for General Gonzalez. Soon, he is being pursued by two sets of mobsters, the police, and three beautiful women. In addition to detailing the operations of a movie palace and life in an apartment hotel, the book satirizes sensationalism in the press and the cult following of movie stars.

187. Caspary, Vera. *The Dreamers*. New York: Pocket Books, 1975. 361pp.

The "dreamers" of the title are three sisters Norma, Amy, and Ernestine Miller and this book traces the course of their lives from the 1920s to the 1970s. Although significantly set in Chicago, where the girls grow up, other settings include New York City and Connecticut. The girls' romantic fantasies influence their choice of life partners in ways that bring them unhappiness. Norma, the beauty, dreams of a rich husband and gets one, but his obsession with work, to the exclusion even of sex, pushes her into the arms of an earlier beau. Discovery and divorce quickly follow and she lives regretting the loss of her pampered life. Unlike Norma, Amy and Ernestine establish careers, Amy as a commercial artist and Ernestine as a teacher. Amy's dream of a man who is cultured and European is fulfilled, but at the cost of all her hard won financial independence since she ends up supporting her husband's unsuccessful audio-recording business. Serious-minded, plain Ernestine is a lesbian and longs for a passionate, expressive woman. She has several long-term relationships with such women, often sacrificing her own best interests. Most of the descriptions of Chicago are of domestic life in middle and upper-middle-class households. One Miller relative is a wealthy businessman and there are several descriptions of his residence and the entertainments he hosts.

188. Caspary Vera. *Evvie*. New York: Harper and Brothers, 1960. 341pp.

The novel explores the lives of two, independent, young women thrilled by the new freedoms of the 1920s. Louise Ashton and Evelyn "Evvie" Goodman share a stable that has been turned into an apartment on the Near North Side in a neighborhood of mansions. Twenty-three year old

Louise works writing copy and developing campaigns for an advertising firm. Evvie, the daughter of a wealthy Jewish banker, has studied dance and toured with a company, and now focuses on painting. The two have an active social life and Louise, in particular, dates a wide variety of men. In matters of sex, they consider themselves more progressive than some of their peers who have a "prewar" mindset and do not understand the new discoveries of human psychology. Both are devoted to art and culture and are knowledgeable about the latest trends in writing, music, and painting. When Evvie is murdered, news stories present their unchaperoned lives in scandalous terms and police claim Evvie had affairs with married men and gangsters. Set in the 1920s, but written in 1960, the book tells the reader as much about cultural attitudes toward women and social convention of the later time-period as it does about the 1920s. The novel's action is firmly rooted in a sense of place and many Chicago locations are detailed, as well as modes of dress, domestic furnishings, and forms of entertainment.

189. Caspary, Vera. *Music in the Street*. New York: Grosset and Dunlap, 1930. 306pp.

     In this novel about coming of age in the 1920s, eighteen-year-old Mae Thorpe moves to Chicago after she graduates from high school and does not get the marriage offer she had expected from the son of the local automobile dealer. She lives in the Rolfe House, a residence for unmarried working women with strict rules and the novel describes the women, their social interactions, and their clothing and grooming habits. For a time, Mae dates Olyn Bradshaw, a commercial artist with a belief in phrenology. When she meets attractive Boyd Wheeler, a graduate of the University Chicago who works as a salesman, drives a Chrysler, and talks of his family's house in Oak Park and his trips to Europe, Mae forgets about Olyn and decides she will do anything to deepen her relationship with Boyd, including, after much hesitation, entering into a sexual relationship with him. They have liaisons in cheap hotels and rented rooms and Mae must fool the Rolfe House manageress about her nighttime whereabouts. Her subterfuge becomes more complicated after her sister Agnes moves to Chicago to share her room. Then, Boyd abandons Mae and marries the daughter of his boss. Soon afterwards, Agnes marries a musician and Mae begins sharing an apartment with a Rolfe House woman in an old subdivided mansion downtown. When Boyd reappears he renews their romance on the promise that he is getting a divorce. Only a few weeks after Mae realizes Boyd will never leave his wealthy wife and that she is no longer infatuated with him, she discovers that she is pregnant. In the aftermath of an abortion, she marries her long time boss, Mr. Moses, who has achieved middle-class affluence, and has demonstrated his deep regard for Mae in numerous ways. After settling into life as a sedate householder, Mae begins to feel ill and discovers she is still pregnant. When her plans to flee are thwarted, Moses promises to raise Mae's child by another man as his own. In addition to exploring the social implications of new sexual freedoms, the novel is filled with details of clothing, food, forms of socializing, and domestic furnishings.

190. Caspary, Vera. *Thelma*. Boston: Little, Brown, 1952. 342pp.

     Most of this novel about yearning for affluence and social acceptance is set in Chicago. Thelma Raissler grew up in a small Wisconsin town with her widowed mother, a hotel chambermaid. Thelma's father, an unsuccessful traveling salesman for a textile firm, died young. Following her childhood dream of living in a well-appointed house and being treated like a lady, Thelma follows a school friend to Chicago and finds a husband from a respectable family. She forces him to give up his literary ambitions to work in advertising. They eventually live on the margin of the Gold Coast in a household that fulfills Thelma's childhood dreams, at which point her ambitions shift. Thelma dreams her daughter Constance will enter the first rank of social acceptance and sends her to one of the best private schools. Constance does marry an affluent, international businessman at Thelma's urging. Soon afterwards, however, Constance begins an affair with the man she had wanted to marry in the first place and Thelma's world implodes when she alienates her daughter and husband by trying to get a sizable alimony settlement for Constance. By the end of the novel, Thelma lives alone in an apartment hotel of dated elegance. Through detailed descriptions of the objects of Thelma's striving, the novel presents the types of dwellings, kinds of food, and sorts of social events that constituted an upper-class life in Chicago in the 1920s through 1940s.

191. Caspary, Vera. *Thicker Than Water*. New York: Grosset and Dunlap, 1932. 426pp.

The Piera family, Portuguese Jews, first came to America in 1690 and settled in New York City. Much later, a branch settled in Chicago and this novel relates their struggles with assimilation in the late nineteenth and early twentieth centuries. Unlike New York, Chicago has no community of Portuguese Jews, and, in 1885, the prospect of intermarriage disturbs family matriarch Becka da Silva. However, her nieces Rosalia and Melanie, and her nephew Saul, all marry German Jews. Rosalia, who married late (she was considered a spinster at twenty-nine), chose Adolph Reisinger, a businessman and also a published poet, who appealed to Rosalia's intellectual side. Unfortunately, he is also a womanizer who dates chorus girls and frequents gambling parlors and other places of low entertainment. Change and assimilation are the major concerns all the characters share as they mingle with Czechs, Germans, Poles, and Russians. The novel also traces the changing position of women in society as some of the female characters take active roles in business. The novel ends in 1931 and the Pieras have survived World War I and the Depression, and although no male heirs are left to carry the family name, they are still proud of the continuing heritage that lives through their most recent descendants.

192. Caspary, Vera. *The White Girl*. New York: Sears, 1929. 305pp.

In this novel about racism, protagonist Solaria Cox is African-American, but she is so light-skinned that people assume she is white. The first sixty-eight pages of the book depict the racial prejudice with which she must deal in 1920s Chicago before she moves to New York City where the rest of the novel is set. Cox is the daughter of Desborough who has been the janitor for Judge Nixon on Oak Street for decades and Desborough houses his family in Nixon's basement. Cox works for a dress manufacturer where everyone knows her origins; she manages the stockroom and dresses the models. When she has a chance in office emergencies, she proves herself to be a competent typist and an attractive model. However, she will never be promoted and when buyers from outside Chicago visit, they are warned-off from thinking Cox is white. After Desborough succumbs to a heart attack, Cox must move with her mother to Prairie Avenue, a much less affluent area than Oak Street and one filled with other African-Americans. In this setting, she receives two marriage proposals. Eggers Benedict, a jazz pianist, is in love with Cox, but she despises him for rejecting support from his family to attend college and become a physician or lawyer. Solaria associates his music with an impoverished African-American culture and she has no appreciation for the successes that eventually propel him to New York City. Her other marriage prospect, Toby Linthicum, is the son of one of the wealthiest African-Americans in Chicago. However, in addition to the fact that he is black-skinned and fat, she does not love him and has no desire to marry only for financial comfort. When Mr. Winkelberg embraces and kisses her in the stockroom at work she realizes she must quit her job and soon afterwards leaves Chicago for New York City to live where she can choose to live as a Caucasian. The Chicago section of this novel describes "black and tan clubs" (where racially mixed audiences come to hear such stars as Ethel Waters), African-American neighborhoods, and day-to-day office life.

193. Cather, Willa. *Lucy Gayheart*. New York: Alfred A. Knopf, 1935. 231pp.

Lucy Gayheart moves to Chicago to study piano with Professor Auerbach after a childhood in Haverford, Nebraska. The novel captures the importance of music in the city and depicts early 1900s artistic circles centered on Michigan Avenue and around the Arts Building. Because Lucy also visits her hometown to see family members and childhood friends, the attitudes emerge of small-town people toward Chicago, and the prospect of achievement in the larger world. Lucy lives independently above a German bakery and meets Clement Sebastian, a famous singer with a studio on Michigan Avenue. Clement is Lucy's entrée to artistic life as they socialize and attend concerts. Lucy has soon fallen innocently in love with Clement and when he admits his love for her, despite being married, he pledges he will never express his feelings physically. Because of this relationship, Lucy breaks off her engagement to Harry Gordon, a boy from her hometown. Shortly afterward she discovers that Clement will be in Europe for an extended period of time. Then, Clement drowns in an accident while on tour. Lucy, unable to emerge from mourning in a city where every street corner seems to be associated with Clement, returns to her childhood home where she also drowns in an accident. As well as being a renowned work of literary fiction, the novel details student and artistic life in Chicago shortly after the turn of the twentieth century.

194. Cather, Willa. *The Song of the Lark*. Boston: Houghton Mifflin, Riverside Press, 1915. 490pp.

Two important sections of this novel about the artist's life are set in Chicago. Thea Kronberg grows up in Moonstone in the sand hill country of Colorado, the daughter of Swedish immigrants, whose father Peter is a Methodist minister. Although Thea is entirely out of place in the gossip-filled small town of Moonstone and the large, impoverished Kronberg family, she benefits from the direct contact with nature and her family's disregard for social conventions that permits her a social life centered on middle-aged men: town physician Dr. Howard Archie, railroad man Ray Kennedy, music teacher Professor Wunsch, and Mexican paperhanger and painter John Tellamantez. When Kennedy dies in an accident Kronberg receives enough money from his life insurance policy to fund a winter's study in Chicago. Although she has a difficult time adjusting to the city, her piano teacher Andor Harsanyi treats her as a fellow artist and convinces her to study voice with Madison Bowers, who knows well-connected people, including his wealthy student Philip Frederick Ottenburg, the heir to a brewing fortune. After a trip to Arizona, funded by Ottenburg, that has important artistic and personal repercussions for Kronberg, most of the novel's remaining chapters are set in New York City after Kronberg has become famous. In Chicago, Kronberg visits the Art Institute, attends Auditorium concerts, and dines out in the Pullman Building. Descriptions of her living arrangements probably reflect conditions for single women in the late nineteenth century. In addition to describing the personality and sacrifices of an artist, the novel touches on the challenges women faced during the time period.

195. Catherwood, Mary Hartwell. *The Dogberry Bunch*. Boston: Lothrop, 1879. 86pp.

In this juvenile novel, originally serialized in a magazine, the orphaned Dogberry children work to remain together after their parents' deaths. The Dogberrys—seven in number and ranging in age from three to eighteen—have several adventures before moving to Chicago after their family home burns down. The city represents the future to them—one in which each of them will be able to follow their dreams.

196. Chamales, Tom T. *Go Naked in the World*. New York: Scribner, 1959. 461pp.

Although Major Nick Stratton saw harrowing active duty in World War II and was twice wounded, he returns to his family in Winnetka with reluctance, knowing that his father, Pete Stratton, will insist that he join the family's multi-state movie theater business. A Greek immigrant, the older Stratton began working at eleven-years-old and has a boosterish attitude toward the United States that his son and other members of the younger generation (including Nick's cousin Pierro) cannot fully embrace. After exposure to the harsh realities of warfare, they seek more than material success, although they concede that Pete Stratton has been unselfish in using his money to help his extended family and to assist the residents of his hometown back in Greece. As twenty-three-year-old Nick tries to readjust to life as a civilian and cope with his father's expectations, Pete schemes to force out his business partners so that he and his son will solely own his firm. Then, Nick unintentionally betrays his father when he begins an affair with a beautiful woman at a cocktail lounge, who turns out to be a prostitute who has had Pete Stratton as a repeat client. The novel touches on life in the Chicago Greek community, but more particularly on the life of affluent businessmen in the city who own restaurants and nightclubs and are part of a network of suppliers of goods and services that is spread across the country.

197. Chance, Frank L. *The Bride and the Pennant; The Greatest Story in the History of America's National Game, True to Life—Intensely Interesting*. Preface by Charles A. Comiskey. Chicago: Laird and Lee, Publishers, 1910. 182pp.

Although sections of this novel are set in New Orleans and New York, most of the action transpires in Chicago. When undergraduate baseball player Harry Sherman fails out of the University of Chicago he tries out for the imaginary Chicago "Bears" and works himself into a pitcher's position. His sporting success is threatened by troubles in his romance with Lucille Merriam, but after lengthy practice on his slow ball and reconciliation with Lucille, he becomes a star pitcher. Written by the coach of the Chicago "Cubs," the novel is a primer of baseball terminology and technique with off-field plot elements.

198. Chandler, Peter. *Bucks*. New York: Avon Books, 1980. 262pp.

This crime novel also addresses issues of ethnic prejudice in 1970s Chicago through the story of Gianfranco Bardolucci. A Sicilian-American, Bardolucci has family connections to the Mafia, but wants to succeed on his own in the business world. However, in addition to business competitors, he must address the false accusations leveled against him by newsmen of Mafia ties. He finally admits defeat and begins a life of crime by planning a multi-million-dollar theft from Chicago's Regency Security Company.

199. Chandler, St. Lawrence, Marquis of Eckersley. *A Human Note*. Illustrated by Jay LaBrun Jenkins. Kansas City, Mo.: Hudson Press, 1908. 208p.

Much of this society novel is set in early-twentieth-century Chicago. The "human note" of the title is Fred Hoxley, son of a wealthy margarine manufacturer (here called butterine). A dupe of the Socialist Party in Chicago, Hoxley persuades his father to send him on a market research trip to Europe so that he can connect with Russian socialists. However, he falls into the hands of aristocrats in St. Petersburg who tattoo a negotiable bank note for 100,000 rubles on his back.

Upon Hoxley's return to Chicago factions with various motivations pursue him throughout the city. The chase scenes provide physical descriptions of the city, but the novel's strength is in presenting social settings and behavior characteristic of the period.

200. Channon, Henry. *Joan Kennedy*. New York: Dutton, 1929. 255pp.

Joan Kennedy, the daughter of impoverished English nobility, grew up in Wiltshire, near Bexenham, England, in her family's ancestral home. The man she was engaged to marry, Hugo Vivian, is killed in World War I. After the war, living in London, she is pursued by a wealthy American, Ralph Kennedy. She had nursed Ralph as a volunteer in a military hospital and she had become truly attracted to him. At first, she does not think the marriage means she will have to give up living in England, for Ralph has been urged by his father to learn the banking business there. However, when the couple goes to America for the funeral of Ralph's father, she is forced to emigrate, for the elder Kennedy's will specifies that his heir must live in the United States. Roughly half the novel deals with the adjustments Joan must make to her new life in the city, referred to as El Dorado, but, as many references make clear, it is Chicago. Initially, Joan tries to get involved in the life of the Kennedys, but finds their focus on socializing and shopping uninteresting. Eventually, she builds a social life around a circle that includes prominent scholars, community leaders, and philanthropists who are distinguished not just for their affluence, but the contributions they make to society. Because her environment is so new to her, she constantly receives explanations about how things are done in the United States. Through these explanations and Joan's own observations, the reader can learn a great deal about upper-class social life in Chicago in the 1920s.

201. Channon, Henry *Paradise City*. New York: Dutton, 1931. 246pp.

Paradise City, a small town on the Green River in Wisconsin, is transformed in the late nineteenth century when the town mill is purchased to be retrofitted as the center of operations for a large corporation. Previously, the main contact the townspeople had with the outside world had been through the summer people who came from Chicago to live in grand houses they had built for themselves on a nearby lake. In the economic boom, not only the children of the local doctor and the local judge, but those of less respectable characters, like the owner of the stable, have access to money that changes their lives and aspirations. The novel tells the stories of eight of these young people as they find places for themselves in the larger world. Surprisingly, several of them settle in France and Italy, but others, through marriage, or business acumen, make names for themselves in Chicago society circles and socialize with some of the very people who summer in Paradise City and would have shun them there. Although only small sections of the novel are physically set in Chicago, throughout the book the city is considered the locus of power and affluence where one might go to establish oneself. The Chicago Columbian Exposition and the Iroquois Theater disaster each play important roles in the lives of some of the characters.

202. Chapman, George [Vernon Warren, pseud.]. *The Blue Mauritius*. London: John Gifford, 1954. 189pp.

In this private detective novel Chicago's illegal gambling rings, controlled by organized criminals play a central role. Mark Brandon, who owns a detective agency and employs a secretary and assistant, has fallen on hard times. On the day he decides to close his office for a while, he is approached by a well-dressed man who asks him to steal a rare postage stamp, a blue Mauritius. Brandon refuses despite the man's offer of tens of thousands of dollars for committing the crime. By a coincidence, when Brandon flies to New York City to propose to his girlfriend, reporter Sue Denning, he meets the dealer who sold the stamp to its current owner, Douglas Craig. Now that Brandon knows the intended victim of the stamp theft he feels obligated to warn him. When he returns to Chicago with Sue he discovers he is too late, for he finds Craig murdered in his Gold Coast apartment. Craig's daughter, Janis hires him to discover the killer. Either of Craig's ne'er do well sons seem likely culprits until Brandon discovers that one, Alexander Craig, has significant gambling debts. Then, Sue is kidnapped by thugs employed by gangster Al Rickard, a gambling ring leader, and it is only a matter of time before Brandon solves the case. Even though the book is more concerned with action than setting, addresses and building descriptions are included to establish locations. Janis' house on Lake Shore Drive merits a lengthier description. Moved in pieces by freight car from Los Angeles and reassembled, the structure revolts Brandon as ostentatious display. Despite the fact that Sue is a reporter, she is relegated to domestic tasks when not a kidnap victim or hostage. All of the characters are Caucasians, except for a Filipino houseboy who is described in racist terms.

203. Chapman, George [Vernon Warren, pseud.]. *Brandon Returns*. London: John Gifford, 1954. 191pp.

Chicago private investigator Mark Brandon considers millionaire Edgar J. Sparks' fear of assassination unrealistic, but willingly accepts employment with Sparks. Then, Sparks is actually killed and Brandon must work for his money.

204. Chapman, George Warren [Vernon Warren, pseud.]. *Brandon Takes Over*. London: John Gifford, 1953. 192pp.

The eponymous Mark Brandon is a Chicago private detective featured in several pulp novels. In this adventure, Brandon's partner is shot by gangsters and he traces their violence back to a major figure in Chicago's illegal drug trade. Written by an English author, the novel demonstrates little familiarity with Chicago.

205. Chappell, Fred A. *Bill and Brocky, a Story of Boy Life in Chicago Especially Adapted to the Understanding of Old Boys*. Chicago: Harrison, Chappell and Davis, 1892. 99pp.

An attempt to evoke the camaraderie of pre-adolescent boys in Chicago, this book's main characters are the eponymous Bill and Brocky. The two boys have dissimilar backgrounds. Bill's parents are solidly middle-class with all the physical and cultural trappings that entails in nineteenth-century Chicago. His friend Brocky is orphaned and literally lives in a packing crate. The two are part of a group of boys of similar ages who seek adventure and build a rather alarming clubhouse for themselves by tunneling into a lumber mill sawdust pile. Bill and Brocky's biggest adventure comes when they run away after a chain of events set in motion by teasing a rule-abiding boy, Reginald, who gets revenge on Bill by revealing his involvement in mischief. Fearing punishment, Bill sets off with Brocky and the story comes to a happy end when the boys find a benefactor who adopts Brocky. Although mostly concerned with the boys' activities, the book seems to be an accurate description of play in turn-of-the-century Chicago and includes telling details about street life in the city.

206. Charteris, Leslie. *Call for the Saint*. Garden City, N.Y.: Crime Club / Doubleday, 1948. 190pp.

One of the two novellas in this book, *King of the Beggars*, is set in Chicago. The main character, Simon Templar, appears in a series of detective novels. In this book, Templar investigates the robbing and killing of Chicago's beggars. An elaborate protection racket emerges headed by the mannish proprietress of a flophouse. Although there are references to the Pump Room and a few other Chicago landmarks, the novel is less concerned with setting than with Templar's investigation into the identity of the "King of the Beggars." Stock characters include some thuggish, illiterate gangsters, a society hostess and philanthropist, and a beautiful actress on tour in Chicago.

207. Chatfield-Taylor, Hobart Chatfield. *An American Peeress*. Chicago: McClurg, 1894. 293pp.

This anglophile romance novel also celebrates the American girl, as best epitomized by a Chicagoan. Hugh Vincent, an Englishman, educated at Eton and Sandhurst, and a member of the Welsh Guards immigrates to the United States after being jilted by his fiancée. Settling in Chicago, he works his way up at the James Morse Boot and Shoe Manufacturing Company, advancing to chief buyer and fiancé of Laura Morse, the owner's daughter. The Morses live in the Chicago suburb of Highland Glen where Morse, a self-made man, has created his own tightly-controlled universe to which much description is devoted. Shortly before the young couple marries, Hugh is notified that, subsequent to the death of his uncle, he will assume the title Earl of Warrington. Fearful of intimidating Laura, he waits until their wedding day to announce that she is now Countess of Warrington. The rest of the novel depicts Laura, the simple, but attractive, Chicago girl, living as a Countess and interacting with members of English society. Laura's genuineness is contrasted with the artificiality and affected behavior of Madge, Hugh's former love, who is a fixture in Hugh and Laura's social circle due to the wealth of her husband. Through many scenes at places like the Henley Regatta and the races at Goodwood, Laura's behavior is favorably contrasted with that of Madge. While the physical setting of the novel shifts away from Chicago, the city remains a symbol throughout of all that is most typical about the United States, including the self-made man and the unaffected, naturally courteous American girl.

208. Chatfield-Taylor, Hobart Chatfield. *Two Women & a Fool*. Illustrated by Charles Dana Gibson. Chicago: Stone and Kimball, 1895. 232pp.

The present of this novel is Chicago in the 1890s, however the main character and narrative voice, Guy Wharton, recounts earlier scenes of his affair with actress Moira Marston that occurred in Paris and London. Wharton, an artist, met Moira and Dorothy Temple when they were all students at Northwestern University. While studying in Paris, he became reacquainted with Moira, the daughter of a wealthy Chicago brewer, and fell in love. However, he grew disenchanted as he witnessed Moira's obsequious behavior toward aristocrats. Returning to Chicago, he became a society portrait painter and was reintroduced to Dorothy Temple. In temperament, Dorothy is Moira's opposite; instead of living for pleasure and adulation over her beauty, Dorothy devotes herself to good works and volunteers at a settlement house. Recognizing her positive influence on his character, Guy is inspired to thoughts of marriage, until Moira turns up in Chicago with her light opera company and he comes under the sway of her unhealthy influence. The Chicago scenes include a visit to Dorothy's settlement house, romantic interludes on World's Fair lagoons, and remarks about the city's tall buildings and elevators. The novel reveals a great deal about social attitudes toward women, marriage, and the theater, as well the veneration of European culture typical of 1890s upper-class Americans.

209. Chatfield-Taylor, Hobart Chatfield. *The Vice of Fools.* Illustrated by Raymond M. Crosby. Chicago: Herbert S. Stone, 1897. 310pp.

Through this narrative, Chatfield-Taylor sets out to prove his book's epigraph, written by Alexander Pope, that claims that pride is "the never failing vice of fools." The setting is primarily that of Washington, D. C., however the plot concerns the family of the Secretary of War whose home state is Illinois. In Chatfield-Taylor's account, bureaucrats and elected officials find opportunities in Washington to enter a social arena dominated by international culture, as represented by members of the diplomatic corps, that would have been forever unobtainable to them had they remained in their provincial hometowns. The plot centers on the Secretary of War's beautiful daughter as she chooses an appropriate husband. She marries out of pride, selecting a man she knows will bring her political power and wealth. However, she later realizes the true nature of love and she and her husband give up political and social life to devote themselves to philanthropy. Although the characters talk a great deal about the role of women in society, an enlarged role for them is never advocated. The Chicago portion of the novel focuses on a strike and attacks labor organizing, applauding the activation of the militia.

210. Chatfield-Taylor, Hobart Chatfield. *With Edge Tools.* Chicago: McClurg, 1891. 315pp.

When a New York society figure visits Chicago he is included in social events and meets Chicagoans who insist on comparing the city to other places, and the slight plot focuses on an inappropriate romance. Duncan Grahame, a well-connected New Yorker, who is not quite rich enough and must still work, is employed by a Wall Street firm brokering a deal between a Chicago elevator syndicate and British investors. During a business trip to Chicago, he visits old friend Harold Wainwright, and through him meets Marion Sanderson. Although Sanderson is married, the strong attraction between her and Grahame inspires an extended flirtation expressed through bantering one-upmanship over current intellectual and social matters, including evolution and Darwinism. The banter is set against Chicago social events, including cotillions, balls, musical evenings, teas, the opera, a ladies' literary society meeting, and Derby Day. When Grahame finally declares his love, Sanderson is frightened by the way her dream of true love seems about to come true in contravention of social mores. She remains faithful to her husband and Grahame returns to New York. When Grahame returns to Chicago and Sanderson realizes her feelings for him have continued strong she goes so far as to arrange a private assignation at her house. Fortunately, her husband returns unexpectedly due to a missed train and ends up having dinner with Grahame and his wife. In this setting, Sanderson comes to despise Grahame for the way he treats her husband, and she rejects him, and apologizes to her husband for her guest's condescension toward him and Chicago. Readers must assume that they are to be just as convinced as Sanderson of Chicago's cultural dominance. Although she lived most of her youth in France and England, she will not say bad things about Chicago the way her society friends do and a good deal of the novel is devoted to favorable comparisons of Chicago with other places and paeans to the city's architectural and cultural improvements.

211. Chinn, Laurene. *Believe My Love.* New York: Crown, 1962. 221pp.

Set during the years 1929 through 1931, this novel deals with interracial marriage, liberalism, premarital and extramarital sex, and gender roles. Celia Carter the daughter of a fundamentalist minister embraced the liberal movement at a young age and, as a college student, attends a joint YMCA-YWCA conference in Estes Park, Colorado, as a way of meeting other young liberals. She meets Ralph Howe, a Chinese-American, and their shared interests form the basis of a romance that alarms their acquaintances and family members. The two begin a long distance relationship from their separate campuses, Ralph in Colorado and Celia in Nebraska. Ralph believes they should never marry because of the prejudice Celia will suffer. He is also concerned that racism will prevent him from getting a job in chemical engineering and that he will never be able to support Celia. When Celia finishes college she moves to Chicago. After months of disheartening urban experiences, she gets a job in the personnel office of a large electric plant and begins seeing personnel research as her career. Ralph also finishes college, secures an internship, and later a job. The two cannot ignore their feelings for each other, as much as they try, and they eventually have an intense sexual experience and marry, knowing that Celia is carrying Ralph's baby. The novel does not include much physical description of Chicago, but does give a sense of the lower-middle-class life experienced by young people moving to the city for their first jobs. Descriptions include living arrangements, domestic interiors, and pastimes. Celia attends lectures, including some given by Havelock Ellis and Reinhold Niebuhr, and spends long hours at the public library, as well as going to art galleries and concerts.

212. Churchill, William Arnold [Arthur Walcott, pseud.]. and William Arnold Kirschberger. *Uncertain Voyage*. New York: Atwood and Knight, 1936. 384pp.

This tale of adultery and suicide is set in 1920s Chicago and was written as an attack on a social set centered on Chicago's North Shore Country Club who the author blamed for the corruption of his wife. Written pseudonymously as a firsthand narrative, the protagonist, Arthur Walcott, presents himself as cultured and moral, the exception in a wealthy society crowd, whose members have no sexual mores. While Walcott remains steadfast in his fidelity to his wife Anita, she is influenced by the environment and has an affair with a member of the circle, Ralph Gilbert. When Gilbert suddenly dies, grief-stricken Anita cannot conceal her infidelity. Society figures and situations are so thinly fictionalized that some of the wealthy people portrayed were able to have this book entirely suppressed when it was first published.

213. Clark, Christopher. *Good Is for Angels*. New York: Harper and Brothers, 1950. 237pp.

This story of working-class Chicago life set in the late 1940s presents Elizabeth Litke as an indomitable figure who survives each challenge that confronts her. Almost all of her difficulties stem from her family. Years before, her husband left her for another woman and she was left to raise four children on her own. To support her household, she took in distant relatives as boarders, worked as a cleaning woman, and sent her oldest son, seventeen-year-old Harry, to work. Years later she takes satisfaction in the marriages of Harry and her second oldest child, Benny, but is concerned about her two children still living at home, twenty-three-year-old Alan and nineteen-year-old Margery. Her household also includes Mrs. Connie "Ella" Redpath, a forty-two-year-old niece with an undesirable reputation for loose living. The mother of three children she placed in an orphanage after her husband left her, Ella is desperately trying to find a man to support her in old age. During the course of the novel, Margery marries John Mason, a man from the pharmaceutical plant where she works, and Ella weds Joe Flynn, an office worker from the laundry where she is employed. Litke must overlook the way Mason treats Margery and eventually move in with the couple. She must also cope with the knowledge that Flynn murdered Ella's oldest son Billy, a petty, blackmailing criminal, as well as the fact that Ella perjured herself at Flynn's trial to guarantee a comfortable life for herself living on Flynn's salary. While the novel makes a significant contribution in presenting 1940s working-class domestic life, the book is also of interest for exploring gender roles and aspects of homosexuality. Along with other young men, Billy preys upon homosexual men, blackmailing them with threats of legal action. While living with Ella and Joe Flynn, Billy discovers Flynn is a repressed homosexual and Flynn's murder of Billy stems from his fears of an extended period of blackmail and eventual exposure.

214. Clark, Edward C. *The Fatal Element*. New York: Empire, 1934. 304pp.

In this police detective novel, artist Edward Boughton is murdered and the police are aided by a reporter in solving the crime. The crime is a variation on a locked door mystery. Here Boughton is found murdered in his studio and the absence of footprints in the surrounding snow makes it seem impossible for the murderer to have entered and left. The reader is introduced to the 1930s worlds of a Chicago police department and newspaper office.

215. Clark, Herma. *The Elegant Eighties: When Chicago Was Young*. Forward by John T. McCutcheon. Chicago: McClurg, 1941. 258pp.

Clark worked as the secretary of William Blair, Chicago's first hardware wholesaler, and after his death, as personal secretary to his widow, Mrs. Sarah Blair. Through Mrs. Blair and her friends, Clark learned about Chicago in the decades of the 1850s through 1880s. A number of years after Mrs. Blair's death Clark began creating fictionalized accounts of Chicago social history, using an epistolary format. Clark first published her "letters" in the *Chicago Tribune*. This collection of her work covers January 1, 1880 to January 1, 1890. Although the main characters, correspondents Martha Freeman Esmond and her cousin Julia Boyd, are fictional composites of Mrs. Blair and her friends, many actual people and social events are impressionistically presented. The book includes photographs of some of the historic figures.

216. Claro, Joe. *My Bodyguard*. New York: Scholastic Book Services, 1980. 94pp.

In this school novel for children, Cliff Peache, the son of an expensive hotel's manager, makes the transition from private elementary school to a Chicago public school. His arrival in the hotel's limousine made Cliff so noticeable that every school bully sets their sights on him. He decides that his only option is to hire one of the older students as his bodyguard. Although primarily focusing on school culture, the book also reveals the workings of a large Chicago hotel. The book is a novelization of a motion picture of the same title, released by Twentieth Century Fox Film Corporation in 1980.

217. Clason, Clyde B. *Dragon's Cave: A Theocritus Lucius Westborough Story*. Garden City, N.Y.: Crime Club / Doubleday, Doran, 1939. 269pp.

When Jason Wright, the majority shareholder of an electrotyping and engraving factory, is found murdered in his house on Crestview Court (between Center and Fullerton Streets, west of Lincoln Park), Theocritus Lucius Westborough, professor of classical history and amateur detective, investigates at the behest of his friend Lieutenant John Mack of the Chicago police force. The affluent Wright collected medieval weaponry and was apparently killed by a halberd inside his trophy room. Since he resided with his wife and unmarried adult children, they are all immediate suspects. The way they and other suspects are described reveals a great deal about attitudes toward women, wealthy people, and ethnic minorities. There are also references to psychoanalysis throughout the book. In addition to the interiors of very affluent households in Lincoln Park and on Lake Shore Drive, the novel describes several "theme" restaurants, including one decorated in mock Tudor fashion and another with Bavarian interiors and waiters.

218. Clason, Clyde B. *The Fifth Tumbler*. Garden City, N.Y.: Crime Club / Doubleday, Doran, 1936. 303pp.

A hotel murder mystery, this is the first of Clason's books to feature Theocritus Lucius Westborough, a professor of classical history, who solves crimes by applying logic. The victim, wealthy Elmo Swink, was staying on the third floor of Chicago's Hotel Equable, when he was murdered by someone with a sophisticated knowledge of poisonous gas. Westborough and the police investigate the guests on the floor and details about hotel routine and staffing emerge. Once Westborough discovers a woman was being blackmailed over her past and an emerald is missing he is on the way to solving Swink's murder.

219. Clason, Clyde B. *The Man from Tibet*. Garden City, N.Y.: Crime Club / Doubleday, Doran, 1938. 302pp.

This locked room mystery is set in a Sheridan Road mansion in 1930s Chicago. Like a number of Chicago mysteries, one of the book's main characters is a wealthy Chicagoan preoccupied with collecting antiquities. Antiquarian Adam Merriweather collects Tibetan antiquities (although he has such distaste for Asian people that he will not shake hands with one). His Tibetan retainer, named Chang, assists him and his brother, Dr. Jedidiah Merriweather, a famous archaeologist. As the head of Merriweather Steel, Adam has almost unlimited resources, and when Jack Reffner approaches him with an eighth-century, Tibetan scroll filled with magical inscriptions, he purchases the item on the spot. Soon after the transaction, Reffner is found dead in his hotel room and Dr. Theocritus Lucius Westborough is called in because of the Sanskrit writing at the scene. When the police discover Adam Merriweather visited Reffner shortly before his death, he becomes the prime suspect and, through a ruse, they get Merriweather to invite Westborough to be his household guest. During the stay, Merriweather is murdered in his locked study, and only a scholar like Westborough can solve the mystery. The author imparts a great deal of information about Tibet and Tibetan Buddhism, but gives little sense of Chicago.

220. Clason, Clyde B. *The Purple Parrot: A Theocritus Lucius Westborough Story*. Garden City, N.Y.: Crime Club / Doubleday, Doran, 1937. 319pp.

In this murder mystery featuring amateur detective Dr. Theocritus Lucius Westborough, the scholar must solve a locked door mystery and exonerate the beautiful granddaughter of the victim. Independently wealthy Hezekiah Morse had, before his murder, lived near the lakefront at 49 Division Street in a mansion with servants and his collection of rare books. Despite this staid domestic setting, Morse, an immigrant from New Zealand, had made his fortune in Chicago through illegal means involving graft and gangsters. Although the book refers to specific Chicago locations, little physical description of the city is included. The novel presents social attitudes of the time toward wealth and the pursuits of the leisure class.

221. Cleaver, Vera and Bill Cleaver. *The Mimosa Tree*. Philadelphia: Lippincott, 1970. 125pp.

In this children's book an Appalachian family moves to a frightening, 1960s Chicago. Partially blind Dormann Proffitt has experienced a string of agricultural failures on his twenty-two acre farm near Goose Elk, North Carolina, culminating in the death of his last hog. Although Proffitt believes the Cricher family on the valley farm below his are to blame, Zollie, his new wife and stepmother to his five children, urges him not to pursue the matter, but to relocate to Chicago where Zollie's sister, Juanita, works in a hotel. Once the Proffitts get to the city, Juanita finds them an apartment above hers in an unspecified impoverished neighborhood. However, soon after getting the oldest Proffitt child, fourteen-year-old Marvella, a job in a nearby pawnshop, Zollie and Juanita disappear. Thrown into a life they do not understand, a youngster named Frank, who lives in the building across the alley, becomes their guide. A petty thief, Frank teaches Marvella and her brothers to pick pockets to get money for food and rent, although Frank takes a hefty percentage. After some of the Proffitt children witness Frank push his own mother in front of a bus, Marvella decides that she must overcome her fears and drive the family back to Goose Elk. Their rural, hard-scrabble existence was better than life in a city that has already turned them into petty criminals. At their farm, the Proffitts are surprised to be greeted by the Crichers, who have been censured by the people in Goose Elk for driving the Proffitts out. The remorseful Crichers pledge their help in getting the Proffitts resettled into their old life. In this novel, Chicago has no redeeming qualities. Every person that the Proffitts meet is corrupt or ineffectual, including the government social workers who repeatedly document the Proffitts' poverty and assure them of assistance without ever providing aid.

222. Cobb, Weldon J. *The Victim of a Crime*. Chicago: Weeks, 1893. 369pp.
This book is a later publication of the entry (223) that follows.

223. Cobb, Weldon J. *A World's Fair Mystery*. Chicago: Melbourne, 1892. 369pp.
Years before the action of this novel, Patrice Ringold was orphaned and the considerable estate from which she was to benefit was put into the hands of trustees, lawyer Dolph Lytle and real-estate broker Richard Sheldon. They cheated her out of her inheritance, imprisoned her for years in Mexico, and had her only ally, her father's friend, Adrian Burgoyne, falsely incarcerated for murder. Burgoyne escapes and uses the crowds at the world's fair as camouflage for getting revenge and justice. The action moves from Chicago to Mexico and back to Chicago, but it is mostly set in and around the city and fairgrounds.

224. Cohen, Lester. *The Great Bear*. New York: Boni and Liveright, 1927. 357pp.
This romance novel is set in Chicago's business community between January 1885 and May 1888. Fifty-year-old Thane Pardway, the "Great Bear" of the Chicago Board of Trade, has been affected by his wealth and fame. He lives selfishly and takes advantage of the women who are attracted to him by his wealth. During a long campaign to control the wheat market, a business acquaintance of Pardway dies, asking Pardway to look after his daughter, Agnes Weatherly, who has no immediate relatives. Attracted by Agnes' beauty, Thane takes her into his office as a personal secretary and into his home as her guardian. As he puts his plan in place to corner the wheat market, he also strategizes his sexual conquest of Agnes. Inconveniently, Agnes falls in love with Thane and to his surprise, he realizes how tender his own affections have become. His brother, Daniel Pardway (the department store magnate of Cohen's novel *Sweepings,* entry 225), urges Thane to marry the girl. However, fearing a personal relationship will impair his business focus and end his career as a womanizer, he encourages Agnes to marry an acquaintance closer to her age. The novel presents issues concerning gender roles, describes domestic settings, and imparts a good deal of information about the workings of the commodities market. The novel mentions many locations in Chicago, but provides little physical description of the city; however, the book does explore the public fascination with the titans of the commodities exchange and the central role of Chicago in the world economy.

225. Cohen, Lester. *Sweepings*. New York: Boni and Liveright, 1926. 447pp.

This generational novel begins at the time of the Revolutionary War, but mostly tells the story of two brothers born in the 1830s, Daniel and Thane Pardway, the second generation after the founding of the United States, and Daniel's children, the third generation. The narrative provides evidence for the author's view of social decay, presenting the generation who comes of age around the turn of the twentieth century as at least inept, and potentially corrupt, in a country where Anglophone immigrants, whose ancestors founded the country, are losing control to an Eastern European rabble. After spending their youth in adventures, Thane begins investing in stocks and bonds and Daniel becomes a merchant. Thane supports Daniel in opening a Chicago store in the months after the 1871 fire in the Loop. Soon his establishment, the Bazaar, is a great success. By 1901, wealthy, married Daniel is concerned about which of his sons will take over his business. Unmarried Thane co-opts Daniel's oldest son, Eugene, into joining his investment firm. Daniel's second son, Fred, delays his career by going to Princeton, and his third son, Bert, is still in school. So, when daughter Phoebe marries Sam Layton, Daniel convinces his son-in-law to join the management of the Bazaar. Layton quickly self-destructs from the effects of drug abuse and Phoebe begins a very public separation and divorce proceedings. She also begins an affair with impoverished European prince Vladimir Gilititz, a man with no moral standards. After Layton commits suicide, Phoebe eventually marries Gilititz, ignoring Daniel's objections. Throughout all of this, Daniel's general manager, Abe Ullman, an Eastern European Jew who is personally distasteful to Daniel, makes himself indispensable to the firm. When Fred gets out of college and still takes no interest in business, and Bert enters the firm, but proves too weak to take a significant role in management, Daniel issues shares in his company, distributing them equally to his children. Eventually, Daniel is overwhelmed by family shortcomings: Fred has an affair with the lowliest of Daniel's employees and then becomes an alcoholic, Phoebe is divorced from Gilititz with extensive and scandalous coverage of her affairs, and Thane has an affair with a "mulatto" and dies. When he learns that Fred and Phoebe have secretly sold their shares in the Bazaar to Abe Ullman, Daniel has a heart attack and begins a long decline that leads to his death. At the end of the novel Ullman owns ninety-percent of the Bazaar and is about to sell his shares to become a very wealthy man. Freddie, a homeless alcoholic, has just been discovered dead and the Pardway mansion is dark and up for sale.

226. Collins, Charles. *The Sins of Saint Anthony; Tales of the Theatre*. Introduction by Henry Kitchell Webster. Chicago: Covici, 1925. 265pp.

Almost all of these seven short stories from the world of the theater are of romance gone wrong and most are, in part, set in Chicago. The actors and actresses that are the main characters have taken to the stage to escape from poverty or small towns and, although they may occasionally have Broadway engagements, they are more likely to travel a circuit that takes them through Chicago. Some of the Chicago settings include the red-light district, the theater district, and the affluent Near North Side. Drug addiction is a prominent theme in one story.

227. Colter, Cyrus. *The Beach Umbrella*. Iowa City: University of Iowa Press, 1970. 225pp.

All of these fourteen short stories are set in African-American Chicago neighborhoods of the 1950s and 1960s. On the whole the settings are middle and upper-middle-class and the characters, many of whom are college-educated, are not primarily concerned with economic survival. Several of the stories are written from the perspective of women and concern their relationships with their boyfriends and husbands. Characters pay a surprising amount of attention to status identifiers, including clothing, household furnishings, organizational memberships, and the relative lightness of one's skin color.

228. Colter, Cyrus. *Night Studies*. Chicago: Swallow Press, 1979. 774pp.

This novel examines racial issues in the United States of the 1970s, mostly by focusing on a fictitious national organization based in Chicago, the Black People's Congress. Although Chicago is not the only setting, a significant portion of the work is set there. Most of the characters, including the African-Americans, are members of the middle, and upper classes and the book includes descriptions of leisure pursuits, clothing, and domestic interiors. The Black People's Congress primarily advocates for public policy and legislation, however the group also tries to aid individuals impacted by racism and most of these people are poor or working-class and their stories present a view of Chicago much different from that of more affluent characters. Extended historical accounts of the experiences of ancestors are not set in Chicago, but present information on the antebellum slave trade and the Civil War era. One of the major plot lines has to do with an interracial affair that destroys the career of the founder of the Black People's Congress.

229. Colter, Cyrus. *The Rivers of Eros*. Chicago: Swallow Press, 1972. 219pp.

This novel, that illustrates the impact of racial hatred, is mostly set on Chicago's South Side in the early 1970s. The book's various characters have each addressed their racial identities in different ways. Clotilda Pilgrim moved to Chicago with her husband in 1935. Through her now-deceased husband's work at an International Harvester factory and her scrimping and labor as a seamstress, she has been able to build some security for herself in a rented house. She cares for her two grandchildren whose father murdered their mother and she has two boarders. One, Titus Neeley, is a frustrated mailman, who attended college, but was never able to get a job that challenged his intellect. Another boarder, Ambrose Hammer, did not attend college, but has become an independent intellectual, working every day at the Chicago Public Library on his history of African-Americans in the United States. Clotilda, Titus, and Ambrose have responded to racism by working hard at whatever opportunities have presented themselves. They are increasingly surrounded by a younger generation that proclaims the need for rebellion or for simply dropping out of the struggle of living in a racist society by self-anesthesia through drug abuse. After Clotilda discovers that her high school age granddaughter is having sex with Desmond Smith, a married man and drug addict, a tragic event brings an end to her household. Although the novel provides little physical description, the work conveys a good deal of social information about working-class African-American Chicago in the 1970s.

230. Converse, Jane. *Alias Miss Saunders, R.N.* Thorndike, Maine: Thorndike Press, 1962. 266pp.

This romance novel set in a 1960s Chicago hospital captures aspects of work culture. Marie Saunders, born Mariska Szabo, is the daughter of Hungarian immigrants who live in Cicero where her father works in a clothing factory. After a high school boyfriend rejected her when he discovered her family circumstances, Marie devoted her energies to training as a nurse and making a new life for herself. Her professional and social life revolves around Tressler Memorial Hospital; she lives with two other nurses and socializes exclusively with nurses and interns. Like Marie, almost all of the novel's characters have family issues they have had to address, or are addressing, to become self-assured individuals. A major sub-plot involves one of Marie's colleagues, Cheryl Griffin, whose father died in racketeer violence. Cheryl gets herself into trouble by following her father's footsteps and trying to blackmail officials that he had bribed in operating his pinball machine racket. Marie is in love with Dr. Wayne Styles, but considers him unobtainable because he is a member of one of Chicago's most prominent families. As she gets to know him and learns about his family's troubles, she becomes more confident a relationship is possible.

231. Cook, Bruce. *Sex Life*. New York: Evans, 1978. 288pp.

Spanning approximately thirty years, from 1952 to 1978, this novel is mostly set in Chicago and its suburbs, and explores the impact of the sexual revolution. Although the book presents itself as a murder mystery and has a sympathetic police detective, Joseph Melaniphy, the novel is mostly a first-person account of Jack Gawlor's sex life from the time he is seventeen until he is murdered at forty-two. Gawlor is outwardly respectable, having graduated from college, worked his way into an executive position in an advertising agency, and married and fathered two daughters. His sexual explorations, however, become increasingly scandalous and criminal. The novel traces his behavior from his relatively innocent visits to burlesque houses, to his first encounters with a prostitute, through adulterous office affairs, and his purchasing of sexual encounters through pimps to have sex with transvestites and boys. The Chicago venues are mostly jazz clubs, stripper bars, pornographic theaters and gay bars, and social exchanges mostly have to do with sexual flirtation and innuendo.

232. Cook, William Wallace. *Wilby's Dan*. Illustrated by C. B. Falls. New York: Dodd, Mead, 1904. 325pp.

In this morality tale, a boy has the chance to prove that he is not his father's son, so far as having a predisposition toward criminality is concerned. After their mother died, Dan and Alice Wilby are sent to live with their grandfather, Enoch Wilby in Trueville, Illinois (and their father was sent to prison for an unspecified crime). Miserly Enoch immediately sends Alice to the county poor house since she is physically disabled and cannot work. Enoch barely feeds Dan, and makes certain his days are filled with labor. When Enoch is murdered, Dan is suspected and he flees to follow the trail of the killers to Chicago. Through cleverness and heroism, Dan captures the criminal gang and is cleared of the murder charge. His prospects brighten as the physician who was one of his first supporters decides to adopt him and Dan learns that he will receive all of the money Enoch had hidden around his house. Consistent with the morality of the novel, however, Alice dies before she can hear any good news and we then learn that years ago Dan had pushed his sister too high in a swing, breaking her back. Presumably, Dan will always live with his guilt. Although there is little physical description in the novel, about a third of the book is set in Chicago and the city plays a big role as the locus of crime that spreads out to country towns like Trueville.

233. Cooke, Marjorie Benton. *The Girl Who Lived in the Woods*. Illustrated by Margaret West Kinney and Troy Kinney. Chicago: McClurg, 1910. 430pp.

This society novel is concerned with women balancing society with home life and social activism with maternal duties, and records the ways in which a stay in the countryside (Lake Forest) transforms the understandings of three Chicagoans. Anne Harmon and Richard Barrett, Chicagoans born into affluence whose parents were friends, married to satisfy parental expectations. As a result, their marriage was troubled from the start. Richard socialized in bohemian circles and Anne had conservative friends she made through her mother. When a son, Bobby, is born, Anne pays scant attention to him and she and Richard still spend little time at home, socializing in their two, distinct spheres, instead. Then, in a Board of Trade panic, Richard loses his own fortune, along with his wife's (through power of attorney). Richard goes to work in his father's office, sells his city house and moves his household, complete with a staff of servants, to Lake Forest. Even there, the Barretts cannot afford to live in their country house, which they sell to Judge Carteret (one of Anne's conservative friends), retaining only the lodge on the property for their residence. Richard, although still somewhat indifferent to his wife, is immediately jealous of distinguished, forty-five-year-old Carteret's friendship with her, even though the Judge is married. Matters are complicated further by self-described bohemian artist Celia Carne, who has decided to leave the city and rusticate in a cottage near the Barretts' estate. When the Judge moves in, Carne is immediately hostile since the Judge gives harsh sentences to labor organizers. On the other hand, she is quickly smitten with Saxton Graves, the architect the Judge hires to renovate his newly purchased house. Although much of the novel is set in the country (some scenes take place on Halsted when Celia returns to the immigrant district, others in the townhouse of the senior Barretts, and more in the Judge's courtroom), the people in the novel are all preoccupied with their experiences in the city. Anne and Richard come to a new understanding of themselves and their lives in society and fall in love with each other. Under the tutelage of the wise Judge, Celia gains a new appreciation for capitalism and a more sophisticated understanding of Socialism and union activism. From the author's perspective, she also grows into her nature as a woman, developing an understanding and appreciation for children through her encounters with Bobby and becoming more romantic through her interest in Saxton.

234. Coons, Maurice [Armitage Trail, pseud.]. *Scarface*. New York: Clode, 1930. 286pp.

The action of the novel convincingly presents 1920s and 1930s Chicago gangs and the neighborhoods and businesses they patronized, including burlesque houses, poolrooms, gambling parlors, and speakeasies. Central character, Tony Guarino, begins his rise in organized crime when, at eighteen, he kills gang leader Al Spingola over a woman in 1916. The Spingola killing gets national coverage and when Tony suspects he may be implicated, he secretly travels to New York City and enlists in the army. His training in World War I makes him even better prepared to engage in a life of violent crime. He changes his name to protect his family and returns to Chicago, reuniting with the woman over whom he killed Al Spingola. By killing other gang leaders, he builds a large and powerful criminal organization. Near the end of the novel, Tony is brought to trial for one of these killings. However, the judge and key witnesses have been bribed and the jury intimidated, so a not guilty verdict is brought in record time. After the trial, just as Tony finishes taking revenge on his enemies, he narrowly escapes a police trap and a car chase ensues. He kills all of the officers who gave chase, except one. When he realizes that the remaining policeman is his brother (who does not realize Tony's true identity because of the name change), Tony lets his brother kill him. Although specific places are not featured in the novel, the book captures a period of Chicago history when gangsters prevailed. The novel was adapted as a motion picture of the same name (United Artists theatrical release, 1932).

235. Corbett, Elizabeth. *Cecily and the Wide World: A Novel of American Life Today*. New York: Henry Holt, 1916. 344pp.

Although some action takes place in Chicago, physical setting, beyond domestic interiors, has little significance in this book about companionate marriage and the role of women in the household and the world of work. As the wife of Avery Fairchild, a physician in the prosperous imaginary town of Jefferson, Cecily devotes herself to creating a pleasant home life and advancing in society for the good of her husband's career. Dr. Fairchild, however, decides to give up his lucrative practice and devote himself to public health projects focused on the inner-city poor. After a period of training with a public health advocate in New York City, Fairchild decides to move to Chicago and start an anti-tuberculosis society. Cecily, who was neglected during Fairchild's absence, had reflected on the meaning of her marriage and responds to Fairchild's decision with one of her own—she will not follow him. The rest of the novel relates their time apart and what they learn about themselves, marriage, and divorce, and addresses themes of gender and social advocacy.

236. Corbett, Elizabeth. *The House Across the River*. New York: Reynal and Hitchcock, 1934. 274pp.
     This novel, that is both a romance and a murder mystery, is partly set in Chicago and a fictional suburb named Hillport, as well as a remote area of Wisconsin. Elliott Farwell, a Chicago architect, met the woman he married, a French war refugee, in Chicago and knows nothing about her background beyond what she told him. Farwell built a house for his wife in Hillport and the two seem happily settled until Elliott rents a cottage he owns in the same suburb to a French couple. Suddenly Anne decides she wants to spend the summer alone in a remote part of Wisconsin. When one of his tenants is found shot to death, the past that links the French couple to Anne is slowly revealed. Suburban life is described ambivalently in the novel. Husbands who work in the city spend their days and some evenings in Chicago and wives try to get to the city frequently. When they are at home with their children and servants, they must entertain themselves as best as they can with bridge, teas, and club meetings. Most of the characters are upper-middle-class and have social lives that include people from the East Coast. Surprisingly, given the Depression-era setting, the only hardship for the characters seems to be getting along without alcohol in the final days of Prohibition.

237. Corbett, Elizabeth. *The Old Callahan Place*. New York: Appleton-Century, 1966. 311pp.
     This tale of family life centers on Molly Callahan McDermott and is set in Helios, a fictional Chicago suburb. Molly is the eldest daughter of Ed Callahan, an Irish immigrant who had married into a large and well-placed family in the United States and became a success in his own right by establishing a grocery store and a saloon. In the flush of his affluence he built a large, comfortable, family house for his daughter and three sons that becomes a Helios landmark. Tragedy strikes when he dies of cancer at a young age and his youngest son dies of a heart attack soon afterwards. His widow, infantilized by grief, became an invalid and, had it not been for Molly, the family would have collapsed. Molly successfully took up the burden of supporting her school age brothers and incapacitated mother and saved the family home. In the novel, Chicago is the location of jobs and entertainment, as well as the source of luxuries, and professional expertise (particularly when a skilled physician is needed).

238. Corey, Paul Frederick. *County Seat*. Indianapolis: Bobbs-Merrill, 1941. 418pp.
     Chicago plays an important role in this novel, even though most of the book is physically set in Elm, the seat of Moss County, Iowa. Otto Mantz, one of Elm's young people who goes to Chicago to become a success, describes his experiences to his mother on trips back to town. Otto gets a college education at a university in Des Moines and obtains a job with the telephone company in Chicago. For his family and their acquaintances, Chicago represents urban life as a contrast to their substantially agrarian existence. Chicago is also the larger world to them—the place where one goes to "make one's mark." Otto's mother (always Mrs. Mantz) believes that her son will become a success and move her to Chicago, a place she associates with all that is best in modern

America. When Otto tries to describe his office drudgery, the dramatic economic inequalities, and the squalor in which so many people live, Mrs. Mantz blocks him out. Then, the stock market crashes and Otto returns home out of work and Mrs. Mantz is forced to give up her dreams and let Otto work the family farm. Covering the period 1924 through 1930, the novel emphasizes the disconnect between town and city in a rapidly urbanizing country and assesses the Depression as clear evidence of the failure of the worldview that made the American city possible.

239. Corne, Molly E. *Death at a Masquerade*. New York: Mill, 1938. 256pp.

One of a series of murder mysteries featuring Elsie Benson and her police detective friend "Mac" McIntyre, this novel is mostly set inside an upper-middle-class apartment building. Elsie, the wife of a well-known journalist who is often on assignment, was a beautician in a small town in Ohio, before she married. When the women in her Chicago apartment building find out about her past, they hire her to employ her skills for in-home treatments. After a murder is discovered during a building-wide masquerade party, Elsie is an inside source of information for Detective McIntyre. Many people had motives for killing the murder victim, Rose Franklyn, a blackmailer, who had affairs with married men and then extorted money from them. The novel has many descriptions of apartments, most of which have a servant's entrance and a maid.

240. Corne, Molly E. *A Magnet for Murder*. New York: Mill, 1939. 254pp.

At the beginning of this murder mystery, Elsie Benson decides to go to the movies to alleviate her boredom in the absence of her reporter husband, who is on a trip to New York City. In the movie house she realizes that the man next to her has died and she is soon caught up in a homicide investigation when her friend Detective McIntyre takes the case. Although the novel is set in Chicago, most of the action transpires inside the home of the victim, Julius P. Tannin. Tannin, the multimillionaire owner of a pharmaceutical firm and chain of drugstores, resided in a mansion on Michigan Boulevard with a staff of four and five relatives, all of whom had reasons for wishing him dead. The novel raises issues of cultural attitudes toward mental illness, physical deformity, and social class

241. Correll, Charles J. and Freeman F. Gosden. *Sam 'N' Henry*. Illustrated by Samuel Jay Smith. Chicago: Shrewesbury, 1926. 189pp.

In this novelistic equivalent of a "blackface" vaudeville act, two African-American men, Sam Smith and Henry Johnson, travel from their hometown of Birmingham, Alabama to Chicago, after recruitment by a traveling agent for a construction company. Not only have they never been to a city, they have never traveled before and descriptions of their confusion and ignorance are meant to be humorous. When they finally locate the job site (Eighth Street and Michigan Avenue) and start work, they immediately run into trouble and are soon fired. Subsequently, they work for a while packaging mail orders at the Montgomery Ward Company. At one point, the men join an African-American men's lodge, the Jewels of the Crown, and there is an extended description of rituals and costumes. Their socializing consists of drinking and gambling and the lodge officers make a profit on everything. During the course of the novel, Sam gets taken advantage of by a street vendor selling pens, a fortuneteller, a quack physician, and his friend, Henry, who consistently cheats him out of money. In addition to the social description in the novel, some physical description is provided as Henry and Sam take bus and streetcar rides and comment on the buildings and parks.

242. Corrington, John William. *The Bombardier*. New York: Putnam's Sons, 1970. 255pp.

This novel presents ethnic, racial, religious, regional, and generational divisions in the United States as an enduring part of the social fabric. The first section of the novel is set during World War II when five men with very different backgrounds meet in Texas during bombardier training. Among them are: a Jew, an African-American, a Polish immigrant, a socially prominent southerner, and a New York musician. Their wartime experiences form a major portion of the book. Years later, the same men experience the 1968 National Democratic Convention and the ensuing riots in Chicago and the event is recorded from each of their perspectives. The Chicago content is very specific to events in 1968.

243. Corrothers, James David. *The Black Cat Club: Negro Humor & Folklore*. Illustrated by J. K. Bryans. New York: Funk and Wagnalls, 1902. 264pp.

Written as humor, today readers will consider the text a racist document. However, the book provides a means of understanding expressions of African-American culture in the social context of the early twentieth century. Set in Chicago's Levee District around Clark Street, this anecdotal work focuses on the founding and early meetings of the Black Cat Club whose members are African-American men. Club founder Sandy Jenkins is considered a poet and he refers to the club as a literary society. However, even though he reads verses, other club members tap into the long oral tradition of African-American culture to share stories and folklore. As a result, when Sandy visits an African-American seamstress with middle-class pretensions, she objects to the club for presenting African-American's as superstitious and illiterate (after all, the organization is named for a big black cat, which, as a representative of Satan, can help them with "hoodoo"). However, the Black Cats are popular with other Chicagoans. A Dutch immigrant saloon owner invites the club to his establishment. His countrymen, who are the only patrons of his establishment, are fascinated by the Black Cats. The club is also invited to perform at an African-American church where they sing and dance. When they finally engage in a debate, more in keeping with the activities of a literary club, they choose the question of whether it is better to stand one's ground or flee to fight another day. Members of the Board of Trade observe and are deeply amused by the proceedings, especially when violence breaks out among the opposing debaters. The book introduces attitudes toward women and education, and is filled with class distinctions made on the basis of clothing, household furnishings, and the relative lightness of skin color.

244. Coryell, John Russell [Nicholas Carter, pseud.]. *The Crescent Brotherhood; or, Nick Carter's Chicago Double*. New York: Street and Smith, 1899. 205pp.

No additional information available.

245. Coryell, John Russell [Nicholas Carter, pseud.]. *The Twelve Tin Boxes; or, Bob Ferret's Chicago Tangle*. New York: Street and Smith, 1898. 219pp.

No additional information available.

246. Courtney, James [Frank M. Robinson, pseud.]. *The Power*. Philadelphia: Lippincott, 1956. 219pp.

In this 1950s, Cold War era novel, an academic working with the military descends into a feverish paranoiac attack in which he believes he is being forced to commit suicide. Professor William Tanner chairs a team of academics (anthropologist, physicist, biologist, psychologist) sponsored by the U.S. Navy to explore the limits of human mental endurance. When team member,

Professor John Olsen, is found dead, foul play is suspected. Thinking that only a superhuman intellect could have committed the crime, the police and team members suspect Tanner. However, Tanner is suspicious of Adam Hart, his nemesis, who seems to be mounting an attack on Tanner's very identity. Officials claim Tanner's bank account never existed and the record copy of his dissertation is no longer in the campus library. Gradually he realizes that everyone who ever interacted with him has no recollection of the encounter and he feels he is being driven to suicide. In this work, Chicago is a lonely place of all-night coffee shops and bars in which Tanner must pursue his nemesis in solitude.

247. Cowdrey, Robert H. *Foiled. By a Lawyer. A Story of Chicago*. Chicago: Clark and Longley Printers, 1885. 337pp.

The complex, melodramatic plot of this novel concerns a woman's efforts to control a man's fortune. Stewart Graham, nearing sixty, has married school principal Sarah, a woman considerably his junior, after meeting her while summering at a resort. Sarah has a fearful ability to discover people's secrets and motivations by inviting confidences and she is also a skilled actress, who conceals all of her own thoughts. Graham has one daughter, Edith, and Sarah decides the girl should marry as soon as possible. With her out of the house, Sarah will get Stewart to adopt her live-in companion Bertha and give her a one-third share in his estate, and in that way Sarah will gain control of two-thirds of the estate, since Sarah is her creature. When Arthur Howard, the young son of one of Graham's friends appears in Chicago, Sarah sees her chance and engineers his marriage to Edith. However, before she can get Stewart to adopt Bertha, he becomes ill and begins asking for his lawyer. Concerned about changes to his will, Sarah poisons her husband, making it seem like an accidental opiate overdose administered by Arthur. Employing an unscrupulous lawyer to forge a new will she receives most of the estate. Arthur, wrecked emotionally over Stewart's death, recovers to take an interest in the will's unfairness and begins to employ his cleverness and strength of character to achieve legal redress. Although he meets with some success, Mrs. Graham's manipulative skills guarantee that she is still left with money and a measure of control. The fact that the author chose to set the work in Chicago, rather than New York City, may indicate the cultural power of the city as a business center and home for men of wealth.

248. Cowdrey, Robert H. *A Tramp in Society*. Chicago: Schulte, 1891. 289pp.

In novel form, the author presents his philosophy on property rights, land ownership, and economics. When a panhandler approaches millionaire Harold Sears, he reacts with disgust. Then, the tramp reveals that he is Edgar Bartlett the son of Dr. Bartlett of Providence, Rhode Island, whom Sears and his family had known socially. Suddenly accommodating, Sears hands over cash and his card. Bartlett is soon arrested for having stolen the money and in the scuffle loses Sears' card. A detective employed by Sears bails out Bartlett and takes him to the millionaire's residence. Sears hears Bartlett's sad story that includes being sent to prison for begging for bread to feed his children, Kate and Johnny. Bartlett convinces Sears that it is the fault of the capitalist system that there are tramps and not individual moral failure. With a one thousand dollar loan from Sears, Bartlett establishes a mercantile business and becomes a respected merchant and clubman with a considerable fortune. He openly discusses his past as a tramp and lectures on the plight of those who lack property. During a coal strike he confronts the mine owner over his one hundred percent return on his investment, forcing the owner to share more of the profits with the miners. Later, Bartlett purchases the DuPage Farm, an untouched tract that had remained intact as Chicago grew, and he offers free occupancy and use of the land so that tenants can gain the full benefit from their labor.

His philosophy on property rights disturbs landholders and for much of the remainder of the novel Bartlett must fight a land syndicate to hold onto his property. Cowdrey's novel is mostly a tract on economic principals with little physical description of 1880s Chicago. The final section of the book includes numerous contemporary newspaper articles that illustrate the mistreatment of tramps.

249. Craig, M. S. (Mary Shura). *The Shop on Threnody Street*. New York: Coronet Book / Grosset and Dunlap, 1972. 160pp.

In this mystery romance for young adults, Liza Quentin returns to Chicago after college to help an elderly childhood friend, Sophia. Proprietor of a doll shop on Threnody Street, Sophia had enthralled Liza and other neighborhood girls with her artistry and her stories of life in France as a "white Russian émigré," with nobles as relatives. Much of Sophia's adult life has been consumed with efforts to find the rightful heirs to the family fortune and she summons Liza to Chicago to meet the heiress Katya. When Liza reaches the city, Sophia is too ill to speak, but Liza is immediately suspicious of Katya and she begins to investigate, eventually meeting an attractive young man in the process. Liza rediscovers her old neighborhood, reconnects with her father (a retired academic) and her friends (many also from academic households). The book conveys a sense of neighborhood intimacy where people truly know each other, and it includes some references to the counter-culture and to the Vietnam War.

250. Crane, Laura Dent. *The Automobile Girls at Chicago; or, Winning Against Heavy Odds*. Philadelphia: Henry Altemus, 1912. 254pp.

Characters in several of Crane's novels, a group of friends known as the "automobile girls," travel to Chicago for a visit. On the way one of them overhears plotters who are determined to financially destroy a man through wheat futures manipulation. Barbara Thurston travels with her sister Mollie and chaperone, Grace Carter, and overhears the plot just before the train derails (and she saves the life of a man). Uninjured, the group boards another train and is soon in Chicago, being greeted by their hostess Ruth Stuart, the daughter of broker Robert Stuart, whom they are visiting. The Stuarts live on the lake, just off Michigan Avenue in a house so large Mollie mistakes it for the public library. The girls go to the opera and visit the Board of Trade, which Barbara finds totally unnerving. They spend Christmas with the family of Ruth's cousin, Olive Presby, on an estate of hundreds of acres called Treasureholme, thirty miles outside the city. Despite the grandeur of their setting, the Presbys are poor, and must soon recover the ancestral treasure hidden on the property by forebears murdered at Fort Dearborn or lose Treasureholme. As secret passages are explored and an old journal yields a clue, the search heats up. So, however, does a threat to the fortunes of both Mr. Presby and Robert Stuart, and Barbara realizes that the train plotters are the culprits. Unable to influence the plotters (despite having saved the life of one of them during the train wreck), she does solve the mystery of the treasure. In the nick of time the hoard of jewels is rushed into Chicago so that Richard Presby and Robert Stuart can meet the margin call on their wheat futures. Their fortunes are saved and they vow never to trade on futures again.

251. Creasey, John [Anthony Morton, pseud.]. *Affair for the Baron*. New York: Walker, 1967. 191pp.

The plot of this novel involving international espionage and the recovery of stolen jewels takes the characters to New York City, rural Mexico, and San Antonio, as well as Chicago. John Mannering tries to help a beautiful young woman whose father, Professor Alundo, an advocate for peace, is trying to leverage possession of microfilmed plans for a weapon of mass destruction to get world leaders to sign a disarmament agreement. When Mannering kills the brother of Mexican gangster, Mario Ballas, who wants to steal the plans from Alundo, the gangsters believe Mannering has stolen emeralds from the body. The only way he can save his life is by recovering the emeralds. Mannering, known as "the Baron," is an art and antiques dealer with an international reputation for helping both the police and high-class criminals. The Chicago sections of the novel are mostly set in the train station and hotels around the Loop, as well as an expensive, new Lake Shore Drive, high-rise apartment.

252. Cromie, Alice Hamilton. *Lucky to be Alive?* New York: Simon and Schuster, 1978. 317pp.

More than a year after an automobile accident that killed her parents and brother, Tyler Ames is still recovering emotionally and physically (she lost part of her foot in the accident). At her physician's suggestion, she accepts a tutoring job that takes her far out the North Shore, near Lakewood, and into the household of Jonathan Clinton, an internationally famous painter. The huge, modernist Clinton mansion is filled with mysteries, including the circumstances of the first Mrs. Clinton's death and the illness plaguing Jonathan Clinton. By the end of the novel Tyler has helped solved some of the mysteries, regained self-confidence through responding to physical challenges, and begun a romance with Clinton's oldest son, Blase. This young adult novel provides extensive descriptions of an upper-class, 1970s estate on Chicago's North Shore, including information about furnishings, food, and pastimes.

253. Crowley, Mary Catherine. *The City of Wonders: A Souvenir of the World's Fair.* Detroit, Mich.: William Graham, 1894. 162pp.

This account of the Columbian Exposition focuses on the fairgrounds with few references to the city of Chicago. The novel presents the experiences of three young adults, Aleck, Ellen, and Nora Kendrick, and their bachelor uncle, Jack Bennett, who accompanies them from their New York state home and pays for the trip. Presented in the form of a travelogue, Crowley's book covers all aspects of the fairgrounds under broad categories consistent with the major themes of the fair (the history of discovery, technology, natural history, etc.). The Kendricks' agenda is supposedly determined by the relative importance of the sites they visit and they do not view the women's pavilion and the children's pavilion until the last day of their trip. One of the highlights of their stay is a nighttime gondolier ride through the illuminated fairgrounds. With the slightest of plots, the book is primarily a souvenir.

254. Crump, Paul. *Burn, Killer, Burn!* Chicago: Johnson, 1962. 391pp.

Injustice and oppression are facts to be accepted by members of the African-American community on Chicago's South Side in the area of Morgan Park in the 1950s. Protagonist Guy Morgan is the son of an evangelical preacher who abandons Guy's mother after she is crippled in an automobile accident, to have an affair with a younger woman, leaving Guy to care for his mother. Unable to engineer an escape from a life of racism and despair, when Guy is caught up in violence he accepts being framed by the police, believing that he will never have access to justice, and he goes to the electric chair for a crime that he did not commit.

255. Crunden, Allan B. and Robert Morse Crunden. *A Chicago Winter's Tale*. New York: Vantage Press, 1960. 224pp.

Private detective Moritz Dantzeff presents the casebook for the Stafford Detective Agency, his employer, for 1915-1916. Besides the sleuthing of Al Stafford, the agency's owner, all of the cases have in common the repercussion of past events on the present. Almost all of the characters came from non-U.S. countries (Italy, Poland, Moravia, Germany, and Canada). The book uses specific places in Chicago to provide a physical setting; especially ethnic neighborhoods and Goose Island. The Roman Catholic Church and the Democratic Party are the most important social organizations in the novel.

256. Crunden, Allan B. and Robert Morse Crunden. *Roses and Forget-Me-Nots: A Study of Intrigue in Chicago*. New York: Vantage Press, 1957. 129pp.

No additional information available.

257. Cunningham, Jere. *The Visitor*. New York: St. Martin's, 1978. 282pp.

Most of this psychological horror novel takes place near Glenwood, a suburb of Chicago, and several scenes are set in downtown Chicago. Psychiatrist Frank is having difficulties in his relationship with his wife and then his family experiences an even bigger threat as some of his patients begin projecting themselves outside of their bodies. This terrorizes his children, Belinda and Bobby, particularly since one of the patient's projections continue after she has died. Frank works in an institution that caters to very wealthy patients and the novel is filled with cultural references to 1970s consumer goods that convey upper-class social status. Conflicts over gender appropriate roles in the family are a major theme of the novel as Frank argues that his wife Ginny should give up her painting (even though she is about to have a show at one of Manhattan's most prestigious art galleries), because her art diverts her energies away from her role as wife and mother. The novel's bizarre final scene may be read as Ginny's vindication or punishment, depending upon the reader's perspective.

258. Cuppy, Will. *Maroon Tales: University of Chicago Stories*. Chicago: Forbes, 1910. 337pp.

These short stories have a common set of characters and cover their experiences from their freshman to their senior year. Most of the plots have a purely campus focus and involve fraternity life, teasing faculty members, and campus clubs and sports. When the undergraduates leave campus it is for reform-minded projects or settlement house work. In general, the portrayal of the city is of a decidedly lower-class place compared with the environs of the university. Social class plays an important role in interactions amongst the students and extends to the way they treat faculty members, having good-natured disdain for those who got their degrees from "normal schools" (i.e., teachers' colleges).

259. Curtis, Wardon Allan. *The Strange Adventures of Mr. Middleton*. Chicago: Herbert S. Stone, 1903. 311pp.

Impoverished law clerk, twenty-three-year-old Edward Middleton, happens upon Achmed Ben Daoud, Emir of Al-Yam, and prince in the court of the Shahriyar of Al-Yam while returning a borrowed suit on Chicago's South Clark Street. The Emir is gathering stories to entertain the Shahriyar and asks if he can practice them on Middleton. During a series of meetings Middleton hears stories set in Chicago, but tinged with the fabulous and involving séances, mysterious villains, disembodied limbs, astral projection, and giant guinea pigs. At each meeting, Middleton

sented with a gift that subsequently leads to a bizarre adventure and his financial gain. By the end of the novel, he has accumulated enough money to marry his sweetheart, but not before having to deal with Achmed's last gift, an odalisque. In the way he deals with this last present, Middleton demonstrates all of the wisdom and sensitivity his exchanges with the emir have taught him. As a whole, the stories in this volume give some sense of the fantasies and preoccupations of young men working in offices around the Loop in the early twentieth century.

260. Dailey, Janet. *A Lyon's Share*. Janet Dailey Americana Series. New York: Harlequin, 1977. 186pp.

Part of an anticipated fifty-book series in which the author will set one of her romances in each state, this is the Illinois book. However, there is little attempt to establish a physical setting for the action beyond descriptions of the Lyon Construction Company where the main characters work and a modest apartment. Twenty-three-year-old Joan Somers has been secretly in love with her supervisor Brandt Lyon since she began working for his engineering firm three years before. To prevent an inappropriate office romance she has disguised her beauty by wearing her hair in a bun and dressing in form-concealing suits. When Joan and Brandt are stranded by a blizzard in the company offices, the experience ignites emotions that each of them has difficulty concealing. The novel touches on themes of gender roles, particularly as they relate to office settings. Brandt behaves in physically aggressive ways toward Joan and her acceptance and interpretation of this behavior is revealing.

261. Dale, Virginia. *Nan Thursday*. New York: Coward-McCann, 1944. 174pp.

When her partner in the radio singing team, the Melody Sisters, dies in a fall from the balcony of their expensive apartment-hotel suite, Nan Thursday does not believe the coroner's suicide verdict and investigates until she finds the murderer of Poppy Dublin. Thursday had been born into a vaudeville family. When her mother died on the road, four weeks after Thursday's birth, her father returned to the road soon afterwards and married one after another of his stage partners before retiring to the Actors' Home. Discomfited by her upbringing, Thursday was intrigued by Poppy Dublin's traditional childhood and is surprised when her illusions about Dublin's background and small-town life in general are destroyed when she travels to Clearwater, Wisconsin, to give Dublin's personal effects to her mother. The Chicago section of the novel describes apartment-hotel life and gives some indication of the city's nightlife and entertainment circuit during World War II. Although at the beginning of the book Chicago is portrayed as tawdry, after Thursday's experiences in Wisconsin, she is eager to return to the city.

262. D'Amato, Barbara. *The Hands of Healing Murder*. New York: Charter Communications / Grosset and Dunlap, 1980. 248pp.

Forensic pathologist Gerritt DeGraaf assists Chicago police inspector Rob Craddock in solving the murder of Dr. Adam Cotton. Cotton, who had been reading after dinner in a wing chair in his library while family members and dinner guests played bridge at nearby tables, was found dead between rubbers, stabbed with a scalpel through his parietal bone. Most of the people at the party were doctors, so the settings tend to be the Cotton mansion and a hospital, with little to tie the plot to Chicago.

263. Darrow, Clarence. *An Eye for an Eye*. New York: Fox, Duffield, 1905. 213pp.

Told in the first-person by protagonist Jim Jackson, Darrow's novel presents the dehumaniz-
ing struggle to earn a wage that nineteenth-century society's large under-class experience. This
struggle often formed the hidden extenuating circumstance of even the most disturbing crimes.
Jackson got his first job as a fourteen-year-old in the Chicago stockyards. No longer able to tolerate the inhuman working conditions, he gets a job as a railroad switchman, but when he sees a
friend run down and killed by negligence, he cannot force himself to return to work. Then he becomes a potato peddler, a job at which he demonstrates good salesmanship, but he soon realizes he
will never make enough money since the potato wholesalers will only sell him imperfect ones,
rejected for more affluent markets, even though Jackson must pay so much for them that he has to
sell them at the price of perfect potatoes to make any money. After a day of frustration, he accepts
drinks from political party members trying to buy his vote and when he goes home and gets into a
fight with his wife, kills her in an alcohol-induced rage. The rest of the novel demonstrates how
the legal system fails people like Jackson. Although Darrow, the famous trial lawyer, intended to
awaken his readers to a society-wide problem, he used the Chicago setting with which he was
knowledgeable from first-hand observation.

264. Davieson, Sarah. *The Seldens in Chicago*. New York: Brentano's, 1889. 189pp.

When English immigrants are forced to move to Chicago and get the assistance of family
members, contrasts are sharply drawn between social life in the two cultures, yet the options for a
woman in the new world remains the same: marriage. Mr. Selden, a successful textile manufacturer from Leeds, is forced to join his brother in Chicago and resettle his twenty-year-old daughter
Marjorie there, after a bank failure pushes him to the brink of bankruptcy. His brother, Henry Selden, had immigrated years before, is affluent and owns a large Chicago textile firm. However,
when Henry dies of a heart attack, his widow Ursula, fearing Mr. Selden will usurp her son's position in the company, maneuvers him out of the company. Fortunately, he soon gets a job in New
York City and Ursula welcomes Marjory, whom she does not consider a threat, into her household
on Calumet Avenue and even invites her to summer with the family in Hyde Park. Too late, she
discovers that Horace Dean, the successful young businessman she had intended for her daughter
Theresa, has fallen in love with Marjory. Theresa's cunning sister Deborah forges a letter that
temporarily separates the lovers, but by the end of the novel the Seldens have emerged with happier prospects than ever. In this Anglophile work, the English Seldens and their customs and perspectives are favorably contrasted with those of Americans. Celebration of Decoration Day and
Independence Day are described, as well as Sunday recreation and visiting. The Seldens live in a
modest cottage in South Chicago, with one African-American servant girl. Their relatives have a
much more extensive household and a summer house. Protestant religion as practiced by the
American Seldens does not compare favorably with Marjory's Catholicism; it is the most religious
of Ursula's daughters who takes steps to poison the relationship between Horace Dean and Marjory.

265. Davis, Clyde Brion. *Jeremy Bell*. New York: Rinehart, 1947. 313pp.

Set in the 1890s, this novel favorably contrasts small-town life with Chicago. Although only
seventeen-years-old, apprentice blacksmith, Jeremy Bell, and his friend, apprentice miller Sam
Brock, despair of their mundane lives and decide to get jobs in Chicago like Henry Fisk. Although
Fisk is enthusiastic about his Spartan life, Bell and Brock are horrified by the ugliness and relative
poverty of the urban environment. They only stay in the city for a few days before rejecting it,

deciding instead to try lumbering jobs in Arkansas. Their experience in a lumber camp is even worse than in Chicago since they end up in a company town with near slavery conditions before they can escape and return to their hometown. This novel falls into the vast category of works in which Chicago attracts young people seeking opportunity, even though these characters reject the city almost immediately.

266. Davis, Clyde Brion. *Sullivan*. New York: Farrar and Rinehart, 1940. 279pp.

Although much of the present of this novel is set in Mexico and California, the protagonist, Gilbert Sullivan, in traveling and sharing adventures with McKinley Williams, daydreams about his life in Chicago working in the art department of a major newspaper and he tells Williams stories about his life there. Initially, Sullivan experiences 1930s Chicago as a young, unmarried man. After marrying hometown sweetheart Mildred Dockery, the two settle on North Clark Street, near Washington Square (known as a bohemian district at the time for the number of artists, students, and writers living there). The two socialize with other young couples and Mildred begins drinking for the first time in her life. Within the first year together, Sullivan discovers her in bed with the bond salesman from next door. He leaves for the West, but the novel ends with Mildred showing up in California (after receiving letters from Williams) asking for a second chance. Sullivan agrees and the two move back to their hometown, with new appreciation for its virtues, as Sullivan plans to take over his father's building and coal business.

267. Davis, Dorothy Salisbury. *The Evening of the Good Samaritan*. New York: Charles Scribner's Sons, 1961. 430pp.

Chicago here is renamed Trader's City and most of the main characters live in the North Shore neighborhood of Lakewood. Spanning 1936 to 1950, the novel tells the dramatic stories of more than half-a-dozen people who at first seem to have few connections. They include: college professor Jonathan Hogan and his physician son Marcus; the very wealthy physician Alexander Winthrop, whose wealth derives from patent medicine; physician Albert Bergner, wealthy from money inherited from his aristocratic, Jewish, European family; and academics George and Elizabeth Fitzgerald, whose families were Irish aristocrats. Through these and other characters, Davis illustrates the impact of the Depression, New Deal, Socialist politics, Chicago politics, anti-Semitism, investigative journalism, the Irish Diaspora, the public health movement, and World War II on segments of American society. The upper-class characters engage in politics and make efforts to improve social conditions, indirectly, through employing their wealth. Most physical settings are upper-class households of great affluence.

268. Davis, George. *The Opening of a Door*. New York: Harper and Brothers, 1931. 265pp.

This story of a Scottish Canadian immigrant family in Chicago is set in the 1920s in a stable, middle-class milieu, in which family ties provide stability, but limit opportunity. Beginning with the death of George MacDougall, the novel ends as most of his eight children gather for the imminent death of his wife. The MacDougalls lived for many years in Canada, where George established a general store. Prosperous for a time, George's business dwindled, and, in old age, he was forced to move to Chicago, where four of his children had already re-located. In reduced circumstances, living with his invalid wife and some unmarried daughters, in an apartment at 46 Upton Place, George devoted himself to Bible study and solitary walks. Only a few of his children married, mostly in their forties, and several of them have had disappointments in love. The fiancé of one daughter committed suicide and any time this daughter can spare from her job teaching disabled children she uses to study spiritualism. The fiancée of another swindled him out of his money. A few of George's children did establish themselves successfully away from the rest of the family. One married and settled in Cleveland, Ohio, and the most successful, Daniel, moved to San Francisco and established an import business. Only one grandson, the offspring of the Cleveland couple, was born to carry the MacDougall name forward. He attends George's funeral and decides to stay in the city and get to know his family. He obtains an office job in a foundry, and is exposed to family lore and secrets. By the end of the novel, he despairs over a life in proximity to his relatives and decides to leave for college, aided by Daniel who warns his nephew of the distorting influence of family ties. In addition to the funeral of George MacDougall, the novel describes a Christmas celebration, a marriage, and a reunion of most of the MacDougall children. The book touches on social roles of women, Canadian immigration to Chicago, the Scottish immigrant community, and family life.

269. Davis, Timothy Francis Tothill [John Cashman, pseud.]. *The Gentleman from Chicago; Being an Account of the Doings of Thomas Neill Cream, M.D. (M'Gill), 1850-1892*. New York: Harper and Row, 1973. 310pp.

Despite the title, very little of this work of historical fiction is set in Chicago. The first-person narrative of a serial killer, who poses as a physician and poisons women, is set in Glasgow, Quebec, and London. In 1880, the eponymous Thomas Neill Cream establishes himself in Chicago, since he considers it a migration center for the nouveaux riches of the Midwest and West and for the grifters and thieves for whom these people are prey. He sets up an office at 434 West Madison Street on Altgeld Park. He is not in the city long, however, before he has poisoned the husband of the woman with whom he had conducted an affair and is put on trial and later imprisoned in the Illinois State Penitentiary in Joliet, although he engineers his release and later makes his way to London. When he is put on trial for his murders in that city, he becomes the "gentleman from Chicago," perhaps due to Chicago's reputation for lawlessness.

270. Dawson, George H. [Michael Storme, pseud.]. *Hot Dames on Cold Slabs*. New York: Leisure Library, 1952. 128pp.

This is one of a series of books by an English author, which feature a Chicago, tough-guy, detective, named Nick Cranley. In this story, three beautiful women from small towns move to Chicago to find gullible men to support them. Unfortunately, several of their marks are gangsters, not such suckers as they seem. Cranley is left to connect the women's corpses with their killer lovers. The Cranley character is somewhat unusual among tough-guy detectives in that he is married. Despite his beautiful wife, Sheila, however, Nick is like others of his ilk in being a ladies' man. The detail with which the Cranley books describe his sexual conquests prompted fines and suppression in England. Dawson's publishing company (in which he was a partner) was forced to find printers and distributors in the United States. Not all of Cranley's adventures were set in Chicago, but because they were unavailable for review for this project, all of the books featuring Cranley are listed here: *Make Mine a Shroud.* (London: Archer, 1949; N.Y.: Leisure Library, 1952); *Unlucky Virgin.* (London: Archer, 1949; Cleveland, Ohio: Kayewin, 1951); *Make Mine A Harlot* (London: Archer, 1949; Cleveland, Ohio: Kayewin, 1951); *Make Mine Beautiful* (London: Archer, 1949; as *Curtains for Carla*, N.Y.: Leisure Library, 1952); *Make Mine A Virgin* (London: Archer, 1950; as *Carmen Was a Virgin*, N.Y.: Leisure Library, 1952); *Make Mine A Corpse* (London: Archer, 1950; as *A Corpse Spells Danger*, N.Y.: Leisure Library, 1952); *Sucker For A Red-Head* (London: Archer, 1950; as *This Woman is Death*, N.Y.: Leisure Library, 1952); *Satan Buys*

A Wreath (London: Archer, 1951); *Elvira Digs A Grave* (London: Harborough, 1952); *Chicago Terror* (London: Harborough, 1952); *Lovelies Are Never Lonely* (London: Harborough, 1952); *Make Mine A Redhead* (London: Harborough, 1952); *Kiss The Corpse Goodbye* (London: Harborough, 1952); *Baby Don't Say Goodbye* (London: Harborough, 1953); *The Devil Has A Racket* (London: Harborough, 1954).

271. Dean, S. Ella Wood. *Love's Purple Dream*. Chicago: John Forbes, 1911. 343pp.

Sections of this romance are set in Chicago's artistic community. Kate Granley is born and grows up in a New England village where her natural ability as a singer develops. She puts off college to nurse her dying mother, and, during the interval, attracts the attention of the wealthy Mr. Starwell, who wants her to give up any thought of employing her art as a singer, claiming the domestic sphere offers all the opportunities a woman should want. After her mother's death, Granley rejects her wealthy suitor to study voice in Chicago. In the novel, the city is exclusively represented by upper-class artistic circles. Granley is given to comparing the city and artistic life there with European capitals, particularly Paris. She eventually marries a Russian count, and the action shifts to Europe. However, Granley finds true love in the arms of Clifford Bennett, an American, after the sudden death of her nobleman husband.

272. Dell, Floyd. *The Briary-Bush*. New York: Alfred A. Knopf, 1921. 425pp.

In this continuation of the story of Felix Fay (*see* entry 274), Felix arrives in Chicago and begins working as a drama critic. He transforms himself from the thinker and dreamer he had been as a young man, into a man of action. He lives at the Community House, an adjunct of a settlement house, and meets the socially unconventional Rose-Ann, a settlement house worker whom he eventually marries. Once he leaves the Community House for his own apartment on Canal Street, he begins the life of a boulevardier, meeting regularly with a group of other bohemians who drink and philosophize together. After he marries Rose-Ann, he rents a former commercial space on Fifty-seventh Street, in which they create a loft-space, where they host salons for intellectual bohemians. They become disillusioned with their loft living, and dream of an actual house. However, Rose-Ann's professional acting ambitions and Felix's surprising allegiance to traditional gender roles eventually drive them apart. For space away from Rose-Ann, Felix rents a room in a Garfield Boulevard house as a writing studio, and when the couple separates, he lives in a cheap apartment on Wilson Avenue on the Near North Side. In Dell's earlier book, *The Moon Calf* (entry 274), Felix was one of a number of small town intellectuals longing to move to Chicago. In this book Felix and similar characters reach the city and try to establish personae to match their self-images as freethinkers and rebels. Often, they must cope with the realization that they may not be as outrageous or as talented as they believed. The book includes a wealth of social detail about restaurants, theaters, newspaper offices, and socializing among young people in Chicago in the first decades of the twentieth century.

273. Dell, Floyd. *Love Without Money*. New York: Farrar and Rinehart, 1931. 365pp.

In this exploration of love and how lovers fit into the larger society, Chicago is the locus for experimentation. Peter Carr and Gretchen Cedarbloom fall in love as teenagers and construe their relationship as rebellion against their parents. Each of them has rebelled against parental authority in the past and together they leave school and move from their small town to Chicago to get jobs and share an apartment. In the city they witness many kinds of love (the love between friends, filial love, and homosexual love, as well attachments to ideals, money, and success). In the end they choose a traditional approach to life, focusing on financial security and marriage. The novel details aspects of non-mainstream culture in Chicago, as well as social events, while presenting viewpoints on gender roles and the relationship of the individual to society.

274. Dell, Floyd. *Moon-Calf.* New York: Alfred A. Knopf, 1920. 394pp.

In this *bildungsroman*, the protagonist, Felix Fay, does not move to Chicago until the end of the book; however the city, as the intellectual center of the Midwest constitutes the promised land for Felix and the writers and socialists he meets. He lives in a series of Midwestern towns that represent places in Illinois and Iowa, including Maple (Barry, Illinois), Vickley (Quincy, Illinois), and Port Royal (Davenport, Iowa). Dell's book *The Briary-Bush* (entry 272) takes up the story of what happens to Felix when he actually moves to Chicago.

275. Dell, Floyd. *An Unmarried Father.* New York: George H. Doran, 1927. 301pp.

When Norman Overbeck returns to his hometown of Vickley (a fictionalized version of Quincy, Illinois) as a recent Harvard Law School graduate, his life seems set. He enters his father's law firm, becomes engaged to Madge Ferris, and begins to fulfill the other social obligations of small town, middle-class life. Then, he receives a letter postmarked in Chicago announcing his paternity of a child. While confirming that the child is his, he discovers that the mother does not want to raise it. Roundly condemned in Vickley for violating sexual mores, he moves to Chicago to raise his child as a single father. Dell presents Chicago as a place where one can escape convention, although he also shows the difficulties Norman faces even in the city. The book addresses issues of social attitudes toward premarital sex and gender roles in child rearing.

276. Denison, Thomas Stewart. *An Iron Crown: A Tale of the Great Republic.* Chicago: The Author, 1885. 560pp.

This indictment of corporations and the unfair advantages granted to them by politicians for their own personal enrichment is mostly set in New York City. However, in the section set in Chicago the protagonist is shocked at the corrupt businesses he finds there (an employment agency and an advertising sheet, among others), but he also begins to remake his fortune by trading wheat.

277. Derleth, August William. *Any Day Now.* Illustrated by Mathias Noheimer. Chicago: Normandie House, 1938. 134pp.

Renna Gluyk's mother was the most important person in her life and after her death Renna cannot bear to stay in memory-filled Sac Prairie, Wisconsin. She moves first to Milwaukee and then to Chicago to be an independent working girl. However, she cannot leave Sac Prairie entirely behind; she subscribes to her hometown newspaper, telephones her father and her childhood friends there, and visits whenever she can. One particular friend, Joe, who has become a physician, has been her love since she was a girl. However, Renna's mother disapproved of him, thinking that he would never be successful. So, when Joe proposes, Renna automatically rejects him. She quickly realizes her mistake, but cannot bring herself to take back her words. Trying to get over Renna, Joe quickly becomes engaged and marries before going off as a soldier in World War I. After years, during which Renna is filled with anxiety for his safety, he returns only to be killed in an automobile accident. Although there is little physical description of Chicago, the city functions as a place of unease for Renna and the novel implies that part of the loneliness of the city stems from the way it serves as a place of exile for many of its inhabitants.

278. Derleth, August William. *The Prince Goes West*. New York: Meredith Press, 1968. 158pp.

The Mill Street Irregulars, a group of adolescent boys, (Pete, Sim, and Steve) who solve mysteries, and have appeared in other Derleth books for children, are on a fishing trip outside of Sac Prairie, Wisconsin when they rescue a Middle Eastern prince, the same age as them, who had been abducted by Chicago gangsters. While Peter and Sim keep the prince in hiding, Steve stakes out the Drake Hotel where the prince had been staying with his tutor and his father's aide-de-camp. He is able to stay with Sac Prairie architect, Leo Weissenborn, in an apartment on Elm Street and Weissenborn's office is in the Tribune Tower near the Drake. Steve's lobby stake-out confirms the prince's suspicion that the aide-de-camp was involved with the kidnapping and when Steve runs into Mr. Barton, a Secret Service man he knows from other adventures, he realizes that the U.S. government knows about the kidnapping. During his breaks from the hotel lobby, he has lunch with Mr. Weissenborn at the architect's table of the Indian Room at the Black Hawk and dinner at the Cliff Dwellers Club on the top floor of Orchestra Hall, facing the Art Institute. Weissenborn, assuming Steve is playing tourist, introduces him to the city's architecture and history. When Steve returns to Sac Prairie and informs the prince of the aide-de-camp's suspicious behavior, the prince cables his father and he is rescued after a dramatic chase on the Wisconsin River involving the Chicago gangsters and the Secret Service. Although the Chicago setting is limited to downtown, the book describes unusual places not generally accessible to the public.

279. DeRosa, Tina. *Paper Fish*. Chicago: Wine Press, 1980. 137pp.

This fictionalized memoir of life in Chicago's Italian-American community in the 1940s and 1950s focuses on the relationship between a little girl and her grandmother, Doria. Carmolina first appears in the novel in the womb and in the course of the book experiences childhood. Since Doria knows she will not live until Carmolina marries, the novel ends with her dressing Carmolina like a bride, confident that she will carry on family tradition. Carmolina's family lives in a tenement building beside the fish market (the market workers burn the unsold fish during the afternoons, creating a remarkable stench). Her father is a policeman and she has one sister, Doriana, who becomes ill with a fever and loses her mental capacity. When there is talk of Doriana being institutionalized, Carmolina runs away, returning only when she is discovered prostrated by a fever. The novel is mostly focused on family life and has memorable scenes of culture-specific activities like picnicking at the family plot in the graveyard.

280. Dever, Joseph. *Three Priests*. Garden City, N.Y.: Doubleday, 1958. 453pp.

As roommates at St. Brendan's College outside Chicago, Bob Lambert, Vincent Whelton, and Arthur Wagner are not seriously thinking about becoming Roman Catholic priests. In fact, Whelton is contemplating a career in professional baseball and is later offered a chance to play for the New York Giants. Each of them does become a priest in a Chicago diocese, however, and this novel traces their quite different careers in the church, as well as their continued friendship. Most of the focus is on Whelton whose commitment to his work as a parish priest inspires him to found a youth center and an adult education center for people of all faiths, where he works to advocate fair labor practices, the right to join labor unions, and the end of race-based discrimination in the workplace. Wagner, whose uncle is a monsignor, devotes himself to editing a church newspaper and Lambert makes a rapid rise into the church hierarchy and focuses on church politics while practicing canon law. The novel depicts some social problems in 1930s and 1940s Chicago, including poverty, the housing segregation of African-Americans, and the growth of organized crime as a result of the Volstead Act.

281. De Voto, Bernard. *We Accept with Pleasure*. Boston: Little, Brown, 1934. 471pp.

Set in the late 1920s, this novel is filled with characters who are alienated from the larger culture that has become dominated by middle-class tastes funded by newly made fortunes. Chicago represents the middle-brow culture dominating the country. The main characters, many of whom fought in World War I, are a circle of friends and relatives who know each other because they are related or shared college life at Harvard. The relatives are members of either the Ewing or Gale families, who have a long history in New England, and are mostly affluent. Although most of the book is set on the East Coast, particularly in the Boston metropolitan area, and in the Gales' summer compound, several chapters are set in Chicago. One branch of the Gales settled in Illinois and a scion, Loring, has worked as the editor of a liberal newspaper in Chicago since his return to civilian life. He returns to the East Coast, however, after his newspaper is bought by a newly wealthy, Jewish man who wants to silence the newspaper's political editorials. Subsequently, Loring gives in to his distaste for Chicago and leaves to reside among his East Coast relatives. Ted Grayson, a Harvard friend of Gale and Ewing is a Northwestern professor at the beginning of the book, but grates at the meager salary and resents the cultural values of the Midwest. Still suffering emotional after-effects of wartime service, after he is dismissed for publicly declaring his pacifism, he has a nervous breakdown and is taken East by an alliance of Harvard friends. Descriptions of Chicago focus on the city's pollution and ugliness, skewer the empty sensationalism and sensualism of its artistic community, and portray the academic community as filled with small-minded, conservative individuals.

282. De Vries, Peter. *Angels Can't Do Better*. New York: Coward-McCann, 1944. 181pp.

College political science professor Peter Topp runs for alderman of Chicago's eighteenth ward in this novel set in the 1930s. Throughout, Topp must court favor from a political boss named Rago who reads Machiavelli. He campaigns in political meetings, but also restaurants, and bars. To win votes he must do the favors expected of ward heelers (deal with a starling infestation, write love letters for the inarticulate, etc.). He must also navigate the political shoals of his college campus and deal with gangsters.

283. De Vries, Peter. *The Blood of the Lamb*. Boston: Little, Brown, 1961. 246pp.

This autobiographical novel is mostly set on Chicago's South Side in the 1920s and 1930s in a Dutch immigrant community that is centered on the Dutch Reformed Church. Don Wanderhope's life from twelve to middle age becomes a catalog of suffering that confirms his rejection of ancestral piety. Wanderhope's father, who worked as an ice deliveryman and later as a sanitation worker, had rejected the Dutch Reformed Church as inconsistent with human reason before Don's birth. Wanderhope's older brother, Louie, became an atheist in medical school. Seeing nineteen-year-old Louie die from pneumonia drove the pre-teen Wanderhope to reject religion as well. For years, he drew meaning from his ambition for the cultured, upper-middle-class life of a Hyde Park resident, until a negative experience during college disillusions him. Shortly afterwards he is diagnosed with tuberculosis and, while living in a Colorado sanitarium, falls in love with a woman and witnesses her slow death from the disease. After marrying a teenage crush, he finishes his college education, works in advertising, and moves to New York City where his wife commits suicide and his daughter dies of leukemia. In addition to the descriptions of the South Side, the book includes evocative descriptions of Chicago's parks and lakefront.

284. De Vries, Peter. *But Who Wakes the Bugler?* Illustrated by Charles Addams. Boston: Houghton Mifflin, Riverside Press, 1940. 297pp.

This humorous novel catalogs the eccentric behavior of the lodgers at Mr. Thwing's boarding house. One scholarly man, engaged in vaguely academic research, often hosts friends that are exclusively library assistants and former missionaries. An intimidating sea captain with an indecipherable accent is drunk much of the time. Several lodgers operate businesses out of their rooms, including a patent medicine man who cooks his compounds on a hotplate, and an egg deliveryman who candles his eggs on the premises. A former baseball player cannot get over the fact that he accidentally killed a bird with a baseball. Broadly humorous and satirical, the book nevertheless reveals aspects of the cultural time period in which it was written, touching on attitudes toward women and ethnic and racial minorities (Mr. Thwing only employs African-Americans, who live-in), as well as illustrating aspects of boarding house life, a common living situation of the time.

285. De Vries, Peter. *The Glory of the Hummingbird.* Boston: Little, Brown, 1974. 276pp.

After a youth spent in Wabash, Indiana, Jim Tickler decides to seek his fortune in Chicago. Opportunity comes to him in a surprising way when he tries to walk up to cash a check at a drive-up bank teller's window. The teller, Amy Wintermoots, eventually agrees to date Tickler and she turns out to be the daughter of a marketing consultant who employs Tickler. Tickler is soon winning attention for writing jingles and slogans. He appears on a television contest show and wins national attention for his answers and his pledge to turn his winnings over to charity. His performance leads to a new job, and an affair, when he is contacted by the beautiful Mrs. Hamstead, a Chicago socialite who lives in a family mansion on Prairie Avenue and owns a hotdog manufacturing company, and hires him as her chief of marketing. De Vries uses Tickler's experiences to lampoon business culture, advertising culture, and Chicago society.

286. De Vries, Peter. *Into Your Tent I'll Creep.* Boston: Little, Brown, 1971. 244pp.

This novel is mostly set in South Chicago. Through the adventures of Al Banghart, De Vries satirizes women's liberation, the incipient counter-culture, liberal Protestant churches, and the marketing industry. At twenty-three, Banghart is a few years out of high school and has failed to become the popular music star he had envisioned. He has, however, perfected the art of female seduction and when he meets Grace Piano, his French teacher from Chicago's Southeast High School, he presents a winning countenance that attracts her. They begin an affair and marry, establishing a relationship in which the older Piano usually has the upper hand. In fact the union was predicated on Piano's commitment to being the bread-winner and Banghart a house-husband, an idea he readily embraced as liberation from the tedium of working in a hat factory. The arrangement also frees him to pursue the housewife next door and Piano soon admits the arrangement's failure and forces Banghart to re-enter the workforce. Although he mostly sells items and services door-to-door, employing techniques that border on fraud, for a time he enjoys middle-class success working with a record company. When he loses that job and is arrested for indecent exposure, Piano finally divorces him to pursue a relationship with the hipster Protestant minister, Shorty Hopewell. In the course of the novel, Banghart lives in a boarding house, visits a brothel, and becomes obsessed with the idea that he has a venereal disease. In addition to raising issues of gender roles, sexual expression and office life, the novel presents a 1960s culture in which most women are housewives, venereal diseases are not easily cured, and the sexual revolution is on the horizon.

287. De Vries, Peter. *The Vale of Laughter*. Boston: Little, Brown, 1967. 352pp.

In this satire of American culture, Joe Sandwich, is obsessed with being liked and cannot help turning every situation into a comedic exchange, involving words or sight gags. He grows up on the South Side and is too poor to attend college, but is able to ingratiate himself with the affluent Mr. MacNaughton, a stockbroker and father of "Naughty" MacNaughton, a girl he is dating who has become his most appreciative audience. MacNaughton sends Sandwich to business college and gives the young man a job in his firm at which Sandwich is spectacularly bad until he is moved to the research department. The couple settles in Wilton, the suburb of Chicago where the MacNaughton family lives and where the college from which Sandwich graduated is located. The second half of the novel is written from the perspective of Wally Hines, an instructor at the college who researches the psychology of humor, who is implicated in Sandwich's death.

288. Dewey, Thomas B. *The Brave, Bad Girls*. An Inner Sanctum Mystery. New York: Simon and Schuster, 1956. 244pp.

At the center of this novel are two wronged women, Lorraine and Esther. Esther believed the man who was dating her when he said he would marry her and she had sex with him. When he reneged on his promise and she gave birth to his child she used her sister Lorraine's name to avoid scandal. Lorraine, a schoolteacher, is then accused of immoral conduct by influential board member, Roscoe Turner. Coincidentally, a private detective, who appears in a series of Dewey's novels and is known only as Mac, is, for another reason, investigating the man who had wronged Esther. When the man is murdered his task becomes much more complicated. This novel touches on McCarthyism, moral positions on sexual relations outside of marriage, and attitudes toward immigrants.

289. Dewey, Thomas B. *Death and Taxes*. A Red Mask Mystery. New York: Putnam's Sons, 1967. 190pp.

Mac was the last person to see Marco Polo, a Chicago gangster, alive, when he was summoned to a meeting in an Italian restaurant in which Polo owned an interest. The grossly overweight Polo told him that he feared he would die of a heart attack at any time and wanted to make arrangements for his daughter to get one million dollars in cash without having to pay any taxes. At their next meeting, Polo was going to tell Mac the location of the money. As he was leaving the restaurant Polo was shot down gangland style. Now Mac fears that the killer knows what they were talking about and suspects that Mac knows the location of the money.

290. Dewey, Thomas B. *Don't Cry for Long*. An Inner Sanctum Mystery. New York: Simon and Schuster, 1964. 189pp.

Hoping to influence Congressman Farnum's vote, two plotters come up with an elaborate scheme involving his wife and his daughter Patricia. They are able to get Mrs. Farnum, a dipsomaniac, released from the sanitarium where she is being held and induce her to kill the bodyguard Farnum had hired to protect his daughter. They then kidnap Patricia to photograph her while two men force her to have sex. Fortunately, Farnum hired Mac after her bodyguard was shot and he uncovers the plot in time. The theme of underhanded political manipulation involving the press is perhaps reflective of the culture of the era.

291. Dewey, Thomas B. *Draw the Curtain Close*. New York: Jefferson House, 1947. 212pp.

Shortly after he hires Mac to protect his estranged wife, Cynthia, and give her a package, the very wealthy Alex Warfield is killed. When Mac first meets the beautiful young Cynthia, they discover that the package contains a Gutenberg Bible. Cynthia also makes the revelation that her ten year marriage to Warfield had been a financial arrangement. Warfield agreed to forgive a million-dollar debt her father had incurred if Cynthia would marry and live with him for at least ten years. Mac takes on the job of protecting Cynthia from being accused of murdering Warfield, but he is soon trying to figure out why more people are being killed—twelve before the end. Like a number of other Chicago murder mysteries this novel revolves around the idea of a wealthy collector who can buy whatever interests him from books, to women, to expensive gemstones, which is what the criminals in this case are seeking.

292. Dewey, Thomas B. *The Girl Who Wasn't There*. An Inner Sanctum Mystery. New York: Simon and Schuster, 1960. 216pp.

The recently widowed Virgie Henley, who was married to Barry Henley, one of Mac's fellow private investigators, suspects her apartment is being cased after several unexpected callers appear with implausible cover stories. She hires Mac to investigate, but she is murdered almost immediately. Mac carries on out of an obligation to her husband and her memory. The case turns on a swindle worked years earlier by a woman and her accomplices, in which the woman assumed a false identity to get a wealthy man to marry her, so that she could gain control of his fortune.

293. Dewey, Thomas B. *Handle with Fear; A Singer Batts Mystery*. New York: Mill, William Morrow, 1951. 218pp.

Scholarly Singer Batts owns a hotel in Preston, Illinois, and employs Joe Spinder as his factotum. Just before Batts is to travel to Chicago to present a conference paper, hotel guest Nick Andrews seeks their help; he is running from Chicago police, who have falsely accused him of killing his wife, Constancia. He is also being pursued by gangsters. Constancia's strangled body was found in the apartment of her sister Marcella, whose husband Angelo, a foot soldier with the Mafia, believes Nick killed her. When Marcella helped Nick get away, she gave him a suitcase she said was Marcella's that contained a fortune in currency. Batts and Spinder's investigation takes them into the heart of Chicago's Italian-American community and the center of gangster warfare.

294. Dewey, Thomas B. *How Hard to Kill*. New York: Simon and Schuster, 1962. 221pp.

Mac would have been a strong suspect in the murder of wealthy, hard-drinking Dickie Fleming, even if his pocketknife had not been the murder weapon, since he had been openly in love with Dickie's wife, Cathy, before the two were married and he had continued to have an intimate friendship with her. In the end Mac discovers who framed him, but not without a great deal of effort. Physical descriptions of Chicago tend to be shallow and establish setting by simply mentioning addresses, however the novel does present aspects of 1960s Chicago social life, touching on issues of social class, the social acceptance of heavy drinking, and cultural attitudes towards the advertising industry, particularly as it relates to commercial photographers (one important character, Ziggy Paul, uses his photography studio to surreptitiously capture revealing images of his models).

295. Dewey, Thomas B. *The King Killers*. A Red Mask Mystery. New York: Putnam's Sons, 1968. 184pp.

While collecting on an unpaid bill for commission merchant Nat Pines, Chicago private detective Mac gets beaten up in his apartment and awakens to find a murdered man on his sofa and police treating his residence as a crime scene. The last thing he remembers is that he was helping fellow private detective Karl Schneider deflect someone who was following Schneider. Schneider's case involves protecting a tough, seventeen-year-old girl and soon the detectives and the girl are on their way to Orange County California and the headquarters of the paramilitary League for Good Government where the novel concludes. In Chicago, the settings are bars, apartment buildings, and hotels.

296. Dewey, Thomas B. *Portrait of a Dead Heiress*. An Inner Sanctum Mystery. New York: Simon and Schuster, 1965. 187pp.

When twenty-six-year-old Lorrie King commits suicide on the eve of her wedding, her fiancé, gynecologist Dr. Peter Kramm, hires Mac to investigate. From the outset, Mac is puzzled by why police detective Saunders is also still pursuing the case when the official ruling was suicide. He thinks that Lorrie's close friend, artist Byron Dillon, may be his best informant. Although Lorrie was wealthy and her Near North Side apartment is described in detail, much of the novel is set in less affluent Chicago settings on the South and Far West Sides. Blackmail, abortion, and homosexuality are all major plot elements. Dillon is homosexual and perceptions of homosexuals are a major theme. Mac visits the residence Dillon shares with a much younger man, as well as bars and other locales frequented by homosexuals. Dillon eventually confesses to killing Dr. Kramm out of his hatred for the way Kramm was replacing Dillon in Lorrie's life.

297. Dewey, Thomas B. *Prey for Me*. An Inner Sanctum Mystery. New York: Simon and Schuster, 1954. 210pp.

When the police find a beautiful young woman murdered in the expensive apartment she rented under an assumed name on Walton Place, the telephone book is open and Mac's detective agency circled. To this lead, the police add the name of Norman Krupp, heir to a department store fortune, who walks in to the apartment to find the police photographing the body of his dead girlfriend. Mac soon finds out that the dead girl was involved with a professional photographer who took nude photographs of her for commercial purposes. Blackmail and stolen identity are underlying motivations for the murder. Social attitudes to women are an important aspect of this novel.

298. Dewey, Thomas B. *A Sad Song Singing*. An Inner Sanctum Mystery. New York: Simon and Schuster, 1963. 192pp.

When Crescentia Fanio's lover, folksinger Richie Darden, said he needed to leave town for a while, he left a locked suitcase in her care. Now, thugs are threatening her life and she follows her lawyer's suggestion that she hire Mac for protection. The first thing Mac wants to do is unlock the suitcase, but Fanio refuses and instead they go into hiding in a Loop hotel, while Mac tries to discover where Darden has gone. His search leads him to towns in rural Illinois and Indiana. In Chicago and the countryside Mac witnesses the prejudice directed against folksingers who were often part of a countercultural movement identified with rights for African-Americans and laborers and they were smeared with the label "Communists." There are also several descriptions that evoke Chicago coffee-house culture of the era.

299. Dewey, Thomas B. *You've Got Him Cold.* An Inner Sanctum Mystery. New York: Simon and Schuster, 1958. 184pp.

Korean War veteran Charles Tavern is on the run from the police when he shows up after hours in Mac's office. Tavern claims that after leaving his apartment in a Chicago housing complex to cool off from a fight with his wife Connie, he returns hours later to find her dead. When the neighbors find him standing in shock over his wife's body, he flees. The only two clues to the murder are the fact that Connie's locked strongbox has been rifled (the contents of which even Tavern had not known), and that Tavern discovered lewd snapshots in his wife's lingerie drawer. Pornography, blackmail, and events from twenty years before eventually cause the deaths of four more people before Mac solves the murder. The Chicago settings are mostly a wide variety of apartment buildings. Social attitudes toward sexuality play an important role in the novel.

300. Dobler, Bruce. *Icepick: A Novel about Life and Death in a Maximum Security Prison.* Boston: Little, Brown, 1974. 460pp.

The "Icepick" of the title is a nickname for the Illinois State Penitentiary in Chicago (ISPIC), a fictional, maximum security prison located on the Chicago Sanitary and Ship Canal near Damen Avenue and the Stevenson Expressway. Dobler touches on the crimes some of the inmates and the conditions in which they and the prison guards, social workers, and psychologists live. However, his main concern is to document the lived experience of incarcerated life in the United States, with all of its violence and injustice. However, the novel is not a reform novel in the traditional sense. Dobler presents characters who are reformers, but demonstrates the bleak prospects for any meaningful institutional change. The main action in the novel is focused around a riot and prison break and the aftermath of these events. Social phenomena of the time period, including the Black Panther and Black Muslim movements (the prison inmates are ninety-percent African-American), the 1970s counterculture, Vietnam War protests, drug culture, and various forms of identity politics are all reflected in prison life.

301. Dockarty, A. J. *Midway Plaisance, the Experience of an Innocent Boy from Vermont in the Famous Midway.* Chicago: Chicago World Book, 1894. 259pp.

This work of juvenile fiction presents a visit to the Columbian Exposition, by Vermonter Ebenezer Slimmens, who travels to the fair with his mother. Presented in journal format, Slimmens' entries comment on days spent roaming the Midway Plaisance at the Fair. He describes the amusement rides, such as the Ferris wheel and Ice-Railway, and also provides colorful comments on the ethnic and national exhibits that were placed on the Midway, such as Street in Cairo, home of the dancer known as Little Egypt. He is also intrigued by fakirs, and the infamous Hoochie coochie dance. Though written in the first person in a simulation of a young boy's writing, adult viewpoints and descriptive phrases are present and reflect the locution and racial prejudices common in the United States of the late nineteenth century. The illustrations and eyewitness descriptions make this work useful for world's fair research and for insights into the broader culture of the period.

302. Donelson, Katharine. *Rodger Latimer's Mistake.* Chicago: Laird and Lee, 1891. 378pp.

This romance novel is set in the imaginary locales of intellectual, university town Edgewood (clearly Evanston) and nearby city Clinton (Chicago). Margaret McVey, the daughter of a university professor, has been in love with Rodger Latimer from her youth and everyone assumes they will marry. Only the issue of where they will reside separates them. When Margaret sticks by her conviction that she can only live in Edgewood, Rodger moves on, takes up residence in Clinton, and marries into society there. Margaret continues to live with her aging father until the death of the first Mrs. Latimer gives Margaret and Rodger the opportunity to reconsider their original choices and correct their mistakes. The novel describes 1880s society life in Chicago, contrasting its superficiality with the high-minded life in Evanston.

303. Donohue, H. E. F. *The Higher Animals: A Romance*. New York: Viking Press, 1965. 273pp.
　　Donohue limns a 1950s Chicago social milieu beset by anomie and alienation. The neighborhood is Hyde Park and most of the characters have some ties to the University of Chicago. For instance, twenty-four-year-old protagonist Daniel Conn, a Korean War veteran, began college but he lacked enough commitment and became a bookshop clerk. Naomi Norris is another young academic hanger-on in the immediate environs of the university. The wealthy Norris studies the physical sciences in a desultory manner while bedding young men, for whom she has little more than physical interest. The novel's action transpires on the day of Daniel's twenty-fifth birthday and centers on his favorite neighborhood bar, the locus for consequential social encounters as the neighborhood is rocked by two unrelated tragedies: a Victorian-era rooming house burns down, and a group of criminal sociopaths, who illustrate the furthest extreme of social alienation, take hostages with fatal results. Donohue presents the many characters in such detail that the book becomes a sociological portrait.

304. Donovan, Cornelius Francis (Rev.). *The Left Hander*. Chicago: Meier, 1925. 301pp.
　　This social reform novel focuses on the activities of Edward Tracy, a cynical lawyer with political ambitions. When he gets involved in the settlement house movement, he finds hope for society and Mary Croston, one of the movement workers, leads him to the Roman Catholic faith and marriage. The novel details many 1920s social problems including bootlegging, narcotics abuse, and social inequities, as well as presenting the deleterious effects of ethnic and racial prejudice. The main social evil the book addresses is anti-Catholicism, particularly as manifested by the Ku Klux Klan. Tracy is active in political clubs and poised to accept a nomination to Congress that he will certainly win, but needs the support of the Klan to do so. He rejects the Klan in a dramatic speech, losing the nomination, but winning Mary Croston's hand in marriage.

305. Dos Passos, John. *Chosen Country*. Boston: Houghton Mifflin, Riverside Press, 1951. 485pp.
　　Only one important section of this novel is set in Chicago. Relating the story of Jay Pignatelli, along with background on his father, the novel covers the time period 1848 to 1930 and ranges from Colorado, France, the Near East, New York City, and Ohio, to Wisconsin. Pignatelli's father was a larger than life character who happened to be a lawyer and Pignatelli is the son of his father's favorite mistress. To avoid scandal, he and his mother spent Pignatelli's childhood in France. When Pignatelli enters adulthood he begins a life of travel, but his adventures end less well than his father's. His romance with the most important woman in his life, Lulie, is set in Chicago.

306. Douglas, Amanda Minnie. *A Little Girl in Old Chicago*. New York: Dodd, Mead, 1904. 324pp.
　　This work of historical fiction for young adults follows a romance set against the backdrop of Chicago's history from the 1830s through the 1870s. Norman Hayne and Ruth Gaynor meet when they are children in the 1830s and fall in love. As a young man Norman works as a private secre-

tary to Mr. Le Moyne, partner in a fur-trading company, and is forced to travel for years at a time to Eastern cities and abroad. Back in Chicago, Ruth becomes the sole support of her household as her father succumbs to a crippling illness. In love with Norman, Ruth feels obligated to marry his brother Dan Hayne, who will aid her father in business. Dan is good at making money, but, verbally and physically abusive, brings Ruth misery. Eventually, he leaves Ruth for another woman, and almost immediately he is killed, along with his new wife, when their ship sinks. Norman, whose employer has died, bequeathing him a large amount of money, returns to Chicago around the same time. After abiding by social expectations for mourning, Ruth and Norman marry and travel abroad for two years seeking a cure for Mr. Gaynor, which they find. The narrative speeds up dramatically after their return, focusing on the Chicago fire, through which Norman loses everything, and his success in rebuilding his fortunes. Most of the history in the first part of the book is national (presidential elections, monetary crises). There are few concrete references to local history except for establishing a clean water supply for the city and widening the Chicago River. However Douglas records foodways and household furnishings and incorporates many historical figures, including Gurdon Hubbard into her narrative, as well as noting trends in immigration and increases in the size of the city.

307. Douglas, Lloyd C. *Green Light*. Boston: Houghton Mifflin, Riverside Press, 1935. 326pp.

This novel about an inspirational Episcopal priest who brings people together and transforms their lives features Dean Harcourt of Chicago's Trinity Cathedral, an Episcopal priest living with the crippling after-effects of polio. Most of the plot has to do with medical ethics and loyalty to one's mentors. When Dr. Bruce Endicott makes a serious mistake that leads to the unnecessary death of a patient, young Paige Newell, to whom Endicott had been an influential mentor, takes the blame and leaves Chicago, living for a time incognito in a small town near Louisville, Kentucky. However, coincidental meetings gradually lead him back to Chicago and into the nexus of Harcourt's influence. As a result, Newell re-enters his profession, weds appropriately, and is forgiven by the dead patient's daughter. General descriptions of Chicago are enriched by very detailed scenes set in the Chicago Art Institute, the art works of which have deep resonance for several of the characters. Researchers may be interested in this articulation of tenets of liberal Protestantism during the early days of the Depression, which plays an important role in the plot.

308. Douglas, Lloyd C. *Invitation to Live*. Boston: Houghton Mifflin, Riverside Press, 1940. 303pp.

This inspirational novel set in the 1930s is one of several featuring Dean Harcourt of Chicago's Trinity Cathedral, who has overcome the challenges of physical disability to head the large church where more than two thousand people attend Sunday sermons. The plot centers on how Harcourt becomes a transformational influence in the lives of a number of young people, mostly women. The first of these is Barbara Breckinridge, a recent college graduate, who had an affluent upbringing and has just inherited a fortune. After hearing one of Harcourt's sermons and having tea with him she is inspired to experience life among the poor—a transformative experience that leads her to reevaluate her priorities. Many of the stories of the novel's characters have something to do with economics and social inequality, although finding an appropriate spouse and having good family relationships is also a concern.

309. Drago, Harry Sinclair and Edmund Goulding. *The Trespasser.* Photographic illustrations. New York: Burt, 1929. 268pp.

Drago's work is a novelization of a film script written by Edmund Goulding for a movie of the same name starring Gloria Swanson (United Artists, 1929) and it presents the difficulties Mary O'Donnell faces in leaving the social limitations of growing up "back of the Yards," as the daughter of a teamster for Swift and Company, who had been a violent alcoholic. Forced out of her job in a State Street department store by the advances of her supervisor, she moves to the North Side, changes her name to Marion Donnell, and graduates from night school. A stenography job in a law office leads to the position of private secretary to firm partner Hector Ferguson. In this setting, she meets Jack Merrick, heir to a manufacturing fortune, and later quits her job to marry him. High melodrama follows when Merrick's family attacks her. She then learns of a bequest from Ferguson and leaves Jack to protect him from scandalous rumors surrounding this inheritance of a fortune from her former supervisor. In despair, Jack goes to Paris and marries a woman he accidentally cripples in an automobile collision. In the denouement everyone is back in Chicago, where Jack discovers Marion secretly had given birth to his son and Marion finds out about the other woman. Social attitudes toward wealth and the status of women in society are a concern throughout the novel.

310. Drago, Harry Sinclair. *Women to Love: A Romance of the Underworld.* New York: Amour Press, 1931. 251pp.

This Mafia novel tells the story of the Conselmo gang, mostly West Side Italians, although one member, Max Strauss, is Jewish (a fact that is made much of, as well as the fact that he can pass in social settings, while the gang leader cannot). The gang are bootleggers, their headquarters are in an Italian restaurant, the Bella Napoli, and their leader is Rocco Conselmo. His wife Scarlet, whose indomitable mother, Maruska, a Hungarian immigrant, lives with the couple, has set up a well-furnished household, dresses Conselmo fashionably, and helps him manage his money. Scarlet wants Conselmo to establish himself socially (he plays the piano and could have trained as an opera singer). He is obsessed with his increasing his gangland power and gets Strauss to act as his wife's consigliere. An affair develops as Conselmo's deals and double-crosses get increasingly Byzantine. When Strauss is found dead, Conselmo is arrested. However, gang members convince Scarlet to confess to the crime (that she actually committed), knowing that with the right story and expensive lawyers she will get off. Forever indebted to the gang, Scarlet is forced to return to life with Conselmo. The Chicago portrayed in this novel is mostly bars and restaurants filled with stereotypical gangland characters.

311. Draper, John Smith. *Shams; or, Uncle Ben's Experience with Hypocrites: A Story of Simple Country Life, Giving a Humorous and Entertaining Picture of Every Day Life and Incidents in the Rural Districts, with Uncle Ben's Trip to the City of Chicago and to California, and His Experience with the Shams and Sharpers of the Metropolitan World.* Chicago: Thompson and Thomas, 1887. 412pp.

The title of this work goes a long way towards summarizing the contents. Following in a tradition of novels in which a naïve, but admirable, rural gentleman travels to an urban area to be shocked and comment on the evils to be found there, Uncle Ben visits Chicago. The city was being celebrated at the time as the epitome of the great American success story, rising from the ashes of the 1871 fire, to achieve renown for innovative architecture and take its place as a dominant center for business, manufacturing, and transportation. Ben finds the city unlivable due to the crowded conditions, soot, and stench. He is also pursued by confidence men who value money above the most basic of virtues and, in Ben's estimation, are only small-scale versions of the well-known capitalists and industrialists of the age.

312. Dreiser, Theodore. *The Genius*. New York: John Lane, 1915.

In this semi-autobiographical novel, the main character, Eugene Witla, leaves the small, Illinois town of his youth to study at the Art Institute and his experiences in Chicago evoke the life of 1890s' bohemians in the city. He becomes the sexual partner of artist's model, Ruby Kenny, but falls in love with Angela Blue, a Wisconsin schoolteacher with conservative values, who does not embrace the sexual freedom of Witla's Chicago circle. Blind to their incompatibility, Witla marries Blue. Most of the book is set in New York City which Eugene sees as the cultural center of the United States and the place in which he needs to make his mark.

313. Dreiser, Theodore. *Jennie Gerhardt*. New York: Harper and Brothers, 1911. 430pp.

Through protagonist Jennie Gerhardt, Dreiser explores the hypocritical sexual morality of the early twentieth century and its tragic implications for women. As an eighteen-year-old, Gerhardt, the daughter of an impoverished German immigrant glass-blower living in Columbus, Ohio, naively becomes the lover of Senator George Sylvester Brander. Although Brander intended to marry her, he dies in Washington, D.C. just as Jennie realizes she is pregnant with his child. She later gives birth to a daughter she names Vesta. Suffering social censure, the family moves to Cleveland, Ohio. Working as a maid, Jennie meets Lester Kane, a thirty-six-year-old businessman and heir to a carriage manufacturing fortune. Kane, a social non-conformist, disdains matrimony and realizes he can possess Jennie without marrying her by providing support for her desperate family. In ignorance of Vesta's existence, Kane establishes Jenny and himself in Chicago in a South Hyde Park house. They come to love each other, but Jennie decides if Kane will not marry her, they must separate, despite how much this hurts her emotionally. Kane goes on to marry a wealthy woman from his social class, but confesses to Jennie on his deathbed that he wronged her and that she was the only woman he truly loved. Although a significant portion of the novel is set in Chicago, Dreiser is mostly concerned about social mores that were not exclusive to the city. He is very specific about Chicago locales and their varying social status and evokes the small town nature of early suburbs such as South Hyde Park.

314. Dreiser, Theodore. *Sister Carrie*. New York: Doubleday, Page, 1900. 557pp.

Through the story of Caroline Meeber, Dreiser presents the plight of late nineteenth century women, who, lacking the social status necessary for establishing independent lives, are forced to become the mistresses of men. Meeber, nicknamed Sister Carrie by her family, arrives in Chicago from small town Columbia City in August of 1889. Impoverished, she plans to live with her married sister on Van Buren Street and support herself. The jobs she finds, however, are menial and spirit breaking. When Charles Drouet, a salesman who she considers to be affluent and sophisticated, begins to take an interest in her, she gradually accepts his assistance, imagining his friendship may lead to marriage. Soon she is living as his mistress. As she becomes more sophisticated, she realizes that Drouet is not as well-established as she thought and she begins spending time with his friend, George Hurstwood, who is much more cultured and intelligent, although he is married. Eventually, she and Hurstwood leave Chicago together for New York City where the rest of the novel is set. An early example of American naturalism, the book provides many social and cultural details and uses actual Chicago places and businesses of the time period as settings. Part of the novel occurs at the time of the Columbian Exposition, which has a role in the development of the work.

315. Dreiser, Theodore. *The Stoic*. Garden City, N.Y.: Doubleday, 1947. 310pp.

In this third and final volume of Dreiser's account of the career of Frank Algernon Cowperwood, the great financier severs his connections with Chicago. Defeated in his attempts to extend his franchise of the street railway system in the city, the sixty-year-old Cowperwood debates retirement. When the young Berenice [sic] Fleming yields to Cowperwood's eight-year-long campaign for her affections, he is reinvigorated. Installing his wife Aileen in an Italianate mansion in New York City, he makes Berenice his ward and travels with her to England to begin work on financing a new branch of the London underground. Only the first few chapters of this work are set in Chicago with the remainder set in New York and London.

316. Dreiser, Theodore. *The Titan*. New York: Boni and Liveright, 1914. 551pp.

Continuing the story of Frank Algernon Cowperwood begun in a Philadelphia setting in *The Financier*, Dreiser presents Chicago in the 1870s and 1880s when construction of private gas lines and streetcar systems proved to be enriching for men like Cowperwood. Much of the book is devoted to Cowperwood's efforts to increase his fortune by establishing corporations. His personal life is also driven by conquest. At age thirty-six, he arrives in the city, a divorced man accompanied by his twenty-six year-old mistress, Aileen, and thinks he will eventually control society as he will the business world. When he makes few inroads on society, he begins to entertain himself with romantic conquests. By the time legislation that would favor his companies is defeated, he has a new mistress and is ready to move to Europe. Dreiser's highly detailed novel presents the business, political, and social history of Chicago in the late nineteenth century.

317. Driver, John Merritte. *Purple Peaks Remote, A Romance of Italy and America*. Chicago: Laird and Lee, 1905. 418pp.

This romance novel is preoccupied with female sexual morality. After graduating from Columbia University Law School, Percival Howard makes a European sojourn during which he meets and falls in love with the tragically wronged Paolina Savelli in Naples. After revealing how she was wronged by men she trusted, Howard pledges his undying love, and accepts her infant daughter, Giovanna, as his ward (to be raised in Italy). Howard returns to the United States to establish a legal partnership in Chicago with his friend and Columbia classmate, Andrew Hollister, believing the late-nineteenth-century city to be a place of great promise. Although the two spend most of their time pursuing love affairs and attending social events, their legal practice flourishes. Hollister is soon engaged to Esther Hardigan, a music student and daughter of a wealthy merchant from Centralia, Illinois. Howard courts the beautiful Agnes Meldrom, a poor girl from Minneapolis who supports herself singing for the Universalist Church and concertizing throughout Chicago where she is proudly compared to Adelina Patti. Both women study with lecherous Professor Henry Slade and much of the plot revolves around whether either woman has fallen to him. Despite her denials to Hollister, Hardigan did fall and dies a sordid death carrying Slade's baby. Agnes remained untouched, but only because she is frigid and can only see men as the means to her social and professional advancement. She soon accepts the proposal of a German baron, and Howard, oddly enough, ends up marrying his ward Giovanna, whose convent life has kept her undeniably chaste. The novel's preoccupation with female sexual morality and cataloging the many threats to which women readily fall, does not prevent the author from including descriptions of

Chicago society and social events, including one of Patti's farewell concerts at McVicker's Auditorium, a reception at the home of Mrs. Potter Palmer, and hotel balls. The book also includes many references to well-known Chicago buildings and businesses.

318. Drought, James. *The Secret*. Norwalk, Conn.: Skylight Press, 1963. 173pp.

Through the course of this coming-of-age novel, the narrator presents his life from the time he is a schoolboy in the 1930s until he is middle-aged, recording the events and realizations that gradually disillusioned him and alienated him from every social institution (family, church, country), leaving him only with the conviction that one must continue fighting against death, despite the certainty of mortality. Except for a brief Korean War section, the rest of the work is set in Illinois, mostly in Chicago. The book is more concerned with the protagonist's thoughts than physical setting; however a number of anecdotes present life in the 1940s and 1950s in and around Chicago, revealing the social control that patriotism, religion, anti-Communism, and capitalism exercised.

319. Dubkin, Leonard. *Wolf Point, an Adventure in History*. New York: Putnam, 1953. 184pp.

Dubkin pursues his fascination with a strip of land named Wolf's Point on the Chicago River near his office in the Merchandise Mart, by exploring the area's history, discovering people from the past who may also have been enchanted by Wolf's Point and presents fictionalized accounts of their connection with the place. Among these are: the Reverend Robert Collyer, an 1860s Unitarian minister; Kitty, the wife of John S. Wright, an 1830s settler of Chicago, and the first school teacher in the settlement; explorer Jean Nicollet in 1633; and an imaginary Delaware Indian woman named Oniata.

320. Du Bois, Shirley Graham. *Jean Baptiste Pointe De Sable, Founder of Chicago*. New York: Messner, 1953. 180pp.

In this biographical novel for young adults, Du Bois presents the life of explorer and trader, De Sable. Reflecting his actual life, very little of this book is actually set in the area that would become Chicago.

321. Duff, Paul James. *Crimson Love; A Realistic Romance of Guilty Passion*. Chicago: Ross Pub. Co., 1895. 169pp.

Set in the 1890s bohemian milieu of a group of young men who work for a small publication, the *Chicago Gong*, this novel espouses romantic and sexual affairs outside the context of marriage in a sensational manner. The protagonist is Tom Freeman, the publication's editor, and his experiences and those of his colleagues reveal what it may have been like to be young and carefree in this era.

322. Duff, Paul James. *Woman's Duplicity: A Story of High Life in Chicago*. Chicago: Stein, 1892. 226pp.

This "novel" is mostly an extended diatribe against sexually immoral women who take advantage of men. Vincent Ashley has a drinking problem. In love with Lucy Heney from afar, he stops drinking and saves money from his office job to buy an oyster house that he turns into a successful business. Finally deeming himself worthy of Lucy, he approaches her and she soon accepts his attentions and expensive gifts. Suddenly, however, she rejects him and marries a wealthy man. Vincent's intense disappointment sends him into a downward spiral and he begins drinking heavily again. Eventually, the support of his friend Max, a lawyer, and his interest in a new woman, May Sillery, gives him the strength to reform and he sells the oyster house to avoid the influence of drinking customers and he begins studying law. Through hard work he becomes successful in his new profession and commences a guarded courtship of May that lasts for years. While outwardly devoted to Vincent she has a sexual affair with her father's clerk and just as she is to marry Vincent, she elopes with the clerk. When he discovers she is pregnant, even though it is with his own child, the clerk is repulsed and, although May has an abortion, the relationship is ruined. May is left scheming to get Vincent back. This disjointed novel provides much narration of Chicago social life, while presenting the distinctly misogynistic views of the author.

323. Du Jardin, Rosamond. *Young & Fair*. Philadelphia: Lippincott, 1963. 187pp.
        Written in the 1960s, a time of intense focus on women's social status, the author raises issues of social standing and opportunities for women in this work of historical fiction for young adults, set in the 1880s. Discovered as a four-year-old during the Chicago fire by adopted mother Kate Powell, Lissa was raised by Kate and her husband Tom in a modest household. In 1883 Kate dies of pneumonia (Tom had predeceased her) and Lissa is forced to support herself as a seventeen-year-old. She eventually gets a job with the Harrison Colby Company, a department store rival of Marshall Field's. She lives in a boarding house where she makes friends, and eventually dates Greg Colby, the son of the department store owner. When Greg proposes marriage, his father rejects Lissa for her lack of social status, until a dramatic revelation proves her to be the heiress to a Kentucky fortune. The novel focuses on the challenges of women in 1880s Chicago, while depicting what it was like to live in a boarding house and work in a major department store.

324. Dunne, Finley Peter. *Mr. Dooley in Peace and in War*. Boston: Small, Maynard, 1898. 260pp.
        These collected sketches from Dunne's nationally syndicated newspaper column were the first in a series of exceptionally popular books. The eponymous Martin Dooley is a saloon owner on Chicago's South Side who is an Irish immigrant and resident of "Archey Road" (Archer Avenue). Dooley speaks in the Irish dialect of his countrymen and although he frequently comments on national politics and events, he also discourses on Chicago politics and sets many of his anecdotes in the city.

325. Dunne, Finley Peter. *Mr. Dooley in the Hearts of His Countrymen*. Boston: Small, Maynard, 1899. 285pp.
        In his second book featuring Mr. Dooley, Dunne mostly focuses on everyday topics, such as a church picnic, political meeting, and a heat wave.

326. Dunne, Finley Peter. *Mr. Dooley on Making a Will and Other Necessary Evils*. New York: Charles Scribner's Sons, 1919. 221pp.
        The final book Dunne published, this work satirizes American political figures, as well as international notables such as Kaiser Wilhelm and King George.

327. Dunne, Finley Peter. *Mr. Dooley Says*. New York: Charles Scribner's Sons, 1910. 239pp.
        In addition to commenting on Turkey, The Hague, and ocean travel, Martin Dooley addresses bachelorhood, divorce, and women's suffrage in these sketches.

328. Dunne, Finley Peter. *Mr. Dooley's Opinions*. New York: Russell, 1901. 212pp.
This transitional volume in Dunne's work includes material written around the time he was resigning from the *Chicago Journal* and moving to New York City. In many of the pieces Martin Dooley's viewpoint is no longer rooted in Chicago, becoming more cosmopolitan and centered on New York City.

329. Dunne, Finley Peter. *Mr. Dooley's Philosophy*. Illustrated by William Nicholson, E. W. Kemble, and F. Opper. New York: Russell, 1900. 263pp.
Martin Dooley's take on news items and world events include commentary on China, the Paris Exposition, and African-Americans. Dunne's most famous essay is included in this volume; a book review satirizing Theodore Roosevelt's Spanish-American War memoir entitled The *Rough Riders*.

330. Dunne, Finley Peter. *Observations by Mr. Dooley*. New York: Russell, 1902. 279pp.
Dooley discourses here on Sherlock Holmes, King Edward's Coronation, swearing, and immigration.

331. Dunne, Finley Peter. *What Dooley Says*. Chicago: Kazmar, 1899. 235pp.
Some of this work duplicates material in *Mr. Dooley in the Hearts of His Countrymen*; however other pieces only appear here in book form. Several items are on Chicago politics and one describes courtship, a christening, and the reaction to women wearing bloomers in Dooley's Chicago neighborhood.

332. Durkin, James Aloysius. *The Auto Bandits of Chicago: A Correct Account of the Greatest Detective Work in the History of Chicago's Police Force*. Chicago: Charles C. Thompson, 1913. 190pp.
No additional information available.

333. Dybek, Stuart. *Childhood and Other Neighborhoods*. New York: Viking Press, 1980. 201pp.
The short stories in this collection are all set in immigrant communities of 1940s and 1950s Chicago dominated by people from Czechoslovakia, Poland, Ukraine, and Russia, as well as African-Americans and Mexicans. Many of the stories are told from the perspective of children, although one protagonist works in an ice cream factory and another is a social worker. However, the plots are often built on extraordinary situations, the stories detail everyday life on the street and in tenement buildings.

334. Eagle, John. *The Hoodlums*. New York: Avon Publications, 1953. 139pp.
This pulp fiction work portrays a 1950s Chicago of dark streets, seedy saloons, and slovenly domestic arrangements in which organized crime is a career option chosen by young men and women like protagonists Kirk and his wife Lisette. Kirk has already been imprisoned, but will still commit any crime for money. Although he believes women should live by a higher moral code, Lisette actually drags him further into a life of crime through her connections with Chicago gangs. Through gang influence, Kirk's crimes begin to include physical violence and brutality. Marijuana use is one cultural detail that stands out in this description, as is a particular view of the influential role of women in hoodlum society.

335. Ebel, Camille Layer. *The Land of Plenty*. New York: Vantage Press, 1960. 283pp.

Much of Chicago history from 1865 to the Spanish-American war is told from the perspective of young Czech immigrant, Nita Kucer, who arrives in the city with her parents as a three-year-old after the Civil War. While presenting some of the struggles faced by immigrants in general (ethnic identity versus assimilation), the book presents Czech cultural tradition through recording everyday life for Nita's family and neighbors.

336. Eberhart, Mignon Good. *The Dark Garden*. Garden City, N.Y.: Crime Club / Doubleday, Doran, 1933. 312pp.

In the aftermath of the Depression, Katie Warren loses her business selling bonds and is reduced to living on the charity of Mina Petrie, the now elderly woman, who was the best friend of Katie's mother and was determined to adopt her when she was orphaned as a child. However, Charlotte Weinberg, Mina's cousin and paid companion, stopped that from happening in order to maintain her son Steven's status as principal heir to Mina's estate. Then, on a foggy, icy night, Katie runs over Mina in the driveway of her Lake Shore Drive estate. Although, Mina had apparently been killed and moved into the driveway, Katie remains the prime suspect. Police Detective Crafft finds many puzzling facts and becomes her supporter. By the end of the novel, Katie has been cleared of wrongdoing and her future looks financially secure, but only because she gives up her single life for marriage. The novel reveals a good deal about family relationships and the social status of women in the time period.

337. Eberhart, Mignon Good. *Dead Men's Plans*. New York: Random House, 1952. 246pp.

On the day that Reg Minary returns to his family home on Game Street near Astor and North State Streets, family tensions are rampant. Reg married a French girl, Zelie, while on his grand tour after college. The couple was in Egypt when they found out that Reg's father had died two months before but they did not interrupt their honeymoon. Reg's sister Amy is eager for Reg's return, because she wants him to agree to sell the family Great Lakes shipping business. Their stepsister Sewal, who is engaged to marry Steve Forsyth, the director of the shipping firm, is opposed to the sale because it will mean the breaking up of a family firm with a long-standing reputation. Then Reg is found shot to death on the grounds of the family estate and Sewal's detective work is crucial to solving the murder. The novel is set in the upper-class Minary household and in the surrounding affluent, residential neighborhood.

338. Eberhart, Mignon Good. *Fair Warning*. Garden City, N.Y.: Doubleday, Doran, 1936. 304pp.

Marcia Trench's three-year-old marriage to Ivan Godden has been complicated by living in the same household with his controlling, unmarried sister, Beatrice, and Ivan's tendency to slight his wife in deference to Beatrice. Even the neighbors in the affluent, suburban Chicago neighborhood of Brayton have noticed. Particularly, Dr. Blakie, the family physician, and the Copleys, a family who lives next door and consists of a mother and her twin, thirty-year-old children Robert and Verity. Robert and Marcia gradually fall in love and when Ivan is stabbed to death, she is accused of murder. As the investigation proceeds Robert Copley is implicated, due to their affair. Dr. Blakie then eerily announces his love for Marcia and, in a dramatic conclusion, is revealed as the murderer. Most of the action of the novel transpires in the affluent, servant-maintained households of the Goddens and Copleys and the reader learns a great deal about life in such settings.

339. Eberhart, Mignon Good. *The Glass Slipper*. Garden City, N.Y.: Doubleday, Doran, 1938. 275pp.

When Rue, a twenty-six-year-old nurse marries forty-year-old Dr. Brule Hatterick, a wealthy and socially prominent man, she knows she will face many challenges in adjusting to a life managing a large household with servants. The task is complicated by Hatterick household residents Madge and Steven Hendrie. Rue first came into the household as the nurse to Hatterick's dying wife Crystal. Madge is the daughter of Crystal and Hendrie, her invalid half-brother and they openly resent Rue as a usurper of Crystal's place. A few months after her marriage, Dr. Andrew Crittenden, Brule's young protégé, lets Rue know she is suspected of murder in Crystal's death and that he is in love with her and wants her to flee to Canada with him. Knowing she is innocent, Rue tries to defend herself, as a nightmarish period begins during which she does not know whom to trust. Most of the physical setting of the novel is within exclusive clubs and expensive houses.

340. Eberhart, Mignon Good. *The Hangman's Whip*. Garden City, N.Y.: Doubleday, Doran, 1940. 275pp.

This atmospheric murder mystery has a troubled marriage at its center. Richard Bohan has been married to Eve for three years and feels unsatisfied. When he realizes his love for Search Abbott and his wife is agreeable to divorce, he and Search look forward to their new lives. Then, inexplicably, Eve changes her mind and soon after she is a murder victim. Search becomes the prime suspect and begins living with the terror that she will be found guilty, despite her innocence.

341. Eberhart, Mignon Good. *Hasty Wedding*. Garden City, N.Y.: Doubleday, Doran, 1938. 301pp.

As with other Eberhart mysteries, the physical environment here is domestic—expensive houses and apartments—and richly described with details about food, drink, and clothing. The entire plot focuses on solving the murder of Ronald Drew, briefly, but intensely, a suitor of heiress Dorcas Whipple. Dorcas' family insisted she reject Drew in order to marry Jevan Locke, a man she had known since childhood and the scion of a well-known Chicago family. In response to a telephone call from Drew, Dorcas goes to his apartment on the night before her wedding and is subjected to a tawdry scene in which he pleads with her and then attempts to force himself on her. She flees, leaving him alive, but when Drew is found dead the next day, the police believe she murdered him. The Victorian-period, Whipple family mansion located on the Near North Shore, the contents of the house, and its staff play a major role in the plot.

342. Eberhart, Mignon Good. *The House on the Roof*. Garden City, N.Y.: Doubleday, Doran, 1935. 302pp.

In this novel Eberhart presents Chicago as a cosmopolitan rival to New York or Paris. Her murder mystery focuses on the sniper shooting of retired international opera singer, Mary Monroe, in a penthouse constructed on the roof of an apartment building off Lake Shore Drive at 18 Eden Street. The shooting is witnessed by Deborah Cavert who had been invited to tea to hear something important that Monroe had to tell her. The singer is shot before divulging her secret and the rest of the novel is devoted to solving what Mary had to tell Deborah, as well as finding out who murdered Mary and committed two subsequent killings in the building. Deborah, had just moved into Monroe's building after her father, invalided by a heart condition, moves to Florida. The Cavert family, consisting of Deborah's father, John, and aunt, Juliet, had lost a great deal of their money only few years before when John's investment firm collapsed. John's health failed and only Juliet's efforts salvaged enough financial resources for them to continue to live comfortably. The novel is filled with social details, including gender roles, apartment house living, and private gambling parlors. Looming in the background of the story are the towers of the 1933 Chicago Exposition, which is described briefly.

343. Eberhart, Mignon Good. *Postmark Murder*. New York: Random House, 1956. 305pp.

An unsettled estate, World War II, and Polish nationals play important roles in this murder mystery. Laura March's father, a bank manager, had financed inventor Conrad Stanley, a Polish immigrant, who established a factory and became wealthy. When March's father was killed in World War II, Stanley supported her. Years later, when Stanley died, he willed half of his money to a Polish nephew, Conrad Stanislowski, who could not be located. Instead, Stanislowski's daughter, Jonny, is rescued from a Polish orphanage and brought to Chicago, where Laura takes care of her on her modest income. A man claiming to be Stanislowski shows up but wants his presence in Chicago kept secret. Shortly afterwards he is found murdered; another murder follows in which Laura is directly implicated. Fortunately, Matt Cosden, the young man who was Stanley's lawyer, helps her find out what really happened. The book has various Chicago settings, mostly in apartments ranging widely in degrees of affluence.

344. Eckert, Allan W. *The HAB Theory*. Boston: Little, Brown, 1976. 566p.

Significant portions of this novel are set in Chicago, but physical setting has little importance to the plot which concerns a hypothesis by Herbert Allan Boardman (HAB) that an irregularity in the rotation of the earth will bring about a cataclysm destroying large parts of the planet. Boardman is a Chicago academic and John Grant, the famous writer who tries to investigate the theory, is from Skokie. Some significant portions of the novel's plot occur in Chicago, including Boardman's attempt on the life of the President of the United States.

345. Eddy, Arthur Jerome. *Ganton & Co.; A Story of Chicago Commercial and Social Life*. Chicago: McClurg, 1908. 415pp.

This novel, set in the world of Chicago's meat packing industry, focuses on the firm of Ganton & Company, an international business founded and owned by John Ganton. In his meat packing facility, sixty thousand animals are killed a day. Although primarily a story about how Ganton deals with labor unrest, the novel also provides details about Ganton's household, daily life, relationships with family members (including his wife and sons), and his social life (that includes functions at the private "Park Club"). His wife, "Mrs. Jack" interacts with other wives and jockeys with them for social prestige. An important pawn in Mrs. Jack's arsenal is her second eldest son Will, who has been given a management position at Ganton and Company. However, Will is essentially a seat-filler with no facility for business and spends a good deal of his time socializing at his golf club, where he also lives. When he falls in love with May Keating, the daughter of Ganton's enemy, "Jem" Keating, Ganton declares that he will cut Will off without a penny should he decide to marry May. Ganton is already estranged from his older son, John Jr., who went to college and wanted to become a scholar. John Jr. is currently being forced to stay in England and learn the banking industry, after which he will be required to work at least a year in his father's business. After it looks like Ganton has defeated strikers at his company, he falls ill and, after an operation, dies. Although he has a chance to reconcile with his sons, he does not. However, he leaves the bulk of his estate to his older son, and when John Jr. returns to Chicago, he makes certain that his brother can marry May Keating without losing his inheritance. This novel about Chicago plutocrats is consistent in its admiration for such characters, despite Ganton's occasional bad behavior. In contrast, the strikers and the union organizers at the Ganton factory are portrayed harshly. Physical descriptions in the novel tend toward the stereotypical with few mentions of specific places in Chicago.

346. Edgley, Leslie. *The Runaway Pigeon*. Garden City, N.Y.: Crime Club / Doubleday, 1953. 188pp.

Wilfred Piper, an employee of the expensive Chicago jewelry store Talbot & Talbot, is a mild-mannered man who lives a very regular existence until he awakens in an abandoned, California ranch house and finds he is wanted for murder and a major jewel theft. He has to call upon parts of his character he never knew he had to find the real culprit. Fortunately, he is aided by Lila Helburn, a Hollywood costume designer, who picks him up as a hitchhiker and gives him a ride from Palm Springs all the way back to Chicago, dispensing wisdom and martinis throughout the trip. She then assists his detective work in Chicago. The novel satirizes suburban life (Piper lives in a suburb named Ridgewood), and implicitly addresses ideas of male and female gender roles. Most of the Chicago physical settings are expensive apartments and hotels.

347. Ellis, Edward Sylvester [H. R. Gordon, pseud.]. *Black Partridge, or The Fall of Fort Dearborn*. New York: Dutton, 1906. 302pp.

In this adventure story for boys, sixteen-year-old Auric Kingdon, son of the commandant of Fort Wayne, and his peer, Jethro Judd of Fort Dearborn, witness the besiegement and surrender of Fort Dearborn. In August 1812 the boys had planned to meet equidistant between their forts. However, Jethro arrives at their meeting to announce he has escaped the besieged Fort Dearborn. He brings news that military commanders have decided to surrender the Fort. Only trading post agent John Kinzie is resisting, afraid the Fort's settlers will be attacked by the encampment of six hundred Indians as they depart. Commissioned to carry a message to the Fort, on the way the boys are captured by Indians. Black Partridge, a powerful sachem and friend of both boys, appears and saves them, ordering them back to Fort Wayne. When they refuse he travels with them to Fort Dearborn. At Fort Dearborn the boys are privy to strategy discussions. In the end, the Fort is abandoned and as Kinzie had predicted, the Indians attack. Kinzie, his family members, and some of the settlers, as well as Auric and Jethro, are the only survivors. Through the intervention of Black Partridge all of them get safe passage out of the area and we learn in an afterward that at the time of the great fire in Chicago, Auric and Jethro are living in the city.

348. Ellison, Jerome. *The Dam*. New York: Random House, 1941. 176pp.

Conditions in Chicago during the Depression are fully articulated in this novel about the value of work. In 1936 John Storm, who had been a successful construction engineer before the crash, is selling egg-beaters door-to-door to support his wife Emily and youngest son Ted. Storm had lost their house and most of their possessions and the family lives in an apartment on Marengo Street, where Emily is forced to feed them chicken feet on a regular basis. John and Ted gather coal that has fallen from railroad trains for heat and tragedy strikes when Ted's best friend Tommy is shot to death by a policeman while the two are hauling a child's wagon filled with broken-up crates for firewood. The Storms' situation is transformed overnight when John gets a Works Project Administration (WPA) job overseeing construction of a new dam at Stony Ridge that will safeguard the canal system around Chicago. With the money he earns, he is able to pay for Ted to take flying lessons (fulfilling Ted's long held dream). Although John faces challenges on the worksite from the untrained WPA workers, he gets the dam completed and looks forward to his next job. The Chicago setting is vague, but conveys the hardships people experienced during the Depression.

349. Ellison, Jerome. *The Prisoner Ate a Hearty Breakfast*. New York: Random House, 1939. 218pp.

Through the story of Shannon Light, an idealist in a morally bankrupt world, Ellison captures the "between-the-wars" generation of the 1920s. A boy during most of World War I, Light avoids the conflict, only to face a different challenge as he is entering manhood. His father is killed in an industrial accident and Light refuses to take any insurance money from his mother to pay for college. Working at a series of menial jobs, he experiences union violence and social prejudices against manual laborers. Entirely focused on becoming an artist, he embraces life experiences, accompanying wealthy classmates to speakeasies and brothels. When he falls in love, he behaves chastely, only to discover his girlfriend is pregnant by a former boyfriend. Light's romance ends in the death of the girl, the victim of a botched abortion. Light manages to graduate from college and enlist as a fighter pilot. Released from the constraints of college and earning his keep, he uses alcohol and the exhilaration of flight to expunge his sorrow, but falls into a self-destructive pattern that results in dismissal. He moves to New York City to become an artist, only to experience the hardships of the Depression and unwittingly falls in with a gangster who promises a job. Although he remains moral and idealistic to the end, he dies at a young age crushed by forces beyond his control. Only the first part of the novel is set in Chicago, but it does capture some of the spirit of the city in the 1920s.

350. Emery, Anne McGuigan. *Dinny Gordon, Freshman*. Philadelphia: Macrae Smith, 1959. 190pp.

In this book for young adults, Rosemont, the suburb where Dinny Gordon and her family live, is thirty miles from Chicago, but many men commute every day for work. One of these is Claude Craybill who recently moved to Rosemont after taking an accounting job with a large Chicago firm. Dinny's family help the Craybills settle into suburban life and in doing so Dinny develops a close friendship with the Craybill's son Clyde, even though she is a freshman and he is a senior. She appreciates his seriousness and begins to develop an interest in classical history that inspires her to extracurricular study and to begin saving money for a trip to Rome when she graduates. While her friends make trips to Chicago to shop and watch movies, Dinny becomes more and more focused on pursuing her intellectual interests. Dinny's clubs and the social activities of her parents give a good impression of suburban social life, even though television has become a prominent part of life it is described as a social activity like going to the movies, since friends gather together and snack and talk while watching.

351. Emery, Anne McGuigan. *Dinny Gordon, Junior*. Philadelphia: Macrae Smith, 1964. 169pp.

This romance novel for young adults is set in suburban Chicago during the early 1960s. At the beginning of the book, Dinny is sorting out her feelings about agreeing to go steady with Curt Beauregard and the degree of her attraction to Tom Jennings. Then, she gets her first job as a clerk at a variety store and deals with her dismissal over a shoplifting incident. She also must deal with prejudice for the first time when a Jewish family, the Goldmans, move to Rosebriar and some residents mobilize against them, despite their affluence. The family's two school age children, Debby and Michael, are excluded from after school activities and Dinny takes a role in getting them accepted.

352. Emery, Anne McGuigan. *Dinny Gordon, Sophomore*. Philadelphia: Macrae Smith, 1961. 185pp.

Dinny Gordon feels increasing pressure to begin dating in this book for young adults. She is attractive and popular and her friends, all of whom are dating, cannot understand why Dinny passes up invitations from boys. The answer lies in Dinny's dreams for a future as a scholar; she is interested in classical archaeology and knows that years of study lie between her and her professional goals and she does not want to get entangled a relationship too early. Set in the Chicago suburb of Rosemont, the city mostly offers Dinny opportunities to visit museums. A major theme of the book is how a female should balance career goals with her own expectation and those of others in regard to romance, marriage, and raising a family.

353. Emery, Anne McGuigan. *A Dream to Touch*. Philadelphia: Macrae Smith, 1958. 190pp.

In this novel for young adults, Emery presents hard-working immigrants and demonstrates the effectiveness of social support networks to aid them in pursuing the American dream. Marya Rose, the daughter of Polish immigrants satisfies her parents' expectations as she finishes her senior year in high school. Musical like her father, a violin teacher in Poland supporting his family in Chicago as an elevator operator, Marya plays violin in a youth orchestra and takes lessons through school and a settlement house. While focused on winning a college scholarship like her brother Jan, Mary also wants to help her parents and younger siblings escape the Victorian-era tenement in which they live on Weed Street before gangs control the neighborhood. She witnessed her boyfriend, Tony Marino, adopt a gangster mentality and believes her younger brother will soon adopt the same outlook. Fortunately, a boy from youth orchestra, Nicky Costanza, understands her goals and supports her. In the end, Marya wins a National Merit Scholarship to Northwestern University and helps her parents find an apartment in a better neighborhood. While Emery portrays 1950s inner-city problems, she conveys the message that hard-working, talented, poor people have effective social support networks to engineer their escape.

354. Emery, Anne McGuigan. *First Love, True Love*. Philadelphia: Westminster Press, 1956. 189pp.

The world of Pat Marlowe is mostly confined to her high school with classes, clubs, and other social activities in this book for young adults. Kenny, the boy she had been dating, has started college and encouraged her to date as she wished. The sixteen-year-old desperately wants a boyfriend, and is soon accepting neighbor Tim Davis' invitations to dates. Initially, considering this socializing to be casual, both of them are surprised when they realize they are falling in love and they decide to go steady. Pat's mother thinks this is a very bad idea and the book is in part about whether or not it is a good thing for a high school girl to go steady. The other issue presented is the degree to which a girl should be focused on her own interests and finding the right balance between her interests and her boyfriends. Although the book takes place in a Chicago suburb, the small town environment seems little influenced by the nearby urban city.

355. Emery, Anne McGuigan. *First Orchid for Pat*. Philadelphia: Westminster Press, 1957. 185pp.

In this second young adult novel featuring Pat Marlowe, her boyfriend Tim Davis is in his first year at Crandall College. At the suggestion of their parents, the couple dates other people while they are apart and Pat makes new friends who are more affluent than her middle-class family. Her new friends have cars, go with their families on long vacations to Europe, and get orchid corsages for special occasions. Through the course of the novel, Pat examines her values and strikes a balance between developing her own interest in theater and taste in clothing and domestic goods while still taking an interest in Tim and supporting his interests. Pat and her friends are more likely to go into Evanston, the next suburb over from them, than to Chicago, which mostly acts a transportation hub and work-day destination for many of their parents.

356. Emery, Anne McGuigan. *First Love Farewell*. Philadelphia: Westminster Press, 1958. 171pp.

In her first year after graduating from high school, Pat Marlowe experiences college life, begins to develop her independence and skill as an actress, and ends her relationship with Tim Davis, the man she had planned to marry at the end of her freshman year in college. Pat attends Northwestern University and all of the action takes place in the Chicago metropolitan area. Pat continues to live in her girlhood home located in Allandale, which is only three miles from Evanston. Except as a place for attending theater and for getting trains outside the region, Chicago does not play a major role in the novel. Much of this young adult novel deals with the appropriate degree of independence a young woman should have while still ceding the appropriate amount of fealty to the man in her life.

357. Emery, Anne McGuigan. *Going Steady*. Philadelphia: Westminster Press, 1950. 189pp.

Sally Burnaby and her boyfriend Scott begin to go steady after he presents her with his literary club pin at senior prom. In the summer after they graduate from high school, Sally realizes they have different tastes in home furnishings, movies, and books. However, as couples in her acquaintance begin to marry and she becomes concerned about future dating prospects as the supply of single men dwindles, Sally pushes Scott to propose. Refusing to listen to parental objections, they begin to realize what they are giving up by not going to college. Both of them have affluent upper-middle-class families and when they visit the apartment of a young married couple, they are appalled to think they will live in such conditions. The engagement is broken and each of them begins looking forward to college. In addition to presenting 1950s' views on dating and marriage, the book for young adults provides many descriptions of leisure activities and parties. On one of their dates, Scott and Sally drive into Chicago to enjoy Buckingham Fountain at night.

358. Emery, Anne McGuigan. *The Losing Game*. Philadelphia: Westminster Press, 1965. 140pp.

In Sue Morgan's junior year in high school she decides that she is no longer is most concerned about being in "The Popular Crowd" and intends to concentrate on her school work and one extracurricular activity—journalism. She faces a crisis when she is writing about honesty and integrity and some of her friends are discovered cheating. This young adult book, a sequel to *The Popular Crowd*, is set in Eden Heights, an imaginary northern suburb of Chicago.

359. Emery Anne McGuigan. *Married on Wednesday; A Junior Novel*. Philadelphia: Macrae Smith, 1957. 224pp.

Family life in the 1950s is the theme of this young adult novel that explores the boundaries newlyweds must cross to establish their own lives. While students at Northwestern University, Kay Chandler and Kenny Dixon fall in love and marry. Their wedded existence is complicated by their parents' continuing attempts to help them out by looking out for them and making decisions on their behalf. By the end of the novel Kay and Kenny have begun functioning as an adult couple.

360. Emery, Anne McGuigan. *The Popular Crowd.* Philadelphia: Westminster Press, 1961. 170pp.

As a sophomore in high school, Sue Morgan's life changes dramatically when she becomes one of the most popular girls in her class and begins dating the school's football hero. Sue lives in Eden Heights, a northern suburb of Chicago and her father manages one of Chicago's largest department stores. Sue's attractiveness and her family's affluence and social distinction are factors in her popularity, but so, too, is her brother. He won a football scholarship to Ohio State University and plays in the starting lineup. When her brother flunks out of school, Sue's popularity wanes and she begins to understand all she gave up in mimicking the interests and behavior of the popular crowd. One issue with which this young adult novel deals is adolescent sexuality, as Sue must decide whether to give in to her boyfriend's advances.

361. Emery, Anne McGuigan. *Senior Year.* Illustrated by Beth Krush. Philadelphia: Westminster Press, 1949. 208pp.

In this young adult novel about high school life in the late 1940s in a Chicago suburb, Sally Burnaby begins to experience some of the issues faced by adults. Her best friend moves away and her boyfriend starts dating someone else. Then, to save money for college she starts giving up some of her social life to babysit. When she finds a new boyfriend, he turns out to be irresponsible and she is forced to break up with him after he takes her and a group of friends to a roadhouse to drink beer, keeps them out late, and speeds while driving home. Illness also becomes a presence in her life when a friend's mother has a heart attack and her own younger sister is hospitalized with rheumatic fever. By the end of the novel she thinks it would not be such a bad thing to live at home and attends a nearby college, rather than going away for school and dealing with life challenges on her own.

362. Emery, Anne McGuigan. *Sorority Girl.* Illustrated by Richard Horwitz. Philadelphia: Westminster Press, 1952. 191pp.

High school junior Jean Burnaby is preoccupied with high school sororities and fraternities in this novel for young adults set in a Chicago suburb. After becoming a sorority member and seeing the impact club life has in determining the friends she chooses and the boys she dates, Jean decides exclusive social organizations are divisive to school spirit and impose false standards in judging others. She resigns her sorority membership before the end of the school year. Although this novel provides a detailed account of the life of a public high school girl in the 1950s, the novel's action could just as well have been set in any American town and has little content specific to a Chicago suburb.

363. Emery, Anne McGuigan. *That Archer Girl.* Philadelphia: Westminster Press, 1959. 175pp.

The action of this young adult novel takes place during the holiday season as Anne Archer strategizes over her social life with a commanding officer's concern about achieving victory. The cherished daughter in a family that owns a chain of ten successful department stores, she has the advantages of wealth and social prominence—the Archers are one of the oldest and most prominent families in Lakeville, an exclusive North Shore suburb of Chicago. Anne is a senior at the local, private girl's school, Auburn Academy, and drives a Thunderbird convertible her parents gave her for her sixteenth birthday. This record of Anne's interactions with others and her private thoughts, demonstrate why she may have an unhappy life, despite her advantages, if she does not become less selfish and begin to talk love seriously, rather than always being concerned about her next conquest. The book presents viewpoints of Anne's parents and friends that convey 1950s understandings of gender appropriate behavior, social expectations, and material culture aspects of establishing and maintaining social dominance.

364. Eng, Rita. *Ruthie*. New York: Simon and Schuster, 1960. 247pp.

When thirty-nine-year-old Ruthie Harkness of Minneapolis hears of the death of her college friend Mary Louise Winterhalter in Chicago, she decides to take advantage of a business trip her husband Roy had scheduled to the city. Although she tells everyone she is traveling to learn more of Mary Louise, with whom she had fallen out of touch, she is really motivated by an increasingly desperate sense of frustration and boredom with her own life as a housewife. In Chicago, Ruthie stays with another college friend, Ethelyn Campbell, and learns almost immediately that Mary Louise had died from a botched abortion. The trip becomes an unexpected agent of change for Ruthie when she discovers that Roy and Ethelyn have been having an affair. The novel addresses gender and marital roles of the time and ends with a rapprochement between Ruthie and Roy and the expectation that Ruthie will be a happier housewife in future.

365. Ernst, Paul Frederick [Ernest Jason Fredericks, pseud.]. *Lost Friday*. London, U.K.: Robert Hale, 1959. 189pp.

In this work of pulp fiction, an insurance company detective, Sam Cates, is waylaid on his trip to Chicago to investigate an extortion case. After being knocked unconscious, he awakens in an empty Elgin warehouse to find his briefcase and wallet stolen. Chicago is only superficially described as a backdrop for the action (by an author who was apparently British) as Cates recovers proof of his identity and solves the extortion case.

366. Essipoff, Marie Armstrong. *My First Husband*. New York: Greenberg, 1932. 308pp.

Written from within the Chicago literary community of the 1910s and 1920s, in the form of a memoir, the narrator includes many details about social life in the midst of her account of an affair and troubled marriage. When Ann, a recent Northwestern University graduate, begins a career as a journalist, she is soon fascinated with, and quickly dating, Eric Mayer, considered one of Chicago's most promising writers. A great deal is made of the fact that Mayer is Jewish and Ann Episcopalian and that Mayer goes out of his way to shock people. The couples' friends include artists, opera singers, performers, and writers, including Sherwood Anderson, Maxwell Bodenheim, Jascha Heifetz, Anita Loos, and the Marx Brothers. Mayer and Ann get very involved in Chicago's little theater movement and several intentionally shocking productions are described. Financial pressures push Eric into writing short stories for magazines and he eventually earns a national reputation. When he publishes his first novel, *Karl Langster*, a love story in which extramarital sex plays a large part, the book is sensationally successful. Ann finds more modest success editing a literary magazine and later starts a literary newspaper. When Ann discovers Eric's affair, Mayer asks for two days per week with his mistress and after much emotional self-searching, Ann decides to try this system and become friends with Mayer's mistress, Esther. Eventually, however, Mayer moves to New York City with Esther and Ann takes a furnished apartment on Sheridan Avenue, continuing to write and beginning a radio show on books and theater, before she, too moves to New York City and re-marries.

367. Everett, Henry L. *The People's Program; The Twentieth Century is Theirs, A Romance of the Expectations of the Present Generation*. New York: Workmen's Publishing, 1892. 213pp.

This utopian novel promotes the idea of young, college-educated people joining together and bringing a combination of rational planning and Christianity to the plight of exploited laborers. A movement called the Geometrical League begins when two young Americans, George Streeter and James Emmett, meet while they are traveling in Europe. They quickly realize they have a shared perspective on the world's social problems. Streeter's ideas attract the support of the German royal family, who also adopt him. The league, which is named for the membership expansion method of each new member getting ten new members to join, is soon publishing a newspaper, the *Deutscher Student*, and later hosts a large gathering of young people. When Streeter and Emmett return to the United States, they decide to base their organization in Chicago. Although the book includes slight physical description of the city, references are made to the Columbian Exposition. The tenets of the Geometrical League remain vague, but touch on some of the social challenges of the time, including women's suffrage, model housing, strengthening the federal government, applying scientific management and government controls to agricultural production, and the international regulation of currency.

368. Ewing, Annemarie. *Little Gate*. New York: Rinehart, 1947. 278pp.

The jazz music scene of 1920s Chicago provides seventeen-year-old Joe Geddes an escape from life in Muscatine, Iowa, working at the local Heinz ketchup factory. A self-taught saxophonist, Geddes leaves Muscatine earlier than he planned when Rose Dubrowsky, a girl he has befriended, claims to be pregnant with his child. Aided by his African-American friends (he is Caucasian), Joe goes to Chicago and finds work playing with jazz bands, establishing himself after several years as a Chicago musician. He is settled in his life until Rose shows up. She reveals that she was never actually pregnant, but seeks revenge over his leaving her behind in Muscatine. She has muscle behind her since she is connected to a powerful gangster organization. Joe leaves within hours for New York City and eventually his girlfriend, a singer named Irene Jaynes, follows him, as do some of his Chicago friends and before long he has formed his own band. After several cross-country tours and a successful record, he is poised to start his own radio show when he realizes that his incipient commercial success has already robbed him of important aspects of his musical life and his ability to employ African-Americans. He gives up on the radio show to continue as a band-leader. The Chicago section of the novel (about seventy pages) demonstrates the city's importance in the development of jazz music and portrays a musical community blind to issues of race and ethnicity. A number of specific music venues in the city are named and the novel also captures a burgeoning youth culture centered on jazz music.

369. Fair, Ronald L. *Hog Butcher*. New York: Harcourt, Brace and World, 1966. 182pp.

In this novel about the racism experienced by African-Americans in Chicago in the 1960s, two policemen responding to a robbery shoot down Nathaniel Hamilton, a young man in whom his neighborhood was proud because he had been offered twenty athletic scholarships and would be starting college in the fall. The only witnesses are two boys, Wilford and Earl. In the course of the novel the entire neighborhood is intimidated by the police so that the true story of Hamilton's murder will not come out. However, when Earl tells the truth at the coroner's inquest, his courage may have an impact.

370. Fair, Ronald. *We Can't Breathe*. New York: Harper and Row, 1972. 216pp.

Fair presents a fictionalized version of his life growing up in one of Chicago's African-American ghettos in the 1940s. Protagonist Ernie spends most of his time with boys his age named Willie, Jake, and Sam. They scavenge the junkyard and vacant lots for trash they can resell, and play organized games of basketball, football, and softball, although their playing grounds are usually muddy lots and their equipment improvised. Fueled by immense anger against the larger culture that oppresses them, the boys occasionally strike out against whites, committing petty theft and tricking business owners. Because books and education are considered the province of whites, the boys all have conflicted relationships with school and print culture in general. By the end of the book, the fourteen-year-old Ernie has already been exposed to gangsters and seen men gunned down in the street.

371. Fair, Ronald. *World of Nothing: Two Novellas*. New York: Harper and Row, 1970. 133pp.

The two stories in this volume illuminate life in Chicago's African-American ghetto in the 1960s. In "Jerome," the illegitimate of son of Episcopal priest Father Jennings has powers variously described as demonic or angelic. His mother Lula was only thirteen-years-old when Jerome was conceived and she must struggle against Father Jennings plot to have her son institutionalized. The other story, "World of Nothing," consists of a first-person narrative that captures the social life and desperation of ghetto life. Domestic settings are mostly in public housing, many of the characters have substance abuse problems, and traditions and perspectives of African-American culture in the Deep South have a major influence.

372. Fairbank, Janet Ayer. *In Town, & Other Conversations*. Illustrated by Rebecca Kruttschnitt. Cover Design by J. O. Smith. Chicago: McClurg, 1910. 222pp.

This attempt to capture upper-class Chicago society around 1910 has no narrative, but consists entirely of conversational exchanges over the tea table of the widowed Mrs. Fletcher with brief descriptions of the speakers. Although many of the subjects may seem trivial, the cultural values they reflect can provide insight on affluent early twentieth-century Chicagoans. A great deal of attention is paid to gender roles and proper behavior at social events, such as house parties and horse shows.

373. Fairbank, Janet Ayer. *The Smiths*. Indianapolis: Bobbs-Merrill, 1925. 433pp.

This family saga set in Chicago covers the years of the 1860s through the 1890s in three sections: the founding of industries and businesses during and after the Civil War; the aftermath of the fire of 1871 and the struggle to rebuild the city; and the Columbian Exposition era. Economic, political, and (primarily) social developments in Chicago are presented through the stories of Peter and Anna Smith, their friends—Peter's business partner Titus Jefferson, the banker Josephus Baker, the lawyer Daniel Lunt—and the Smith children and those of their friends. Peter Smith founded an iron factory after the Civil War, at just the right moment to take advantage of the development of the steel industry in the United States and made a fortune (after years of struggle) that funded a Prairie Avenue mansion and a comfortable life for his descendants. He spends the last years of his life collecting art and his children are able to pursue careers in banking, politics, and Chicago society. Although Peter's wife is the scion of an important New York family, the Cortlandts, Peter has never wanted any advantages to stem from the connection. It is inevitable that the supposed evil of inherited wealth becomes a major theme of the book as the children of Peter and Anna become adults. In addition to documenting the social history of Chicago, Fairbanks contrasts the city with other places (New York City, fashionable summer resorts, and Europe) through her affluent characters travels and articulates what makes Chicago distinctive.

374. Fairbank, Janet Ayer. *Rich Man, Poor Man*. Boston: Houghton Mifflin, 1936. 626pp.

Fairbank continues her Smith family saga in this volume that begins in 1912 and ends in 1929. Most of the work covers 1912 to 1915 and the focus is on Hendricks Cortlandt Smith, Jr., who has just finished Harvard at the beginning of the novel. An enthusiastic supporter of Teddy Roosevelt's presidential campaign, he eagerly returns to Chicago to witness the Republican national convention, outraging his father, a Taft supporter. A rift develops that is formalized when Smith is disinherited. Forced into an adult independence earlier than he intended, he soon marries Barbara Jackson, a self-educated, politicized young woman from Kansas. Fortunately, his grandmother, Mrs. Peter Smith, has always favored Smith and her wedding gift is enough steel stock to provide him with an adequate private income. Although he does get a job as a newspaper reporter and Barbara soon has a baby girl, the two never settle down into upper-middle-class married life. Barbara is too political to devote herself to household matters, cares nothing for social events or the affluence of her in-laws, and is soon using her public speaking skills in the suffragette movement. The World War I era brings the death of Mrs. Peter Smith, who had been the center of the family and a link to an earlier Chicago now seen as irrelevant to the present-day Smiths, and the rift between Barbara and Smith brings their divorce. Fairbank presents highly detailed accounts of political meetings and conventions, records upper-class domestic life and its food and clothing, and captures family tensions raised by national politics. Through the character of Barbara, she elucidates issues of gender and social class. Although much of the novel is set in Chicago, the Smiths summer in Bar Harbor and travel to New York City and France.

375. Farrell, James T. (James Thomas). *An American Dream Girl*. New York: Vanguard Press, 1950. 302pp.

Mostly set in the 1920s, not all of the short stories in this book are set in Chicago, however many of the stories from outside the city present Chicago characters remembering their lives in Chicago. The characters tend to be working-class and live on the South Side. Among the professions represented are trolley car motorman, freight transporter, and dispatcher. Characters include several schoolboy athletes, young people finding their way as adults with difficulty, and middle-aged men and women dealing with the loss of youth and the prospects of age. A number of the stories touch on themes of ethnic prejudice and racial violence and women are always objectified and often presented as commodities (in brothels, dance halls, or, as in the title story, in advertising).

376. Farrell, James T. (James Thomas). *Boarding House Blues*. New York: Paperback Library, 1961. 220pp.

The setting of a boarding house on Chicago's Near North Side during the Depression gives Farrell a chance to present a series of character sketches with little in the way of plot to connect them. The central character is Bridget O'Dair, the boarding house manager. Characters from some of Farrell's other works, such as Danny O'Neill (from the O'Neill O'Flaherty series) and Ed Lanson (Ellen Rogers) also appear.

377. Farrell, James T. (James Thomas). *Calico Shoes*. New York: Vanguard Press, 1934. 303pp.

All of these sixteen short stories are set in Chicago and convincingly depict lower-middle-class Irish, Polish, or Lithuanian characters. Plot conflicts stem from romantic and sexual relations that cause animosity between friends, children and parents, and men and women. Syphilis is a dreaded disease that several characters contract, including a couple who seem happily married on their way up the ladder to upper-middle-class respectability. One story details a white homosexual man's affairs with African-American men. Some of the most poignant stories depict hopeless, unmarried women who exist in a culture in which only marriage and children can earn them respectability and financial security. The characters attend parochial school or university and work as bond salesmen, boxers, gas station attendants, janitors, teamsters, and soda jerks. Settings include apartment houses, private parties, the beach, brothels, public dance halls, and hotel ballrooms. The drug of choice is gin and Prohibition presents difficulties for the alcoholics. Because of the importance of clothes and cars for establishing social status enabling sexual conquests, descriptions of material culture are especially rich. Farrell also evokes physical settings from the campus of the University of Chicago, to the lakefront, to public parks, and the depressed neighborhoods near the slaughterhouses.

378. Farrell, James T. (James Thomas). *A Brand New Life*. Garden City, N.Y.: Doubleday, 1968. 371pp.

A newly divorced woman arrives in 1920s Chicago hoping to create a new life for herself. Anne Duncan Daniels from Valley City boarded a train Chicago in February 1928, immediately after she and her husband Zeke divorced. She uses part of her one hundred dollars per month alimony to rent a room in The Lancaster Arms apartment hotel on the North Side on Winchester Street. A waitress before her six-year marriage, she has no immediate goals, except to escape into the anonymity of the city and, eventually, find a man unlike Zeke, who sometimes hit her. Almost immediately she and fellow Lancaster Arms tenant Roger Raymond begin an affair and are soon living together. Roger sells advertising space in a telephone company directory. However, having run away from home at seventeen to join the U.S. Navy, he has traveled widely and prides himself on his intellectual and artistic interests fed by hours spent reading at the Chicago Public Library and viewing works at the Art Institute. Focusing on the interactions of these characters and their thoughts and changing perceptions, Farrell presents issues of gender and evokes lower-middle-class life in the 1920s, describing food, pastimes, restaurants, dance halls, and clothing. Physical settings tend to be in Lincoln Park and the Loop.

379. Farrell, James T. (James Thomas). *Can All this Grandeur Perish?* New York: Vanguard Press, 1937. 308pp.

In these short stories, Farrell evokes life for Chicagoans of several social levels during the Depression era. In "Can All This Grandeur Perish," Tom Gregory and members of his social circle who attend his New Year's Day open house, are insulated from the impact of the Depression. Gregory, for instance, had established a wholesale grocery business and sold out just before the stock market crash. Similarly, the characters in "Mendel and His Wife" are Chicagoans living in Paris able to concern themselves with literary and artistic matters because of a monthly allowance from home and their ability to find a constantly changing circle of Americans to host them and lend them money. In "The Professor," Paul Saxon earns a comfortable living as a teacher and editor and finishes his work around midday. For Saxon the mass of underfed humanity passing out of factory gates constitutes a metaphor to be worked into his writings and a reminder that he must try to take his life more seriously. In other short stories, characters are in less control of their lives; a couple living on social assistance, inspired by the Lindberg kidnapping, ransom a lost dog, and are sentenced to a maximum jail term; and a pregnant seventeen-year-old girl has an abortion and unrealistically pledges to never love again. The stories work together to present dramatically different perspectives on the impact of the economy on the lives of Chicagoans.

380. Farrell, James T. (James Thomas). *Childhood Is Not Forever*. Garden City, N.Y.: Doubleday, 1969. 300pp.

This collection of semi-autobiographical short stories includes works mostly set in the late 1940s and 1950s. The title story, and several others, including the novella-length "Native Returns" are set in Chicago and have the common theme of characters who grew up in the city in the 1920s returning after establishing themselves in the larger world and dealing with changes in the city and their own relation to the place.

381. Farrell, James T. (James Thomas). *A Dangerous Woman and Other Stories*. New York: Vanguard Press, 1957. 160pp.

Although a few of these short stories are set in Europe, most are set in 1920s and 1930s Chicago and deal with either the control sexual desire gives women over men, or the challenge of achieving a meaningful life as an individual powerless in the face of social prejudices and economic constraints. The story of Milt Coggswell's life told in "Momento Mori" is typical of the volume. Milt, the son of a violent alcoholic carpenter who died young, lives his whole life respectably, working for decades as an expressman, marrying and raising a family, and remaining faithful to the Roman Catholic Church. However, he never experiences a moment of joy, is plagued by weariness and ill health, and is killed randomly in a traffic accident. Norman Allen's life is also a story of futility. Born an African-American in prejudiced Chicago, he overcomes a life of harsh poverty, limited opportunity, and racial hatred, by working his way through college and university, eventually earning a doctorate and a position of respect in an African-American college, only to be plagued by the "sweet voices of white women" to the point of a nervous breakdown and diagnosis of schizophrenia. Less evocative of place than some of Farrell's other short story collections, this work presents lower-class culture in the 1920s and 1930s.

382. Farrell, James T. (James Thomas). *The Dunne Family*. Garden City, N.Y.: Doubleday, 1976. 326pp.

Farrell's story of Irish immigrant experience in Chicago presents three generations. Grace Hogan Dunne, now confined to a wheel-chair, arrived in the United States in the 1860s and settled with her husband in Chicago. From the novel's present, the 1930s, she reflects on her life and witnesses the lives of her children. The oldest, Richard, was for thirty years the main support of his family, earning his living as a salesman, but as the Depression worsens, he becomes increasingly anxious and, in his sixties, finds few opportunities. His younger brother Larry, has always been prone to idleness and dependence and even the hardships of the Depression have done nothing to energize him. The two daughters in the family are Jenny and Nora. Jenny was beautiful in her youth and had a wealthy suitor, but thought she needed to stay at home and take care of her mother and brothers. The youngest sister, Nora married a man of whom the Dunnes did not approve, but her financially successful marriage becomes a resource for the Dunnes. Nora's son, Eddie Ryan, as the youngest on the family tree, will become the family's legacy, although he has no visions of establishing a fortune or building a dynasty, but only wants to become a writer. The novel does much to illuminate Irish immigrant family life in Chicago in the 1930s.

383. Farrell, James T. (James Thomas). *Ellen Rogers*. New York: Vanguard Press, 1941. 429pp.

Nineteen-year-old Ellen Rogers lives with her father (her mother died when Ellen was still an infant) in a comfortable, newly furnished, maid-attended, apartment on East Sixty-seventh Street near Jackson Park, where she is free to pursue interests like horse-back riding and piano lessons. However, Ellen is bored most of the time. She has graduated from high school and embraced in desultory fashion her father's plan to send her to the University of Chicago. Her time in the summer of 1925 is spent taking long walks and going on dates to dances and the movies, but none of her escorts really interest her and she amuses herself by treating them badly. When she meets Edmond "Hellfire" Lanson, the boyfriend of a schoolgirl chum, tables are turned and she is fascinated. Lanson is unlike the other boys she dates. He is not going to college and has no job or prospects. He also enjoys being outrageous and talks like a character out of a novel. Over the course of the book, she falls ever more deeply in love with him, only to be treated badly, until he finally leaves Chicago. Edmond grew up in the working-class neighborhood in which Farrell did and his way of treating women, borrowing money from them and then abandoning them has a component of class resentment. Physical settings are not particularly well-described in the novel, but many dating activities, like going to jazz clubs and restaurants are.

384. Farrell, James T. (James Thomas). *The Face of Time*. New York: Vanguard Press, 1953. 366pp.

This, the fifth and final volume of the O'Neill-O'Flaherty series of novels, actually covers a time period prior to the other books, summer of 1909 to December of 1910, when Danny O'Neill, a central character in the other novels, is only five-years-old. Some of the major issues with which the book deals are the dynamics of assimilation for the Irish-American O'Neill family as they settle on Chicago's South Side, and the emotions associated with one generation supplanting another. Danny's father Jim, is having financial difficulties and sends Danny to live with his grandfather, Tom O'Flaherty, in a household on Washington Square that includes several unmarried aunts and uncles. While living there, Danny witnesses the drama of Tom's final illness and death, and the interactions of family members in the face of Tom's inevitable demise.

385. Farrell, James T. (James Thomas). *Father and Son*. New York: Vanguard Press, 1940. 616pp.

The third book in the O'Neill-O'Flaherty series deals with Danny O'Neill's relationship with his father Jim O'Neill. Danny grew up in the household of his maternal grandfather, Tom O'Flaherty, since the O'Neills' economic struggles made it too difficult to care for Danny, the youngest son. Now, in 1918, Danny experiences O'Neill family life and hardship, deals with his father's death, and later works in his first job at the teamster firm that had employed his father. Danny's challenges in communicating with his father, siblings, and co-workers foster a sense of alienation that inspire him to find a way to aspire to a more intellectually satisfying life and social setting.

386. Farrell, James T. (James Thomas). *Fellow Countrymen; Collected Stories*. London, U.K.: Constable, 1937. 439pp.

This publication, released in England, is similar to *The Short Stories of James T. Farrell*, drawing on the contents of *Calico Shoes*, *Guillotine Party*, and *Can All This Grandeur Perish?* each of which is separately described here.

387. Farrell, James T. (James Thomas). *Gas-House McGinty*. New York: Vanguard Press, 1933. 364pp.

Farrell's second book is based on the experiences of his father and himself working for the Amalgamated Express Company of Chicago and depicts working-class life. The setting for most of the novel is the "gas-house" of the Continental Express Company where trucks are serviced and the dispatcher, Ambrose J. McGinty, rules. McGinty's house is a minor setting and Mike Boylan's Prohibition-era barroom plays a major role in the life of many of the characters.

388. Farrell, James T. (James Thomas). *Guillotine Party and Other Stories*. New York: Vanguard Press, 1935. 305pp.

Most of the short stories in this volume are set in Chicago in the 1920s and 1930s and present life on the city's South Side. The characters are mainly from the Irish-Catholic community and in their final years of high school or first years as adults, finding their way in the world. For most of them, their choices are shaped by the prejudices (political, religious, racial, and ethnic) with which they grew up. The few young people whose perspectives are broadened by introspection and a university education are usually forced by economic realities to keep quiet about their new understandings. In addition to capturing the rhythm and slang of lower-class speech, Farrell successfully conveys a sense of place, in scenes set in parks, beaches, schools, businesses, households, speakeasies, and brothels. His depictions of ethnic and racial hatred, economic despair, and aspects of the immigrant experience are particularly memorable.

389. Farrell, James T. (James Thomas). *Judgment Day*. New York: Vanguard Press, 1935. 465pp.

This third volume in the Studs Lonigan trilogy is set in 1931 in a Chicago that has undergone a dramatic transformation from the city portrayed in the earlier novels. Studs is no longer a fit, carefree, envied young man. At the beginning of the book he is recovering from pneumonia that leaves him weakened throughout the rest of the book. His father's construction business, upon which the whole family had depended, has no work. Studs, who is forced to marry his fiancée earlier than he expected when she becomes pregnant, must find a job in a market in which millions are looking for work. All of the money he had saved in his youth is gone in bad investments and failed banks. The Lonigans' neighborhood has also been transformed by the economic climate and has become part of Chicago's African-American ghetto. Both Studs and his father spend more and more time trying to reconnect with their irretrievable pasts. The novel conveys the emotional and physical impact of the Depression on Chicago, a city that had enjoyed decade after decade of expansion and growth since the 1871 fire.

390. Farrell, James T. (James Thomas). *Judith*. Athens, Ohio: Duane Schneider, 1969. 363pp.

The short stories in this volume are set in New York City and Europe, as well as in Chicago. With the exception of one story in which Eddie Ryan, the author's alter ego, returns to Chicago as a successful writer, the Chicago stories are mostly set in working-class milieus, particularly among teamsters. The final story in the volume is about a boy's experiences in a private Catholic middle school as he becomes friends with one of the teaching nuns.

391. Farrell, James T. (James Thomas). *The Life Adventurous and Other Stories*. New York: Vanguard Press, 1947. 313pp.

Most of these short stories are set in 1920s Chicago on the South Side or on the Near North Side. In general the characters are young men who are looking for love, a vocation, or a social institution or movement through which they can find meaning. Although they were raised in the Roman Catholic Church and attended parochial schools, the church no longer provides a viable source of meaning and the characters who have become priests, nuns, or monks still experience a sense of dislocation. Several of the characters are members of the Communist Party and experience its flaws, as do the men who try to finding meaning in their jobs (usually as freight dispatchers). Some historical events of the time period are described, including the public celebrations after the election of President Coolidge and the rent moratorium protests. Many of the characters are conflicted over sexual expression and the greater openness of sexuality in the 1920s is not universally welcomed.

392. Farrell, James T. (James Thomas). *Lonely for the Future*. Garden City, N.Y.: Doubleday, 1966. 263pp.

In this novel, Eddie Ryan, a character in a series of Farrell novels, grows up and enters young adulthood. Ryan's neighborhood is near the elevated station at Fifty-seventh and Cottage Grove Avenue and his most important friend is George Raymond who moves to Chicago from Kickapoo, Illinois when he is fourteen and Ryan is fifteen. Ryan has alienated all of the other neighborhood boys through his conflict with a rich boy who then blackballs him from neighborhood social life. Parochial school boys, both Ryan and Raymond are intelligent, but have difficulty accepting authority. They begin frequenting the Bug Club, the Wild Onion, and the Bohemian Forum when they are in their teens and by the time they have graduated from high school, decide to start their own intellectual/social club on the South Side. Power struggles and rivalry over women lead to hostilities that end in a dramatic boxing match between Raymond and one of his rivals. By the end of the novel both Ryan and Raymond have decided that Chicago has nothing more to offer them and they leave for New York City where Ryan hopes to become a writer and Raymond hopes to make his mark. Most of the novel is set in 1927 on the South Side and deals with the theme of culturally alienated young men from the working class with intellectual proclivities. In general women are treated very badly in the novel as sexual conveniences.

393. Farrell, James T. (James Thomas). *More Fellow-Countrymen*. London, U.K.: Routledge, 1946. 223pp.

In addition to Chicago, these short stories are set in Paris and New York City. The Chicago stories ("The Sport of Kings," "Monday is Another Day," "The Only Son," "The Fate of A Hero," "A Teamster's Payday," "Autumn Afternoon," "The Hyland Family"), mostly deal with family life on Chicago's South Side and conflicts over accepted social values based on adherence to politics or religion in contrast with intellectual self-examination.

394. Farrell, James T. (James Thomas). *My Days of Anger.* New York: Vanguard Press, 1943. 403pp.

In this fourth volume in the O'Neill-O'Flaherty series, spanning 1924 to 1927, Danny O'Neill begins studying at St. Vincent's Law School and the University of Chicago and copes with the end of his childhood. His grandmother, the key figure in his household during his youth, is dying and he begins to realize that he must quit college and move to New York City to become a writer. Through the friends he makes at the university, Danny's social world broadens and he experiences other parts of Chicago than the South Side in which he had grown up. At the same time his interactions with blue-collar family members and high school classmates who are now in the workplace, heighten his sense of cultural alienation until he decides he must make a definitive break with Catholicism and Chicago.

395. Farrell, James T. (James Thomas). *New Year's Eve, 1929.* New York: Smith, 1967. 144pp.

In this account of a day in the life of Beatrice Burns, Farrell captures the dying embers of the roaring 1920s as the Depression begins to deepen. Burns, who had worked as a nurse, is part of a social circle that includes writers and painters most of whom live in an area on the South Side known as the Fifty-seventh Street Art Colony. Although she takes great satisfaction in identifying herself as part of the bohemian setting, Farrell exposes the inaccuracies of her self-perception, showing Burns to be a hanger-on. Dying of lung disease, she throws herself into celebrating the New Year at an alcohol-fueled party at the center of her neighborhood, located at Fifty-seventh and Harper Streets. Although she has a sexual relationship with a man who wants to marry her, she does not consider him fast enough and yearns for an emotionally fraught relationship of the sort her artist acquaintances have and on which she spends most of her time spying at the party. Through Burns and her friends, Farrell articulates cultural values and captures aspects of daily life among cultured, educated—but poor—young people in 1929. A surprising number of young men in this setting are concerned about an imminent world war.

396. Farrell, James T. (James Thomas). *No Star Is Lost.* New York: Vanguard Press, 1938. 637pp.

This story of the domestic life of a working-class Irish immigrant family on Chicago's South Side is set in 1914 and 1915 and is mostly told through the perspective of Danny O'Neill, his mother Lizzie, and his Aunt Margaret O'Flaherty. Lizzie, the wife of Jim O'Neill, tries to manage an ever-growing household of children near Twenty-fifth and LaSalle Streets. She resents the interracial neighborhood and the tensions that inspire street fights between black and white children. Jim does not make enough money to support them, so Danny has been sent to live in his widowed, maternal grandmother's household near Fifty-first Street and Prairie Avenue, along with his unmarried Uncle Ned and Aunt Margaret. When his older brother Bill steals a letter to Margaret that he knows contains money from her boyfriend, lumberman Lorry Robinson, Margaret, unaware of the theft, believes Robinson has abandoned her and falls prey to alcoholism. Shortly after she is found naked in the kitchen with all the gas jets turned on, she is institutionalized for alcoholism treatment. The social disgrace in the close-knit neighborhood of Irish Catholic families prompts the O'Flahertys to relocate to the somewhat different neighborhood of Fifty-eighth Street and Prairie Avenue where Danny attends a new school at which his classmates will not tease him about his aunt. On his first day in the new neighborhood he meets Studs Lonigan, a character Farrell develops in other books. Farrell's account is larded with details of domestic life and the frustrations of working-class characters. Racism and ethnic-based prejudices are openly expressed and even remote political events get vented in verbal and physical violence.

397. Farrell, James T. (James Thomas). *$1000 A Week and Other Stories*. New York: Vanguard Press, 1942. 226pp.

Many of the short stories in this volume are set in Chicago during the Depression and frequently deal with educated people from the working class finding hope in the perspective of the Communist Party. Other stories deal with professional athletes and on-the-job experiences of working-class men.

398. Farrell, James T. (James Thomas). *The Road Between*. New York: Vanguard Press, 1949. 463pp.

Bernard Carr is living in New York City struggling to establish himself as a writer while dealing with financial constraints in 1932 in the midst of the Depression. Months after his marriage to twenty-one-year-old Elizabeth, a girl he knew from his Chicago youth, he is awaiting reaction to the publication of his first novel *The Father*. His hopes are dashed when sales of the book fail to cover his advance. Elizabeth makes his situation more precarious by her unthinking need for luxury, stemming from her affluent upbringing. The death of Bernard's father in Chicago provides a face-saving excuse for Bernard to return to his hometown. However, he must then deal with his family and the hostility of Elizabeth's father. The novel captures Depression-era, lower-middle-class life in Chicago and the plight of alienated intellectual young people. This novel is the second in Farrell's Bernard Carr trilogy.

399. Farrell, James T. (James Thomas). *The Short Stories of James T. Farrell*. New York: Vanguard Press, 1934. 534pp.

This volume brings together the contents of *Calico Shoes*, *Guillotine Party*, and *Can All This Grandeur Perish?*, each of which is separately described here.

400. Farrell, James T. (James Thomas). *Side Street, And Other Stories*. New York: Paperback Library, 1961. 224pp.

Of the sixteen short stories in this volume, six ("Aunt Louise," "Blisters," "High School," "Husband and Wife," "An Old Sweetheart," and "Shanley") have Chicago backgrounds. As in other Farrell stories the settings tend to be on Chicago's South Side and feature working-class characters.

401. Farrell, James T. (James Thomas). *The Silence of History*. Garden City, N.Y.: Doubleday, 1963. 372pp.

This first novel in Farrell's *A Universe of Time* series is set in July 1926 and is concerned with Eddie Ryan's mental life as he decides to stop working as a gas station attendant to spend more time studying. His top grades for his freshman year classes at the University of Chicago have fueled his desire for a life of the mind. Despite his inward focus, Ryan describes campus life, and his interactions with family and high school friends in South Side neighborhoods.

402. Farrell, James T. (James Thomas). *Sound of a City*. New York: Paperback Library, 1962. 176pp.

Although not all of these short stories are set in Chicago (settings also include New York City, Paris, and other locations in Europe), a significant number of works have Chicago settings. The Chicago stories document the work life of teamsters, married life for the working class, and the social life of adolescent boys attending private Catholic schools. The stories are set on the South Side and near Washington Square prior to World War II.

403. Farrell, James T. (James Thomas). *Studs Lonigan: A Trilogy*. New York: Vanguard Press, 1935. 465pp.

This publication brings together the three novels featuring Studs Lonigan and previously published separately all of which are described under their individual titles (*Judgment Day*, *Young Lonigan*, and *The Young Manhood of Studs Lonigan*).

404. Farrell, James T. (James Thomas). *This Man and This Woman*. New York: Vanguard Press, 1951. 205pp.

Peg and Walter Callahan have lived together as husband and wife for thirty-nine years. Their two children Dorothy and Jack are both married with children and their own households. Left alone together in their tiny, working-class apartment, the couple longs for their vanished youths and fears the inevitability of illness and death. At sixty-three-years-old, Walt still works for the teamster firm that hired him at seventeen. He was promoted to dispatcher decades before and to his alarm, increasingly has difficulties on the job stemming from tiredness and difficulty concentrating, despite the fact that his retirement is seven years away. On the whole, however, his outlook is positive and he takes satisfaction in his children and grandchildren. Peg, however, shrewish and neurotic most of her life, has been sliding into mental illness, and with the provocation of imagined demons urging her to kill before she is killed, murders Walter. The novel includes descriptions of lower-middle-class life and work culture, and implicitly expresses attitudes toward aging, gender, and mental illness.

405. Farrell, James T. (James Thomas). *To Whom It May Concern*. N.Y.: Vanguard Press, 1944. 204pp.

Eight of the thirteen short stories in this volume are set in South Side Chicago in the 1930s. They alternate between dealing with working-class family life as played out on Sunday afternoons and work life, mostly as led by teamsters. One story also deals with the pathos of a high school football player experiencing a knee injury that dashes all his hopes.

406. Farrell, James T. (James Thomas). *A World I Never Made*. N.Y.: Vanguard Press, 1936. 508pp.

Danny O'Neill is seven-years-old in this novel that spans August to December, 1911. His developing awareness of himself as an individual helps him realize how alienated he is from both the working-class O'Neill household and the middle-class O'Flaherty household ruled by his maternal grandmother where he lives due to the poverty of the O'Neills.

407. Farrell, James T. (James Thomas). *Yet Other Waters*. New York: Vanguard Press, 1952. 414pp.

The third and final volume of Farrell's Bernard Carr series is set in New York City, where Carr lives, and Chicago, to which he returns as his mother grows ill and dies. Carr's excitement with New York City and the Communist Party had waned and returning to Chicago helps him understand his family and the South Chicago neighborhood in which he grew up. This new understanding helps him develop closer relationships with his wife and young son, as well as reawakening his interest in writing about the city, an endeavor that will bring professional success. The

Chicago scenes are all set in South Chicago and, in addition to outright description, comparisons and contrasts are made with New York City.

408. Farrell, James T. (James Thomas). *Young Lonigan: A Boyhood in Chicago Streets*. New York: Vanguard Press, 1932. 308pp.

The first in the trilogy of books featuring Studs Lonigan, most of this book's action takes place in the summer after Lonigan graduates from elementary school when he is just about to turn fifteen-years-old. Lonigan's father is a contractor and the family is lower-middle-class. They live in a predominantly Irish, South Side neighborhood and Lonigan and his friends are preoccupied with athletic contests, including boxing. Once Lonigan beats up a neighborhood bully named "Weary" Reilly, his career as a young man is made and he takes on more and more of the character and behavior of a street tough, including experimentation with sex and bootleg alcohol. In addition to the streets of Lonigan's neighborhood, Farrell describes pool rooms, bars, beaches, parks, and the adjoining Jewish neighborhood.

409. Farrell, James T. (James Thomas). *The Young Manhood of Studs Lonigan*. New York: Vanguard Press, 1934. 412pp.

Covering the years 1917 to 1929, Lonigan graduates from high school, tries to get into the army before he is old enough to enlist, and later goes to work for his father as a house painter. Lonigan engages in few socially respectable activities, except for attending Roman Catholic Church services and playing football. The South Side neighborhood in which he lives is in the process of steady decay away from middle-class respectability and Lonigan spends more and more time drinking as time passes. The last football game he plays ends in a gang fight. He ruins his first real love affair after he infects his partner with a venereal disease he picked up in a casual sexual encounter. He also attempts a robbery with some of his gang and helps them torture an African-American child during a period of racial tension. As in his earlier book featuring Lonigan, Farrell presents not only the consciousness of Lonigan, but the physical and cultural environment in which he exists, establishing Lonigan's personal decline in the context of larger cultural patterns.

410. Farson, James Scott Negley. *Daphne's In Love*. New York: Century, 1927. 309pp.

Single young women in the 1920s, Daphne and Ivy work as secretaries at the Eureka Motor Truck Company and live in a boarding house on Chicago Avenue. The two converse about clothing, their figures, men, and their future. When Daphne is introduced to wealthy Taffy LeDoux, she tries to take an interest in him, and the two date when LeDoux is not in New York or Europe, however Daphne finally realizes that she cannot force herself to love him and instead falls in love with Steve Brinton, a salesman at Eureka. The novel provides many details about the life of young, working women in 1920s Chicago. There are descriptions of the new studio apartments with their fold-up beds and tables, the changing sexual mores that place the burden on women to give into "petting" at the end of any date, socializing in private apartments away from the eyes of chaperones and the public, and the impact of World War I on the perspectives of young men.

411. Farson, Negley. *Fugitive Love*. New York: Century, 1929. 267pp.

In this novel about 1920s Chicago, a young woman successfully thwarts her father's power over her, despite his corrupt political power in the city. Nineteen-year-old Jenny Cain lives with her father Hickey in an industrial waste land around a small body of water called Corey's Wharf in

West Chicago. Hickey is a corrupt building contractor with secret ties to political boss Chauncey O'Malley who steers all manner of building contracts Hickey's way, to their mutual benefit. Jenny's mother ran away when Jenny was a child and Jenny's life has been entirely controlled by Hickey. While living with her father and his construction crew in rural Illinois where they are building a road, Jenny falls in love with Torsten Aberg, one of her father's supervisors. The relationship is complicated by her father's commitment to O'Malley and the fact that Aberg had murdered a man in San Francisco years before. After a violent confrontation with O'Malley, Aberg flees and Jenny absconds to Chicago, where she uses a friend of Aberg to establish contact with the fugitive. She sells a bran supplement marketed in patent medicine fashion for pocket money while living with a non-conformist society figure, the beautiful young Tony Dell, who helps her make the society contacts that turn bran into a fad. Dell finds out that the man Aberg thought he had murdered is still alive and that O'Malley has hired a Mafioso to kill Aberg. Dell comes up with an elaborate plot to help them escape the gunman. Although half of this novel is set in rural Illinois, the Chicago sections are revealing for showing a polluted, over-populated, corrupt city, enlivened only by the artificiality of the high-society nightlife and absurd social events like "bran luncheons."

412. Fast, Howard. *The American, A Middle Western Legend.* New York: Duell, Sloane, Pierce, 1946. 337pp.

   Although much of the Illinois section of this fictionalized biography of John Peter Altgeld is set in Springfield, a number of significant scenes transpire in Chicago in 1887, 1893, 1895, and 1902. In describing the execution and funerals of the men implicated in the Haymarket riot, the pardoning of some of the Haymarket rioters, the Pullman strike, and the Chicago Democratic convention of 1896, Fast details physical and social settings to convey a sense of Altgeld's life in Chicago in the late nineteenth century.

413. Fearing, Blanche [Raymond Russell, pseud.]. *Asleep and Awake.* Chicago: Charles H. Kerr, 1893. 199pp.

   This romance novel includes lengthy perorations on the meaning of life and love. Chicagoan Raymond Russell, an upper-class young man who lives with his widowed mother, seeks diversion through a sojourn in the country town where Leonore Brooks, an innocent young woman of twenty-two, lives. Leonore happily and unselfconsciously enjoys the natural world around her until Russell awakens her intellect and she begins reading the old books of her grandfather. Newly dissatisfied with her life, she longs for further contact with Russell, who had returned to the city. Rejecting her country suitor, Hiram Gibbs, Brooks arrives in Chicago without a job and after living on a sparse diet for months, falls ill as winter approaches. Twenty-five-year-old Adel finds her and nurses her back to health. Eventually, Adel reveals that she fell into a life of prostitution because of Raymond Russell who claimed he loved her but could not marry, because of family opposition. Russell convinced Adel to live as his common law wife and the two had a child. However, the relationship collapsed and subsequently the baby died in an accident. Adel tries to use Brooks to mete out revenge on Russell, but Brooks goes mad and is returned to the country to live in an insane asylum where Russell discovers her and tells his side of Adel's tragic story. Brooks dies soon afterwards. Chicago in the novel is a place where anonymity and the poverty of single women work in the favor of men who take advantage of them.

414. Fearing, Blanche. *Roberta*. Chicago: Charles H. Kerr, 1895. 424pp.

Covering the 1870s to 1890s, this moralistic tale recounts the story of Roberta "Berta" Green. Berta is born into a poor family and her father dies when she is fourteen. Her mother supports a houseful of children taking in laundry and Berta, as the oldest, is forced into a sweatshop where she succumbs to typhoid. Confined in a hospital charity ward, she is visited by Mrs. Evalyn Fay, who promises to adopt Berta and support the Green family. Fay is a swindler, however, and she and her son view Berta as an innocent-looking accomplice. To permanently attach Berta to them, Fay's son makes romantic overtures and a sham marriage is held, after which Berta becomes pregnant. Before the birth, the Fays are arrested and Berta must put her baby up for adoption. After further suffering for Berta, the paroled Fays reappear, and during an emotional exchange, a firearm accidentally discharges. Berta flees to the "murderess" shouts of Mrs. Fay and goes into hiding in a slum, where she meets an evangelist, and is inspired to devote her life and modest savings to helping children. While visiting the Columbian Exposition, however, she is arrested and charged with the death of Fay. Lawyer Paul Graham earns her acquittal, and reveals that he has loved her since they were children living in the same neighborhood. The two marry and leave the city to live in material comfort, with Berta continuing to find ways to give of herself to others. Throughout the book suffering is presented as an opportunity for personal growth and the model for morality is the love of mother for child. Chicago is described as a frightening place with perilous environments, however, the Columbian Exposition represents a perfect city in which Berta can believe.

415. Ferber, Edna. *Buttered Side Down*. New York: Frederick A. Stokes, 1912. 230pp.

Almost all of the short stories in this collection are set in Chicago and deal with the experiences of women, who have reached their twenties and begun to accept the constraints and opportunities of unmarried life in the city. Most of the women work as specialty sales clerks (men's gloves, corsets, etc.). The narratives often include celebrations of Chicago. The protagonist in one story is a woman too poor to buy food who passes display windows of grocers filled with exotic gourmet comestibles. In another story, a woman describes the pleasure she takes in watching the great variety of humanity that passes by the corner of Clark and Randolph Streets.

416. Ferber, Edna. *Cheerful, by Request*. Garden City, N.Y.: Doubleday, Page, 1918. 366pp.

Six of the twelve short stories in this volume are set in Chicago. Several of the stories deal with young men and women who grew up in small towns moving to the city and trying to find a place for themselves in the urban setting. A few stories treat the plight of the single woman as she ages and realizes that she will never marry. The women are a head housekeeper in a hotel, a head department store clerk, and an oldest daughter who must care for an invalid mother and manage a household of unmarried brothers.

417. Ferber, Edna. *Fanny Herself*. Illustrated by J. Henry. New York: Frederick A. Stokes, 1917. 323pp.

In this novel about working women, Fanny Brandeis must negotiate among her business and artistic skills and her love for a naturalist to make a life for herself. Brandeis grows up in Winnebago, Wisconsin, the daughter of Jewish general store proprietors, and throughout the novel makes enough of what are characterized as the innate skills of Jews, so as to border on anti-Semitism. Fanny eventually inherits the family business but, convinced she should try for success in the larger world, goes to work as an assistant manager at one of the country's largest mail order companies, Haynes-Cooper in Chicago. Presumably based on Sears-Roebuck, the company is described as a tourist destination, much as the Art Institute. She is quickly successful and establishes a life that includes a Lake Shore Drive apartment. Then, Clarence Heyl from Winnebago seeks her out and reveals his interest in her. He believes she is ignoring her true self that is wrapped up in her Jewish identity and involves an understanding of human psychology, especially society's outcasts, whom she draws so well. Heyl is on his way to New York City to begin writing a newspaper column and encourages Fanny to become a graphic artist but she resists, pointing to her business success. She is in New York City when a large suffragette rally occurs and her drawing of the event wins her wide acclaim when it appears as a newspaper illustration. Complications prevent her from being united with Heyl until he rescues her in the middle of a Colorado blizzard and it seems clear that the two will marry and Fanny will take up a career as a newspaper artist, advocating for the downtrodden through her art. The novel repeatedly speaks about the central role Chicago plays for Midwesterners as a center for culture and commerce. The city is lyrically described with an emphasis on its beauty and vigor, as well as on the contrast between its well-known lakefront and architectural achievements and its hidden squalor.

418. Ferber, Edna. *Gigolo*. Garden City, N.Y.: Doubleday, Page, 1922. 291pp.
    Five of the eight short stories in this collection are set in Chicago. "Afternoon of Faun" depicts the self-absorbed appeal of garage mechanic Nick with whom every woman is enchanted. In "Old Man Minick" some of Chicago's history gets remembered by Minick who, now widowed, decides to move out of his son's house and live in a modest apartment hotel with other men of his generation, yet another step toward ceding his place in the world. The female version of Minick's hotel is featured in "The Sudden Sixties," where Hannah Winter lives continuing her life-long self-sacrifice for her children. "Home Girl" is filled with descriptions of post-World War I material culture, including apartment furnishings, with everything from shelves to beds built in, the availability of prepared foods, and the latest in fashion, all of which the stay at home girl Cora covets and her husband Raymond slaves away to provide, preventing him from ever finishing a promising invention. Together the stories provide a vivid description of lower-middle-class life in 1920s Chicago.

419. Ferber, Edna. *The Girls*. New York: Grosset and Dunlap, 1921. 374pp.
    Through the stories of three generations of women in the Thrift family, Ferber explores changing options available to women and relates Chicago social history. Isaac Thrift appeared in Chicago in 1834, eventually established a real estate business, and in a firm belief that the South Side would become Chicago's premier residential district, invested heavily there after 1871, building a handsome residence for himself near Prairie Avenue and Twenty-ninth. He ended his life envious of other men of his generation who made real estate fortunes. He was also disappointed in his offspring, having only two girls, Charlotte and Carrie. Charlotte has a secret, chaste romance with a working-class boy, Jesse Dick, who is killed in the Civil War, but when the romance is publicly revealed her reputation is ruined and she never marries. Carrie marries Samuel Payson who gives her two daughters and takes over Isaac's business, only to abscond with all of the company's assets. In recovering the assets and reputation of the business Carrie demonstrates business skill, but her daughters, Belle and Lottie, reject a life of business. Belle marries very young to a much older man and sets up a household in Hyde Park and Lottie falls in love with a brilliant novelist, but Carrie disapproves and Lottie goes unmarried. The representative of the youngest generation in the novel, Belle's daughter Charley falls in love with the namesake of

Charlotte's Jesse Dick. World War I brings dramatic change for the Thrift women as Dick is drafted and Lottie goes to France with the Red Cross. Although Ferber's main concern is with choices for women in a sexist society, she provides much social history of Chicago.

420. Ferber, Edna. *Half Portions*. Garden City, N.Y.: Doubleday, Page, 1920. 315pp.

Only two of these nine short stories are set in Chicago. One describes the household of a widower with a dutiful son; another tells the story of a farmer who accedes to his wife's demand that they retire to the city only to rebel.

421. Ferber, Edna. *One Basket; Thirty-One Short Stories*. Chicago: Peoples Book Club, 1947. 581pp.

Many of the short stories in this volume are set in Chicago and deal with people in a variety of circumstances, including those impoverished by the Depression and attempting to maintain their respectability, a middle-aged man living like a boulevardier in establishments around the Loop, affluent young people studying at the University of Chicago, elderly men and women living in apartment hotels on Lake Shore Drive, and arrivals to the city who are retiring from lives spent on the farm or young people from small towns seeking love and fortune.

422. Ferber, Edna. *Show Boat*. Garden City, N.Y.: Doubleday, Page, 1926. 303pp.

Although only a portion of this story, made familiar through stage and film productions, is set in Chicago, that section is well researched and highly evocative. Through the stories of Captain Andy, his wife Parthenia Ann Hawks, their daughter Magnolia Ravenal, and granddaughter Kim Ravenal, Ferber tells the story of the show boat era, the vaudeville circuit, and the later predominance of the New York stage. By the time Magnolia marries Gaylord Ravenal, few show boats are left and when, in 1890, Captain Andy is killed in a riverboat accident, Magnolia sells her share in the boat to move to Chicago with Gaylord and their infant daughter Kim. In the city, Gaylord spends all of his time as a professional gambler and the little family lives in hotels and boarding houses mostly on the North Side near Lincoln Park of varying degrees of comfort, depending upon Gaylord's luck. Much of Gaylord's life centers on South Clark Street and numerous gambling parlors, restaurants, and theaters are mentioned by name. Readers learn about styles of clothing, foodways, and types of entertainment. Once reformers begin attacking Chicago gambling parlors, bordellos, and saloons, Gaylord and his fellow gamblers have nowhere to play and the Ravenals cannot afford even cheap lodgings. Subsequently, Gaylord abandons Magnolia, who begins a long struggle to support herself and Kim through vaudeville performances, singing the songs she learned on the show boat. By the end of the novel Kim has become a success in the "legitimate" theater and is the wife of a well-known producer. Magnolia, who had achieved fame on the disrespectful vaudeville circuit, returns to life on a showboat plying the Mississippi. Ferber took pains to achieve accuracy in describing the small segment of Chicago portrayed in the novel and creates a rich account.

423. Ferber, Edna. *So Big*. Garden City, N.Y.: Doubleday, Page, 1924. 360pp.

Selina Peake abandons the colorful life of her Chicago gambler father for that of a school-teacher in the Dutch settlement of High Prairie, southwest of Chicago (now the Chicago community of Roseland). She later marries Pervus [*sic*] DeJong, a Dutch farmer, and when he dies, she shocks her neighbors by taking over the farm, including selling produce in the Chicago market. Pent up energy from years of watching her husband's faltering agricultural management, fuels the research and hard work through which she makes the farm profitable. She is able to give her son Dirk "So Big" DeJong advantages, like a university education and is gratified when he graduates from Cornell University in architecture and pleased when the two of them can discuss the buildings going up in Chicago in the first decades of the twentieth century. However, when Dirk comes back from fighting in World War I, he wants to make money and acquire social status more quickly than he would as an architect. He becomes a bond salesman and moves in very affluent social circles. Selina finds her son's choices disappointing, because she feels he is robbing himself of the gratification of a vocation that she found on the farm and is wrongheaded in valuing money and social status above all else, although she is wise enough to respect his freedom and keeps her own counsel. Ferber spends a good deal of time contrasting Dirk's Chicago of businessmen who are focused on New York City with Selina's Chicago of neighborhoods, enlivened by the energy of immigrants, and the novel summarizes the changes in the physical environment of the Chicago metropolitan area from the 1890s to the 1920s.

424. Field, Eugene. *The House: An Episode in the Lives of Reuben Baker, Astronomer, and of His Wife Alice.* New York: Charles Scribner's Sons, 1896. 268pp.

Capturing cultural aspects of the importance of home-owning and trends toward suburbanization, this novel recounts a couple's search for a house and subsequent efforts to refurbish the property. The twenty year goal of Chicago residents Reuben and Alice Baker has been home ownership, however, Baker is an independent astronomer, who has self-published on topics of little interest to anyone and he supports his wife and seven offspring on a modest inherited income. A New England transplant, like his wife, he is a gentleman of leisure, making purchases for his collections of incunabula and medieval armor and writing in his study. He and Alice have held fast to the idea that an inheritance from his Aunt Susan will fund a house purchase at some point. When Susan dies and makes no bequest, Alice negotiates for a long-admired farmhouse on the North Shore with a widowed owner eager to sell, with owner financing and payments approximating the Baker's current rent. The book describes this financing and Baker's efforts to get the down payment from a relative. The bulk of the volume is devoted to humorously describing the influence of neighbors and friends on renovations of the house and grounds, difficulties working with contractors, and other challenges of home ownership. The novel captures what was probably a common experience in Chicago in the 1890s and 1900s as the city expanded and residents moved into suburban houses. Other issues the novel conveys are: gender roles as they relate to business matters; the cultural importance of relatives, friends and neighbors; and the use of New England heritage and high culture to establish social status.

425. Field, Roswell Martin. *The Bondage of Ballinger.* Chicago: Revell, 1903. 214pp

Thomas Ballinger is born into a family distinguished in the history of England and the United States, who for several generations have been notable clergymen. However, Ballinger's love of books and independent study keep him from also joining this profession. He becomes a printer and bookshop proprietor and eventually moves to Chicago with his wife, Hannah, a Quaker who is patient and tolerant of Ballinger's obsession, despite the fact that it keeps them in poverty. Fortunately, in Chicago, Ballinger meets Helen Bascom, heiress to a fortune and teaches her from the time she is a child to love books. She in turn becomes his patron, saving him from destitution. Although Ballinger comments on book culture in the city and Helen's father is portrayed as a typical, if notably philanthropic, businessman, the Chicago setting has little real significance in the story.

Bascom gives Ballinger a job in a library he has built and endowed and the newly emerging practices of professional librarianship are critiqued.

426. Field, Roswell Martin. *Little Miss Dee*. Chicago: Revell, 1904. 241pp.

Although the city in this family tale is unnamed one can infer from Field's biography and other work that the place is Chicago. Agatha Dee grows up accepting the burden of being a Dee, since her father has no sons and she feels an obligation to perpetuate the family name. So, she adopts a boy she names Archibald. The story catalogs her sacrifices for the family name and her son. To give Archibald the opportunity he deserves, she gives up the family house to live in a boarding house, funding Archibald as he trains as a lawyer, gets elected to the right clubs, marries a socially prominent woman and eventually becomes a law firm partner. Agatha provides emotional support from her modest, boarding house room. As she is on the verge of independence, through a bequest from the man she would have married had she been willing to give up her family name, she discovers Archibald is deeply in debt through imprudent speculation. She signs over the bequest and continues to live a humble, retiring life in a rented room while Archibald and his wife rise to the highest levels of Chicago society. The novel touches on issues of social class and the limited opportunities for women in the late nineteenth century.

427. Finley, Martha. *Elsie at the World's Fair*. New York: Dodd, Mead, 1894. 259pp.

One of the later installments in the Elsie series, depicting life in the South after the Civil War, in this young adult book, set in 1893, Elsie is a grandmother with two sons that have just started practicing as physicians. Her extended family, including her father, as well as family friends travel to the World's Fair for the opening ceremonies, most on board the family yacht, traveling up the coast and through the canals and Great Lakes. The numerous young people in the party give their elders many opportunities to explain the sights. When they arrive at the fair, the description becomes even more detailed. As well as information, Elsie and her peers impart Bible lessons, moral instruction, and observations on American history. In addition to the staged drama of such exhibitions as Buffalo Bill's Wild West Show, members of the family witness the burning of a building and the death of sixteen firemen. Elsie's party unexpectedly meets friends, including some who live abroad, and romance is in the air. Two men ask to marry Lulu, one of Elsie's granddaughters, but her father declares the fifteen-year-old too young for betrothal. However, a friend, Annis Keith, visiting from Elsie's hometown, accepts the proposal of Ronald Lilburn and the visit to the World's Fair ends with an onboard wedding. Although few traveled by private yacht to the fair, people did arrive in extended family groups and the descriptions of the social impact of the fair, in which family members become closer, are valuable. Furthermore, of course, many aspects of the cultural values of the time are presented in the extended instructional monologues in the book.

428. Fisher, Vardis. *We Are Betrayed*. Garden City, N.Y.: Doubleday, Doran / Caldwell, Idaho: Caxton Printers, 1935. 369pp.

In this tale of a self-destructive academic, Chicago serves as an intellectual center. As a married undergraduate at Salt Lake City College in 1919, Vridar Hunter tries to accept the human condition aided by philosophy and literature. He married his hometown sweetheart, Neola, who is beautiful, in touch with herself, and untroubled by the larger meaning of existence. She alternately inspires Vridar's love and hatred. Despite his emotional and psychological distress, he is offered a teaching position at Salt Lake on the condition of obtaining a higher degree in Chicago (seemingly at the University of Chicago). Separated from Neola by his periods of study in Chicago, he finds a new source of personal torture when he discovers intellectual women. After the couple has a baby, Vridar thinks he can find meaning in fatherhood and moves Neola to Chicago where he works as a building superintendent in exchange for housing. Even after the birth of a second son, he draws only minor satisfaction from fatherhood and begins a relationship with Athene Marvell, an intellectual soul mate fitted to support his academic career. Preoccupied by alternating desire for Neola and Athene, he becomes increasingly disaffected with the consolations of philosophy and literature and begins to experience mental breakdowns. Unable to deal with the situation and unable to leave, Neola eventually commits suicide. Chicago plays an important role in the novel as a center for academic and intellectual life for Midwesterners. Devoted to capturing Vridar's emotional and intellectual life, often to the exclusion of concerns about physical setting, the book does include evocative descriptions of Vridar's walks through the city and accounts of Chicago residents. Vridar also frequents Washington Square Park, attracted to the atmosphere, as much as to the content of any of the speeches he hears there. The novel tells the reader a great deal about male attitudes toward women and sexuality.

429. Flavin, Martin. *Journey in the Dark*. New York: Harper and Brothers, 1943. 432pp.

Obsession with social class, as represented by members of his hometown's most prominent family, shapes a man's entire life in this novel. Growing up in Wyattville, Iowa, in the 1890s, Sam Braden falls in love with Eileen Wyatt, for whose family the town was named. Eileen rejects Braden for his lack of prospects and he decides to become wealthy and model his personality on self-assured, worry-free Neill Wyatt, Eileen's brother and heir to the Wyatt fortune. Braden relocates to Chicago as a place of opportunity and finds the city wondrous. Entering a paper company in a lowly capacity, he learns the business and becomes an investor in a wallpaper manufacturing firm. Eventually, he owns the firm and later sells the business at a huge profit. Through work, frugality, and shrewdness he builds a fortune by the time he is fifty. He and Eileen eventually marry and even after she divorces him, he continues to be obsessed by her and Neill. Despite his love for Chicago, he focuses his energy on creating an estate for himself just outside his hometown of Wyattville, and, after witnessing the bankruptcy of the Wyatts, buys their family home. Although Chicago is not vividly presented, the city is important as a place of opportunity for young men like Sam from all over the Midwest.

430. Flinn, John J. *The Mysterious Disappearance of Helen St. Vincent; A Story of the Vanished City*. Chicago: George K. Hazlitt, 1895. 304pp.

This melodramatic romance about a mysterious, intellectual, beauty and her troubled past is set against the backdrop of World's Fair social events. A first-person account by Edmund Powers, a novelist and newspaperman, the story begins in 1892 when the multi-talented Helen St. Vincent (artist, poet, journalist, and novelist) arrives in Chicago with her aunt as chaperone. St. Vincent moves easily in the society of the finest families, who declare her the belle of the ball that opens the Columbian Exposition. She also dominates the attention of the livelier, bohemian society of writers and artists of the circle in which Powers moves. Powers falls in love with St. Vincent and the two have many romantic days and evenings on the fairgrounds. Even though St. Vincent encourages his friendship, she says she is not free to marry because of some mystery in her past. Then, she disappears. Believing her to be in danger, Powers pursues all the leads he has about her, including going to visit her uncle in Boston. The highly melodramatic work includes bizarre coincidences, a bogus marriage, mistaken identities, and false innuendo, before the emotionally abused and physically ill Powers finally hears the truth and is reunited with Helen St. Vincent. The novel's descriptions of Chicago all date to around the time of the fair. However, when the couple returns to the fairgrounds several years later to revisit happy memories, they find abandoned gardens and ruined buildings.

431. Flower, Elliott. *The Best Policy*. Illustrated by George Brehm. Indianapolis: Bobbs-Merrill, 1905. 268pp.
    The twelve short stories in this volume are supposedly set in Chicago at the turn of the twentieth century, although no indication is given of physical setting. The key figure in most of the stories is insurance executive Dave Murray. As a group, the stories show why life insurance is a good thing and provide illustrations of the good character of insurance salesmen. Although published by a commercial publisher, the volume was probably intended as a promotional tool for the insurance industry.

432. Flower, Elliott. *Policeman Flynn*. Illustrated by Frederic Dorr Steele. New York: Century, 1902. 294pp.
    Although this first-person, anecdotal work, is written from the perspective of an Irish immigrant who speaks in dialect, the volume is not concerned with immigrant issues, but with presenting the work and home-life of a Chicago policeman around the turn of the twentieth century. Patrolman Barney Flynn is a married, middle-aged man with highly-developed common-sense that he employs to effectively deal with most situations. Much of his work life is spent walking a beat, and the situations he encounters give a good sense of street life in the city. Flynn must deal with a run-away horse, a haughty carriage driver, and the driver of a new-fangled automobile. He also addresses the public nuisances of "dudes" hanging about outside theaters waiting to flirt with showgirls and young rowdies engaged in petty crime and disorderliness. When he takes on a new beat, youth gangs test him and he must find a way of gaining their respect (he utilizes a fire hose). Flynn believes in using physical intervention. Although he does not use his gun, he does employ a billy club, supports police-sponsored boxing matches, and encourages his daughter, a young school teacher, to use corporal punishment in the classroom. His law enforcement is balanced with common-sense when it comes to the impoverished and, fortunately, in his home-life he maintains the upper hand by using practical psychology and not violence (especially when it comes to cajoling his wife out of what he typically considers to be foolish notion).

433. Flower, Elliott. *Slaves of Success*. Illustrated by Jay Hambidge. Boston: Page; Colonial Press, 1905. 304pp.
    In this political novel Chicago is the center of party politics and the site of meetings, although the city itself has little presence as a physical location. When Azro Craig is elected to the legislature in a country district where people are weary of machine politics, he is immediately targeted by Chicago politicians, especially Jack Wade, all of whom want his votes and attempt to bring him into the party machine. At first Craig is duped, but in the end he gets the upper hand.

434. Flower, Elliott. *The Spoilsmen*. Boston: Page, 1903. 324pp.
    This account of Chicago politics around 1900 is focused on the political machine and the way it attempts to destroy essentially good men with very different backgrounds. Using imaginary wards, as the foreword indicates, the intent is to characterize an entire political culture. The story begins when a political boss selects two men to be nominated to win election as aldermen. One, Joe Mason, is a hardware store owner who has been active in ward politics by using the political

club to help people in his neighborhood. The other man Harold Darnell, is a lawyer with political ambitions and the son of an affluent man. Most of the novel is concerned with the pressures placed on these two men once they take office and votes on franchises and right of ways for street car companies and natural gas lines come before the city council. Darnell's social and financial resources aid him in maintaining his independence, although he soon realizes that he will never be able to get elected to another office. Mason is more susceptible and only Darnell's friendship and influence with important businessmen help him keep his home and family intact.

435. Foran, Martin Ambrose. *The Other Side, A Social Study Based on Fact.* Cleveland, Ohio: Ingham, Clarke, Booksellers / Washington, D.C.: Gray and Clarkson, Printers and 1886. 461pp.

This work of social commentary uses a thinly developed plot on which to hang extensive observations and theories about social conditions and proposals for reform. Irene and Richard Arbyght live on the farm Irene inherited from her family in northeastern Pennsylvania. When she and her husband are in their thirties she decides that she is holding back Richard, making him be a farmer when he is actually a businessman. Once he finds a business opportunity in Chicago, she sells the farm and they make preparations to relocate. On his way to complete his transaction, Richard is murdered and robbed of the farm sale proceeds. Years later his son Richard actually makes it to Chicago to work as a cooper in a Chicago meat packing plant. In Pennsylvania, as an agrarian laborer he had been treated with respect and made an adequate wage. In Chicago, he is forced to work long hours under unhealthy conditions, is only paid irregularly, and is forced to buy goods from the dishonest company store. At great personal risk he organizes his fellow laborers and successfully strikes for wage increases. Subsequently, he begins his own company based on his theories of profit sharing. By the end of the novel the company he founded is struggling, but healthy. A subplot involves finding his father's murder and recovering the stolen money. The novel details daily life in the 1880s for Chicago laborers and the inequities they faced.

436. Forbes, Murray. *Hollow Triumph.* Chicago: Ziff-Davis, 1946. 339pp.

This bizarre novel about a psychopath who takes over the life of another man provides details about upper-class life in Chicago. Henry Mueller's only concern is acquiring wealth so that he can exercise his will over others. The son of German immigrants, he grew up Pittsburgh, attended college, and completed two years of medical school before realizing that a medical practice would never bring him enough money. He quickly makes a good deal of money as a con man before he is arrested. He uses his four years in prison to study psychoanalysis and perfect influencing others. Starting life over in Chicago he accidentally discovers that he resembles Nobel-winning psychiatrist, Dr. Viktor Bartok. He kills Bartok and takes over his life, occasionally having to kill again to protect his secret. His conscience is finally awakened and in World War II he successfully carries on Bartok's research on treating shell-shocked veterans, earning a citation and medal. By this time, however, his conscience is out of control and he descends into madness and dies, an accidental suicide. The novel illustrates cultural attitudes toward psychoanalysis and the mentally ill. As Mueller takes over Dr. Bartok's life, the novel goes into great detail about the comforts he suddenly enjoys as a member of Chicago's upper class.

437. Forbes, DeLoris (Florine) Stanton [Stanton Forbes, pseud.]. *The Sad, Sudden Death of My Fair Lady.* Garden City, N.Y.: Crime Club / Doubleday, 1971. 161pp.

This novel set during the 1933 Chicago World's Fair provides descriptions of the fair, but focuses on the impact of the event on the lives of a working-class family. The first-person narrator,

Buddy Carmody, is a seventeen-year-old recent high school graduate. The son of Irish Catholics, his father, Donal, immigrated as an adult and married his mother, Beulah, whose family had been established in Chicago for a generation. During Buddy's first summer of adulthood, he learns many truths about his parents, the most important of which is that his father has long been a philanderer and has not been out of town looking for work for the last six months as he claimed, but in hiding from the Mafia-connected brother of a woman he has gotten pregnant. To support the household, Beulah takes in boarders and quickly has a houseful of entertainers working at the Hindustani Palace at the fair. The most exotic tenants are Lurlane Salome and her daughter Tamara. Lurlane performs a dance involving veils and a cobra and Tamara a suggestive "toe dance." After Donal emerges of hiding, he is soon spending a great deal of time with Lurlane. When Lurlane is murdered Donal is convicted of the crime, one that he did not commit. The novel presents many details about food and clothing, as well as the then current fascination with gangsters like John Dillinger in the midst of the Depression.

438. Forrest, Leon. *The Bloodworth Orphans*. New York: Random House, 1977. 383pp.

Place is of little consequence in this novel that presents the impact of racism on an African-American family over the course of American history. A number of characters are part of the great migration to Chicago from the South and some of the novel's action transpires in the city. The central character, Nathaniel Witherspoon, has a cosmic viewpoint that he expresses through a folkloric narrative that draws upon the Bible.

439. Forrest, Leon. *There Is a Tree More Ancient Than Eden*. New York: Random House, 1973. 163pp.

Some scenes in this work are set on Chicago's South Side, but the work is not structured to convey a sense of place since the author is more concerned with using the inner, dream-like reflections of his character Nathaniel Witherspoon to convey the tragedy of racial hatred over the course of American history.

440. Fowler, Bertram B. [Jack Baynes, pseud.]. *Meet Morocco Jones; In the Case of the Syndicate Hoods*. Greenwich, Conn.: Crest Original / Fawcett Publications, 1957. 144pp.

In this pulp fiction gangster novel, Morocco Jones is employed by a Chicago detective agency, having previously been a European counter-espionage agent for the United States government. His Communist enemies issue a contract on his life to be executed by Chicago Mafioso's and he must use all of his skills as a spy and fighter to save himself.

441. Fox, Fannie Ferber. *Chocolate or Vanilla*. New York: Alfred A. Knopf, 1935. 274pp.

Many of the eleven short stories in this volume are set in 1930s Chicago. Often, characters in the stories have moved to the city from Appleton, Wisconsin and most plots involve newly married couples settling in the city. The households tend to be middle-class and many characters are absorbed in acquiring clothing and household furnishings. For female characters children are an unwelcome intrusion into their households. Social events include a fiftieth-wedding anniversary, ladies' luncheon parties, and a mixed-sex golf outing. In general, the Chicago settings are on the South Side and the social life there makes the area seem more like a small town than a part of the big city.

442. Fox, May Virginia. *Ambush at Fort Dearborn*. New York: St. Martin's, 1962. 173pp.

In this iteration for children of the history of early settlement around Chicago and of the massacre at Fort Dearborn, the focus is on a family who escape the area before the massacre because of their friendship with Tamrack, a young Potawatomi tribesman who they nursed through an illness. The main character, Tom Malen, arrives on the frontier with his parents and sister so his father can take up a land claim, only to find turmoil. The family gives up their original destination and settles within a short ride of Fort Dearborn where they benefit from living in a community with other settlers, until the massacre disrupts their lives.

443. Fraser, John Arthur [Hawkshaw, pseud.]. *A Wayward Girl's Fate*. Chicago: Eagle, 1890. 243pp.

This convoluted, melodramatic, sensational novel focuses on an innocent, young heiress who is rescued from numerous villains by an attractive, rich, young man. Mattie Fleming will come into a fortune when she is of legal age. She arrives in Chicago with her mother Tessie Fleming and Jabez Blitherton, who stole Tessie away from her husband and embezzled money from his employer at the Presbyterian Church in Yonkers, New York, where he was a volunteer. In Chicago, he quickly makes a fortune on the floor of the Board of Trade, but also schemes to get control of Mattie's inheritance. A boarding student at an exclusive, private school, Mattie is safe until she is about to come of age. Then, Blitherton hires private detective Dick Stains to kidnap her. Tessie Fleming's brother Bradwell also wants the money and Stains agrees to double-cross Blitherton and secure Mattie for Bradwell. Mattie unwittingly foils the plot by responding to a newspaper advertisement for actresses. In doing so, she falls into the clutches of Maud Passidy, a devious madam entrapping innocent girls for her brothel. Fortunately, Mattie and Passidy are followed by Detective William Kernell, who has been trying to get evidence against Passidy to prosecute her. Soon Blitherton, Tessie, Kernell, and young Ray Rivers, an attractive and affluent actor who had fallen in love with Mattie after only one meeting, are all searching for her separately. Fortunately, Rivers has the perspicacity and means to engage Pinkerton detectives and rescues Mattie from a brothel in the horrible "Wisconsin Dens," in the midst of the lumber camps. Mattie and Ray marry and become box office lovers. Although there is little physical description of Chicago in the novel it is of interest that this particular city was chosen as the setting for this lurid tale of deceit, crime, the white slave trade, and mayhem.

444. Freeman, Martin J. *The Case of the Blind Mouse*. A Dutton Clue Mystery. New York: Dutton, 1935. 256pp.

A private detective and female journalist work together to solve the mystery of a kidnapping and murder in this Depression-era novel. Judy Marlow Evans, the radio singer known as "America's Hometown Sweetheart," had been ill with throat cancer and was expected to die, but not on the same night her husband Eugene Evans is kidnapped. Their manager Jim Dressen witnesses these events. Fearful Eugene's life will be endangered by early newspaper coverage, Dressen decides to give Peggy Weaver, a reporter for *The Bee*, an exclusive. Fortunately, her boyfriend, Jerry Todd, is a private investigator. As the story unfolds the reader gets a behind the scenes look at the radio industry, as well as the world of 1930s journalism and Chicago gangsters. Most of the action takes place in apartments and hotels, as well as on the streets of a misty, foggy, autumnal Chicago in subjection to the Depression, symbolically represented by the Century of Progress Exposition buildings that are disappearing under the wrecking ball. One of the most frequently mentioned neighborhoods is that around Fifty-third and Woodlawn, where the Evans house is located.

445. French, Alice [Octave Thanet, pseud.]. *The Man of the Hour*. Illustrated by Lucius Wolcott Hitchcock. New York: Grosset and Dunlap, 1905. 477pp.

Much of this novel is set in Fairport, Iowa to which a number of families with long histories in the East have relocated and established themselves as the most socially prominent community members. The wealthiest man in town, Josiah Winslow, owns a factory that produces plows and carriages. After the death of his first wife, he married a Russian woman, Olga Galitsuin, who gave him a son, John-Ivan Winslow. Olga has a strong loyalty to her heritage and the novel explores the impact of John-Ivan's duel heritage on his temperament. Olga dies in Switzerland and not long afterwards Winslow marries a New Englander who has a daughter John-Ivan's age named Peggy and the two have a childhood crush. After graduating from Harvard, John-Ivan settles in Chicago where he supports labor unions and the settlement house movement. Eventually, however, he is drawn back to Fairport out of loyalty to his father's memory and out of love for Peggy. Chicago in the book is a place where upper-class people go shopping and working-class people live in poverty.

446. Friedman, I. K. (Isaac Kahn). *The Autobiography of a Beggar: Prefaced by Some of the Humorous Adventures & Incidents related in The Beggar's Club*. Boston: Small, Maynard, 1903. 350pp.

Chicago hobos meet to discuss their lives and share anecdotes. The tales, related in dialect, usually have little physical description of Chicago, although street names or businesses are sometimes mentioned. Not all of the tales are set in the city, since during the summer the beggars leave to sojourn in the countryside. One section is an "autobiography" solicited by an anthropologist. Most stories relate chicanery, such as stealing a Persian cat, that more often than not does not have the payoff that the hobo protagonists expect.

447. Friedman, I. K. (Isaac Kahn). *By Bread Alone*. New York: McClure, Phillips and Co, 1901. 481pp.

After a successful Protestant minister has a mystical experience, he resigns his fashionable church ministry and begins working in a steel mill to better understand the plight of the working poor. Attractive, self-assured, well-spoken Blair Carrhart [*sic*] had a brilliant career ahead of him as a society minister and was engaged to marry Evangeline Marvin, daughter of a steel magnate. He gives up his comfortable life and breaks off his engagement when he moves into a worker neighborhood and obtains employment in the Marvin steel factory. Unaccustomed to worker living conditions or manual labor, he experiences physical challenges and the novel goes into detail about the living and working conditions. Carrhart is surprised by the ethnic rivalries that divide the Poles, Croats, Germans, and other groups working in the mills. He is also startled to find that physical impulses, particularly anger, now sometime take control of him in his new environment. However, he continues to focus on his mission, preaching the gospel of an "altruistic Cooperative Commonwealth." Although he initially finds an audience for his vision, he has a good deal of competition from union organizers and communists and from the social weight of the Roman Catholic Church and the capitalist hegemony. When a strike begins it turns bloody as Marvin persuades the governor to let state troops turn a Gatling gun on the strikers. Carrhart is wounded and Evangeline seeks him out and urges him to give up his efforts at the mill. After an assassination attempt on Marvin's life carried out by one of Carrhart's close worker friends, Carrhart realizes that his efforts have achieved nothing and blames himself for making the lives of the workers even worse. In the novel's final scene he and Evangeline ride away from the mill Carrhart announces his new conviction that he should enter politics in order to reform society through legislation.

448. Friedman, I. K. (Isaac Kahn). *The Lucky Number*. Chicago: Way and Williams, 1896. 217pp.

The ten short stories in this volume are all set in Chicago and the characters and or incidents in each have some connection to a seedy bar named "The Lucky Number," located in one of Chicago's 1890s slums. The stories are of the sort that people would tell each other in such a setting. Among the plot devices are a switch of infants that gives a child of poverty the chance to grow up in a wealthy household and the legitimate heir to flourish on the streets, a man with a genius for music cannot escape poverty and then is falsely accused of a crime, and a gambler lives a whole life of hope in the time it takes a roulette wheel to come to rest on his losing number. Although the book has little physical description of the city, the work captures attitudes prevalent at the time towards some cultures and ethnicities (Jews and French and Italian immigrants).

449. Friedman, I. K. (Isaac Kahn). *Poor People*. Boston: Houghton Mifflin, 1900. 244pp.

Friedman presents a detailed account of tenement life for immigrant families, most of whom are German and Irish. Although the men are forced to support themselves through manual labor and the women through sewing and working in department stores, many of the immigrants are cultured and are painters or musicians, others have skilled trades, such as watch making. When Jane Wilson, the daughter of one family marries into the upper-middle-class Rounds family, she moves her parents, Thomas and Mathilda, into a flat in her new suburban house. Soon made uncomfortable by their rude, social-climbing in-laws they move back to the tenement where they had a more authentic social life. Friedman is concerned with the domestic life of the immigrants he describes and provides little description of Chicago. The life of the poor immigrant is clearly valorized, and the novel provides many social details.

450. Friedman, I. K. (Isaac Kahn). *The Radical*. New York: Appleton, 1907. 362pp.

Most of this political novel is set in Springfield, Illinois and Washington, D.C., although the politicians are Chicagoans and their party is centered there. In a political rivalry between Addison Hammersmith, a mother's boy and scion of wealth, and Bruce McCallister, the son of a butcher with a superior intellect and strong will, McCallister gets political boss Buck O'Brien's patronage and is elected to the U.S. Senate. However, his relationship with Hammersmith is complicated by his love for Hammersmith's sister. The novel deals with social class and the system of political patronage active in Chicago in the early twentieth century.

451. Friend, Oscar J. [Owen Fox Jerome, pseud.]. *The Murder at Avalon Arms*. New York: Edward J. Clode, 1931. 309pp.

Set in an upper-class Chicago milieu in which the Depression has no impact, this murder mystery features a competent police detective. Harry Lethrop, a young lawyer and son of a prominent and wealthy judge, is horse-back riding in Lincoln Park when he rescues a beautiful young woman, Christine Vincennes, who is being physically accosted by a man who seems to be her chauffeur. After running off the chauffeur, Lethrop agrees to drive Vincennes to an apartment building where she has been summoned by a note to meet with her father. While investigating her long absence, Lethrop finds himself alone in a room with a murdered man only a few minutes before the police arrive and take him into custody for the crime. Fortunately for Lethrop, Chicago police detective Philip MacCray is assigned to the case. MacCray uses his brilliant logic and deductive reasoning to find the real culprit. He also links the murder to one that had occurred ten months before in the city. Even though one main character owns a Chicago gambling parlor, this mystery, unlike many of the period, does not have gangsters. Set firmly in upper-class milieus, the physical settings tend to be Lake Shore Drive mansions and expensive apartment buildings with domestic establishments that include servants and butlers, many of them British.

452. Friend, Oscar J. [Owen Fox Jerome, pseud.]. *The Red Kite Clue.* New York: Edward J. Clode, 1928. 303pp.

When a disillusioned society figure turned art thief is forced to solve a murder his life is transformed in this 1920s era novel. Wealthy, young society figure Artemus Gordon served in the trench-warfare of World War I and returned to Chicago thoroughly disillusioned with Western civilization. A trained physician who had intended to serve humanity, instead he decides to simply live off an inherited income in a mansion designed by his deceased architect father. Outwardly Graham is a rich carefree bachelor noted for his elegant dinner parties and important friends that include society figures, wealthy businessmen, artists, and scholars. In secret, however, Graham is the "Vandal" an art thief who has baffled and intrigued the police by his clever execution of his crimes and outraged society by stealing from famous collectors and art museums. When renowned archeologist Charles Vandeventer is found murdered, Graham fears the Vandal will be blamed and tries to solve the crime. Soon dapper Chicago detective Philip MacCray, perennially critical of Chicago's filthiness, is on the case and a ruthless Chinese gang, the "Red Kite," is on the scene trying to recover a religious artifact stolen from Vandeventer on the night of his death. Graham's adventure, involving rescuing a young lady for whom he realizes romantic feelings, reawakens his humanity and by the end of the novel he is committed to practicing medicine, marrying, and returning the art works he stole. The novel describes high society parties and touches on attitudes toward Asians and women. The Chicago of the book is filled with people who appreciate art, witty conversation, and antiquities. They hate Chicago's crudeness, but resign themselves to living in the city. Lincoln Park is a prominently featured setting.

453. Friermood, Elisabeth Hamilton. *Peppers' Paradise.* Garden City, N.Y.: Doubleday, 1969. 259pp.

In this novel for young adults set in 1927 and 1928, the author carefully provides details about clothing, food, social manners, pastimes, and current events. Although only one chapter of the novel is physically set in Chicago, the city dominates the imaginary town of Endicott, the setting for the rest of the work. Town residents get their news from the *Chicago Tribune* and make frequent trips to the city. The town is close enough to the city that bootlegging gangsters sometimes commit crimes in Endicott. Seventeen-year-old Kitty Pepper is a high school junior and planning her future. Her family owns all four of the movie theaters in Endicott. Kitty has helped manage one of them, Pepper's Paradise, a movie palace with live entertainment as well as films, for several years and wants to continue after graduation. However, the family business is threatened by the incipient growth of radio. Then, Kitty and her grandparents see the future of the movie industry when they visit Chicago to see *The Jazz Singer.* The trip also inspires her decision to attend the University of Chicago. In addition to presenting a history of the growth of the movie industry and raising both sides of the debate over Prohibition (one of Kitty's uncles is an alcoholic and the bootleggers are responsible for robbing one of the Peppers' theaters and killing the manager), the book demonstrates the degree to which Chicago shaped the lives of Midwesterners.

454. Fuessle, Newton A. (Newton Augustus). *The Flail*. New York: Moffat, Yard, 1919. 328pp.

This story of a German immigrant's rise in American society, seemingly a positive portrayal during an age when immigrants were encouraged to assimilate rapidly, actually captures World War I xenophobia. Rudolph Dohmer realizes how foreign he is when, as a twelve-year-old, he visits a non German, upper-class household. He immediately commits himself to becoming fully American. The novel implicitly claims, however, that his racial inheritance (traits of arrogance, greed, and ruthlessness) cannot be left entirely behind. Dohmer makes a new commitment to school and wins a medal for his Americanism essay. He graduates from high school and begins working in a bank in the Loop to earn his college tuition. After graduating, he works for a Chicago newspaper and in 1913 moves to New York City for a business position with a salary beyond his dreams and marries a girl, who, in his childhood, he had considered far above him. However, right to the end of the book he remains a character the reader is meant to despise. The Chicago section of the novel dealing with Rudolph's boyhood neighborhood around Belmont Avenue provides a great deal of information about the German immigrant community and ethnic tensions in a variety of social settings.

455. Fuessle, Newton A. (Newton Augustus). *Gold Shod*. New York: Boni and Liveright, 1921. 243pp.

Engagement in business and the accumulation of wealth is considered antithetical to artistic concerns in this novel about a man who denies his artistic impulses. The story begins in Elyria, Ohio, where Glinden's grandfather and father abandoned their interest in music and art for the love of women interested in material success. After both men die, the four-year-old Fielding is in the hands of their widows. The women move to Chicago and establish themselves in a house in Wicker Park with the idea that the industry of the burgeoning city will inspire Glinden to become a manager or financier. Instead, Glinden is a dreamy, artistic boy who wants to go the Art Institute. Prevented doing so by his grandmother, he becomes a copywriter, moving from job to job in the offices of industry publications until he is working for a shoe industry newspaper. His life is transformed after he meets a girl from Detroit at a Calumet Club dance and around the same time he is encouraged by a school friend to apply for a job at an automobile works in Detroit. Fielding decides to leave Chicago to get the job and pursue the girl. Although none of the remaining novel is set in Chicago, while Glinden lives in Detroit and New York, becoming wealthier and more powerful with each year, he dreams of his days in Chicago and the evenings he spent walking the streets of Wicker Park listening to the piano music coming from the houses and dreaming of a life as an artist, writer, or musician; establishing the city as a center for artistic endeavor. The section of the novel physically set in Chicago includes general description of the city and some specific locales and places, including a bohemian district on the South Side, the red-light light district of Custom House Place, Kohl and Middleton's dime museum, Orchestra Hall, and the Art Institute.

456. Fuller, Henry Blake. *Bertram Cope's Year*. Chicago: Aldenbrink Press, 1919. 314pp.

Although named Churchton, the setting for this novel about academic life is Northwestern University. Slender, attractive Bertram Cope arrives on campus as a young instructor to find that men and women alternately want to monopolize his time. Medora Phillips, who presides over one social circle, soon has Cope targeted for Amy Leffingwell, and when that prospect ends with Leffingwell's marriage, Phillips forwards her niece, Carolyn Thorpe, as a fiancée. Basil Randolph takes an interest in Bertram, as well. He encourages Bertram's friendship with Arthur LeMoyne, a friend from Bertram's past who arrives to share an apartment with him. At the end of the school year, Bertram escapes the hothouse atmosphere, leaving with his parents for summer vacation and then a teaching post in the East. Reflecting on his departure, Phillips is convinced that Carolyn and Bertram will marry within the year and Randolph is equally convinced that Bertram will be keeping house with LeMoyne. The novel is notable for openly describing exclusive male friendships and their acceptance in a Chicago social milieu.

457. Fuller, Henry Blake. *The Cliff-Dwellers*. Illustrated by Thure de Thulstrup. New York: Harper and Brothers, 1893. 324pp.

This well-known, realist novel presents the author's understanding of the cultural relevance of Chicago in the early 1890s. In a post-Civil War society, in which the acquisition of wealth has become the dominant value, Chicago's sky-scrapers serve as powerful symbols. Fuller sets his novel in a such a building—the Clifton—where four thousand people work in a complex hierarchy of rank based upon occupation. Chicago and the Clifton are viewed through the eyes of George Ogden, a Bostonian who has relocated to the city. Ogden's values draw upon antebellum culture and are deep-seated. He does not embrace the materialism he finds in Chicago. In fact, when he marries he chooses Jessie Bradley because she has a more fully developed character than wealthy Abbie Brainard. However, Ogden is caught up in the web of materialism anyway, for Jessie can dream of nothing but living in the charmed circle of Arthur J. Ingles and his wife Cecilia, some of the wealthiest Chicagoans. The social web that binds the characters in the novel forces them into roles in the same way that the physical structure of the Clifton, with its nested rooms, does. In the end, even Ogden is drawn into behaving counter to his hyper-civilized nature. The novel presents a detailed account of social life in Chicago around the time of the Columbian Exposition.

458. Fuller, Henry Blake. *Not on the Screen*. New York: Alfred A. Knopf, 1930. 276pp.

In this novel about a young man moving to the city to satisfy his ambition, a woman undertakes giving him the necessary social polish to make him a suitable beau. Although the narrative is not concerned about establishing place, the prologue identifies the Chicago setting. Embert Howell arrives from a small Midwestern town, driven by ambition. He is soon working as a successful bond salesman. His financial success does not qualify him to court Evelyn Trent, however. She and her mother are established society fixtures, although their finances are on a gentle decline. They still live in a grand house, but in a neighborhood increasingly filled with businesses and boarding houses. Evelyn's mother, Catherine, counting on a good marriage for her daughter, does not see Embert as a viable suitor. However, Evelyn believes that Embert, after he has passed through her personal finishing school may prove himself to be quite satisfactory. Without letting him know what she is doing, Evelyn engineers his attendance at typical social events of the day to polish his social skills. Step-by-step he makes the changes that advance him in society (moving from his hotel room to an apartment hotel, purchasing an automobile, and joining a gentleman's club). Although the novel contains little physical description, the accounts of social events (prize fights, church charity bazaars, opera performance, teas, club events, football matches, and country outings), as well as Catherine's assessments of Embert and his increasing respectability, provide a good overview of upper-middle-class society and the qualities that contributed to status in a socially fluid urban environment.

459. Fuller, Henry Blake. *On the Stairs*. Boston: Houghton Mifflin, Riverside Press, 1918. 265pp.

In this celebration of Chicago's emergence as a world-class city, Fuller contrasts the lives of two men over forty years, from 1873 to 1916, to illustrate the city's rise. Raymond Prince and

Johnny McComas are presented as very different types of men. Raymond has a grandfather who founded Mid-Continent Bank and a father who started a building supplies company. Although Raymond starts working in the bank to meet family expectations he disdains American business culture, and pursues his interests in the art, literature, and music of European culture more avidly than his vocation. A competent pianist in demand for social events, Raymond meets Johnny McComas at one such event. Johnny, a product of suburban Chicago, is enthusiastic about Chicago's emerging cultural life and when he gets a job at Mid-Continent, enjoys the business world. To vent his distaste for his job, Raymond takes a year-long, European tour. Johnny spends all his time advancing his career and marries well, later obtaining capital from his father-in-law to open his own bank. Raymond disdains Johnny as a throwback to an earlier form of civilization inferior to the refinement of European culture. When Raymond comes into his inheritance he lives abroad and marries a French woman, but the rest of the novel catalogs his losses (his bank, his family home, his wife—who marries the widowed McComas, and his son who marries McComas' daughter). The story of McComas rise is paralleled by Chicago's rise as an epitome of American business and culture. Much of the latter half of the novel describes the social organizations and events that establish Chicago as a city as significant as London or Paris.

460. Fuller, Henry Blake. *Under the Skylights*. New York: Appleton, 1901. 382pp.
    Physical setting is not important in this work, composed of three novellas with some overlapping characters, however the book is generally considered to be a roman à clef based on Fuller's experiences in Chicago artistic circles. The first section, "The Downfall of Abner Joyce," traces what happens when Joyce publishes his first book and is taken up by Chicago bohemia. In "Little O'Grady vs. The Grindstone," art patron Eudoxia Pence gets her wealthy husband to influence The Grindstone Bank Board to put her on the board of directors so that she can oversee the redecoration of the bank and employ an artist protégé. In the third section, "Dr. Gowdy and the Squash," arbiters of artistic taste are confronted by paintings of squash produced by a self-taught country artist named Jared Stiles, who gets taken up by hotels and department stores.

461. Fuller, Henry Blake. *With the Procession*. New York: Harper and Brothers, 1895. 336pp.
    Through the story of David Marshall's family, Fuller explores the status anxiety and social displacement experienced by affluent Chicago families living in the city before the Civil War. The dramatic growth in business and population after the war and the 1871 fire brought large numbers of ambitious men and women with social aspirations to the city. David Marshall's wholesale grocery business was well-established by the 1860s, but the fire brought a financial crisis. The firm would have closed had easterner Gilbert Belden not invested a significant amount of cash. In return the family business had to be renamed Marshall and Belden, and Gilbert remained a distasteful presence for the Marshall family. In 1893, with the return of Truesdale, the family's oldest son, from an extended cultural tour of Europe and the social awakening of Jane, Marshall's oldest, unmarried daughter, the family suddenly realizes the extent to which they have been marginalized socially. Fortunately, David has been a friend of social arbiter Mrs. Susan Bates for many years. Living in a Lake Shore Drive mansion staffed by liveried servants, Bates' guest lists determine who is in society. Although she aids the Marshalls, she excludes the Beldens, fanning the enmity between the families and destroying the firm. The Marshalls regain their social status, but lose important parts of their identity, symbolized by the loss of their family home, which is torn down to make way for a skyscraper. They move into a characterless mansion and bask in the social glow brought by their youngest daughter's marriage into a prominent English family. Finally, David's

personal fortune increases dramatically through the efforts of his youngest son. Despite regaining their fortune and reestablishing their social status the Marshalls are left unhappy and longing for pre-fire Chicago. The novel encapsulates Chicago social history and describes a wide range of social events and domestic interiors.

462. Gaines Diana. *The Knife and the Needle*. Garden City, N.Y.: Doubleday, 1962. 336pp.

This romance novel covers a wide range of social issues faced by women in the nineteen-teens and twenties. Through flashbacks from the present of 1929, readers learn of the romance between Italian-Jewish Sal Scott and Kay Quimby. Before Scott left for medical service in World War I, the couple were certain they would marry and their romance became physical. After Scott left for Europe, Kay realized she was pregnant and handled a frightening abortion on her own. In the aftermath, Kay married medical researcher and surgeon Orrin Quimby. Although the couple had several children, Quimby is the head of a private clinic and has no time for his family or wife. With her children in school, Kay occupies herself with tedious meetings of women's clubs, and charitable boards. Emotionally vulnerable, when Scott returns to Chicago, an affair commences. Most of the scenes are domestic and socializing tends to be conducted at large, alcohol-sodden parties. Social attitudes toward family life, professions, the social status of women, extramarital affairs, and abortion are touched upon. By the end of the novel, Orrin has agreed to Kay's plan to start her own business designing specialty packaging for department stores as a solution to her feelings of being unfulfilled within her marriage.

463. Gaines, Diana. *Marry in Anger*. Garden City, N.Y.: Doubleday, 1958. 309pp.

In this Depression-era romance novel, a girl whose family lost everything marries a wealthy man and finds love in the process. Gillian March, the daughter of a chemical engineer had an affluent life, even after her father's premature death while she was in high school. However, after the 1929 stock market crash she had to change schools from Vassar to the University of Chicago, and work as an advertising copy writer to finance her education. A girlish crush of her former life, Tom Ballew, heir to a department store fortune, suffered no such reverses. He graduated from Harvard and then spent a colorful year in Europe before returning to Chicago for medical school at Northwestern University, He and Gillian renew their acquaintance and she is soon invited to the Ballew's North Shore estate. There, Gillian is deflowered in a passionate moment quickly followed by remorse. Tom proposes, even though he is in love with his older brother's wife. After a tumultuous engagement, Tom and Gillian agree to stay married for at least a year. Most of the action of the book covers the year 1933-34 and shows how the two gradually fall in love. Physical settings include Chicago suburbs and Michigan, with frequent references to places in the city. The Ballews own a penthouse apartment near the Merchandise Mart, a large apartment on Goethe Street, and another more modest apartment on the Near North Side where Tom and Gillian live. The importance of a career, even for affluent men and women, is a theme. Homosexuality is touched upon and one of the main characters is revealed to be a lesbian at the end of the novel.

464. Gaines, Diana. *Tasker Martin*. New York: Random House, 1950. 342pp.

The present of this novel is 1947, however most of the book consists of flashbacks that range over the 1920s and 1930s and create a portrait of Chicago's gangster era, a time when men were making and losing huge fortunes. The opening scene is at a party in Barrington, Illinois, at the estate of Virginia "Gin" Bishop in honor of forty-seven-year-old Tasker Martin, a railroad magnate. Gin is an international society hostess and her party symbolically announces her romantic alliance with the still married Tasker, whose wife is suing for divorce. An alliance with Gin could finally bring Tasker entrée to society; although an important businessman for decades, his family origins were modest. When Tasker mysteriously disappears after the party the narrative shifts to an extended flashback that relates his biography from the perspectives of his business associates, lawyer, physician, and lovers. Tasker returns, surprising those who assumed him to be a victim of a gangland assassination. In fact he had been compelled by some subconscious need to earn his living as a farmhand. Through the experience, Tasker begins to value manual labor and appreciate the needs of humble people on farms and in small towns. He decides to retain money-losing railroad routes to serve the people along them. He also decides to sell his estate and buy a farm. Written after the disillusionment of the Depression and World War II, the novel can be read as a rejection of capitalism and urban values in favor of a return to agrarian self-sufficiency. Descriptions of Chicago are very detailed and include domestic establishments, public entertainment, restaurants, and nightclubs.

465. Gale, Zona. *Birth*. New York: Macmillan, 1918. 402pp.

This novel is mostly set in Burage, Wisconsin, however Chicago is a dominant symbolic presence. Michael Pitt, a traveling salesman, meets and marries Barbara Ellsworth, a young, orphaned woman without family after the recent death of her uncle. Pitt takes over her uncle's painting and paperhanging business to pay off debts and support Barbara. The couple marries and their Chicago honeymoon fires Barbara's longing for urban life. Pitt's kindness and the baby she has with him become chains binding her to Burage. Although she has a pleasant social life in the town and many friends, she finally abandons her husband and son to try to enter the theater world of Chicago. Realizing that he will never make enough money to provide a better life for his son, Jeffrey, or re-attract Barbara, Pitt sells everything, leaves Jeffrey in the care of friends, and participates in the Alaskan gold rush. He comes close to making his fortune, but returns to Burage empty-handed to take up his paperhanging business again. From then on, he devotes himself to Jeffrey and his son's ambition to study art at the Chicago Art Institute. When the financial challenge is too great, Jeffrey gets to the city with the monetary support of Miss Arrowsmith, the spinster daughter of one of Burage's best families. Once in the city, Jeffrey decides to earn his own way with a job in a wallpaper-manufacturing firm. Although his job is prosaic, in the energy of the city he experiences a rebirth that promises to stimulate him towards a significant life in the world beyond Burage's pettiness.

466. Garfield, Brian (Wynne). *Death Sentence*. New York: Evans, 1975. 209pp.

The Chicago of this novel is crime-ridden and citizens get little aid from the corrupt police department and ineffective judicial system. After Manhattan accountant Paul Benjamin is transferred to the city by his firm he continues the vigilantism he began in New York after his wife and daughter were killed by robbers. Armed with a concealed pistol, Benjamin roams the early morning streets gunning down criminals in the act. On his late night patrol he visits neighborhoods that were particularly crime-ridden in the 1970s. Through bar-room conversations with journalists and dates with a young female lawyer in the district attorney's office, Benjamin hears a good deal about crime, politics, and the criminal justice system in Chicago. While frustration over crime is a central theme, the novel does put out some of the dangers of vigilantism.

467. Garland, Hamlin. *Mart Haney's Mate; or, Money Magic*. New York: Harper and Brothers, 1907. 280pp.

Only a few chapters of this book are set in Chicago, but they present a surprising glimpse of the acceptance of nouveaux riches westerners from Colorado by Chicago's academic and artistic circles. Marshall Haney, who has earned the sobriquet "the gambling prince of Cripple Creek," arrives in Chicago with his beautiful young bride on their honeymoon tour. Letters of introduction garner them invitations and they reciprocate with dinner parties. The couple takes a surprisingly active interest in visiting artists' studios and their new Chicago acquaintances openly relish the westerners' novel backgrounds and are titillated to watch the obsequious reactions their wealth garners.

468. Garland, Hamlin. *Rose of Dutcher's Coolly*. Chicago: Stone and Kimball, 1895. 403pp.

Raised by her father on a remote Wisconsin farm, Rose Dutcher is too intellectual to be contented with housework and agricultural labor. After graduating from the University of Wisconsin, she convinces her father to support her in Chicago for a while. On a modest allowance she establishes herself through her beauty, natural charm, and imagination. She wins numerous friends and the attention of a wealthy, attractive young man who could give her a life of comfort. Several society families want to establish her in their social circle, and Warren Mason, a distinguished writer twenty years her senior, is intrigued by her complex personality. During her first year in the city, Rose makes many decisions about who she is and how she wants to live. She does not want to lose her personality and interests in a traditional marriage. She also does not want to cut herself off from her father and origins by becoming a society lady. In the end she is eager to accept the companionate marriage offered by Mason. In addition to dealing with the issue of women's role in society and the nature of marriage, Garland says a great deal about Chicago. Rose's new friends describe the city with admiration, summarize aspects of its distinctiveness and characterize the place, claiming that Chicagoans are no longer obsessed with wresting the necessities of physical comfort through their labor. Instead, the economy is strong enough that a large number of people can practice cultured professions, or are wealthy enough to have leisure to be full-time connoisseurs of art, literature, and music. An underlying theme of the novel is that Chicago has become a cultural center to rival the cities of the East.

469. Gatchell, Charles. *What a Woman Did*. Chicago: Era, 1900. 337pp.

The first-person narrator of this novel is the wife (name never given) of John (surname also never given). The story is about her cleverness in household management, evidenced most clearly in her response to the diagnosis of her husband's lung ailment (phthisis) and the impact of Chicago's polluted air on the condition. When the family physician recommends a two-year stay in Colorado, John immediately decides such a trip is impossible because he will lose his job and he does not have money to cover the cost of such a trip. His wife gathers information (discovering that a long summer trip to Wisconsin could heal her husband's condition), arranges a work leave, gets a bargain on a delivery wagon to be used as transportation and housing, and acquires a horse formerly employed in the street car system (which is being converted to electric). She even finds temporary tenants for their apartment at Grand Boulevard and Fifty-first Street. By the time she approaches her husband, he cannot object to her well-developed plan. John recovers his health and when they return to the city his wife creates a balcony sleeping porch so that John continues to thrive, bolstered by summer camping trips. Later the couple acquire a house in Kenwood also with a sleeping porch. Although most of the novel describes the camping trip, some sense of domestic life in late-nineteenth-century Chicago is conveyed, as well as the relative size of the city when traversed by horse. An analysis of urban air quality and the causes of pollution are also detailed.

470. Gault, William Campbell. *Quarterback Gamble*. New York: Dutton, 1970. 137pp.

Tom "Jug" Elroy was still in junior high school when his professional football playing father died of a heart attack. The rest of this story for young adults briefly recounts Elroy's college years and first few years playing for the Chicago Miners professional football team. Although Elroy plays for a Chicago team, the city is not much of a presence in the book.

471. Gault, William Campbell. *Wild Willie, Wide Receiver*. New York: Dutton, 1974. 147pp.

When native Alabaman Matt Tulley, coach of the Chicago Miners football team, finds out that his father-in-law, team owner Alan Fiske, has signed African-American player Willie Waggen from South Chicago, Tulley has his doubts, considering that Waggen is more showman than effective player. Through contact with Waggen, Tulley gains an understanding of the effects of racism and poverty and by the end of the book has gained respect for Waggen's team spirit. Although much of the book transpires on football fields, scenes in apartments and restaurants provide examples of the prevalence of racism.

472. Gerson, Noel B. (Noel Bertram). *The Sunday Heroes*. New York: William Morrow, 1972. 288pp.

In this football novel, an assistant manager must deal with a series of crises that reveal a good deal about cultural values of the time period. Robin Stephens is in his first year as the Cougar's assistant general manager when the general manager suffers a heart attack. Newly important, when it is learned that Stephens had been having casual sex with the wife of a Cougar team member, he is forced by the team owner to marry the woman, after the couple divorces, to avoid scandal. In fact much of his time is spent trying to protect team members from negative fan reaction. He forestalls any news leaks when two bisexual team members are discovered to be having an affair, when amphetamines are being used in the locker room, and when financial improprieties by the team's public relations manager are discovered. Physical descriptions of Chicago are mostly restricted to accounts of apartments and hotels, as well as some references to restaurants and nightclubs. A minor theme is the novelty for Stephens of a racially integrated team and office staff.

473. Gerson, Noel B. (Noel Bertram) [Leon Phillips, pseud.]. *When the Wind Blows*. New York: Farrar, Straus and Cudahy, 1956. 311pp.

In this Depression-era novel about the boundaries of social class, immature Paul Dawson marries an insurance secretary from Hyde Park named Helga Bjornson. Dawson, the son of Gordon Dawson, a businessman with a mansion on South Shore Drive near Jackson Park, rejects his father's proposal that he enter the family firm. However, when he decides to marry Helga, he barely acknowledges the challenges she will face living on his salary as a journalist and as an unwelcome addition to the Dawson family. Her clear-headedness saves their relationship. When the Dawson family firm runs into financial difficulties that may evidence negligence or malfeasance, Dawson's uncle commits suicide. Paul responds to the crisis by quitting his job as a reporter to stand by his father. In addition to the Hyde Park tenement where the Bjornsons live and the Dawson's mansion, action is set at the Balloon Room at the Congress Hotel, the Cape Cod Room at the Drake Hotel, tennis and social events at the Meridian Club. The Dawsons' ceremonial Sunday dinners are contrasted with meals in Hyde Park diners and spaghetti restaurants and the grittiness of covering stockyard fires.

474. Gerstenberg, Alice. *Unquenched Fire*. Boston: Small, Maynard, 1912. 417pp.

A young society woman must navigate between social expectations for her life and her own interests and wishes. Jane Carrington's father made his fortune manufacturing plows and her mother established the family in Chicago society. However, the thought of filling the social role her parents created for her fills Jane with dread. As a debutante she has been able to gently flaunt the dictates of fashion and behavior, but three years have passed and everyone expects her to become a young, married matron. When she rejects shallow, but wealthy, Walter Scribner's proposal, her mother is outraged. After Jane's father refuses to support her dream of becoming an actress she decides she has no choice but to accept Scribner's renewed proposal. During the yearlong engagement Jane continues to chafe, however, and she finally devises a way to escape to New York City. After a period of disappointments, she establishes herself on the stage and marries writer Bryce Gordon, who she can respect for his intellect and achievements. The book contains descriptions of Chicago social events and articulates a version of the behavior expected of Chicago society women. Despite the book's argument that women should be able to find meaning in life outside the roles of mother and wife, by the end of the book Jane has realized that she will gladly submit to the will of her husband, even if that means giving up the stage.

475. Gillian, Michael. *Warrant for a Wanton*. New York: Mill, 1952. 246pp.

In this murder mystery, Leith Hadley has already been sentenced to death for the murder of his father's business partner, Burt Winslow. At the sentencing he fled the courtroom and for the first time since the murder, for which he was immediately incarcerated, he has a chance to investigate the crime. He gets no further than the neighborhood around Clark Street and Fullerton Parkway before he needs to find cover from the police. When he gains entry into an apartment, Leith finds Christine Shaw unconscious from an overdose of sleeping pills. A World War II veteran, he is able to save her life. In return, she saws off his handcuffs disguises him with her cosmetology techniques (she works in a beauty parlor), and helps him solve the murder. All of the evidence against Leigh had been circumstantial. He was discovered blacked-out in the murdered man's vacation cottage. Subject to blackouts when he drinks, and abstemious as a result, he does not know what had happened in the preceding hours. In addition to small businesses, apartment buildings, and Belmont Harbor, the novelist establishes the setting by describing the Irving Park Road neighborhood and other areas on the North Side. One underlying theme of the novel is the plight of returned veterans re-establishing their lives.

476. Givins, Robert Cartwright [Snivig C. Trebor, pseud.]. *Jerry Bleeker; or, Is Marriage a Failure?* The Pastime Series, vol. 30. Chicago: Laird and Lee, 1889. 206pp.

Only part of this novel is set in Chicago and it is mostly concerned with the city as a venue for securing a divorce. Heroine Phoebe Parry of Vincennes, Ohio, a pretty girl with many suitors, decides to reject everyone's advice and marry the village rake. She soon rues her choice and wants a divorce. Jeremiah "Jerry" Bleeker, a reform-minded lawyer, represents her during the lengthy proceedings. In addition to descriptions of Chicago divorce courts, the novel includes digressions on temperance, and the nature of marriage. Phoebe secures her divorce, but by the time the decree is finalized, she and Jerry have fallen in love and they marry soon afterwards.

477. Givins, Robert Cartwright [Snivig C. Trebor, pseud.]. *Land Poor: A Chicago Parable*. Chicago: Franklin, 1884. 117pp.

Spurred by the dream of greater financial security, Barnabee Smith, a poorly paid school teacher, moves his family to a land claim on the DuPage River near Naperville in the newly created state of Illinois (1818). Because he is not a farmer, he does not realize the fecundity of his land and with poor techniques struggles to earn a living from it. When a land agent offers to exchange Smith's claim for a piece of land near Chicago (that is actually worthless), the clueless Smith agrees, attracted by the prospect of Chicago's growth. His new land is not arable and his poverty deepens until a manufacturing concern offers him $2,000,000 for his tract. Cartwright uses his story to present the pros and cons of Communism and set the stage for the conclusion that "...the basis of all security is LAND."

478. Givins, Robert C. [Snivig C. Trebor, pseud.]. *The Millionaire Tramp*. Chicago: Cook County Review, 1886. 181pp.

Charles Landsdowne, sole heir to his father's English estate, is falsely accused of killing the oldest son of the Margates, a family with which the Landsdownes have feuded for hundreds of years. Believing circumstantial evidence will convict him, Charles flees England, under the assumed name of James Darrow. Before he flees, he leaves a message for romantic interest Lillie Margate, the sister of the deceased, stating his innocence. Landsdowne eventually travels to Chicago where he lives in the city's parks with tramps. One of the tramps, Old Tom, befriends him, cautions him about the evils of alcohol, and exposes the influence of saloon owners and distillers on city politics around the country. Landsdowne works hard and can eventually afford a room where he shelters Old Tom, who dies during the winter. In return for his kindness, Tom had given Landsdowne a quit-claim deed for land in Maine that turns out to be worth eight hundred thousand dollars, although to avoid attention, Landsdowne continues to live modestly in Chicago. In the meantime, Lillie Margate works to prove Landsdowne's innocence. On a trip to the United States she meets Landsdowne through a bizarre coincidence and the two renew their relationship. Soon after her return to England, Lillie finds new evidence that clears Landsdowne who resumes his old life. Although the novel is only partly set in Chicago, the book is of interest for its temperance message and for declaring Chicago to be a haven for the dispossessed and the site of a potential flashpoint for a Socialistic revolution that will overturn society.

479. Givens, Robert C. [Snivig C. Trebor, pseud.]. *The Unwritten Will: A Romance*. Chicago: Rhodes and McClure, 1886. 214pp.

Henry Norwood, falling under the influence of an older businessman and eager to rapidly accumulate a fortune so that he can marry his sweetheart, Kate Ogleby, uses a client's money to cover a margin on some Erie Canal stocks he has in his account. His timing is slightly off and he loses the stock, after which he immediately turns himself over to the police for malfeasance. After serving his sentence, Norwood decides to leave the East Coast, where he is in disgrace, and relocate to Chicago. He redeems his reputation through a law partnership and lays the foundation of a real estate fortune, buying and selling properties during the great building boom of the 1860s. He engineers a chance to reconnect with Kate by traveling on the same ship with her and her ailing father to San Francisco, disguised as a Mexican. When the ship sinks, he and Kate are in the survival party that ends up on deserted island for several weeks. Henry gradually loses his disguise and is reconciled to Kate, who after the death of her father on board the ship, has inherited a considerable fortune. Henry stands in line to inherit another fortune from his mother, since his law partner has successfully prosecuted a man who had cheated Henry's mother out of an estate. Although the lovers travel to Chicago after they are rescued, in a postscript we learn that they went on to settle in San Francisco. Chicago in this novel is a place of opportunity to lose one's past and create a new life through one's own endeavors. It is also a cash machine as rising property values make earning a fortune through savvy land speculation easy

480. Glasmon, Kubec and John Bright. *The Public Enemy*. New York: Grosset and Dunlap, 1931. 280pp.
    The insidious influence of organized crime on an Irish immigrant family heightens during Prohibition and brings a tragic death. Irishman Michael Powers, Sr. supports his family in a Chicago tenement near the stockyards on his income as a policeman. His oldest son and namesake Michael is serious about his studies and wants to become a lawyer. His youngest son, Tommy, hangs out in the social club of gangster "Putty Nose" Considine, at whose instigation, Tommy commits his first crimes. When Michael Sr. is gunned down, the two boys are left to support their mother, although they are too young to do so legally. Michael uses a false birth certificate to get work driving streetcars and Tommy gets involved in more serious crime. When the United States enters World War I, Michael patriotically enlists, leaving Tommy to provide for Mrs. Powers. As Prohibition begins, Tommy starts working with bootlegger Paddy Ryan who is connected with the Democratic political machine. Tommy gets a job in the sanitation department and by the time Michael, recovering from serious injuries, comes home a war hero, Tommy has become a genuine gangster. Michael confronts Tommy about his crimes, but accepts when Ryan arranges for a legitimate job and cash to finance his studies. As more gangs develop, bootlegging warfare begins and before long Tommy is shot and his body dumped on the street in front of the Powers' house. The novel provides many details about the mechanics of bootlegging operations, crooked politicians, and federal agents. In addition, there is a lengthy description of an African-American nightclub and visits to Polish and Italian restaurants, highlighting the food's novelty for the Irish protagonists. All cultural groups are portrayed as distinct from each other, with only commercial interaction.

481. Glaspell, Susan. *The Glory of the Conquered: The Story of a Great Love*. New York: Frederick A. Stokes, 1909. 376pp.
    A young woman discovers how fortunate she has been when she learns about the life of a woman forced to live in Chicago. Twenty-five-year-old Katie Jones lives with her brother Wayne, an army officer, on an unnamed military post in the Mississippi River Valley. She enjoys a middle-class affluence that includes trips abroad and to New York City and Washington, D.C. and is being courted by a respectable young man. Katie's life changes when she saves an anonymous young woman from committing suicide. Katie presents the woman to her family household as Ann Forrester, a visiting friend. Ann grew up in Centralia, Illinois, the daughter of a harsh clergyman, and ran away to Chicago when she was sixteen. She experienced a Chicago filled with women who could not support themselves. After she is wronged by a man she attempts suicide. When Ann runs away from her rescuer's household, Katie searches for her in Chicago and experiences for herself a city ruled by a harsh capitalism. In such an environment, Katie longs for a society more concerned with creating fuller lives for everyone, rather than the enrichment of a small percentage of the population. She also reflects on the impact of one's social environment on one's emotional development and realizes that she owes her sunny disposition to the family love she has experienced. Eventually, Katie learns Ann was discovered seriously ill in Paris by Katie's brother.

Wayne cares for her, takes her to New York City, and eventually falls in love with her. The next time Katie meets Ann, she finds her transformed by Wayne's love. Although much of this novel is not set in Chicago, the city plays an important role and is described in enough detail to support the novel's indictment of some of the evils of American capitalism.

482. Glazer, Mitchell [Miami Mitch, pseud.]. Dan Ackroyd, John Landis. *The Blues Brothers*. New York: A Jove Book, 1980. 245pp.

In this adaptation of a motion picture screenplay of the same name (Universal Pictures, 1980) two brothers try to save the orphanage in which they grew up. Elwood and Jake Blues were raised in St. Helen of the Blessed Shroud Orphanage and had a brief moment of fame in northern Illinois with their band, The Blues Brothers. The band broke up when Jake went to jail. Released after serving three years, Jake reconstitutes the band in the hope of raising money to save the orphanage from being sold for nonpayment of taxes. A sub-plot involves neo-Nazis who want to acquire the orphanage because of its resemblance to the beer hall in which Hitler held his early meetings. Although not exclusively set in Chicago (some of the plot transpires in Calumet City, Joliet, and Urbana-Champaign, as well). Jake and Elwood live in a blighted area of Chicago that is portrayed as gritty and surrounded by industrial wasteland.

483. Gleeson, William. *Can Such Things Be: A Story of a White Slave*. Chicago: The Author, 1915. 325pp.

Gleeson's social reform novel exposes the methods by which innocent country girls become white slaves, and the complicity of police and politicians in the process. Martha Hill, the child of Irish immigrant parents, lives in a Michigan village. When her father Robert's rheumatism prevents him from work, Martha decides to get a job in Chicago to support the family that includes seven children. On her first day in the city she meets a helpful young man who takes her to dinner, during which she is drugged. She is taken to the brothel of Madam Blomgarten and her companion is paid his finder's fee. A prisoner in a barred room, all of her clothing taken from her, Martha is forced to work for her keep by entertaining men. Although her brother searches for her and contacts the police, the policeman who locates her accepts a bribe to keep her location secret. Finally, Matthew Howard, a Hill neighbor, travels to Chicago on business and is taken out on the town by a businessman eager for his trade. Horrified at the nightlife depravity, he is even more shocked when he discovers Martha. When he and Martha's brother try to free her, they are thwarted and a short time later discover she has died. Howard pays for a touching funeral and memorial to Martha and her brother wreaks vengeance on Madam Blomgarten and the man who entrapped Martha. Whether an accurate portrayal or merely sensational, the novel conveys the perceived dangers a female would encounter when traveling without a chaperone to Chicago.

484. Gleeson, William. *Vice and Virtue a Story of Our Times*. Illustrated by F. A. Gibson. Chicago: Mecklenberg, 1913. 603pp.

In a preface, the author declares his intent to illustrate the evils of urban life—particularly the power of saloon owners and ward politicians. This lengthy novel has many characters, each introduced to illustrate some point, but the main figures are Michael Scully, Owen Hooligan, Florence Burdett, and Alderman Great. Saloon owner Hooligan has the means to influence voters for Alderman Great. Great rewards Hooligan with jobs and contracts. One of the evil aspects of Hooligan's neighborhood influence, alcohol abuse, is revealed when the Murphys accidentally set fire to their apartment after creating a drunken scene at Hooligan's. Michael Scully heroically saves the Murphys' son, Tony, and the fire inspires him to pledge abstinence and get away from Chicago, where he sees no future except many nights spent in Hooligan's. He heads west and thwarts the mugging of well-known Western rancher, John Monroe. Monroe employs Scully on his Montana ranch and, after witnessing many evidences of Scully's character, lets Scully marry his daughter, in effect making him his heir. Florence Burdett does not have as happy an experience entering adulthood. She graduates with honors from school but no jobs are available except in a department store where Florence discovers the perils of life for working women, who rely upon male managers to let them make enough money to support themselves. Florence resists inappropriate overtures, but is powerless before Alderman Great's attention. Tempted by all that he can offer to benefit her family, Florence spends unchaperoned time with him. After he earns her trust, the alderman drugs her and she wakes on a ship bound for Europe. Realizing that her reputation has already been ruined and the extent of her powerlessness, Florence gives up and becomes the Alderman's well-provided for mistress. When Mrs. Great dies, and can no longer be harmed by scandal, Florence impulsively attacks and kills Alderman Great with his own gun. Arrested immediately, she says nothing in her own defense. Scully, a county sheriff, reads of the case, investigates, provides legal support that results a not-guilty verdict, and reunites her with her family. At the end of the novel, Florence leaves Chicago to begin life near Scully in Montana. Appointed school principal, Florence also soon has a fiancé. The author provides a thorough description of Chicago social life and working-class entertainments (company outings, funerals, opera, and theater performances) in the 1890s, as well as depicting the plight of women and the working class in general whose only defense against systemic problems is violence or relocation.

485. Godley, Robert [Franklin James, pseud.]. *Killer in the Kitchen*. New York: Lantern Press, 1947. 281pp.

In this novel set in World War II Chicago, the toughest character and the one who solves the crime is twenty-five-year-old Madelon Richards. Her first husband was killed at Pearl Harbor and her second husband is missing in Burma. She has been called to Chicago from her father's Texas ranch to take care of business matters on her husband's behalf. Her visit takes a dramatic turn when an employee of one of the Richards' businesses is found decapitated. The victim, Otto Schubert, a German immigrant, is soon discovered to have connections to organized crime and Richards finds herself in the company of one gangster after another. Most of the physical settings are thinly described and incidental to the plot. The novel touches on issues of female gender roles by presenting such a strong female character.

486. Goetzinger, Clara Palmer. *Smoldering Flames; Adventures and Emotions of a Flapper*. Chicago: Zuriel, 1928. 314pp.

In the form of a diary, Nan Livingstone relates her years as a flapper, over a time period from approximately 1922 to 1927, beginning when she was sixteen. Nan is the daughter of a French woman and a father who is a bank president and member of one of the Mid-Atlantic's oldest, aristocratic families—the Livingstones. After Livingstone's death, Nan moves with her mother to Chicago where they reside on Lake Shore Drive, in a floor-through apartment. Although Nan describes her forty-two-year-old mother's efforts to look younger and attract a new husband, her main concern is with her own affairs. She revels in being loved by a wide range of men ranging in age from boys five years her senior to men several decades older than she. The social events where she is courted include opera performances and dinners, charity balls, and studio parties where models, actors, and artists mingle with society people. Although Nan describes the out-of-wedlock pregnancy of one of her acquaintances and a police raid on one of the studio parties, most of the scandalous behavior of herself and her friends is relatively innocent. She eventually marries a much older man who soon dies of alcoholism and leaves her a small fortune. When she marries again, her husband is similar in age and becomes her soul-mate. Her flapper days over, by the end of the book she is a doting mother. The novel is a good source for description of 1920s social behavior and captures upper-class attitudes toward love and the role of women in society. The new freedom for women that Nan describes focuses exclusively on unchaperoned dates with men and has nothing to do with an enlarged role in non-domestic contexts.

487. Gooch, Fani Pusey. *Miss Mordeck's Father*. New York: Dodd, Mead, 1890. 288pp.

Returning by train to Chicago where she resides with her parents Browné Modeck is approached by young Shreve Chilson, as though she were an intimate friend, even though she has never met him. Repulsed by his behavior, she is also titillated, and eventually consults books on mental illness to determine what malady afflicts Chilson. The mystery is solved when she meets her double, Nadia Dunbar, Chilson's fiancée. Browné is so taken by the exactness of the resemblance that she hosts a ball at which she and Nadia cause a sensation by appearing in the same gown. Chilson finds the resemblance more sinister and secretly begins to explore the family background of each girl. He had always been somewhat concerned about the instability of the Dunbar household from which Colonel Dunbar, a gambler, is absent for months at a time. He then discovers from Browné that her multimillionaire father is mysteriously absent from time to time and occasionally suffers physical and mental collapse. Chilson eventually accumulates proof that Mordeck suffers from a psychological condition in which he has a double identity, with each distinct personality unknown to the other. The novel is much more concerned with exploring the maladies of the human mind than the physical realities of Chicago. However, the affluent Mordeck household on Michigan Avenue is described, as well as the Chicago Public Library, the art community of the city, and skating parties in Lincoln Park.

488. Gordon, Mildred and Gordon Gordon [The Gordons, pseud.]. *Case File: FBI*. Garden City, N.Y.: Crime Club / Doubleday, 1953. 189pp.

When FBI agent Zack Stewart is murdered by an unseen gunman, his fellow agent, John (Rip) Ripley, gets assigned to find the culprit. His only leads are the cases on which Zack had been working: a bank robbery and fatal shooting, a car theft linked to a syndicate, and an extortion attempt. Assuming that one of the cases will lead him to Zack's murderer, Rip focuses on solving each. The author is more concerned with conveying information about investigative procedures and criminal psychology than providing much physical detail to establish settings. A few specific addresses and restaurants are mentioned, including the Palmer House. Most of the characters are not that distinct from those in other such books; however, one, a former lawyer of Al Capone, is clearly a Chicagoan. The Cold War and Korean War are explicitly referenced throughout the book. From a cultural perspective, the characters' concerns about their reputation with "the neighbors" and the lengths to which women need to be concerned about being seen with strange men are notable.

489. Graham, Marie. *A Devout Bluebeard*. New York: Abbey Press, 1900. 300pp.

This social satire concerning organized religion (Presbyterianism here) is also a social history of Chicago from the late 1860s through the 1880s. The "bluebeard" of the title is Richard Maxton who moves to Chicago after working as a missionary in Africa, where his first wife Harriet Newell

Raynor dies. He moves to the city with new wife, Petronella Van Bloom, a New Yorker of notable social antecedents. Maxton establishes a firm manufacturing agricultural implements that is immediately successful and he begins accumulating a fortune. Petronella ignores how crude Chicago society is in the 1860s and establishes a home and social position for Maxton. Home life is of little interest to Maxton, however, for he spends every free moment on church matters. Petronella soon dies in childbirth. After the great fire, Maxton's losses are few since he had invested in the West Side. His next wife, Lulu Fields, ignores her husband's religious convictions and focuses on socializing. The social cachet of church work, however, means that she increasingly focuses on organizing church social life, founding and directing committees. His final wife, Parthenia Revere, outlives Maxton and inherits his fortune, since she demonstrates that religious practice is more important than church politics. In addition to descriptions of social activities, the author makes a point of summarizing social history and practices in Chicago during the nineteenth century.

490. Granger, Bill. *Public Murders*. New York: Jove, 1980. 275pp.

Most of the action in this police detective novel is set in Old Town, the Loop, and Grant Park. As the police try to solve the murders of two young women in the park, they work on other criminal investigations that reveal the lack of safety and seediness of the city's downtown neighborhoods. Although the novel includes descriptions of detective investigations, the police often employ intimidation and physical violence and the murders are not solved until a policewoman is used as bait. The killer turns out to be a Slavic immigrant who works as a janitor and killed women he mistakenly thought were prostitutes. One scene is set in a pornographic movie theater.

491. Granville, Austyn, and William Wilson Knott. *If the Devil Came to Chicago: A Plea for the Misrepresented by One Who Knows What It Is to Be Misrepresented Himself*. Illustrated by F. Holme. Chicago: Bow-Knot, 1894. 352pp.

Written in open response to a work by William T. Stead, an English journalist, who attacked the city of Chicago in a book titled *If Christ Came to Chicago* (London, U.K.: Review of Reviews, 1894), the author imagines the Devil visiting the city and trying to tempt Chicagoans into transgressions. Satan's primary interactions are with the protagonist, Granville, a journalist, whom he tries to catch off guard by assuming various guises. Granville, a journalist, takes on claims about working conditions, relief for the poor, and attacks on public figures (such as Marshall Field, Philip Armour, and George Pullman) and city officials. His arguments often take the form of declaring that Chicago has laws and social institutions in place, but that conditions are dictated by the wrong doing of individuals and should not be blamed on anything peculiar about the city since desperate poverty, poor working conditions, and prostitution can be found in any city in the world. He also portrays men Stead described as the predatory rich as benefactors of the public good, since they enabled public improvements (such as streetcars and public utilities) that benefit everyone. In an appendix to his book, Granville lists all of Chicago's churches.

492. Greeley, Andrew Moran. *Death in April*. New York: McGraw-Hill, 1980. 246pp.

In this romance novel a journalist saves a woman from unjust legal prosecution and rescues her from a Chicago with dangerously corrupt social structures. Twenty years after breaking his engagement with Lynnie, James O'Neill seeks her out on a layover in Chicago. O'Neill's poor, Irish-American, immigrant parents were scandalized when his childhood friendship with Lynnie, the daughter of a wealthy judge whose money came from bootlegging, deepened into a romance. The couple became engaged anyway, but O'Neill ended the relationship when he realized that

Lynnie wanted him to stay in Chicago and take a job in her father's law firm; he wanted to be a writer and journalist, covering stories internationally. O'Neill becomes a successful war correspondent and novelist, and begins to dream about Lynnie and realizes that despite two marriages she had always been his true love. When he finds Lynnie, she has been widowed for some time and is still in love with him, but before the two can reunite, they must address accusations by a corrupt politician that could put her in jail. She had made her late husband's real estate business a huge success, in part through land deals with the state, that are now being questioned. The novel portrays the corruption of the political system, the media, and the Roman Catholic Church and when O'Neill threatens an exposé the charges are dropped and the two leave for Paris and O'Neill's home. The novel includes some physical description of Chicago (particularly of Lincoln Park and Hyde Park), but the novel is mostly concerned with social structures. Readers may be shocked by the novel's sexism and the physical violence that Lynnie accepts from O'Neill.

493. Greene, Bob and Paul Galloway [Mike Holiday, pseud.]. *Bagtime*. New York: Popular Library, 1977. 283pp.

The popularity of Greene's column of the same name that appeared in the *Chicago Sun Times*, led to the publication of this book that recounts the adventures of Mike Holiday as he tries to find himself. Holiday, a college graduate and cellist, is recently divorced and working as a bag boy in a Treasure Island grocery store on Wells Street. The plot consists of a series of adventures ranging from the almost believable (like meeting Chicago celebrities such as Hugh Hefner, Jane Pauley, Studs Terkel, and Norm Van Lier) to the outlandish (the kidnapping of his cat à la Patty Hearst and the armed high-jacking of a bus on which he is a passenger). The book provides some insight into the cultural concerns of Chicagoans in the 1970s.

494. Greenlee, Sam. *The Spook Who Sat by the Door*. New York: Richard W. Baron, 1969. 248pp.

Although the majority of this book is set in Chicago, the novelist is concerned with articulating views on racism and presents little physical or socio-cultural description specific to the city. The plot concerns the elaborate, insurrectionist mission of Dan Freeman to redress generations of African-American mistreatment through violence. Freeman learned early in life the secret of using the misperceptions of racists against them. His skill carries him from a Chicago ghetto to the University of Michigan and to a master's degree program at the University of Chicago. Athletic by nature, his Korean War military service enables him to add discipline and tactical methods to his skill set. When he learns that the Central Intelligence Agency is being forced to recruit African-Americans he resigns his ghetto-based social worker job and within five years has become the CIA director's assistant. His assimilation, however, is only a pose he uses to develop more skills and learn the techniques of espionage. By the time he returns to Chicago, ostensibly to become the director of a non-profit focused on ghetto social problems, he is ready to activate an insurrectionist plot against American society based in twelve cities. His army is a federation of street gangs and his funding comes from a bank robbery. Although the author clearly sees New York City as the capital of African-American culture, the novel rehearses the history and demographics of Chicago to make it clear that that city is the only clear choice for the base of Freeman's insurrection.

495. Grimm, George. *Pluck*. Milwaukee, Wis.: Germania, 1904. 284pp.

In an epigraph the author declares his intent to capture aspects of the German-American immigrant experience through his protagonist, Phillip Bertram. Forced by his family's poverty to leave Germany as an eleven-year-old, during his voyage to America a smallpox epidemic on the ship overwhelms Dr. Lawrence and he has Bertram nurse his own daughter, Bessie, while taking care of his many other patients. A long time passes before Bertram's story has anything to do with Chicago. He spends four years in New York City where he must deal with false accusations of criminal activity, a year in Philadelphia, and by the 1850s he and a New York City friend, Jack O'Donnell, buy three hundred and twenty acres of land in Wisconsin. They are almost finished harvesting all of the timber on the land and establishing farmland when they respond to Lincoln's call for volunteers. To enlist they must go to Chicago. After he falls ill in the South, Bertram is transported to a Chicago hospital to recover and is reunited with Dr. Lawrence. Bessie Lawrence nurses Bertram back to health and they are soon engaged to marry. Even though Lawrence has significant property holdings in Chicago, Bertram, Bessie, and Dr. Lawrence all resettle on the Wisconsin farm and an agricultural life is held up as superior to city living. The author throughout vaunts the positive qualities of German-American immigrants.

496. Gruber, Frank [John K. Vedder, pseud.]. *The Last Doorbell*. New York: Henry Holt, 1941. 294pp.

This murder mystery is set in the offices of a dubious publishing house, Business Journals, Inc., in the Dockery Building on Wells Street near Harrison. Frank Sargent who has been working unhappily with a company conducting door-to-door polls, is given a job editing a trade publication for turkey growers by publisher Ben Chapman, almost as soon as he enters the office. Other publications include trade journals for skating rink owners, slot machine owners, and exterminators. Sargent, a bachelor, lives in the Ajax Hotel on North Avenue near Halsted, but dreams of earning enough money to get married (even if he has yet to pick a bride). When Daniel Sligo, a member of the Business Journals staff, is murdered, Sargent investigates and uncovers a secret marriage and a missing stock certificate. Although some specific locations are included, physical setting is less detailed than the generalized milieu of a single young man in Chicago in 1940.

497. Gruber, Frank. *The Leather Duke*. A Murray Hill Mystery. New York: Rinehart, 1949. 247pp.

Door to door book salesmen Johnny Fletcher and Sam Cragg are thrown into desperate financial circumstances when their book supplier goes bankrupt and they are forced to work in a Chicago shoe leather factory. When Cragg finds the murdered body of a fellow laborer they get involved in solving the crime. In the process, they become acquainted with Chicago police detectives, as well as with Elliott Towner the son of Harry Towner (the Leather Duke), who owns the factory and other business properties. In the course of their investigation they go to seedy bars and Towner's private club and residence. The murder is Mafia related and the book includes a condensed history of organized crime. Extended descriptions are also presented of the Chicago Italian-American community, gambling, and leather factory jobs. At various points in the novel, Fletcher and Cragg point out the inequities of factory labor.

498. Gruber, Frank. *The Navy Colt*. A Johnny Fletcher Mystery. New York: Farrar and Rinehart, 1941. 278pp.

Johnny Fletcher and his friend in adversity, Sam Cragg, are idling away the day on West Madison Street, an area they refer to as "Hobohemia," when they are approached by a well-dressed, beautiful young woman, Hilda Nelson, who offers them ten dollars for punching James Maxwell in the nose. They carry out the assignment, only to discover that Maxwell has been found dead and they are the suspects. To clear themselves, they investigate the crime and find themselves piecing together events from sixty years before when Jesse James robbed a bank in North-field, Minnesota. Most of the Chicago sections of the book are set in flophouses and seedy busi-nesses, although the pair make several visits to an office in the Merchandise Mart. As a reflection of the Depression-era time period, the scenes at a wrestling match, a mail order school for aspiring screenwriters, and a club for amateur writers hoping to sell magazine fiction, are all of interest.

499. Gruber, Frank. *The Scarlet Feather*. A Johnny Fletcher Mystery. New York: Rinehart, 1948. 249pp.

While walking in Lincoln Park, Johnny Fletcher and his body-builder sidekick, Sam Cragg, witness a girl shedding her mink coat in the frigid December weather and plunging into a lagoon. Johnny rescues her and discovers that she is Lois Tancred, the daughter of a wealthy stockbroker, who was driven to desperation by a blackmailer. When the blackmailer is found dead at a poultry show, Johnny and Sam uncover a high stakes cockfighting ring that involves wealthy, society fig-ures.

500. Gruber, Frank [Stephen Acre, pseud.]. *The Yellow Overcoat*. New York: Dodd, Mead, 1942. 232pp.

A completely broke Joe Devlin inherits his uncle's Chicago mail order business, a course in criminology operated as an "institute" from offices in the oldest building in the Loop. Soon, Dev-lin is tied up in several mysteries, one of which concerns a man who is paying him four hundred dollars to find a yellow overcoat worth less than forty dollars. He is also framed for cheating at cards by the chief of police (a graduate of the correspondence course). The novel is mostly set in hotels and office buildings in 1930s Chicago, although Devlin travels to Minnesota, following clues. The most important mystery he solves in the book is who stole fifty thousand dollars from his uncle's apartment. The novel satirizes both the huge correspondence course industry of the time period and private detective agencies.

501. Guest, Judith. *Ordinary People*. New York: Viking, 1976. 263pp.

This story of middle-class family life is set in Lake Forest, Illinois and depicts how the Jar-retts deal with the accidental death of oldest son Jordan in a boating mishap. After eighteen-year-old Conrad Jarrett attempts suicide, understanding his action and aiding his recovery demand the attention of his parents. The story is told from varying perspectives. In addition to Conrad's view-point, those of his father Calvin and mother Beth are included. The novel is mostly concerned with family dynamics and interpersonal exchanges. The city of Chicago is a dominant presence in the awareness of the characters, but has little importance as a physical setting.

502. Gunther, John. *The Golden Fleece*. New York: Harper and Brothers, 1929. 421pp.

In this coming of age novel, an affluent young woman embraces the independence of earning an income and decides how to integrate her traditional viewpoints with 1920s society. Although Joan Tilford's mother died when she was three, as a twenty-one-year-old she can look back on a full, comfortable life. Her father is the principal of a family law firm that has been in business since the eighteenth century and has provided well for Joan and her sister. The Tilfords live in an architect-designed house at 8000 Sheridan Road and have a summer house in Maine. In addition to the family business, Tilford owns a downtown apartment building with hundreds of units. At the end of her college career, Joan contemplates an extended trip to Europe, but gets side-tracked when she meets reporter and public intellectual, Philip Hubbard. The plot covers the next two years in her life as she starts a subscription library and sorts out her thinking about sexuality. She decides to hold onto her traditional views about sexuality and married life (views that she identifies as Puritanism, referencing her family's New England heritage), even though it means giving up Hubbard. He has already had a series of affairs and will clearly never settle down to traditional family life. As Joan transitions to adulthood, her father falls in love with a beautiful Swedish violinist, Hilda Jacobsen, several decades his junior and has an extended affair with her when the violinist refuses to marry. Eventually, Joan does have a new stepmother and is finally headed off to Europe after a definitive break with Hubbard. The novel is filled with social events and domestic settings that provide good illustration of cultured, upper-middle-class life in Chicago in the 1920s.

503. Gunther, John. *The Red Pavilion*. New York: Harper and Brothers 1926. 269pp.

Set in the 1920s, this novel deals with a group of college friends establishing lives for themselves in the years after they graduate from the University of Chicago. Almost all of the characters are in relationships, but the couple that gets most scrutiny is Richard Northway and his wife Shirley. A sculptor, Shirley, came from a wealthy family who could support her financially and emotionally. Her husband, Richard, had an entirely different family life. His father died in an insane asylum in 1915, leaving Richard to support himself while completing college. In the present of the novel he has been working in a brokerage house for approximately ten years and makes an attractive living, but unlike Shirley, he has not followed his passion—studying chemistry—having only a garage laboratory for occasional experiments. While Richard devoted himself to creating financial security for himself and Shirley, she began to find her life with him a distraction from her art and separated from him to work in Europe. During the action of the novel she returns and the Northways work to negotiate their identities as a couple and as individuals. Gunther's characters were too young to be directly involved in World War I and came to adulthood in a period of economic prosperity. He conveys their preoccupations, describes domestic arrangements, and recounts bohemian tinged socializing. The Northways live at 619 Bryn Mawr near Sheridan Road, and many of their acquaintances live in the same area. The other geographical focus for them is Hyde Park. The novel includes vivid evocations of the city of Chicago, particularly as characters soulfully walk about the metropolis. At one point, Richard Northway walks far enough west to escape the city's environs.

504. Haas, Joseph. *Vendetta*. Chicago: Henry Regnery, 1975. 219pp.

John Krieg works as a valued journalist on the staff of a major Chicago newspaper supporting an attractive suburban life for his wife and two young children in Maple Hills. Occasionally he has reveries in which he thinks of the unsettling excitement in his distant past when he was a skilled soldier in the Korean conflict, and in the pay of the British East African police force in the mid-1950s responsible for reprisals against the rebelling Mau Mau tribe and personally involved in killing forty-four people. Then, in a racially tense 1970s Chicago summer, the past intrudes more insistently on his middle-class life, as he learns of the murders of the men who were on his police squad, as well as the dramatic butchering of their family members. Soon, he realizes that a Mau Mau has his family under surveillance. Even though he sends them to Iowa, they are slowly and painfully murdered, and he is forced to play an extended cat and mouse game with the killer on the streets of Chicago. As Krieg searches for the killer, he lives in an African-American section of Hyde Park and covers the rioting by African-Americans that breaks out in other city neighborhoods. Toward the end of the novel, after he is injured in a confrontation, an African-American prostitute takes him into her apartment and helps him recover, providing the author with an opportunity to introduce an African-American perspective on living with racism. Taken as a whole the book presents one view of Chicago in the throes of racial violence as ghettos are being bulldozed to be replaced by public housing projects.

505. Hailey, Arthur. *Airport.* Garden City, N.Y: Doubleday, 1968. 440pp.

Like Chicago novels set inside major department stores, this book outlines the work culture of a 1960s airport, Lincoln International, which is clearly a slightly disguised O'Hare International Airport. The major characters are administrators, from the general manager, to the maintenance supervisor, all of whom are faced with dramatic challenges over the course of one day during the great blizzard of 1967 that was one of the worst in Chicago's history. Although there are references to aspects of some of the characters' lives who live in the city, Chicago mostly plays a role in regard to the conflict between the needs of the airport as demand for air travel grows and airplanes become larger, and the quality of life in communities near the airport and on flight paths. These issues are rehearsed in a series of exchanges between Lincoln Airport's general manager, Mel Bakersfield, and a lawyer and resident of nearby suburb Meadowood, Elliott Fremantle. In another plotline, issues surrounding abortion are raised in the story of tough-guy, married Vernon Demarest, and the single stewardess Gwen Meighen who is pregnant as a result of her affair with Demarest. Airline industry issues are also touched upon including the lack of airport security, the difficulties of customs regulations enforcement, and the temptations posed by flight insurance.

506. Hale, Arlene. *Chicago Nurse.* New York: Ace, 1965. 127pp.

After her marriage plans fall through less than two weeks before the wedding, Delora Lambert leaves her hometown to start a new life in Chicago. Her job as a nurse brings with it a whole set of new acquaintances, and before long two handsome men are giving her their attention. The hospital setting dominates this novel in which Chicago is presented as a place of opportunity where people can leave behind their past lives.

507. Hale, Edward Everett, ed. *Six of One by Half a Dozen of the Other; An Every Day Novel by Harriet Beecher Stowe, Adeline D. T. Whitney, Lucretia P. Hale, Frederic W. Loring, Frederic B. Perkins, and Edward E. Hale.* Boston: Roberts Brothers, 1872. 245pp.

This romance novel featuring six main characters, three female and three male, was written by the six authors listed in the title. The work has a number of settings, but ends dramatically in Chicago. Jeff Fleming, Nettie Sylva, Horace Vanzandt, Jane Burgess, Rachel Holley, and Mark Hinsdale all grew up together in Greyford, Connecticut. Youthful flirtations that could mature into marriage proposals are interrupted by quarrels, visits to relatives, and career decisions (on the part of the men) scattering some of the young people to New York City, Boston, and Hartford, Connecticut. In the last seventy pages of the book everyone is reunited in Chicago in 1870. One character refers to the city as "the central ganglion of the world's nervous system." Mark Hinsdale arrives to work as the head librarian of the Johnsonian library at a "substantial salary" and lives on the West Side. Horace Vanzandt continues his career in the lumber industry, getting a position in one of Chicago's large lumber-yards. Rachel Holley arrives with wealthy relatives to live in a newly constructed house on Erie Street. Nettie Sylva, also with relatives, stays at the Sherman House. The Greyford friends have excursions to see the sites of Chicago, including Hyde Park, Riverside, the stock-yards, various elevators, the city waterworks, and the Chicago Historical Library. They also go to the North Side to hear Robert Collyer preach at Unity Church. Jeff Fleming is the last to rejoin the group and as his train approaches, he sees the city in flames. Drama ensues as the separated friends seek each other in the burning city. As an aftermath, proposals are made and marriages are in prospect. The novel presents a tourist's view of Chicago and a dramatization of the fire probably drawn from newspaper accounts, and written soon after the event.

508. Hale, Helen. *Where Life Is Real*. Cincinnati, Ohio: Jennings, Graham, 1906.
No further information is available about this collection of short stories which first appeared in Chicago newspapers.

509. Hall, Grace Darling, and Ernesto Giuseppe Merlanti. *Honor Divided*. New York: Fleming H. Revell, 1935. 224pp.
This novel about the Italian-American immigrant experience presents the story of the Sicilian Torchiani family. Tony and Maria Torchiani relocate with their sons Mario and Alberto in 1902. Childhood friends already in Chicago have found the family an apartment and a foundry job for Tony. Although the initial transition is smooth, over time nothing quite works out. Wages are higher in America, but expenses are greater, and just as Tony begins to save money, he gets laid off. After more years of labor he finally saves almost enough for a vegetable stand when Maria becomes pregnant and medical expenses must be paid. Just as he has recovered his finances, the baby dies and Maria becomes ill. Soon after, Tony loses his job entirely and only after stressful months finds work as a janitor, with pay that just meets basic living expenses. By this time Mario, the oldest son, has quit school after being twice held back in seventh grade. Defying his parents, he lies about his age and gets a foundry job. His financial contributions help, but he really makes a difference when he becomes a gangster, an identity he keeps a secret from his family. An associate of an important bootlegger, he soon earns the moniker, "Mario, the Enforcer." Younger son Alberto, by contrast, goes to college and becomes a lawyer. He struggles for several years because of prejudice against Italians, but finally gets a job with a Detroit law firm and is eventually elected to the bench. Through his romance with Carlotta Benevenuti, the daughter of Northern Italian merchants, the novel takes up the issue of prejudices within the Italian immigrant community based upon social origin and regional affiliation. The dramatic climax of the novel comes when Mario, accused of a gangland murder, is tried in Alberto's court. Since he pleads guilty, Mario must sentence his brother to life in prison if he is not to violate his office. While the novel attempts a rich portrait of social life in the Italian immigrant community, it includes little physical description. References are made to the Italian neighborhood centered on Taylor and Halsted streets and to Hull House and the role it plays for Maria, Mario, and Alberto.

510. Halper, Albert. *The Chute*. New York: Viking Press, 1937. 558pp.
Paul Sussman, the son of Sam, a tobacconist, fills orders at the Golden Rule Mail Order Company. His sister Rae wants to help him by giving him money to go to architectural school, but abandons this project when she falls in love and begins to save for her marriage. Paul falls in love with Rosanna Puccini, a packager at Golden Rule, however, his Jewish parents object to this alliance with a "goy" and his inability to win financial independence means he must obey them. Halper evokes the grim reality of people like Paul and his acquaintances who work at unsatisfying jobs, while at the same time he reveals the power of the company owners, union, and political bosses, displaying the ways socio-economics, ethnicity, and religion shape every aspect of working-class people's lives.

511. Halper, Albert. *The Foundry*. New York: Viking Press, 1934. 499pp.

One year at the Fort Dearborn Electrotype Foundry in Chicago is captured in this novel about factory work (autumn 1928 to autumn 1929). The lives of a whole range of characters are detailed, from the foundry owners to the newest apprentice. Although the main focus is work life, some aspects of the characters' home life are conveyed (one character boards with a widow who he eventually marries; another man buys a piece of land outside the city, constructs a Sears garage kit on the property and moves into it with his wife as their new home; and one of the firm's partners is troubled by the end of a love affair and commits suicide). Workplace challenges include efficiency studies and the rising power of the union that forces difficult collective bargaining agreements. A few entertainments are described, including a group outing to a vaudeville theater and a company picnic. Halper evokes a workplace environment that, by the time he published his novel, was dramatically disrupted by the Depression and he leaves a nuanced record of late 1920s social history.

512. Halper, Albert. *The Golden Watch*. Illustrated by Aaron Bohrod. New York: Holt, 1953. 246pp.

Set in Chicago in the first decade of the twentieth century, this episodic novel consists of incidents in the life of David, a boy growing up on Chicago's West Side, and continues through his high school graduation. Although some of the events are tragic (a young man living in a nearby boarding house starves to death and a man who has endeared himself to the neighborhood is taken back to the insane asylum from which he had escaped), the general tone is one of fond nostalgia. David's family is Jewish and he has an extensive network of relatives who visit occasionally from other cities. He is near the middle of a family of seven children and his father is an unsuccessful grocer who operates his business out of a rented building on Lake Street, on the top floors of which he houses his family. The novel illustrates the intimacy of neighborhood life and the pressures to conform to social norms. Job training and scholarship programs that would become common later are not in place and David and his brothers' only options are to engage in some form of mercantilism to earn a living. The physical constraints accompanying genteel poverty are made obvious without being explicitly stated and include anxiety over money, reduced access to health care, and extremely limited leisure time.

513. Halper, Albert. *The Little People*. New York: Harper and Brothers, 1942. 402pp.

This novel depicts a large department store, Richard T. Sutton and Company, located in the Loop on State Street, during the Depression. Its more than four hundred pages present a surprising amount of detail about the store, its merchandise, internal operations, and the people who work there. At the outset, the store has much in common with those of the late nineteenth century in terms of architecture and operations, but near the end of the novel it moves into a brand-new facility on Michigan Avenue. Although most of the novel is set inside the store, enough description is given of employee work commutes and domestic establishments to illustrate working-class life. Socializing in dance halls, saloons, movie theaters, and apartments is described, as well as the personal troubles and minor achievements that motivate the novel's characters. Whether at the store or outside of work, race, ethnicity, and social class have a major impact, shaping home environments and the interactions of staff members with each other, management, and customers. For instance, one of the African-American employees is fired because her skin is considered too dark to be presentable on the sales floor.

514. Halper, Albert. *On the Shore; A Young Writer Remembering Chicago*. New York: Viking Press, 1934. 257pp.

Through these fifteen semi-autobiographical short stories about his family told from the viewpoint of a boy, Halper captures immigrant Chicago of the early twentieth century. The protagonist's father owns a grocery store on Lake Street where the boy spends time, as well as at Randolph Street wholesale market, the lake shore, and Union Park. Ethnicities in the book tend to be Slavic, Irish, German, Swedish, and Dutch. African-Americans appear on the margins of the lives of the people in these stories, although a little boy witnesses the murder of an African-American man and the prompt cover-up of the crime.

515. Halper, Albert. *Sons of the Fathers*. New York: Harper and Brothers, 1940. 431pp.

Twenty years before the story's action Saul Bergmann fled Russia to avoid conscription into the Russian army. Settling in Chicago, he opened a grocery store on Kedzie Avenue, became a part of the immigrant neighborhood, and remained faithful to his Jewish faith, attending temple and socializing with other Russian Jews. When the United States enters World War I, everything changes. New animosities are aroused among ethnic groups and Saul's sons Ben and Milton need to decide whether to accept conscription. A number of characters, including Saul, articulate anti-war, isolationist positions and rail at the intimate link between capitalist expansion and war. Eventually, Milton enlists to try for a commission in the ordnance corps. Ben, however, believing that agricultural laborers will be exempt from the draft, farms land in an isolated part of Montana. Milton is killed in the final weeks of the war and Bergmann family members gather on Armistice Day to pray for him, while their neighborhood rings with the shouts of victory. Halper vividly evokes neighborhood life and the emotional toll of a European war on a neighborhood of European immigrants.

516. Ham, Roswell G. *Account Overdue*. London, U.K.: Neville Spearman, 1953. 215pp.

Originally published in the United States as *The Gifted* (see entry 517).

517. Ham, Roswell. *The Gifted*. New York: Avon Books, 1952. 191pp.

Although the main action of this novel occurs at a Chicago New Year's Eve party ushering in 1952, the social history of the previous thirty years is presented through the novel's flashbacks. Most of the ten people attending the party are members of "The Group," a circle of friends at whose center is Bill Cabot. In their thirties, educated at private schools and colleges, and possessed of comfortable incomes (whether earned or inherited), The Group lives and socializes in a region with the boundaries of Lincoln Park, North State Street, Lake Shore Drive, and the Drake Hotel. Approximately the first half of the novel details the backgrounds of each person attending the party. Most of the characters are Chicago natives, and their life stories include parents with meat packing fortunes or other connections typical of Chicago. The main concern of the characters is mostly with sexual and marital relations. Homosexuality and cross-dressing are touched upon and attitudes toward premarital and extramarital sex and out-of-wedlock pregnancy are revealed.

518. Hansen, Harry. *Your Life Lies Before You*. New York: Harcourt, Brace, 1935. 305pp.

In this coming-of-age novel, a young, small-town newspaper reporter moves to Chicago and explores opportunities that lead him to self-understanding. David Kinsman's hometown is on the Mississippi River. Still living with his parents as a twenty-one-year-old, Kinsman works as a riverboat reporter. The newsmen in his office and almost everyone in town consider Chicago to be the center of the Midwest and the source of information and entertainment. Avocationally, Kinsman is interested in music and, in that field as well, Chicago is the focus. Stella Sylvester, the daughter of his violin teacher with whom he is infatuated, is sent to study music in Chicago and David decides he must also attempt success in the larger world and he obtains a letter of introduction to Chicago reporter "Pop" Finlay, whose wife operates a boarding house in their residence for writers. David boards with the Finlays in their large, converted brownstone on the South Side in the Grand Boulevard District and gets his first job as a picture chaser for the *Chicago Bulletin*. When tragedies strike, he must secure photographs for story illustrations, even if he has to steal them from family members. He socializes with Stella, who lives in a mansion converted to a boarding house and dates women in his own boarding house, particularly Paula Harley, who teaches him about the settlement house movement. While Stella thinks David is ignoring his musical gift, Paula believes he should devote himself to studying law to aid the under-privileged. David willingly disrupts his city life at Stella's request, when she invites him to a Midwestern choral festival with a massed male chorus of two thousand voices that will be held in their town, where her father will conduct one of his own compositions in which Stella will solo. Taking a leave of absence from his job, David returns with Stella for the rehearsal weeks, gets his hometown job back, and again takes violin lessons from Professor Sylvester. Although the concert is a great success, soon afterwards Stella sickens from a virus and dies, then Professor Sylvester has a nervous breakdown. Bereft of Stella and his teacher, David soon tires of his hometown and at the end of the book plans to return to Chicago. The novel illustrates the position of Chicago as a center for social idealism, art, and music, while presenting examples of the lives given over to their service.

519. Hanson, Harvey. *Game Time*. New York: Watts, 1975. 87pp.

Through the eyes of the thirteen-year-old, African-American protagonist of this novel for children, prejudice in 1970s Chicago is explored. Skip Howard lives with his parents at 704 East Fifty-first Street near the intersection with Vincennes. To earn the money to give him every possible opportunity, his mother operates a beauty parlor out of the living room and his father works two eight-hour jobs, one in a factory and one as a night watchman. Skip is good in school and his parents have also paid for music and dance lessons. Although his parents want him to become a lawyer or physician, secretly Skip prefers to think of himself as a future musician or actor. His social life is difficult since his skin color is very dark and attracts negative comments from other African-American children. Furthermore, as a good boy, he would never fit into the gang culture of his peers who spend time on neighborhood streets. He is an organist for his church and attends church camp, but he gets more of a chance to learn about life outside his home neighborhood when he represents his school in a speech contest and when his parents force him to learn to swim by getting him a Hyde Park YMCA membership. In Hyde Park, he meets boys who are part of the African-American middle-class and begins to realize that there are other boys interested in school and music and that there is a life for African-Americans outside the ghetto.

520. Hapgood, Hutchins. *An Anarchist Woman*. New York: Duffield, 1909. 308pp.

In a preface, the author describes his novel as a "natural history" of anarchism and the work is written like a sociological report in which the main characters talk about their lives. Marie, the eponymous anarchist woman, is the daughter of an alcoholic German machinist and an abusive, French-German mother. Born in 1884 on Chicago's West Side, Marie had a miserable life, being forced to work at twelve, until, as a seventeen-year-old maid, she meets Katie, a German cook. Katie impresses Marie for her self-respect, for embracing life, and for ignoring social conventions, particularly those concerning sex. While working in the same household they meet Terry, a thirty-five-year-old Irish idealist who is the brother of their employer. Terry believes there is no honest labor in a capitalist society. To work for a wage is to be enslaved to a wealthy capitalist and to be a manager in such a system is to be a slave master. The three create a communal household with Katie paying the rent and they live in this fashion over a seven-year period, with the house becoming a meeting place for free-thinkers. Terry devotes himself to self-understanding and social analysis, as he tries to raise the self-awareness of those around him. He presents speeches at the Chicago Social Science League and meets with Emma Goldman, Peter Kropotkin, and Bill Haywood on their visits to Chicago. Through his influence, Marie rejects the conventions of marriage, briefly works as a prostitute, and later enters into an open sexual relationship with Terry. The two eventually disagree over Terry's unwillingness to endorse any human society, and Marie's need to embrace life and humanity. She leaves Chicago for California, to live a natural existence in the wild with like-minded people who fish and forage for their food. Eventually she enters domestic service in San Francisco, having become a self-aware, confident person like Katie. The novel provides an extensive description of anarchist culture as it may have existed in Chicago and the social conditions, including the challenges faced by new immigrants, which made Chicago receptive to new social and political movements. In addition to a discussion of prostitution, several characters use illicit drugs.

521. Harris, Frank. *The Bomb*. New York: Mitchell Kennerley, 1909. 312pp.

In this fictionalized account of the 1886 Haymarket Riot, told through the voice of a first-person protagonist, Harris tries to portray as accurately as possible the events leading up to the bombing and the motivations of the participants. Harris' presentation of the bomber, his associates, and the major figures in anarchist and socialist movements in sympathetic and even heroic terms, would have seemed outrageous to an American audience in the years immediately following the incident. However, by the time Harris published his book, attitudes had changed dramatically. Illinois Governor John P. Altgeld had pardoned the two surviving "conspirators" and condemned the trial as a miscarriage of justice. Harris was not in Chicago during the riots, but lived in Chicago to gather information on which to base his account. Protagonist Rudolph Schnaubelt, an actual historical figure who disappeared after the riot, threw the bomb in Harris' account, even though his research never provided enough evidence to identify the bomb thrower. A German immigrant, Schnaubelt arrives in Manhattan and finds work as a laborer, only to be mistreated and cheated. His avocation of writing newspaper articles about the experience of working men for German-American newspapers, leads to a job in Chicago with the *Arbeiter Zeitung*. After witnessing the beatings and shootings inflicted by policemen on men, women, and children attending worker assemblies, he embraces the position of Louis Lingg, the bomb creator, that sometimes the only response to violence is violence. Harris highlights the role of the Chicago press, in intensifying hostility toward immigrant workers and includes brief, telling accounts of the kinds of suffering that were considered commonplace at the time, including job-related deaths due to grossly unsafe working conditions. His account of social life among Chicago immigrant workers is convincing, as is his evocation of the various philosophical positions taken by highly educated and cultured men motivated by personal integrity to work for the good of everyone in a society that respected only the concerns of wealth and selfish personal enrichment.

522. Harrison William. *In a Wild Sanctuary*. New York: William Morrow, 1969. 320pp.

Four young men—Adler, Clive, Pless, and Stoker—culturally alienated during the Vietnam War, and each social misfits for different reasons, make a suicide pact as undergraduates at the University of Chicago. As an act of defiance toward a social order that will co-opt their intelligence and creativity for evil ends, they agree to commit suicide and die leaving no explanation. After the first two deaths, Stoker's father Marty, a Vietnam veteran, identifies the ring leader of the pact and prevents further deaths. Much of the novel is set outside Chicago as the boys have flashbacks about their childhoods and take a trip with each other, meeting in Las Vegas, and traveling back to school together. The Chicago sections focus on undergraduate life and are often dominated by sexual matters (fantasies as well as intercourse). Although the young men vaunt political rhetoric, the novel implies that psychosexual pathology (including repressed homosexuality and masochism) really motivates their actions.

523. Hart, Frank J. *The Speed Boy: A Story of the Big League*. Illustrated by Charles Copeland. Chicago: Lakewood House, 1938. 226pp.

Always told that professional sports are ungentlemanly endeavors to be avoided by college students and the college-educated, a new college graduate warily enters the world of professional baseball. Jack Kelway is recruited for the Chicago White Sox after the last baseball game of his college career. A product of suburban Chicago, Kelway likes the idea of promoting his city through winning baseball games, but has long heard college coaches and professors denigrate professional sports. He confers with his friend Alan Graham who had been expelled from college for playing summer baseball with a professional team, and with Alan's encouragement accepts a contract with the White Sox. During most of this young adult novel Jack is on the road, in training camp, or winning games. The novel covers an entire season's play, at the end of which the White Sox are the national champions, due in part to Jack's pitching. The main message is that professional sports are not disreputable. By the end of the book, Jack's performance has so impressed a professor at Alan's former college that he pledges to try to get the rules preventing college athletes from playing baseball in summer with professional teams abolished.

524. Hawkins, Odie. *Chicago Hustle*. Los Angeles: Holloway House, 1977. 224pp.

Characters with names like "Monkeydude" populate this novel set on Chicago's South Side in the 1970s in a neighborhood near Forth-seventh Street and Indiana Avenue. The main character, con man Elijah Brookes, works a series of successful scams and commits a number of small crimes, accumulating funds to start a legitimate business. Even after he opens his business, however, he cannot resist robbing an illegal gambling parlor using a gun-carrying buddy. He is caught, and sentenced to a year in prison; a thirty-one-year-old when he gets out, he can only get a job as a custodian and borrows money from a drug dealer to start living the high life for which his illegal activities had formerly paid. When he cannot pay the money back his life is in danger. The novel is filled with descriptions of social venues, including nightclubs and restaurants. Through explicit descriptions of sexual intercourse and Elijah's attitudes toward women, gender issues are touched upon.

525. Hawthorne, Julian. *Humors of the Fair*. Illustrated by Will E. Chapin. Chicago: Weeks, 1893. 205pp.

This highly opinionated first-person account of the fair is written from the perspective of a "Connecticut Yankee." The work differs from many physical descriptions of the fair in focusing on the people working, visiting, and on exhibit at the fair. Workers include the "Chair Wheelers," responsible for pushing visitors around in hired wicker wheelchairs; the "Gatemen," who take tickets; and the "Columbian Guards," who answer questions. The visitors represent the common man in the United States and the narrator remarks on the skepticism with which attendees greet every aspect of the fair (for instance, one visitor claims that the Zulus are actually costumed African-Americans). Not surprisingly, the narrator spends a great deal of time making observations about the inhabitants of the world villages on display at the fair and describes acquaintanceships that spring up between the visitors and those on exhibit. The only plot element in the novel is a flirtation between the narrator and Hildegaard [sic], a young woman he has known for the past seventeen years, since she was a child. In the narrator's eyes, Hildegaard epitomizes the American girl—she has healthy appetites, a capacity for enjoying both the country and the city, and intelligence. Although Hildegaard's observations on the fair are treated with esteem, it is the narrator's criticism of the fine art exhibits that take precedence. The novel concludes with a description of a nighttime electrical illumination and Hildegaard's reaction, which leads to the narrator's paean celebrating the fair and praising the nation responsible for its creation.

526. Hecht, Ben. *Broken Necks, Containing More "1001 Afternoons."* Chicago: Pascal Covici, Publisher, 1926. 344pp.

Mostly previously published in the *Chicago Daily News*, these thirty short stories and sketches reflect Hecht's perspective on 1920s Chicago and touch on racial prejudice, the influence of movies and jazz culture, and the continuing novelty of skyscrapers.

527. Hecht, Ben. *Count Bruga*. New York: Boni and Liveright, 1926. 319pp.

Written in the form of a detective story in which the main character incidentally solves the question of what happened to a magician named Pannini, this book is a thinly fictionalized take on the biography of Maxwell Bodenheim. The two writers had been friends in Chicago and this satirical work brought about the final rupture in their acquaintanceship. Like Bodenheim, the main character here, Jules Ganz, comes to Chicago to make his name, even though for Ganz that involves assuming the title Count Bruga. Ganz' search for literary fame is aided by his skill, but thwarted by his love of food and drink and he fritters away his talent. Although Bodenheim was outraged by the book, readers will glean a sense of literary Chicago in the 1920s.

528. Hecht, Ben. *Erik Dorn*. New York: Putnam's Sons, 1921. 409pp.

Considered a key work of the Chicago renaissance that established Hecht's reputation, this book evokes the cultural currents of the World War I era, drawing upon Hecht's own experiences as a Chicago journalist and war correspondent. Dorn, a man in his thirties, is filled with a self-acknowledged ennui, from which he feels unable to escape; neither his career as a journalist, nor his marriage satisfy him or provide meaning. An affair with Rachel Laskin turns into a selfish exercise to feel something other than boredom and even his murder of George Hazlitt, the lawyer who actually does love Rachel, is less an expression of jealousy, than an attempt at a passionate act that fails for its lack of emotional content. Even the demands of wartime journalism fail to rouse Dorn from his boredom and he returns to Chicago to find his wife gone, his lover Rachel irremediably alienated, and his job a torture after the excitement of wartime assignments. In Dorn, Hecht characterized his generation.

529. Hecht, Ben. *Gargoyles*. New York: Boni and Liveright, 1922. 346pp.

This attack on sexual hypocrisy focuses on the experience of George Basine, a young man living in Chicago with his two sisters and parents. Even though Basine sometimes acts on his sexual impulses by hiring prostitutes, in general he separates his feelings from the rest of his life and shares a social code of behavior in which such feelings are denied. With the approach of World War I, Basine becomes an obsessed war bond salesman. Basine's passions, which may have been consumed in sexual expression, are vented instead in hating Germans and he never develops a fully integrated personality.

530. Hecht, Ben. *Humpty Dumpty*. New York: Boni and Liveright, 1924. 383pp.

Considered a rewrite of Erik Dorn by critics, this semi-autobiographical novel's hero is Kent Savaron, who decides to leave his Wisconsin hometown to pursue his literary ambitions in Chicago. The plot traces his attempts to establish a career in journalism, and deal with the demands of friendship and marriage. The book evokes 1920s Chicago.

531. Hecht, Ben. *A Thousand and One Afternoons in Chicago*. Designed and illustrated by Herman Rosse. Chicago: Covici-McGee, 1922. 289pp.

This collection of pieces ran in the *Chicago Daily News* as a column with the same name and presents Hecht's impressions of Chicago garnered from walking its streets, patronizing its businesses, and attending public events. Any accounts of domestic life are usually presented in the context of a crime. Each piece tells a story, based on a real life person or event, but so thoroughly translated through Hecht as to be unclassifiable as reportage.

532. Heed, Rufus. *Ghosts Never Die*. New York: Vantage Press, 1954. 180pp.

In this family murder mystery, Laverne has found out that her brother-in-law Drake Maxwell is having an affair with the Latina interior decorator she hired to do over her apartment. She feels responsible since Drake met Lupe through her and tries to get Gregory Kent, Drake's best friend, to talk Drake out of the affair. Kent is described as the only holder of a doctorate on a police force in the United States. He is also an epicurean and a physician. Then, Drake dies at a dinner party and Kent solves the murder. Set in 1950s Chicago, the novel contrasts interiors, wardrobes, and menus of educated and reliable people with those characterized as social upstarts like Lupe, whose love of colorful décor and clothing was Laverne's first reliable warning that she was not trustworthy.

533. Heeler, Ward [pseud.]. *The Election: Chicago-Style*. Chicago: Feature, 1977. 166pp.

This paperback exposé, written in the form of a novel, was supposedly authored anonymously by a Chicago judge frustrated with polling abuses. No further information available.

534. Herber, William. *The Almost Dead*. A Main Line Mystery. Philadelphia: Lippincott, 1957. 222pp.

Only the first part of this 1950s novel that evokes both the Red Scare and tedium of a culture centered on the "man in the gray-flannel suit" is set in Chicago. Stacy Andrews, a corporate lawyer working for a large firm in the Loop, is one such conservatively garbed man at the beginning of the novel. An ex-Marine who was twice enlisted, the twenty-nine-year-old Andrews has only worked as a lawyer for a few years, but decides to give up his lucrative job to try to find a more exciting position. On the day he resigns, he leaves his office to happen upon a mysterious street confrontation that leads him into a job involving international intrigue. A German, Jewish-refugee, financier hires Andrews to represent him in Paris delivering microfilm of secret documents to Communist kidnappers to gain the release of his wife. The adventure brings Andrews to a near brush with death and emboldens him to declare his love for Ellen Dorman, an attractive colleague from his old law firm. In addition to descriptions of the Loop, the Near North Side and an opulent, modern, Lake Shore Drive apartment tower, the novel includes details about Andrews' rather squalid living conditions on North Clark Street.

535. Herber, William. *Death Paints a Portrait*. A Main Line Mystery. Philadelphia: Lippincott, 1958. 223pp.

Peter Stark and his partner Charley Bowen had worked to create a successful advertising business, then Charley began drinking and Stark, trying to manage single-handedly, quickly lost the business. Fortunately, Bowen's girlfriend Nita Novak helps Stark find a job as the public relations agent for Peter Van Gelder's Chicago art gallery, one of the most successful in the country. Soon after taking the job, however, Mrs. Van Gelder is poisoned; shortly afterwards Van Gelder's receptionist is stabbed to death. The police suspect Stark and he must try to solve the crimes in self-defense. In addition to Chicago art circles, the novel presents characters that frequent Rush Street bars, introducing a seamy nightlife populated by dissolute young people. The criminal in the novel is a man-hating woman reflecting cultural attitudes of the time period.

536. Herber, William. *King-Sized Murder*. A Main Line Mystery. Philadelphia: Lippincott, 1954. 222pp.

In this crime novel, Chicago private detective James Rehm takes on a simple blackmail case only to be forced into solving a series of murders in which he seems to be implicated. The first murder victim is his client, although that man was merely acting on behalf of a beautiful young woman, Dorothy Haggis, who is being blackmailed over lewd photographs depicting sex acts between her and her estranged husband. When Rehm pieces together the story, he finds thugs and organized crime at the center of the tale and he is able to play Gino Gabaldi, a small-time hoodlum, against Gabaldi's boss, Sam Butler. Slurs over Italian ethnicity and sexual orientation are prominent in many scenes. In his pursuit of the criminals Rehm visits a number of Chicago neighborhoods and though his descriptions are cursory he does sum each of them up, giving a sense of the city in the 1950s.

537. Herber, William. *Live Bait for Murder*. A Main Line Mystery. Philadelphia: Lippincott, 1955. 221pp.

In this Cold War espionage novel Russia's atomic secrets have been stolen and the United States has a chance to get them before the Russians retrieve them. Army veteran Jimmy Rehm, a Chicago private detective, is called back into government service to aid U.S. efforts. Rehm is just about to marry a wealthy, beautiful woman and resents the intrusion on his life. Approximately half of the novel is set in Chicago, with the remainder set aboard trains, in New Orleans, and in Mississippi. The Chicago Museum of Industrial Science serves as one backdrop for espionage activities that involve disguises and altered identification documents. In addition to Chicago's portrayal as an important base for government espionage, the city is shown to be a mercantile hub. Rehm is first disguised as a swimwear salesman and, following the practice of the time, he uses his hotel room to sell swimwear to Chicago department store buyers and uses a beautiful female model while plying the buyers with alcohol.

538. Herbst, Josephine. *Somewhere the Tempest Fell*. New York: Charles Scribner's Sons, 1947. 344pp.

When a jazz trumpeter with organized crime connections begins dating his daughter, an affluent mystery writer begins to realize how insulated his life and those of his friends have become. Adam Snow began writing commercially successful novels after serving in World War I and for many years lived as an expatriate in Italy. Forced back to the United States by World War II, he lives in an upper-class Chicago milieu that includes his wife, children, and a small circle of old friends, including journalist Ralph Johns and his wife's uncle, Henry Rodney, a society interior designer. When Steve Bright begins dating Snow's daughter he is immediately out of place. Appearing to be a man on the make, he engenders a range of reactions from Snow that become refined as he investigates Bright with the assistance of Johns. The daily activities of Snow, his friends, and acquaintances are described in some detail to show how they have distanced themselves from the grittier life of Bright. Snow's preoccupation is his fiction—a friend paints, a woman is absorbed by relationships with much younger men, and the journalist Johns lives only for his news stories, distancing himself from any emotional reaction to the people about whom he writes. The focus on domestic activities and the interior life of characters creates a very rich portrait of life in Chicago among educated, financially secure people.

539. Herrick, Robert. *Chimes*. New York: Macmillan, 1926. 310pp.

Herrick, a University of Chicago faculty member, presents a history of the institution (Eureka University here) from its founding in 1891 through World War I from the point of view of the fictional character Beaman Clavercin. Clavercin arrives on campus, recently graduated from Harvard University, and his experiences at a school with such a long history and traditions informs his observations of Eureka, which initially tend to focus on Eureka's unhealthily rapid growth, the materialistic philosophy of its founders, and the lack of traditions. Much of the novel deals with institutional politics as some of the faculty try to instill standards from the Western academic tradition to countermand the administration's image of the university as a kind of factory turning out educated youths.

540. Herrick, Robert. *The Common Lot*. New York: Macmillan, 1904. 426pp.

In this critique of wealth, Jackson Hart is to inherit his uncle's fortune and his uncle has also paid for Hart's study of architecture at Cornell University and at the Ecole des Beaux Arts. Hart assumes he will be a wealthy man, but when his uncle dies, he leaves Hart only ten thousand dollars and Hart begins to practice architecture with Chicago's most prestigious firm. While he appears to have a satisfying career ahead of him that will earn him respect, while performing a useful social function, he is obsessed with money. His greed so preoccupies him that he overlooks a contractor's shortcuts in constructing an apartment building. Soon after tenants move in, the building burns to the ground, killing several people. The experience awakens Hart's sense of social responsibility and he decides to work to become an asset to society. In addition to the Chicago physical setting, Herrick's book presents debates over social values and appraises the motivations of wealthy Chicagoans admired for their fortunes.

541. Herrick, Robert. *The Gospel of Freedom*. New York: Macmillan, 1898. 287pp.

Although this novel addresses issues of gender, the focus is on even broader social values. Althea Anthon inherits a fortune from her father, a Chicago manufacturer. Inspired by a Harvard professor, she relocates to Paris to participate in the arts community. She is soon disillusioned with the underlying materialism of the artistic endeavor, dependent as it is on a system of patronage. Admiration of her father's clear-cut work ethic brings her back to Chicago and she marries a young businessman, only to discover that he has no principles beyond his materialism. She finally divorces him and devotes herself to a life of philanthropy. Although only part of this novel is set in Chicago, the book presents aspects of upper-class Chicago life in the late nineteenth century.

542. Herrick, Robert. *Homely Lilla*. New York: Harcourt, Brace, 1923. 293pp.

This novel contrasts urban and rural environments and explores female gender roles as they begin to change in the World War I era. Lilla grew up in Wyoming with few social constraints. When she was thirteen, her father died and her mother, who had grown up on the East Coast, decides to move to Chicago in hopes of finding a more social environment than Wyoming can offer. She establishes a household in suburban Lawndale, where Lilla chafes at social norms, but conforms by dressing well, attending church, and graduating high school. She begins college, but transfers to a normal school course to become a schoolteacher. In her first job, school principal Dr. Gordon James courts and eventually marries her. An ambitious man, James soon gets elected to statewide administration posts. Around the outbreak of World War I, Lilla learns about his affair with his young secretary. To avoid divorce, James enlists in the army. Lilla's mother dies soon afterwards and Lilla is free for the first time in her adult life. She buys a horse ranch in Idaho and moves there with her son. Eventually she falls in love with local rancher, John Slawn. James, who had a comfortable war in government jobs, turns up in Idaho asking to be reconciled. When Lilla rejects him, he confesses that he has no job and has spent all his money. Defying convention, she sends him away, and pursues her relationship with John Slawn. Lilla clearly epitomizes the author's conception of the much talked about "new woman" of the time period—self-confident, healthy, natural, and not conforming to popularly held standards of appearance or behavior for women.

543. Herrick, Robert. *Love's Dilemmas*. Chicago: Stone, 1898. 193pp.

Only two of these six short stories are set in upper-class Chicago society and deal with aspects of romance and marriage. In one story, the lovers are separated by a work assignment soon after they meet and must try to adapt letter-writing to convey their deep feelings. Another story illustrates the behind-the-scenes impact of women on the careers of their husbands. Aspects of Chicago social life include literary clubs, book discussion groups, suburban life, and the ability to afford extended travel in Europe.

544. Herrick, Robert. *The Memoirs of an American Citizen*. Illustrated by F.B. Masters. New York: Macmillan, 1905. 351pp.

This fictional memoir of Edward "Van" Harrington's life begins when he arrives as a boy in 1880 Chicago with nothing. From his first job as a grocery wagon driver, over the years he becomes a wealthy meat packer, and later a United Sates senator. Impaneled on the jury trying the accused Haymarket riot conspirators, he describes the bombing and subsequent hysteria in addition to frankly presenting the trial as a miscarriage of justice. However, the experience does not change his personal life. He does not become a reformer or work for improvements for the working poor. Instead, he accepts kudos for his role on the jury, and returns to work increasing his network of business contacts through the novel's end in 1905. In the experiences and reflections of Harrington, Herrick presents the socio-economic conditions that made a few men wealthy and powerful in late-nineteenth-century Chicago, as well as capturing the opinions and attitudes of such people.

545. Herrick, Robert. *One Woman's Life*. New York: Macmillan, 1913. 405pp.

For protagonist Millie Ridge, the Haymarket Riot forces an awareness of the social problems she had formerly ignored. Millie grew up on the West Side of Chicago, but as a sixteen-year-old began to yearn for social prominence and was able to get her family to move to a more fashionable neighborhood. However, instead of marrying a wealthy man, she wed a struggling artist, who took her to New York and Paris, even though he remained poor. She makes a second marriage that brings her back to Chicago and, newly socially aware after the Haymarket Riot, she interests herself in the trial and becomes a courtroom spectator. This leads to a sentimental attachment to Louis Lingg, the maker of the bomb thrown during the riot. However, by the time Lingg is found dead in his cell, Ridge has once again become preoccupied with her private life. Through the life of Millie Ridge, the novel illustrates the shallowness of a social climber and the ways such people trivialize social problems.

546. Herrick, Robert. *Waste*. New York: Harcourt, Brace, 1924. 449pp.

Only portions of this novel tracing more than forty years of United States cultural history are set in Chicago. Protagonist Jarvis Thornton is a New York based architect with a philosophical bent who spends extended periods of time in Chicago. His sojourn in the city around the time of the Columbian Exposition is described in some detail, as well as the aftermath of the fair in labor unrest and the destruction of the fairgrounds. The novelist uses the exposition as a symbol of cultural excesses that will eventually lead to nationwide economic collapse.

547. Herrick, Robert. *The Web of Life*. New York: Macmillan, 1900. 356pp.

As in other of his novels, Herrick here explores themes of social responsibility and engagement. However, unlike some of his work, this story includes extensive descriptions of Chicago events and presents more varied social settings. Protagonist Howard Sommers moves from Ohio to Chicago to become part of a medical practice serving an affluent clientele. The skilled young surgeon responds deeply to the economic depression that followed the Columbian Exposition and establishes a medical practice to assist the poor. He does not make a success of his project, in part because his patients identify his condescending self-sacrifice, and in part because they distrust scientific medicine. He eventually abandons his practice and takes up residence in one of the abandoned World's Fair ticket booths. From this abode, he devotes himself to loving Alves Preston, the wife of a derelict laborer. Fearing that she is holding him back, Alves eventually commits suicide, after which Sommers leaves Chicago to practice military medicine in Cuba during the Spanish-American War. When he returns to the city, he marries heiress Louise Hitchcock and establishes a middle-class medical practice, claiming that he has removed himself from the evils of working for a profit, since he is not dependent on his earnings.

548. Herter, Lori. *No Time for Love*. Candlelight Romance, 574. New York: Dell, 1980. 187pp.

This romance novel for middle-aged women features Lorelei Lawrence, a violinist with The Chicago Philharmonic Orchestra. Lawrence has stopped longing for love, focusing on the demands of her profession. When she is promoted to second chair, her new physical proximity to violinist Peter Sutherland, leads to romance. The novel's narrow focus prevents a very full use of the Chicago setting.

549. Hill, Agnes Leonard (Scanland). *Heights and Depths*. Chicago: Sumner, 1871. 271pp.

This novel for young adults is a morality tale that teaches the importance of gentlemanly behavior for boys and the benefits of domestic skills for girls. At the beginning of the novel twelve-year-old Janet Soyer lives with her eighteen-year-old sister Lizzie and alcoholic teamster father Michael. Her mother is confined to an insane asylum after the death of infant Nell. After Michael dies in a drunken accident, Janet must find a way to support the household. Too young to secure a regular job, her recently married Sunday schoolteacher, Mrs. Ruth Langdon, agrees to hire her sister Lizzie. Eventually, Janet is also taken into the Langdon household. Despite her admiration for Mrs. Langdon, she finds middle-class family life, that includes unmarried sisters and other relatives, socially difficult. However, when she decides to live in the boarding house run by the slovenly Mrs. Mulaney and enjoy some independence, she comes to regret her decision and pleads to return to the discipline of well-ordered, middle-class domesticity. Soon returning to the Langdons, Mrs. Langdon helps her open an "infant school." The novel provides no physical description of Chicago, but details the operations of several very different households.

550. Hinrichsen, William H. *Plots and Penalties*. Chicago: Rhodes and McClure, 1902. 458pp.

These short stories, originally published in the *Chicago Sunday Inter-Ocean*, are all fictional accounts of actual political and legislative events in Illinois history. Many of the works are set in Springfield, however, the offices of Chicago lawyers and political committees are frequently mentioned.

551. Hix, J. Emile. *Can a Man Live Forever?* Chicago: Western News, 1898. 143pp.

In this futurist novel set in the early twentieth century, a national institute of science holds organizational meetings in Chicago. Created by a legislative act in 1900, the institute gets organized with international publicity at Windermere Hotel. The rather extensive list of people appointed to various divisions of the institute includes many Chicagoans, as well as such historical figures as Thomas A. Edison. Even though the institute moves to Pueblo, New Mexico, the founding in Chicago is considered so significant that wealthy Chicagoan P. D. Armour donates money for a lake-front monument. Expressing an intense faith in the abilities of science to overcome human ills, much of the book is devoted to the rapid achievements of the institute: in 1901 money, land, and labor problems are solved; shortly after this construction begins on macadamized roads and electric powered trains; by 1904 crimes are no longer being committed since the institute has helped civilization progress beyond such behavior. The institute's first major discovery is a method for doubling longevity through a blood purification procedure that, once it is perfected, will give perpetual life for anyone who submits to the treatment. Clearly the identification of Chicago with scientific industrial manufacturing and forward-thinking inspired the city's use as the venue for the organizational meetings of the institute.

552. Hjerstedt, Gunard [Day Keene, pseud.]. *Chicago 11*. New York: Dell, 1966. 220pp.

When a woman is raped by a gang of men in a Chicago apartment building, a number of lives are affected. In the immediate aftermath, a male resident responding to the victim's screams is stabbed; however the continuing impact on the building tends to bring the residents together in new ways as they realize how interdependent they are for each other's protection. Unfortunately the police investigation also uncovers the criminal pasts of several residents connected to Prohibition-era organized crime. The 1960s Chicago in this novel is a dark, frightening place that is connected to a long tradition of crime and violence in the city.

553. Hjerstedt, Gunard [Day Keene, pseud.]. *To Kiss or Kill*. New York: Fawcett, 1951. 169pp.

Barney Mandell, a heavy-weight fighter, married to a beautiful, wealthy woman, Gale Ebbling, checked himself into a sanatorium when he started hearing voices. Told that he has recovered, and released from the hospital after two years, he is surprised when his wife is not there to greet him. Within twenty-four hours he awakes in his room and finds a blonde woman, Cherry Marvin, naked and dead on his bathroom floor. Although he remembers talking to her in a bar the previous night, he has no memory of anything else except that she said she had always wanted to have sex with a prizefighter. The men who investigate the crime are Jim Graziano, the house detective at the furnished hotel where Barney lives, and Chicago Police Inspector Carlton. However, the FBI is soon involved for surprising reasons involving a wealthy uncle Mandell never knew. The Chicago of this novel is set in barrooms, furnished hotels, and neighborhoods of low entertainments and pawnshops.

554. Holley, Marietta. *Samantha at the World's Fair, by Josiah Allen's Wife*. Illustrated by Baron C. de Grimm. New York: Funk and Wagnalls, 1893. 694pp.

One of a series of books featuring "Josiah Allen's wife," in this work the Allens travel to the Columbian Exposition. Besides Josiah and Samantha Allen, the party includes their son Thomas Jefferson, daughter-in-law Maggie, and nephew Christopher Columbus. The first one hundred pages are set in the Allens' hometown of Jonesboro, New York, where relatives visit on their way to and from the fair, and townsmen describe their World's Fair experience. One lengthy chapter articulates both sides of the debate over whether the fairgrounds should be open on Sunday, a controversy at the time. Samantha interjects her negative opinions about fairgoers who buy entirely new wardrobes for the trip, try to camp in a tent to save money, and spend too much money on souvenirs. With everyone they know having gone or going to the fair, the Allens decide they must make the journey, as well. Arriving by train, they stay in a boarding house and their fellow boarders and boarding house life are described. One of the regular residents delivers lengthy monologues about the importance of Chicago, filling his perorations with facts and figures about population and industry. As in other novels of this kind, the fairgrounds are fully described and several notables the Allens meet are mentioned. The work is distinctive for Samantha's convictions on women's rights and her subtle attacks on Josiah's male chauvinism. In the most amusing of these Josiah becomes enraged when a male ostrich is pointed out who freely participates in "women's work" by keeping the eggs in a nest warm. There is little description of Chicago beyond the fairgrounds. In addition to inspiring dreams of other trips, the fair inspires romances for a number of the Allens' acquaintances.

555. Holmes, M. E. Mrs. *A Desperate Woman*. Chicago: Laird and Lee 1886. 174pp.

This convoluted melodrama is physically set in Chicago, although it includes no distinctive physical descriptions. Innocent, young Myrtle Blake works in a Chicago pencil factory to support her dying mother. When her father died several years before, to everyone's surprise, he left no money and mother and daughter went from affluence to poverty. Myrtle's situation worsens when Bryce Willard, agent for the tenement owner Ansel Grey, evicts her and her mother. The shock kills Mrs. Blake and while Myrtle is emotionally prostrated, Willard tries to force her to marry him. Fortunately, Grey appears, fires Willard immediately, and promptly falls in love with Myrtle. Willard vows revenge and is aided by Blanche Vansant, Grey's secretary who is secretly in love with him. Despite saving Myrtle, Grey has a questionable character, evidenced by his cheating Myrtle's father out of his money and having him falsely imprisoned. The highly melodramatic plot includes a second-nephew to Grey, named Percy, with identical looks who is good. There are also false weddings, stabbings, imprisonment in an insane asylum, and many characters who appear dead, only to reappear alive. This happens twice to Myrtle's father who eventually goes mad after a train crash, wanders in the West, is discovered by Ansel Grey, nursed back to health after an Indian attack and lives to forgive Ansel, freeing Myrtle from guilt over falling in love with Percy and her father's interdiction that she have nothing to do with anyone related to Ansel Grey. Although the plot is filled with unbelievable coincidences and behavior, the author evokes some of the helplessness of laborers and women and captures the milieu of working-class Chicago.

556. Holt, Alfred Hubbard. *Hubbard's Trail*. Chicago: Erle Press, 1952. 319pp.

This fictionalized biography of Gurdon S. Hubbard, a man important to the settlement of Illinois and the development of Chicago, begins with Hubbard's first appearance in Illinois as a sixteen-year-old in 1818 as an employee of John Jacob Astor's American Fur Company. He was eventually named superintendent of the Illinois River Trading Posts, but as Illinois transitioned from a frontier to agrarian state, the fur trade came to an end and Hubbard moved to Chicago where he became a meat packer and, later, got involved in other businesses, including banking, importing, insurance, and shipping. The Chicago fire wiped out his fortune and by the end of the novel he is ill, losing his eyesight, and too old to start over. The Chicago section gives some sense of social life before the Civil War and includes vignettes of individuals who would become nationally prominent, such as John Kinzie and Abraham Lincoln.

557. Holt, Isabella. *Aunt Jessie*. Indianapolis: Bobbs-Merrill, 1942. 292pp.

Covering the period 1912 through the World War II era, this novel presents cultural and social history through the Kendall family, dealing with the impact of changing cultural values. Walter Kendall and his wife Ann each come from wealthy families and have devoted themselves to the arts—Walter is a painter and Ann a patroness of poets and artists. Ann is particularly devoted to Walter's cousin Alastair. After a disastrous review of Alastair's gallery exhibitions in Chicago and in New York the year following at the Armory Show, Ann and Alastair decide to spend time in Paris, in the hope that Alastair will be inspired by new artistic trends. In her absence, Jessie arranges for Alastair's sister, Aunt Jessie, to look after her three children (Theodosia, Benjy, and Alastair) and her house on Erie Street. Jessie has lived in rural seclusion for years, after a disastrous marriage. In contrast to her brother, she upholds earlier, Victorian, social values and her influence is a counterweight to the liberal, bohemian values of Ann and Walter. Ann eventually divorces Walter, marries a Swiss poet and takes up residence in Europe. Unable to count on the independent incomes on which their parents relied, the Kendall children enter the workforce. Theodosia supports herself as a commercial artist. Jessie marries for love to a wealthy Chicago banker and Benjy gets a job in his firm, rising to ever greater levels of affluence. The novel presents the social expectations of upper-class Chicagoans and the way cultural values are maintained through subtle censure. Although much of the action occurs before 1929, when the Depression comes, the affluence of the extended Kendall family seems hardly impaired.

558. Holt, Isabella. *The Marriotts and the Powells: A Tribal Chronicle*. New York: Macmillan, 1921. 328pp.

One of a series of novels about members of a Midwestern family, this work deals with the second and third generation of the Marriotts, whose Chicago branch was established by Joshua and his headstrong wife Lucinda. Joshua established a factory and while he fought in the Civil

War, Lucinda convinced him to let her invest in real estate, contributing significantly to the holdings that would make them wealthy in the 1880s. By the early 1900s, when this story begins, Lucinda is dead and Joshua is a daydreaming old man. His oldest son, Tolman, manages family businesses and has several, strong-willed children, including Josie and Fanning. Joshua's youngest son, Edgar, was poised to become a United States senator, until his wife petitioned him for divorce. Disgraced by the scandal, he had a nervous breakdown, and lives as a semi-invalid in his father's house with his son Edgar, II. In 1905, New England relatives come for a visit. Amy, the daughter of Joshua's brother Ezra and her husband Vesey Powell, travel with their children, Herbert, Marriott (Mat), and Diantha. Powell, a salesman of shady investments, was driven out of their hometown and hopes that Marriott money will make one of his schemes successful. Although the Marriotts see through Powell, Tolman and Edgar take an interest in their relative Amy and her children. As heredity and the development of character become an interest of Edgar's, he brings Fanning, Josie, Mat, and Diantha together to observe their interactions. However, Edgar is most interested in Diantha. He watches as she falls in love with Fanning. Then, long after her hopes are dashed, in part by family opposition, she ends up marrying Edgar's son. Although political views concerning the distribution of wealth, management of natural resources, and, later, entrance into World War I, are introduced to create tensions among characters, they are shallowly described in what is essentially a romance novel. The novel includes descriptions of social attitudes, events, and clothing, but physical setting, except for establishing the location of various houses and neighborhoods, is relatively unimportant in the work.

559. Holt, Isabella. *A Visit to Pay*. Indianapolis: Bobbs-Merrill, 1939. 329pp.
This story of family life focuses on two generations of the Converses. Cousins, Emily and Paulina, were known as great beauties in society. Similar in appearance, they married very different men. Emily wed the respectable businessman Walter Morlock who has family connections and intelligence befitting the tycoon he becomes. Paulina married out of love to Bertram Sadler. Sadler, an embezzler, is caught and jailed and Paulina dies, perhaps out of disillusionment. After the tragic, early death, Emily looks after her cousin's son, Martin Sadler, and later has her husband offer to pay for his education at Harvard. Instead, Martin decides to live with his stepmother, Katherine, a beautiful, but untalented actress. Several years pass until Emily's daughter Peggy, the same age as Martin, and still fond of him, seeks him out with her school chum "Towny" Abercrombie in tow for company. Martin is immediately smitten with Towny, a Chicago debutante. Inspired by his pursuit of Towny, Martin gets a radio job in the midst of the Depression that soon leads to a well-paid, script-writing position. However, Martin soon realizes that he will never measure up to Towny's Lake Forest standards and, indeed, she soon marries a Yale graduate. Peggy then gets her chance at Martin. When he runs into trouble with the sponsor of the radio show for which he is writing, Peggy saves the day through her father's influence. Martin finally acknowledges Peggy's devotion and marries her. The novel includes details about daily life in Chicago during the Depression, particularly about the Sadlers' rented abode in the city, a converted stable off Rush Street.

560. Homewood, Charles [Harry Homewood, pseud.]. *A Matter of Size*. Chicago: O'Hara, 1975. 154pp.
In this novel of international espionage, a Chicago firm is being forced by the Soviet government to manufacture micro-circuitry for computers. Fred Hennessey, a Chicago newspaper columnist and former Secret Service agent, is pressed into gathering information. The situation becomes

much more dangerous than anticipated since some of the city's powerful organized crime figures are involved. Enough description of Chicago is included to provide a convincing backdrop for the action-filled plot.

561. Horan, Kenneth. *It's Not My Problem*. New York: Doubleday Doran, 1938. 266pp.

This first-person account of suburban domestic life is written in diary format, beginning on New Year's Eve and ending on New Year's Day, one year later. Set in the late 1930s, the Depression is waning but the social effects are still a matter of comment for the upper-middle-class family members in the novel. The narrator, a mother of two boarding school students (a boy and a girl), is married to a physician. The unnamed Chicago suburb in which she lives seems to be Evanston. The contributor of a book column to a Chicago newspaper, she also writes novels, one of which appears in print during the course of the book. A graduate of Vassar College, much of the wry humor of the book focuses on the contrast between domestic work (painting closets, gardening, managing an overly familiar domestic) and literary endeavors that bring her honors. She meets the most famous authors of the day (including Aldous Huxley and H. G. Wells) and is invited to teach at a writer's conference on a program with Carl Sandburg and Allen Tate. She considers the household to be suffering from privation since she has only one servant, but the house is large enough to host a party for five hundred people. Much of her life is devoted to socializing. In addition to book readings, lectures, and signings she is involved in a range of organizations. It is clear from the number of literary organizations that book culture is strong during the time period. The book details domestic life in the 1930s and includes some extended descriptions of Chicago. The city plays an important role as the home of social organizations and the venue for literary and musical events for the protagonist and members of her family.

562. Horton, George. *The Long Straight Road*. Illustrated by Troy and Margaret West Kinney. Indianapolis: Bowen-Merrill, 1902. 401pp.

This somewhat misogynistic novel conveys cultural attitudes toward women in the early-twentieth century. Realtor Harry Chapin is a well-connected young man whose uncle was a senator. When his friend, prominent lawyer Edward Crissey, hosts a dinner party, Nellie Aikin, a department store clothing model, is among the guests, Chapin is immediately smitten and they marry within months. Despite Chapin's devotion to his wife, the marriage is far from happy. Nellie finds her husband dull and uninterested in the cultural activities she wishes to pursue with her new leisure. Even though they move into a floor-through apartment in a three-flat building on George Avenue, a block off the lake, she takes no interest in creating a home or starting a family. The Chapin marriage is contrasted unfavorably with that of Edward and Dorothy Crissey and with their upstairs neighbors, the German immigrant Roths, who have several children and a robust family life. Nellie whiles away afternoons with French lessons and joins the Garden City Club where she meets wealthy older men, including an unscrupulous businessman who gets her to agree to use her feminine charms to get Crissey, a city council member, to vote favorably for one of the businessman's projects. Horton pays a great deal of attention to physical and social settings, and there are extended descriptions of an Italian restaurant (presented as the ultimate in bohemian experiences), a theater party, and a social club meeting. A number of atmospheric descriptions of the Chicago sketch the city in various seasons.

563. Hough, Emerson. *John Rawn: Prominent Citizen*. Illustrated by M. Leone Bracker. Indianapolis: Bobbs-Merrill, 1912. 385pp.

In this social and political satire, Chicago is the locus of new products and manufacturing methods transforming the United States. John Rawn, who has spent twenty years working as a railroad clerk in St. Louis, is distinguished only by his sense of entitlement and disregard for his fellows. Quite suddenly he decides to establish himself as one of the country's most influential capitalists. The forty-nine-year-old Rawn claims he has an invention that can transmit and receive electricity without wires and is able to convince wealthy investors to establish the International Power Company with offices in Chicago and Rawn as president earning one hundred thousand dollars a year. He makes certain that his college educated son-in-law, Charles Halsey is the one to take his untested invention and turn it into a working model. Rawn continues to find investors and establish political influence for his company, convincing others that they should value him as highly as he values himself. Building a fortune with ease, he spends most of his time establishing himself in society through charitable gifts and acquiring the trappings of wealth (i.e. a newly constructed Lake Shore Drive mansion in the most fashionable blend of styles, a collection of antiques, and servants). Rawn's fortune disappears as suddenly as it was made when his invention never produces electricity and in the aftermath, the stock market collapses. Rawn is relatively unaffected—his self-delusion remains as strong as ever. There is little physical description of Chicago in this novel, but much generalized description of the lives of Chicago millionaires, and of Samuel Insull, upon whom the Rawn character seems to be partly based (although Insull's fall would not come until more than a decade after Hough's book was published).

564. Hough, Emerson. *The Man Next Door*. New York: David Appleton, 1917. 309pp.

In this novel about social climbing in Chicago in the nineteen-teens, the climbers are valued much more highly than established members of society. When illiterate and recently widowed cowboy Colonel John William Wright sells his Wyoming ranch for four million dollars to a syndicate interested in his water rights, his goal is making certain his daughter Bonnie Bell has every opportunity in life. He sends her to Smith College and after she graduates the two move to Chicago to launch Bonnie in society. By chance Bonnie chooses lakefront land adjacent to the house of David Abraham Wisner, one of Chicago's wealthiest men. The Wrights soon learn that Wisner had been the major financer of the syndicate that bought the Wright ranch. As the Wrights construct their house, the Wisners build a high brick wall. Subjected to this and other insulting lapses of neighborliness, the Wrights note the Wisners' steady decline in fortune with satisfaction. A lifelong rancher, Wright has no special knowledge of investments, but does have common sense that aids him in effortlessly making wise investments in emerging industries, dramatically increasing his fortune, and bringing him to the attention of influential men. He is soon elected an alderman and Bonnie discovers that her mother's Maryland ancestry is old and distinguished, qualifying her for membership in ancestral societies, like The Colonial Dames, that people like the Wisners cannot join. After a series of farcical encounters involving mistaken identities, Bonnie Bell and the Wisners' son James eventually elope and secretly marry. The Chicago society of the novel is filled with nouveaux riches who appreciate the vitality and common sense of the Wrights.

565. Howard, Fred (Fred Steven). *Charlie Flowers & the Melody Gardens*. New York: Liveright, 1972. 218pp.

Expressing misogynistic views, this novel of Chicago in the 1920s and 1930s tells the story of a young man consistently treated badly by women. Charlie Flowers' parents were vaudevillians and, after his mother killed herself while committed to an insane asylum, as a four-year-old, Charlie's guardianship was contested. Flowers' father wanted to take his son with him on the road, but his grandmother, a boarding house owner, was urged on by her friend and tenant Mabel to get full custody. The boarding house where Flowers' lives on the Near North Side is next to the Melody Gardens, a restaurant and beer garden. When the establishment burns down most of the boarding house is destroyed. By this time Flowers' grandmother is under the control of Mabel, who goes on to inherit the entire estate with only a pittance given to Flowers. Forced to drop out of school, Flowers gets a series of jobs ranging from dishwasher, errand boy, to stockroom worker in an expensive department store. Eventually, he falls in love with Maggie Werner, a clothing sales clerk whom he marries. Werner is another schemer and she engineers Flowers into a divorce after their infant son dies, so that she can marry another man she thinks will become affluent. By the end of the novel, at the age of twenty-six, Flowers has enlisted in the navy as World War II is declared and he prepares to leave Chicago. Through descriptions of living conditions and workplaces, the novel captures the life of the working poor in the 1920s and 1930s. The plot touches on alcoholism, anti-Semitism, homosexuality, and mental illness.

566. Howland, Bette. *Blue in Chicago*. New York: Harper and Row, 1978. 183pp.

This series of six short stories explores aspects of Jewish family life and life in Chicago in general in the 1970s. The first-person narrator is a young, divorced woman living in a violent, and racially divided, Hyde Park, ignoring the concerns of her extended family, most of whom have moved to the suburbs. Her contact with her family is often through gatherings at major life events: weddings and funerals. She also visits her elderly grandmother, who lives in a neighborhood less violent, but almost as scary as Hyde Park—Uptown, near the Argyle train stop. The stories deal indirectly with the issues of racism, ageism, and sexism, and problems within the criminal justice system. Descriptions of houses, apartment buildings, and neighborhoods give a good sense of daily life. Although many of the protagonist's relatives immigrated from Europe, the book talks about more recent in-migration, particularly from Appalachia, and the poverty and continued displacement of these people. Status anxiety, in part inspired by an economy in recession, is also a major theme. The narrator's parents, aunts, and uncles, were mostly uneducated and worked as manual laborers or in service occupations, saving to give their children a better future. Now, their offspring have college educations, but can find no jobs in their professions.

567. Hudson, Jay William. *Nowhere Else in the World*. New York: David Appleton, 1923. 383pp.

Set in the 1920s, in the course of this novel a returning veteran, who has seen something of the world and believes he has material for a novel, finishes his book only to have it rejected and to come to the realization that he overlooked his best subject—Chicago. Steven Kent's father pays for him to study in Paris and earn his doctorate in literature after his World War I service. When an economic downturn weakens his father's construction business Kent's allowance ends and he is forced to teach at a remote, undistinguished Midwestern university. Coming to despise academic life, Kent moves to Chicago to live in the boarding house of a college friend near Humboldt Park and gets a job as a newsletter editor for the Progress Club, while finishing his novel. When his book is rejected for being too idealistic and out of touch with American audiences, he verges on a nervous breakdown before choosing to write about Chicago, a city that has come to epitomize for him all that is best about his native country. His realistic Chicago novel is published and promises to be a great success. The novel is filled with comparisons between Chicago and other cities in the

United States and the world that present a rationale for the city's importance in American and world culture.

568. Hufford, Susan. *Going All the Way*. New York: New American Library; A Signet Book / Times Mirror, 1980. 359pp.

As they are graduating from college in 1963, six friends pledge to hold a reunion ten years hence. The very different experiences of each of the six, one of whom lives in Chicago, form the bulk of the novel.

569. Hughes, Langston. *Not Without Laughter*. New York: Alfred A. Knopf, 1930. 324pp.

In this semi-autobiographical novel, Hughes fictionalizes aspects of his life to make them more typical of the African-American experience. His alter ego, Sandy Rogers, grows up in the fictional town of Stanton, Kansas. His father, Jimboy, lives apart from Sandy's mother Annjee, visiting only occasionally from Detroit. When Sandy's mother eventually leaves to live with Jimboy, Sandy lives with his grandmother and when she dies he moves in with a social climbing aunt, Tempy Siles, whose husband is a railroad mail clerk. Sandy's life in the Siles household is unhappy; when Jimboy is drafted into the Army to fight in World War I, he eagerly moves to Chicago with his mother. The Chicago section describes the city from the perspective of a teenaged newcomer.

570. Hutchens, Paul. *Romance of Fire*. Wheaton, Ill.: Van Kampen Press, 1934. 197pp.

This damsel in distress novel begins a few days after the death of Betty Dreanard's mother. Stranded in the mansion of her gangster stepfather, Jaird Barloman, she gets help from the cook to flee. Through a case of mistaken identity, she is taken to the home of the Mrs. and Rev. Walker T. Raynor, Christian evangelists who operate a Chicago mission and have been expecting a young woman pianist. Fortunately, Betty can play the piano and the other girl has been delayed by a death in her family. Shortly after settling in, however, Betty discovers she is being sought by the police as the murderer of Barloman. To escape pursuit, she travels with the Raynors on a revival mission to Colorado and meets a young man who becomes her protector and, much later, her husband. His protection is needed from both the false accusations of the police and from criminals who are trying to get control of a gold mine in which her deceased father had an interest and of which she has now unwittingly become the principal shareholder. Sermon texts railing against modernism and Chicago are included in this book and when a fire burns down part of the city, the evangelists rejoice over this proof of God's punishment of Chicago's corruption

571. Hutchens, Paul. *The Sugar Creek Gang in Chicago*. Grand Rapids, Mich.: Eerdmans, 1941. 88pp.

One of many children's novels featuring a group of boys from the imaginary town of Sugar Creek that Hutchens based on the area of Indiana in which he grew up, in this book, the gang's Little Jim has been invited to sing at a Labor Day Youth Rally in Chicago. With the financial aid of Old Man Paddler the entire gang is able to take the trip, with Paddler's nephew, Barry Boyland, as chaperone. The boys travel by airplane and visit tourist sites, including Adler Planetarium, Brookland Zoo, Field Museum, and Shedd Aquarium. Each of these visits inspires biblical references and the boys also visit a rescue mission (Pacific Garden Mission) and the Moody Bible Institute. A crisis strikes when Big Bob Till, who is from their hometown, follows them, and, in trying to strike Big Jim, loses his balance on the El train platform and falls, seriously injuring himself. The boys escort him to the hospital and Big Jim saves his life with a blood transfusion.

572. Hutcheson, Frank. *Barkeep Stories*. The Melbourne Series; no. 48. Chicago: Weeks, 1896. 212pp.

This work consists of sketches originally published in the *Chicago Daily News*. No further information is available.

573. Jackson, Charles Tenney. *The Midlanders*. Illustrated by Arthur William Brown. Indianapolis: Bobbs-Merrill, 1912. 386pp.

Set mostly in Rome, Iowa, the story tells of Aurelie, an orphan, abducted in New Orleans by eccentric, Confederate Civil War veterans and raised in an impoverished family headed by a religious zealot. Without her awareness the local newspaper editor enters Aurelie in a Chicago newspaper beauty contest. She wins and becomes a sensation, receiving offers to endorse products, become an actress, work as a stenographer, and marry. In love with Harlan Van Hart, a local man whose family does not believe she is good enough for him, Aurelie eventually goes off with a theater company intent on making the most of her celebrity, even though her heart remains true to Harlan. After a disastrous Midwestern tour, she becomes a sensation on the Chicago stage in a comic role for which she can use her own personality. Although there is talk of taking her to New York, a violent conflict over property rights forces her back to Rome and into the arms of Harlan. Chicago's news outlets and symbolic power as a place where riches and fame can be won dominate Rome, Iowa and the entire region, throughout the novel.

574. Jackson, Charles Tenney. *My Brother's Keeper*. Illustrated by Arthur William Brown. Indianapolis: Bobbs-Merrill, 1910. 324pp.

The proper relationship between the educated and affluent and the poor and underprivileged is the main concern of this reform novel. Herford Rand, heir to a textile fortune, has been disowned by his father Stephen Rand, a retired Supreme Court Justice. The elder Rand had insisted that Herford be educated as a Presbyterian minister. However, he was defrocked before his career began after he purchased Demetra, an eight-year-old gypsy girl, from her family in Europe so that she could be trained as a professional singer. Scandalized by imagined intimacies, the church and his father disowned Herford. Since then, he has supported himself as a sailor, smuggler, and laborer. He appears in Chicago, a forty-year-old-man, pursued for his role in killing a camp guard during a strike in Cripple Creek, Colorado. He finds Demetra married to sociology professor Dr. Ennisley Corbett and in residence in Stephen Rand's house, as another form of Stephen's support for Corbett's settlement house. Stephen refuses to see him, but Rand finds a protector in family friend John Bride (who shelters him) and aid from Demetra as the two try to get Stephen to reconcile with his son. The tentative relationship is destroyed after police and mill guards are bombed by some of Corbett's settlement school students. One of the bombers, Ludovic, appears in Chicago and Corbett is forced to choose between providing assistance, or protecting himself. With his entire career in jeopardy he chooses professional survival. When Ludovic appears in Stephen's house and is about to be captured, Rand claims Ludovic (who turns out to be Demetra's long estranged brother) is an anarchist friend of his, demonstrating his pragmatic approach to aiding laborers. A dramatic escape by boat ensues that Rand does not survive. Although the novel raises social issues (unionism, labor conflict, child labor, the settlement movement, and immigration), it is essentially a romance novel. The use of Chicago as a setting stems more from the idea of the city as the home of wealthy industrialists and intellectuals working on labor reform than out of a concern to accurately portray the city.

575. Jackson, Margaret Weymouth. *Beggars Can Choose*. Indianapolis: Bobbs-Merrill, 1928. 319pp.

  In this novel about married life between a woman from an affluent family and a man with a humble background and modest income, Chicago's bohemia is the social venue in which such a relationship can work. Ernestine Briceland first met Will Todd when he was an eight-year-old accompanying his carpenter father on a job for her father. They meet again more than a decade later shortly after Ernestine graduates from an exclusive, private girls' school. Will is a cartoonist on the staff of the *Chicago Sun* and before long the couple realizes their love for each other. Twenty-year-old Ernestine knows her wealthy family is ancestor-proud and concerned about social status. She convinces Will to marry her at a civil ceremony. When they announce the marriage Ernestine's father banishes them from the family circle. Throughout the rest of the book Will and Ernestine adjust to the limitations and barriers of social class as they pass through major crises. In this novel, the upper class is identified with planning and management skills that Ernestine brings to her marriage and the lower classes with being in touch with feelings and open to artistic inspiration that Will brings to his cartooning. The book makes plain the health implications of living in poverty, in part through noting the health benefits the wealthy enjoy by living near the lake. Will and Ernestine can only afford an inland housing development and once they have children Ernestine protects them by accepting vacations at the summer houses of more affluent friends. Much is made of Will's raffish social circle of journalists and writers, a bohemian milieu epitomized by a Greek restaurant and the Mafia-connected family that operates the establishment. One of the major themes of the book is the importance of marrying for love, rather than anticipated financial security.

576. Jackson, Margaret Weymouth. *Sarah Thornton*. Indianapolis: Bobbs-Merrill, 1933. 310pp.

  Sarah, the daughter of a physician with a large family, grows up in Chicago's Avondale neighborhood, at the time a Swedish immigrant community, and falls in love at seventeen with Kurt Mueller. For the next twenty-five years she remains faithful to Kurt, but the two cannot marry for a series of reasons including his mother's objections to the match (he is an only child). After Kurt's father dies, the difficulties increase because of his mother's increased dependence upon him. He becomes a successful businessman like his father and at the time of World War I is an executive with the Germania Insurance Company. In 1915 with the outbreak of hostilities, he returns with his mother to their homeland where he enlists with the Prussian Army. Sarah and Kurt are separated with no means of remaining in contact. Finally, at the end of the war Kurt returns to marry the forty-two-year-old Sarah. In addition to touching on attitudes toward courtship, marriage, and the place of women in society, the novel presents an overview of Chicago history from 1901 to 1919 and, through the character of Sarah's father, voices positions on topics of political debate, such as rights of way for private utility companies, tariffs, and immigration quotas. The extended family relationships of the Thorntons and their ties to their neighborhood illustrate the social life of middle-class Chicagoans in the time period.

577. Jakes, John [Jay Scotland, pseud.]. *The Seventh Man*. New York: Mystery House, 1958. 221pp.

In this mystery novel, a journalist becomes a hero when he discovers the identity of the "seventh man," the representative of an Eastern syndicate of gangsters intent on taking over organized crime in Chicago. The journalist, Harry Diamond, writes a gossip column and when he describes gangster Al Asperito's evening out with Linda Dwight, the wife of another gangster, his girlfriend Rosemary McClennen, a war widow with a young son, is immediately worried. Within twenty-four hours Diamond's life has been threatened and he is shot at. When he confronts Asperito, however, the criminal denies any involvement and then is shot before Diamond's eyes. As he is dying, Asperito describes a meeting of all the Chicago crime bosses at which they are told through an anonymous letter that an Eastern syndicate is taking over all of their operations. Asperito is only the first to die, and Diamond makes a deal with a police detective to have insider access in pursuing the story in return for his assistance with uncovering the plot. The author includes atmospheric descriptions of Chicago, evocative 1950s details about cars, clothing, and food, and incorporates slang and idioms of the time period. The Korean War is a presence for a number of characters, from war widow Rosemary whose husband's airplane was shot down, to Diamond himself who is a veteran.

578. James, Alice. *Decision to Love*. New York: Dell, 1972. 154pp.

Susan Lorimer flees the constraints of life in a small mining town, poverty, and family tragedy when she moves to Chicago. Pledging that she will never be impoverished again, she believes her job as a department store nurse in Chicago's most prestigious emporium holds out the promise of living in stylish comfort. Even in such an alluring environment, her dreams are modest, but when store owner Walter Hadley proposes marriage, Susan begins to think about a life of leisure and convinces herself that she can learn to love the older man, who is both attractive and kind. When Dr. Peter Harrison warns her that if she accepts Hadley she will be throwing away a personally rewarding life of service for an empty life of consumption and a loveless marriage, she dismisses his reasoning. After she plays an important role in a medical emergency she begins to appreciate Harrison's position and becomes more closely involved with the young and handsome doctor. The novel touches on the social status of women and consumerism, and illustrates the work culture of a major department store.

579. Janifer, Laurence M[ark]. [Larry M. Harris, pseud.]. *The Pickled Poodles; A Novel Based on the Characters Created by Craig Rice*. New York: Random House, 1960. 217pp.

An associate of the literary firm that represented Craig Rice, Harris revived Rice's popular characters of John J. Malone, and Jake and Helene Justus after their creator's death, in this mystery novel in which a Chicago television newsman, Jason Beck is being blackmailed. Beck, a notorious practical joker, believes one of his jokes caused a death years before in Topeka, Kansas. The blackmailer seems to know about the accident. Malone's investigation takes him back to Topeka, and he is soon also trying to figure out the murder of Beck's personal secretary, as well as what to do with several dipsomaniac poodles. Physical settings have little importance in this book, although several Chicago landmarks are mentioned.

580. Johnson, Charles Richard. *Faith and the Good Thing*. New York: Viking Press, 1974. 196pp.

Faith Cross is eighteen years old when her mother Lavidia dies (her father Todd had died years before). Faith has lived her whole life in rural Hatten County, Georgia, and is driven by her mother's death to set out on a quest for "the Good Thing"—that unnamable experience, understanding, possession, or goal that will make life worth living. Encouraged by the local swamp-dwelling witch, Faith moves to Chicago and has a series of experiences stemming from her poverty. After she is raped and forced into prostitution to support herself, she lives in a Stony Island hotel. Eventually, she enters into a loveless marriage in exchange for what most people would consider the Good Thing, a comfortable middle-class life. Then, her childhood sweetheart reappears after years in which she thought he was forever lost. Their love is consummated, but he has committed himself to a life of art that leaves no room for a committed relationship and abandons her while she is pregnant with his child. Driven from home by her husband, Faith returns to Stony Island where the final tragedy of her life is enacted. Although the novel alternates supernatural fabulism with philosophical discourse, it also conveys a sense of Chicago as a focus for ambitions of many kinds and includes some vivid descriptions of city neighborhoods and streets. The work also touches on themes of race and gender.

581. Johnson, Curt (Curtis Lee). *Nobody's Perfect.* Illustrated by David Dynes. Pomeroy, Ohio: Carpenter Press, 1974. 236pp.

Gasserpod P. Slocum is an assistant to sixty-six-year-old Ellis Schoenbatic, a writer and publisher of a "little" magazine, although that mostly means stapling the magazine together and performing other menial tasks. In this picaresque tale the two are on a cross-country attempt to line up grant money for their publication *Flagrante Delicto.* During their stay in Chicago, they have a long, boozy encounter with a thirty-five-year-old man who claims to be the literary heir of Ben Hecht and attend an art opening celebrating various forms of performance art. Chicago is a city under siege by Yippies and other young anti-war protesters and counter-cultural types with policeman on every corner.

582. Johnston, William [Susan Claudia, pseud.]. *Mrs. Barthelme's Madness.* New York: Putnam's Sons, 1976. 281pp.

In this psychological thriller set in modern day Chicago, Rachel Barthelme has an emotionally disturbing experience on Halloween when she runs down a child with her automobile. She complicates matters by fleeing. When she later reports the accident, the police are unable to find any evidence of what she describes and no child is reported missing. Having already come to the conclusion that her marriage was a failure and her life unsatisfying, as her businessman husband, family members, and friends begin to doubt her sanity, she does as well. By recording the life upon which Rachel's hold is so fragile, the novel provides a good description of upper-middle-class life in the city in the 1970s.

583. Jones, Ira. L. *The Richer—The Poorer.* Illustrated by Thomas B. Thompson. Chicago: Fiction, 1902. 321pp.

Much of this novel, which has a fantastical plot involving an inherited gold mine, missing relative, dramatic flood, and wealthy suitor is set in Ohio and Kentucky. However, after young and beautiful Becky Morris is rescued from the flood engorged Ohio River, by Prov, a fisherman who is a natural philosopher with a utopian vision, many of the main characters end up in Chicago. As Prov nurses Becky back to health, she comes to admire his self-reliant life and embrace his philosophical convictions, which have a great deal to do with the redistribution of wealth and the reformation of society to benefit all its members, rather than only the rich and powerful. At the same time, a wealthy young man named George pays admiring visits, but newly awakened to the evils of wealth she rejects him out of hand. Increasingly caught up in Prov's vision, Becky joins him on a crusade to bring his Humanarchy to the attention of Chicagoans, since they are more impressionable and open to new ideas than residents of other cities. George finds the "gone to Chicago" note Prov leaves on his cottage door and follows Becky and Prov to the city. Becky and Prov's crusade brings them a good deal of attention, but when they are taken up by striking workmen they are accused of instigating labor unrest by the authorities. George finds them by reading newspaper accounts and helps them get out of prison. Set upon by a mob, George ends up in hospital and it is there that Becky is reunited with the aunt and uncle who raised her. In the remarkable conclusion, Prov turns out to be the missing brother of Becky's aunt and when George pledges financial support to help Becky spread the message of the Humanarchy she accepts his marriage proposal. Although physical description of the city is mostly related from the skewed perspective of Becky's aunt, the author, a Chicagoan, includes a number of telling details about social and political life in the city.

584. Jones, Jack. *The Animal*. New York: William Morrow, 1975. 220pp.

The protagonist of this first-person narrative, Jo-Jo Jenkins, grows up in the Watts section of Los Angeles and eventually plays football professionally, working for a time for a Chicago team. Not much is made of the Chicago setting; however the African-American neighborhoods are paralleled with those found in Los Angeles and other urban areas. The book's plot and characters illustrate the effects of racial hatred on individuals.

585. Judson, Clara Ingram. *Alice Ann*. Illustrated by John M. Foster. Newark, N.J.: Barse, 1928. 300pp.

This book for children is set in 1920s suburban Lakeshore, a place of middle-class affluence in which young people have the opportunity to develop their interests and pursue extensive leisure activities, particularly in the summer, during which this novel takes place. Protagonist Alice Ann Lloyd and her friends do not use their time selfishly, however. When their summer plans to utilize a neighborhood vacant lot for recreation fall through, they work together to establish a city-wide summer program for youth. Although the characters and plot are clearly idealized for didactic purposes, the novel does present the material culture and leisure activities of middle-class Chicagoans before the Depression.

586. Judson, Clara Ingram. *The Green Ginger Jar: A Chinatown Mystery*. Illustrated by Paul Brown. Boston: Houghton Mifflin, Riverside Press, 1949. 210pp.

Chicago's Chinatown is the setting for this children's book calculated to teach racial tolerance. The plot centers on Ai-mei, a twelve-year-old Chinese-American who tries to get back a ginger jar that she mistakenly gave away, thinking it worthless. In fact the jar was a valuable heirloom intended to finance her brother's college education. Although the novel tries to instill sensitivity, it really does not avoid many of the stereotypes of the time, including those centered on gender roles.

587. Judson, Clara Ingram. *The Lost Violin; They Came from Bohemia*. Illustrated by Margaret Bradfield. Boston: Houghton Mifflin, Riverside Press, 1947. 204pp.

Set in 1893 at the time of the Columbian Exposition, this mystery novel for young people deals with the immigrant experience by presenting the story of the Kovec family, Bohemians from Czechoslovakia. The young daughter in the family, Anna, is a violinist and her violin, the family's only prized possession, disappears on the day they arrive in Chicago. The Kovecs' determination to recover the violin force them into adventures that help them adapt to customs, situations, and surroundings that are new to them. The interplay between the Kovecs' cultural assumptions and those of 1890s Chicagoans provide a useful record of both and the book includes descriptions of the World's Fair buildings and grounds and of 1890s Chicago in general.

588. Kaminsky, Stuart M. *You Bet Your Life*. New York: St. Martin's, 1978. 215pp.

Los Angeles detective Toby Peters is hired by Louis B. Mayer to help one of his actors, Chico Marx, who is being pursued by the Chicago mob for a gambling debt that Chico says he does not owe and that he does not have the cash to pay. After securing the blessing of Al Capone, at this point an addled Florida retiree, Peters travels to Chicago in January 1941 to gather information. Soon, he becomes convinced that a local grafter impersonated Chico, a known gambler, to cover his own losses. The Marx brothers arrive in Chicago to support Chico when he appears before the mobsters only for Peters to find that a corrupt policeman was at the center of the plot and a series of narrow escapes follow before justice is wrought. The novel provides characterizations of a number of famous gangsters, as well as the Marx brothers, but makes relatively shallow use of Chicago as a physical setting.

589. Kantor, MacKinlay. *Diversey*. New York: Coward-McCann, 1928. 345pp.

When a young journalist moves to Chicago from his small hometown, he does not get a newspaper job, but does have affairs with beautiful women and befriends both a journalist he idolizes and a powerful gangster. Marry Javlyn was a success in Clay City, Iowa, but relocates to Chicago in search of fame and fortune. He moves into a boarding house (near Diversey Parkway and Cambridge Avenue) and watches his savings dwindle as he searches for a job. However, he is soon having an affair with Josephine Ruska, the beautiful blonde who lives across the hallway and is socializing with his hero, a famed Midwestern journalist, known even socially by his byline "J.R.P." His connection to each of them leads to troubled reflection over social class and cultural attainment. He thinks he loves Ruska, but she grew up in a rough area of Chicago, has no intellectual interests, and is happy in a hard-drinking social circle whose members' speech and habits grate on Javlyn. He is much happier intellectually in the bohemian circle of J.R.P. where ideas and events are discussed, although he finds the women, particularly Doris Halt, with whom he has an affair, emotionally unavailable. His contacts in neither of these circles lead to a job, but another boarding house acquaintance does help him with his search. Initially, Javlyn simply runs innocent errands for boarder Steve Gold and cooks his dinner for large tips. He soon learns that Gold is a gangster in hiding. After Javlyn is shot by an intruder who mistakes him for Gold, the gangster uses his influence to get Javlyn a do-nothing job in City Hall that enables him to live well, briefly, until Gold is shot and killed. Kantor expands rich social details by providing brief character sketches that detail the backgrounds of many of the people with whom Javlyn comes into contact. One of the major themes of the novel is the degree to which social mobility is possible, even in a large city that fosters anonymity.

590. Kantor, MacKinlay. *El Goes South*. New York: Coward-McCann, 1930. 297pp.

The author depicts lower-middle-class life in Rogers Park in the late 1920s through the lives of the Troutwine family. Lester, forty-four years old and widowed for fifteen years, has worked at a major department store, Hirschfield's, for twenty-four years in a basement office as a claims correspondent. Troutwine's four children include Charlotte, a beauty counselor; Theodore, who sells radios, but wants to be an announcer; Pauline, a graphic artist for furniture catalogs; and, Douglas, a compositor for the Dixie Flyer company. All in their early twenties, Troutwine's children date within different social sets, and to their surprise, Troutwine begins a romance with a twenty-eight-year-old police detective widow that leads to marriage. When the newlyweds move in together, each of the children reacts differently. However, when sexual tensions arise between the young widow and one of her stepsons, tragedy for everyone is narrowly avoided. The novel presents a great deal of social and physical details of daily life.

591. Kantor, MacKinlay. *I Love You, Irene*. Garden City, N.Y.: Doubleday, 1972. 347pp.

In this fictionalized autobiography, the author draws the plot from his actual experience arriving in Chicago as a young man and establishing himself there as a journalist and writer. Kantor refers directly to actual people he knew and his published works. As the title indicates, Kantor's love life constitutes a major part of the book. Physical settings include department stores, newspaper offices, boarding houses, and Chicago streets.

592. Karlins, Marvin. *The Last Man Is Out*. Englewood Cliffs, N.J.: Prentice-Hall, 1969. 217pp.

This humorous futuristic science fiction work is set in Chicago in the year 2002. Matt Paradise, a college professor, inherits a big league baseball team with a major string attached—he must pitch every fourth game. Although he has no skills as a pitcher, he is able to take advantage of his friendship with a former professor who is a computer expert. Utilizing computing, Paradise positions his team as a major contender in the World Series. The Chicago setting is of slight significance.

593. Keeler, Harry Stephen. *The Amazing Web*. New York: Dutton, 1930. 320pp.

The central story in this complexly plotted work is Chicago lawyer David Crosby's love for Lindell Trent, a maid. The two met when Crosby defended Lindell against the charge of stealing her mistress's diamond ring. After reviewing the evidence, he decided Trent should plead guilty in return for a relatively short sentence. Some time later he has contact with Trent's accuser and hears that he could have proven Lindell's innocence if only he had asked the right questions. In hope of a retrial, he tries to contact Trent, only to find that she has been released for saving a prison visitor's life and returned to Australia. With very few clues, he tries to trace her, but because she has changed her name, is unsuccessful. He final chance for evidence seems to be retrieving a handbag from a deserted South Pacific island and his bizarre planning for this mission takes up a good deal of the plot. In defending a society murderer, Crosby gets falsely accused of larceny and Trent appears as a key witness to prove the murderer and Crosby's innocence. Crosby is able to win the case, gain national attention, and reconcile with Trent. Chicago is portrayed as a place where surprising coincidences are possible as people arrive there from all over the world and through these chance connections the entire course of one's life can be changed.

594. Keeler, Harry Stephen. *Behind That Mask: A Detective Novel*. New York: Dutton, 1938. 287pp.

When Jack Kenwood is murdered on Halloween by a man in an Indian mask, Yin Yi, a Chinese wax modeler, is taken into custody. Kenwood's calendar had shown an appointment with Yi for approximately the time of the murder and Yi had the previous day demanded five hundred dollars from Kenwood to settle a claim. Terry O'Rourke of the Chicago Detective Bureau investigates and finds that matters are not as straightforward as they seem. Aspects of the case include numerology, air travel between Indianapolis and Chicago, an affair between Yi and a married Caucasian woman, and prejudice against Asians. Although the physical description of places is scant, the multi-ethnic makeup of the city (Scotsmen, Germans, Chinese, Japanese, Filipinos, and African-Americans) is prominently highlighted and many Chicago places are mentioned.

595. Keeler, Harry Stephen. *The Box from Japan*. New York: Dutton, 1932. 765pp.

Keeler sets this novel a decade into the future (1942) so that he can speculate on how trends he was noticing in 1932 played out. At the center of the story is the development of the color television. Carr Halsey's uncle, Roger Halsey, is the head of the American Projectiscope Company. Carr has ignored Roger's urgings to enter the firm, preferring his job as a sports journalist. However, he stands to make a large sum of money from American Projectiscope stock Roger gave him if the company wins a legal dispute. In addition to discovering why a box he purchased at an unclaimed freight auction is so important to the men trying to steal it, Carr must solve a murder that hinges on a rare dye. Color blindness, optics, and genetics all play a role in this lengthy book that mentions numerous Chicago addresses and locations. Racism and discussions about race play a role in the book.

596. Keeler, Harry Stephen. *The Case of the Barking Clock*. New York: Phoenix Press, 1947. 255pp.

When an innocent man is on death row for murder, his girlfriend secures a key piece of evidence that may clear him, but needs to employ Tuddleton T. Trotter, the human encyclopedia, to interpret the evidence and make a last-minute clemency appeal. Joe Czeszcziczki was found guilty of murdering State's Attorney Ibstone. His final appeal for clemency has been denied and there are only hours before his execution. Then, his girlfriend Jadwiga Karlowicz receives an anonymous letter from a newspaper pressman in Chicago claiming he knows the real murderer. The letter provides hope, but gives no details. Trotter pieces together the needed information and stops the execution. Much of the book is set in the fictitious "Central City" (presumably Springfield), but some of the flashbacks, and meetings with key witnesses, as well as Trotter's dramatic meetings with Governor Moorgate at the Patner (i.e., Palmer) House, occur in Chicago.

597. Keeler, Harry Stephen. *The Case of the Jeweled Ragpicker*. New York: Phoenix Press, 1948. 256pp.

A murder case that has gone unsolved by the police for thirty years is finally solved through interviews with key informants and the power of deduction. Joe, a rag picker, is found murdered at the South Side Hotel DeRomanorum, a jeweled dagger skewering an ace of spades playing card to his back. Police detective Sergeant Frank DuShane, finds the setting appropriate for a murder. The once grand hotel, with its classical scenes, Latin mottoes, and Roman bath (now a laundry room) was built as a folly by a society figure with more wealth than business sense. The establishment has gradually turned into a "no tell motel." DuShane fails to solve the case, and thirty years later, articles are still being written about the unsolved mystery in pulp magazines. When Bill Chattock, wine chemist and temporary driver for Angus McWhorter, "owner and proprietor of MacWhorter's Mammoth Motorized Shows" sees one such article, he decides to solve the case. Chattock's father had learned the facts of the case from a girlfriend and left an encoded account among his effects when he died. Chattock pieces together the solution as his traveling show's route takes him to towns where he meets key informants and gathers evidence. Even though only the murder scene is set in Chicago, the novel is filled with descriptions of Chicago characters.

598. Keeler, Harry Stephen. *The Case of the Lavender Gripsack*. New York: Phoenix, 1944. 256pp.

In this courtroom drama a woman got her chance to study law when a relative agreed to lend her the money with her share in a business as collateral and the stipulation that she had to win her first case. Unfortunately, Elsa Colby's first case is defending "John Doe" against the charge that he murdered a night watchman. At the outset, it seems impossible that Colby will get an acquittal for her client, a criminal who has been convicted numerous times and has achieved public notoriety. To make the situation even worse, an archbishop is a key prosecution witness. Although the novel is set entirely inside a courtroom, the witnesses are a colorful lot of Chicago characters, including Chinese gang members, a "negress scrubwoman" who is paid to weep at African-American funerals, Baldy Venus who has a tattoo of Venus on his bald pate, as well as a number of tough talking men. The Chicago scenes the witnesses describe tend to be set in the city's underbelly. Despite the odds, Colby wins her case in this portrayal of a tough, capable woman, unusual for the time period.

599. Keeler, Harry Stephen. *The Chameleon: A Mystery-Adventure Novel*. New York: Dutton, 1939. 299pp.

Main character Rowland Quirk, a "character impersonator," is eager to collect a one hundred thousand dollar reward offered by the Sandringham trust for the return of Gilrick Sandringham, a homicidal paranoiac, to Birkdale Insane Asylum. He also schemes to get the reward money without paying his one hundred thousand dollar debt to Gustav Shrik, who holds a promissory note from Quirk for the same amount as the reward. To get assistance with his plot he talks with numerous people in Chicago, each time using an alias that is embroidered with a wealth of fictional personal details. In between, he stops by the offices of satire magazines and dashes off stories that he sells on the spot to finance the bribes that he must pay in his encounters around the city to newspapermen, academics, physicians, psychiatrists, and others. On one occasion he collects a fee for presenting a guest lecture in the guise of a famous philosopher. With the money he accumulates, Quirk gets an underworld figure to sell him safe-breaking tools and he retrieves the promissory note from Shrik's safe. Assured that the entire reward will be his, Quirk's promise to a nun, Sister Agatha, that her convent will benefit when he returns Sandringham to Birkdale, seems insincere. However, Quirk, of course, turns out to be the escaped Sandringham, who had been trying to get some of the money in the trust out of the hands of the trustees by getting them to pay out the reward. When Quirk involves Sister Agatha in getting him back to Birkdale, he guarantees her convent the reward and in return the convent begins devoting itself to his well-being. Although the novel does not have a great deal of physical description, Quirk has encounters with a broad range of Chicagoans, each of whom is meant to encapsulate particular Chicago types.

600. Keeler, Harry Stephen. *The Face of the Man from Saturn*. New York: Dutton, 1933. 254pp.

Jimmie Kentland, a reporter on the *Chicago Sun* who hopes to get his big break while temporarily subbing for the nighttime city editor, is disappointed until he discovers a barely literate note on his desk directing him to a specific address and he quickly finds himself on the way to a scoop. On the way there, his cab runs down a beautiful young woman. Although he wants to accompany her to a hospital, he decides to follow up with her later and hurries on to his address, only to find a seemingly empty Asian antiques store. However, in the center of the shop is a corpse pinned to the floor with an ornate dagger. The only clue to the crime is the fact that a picture on the wall entitled "The Man from Saturn" has had its face cut out. With a great deal of effort Kentland discovers the meaning of the clue and uncovers the secret of a sabotage plot to blow up the *Chicago Times-Star* building, the originals of which are buried in the Des Plaines River bed. By the end of the novel, Kentland has foiled the sabotage plot, gotten his scoop, and won the hand of the beautiful girl his cab had run down. Throughout the book 1930s Chicago settings form the backdrop.

601. Keeler, Henry Stephen. *Find the Clock: A Detective Mystery of Newspaper Life.* New York: Dutton, 1927. 338pp.

Jeff Darrell, a star reporter with the *Chicago Call*, came close to a scoop by capturing Carl von Tresseler, the "Blond Beast of Bremen," wanted for murdering his wealthy wife, but at the last minute von Tresseler escaped. Von Tresseler had been in charge of the brutal, German prison camp where Darrell had been held during World War I and he wants to be personally involved in bringing the man to justice. While he is still punishing himself over the escape, the *Call* hires a reporter from San Francisco with a national following to write the stories for which only Darrell, with his knowledge of Chicago streets and his connections to informants, can provide the information. Resenting the arrangement, Darrell is uncooperative as he follows up leads to a complicated life insurance fraud that involves the deaths of some of his Chinese informants and that gives him a second chance at the "Blond Beast of Bremen." One character in the novel is a physician who provides drugs to addicts who can pay his price and who operates a phony insane asylum. As with other Keeler novels, double identities abound. In general, the novel includes descriptions of gangsters and ethnic neighborhoods, focusing on the exoticism of language and behavior to the point of caricature.

602. Keeler, Harry Stephen. *Finger, Finger: A Mystery Novel.* New York: Dutton, 1938. 536pp.

The overarching plot in this book (as with all Keeler books, there are many), is one of international espionage in which Japanese agents based in New York City try to steal the "Thirteenth Coin of Confucius," an antiquity with talismanic power for the Chinese people that could be used to strengthen Chinese nationalism to the detriment of Japan. The solution of a Chicago murder is related to this plot and much of the book is set in Chicago where Jack Kenwood, publisher of *Ultrapolitan* magazine, and his assistant, David Rand, solve the crime. Many Chicago addresses and places are mentioned and ethnic and racially defined neighborhoods provide settings and supply characters. Keeler has an opportunity to present racist observations about people from Japan, China, Ireland, and Africa.

603. Keeler, Harry Stephen. *The Five Silver Buddhas: A Mystery Novel.* New York: Dutton, 1935. 281pp.

When Penn Harding, an unemployed newspaperman, buys at an auction one of five silver Buddha charms, reputed to bring good luck, he hopes for good fortune in proposing to Neva Edgecomb and dealing with her father, the wealthy steelmaker, Bradley Edgecomb. After paying far more that he can afford (five and one-half dollars) for the silver charm in a bidding war, he goes to a Chinese laundry to pick up his shirts. Displaying his new charm to the attendant for information, he discovers the Buddha with its hands over its eyes will bring bad luck. He proposes to Neva anyway and she accepts on the condition that he gets a newspaper job. He decides that the story of the charms could give him a scoop and land him a job. The bulk of the novel describes what he discovers about the bad luck that befalls the other charm buyers. Their elaborate misfortune causes the reader to anticipate Edgecomb's bad luck. However, as he points out, sometimes the fifth one is a charm. He wins over his father-in-law by assisting him in a secret business negotiation over a new manufacturing process to make steel harder than diamonds. He also gets his scoop on the charms after discovering that they were stolen from the Art Institute. Throughout the novel there are Chicago themes (organized crime, large-scale manufacturing, the newspaper business), as well as descriptions of Chicago neighborhoods, like Rogers Park, Little Italy, Chinatown, and Washington Square (where effeminate men wearing make-up are described with great distaste). There is strongly pronounced racism against the "yellow races" throughout the novel that is expressed with the most vituperation in the context of the steel negotiations when a final showdown between the yellow and white races is anticipated in which the hardened steel will give the white races a crucial advantage.

604. Keeler, Harry Stephen. *The Fourth King*. New York: Dutton, 1930. 317pp.

Stockbroker J. Hamilton Eaves has earned a fortune in Chicago by capitalizing dubious inventions. When he receives a threat through the mail, he manipulates an honest and well-trained engineer on his staff, Jason Folwell, to impersonate him and take the brunt of any attacks, or evade them through his physical strength and intelligence. When Eaves is murdered anyway, Folwell must solve the mystery since he is charged with the crime. Three other men, all of whom received threats similar to that mailed to Eaves, also died mysteriously, and the circumstances provide further clues for Folwell. Aided by his fiancée, Avery Reardon, he gathers evidence all over the city, benefiting from his extensive study of Chicago's geography. The author seems to be demonstrating his own expertise in this area and describes a number of neighborhoods, often populated by single ethnic groups—the most important to the plot is populated by Russians. Various technologies, accurately described or not, play important roles in the plot, including the transport of gases and telephony.

605. Keeler, Harry Stephen. *The Green Jade Hand: In Which a New and Quite Different Type of Detective Unravels a Mystery Staged in Chicago, Bagdad on the Lakes, London of the West*. New York: Dutton, 1930. 327pp.

Similar to other Keeler murder mysteries set in Chicago and involving an antiquity—a rare book—this work is distinctive for having a developmentally disabled man solve the murder. The man, Simon Grundt, lives on the streets during the day and sleeps in a police station. Along with Chinese characters, Keeler includes Bohemian immigrants who are members of the Bohemian Society, and talks about that community's background. Although Grundt solves the crime, much of the investigation in the novel is conducted by Chicago police detectives.

606. Keeler, Harry Stephen. *Man with the Crimson Box*. New York: Dutton, 1940. 317pp.

Wah Lee, the son of a wealthy Chinese restaurateur, was kidnapped, but even after a large ransom had been paid, he was not released. A headless body that was supposed to be Lee's was found and a gangster named Gus McGurk stands accused of the kidnapping and murder. Later a skull was recovered by a workman that is tentatively identified as Lee's. Prosecutor Louis Vann's whole murder case is built on the skull, but it disappears from his office safe. When the skull turns up again, it is found in a crimson box carried by a man who supposedly has amnesia, but has a wild explanation for how the box came into his possession. A crucial twist in the plot features an effeminate, rouge-wearing, radio hypnotist nicknamed "Gertrude." In addition to the author's racist attitudes toward African-Americans and Asians, this book contains numerous derogatory remarks about effeminate men. The novel takes place in many specific locations in downtown Chicago and Jackson Park, Goose Island, and Chicago's "Rialto."

607. Keeler, Harry Stephen. *The Man with the Wooden Spectacles*. New York: Dutton, 1941. 378pp.

This novel continues and embellishes the story in *The Man with the Crimson Box*. At the center of the plot is a female lawyer, Elsa Colby, who unwittingly assists in destroying evidence, but eventually finds a signed confession that solves the case. One of the book's main evil doers is Silas Moffitt a real estate investor who successfully bribes public officials, including judges. As with other Keeler novels, mistaken identities (even when it comes to skulls) and people in disguise play a large part. Criminal gangs and corrupt public officials add plot elements familiar from many other Chicago novels.

608. Keeler, Harry Stephen. *The Matilda Hunter Murder*. New York: Dutton, 1931. 741pp.

When Jeremy Evans' aunt, Matilda Hunter, dies in his office after relating a mystifying tale told to her by one of her boarders before his disappearance, Evans calls in amateur investigator Tuddleton Trotter. In Hunter's story, Japan is supposedly plotting a war against the United States and has already created several flu epidemics. Now they are trying to get a z-ray machine from her boarder. Frightened by the machine, Hunter brought it to Evans' office. When he left the room and came back Hunter was dead, apparently killed by the z-ray contraption. The police suspect Evans since Hunter recently took out a life insurance policy with Evans as beneficiary and Evans wants to marry an affluent woman whose parents disapprove of his poverty. Trotter finds a more logical explanation for Hunter's death than a z-ray machine and helps establish the legitimacy of Evans' claim on an estate of a distant relation. The estate seems to be at the center of a number of murders in addition to Hunter's as someone is killing off heirs. Trotter realizes that the z-ray machine is a red herring concealing a bar of platinum stolen from the bank vault of Evans' dead relation and Evans unexpectedly finds himself the heir to a platinum mine, easing the way for his marriage. As usual in Keeler novels, the narrative employs broad racial stereotypes. Evan's African-American maid is named Lily White and the Blue Moon is a taxi dance operation strictly for "Orientals" who can dance with Caucasian women in embraces that the author considers both grotesquely humorous (because of the height differences) and scandalous. Among the Chicago settings are North State Parkway, the neighborhood around Division and Lasalle, Lincoln Park, and Devonshire Street.

609. Keeler, Harry Stephen. *The Mysterious Mr. I*. London, U.K.: Ward, Lock, 1937. 308pp.

To assist the abbess of a convent, Sister Agatha, McAllister Thane solves a mysterious death that resulted in T. Parker Yocum inheriting six thousand pounds sterling from his cousin, Trell Yocum. T. Parker was the one to identify the body of his cousin. Thane realizes that the body was not Yocum's on the basis of the police evidence gathered at the time of the murder several years before and from an examination of a skull in the possession of Sister Agatha. As with many Keeler novels, the plot is complex, although the Chicago setting includes surprising details, such as businesses like an all-night dental office, a large numismatics shop, and the services and furnishings of bachelor apartments. This novel has a sequel, *The Chameleon*, discussed above (entry 599).

610. Keeler, Harry Stephen. *The Mystery of the Fiddling Cracksman*. A Dutton Clue Mystery. New York: Dutton, 1934. 317pp.

After successfully publishing his first novel, Billy Hemple returns to Chicago with enough money to pursue Laral [*sic*] Craig, the wealthy girl he loves. His visit is complicated by a mystery. An intruder has broken into four houses owned by four different men, each named John Craig.

The intruder did no damage, but simply played his violin in each residence. Laral believes her father, another John Craig, will be the next to have his house broken into. The solution to the mystery involves jewels from an imaginary country named Ulania located in the Black Forest and the acoustical properties of a violin tuned to open a lock. Settings include jewelers' shops in Chinatown and expensive apartments and houses. Laral Craig writes plays and there is some description of the Chicago theater scene. The Depression has had a tragic impact on the lives of some of the characters in the novel.

611. Keeler, Harry Stephen. *Riddle of the Traveling Skull*. New York: Dutton, 1934. 288pp.

The mystery in this novel concerns a skull and a young man who must find a solution if he is still to marry his fiancée, who happens to be the daughter of his boss. Twenty-nine-year-old Clay Calthorpe works for Roger Pelton, a wealthy candy manufacturer. He is returning home from the Philippines, where he had successfully negotiated a contract for an exclusive supply of a native berry that will provide a new candy with an innovative color and taste, when he realizes that his bag must have been exchanged with another on the Chicago elevated train. The bag in his possession contains a skull with a hole drilled in it and a metal plate affixed reading "No. 82, 9-17-'14." Inside the cranium are carbon copies of a poem and bullet fragments. When he tells his twenty-year-old fiancée Doris and her father Roger Pelton of his bizarre discovery, Roger becomes ill and the next day declares that Calthorpe and Doris cannot marry. When he responds to a telephone call for a meeting to exchange the bag for his own, he is mugged by a "scar-faced Chinaman." Calthorpe soon discovers that the skull's hole is an example of "trephining" (more commonly known as trepanning) with the tag indicating the number of an operation, and that the "Chinaman" is a gangster known to the police. By intercepting a telephone call intended for Roger Pelton, Calthorpe also learns that a blackmailer is asking for twenty thousand dollars in return for the skull. In the course of his investigation, Calthorpe visits a number of Chicago neighborhoods and parks, although as with other Keeler novels, the descriptions are not very evocative.

612. Keeler, Harry Stephen. *The Riddle of the Yellow Zuri, A Mystery Novel*. A Dutton Clue Mystery. New York: Dutton, 1930. 294pp.

Clifford Carson is a mining engineer who recently became an agent for the Federal Bureau of Investigation to investigate fraudulent mining stocks when his fiancée Marcia Desmond sends Jake Jennings to him. Jennings is looking for a rare yellow Zuri snake that has gone missing in Chicago and wants Marcia's father Angus Desmond, a famous herpetologist, to help locate the snake. However Angus is also missing. The plot also involves a missing twenty thousand dollar bank note, a real estate company's attempts to secure title to a tract of land in the Chicago neighborhood of Ravenswood, members of the Sicilian Mafia, and an invention for a safe that will incapacitate any thief. The novel's characters (as well as the author) seem obsessed by stock certificates for land and mining companies and, despite the setting in the early days of the Depression, a land rush seems to be in full-swing in Chicago. Cross-dressing plays a role in the book since a character known as Kate Barwick, who also disguises herself as Madame Mercedes, "the Handcuff Queen," turns out to be the missing Angus Desmond.

613. Keeler, Harry Stephen. *The Sharkskin Book, A Mystery Novel*. New York: Dutton, 1941. 286pp.

This complex novel has several plots and subplots, all connected by a book bound in sharkskin that passes through several hands over the course of the novel. In the Chicago section (other locales include Niagara City, New York, and Nebraska City), the book, a compilation of Chinese wisdom entitled *The Way Out*, is in the hands of gangster Swig Mullarkey, whose hangout is in "Little Sicily." Swig operates a tavern that features a wall of bars behind which overweight female prostitutes try to entice customers. Incongruously, Mullarkey's "office" has been furnished like a gentleman's library, even if the furniture is Chippendale via Montgomery Ward (a Chicago catalog retailer). It is there that Joe Long-Buffalo seeks him out in the hope of locating Swig's brother, Slick Mullarkey, who is also Joe's brother-in-law. Raised in England with his sister, upon the death of their father, they were adopted by an American physician and grew up on a Michigan farm. Upon the physician's death they inherited the farm and now want to sell it. However, Slick Mullarkey, hiding out after escaping from prison, married Joe's sister under false pretenses. Since Mullarkey is part owner of the farm, they must get a quitclaim. In addition to Keeler's usual racist attitudes toward Italians and Asians, this book includes negative depictions of Native Americans.

614. Keeler, Harry Stephen. *Sing Sing Nights*. New York: Dutton, 1928. 397pp.

Imprisoned in Sing Sing, criminals entertain each other by telling crime stories to pass the time and two novella-length ones are set in Chicago. "The Strange Adventure of the Giant Moth," concerns a jewelry theft during a society masquerade ball held in a mansion at 1400 Lake Shore Drive. The story incorporates descriptions of the mansion, Lincoln Park, a residential area around St. Clair Street, an area of Monroe Street with dance pavilions and costume shops, and the costumes of guests (two of which turn out to be yellow moths). The two main characters are Asian—gangster Moonface Eddy Chang, a Chinese man, and household servant Ushi Yatsura, a Japanese man—and the story becomes a vehicle for racist comments about Chinese and Japanese peoples. In "The Strange Adventure of the Twelve Coins," Jason Barton, a *Chicago Dispatch* reporter, gets a scoop for his newspaper by interviewing a Chinese princess on an extended visit to the city. A transcription of his interview takes up many pages of the story and includes a long discussion of "the race question" which is described as the biggest issue facing humans. Surprisingly, for a Keeler plot, a romance develops between Barton and the princess. However, this is thwarted by the Chinese ambassador who is able to get the princess deported under the United States Chinese Exclusion Act. The story's main plot revolves around the murder of a Chinese laundry man, twelve missing gold coins of great cultural significance, and Barton's successful efforts to locate the coins.

615. Keeler, Harry Stephen. *The Skull of the Waltzing Clown*. A Dutton Clue Mystery. New York: Dutton, 1935. 247pp.

In this crime mystery, George Stannard is returning from Hawaii to his home in Boston and stops on the way at his estranged Uncle Simon Stannard's house at 16 Russell Square in Chicago. George is a traveling salesman for a shirt company and his uncle owns a money-making short story magazine that he publishes from his house. Soon after meeting his nephew, Simon announces that he is running for mayor of Chicago as a member of the Dissatisfaction Party (created on the theory that everyone is dissatisfied with the current political parties). Holding over George's head an old financial obligation of his father's, Simon gets his nephew's assistance in gathering information, utilizing contacts George has made during his trips as a traveling salesman. The information Simon wants is presented as a series of questions that seem unrelated, but when answered will solve the mystery of a skull that Simon illegitimately has in his possession. Evidence in a violent crime case, the skull could also help Simon perpetrate insurance fraud. As is typical of Keeler, a good deal of racist rant is presented in an offhand way and there is little physical setting to the novel that mostly consists of dialogue between Simon and George, the first-person narrator.

616. Keeler, Harry Stephen. *The Spectacles of Mr. Cagliostro*. London, U.K.: Hutchinson, 1929. 384pp.

Multimillionaire Digby Middleton tries to protect his son Jerry from the schemes of his half-brother Lionel Catesby by bequeathing him a mere seventy five dollars a month. However, Digby underestimated the evil of his business manager, who uses Catesby as his pawn and enlists Chicago organized crime figures to provide the muscle for his elaborate plan to gain control of the Middleton fortune. An extended portion of the novel is set in the Birkdale insane asylum in suburban Chicago where Jerry is held and the novel decries the treatment of the mentally ill and calls for reform. The novel also speculates on matters of genetics. Numerous locations and addresses in Chicago are used to establish the setting for other sections of the novel.

617. Keeler, Harry Stephen. *Thieves' Nights, the Chronicles of De Lancey, King of Thieves*. New York: Dutton, 1929. 321pp.

This novel involves a misappropriated fortune and a whole series of concealed and mistaken identities. All his life Ward Sharlow has been carrying a letter from his deceased stepfather that can only be opened on a specific date in September 1929. Three days before he is to open the letter, wealthy John T. Atwood of North Wacker Drive, owner of the Atwood Safety Catch Company, manufacturers of a device for passenger elevators, offers him ten thousand dollars to impersonate his son Calvin Atwood, who drowned recently in an accident. Atwood had seen Sharlow on the street and found his resemblance to Calvin remarkable. The impoverished Sharlow agrees and begins residing in the Atwood residence, however after only a day Atwood dies. As mourning begins and preparations get underway to settle the estate, Sharlow is torn about whether or not to reveal his true identity. Then the day arrives for him to open the letter the contents of which describe how John T. Atwood cheated Sharlow's stepfather out of an invention. To revenge his stepfather, Sharlow maintains his identity as Calvin only for two more Calvins to appear on the scene, as well as a chorus girl presenting a breach of promise suit against Calvin Atwood, an Indian prince determined to buy an emerald from the Atwood estate, and a jewel thief—De Lancey, "King of Thieves."

618. Keeler, Harry. *The Voice of the Seven Sparrows*. New York: Dutton, 1928. 304pp.

A substantial portion of this convoluted novel is set in Chicago; other settings include New York City, New Orleans, and an oceangoing ship. When Beatrice Mannerby, half-owner of the *Chicago Morning Leader*, disappears, twenty-nine-year-old reporter Absalom Smith goes on assignment to discover what happened to her. His inquiry takes him into the Chinese community in which he runs up against the Seven Sparrow T'ong (more commonly Tong). As with many Keeler novels racism is implicit. Here mixed race parentage is a major issue and, again, as in other Keeler novels, disguised identities are a major theme. The Chicago section of the novel is set in the world of newspaper offices, apartment hotels, and private clubs with little general description of the city.

619. Keeler, Harry Stephen. *The Washington Square Enigma, A Mystery Novel*. New York: Dutton, 1933. 247pp.

When a San Francisco bank teller gives a promissory note to the wrong man, he travels halfway across the country to try to retrieve the financial instrument. Ford Harling uses all of his resources to track the promissory note recipient to Chicago. With no further leads, he has almost given up hope when, in a deserted house, he finds the body of an expensively dressed man killed with a hat pin through the eye. In a bizarre coincidence, the man is the one he has been seeking. Fortunately, he is able to get the help of wealthy, young Trudel Vanderhuyden, whose life he had saved in San Francisco. Her too zealously faithful Filipino houseboy turns out to be the murderer. In addition to depicting the plight of the unemployed and homeless around Washington Square, this novel includes a number of scenes set in more affluent, Near North neighborhoods, such as Lake Shore Drive and North Clark Street.

620. Keeler, Harry Stephen. *The Wonderful Scheme of Mr. Christopher Thorne*. New York: Dutton, 1936. 503pp.

Ostensibly Christopher Thorne is a money lender, but there is a mystery concerning his true identity, his connection to the Marceau murder that was a major plot line in two of Keeler's earlier books, and where he obtained the money he is lending. A subplot in this book of many plots and subplots is Thorne's concern over the engagement of his daughter Alicia to Phillip Erskine, one of his clerks. Mixed races (African-American and American Indian) are a source of continual fascination and comment on the part of Thorne. As with other Keeler books physical settings are of little interest, although addresses and places in Chicago are mentioned. In addition to Chicago, some of the book's action is set in New Orleans and New York City.

621. Keeler, Harry Stephen. *X. Jones of Scotland Yard*. New York: Dutton, 1936. 448pp.

The second of a series of books dealing with the Marceau murder that occurred in England, here Xenius Jones, a former detective at Scotland Yard who had worked on the case for two years, follows leads to Chicago. His interest is initially in one of the claimants to the Marceau fortune, Joe Scarnisi, a Chicago bootlegger and gangster. The book takes the form of collected evidence, including letters, legal testimony, and other documents, that Jones analyzes, demonstrating the methods of crime detection. The physical settings for the action described in the evidence range all over the world.

622. Keenan, Henry Francis. *The Money-Makers: A Social Parable*. New York: David Appleton, 1885. 337pp.

In writing this book Keenan was primarily concerned with responding to John Hayes' anti-union novel, *The Breadwinners*. Hayes had portrayed laborers as marginally human brutes and Keenan illustrates the ways in which laborers are degraded by the economic system. Keenan sets his novel in a city he calls Valedo, but the place is a thinly disguised Chicago and a large percentage of the book deals with the Pullman strike of 1884. The novel follows two young journalists, Archibald Hilliard and Fred Carew, each of whom receive a significant amount of money after preventing the wreck of a wealthy man's carriage. Hilliard uses inside information he accesses as a journalist to invest in the stock market and make a fortune. Carew gives his reward to his impoverished family and continues working as a journalist, dedicating himself to fairly reporting both sides of labor disputes. Keenan openly describes his work as a parable, but he creates realistic characters and accurate descriptions of social life.

623. Kelly, Regina Zimmerman. *Beaver Trail*. New York: Lothrop, Lee and Shepard, 1955. 237pp.

Eleven-year-old Jimmy Russell, recently orphaned, becomes the ward of his uncle James Russell, who takes him to the Northwest Territory in hopes of establishing a farm near Fort Dearborn. To earn transportation to the settlement, they first work for the American Fur Company, based on Mackinac Island. Their experiences working for their passage takes up a good deal of this book for children. When they finally arrive at Fort Dearborn, Jimmy is apprenticed to John Kinzie and, since autumn is approaching, James Russell continues to work as a fur trapper until he can stake his claim in the spring. Their life at Fort Dearborn is soon disrupted, however by the massacre at the fort, which both Russells separately escape. Jimmy is held prisoner in the village of Black Partridge for months until he is ransomed at John Kinzie's old trading post and finds, to his great surprise, that his uncle is living nearby. This historical novel for children provides detailed information about fur trading and its relationship to the settlement of the Northwest Territory, while attempting cultural sensitivity in describing the conflict between Indians and European settlers.

624. Kelly, Regina Zimmerman. *Chicago: Big-Shouldered City*. Chicago: Reilly and Lee, 1962. 158pp.

In this book for children, Kelly presents some major events of Chicago history through the experiences of several generations of the fictional Stuart family, the first members of which move to Chicago from Detroit in 1811. The book includes accounts of the massacre at Fort Dearborn, Lincoln's presidential nomination, the Chicago fire, and the Columbian Exposition.

625. Kencarden, Stuart. *A Mother of Unborn Generations*. New York: Broadway, 1912. 214pp.

This novel features a female physician who inspires a young man to finish medical school. John Langworth had begun medical school in New York City. Younger than his friends, when they graduated he could not stand to be left alone and returned to his parents' Montana ranch. On a trip back East, he stops in Chicago to look up one of his old friends, Dr. Caldwell Winngrath. He finds a Dr. Winngrath, but the physician turns out to be a woman, the widow of the friend Langworth sought. Immediately impressed by Annetta Winngrath, within a few weeks Langworth decides to settle in Chicago and complete his medical education. The two marry, have a child, and benefit from Langworth's lucrative practice. Their happiness is destroyed when Hilkley Tweedwell appears and threatens to expose a secret of Annetta's. For months Hilkley preys upon Annetta, trying to blackmail her into providing him with sexual favors. She finally confesses to John that she had been a chorus girl in New York City. After hearing of the poverty in which she had grown up and the way she had been misled by men, he pledges to remain by her side. However, she fears he will have no control over how he feels and over time a change in their relationship will occur. To free both of them, she mortally shoots herself, with enough skill that she has time for a deathbed farewell. John, considering Annetta's story further evidence of the corruption of the eastern United States, leaves with his infant daughter for the West. Chicago functions symbolically in the novel as a place that is freer and less corrupt than the East, but is still too much influenced by it.

626. Kennedy, Adam. *The Scaffold*. New York: Trident Press, 1971. 346pp.

Using flashbacks, this novel covers a period of approximately twenty years in the life of Floyd Lucas and his intimates, a circle that includes wives, ex-wives, lovers, and illegitimate children. A foundling, Lucas' adoptive parents died in an automobile crash when he was eighteen, leaving him wealthy enough that he has spent his life traveling and enjoying art, culture, and numerous affairs. If Lucas has any home it is Chicago where the legal firm managing his investments is located. He returns to the city twice a year and one visit, during which a former lover commits suicide with a pistol in front of his eyes, is recounted in some detail by referencing expensive hotels and restaurants. Much of the novel is set in Mexico. Chicago is also important as a cultural center to other characters who live in the Midwest.

627. Kennedy, Adam. *Somebody Else's Wife*. New York: Simon and Schuster, 1974. 349pp.

A journalist returns to Chicago after being held for ten years in a mental institution for killing his wife and her lover. Chet Rector, now thirty-seven-years-old, had received a job offer from the *Chicago Courier*, but after meeting with his new supervisor turns down the position and moves into a flop house to make his remaining cash last as long as possible. Fortunately, the same friend who had found him the *Courier* job sends Grady Bostwick to him. Bostwick, a wealthy Chicago businessman, supposedly wants Rector to write materials for a public relations campaign to launch a new company. Before long, however, Bostwick reveals that he wants Rector to start an affair with his current wife (Helen, his fourth), so that he can get a divorce and marry another woman. Rector refuses until he finds himself falling in love with Helen. The affair develops through a series of romantic liaisons conducted while Grady is out of town. At Helen's instigation the two soon leave for the Virgin Islands. In the novel's dramatic conclusion we realize that Helen executed a plot to abscond with a significant part of Grady's fortune for which he violently pursues her. The novel's Chicago content includes extended descriptions of restaurants and apartment buildings on the Near North Side, as well as social interactions that capture some aspects of gender relations in the 1970s.

628. Kennedy, Mark. *The Pecking Order*. New York: Appleton-Century-Crofts, 1953. 278pp.

A tragic day in the life of an adolescent African-American reveals the dangers of racism. Thirteen-year-old Bruce Ashford Freeman joins some of his classmates and their ringleader, B. J., convinces them to form a gang named the "Warriors." One of their first destinations is the apartment of B. J.'s sister who works as a prostitute. Later, they steal cookies from an A & P, climb to the roof of a condemned, burned-out tenement, and ingratiate themselves with a group of men to be rewarded with pot and wine. Near the end of the afternoon they travel to Hyde Park, portrayed here as an all-white neighborhood. After being warned off by a policeman, they get into an altercation with some whites and, fearful that they are being pursued, end up stealing an automobile to ease their escape. A series of tragedies follow that leave all the Warriors dead except for Bruce. The novel includes descriptions of impoverished domestic interiors, family life, and neighborhoods. Many of the adults in the novels grew up in the rural South and carry their regional food ways and traditions with them to the frustration of their children, who have embraced a national urban culture. One of the implicit themes of the book is internalized racism expressed through the higher cultural status accorded to light-skinned blacks within African-American culture.

629. Kent, Mona. *Mirror, Mirror, on the Wall*. New York: Rinehart, 1949. 307pp.

This novel touches on issues of women's social independence in the 1930s and the history of commercial radio broadcasting in Chicago. The author created a nationally syndicated radio serial and this work is clearly based on her experiences. Delilah "Dell" Hershey grew up on a farm, but her parents willingly made sacrifices so that their four girls could attend college. In college, Dell meets Gerald Thornton and falls in love, in part because of her false impression that he is a so-phisticated, affluent Chicagoan. After they marry and move to Chicago, Dell realizes that although the Thorntons are wealthy, they do not have the personal strengths she associates with social prominence. Married in 1929, Gerald has a falling out with his parents soon afterwards and finan-cial difficulties quickly follow. Residing in a basement apartment on Chicago's Near North Side, Dell realizes she must take over household finances. On a secretarial job with an advertising agency she is responsible for typing soap opera scripts. Soon she has taught herself script-writing and by 1932 has her own soap opera. Dell is obligated to socialize with work colleagues (many of them attractive men) and frequents Prohibition-era speakeasies. Although she has a son with Ger-ald, he resents her success and commits suicide halfway through the novel. Dell rebuilds her life in New York City, where much of the rest of the novel takes place, and pursues her love for voice actor Peter Madison. Unfortunately, her son Gerald has many of the character flaws of her hus-band and although the present of the novel is in the 1940s when Dell has professional achievement and financial security to bolster her, she keeps revisiting her memories of her early days in Chi-cago.

630. King, Charles. *Foes in Ambush*. Philadelphia: Lippincott, 1893. 263pp.

Less than ten pages of this novel are set in Chicago. Lieutenant Drummond and his new bride, the former Edith Wing, are from Chicago and they spend most of their honeymoon on the Arizona frontier in dramatic warfare against Indians. Near the end of the book Drummond returns to Chi-cago with his company in order to save the city from railway strikers who have terrorized the pop-ulace. None of the civic authorities have been able to gain control of the situation and only Drum-mond's railway carriages of rifles and a Gatling gun have the power to end the standoff. This cel-ebration of violence against labor organizers may seem surprising to modern readers, given later valorization of the labor movement.

631. King, Charles. *A Tame Surrender: A Story of the Chicago Strike*. Philadelphia: Lippincott, 1896, 277pp.

Most of this romance novel is set just before and during the Pullman strike of 1894 and de-fends the rights of capitalists to take extreme actions against labor organizers. Florence Allison met Floyd Forrest while on holiday with her family in Europe. After returning to Chicago, Forrest appears on a "special assignment" that keeps him occupied in the Pullman Building all day. Alli-son soon learns that he is the key figure in the company's strategy to end the strike without ceding to any worker demands. Alison and Forrest socialize mostly by attending society balls and din-ners.

632. Kinzie, John H. Mrs. *Wau-Bun, the "Early Day" in the North-West*. New York: Derby and Jackson, 1856. 498pp.

For decades considered a historical account of the Northwest Territory in the 1830s, since the 1930s this work has rightfully been treated as a fictional work inspired by real-life experiences. Much of the book deals with Juliette and John Kinzie's travel from Wisconsin to Detroit, where they settle and try to establish a home. However, the couple makes an extended visit to the settle-ment at Chicago, where John, who is related to the famous John Kinzie, important to Chicago history, has living relatives. Their visit to Chicago is dominated by an account of the Fort Dear-born massacre, related by an eyewitness, but does give some sense of pioneer life in the settle-ment.

633. Kirk, Hyland C. *The Revolt of the Brutes; A Fantasy of the Chicago Fair*. New York: Dillingham, 1893. 123pp.

Written by a reformer concerned with the mistreatment of animals, this allegorical work is set at the Columbian Exposition in Chicago. The narrow focus is on an imagined convention of animals brought together by the exposition. The author parallels the animals' effort to organize for their rights with the activism of other groups, including women, fraternal organizations (the Odd Fellows and Masons), religious organizations (the Mormons and Roman Catholics), and the threat the animals pose to American society with that posed by anarchists, American Indians, and the Chinese. The volume is heavily illustrated with drawings of animals, but has no images depicting Chicago.

634. Kirkland, Joseph. *The Captain of Company K*. Chicago: Dibble, 1891. 351pp.

Chicago during the Civil War sets the backdrop for this romance novel that illustrates some aspects of the conflict's impact on the city. A minister's daughter, Sally Penrose, is fond of William Fargeon "merchant, philanthropist, Sunday-school, superintendent, temperance orator," but before their courtship develops, he is inspired by an 1861 Wigwam auditorium rally to enlist in Company K and is soon elected a company captain. While in training at Cairo, Illinois, Fargeon gets a leave, returns to Chicago, and begins courting Sally, mostly in the parsonage with Penrose family members present. Occasionally, the couple strolls by themselves along the plank walk beside Lake Michigan. Some of Fargeon's Chicago leave is spent at the store he owns and there is a description of the impact of the war on the Chicago economy. Fargeon's absence has put his business in such poor condition that he is convinced to sell it to a rival, mostly for the cancellation of debts. When Fargeon returns to his regiment, attention is paid to newspaper coverage, particularly the ways local heroes are created by reports of regiment activities. Sally and Parson Penrose are part of a Chicago delegation that travels by steamboat to the battle of Shiloh and the Penroses are on hand to nurse Fargeon after he is injured and one of his legs is amputated. When they return to Chicago, Sally discovers that she has inherited a fortune and she and Fargeon can marry despite the loss of his business. The novel is unusual for the time period in presenting, without judgment, a household in which the man will not be supporting his wife.

635. Klasne, William. *Street Cops*. Englewood Cliffs, N.J.: Prentice-Hall, 1980. 234pp.

When Officer Clarich leaves the police academy and begins walking a beat in the Lakefront District, he is immediately confronted by a moral dilemma. His fellow officers supplement their pay by shaking down members of the public. Reporting their behavior from within the close-knit ranks of the force is not an option. Eventually, Clarich feels pressured to engage in the same chicanery and subjects himself to extended self-appraisal. Written by a former policeman, the novel presents a catalog of police misbehavior, but the book's focus on the police force means it has little general description of Chicago.

636. Knebel, Fletcher and Charles W. Bailey II. *Convention*. New York: Harper and Row, 1964. 343pp.

The authors, real-life political reporters, present a fictionalized Republican National Convention held in Chicago. Up to the convention, Secretary of the Treasury Charles B. Manchester is the leading presidential candidate, however as he presents his platform, his supporters turn against him and the party is left in turmoil. This novel is tightly focused on political intrigue and the emotions of a political convention with Chicago serving as a shallow backdrop.

637. Knott, William Wilson and Austyn Granville. *Stolen Sweets, or W. W. W. & W: A Romance with a Moral, the Acme of Realistic Fiction.* Chicago: Bow Knot, 1891. 368pp.

The characters in this melodramatic romance are surprisingly mobile in an age of steamship and locomotive, but they always return to Chicago. Roy Felton of New York falls in love with Agnes McMillan, the sister of his college friend Arthur and daughter of a Chicago judge. Their love has little hope because Roy's mother, who controls the fortune his father left him, wants him to become a Protestant minister and believes clergymen should not marry. Agnes' father wants her to marry the Italian Count Zufrani. When the judge openly rejects Roy, the couple elopes and takes a lengthy wedding trip on the West Coast. Agnes and Roy secretly return to Chicago and stay at the Palmer House, accompanied by Agnes' maid, a Frenchwoman named Polly. Determined to separate the couple, Polly gets Zufrani to come to the apartment and aids Roy in breaking in upon the Count and Agnes. Mistakenly believing that he has been betrayed, Roy is heartbroken and Agnes collapses. At this moment, Arthur appears. To pay a gambling debt he forged Judge McMillan's signature on a check for $10,000. To save his friend, Roy falsely claims that he forged the check and goes to prison. The Judge takes this opportunity to have the delirious Agnes sign divorce papers. Roy's mother eventually gets Roy out of prison with the help of the governor of Illinois, who is Arthur's uncle. Soon upon his return to New York, Roy inherits his deceased aunt's fortune and upon the death of his mother, comes into his father's fortune. Agnes, in the meantime, suffering from emotional exhaustion, is taken to Europe by her parents. There she gives birth to Roy's son and finally revives for the sake of the child. The deeply unhappy Roy cannot get over his love for Agnes and makes a South Sea voyage to Mauna Loa, where he disappears in a volcanic eruption and is declared dead, Agnes is his sole beneficiary and becomes an independently wealthy woman. The novel then, mysteriously, takes up the story of Harold Ferner, an American actor in Europe. Ferner, a great success on the stage and a friend of the Duke of Wales, has a surprising number of amorous adventures involving beautiful European noblewomen. Returning for a season in New York City, he is in the middle of a dramatic scene, when Agnes recognizes him as Roy. He had fallen into a cave in Mauna Loa, and was cared for by the daughter of a disgraced chief. He then traveled to Europe to revenge himself on the female sex in return for the pain he had suffered at Agnes' hands. However, he has since seen the error of his ways. At this point, Polly, Agnes' former maid, breaks into the room, confesses that she had plotted to break up Roy and Agnes because she loved Roy, and since she is dying is there to beg forgiveness. Agnes and Roy are reunited and move back to Chicago to be remarried and build a palatial home. In addition to revealing cultural concerns about social identity in an anonymous urban environment, the novel presents women as entirely emotional creatures who can arouse feelings in men that entirely control their actions.

638. Komroff, Manuel. *Coronet.* 2 vols. New York: Coward McCann, 1929. 677pp.

This work traces more than three hundred years in the history of a coronet commissioned by French Count de Senlis from the Italian goldsmith, Cappini, in 1600. The final owner of the coronet is George Mallet, a Chicago meat packer. The novel addresses the idea of social position in Chicago where wealth alone establishes social status and after the distinguished lives previously connected to the coronet, the final owner makes a sorry contrast.

639. Krautter, Elisa Bialk [Elisa Bialk, pseud.]. *On What Strange Stuff*. Garden City, N.Y.: Doubleday, Doran, 1935. 301pp.

In the prologue to this book the reader is alerted to the fact that the novel is an extended meditation on the nature of human ambition told through the lives of seven people. Among the characters is Gracie Rose, who grew up on the West Side and early decided to marry a powerful man. The beautiful Gracie is just sixteen when she gets a job with orchestra leader Jack Dell, as his personal secretary and fan club administrator. Through her work she meets the rich and famous and is soon dating Ben Streeter, a famous actor. Another character, Julia Nagoda, grew up in Bucktown, Chicago's Polish section, and wants to escape from her ethnic enclave. Among the male characters, Ed Dossinger wants a political career; hardworking James O'Donnell is focused on becoming a lawyer; Ben Adler, an actor; Peter Van Heusen, an artist; and Philip Gregory, a musician. Tracing each character's life over the period of three years and, looking at how some of the lives intersect, Krautter presents a complex social history of the early years of the 1930s, describing neighborhoods, clothing, restaurants, public entertainments, and implicitly presenting information about gender relations, social status, and values of lower and middle-class Chicagoans.

640. Krautter, Elisa Bialk. *Taffy's Foal*. Illustrated by William Moyers. Boston: Houghton Mifflin, 1949. 179pp.

This book teaches children to accept death and change, by presenting the story of Nancy. After her mother died when she was a toddler, her father, the owner of a Chicago furniture company, decided Nancy should live with her grandmother on a Kentucky horse farm. Nancy loves her life in Kentucky and her horse, a mare named Taffy. However, when her father remarries and wants to establish a home, ten-year-old Nancy must relocate to Chicago. She is sad about leaving Taffy, who is pregnant, but is determined to be positive about the move. Her father's apartment is in a doorman building on North Michigan Avenue with views of the famous buildings in the Loop. Nancy is enrolled at a private school for girls. Although she is shy, her teacher encourages her to share her interests and all Nancy talks about is Taffy. On the basis of this, her teacher suggests to Nancy's father that Taffy could be boarded at a stable in the Chicago metropolitan area. A short time afterwards Taffy is moved and soon gives birth to a colt Nancy names Starbright. Starbright is healthy, but Taffy dies from foaling complications. After some emotional struggle, Nancy eventually accepts Taffy's death. The book gives some indication of daily life in an upper-middle-class household in Chicago in the 1940s, but does not provide much description of the city.

641. Kurtz, Ann. *Pendy*. Charlotte, N.C.: Heritage House, 1960. 274pp.

Most of this novel is set in Chicago and deals with Pendina "Pendy" Verinoff's efforts to support her family. The oldest child in a Russian immigrant family, Pendy's father Nicholas was born a nobleman and her mother Clare the daughter of a wealthy landowner. However, Nicholas was disinherited for marrying Clare, a commoner, and with no practical skills the couple goes from failed enterprise to failed enterprise. They arrive in America through a relative's decision to establish Nicholas in business in Canada. After years of saving, he finally raises enough money to pay for the passage of his family, but by the time they arrive, his business has failed and they must move to Minneapolis. After more financial struggle, they are forced to relocate again to Chicago so that Nicholas can take up another job found by a charitable relative. In the midst of poverty and dislocation, Pendy holds the family together by taking care of her sisters and brothers. Nicholas becomes an invalid when Pendy is sixteen and she gets a department store job. Through energy, intelligence, and an innate understanding of human psychology she works her way up from counter girl to ever better positions, finally becoming a company representative demonstrating products. She begins to dream of becoming an actress and marrying her true love, the actor Ivor. However, she realizes that she will never make enough money to raise her family out of poverty and sacrifices her own wishes to marry a wealthy businessman. Much of the book is devoted to presenting the worlds of department stores and nineteenth-century salesmen (the novel is primarily set in the 1890s), including the material culture of the stores and the clothing, language usage, and modes of behavior used to establish social distinctions. The novel also includes descriptions of neighborhoods and the social interactions among groups of immigrants.

642. Lait, Jack. *The Beast of the City.* New York: Grosset and Dunlap, 1932. 218pp.

In this novelization of W. R. Burnett's film of the same name (Metro-Goldwyn-Mayer, 1932), Chicago Chief of Police Jim Fitzpatrick prides himself on his wholehearted battle against organized crime, his honesty, and his younger brother Ed, who followed him into the Chicago police department. However, bootlegger Giuseppe Belmonte avenges Jim's attacks by corrupting Ed with the assistance of stunning Daisy Beaumont. Quickly embracing a life of crime, Ed plots the theft of two hundred and fifty dollars that Jim has told him is being moved from one bank branch to another. The theft goes awry when Ed is double-crossed and a policeman and little girl get shot in the confusion. Outraged to discover Ed's involvement, Jim does not hesitate to charge him, but Belmonte, wanting to show Jim his power, uses his influence to get Ed acquitted. After a celebratory party hosted by Belmonte, the man who double-crossed Ed is found knifed. Assuming Belmonte and Ed were involved in the murder Jim renews his investigation of both of them. The climax of the novel comes when both Daisy and Jim's son Mickey are kidnapped by Belmonte's men. In the dramatic conclusion Ed saves Daisy and Mickey, but is mortally wounded and his reconciliation with Jim is necessarily posthumous. The Chicago physical settings in the novel are the merest backdrops as are the mentions of North Woods, Glendale, and Cannondale.

643. Lait, Jack. *Beef, Iron and Wine.* Garden City, New York: Doubleday, Page, 1916. 316pp.

This volume contains short stories, some of which have shared characters and run to novella length. Set on Chicago streets in the nineteen-teens, Some of the characters are reporters, but there are also beggars (some as young as five-years-old), chorus girls, policemen, vagrants, vaudeville performers, and a variety of criminals from scam artists to escaped convicts.

644. Lait, Jack. *Gus the Bus and Evelyn, the Exquisite Checker.* Garden City, N.Y.: Doubleday, Page, 1917. 342pp

The episodic nature of this work stems from the fact that the chapters appeared as columns in the *Chicago Herald*. The novel presents a humorously sympathetic view of the experiences of German immigrant Augustus Siegfried Schimmelhaus, the eponymous Gus of the title. A busboy at a Chicago restaurant, he has a crush on Evelyn, the restaurant billing clerk. In addition to presenting physical and cultural details about a pre-World War I restaurant, the book indicates what social life was like for working-class Chicagoans during the time period. Most of Gus and Evelyn's free time is late at night after the restaurant has closed, and they frequent dance halls, nightclubs and all-night movie theaters. Because Gus's family continues to live in Schleswig-Holstein, the outbreak of hostilities that lead to World War I are a great worry to him. In the end, when he must choose between his allegiance to the country of his origin and the United States, he chooses the latter and enlists as a soldier. Readers will note the wide variety of petty criminal activity in the novel, ranging from hucksterism to armed robbery.

645. Lait, Jack. *Put on the Spot.* New York: Grosset and Dunlap, 1930. 212pp.

In this novel about Chicago gangland warfare, Chicago's mayor actively schemes with police and negotiates with gangsters to find some way to end a period of violence and keep his office. When Edgewater Kid is slain by machine-gun fire, the murder is blamed on Kinky King, boss of the West Side mob, since the Kid, a member of the North Side mob headed by Goldie Gorio, had stolen the affections of Polack Annie away from him. When King is found dead, the avenger is assumed to be Gorio. Without proof and knowing Gorio's power, the mayor arrests Polack Annie for the King murder. In retaliation, Gorio's gang knocks out electrical power to downtown Chicago, shatters department store windows, and breaks Annie out of jail. Civic leaders begin to call for martial law as the mayor tries to get Typewriter Gleason's South Side gang to kill Gorio and his mob. In the meantime, Gorio has retired to his country estate for safety and to make a play for Annie. She complies after confessing that she killed King. Back at Gorio's city hideout one survivor escapes as Gleason's men kill Gorio's. The survivor makes it to the country to warn Gorio and from him Annie learns that Gorio killed the Kid to get her. Just as Annie takes her revenge by shooting Gorio, the police break in. They let Annie go free so they can take credit for slaying Gorio. The book includes almost no physical description of Chicago, although there are references to famous gangsters and their escapades and an appendix contains a glossary of underworld slang.

646. Lake, Joe Barry [Joe Barry, pseud.]. *The Fall Guy.* New York: Mystery House, 1945. 256pp.

In this private detective novel, three members of the same family separately try to hire the same detective. Rush Henry, a World War II military intelligence officer, is discharged early after a serious injury left him with a metal plate in his shoulder. Although he had been an investigative reporter with the *Chicago Express* before the war, upon his return, his old editor successfully persuaded him to become a private detective—an occupation that would be much more lucrative than journalism. In his new career, three members of the wealthy Germaine family each try to hire him. At first it seems as though a patent for a repeating rifle is at the heart of the case, but Henry soon discovers that a number of people, some of them gangsters, are trying to gain possession of some highly valuable emeralds. The novel consists mostly of dialogue and, with the exception of general addresses and references to neighborhoods, has little in the way of physical setting.

647. Lake, Joe Barry [Joe Barry, pseud.]. *The Third Degree.* New York: Mystery House, 1943. 256pp.

In this World War II espionage novel, Rush Henry, former Chicago crime reporter and current undercover agent for Army Intelligence, is sent to Detroit to investigate the source of fake birth certificates that are plaguing the Army. When he encounters a Chicago gangster in Detroit he realizes the operation has a base in his home city as well. Henry's search takes him into mansions and expensive apartment hotels in Chicago, as well as a yacht on the lake. He eventually finds the mastermind, a German sympathizer with connections to Hitler, and locates the records of the false documents.

648. Lake, Joe Barry. *Three for the Money.* Kingston, N.Y.: Handi-Book Editions / Quinn, 1950. 123pp.

When police find Sammy Burns knifed at Chicago's airport, actress Vikki Lake, a witness to the discovery, hires private investigator Bill August to protect her from police investigation, claiming she does not want her millionaire fiancé to find out certain things about her. August eventually discovers that Lake was being blackmailed by fellow actor Jack Cary, so that he would not reveal that she was already married. This brief novel is mostly focused on August's investigation and includes little description of physical settings.

649. Lake, Joe Barry. *The Triple Cross; a Rush Henry Mystery*. New York: Mystery House, 1946. 256pp.

Chicago detective Rush Henry is almost killed three times in this mystery novel that opens with him in a Des Moines hospital with a head wound and partial amnesia. His condition means that when he returns to Chicago his assistants must explain a good deal about his life in the city to him, although the Chicago locale is still somewhat shallowly portrayed. The mystery that Rush eventually solves involves what really happened when a yacht sank decades before and the true identity of the beautiful young woman who became millionaire George Michael Simon's heir.

650. Lally, John Patrick. *Anne Herrick*. Chicago: Burt, 1934. 251pp.

Set in Depression-era Chicago, this novel illustrates the emotional strain and physical discomforts experienced by impoverished white-collar workers, as well as specifically highlighting the challenges faced by Chicago public schoolteachers. Anne Herrick, the daughter of a schoolteacher, is just beginning her own teaching career when the Depression strikes. As the economic situation worsens, schools are unable to pay their teachers and Anne must find a way to support her parents and sister, with whom she lives in a mortgaged house in Rogers Park. Anne still has debts from the last year of her education at the University of Chicago and from the first courses she is taking toward her graduate degree. When her sixty-year-old father dies from pneumonia, his medical expenses are enough to capsize the family and they lose the family house. Despite the Depression, Anne's romantic life proceeds. She has two suitors, Peter Nash, a fellow teacher, and Dick Hardy, an electrical engineer she met at the University of Chicago. Believing that she must allow her family's well-being a place in her marriage considerations, she eventually chooses Hardy over Nash, convincing herself that she really is in love with him. When Hardy patents an invention for improved radio technology, Anne's financial worries end. However, she undergoes new emotional trials when her love for Peter becomes too strong to ignore. A melodramatic climax resolves the emotional stress. The novel presents a compelling portrait of the trials faced by Chicagoans during the Depression.

651. Lamb, Martha Joanna. *Spicy*. New York: Appleton, 1873. 178pp.

This romance novel presents the years 1862 to 1871 in the lives of Mrs. Medley Belmore and her sixteen-year-old sister, Spicy Merriman. At the beginning of the novel, Belmore is recently married and has a baby. Her husband, General Belmore, is away fighting in the Civil War. The sisters live in a rented house that is large and old-fashioned. When they find letters in the house that describe a romance of a decade before, they concern themselves with finding out who wrote them and how the writer's life turned out. Solving the mystery becomes vital when mysterious events begin taking place in the house, including the theft of Belmore's jewels and the disappearance of one of the servants. The account of life in the Belmore household is punctuated by descriptions of historical events, such as the two sanitary fairs Chicago women conducted to raise money for wounded Civil War soldiers, the assassination of President Lincoln and his funeral procession through Chicago, and the fire of 1871. The novel gives a good sense of a middle-class household in the 1860s, portraying the relationship between householders and servants, merchants, and tradesmen. In the early part of the book, before the return of General Belmore from the battlefield, the work illustrates the challenges an all-female household faces in terms of physical safety.

652. Lamensdorf, Leonard. *Kane's World*. New York: Simon and Schuster, 1968. 378pp.

As the title implies, this novel limns the world of Norman Kane, a Jewish real estate developer. For years Kane has been developing land in Chicago and making a good profit. He already owns ten apartment buildings on the lake, but has long wanted to establish his legacy by developing the remaining premier parcels of lakefront, which are owned by the feuding Kincaid family. Kane purchased the first parcel years earlier; when he gets inside information that the youngest of the Kincaids, Delbert, has been given a six-month option on the entire remaining tract, Kane begins maneuvering to make the purchase. The novel traces all of the deals Kane strikes in order to: get Delbert to agree to sell, get financing from investors for the purchase and construction, get the property rezoned for the six office towers Kane wants to build, secure a famous architect, and rent space in the new buildings prior to construction. Kane's interactions highlight ethnic and class-based prejudices, illustrate various levels of Chicago's power base, and reveal the motivations that drive someone like Kane. Physical descriptions of Chicago focus on some of the architectural and planning mistakes that made parts of the city undesirable by the 1960s.

653. Lardner, Ring. *Gullible's Travels*. Illustrated by May Wilson Preston. Indianapolis: Bobbs-Merrill, 1917. 255pp.

The narrative voice in these five humorous stories is that of a Chicago husband who has made money in the stock market and must now suffer his wife's efforts to spend his wealth. While they continue to play poker with some of their old friends and go out to vaudeville shows and the movies, "the Missus" tries to climb a few rungs on the social ladder through opera attendance, a trip to Palm Beach, and membership in a society bridge club. Beyond naming some landmarks, such as the Auditorium, the stories make little of the Chicago physical setting. However, the narrator's plain-speaking reveals cultural attitudes of the time period.

654. Lardner, Ring. *You Know Me Al: A Busher's Letters*. New York: Scribner, 1925. 247pp.

This humorous, epistolary work features letters from Jack Keefe, a rookie baseball player. Not surprisingly, a good deal of the content of the missives has to do with baseball. However, Keefe also tells about his living situation, social life, and life as a newlywed, giving some sense of lower-middle-class life in Chicago during the 1920s.

655. Lardner, Ring. *Own Your Own Home*. Illustrated by Fontaine Fox. Indianapolis: Bobbs-Merrill, 1919. 123pp.

In this epistolary novel, Fred A. Gross writes his brother Charlie to describe his experiences in building a house in the suburbs of Chicago. His wife Grace instigated the project and the story includes every aspect of house building from obtaining financing and land, to haggling with the architect and dealing with contractors.

656. Larsen, Nella. *Passing*. New York: Alfred A. Knopf, 1929. 215pp.

As the title indicates, this novel is about concealing one's African-American heritage to pass as Caucasian. Irene Redfield and Clare Kendry knew each other as girls in Chicago, but both have moved away from the city to escape racial prejudice. Redfield is married to a physician and lives in the middle-class respectability that Harlem offers economically successful African-Americans. Kendry, raised as white by her father's sisters after being orphaned, married a white businessman who does not know her mixed race and has mostly lived in Europe. Both happen to visit Chicago at the same time and become reacquainted by accident. When Kendry and her husband later spend an extended period of time in New York, Kendry pursues a friendship with Redfield that ends disastrously. The novel provides a sense of the extent of racial prejudice in Chicago and reveals some aspects of life in the city for African-Americans.

657. Larsen, Nella. *Quicksand*. New York: Alfred A. Knopf, 1928. 301pp.

This novel about racial identity in the United States, set in the 1920s, has some Chicago content. Protagonist Helga Crane was born and grew up in the city, the daughter of a Danish woman and an African-American man, who abandoned Crane's mother. Helga was orphaned at fifteen and sent away to school in the Deep South by her mother's brother. She does well in African-American schools, graduates, and becomes a teacher, but grows dissatisfied with a segregated environment. She returns to Chicago only to find racism and a lack of opportunity for educated African-Americans. She soon leaves for New York City where she lives in Harlem and is able to build a life for herself, although her internalized racism so controls her thinking and shapes all of her decisions that she ends up marrying an African-American preacher and living a servile life, exhausted by repeated pregnancies. Chicago in the novel is contrasted unfavorably with New York City and portrayed as dominated by racism.

658. Latimer, Jonathan Wyatt. *Headed for a Hearse*. Garden City, N.Y.: Crime Club / Doubleday, Doran, 1935. 306pp.

With only days left until his execution, wealthy Robert Westland, convicted of murder and on death row, is finally roused to hire a private investigator in the hope of finding the real culprit. Westland had been estranged from his wife at the time she was murdered, but still went into shock over her death and was in an emotionally confused state throughout the trial. Only six days away from execution, he employs his considerable wealth to bribe the prison warden for special privileges, hire shady lawyer Charles Finklestein, and retain private investigator William Crane. Most of the characters are affluent, or have expensive tastes, and clearly part of the appeal of this novel to Depression-era readers was the vicarious enjoyment of elaborately described meals and expensive apartments, clothing, entertainments, and nightclubs. Interestingly, most of the restaurants and nightclubs have some sort of gimmick (like recreating an interior from the *Normandie*, or authentic German, Italian, or French interiors) and presumably reflect the actual nightlife of Chicago in the 1930s.

659. Latimer, Jonathan. *The Lady in the Morgue*. Garden City, N.Y.: Crime Club / Doubleday, Doran, 1936. 296pp.

When a woman is murdered and her corpse stolen, the men attempting to recover her body have varying motivations. Private detective William Crane was hired on contract by a nationwide detective agency owned by Colonel Black to identify the corpse of a beautiful young woman. His job quickly becomes more complicated and dangerous when the discovery is made that the body was stolen from the Cook County Morgue and the morgue attendant was murdered just after Crane visits. As a prime suspect in these crimes, Crane is subjected to violence by the police, gangster Frankie French, and Teamster Union official Mike Paletta. The police want a confession, French thinks the missing body may be used to get him into trouble, and Paletta thinks the corpse may be the body of his wife. Soon other claimants to the body turn up, including jazz orchestra musician Peter Udoni and Chauncey Courtland, nephew of the man retaining Black's firm. The complexity of the case and wealth of the Courtlands mean that Crane's efforts are reinforced by two more of Black's detectives. All of them move into a two-bedroom suite in an expensive hotel and enjoy meals and alcohol on their client's account while following leads that take them to seedy hotels, bars, and taxi-dance halls. To establish the setting, the author details clothing, food, and interiors and presents dialogue and characters not integral to the plot. Consistent with the prejudices of the time, there are racist presentations of African-Americans and Filipinos. The novel takes place during the summer and the effect of the heat on city residents before air-conditioning is treated repeatedly.

660. Latimer, Jonathan. *Sinners and Shrouds*. An Inner Sanctum Mystery. New York: Simon and Schuster, 1955. 250pp.

When his divorce decree comes through, Sam Clay goes out on the town to celebrate, becoming so drunk that he remembers nothing of a thirteen hour time period. When he comes to, he finds himself in bed beside the murdered corpse of affluent society columnist Mary Trevor. He flees her bedroom in horrified confusion only to find out a few hours later that he has been assigned to report on the case for his newspaper. Secretly, the managing editor, Edwin Justin Standish, also wants Clay to solve the case before the police, since Standish had clandestinely dated Trevor and is fearful of suspicion falling on him, along with the accompanying scandal. Before long Clay finds another dead young woman and realizes that when he discovers who the women knew in common, he will find the murderer. Bigamy and blackmail are motivations for the murders and new technologies of the time period, such as voice recorders, play an important role. The novel includes descriptions of newsrooms and journalistic practice, police stations, and a brothel.

661. Laughlin, Clara Elizabeth. *Felicity: The Making of a Comedienne*. Illustrated by Alice Barber Stevens. New York: Charles Scribner's Sons, 1907. 426pp.

Covering the time period 1869 through 1898 in the life of Felicity Fergus, who becomes an internationally known actress, this novel is set in Chicago, Massachusetts, New York City, and Louisiana. Felicity's mother died shortly after giving birth and her father died of fever as a hospital volunteer during the Civil War. Felicity's life is transformed when her amateur theatrical performance attracts a famous visiting actor. The Ferguses' next door neighbors, the Allstons, are related to Phineas Morton, a nationally known actor. When Morton sees talent in Felicity he offers to take her into his acting company as a student. After Felicity has matured into a skilled actress, several of the most important events in her life transpire in Chicago. Her friend and mentor Adelaide Walters dies in the city and is buried in Graceland Cemetery. The grieving Felicity is taken out to dinner at several landmark Chicago restaurants to be comforted and when the neighborhood friend of her childhood, Morton Allston, hears of her bereavement, he has her to dinner in his Chicago house. Allston is on hand again when Felicity experiences an even more tragic death in 1895. She had married fellow actor Vincent Delano and the actor is killed when he shields her from the bullet of a drunken rogue. The wake is held in Morton Allston's house and three years later, Allston and Felicity wed. In addition to hotels, restaurants, and theaters, Felicity visits landmarks near the Loop, and Michigan Avenue. She is also forced to walk along the border of the red-light district on Wabash. Given the author's theme of post-Civil War reconciliation, Chicago clearly has major symbolic importance for her.

662. Laughlin, Clara Elizabeth. *Just Folks*. New York: Macmillan, 1910. 377pp.

This novel articulates the problems that arise from the low social status of women in the early twentieth century and presents these problems as the common ground that unites women of all social classes. Soon after taking a job as a juvenile court probation officer, Beth Tully, daughter of a deceased judge, moves into the neighborhood of the working-class people she has the mission to serve. She takes a room in the tiny apartment of Liza Allen, a dressmaker on Maxwell Street whose life has been filled with sorrow. Years before, Allen's fiancé left her when she thought it was more important to use her savings to pay a debt incurred by her brother than to contribute to establishing a household. In the fire of 1871 she lost the small business she had established and for the past seventeen years she has cared for her incapacitated brother, who suffers from the effects of life-long alcoholism. Allen's stories are characteristic of other women Tully encounters and these stories make up the bulk of the book. In most of them women subject their own will to that of seriously flawed men. Out of love they labor with great industry to take advantage of the incredibly modest economic opportunities available to them. The plight of children who have no legal rights and are denied schooling and leisure is conveyed through the stories, as well. As Beth tries to make practical improvements in the lives of her fellow slum-dwellers, she is drawn closer to her fiancé, Hart Ferris, a crusading newspaperman who exposes conditions in the slums. The couple had decided not to marry until Ferris made enough money to rent a middle-class apartment, but after their experiences in the Maxwell Street ghetto, the couple decides not to postpone marriage and chooses to live in modest accommodations there. In addition to issues of social class, gender, and age, the novel deals with the impact of ethnicity and religion on acculturation.

663. Laughlin, Clara Elizabeth. *The Penny Philanthropist: A Story That Could Be True*. Illustrated by Victor Semon Pérard. New York: Fleming H. Revell, 1912. 217pp.

At a time when Irish political bosses helped their constituents secure jobs and introduced philanthropists to those in need of charity, Peggy, an eighteen-year-old Irish orphan who runs a newsstand, performs some of the same functions without having any political or economic power. She, and three younger siblings whom she supports, live in the basement of a townhouse on Halsted Street, in the center of the immigrant neighborhood known as Whitechapel. Peggy has befriended Andrew Kimbalton, the owner of the nearby factory where many of the people who rely on Peggy work. One aspect of Peggy's activity involves giving a penny every day directly to whomever needs it. However, many problems are too large to be aided by a penny and she also helps people by connecting them with more affluent benefactors. For example, after she meets Tom Oliphant and learns he has not been able to find an accountant job since his father was falsely convicted of embezzlement, she convinces Kimbalton to hire him. Then, when she realizes that Oliphant has unwittingly befriended a union agitator, she introduces Oliphant to a police detective and Oliphant helps derail a bombing the agitators had planned in order to kill Kimbalton. Realizing his close escape from death, Kimbalton intervenes on behalf of Oliphant's father and improves Peggy's living quarters and expands her business, in accordance with her wishes, into a sort of reading room for her acquaintances who have nowhere to go during the day. Through description and dialogue the novel presents a convincing portrait of the Whitechapel district in the early twentieth century while raising issues of ethnicity, gender, and social class.

664. Lawrence, Catherine Ann. *The Narrowing Wind*. New York: Dodd, Mead, 1944. 214pp.

Dealing with challenges faced by working-class women in the 1940s, this novel focuses on the experiences of a young woman as she gets a job in the city during World War II and makes the transition from rural to urban life. The daughter of Irish immigrants who work on an Illinois farm, Shane Kearney was forced to leave school after eighth grade to work odd jobs to help with household expenses. As she reaches her late teens, Shane realizes she must get a factory job in the city if she is ever to save money for her own future, and continue to assist her parents. She finds work assembling tachometers for the Story-McNeil Company at the intersection of Diversey and Western Avenues. Her fifty-five mile commute takes two and a half hours each way. Shane's adjustment to factory life and her fellow workers illustrates how ethnicity is a major factor in social interactions among characters from Armenia, France, Germany, Hungary, Poland, and Sweden. Although Shane longs to move to Chicago, her older sister Katie's example is ever before her. Katie moved to Chicago and married, only to be abandoned by her husband Bert after supporting a household and two children on a limited income became unbearable. When Katie moves back to the farm, Shane takes over her sister's apartment and is soon sharing it with a girlfriend from the factory. The rest of the novel is devoted to Shane's first romances and increasing ambition to compete for the supervisory jobs held by men. The novel documents working-class life in Chicago in the 1940s and prejudices based on ethnicity, rural origins, and gender.

665. Lawson, Don. *A Brand for the Burning*. London, U.K.: Abelard-Schuman, 1961. 254pp.

Through the family of "Mutter" Brosi, the author encapsulates more than two decades of cultural history from the years after World War I through World War II. Grandmother Brosi, known, even as a young woman, as "Mutter" or "mother," emigrated from Switzerland to Chicago with her husband Conrad in the 1880s. She convinced her husband to move to the western suburbs of Chicago and take a job with an established Swiss immigrant, Jacob Braun, who owned a successful dairy. She then used Conrad's earnings to buy land in the area, in the imaginary suburb of Maple Grove, that she sold at fair prices to Swiss people from her home canton. Eventually, her daughters, Christina and Greta, marry Swedish brothers, Pike and Bill Erikson. Pike settled down immediately after high school and built a successful lumber and coal business, but Bill engaged in a range of ventures that never panned out. After serving in World War I, he sold building lots he owned with his brother, but marketed them with a low down-payment scheme so that when the stock market crashed the business was wiped out. He left Maple Grove in disgrace, but returned in desperate straits to take a supervisory job in the local camp of the Civilian Conservation Corps. By the time World War II approaches, the novel's plot focuses on Mark Erikson, Pike's son, and is mostly set in Iowa and England as Mark goes through college and is drafted into the army. Unlike many other novels set in Chicago suburbs, here the draw of downtown neighborhoods is less apparent, perhaps because Maple Grove maintains some integrity as a small town.

666. Lawson, Robert. *The Great Wheel*. New York: Viking Press, 1957. 188pp.

In this illustrated work for children, Lawson addresses themes of the immigrant experience and social class, as well as describing the Columbian Exposition. Growing up in Ireland, Cornelius "Conn" Kilroy is satisfied with village life, but his fortune-reading grandmother reveals that his destiny is in the West. So, as an eighteen-year-old, when his wealthy New York City uncle, a sewer contractor on municipal projects, contacts him and suggests he should come to learn his business, Conn sets out for America. Once he arrives in New York, however, he decides to travel on to Chicago to help in the construction of G.W.G. Ferris's Great Wheel at the Columbian Exposition. The rest of the book recounts his experiences on the fairgrounds. After the wheel is complete, he works as an attendant and is reunited with a young German woman, Trudy Zillheimer, who was on the same immigrant ship as him, when she attends the fair. By the end of the novel he has realized that closeness to the land is more important to him than the chance at wealth he has in learning his uncle's sewer business. So, he moves to Wisconsin to marry Trudy, work on the dairy farm of her uncle and learn traditional cheese-making. The book provides detailed information about the Ferris wheel, as well as an overview of the exposition, while presenting a view of the important contribution immigrants have made to the vitality of the United States.

667. Lee, Ella Dolbear. *Jean Mary Solves the Mystery*. New York: Burt, 1933. 256pp.

Sections of this novel, focused on lost identity, are set in Lake Forest, Illinois. The book describes a set of affluent young people whose main residences are on the North Shore. They socialize at their country houses and in the city, but spend much of the year in other parts of the country and abroad. At the beginning of the novel Aline Bennett is living outside Philadelphia as an adoptee of her mean-spirited aunt; her parentage has been kept secret. At fifteen, she can no longer stand her Aunt's cruelties and runs away. When she is saved from accidental drowning by a summering brother and sister, Anthony Gale and Mrs. Heath (whose first name is never revealed), Mrs. Heath decides to adopt Aline and she is soon off to finishing school in Switzerland. In the meantime, Gale travels to England to unravel a mystery about his family's origins that dates back to the seventeenth century. When Mrs. Heath dies, Aline (who has changed her name to Nancy Lou), begins teaching at a private school in Lake Forest, which is where she is reunited with Gale, who has resolved the mystery of his past and become John Kent. The portrayal of the Chicago metropolitan area in the novel as a base for the very affluent is particularly interesting since it was written in the early years of the Depression.

668. Lee, Jennette (Perry). *Mr. Achilles*. New York: Dodd, Mead, 1912. 261pp.

In this melodramatic novel, the friendship between a Greek immigrant and the daughter of a newly rich Chicago industrialist is calculated to counter negative portrayals of the nouveaux riches and of immigrants common in the time period. The industrialist's daughter, twelve-year-old Betty Harris, is a natural intellectual with an interest in classical culture. When a Greek-immigrant fruit merchant, Achilles Alexandrakis, accidentally meets Betty, he also considers her extraordinary because she shows an interest in the history and culture of Greece. Betty's mother is unusual in another way, in that she is able to overlook Alexandrakis' lower-class appearance and appreciate his inner cultivation. When he appears at the Harris residence while Mrs. Harris is hosting the North Side Halcyon Club, a society for affluent ladies devoted to topics of art and culture, she invites Alexandrakis to speak to the group, at great risk to her social standing, when the scheduled classical scholar does not appear. He rewards Mrs. Harris' boldness by doing an excellent job. Soon afterwards Betty is kidnapped and Alexandrakis devotes himself to her rescue, eventually succeeding where the police have failed. In addition to addressing prejudice, the novel touches on the epidemic of kidnappings that plagued wealthy families in the early twentieth century.

669. Lee, Norman [Mark Corrigan, pseud.]. *Dumb as They Come*. London, U.K.: Angus and Robertson, 1957. 224pp.

One of a series of books presented as first-person accounts of the adventures of international private investigator Mark Corrigan. In this story Corrigan aids an attractive blonde Chicago actress accused of murder.

670. Leiber, Fritz Reuter. *The Sinful Ones*. New York: Universal, 1950. 319pp.

The main character in this work of science fiction becomes convinced that the entire world is a machine in which human free will is an illusion. Originally published as part of a two-in-one paperback volume, the novel was partnered with erotica about a female toreador, demonstrating that the frank sexuality of Leiber's work overwhelmed any consideration of literary merit in the repressed 1950s. Leiber's tale is dependent upon recording in great detail aspects of daily life, including modes of dress, household and office furnishings, street scenes, office interactions, and so forth, in order to establish main character Carr Mackey's increasing terror over the perception that the world he experiences is actually part of a huge automaton and that every person with which he interacts are parts of the machine. When he steps slightly outside his frame of reference with the encouragement of Jane Zabel, he enters a parallel universe that is the opposite of the automaton. Instead of being connected in the universal machine, he and his fellows are in mortal competition. In addition to details of life in Chicago in the late 1940s, Leiber includes descriptions of public monuments and buildings, such as the Chicago Public Library, the Art Institute, the Tribune Tower, the Wrigley Building, and Taft's Great Lakes fountain.

671. Lengel, William Charles. *Candles in the Wind*. New York: Ives Washburn, 1937. 296pp.

In this romance novel, set at the turn of the twentieth century, some women have begun to embrace new social freedoms and form liaisons for the sake of romance, not marriage. The characters are connected to the millinery industry and the main employer is the House of Fields. Founder George Fields, a ladies' man, chose to marry a woman who was the opposite of his paramours; Grace Jordan, a plain schoolteacher in her late twenties. When Fields died prematurely, Samuel Harper, a consulting efficiency expert, saw his opportunity to inveigle himself permanently into the lucrative business and, as soon as seemed decent, courted and married the childless widow Grace, now in her late thirties. Harper soon discovers Grace's infatuation with Fields' most successful salesman, Peter Madigan. Peter is devoted to his invalid wife, but his magnetic charm draws women to him. Grace finds opportunities to invite Peter to her house and through these visits, Jane Owain, a Welsh servant, becomes smitten with him as well. She gets a job as a hat model at Fields, and is soon featured in advertisements. As Grace sees the attraction between Jane and Peter develop, she alerts Peter that Jane is a fallen woman (she had a baby out of wedlock in Wales). Peter pities Jane rather than despises her and begins to think ill of Grace and of Samuel, who finds petty ways to express his jealousy of Peter's successes. Before long, Peter becomes determined to take the House of Fields away from the Harpers. When they refuse to sell, he establishes his own firm, which is immediately successful. As the Harpers watch their business wane, Grace reveals that an artist turned an innocent portrait sitting with Jane into a nude. Peter is unconcerned and when the picture is exhibited it establishes Jane as a beauty and makes the artist famous. However, Grace contacts the immigration authorities and they begin deliberations on deporting Jane as an immoral woman. Peter laughs off the threat and takes Jane on a buying trip to Paris where he receives news of his wife's death. Now free to marry, Peter becomes preoccupied with business. Then, Jane falls ill and when she receives a letter from the immigration authorities she is too frightened to open it. When she seeks Peter's emotional support, she finds him with another woman. Exhausted by her illness and stunned by her discovery, she dies in the street with the letter unopened in her hand. Her funeral is elaborate and well-attended, populated by many remorseful people. Lengel's novel does not clearly establish a Chicago physical setting, focusing instead on his characters and their dialogue to ground his plot.

672. Levin, Meyer. *Citizens*. New York: Viking Press, 1940. 650pp.

When physician Mitch Wilner is persuaded by his wife to visit the site of a steel mill strike in an area between Gary and Chicago known as Steel Harbor, Wilner concedes reluctantly. His life is focused on his work and research and he begrudges any time taken away from these activities. His wife Sylvia has been taking enrichment courses at a local college and met sociologists and other young people very involved with the issues raised by the strike. When they reach Steel Harbor, the Wilners find a large number of strikers and strike supporters picnicking. The strikers, who have been prevented from picketing by police, are spurred on by their supporters, but as the group gathers, the police begin firing on them and Dr. Wilner suddenly finds himself treating fatally wounded men. The event raises Wilner's awareness of labor issues and the callous disregard of life by police and officials. Most of the book is occupied with Wilner's attempts to find out what happened to the wounded and his later appearances as a witness at trials and hearings, but Levin fleshes out his story by relating the life stories of a number of the slain workers. In doing so, Levin touches on the steel industry, labor/management relations, domestic life of the working poor, and life within the African-American, German, Irish, and Polish immigrant communities. The book as a whole illustrates prejudices against alternative political groups, Jews, Catholics, and union organizers.

673. Levin, Meyer. *Compulsion*. New York: Simon and Schuster, 1956. 495pp.

Levin's fictionalized version of the Leopold-Loeb case (in which two young Chicago men, possessed of all the signifiers of social status, violate all standards of morality by kidnapping a fourteen-year-old boy, attempting to collect ransom money, then murdering the boy and mutilating his body in a sexually deviant fashion) is told through the eyes of a cub reporter acquainted with the young men. In the vein of many social commentators at the time, the investigative reporting of the novel that looks into family and social relations of the criminals, tries to explain how young men who are wealthy and intelligent, and therefore at the acme of social status, could commit such a degraded crime. Levin uses most of the facts of the actual case, while changing the names of everyone involved, including defense lawyer Clarence Darrow, for whom a good deal of admiration is expressed for trying to get the murderers a fair trial amidst great public hostility.

674. Levin, Meyer. *Frankie and Johnnie*. New York: John Day, 1930. 212pp.

Levin details a first romance and reveals cultural attitudes to sexuality, romance, and marriage in the 1920s. The narrative is mostly composed of the inner thoughts of the lovers as their attitude towards each other change over time. Frances, or Frankie, a high school senior, is the sister of Johnnie's best friend Steve. Johnnie has graduated and is working at a hardware mail order fulfillment house. As the two begin to go on dates, each becomes curious about the other's body. Their relationship continues to be chaste, but their kissing and cuddling starts to take place in more isolated spots, like parked cars and moonlit beaches, as their relationship is openly accepted by friends and family. Although he never tells Frankie, Johnnie becomes frustrated over not having sex. He also begins to think about the practical aspects of marriage, speculating on how much money he needs to make. When Frankie graduates and gets a switchboard job, Johnnie gets a better paid job as a car mechanic, and becomes more optimistic about the future. When Frankie breaks off the romance, Johnnie continues to feel passionately about her, a passion expressed in thoughts of murder and suicide. Frankie misses Johnnie, but begins dating more eligible men and dreaming of a moment she has not yet had when she will kiss a man and immediately know he is "the One." By the end of the novel, from their fantasies, it is clear that the couple no longer has anything in common. Although the book is preoccupied with capturing the thoughts and feelings of the lovers, the Chicago setting is important, and includes descriptions of social activities, including parties, ice cream parlor dates, and seeing movies or live musical performances (such as those by the Paul Whiteman Orchestra) at the Tivoli, Chicago, and Oriental. The couples' lack of privacy stemming from cultural factors is also made clear. Frankie and Johnnie each live in apartments with their parents and Johnnie usually makes telephone calls to Frankie from public telephones. Automobiles are important as opportunities for privacy and Johnnie often gets to borrow his father's Chevrolet.

675. Levin, Meyer. *The Harvest*. New York: Simon and Schuster, 1978. 670pp.

Mostly a historical novel about the founding of Israel during the 1930s and 1940s, the third of the book set in Chicago deals with Mati Chaimovitch's story. As a twenty-year-old, Mati travels from Palestine to study at the University of Chicago on a grant arranged by an American scholar, Horace Rappaport, who had visited Palestine and married one of Mati's teachers. Mati's experiences in the United States raise issues of assimilation as he is exposed to Reform Judaism and to the personal adjustments American Jews make in order to succeed in business or society. Mati himself is forced to negotiate between religious teaching and secular life when he must choose between two women: the free-spirited and sexually available Andrea; and Dena Kossof, a traditional girl from the Zionist youth group in which he participates. After Mati's mother dies and his brother is killed in an Arab attack, Mati returns to Palestine and must decide whether to become the manager of the family citrus farm or return to Chicago and finish his degree. He does go back to Chicago and takes an even more public role as emissary from Palestine to Jewish groups in the city. He also learns to fly and eventually marries Dena. The book depicts Jewish participation in Chicago's intellectual and upper-middle-class circles in the 1930s, although most of the novel is set in London and Palestine.

676. Levin, Meyer. *The Old Bunch*. New York: Viking Press, 1937. 964pp.

Using more than twenty main characters, "the old bunch," Levin constructs a complex narrative that captures Jewish life in Chicago from 1921 to 1934. The characters are adolescents at the beginning of the story and fully experience jazz age Chicago, featuring titillating new sexual freedoms (represented by flappers), the dangers to the public presented by warring gangsters, political bossism, and the challenges and promise of labor organizing. The Chicago World's Fair of 1933 plays a major role in the later part of the book.

677. Levin, Meyer. *Reporter*. New York: John Day, 1929. 409pp.

This novel details the life of an anonymous reporter for the *Chicago Daily Press* as he gathers information and writes stories, some of which are included in the text of the novel. He has no life outside of work, having previously been romantically involved with a young woman, only to discover that she is pregnant by another man. Two big news stories dominate the reporter's work: an episode of gangland warfare, and the "society theft" of a valuable pearl necklace that was supposedly stolen by a millionaire's son. He is delighted when he gets to cover part of the Scopes trial, interview Clarence Darrow, and try to expose the sanctimony of fundamentalists. The reporter also writes celebrity interviews occasioned by the Chicago visits of Calvin Coolidge, and D. W. Griffith. Griffith is in town to film a movie version of Edwin Balmer's *That Royle Girl* (entry 83) and the reporter watches some of the filming. This privileged access is typical throughout the book: merely because of his profession he observes an autopsy, has access to prison cells, and gets into people's houses by simply announcing himself. Although he writes many unsavory human interest stories, he escapes the label "scurrilous" by his devotion to the power of investigative reporting to correct societal wrongs. The novel has no dramatic conclusion. Instead, the reader leaves the reporter as he tries to decide among a series of leads to follow. The book is rich in details about neighborhoods, businesses, and daily life in apartments and modest houses.

678. Lewin, Michael Z. *The Enemies Within*. New York: Alfred A. Knopf, 1974. 225pp.

Private detective Albert Samson has the unenviable reputation of being the least expensive and impressive member of his profession in Indianapolis. However, a shady antiques dealer with the assumed name of M. Bennett Willson hires Samson to protect him from the inquiries of a private detective from Chicago named Artie Bartholomew. When it turns out that Willson lives with a woman who disguises herself as a man, Samson's interest is piqued and he begins his own investigation. The tale involves incest, illegitimacy, abortion, and murder. Chicago is of past importance to several characters and Samson spends time in the city tracing leads. Living situations are described, although the novel is most concerned with characterization.

679. Lewis, Edwin Herbert. *Those About Trench*. New York: Macmillan, 1916. 326pp.

Dr. Isham Trench, a twenty-nine-year-old man, inherited a fortune when his parents died in a shipwreck. He has devoted himself to caring for the babies and children of the Halsted Street neighborhood, teaching medicine at Lister College, and providing housing in his residence for medical students from abroad who would experience prejudice in the housing market. While Trench is dryly pragmatic, not even wishing to have children because there are too many births in the world already, the book is highly romantic and is filled with unlikely coincidences. Trench's medical cases illuminate medical problems stemming from social conditions affecting women and children. Although many of these relate to working and living conditions, the book also touches on the problems experienced by women forced to live as single mothers when they are abandoned by the fathers of their children. Although mostly concerned with conveying a moral message, the novel details living and social conditions in the Halsted Street neighborhood in the early twentieth century and touches on issues of racial and ethnic prejudice and the social status of women.

680. Linn, James Weber. *The Second Generation*. New York: Macmillan, 1902. 305pp.

In this novel about political corruption and the power of the free press, the protagonist, Jerome Kent begins his job at the *Chicago Eagle* and explores the city. From small-town Scannell, Indiana, Kent's father was the publisher and editor of the local newspaper, and Kent witnessed his fight twenty years before to expose the corrupt local political boss Congressman Christopher Wheeler. In a public confrontation, Wheeler hits Kent's father, in response to the accusation that he sold his vote to an oil corporation, and Kent's father later dies of the injury. Afterwards, Henry Northrup, a friend of Kent's father who is the proprietor of the *Chicago Eagle*, mentors Jerome Kent, provides him with social opportunities unusual to a young reporter, and secretly encourages him to expose Wheeler, now a politically-powerful, millionaire-banker in the city. In a coincidence, Kent finds Wheeler injured in the street from a mugging. He helps Wheeler home and then, hoping for a "scoop," rushes back to the crime scene. Wheeler's wallet is there, emptied of everything except papers that provide evidence of Wheeler's efforts to bribe legislators to vote for a measure beneficial to an oil company. His scoop becomes complicated when he falls in love with Wheeler's daughter, and is later falsely arrested and convicted of assaulting and robbing Wheeler. In the end, Wheeler's own evil defeats him. The early sections of the novel describe Chicago, social events, and work life in a city newsroom.

681. Linn, James Weber. *This Was Life*. Indianapolis: Bobbs-Merrill, 1936. 304pp.

While mostly concerned about life on the campus of the University of Chicago in 1893, unlike many college novels of this period that have an on-campus focus, in this book students spend some time exploring the city and making friends and acquaintances. In part, this is because so many of the students are Chicago residents. Protagonist Jerry Grant, the son of a minister, clearly exemplifies the author's conception of a young scholar and athlete. Grant enthusiastically studies Greek, but is also on the football team and boxes. The novel also presents a vision of social hierarchy in which New Englanders and the Harvard educated are accorded highest social status. Grant socializes freely on the campus, which has a student body of only one thousand students, and dates Dorothy Keith, a fellow student whose family gave the money for the dormitory in which he lives. One of his father's parishioners is a newspaper city editor and Jerry spends some time around the newspaper office and on the trail of stories (he witnesses a shooting, a deadly apartment building fire, and investigates the murder of a university student). The book rehearses some of the issues pertinent to the early development of the university (fraternities, coeducation, and the high percentage of junior faculty) and describes a number of restaurants and saloons of the time period, ranging from the disreputable to the most socially respectable.

682. Linn, James Weber. *Winds Over the Campus.* Indianapolis: Bobbs-Merrill, 1936. 344pp.

Jerome Grant has been a professor at the same university for thirty-two years and is facing new challenges in this Depression-era novel. One of his students, Vincent Lamar, is a Communist at a time when local newspapers are eager to find Communist sympathizers in order to smear the publicly-funded university. When Lamar gets into an altercation with a policeman as he is handing out the *Daily Worker,* the newspapers immediately pick up the story of a violent Communist student. When Lamar escapes and flees to Grant, he is in the position of protecting the university by encouraging Lamar to suppress his political views, taking a politically expedient stance against his long-held commitment to intellectual freedom. In another case, Grant helps a young woman, whom he believes to be a mulatto, by supporting her when she is accused of marijuana use. When she is expelled she threatens him with false accusations, and when she later commits suicide he is the first to find her and burns the suicide note that would have destroyed his reputation. Increasing demands by the local press for a legislative inquiry on Communism at the university eventually leads to a hearing during which students form a pacifist organization and, in a dramatic climax to the novel, Lamar is shot by a policeman. Professor Grant's reflections throughout the novel on the changing purpose of the university and the changing nature of manliness, which has come to incorporate more emotional honesty, are fully expressed in the final pages of the book. As a city with so many institutions of higher education, this depiction of major social issues associated with universities captures an important aspect of Chicago life.

683. Linton, Adelin Sumner Briggs [Aldin Vinton, pseud.]. *Mystery in Green.* New York: Phoenix Press, 1937. 284pp.

In this murder mystery, Chicago journalist Jim McBride assists police detective Daggett after the corpse of a murder victim is discovered at the entrance to the Oak Park apartment building where he lives with his mother. The victim, Jonathan Crane, a stockbroker, had lived in an Astor Street mansion and was known for his fabulous gem collection and beautiful wife. McBride's initial investigation turns up Crane's dealings with antiquities dealer Augustus Schultz (a German American with a business on North Clark Street); Jewish fur dealer Jacob Rakowitz; and Benedetto "Pirani" Montebruzzi. Montebruzzi turns out to be a relative of Mrs. Crane and sold items to Schultz, including a stunning emerald that Crane had purchased just before his death. Crane's impoverished nephew, Tony Paige, becomes a suspect as well, when he is revealed to be the wealthy victim's primary heir. In addition to the Crane mansion, settings include a Scottish restaurant, the opera, and an apartment building on Surf Street with a Pullman kitchenette. The case is solved when a butler is revealed to be Mrs. Crane's first husband in disguise.

684. Little, Paul H. (Paula Hugo Little) [Kenneth Harding, pseud.]. *Pushers*. Atlanta, Ga.: Pendulum Books, 1968. 224pp.

This erotic novel is set in the world of women chess players in Chicago. No further information is available.

685. Little, Paul H. (Paula Hugo Little) [Marie De Jourlet, pseud.]. *Trials of Windhaven*. Los Angeles: Pinnacle Books, 1980. 421pp.

Set in 1869-1871, this is the sixth volume of the Windhaven saga which chronicles the Bouchard family of Alabama. The novel is concerned with Southern Reconstruction and contrasts the economic opportunities of Chicago with the devastation of the South and the hardships of cattle ranching in Texas, where some members of the Bouchard family relocated prior to the Civil War. Laurette Douglas, a Bouchard niece, is excited by the growth of her husband's department store business, but more concerned about establishing social status in Chicago. One of the final chapters of the book describes her experiences during the Chicago fire. Less than thirty pages of the novel are physically set in Chicago, but the city is important as a symbol of opportunity.

686. Lobell, William. *The Steed Success*. New York: Reader Press, 1949. 758pp.

Part satire and part social history, this book traces the career of Oscar Carlson, born to two German immigrants who met while fleeing the great Chicago fire. At the peak of his career, Carlson is the head of a network of food producers and distributors, and owns an advertising agency that popularizes processed foodstuffs. Because of his lisp and tendency to drool while looking at pictures, Carlson's father thought him an idiot. His early years were spent in Chicago going to school and later working for a delicatessen. As he matured, his business acumen soon revealed itself and by 1915 he had established a New York advertising agency. The Chicago business community in which Carlson is prominent in the first decade of the twentieth century is still small and cliquish and Carlson is one of the first members of the Loop Athletic Club. Written after the Depression, when corporations had taken over the food industry, destroying the family farm, this novel satirizes an American consumer society that was about to grow dramatically and increase its control over life in the United States and most of the Western world.

687. London, Jack. *The Iron Heel*. New York: Grosset and Dunlap, 1907. 354pp.

London used this futurist novel to articulate his political views and promote Socialism. The narrative is presented as a firsthand account of the political turmoil of the decades 1912–1932 in the United States that led to a new social order named the Brotherhood of Man. The present, in which the narrative is being published for the first time, is seven hundred years in the future. The contents are the journal of Avis Everhard, the wife of Ernst Everhard, a key political leader. Much of the novel is set in California, where Avis lives with her father in a small university town. However, Chicago is important symbolically as the city that experienced the worst labor violence during the capitalist regime. Also, the revolutionary overthrow of the government begins in Chicago, where the first worker commune is organized.

688. Loose, Harry J. *The Shamus: A True Tale of Thiefdom and an Exposé of the Real System in Crime*. Boston: Christopher Publishing House, 1920. 296pp.

   Written by a detective in the Chicago Police Department, this novel is set in the city's Sixty-first Precinct and mostly records the activities of Jewish criminals and the police who try to capture them. A few major crimes are described, including a safe break-in that nets forty thousand dollars, and a murder, but many of the crimes are small-scale and remarkable mostly for their variety. Written in the language of the streets, the slang of both criminals and police is included and defined. Street life in the city and the establishments where criminals meet (mostly lunchrooms and saloons) are detailed.

689. Lorenz, Tom. *Guys Like Us*. New York: Viking Press, 1980. 255pp.

   Although set in Chicago, this novel has little physical description beyond domestic interiors; the book is mostly concerned with presenting male culture and the final days of the 1970s counterculture. Buddy Barnes married Jo Reed, the daughter of an industrialist, with little forethought. Both of them shared an anti-materialist outlook and moved into a West Side apartment that they furnished with Salvation Army furniture. However, nearly a decade has passed and as Barnes turns thirty, Jo decides she needs a change from working low-wage jobs to support their household. Even Barnes' friends have tired of his irresponsible behavior. Having lost job after job, Barnes has most recently been fired from a position mowing lawns for the parks department. The only task to which he has consistently dedicated himself is playing softball with his friends on the Chicago Sticks team. After Jo leaves him, Barnes becomes even more focused on softball, somehow believing that if he helps the Sticks win the city championship he will win Jo back. The team wins, but Jo does not reconcile, heading instead for San Francisco. The novel documents male, working-class social interaction and bar culture of the late 1970s.

690. Lorimer, George Horace. *Letters from a Self-Made Merchant to His Son*. Boston: Small, Maynard, 1901. 312pp.

   John Graham, the founder and director of the pork processing firm, the House of Graham, writes a series of letters to his son Pierrepont who finishes Harvard College, begins to establish himself socially, and works at his first job. Intended to be humorous, written in dialect with colloquialisms, the letters are filled with anecdotes and homespun observations of a stereotypical Chicago pork packer. In the course of the novel, the elder Graham travels to various branches of his firm, including one in London, as well as to resorts in Hot Springs, Arkansas, and Karlsbad, Austria. Pierrepont travels as well, as a salesman for his father's company, far from resort areas in remote locales in Kentucky and Indiana. The contents almost exclusively present social interactions and contain little physical description or settings.

691. Lorimer, George Horace. *Old Gorgon Graham; More Letters from a Self-Made Merchant to His Son*. New York: Doubleday, Page, 1904. 308pp.

   In this sequel to Lorimer's earlier book of letters between Graham and his son, Pierrepont, the latter marries and is somewhat later promoted to the position of general manager as his father's ill-health worsens. Although references are made to Chicago and Chicago characters, the half-mile pork processing facility of the Grahams and the management of the firm's ten thousand employees gets the fullest description. Because the text consists of so much advice and instruction, it captures cultural attitudes of the time period.

692. Lory, Robert Edward [V. J. Santiago, pseud.]. *Chicago, Knock, Knock, You're Dead.* Vigilante, no. 4. New York: Pinnacle Books, 1976. 184pp.

This work of formula fiction is the fourth in a series of books set in various American cities in which Joe Madden revenges the brutal murder of his wife on organized criminals. As with other books in the series the setting is of less interest than high speed automobile chases, desperate escapes, and violent confrontations.

693. Loux, DuBois Henry. *Ongon: A Tale of Early Chicago.* New York: C. Francis Press, 1902. 182pp.

It is difficult to determine a clear plot in this novel, besides a romance between John Trenton and Catherine Dale, a painter and admirer of the Indians. One of her Indian subjects is Ongon, generally acknowledged to be a remarkable chief, but he is not actually an Indian, as he was captured as a child and then given some tincture that changed his skin color. The novel contains much discussion of the machinations that led the Indians to cede their land in Illinois. At the time of the novel, 1833, Chicago has been founded, but is still a trading post and the novel is supposedly based on research in historical sources.

694. Lovett, Robert Morss. *A Wingéd Victory.* New York: Duffield, 1907. 431pp.

From an early age Dora Glenn lives through situations that dramatize the plight of women in the American culture of the late-nineteenth through the early-twentieth centuries. After the death of her mother, twelve-year-old Dora could have gone to live a Chicago mansion with her aunt, as her sister Linda chose to do, but she felt an obligation to care for her developmentally disabled, six-year-old brother Peter. So, against her father's wishes she stays in the ramshackle family homestead on one hundred acres north of Chicago near Eggleston. Dora goes to a one-room school and dresses in frequently mended clothing. Her only consolation is her friendship with Leverett Raymond, the son of a wealthy Chicago businessman who was forced to leave Exeter Academy for drunkenness and must live at his family's country house to do penance. As an adolescent, Peter is mortally injured while employed by an ice-cutting company, and Dora is freed from her father's household. She is given the settlement money from her brother's death to attend the same suburban college as Raymond (seemingly Northwestern University). She studies medicine to the distaste of most people she knows, since they consider it an inappropriate profession for a woman. Dora develops a social life, revolving around her friend Constance Dare and young people in Dare's circle. With them, she explores Chicago, attending concerts and plays and experiencing the city's bohemian side, eating at Italian restaurants and attending Yiddish theater productions. Her caring nature soon draws her into a relationship with an awkward young poet named Vance Sterling. Throughout college Dora aids Sterling with class work and his social skills. She eventually marries him after he begins teaching poetry in a settlement house where Dora also volunteers. After several years of desperate poverty, Sterling has a play produced in New York City and he is suddenly financially secure and socially acceptable. Sterling changes, however, abandoning his social ideals, and becoming absorbed in the social whirl to which Dora's sister Linda can give him entrée. Dora continues her nurses' training in opposition to her husband's and sister's wishes. When Sterling eventually realizes the depth of his betrayal of Dora, he commits suicide and opens the way for Leverett Raymond to win her hand in marriage. The novel makes clear the varieties of living available within the Chicago metropolitan area in the early twentieth century, from rural to suburban, all accessible by train and kept informed by a number of daily Chicago newspapers.

Through Dora, her sister, and her friends, the novel illustrates the challenges of women in the time period in establishing an identity within the family and society.

695. Lucas, Cleo. *I Jerry Take Thee Joan*. Garden City, N.Y.: Doubleday, Doran, 1931. 297pp.

In this Depression-era romance novel, Joan Prentice, twenty-one-year-old daughter of a Chicago millionaire who owns a packaged food company, has always socialized within the upper echelon of society. When Dick Taylor, the son of her father's former business partner, whom everyone assumes she will marry, takes her slumming to a party in the apartment of a journalist, she meets thirty-two-year-old Jerry Corbett, the drama critic for the *Daily Press*, and she is immediately intrigued to meet someone who works for a living and socializes with writers and theater people. The Prentices live in a lakefront mansion, off Wellington Street, in a house Mr. Prentice had built before Joan was born and in which her mother had died soon after her birth. Most of Joan's set live in Lake Forest, a newly fashionable neighborhood. Joan's youth and protected life have left her emotionally immature and she openly declares her infatuation with Jerry in the days after they first meet. Jerry, who typically begins drinking at breakfast, is also openly emotional and soon proposes to Joan, realizing that he has not been in love since college, when Claire Hempsted rejected him. Although Jerry is drunk most of the time and even passes out, dressed in his tuxedo, on the way to Joan's announcement party, the culture of drinking in this Prohibition-era novel is so pervasive that no one tries to prevent the marriage except for Dick Taylor. At the wedding, Jerry is drunk enough to muff the wedding vows and Prentice's friends and relatives put on a brave face. Although Jerry seems to truly love Joan, his drunkenness impairs his judgment, especially when Claire Hempsted is in town starring in a new play and he openly accepts her advances. In despair over her situation, Joan walks into the lake; although she is rescued by Dick Taylor, she succumbs to pneumonia. Jerry, who was in a drunken stupor, only appears to witness her final moments, and afterwards heads out to get a drink. The acceptability of drunkenness and the availability of alcohol during Prohibition are of interest, as well as social attitudes towards affluence during the Depression.

696. Lund, Roslyn Rosen. *The Sharing*. New York: William Morrow, 1978. 216pp.

In this novel about widowhood and Jewish family life, forty-five-year-old Sophie Mandel is forced to make a new life for herself after her husband Bill's premature death, and to fight for assets misappropriated by Bill's brothers. Sophie lives in Winnetka, but works in Chicago as a caregiver in a home for emotionally disturbed children while working on her master's degree in social work. Her social life, too, is focused on Chicago where she has friends on the Near North Side and participates in social groups organized for recently divorced or widowed men and women. Sophie's financial and legal struggles, the social status of her work, and her social interactions with men all contribute to a picture of the social status of women in the 1970s. Descriptions of restaurants, bars, and residences give a sense of daily life in Chicago during the time period.

697. Lytle, H. M. *The Tragedies of the White Slaves: True Stories of the White Slavery Taken from Actual Life; Each One Dealing with a Different Method by Which White Slaves Have Become Innocent Victims to Destruction*. Chicago: Charles C. Thompson, 1910. 193pp.

Although advocating social reform, this book's fictional accounts seem intended to have prurient appeal (and are accompanied by suggestive illustrations). The author relates the stories of ten different young women as representing the ways in which women are victimized and fall into lives of prostitution. The common thread is the danger of the dance hall, although readers today may see the economic factors underlying the social problems described. The book's women include immigrants, a switchboard operator, a factory girl, a country girl, and a young mother. The novel presents dialogue that captures slang of the time period and describes food, drink, clothing, living arrangements, and social settings of early-twentieth-century Chicago.

698. MacDonald, John D. *One Fearful Yellow Eye.* A Fawcett Gold Medal Book. Greenwich, Conn.: Fawcett Publications, 1966. 224pp.

Four years before the action of this story, Florida resident Travis McGee had found a woman, Glory Doyle, sleeping on the beach. She had been crushed by a series of tragedies, including bankruptcy, after the murder/suicide of her children at the hands of her husband. McGee helped Glory regain her hope for the future and get a job. She was able to truly begin a new life when she met a vacationing Chicago physician, Dr. Fortner Geiss, whom she subsequently married. Geiss died after a long illness and Glory has summoned McGee to Chicago to help her figure out why Geiss liquidated all of his assets and why she is being pursued by creditors. It soon becomes apparent that extortionists were pursuing Geiss, threatening to expose his past sexual dalliances. Not until the end of the novel does the reader learn that the blackmailers are former Nazis. The novel includes references to, and scenes of, sexual abuse and rape, as well as accounts of emotionally and psychologically disturbed women that reflect the psychological assumptions of the time period about female sexuality. Furthermore, LSD is used in a therapeutic context. McGee stays at the Drake and has most frequent contact with upper-middle-class people; however he does visit some lower-middle-class environs, as well. He occasionally makes general observations about Chicago that convey the troubled city it was at the time. For instance, he comments on the pollution residue on his clothing and the ghettos that seem like an unsolvable social problem. Cultural historians will be interested in the novel's treatment of female sexuality and the concern about war criminals as a continuing source of evil.

699. MacHarg, William Briggs. *Peewee.* Chicago: Reilly and Lee, 1922. 276pp

In this melodramatic story, a boy living on the streets discovers his father's identity and is eventually accepted into his father's affluent household. Eight-year-old H. "Peewee" Seabury earns money for food by selling newspapers and is easily located by the private detective sent to find him by his dying mother. Before he ran away, Peewee lived in an orphanage and had no contact with either of his parents. So, when the detective takes him to the sickroom of a dying woman claiming to be his mother, he has little emotional reaction. She gives him a paper with the name and address of his father. Initially, Peewee is skeptical about seeking his father, since the parents of other children he has known were just drunken thugs. However, Peewee recognizes the name his mother gave him, Markyn, as a name he has seen on the sides of trucks from a large cartage firm. So, he goes to the Lincoln Park address the woman gave him and bit by bit, with a child's limited understanding, pieces together the story of his mother, Helen Lampert, and her affair with his father, Walter Wendell Markyn. Peewee does not try to approach anyone in the house at Sixteen North State Street and continues his life on the street until his grandfather Lampert finds him. Lampert had worked as a supervisor for the Markyn until he began to ask what the Markyns were going to do for his daughter. Dismissed from his job, he sees Peewee as a meal ticket with the Markyns. As soon as Peewee divines his intent, he flees. In hiding from Lampert, he cannot sell newspapers for food and goes hungry for several days. Then a boy befriends him and takes him to a house on Lincoln Park that turns out to be that of the father of Wendell Markyn's wife. Through him, Peewee is eventually united with his father and accepted by Mrs. Markyn as a stepson. The novel gives a sense of the life of children living on the streets and the implications of repressive social codes governing sexuality.

700. MacHarg, William Briggs and Edwin Balmer. *The Blind Man's Eyes*. Illustrated by Wilson C. Dexter. New York: Burt, 1916. 367pp.

This tale set in the upper-class milieu of millionaire capitalists involves faked murders, concealed identities, and secret financial schemes. A blind, millionaire lawyer from Chicago, Basil Santoine is traveling by private railroad car from Seattle with his daughter Harriet and her fiancé Avery when he is viciously attacked while the train is snowbound. A mysterious man named Eaton is detained, but, after questioning him, Santoine is convinced that Eaton was not his attacker. However, Eaton is still a suspect in another crime. The powerful Santoine is able to get Eaton released into his custody. Near Chicago the train is brought to a halt and chauffeured limousines take the party to Santoine's estate on Lake Michigan, north of Chicago. After another murder and the rifling of Santoine's safe, Eaton's true identity is revealed to be that of Hugh Overton. Overton had been convicted of the death of financier Matthew Latron, but escaped and fled the country. When Santoine reviews the evidence, he realizes that Overton is not guilty and that his daughter's fiancé, Avery, must be the culprit. When Santoine confronts Avery, he reveals that no murder had actually taken place. Latron wanted to disappear; he faked his own death and arranged for Overton to be accused. Latron has actually been in hiding with some accomplices, plotting to prevent the vaguely described corporate restructuring of several railroad companies for which Santoine has been working. Santoine's investigation clears Overton with the police and with Avery disgraced and sure to be convicted of his wrongdoing, it looks like Overton, in whom Harriet has developed romantic interests, will replace Avery as her fiancé. The novel reflects cultural attitudes toward Chicago as the home of wealthy capitalists whose financial machinations, conducted without government oversight, have nationwide impacts.

701. MacHarg, William Briggs and Edwin Balmer. *The Indian Drum*. New York: Grosset and Dunlap, 1917. 367pp

This melodramatic tale concerns a young man's efforts to uncover his true identity. Alan Conrad grew up in Kansas knowing that the farm family with whom he lived was getting paid to take care of him by an anonymous Chicagoan. As a twenty-three-year-old, Conrad is summoned to Chicago by telegram. He arrives to find that the man who wired him, Benjamin Corvet, a wealthy partner of a Great Lakes shipping firm, disappeared the day after sending his telegram. Before his disappearance, he made arrangements to transfer all of his assets to Conrad, without specifying what, if any, relationship existed between them. Through his own investigation Conrad realizes that the mystery of his identity is tied to an 1895 shipwreck on the Great Lakes. Corvet's Chippewa servant, Judah Wassaquam, came from the area of the shipwreck and travels with Conrad to aid his information gathering. During his expedition, he comes upon Benjamin Corvet on a sinking ship. Covert dies, but not before relating a complicated story revealing that his business partner, Henry Spearman, had murdered Conrad's father, Captain Caleb Stafford, and been responsible for sinking Stafford's ship with all hands onboard. Most of the book is set in Chicago, although the descriptions are primarily of upper-class households, staffed with servants, and private clubs. However, there are a number of evocative descriptions of the city in winter that emphasize the relationship between the city and the lake. The Indian drum of the title is a legendary drum with supernatural powers to announce the death of those who perish on the lake. The drum was heard before the sinking of both Stafford's and Corvet's ships.

702. MacHarg, William Briggs and Edwin Balmer. *The Surakarta*. Illustrated by Lester Ralph. Boston: Small, Maynard, 1913. 369pp.

Many characters in this romance mystery have traveled extensively, particularly in Asia, making Chicagoans seem very cosmopolitan. Ward Hereford administers the Matthew Regan estate for the benefit of the deceased meat packer's daughter, Lorine Regan, providing her with an income of a half-million dollars each year. Hereford is alarmed when she announces her betrothal to the Malay sultan of Surakarta, a subdivision of Java, with the proviso that the potentate will give up his harem of one hundred and fifty wives. As a guarantee of his intentions the sultan sends an extraordinary emerald to Regan. Soon after Hereford formally receives the emerald, the stone disappears. Hereford is a suspect and calls upon Detective McAdams and his eccentric elderly German friend Max Schimmel for their assistance in solving the case within twenty-four hours, after which the Surakartans are determined to have the emerald or execute Hereford. With Hereford's life threatened, Regan acknowledges her love for him and by the end of the novel it is clear that the two will marry. The book is filled with racial and ethnic stereotyping in which Asians are portrayed negatively. In addition to the Surakartans, there is a Chinese "boy" whom Max employs as his personal servant in a manner reminiscent of slavery. Although there is some description of Hereford's elegant Lincoln Park apartment, the book does not include much physical description of Chicago nor are there accounts of social events that could be considered particular to the city.

703. MacQueen, James. [James G. Edwards, pseud.]. *But the Patient Died*. Garden City, N.Y.: Crime Club / Doubleday, 1948. 189pp.

Much of this novel is set inside a large private hospital, Monmouth Memorial, and the book details staffing, layout, services and the hierarchical structure that fosters animosities. An attempted murder is discovered at the facility and soon afterwards a fatal shooting transpires. The investigation is conducted mostly at the hospital, although a large "gentleman's farm" outside Winnetka is described and is crucial to the plot, as is a Mafia-owned nightclub named "Club Tosca." Practically no description of Chicago in general is included.

704. MacQueen, James [James G. Edwards, pseud.]. *F Corridor: A New Hospital Mystery*. Garden City, N.Y.: Crime Club / Doubleday, Doran, 1936. 275pp.

One of a series of books featuring a physician who aids the Chicago Police Department, this novel is almost exclusively set in a Chicago hospital and reveals health sciences culture of the 1930s. After a beautiful young woman, Luella Ring, is hospitalized, a series of murders are committed. Among the victims are Ring's physician, an intern, and her husband. Dr. Paul Ravel and Inspector Bondurant solve the crimes that are committed using the poison aconite.

705. MacQueen, James [Jay McHugh, pseud.]. *Sex Is Such Fun*. New York: Godwin, 1937. 284pp.

The author chose to set his satire about sexual mores in American culture in the Chicago suburb of Glenview. The area is thrown into disarray when an unknown introduces his newly discovered potent aphrodisiac into Glenview society. No additional information is available.

706. Maitland, James. *Suppressed Sensations, or Leaves from the Note Book of a Chicago Reporter*. Chicago: Rand, McNally, 1879. 254pp.

This collection of short stories set in the mid to late 1870s reveals the underside of Chicago from the perspective of a reporter. Plot elements include: a jealous wife's murder of her wealthy husband; a physician dealing with the aftermath of poisoning the husband of his lover; the destructive effects of a gambler's addiction on his beautiful and wealthy wife; the death of a found-ling kidnapped for a large ransom by a the wife of a former secessionist and United States senator; the use of a murder victim's skull to destroy the life of the murderer decades after the crime; the deaths of an alcoholic Scottish immigrant and the woman who had emigrated from Scotland to be with him; and an apparition frightening a murderer to death in Chicago's Polish community.

707. Maling, Arthur. *Bent Man*. New York: Harper and Row, 1975. 227pp.

This 1970s novel is populated by criminals whose crimes range from fraud to murder. At forty-two, Walter Jackson has just learned that he has Hodgkin's disease, from which he will die in the very near future. In some ways, however, he feels like his life ended years before when, as a professional football player, he was implicated in throwing the outcome of a game. In the after-math, he lost his job (he now works as an insurance salesman) and his wife, Olive divorced him. Olive later married a wealthy Southern Californian, Delmore Livingston, who eventually adopted Steve, the son Jackson had with Olive. When Jackson is approached by an FBI agent looking for nineteen-year-old Steve, Jackson slowly gets involved again in his son's life. Steve has been dat-ing Georgette Himes, a jewel thief, and almost as soon as they arrive in Chicago Georgette is mur-dered. Concerned for Steve, Delmore and Olive travel to Chicago and join forces with Walter to help the authorities track down the head of the jewel theft ring, Pepper Himes, who murdered Georgette and has targeted Steve. Their task is complicated by Pepper's ties to organized crime. Jackson lives in Lincoln Park and takes farewell walks through the neighborhood and other parts of the city. Other characters live in Old Town and Lake Forest.

708. Maling, Arthur. *Decoy*. New York: Harper and Row, 1969. 199pp.

This book portrays Chicago as a bleak, winter-dominated landscape, whose residents dream of escaping to a warm climate. International crime syndicates have taken over the city, making huge profits under the guise of legitimate businesses, focusing on real estate transactions, produce smuggling, and tax evasion. The unnamed protagonist and first-person narrator of the story is the part-owner of a struggling trucking firm. He needs to defend himself from the wrath of a syndicate when his half-brother Carl Rogers sends him as a courier to Mexico. Prior to the trip, the narrator had no idea that Carl is anything other than a legitimate real estate broker. When Carl cheats his partners and absconds with two million dollars, the narrator is made painfully aware of the brutal-ity of Carl's business partners and their criminality. Narrowly surviving his first encounter with them, in the rest of the novel, the narrator tries to find Carl. Upon returning to Chicago he hires a bodyguard, but still only narrowly escapes a car bomb. Before long he is headed back to Mexico with undercover Treasury Department agents. Specific locations in Chicago are mentioned, mostly bars and hotels, as well as neighborhoods such as Maywood and Oak Park.

709. Maling, Arthur. *Dingdong*. New York: Harper and Row, 1974. 245pp.

The main characters in this novel are actors and models and their hand-to-mouth existences in Chicago are amply illustrated. Mike Wiley, the protagonist, is living with Genevieve "Cat" Royce when he runs into his old girlfriend, Holly Simmons, now a successful actress. He has little time to renew his acquaintance, however, when he learns that his mother has been run down by a car in Corpus Christi. As she is dying she tells him that his uncle Burton Markham, a murderer, has been paroled from prison, and is looking for Wiley's cousin Hal. Soon after Markham's return to Chi-cago he shows up at Wiley's apartment with a thug named Dingdong. They subject him to enough physical abuse to make him telephone Hal and get him to agree to a meeting. When Hal does not appear, Wiley must once again deal the wrathful gangsters. By physically intimidating his girlfriends, Simmons and Royce, and threatening even greater violence, they get Wiley to agree to go to Switzerland and smuggle money from a secret account back into the country. Hal had beaten them to the money however, and Wiley must return to Chicago empty-handed to face the violent criminals. Despite the stereotypical criminals and violence, the novel does a good job at evoking the economically marginal life of young actors in Chicago in the 1970s.

710. Maling Arthur. *Go-Between*. New York: Harper and Row, 1970. 204pp.

In this novel set in the late-1960s, Chicago is the center for powerful international corporations. The unnamed first-person narrator was a professional golfer before an automobile accident killed his wife and seriously damaged his hand. Remaking a life for himself took a long time and childhood friend Pete Lambert played an important role. So, when Pete steals a confidential document from the office of Oliver Lambert, Oliver contacts the narrator to help him track down Pete and prevent him from going to jail for trying to blackmail Oliver for five hundred thousand dollars. Oliver is Pete's estranged father who had divorced Pete's mother when he was still a child. He is also the owner of an international corporation and a man of wealth and power. The search for Pete and the missing papers soon focuses on Pete's accomplice, Harry Scott, a violent man, and involves travel to Houston and the Virgin Islands. Because the narrator had such difficulty coping with his life after his accident and is still recovering, the novel provides many details about his daily life in a high-rise apartment building on the Near North Side, and about his nearby bartending job. Divorce plays a major role in the novel. Oliver's divorce from Pete's mother seriously distorted the young man's personality. The protagonist has a chance to be a positive influence for a child of a broken home when he begins a relationship with the woman across the hallway from his apartment who has separated from her husband and has a young son.

711. Maling, Arthur. *The Koberg Link*. New York: Harper and Row, 1979. 244pp.

Approximately half of this novel is set in 1970s Chicago and depicts the city as a place of corporate headquarters at the center of the business world. When New York stockbroker Brock Potter's secretary tells him that she does not like the father of her niece's fiancé, Bob McDonald, Potter is dismissive. However, when Bob is murdered, Potter begins his own investigation, puzzled by a link between the murder and the sudden rise of Koberg Chemical Company stocks (Bob was the alienated grandson of Koberg matriarch Elissa Koberg). The Chicagoans Brock meets would be at the highest echelon of society anywhere and among them are titled aristocrats. Food, drink, clothing, restaurants, and expensive residences are all described to establish the setting. Although specific Chicago locales are occasionally mentioned, the novel presents an international set that frequently travels to New York, Paris, and famous resorts. Potter is shot outside his room at the Drake, but recovers to solve the mystery and see that Andrea and Bob's unborn baby become the sole beneficiaries of the Koberg estate.

712. Maling, Arthur. *Ripoff*. New York: Harper and Row, 1976. 248pp.

This novel deals with criminal activity in Chicago's corporate world in the 1970s. New Yorker Brock Potter, a Wall Street stockbroker, receives an anonymous tip about Chicago's Interlake General Life Insurance Company and then the firm's assistant treasurer is found shot to death. Brock heads to Chicago to investigate, with little success. When one of his assistants is gunned down in New York City by a Chicago Mafia hit-man, Brock realizes that his assassination has been ordered. Chicago is only one locale in which Brock gathers evidence to turn over to the

FBI; he travels to Boston, Maine, and Canada, as well, while being pursued by gunmen. Most of Brock's Chicago trips are spent inside office buildings and expensive hotels and apartments, but he does observe the rapid transformation of the city's lake shore areas as houses and small apartment buildings are torn down to be replaced by high rise luxury buildings.

713. Maloff, Saul. *Happy Families*. New York: Charles Scribner's Sons, 1968. 375pp.

In this 1960s novel, cultural changes in family dynamics and attitudes toward aging predominate. Robert Kalb fled New York City to live in Chicago after a painful divorce from his wife. His daughter Jenny's psychoses seemed to center on him as she reached adolescence, so he thought it best to relocate. In Chicago, Kalb works for a publishing company specializing in various sex and marriage manuals published under several imprints. Unable to visit his daughter, each afternoon he watches girls leaving school, each year observing the next older class so that he can imagine how Jenny is maturing. By the time he is watching seventeen-year-olds, one of them initiates an affair with him. Around this time he learns that Jenny is missing and he returns to New York to search for her. The Chicago section of this book is relatively brief and mostly focused on Kalb's workplace and the transitory nature of his living arrangements.

714. Malzberg, Barry N. (Nathaniel) [Mike Barry, pseud.]. *Chicago Slaughter*. Lone Wolf Series, no. 6. New York: Berkeley Medallion, 1974. 192pp.

This book is one of a series of fourteen action-adventure novels written by Malzberg that are similar to Don Pendleton's Executioner series in that the protagonist travels from city to city avenging himself against organized crime. The protagonist in this case is Martin Wulff, a detective with the New York City Police Department until his girlfriend deliberately overdosed on illegal drugs. Wulff is on a vendetta to destroy the drug trade and find the key Mafia figures in Chicago to eradicate them.

715. Marion, Frances. *The Secret Six*. New York: Grosset, 1931. 129pp.

This book is a novelization of a motion picture with the same title starring Ralph Bellamy, Wallace Beery, Clark Gable, and Jean Harlow (Metro-Goldwyn-Mayer, 1931). Bootlegger and café owner, Johnny Franks, recruits packing house worker Louis Scorpio to join his gang. Scorpio eventually out-maneuvers Franks for control of the gang, increases his operations by defeating a rival gang, and becomes wealthy. Finally, six businessmen form a coalition to secretly rid the city of Scorpio. With the help of crusading journalists Carl Luckner and Hank Rogers, Scorpio is tried and sent to the electric chair. This Prohibition-era work vaunts the role of a courageous citizenry and investigative journalists in defeating organized crime in a city in which law enforcement and representatives of the court system are corrupt.

716. Marlowe, Derek. *The Rich Boy from Chicago*. New York: St. Martin's, 1979. 440pp.

In this work of historical fiction the protagonist's life is dramatically affected by two violent events in the history of Chicago. Frederick Geddes is the only son of a self-made millionaire who had grown up poor in the immigrant ghetto on Maxwell Street. The course of Geddes' life is dramatically altered when he is twelve-years-old. Waiting outside the Harvard Preparatory School in Chicago for his father's chauffeur, he is approached by acquaintance Richard Loeb who, with increasing insistence, offers Geddes a ride. After repeated refusals, Geddes' chauffeur finally arrives. A short time later, Geddes realizes how close he had come to being the murder victim of Loeb and his accomplice Nathan Leopold. When his father hears of the incident he sells his house in Chicago and moves to New York. The young Geddes turns his back on his Jewish ancestry in reaction to the behavior of Leopold and Loeb, who before their crime had been held up to him as admirable Jews, and devotes himself to the pleasures of high society in New York, England, France, and Italy. After his father's death, however, he decides to redeem his life by taking a job at the bottom of the Chicago branch of his father's firm. He succeeds in working his way up the organization, eventually managing the office, only to be violently killed during the riots that took place during the 1968 Democratic Convention.

717. Marshall, James. *Ordeal by Glory*. New York: Robert M. McBride, 1927. 288pp.

Although the main character in this historical novel is named John Hoyer, the book is actually a fictionalized account of Illinois governor John Peter Altgeld's life. As such, the book is only partly set in Chicago, a city where Hoyer builds a real estate fortune, most of which he risks on constructing a skyscraper, a project that nearly defeats him. The book also devotes some attention to the Haymarket Riot, as Hoyer agonizes over whether or not to issue pardons in the case.

718. Marshall, Sidney. *Some Like It Hot*. New York: William Morrow, 1941. 278pp.

Scott Bennett, a radio actor is pleased but puzzled when talent agent Doris Thornton telephones to offer him a part in the radio serial "Unwanted Wife." Not until after Bennett finds director Arnold Mattsen murdered and is being pursued by the police and the murderer, does he realize that the radio role was only a set-up to implicate him. In order to keep himself out of prison and save his life, he must solve the mystery of who killed Mattsen. Before long, Bennett finds his former wife Marcia murdered. Then he discovers fellow radio actor Gentry West dead, with a suicide note claiming that he killed himself in remorse for slaying Mattsen that is obviously false and frames Bennett. Knowing the note is false, Scott adds West's murder to the list of crimes he must solve. The radio folk in the book include divorcees, a gay man, an alcoholic, embezzlers, and, of course, a murderer. Chicago is evoked through car chases on downtown streets, descriptions of apartments, nightlife, Lake Shore Drive mansions, restaurants, and air travel between the city and Detroit. Some description is also given of radio talent agencies, radio studios, and the casting process.

719. Mason, Edith Huntington. *The Politician*. Illustrated by The Kinneys. Chicago: McClurg, 1910. 409pp.

This romance novel is set during the 1904 Chicago Republican National Convention that nominated Theodore Roosevelt. The excitement of young people gathering from all over the country and the inevitable romances that develop are represented in the experience of James Vernon Ellis, a New Yorker with fervid political ambitions. When he meets Chicago debutante Harriet Rand, he realizes what an asset she could be to his career. Her politics are harmonious with his own, and, in addition to wealth, she would bring social prestige, personal charm, and her attractive appearance. Their romance flourishes against the backdrop of the convention. In the end, however, Ellis weighs his self-interest against fairness to Rand and decides he could never take enough time away from his career to devote to a wife and home, thus giving up on the idea of marriage. This book is unusual in presenting a woman's view of what should be expected of a husband. A number of ideas about women's place in society and politics in general are presented through dialogue in the novel and the social events described.

720. Masselink, Ben. *The Crackerjack Marines*. Boston: Little, Brown, 1959. 275pp.

Ne'er-do-well George Toliver was forced to leave college for attending too few classes, and forced to work in a pea processing plant before enlisting in the Marine Corps at the outbreak of World War II. The war is the making of him, not on the battlefield, but as a recruiting officer in Chicago, where he gets to attend fund raising dinners and movie premieres, and escort girl bands and all-girl baseball teams in parades. In a city depleted of young men, Toliver, in his dress whites, is a popular date with women ranging from a Winnetka debutante to a bohemian Christmas card artist. Toliver's adventures capture a World War II Chicago that is a non-stop party as young people attempt, if only briefly, to wipe out the memory of their friends dying on the front where they, too, may soon be headed.

721. Masters, Edgar Lee. *Children of the Market Place*. New York: Macmillan, 1922. 469pp.

This novel presents a truncated account of the history of Illinois and Chicago, the career of Stephen Douglas, and the development of abolitionism in the period from 1833 to 1861. First-person narrator James Miles, an Englishman of means educated at Eton and Oxford, travels to the Illinois frontier in 1833 to take possession of his father's estate situated in Jacksonville, and there he is awakened to the abolitionist cause through his connection with a mulatto named Zoë. He becomes a friend of Stephen Douglas, who he assists in political campaigns. Eventually, Miles sells his rural lands and invests in Chicago real estate. Although he travels a great deal in Illinois, the Deep South, Washington, D.C., New York City, and New Orleans, Chicago is his home and he describes the city's development and events, such as the 1860 Democratic Convention in some detail. Masters' account of Chicago illustrates the city's importance in the Midwest as a center for political debate and as a transportation nexus.

722. Masters, Edgar Lee. *Mirage*. New York: Boni and Liveright, 1924. 427pp.

At the beginning of this novel, Skeeters Kirby is still living at a cabin on the Rock River, but most of the novel is set in New York City and Long Island. Chicago in the novel represents Kirby's young adulthood, of which he has fond memories. He stays in the city for a few days on his way east, but during his lengthy ruminations about what he should do with his life, he never seriously considers returning to the city. For him, and for other characters in the novel, Chicago is a stopping point from small towns in the Midwest as they prepare to move to New York City.

723. Masters, Edgar Lee. *Nuptial Flight*. New York: Boni and Liveright, 1923. 376pp.

This saga of the Creighton and Houghton families begins in 1849 when the families, unknown to each other in their hometown of Louisville, Kentucky, move to Illinois. Over three generations the families become intertwined. Although the novel is mostly set in small-town Whitehall, Illinois, Alfred Houghton, a professional musician, moves to Chicago for a teaching position, after marrying a woman almost twice his age. She tries to enhance his artistic life by finding a property in a bohemian community on the Des Plaines River outside the city. However, Alfred rejects the isolation and eventually begins a disastrous romance. He tries to find escape and anonymity in the city but repeatedly must confront social expectations and the legal system that his wife employs to protect her rights and extend her hold over him. Although the Chicago setting is never fully developed, several locales on the South Side and the lakefront are specifically mentioned.

724. Masters, Edgar Lee. *Skeeters Kirby*. New York: Macmillan, 1923. 394pp.

In this novel, Arthur "Skeeters" Kirby tells the story of his late adolescence in Marshallville, Illinois and his young adulthood in Chicago, where he first arrives at the age of twenty-two. At the insistence of his father, a lawyer and politician, Skeeters pursued a legal education. However, he is really interested in writing and wants to become a newspaperman. The only newspaper job he is able to find is as a typesetter. Dissatisfied, he begins collecting delinquent payments for a bank and is suddenly making enough money to enable frequent theater and vaudeville attendance and dinner dates with women. With some friends he rents a stylish apartment on the South Side and pays for a daily maid service that includes meals. After a time he starts his own law office, joins clubs to further his career and social life, and begins romancing Martha Fiske, the daughter of industrialist and financier Henry Fiske. His romance is not whole-hearted since he is actually in love with another woman, Alicia, and is somewhat relieved when Henry Fiske finally decides that he would not be an appropriate son-in-law. Skeeters marries Alicia only to find out that she continues to have affairs and has had a hysterectomy. Skeeters' growing disillusionment with the city and its morality refocuses his attention. He leaves the city for a wilderness cabin on the Rock River where he writes a novel and meets Becky Norris, a woman who shares his literary interests and values. After giving Alicia a divorce and most of his money, he rejects Chicago. As a thirty-three-year-old, Skeeter has become self-assured and confident in his values and that he will be united with his soul mate. The novel presents a good deal of information about Chicago domestic life in apartments and boarding houses, gives some description of nightlife in the early part of the twentieth century, and raises issues of gender and social status.

725. Maupin, Robert Lee [Iceberg Slim, pseud.]. *Airtight Willie & Me*. Los Angeles: Holloway House, 1979. 245pp.

Although not all of these short stories (some novella-length) are set in Chicago, most of the characters have some connection to the city, even if the action occurs in Cleveland, Milwaukee, Houston, or Galveston. The African-American characters are drug dealers, prostitutes, pimps, or their clients, and speak in urban ghetto, slang-filled dialects.

726. Maupin, Robert Lee [Robert Beck, pseud.]. *Mama Black Widow*. Los Angeles: Holloway House, 1969. 312pp.

Unlike some of Beck's other intensely heterosexual books, this novel's protagonist, Otis Tilson (known as Mama Black Widow), is homosexual, and the book is set in a doubly marginalized community—openly gay and African-American. Most of the book's action transpires in Chicago, although a number of the characters have moved to the city from the Deep South and aspects of rural culture, including a belief in the efficacy of spells cast by practitioners of black magic, play a role.

727. Maupin, Robert Lee [Iceberg Slim, pseud.]. *Trick Baby: The Story of a White Negro*. Los Angeles: Holloway House, 1967. 312pp.

Set in South Chicago in the African-American community, this novel takes place before the civil rights movement had a significant impact. Written in the dialect of black ghetto residents, it deals with the adventures of "White Folks," a grifter so nicknamed because of his light skin. The son of a light-skinned, African-American woman and a Caucasian man, he can fit into the social group of either of his parents. Another grifter named "Blue" Leon Howard sees the advantages of teaming up with White Folks, and the novel recounts their adventures. The author drew on his own experiences as a South Chicago criminal in creating the story that presents a rich narrative record of life in a segment of Chicago's African-American community in the 1950s and 1960s. A glossary of slang words and terms by the author is included, although it is not comprehensive.

728. Maxwell, William. *The Folded Leaf.* New York: Book Find Club, 1945. 310pp.

Set in 1920s Chicago, Maxwell evokes boyhood and school life through the story of a friendship that forms between two boys who feel out of place in the city. Lymie Peters lives with his father in a dirty furnished apartment and eats meals at diners where his father tries to pick up waitresses. He has fading memories of his mother, but a clear image of his childhood home in a large, old Victorian house his father sold after his mother's death. Charles "Spud" Latham is also living in exile from his childhood home, albeit in much more comfortable circumstances. Spud moved with his family from a small town in Wisconsin, where their large house overlooked the lake. He is nostalgic for the house and misses his friends from home. Spud's frustration, his anger with his father over the move to the city, and his resentment over the comparative affluence of his classmates find an outlet in fights he initiates with other boys. Through his friendship with Lymie he achieves a level of social integration and channels his anti-social behavior into organized boxing matches.

729. Mayer, Jane Rothschild. *The Year of the White Trees.* New York: Random House, 1958. 282pp.

This romance novel tells the story of Anneira Veck's love affair with Ellis Springbok. Twenty-five-year-old Veck is the daughter of a wealthy Chicago family and Springbok is a violinist. One of the author's main themes is the clash between musical circles and affluent business circles in Chicago. Before meeting Springbok, Veck was having an affair with a fellow schoolteacher, but he is married with three children and neither of them are comfortable with the difference in their social class (he has never had enough money). Although she does not at first realize it, Springbok is also married. He is no longer in love with his wife and has separated from her. Through his involvement with Veck, he realizes that he cannot let romance affect his career. His complicated travel and household arrangements need to be managed and this can best be done by his wife and staff. Having a smooth-running professional life finally outweighs his love for Anneira Veck. Anneira also finds the affair unsatisfactory since seeing Springbok only a few times a year is not emotionally satisfying. She begins to think that even a loveless marriage would be preferable to continuing to live with her mother. The novel includes descriptions of domestic settings and reveals cultural attitudes toward romance and marriage.

730. Mayer, Jane Rothschild and Clara Spiegel [Clare Jaynes, joint pseud.]. *Instruct My Sorrows.* New York: Random House, 1942. 383pp.

When a relatively young woman's husband dies, she must adjust to social expectations while trying to build a new life. In 1940 Jessica Drummond loses her forty-year-old husband Paul to heart disease. Married when she was eighteen, Jessica finds herself a thirty-three-year-old widow with fourteen-year-old twin sons named Keith and Kim. Jessica's very conventional mother expects her to go into mourning; her parents-in-law think she will remain faithful to Paul's memory; and Paul's friends believe she should continue to socialize exclusively with them. Fortunately, Jessica has no concerns about money; she continues living on a "gentleman's farm" near Chicago and sends her sons to Andover and Exeter. An attractive woman, she must cope with the advances of a friend of Paul's and an unwanted proposal from Paul's estate lawyer. After a few years, she meets and falls in love with someone entirely outside her social circle, a well-regarded, world-traveling geologist named Scott Landis. When she begins a sexual relationship with Scott, she is plagued by concerns over the reaction of people within her social set were they to find out. While Scott is socially unconventional, he is concerned about Jessica's feelings and her compulsion to follow social conventions. His job is dangerous and would require long periods of separation. Although he knows he is protecting her by not wanting to marry, by the end of the novel it seems his love will win out and the two will wed to satisfy her social and emotional needs. Although there is not much physical description of Chicago, the novel does evoke the material culture and social customs of upper-class Chicagoans of the 1940s. The narrative includes descriptions of clothing, food, social events and commercial radio (some of Jessica's friends own a radio station and she sometimes writes theme music for shows).

731. Mayer, Jane Rothschild and Clara Spiegel [Claire Jaynes, joint pseud.]. *My Reputation.* Cleveland, Ohio: World, 1944. 288pp.
　　This title is a reprint of the author's earlier work, *Instruct My Sorrows* (entry 730)

732. Mayer, Jane Rothschild and Clara Spiegel [Claire Jaynes, joint pseud.]. *These Are the Times.* New York: Random House, 1944. 273pp.
　　This novel about gender roles, social responsibility, and married life is set in World War II Chicago. When thirty-eight-year-old John Kenyon is offered an important post in the Army Medical Corps, his wife Judith opposes his acceptance. An orthopedic surgeon in one of Chicago's major hospitals, his practice has increased dramatically as other doctors have become involved in the war effort. Judith is gratified by his important patients and increased income. Since they are childless, she has become intimately involved in his practice, even accompanying him on his rounds (he still makes house calls). Although she openly expresses concern for his safety in a military field hospital, she is secretly worried about how an extended absence would damage his practice and how empty her own life would become while she is not serving as his unofficial secretary. She is also aware that in his absence John might fall in love with someone else, or simply lose interest in her. The novel openly maintains a patriotic message, insisting that everyone must make sacrifices for their country, but the social implications of the enforced separation between husbands and wives during wartime are vividly presented. In the end, Judith gets her way and John does not go to war; however he comes to despise her possessiveness, particularly after she sends a young associate of his on a call that he should have taken and the associate is killed in an automobile accident. Afterward, finding the relationship unbearable, he separates from her. Although the novel mentions places in Chicago, most of the physical and social settings described are the interiors of expensive apartment buildings, private medical practices, and hospitals.

733. Mazzaro, Ed. *Chicago Deadline.* London, U.K.: New English Library, 1978. 176pp.
　　No additional information available.

734. McAlpine, Dale K. *Marie Naimska: A Saga of Chicago.* Philadelphia: Dorrance, 1954. 242pp.
　　In this story about Polish and Irish immigrants to Chicago in the late-nineteenth-century, the city symbolizes freedom and political idealism. Jan Naimski, the scion of Warsaw bankers, is frustrated by Russian control of Poland that is causing widening class inequalities and lack of economic opportunity. He decides to emigrate and in 1899 marries Rose Palleski, daughter of the dir-

ector of the Warsaw Opera. When they arrive in Chicago, the Naimskis settle among family friends in the Polish district, where a house has been prepared for them, and Jan is given a job in a Polish-American bank. Both Jan and Rose are delighted by the Art Institute and the orchestra concerts. They soon have a child they name Marie. Their experiences are contrasted with less affluent Polish immigrants, some of whom must perform mind-numbing work in the stockyards and others who fall into the vices of drink and casual sex. An Irish immigrant builder, Michael Cadulahay, enters their circle after becoming acquainted with Jan at the bank and the families soon become close. After their daughter Marie's triumphal return to Poland as an opera singer, and the deaths of Michael and his wife on the *Titanic*, Marie marries Jack Cadulahay, uniting the two families with such different backgrounds. In addition to presenting aspects of Chicago history up to 1920, the book vaunts the political and economic system of the United States and its superiority over the systems of other countries.

735. McConaughy, J. W. and Edward Sheldon. *The Boss*. New York: Fly, 1911. 316pp.

In this story of Chicago's political machine, protagonist Michael "Shindy Mike" Regan rises from childhood poverty in the Fourth Ward to wealth and influence. At twenty-nine, Regan is already the boss of the Fourth Ward and owner of the tavern he inherited from his father. Using his political power, he forces all the city's saloons to buy only his beer which he gets through a favorable deal with a brewer. Before long he also owns a cigar factory and later a construction company that gets all the city contracts. His real goal is wheat contracting and Regan uses his control over workers to gain interest in a series of companies as he closes in on the long-established Griswald Company. He happens to meet Emily Griswald, a college-educated settlement worker in the Fourth Ward and falls in love with her. Instead of taking over the Griswald Company outright, Regan offers Emily's father and brother a deal in which they can retain a fifty-percent control of their business if Emily marries him. Emily agrees because she cannot stand what would happen to the laborers she has been trying to help if Regan takes over entire ownership of the company. At thirty-eight, Regan seems to have gained everything he ever desired, however, he continues to pay his laborers sub-par wages and force them to drink in his saloons. The Griswalds revenge themselves on Regan through labor organizing and soon have the civic and church authorities behind them. Regan tries to hold onto his control until the very end, but when Emily leaves him, he realizes that the upper classes are in power not only because of their genealogy or their money, but because of their moral code. None of the Griswalds would have treated workers the way he has done. In remorse, Regan attempts to redress some of the wrongs he committed and acknowledges that he will never be good enough for Emily. This novel is interesting for a plot that runs counter to many novels of the time period that celebrated working-class men who gained wealth and power.

736. McCord, Joseph. *The Piper's Tune*. Philadelphia: Macrae Smith, 1938. 304pp.

This novel about romance and coming of age features a female character with the social independence that wealth can endow. When young Caradad Vardell inherits her family's ranch in Oklahoma, she sells it after oil is discovered on the property and sets out to see the world. On her way east, she stops in Chicago to see a childhood friend on whom she had a crush, Terry Cantine. Cantine sells investment securities and is in some sort of trouble that Caradad cannot make out; he is also in a relationship with a young widow, Mrs. Greenway (always so denoted). Through Terry, Caradad meets several wealthy and eligible young men, and begins to take an interest in one of them, John Severance, whose level-headedness and genuineness she appreciates as much as his appearance and elegance. However, when Mrs. Greenway confides that Terry had used other people's money to purchase stock that is now worthless and is about to be arrested, Caradad cannot let go of her early emotions for him and devotes herself to helping him. She has kept her wealth a secret, but as a millionaire she can easily repay Terry's fifteen thousand dollar debt. The two become engaged and Caradad leases a penthouse apartment complete with a butler when Terry says he needs the establishment to entertain investors. However, Caradad soon realizes that Terry cannot be faithful to his business associates or her and makes a clean break with him. She recognizes her feelings for John Severance as those of a mature woman based on his superior personal qualities and not the schoolgirl crush she had for Terry. By the end of the novel, it seems certain that Caradad and John will marry and begin to explore the world together. All of the description of the novel focuses on wealthy Chicagoans and the luxuries they can afford, with little physical description of the city.

737. McCutcheon, George Barr. *Jane Cable*. New York: Dodd, Mead, 1906. 336pp.

A woman's scheme to get her husband to be faithful to her works incredibly well until an evil man threatens to reveal her secret and put a tawdry, untrue spin on it. Soon after David and Frances Cable marry, David tires of domestic life and heads west to find his fortune. The abandoned Frances adopts a foundling hospital orphan, with the assistance of the shady lawyer James Bansemer and his assistant Elias Droom. By presenting the baby as David's daughter, she is able to get him to return and become a conscientious husband. He becomes so devoted that over a twenty year period he works his way up from manual laborer with a railroad company to the highest position on the Chicago-based Pacific, Lakes, and Atlantic Railroad. As a forty-year-old, Frances, ten years David's junior, can enjoy her husband's affluence as a society beauty and their daughter, Jane, is poised to marry well. Then, in a bizarre coincidence, Jane chooses Graydon Bansemer, the son of lawyer James Bansemer as her fiancé. Because Graydon is a recent Yale graduate with a promising future in finance, David Cable is supportive, even though he has doubts about Graydon's father and knows he was involved in a financial scandal in New York City. Frances Cable is soon being blackmailed by James who claims he will publicly end his son's engagement and announce that Jane is the offspring of one of Frances' extramarital affairs. At almost the same time, Denis Halbert, the man who had uncovered Bansemer's New York crimes, appears in Chicago to drive him out of the city. Rather than submit to blackmail, Frances decides to reveal her secret and David eventually forgives her. Jane's true ancestry proves to be distinguished and her social status advances dramatically. Although the novel describes social events and characterizes the respectability of various neighborhoods, it is mostly concerned with issues of social status, the fluidity of status in Chicago, and the ease with which a social façade may conceal character flaws and even criminal behavior. Throughout the novel specific Chicago establishments are mentioned by name, including Hooley's Theatre and Rector's restaurant.

738. McCutcheon, George Barr. *The Sherrods*. Illustrated by C. D. Williams. New York: Dodd, Mead, 1903. 343pp.

Childhood sweethearts Dudley "Jud" Sherrod and Justine Van are the children of two affluent men in Glenville, Indiana—John Sherrod and Captain James Van—each of whom invested in Arizona mining stocks and experience financial disaster. John Sherrod shoots himself immediately to avoid disgrace. His widow goes mad and only lives for another year. James Van and his wife are both dead within two years, leaving Justine to continue to live alone, supporting herself on the pittance of a one-room schoolteacher's salary. Jud ends up working for the man who foreclosed on the mortgage to the Sherrod estate. Despite their poverty, Jud and Justine marry, but when a visitor from Chicago admires Jud's artwork he moves to the city to try to establish a market for his art. His absence refuels the hopes of Jud's childhood rival, Gene Crawley. A bully previously, Crawley helps Justine with farm work and with calculation wins her trust. In the meantime, Jud becomes a newspaper artist and soon has his own admirer, Celeste Wood, the daughter of a wealthy man. Challenged by social life in the city, Jud depends upon Wood's advice and rarely goes into society without her. Too late, he realizes that Wood loves him and has led her friends and family to believe they will wed. Unable to hurt Wood and leave the Chicago life she enabled, he enters into a bigamous marriage with her. A tragic denouement is inevitable, but surprisingly, Wood and Justine unite to support each other and Justine's future as a single woman in Chicago looks hopeful. In addition to the common theme of a young person relocating to Chicago to establish a career, this novel dwells on the heady opportunities of anonymity that the city offers to create an entirely new identity. Although the novel references Chicago neighborhoods and institutions (particularly the Art Institute and Lake Shore Athletic Club), the book conveys little about life in the city.

739. McCutcheon, John T. *Dawson '11, Fortune Hunter*. New York: Dodd, Mead, 1912. 159pp.

A 1911 college graduate, Charley Dawson, tries to establish himself in Chicago in this epistolary novel in which the protagonist relates his adventures in disarming fashion in letters he writes to his mother. Dawson gets a job in a large commercial firm and is soon promoted to requisitions clerk. The novel provides some details about office life and boarding house life, but is more concerned with universal themes such as maintaining a sense of personal ethics and remembering one's family. Scadsworth Alcott, lacks personal and business scruples, and provides a counterexample of the sort of young man one should not grow into, one without personal or business ethics. While Dawson begins to succeed in business and romance, Allcott fails.

740. McCutcheon, John T. *The Restless Age*. Illustrated by the Author. Indianapolis: Bobbs-Merrill, 1921. 218pp.

The impact of the beginnings of agribusiness is an underlying theme of this novel that also contrasts the city unfavorably with the country. Twenty-three-year-old Tom Wickham fought overseas in World War I and when he returns to his father's farm near Grangefield, Illinois, he thinks he will be driven insane with boredom. In deciding to leave for Chicago, he knows he is crushing his father's hopes and jeopardizing his romantic friendship with Emily Harbridge, whose father owns the neighboring farm. On his very first day in Chicago, a beautiful young woman steals his wallet after slipping a sedative into his drink. He is forced into work for a cab company to pay off a fare. The punishment leads to a full-time job, through which he meets wealthy young Lucille Morland. They have a brief, intense romance, but Lucille lets him down twice. He gets a white-collar job working in the wholesale food company of Morland's father and thinks that he is on the verge of success in the city. Before long, however, he is reminded once again of Lucille's fundamental selfishness and is filled with remorse for working for Morland, whose business and speculation in agricultural futures endangers the livelihood of men like Wickham's father. Leaving the city in disgust, Wickham returns to Grangefield to become engaged to Emily Harbridge and work on his father's farm. Although the book does not describe Chicago in any evocative way, the city symbolizes the evils of the jazz age with immodest women, bootleg alcohol, and greed-driven plutocrats. At several junctures the book adopts a pedagogical tone, informing readers about the plight of the farmer and the evils of drink.

741. McDougall, Ella L. Randall. *From Side Streets and Boulevards: A Collection of Chicago Stories*. Chicago: Donnelley and Sons, 1893. 352pp.

This book consists of two novellas, a short story, and some poems, all of which are, in part, set in Chicago. The longest work, "Vagabond for a Year," tells the story of Crissy Trevanion. Her father is the alcoholic younger son of a wealthy Englishman. A literary man, he is kind and loving when he is sober, but is to be avoided when he is drunk. To get her safely out of the household, she is sent to apprentice in an acting troupe and pose as the daughter of the troupe's proprietors, Mr. and Mrs. Burton. Most of the novella tells of Crissy's adventures as a traveling player. When she rejoins her family, they have moved to Chicago and her father is very ill. Mr. Trevanion finds out on his deathbed that he has inherited a fortune, and when he dies his family rids themselves of an alcoholic, while gaining a fortune. George, a member of the Burton acting company and devoted to Crissy, marries her when he returns from the Civil War. They make their permanent home in Chicago, a city that fascinates Crissy. The story includes some description of theater life in Chicago in the 1860s.

The other novella, "All on a Christmas Eve," features an Irish immigrant, Anne, who was forced come to America with her family, leaving behind her lover, Dave. They pledge faithfulness, but years pass without them seeing each other. Working as a servant, her family dead, Anne socializes within a small circle of other Irish immigrants, among them an older couple, Mr. and Mrs. John Malone. John's real estate investments have made the Malones affluent and not long after Mrs. Malone dies of a lingering illness, John asks Anne to marry him. They marry for practical reasons, instead of love, but Anne believes that she has no choice. The marriage is happy enough and they soon have a baby boy. Then, in a strange coincidence, John returns from a business trip to New York City with Dave, who he employs as a bartender in his saloon. The couple's renewed love has a tragic outcome. Readers will find little physical description of Chicago, except for a portrayal of the theater district and the Irish neighborhood.

742. McDougall, Ella L. Randall [Preserved Wheeler, pseud.]. *One Schoolma'am Less*. Chicago: Donnelley and Sons, 1895. 217pp.

This polemic against the hiring practices of the Chicago City Schools is written in the form of a novel. In the 1890s, protagonist Minnie Morton gets help from her struggling family to obtain a teacher's license and a teaching position. However, changes in certification requirements, the vagaries of bureaucratic administration, and work-place prejudices, eventually force Morton to give up her dream of a career as a schoolteacher.

743. McEvoy, Joseph Patrick. *Mister Noodle: An Extravaganza*. New York: Simon and Schuster, 1931. 186pp.

The story of Charlie "Chic" Kiley from Gum Springs, Illinois, is told through letters to his mother, news clippings, telegrams, and transcripts of conversations. Kiley takes drawing classes at the Art Institute and works in the art department of the *Chicago Star*. Overnight he becomes a nationally known comic strip artist when he introduces *Mister Noodle*, a strip composed only of profiles (since that is all Kiley can draw). He also effortlessly achieves social status in Chicago, receiving memberships in the Chicago Athletic, Forty, and Midday Lunch clubs. With his newfound financial security he is able to marry his girlfriend and he soon has a one hundred thousand dollar per year contract for his syndicated strip. However, when he relocates to the syndicate's offices in New York City he succumbs to the temptations of beautiful women, nightclub entertainments, and drink. When an actress falls from the balcony of his penthouse the scandal fills the

Midwest with moral indignation and his comic strip gets cancelled. Only when he returns to Chicago and reconnects with his small town does he get the inspiration for a new comic strip and rediscover success. This satire of the syndicated comic strip industry makes pointed comparisons between Chicago and New York to the detriment of the latter.

744. McGivern, William P. [Bill Peters, pseud.]. *Blondes Die Young*. Red Badge Detective Series. New York: Dodd, Mead, 1952. 240pp.

This novel is distinctive for portraying the 1950s bohemian culture of the Near North Side with jazz clubs, wine parties, crash pads, and marijuana use, before the youth movement became officially designated "Beat" culture. The plot focuses on private detective Bill Canalli's efforts to find the killer of Jane Nelson, a show-girl connected to organized crime. Canalli is from Philadelphia, where he met Nelson, and a small section of the novel is set there.

745. McGivern, William P. *But Death Runs Faster*. Red Badge Detective Series. New York: Dodd, Mead, 1948. 231pp.

Chicago in this 1940s novel is a center of the advertising and publishing industries. First-person protagonist Steven Blake, a successful mystery novelist, is lured to Chicago from Los Angeles by a high salaried position editing a new detective magazine. His affluence enables him to quickly secure an apartment despite the tight housing market, in the 4800 block of Winthrop Avenue, on Chicago's North Side. He also rapidly establishes his personal life by dating both his secretary, and the publishing firm's accountant. However, things start going wrong when he hires Byron Crofield as assistant editor. Crofield proves to be opinionated, foppish, and overtly flirtatious with women. He is soon murdered, after hosting a party during which he became drunkenly obnoxious. Blake's distaste for Crofield and the fact that he punched him make him a prime suspect, until his secretary confesses. Blake knows she is just trying to protect him and spends the rest of the novel identifying the real killer. In addition to describing office life and alcohol-focused socializing, the novel depicts elegant apartment interiors and two bars: Harry's an elegant Michigan Avenue establishment favored by advertising men and publishers; and the Zebra, a dive Crofield frequents, that caters to men seeking prostitutes. Post-war Chicago is portrayed as a place of opportunity to enter new white-collar industries. Women are a presence in the workforce and some have high-paying jobs.

746. McGivern, William P. *Heaven Ran Last*. A Red Badge Mystery. New York: Dodd, Mead, 1949. 247pp.

In this crime novel set in 1940s Chicago Johnny Ford, a twenty-nine-year-old bookie who takes telephone bets commits a crime of passion. Ford has a slight physical defect that exempted him from the draft, but did not impair his appeal to women with husbands serving overseas. He becomes passionately involved with married Alice Olsen, and when her husband Frank is discharged cannot give Alice up. He finds an ingenious way to incriminate Frank for a murder he committed. The rest of the novel reveals how Chicago Police Detective Inspector Harrigan catches Ford. The characters are all lower-middle-class. Alice works as a secretary for an insurance company and lives in a small apartment in a converted house in the 6000 block of Winthrop Avenue off Sheridan Road. Ford lives in a Loop hotel and spends most of his time in bars and card parlors around the Loop. To establish the setting, the novel provides a good deal of information about his social life (as a bookie Ford knows politicians, policemen, and judges and has business connections with gangsters), clothing, food, and drinking habits.

747. McGivern, William P. *Very Cold for May*. A Red Badge Mystery. New York: Dodd, Mead, 1950. 246pp.

Although World War II is over, the conflict has a range of lingering effects on individual Chicagoans. The woman at the center of this story, May Laval, was a famous hostess during the war years, entertaining generals, industrialists, journalists and politicians at alcohol-fueled parties at which men vied to celebrate her beauty. The stock market tips she got dramatically increased the wealth she had garnered from previous marriages, but now fails to assuage her disappointment over falling out of the limelight. When she announces that she is turning her war-years journal into a book, not all of the attention she gets is welcome. Dan Riordan in particular is afraid she will reveal how he cheated the government by manufacturing rifle barrels with thin-gauge steel. May's old friend, Jake Harrison, a former newspaperman, is now working for a Chicago public relations firm retained by Riordan in anticipation of appearing before a Senate investigative committee. When May is murdered shortly after she shows Jake her leather-bound journal, Jake gets involved in the police investigation. In addition to attitudes toward war-time profiteering and the public relations business, the novel reveals a good deal about hard-drinking social life, office culture, and clothing styles for men and women in the post-war years. Geographically, most of the novel is set in the Loop and on the South Side. Disparaging remarks are made about the Near North Side and its occupants, who are described as office girls, artists, writers, and homosexuals, living in once grand houses now divided into studio apartments.

748. McGovern, John. *Daniel Trentworthy: A Tale of the Great Fire of Chicago*. Chicago: Rand, McNally, 1889. 281pp.

Daniel Trentworthy's father had been a famous speculator and bank president before a reversal made him a debtor and he committed suicide. Studying at Harvard at the time, Daniel is told by the college president to go to booming Chicago to win his fortune. Daniel finds jobs, if not his fortune, in late-1860s Chicago, working as a building inspector, fireman, and proofreader for a printer. Then he falls in love with Mary Holebrooke, and his association with the Holebrookes leads him to a job with Ralph Errington. Errington is making a fortune building wood frame houses all over Chicago and Mary soon becomes his wife. Daniel's disappointment is eased through continued socializing with Mrs. Holebrooke and Mary's sister Mercy. Through his work in running a smelting plant for Errington, Daniel saves money and buys a house. However, he cannot get over his love for Mary or return Mercy's love. The novel describes the boom that led up to the fire, claiming that political corruption had created the circumstances that led to the conflagration in which Mary and Errington die. In a peroration the novelist summarizes the rebuilding of Chicago and Daniel's success in building his fortune.

749. McGovern, John. *David Lockwin: The People's Idol*. Chicago: Donohue, Henneberry, 1889. 297pp.

This bizarre, melodramatic novel, presents the author's version of the evils of politics. When David Lockwood marries heiress Esther Wandrell he is a rising political star who has demonstrated his goodness by taking in a foundling boy. In running for Congress at the urging of his friend Dr. Irenaeus Tarpion, Lockwood, a political machine candidate, pays bribes and engages in low-dealing against an outsider candidate, Walter B. Corkey, a retired seaman who bills himself as the workingman's friend. Although Lockwood wins the election, his adopted son succumbs to diphtheria in the midst of the campaign and Lockwood blames himself for a lack of attentiveness. In utter despair over the death and his behavior in the election, Lockwood sets in motion a strange plan while returning from a congressional session. He arranges to meet with his political rival Corkey on a lake steamer, having paid in advance for the ship to be scuttled, so that he can take up a new life as Robert Chalmers, move to New York City and try to forget his life in Chicago. His plan goes slightly awry and, even though more than one hundred and eighty people die, Corkey survives and Lockwood barely does. From afar, Lockwood suffers as he hears of his widow's grief and tries to get her to accept his attentions as Robert Chalmers. He fails, although he does prevent her from marrying a scoundrel, before taking his own life. The novel provides little physical description of Chicago, although accounts of barroom campaigning and domestic scenes give a sense of the city in the 1890s.

750. McGrath, Tom, Lieutenant. *Copper*. Boston: Bruce Humphries, 1941. 317pp.

Mike Casey is an idealistic young man when he joins the Chicago police department, but his cases show him the dark side of humanity and he rails against immigrants, criminals, and "perverts." He also quickly learns that police work often has less to do with the law, than it does with political influence and outright bribery. Many cases are related in detail, as well as the history of Casey's career, that changes dramatically depending upon which politicians are in office (i.e., from powerful detective to mere beat walker). From Casey's point of view, the city is being destroyed by a reputation for lawlessness that attracts increasing numbers of criminals. Although he prides himself on doing good police work, becomes a well-known detective, and gets injured several times in the line of duty, he also drinks on the job and sometimes engages in vigilantism. Prohibition, the Red Scare, and World War I are all presented through their impact on Casey's police work. Finally, reformer Tim Mannion gets elected mayor and Casey becomes his right hand man in cleaning up the city. Although Mannion is assassinated, the book ends with Casey's observation that the right thinking policemen Mannion put in place remained in their positions and criminal enforcement was therefore permanently changed by his career.

751. McInerny, Ralph M. *Bishop As Pawn: A Father Dowling Mystery*. New York: Vanguard Press, 1978. 219pp.

Soon after a sniper's bullet kills Billy Murkin in Father Dowling's rectory, Bishop Rooney of the Archdiocese of Chicago is kidnapped. Dowling uncovers the connection between the two events and a plot involving industrial espionage in this third book in the Father Dowling series set in the West Chicago suburb of Fox River.

752. McInerny, Ralph. *Lying Three: A Father Dowling Mystery*. New York: Vanguard Press, 1979. 250pp.

Chicago suburb Fox River would seem to have few connections to the world of international politics. However, when the town's most outspoken Zionist, Aaron Leib, is murdered on the golf course of the Fox River Country Club, Father Dowling's investigation uncovers several links to the world of international terrorism through small arms sales and lobbying efforts. Although some scenes are set in Chicago, most of the novel is set in the suburbs in this fourth book in the Father Dowling series.

753. McInerny, Ralph M. *The Seventh Station: A Father Dowling Mystery*. New York: Vanguard Press, 1977. 212pp.

This murder mystery is set in the imaginary Chicago suburb of Fox River and features Father Dowling, formerly of Chicago and the protagonist of a series of works of detective fiction. Urban sprawl has begun making incursions on Fox River in this tale of murder, mostly set in a Franciscan retreat house.

754. McKay, Allis (aka Allis McKay Klamm). *Woman About Town*. New York: Macmillan, 1938. 278pp.

This story, set in the late 1920s, captures an American society still adjusting to rapid change in social behavior and roles for women. Leila Gersten is a divorced woman at a time when many people still believe divorce is a disgraceful attack on civic institutions and morality. Her former husband, Michael, is a theater designer and Leila is a commercial artist. Michael envisioned the two of them becoming great successes in their careers and only then starting a family. So, most of their time was spent at work and their evenings were devoted to the kind of socializing that would advance their careers, whether enjoyable, or not. As Leila succeeded and Michael did not, their mutual friends began to talk about his inferiority complex. He left Leila for a blonde who was more beautiful than her and who did not have a career to compete with his. Leila lives in an apartment hotel with maid service on the Near North Side, within a short walk to Lincoln Park. She wears beautiful clothes, has a likable job from which she earns a good income, and has an active social life filled with parties and dining out. Her friends tease her about still wanting to become an Oak Park matron, but she really is dissatisfied. Much of the novel tells the story of her romance with a new artist at her agency, Don Atkinson. Just as Leila has allowed herself to begin thinking ahead of settling down to married life again, Atkinson receives a job offer in New York City. Although he gives her the opportunity to go with him, after careful analysis, she concludes that he is only doing the honorable thing. So, she lets go of her fantasies of having children with him, participates in all the farewell parties in his honor, and moves to a new, and even more elegant apartment, closer to the lake. The novel details restaurants, nightclubs, speakeasies, and the apartment furnishings, clothing, and food that constitute an affluent middle-class life in the boom times of the late 1920s. Taken as a whole, the work is a celebration of the excitement and physical comfort of Chicago, written after the 1929 stock market crash and possessing a sense of longing and elegy for the boom times.

755. Meadowcroft, Enid La Monte. *By Secret Railway*. New York: Thomas Y. Crowell, 1948. 275pp.

In this work of historical fiction for children, mostly set in 1860s Chicago, the author illustrates the issues that fueled the Secession Crisis. Twelve-year-old David Morgan feels compelled to help with his family's finances. His widowed mother maintains a household that includes an elderly grandfather and four young children on proceeds from a small bakeshop operated in the family's sitting room. On the first day David looks for work on the Chicago wharves he meets Jim Clayton, an African-American boy. His father worked at Chicago's Tremont House to earn money to buy his son's freedom. However, Jim discovers that his father died the week before and they will never be reunited. David takes Jim home with him where he is accepted into the household and works with David on the construction of the Wigwam convention hall. They later experience the excitement of the Republican presidential convention of 1860. Soon afterwards, Jim helps David save David's younger brother from drowning and in so doing destroys his letter of manumission. A boarder in the Morgan household hears of the disaster and tricks Jim away from the Morgan's protection, selling him back into slavery. Eventually, the Morgans learn of Jim's plight and David frees him from a Missouri farm. In addition to the 1860 presidential convention, the novel describes rallies in support of Lincoln by the Wide-Awakes and mentions several historical Chicago businesses.

756. Means, Mary and Theodore Saunders [Denis Scott, joint pseud.]. *The Beckoning Shadow*. Indianapolis: Bobbs-Merrill, 1946. 288pp.

Chicago private eye Mike James gets a job through his aunt to work for her next door neighbors, the Bronson family. The Bronsons include two sets of siblings from their father's two marriages and all of them benefit from a productive mine in their hometown of Belleplaine, Illinois. The estranged husband of Martha Bronson has gone missing and James is hired to find him. After traveling across the country in his search, he is shocked to discover Donahue is living in Chicago. Although the case is solved, the Bronsons soon have many other needs for James after a mine explosion, the murder of Harold Bronson, and a murder attempt on another family member. Some of James's detective work is performed in Chicago, although Belleplaine and St. Louis are also important and the descriptions of Chicago are narrowly focused on specific addresses and business.

757. Meeker, Arthur. *The Far Away Music*. Boston: Houghton Mifflin, 1945. 308pp.

This novel contrasts the spirit of frontiersmen with those of settlers who establish businesses. In 1856 Jonathan Trigg returns from the West Coast after a seven year absence to be reunited with his wife, Julia, and her demanding and close-knit family, the Bascombs. He has been gone so long from the modest household he established at 80 State Street that his children have been told he died in California. The novel is written mostly from the perspective of his youngest daughter, Loulie, and ends with the marriage of his oldest daughter, eighteen-year-old Sissie (the middle daughter is named Nancy). Trigg, a man of humble origins, left to join the California gold rush because he felt out of place around his affluent in-laws. In his absence, various members of the Bascomb clan have become even more successful, owning interests in iron mines, shipping firms, and the wheat exchange. Although Trigg came close, he did not win a fortune in the gold fields; however, he did learn patience and humility from his hardships. Most of the novel's action develops around the appearance in Chicago of California acquaintances of Trigg's—Zepherine Amberley and her nephew Ted. These two do not share the East Coast social conventions of the Bascombs and have a surprisingly unsettling effect. The most unsettled of all is Sissy, who is so attracted to Ted that she begins to doubt that she should marry her fiancé, Aaron. However, Ted has the frontier spirit of Trigg and after a while leaves for San Francisco, removing himself from the picture. At the end of the novel, Trigg leaves once again, but this time for the east and Buffalo to be near the places he had known as a youth. The novel's plot is conveyed through accounts of social events and conversations that capture the attitudes and outlook of the Bascombs, upper-class Chicagoans. Plentiful descriptions of clothing, food, and household furnishings establish a clear physical setting for the novel and the time period. Important Chicago events and developments are mentioned and the national political debate over slavery and the threat of secession gets rehearsed.

758. Meeker, Arthur. *Prairie Avenue*. New York: Alfred A. Knopf, 1949. 318pp.

This fictionalized cultural history of Chicago's Prairie Avenue, the street on which the city's most prosperous businessmen constructed their mansions, covers the period from 1885 through 1918. The novel details clothing, food, furniture, social events, conversation, and their changes over time. When protagonist, twelve-year-old Ned Ramsay is sent to live with his Uncle Hiram and Aunt Lydia Stack in their Prairie Avenue mansion, his peripatetic parents have just experienced another of their financial reversals. Mr. Ramsay is a speculator in the grain market and his resources fluctuate widely. The Stacks, on the other hand, have a comfortable fortune earned by Hiram in the lumber business. Similar in age to one of the Stack children, Almira, Ned is quickly accepted family and becomes a particular favorite of his Aunt Lydia, about whom he is intensely curious. She is a great beauty who has achieved social prominence, but has mysterious origins (was she really an escort or is this just malicious gossip?). He is especially puzzled that she is too weakened by a heart condition to climb the stairs that lead to the master bedroom, but holds court in her first-floor, sitting room, visited by the city's most respectable gentlemen, but never any women. Ned also becomes intimate with the Abner Kennerley household through his friendship with Celia Kennerley. Abner made his fortune as a food wholesaler and is said to be the richest man in Chicago. As Ned becomes familiar with the Stacks and Kennerleys his curiosity and un-usual sophistication, developed through his travels with his parents and experiences with their tra-vails, make him a perceptive observer. He realizes that Mrs. Kennerley, known for her high spirits (attributed to being a Southern woman from Charleston) is actually an alcoholic and that Lydia and Abner Kennerley are having an affair. On the tragic day of his Uncle Hiram's death, Ned ac-curately concludes that Hiram committed suicide. Rushed away by his parents, who are once again solvent, Ned returns to Chicago three more times: for a year to work as a music critic in 1895 after the death of his parents; in 1904 after the success of one of his novels; and in 1918 at the behest of his Aunt Lydia who is on her deathbed. At each juncture he observes his Prairie Avenue acquain-tances facing new challenges and notes the changes in the neighborhood. By his final trip, many of the grand houses on the Avenue have been torn down and few of those remaining are still resi-dences. The author's intimate knowledge of this Chicago neighborhood and its notable residents makes this novel a useful resource for cultural historians.

759. Merwin, Bannister. *The Girl and the Bill*. Illustrated by Troy Kinney, Margaret West Kinney, and Harrison Fisher. New York: Dodd, Mead, 1909. 371pp.

   In this romance novel, Robert Orme is an easterner in Chicago for a business meeting that is delayed. He is filled with admiration for the city's drive and excitement and gets involved in a mystery as well as establishing a relationship with a beautiful young woman. The mystery centers on a defaced bill he receives as change from a haberdasher. The currency has the inked message "Remember person you pay this to" and a cryptogram. As he puzzles over this message, he gets drawn into international intrigue concerning a purloined treaty between the United States and Germany that he recovers after dealing with a mysterious South American and keeps out of the hands of the Japanese ambassador, an adversary of the United States. When he finally delivers the documents into the hands of the secretary of state, the girl he has been running into all over the city, but to whom he never gets properly introduced, turns out to be the high-ranking official's daughter. Most of the action takes place in expensive domestic environments and private clubs, conveying a sense that Chicago has a large, well-defined, upper class.

760. Merwin, Samuel. *Goldie Green*. Indianapolis: Bobbs-Merrill, 1922. 341pp.

   Set in the 1920s, an era protagonist Marigold "Goldie" Green designates the age of the girl, much of the action occurs in the imaginary Chicago suburb of Sunbury, with significant portions set in Chicago, where Sunbury residents tend to work and socialize. Through the experiences of nineteen-year-old Goldie, Merwin presents the challenges faced by women in a sexist society and celebrates new opportunities. Goldie lives with her family and works as a ticket agent, but unlike her family, she has ambition and an analytical approach to life. Her lower-middle-class family is dependent upon the earnings of her accountant father, Henry, who is subservient to his dominating wife, who tends to over spend on clothing and meaningless trappings of social class. Goldie's twenty-four-year-old brother Percy, also an accountant, is as ambitionless as his father and spends his free time at the Y.M.C.A. Sixteen-year-old Anderson has no discernible interests beyond his personal pleasures and the Green's twin, eleven-year-old girls have not yet begun to manifest any personality. Although Goldie seems to be a "flapper" of the sort Mrs. Green despises and the Y.M.C.A. warns Percy about, in fact she is business-minded. A chance encounter leads to an automobile insurance franchise and she becomes Sunbury's first business woman. Within a year she is the general manager of a large movie theater and, by the end of the novel, is poised to manage a whole chain of theaters. Motivated by solving business problems more than by personal financial gain, Goldie helps her family and even purchases a house for them, even though she knows she is fostering their continued dependence upon her. She is offered the traditional, dependent role, of wife by a wealthy Chicago lawyer, twenty-seven years her senior, and has in prospect a marriage to a man who has wealth of the sort that ranks nationally. Instead, she decides on a companionate marriage to a man of her own age without financial resources, who studied art and has become a designer for her theater. Chicago in the novel is the cultural and business center for people in Sunbury, a separate entity, but almost a continuation of their town.

761. Merwin, Samuel. *Henry Is Twenty: A Further Episodic History of Henry Calverly 3rd*. Illustrated by Stockton Mulford. Indianapolis: Bobbs-Merrill, 1918. 385pp.

The imaginary Sunbury, Illinois in which most of the novel is set is a close-in suburb of Chicago. Henry Calverly, 3rd, first introduced in *Temperamental Henry* is about to receive the inheritance held in trust for him by his uncle. Henry, still ruled by his temperament, is at his best only when he is writing. His local newspaper assignments rarely pique his interest enough to bring out his skill. When he writes about a businessman's picnic, accurately skewering the town's leaders with their short-comings and malfeasances, his newspaper editor is delighted by the writing, but heavily edits the piece to forestall libel suits. Outraged, Henry quits to join a struggling rival newspaper, *The Sunbury Weekly Gleaner*, convincing his uncle to give him a third of his anticipated inheritance to invest in the publication. Energized by the incident, Henry facilely writes a series of stories humorously dissecting Sunbury life that sells newspapers, however, the *Gleaner's* owner is too far in debt to be aided by the increased sales. So, Henry and his friend Humphrey Weaver get the business and its equipment cheaply. At the same time, Henry begins wooing Ciceley Hamlin daughter of a wealthy woman whose stepfather is a retired, nationally known U.S. senator. Henry's poverty, made increasingly dire by a libel suit and the impending failure of the *Gleaner*, is the major impediment to the marriage. Fortunately, a visiting New York publisher sees Henry's stories and offers him a contract to publish them in a national magazine and as a book. The novel ends with Henry about to enter adulthood as a published author and husband. Throughout the book Chicago functions as a geographical continuation of Sunbury where business offices are located as well as commercialized social and cultural venues (as opposed to social and cultural venues in Sunbury that are in people's homes).

762. Merwin, Samuel. *The Passionate Pilgrim, Being the Narrative of an Oddly Dramatic Year in the Life of Henry Calverly, 3rd*. Indianapolis: Bobbs-Merrill, 1919. 403pp.

Very little of this third book in the Henry Calverly series is set in either Sunbury or Chicago. When Madame Watt murdered Senator Watt during a luncheon with her daughter Ciceley, Henry's wife, Henry's life in Sunbury quickly came to an end. By the time of the murder trial Henry was famous for his book of short stories set in a fictional version of Sunbury. Fearing what being the crucial witness in the prosecution's case will do to Ciceley, Henry absconds with her to a remote, rural area. They are eventually arrested and Henry charged and convicted of obstruction of justice. As Henry feared, Ciceley dies from emotional strain before she can testify. The acquitted Madame Watt builds a castle for herself on the North Shore. Under an assumed name, Henry works for a newspaper in an unnamed town and rejects money from the Watt fortune. He later completes a successful biography of a corporate titan and marries the titan's daughter/heiress. The book recounts some of Henry's past in Sunbury and Chicago and includes a dramatic visit to Madame Watt in her castle.

763. Merwin, Samuel. *Temperamental Henry: An Episodic History of the Early Life and the Young Loves of Henry Calverly, 3rd.* Illustrated by Stockton Mulford. Indianapolis: Bobbs-Merrill, 1917. 382pp.

In the early 1890s, Henry Calverly, 3rd has few prospects as an eighteen-year-old high school dropout living with his widowed mother in a boarding house in Sunbury, Illinois, a suburb of Chicago. Then, he begins dating Clemency Snow, the daughter of William B. Snow, Sunbury's wealthiest man with an entire office building in Chicago. To make himself a competitive suitor, he teams up with a peer, Banning Widdicombe, who has a strong business sense that enables him to find endless opportunities to make money. Because Henry is known to have a good singing voice and can play guitar and piano, Widdicombe convinces the hospital board to hire the two of them to produce a musical benefit with Henry directing and Widdicombe doing not much of anything. The benefit is a success, but Henry squanders his money. After his mother dies his uncle tries to get Henry to accept maturity and he finally gets a job in a newspaper office. Sunbury is one of several North Shore towns connected to Chicago by Lake Shore Drive and railway service that are suburban residential communities with a few shops. Many residents work in Chicago and a significant part of their commercial and social life is focused on the city. Readers will note the extent to which musical performance was important during this time period before radio and moving pictures. People attend even amateur musical performances in great numbers and the ability to play an instrument or sing is certain to earn social invitations.

764. Merwin, Samuel. *The Whip Hand: A Tale of the Pine Country.* Illustrated by Frederic Rodrigo Gruger. New York: Doubleday, Page, 1903. 299pp.

In part a tale of three young men and their first years in the workforce, Merwin uses their experiences to vaunt the courage to resist social corruption. Jack Halloran worked his way through college and lived in the Chicago household of the Davies family, doing odd jobs in exchange. He became friends with Margaret Davies and their interest in each other turned romantic once Halloran graduated and moved out of the house to work in a Wisconsin lumber firm. Margaret has become active in the settlement house movement and the two of them often socialize at settlement house events. Their acquaintance, William H. Babcock, is a rival for Margaret's affections. Driven by business ambition, he works for G. Clyde Bigelow the owner of an investment firm who is notorious for his unscrupulous business practices. Bigelow has been purchasing lumber companies and the family firm for which Halloran works is one of the last holdouts. The novel details the underhanded machinations Bigelow uses to get control of lumber firms—methods carried out by his underling Babcock. In the end Halloran, the man with superior values gets the hand of Davies, for which Babcock had also vied, and defeats Bigelow.

765. Merwin, Samuel and Henry Kitchell Webster. *Calumet "K."* Illustrated by H. C. Edwards. New York: Macmillan, 1901. 345pp.

Charlie Bannon of the Minneapolis firm MacBridge & Company is sent to South Chicago to oversee the construction of a two million bushel grain elevator. The novel details the engineering, transportation, and personnel difficulties (union organizing) he confronts, as well as the impact on the wheat market as this huge facility nears completion. In the meantime, a romance develops between Bannon and office girl Hilda, although most of their conversation is work-related and the opportunities for socializing during a six day work week are limited (they even work on Christmas Day). The novel ends with a celebratory dinner and speeches upon the completion of the grain elevator that has enabled the company that paid for its construction to make a fortune in the wheat market. The book documents one aspect of Chicago's economic success—wheat trading and the personal sacrifices made by loyal company employees working in a non-union environment.

766. Merwin, Samuel and Henry Kitchell Webster. *The Short Line War.* New York: Macmillan, 1899. 334pp.

This novel about railroads and business rivalries in the late nineteenth century is partially set in Chicago where the headquarters of the opposing railroads occupy office buildings near the Loop. James Weeks built his railroad in the years after the Civil War. A native of Kentucky who was orphaned at an early age and raised by his grandfather, after fighting with the Union Army, he returned to Kentucky to find his grandfather had died and used the modest inheritance he received to begin investing in railroads. By the 1890s he controls a considerable railroad network. Weeks' railroad line is jeopardized when the C. & S. C. Corporation, headed by William C. Porter, learn of substantial coal deposits along one of Weeks' railway lines and Porter decides to gain control. The opposing sides use a range of tactics, although C. & S. C. tends to use illegal ones, including bribery, violence, and kidnapping. The railroad feud is stabilized when the governor imposes military rule for his own political reasons and the day is won for Weeks when he is able to expose the bribery and corruption of his opponents. Physical locations range widely over Illinois and the Chicago metropolitan area, although a number of Chicago locales are mentioned and Weeks resides on Ashland Avenue on Chicago's West Side.

767. Meyer, Lucy Rider. *Deaconess Stories.* Introduction by Dwight L. Moody. Chicago: Hope Publishing, 1900. 253pp.

These vignettes, set in Chicago's slums around the turn of the century, are intended to give some sense of the work of deaconesses, Christian women devoted to helping others (mostly women and children). Illustrated with photographs, the work is probably only slightly fictionalized. The only systemic problem noted in the stories is alcoholism and Christianity, cleanliness, and manual training are the solutions offered to the dismal conditions described in the book.

768. Meyer, Lucy Rider. *Mary North.* New York: Fleming H. Revell, 1903. 330pp.

In this novel about social injustice and the plight of women, Mary North of Westland, Massachusetts has a happy life until she first takes an emotional interest in men. Orphaned at fourteen, the local physician, Dr. Sheldon, is made her guardian. Dr. and Mrs. Sheldon are kindly and encourage Mary's interest in books and self-culture. A Sheldon nephew, Stephen Bayard, a wealthy young medical student ten years older than Mary is immediately smitten with her, but though Mary would have welcomed his attentions, he follows the family's reticence and continues his studies in Germany. While living in Boston preparing for Vassar entrance exams, Mary naively accepts the attentions of Jules Henri le Cygne. Mary quickly falls in love with him and when he claims he has been recalled to France and must leave immediately, a false marriage follows. After Mary signs over her property, she discovers le Cygne is the villain Billy Sloan. Mary flees to Chicago as the place where her guardians will never discover her disgrace. She finds a department store job, befriends other young clerks, and moves into a boarding house with some of them. However, she soon experiences dire poverty when she is wrongfully fired. The book details working and living conditions for impoverished women, paying close attention to the sufferings of the poor in Chicago's summer heat. In the final months of her pregnancy with Sloan's baby and near physical collapse Mary is reunited with a department store friend and nursed back to health, only to return to Chicago's streets for fear of bringing shame to her friend. Near death again, she is finally discovered by Stephen Bayard who takes her back to Massachusetts. Soon afterward she inherits the Sheldon estate and returns to Chicago to establish a school to train domestic servants and bring respectability to housework. She is supported by Bayard and his private income, although it is uncertain whether she will ever conquer her feelings of self-repugnance and marry him. The novel articulates the dangers and suffering late-nineteenth-century Chicago presented for women, as well as presenting the "professionalization" of domestic service as a possible solution.

769. Miller, Francesca Falk. *The Sands: The Story of Chicago's Front Yard*. Chicago: Valentine-Newman, 1948. 215pp.

This work of historical fiction is about "The Sands," a lakefront area that stretched from the Chicago River north to what is now Oak Street Beach. In theory the land was not under the legal jurisdiction of Chicago or Illinois. In the 1850s Dad Kinny took advantage of this loophole to operate a gambling parlor, saloon, and house of prostitution in a series of makeshift houses and shacks. Frequented by sailors, fishermen, and socially marginal figures, it was an odd place for Sulie West to take up residence. The seventeen-year-old grew up in a respectable family that followed New England manners and tastes. However, Sulie fell in love with Jack Hannon and followed him to his waterside shack, even before his Indiana wife, who would later die, had divorced him. Sulie also overlooks Hannon's criminal activities, conducted on the behalf of Kinny, patiently awaiting his return from prison after he is convicted as an accessory in a murder. When he is released, Hannon is only with Sulie a few years before leaving to fight in the Civil War. When he finally returns, he settles down to life as a fisherman, matching a gradual change in the Sands as Kinny leaves and George Streeter decides the area should become a town named after him. For decades he carries on a fight to keep the land from the city. The struggle becomes less and less tenable as Chicago develops and moneyed interests employ violent tactics to gain control of the Sands. However, Streeter holds on until his death in 1921. Miller focuses on the experiences of women from successive generations as they stand with their men out of love-inspired loyalty. The major events in Chicago's history from 1850 to 1918 are recounted, including the Lincoln funeral cortege, the fire of 1871, and the Columbian Exposition.

770. Millspaugh, Clarence Arthur. *Men Are Not Stars*. New York: Doubleday, Doran, 1938. 365pp.

The life of an unsuccessful, Chicago artist and his family is recounted in this novel that ends with a rejection of urban life. Told from the perspective of the youngest member of the O'Riordan family, Celia Ann, in an extended flashback that covers the years 1908-1910, patriarch Daniel O'Riordan, a painter who ignores the art world's emerging taste for modern art by continuing to paint dramatic historical scenes, is at the center of the narrative. In addition to Celia Ann, the family includes one son, Pat, and two other daughters, Kathleen and Elizabeth. Most of the Chicago section of the novel takes place in the O'Riordan studio and focuses on Daniel's philosophy on art and life and the interactions he has with members of his artistic circle, including Lionel Vestal, Daniel's oldest friend and a naturalist poet; Koger Kennedy, a poet attracted to Eastern spiritualism; and self-proclaimed art critic, Mabel Geers. Daniel has little regard for his family's needs and they begin selling his paintings along busy Chicago sidewalks to get food money. When Daniel realizes he has serious aesthetic differences with his most admired friend, and his work is rejected for an important exhibition, the O'Riordans take to the summer roads of the Midwest, getting commissions for portraits and selling paintings and drawings along the way. As winter approaches, they return to Chicago and Daniel commences what he believes will be his great masterwork, a crucifixion. However, when one member of his circle commits suicide Daniel concludes that he must leave the city with its distorted values and aesthetic and return to his childhood home. So, he moves his family in order to commence a simpler life on a rural farm. The novel is of interest for its description of Chicago artistic circles in the early twentieth century.

771. Milman, Harry Dubois. *Mr. Lake of Chicago.* The Criterion Series. New York: Street and Smith, 1893. 219pp.
    This work imitates Archibald Clavering Gunter's *Mr. Barnes of New York* (New York: Home, 1887). No additional information is available.

772. Mizner, Elizabeth Howard. *Dorinda.* New York: Lothrop, Lee and Shepard, 1944. 303pp.
    This young adult book presents aspects of Chicago history in the 1840s through the story of sixteen-year-old Dorinda Duffield's year-long visit to the city in 1843. Dorinda lives with her family in the countryside along the Wabash River. When her Aunt Adeline writes from Chicago to invite Dorinda to live with her while her husband, Uncle John, is away on an extended business trip, Dorinda is thrilled at the prospect of seeing the booming settlement with a population of two thousand that she has known only from her father's descriptions, based on his trips there to sell agricultural products. Her mother approves of the plan since Dorinda will attend Miss Elliot's school for young ladies. Most of the book is occupied with Dorinda's experiences as she learns about Chicago and its booming industries and civic projects (such as the Navy Pier). The book provides a good deal of cultural history, as well, detailing secondary school pedagogy for girls and fashions in clothing and entertainments. Through the character of Jethro Warren, in whom Dorinda takes a romantic interest, readers learn about economic opportunities in Chicago.

773. Molloy, Paul. *A Pennant for the Kremlin.* Garden City, N.Y.: Doubleday, 1964. 185pp.
    Drawing upon his experiences as a Chicago sports writer, Molloy imagines what would happen if a wealthy man, Armistead E. Childers, unhappy over the Cold War, willed his fortune and the Chicago White Sox to the Soviet Union. This baseball novel is mostly set inside offices and stadiums.

774. Monteleone, Thomas F. *The Time-Swept City.* New York: Popular Library, 1977. 287pp.
    This futurist work envisions a Chicago that has become an integrated organism protected by force fields and a dome in which individualism has been lost and a central computer controls all activity. Even breeding has been taken outside the hands of individuals and delegated to creatures genetically modified to perform the task as efficiently as possible. Security is maintained by humans whose bodies have been robotically enhanced. When one man discovers, via a time capsule

and the contents of a long-buried library, that the entire system was created by humans under attack by alien forces centuries before, rebellion against the control of "Eternal Chicago" seems possible. Readers may be interested in speculating upon why this futurist vision of Chicago emerged in the cultural climate of the late 1970s.

775. Montgomery, Louise. *Mrs. Mahoney of the Tenement*. Illustrated by Florence Scovel Shinn. Boston: Pilgrim Press, 1912. 168pp.

Immigrants from all over Europe live together in a Chicago tenement. They socialize by telling each other stories, often about the troubles of their neighbors, but occasionally folk tales from abroad. Ethnicities represented include Irish, Scots, Poles, Bohemians, and Germans. Frequent themes in the stories are marital challenges (often caused by male alcoholism), the death of children, the waywardness of children, and the strategies for protecting the virtue of young women from predatory males. Most of the women do some kind of paid work in their tenements far into the night (often taking in laundry or sewing). Despite the harsh, overcrowded conditions, and poor environment (stench from the stockyards and soot from factories) the book tacitly asserts that the tenants form a community of mutual assistance. The book ends with the story of a young society girl working as a caseworker who gets her comeuppance when she removes a gravely ill elderly man to the hospital, separating him from the aged wife who has been taking care of him. Within a few days the tenants have banded together and raised ten dollars through twenty-five cent donations to bring him back home.

776. Montross, Lois. *No Stranger to My Heart*. New York: Appleton-Century, 1937. 281pp.

As a young woman experiences living on her own in the city and the early years of married life, she negotiates an identity for herself outside those typically available to females in the time period. The daughter of a minister in small-town Jeremiah, Illinois, Alison Pray, wearied by the fact that every aspect of her family's life is the subject of gossip, runs away to Chicago at the age of twenty-one. Having finished one year of business college, she gets a secretarial job in the office of Chester Kearney, a young man who is editor of *Captain Twinifort's Magazine for Boys* (he prides himself on the two-million-copy circulation). The attractive Kearney proposes, but Alison is not in love and rejects him. When her sister Fredi also runs away from Jeremiah, she lives with Alison in her boarding house room, but can only find work dancing in the chorus of Scapelli's "Circus Tent," a nightclub. In the meantime, Alison meets Dolf Norman through Kearney and begins dating the young lawyer. Before long they marry and settle in the small town of Beckley, Illinois, where Dolf grew up and his family is prominent. Despite some social triumphs in Beckley, Alison finds life too much like Jeremiah and she makes a long trip to Chicago to sort out her feelings. When Dolf follows three weeks later, the two of them realize that Alison thought Dolf wanted a country club society matron as a wife and had become unhappy trying to play that role; and Dolf thought that Alison truly wanted to be a society matron. When they realize that Dolf fell in love with Alison because of her free spirit, they return to Beckley with their love renewed. The sections set in Chicago describe 1930s boarding houses, furnished apartments, office life, and a nightclub.

777. Montross, Lynn. *East of Eden*. New York: Harper and Brothers, 1925. 299pp.

Only a few brief sections of this novel that tells of a 1921 effort of farmers to organize a grain growers association are physically set in Chicago. However, the city is such a force in the novel that it almost seems like one of the characters. Taciturn Fred Derring represents the farmers in his area at the meeting that establishes the U.S. Grain Growers, Inc. and risks his farm to make the organization work. He associates Chicago with the Board of Trade and the banks that have begun taking over mortgaged farms. His children, eighteen-year-old Louisa and twenty-three-year-old Augie, see the city as the only place that will give them an opportunity to live away from the crushing burden of farm work, family obligation, and small-town social control. Augie, who left school at thirteen to work on the farm with his father, leaves for the city to follow his ambition of becoming an automobile mechanic. When it seems that Derring will lose part of his farm, Augie returns from the city. He gives Louisa enough money to attend business college and the remainder of his savings to his father, who is then able to keep the farm intact. Each day all members of the Derring family observe expensive automobiles with well-dressed people glide by on their way to Chicago. Only Ida, Fred's wife, takes the practical approach of selling farm goods to the city-dwellers from a roadside stand. The novel rehearses the plight of family farms while presenting all that Chicago symbolized for rural agrarian people of the time period.

778. Montross, Lynn and Lois Montross. *Town and Gown*. New York: George H. Doran, 1923. 283pp.

This collection of short stories evokes life at the University of Illinois at Chicago in the early 1920s. Many of the stories have characters in common and although most are told from the perspective of students, several of them deal with faculty members. For instance, Agnes Watson, dean of women, is obsessed with preventing students from having sex. The product of eastern colleges, she cannot adjust to the vulgar behavior of Midwestern university students and is shocked at the way music and dancing from Chicago's "black and tan" clubs infiltrates the campus. The student stories have the shared theme of finding one's place on campus and in the world. Peter Warshaw, the son of a small town doctor, initially becomes a "swell" under the influence of university life. He entirely changes his wardrobe, mannerisms, and speech to match those of his affluent new friends. However, he becomes frustrated with their shallowness and transforms himself once again to fit in with intellectuals and political radicals. By his senior year, he has rejected outside influences and realized that he will follow in his father's footsteps, return to his small town, and eventually take over his father's practice. Other young men win distinction on campus from their success with women, their cars, or their clothing. The coeds struggle to win social distinction through sororities and maintain the purity that will win them a husband while at the same time being flirtatious enough to keep men interested. Although many of the students are from outside Chicago, several stories describe the challenges of Chicago students who can be aided socially by their family's affluence or threatened by even minor socio-economic failings of their families. The plight of foreign students is featured in several stories. They are characterized as much more sophisticated and socially accomplished than their classmates and Chicagoans in general, but treated as socially inferior since they are not Americans. The book includes extensive descriptions of material culture (clothing, room furnishings) and social events, including dances, fraternity and sorority dinners, and meals at faculty houses. There is also an extended description of a vaudeville show off-campus at a Chicago theater.

779. Moody, Minnie Hite. *Once Again in Chicago*. New York: King, 1933. 268pp.

Henry and Mattie, who met and fell in love at the 1893 Columbian Exposition, reunite at the 1933 Chicago World's Fair after having had no contact with each other for forty years. Mattie had traveled with her grandparents in 1893 and her grandfather had become ill upon arriving in Chicago. Mattie had only a short time to visit the fair before her grandfather's condition worsened and he soon died. Walking along the lake, she had met Henry and they had immediately fallen in love. Henry had impulsively proposed. However, her grandparents had earlier decided that orphaned Mattie should marry Joel Thornton, the owner of a good deal of prime farm land. When her grandfather died, Mattie had no time to meet Henry to say farewell and make plans for continued contact. Rushed back to her hometown of Prairieville, Illinois, Mattie felt obligated to carry through on her grandfather's wishes. When she did not hear from Henry, she married Thornton and soon had a child. As the years passed, she never traveled outside of Prairieville. However, several months after Joel Thornton's death she begins planning to attend the 1933 World's Fair, angering her five children. When she arrives in Chicago she sees the city from the perspective of her memories from almost forty years before. Although she does not think it really possible, she hopes she will meet Henry at the fair and on the first evening, walking along the lake, she does. When she is reunited with Henry, she learns that he had written to her and they realize that their letters had been intercepted by Thornton and Mattie's grandmother. In their conversations, they share the events that filled their lives apart (Henry lost his arm in a corn shredder while a young man, his wife died in childbirth, and both of them experienced the death of a child from illness). They also reminisce about the Columbian Exposition and make plans to marry. Mattie, increasingly concerned about the practicalities of a new life that would include a daughter-in-law unlikely to welcome her, makes a final decision when Henry suddenly becomes ill. She stays with him long enough to believe he will recover, then, leaving a note with her address, returns to her children. Much of this novel is concerned with the interior life of Mattie, but the book does present a good deal of information about what it would have been like to be a fair visitor to Chicago in 1893 and 1931.

780. Mooney, James. [Le Jemlys, pseud.]. *Lawyer Manton of Chicago: A Detective Story of Thrilling Interest.* Chicago: Eagle, 1888. 201pp.

This elaborately plotted suspense novel plays with the theme of social misrepresentation and disguise, a concern of nineteenth-century urban Americans as they left the social setting of small towns for the anonymity of the city. The central plot device is the kidnapping of lawyer Robert Manton. Early in private detective Fenton Chase's investigation he realizes the culprit is probably physician Julian Oswald, who wants to marry Manton's sister Ora. Manton opposed the match and he and Oswald quarreled over the matter. Soon after Chase begins trailing Oswald the doctor's henchmen dump him bound into Lake Michigan. Fortunately, he lands on a shipwreck and is able to stay above water long enough to remove his bonds. Chase afterwards uses a series of disguises as he tries to recover Manton. He begins to realize that more people than Oswald were involved in the abduction, including Leon Dacre, the beautiful and wealthy Lucille Duchon, the even more beautiful and wealthy Hortense Faxon, and Major Dalton. After being trapped and almost burned to death, Chase recovers a body in Benton Harbor, Michigan that he believes is Manton and has Oswald arrested. However, during Oswald's trial Chase confronts Lucille Duchon, who leads him to the real murderer, Major Dalton. Dalton, aka Leon Dacre, is actually Leon Oswald, the twin brother of Dr. Oswald. He confesses his crimes while slowly dying after shooting himself. When Chase discovers Leon Oswald's box of disguises he finds a box of contact lenses, dyed in different colors, and comes to understand why Oswald's disguises were so successful. After the corpse Chase found is determined not to be Manton, the lawyer is recovered alive, restored to health, and reunited with Hortense; and Dr. Oswald is betrothed to Ora. Although a number of Chicago addresses are mentioned in the novel, as well as some businesses (such as the Palmer House), physical settings are of little importance in the book.

781. Mooney, James [Le Jemlys; Symmes M. Jelley, pseuds.]. *Shadowed to Europe: A Chicago Detective on Two Continents*. Illustrated by True Williams. Chicago: Belford, Clarke, 1885. 357pp.

Like other novels by Mooney, this one is mostly concerned with social presentation and the concealment of one's identity. The central plot element is a robbery. Pauline Barr, an attractive, young widow is about to invest almost all of her assets in real estate. Accompanied by her lawyer Victor Price, she is robbed at Wells Street station. Price calls in detectives from the Mooney and Boland firm, the principal of which, James Mooney, is an old acquaintance. As Mooney investigates the three men in the vicinity at the time of the robbery, he decides the attractive Eugene Lamont, with whom Price and Barr had been conversing, is the culprit. The narrative proceeds through Mooney's detective reports that detail visits to gambling houses, bordellos, and saloons. Gathering evidence takes a long time, even after Lamont suddenly establishes a wholesale cloth business that is a huge financial success. When he flees with the money from unfulfilled orders, a chase across the United States, Canada, and England ensues. Mooney finally captures Lamont in Paris and brings him back for trial in Chicago. Pauline Barr prosecutes him only with great reluctance and two beautiful women come to his aid. For social historians, accounts of 1870s entertainment venues will have most value. Students of police procedurals will find this an early example of the genre.

782. Moore, Ward. *Breathe the Air Again*. New York: Harper Brothers 1942. 445pp.

The early days of the labor movement in the United States are presented through the adventures of Simon Epstein, a working-class offspring of Jewish immigrants who settled in Los Angeles, California. The novel covers the years 1926-1929, the years when the protagonist is seventeen through approximately twenty. When their father is injured in an accident, Simon and his brother Rudolph are forced to drop out of school and find jobs. They work for Los Angeles' largest department store, the Sentry Company. Rudolph quickly settles into the structured work life, but Epstein chafes at being trapped in a low-wage position. He decides to leave for Chicago, a city ballyhooed for its growth and active labor movement. His journey takes up almost half the book since he must precariously ride the rails and occasionally work to earn food money. Through reading and the men he meets, including labor organizer Vincent Staim, he learns more about the labor movement and socialist theory. When Epstein finally arrives in Chicago he finds a job in a steel foundry, but his intellectual curiosity propels him into the bohemian society of the Near North Side where he rents a room on Cass Street and meets a series of liberal-minded, educated young people. Bookshops in the area are meeting places and Epstein gets to know several store owners, as well as young women with relaxed views on sexual morality. Epstein only leaves the city after he loses his job because he marched on a picket line to help Staim who is organizing domestics in a new Chicago suburb, named Chicago Riviera. After Epstein leaves Chicago he works on an Oklahoma farm for an extended period before returning to his family in Los Angeles. Although only about one hundred pages are set in Chicago, they detail a newcomers view of the city in the 1920s, detail Near North Side social life.

783. Morgan, Al (Albert Edward). *The Whole World Is Watching*. New York: Stein and Day, 1972. 252pp.

This fictionalized account of the 1968 Democratic National Convention presents the riots from the perspective of a television show producer and his staff. The author, himself the producer of the popular *Today* show, articulates the social issues underlying the riots, while relating the substance of the actual events.

784. Morris, Henry O. *Waiting for the Signal*. Chicago: Schulte, 1897. 407pp.
    This thinly fictionalized political tract presents the philosophy and strategy of organized labor in the 1890s through protagonist Wesley Stearns, who works as a journalist for the *Chicago Biograph*. Stearns' father, John, the captain of a lake steamer, had been involved in the Seaman's Union and was killed in strike-related violence in Cleveland, Ohio. So, underlying all of Stearns' efforts is filial piety, adding an undercurrent of Victorian sentimentality to his commitment to the Universal Brotherhood of Man.

785. Morris, Ira Victor. *The Chicago Story*. Garden City N.Y.: Doubleday, 1952. 347pp.
    The Chicago story of the title is that of the stockyards and is related through the experiences of Adolph Konrad and his family. A German immigrant, by the beginning of the novel in 1905, Konrad has built an international meat packing business that includes cattle production, transportation, meat processing, and distribution. The father of two sons, Rupert and William, he is confident that his achievement will be preserved. However, Rupert, who studied philosophy at Harvard, wants no part in "butchery" and after marrying the vegetarian daughter of one of his philosophy professors becomes a career diplomat. William marries into one of Chicago's wealthiest and most respected families and expends his energies on establishing himself in society. Adolph is left to deal with the unionization of his enterprises and efforts to convert his family-owned business into a corporation with publicly traded stock. After the expected affairs and family scandals, this novel concludes in 1950 with Adolph on his deathbed. Fortunately, his grandson Frank, a war hero and MIT trained chemical engineer, is poised to take over his grandfather's legacy. The novel summarizes a good deal of history concerning the development of the meat processing industry and the social tensions created by the astonishing fortunes accumulated by the packing house families.

786. Motley, Willard. *Knock on Any Door*. New York: David Appleton-Century, 1947. 504pp.
    Motley illustrates the blighting influence of poverty through the story of Nick Romano. When Romano's twelfth birthday is celebrated his father is the proprietor of a food shop and his family is lives in lower-middle-class comfort. Romano is an altar boy and under the cheerful, caring guidance of a priest dreams of a life dedicated to the Church. Within a year the business is gone, the Romano house and contents sold, and the family relocated to a slum apartment. In their new neighborhood the priests are harsh patrolmen against vice, and poverty brings a hunger which makes it seem reasonable to do anything for relief. Sentenced to reform school for a petty crime that he did not commit, by the time Nick is released he can no longer tolerate the poorly run school he is to attend. A desire for camaraderie and his alcoholic need for liquor propel him into a gang and criminal activity until, in disillusionment and despair, he shoots a policeman, is sentenced to death, and is executed. The Depression-era Chicago of the book is a place of no opportunity in which survival requires compromising one's human dignity.

787. Motley, Willard. *Let No Man Write My Epitaph*. New York: Random House, 1958. 467pp.
    This continuation of Nick Romano's story begun in *Knock on Any Door* is also set in the Chicago slums and deals with the corruption of Romano's son, born out of wedlock, and named for his father. The neighborhood on West Madison in which Romano grew up in the 1930s and in which his son lives in the 1940s and 1950s has changed dramatically. The area is now more di-

verse, has fewer recent immigrants and is dominated by people of color. A new focus of vice has also taken over—illicit drugs. Nellie, the mother of Romano, Jr., cares for him conscientiously in his youth, working long hours as a waitress. However, her struggles to forget sexual abuse in childhood and the electric chair execution of her lover drive her from alcohol abuse to drug addiction. A loose collective of alcoholic men who have lived with Nellie look out for Romano, Jr. and he stays in school and becomes interested in literature, poetry and art. However, the neighborhood and the influence of friends becomes too much and he succumbs to drug addiction. In addition to portrayals of people of color, the novel includes depictions of predatory homosexuals. The Chicago of the novel is a broken place in which it is impossible to live with decency, due to poverty and the predation of those who benefit financially from vice.

788. Motley, Willard. *We Fished All Night*. New York: Appleton-Century-Crofts, 1951. 560pp.

Intent on portraying World War II and its aftermath as a revelation of American political corruption and capitalist greed, Motley focuses on Chicago as the nexus of the country's industrial and transportation system. He dramatizes his story through the lives of three Chicagoans. Chet Kosinski, the son of Polish immigrants, grew up in poverty on North Clark Street, near Grand Avenue. Longing to escape his origins, he studies acting, takes the stage name Don Lockwood, and believes his performance in the role of Hamlet with a North LaSalle Street theater group will be his breakthrough. Then, he is drafted and experiences disillusionment after the battlefield death of a friend and his own physical suffering from battle injuries. When he returns to Chicago, he is primed to become an agent of a corrupt political machine. Aaron Levin is still in high school when war breaks out. From his earliest youth all of his Russian-immigrant, Jewish father's hopes for the future have focused on Levin. Despite his father's urgings that he become a businessman or enter a profession, Levin is interested only in ideas and art. He grudgingly plays football, but spends all of his free time writing poetry. After the military draft begins, Levin succumbs to family pressure to enlist and fight for his people, the Jews, to redress the suffering his father experienced during a pogrom. Too sensitive for the military, he suffers a nervous breakdown, undergoes electric shock therapy, and converts for a while to Roman Catholicism. He returns to Chicago unable to find peace from his disordered mind. Jim O'Keefe is a married man and labor organizer who has been successful in his strike against the Haines Company (the firm that symbolizes corporate greed in the novel). He enlists out of idealism, but after killing men in battle and trying to find solace in the arms of a prostitute, returns to Chicago guilt-ridden and unable to take his ideals seriously. The bulk of the novel is set in Chicago and presents a highly-detailed account of working-class life in the city during the 1940s, and the increasing tensions over the African-American presence in the city.

789. Moyer, Clarissa Mabel Blank [Clair Blank, pseud.]. *Beverly Gray at the World's Fair*. New York: Blue Ribbon Books, 1935. 250pp.

One of a series of mystery novels for girls featuring Beverly Gray, in this book Beverly has recently graduated from college and is living in New York City with some of her sorority sisters. When one of them goes off to study in Paris, the rest decide to take their own month-long trip to the 1933 Century of Progress Exposition in Chicago. While visiting the city, Beverly witnesses a murder and solves the crime. The book describes the exposition and the city from a tourist's perspective and conveys the material culture of the 1930s.

790. Mundis, Jerrold. *Gerhardt's Children*. New York: Atheneum, 1976. 305pp.

This family saga deals with five generations of a German Catholic family with ties to Chicago. Told in the first person by the writer of the family, Garvin, who is inspired to record his memories during the prolonged death from cancer of his cousin Naomi (who was raised as his sister), this book is more concerned with psycho-social dynamics than setting. However, many sections of the novel are set in Chicago, the city to which family matriarch Idalla emigrated on her own as a sixteen-year-old in 1890. She married, raised eight children, and, widowed early, controlled her offspring's lives. The effects of her control are a major theme of the novel. By the 1950s, when Idalla dies, most of her family (two hundred descendants) lives elsewhere in the country and even those in the Chicago area live in suburbs like Geneva. In the present of the novel, Chicago is plagued by urban problems that seem unconquerable.

791. Nablo James Benson. *The Long November*. New York: Dutton, 1946. 223pp.

Roughly twenty pages of this novel are set in Depression-era Chicago. As Canadian Joe Mack lies wounded behind enemy lines in Italy during World War II, he feverishly reviews his life. Broke and with no prospect of work in Canada, Mack had gone to Chicago. After living on the streets for a while he got help from the Salvation Army and found a brewery job. After a period of struggle his future looked bright after a promotion to a sales job on Chicago's Near North Side and he began dating an heiress. Then, a jilted lover reported his illegal status to the U.S. Immigration Department and he was deported. In addition to portraying life on the streets in Chicago, the book gives some sense of work life in a brewing company. Anti-Semitism in Chicago is a major plot element.

792. Nathan, Robert Louis. *Coal Mine No. 7*. New York: St. Martin's, 1980. 279pp.

The first eighty-five pages of this novel are set in Chicago in 1948, with most of the remainder of the book set in Vergennes, Illinois. At seventeen, developmentally disabled Seth has been forced out of school. Three years earlier his dream of rabbinical training was crushed when his rabbi refused to bar mitzvah him because of his inability to learn Hebrew. Seth is unable to get a job until Robert Adams, an African-American coal deliveryman, befriends him. Adams helps him get a job in a candy shop owned by an elderly Jewish merchant, a hold out in a neighborhood near Thirty-ninth Street and Drexel Boulevard that is now entirely African-American. He moves in with the Adams family, eventually marrying Arley Adams and later relocating to live with Robert Adams' brother Samuel in Vergennes where he can get a job in Coal Mine No. 7. After an accident, Seth's visions of God, which he has experienced since childhood, become stronger and he becomes a prophet of universal brotherhood. In addition to portraying life in one of Chicago's African-American neighborhoods and touching on issues of housing and employment, the novel presents anti-Semitism and the prejudice experienced by the developmentally disabled.

793. Nearing, Scott. *Free Born, An Unpublishable Novel*. New York: Urquhart Press, 1932. 237pp.

In this novel that proposes unionization and Communism as the solutions to the violent suppression of the working class, protagonist Jim Rogers matures from an eight-year-old boy to a man in his early twenties and moves from rural Georgia to Chicago. As an African-American, growing up before World War I, Jim experiences horrific violence in the Deep South. The all-black school he attends is burned down by whites; his best friend, and, later, his parents, are lynched; and his girlfriend is kidnapped, raped, and murdered. As the only witnesses to his girlfriend's abduction, he and his brother are forcibly transported to Chicago. Although Rogers finds exciting educational opportunities in the city and begins college classes alongside whites, the only jobs available to him consist of low-paid, manual labor. He also experiences segregation that restricts him to the South Side and prevents him from entering many restaurants and businesses. Rogers lives through several historical events including: the 1919 Chicago race riots; the dismissal of African-American workers after the end of World War I as white soldiers returned to the city; and the Mother Africa movement led by Marcus Garvey. After years of being out of work during the Depression and the death of his sister Sue from exhaustion and influenza, he meets union organizer Jane Wilson who provides him with a new interpretive framework to understand his experiences. Through Wilson he becomes involved in the union movement, the Negro Labor Congress, and the Communist Party. When he tries to organize Chicago African-Americans who were dragooned into being strike-breakers in the Pennsylvania coal fields, he is charged with attempted murder and sentenced to five years in prison. The Chicago section of the novel (approximately ninety pages) details life in the African-American ghetto, the impact of historical events from 1917 to 1925, the Great Migration of African-Americans into Chicago, and the backlash they experienced in the aftermath of World War I and the Depression.

794. Nelson, Shirley. *The Last Year of the War*. New York: Harper and Row, 1978. 255pp.

In the last year of World War II, Jo Fuller leaves her hometown outside of Boston for her first year at Calvary Bible College, located in the South Side slums of Chicago. Jo's life is focused on her own spiritual development, her school classes, and the new friends she makes. Although all of the students at Calvary have assignments in the outer world, like visiting Cook County jail inmates, they strictly follow the admonition to be in the world, but not of the world. The city has little reality for Jo, except as a threat to personal morality, and the venue of frightening exchanges with sinners. The only place Jo repeatedly mentions is the Newberry Library. Much of Jo's personal struggle centers on her acceptance of her older brother's battlefield death. Jo is not the only student who must deal with a war death and the book gives a clear sense of the lingering emotional impact of the war.

795. Neville, Edith. *Alice Ashland: A Romance of the World's Fair*. N.Y.: Peter Fenelon Collier, 1893. 216pp.

The action of this melodramatic romance novel is set into motion by the Columbian Exposition. Wealthy Major Craven, his wife Mary, and brother-in-law Wilfred Nevin, set out from Peekskill, New York to the Evanston house Craven has rented complete with a staff, horses, and a carriage. On her visit to the fairgrounds, Mary meets Harold Neale, her first boyfriend, who has been living in the west, seeking his fortune and invites him to a dinner party. In the meantime, Wilfred, stops a runaway carriage whose occupants are sixteen-year-old Alice Ashland, the orphaned niece and sole heir of a California millionaire, and one of her elderly guardians. Brought to the fair to find a suitable husband, her guardians immediately perceive Wilfred as the right choice, urging him to court Alice (so long as he pledges to pay ten thousand dollars after he marries). Mary Craven is also eager that ne'er-do-well Wilfred marry Alice and tries to impress the girl and her guardians. When Alice's chaperone falls ill, Mary insists that the girl move into the Evanston house. To Mary's alarm, when Harold visits for dinner, a love match immediately springs up between him and Alice. Mary mortifies Alice by telling her that Harold found her open interest in him distasteful. Harold does not discover the lie before his return to Peekskill to care for his ailing mother. Almost as soon as Alice and Wilfred are engaged, a long-lost cousin of Alice's, Thomas

Ashland, shows up with proof that the money in her trust is rightfully his. Thomas is a good fellow, and investigates the trust accounts, revealing the dishonesty of Alice's guardians. In the meantime, Wilfred breaks off the engagement now that Alice is not an heiress and Alice realizes how Mary and Wilfred manipulated her. Alice and Thomas return to California and by a coincidence she stays in the same seaside boarding house where Mrs. Neale is recovering. When Harold comes to visit his mother, the two are reconciled, but Thomas, who had fallen in love with Alice, becomes wild with jealousy. An alcoholic, while in a drunken rage, he confronts Alice, threatening to kill her. Alice narrowly escapes into Harold's arms and Thomas shoots himself, restoring Alice to the heiress status she had and soon she is happily engaged to Harold. Although the novel is not exclusively set in Chicago, the city is its most important locale, functioning as a setting where people from all parts of the country gather for the world's fair to rediscover old acquaintances and new loves. During her time in Chicago, Alice attends balls hosted by the Potter Palmers and the locales mentioned besides the fair, include Garfield Park and Jackson Park.

796. Newman, Charles. *New Axis; or, The "Little Ed" Stories, An Exhibition.* Boston: Houghton Mifflin, Riverside Press, 1966. 175pp.

These stories, set in a Chicago suburb that started out as Horseradishville and is now called King's Kove, cover several decades in the life of Ed and his family. The focus is domestic and rarely extends beyond the neighborhood. Cold War talk of Communism and, later, the space race are remote echoes in the affluent suburb. The African-American struggle for civil rights also has little resonance in an area with no people of color (although ethnic prejudice is present). The only tragedy is a polio epidemic which cripples a neighbor boy. Chicago does not have much presence in the life of Ed. His father works in the Oil Building, but Little Ed only travels to the city with his father to get his haircut. As a whole the collection of stories conveys what it was like to grow up in the Chicago suburbs in the 1950s.

797. Newman Charles. *The Promise Keeper, A Tephramancy: Divers Narratives on the Economics of Current Morals in Lieu of a Psychology, Here Embodied in an Approved Text Working Often in Spite of Itself; Certain Profane Stoical Paradoxes Explained, Literary Amusements Liberally Interspersed, Partitioned with Documents & Conditioned by Imagoes, Hearty Family-Type Fare, Modern Decor, Free Parking.* New York: Simon and Schuster, 1971. 249pp.

This satire of 1970s American society is set in Chicago. Although Sam Hooper occupies a position of enfranchisement as a promising young stockbroker, he cannot resign himself to the senselessness of his existence. He tries to address his feelings through meetings with a company psychiatrist, having an affair with the wife of an art photographer, and becoming preoccupied with an account of navigating the world by sailing ship. Since the author's project is satire, the exaggerated descriptions of social interactions and domestic arrangements may not give a true sense of 1970s Chicago, but Hooper's disenchantment and the author's choice of Chicago to epitomize American society are of interest.

798. Nichols, Edward Jay. *Hunky Johnny.* Boston: Houghton Mifflin, Riverside Press Cambridge, 1945. 246pp.

This novel concerning ethnic prejudice is set in 1930s Chicago and Gary, Indiana. Protagonist John Opalko must deal with his family and social circle's disdain for the fact that he is breaking away from them by attending the University of Chicago and dating WASPs. Although he experiences some prejudice for being of Czechoslovakian heritage, he has internalized cultural stereotypes and struggles to overcome the negative feelings he has about himself and his heritage. His situation is complicated by the fact that his father operates a bar in Gary—illegal with Prohibition still in place—and his brother works for the Mafia. As a college graduate looking for work in the Depression, he finds no opportunities for white-collar work and puts himself at odds with his father and brother when they insist he join the family business. Johnny's relationship with Jean Howland, a young woman from Shaker Heights, Ohio, who was a classmate at the University of Chicago, helps him get perspective on his life. When family illness forces Jean back to Ohio, it seems likely that Johnny will leave with her. The novel is filled with visual descriptions of food, apartment furnishings, clothing, automobiles, and bars. Prejudice based on race and ethnicity includes Mexicans, Jews, and Italians, as well as Czechs.

799. Nielsen, Helen. *Gold Coast Nocturne*. New York: Ives Washburn, 1951. 203pp.

Casey Morrow, recently discharged from the army, is passing through Chicago when he meets a beautiful young woman in a bar who offers him five thousand dollars to marry her. The next day, after he awakens from a drunken stupor, he learns that the woman was Phyllis Brunner the daughter of Darius Brunner, II, one of Chicago's wealthy financier's, who has just been murdered. Soon she is paying him to investigate who murdered her father. The murder mystery makes cursory use of Chicago as a setting.

800. Norris, Frank. *The Pit: A Story of Chicago*. New York: Doubleday, Page, 1903. 421pp.

Although this work reveals the social costs of market speculation in basic foodstuffs (in this case wheat), Norris is mostly interested in the psychological impact on one of the men who controls the market for a time, Curtis Jadwin. Jadwin's real estate fortune, made in the decades after the Chicago fire, is secure. A colleague influences him to start speculating in wheat, on a small scale, and as a supplement to his other business investments. The excitement on the floor of the Chicago Board of Trade's pit, draws in Jadwin, and Norris illustrates the way in which speculating has an emotional aspect that parallels gambling. Soon Jadwin and his associates devote themselves to controlling the entire spring wheat crop. When he succeeds, he becomes enthralled with his feeling of power and decides to hold his position through the summer. In doing so, he bankrupts himself and his associates (including his father-in-law, who commits suicide), and nearly destroys his health and his marriage. As with other business novels of this type, physical setting is less important than social forces, however, Norris illustrates the economic power resident in Chicago.

801. Norris, Hoke. *It's Not Far, But I Don't Know the Way*. Chicago: Swallow Press, 1969. 155pp.

Reporter David Elliot recently relocated to Chicago to be near his brother, Bert, who is finishing his surgical residency. When Elliot attends a Chicago Symphony Orchestra concert one afternoon, he meets an old lover, Joyce Harper, whom he had last seen in his hometown, in the rural Deep South, where his father had been a conservative Baptist minister. Through flashbacks, we learn that although Harper was pregnant with Elliot's child, she decided not to marry him and had an abortion. When they meet years later as thirty-somethings, Elliot has seen more of the world and has a broader moral perspective that is not constrained by a strict adherence to his father's religiosity. On the first night they are reunited, the two attend a cocktail party in Old Town, hosted by two lesbians, and populated by a diverse, artistic crowd of 1960s bohemians. Their reunion, however, quickly turns into a final farewell after Harper reveals that she is undergoing a hopeless series of chemotherapy treatments after a double mastectomy. Although the novel includes descriptions of Chicago, the book also contains several extended flashbacks to the Deep South. Chicago is portrayed as a place where it is possible to achieve a moral freedom made more difficult in rural areas and hometowns and one in which the scientific and medical communities offer a different kind of hope than the religion of Elliot's youth.

802. North, Sterling. *Seven Against the Years*. New York: Macmillan, 1939. 326pp.

Set during the Depression, North traces the first ten years after college graduation of seven young men who were fraternity brothers at the University of Chicago. Not all of their stories transpire in Chicago but four characters are intimately connected with the city. Frederick Oswald Blucher is the heir to a fortune built in the 1870s and 1880s from breweries and meat packing plants. His story recaps the history of the Chicago industrialists and their heirs. John Wesley Copeland's Chicago is dramatically different. A fervent Methodist, he is employed by the city as a relief case worker. Demetrius Dardanus, the son of a wealthy man in Greece, was forced by war to emigrate as a twelve-year-old and live with an uncle in Chicago, earning his living by menial labor, before devoting himself to marginally successful business schemes focused on the Greek community. Mark Harbord, a poet and novelist, forced to earn his living as a newspaper reporter, has the most comprehensive perspective on the city, moving freely between the worlds of Blucher and Dardanus, as well as exploring the African-American community, organized crime, and the world of Jewish immigrants. North presents Chicago as a nexus of transportation, industry, and culture that symbolizes the failings of the United States as well as its hope for the future.

803. North, Sterling. *Tiger*. Chicago: Reilly and Lee, 1933. 314pp.

In the depths of the Depression, nineteen-year-old Jerry Hartford is responsible for her widowed mother Sarah and a young niece and nephew. Jerry's sister Mary Ann died after months of worrying over her husband, Peter Baird, a mining engineer who disappeared in the Amazon. When Joe Middleton, the president of Middleton Radio Company, offers Jerry a job as his executive secretary at a salary higher than she has ever made, her anxiety over money is seemingly over. Then, she discovers that Middleton, a forty-year-old married man, chose Jerry for her physical attributes and not her typing. Soon he is buying her expensive clothing and taking her on yachting trips. He offers her a trust fund, a house, and medical care for her ailing nephew if only she will be his lover. Jerry is appalled at the prospect of hurting Mrs. Middleton and once she realizes Middleton's connections to organized crime and liquor smuggling, she is even more determined to fight him. She has an ally in another of Middleton's secretaries, Harriet Wilson, who has already been wronged by him and when Peter Baird unexpectedly returns from South America her efforts are strengthened. After being kidnapped and escaping from Middleton's Lake Geneva weekend house, that doubles as a stronghold with paid assassins and sound-proofed rooms, Jerry, Peter, and Harriet successfully negotiate financial settlements from Middleton with the evidence they have collected. Depression-era Chicago still offers affluent mansions and expensive shops and restaurants, but for workers like Jerry the city means roach-infested rented rooms and the bad air that exacerbates her nephew's lung condition. The novel does includes atmospheric descriptions of the magic of the lakefront, the beauty of the city lights at night, and skyscrapers that represent the power of commerce.

804. Noyes, Henry. *Hand Over Fist*. Boston: South End Press, 1980. 322pp.

Set on Chicago's North Side in the 1950s, this novel presents the author's views on the racism and greed that created African-American ghettos. Kathryn Bianchi, a lower-middle-class Sicilian immigrant, embarks on the career of landlord, with moral support from her wealthy son-in-law, Anselmo, whose father is a Mafia gangster who bolsters his son's legitimate real estate business with Mafia influence. Kathryn had saved money from her husband's earnings in a factory and eventually bought a house on Hemlock Street, in an Italian-American neighborhood, where the couple raised four children. Now that Kathryn has seen her daughter's opulent life with Anselmo in a Lake Shore Drive apartment, she dreams of establishing a real estate business to raise her standard of living and escape from her Hemlock Street neighborhood that is rapidly changing for the worse. All of these concerns are secondary, however, to establishing Luigi, her youngest son who is currently fighting in Korea, in a business. Her first building, on Pioneer Street, is occupied entirely by African-Americans, and produces steady rental income, inflated by pricing far above the Chicago Housing Authority's listed rent guidelines. When one of the basement tenants, Anna Mae Green, discovers the overcharges, she spreads word among all the tenants and threatens a lawsuit. On Anselmo's advice, Kathryn hires a thug to assist her in rent collection and begins looking for a second building in her own neighborhood that she will cut up into small apartments and rent to African-Americans. By the end of the novel she has alienated people in her own neighborhood, family members, and her husband. A final confrontation with Anna Green ends in tragedy. The book presents a period of dramatic housing changes in which buildings were being converted into high density structures for low income tenants, as well as showing the impact of internal migration of African-Americans from the Deep South that fueled racial hatred.

805. Oates, Joyce Carol. *Wonderland*. New York: Vanguard Press, 1971. 512pp.

Approximately half this novel about the relationship between family and the development of personality is set in Chicago. Jesse Harte's life is shaped by a tragic event in his fourteenth year. He returns to his family's house in Yewville, New York to find that his father is armed, has shot the rest of his family, and is waiting on him. He escapes and his father shoots himself. After living with his grandfather and then an uncle, Jesse is adopted by Dr. Karl Pedersen of Lockville, New York, who, although a respected surgeon, is emotionally disturbed and disowns Jesse as he is setting off for college after a family conflict. In college, Jesse begins to create a life for himself, falls in love, studies medicine, and goes onto a surgical residency in Chicago, eventually founding his own successful practice. However, he is transformed by new tragedy when he must deal with an emotionally disturbed daughter. Oates' writing is tightly focused on the inner life of her characters and is not concerned with conveying much about Chicago.

806. O'Brien, Howard Vincent. *An Abandoned Woman*. Garden City, N.Y.: Doubleday, Doran, 1930. 310pp.

In this society novel, the impact of World War I is still being felt in matters of social status, roles for women, and attitudes toward sexuality. As the wife of Stephen Hilliard, Joan has the comforts of a wealthy suburban matron, with two children and a stable of horses. However, she feels no sense of purpose until an old romantic interest, Val Morlas, an artist, returns to Chicago from Paris. He introduces her to artistic and bohemian life in the city and gives her a purpose, for he is struggling young man and she can be his muse and patron. She eventually travels with him to England and Paris. Then, however, he becomes a success and her sense of purpose wanes again until the financial collapse of 1929, when Stephen is ruined and she tries to return to his side. The novel articulates issues of divorce, companionate marriage, and relations between the sexes, as well as describing life in several very different types of social circles in 1920s Chicago.

807. O'Brien, Howard Vincent [Clyde Perrin, pseud.]. *The Green Scarf: A Business Romance Having to Do with a Man Who Is Determined to Win Success without the Help of Wealth or Family Prestige*. Chicago: McClurg, Donohue, 1924. 323pp.

When Thomas Elgin Cass graduates from Yale in 1914, he could, like many of his classmates, take advantage of family wealth and connections to establish himself in a career. Without much reflection, however, he decides to rely only on his skills. He takes a job in Chicago in the advertising office of a paint company. Raised in Cleveland, Cass never visited Chicago and a significant portion of the novel consists of his reactions and observations, as well as more general descriptions of office life and business culture. One of his supervisors is a woman and this is the first time he has interacted with a female who has responsibilities outside a domestic setting. He is soon in love with her. Moved from position to position within the company, by its owner John W. Burroughs, who sees Cass as a potential manager, the young man does learn the business. However, he also sees injustice in the factory system. When he proposes a new, scientific management plan, Burroughs is unconvinced, even though his workers have struck in the midst of World War I when the factory's profitability is burgeoning. The conflict is resolved when his father buys the company and gives it to Cass. The novel focuses on gender roles, unionism, labor relations, and the correct relationship between capital and labor.

808. O'Brien, Howard Vincent. *New Men for Old*. New York: Mitchell Kennerley, 1914. 320pp.

Harlan Chandos, the scion of an old Chicago family, returns from Paris at the behest of his recently deceased father's lawyers who tell him that his father died penniless. Chandos, thirty-two-years-old, has spent very little time in Chicago and has never worked. He graduated from Yale and then studied art abroad. Forced to end his life as a dilettante, he gets an illustrator job in an advertising firm and, in an unlikely coincidence, writes copy for the Gresham Food Products Company, the firm owned by the father of Dorothy Gresham, the woman with whom he is in love. The copy attracts the attention of Mr. Gresham (who is always denominated in this way) and soon Chandos is working at the Gresham factory. As he becomes familiar with the operation, he expresses concerns about the safety of some food products and about working conditions and wages. Although opposed to any impact on profitability, Mr. Gresham develops confidence in Chandos and makes him general manager when he must go abroad for his health, indicating that Chandos has successfully transitioned from an artistic dilettante to a level-headed businessman worthy of Dorothy Gresham. Set in early-twentieth-century Chicago the book raises social reform issues (fair wages and profit-sharing) and touches on trade unionism and the city beautiful movement. Physical descriptions include Chicago architecture, domestic furnishings, and clothing.

809. O'Brien, Howard Vincent. *The Terms of Conquest*. Boston: Little, Brown, 1923. 357pp.

Although Homer Gaunt spent most of his life up until he was twenty-three-years-old in Cold Harbor, Michigan, as the novel reminds us several times, he is of Puritan stock and his father, an engineer, was raised in Salem, Massachusetts. Orphaned as a boy, Gaunt relied upon the charitable institutions of Cold Harbor, but when he reaches young manhood, he can no longer tolerate the complacency of his fellow townsmen and, leaving behind his wife Ivy and his infant son, relocates to Chicago to follow his ambition to be more than a printer's devil. Unfortunately, he arrives in the depths of the depression that followed the Columbian exposition. Unable to find a job, he is soon reduced to sleeping on the street. When he does get work as a railroad switchman, it does not last after union unrest turns into a long, bloody strike. Gaunt is caught up in an armed confrontation and by saving Fiske O'Dea, an undercover detective and political operative, establishes a debt that

O'Dea repays over the course of the novel. Gaunt is also aided by Eleanor Miner. The two met in Cold Harbor and, had their socio-economic statuses not been so different, may have married. However, Miner wed the wealthy Watson Miner and when Eleanor moves with him to Chicago, she helps Gaunt get a job in Miner's printing company. Through his work and the insider information he gets from O'Dea and his political friends (buy Union Pacific railroad stock, fight in the Spanish-American War) Gaunt rises in the business world and becomes a wealthy man. By the end of the novel, however, as a forty-five-year-old, his wife is an invalid, he has a mutually acknowledged love for the widowed Eleanor that he cannot pursue, and is disappointed in his son, a World War I conscientious objector and expatriate supporter of the Russian Revolution. The novel's preoccupation with presenting early-twentieth-century social and economic thought through Gaunt's life diminishes descriptions of Chicago.

810. O'Brien, Howard Vincent [Clyde Perrin, pseud.]. *The Thunderbolt*. Chicago: McClurg, 1923. 283pp.

In this satire of business and advertising culture during the kinetic years leading up to the Depression, twenty-eight-year-old Barnaby Lamb transforms himself into "The Thunderbolt," a business dynamo. Fired from an advertising firm for no good reason, Barnaby is mystified, especially since he has devoted himself to endless study and self-improvement. Spurred to take some dramatic step by the fact that his beloved, Peggy Whitredge, daughter of a manufacturing millionaire, is about to marry the wealthy Douglas MacKenzie, he turns for advice to Peter Wye, an erudite tinkerer who suggests that Lamb always model his behavior on the thunderbolt, being showily confident without concern for convention or the estimation of others, since he will never get anywhere working hard and quietly employing his vast amount of knowledge. Behaving audaciously, Lamb immediately gets a job with substantial compensation in a prestigious advertising firm. His new confidence transforms his relationship to Whitredge and he edges out his rival. The novel presents Chicago as an important center of the advertising industry. Occasional descriptions of restaurants, bars, domestic interiors, and public landmarks give some sense of the city in the 1920s; however the main focus is on articulating a personal philosophy for self-advancement drawn from popularized versions of Freudian psychology and the numerous self-help books of the time period.

811. O'Brien, Howard Vincent. *What a Man Wants*. Garden City, N.Y.: Doubleday, Page, 1925. 344pp.

Ammiel Spottswood dies after an illness that his family thinks was brought on by his grandson and namesake pushing him off the Navy Pier. Believing that the boy has a quality that none of his other grandchildren has, during his illness he decides to give his namesake a special bequest that is not revealed until the end of the novel. He seemingly divides his money among the other family members, giving Ammiel a token. As the lives of his siblings are destroyed in various ways, Ammiel develops the human qualities that make him a valuable friend, an able businessman, and a good brother. At the end of the novel he is told by his grandfather's executor that the old man had been far wealthier than anyone knew and that the bulk of his fortune had been held in trust to see if Ammiel would become the sort of person he had: someone for whom money was only a tool. The novel has few overt references to Chicago.

812. O'Connor, Richard. *Guns of Chickamauga*. Garden City, N.Y.: Doubleday, 1955. 288pp.

The early pages of this novel are set in Chicago during the Civil War. Protagonist Matthew Wayne, a political reporter for the Chicago *Sentinel*, lives in a boarding house and his narrative includes enough description of the establishment to give a sense of life in such a residence. The main focus, however, is on Wayne's work life. The disreputable editor of the *Sentinel*, Jed Hopkins, is an ally of wealthy entrepreneur Henry J. Harper, who may secretly own the newspaper and has consistently bailed out the newspaper to keep it from failing. His financial commitment has enabled Harper to dictate editorial policy making the newspaper one of the country's most rabid Radical Republican publications. Harper's stance is less about political conviction than wartime profits. Concerned about mistiming his investment strategies, Harper sends Wayne to observe the movements of the Army of Cumberland, believing that General Rosecrans' troops could force a Confederate surrender. Wayne is to make his reports to Harper personally and not the newspaper and before long Wayne realizes Harper is part of a circle of war profiteers involved in selling contraband Confederate money. Although less than forty pages of the book is set in Chicago is does give a good sense of the economic consequences of the war on the city.

813. O'Connor, Richard [Patrick Wayland, pseud.]. *The Waiting Game*. Garden City, N.Y.: Crime Club / Doubleday, 1965. 188pp.

In this Cold War espionage novel, Tamara Kuprinskaya, a ballerina with the Kiev Youth Ballet, is duped into thinking she will be reunited with a relative who had settled in the United States before World War II if she defects. In fact, Kuprinskaya is to be brain-washed into becoming a spy for an anti-Communist group operated by Chicago millionaire Morgan Gilchrist. Lloyd Nicholson is an agent for another privately financed anti-Communist group, Counterstroke, engaged in high-level espionage and counterespionage tacitly encouraged by the U.S. government. His mission is to retrieve the girl before an international incident and by the end of the novel, he succeeds. Although much of the book is set in and around Chicago, the physical setting is generally of minor importance. However, there is an extended description of Rush Street and its bars that capture their 1960s, anything goes seediness.

814. O'Donnell, Simon. *The Runaway Wife; or, Love and Vengeance*. Chicago: Laird and Lee, 1889. 172pp.

Supposedly based on a true-life case and written by a captain of the Chicago Police Department, the runaway wife of the title is Elizabeth Drumley who ran away from Todmorden, England with a schoolmaster, Albert Greenleaf, abandoning her husband Joe and their two children. Receiving word that his wife is in Chicago, Joe arrives in the city in 1867, having used up all his resources, to come take her back. However, Elizabeth is no longer in Chicago, having fled Greenleaf after he proposed that she become a prostitute. In fleeing him, she was duped by another man and is now a white slave in Wisconsin. She escapes with the help of Bowery Joe Horton, whose assistance turns out to be selfish; he believes he can employ her beauty to commit jewel thefts. Her husband Joe is finally reunited with her after she has been imprisoned for a theft. To his dismay, she refuses to return to England, believing that there she would forever live in disgrace in the eyes of her former acquaintances. Instead, she returns to her life of crime for as long as she can before throwing herself off a lake steamer. The only satisfaction Joe gets is in killing Greenleaf, the man who corrupted her, a crime for which he is executed.

815. O'Hara, John. *Pal Joey*. New York: Grosset and Dunlap, 1939. 195pp.

Through letters, O'Hara presents a character, Joey, who sings in Chicago nightclubs while scheming to achieve the break that will propel him to fame as an entertainer. In the meantime, he distorts the truth to win over women and manipulate himself into easy jobs. The composer/lyricist team Rodgers and Hart based a successful musical on the book and a film version with the same title was released in 1957 starring Frank Sinatra (Columbia Pictures).

816. Okun, Lawrence Eugene. *On the 8th Day*. Millbrae, Calif.: Celestial Arts, 1980. 217pp.

Author Bill Conover, already famous at thirty-four for several investigative books, is in Lake Tahoe doing research for a golf book when he notices a very successful young gambler. At first he thinks the woman, Julie Brubaker, is cheating. After he meets her, she proves she has telekinetic powers. When Conover returns to the golf course, he is astounded by twenty-four-year-old Tom Benson, whose unlikely performance he finds just as puzzling as Brubaker's. When he discovers that both young people are from Chicago, he begins investigating and finds other men and women their age from Chicago who also have remarkable skills and decides to write his next book about them. His research uncovers a genetic experiment conducted by a Chicago physician. As Conover gathers evidence in Chicago archives, the young people begin disappearing, leading to a dramatic climax in which Conover helps save Brubaker, Benson, and other people in the cohort. The book references universities in Chicago, and the genetic project is tied to the Manhattan Project but the book provides little physical description of Chicago.

817. Olesker, J. Bradford. *No Place Like Home*. New York: Putnam's Sons, 1976. 185pp.

In this police procedural detective novel, the Homicide Division of the Chicago Police Department tracks down a serial murderer who is not stopped until he has killed five residents of a North Shore high-rise. Although the team of detectives headed by Lieutenant David Colt is multi-ethnic and racially diverse, cultural differences are openly commented upon in a way that may offend present-day readers. Much of the novel is set within the affluent apartment complex where the murders transpire and the author clearly sees this style of life as distinctive enough to warrant detailed accounts of building operations, staffing, relations among tenants, and apartment layouts and interior decoration, conveying a sense of what it would have been like to live in such circumstances in the 1970s. The fact that a nationally-known Korean War hero and top-ranked baseball player is the murderer raises issues of cultural attitudes toward war and professional sports.

818. Olsen, Tillie. *Yonnondio: From the Thirties*. New York: Delacorte Press/Seymour Lawrence, 1974. 196pp.

This impressionistic novel captures the lived experience of crushing poverty from the perspective of Mazie Holbrook, a girl who ages from around six to eight-years-old in three different environments in the 1920s: the coal-mining town of Rascoe, Wyoming; a tenant farm in the Dakotas; and a partially finished house in Chicago's packing-house district. In each setting, her father, Jim Holbrook, labors at sickening jobs that earn him almost nothing to support his wife and four children (Mazie has three younger brothers). He leaves the coal mine when he begins to get paid less and less money and more company script—good only at the company store. For a short time the family rejoices in their rural life in the Dakotas, but despite their hard work, at the end of a growing season they are actually in debt to the farm owner. In Chicago, the only job Jim can get initially is excavating for sewer lines that leaves him ill from constantly being wet. He gets a job in a meat processing plant just as summer begins and barely survives temperatures that are ten to fifteen degrees hotter than the hundred plus temperatures outside. Mazie witnesses drunken violence and her mother's miscarriage. The Chicago section is interesting for portraying the competition for the most degrading jobs in a heavily populated area, suffering brought by summer weather, and the pointlessness of public health information when there is no money to meet the most basic needs.

819. Osborn, Catherine B. and Margaret Waterman. *Papa Gorski*. New York: Harcourt, Brace and World, 1969. 273pp.

This parody of French classic *Père Goriot* by Honoré Balzac is set in a Chicago boarding house near downtown and the campus of the imaginary Lake Michigan University in 1965. The house is managed by Italian widower Mrs. Velotta and has a diverse cast of tenants, though most are unmarried men. Additional boarders from the area, mostly businessmen and university students, also take their meals at Velotta Manor. Three boarders receive the fullest treatment: African-American Frank Vance, Eugene Robertson, and Papa Gorski. Vance is a great favorite of everyone because he is friendly and willingly loans money. However, he is also a mysterious figure coming and going at odd hours and is eventually dramatically revealed to be a drug dealer. Eugene Robertson is a doctoral student in political science from a small town, Alma Junction, Michigan. He is ambitious and follows up on some distant family connections to get introduced into Chicago's high society where he immediately happens upon the true identity of Papa Gorski, who had been a figure of fun in the boarding house. The elegantly clothed gentleman with his Swiss watch and expensive oil paintings is visited by attractive young women, causing the boarders to believe he is a roué. Robertson discovers that the women are his daughters. An immigrant, he had worked himself up from nothing and when his daughters married into Chicago society he gave each of them checks for $500,000, leaving himself with only a modest retirement income. As they continued to climb in society they rejected him and he was reduced to living in a boarding house. Robertson, who begins to socialize with one of the daughters, also builds a friendship with Gorski and gets involved in their lives. The novel provides an outsider view of Chicago society and a very detailed account of boarding house life.

820. Ozaki, Milton K. [Robert O. Saber, pseud.]. *The Affair of the Frigid Blonde*. A Handi-Book Mystery. Kingston, N.Y.: Quinn, 1950. 127pp.

In this private-eye pulp novel, Frank Laughton, a successful insecticide manufacturer had exchanged identities with an artist. When he wants to return to his former life and his beautiful wife, he hires private detective Bob Stille to find the erstwhile artist. Laughton's wife is an eye-catching blonde who is always pursuing her own agenda for financial gain, has her own scheme that does not involve being reunited with the real Laughton. As with other Ozaki novels, settings tend to be bars, late-night hangouts, and apartments shrouded in nighttime darkness.

821. Ozaki, Milton K. [Robert O. Saber, pseud.]. *The Black Dark Murders*. Kingston, N.Y.: Handi-Book Editions, 1949. 158pp.

One of a series of novels featuring the co-owners of the Keene and Cooper Private Detective Agency, this book plays on the titillation of coeds living independent lives on a college campus. Phil Keene is called onto the case by a wealthy businessman whose daughter is attending a Chicago college where a girl has recently been knifed. Keene poses as a prospective student to interview professors and coeds. Two more murders are committed before Hal Cooper, Keene's partner, solves the case using forensic evidence gathered utilizing a knowledge of ultraviolet light provided by physics professor John Barber. The police share information about the murders, as well as their theory that a sex fiend is the culprit. Suspicion is focused on the effeminate Allen Beck, boyfriend of the first murder victim, as well as Roger Morse, the chair of the English Department who affects British mannerisms and is notorious for his womanizing. The cast of characters also includes Ann Seymour, a thirty-five-year-old woman bored with living as the wife of a college professor; music student Rita Rand, who is always in search of men to support her expensive tastes; and man-hating art professor Natalie Apyan. In addition to depicting 1940s campus life, the novel conveys a good sense of social attitudes to independent young women and academics.

822. Ozaki, Milton K. *Case of the Cop's Wife*. New York: Fawcett Publications, Gold Medal Books, 1958. 141pp.

On the first day of Chicago police Lieutenant Robert Fury's paternity leave, his pregnant wife, Mary Ellen, journeys to the Loop for a doctor's appointment. Unfortunately, she is in her car in the exact spot where a criminal has agreed to rendezvous with his getaway driver and ends up being kidnapped and taken to a Wisconsin farm as protection. The criminals developed a well-thought out plan to steal money being delivered to the Revens Department store, one of the city's largest, on the day a sale is to begin. Mastermind Wally Hirsch developed the plan based on information from his girlfriend Helen Harashek who worked at the store. However, the criminals he was able to assemble (fifty-year-old Jim Hoops and Mexican immigrant Salvio Morales) were not up to the task. They panic and shoot two police officers who had been tipped off by Mafioso Sam Nazarian. The novel gives some sense of the camaraderie of the Chicago police department and the easy access Chicago newspapermen have there. However, the book provides little sense of place except for expressing racist attitudes towards Mexican immigrants who have settled on Clark Street. Mary Ellen is the daughter of a wealthy society figure and there are references to the family's Lake Shore Drive apartment that serves as their base in the city, although they are often in New York and abroad.

823. Ozaki, Milton K. [Robert O. Saber, pseud.]. *Chicago Woman (The Dove)*. New York: Pyramid Books, 1953. 158pp.

No additional information available.

824. Ozaki, Milton K. *The Cuckoo Clock*. Chicago: Ziff-Davis, 1946. 261pp.

In this work of detective fiction, Benedict "Bendy" Brinks, the twenty-three-year-old psychology graduate student of Professor Androcles Caldwell of Chicago's North University takes the lead role in solving the locked-door murder of Justine (a man always referred to by his last name), owner of and chief beautician at Monsieur Justine's at the corner of State and Elm Streets. In addition to Mary Underwood, his supposed fiancée, at the time of his death, Justine had currently or recently been involved with seven women and in most of the novel Brinks is involved in interviewing the various women, sometimes under the guise of a date. The novel touches on attitudes toward beauty culture, male/female gender roles, and artwork featuring nude women. Brinks' investigations take him to the residences of single women and physical descriptions of their apartments, as well as accounts of their relationships with their female roommates reveal a good deal about typical living arrangements available to single women in 1940s Chicago. As with other detective novels featuring Brinks and Caldwell, this one includes the inept Chicago Police Lieutenant Phelan and hinges on the ability of the academics to employ their knowledge of human psychology. In this book, the killer is revealed when she unwittingly submits to a word association test.

825. Ozaki, Milton K. [Robert O. Saber, pseud.]. *A Dame Called Murder*. Hasbrouck Heights, N.J.: Graphic, 1955. 190pp.

In this 1950s pulp novel while Chicago private detective Max Keene is being paid by Handy Andy Cafeteria to make certain none of their cashiers is stealing from the till, he witnesses a murder. His investigation leads him to a shoplifting ring operated by an organized crime syndicate employing poor Chicagoans. He deals with Attorney Barone, whose entire practice consists of defending low-level criminals and sociopaths. Keene also must deal with a corrupt, beautiful woman. The book presents organized crime as a pervasive feature of Chicago life and describes businesses typical of the 1950s (a cafeteria and striptease parlor) in some detail.

826. Ozaki, Milton K. [Robert O. Saber, pseud.]. *The Dove*. Kingston, N.Y.: Quinn, 1951. 150pp.
Same as *Chicago Woman (The Dove)*. No additional information is available.

827. Ozaki, Milton K. *Dressed to Kill*. Cover Illustrated by Walter Popp. Hasbrouck Heights, N.J.: Graphic Books, 1954. 189pp.

Rusty Forbes, a down and out Chicago private detective, has one fail-safe way of making a few dollars: he recovers stolen cars for insurance companies. After picking up a stolen Cadillac being driven by the beautiful Giselle Kent, he is panicked when he finds the corpse of Eddie Sands, manager of the Silver Cloud nightclub, in the trunk. Piecing together the meaning of the errands on which Kent has been sent by gangster Arthur J. Richmond, Forbes realizes that he has come across a major fencing operation. Wanting to avoid any implication in Sands death, he meets with Richmond, who realizes his identity, and arranges for the police to find him in the arms of Fia Sprite, a prostitute Richmond hired to claim to be Sands girlfriend and to testify that Forbes had killed Sands to get her for himself. Forbes is able to provide enough information to the police that they realize his innocence and the detective then aids them in bringing Richmond's fencing ring to justice (as personal revenge when Giselle Kent is found murdered). The novel has many references to Chicago locales, although they are mostly bars and cheap hotel apartments. The criminal activity in the novel is interesting for revealing the dominance of interstate trucking in the transportation of goods by the 1950s since all of the fenced items come from stolen trucks. In addition, police corruption plays a major role, as does the activities of a Mafia lawyer in strategizing with the criminals and defending them.

828. Ozaki, Milton K. [Robert O. Saber, pseud.]. *Dummy for Death*.
The content of this book is the same as *The Dummy Murder Case*. No additional information is available.

829. Ozaki, Milton K. *The Dummy Murder Case*. Hasbrouck Heights, N.J.: Graphic, 1951. 190pp.

This murder mystery is set on a college campus and features Professor Androcles Caldwell and Bendy Brinks, the amateur detectives who appear in other Ozaki mysteries. Psychology professor Caldwell sets up an elaborate class demonstration as part of his discussion of human perception. He gets friends of his assistant, Bendy Brinks to pretend to shoot a young woman who falls off a pier. Through Caldwell's friendship with Lieutenant Phelan of the Chicago Police force, the professor is able to get actual policeman to appear on the scene and dredge the lake for the body. All they are supposed to find is a mannequin; instead, they find a murdered woman whose apartment is full of unused gift wrap from some of Chicago's most expensive stores and wrapped boxes that are empty, giving Caldwell and Brinks a new mystery to solve.

830. Ozaki, Milton K. *A Fiend in Need*. Chicago: Ziff-Davis, 1947. 232pp.

The worlds of the Chicago Police Department and academia, represented by imaginary North University, collide during a murder investigation in a high-rise apartment building near the intersection of Rush and Goethe Streets. Narrator Benedict Brinks is a master's degree student in psychology and the lab assistant and live-in factotum of fifty-six-year-old Professor Androcles Caldwell, whose research focuses on response conditioning. On their way to visit Professor John Niles Thomson from the Department of Comparative Literature, they find a murder victim in the elevator of Thomson's building and are impelled to investigate upon witnessing the incompetence of the police. The novel goes into great detail about Thomson's apartment building, the residents' lives, and their domestic interiors. Gender roles and sexual behavior are presented in titillating fashion and homosexuality is discussed openly, if derisively. The culprit is a popular writer and lecturer who is a matinee idol for attendees of women's club events; he also secretly operates a successful bookstore that markets prurient material to pseudo-intellectuals.

831. Ozaki, Milton K. *Maid for Murder*. Bound with Chase, James Hadley, *Dead Ringer*. New York: Ace Double Novel Books, 1955. 141pp.

In this tough-guy detective novel set in 1950s Chicago, private-eye Carl Guard is hired to find Elberta Ryerson who vanished with a new automobile after making one payment. Instead, he discovers that someone is making sexy audio-tapes featuring sports stars and movie celebrities. Then he finds Ryerson working for the Chicago branch of a national talent agency and thinks he has a lead on a much larger illegal business. Before he can investigate, he wakes up in bed with Ryerson, who has been murdered, and finds himself accused of the crime. Blackmail, a pornography ring, and unpleasant men preying on ill-paid starlets are all part of the plot which has physical settings on the Near North Side of Chicago. The scandal press of the 1950s is a major feature of the novel.

832. Ozaki, Milton K. *Never Say Die*. New York: Wyn, Ace Books, 1956. 138pp.

Aging millionaire roué Horatius Field hires Chicago detective Bob Wherry to rid his life of his current fling, Helen Nebb, by confronting her with the names of all the men she has suckered in the preceding year. Twenty-eight-year-old Wherry served in the Marines and has been a private eye since he returned to civilian life at the age of twenty-two. Nebb does not scare off so easily and she is eventually found murdered. Wherry is accused of the crime by the police and when a purse containing valuable jewelry connected with Nebb is found in his apartment, he realizes he is being framed. The rest of the novel is devoted to Wherry's attempts to discover the true murderer and clear his name. His informants are "b-girls" who work in the nightclubs and stripper joints around Clark Street. These clubs are described, as well as apartments, sometimes in expensive buildings along the lakefront, where the girls are kept by wealthy men. By the end of the book Wherry has uncovered an elaborate casino operation run by Tom Tully that used remodeled transport planes flying out of Chicago's O'Hare airport. Tully was being cheated by several of his beautiful hostesses who stole expensive jewelry from clients.

833. Ozaki, Milton K. [Robert O. Saber, pseud.]. *The Scented Flesh*. Kingston, N.Y.: Quinn, 1951. 127pp.

Chicago private detective Carl Good is hired by Sidney Shepherd of Hickok, Iowa to find his nineteen-year-old-daughter Sylvia. After less than twenty-four hours on the case, Good wakes to find himself in bed with the corpse of a beautiful, young, naked woman who has been stabbed to death. Good flees, but the following day an effeminate thug appears in his office to deliver photographs of Good and the dead woman along with a threatening note warning him to forget about Sylvia. With the help of his lawyer friend, Morrie Tannenbaum, Good solves the crime, pursuing leads in the world of white slavery and organized prostitution in 1950s Chicago. He also uncovers the market in babies born to unwed mothers and sold to childless couples. Many of the establishments he explores are saloons on State Street and pseudo-rooming houses on Rush Street, uncovering police department corruption along the way. The Chicago of the novel is filled with official corruption and vice. The novel touches on homosexuality in homophobic terms as part of the seedy, vice-ridden, under-world Good navigates.

834. Ozaki, Milton K. [Robert O. Saber, pseud.]. *Sucker Bait*. Hasbrouck Heights, N.J.: Graphic, 1955. 190pp.

Set in 1950s Chicago, this book's milieu is the world of private detectives, tough-guy policemen who take bribes and violate individual rights, and beautiful women able to get large amounts of money from wealthy "suckers." Private detective Carl Good does a favor for fellow detective Jim Peterson by covering him as he shadows someone. In the process, Good is knocked unconscious and from blood he finds on the pavement, he fears for Peterson's safety. Good is soon investigating Peterson's murder and quickly discovers a connection to the Purple Door Club, a private membership club with a one thousand dollar membership fee where wealthy men gamble for the services of young prostitutes. Before Good can make much progress, he finds himself accused of murdering a woman he had dated only once. By the end of the novel he has uncovered a gang who uses the Purple Door Club in blackmail schemes and cleared himself of the murder charge.

835. Ozaki, Milton K. [Robert O. Saber, pseud.]. *A Time for Murder*. Hasbrouck Heights, N.J.: Graphic Books, 1956. 189pp.

This novel featuring Chicago private detective Max Keene directly addresses police corruption. In other Ozaki novels, some Chicago police are crooked and protect criminals in exchange for kickbacks, but in this book Lieutenant Detective Timothy Flynn is directly responsible for illegal gambling operations and prostitution rings and is not above arranging murders to cover up his crimes. As with many other Ozaki novels, 1950s Chicago is an after-hours city filled with crime and corruption.

836. Ozaki, Milton K. [Robert O. Saber, pseud.]. *Too Young to Die*. Hasbrouck Heights, N.J.: Graphic Books, 1954. 190pp.

Chicago private detective Carl Good is framed for murder and must rely on his criminal lawyer friend Morrie Tannenbaum to get him out on bail so he can clear his name. The plot involves organized crime and the illicit sale of morphine.

837. Paine, Lauran Bosworth [Mark Carrel, pseud.]. *A Sword of Silk*. London, U.K.: Robert Hale, 1967. 191pp.

This work of pulp fiction written by a prolific author known for his Westerns, involves the illicit drug trade. Sergeant Blake of the Chicago Police Department investigates with the help of New York attorney Andrew McCall, while avoiding the violent death promised by a powerful drug dealer.

838. Palumbo, Dennis James. *City Wars*. New York: Bantam Books, 1979. 152pp.

This post-apocalyptic novel takes place after a nuclear war. National governments are no longer in power on the North American Continent; instead, city states are the only governing bodies and they attempt to extend their control through armed aggression. Largely set in a futuristic Chicago under attack by New York City, the Chicago municipal government is proving ineffective as internal power struggles are thwarting a coherent response and protagonists Jake Bowman and Cassandra Ingram despair of any action but fleeing to save themselves.

839. Paradise, Viola. *The Pacer*. New York: Dutton, 1927. 278pp.

Set in 1920s Chicago, this novel presents middle-class and working-class women who can choose social roles beyond those of wife and mother to achieve personal fulfillment. Protagonist Judith Hazlitt was orphaned at an early age, raised by her Aunt Carrie in a South Side apartment, and supported by Carrie's earnings as a seamstress. As Judith is to begin her senior year in high school and has started looking forward to college, Carrie falls seriously ill from breast cancer. Her life is saved, but medical expenses exhaust years of savings and push Carrie into serious debt. Judith's school principal's offers assistance and the prospects of loans and scholarships so that Judith can still attend college, but knowing her aunt would consider such arrangements charity, she begins working in a pickle cannery as a sixteen-year-old. Most of the immigrant workforce has no goals, but Judith is inspired by a Jewish Russian woman, Rosie Cohen, determined to study at the university at any cost. Surprisingly, in setting goals, Judith chooses matrimony, not college. Conveniently Joseph Gunner, the owner of the pickle cannery, an attractive twenty-eight-year-old is enchanted with her and the two soon wed. Judith does not find housewifery or motherhood fulfilling, and a year after her son's birth begins attending the University of Chicago. On campus she befriends independent, intelligent women and undergoes an emotional crisis when she falls in love with poet Eugene Wile. By the end of the novel she and her husband have experienced personal growth that gives both of them a new perspective on love and marriage. Chicago, in the novel, is a place filled with opportunity for women and immigrants (Aunt Carrie succeeds as a dress designer with a large firm and Rosie finally gets to attend college).

840. Parker, Mary Moncure. *A Girl of Chicago*. New York: Tennyson Neely, 1901. 140pp.

An aspect of the nouveaux riches social pretensions in this novel is marriage to European nobility. Soap producer Edward Gordon Allene had modest origins and became a millionaire through luck and self-interest. His wife is an exceptional snob who insisted Allan change his name to Allene, devised a meaningless Latin family motto, and furnished their house in an overblown luxury intended to impress. For her daughter, Medora, she established the goal of marriage to a European nobleman. She considers the likeliest candidate on the Chicago market to be Lord Carnleigh. Poor and a womanizer, any respectable English woman keeps him at a distance, but to Americans he is attractive, well-mannered, and titled. Although Medora is sarcastic and egotistical, she is in love with a good man, Will Porter, the son of a business associate of her father's whom he treated uncharitably. Will is hard working, but does not covet wealth, and lives simply. He reciprocates Medora's love and is heartbroken when her mother arranges Medora's engagement to Carnleigh. Just as the marriage seems inevitable, Carnleigh's brother appears to privately confront Carnleigh over his treatment of a young, beautiful, well-educated, impoverished woman in England. Carnleigh thought he had wed the woman in a staged, invalid marriage, lived with her for a time and then abandoned her. In fact, a real clergyman who hated Carnleigh performed the valid ceremony and the woman has since given birth to Lord Carnleigh's son. Carnleigh, now in love with Medora, confesses and pleads with Medora to wait for him to divorce his wife. Horrified at his mistreatment of the English woman Medora rejects him. Subsequently, Carnleigh shoots himself and the emotional strain weakens Medora into a life-threatening illness. Out of concern for her daughter, Mrs. Allene relents and by the end of the novel Will and Medora are engaged and Medora has begun to recover her health, a wiser and more mature woman. In addition to being a critique of a social trend to apishly venerate European nobility, the novel skewers upper-class pretension among Chicagoans and describes social events, like women's tea parties, in some detail.

841. Parrish, Randall. *The Case and the Girl*. New York: Alfred A. Knopf, 1922. 343pp.

Matthew West, a veteran recently returned from France to Chicago and residing at the University Club, feels mysteriously compelled to respond to a personals advertisement and soon finds himself in love with an heiress, Nathalie Coolidge. However, she disappears, her place taken by a double, of whose alarming existence Nathalie had informed West. As he tries to find the real Nathalie and prevent a band of criminals led by gangster "Red" Hogan, from stealing the Coolidge fortune, West gets help from an army friend now on the Chicago police force. In addition to the kidnapping years before of Nathalie's twin sister, of whose existence only three people had knowledge (Nathalie's mother died in childbirth), the plot involves drugged abductions, confinements in gangster hangouts, and an attempt to drown Nathalie and West on a sinking yacht. Although some areas of Chicago are specified, this thriller conveys nothing of consequence about the city.

842. Parrish, Randall. *Gordon Craig; Soldier of Fortune*. Illustrated by Alonzo Kimball. Chicago: McClurg, 1912. 366p.

Gordon Craig, a recent veteran of the Spanish-American War, is sent to Alabama to impersonate an heir and secure a fortune by men he believes are lawyers acting in the interest of the legitimate heir. Craig is hired in Chicago and the first section of the novel is set there, although the descriptions are shallow.

843. Parrish, Robert. *My Uncle and Miss Elizabeth*. New York: Beechhurst Press, 1948. 221pp.

In this stream of consciousness work of fiction, a literary young man, known only as Mr. Chapel, gives an account of living with his uncle in a 1930s apartment. The household includes a third unmarried man, Mr. Farrer, who, unlike the narrator and his uncle has a romantic relationship with a woman, Miss Elizabeth. The cast of characters, almost all of whom were educated at the University of Illinois, includes a former apartment-mate of the uncle, Mr. Parkington, now married to a wealthy, free-thinking woman; and a quirky, University of Illinois professor. Chicago remains fairly anonymous in the novel which focuses on personality quirks of the uncle, who has a very regimented life and easily becomes emotionally upset. Nighttime visits by Miss Elizabeth do not fit into any conceivable orderliness to his mind. For a time, he pretends not to notice, even when he accidentally spots her in red pajamas, and also when Mr. Farrer's bed collapses and upon investigating the uncle sees her unsuccessfully concealed in the bedding. However, one fateful day she incontrovertibly obtrudes herself and the household is temporarily under threat, until the uncle happens upon another young man to share the expenses. The house-proud, canary-owning, bachelor uncle and his literary nephew, the novel's narrator, who is given to extended illnesses and neuroses, may or may not be homosexuals. The uncle's life revolves around his office, the YMCA, and golf (in season). Few Chicago establishments are mentioned except for an unnamed cabaret and the Iroquois Club.

844. Parrish, Randall. *When Wilderness Was King: A Tale of the Illinois Country*. Chicago: McClurg, 1904.

Set during the War of 1812, the novel provides a description of Fort Dearborn and the massacre of the settlers there. Twenty-year-old John Wayland is dispatched by his father to retrieve orphaned Elsa Matherson from Fort Dearborn and deliver her to the Wayland household on the Upper Maumee River to be raised as a member of the family. When Matherson turns out to be seventeen-years-old, a romance develops in the midst of the couple's hardships. This work of fiction presents summary descriptions of the history of Fort Dearborn and the tragic events of 1812.

845. Patchin, Frank. *The Range and Grange Hustlers at Chicago; or, The Conspiracy of the Wheat Pit*. Philadelphia: Altemus, 1913. 249pp.

This work is one of four novels featuring a group of boys known as the Range and Grange Hustlers (Patchin wrote other series for children as well, including the Pony Rider series). The novel introduces the Chicago Board of Trade illustrating how the price of wheat can be manipulated by selfish men with world-wide consequences. Chicago is portrayed as the center of economic activity of great significance.

846. Patterson, Eleanor Medill [aka Eleanor Gizycka]. *Fall Flight*. New York: Minton, Balch, 1928. 277pp.

Only the first fifty pages of this novel are set in Chicago, however the book scandalized Chicagoans by skewering a few of the city's real-life social climbers and society figures. Susan Shawn epitomizes this class. Born in Cleveland, Ohio, Susan eloped to Chicago as a sixteen-year-old with a dentist ten years her senior. The first years of her marriage were spent in poverty, in part because her ambitionless husband spent his free time in saloons. When Susan inherits money from her grandmother the income provides respectability and she sets her feet on the path of social advancement, despite the dragging weight of her husband and too-common fourteen-year-old daughter, Daisy. Tuberculosis frees her of her husband and soon after his death she meets Oliver Redmond, a wealthy foreign service officer who becomes her second husband. The inconvenient Daisy is parked with former neighbors, the Schultzes. Their middle-class social life focused on family and outdoor pleasures entrances Daisy, as does Oscar, one of the Schultz sons, who is studying medicine. Unfortunately, when Redmond is named American Ambassador to Russia, Susan recalls Daisy in the hope of marrying her to a nobleman to advance her own social status. Dazzled by the Russian court, starry-eyed Daisy is easy prey for a dishonorable Russian prince, made desirable by her mother's disapproval of him. An unhappy marriage follows soon after the death of Susan and, through the excesses of the prince, Daisy loses the money Redmond had settled upon her. She escapes with her youth and is reunited with Oscar in Vienna, where he has been studying. By the end of the novel the two are about to embark for Chicago.

847. Patterson, Joseph Medill. *Little Brother of the Rich*. Chicago: Reilly, Britton, 1908. 361pp.

This romance novel also addresses the morality of accumulating wealth. Paul Potter and Sylvia Castle grow up in the same small town, Darbyville, Indiana, and become sweethearts. When Paul goes off to Yale University, he befriends scions of some of New York's wealthiest families. However, he still proposes marriage to Sylvia. Her father, banker John Castle, insists that Paul promises to return to Darbyville when he marries Sylvia and eventually take control of Castle's bank. Paul agrees, but when Sylvia realizes the opportunities Paul is giving up in New York City she breaks the engagement. Shortly afterwards, Castle's bank fails amidst the scandalous revelation that he lost his personal fortune in speculation and then used bank funds to try to recover his losses. Castle dies in disgrace and Sylvia relocates to Chicago to escape Darbyville's hostility, finding work in a department store. She lives in a boarding house and the novel goes into great detail about her work and social life in 1890s Chicago. While Sylvia struggles, Paul begins his New York City career buoyed by wealthy friends. The paths of the two cross again after Sylvia joins an acting company that tours the theater circuit and eventually appears in New York City. The rest of the novel traces the forces that work for and against a renewal of their romance. Although relatively brief, the pages that deal with Sylvia's experiences in Chicago, presented in the form of her journal entries, illustrate some of the difficulties single women faced when they tried to establish themselves in the city in the 1890s.

848. Patterson, Joseph Medill. *Rebellion*. Illustrated by Walter Dean Goldbeck. Chicago: Reilly and Britton, 1911. 355pp.

Dealing with women's role in society, this book also addresses the unequal sacrifices that women must make in order to abide by Roman Catholic teachings on marriage. Georgia marries Jim Connor, of Irish descent like herself, because he is pleasant and attractive and she feels obligated by Church teaching to marry. Over time Connor starts working for a political boss in exchange for perks, but very little money, most of which he spends on alcohol; he is the son and grandson of alcoholics. Georgia provides most of the income for the household working as an insurance office stenographer. When she is promoted she throws Connor out over her mother's protests on the grounds of Church teaching. Georgia starts skipping mass and attending Sunday Evening Ethical Society meetings, instead. She begins to accept the friendship of Mason Stevens, Jr. from the insurance agency. The thirty-year-old Stevens lives a sober, frugal life entirely centered on work. He quickly becomes infatuated with Georgia, although she cautions him that they can only be friends since the Church will not allow her to divorce and remarry. Connor returns from working in Oklahoma tanned, fit, and sober. He begs forgiveness and Georgia's brother and mother urge her to reconcile. However, she is in love with Stevens and does not believe that Connor will stay away from alcohol. A crisis comes when Stevens asks Georgia to get a divorce, marry him in a civil ceremony, and relocate with him. While still considering his proposal, Georgia is diagnosed with typhoid fever. The health crisis returns her to the Church and she swears off agnosticism, materialism, and sociological analysis. She reconciles with Connor and after discovering that Stevens had secretly paid her hospital bills pledges to pay back the money by taking in a lodger. This requires letting Connor move out of the living room and return to her bed, where he forces himself on her. Pregnant and unable to work, she is now dependent on Connor who has begun drinking again. When her baby is born, he has a health defect inherited from his alcoholic father and dies before his first birthday. Georgia separates from Connor and becomes a partner in a stenography business. Her practicality, hard work, and sharp business sense brings success to the firm. When Stevens reappears she confidently accepts his marriage proposal and after an uncontested divorce marries in a civil ceremony and moves to Kansas. Although her priest believes she has been defeated by secularism and Darwinism, she is confident that God talks to individuals, not through priests. Despite a didactic intent, the book includes a great deal of Chicago description. In addition to the sociological description of amateur baseball leagues, office life, political clubs, saloon culture, and the influence of the Church, there is physical description of apartment and rooming house living, advertisements, clothing, public transportation, horse wagons, German beer gardens, and bands. Neighborhood descriptions are not detailed and primarily focus on Lincoln Park and the Loop. Chicago as a whole plays an important symbolic role, for Georgia takes strength from it as a city unafraid of violating tradition, just as she is called to do.

849. Paulsen, Gary. *Meteorite Track 291*. New York: Dell Books / G/M Publishing, 1979. 221pp.

This science fiction novel is partly set in a 1970s Chicago under threat of total annihilation by a meteor strike. A satellite tracking station engineer in southern California named Richard Foreman is the first to realize that a huge meteorite is headed for the earth and will hit Chicago with a tremendous impact that will bring destruction for a one hundred mile area. Since he reports to the military, he quickly encounters a general who thinks a meteor strike made to look like an atomic bomb explosion might not be a bad thing if it can be used to end the stalemate of the Cold War. Foreman is quickly put under armed guard. His desperation to warn Chicagoans fuels a courageous escape. After some airplane trips to throw off the authorities, he ends up driving cross-country and in the final fifty pages of the novel arrives in Chicago and enlists investigative reporter Sharon Connolly to warn Chicagoans. Of course, no one pays attention. The book includes little physical description of the city.

850. Payne Philip. *Duchess of Few Clothes: A Comedy*. Chicago: Rand, McNally, 1904. 341pp.

Through a plot involving the owner, employees, and guests of the Pantheon, a luxurious Chicago hotel, the author presents his ideas about the distinct topics of capitalism and marriage. Alonzo Alexander Farson constructed the Pantheon to celebrate his sixtieth birthday. He spends most of his time traveling with his daughter, Genevra, or at home in California, but a few weeks each year, they stay in their hotel. The action of the novel transpires over one of their stays in which Valentine Quarles, a thirty-three-year-old millionaire who got his start in the stockyards, is determined to marry Genevra to advance socially. He is surprised to find his college classmate, Ned Hazard working as the hotel violinist. Hazard, heir to a New England textile firm, realized after his father's death that he would have a difficult time rebuilding the family business after his mother had gutted the firm to fund her art collecting and charitable activities and allowed it to lapse into bankruptcy. Hazard attracts Genevra and she gets her father to pay for private violin lessons from Hazard, who is less than enthusiastic, but is enticed by Genevra's Stradivarius. Ned considers both the Farsons unrefined and has his eye on hotel cigar girl Elsinore Vantage who grew up poor on a Michigan farm but has highly developed cultural tastes consistent with her ambition to become an opera singer. However, Farson becomes infatuated with Vantage and proposes. She recognizes that he is truly in love and will marry him so long as Genevra will accept her. Genevra is vicious and devises a plan to discredit Vantage. Quarles steps in to rescue Vantage and by the end of the novel the two are engaged. Ned is urged by both Vantage and Quarles to marry Genevra, but he remains "too finical" and will likely continue to be poor and unwed. The novel satirizes the nouveaux riches of Chicago, but not viciously. Although Farson is portrayed as silly in his Napoleonic pretensions, Quarles portrays him as socially creditable for using his wealth to create jobs and maintain the social order. Ned, on the other hand may see himself as a democrat, but finds the behavior of working men as distasteful as the false refinement of the Farsons. He gave up his opportunity to help others when he refused to revitalize his father's mills and will seemingly remain at odds with society in a less than useful way.

851. Payne, Will. *The Automatic Capitalists*. Illustrated by Leslie L. Benson. Boston: Richard G. Badger, Gorham Press, 1909. 150pp.

This humorous account of the attempts of Marcus Barrington and Theodore Benton to avoid legal action and bankruptcy through elaborate machinations involving deception and stock manipulation depends upon the caricature of behavior and has little description of Chicago. However, the city is presented as a commercial center filled with brokerage houses and investors. Most of the action is set in offices in the Loop. Barrington and Benton's efforts fail when a cabal of investors decides to ruin them. One of the most prominently mentioned genuine financial instruments to be mentioned are gas bonds. The tone of the novel is good-humored

852. Payne, Will. *Jerry the Dreamer*. New York: Harper and Brothers, 1896. 299pp.

In this coming of age story, Jerry Drew leaves his hometown, Tampico, Illinois, for Chicago hoping to make a career as a journalist on one the city's nationally known daily newspapers. Drew not only establishes himself as newspaperman, he also falls in love and marries Georgia House the beautiful daughter of a wealthy and powerful judge. However, his successes are tempered by complications. In order to maintain his position with the prominent *Evening Call* he must agree not to write stories about the plight of workingmen; stories to which he is deeply committed. Furthermore, Georgia's father does not approve of the match and the couple ends up eloping, putting Georgia in a difficult situation for which Drew feels responsible. When he secretly continues to write for a socialist newspaper, he jeopardizes his career and happiness with Georgia. One of the characters in the novel is an architect and the book includes comments on architectural theory relevant to the development of Chicago.

853. Payne, Will. *The Losing Game*. Illustrated by F. R. Gruger. New York: Dillingham, 1910. 352pp.

This novel about stock manipulation is partly set in Chicago. The main characters, twenty-six-year-old Emma Raymond and John Pound, meet in a brokerage office in Chicago on La Salle Street. They immediately spot each other as corrupt characters and soon reveal past criminal activity. Pound has experience intercepting telegraph messages and, soon, he and Emma, a telegrapher, have devised a plan for defrauding investors. During most of the novel the couple lives in St. Paul, Minnesota, as Pound builds a network of brokerage offices throughout the Midwest to be exclusively served by his telegraph lines. By the end of the novel Emma has divorced Pound and gained control of his assets. In addition to providing a great deal of information about stock transactions, the novel is of interest for the protagonist's misogynist attitude toward women.

854. Payne, Philip. *The Mills of Man*. Chicago: Rand, McNally and Co, 1903. 476pp.

The Chicago characters in this novel are at the top of the late-nineteenth-century socio-economic ladder. As a forty-year-old Victoria Corliss learns that she has only six months to live. Rather than bemoan her fate, she reviews the successes of her life and decides to embrace the "Puritan" morality of her youth and die a good wife and mother. The daughter of a U.S. Senator, she won acclaim in Washington society for her intelligent and witty conversation. As the wife of politician Walter Corliss, she became a dominant force in New York and Newport society. When she returns to Chicago after a season in Washington, she resolves to dedicate herself to her father's re-election and her husband's campaign for political control of Chicago and Illinois. She tires herself out by attending and hosting social functions and interacting with people for whom she has no respect, only to find out that for years both her husband and father have accepted bribes from capitalists and corporations. After the crisis of the revelation, Victoria decides she can take satisfaction in her own moral convictions, even though she is disappointed in the limited role she was able to play as a woman. Hildegard Browne, a younger woman, works as a reporter and earns Victoria's interest and approval for taking advantage of new social opportunities. Chicago has little real presence in the novel, although the city is presented as nationally significant politically.

855. Payne, Will. *The Money Captain*. Chicago: Herbert S. Stone, 1898. 323p.

   This 1890s account of Chicago focuses on the world of corporate business showing the way in which all of urban society is affected by the captains of finance. Archibald Dexter, an easterner who had come to Chicago years before, developed a monopoly on supplying gas to the city. A bill is under consideration in the city council to allow competition from a new gas company and the stock market is in turmoil. The novel demonstrates the impact of the crisis on several levels of society, including the owners of brokerage firms, bankers, and one of Dexter's employees, Victor Nidstrom, a young man with a wife and toddler to support. Newspaper publisher Hamilton J. Liggett investigates the new company and discovers Dexter employees are listed as owners. He accuses Dexter of setting up a dummy corporation to manipulate the markets and later gathers evidence that Dexter bribed a corrupt alderman. Just as Liggett is about to publish his story, Dexter brings a libel suit against him; just defending himself against the suit could bankrupt him with legal fees. However, Liggett publishes the story. The day before the libel trial is to begin, Dexter dies of apoplexy and his machinations die with him, but the money he generated for investors remains, as does the fortune he leaves for his niece. The novel is tightly focused on the struggles of financial titans and their less than moral approach to business with no general description of Chicago (except for a disreputable saloon in which every patron is cheated but remains exempt from prosecution since an alderman owns the establishment).

856. Payne, Will. *Mr. Salt*. Illustrated by Charles H. White. Boston: Houghton Mifflin, 1903. 330pp.

   This novel defending corporate capitalism features a controversial hero, Henry Salt, the president of the Illinois Coal and Iron Company. As the work opens, Salt is battling to keep his position as a major stockholder in his firm, who is a conservative Chicago capitalist, leads a shareholder revolt. The year is 1893 and the city and country is in the midst of an economic crisis as the Columbian Exposition is about to open. The views of conservative capitalists are rehearsed several times in the novel and so are the perspectives of wage laborers in the guise of Fred Haward who talks of the deleterious effects of Salt's actions on working men. Salt, however, is committed to establishing successful businesses rather than simply increasing his own wealth. In fact, he risks his fortune repeatedly in the novel in the interest of creating rational business structures, which in the perspective of the novel, means building corporations that include raw materials, factories, and transportation. Although it takes all of the novel's three hundred-plus pages and relatively frequent iterations of arguments against corporations and Salt's techniques, by the end of the novel both Salt's main opponents have embraced incorporation as a natural force in human affairs. The decision is not whether to oppose incorporation, but how to adapt to the organizational structure. In the final scene of the novel, Salt drives a luxurious automobile that one character regards as an apt symbol of the impulse of Western civilization towards corporate growth. One can find a place in the vehicle, or be crushed under its wheels. Although the novel is primarily a dramatization of arguments for and against corporations, a love story also runs through the book. Esther Ross, a girl from the stenographers' pool at the beginning of the novel, supports Salt in a number of crises and demonstrates the power of a woman's love to redeem the actions of a hard-minded businessman. By the end of the book, Salt, several decades her senior, has married her and put her in charge of a charitable foundation funded by his wealth. Esther's sister Elizabeth, the recipient of a loan from Salt to fund her operatic training, has become a world famous singer, demonstrating the importance of Salt and his kind for the arts. Although the novel does not contain a great deal of physical description (even though specific locations are provided for places such as Salt's office in the La-Salle Building) it does encapsulate elements of Chicago history from 1893 through the turn of the century and includes accounts of labor unrest, particularly during the Pullman strike, the burning of the Columbian Exposition buildings, and the local impact of national politics, especially during the elections of McKinley and Cleveland.

857. Payne, Will. *On Fortune's Road: Stories of Business*. Chicago: McClurg, 1902. 290pp.

Six of these seven short stories are set in Chicago and the seventh is set in a nearby industrial suburb. Although several forms of business are presented, the common theme is the impact of speculation in the commodities market and the governing morality of each against each in the struggle for wealth. The impact of greed on working class people is presented, but on the whole the stories focus on capitalists and their families. Women are universally presented as ignorant of business and entirely dependent upon the efforts of men. Wealth in the stories is won through skillful manipulation and often lost in sudden market reverses. The physical description of the city focuses on office buildings, brokerage houses, banks, and the Chicago Board of Trade.

858. Payne, Will. *The Scarred Chin*. New York: Dodd, Mead, 1920. 310pp.

In a period of economic growth in Chicago during the late nineteen-teens "money captain" Alfred Dinsmore and J. Wesley Tully, the owner of a newspaper are at odds over personal grievances, as are most of the other vindictive main characters. Dinsmore, with fifteen million dollars and a house in the North Shore suburb of Highland Park, is socially superior to Tully, who inherited money, attended Harvard University, and wrested a modest fortune of a million dollars out of dealing in Chicago real estate. Tully lives in the less socially desirable suburb of Elsmoore, just south of Highland Village. Committed in a socially fashionable way to reform and eager to advance in society, Tully buys a newspaper to showcase his ideas and his wife's social events. A dandy, Tully is humiliated at his private club when Dinsmore comments on his clothing. In response, with the help of his reporters, Tully finds slightly embarrassing information to publish about Dinsmore's company and his presidency of the Highland Village board of trustees. However, he blindly signs off on an editorial page letter concocted by his managing editor Charles Purcell, who resents Tully for his wealth. In response, Dinsmore files a lawsuit that could do Tully serious financial harm. Purcell is also a petty blackmailer; when an African-American servant with a grievance against Dinsmore, claims that Dinsmore got his start with money from an armed robbery during which a teller was killed, Purcell enlists a crooked lawyer, Lawrence McMurtry, and the Morden Private Detective Agency. McMurtry soon devises a blackmail plot that could net the accomplices a million dollars. They are defeated when their eyewitness repeatedly emphasizes the perpetrator's scarred chin and Dinsmore shaves his beard revealing a smooth chin. When Dinsmore reveals that the true culprit of the murder was his mentally ill older brother, whom he has protected and cared for during the intervening thirty years, his wife and daughter come to see him in a new and flattering light. The novel portrays honorable, hard-working men of wealth and contrasts them with men engaged in purely self-serving efforts to accumulate riches through chicanery. A variety of settings are used to tell the story, including domestic establishments, private clubs, offices, and saloons.

859. Payne, Will. *The Story of Eva.* Boston: Houghton Mifflin, Riverside Press, 1901. 340pp.

Twenty-four-year-old Eva Soden grew up in Hopeville, Nebraska and married a traveling salesman, won over by his experience of the world, manners, clothes, and physical attractiveness. After the couple moves to Chicago, Eva discovers that her husband is not faithful to her while on his travels. To maintain her sense of self-worth she leaves him while he is on a sales trip. Her guide to the city is a distant cousin, Sarah White, who helps her get a job at the Economy Publishing Company. The novel details office life in a large publishing firm and the workplace difficulties women can experience dealing with men as peers and supervisors. When Sarah eventually leaves the city, Eva has no one to guide her and once again falls under the control of a man, even though it seems to be a love match. The book gives a clear sense of the life of working women of the time, detailing not only office interactions, but social opportunities and living arrangements.

860. Pearce, John Irving. *The Strange Case of Eric Marotté: A Modern Historical Problem-Romance of Chicago.* Illustrated by Carle J. Blenner and Norman Tolson. Chicago: Pettibone, 1913. 366pp.

As a foundling raised by an African-American couple on Goose Island, John's closest friendship is with Gretchen Hummelmueller, the daughter of a German brewer. The friendship between the olive-skinned John and Gretchen is made acceptable when John becomes a city-wide celebrity for saving her when she is caught in a lumberyard fire. The grateful Hummelmueller puts ten thousand dollars in trust for John and when he graduates valedictorian of his high school class he is able to pay his expenses at Yale University with the income. After his graduation, John returns to Chicago to learn the operations of a machine shop, and then uses the principal of the trust to establish his own successful business. Even though he is now able to provide for Gretchen, John resists marrying her, for fear of damaging her socially by his supposedly black skin. Finally, through a bizarre coincidence, John discovers the truth of his origins. As a baby, a bear removed him from his father's Canadian lumber camp. He was recovered by a man fleeing Canada, but the woman with whom he fell in stole John when she decided to break up. Eventually tiring of the baby, she left John with another man who delivered him to the doorstep of his adopted parents because he could tell from the orderliness of their cottage that they were good people. When John is reunited with his true parents, he discovers that he is French-Canadian and his real name is Eric Marotté. Freed from the social prison of black skin, he also discovers he is the heir to a lumber fortune. He immediately marries Gretchen and the two leave for Montréal. The author provides a great deal of physical description of Goose Island and other neighborhoods in which impoverished people live. He also discourses extensively on the conditions of black people in Chicago in the 1870s through 1890s. His stand that "Negroes" need to take responsibility for their lot and work hard to utilize opportunities in Chicago to better their lives may rankle twenty-first century readers.

861. Peattie, Elia Wilkinson. *The Judge*. Chicago; New York: Rand, McNally, 1890. 286pp.

This murder mystery includes an adopted son of a wealthy man, a romance, and the bizarre killing of household pets. On the night that Harry Leiter proposes to Margaret Barthwait, Leiter's adopted father is murdered and soon afterwards Leiter is charged with the crime. Journalist Dennis Pond investigates the case and aids Leiter's defense. Physical setting is relatively unimportant in the novel, although the upper-class households of the characters are on the North Side of Chicago. From the standpoint of social history the novel is of interest for contrasting the robust state's attorney William Wendell McCook, a rival for Margaret's hand, with Leiter, who is described as an effete bohemian who has never really entered manhood. Leiter's tribulations make a man of him, and Margaret achieves a new maturity when she realizes her father is mentally ill and secretly tries to restore his wits by taking him in disguise to the countryside and getting him to work at farm tasks. He recovers enough to remember and record his crimes (the killing of pets and of Leiter's father) before dying.

862. Peattie, Elia Wilkinson. *Lotta Embury's Career*. Boston: Houghton Mifflin, Riverside Press, 1915. 214pp.

In this young adult book, Lotta Embury has just finished her sophomore year in high school when her Aunt Catherine Summerwood, who is unmarried and a part of the Emburys' Maitland, Iowa household, makes a dramatic announcement. She has sold jewelry and land to assemble enough money to take Lotta to Chicago to study with famed Danish violinist Gunnar Heegard. At her first meeting with Heegard he lets Lotta know she will never be a musician. She is crushed, but mostly sorry for her aunt, and tries to remedy the difficult situation by selling her violin to pay for a business college course with the idea of getting a job and repaying her aunt. While studying, she lives in the Anna Louisa Home for Self-Supporting Women, and makes friends with a commercial artist, as well as the Heegards. Although Lotta demonstrates that she could survive in the city, she believes life only has meaning in the context of one's family and hometown. When her father is paralyzed by a stroke, she returns to take over his failing hardware business, transforming the concern into a household supply store that begins to attract female clients for the first time. Chicago in the novel is a focus for aspiration, but is portrayed as a hard place to live where most people must work all the time and do not live the life of the boulevardier most people know as tourists.

863. Peattie, Elia Wilkinson. *The Precipice*. Illustrated by Howard E. Smith. Boston: Houghton Mifflin, 1914. 417pp.

Through Kate Barrington, Peattie explores the life choices available to Chicago women at the beginning of the twentieth century. Kate, the daughter of a physician in Silvertree, Illinois, witnessed her mother continually abnegating her own wishes to serve the needs of her husband and devote herself to creating a well-maintained household. After she graduates from the University of Chicago, her family expects her to marry, but Kate rejects a wealthy suitor, because she cannot imagine herself in the servile, traditional role of housewife. She rejects a number of other models as represented by friends and acquaintances, as well. One classmate has a companionate marriage with a promising young scientist, but the couple has streamlined their household affairs to such an extent that they truly have no home life. Another acquaintance has so devoted herself to scholarship that she has entered a perpetual academic spinsterhood. Her opposite is a young woman who has developed a siren persona, employing feminine charms to get whatever she desires. Kate finally decides to devote herself to her job with the Children's Protective League an actual organization founded by Julia Lathrop that grew into the nation's first Children's Bureau. Kate models herself on Julia Lathrop and Jane Addams; embracing the concept of the civic family, she does not limit herself to a single household, but uses her maternal abilities for the public good. At the end of the novel, the President of the United States offers Kate the directorship of the newly created federal Bureau of Children. The offer seemingly forces her to choose between a marrying Karl Wander, a mine owner in the Far West, and her independence. However, she and Wander decide to marry and live apart, each devoted to their work lives, hoping to be united in the future. Chicago in the novel offers the chance for social experimentation due to the conjunction of work opportunities and a large, educated population. Although the novel contains little physical description of the city, it does describe aspects of social life in the academic community and the settlement house movement.

864. Peattie, Louise Redfield. *Fugitive*. Indianapolis: Bobbs-Merrill, 1935. 295pp.

In this Depression-era romance novel, a mysterious, aristocratic woman steals the heart of Dominique Alexander, an art dealer reduced to teaching art history in an evening studies program. He saves the life of a woman who attempts suicide in the room next to his at the rooming house where he lives. The woman, who refuses to give her name, has escaped her affluent life, to do away with herself in anonymity. Alexander takes her to the farm of a family he knows. She recovers her health and entrances Alexander. The country idyll is destroyed when newspapers publish her picture, identified as Viola Gorman, along with that of her disgraced husband Howard, extradited from Corsica to face trial for embezzlement with attempt to defraud. Viola, the daughter of an impoverished English aristocrat, had married the wealthy Gorman out of a sense of duty and she returns to stand by him in his Prairie Avenue mansion for the same reason. Alexander tries to get Viola to leave her husband and salvage her life, but she refuses and is killed by a stone thrown by one of the rioting socialist activists who storm the Gorman mansion when they discover Gorman has been released on bail and suspect he will be found not guilty. Although set in Chicago, the novel provides little description of the city and expresses admiration for the refined feelings of European aristocrats, as represented by Alexander (the unrecognized heir of a Parisian nobleman) and the English aristocrat, Viola.

865. Peck, Richard. *Don't Look and It Won't Hurt*. New York: Holt, Rinehart and Winston, 1972. 173pp.

Most of this novel is set in the fictional town of Claypitts [*sic*], Illinois during the early 1970s and deals with issues faced by women in a sexist society. Carol Patterson lives in a single-parent household with her two sisters and mother. Carol's father abandoned the family years ago and her mother supports them by working as a hostess at a truck-stop. Carol's older sister Ellen has an affair with a college-age boy who is supposedly helping draftees escape to Canada. Shortly after he is arrested for drug-dealing, Ellen realizes she is pregnant and subsequently relocates to Chicago to live in a home for unwed mothers until she has the baby, which will be put up for adoption. Carol eventually runs away to visit her sister and briefly relates her impressions of the city as someone from a small town. Ellen convinces herself that she never wants to leave Chicago, but Carol has a more measured view of the place, which although only four hundred miles from Claypitts, seems like a different world.

866. Pendleton, Don. *The Executioner: Chicago Wipe-Out*. New York: Pinnacle Books, 1971. 187pp.

This is the eighth in a series of books featuring Mack Bolan, a veteran of Korea and Vietnam who has dedicated himself to destroying organized crime in the United States, earning the sobriquet the Executioner. Here Bolan uncovers the Mafia's master plan to dominate American life from a headquarters in Chicago. He heads to the city to assassinate the masterminds. As with other action-adventure novels in this series, physical setting gets lost in the emphasis on dramatic automobile chases and violent confrontations.

867. Petrakis, Harry Mark. *A Dream of Kings*. New York: David McKay, 1966. 180pp.

In his story of Leonidas Matsoukas' desperate attempt to raise enough money for airplane tickets to take his invalid son Stavros back to Greece, where he believes the sun will cure the boy, Petrakis creates a picture of the Greek immigrant community in Chicago. Matsoukas' skills, though acknowledged within his community, would not typically earn him a living in American society. He uses astrology, omen analysis, and palmistry to counsel people. He also coaches wrestlers, teaches vocabulary, and writes poems. Unfortunately, he believes in his own abilities to read omens and keeps gambling in the hope of getting the money needed for his son's trip. Found cheating, he is banned from gambling parlors in the neighborhood and beaten up by a Turk. In disgrace, and realizing that he will never get the money for his son in time, he steals it from his mother-in-law, and, in a dramatic final scene, boards the plane with his dying son. As with other work by Petrakis, classical mythology underlies the twentieth-century story.

868. Petrakis, Harry Mark. *In the Land of Morning*. New York: David McKay, 1973. 290pp.

After serving in Vietnam, twenty-four-year-old Alex Rifakis returns to the Greek neighborhood where he grew up to find a changed world. Chicago is undergoing rapid transformation as whole neighborhoods are torn down. Impoverished African-American and Puerto-Rican neighborhoods have grown larger and are encroaching on Rifakis' neighborhood. His father, Manouso, a gambler who lost the family business to the local gangster, Antonios Gallos, is dead. His sister suffers from systemic arthritis and yearns for marriage, although she realizes that her adherence to traditional social customs and styles of dress in a society filled with mini-skirted, sexually available, young women will probably keep her single. Alex' mother, Asmene, follows the daily liturgy of the Greek Orthodox Church, but is the mistress of Gallos. Soon after his return, Alex becomes reacquainted with Ellie Naoum, the daughter of his parish priest, whose husband was killed in Vietnam. The two immediately commence an emotional and sexual relationship. Meanwhile, disturbed by Asmene's refusal to return to his bed now that Alex has returned, Gallos realizes he is in love with Asmene and decides to legitimate the relationship through marriage. When she accepts, he begins selling his assets, businesses both legitimate and criminal, and planning his life in Greece with Asmene. Before Asmene announces the betrothal, Alex discovers the scandalous relationship she has had and slays Gallos in his bath. Even though the crime will go uninvestigated as a gangland murder, Alex moves to Phoenix and Ellie soon follows him. In addition to referencing the social problems of the 1970s, the novel depicts the impact of urban renewal on neighborhood life in Chicago and the city appears as a moribund body from which vital young people like Alex and Ellie should escape.

869. Petrakis, Harry Mark. *Lion at My Heart*. Boston: Little, Brown, 1959. 238pp.

This novel set in Chicago's Greek community in the 1950s deals with the theme of cultural assimilation, as well as the more universal topic of aging and generational transition. Angelo Varinakis, a Greek immigrant is admired for his capacity for work, ability to inspire his work crew in the steel mill, and his physical strength. After his wife's death when his two sons were just boys, Angelo raised them by himself in the house he bought for them on Dart Street. Now, his oldest son, Mike, is a twenty-six-year-old World War II veteran and works in the same steel mill as his father. Tony, is twenty-one and about to graduate from college. When Mike chooses a beautiful, young Irish woman, Sheila, as his fiancée, Angelo vociferously denies his blessing on the match, accusing Mike of violating centuries of family history and tradition. Mike weds Sheila anyway in a civil ceremony. Later, Angelo discovers that Sheila was pregnant with Mike's child when they married and when Sheila has a life-threatening miscarriage, he refuses to go to the hospital, claiming the couple is being punished for their sin. In Tony's presence, the family priest reminds Angelo of his long career as a philanderer, pursued even while his wife was ill, and Tony comes to a new understanding of his father. Tony violates cultural tradition in another way, when he falls in love with Marika, the daughter of family friends, the Bratsos, who had arranged a marriage for their daughter with a local businessman. However, Angelo helps Tony secure his match. The novel deals with the difficulties of finding a balance between maintaining cultural traditions and assimilating as immigrants in a new country. The story also touches on institutions that hold the immigrant Greek community together, including the Greek Orthodox Church, and describes food ways and social events that center on story-telling and traditional dancing. There is some physical description of the neighborhood that is dominated by the steel-mill and the Greek-owned coffee shops and small grocery stores that provide necessities and social life.

870. Petrakis, Harry Mark. *Nick the Greek*. Garden City, N.Y.: Doubleday, 1979. 302pp.

This work of historical fiction covers the years 1919-1966, although the main focus is on 1920s Chicago. Nicholas Dandolos arrives in Chicago in 1919 with family money to establish an import business. However, he soon loses the money in the gambling parlors on South Halsted Street. Through the course of the novel, he wins fortunes gambling, gains a national reputation, and is frequently asked to compete in poker games all over the continent. Through his addiction to gambling, he loses Marina Rantoulis, the woman he loves, and becomes obligated to organized crime figures. After he is forced to act as a decoy to set up the massacre of the O'Donnel gang, he must leave Chicago, and he ends his life gambling in Las Vegas. Although set in Chicago's Greek community, the main emphasis is on describing the culture of gambling. Through Marina's character the novel touches on feminist issues (she is involved in the suffrage movement and tries to establish rights for herself as an individual in opposition to traditional male-dominated Greek culture).

871. Petrakis, Harry Mark. *The Odyssey of Kostas Volakis*. New York: David McKay, 1963. 271pp.

In 1919, Kostas Volakis knows that Crete holds no future for him and consents to marry plain Katerina Peterakis since her dowry is large enough to pay for both of them to go to the United States and join relatives in Chicago. The rest of the novel, covering the years up to 1954, traces their experiences in the Greek immigrant community. Their hard work and personal tragedies are balanced by moments of love and friendship. As newcomers they are sickened by the ugliness of Chicago and stay only because Katerina becomes pregnant. Eventually, Volakis is a part-owner in a restaurant and accepts that the future of his family, through his American sons, is in the United States. Two of Volakis great tragedies are the death by pneumonia of his first child and the murder of his oldest son by his youngest son in a drunken rage. Two of Volakis best friends, Father Marlas and Dr. Barbaris help him through many of his trials. The novel illustrates how immigrants are forced to assimilate by having children who are native-born citizens of the United States.

872. Petrakis, Harry Mark. *Pericles on 31st Street*. Chicago: Quadrangle Books, 1965. 213pp.

As with other short story collections by Petrakis, this volume evokes the Chicago Greek community. Settings include taverns, coffee shops, grocery stores, ice houses, and Orthodox churches. Several of the stories are retellings of classical myths.

873. Petrakis, Harry Mark. *A Petrakis Reader*. Garden City, N.Y.: Doubleday, 1978. 384pp.

The twenty-eight short stories in this collection were previously published between 1957 and the 1970s. Many of the works are set in Chicago and capture family and community life among Greek immigrants. Workplaces include a lunch counter, ice depot, candy store, library, and saloon. Much of the focus is on relationships between men and women.

874. Petrakis, Harry Mark. *The Waves of Night, and Other Stories*. New York: David McKay, 1969. 230pp.

The eleven stories in this work are set in the Greek community in Chicago, mostly within the male culture of coffee shops and diners. Although many of the characters own or work in such establishments, other men work as railroad guards, steel hands, advertising copywriters, and truck drivers. Women have a great deal of negative power in the stories. A man believes he has fallen in love with one woman only to discover she is a prostitute. Another man who had lived as a bachelor for many years marries only to fall seriously ill and believe his wife has robbed him of his health. A third man avoids marriage because he knows his mother will expect to live with him and his wife, draining the household finances until her death.

875. Pflaum, Melanie. *The Gentle Tyrants*. New York: Carlton Press, 1969. 274pp.

This fictionalized account of the experiences of an immigrant family was written by the granddaughter of French immigrant, Pierre des Pres. De Pres arrives in the United States with no intention of settling permanently; he only wants to save enough money to return to France in comfortable economic circumstances. However, he arrives in Chicago around the time of the 1871 fire and starts a business scavenging scrap metal. His success and growing family keep him in the United States as he sees his business expand to a multi-million dollar undertaking and he realizes his American-born offspring have no interest in living in France. The novel captures aspects of the immigrant experience over three generations, while presenting the history of Chicago over seventy-five years. In addition to covering events like the Haymarket Riot and the impact of the world wars and the Depression on Chicago, the novel conveys a good deal of social history concerning the economic boom years of the 1920s and the suffrage and women's liberation movements.

876. Phelon, William A. *Chimmie Fadden Out West: A Sequel to Chimmie Fadden*. Chicago: Weeks, 1896. 171pp.

This work takes a New York City Bowery character named James "Chimmie" Fadden created by Edward W. Townsend and transplants him to Chicago. The entire book is written in first-person, Irish dialect as Fadden comments on his exploration of Chicago. One of his first activities is a lake steamer excursion sponsored by a social club called the Ivy Monarchs which has their club-house on Blue Island Avenue near Halsted. He later goes to a masquerade ball on Blue Island Avenue sponsored by the French Club and to Chinatown where he witnesses an opium den. He has several opportunities to observe policemen and the operation of the local court, although the crimes tend to be petty theft. Fadden is also a theft victim and the butt of elaborate jokes played upon him by Chicagoans. In general, Fadden's experiences evoke popular perceptions of the city in the 1890s, including having a large African-American population, numerous elevators and sky-scrapers, and a large, fast-moving public transportation network. Fadden's account catalogs day and nighttime diversions in Chicago in the 1890s (many of them on Wabash Avenue and Dearborn and Clark streets), some of which border on the scandalous and occasionally bring a police response.

877. Phillip, Quentin Morrow. *We Who Died Last Night*. St. Meinrad, Ind.: Grail, 1941. 299pp.

This religious novel explores the rewards and trials of living in accordance with Roman Catholic teachings in the secular world of twentieth-century Chicago. After thirty-year-old Anton Lippert was bankrupted by the Depression, his wife Loretta abandoned him, leaving surreptitiously and taking their children with her. Falling into despair, Lippert began living on the streets of Chicago. He developed a wide circle of acquaintants, and when one freezes to death, he resolves to regain control of his life. After obtaining a small loan from his old friend, Catherine "Kit" Eillison, he employs the money wisely and begins the process of achieving financial stability. In writing about Lippert's transformation, the author minutely details Lippert's activities, providing a good sense of life in the city during the 1930s. A crisis comes when he must acknowledge that he and his secretary Grace Smith are in love with each other. Later, he and Kit Ellison also recognize their love. Due to his Catholic morality, he must reject these opportunities for a loving relation-ship. His wife obtained a civil divorce decree, but in the eyes of the Church Lippert knows he is still married. In a bizarre coincidence, Loretta married an industrialist for whom Lippert works as a salesman. To live as a Catholic, Lippert cannot accept divorce and he must reject the prospect of a married domestic life in the future, no matter how much he loves Smith or Eillison. In addition to evoking the challenges working class people faced during the Depression, the novel touches on issues of race (one of Lippert's acquaintances is African-American and another is Mexican) and gender.

878. Phillips, David Graham. *Golden Fleece: The American Adventures of a Fortune Hunting Earl*. Illustrated by Harrison Fisher. New York: McClure, Phillips, 1903. 326pp.

This satire of upper-class culture lampoons nouveaux riches Americans marrying off their daughters to impoverished European nobility and the Anglophilia of Americans in general. When George, Lord of Surrey announces his engagement to New Yorker, Helen Dowie, Arthur, Earl of Frotheringham, is imposed upon by his family to attend the wedding and find an American heiress to replenish the family fortune. Frotheringham goes despite the fact that he is in love with Surrey's sister, Gwen. On shipboard, Frotheringham meets Mr. Barney, a Chicago merchant, and after an extended stay in New York in the first two hundred and fifty pages of the novel, Frotheringham arrives in Chicago at Barney's invitation. He observes many differences between the city and its upper-class inhabitants and New Yorker. When Frotheringham realizes that even wealthy Chica-goans work, he acknowledges that he is too accustomed to a life of leisure to ever fit in. The Bar-ney family identifies title-mad, wealthy families for him and soon Frotheringham is courting Jeanne Hooper, the daughter of meat packing magnate Amzi Hooper. Amzi angrily breaks off the engagement when Frotheringham's lawyer proposes the specific sum of money expected as a marriage settlement. Fortunately, Surrey's father-in-law dies suddenly and his American wife inherits a fortune large enough for George to settle an amount on his sister Gwen large enough for her to marry Frotheringham, who quickly returns to England. The novel is preoccupied with social customs and provides little physical description of Chicago.

879. Phillips, David Graham. *The Plum Tree*. Illustrated by E. M. Ashe. Indianapolis: Bobbs-Merrill, 1905. 389pp.

The tree of the title is filled with political plums—positions that garner financial tribute from corporations—and the novel tells the story of Harvey Sayler, who finds a way to climb in search of the biggest plums. The young Sayler is an impoverished lawyer, when political boss Bill Dominick offers to make him the party candidate for state assemblyman. In office, he votes his conscience on a bill that would exempt railroads from paying taxes and experiences Dominick's wrath. Years pass before Sayler devises a plan to ally himself with Roebuck Gas and Electric Company and use their wealth and power against Dominick to gain control of his political party and eventually win a seat a U.S. Senate seat. The novel has several sections that are set in Chicago, where important political conventions and party meetings transpire. The narrative's tight focus on political machinations means that physical setting is of minor importance.

880. Phillips, David Graham. *The Second Generation*. New York: Appleton, 1907.

Through his story of the Ranger and Whitney families, who jointly own the Ranger-Whitney flour mills, Phillips presents his views on the dangers of inherited wealth. Hiram Ranger and his wife Ellen still live near the mills outside Chicago and continue to work, Hiram on the floor of the mill and Ellen in her household. When Hiram's physician warns him of his impending death, he takes immediate steps to prevent his son Arthur, from becoming a gentleman of leisure, by ending his allowance and insisting he drop out of Harvard to work in the flour mill. In contrast to the Rangers, the Whitney family, have used their wealth to establish themselves in society. Hiram's decision affects them, since Arthur was to marry Janet Whitney. Over time, Arthur's work sensitizes him to labor issues and he ends his engagement to Janet after becoming acquainted with Madelene Schulze, whom he admires for her beauty and social engagement, since she has studied medicine and devoted herself to improving public health. Arthur's sister, Adelaide, also rejects a wealthy suitor to choose Dory Hargrave, the son of a local college president, who is committed to broadening access to higher education. When Hargrave's father reinforces Hiram Ranger's concerns about inherited wealth, he bequeaths the bulk of his fortune to Hargrave's Tecumseh Agricultural and Classical University. The money will provide scholarships to generations of poor, hardworking students, many of them the offspring of Ranger-Whitney mill workers. While the Rangers are dealing with the curse of wealth, the Whitneys blindly pursue their social ambitions. Janet Whitney marries a French nobleman and Roger Whitney devotes himself to amassing a new fortune, independent of his father, Charles Whitney. When Charles dies, in somewhat reduced circumstances, his widow, the striving Matilda Whitney, struggles to save face. Phillips' didactic concerns mean that physical setting is not important in the novel, but his tale is set in Chicago, a city with a reputation for families who overnight accumulated vast fortunes and tried to establish dynasties.

881. Pickard, William John. *A Spider Phaeton and Other Stories*. Chicago: Will Ransom, 1924. 163pp.

Several of the short stories in this volume are set in Chicago. In "A Spider Phaeton," Joseph Eliot, a young reporter, is thrilled to be invited to the Lake Forest, Illinois country house of celebrated society woman Charlotte Chesterfield Kingsley. Suspecting the invitation was a mistake, he nevertheless embraces this chance to meet prominent people, and makes elaborate preparations based on his reading English novels. He even arranges for a horse-drawn, spider phaeton, carriage and coachman. Although he makes a great impression, he feels like an imposter and when he finally asks why he was invited, he learns it was at the insistence of his Italian immigrant fiancée, Mrs. Kingsley's hairstylist, who arrives as herself, without elaborate clothing or airs. Another Chicagoan revisits scenes most deeply associated with his former fiancée, following the advice of an African-American porter on how he can get over his broken engagement. After he revisits the lakefront, and the Northwestern Railroad Station, he happens upon his former love at the River View Amusement Park. The other story with a Chicago setting, "Mr. Jeckel's Wife," is set in a Prohibition-era cabaret and includes descriptions of the costumes and entertainment, as well as the nature of the beverages served; the story is about a wife's plot to get her husband to be faithful to her. All of these short stories provide glimpses into the social life of lower-middle-class Chicagoans during the early 1920s and the class based divisions that separate them from other socio-economic groups.

882. Piercy Marge. *Going Down Fast*. New York: Trident Press, 1969. 349pp.

Set in the late 1960s on the South Side near the University of Chicago, this novel captures strife over urban renewal while evoking the counter-culture of the time period. Many of the main characters live in what is referred to as the Black Belt, the primary focus of the University's renewal project, however the people who live there are from a variety of ethnic and social backgrounds. There are Jewish schoolteachers, young professors from affluent backgrounds, and young people who make art and love and live on money begged from family and friends. These and other characters rehearse aspects of the rhetoric against urban renewal. While much of the characters' interactions center on strategizing to save their neighborhood and their homes, there are also several love stories and intense friendships. The physical background of the novel, filled with cranes, partially demolished buildings, earth-moving equipment, and excavation sites is highly evocative.

883. Pinkerton, Frank (Allan Frank). *Claude Melnotte as a Detective, and Other Stories*. Chicago: Keen, Cooke, 1875. 282pp.

The first, novella-length story in this volume of fictionalized accounts of a real private detective's cases is set in 1850s Chicago. A resident hotel with an exclusive clientele, the Clifton House, on Wabash Avenue, has been plagued by thefts. Pinkerton sends one of his employees, a Bavarian, on an undercover mission to live in the hotel. Pinkerton considers his employee ideal for the task since he can be disguised as a German prince on a tour of the United States. Readers get a good idea of the nature of expensive hotels of the time period through the descriptions of the staff and the interactions amongst the guests. The prince and hotel guests also attend several balls and other social events leading up to Christmas and the acme of the social season.

884. Pinkerton, Frank (Allan Frank). *The Detective and the Somnambulist and The Murderer and the Fortune Teller*. Chicago: Keen, Cooke, 1875. 241pp.

This volume contains two novellas; approximately one-third of the second is set in Chicago and is particularly interesting for describing a fortune-telling parlor in great detail and even including a drawing of same.

885. Pinkerton, Frank (Allan Frank). *Dyke Darrel, The Railroad Detective; or, The Crime of the Midnight Express*. Chicago: Fred C. Laird, 1886. 121pp.

During the robbery of the Central Railroad's midnight express Darrel's friend Arnold Nicholson, a messenger, is murdered and Darrell must apprehend the culprits without letting personal emotions overwhelm his judgment. He is supported by his sister Nell, who nobly accedes to the cancellation of the trip East with her brother to which she had been looking forward. Although the Darrels live in an Illinois town more than an hour from Chicago, most of Dyke's detective work is set in Chicago referred to here as "the Gotham of the West." His work is impeded by the animosity of Martin Skidway and Skidway's aunt, Madge Scarlet, who have a long-held grievance against Darrel for sending Scarlet's husband to prison, where he died. During the course of the novel Nell is abducted by outwardly respectable New Yorker, Harper Elliston, who tries to kill Darrel since the detective is too close to revealing that Elliston was one of the men involved in the train robbery. The novel includes little description of settings, devoting itself to dialogue, action, and travel (by the end of the novel many of the main characters are in New York City. Several characters use aliases and disguises in the novel and Darrel must use forensic evidence to solve the crime.

886. Pinkerton, Frank (Allan Frank). *Jim Cummings; or, the Great Adams Express Robbery*. Chicago: Laird and Lee, 1887. 152pp.

In this fictionalized account of the Great Adams Express Robbery, Fred Wittrock, alias Jim Cummings, lives in Chicago and uses a coal delivery business as a cover for his criminal activities. His nemesis, William Pinkerton of the Pinkerton Detective Agency is also located in Chicago. However, the train robbery occurs outside St. Louis, Missouri, and most of the action of the novel transpires in Kansas, including Jefferson City, Kansas City, Leavenworth, and the Indian Territory. Settings include a distillery, a cooperage, a fortune telling parlor, and a ranch. The work includes references to African-Americans and Native Americans that reflect attitudes current at the time. Chicago receives little description, but is the headquarters for both the criminals and law enforcement personnel in the novel.

887. Pinkerton, Myron. *The Stolen Will; or The Rokewood Tragedy*. Chicago: Laird and Lee 1887. 138pp.

Although this is one of a series of books detailing the exploits of Captain Turtle, "the famous Chicago detective," only a few pages, detailing Turtle's capture of a forger, are physically set in Chicago. The main action of the book is set in Virginia and West Virginia and details Turtle's search for an heiress on the run for twenty years because she was, as Turtle demonstrates, falsely accused of murdering her husband.

888. Plagemann, Bentz. *The Heart of Silence*. New York: William Morrow, 1967. 159pp.

This family drama focuses on the upper-class Carstairs and their attitude to religious fervor. The Carstairs fortune was earned in the era of grandfather Jack Carstairs, who was a land speculator. His son, Patrick, married a senator's daughter. As members of an upper-class dominated by Protestants, the Carstairs have grown accustomed to downplaying their Roman Catholicism and are puzzled and then alarmed by youngest son's Paul religiosity. However, Paul's college career, where he is a popular student and dates girls, seems normal enough until he disappears in Mexico. Fifteen years pass until, in 1950, his older brother James sets out to find Paul. After a period of little progress he encounters Nancy, a college girlfriend of Paul's, who is also seeking him. Although they finally discover Paul living as a hermit in an abandoned monastery, they cannot persuade him to return to his life in the United States and must acknowledge the depth of his faith. The novel touches on attitudes toward Roman Catholicism in upper-class Chicago society of the 1940s and 1950s.

889. Plum, Mary. *The Killing of Judge MacFarlane*. New York: Harper and Brothers 1930. 292pp.

This murder set in Depression-era Chicago touches on the social phenomenon of English expatriates in the United States driven abroad by financial conditions in England. One of these, Gerald Louis Gilfillan Gillespie, works as a banker with a modest income and, unlike his acquaintances from his days at Oxford, does not live in affluent society in Lake Forest or on the North Side, but in a small apartment just above the Loop. Just as he is bemoaning the boredom of his life, he returns to his apartment to find a corpse on the floor. The police quickly identify the body as that of gangster "Brick" Carrio; soon afterwards, Gillespie meets Judge MacFarlane, who has earned a reputation in Chicago for fighting organized crime. Gillespie also meets MacFarlane's daughter Claire and his assistant Tugs Schrader. When he is the one to discover the murdered Judge in the street, he breaks the news to the MacFarlane household and is soon taking the role of Claire's protector. A romance develops and by the end of the novel, when, with the aid of detective John Smith, the murders have been solved, Gillespie proposes to Claire. A younger son, Gillespie had left England due to bleak financial prospects, but he has just learned of his older brother's death and he and Claire will live in England, proprietors of his family's ancestral home. The Chicago setting consists of some reference to neighborhoods, and rather stereotypical presentations of policemen and gangsters.

890. Plum, Mary. *Murder at the World's Fair*. New York: Harper and Brothers, 1933. 255pp.

When Charles Graham happens upon a murder victim while visiting the 1933 Chicago World's Fair, he immediately calls for assistance from his acquaintance, Chicago private detective John Smith. By the time the murder is solved, the killing is considered justified, for the dead man had led a mob of peasants who had taken over the estate of Russian Prince Dobro Zarloff during the Russian Revolution and helped smuggle jewels out of Russia that were sold to fund the Soviet government. The novel includes descriptions of the fairgrounds, staffing, and the transformation of the city by fairgoers.

891. Pollard, Percival. *Cape of Storms, a Novel*. Chicago: Echo, 1895. 216pp.

In this romance novel, two young people leave their small hometown of Lincolnville, have experiences separately in the larger world, and return to marry and settle down. Dorothy wants to travel before getting married and leaves on an extended trip to Europe with her mother, while Lancaster relocates to Chicago to become an artist. Although Lancaster begins studio courses at the Art Institute, he quickly realizes that he will have to support himself as an illustrator. At the *Torch* newspaper, he makes a good salary as a staff artist and meets Daniel Grant Belden, a connoisseur known for his bohemian outlook and Sunday evening salon. Lancaster enjoys Belden's friends, even the worldly Mrs. Annie McCallum Stewart, the daughter of a well-known physician who has married well and is in the forefront of society. Lancaster's time fills up with gallery openings, the opera, and even horse races. After her extended stay in Europe, Dorothy insists that her family have a season in Chicago and she meets Lancaster at one of Mrs. Stewart's salons. Unfortunately, the encounter occurs just after a society gossip has revealed that she saw Dorothy and an older man on a deserted road at night. Believing herself to be compromised, when Lancaster asks Dorothy if they will marry she tells him to forget her. Lancaster takes all of his savings and leaves for Europe, where he becomes a great success as an illustrator. In due time, he meets the widowed Mrs. Stewart, who criticizes him for not pursuing Dorothy. Returning to Chicago for an exhibition of his work, he visits Dorothy, and the pair, matured by their adventures in the world, acknowledges their feelings for each other and their desire for domestic life. They marry and return to Lincolnville to establish a home. Throughout the novel, Chicago is represented as a cultural and social center of distinction, even if some participants in each realm are insincere and jaded.

892. Postgate, John T. *The Stolen Laces: An Episode in the History of Chicago Crime; From the Diary of Ex-Chief Denis Simmons, of the Chicago Police.* The Pinkerton Detective Series, vol. 28. Chicago: Laird and Lee, Publishers. 1889. 175pp.

Lawyer Henry Claypoole and his wife Alice cause great agitation in the respectable West Adams Street boarding house in which they live because Alice entertains a steady stream of teen-aged men in her room. The proprietress will not involve herself in the situation so an elderly spinster, Henrietta Goggles, takes matters into her own hands. Through her spying she overhears evidence that the youths are thieves and Henry Claypoole their fence. Before she can reveal this disturbing information, she collapses of "brain fever" and is taken to an insane asylum. Detective Denis Simmons eventually uncovers the crime ring, but when Henry Claypoole flees, another man brings him to justice. Claypoole had gained control over Alice, but she was not his wife. Her real husband, George Duryea, pursues Claypoole to Atlanta and challenges him to a duel during which he kills him. The novel provides unusually detailed accounts of boarding house life in the 1880s.

893. Postgate, John William. *The Mystery of Paul Chadwick: A Bachelor's Story.* Chicago: Laird and Lee, 1896. 248pp.

In this novel set in 1890s Chicago, a confirmed bachelor, marries a divorced woman, who is the subject of gossip and feverish speculation on the part of his friends, revealing cultural attitudes toward divorce in the time period. Lawyer Paul Chadwick is forty-three and has established himself in his profession and in political circles. While giving a lecture he espies Helen Barton, although he is not introduced. The following day she appears in his office hoping to engage him as her divorce lawyer. Realizing his immediate attraction to her, Chadwick sends her to another lawyer. Chadwick lives in an upper-middle-class boarding house operated by Mme. Dupierre where his friend Robert Mortimer, the narrator of the novel, also lives. Mortimer and Dupierre gossip about Chadwick's lovesickness and their suspicions of Helen Barton. They are very surprised when Barton moves into the boarding house and spy on her to protect their friend. At first Barton seems to be an adventuress and then Mortimer realizes that it is her brother who is the scoundrel. After Barton and Chadwick marry, Mortimer is surprised when Barton's behavior again seems inappropriate. Fortunately, when the full truth is revealed, she is found blameless again. Maintaining a good name and the fear that scoundrels can manipulate their appearance and reputation to appear to be who they are not is the theme running throughout the novel that has a complicated and melodramatic plot. Although the book does not include much physical description of Chicago, the work does convey a great deal of information about aspects of upper-class boarding house life, and social attitudes toward marriage and divorce.

894. Postgate, John William. *A Woman's Devotion; or, The Mixed Marriage.* Chicago: Rand, McNally, 1887. 270pp.

This fictionalized account of a Chicago area murder in which a farmer was killed by a woman (possibly his wife) disguises all of the principal characters and presents the locale as Montcalm (probably the former Mont Clare area of what is now Chicago). The work uses a journalistic style and is focused on conflicting testimony and the difference of opinion by two detectives—Thomas Hood and Joseph Paxton—over the perpetrator. In addition to presenting the basic facts of a well-known case, and protecting himself from a libel action, the author has little interest in physical setting and the reader gets little real sense of Chicago, except for the degree to which farmland remained quite near the city center in the late 1880s.

895. Potter, Jack. [John Hart, pseud.]. *The Heavy Day.* Springfield, Ill.: The Author, 1953. 127pp.

In this subtle indictment of corporate life, forty-five-year-old George Mazur consistently feels angry and dissatisfied, but refuses to examine the true source of his unhappiness. He lives with his wife and their two children in the Indian Trail district, close to Clybourn Station, and works as a personnel officer for a national corporation with offices in the Acme Building in the Loop. The novel presents Mazur's life in great detail, cataloging his activities over several days, including his commute, newspaper reading habits, clothing, reaction to the heat of July, and diet. After a Friday workday, Mazur has drinks and sex with Clara Winters, a secretary from his workplace, at her apartment. As an alibi, he afterwards joins his cronies at the Wunderbar where he plays poker until one o'clock in the morning. His weekend is filled with golf, social obligations, and appointments. Monday is the company picnic at a country club and Mazur makes a fool of himself, getting caught shooting craps by his boss, becoming publicly drunk, and arguing with a junior colleague over Clara Winters. However, he redeems himself at the company's weekly department head meeting. The novel ends with Mazur, self-satisfied though he may be, feeling irritable, but blaming the heat. In addition to descriptions of clothing, food, drinks, and buildings, Mazur's interactions with service providers (an African-American shoe shine boy, a barber, an optometrist, and a gas station attendant) are interesting for revealing his attitudes to social inferiors and his political leanings. As a whole the novel presents an ethnographic portrait of a Chicago type, the upper-middle-class corporate manager.

896. Potter, Margaret Horton Black. *The Fire of Spring.* Illustrated by Sydney Adamson. New York: David Appleton, 1905. 357pp.

This melodramatic romance novel is set in the greater Chicago metropolitan area in the late 1900s and skewers the manners and morality of Chicago's nouveaux riches. Mrs. Merrill is eager to marry her eighteen-year-old daughter Virginia to Charles Van Studdiford, a man of thirty-five who owns a plow factory in suburban Grangeford. Many women have vied for Studdiford and most of Chicago believed that the widowed Muriel Howard won him. So, Mrs. Merrill takes great satisfaction in her coup. Virginia, however, is an innocent. She is excited by the lavish wedding preparations, but when she settles down to life with Studdiford, she regrets her marriage to the bald millionaire. Virginia is thrilled when she becomes pregnant and looks forward to finding an outlet for her emotional life in the baby; however, the infant soon dies. When Studdiford's cousin,

Philip Atkinson, an incompetent in business, but a skilled womanizer, begins paying attention to her, she cannot resist him. Studdiford, realizing the situation, drives a carriage bearing himself and Atkinson in front of an oncoming train, thinking they have an equal chance at survival. After he survives and his cousin is killed, emotions between himself and Virginia reach a breaking point and Virginia separates from him and asks for a divorce. Although he claims to still love her and will not divorce, he allows Muriel Howard to move into his household. Eventually, a worldlier, chastened Virginia reunites with the husband to whom she is bound by law. Throughout the novel, contrasts are made between the morality of the upper and middle-classes.

897. Potter, Margaret Horton Black. *The Golden Ladder*. New York: Harper and Brothers, 1908. 434pp.

Potter's morality tale shows the corrupting influence of a money-obsessed Chicago through the stories of Kitty Clephane and John Kildare. Kildare arrives in the city in 1900 from a small-town in Wisconsin, twenty-four years old and filled with ambitions that are slowly crushed. He becomes the prey of Kitty, his landlady's daughter, who uses him to develop her skills to entrap men to gain money and power. The Clephane family is from Kentucky and the author implicates the South and the Clephane family's Irish ethnicity in presenting the evil Kitty. In addition, one of the Clephanes' boarders is a French actress who delights in helping Kitty develop her coquetry and foster her interest in the stage. After ensnaring Kildare, Kitty joins an acting troupe and moves to New York City. Kildare, who has begun playing the stock market under the guidance of a brokerage house friend, builds a fortune in order to win Kitty back. However, by the time the two meet again, Kitty has been thrown out by her New York society boyfriend and is already showing the physical marks of her dissipated life. Now a millionaire, Kildare realizes that he has risen too far in the world to marry a woman with such a bad reputation. Approximately half of this novel is set in Chicago and illustrates boarding house and office life and the restaurants, saloons, and theater parties of the lower-middle-class in the city around the turn of the twentieth century.

898. Potter, Margaret Horton Black. [Robert Dolly Williams, pseud.]. *A Social Lion*. Chicago: Donnelley and Sons, 1899. 432pp.

Chicagoan Herbert Stagmar is a respected author, a society figure, and a wealthy man. He lives in fear, however, that a past alliance will be discovered and bring him social disgrace. Surprisingly, the disgrace he fears is not about his untraditional origins. He is the son of a wealthy young man, but his father never married his much older mother, or acknowledged Herbert as his son. At the age of three Herbert's mother abandoned him to live on the streets as best he could. Fascinated with words he early taught himself to read and after working as a newsboy, became a print shop apprentice and, later, a printer. Soon he was publishing articles and stories, although the novels he wrote were rejected. Pursuing some of the enthusiasms of young men: theater and beautiful women, he became an admirer of actress Helen Howard. To his surprise, after his courtship, she chooses him over her many male admirers, and they marry. However, even as he begins selling novels and winning a national reputation, Helen becomes dissatisfied with married life and caring for their daughter Joan and leaves to become a dance hall performer, popular with the men, but a social pariah. Joan was sent to live in a convent in California and Helen and Herbert never divorced since Helen was a Catholic. Successful investments make Herbert a wealthy man and he begins a rapid ascent in society. Years later, Helen is performing in Chicago when she injures herself and will never dance again. Herbert aids her and decides to bring their daughter, Joan, now seventeen, to live in Chicago, but still wants any connection between himself and Helen kept secret. Herbert presents Joan in her debutante year as his niece. She quickly has admirers, including Malcolm van Alyne, the heir of one of the most prominent of Chicago families. However, Joan is more interested in the slightly disreputable, if well-connected, Robert Courtenay, although Courtenay is married and also a courtier to her mother. Not many months after Courtenay's wife dies, Joan breaks off her engagement with Malcolm in the hope of marrying Courtenay. Many other subplots fill this society novel. They involve commodities theft, insurance fraud, arson, and a society clergyman having an out of wedlock child with Helen. The dramatic conclusion of the novel comes after a fire nearly kills Helen and Herbert decides to acknowledge her and present her in society as his wife. He is, as he had predicted, ostracized (a matter of no concern to Helen, but of great import to Joan). Courtenay and Joan to live as affluent vagabonds outside society and Herbert and Helen leave Chicago for a new life in Europe.

899. Powers, J. F. (James Farl). *Morte D'Urban*. Garden City, N.Y.: Doubleday, 1962. 336pp.

Much of this novel is physically set in rural Minnesota to which Father Urban, a worldly Catholic priest who has achieved popularity as a public speaker is exiled by Father Boniface, his superior. A member of the Order of St. Clement, which is headquartered in Chicago, Urban had thought there was nothing standing in the way of his becoming the head of the order, especially since he has attracted two major donors, one of whom, Billy Cosgrove, has already moved the order into a lakefront building with spaces as lavish as corporate offices. Urban enjoys taking advantage of Chicago's pricey restaurants and cultural offerings and is eager for the day when he will live an even more comfortable life as the head of the order and transform it into something like a private club choosing novitiates with the right looks and personalities. From small-town Minnesota, Urban longs for his return to Chicago; however, by the time he is finally installed as head of the order the worldliness of Chicago no longer holds any appeal.

900. Powers, John R. *Do Black Patent-Leather Shoes Really Reflect Up?: A Fictionalized Memoir*. Chicago: Henry Regnery, 1975. 227pp.

In this sequel to his novel *The Last Catholic in America*, Eddy Ryan attends Chicago's Bremmer High School, a private Roman Catholic institution on the city's South Side where Ryan lives with his family. Much of the book records school life in a Catholic boys' school in the early 1960s. However, as Ryan begins dating and gets his own automobile, the narrative incorporates more description of his neighborhood. Powers depicts a homogenous social life in which everyone is white and Roman Catholic and usually tries to fit in socially. The larger city plays an insignificant role in the lives of Ryan family and classmates.

901. Powers, John R. *The Last Catholic in America: A Fictionalized Memoir*. New York: Saturday Review Press, 1973. 228pp.

In a nostalgic return to the neighborhood in which he grew up, Eddie Ryan, a middle-aged, businessman, living in New York City, who is no longer a Roman Catholic, reminisces about the South Chicago area known as Seven Holy Tombs as it existed in the 1950s when he was a schoolboy. Established in the 1920s, and surrounded by seven cemeteries, the neighborhood blossomed during the post-World War II housing shortage when returning soldiers moved there with their brides and young families to live in small houses and apartment buildings. In this predominantly Catholic neighborhood, Ryan attended parochial school and lived in a society in which the Church was the center of social life. The book describes his school life and preparation for first communion, but the narrative also presents the secular influences from friendships with neighborhood children absorbed in 1950s popular culture, the local Cub Scout troop, and playing sports. The reminiscences end as Ryan is finishing eighth grade, so the nostalgic account retains an innocent quality. One of the qualities of Seven Holy Tombs is feeling of separateness from the rest of Chicago. So, little of the novel occurs outside the neighborhood, although the reader gets a very complete sense of this particular section of the city during the 1950s.

902. Powers, John R. *The Unoriginal Sinner and the Ice-Cream God*. Chicago: Contemporary Books, 1977. 330pp.

Continuing his evocation of South Side, Irish-Catholic Chicago, Powers' protagonist in this novel, Tim Conroy, graduates from high school in the 1960s. Avoiding any risk of getting drafted to fight in Vietnam, Conroy, who earned poor grades, successfully applies to non-competitive Engrim University, a commuter school housed in an eighteen-story building that was once a hotel, on the Near North Side. Conroy's interactions with fellow students, who are facing young adult experiences (romance, marriage, parenthood, and job searches) as well as negotiating the political and cultural issues of the time period, form the bulk of the book. He also engages in philosophical exchanges with a gas station owner and mechanic in his neighborhood named Caepan whose death at the end of the novel brings closure to the narrative. As with Powers' other books, this one is written in a nostalgic tone that underlies complete descriptions of streets, businesses, and people.

903. Pratt, Mrs. Eleanor Blake Atkinson [aka Eleanor Blake]. *The Jade Green Cats*. New York: Robert M. McBride, 1931. 244pp.

In this murder mystery, a pair of Chicago journalists, John Kymmerly and Dawn Corson, covers the murder of Dr. Amos Cartwright in his West Madison Street office in the hope of getting a scoop. Corson, a society reporter, does not often write hard news, but is in love with Kymmerly and eager to find any excuse to spend time with him. Although the murder takes place in Chicago and details are provided about the operations of a 1920s office building in the Loop, much of the novel takes place in the metropolitan area. Cartwright lived in Evanston, Illinois and the author tries to derive humor from the attitudes of Chicagoans, particularly Chicago policemen towards the wealthy suburb. Part of the investigation also takes place in Desplaines, Illinois, where the police's prime suspect, Annie Thompson, raises delphiniums as a profession. Chicago scenes, in addition to the newsroom and police department, include a séance. The reporters eventually discover that radium sulfate sealed into two cat bookends is at the center of the case that involves international espionage.

904. Pratt, Mrs. Eleanor Blake Atkinson [Eleanor Blake, pseud.]. *Wherever I Choose*. New York: Putnam's Sons, 1938. 271pp.

Bergit Marison grows up on her family's farm in a lakeside resort area north of Chicago. Her intellectual curiosity and tastes inspire frustration with her family and life on the farm and her parents approve her plan to save money from babysitting the children of summer residents in order to go to business school in Chicago. Arriving in Chicago near the end of World War I, Bergit lives with an aunt and uncle in South Chicago near Washington Park. Even though she graduates near the top of her business school class, without a man's influence she can only get typing pool jobs. She resigns herself to letting Joseph C. Thorne date her in return for a job in the advertising agency where he works. Although she does not love him, she eventually marries him out of a desire for middle-class comfort. When her friends begin moving into houses she longs for a house as well and convinces Thorne to get a mortgage on a dwelling in Winnetka, off Sheridan Road. Several years pass as the Thornes go ever more deeply into debt obtaining automobiles and appliances to satisfy Bergit. As Bergit advances in the agency she begins an affair with Geoff Mallard, a commercial artist working on agency contracts, who is also the husband of a friend of hers. When she confesses to the affair of which Joe had suspected her, he at first believes that their marriage cannot continue. However, he surprises her by investing in her father's farm, and as the Depression approaches, it looks like Bergit will go back to life in the country, but this time with knowledge of the corrupting influence of city life and as the wife of a loving husband. Throughout the novel, the importance of traditional married life is touted. Published after the Depression, the novel critiques the debt-ridden households of the 1920s typical of young urbanites. The novel provides many details of office life and leisure pastimes in Chicago during the 1920s.

905. Pugh, Charles. *The Hospital Plot*. Port Washington, N.Y.: Ashley Books, 1978. 269pp.

Inspired by actual cases of forced sterilization, the "plot" of this novel is one in which a white physician schemes to create a secret, nationwide program to sterilize African-Americans. Twenty-nine-year-old African-American artist, Aaron Chapman uncovers the plot through his wife Rita, who is a nurse in the hospital where the evil Dr. McCloskey plans his campaign. The novel sketches the physical and mental racial divisions in Chicago. Through protagonist Chapman, who has attained an upper-middle-class standard of living in a Near North Side neighborhood, that is a buffer zone between white and black areas, the story also presents the psychological challenges faced by African-Americans who have broken free of the ghetto and struggle to maintain a cultural identity that embraces their origins. The novel also depicts the treatment of African-Americans in institutional settings, such as hospitals, police stations, and courtrooms.

906. Purdy, James. *Ace Chisholm and the Works*. New York: Farrar, Straus, 1967. 241pp.

This Depression-era novel is set on Chicago's South Side in the neighborhood around Fifty-fifth Street near Washington Park. Protagonist Ace Chisholm moved to the city from a small town in Michigan to become a poet. Although he has written many pages of a narrative poem, he has yet to be recognized for the effort. However, his physical appearance and personality have attracted a circle of male and female courtiers and the novel records his relationships with these friends and lovers, one of which ends tragically. The book openly describes homosexual relationships, an abortion, venereal disease, and male prostitution. African-Americans from the Deep South are a major presence in Chisholm's neighborhood.

907. Quammen, David. *To Walk the Line*. New York: Alfred A. Knopf, 1970. 236pp.

In this fictionalized memoir, Quammen presents his experiences while on a 1968 summer vacation from Yale doing volunteer work in the African-American ghetto of Knox, centered near Lexington and Pullman streets. Quammen's alter ego in the novel is John Scully, a senior-year Yale dropout. He lives in an apartment with Dan, who is struggling to be ordained a Jesuit; Bruce Tanner, who grew up in affluence in Winnetka and represents the Worker-Student Alliance; Columbia University drop-out and neo-Marxist, Frank Rapp; and counter-cultural Kooch, whose perfectly natural friendliness and empathy has earned him friends in the African-American community despite the fact that he is white. Not knowing how to promote racial harmony, Scully decides to befriend high school student Tyrone Williams, leader of a black militant group. To earn the respect of Williams and his friends Scully must "walk the line"—carry out the tests of courage, faith, and strength that they devise. Scully's experiences present the nature of life in racially divided Chicago in the 1960s.

908. Quick, Herbert. *Aladdin & Co.: A Romance of Yankee Magic.* New York: Grosset, 1904. 337pp.

Only about forty pages of this novel are set in Chicago. The main characters, James Elkins and Albert Barslow, acquainted in their boyhoods, are reunited at their unspecified political party's convention in Chicago and devise a scheme to get rich by constructing a railroad line through their hometown, Lattimore. Albert is accompanied to the convention by his sister, Alice Barslow, who meets the man she will marry later in the novel. As in other books, Chicago serves as a meeting place for people who might not otherwise come together.

909. Quick, Herbert. *The Broken Lance.* Illustrated by C. D. Williams. Indianapolis: Bobbs-Merrill, 1907. 546pp.

This early-twentieth-century novel rehearses the author's views on labor reform through the story of Christ-like Emerson Courtright. Courtright begins his career as a schoolteacher, but develops his skill as an orator and becomes a popular minister in an imaginary suburb of Chicago named Lattimore. As his commitment to social justice grows he alienates the affluent members of his congregation, especially when more and more laborers become church members. Turned out of his pulpit, he ends up in the meat packing district of Chicago supporting the laborers in their fight against unfair employment practices. Courtright eventually succumbs to illness and receives a funeral oration in a union hall. The novel describes working-class neighborhoods, as well as newspaper offices (one of Courtright's supporters is a journalist named Morgan Yeager) and the world of grand opera where one of his former students, Olive Bloodgood, is a star.

910. Quinlan, Sterling. *The Merger.* Garden City, N.Y.: Doubleday, 1958. 331pp.

This 1950s business novel traces the merger of National Dynamics Corporation and Interstate Broadcasting, who had owned and operated two rival Chicago television stations. The rivalries and shifting loyalties in the ensuing power struggle form the plot of the novel, told mostly from the perspective of program director, Les Madigan. The reader learns about programming, philosophies on news coverage, and advertising, as well as getting an insight into corporate culture of the time period. The novel is almost exclusively set in Loop offices, although some scenes are set in neighborhood restaurants and bars.

911. Randolph, Georgiana Ann [Craig Rice, pseud.]. *The Big Midget Murders.* An Inner Sanctum Mystery. New York: Simon and Schuster, 1942. 365pp.

Jake Justus and his wife Helene return in this sequel to *The Right Murder.* Jake has remodeled "The Casino" which he won in a bet from Mona McClane in a previous book and it now includes a nightclub and a theater. To complete the remodeling, Jake borrowed heavily and is hoping that his new act, Jay Otto, a "midget" comedian, will fill his establishment and help him pay off his loans. When Otto is found dead, Jake and Helene search for his killer. The novel details show business life, including the kinds of acts popular at the time, and the apartments and furnished hotels where the performers and the affluent friends of Jake and Helene live.

912. Randolph, Georgiana Ann [Craig Rice, pseud.]. *But the Doctor Died.* New York: Lancer Books, 1967. 158pp.

In a twist on Rice's typical mystery novel featuring John J. Malone, a Chicago criminal lawyer, Helene Justice refuses to cooperate with him when her husband Jake is accused of murdering a famous psychiatrist. The solution focuses on international intrigue.

913. Randolph, Georgiana Ann [Craig Rice, pseud.]. *The Corpse Steps Out*. An Inner Sanctum Mystery. New York: Simon and Schuster, 1940. 305pp.

Nelle Brown, a twenty-three-year-old radio star for whom Jake Justus has been working as press-agent and manager, has been blackmailed by ex-lover Paul March. However, when she goes to his apartment to find incriminating letters, she discovers the murdered March. Brown is the wife of Henry Gibson Gifford, who was a millionaire socialite prior to 1929. Gifford lost his mind along with his money, leaving the tough-minded Brown to use her career to support them and help him preserve his illusions of still being wealthy. When March's body disappears and the letters are still missing, Justus turns to socialite Helene Brand and renowned criminal lawyer John J. Malone as he has in the past. Two more murders are committed before the trio solves the case. Much of the action of the novel transpires in the Loop and on the Near North Side. The culture of radio broadcasting is a major presence in the novel, as is bar culture.

914. Randolph, Georgiana Ann [Craig Rice, pseud.]. *8 Faces at 3*. An Inner Sanctum Mystery. New York: Simon and Schuster, 1939. 308pp.

Beautiful, young Holly Inglehart is about to elope with popular Chicago band leader Dick Dayton when she is accused of murdering Alexandra Inglehart, the elderly aunt with whom she lived in a lakeshore mansion in Chicago suburb, Maple Grove. Fortunately, former journalist and amateur detective Jake Justus is Dayton's press agent and investigates with the assistance of Helene Brand, an Inglehart relative with whom Jake is immediately smitten. The Ingleharts are wealthy, and class hostility plays a role in Holly's prosecution by a Jewish district attorney from a less fortunate background. The novel also touches on the social status of entertainers and gender roles. The consumption of alcohol in large quantities is a prominent social activity in this account of Chicago in the late 1930s.

915. Randolph, Georgiana Ann [Craig Rice, pseud.]. *The Fourth Postman*. An Inner Sanctum Mystery. New York: Simon and Schuster, 1948. 243pp.

John J. Malone is hired to defend wealthy, but eccentric, Rodney Fairfaxx against the charge that he murdered three mailmen in front of his house, near the corner of North State Parkway and Astor Place. Each day Rodney expects a letter from his fiancée who died on the *Titanic* decades before. His nephew, Kenneth Fairfaxx, and the police believe the frustrations of his delusion have become unbearable for the old man, driving him to violence. However, Malone is able to exonerate his client. The book includes speculation on the redistribution of wealth and the philanthropic impulse, as well as touching on the impact of changing land use in Chicago, as demand for apartment houses increase.

916. Randolph, Georgiana Ann [Craig Rice, pseud.]. *Knocked for a Loop*. An Inner Sanctum Mystery. New York: Simon and Schuster, 1957. 219pp.

First lawyer John J. Malone finds the corpse of wealthy financier Leonard Estapoole in his office with enough evidence scattered around to frame him. Then, Estapoole's kidnapped stepchild Alberta Commanday is delivered to him. As jail time looms, Malone again relies on the help of his friends Helene and Jake Justus, who are television producers in this novel. The book includes descriptions of Lake Forest as well as Chicago.

917. Randolph, Georgiana Ann [Craig Rice, pseud.]. *The Lucky Stiff.* An Inner Sanctum Mystery. New York: Simon and Schuster, 1945. 251pp.

Set in 1940s Chicago, mostly in the neighborhoods around North Clark Street, this book is another in Rice's series of books featuring Jake and Helene Justus and their friend, criminal lawyer John J. Malone. The mystery in this book centers on Anna Marie St. Clair, the mistress of Big Joe Childers, a mobster. Childers is married to Eva Childers and is also having an affair with lounge singer Milly Dale. When St. Clair is found standing over Big Joe's dead body with a gun in her hand, the police assume she is the murderer. At the beginning of the novel St. Clair is on death row, only hours away from her execution. When orders for her release come through at the last moment, she learns that gangster Ike Malloy has made a deathbed confession to killing Childers. St. Clair's cool-headed reaction is to force the officials to fake her execution and release her secretly so that she can find out why she was framed. She is aided by Jake, Helene, and Malone. Much of the novel is set in nightclubs and bars. However, Eva Childers aspires to become a society woman and there are some scenes that illustrate social climbing during the time period. As in many of Rice's novels alcohol consumption plays a major role. The limited social roles available for strong, self-possessed women like St. Clair becomes an important theme.

918. Randolph, Georgiana Ann [Craig Rice, pseud.]. *My Kingdom for a Hearse.* An Inner Sanctum Mystery. New York: Simon and Schuster, 1957. 249pp.

Another in the series of novels featuring John J. Malone and Helene and Jack Justus, in this book Helene and Jack have started their own television production company to create commercials. One of their clients, a cosmetics firm owned by Hazel Swackhammer, is in trouble and the couple contacts Malone to help investigate. The mystery is who has sent body parts to the cosmetics firm. Each part is from a model whose best features were used in creating a composite image for the representative of the company, Delora Deanne. As Malone tries to solve the crime and prevent further deaths, he finds out about the cosmetics and advertising industries, and visits a number of apartment buildings of varying levels of luxury, as well as the studio of a photographer.

919. Randolph, Georgiana Ann [Craig Rice, pseud.]. *The Name is Malone: Ten Stories Complete and Unabridged.* New York: Pyramid Books, 1958. 192pp.

These previously uncollected short stories were printed in pulp magazines from the 1940s to 1950s and were published as a tribute to the author. All of the works feature Chicago criminal lawyer John J. Malone, a popular Rice creation.

920. Randolph, Georgiana Ann [Craig Rice, pseud.]. *The Right Murder.* An Inner Sanctum Mystery. New York: Simon and Schuster, 1941. 311pp.

In this sequel to Rice's *The Wrong Murder*, Jake and Helene Justus return from their Bermuda honeymoon separately after having a major disagreement that ended in Jake calling Helene (an heiress) a spoiled rich girl. She returns to Chicago to solve the murder of which Mona McClane is accused; shortly afterwards Jake shows up with the same mission and both of them want the assistance of Malone. In the meantime two more murders occur that Malone must solve. The book includes descriptions of 1930s Chicago, including a Lake Shore Drive mansion, expensive apartment buildings, "black and tan" clubs, where African-Americans and whites mingle, and other nightclubs and bars.

921. Randolph, Georgiana Ann [Craig Rice, pseud.]. *The Wrong Murder*. An Inner Sanctum Mystery. New York: Simon and Schuster, 1940. 311pp.

At the wedding reception for Jake and Helene Justus, scandalous society figure Mona McClane makes a wager with Jake that delays his honeymoon. Mona has been married five or six times—even she cannot remember—and her husbands have occasionally been aristocrats. She has also gone big game hunting, been on exploring expeditions, and made a transatlantic solo flight. Mona brings conversation to a halt when she announces that she has always wanted to commit a murder and has one planned. If Jake, who has solved two murder mysteries in the past, is able to implicate her, she will sign over to him "The Casino," a nightclub and one of the many properties she owns. Since he is marrying an heiress and is in between jobs as a public relations manager for entertainers, he fantasizes about his future income from the Casino, although he is drunk at the time. During the course of the novel, Jake, Helene, and side-kick John J. Malone solve another murder (thus the "wrong" murder of the title) that takes them all around Chicago and draws upon Jake's earlier career as a reporter. The novelist makes significant efforts to establish a convincing Chicago setting and describes street scenes, neighborhoods, domestic establishments, restaurants, and nightclubs.

922. Rapp, William Jourdan. *Poolroom*. New York: Lee Furman, 1938. 312pp.

Joe Dugan first gets involved in the world of off-track betting in Kansas City where he works for Doc Taylor. He moves to Chicago to work in the nerve center of off-track betting at the National Wire Service, the firm that supplies race information to poolroom betting parlors around the country. After Dugan starts his own successful service, Taylor tries to take advantage of their acquaintanceship to buy Dugan out. When he refuses, Taylor uses increasingly violent intimidation to get his way, including threatening notes, kidnapping, and a bomb. Taylor's most effective tool is his mistress Diane, who he presents as his niece. Dugan's co-worker Jane Clayton sees through Diane and is eventually able to free Dugan of Taylor's influence, winning his heart along the way. This romance novel is tightly focused on the world of gambling and provides a great deal of information about its structure in the 1920s, showing the influence of Chicago and the Arlington race track outside the city.

923. Raskin, Ellen. *The Westing Game*. New York: Dutton, 1978. 185pp.

This novel for young adults is set in a five-story, glass-walled apartment building called Sunset Towers on Lake Shore Drive near the Westing mansion. Sam Westing made his fortune in paper manufacturing and when he dies, sixteen residents of Sunset Towers are told they are all his cousins. Furthermore, one of them is his murderer and one of them his heir. The residents are paired into two-person teams and charged with solving the puzzle. The novel conveys a sense of urban, apartment living and touches on cultural diversity (residents include, Chinese-Americans, Greek-Americans, and Polish-Americans) while gently conveying a moral message about family relationships and honesty.

924. Rathborne, St. George Henry. *The Bachelor of the Midway*. New York: Mascot, 1894. 314pp.

This romance novel of intrigue and suspense is mostly set during the Columbian Exposition when people from all over the United States and the world traveled to Chicago. In this book, Canadians Alec Craig and Claude Wycherley save the day when a Turk seeks revenge on Samson Cereal, the appropriately named grain king of Chicago. Twenty years before, Cereal fell in love with a slave girl intended for the harem of a Turkish pasha. He successfully abducted the girl and she became his wife. In 1894 a plot is afoot by Turks to kidnap Cereal's daughter as revenge. Although the book touches on cultural attitudes toward wealthy Chicagoans and includes some description away from the fairgrounds, the main focus is on the exposition.

925. Raymond, Clifford. *The Honorable John Hale: A Comedy of American Politics*. Indianapolis: Bobbs-Merrill, 1946. 370pp.

This satire of state and local politics uses as a foil, the naive, John Hale, the son of the head of a corporate law firm whose clients are railroads and public utilities. The young Hale grew up on the North Shore and graduated from Harvard and his family and friends consider his interest in politics an eccentricity. The author uses the characters of career politician Joseph Joyliff and the governor of Illinois to represent the worst type of politicians in contrast with whom Hale's innocence seems noble. Most of the novel is set in Springfield, Illinois; however, Hale visits his parents' house fairly frequently and is courted there by the determined young reformer, Julia Warren, the daughter of a wealthy man. Warren is a settlement house worker with causes she thinks Hale can advance and she succeeds in becoming Hale's fiancée. Inspired by the matrimonial alliance, the fathers of the bride and groom form a business alliance to produce automobiles that will increase the wealth of both families exponentially. Hale holds political office intermittently, eventually entering national politics. Julia becomes disenchanted with him by the time he is in his fifties, even though he seems about to get a presidential nomination. She decides to divorce him, knowing the scandal will prevent the nomination. In addition to Julia's settlement house work, the novel discusses the growth of the city and loss of the North Shore estates to apartment buildings, but the novel's main focus is political satire and physical setting is only of importance in showing that the Warrens and Hales hew to a particular type of wealthy Chicago family.

926. Raymond, Clifford. *The Men on the Dead Man's Chest*. Indianapolis: Bobbs-Merrill, 1930. 255pp.

In the aftermath of a 1928 shooting, in a North Side speakeasy disguised as a restaurant named the Dutch Mill, police lieutenant John Stanton follows leads that connect the crime to murders committed in Wisconsin, San Francisco, and France. Stanton travels within the United States and Europe to gather information. The novel uses slang from the 1920s and is written with footnotes to give the impression of being a documented report. The crimes seem to be connected to a last will and testament, but all of the major suspects have been killed by the end of the novel and no clear explanation is forwarded to solve the puzzle. The work is only set in Chicago in part, although it is clearly meant to capture the feel of the Prohibition-era city and the tough-guy policemen battling crime.

927. Raymond, Clifford. *Our Very Best People*. Indianapolis: Bobbs-Merrill, 1931. 313pp.

This society novel satirizes the foibles of upper-class Chicagoans during the Depression. The Howelings are some of Chicago's "very best people," having never engaged in meat packing, merchandising, or politics. Instead, their money comes from lumber and manufacturing plows. The current patriarch is lawyer Hubert Trotter Howeling, a fifty-five-year-old bachelor who spends most of his time attending meetings of the corporate and charitable boards on which he sits. He sees himself as an aristocrat, although his sisters Georgiana and Dolly are more interested in real nobility—British royalty. Hubert and a number of his well-to-do friends must deal with gangster Con Amore who insists that they make donations to such groups as the Association Opposed to Militarism, the Friends of Haiti, the Mexican Harmony Alliance, the Universal Fellowship, and the World Foundation for Peace, all of which tax-exempt organizations he and his fellow gangsters control. When the situation gets too difficult, Hubert and his sisters decide to travel to England, live in a country house, and pass themselves off as descendants of notable Englishmen. The novel mentions Chicago landmarks and locales. Some of the topics of the day that get humorous treatment are raw vegetable diets, gangsters, and the federal income tax.

928. Raymond, Evelyn. *The Sun Maid: A Story of Fort Dearborn*. New York: Dutton, 1900. 326pp.

During the days leading up to the Fort Dearborn massacre of 1812, a young child, Kitty Briscoe (the "Sun Maid" of the title), wanders off and is discovered by Black Partridge. Confident that the settlers and soldiers at the fort will be killed and frustrated that they are ignoring his warning, the Indian chief decides to save the girl by taking her back to his village and presenting her to a woman whose child has died. Briscoe grows up with the Indians, but eventually returns to Fort Dearborn. The author uses Kitty's life experiences to relate the history of Chicago, including the Black Hawk War of 1832, the Asian cholera epidemic of 1849, the Civil War (in which Kitty's husband and sons are killed), and the fire of 1871, in the aftermath of which Kitty dies.

929. Rayne, Martha Louise. *Against Fate. A True Story*. Chicago: Keen, Cooke, 1876. 251pp.

This religious novel includes sermonizing interludes in which the evils of the city for women are detailed. Jennie Armstrong, from a small town outside Chicago, came upon Ross Farnham after a horse had thrown him near her family's farm. After she aids him, he arranges for his cousin Mrs. Monroe to give Jennie a maid's position. The Armstrongs are very poor, and Jennie hopes to send them money. She leaves for the city with school friends, Lucia Winne and Eva Bartlett. Lucia, a schoolteacher, hopes to get a better job in the city and Eva, wants to experience the city before settling down. When the three reach Chicago they are met by Lucia's brother, Albert, a post office employee who orientates them. With their naïveté as an excuse, the author introduces additional characters from whom the country girls get detailed descriptions of the city. Eva is hired as a model in a dry goods store, and Lucia begins work as a substitute teacher. Jennie discovers that Mrs. Monroe is a proponent of female emancipation and heavily involved in committee and volunteer work. She has refused to bear her husband children and the relationship between her and Jennie is cast in a sinister light by reference to Mrs. Monroe's "morbid desire for a protégé," and the fact that Jennie's room adjoins Mrs. Monroe's bedroom. Lucia, hearing of Jennie's new love for beautiful things, including gifts from Ross, accuses Jennie of becoming a materialist, loving things of the flesh above spiritual pleasures; and Albert warns her that Ross is a womanizer. The gifts from Ross have led Mrs. Armstrong to believe that the two are engaged and when her former beau, Reuben, hears of the situation he decides to travel to Chicago and discover Ross' intentions. When Mrs. Monroe tires of Jennie and petulantly turns her out, Ross is lying in wait nearby. He takes Jennie in and she publicly becomes "Mrs. Farnham," though no wedding transpires. When her father visits Chicago, he discovers the truth, returns home, and shoots himself, after telling Mrs. Armstrong that Jennie is lost to them. When Reuben arrives in the city, he overhears Ross entertaining young men at his club by declaring he will never marry and sharing secrets for corrupting young girls. Enraged Reuben shoots Ross on the spot then shoots himself, though not fatally. Later, when Mrs. Armstrong travels to the city to search for Jennie, she becomes deranged by the crowds and anonymous streets. When she finally discovers Jennie, the girl repents her evil life and her mother regains enough sanity to forgive her with her dying breath. Reuben also forgives Jennie, but the author uses her former friends, Lucia and Eva, to make it clear that a fallen woman can never simply repent and take up a new life. Only Jennie's death at the end of the novel redeems her. Even though the novel is almost wholly set in Chicago, there is little physical description of the city; however as a symbol for all that is evil about urban life, the city plays a major role.

930. Rayner, William. *Seth & Belle & Mr. Quarles and Me: The Bloody Affray at Lakeside Drive.* New York: Simon and Schuster, 1972. 157pp.

Some of the most consequential scenes of this novel are set in Chicago, although most of the book is set in the Far West, particularly Helena, Montana, where Noah "Missouri" Flynn first meets and begins working for Mr. Quarles who owns a saloon and hotel. Quarles later moves to Chicago to establish himself in society by posing as an art connoisseur, commissioning art works that he displays in his Lake Shore Drive mansion. To thrill his society friends with a frontiersman, he invites Flynn to Chicago and secretly invites Flynn's sworn enemy. A shooting occurs and the gullible Flynn is charged with a murder he did not commit. The city is portrayed as a place where confidence men are able to manipulate the details of their past and attain respectability.

931. Rea, M. P. (Margaret Paine). *Compare These Dead!* Garden City, N.Y.: Crime Club / Doubleday, Doran, 1941. 271pp.

This 1940s murder mystery presents aspects of work culture for women engaged in department store retail and the office culture of comparison shoppers. Terry Cavender works as a comparison shopper for the Dunbarton, MacGregor department store. The head of the operation is Brant Anders, an unpleasant man who led Terry's friend Lois Walden on, before marrying another woman. Anders was also a partner with Terry's father in a jewelry business; after a jewel robbery, the firm failed and her father committed suicide. Anders falls to his death through a stained-glass, department store skylight, and an investigation shows he was poisoned before the fall. Lois Walden is accused of the crime, but Cavender helps Police Lieutenant Powledge find the real culprit. Bigamy and blackmail turn out to be at the center of the case. Readers learn a great deal about Chicago department stores and smaller retail establishments during the 1940s.

932. Rea, M. P. (Margaret Paine). *A Curtain for Crime.* New York: Crime Club / Doubleday, Doran, 1941. 269pp.

This murder mystery is set in a large Chicago department store. Linda Thorne, a clerk in the draperies and curtains department, finds the murdered corpse of Carl Brewer, a recent and unpopular hire for a management position, under a pile of curtains. With her knowledge of department store operations and personnel she soon becomes an aid to Police Lieutenant Powledge in his murder investigation. Most of the novel is set inside the store, but Linda shares an apartment with one of her co-workers and there are some accounts of their domestic life and leisure activities, including dates with young men.

933. Rea M. P. (Margaret Paine). *Death of an Angel.* Garden City, N.Y.: Crime Club / Doubleday, Doran, 1943. 266pp.

Set during the Christmas sales season in Chicago's Dunbarton, MacGregor department store, this novel describes retail work culture and seasonal activities of the 1940s. After the death of her father leaves her alone in the small town where she grew up, Noel Thackeray decides to visit her sister Mimi in Chicago and work during the holiday rush season. She gets a job in the toy department of the large Dunbarton, MacGregor store, where Mimi is also working temporarily singing

Christmas carols dressed as an angel. Mimi has had some success getting parts in radio dramas and singing in nightclubs, but Noel is still surprised that her sister lives in an elegantly furnished apartment on Dalton Place in the Near North Side, since this elegance is not in keeping with her income. When Mimi is found poisoned, Chicago Police Lieutenant Powledge has numerous suspects, including a young German woman, Orphah Beeks, whose boyfriend, Judson Carewe, had been stolen by Mimi. Judson, himself is a suspect since he realized he had been two-timed by Mimi. Other men connected to Mimi also have motives. Finally, there is Judson Carewe's sister who resented the money he was giving Mimi (including money he had stolen from his workplace). Eager to discover who murdered her sister, Noel gathers information for Powledge through her department store contacts. In the course of the novel, a number of working-class apartments are described, as well as radio broadcasting offices; however, the main physical setting is the Dunbarton, MacGregor department store. The novel touches on dating relationships of the time period.

934. Read, Opie. *The Bandit's Sweetheart*. Chicago: Thompson and Thomas, 1907. 225pp.

Most of these short stories have unspecified settings in the countryside, in towns, and villages. At least two, however, are set in Chicago. In "Mr. Dog," a man known for his hard-hearted business dealings, riding by a tenement window, in an elevated train car on his way to work, sees a boy each morning. In his imagination he begins to make the boy part of his life and when he does not see the face for several days he investigates and finds that the boy has fallen ill. He then persuades the boy and his mother to move and live in the comfort of his country estate. In "Princess Yepti," a museum visitor becomes intrigued by a man who always seems to be in deep contemplation of one of the mummies. From a museum attendant, he discovers that the man, Ham Bottsford, is so rapt in his attentions that he has to be shaken out of his entranced vigil at closing time each day. Upon questioning the man, the visitor learns that Bottsford was in love with Yepti in an earlier life and is pining for her to return to him. Several months later, the visitor sees a wedding announcement for Bottsford and attends the ceremony to be introduced to the new wife, whom Bottsford believes is Yepti reincarnated. In "Economical," Mrs. Tolliver, a wealthy woman, wants her son John to marry, but also wants him to choose well. Every potential bride is scrutinized with regard to her spending habits. So, when John finds a woman to his liking, he makes certain she passes his mother's test by coaching her ahead of time. Although there are only slight physical descriptions of Chicago in the stories, the focus on establishing a domestic life in the harsh urban setting is a common theme.

935. Read, Opie. *The Captain's Romance, or Tales of the Backwoods*. Chicago: Tennyson Neely, 1896. 319pp.

A few works in this collection of short stories and novellas are set in Chicago. In "The History of the Watch," a man becomes curious about the previous owner of a rare watch with which he has been presented. His quest takes him from address to address in Chicago; to a harness maker, a boarding house manager, a furniture dealer, and a pawn broker before his quest ends when he finds the murderer who had stolen the watch a year before. In "A Young Man's Advice," a reader of *Household Comfort* confronts the editor of the weekly newspaper, telling him that he had become convinced by a column in the paper to marry since it would be cheaper than living alone. He relates his unpleasant experiences before pummeling the editor. "The Professor," "Old Brothers," and "A Chicago Man" are character sketches. The Professor plays piano at a bar in exchange for drinks until a swinging bridge crushes his hand, then he dances for drinks, until a streetcar smashes his foot. With no skills left he is bounced from the bar only to return one cold day to briefly warm up and dies. "Old Brothers" tells the story of an elderly African-American man who had made his way from slavery in the South to freedom in Chicago, only to live on the streets. A kind-hearted man, who helped everyone out, he lost his eyesight saving a handicapped person from a burning tenement. The Chicagoan in "A Chicago Man," Cyrus W. Higglegag, a traveling salesman, employs his skills in a small town and wins a bride. Although the characters and plots are disparate, some of Chicago's popular associations are echoed in the tales (e.g., crime, newspaper columns, swing bridges over the Chicago River, and salesmanship).

936. Read, Opie. *The Colossus*. Chicago: Laird and Lee 1893. 254pp.

In this novel, Chicago represents the epitome of late-nineteenth-century materialism and class stratification as symbolized by the "The Colossus" a huge department store, with its minutely classed workforce and wealth of consumer goods. The protagonist, Henry DeGolyer, was born in New Orleans, the son of an alcoholic painter. His mother died when he was still an infant, so he was raised in an orphanage. He became a newspaperman, spent some time in Costa Rica on assignment, and met Henry Sawyer and his mine-owning uncle. When the uncle dies, Sawyer discovers a document proving that he is the son of a famous Chicago businessman and he excitedly invites DeGolyer to accompany him to Chicago. During the trip from Costa Rica, Sawyer becomes ill, and thinking he is about to die, gets DeGolyer to exchange identities with him. When DeGolyer arrives in Chicago, he discovers that his "father" is George Witherspoon, the owner of "The Colossus." As a newcomer to Chicago, DeGolyer is taken on tours and presented to society. When Witherspoon reveals that DeGolyer is to be trained and eventually take his place in the department store, DeGolyer convinces Witherspoon that his real calling is as a journalist. DeGolyer wanted to return to being a reporter, but Witherspoon buys a newspaper and makes him the publisher and editor. Then, a series of misfortunes draw him away from journalism and to The Colossus, and, as Witherspoon's rheumatism worsens, DeGolyer begins managing the store and sells his newspaper. Visiting New Orleans on a business trip he begins to resign himself to a life of materialism, like Witherspoon's, when he hears someone pointing out a wretched creature as Henry DeGolyer, a former journalist. He discovers that Henry Sawyer had not actually died but had experienced a brain-damaging coma. DeGolyer takes Sawyer to Chicago for treatment and when he is recovered presents him to the Witherspoons. Although the Witherspoons would have DeGolyer continue to live with them or accept a significant reward, he takes nothing and marries Miss Drury, the woman reporter he loves, and whom the Witherspoons found inappropriate. The couple moves to rural Virginia to escape the materialism and class-based society of Chicago.

937. Read, Opie. *Confessions of a Marguerite*. Chicago: Rand, McNally, 1903. 164pp.

Written as first-person narration, in this work, a young woman moves to Chicago to become an artist and faces disillusionment. Born in Fox River, Wisconsin and orphaned at an early age, Marguerite was raised by her uncle who provided for her schooling through a bequest, but when he died while she was still young, left no other resources. So, Marguerite moved to Chicago to become an artist. She is immediately disappointed to find the city filled with second-rate art practitioners from small towns across the Midwest. Her only solace is Silvia who lives in the same building of studio apartments in which she resides on Wabash Avenue. Silvia becomes her guide to the city and the art world, but Marguerite is often near starvation and eviction, particularly once Silvia leaves town to tour as an actress. In desperation, Marguerite tries acting, but she receives inappropriate attention from men that she finds disturbing. Finally, an elderly gentleman employs her to read to him as he works on a philosophy book on "human error." His payments of ten dollars a week enable Marguerite to move into a boarding house, where she meets impoverished bookkeepers, dentists, dramatists, and poets. When the old man dies, she gets the leading part in a boarding house dramatist's play, and tours in small towns, until she gets a letter from Silvia asking Marguerite to come be with her as she lies dying in Chicago. After comforting Silvia in her final days, Marguerite returns to Wisconsin to become a schoolteacher and marry a man of the fields and woods. Her rejection of Chicago is a judgment on the harshness of the life to be found there and the city is characterized as a place which punishes young people with poverty and death.

938. Read, Opie. *Judge Elbridge*. Chicago: Rand, McNally, 1899. 295pp.

Although this novel is preoccupied with morality, Chicago settings and social life are important elements. In the late-nineteenth-century, Judge Elbridge has begun to resign from his commitments in the larger world and settle into domestic life in a large house he constructed on Indiana Avenue. In addition to his wife, the household includes his dependent brother William and three young people in their twenties: his son Howard, and Florence and George Bodney, children of a deceased law partner. Through most of the novel the household is in moral crisis. The judge seems to be going mad and turns against his son, effectively driving him out of the house and forbidding him to marry Florence, a match of which he had earlier approved. George is secretly at fault for causing the discord. He had been stealing money from the Judge's safe in order to feed his gambling addiction. When he realized that the Judge had discovered money was missing, he enlisted his gambling buddy, Goyle, a man with no morals, to aid him. Goyle devised a plot to disguise himself as Howard and appear to steal money from the Judge's safe while George and the Judge watched, drawn to the scene by a pretense. The Judge's world was turned upside down as he exiled his beloved son. He falls into despair, until the truth is revealed near the end of the novel. Settings include gambling houses, saloons, law offices, and the Judge's household. The novel touches on the issues of mental health and family relationships.

939. Read, Opie. *The New Mr. Howarson*. Chicago: Reilly and Britton, 1914. 460pp.

When Professor Hudsic, the leader of the anarchist group the Agents of Justice, decides to assassinate Calvin Whateley, a millionaire capitalist who owns mines and street railways, he realizes that the deed must be committed by a disenchanted, native-born American, not by one of the naturalized immigrants who compose the membership of the Agents. He chooses Mr. Howarson and much of Read's novel presents the aspects of Howarson's life that led to his disenchantment with American capitalism. Read also presents Whateley's story and the rhetoric of the anarchists. In doing so, Read illustrates life in the early twentieth century for Chicago men from very different social classes. Through the course of the novel the anarchists, represented by Howarson and his girlfriend, and the capitalists, represented by Whateley and his daughter, achieve new understandings of the meaning of wealth and poverty. In the end, Read's work becomes a defense of the American capitalist system by focusing on the power of money to do good in the world.

940. Reed, Myrtle. *The Shadow of Victory: A Romance of Fort Dearborn*. New York: Grosset and Dunlap, 1903. 413pp.

This work of historical fiction closely follows earlier novels recounting the Fort Dearborn massacre during the War of 1812, with the exception of the introduction of Beatrice, a niece of John Mackenzie, who becomes the focus of romantic designs on the part of most of the unattached men in the fort. The novel is also distinctive in providing a more believable characterization of Black Partridge and showing more sensitivity to interpreting the relationship between Native

Americans and European settlers, even though the character of Chandonnais, a "half-breed" is introduced to show the dangers of too much intimacy. The author's method of fictionalization often leads her to change the names of historical personages, leading to some confusion for readers.

941. Reilly, Patricia and Harold N. Swanson [Anna Bell Ward, pseud.]. *Big Business Girl: By One of Them*. Chicago: Burt, 1930. 278pp.

This book is a novelization of a motion picture screenplay with the same name and by the same authors. The 1931 Warner Brothers Picture stared Loretta Young in the role of Claire McIntyre. The work explores what happens when McIntyre, a college-educated woman, decides not to marry immediately, but to enter the business world. She has great difficulty finding a job (no one wants to hire a college girl who is expected to be preoccupied with continuing her college social life and marrying). McIntyre finally gets work as a claims adjuster at R. J. Clayton, a large dry cleaning plant. However, after working for only a few months, she realizes that, as a woman, she will never be able to earn a high enough wage. Her boyfriend, Johnny Goodman, has experiences that are quite different. After discovering how fun it is to play in a jazz band, he drops out of college and takes his band to Paris. When he returns to Chicago, he is offended to see Claire socializing with her boss and proposes marriage. Claire wants to continue working and pay Goodman's expenses to finish college and when he refuses, she rejects his proposal and the two have a tiff. Soon afterwards, Claire is suddenly promoted at work and then a rival firm hires her away at an even higher salary. Despite Johnny's reservations about having a wife keeping him, by the end of the novel it looks as though they will marry. In addition to open discussions of gender equality and the role of women in the business world, the novel discusses the impact of labor unions and their connections to organized crime syndicates. Although Claire works hard, she enjoys her evenings and the novel includes descriptions of lakefront restaurants and nightclubs.

942. Renken, Aleda. *The Two Christmases*. St. Louis, Mo.: Concordia, 1974. 96pp.

In this children's book, the Haley children are excited to be spending Christmas with their grandparents in Iowa, all except for stepbrother Sam, who will travel to Chicago to be with his father, who is a professional entertainer. Being in the city without any other children holds no appeal for him compared with the prospect of sledding with favorite uncles and helping to cut down a Christmas tree. However, once he gets to Chicago, Sam does begin to enjoy urban pleasures. He stays in an expensive hotel room, gets to order room service, buys clothes, and has a haircut at the Marshall Fields store. However, things begin to go wrong when a con man picks his pocket. Later, when some boys his age threaten him, he defends himself, but after hearing about the trouble his father cancels his engagements to spend time with him. Although the novel articulates some urban pleasures, they seem unlikely to attract a young boy and the reader is left with the more convincing image of Chicago as a dangerous place in the 1970s.

943. Rhodes, James A. and Dean Jauchius. *The Trial of Mary Todd Lincoln*. Indianapolis: Bobbs-Merrill, 1959. 187pp.

In this work of historical fiction the authors imagine what would have happened had a more forceful defense lawyer been retained in Mary Todd Lincoln's insanity trial. Although primarily a courtroom drama, the book does give some account of Robert Lincoln, a promising young Chicago lawyer, his household, and his social embarrassment over his mother's erratic public behavior and her tendency to spend large amounts of money in shops on lavish dresses.

944. Richardson, George Tilton and Dwight Quint Wilder [Charles Eustace, joint pseud.]. *Letters from a Son to His Self-Made Father: Being the Replies to Letters from a Self-Made Merchant to his Son.* Illustrated by Fred Kulz. Boston: New Hampshire Publishing Corporation, 1903. 289pp.

   In these responses to his father's letters, Pierrepont Graham, the son of a Chicago pork-packer who made his fortune the hard way, describes his frivolous life at Harvard and (once his father is convinced that education has no value for his son) his early days as a laborer, and then a traveling salesman, for his father's company.

945. Richardson, George Tilton and Dwight Quint Wilder [Charles Eustace Merriman, joint pseud.]. *A Self-Made Man's Wife, Her Letters to Her Son: Being the Woman's View of Certain Famous Correspondence.* Illustrated by F. T. Richards. New York: Putnam's Sons, Knickerbocker Press, 1905. 249pp.

   One of the series of epistolary works featuring a Chicago meat packer and his family, this volume includes sixteen letters written by the meat packer's wife. Now that her son Pierrepont has married his mother begins writing him during his honeymoon and through the first year of his marriage offering advice about everything from how to treat his wife to household economics. She includes occasional jibes against her own husband. The work provides a sense of current attitudes about marriage and domestic life.

946. Richardson, John. *Wau-nan-gee; or, The Massacre at Chicago: A Romance of the American Revolution.* New York: Long and Brother, 1852. 126pp. Republished as *Hardscrabble; or, The Fall of Chicago a Tale of Indian Warfare.* New York: de Witt, 1856. 99pp.

   The action of this novel is mostly set in and around Fort Dearborn during the War of 1812. Although the author attests to the historical accuracy of the text, he has introduced a fictitious character, Maria (Heywood) Ronayne, the wife of a fort ensign, who is abducted by Wau-nan-gee, an act that precipitates armed conflict. However, it turns out that Maria went with Wau-nan-gee of her own free will; she had been great friends with the young Indian, and was saddened that he disappeared after she married. Definitive evidence that the two were romantically involved is found in a letter Maria left for a woman friend. Then, Wau-nan-gee appears at the fort and says he has taken Maria to a safe place, not abducted her, and will do what he can to protect the other settlers from the hostile Indians surrounding the fort. When everyone sets out from the fort, however, they are attacked and Ensign Ronayne is among those killed. Maria curses Wau-nan-gee and all Indians, but must continue to rely upon his protection as the novel ends. Although one of many accounts of events at Fort Dearborn, this book was written by a man who was a fifteen-year-old soldier in the War of 1812.

947. Richardson, Merrick Abner. *Chicago's Black Sheep and Bonny McClear's Friends.* Chicago: Giles E. Miller, 1898. 306pp.

   Presented as a reform novel, this work often seems to be mostly about titillation and presents the Chicago Police Department one-dimensionally, as entirely inept and injurious to the process of redeeming criminals. The reclaimed Bonny McClear, alias Dot Steel, alias Miss Peters, is working as a live-in nurse with a Prairie Avenue family until the police arrive to accuse her of robbery and reveal her past work as a prostitute. She is jailed only briefly before the robbery charge is dismissed, but McClear's life as a reformed woman has been destroyed. McClear vows revenge against Police Officer Benham and disappears. For some reason, the police are unsettled by her threat and follow leads to the most disreputable parts of the city to ferret her out. The bulk of the novel describe brothels, dive bars, and disreputable theaters, presenting a catalog of crime and vice in Chicago in the 1890s.

948. Richberg, Donald Randall. *In the Dark*. Chicago: Forbes, 1912. 308pp.

In this romantic suspense novel, Gilbert Winston's life is transformed when he gets involved in the plight of a beautiful woman in distress named Gwen Fenton who is in financial difficulties and being pursued by sinister Jim Curlew. Because Fenton needs protection, Winston allows her to sleep in the room of his sister Dora, who is away on the East Coast. When Dora returns unexpectedly, Winston is put in the uncomfortable position of explaining his actions, when he knows so little about Fenton. Soon the rest of his family, including his married sister Edith and her husband, banker George Carfax, are trying to get him to see the dangers of his situation. The matter is speedily resolved, although with too much publicity from the perspective of the staid Winston, when Curlew is captured by the U.S. Secret Service for purchasing rifles, suspected to be intended for Costa Rican revolutionaries. Winston lives in a house in Hyde Park, Fenton resides in a boarding house near Indiana Avenue and Twentieth Street, and scenes of the novel are set at a German beer garden named Winkler's, a football game, and inside the offices of a banker. The novel revolves around ideas of reputation and social respectability, as well as concealed identities.

949. Richberg, Donald Randall. *A Man of Purpose*. New York: Thomas Y. Crowell, 1922. 329pp.

Written in the form of a diary, this novel covers the years 1900 to 1920 in Rodney Merrill's life as he progresses from a twenty-four-year-old Chicago lawyer to an Illinois gubernatorial candidate, and a government official during World War I. However, Merrill's account is concerned with inner growth, not public achievement. He is most concerned with correct relationships with women and in one chapter claims that non-sexual relationships with women can garner the energy for a man that he needs to fully engage in life's struggle. His relationship with Mary, the woman he marries, remains chaste, despite matrimony, and he considers her the perfect wife. At the same time he has a friendship with Irma, who openly admits she has married the wrong man. Her marriage is filled with emotion that Merrill realizes is best avoided. In the end, Merrill destroys his career as a corporate lawyer by vaunting the rights of laborers in a mining strike. He is jailed by a judge for contempt for trying to voice the mine workers plight and the novel ends suddenly on the day before his release, just after he has learned that Irma has left her husband and declared her love for him. The book is mostly concerned with Merrill's inner life and his belief that his awareness of God's presence has grown through the influence of the women in his life. The novel reveals a great deal about social attitudes toward women during the time period.

950. Richberg, Donald Randall. *The Shadow Men*. Chicago: Forbes, 1911. 312pp.

This novel concerning business ethics is mostly set in Chicago during the early 1900s and takes the form of attorney Jarvis Whitfield telling the story of John Quincey Byford, a man who after unwittingly being the scapegoat for the misrepresentations of people in authority, eventually decides to act as a willing scapegoat and follow his destiny. Although social events, mostly private dinner parties, are described, the novel is preoccupied with recording the complexities of numerous business world frauds. The novel takes the position that the decision-makers and company owners are never held accountable for the crimes they commit. Instead, lower-level functionaries like Byford are tried and imprisoned.

951. Richberg, Eloise O. Randall. *Bunker Hill to Chicago*. Chicago: Dibble, 1893. 151pp.

This book is unusual in a time period when so many novels were written about newly wealthy families moving to the city to advance their social status. Protagonist John Sawyer remains committed to his values, even as his inventions make him a wealthy man, raising him from rural, Pennsylvania blacksmith to Chicago entrepreneur. Sawyer moves his family to Chicago to be closer to the market for a new series of inventions and satisfy his daughters' wish for a livelier social environment. Initially, all of his girls—Drexella, Jane, Laura, and Minnie—want to take advantage of his new wealth to leap into upper-middle-class society. However, he restrains them, buying a frame house on Aberdeen Street, instead of a stone mansion on Michigan Avenue and insisting that his daughters, not servants, maintain the house. He also announces that he will only support them for five years, long enough for them to develop their own means of support. Each daughter chooses a different field of study (medicine, music, dressmaking, and teaching), masters her field, and begins socializing with potential husbands. At the end of five years, each has become engrossed in her profession. Although, given the era in which the novel was written, the novel's assumption that the girls will have careers is surprising, no debate is aired over this contravention of the traditional view that a woman's place is in the home. There is, however, much debate about the qualities of an appropriate husband, and social rank does not figure in the evaluation. In this novel, Chicago is not presented as a place to win a fortune or engage in empty displays of wealth, but as a place that offers opportunities for personal growth through education and social interaction with people from diverse backgrounds.

952. Richert, William. *Aren't You Even Gonna Kiss Me Good-by?* New York: David McKay, 1966. 247pp.

In this novel set in affluent Weston, Illinois, a suburb of Chicago, eighteen-year-old Jimmy Reardon tries to cover a financial shortfall by utilizing his biggest talent—having sexual intercourse. A few months before, he had sex with a sixteen-year-old who looked and subsequently behaved much older. Some weeks after their encounter she called to say she had to get married or have an abortion at the cost of one hundred and ten dollars. Reardon sent the money out of his college fund only to learn that the same operation had also been financed by at least two other men. His father discovered the misappropriation and has threatened to cut off Reardon's allowance unless he repays the money within the next twenty four hours. After exploring every legitimate option of which he can think, Reardon is left with a sixty dollar gap and decides to have sex with a series of women in exchange for cash contributions. What follows is a boozy night spent in and out of bars on the Near North Side with dubious clientele, including pimps, prostitutes, and gay men. The novel presents one interpretation of sexual mores among affluent Chicagoans in the mid-1960s.

953. Rickett, Frances. *An Affair of Doctors*. New York: Arbor House, 1975. 316pp.

This romance novel is set in a Chicago area hospital and focuses on the sexual relationships of physicians. Perry Whittier has been appointed head of medicine at Claremont Community Hospital that is located in a Chicago suburb. He chooses Dr. Stevenson as his chief resident, not realizing Stevenson and his own wife, Susan, are having an affair. He does find out that their babysitter, Caroline Coburn, daughter of the head of surgery, is secretly living with a hospital intern and must decide what to do about it. Other secrets with which he has to deal include the special room one physician has equipped to have sex with female patients, a drug kick back scam, and a contaminated shipment of birth control pills. How Whittier is able to deal with these situations and hold onto his position forms the plot of the novel, most of which is set inside hospitals, although Chicago locations are referenced.

954. Riesenberg, Felix. *P.A.L.: A Novel of the American Scene*. New York: Robert M. McBride, 1925. 340pp

Written during the booming 1920s when businessmen were the heroes of American society, the novel satirizes business culture. The book is written in the form of a memoir about the narrator's work with P. A. L. Tangerman, a nationally famous businessman. Tangerman is a success at self-promotion and public relations, using credit to build huge corporations that have few assets or profits. At the height of his success he moves to Chicago where he sets up a series of headquarters and offices for his dubious products. Chicago locales are mentioned to establish place, but the book is devoted to describing Tangerman's personality and the operation of his businesses. Tangerman uses a mail order fulfillment house, printing operations, and mass-mail facilities that parallel the large-scale operations of actual companies located in the city at the time. When his empire, based paper on credit, collapses, Tangerman is murdered in Chicago. The novel includes several extended passages that poetically encapsulate the cultural significance of Chicago.

955. Riesenberg, Felix. *Red Horses*. New York: Robert M. McBride, 1928. 336pp.

This first-person narrative ostensibly relates the biography of famed businessman P. A. L. Tangerman from the perspective of his only confidante, Dimitri Marakoff, a Russian civil engineer, who in a case of mistaken identity he simply accepts, is given the name D. Markham and an English nationality. The book is, in fact, a satirical indictment of the United States of the 1920s. Tangerman, hires Markham in Seattle as his adjutant because he is a well-mannered, an asset in America, where people are unmannerly. Tangerman's first ventures are cures for basic human failures (constipation, baldness, and bad breath). As he progresses, he offers the secrets of success and happiness through the Mount Healey Institute, which grants degrees, through the doctorate, by mail order. None of what Tangerman sells has substance, for him the best merchandise consists of the perfect label. Markham describes the energy and enthusiasm that flows from Tangerman, while detailing a complex corporate structure funded by worthless stock issues backed by greedy bankers who accept news stories about Tangerman as collateral. When Tangerman moves his operations to Chicago they include his educational institute, publishing house (classics edited to pamphlet length), and health supplement business. Markham regards the Loop as the literal heart of the country with roads bringing essential raw materials into the city and carrying all manner of adulterated, processed, and repackaged products out. Descriptions of Chicago highlight physical squalor unseen by residents who see only the manipulated fancies in Tangerman's publications. Each time Tangerman faces exposure, he is saved by newspaper stories that lend him credibility by simply describing his great wealth. When a jealous woman shoots him to death, auditors find that even his wealth was an illusion, since he literally has no assets. Markham's experiences with Tangerman inspire a desire for tangibles. He gains citizenship under his real name and partners up with an architect to use his civil engineer degree to construct useful buildings. He also moves far away from the rising and falling buildings of Chicago, to live with a view of mountains, reminders of the true, immobile, foundations of the earth.

956. River, W. L. (Walter, Leslie). *Death of a Young Man*. New York: Simon and Schuster, 1927. 206pp.

Set in Hyde Park in the 1920s, this fictional diary contains David Bloch's account of his thoughts and activities in the months following his physician's diagnosis that Bloch has only one year to live. His increasing preoccupation with death finally drives him to suicide. During the course of the book he continues to interact with a series of friends, including his girlfriend Polly Carr who lives near Fifty-eighth and Kimbark. Bloch lives just across from the Midway near the University of Chicago. One of his friends, Fuqua is studying psychology and monitors Bloch's sanity. Fuqua is the son of an Italian-American and takes Bloch to dinner at his mother's house, presenting Bloch with the spectacle of a working-class household of immigrants. In the company of Fuqua and one of his professors, Bloch attends a performance by King Oliver's jazz band at the Lincoln Gardens on Thirty-fifth Street. With Polly, he goes to Edgewater Beach. A discussion of "black and tan" clubs and the propriety of white women visiting them touches on issues of racism, while Bloch's identity as the offspring of a Catholic and Jew and Fuqua's Italian heritage touch on issues of ethnicity and religion. Although told from the perspective of Bloch's feverish mental state, the book does give some sense of life among students and professors in Hyde Park in the 1920s.

957. Roberts, Edith. *The Divorce of Marcia Moore*. Garden City, N.Y.: Doubleday, 1948. 249pp.

In this novel about the human cost of divorce, Marcia Moore complies when her husband Jeff requests a divorce, even though she still loves him and is filled with anxiety over the economic repercussions for herself and two-year-old child, Stevie. Despite her cooperativeness, after the divorce decree, Jeff fails to pay child support. Marcia refuses to pursue the matter and gives up her apartment, sending Stevie to live with her parents. She moves into a YWCA after getting a clerical position. The novel records the personal slights Marcia experiences as a divorced woman and the advice she gets from other divorcees. After working and saving money, Marcia is eventually able to rent a furnished apartment and have Stevie live with her, but the situation is unfair because of the smallness of the apartment and the scant time she has to spend with the child. A friendship develops between Marcia and Jeff's friend Terry Harkness, who was his lawyer in the divorce proceedings. Eventually, they fall in love and Marcia accepts Terry's marriage proposal. Set in a post-World War II Chicago, the book does a good job of setting out the practical aspects of a woman living on her own with a child in the time period. Although most of the narrative is occupied by Marcia's reflections and her conversations with other women, the book does reference Chicago places and businesses.

958. Roberts, Edith. *Little Hell—Big Heaven: a City Arabesque*. Indianapolis: Bobbs-Merrill, 1942. 327pp.

On the verge of the United States' entrance into World War II, members of the wealthy Meade family of Chicago are forced to reassess their priorities and commitments. For years, Spencer Meade has spent a portion of his manufacturing company earnings on charity, most visibly on a boys club in Chicago's "Little Hell." His daughter, Andrea, volunteered at a settlement house in the ghetto in college and met a full-time settlement worker, Glenn Beckett, with whom she fell in love. The Meades, for whom charities have just been social theater and not a commitment to social reform, find the romance unacceptable. However, Beckett is the one who ended the engagement after a weekend visiting the Meades' palatial country estate. Raised in poverty, he could not imagine marrying a woman who benefited from an unfair social system. Andrea married an older society figure to forget Beckett and soon separated from him, realizing the mistake of a loveless marriage. She then took up a life of urban dissipation on Chicago's bohemian Near North Side. Soon a favorite of society columnists, Andrea went out to nightclubs featuring scandalous performances and salons where socialists held forth. Glen Beckett suddenly re-enters her life when he discovers Andrea's bother Philip being held for drunken driving and contacts the Meades and their family lawyer. Philip, a nationally-famous, all-American, halfback in 1940, has, at twenty-two, become a drunken playboy and gambler. Driving while blind drunk, he runs down Lucy Mareska, a girl who has made incredible sacrifices to lift herself out of poverty and study singing. Over the course of the novel she must suffer numerous, Meade-funded operations just so that she can walk and have her marred face returned to some semblance of humanity. The remorseful Philip awakens to a sense of social responsibility, as does his father. However, as characters in the novel get drawn into World War II, it is clear that battlefield and home front privations will bring genuine transformation to the dissipated lives of the Meades and others in their social circle. The novel includes descriptions of 1940s nightlife and elite pastimes, as well as descriptions of life in a Chicago ghetto, primarily populated by Italians.

959. Roberts, Edith. *This Marriage*. Indianapolis: Bobbs-Merrill, 1941. 306pp.
    This novel about companionate marriage, that also includes a ménage á trois, is set in 1930s Chicago among college-educated, young people. Priding themselves on their intelligence and progressive social views, Martin Rivers (a research chemist) and Clare Ainslee (a writer) decide to wed, but only after writing and signing a prenuptial contract to guarantee that they will continue to enjoy personal freedom, including the freedom to have sexual relationships with other people. The contract also promises shared responsibility so that marriage will not become a burden to either one of them. The Martins' lifestyle includes eating at "Bohemian" restaurants and living in a large apartment building with a mixture of academics and laborers. Their friends eye their experiment with admiration, but the novel describes the many challenges the couple faces, especially when they have a baby and Clare is forced to stay at home, first due to the illnesses of pregnancy, and then to care for the baby. Then, Martin has an affair with an actress and, later, a woman from his lab. The novel is mostly concerned with exploring the institution of marriage and less focused on physical description, although it does present social life among educated, lower-middle-class people.

960. Roberts, John Hawley. *Narcissus*. New York: Sears, 1930. 301pp.
    In this society novel, Millwater Crane grows up on a North Shore estate in Highland Park with only his widowed mother, Virginia, his Uncle Stephen, and his tutor, Mr. Tolson, for companionship. Crane is sent to an East Coast boarding school around the beginning of World War I, when his mother volunteers to operate a serviceman's canteen. Although Crane socializes, he always preserves a distance with classmates. In college, he finally tries to befriend another young man, only to feel betrayed by him, and drop out. When he returns to Highland Park, he discovers Virginia has decided to go to Europe in pursuit of a husband. Left to himself, Crane begins exploring Chicago for the first time and takes an apartment on Superior Street just off Michigan Avenue. He socializes with worldly men and attractive women and several society women are eager to seduce Crane, who openly clings to his virginity. After Virginia announces her engagement to a Spanish count, Crane decides to force himself to have sexual relations, only to catch a glimpse of himself in a bathroom mirror before the act and decide not to give up his beauty to any-

one else. The novel captures social activities and extended conversations among educated, upper-class Chicagoans in the 1920s.

961. Robinson, Herbert B. *Chester*. Chicago: Conkey, 1898. 145pp.

George Chester and society men from his club go slumming at a masquerade ball. When George sees Jane Hadding in a gypsy costume, it is love at first sight. As the son of a wealthy banker, recently graduated from college, it is entirely inappropriate for him to think of getting involved with working-class Jane from Clark Street. She grew up on the family farm in Western Illinois, but had to move to the city to live with her married sister after her final living parent died while she was still a child. Although she clearly has no personal responsibility for her poverty, George's father opposes an engagement to Jane. When they marry anyway, he disinherits George and they move to southern Illinois, to the farm of her Uncle Joe. Fortunately, George's sister Virginia remains loyal to George, as does her fiancé, Mr. Rutherford. When George's father dies within a year after Virginia's marriage, Virginia and her husband want to protect George's rights. They make certain he gets half his father's estate and he enters the family firm with his brother-in-law, helping to make it a success. The novel argues for the positive effects of marriage on young men as they become responsible members of society. The book includes a number of extended descriptions of Chicago street life in the 1890s, particularly workers on their way to their jobs, and street vendors.

962. Robinson, Rose. *Exile in the Air*. New York: Crown Publishers, 1969. 159pp.

This young adult novel about the challenges of being an African-American female in 1960s America is partially set in Chicago. Jean Pierce was attending Midwestern University in Chicago on a scholarship, until she participated in a student protest over the Vietnam War in her senior year. Because she was arrested during the incident, the university revoked her scholarship and expelled her. In the months that follow, she lives with her boyfriend, Ferris Boone, in an apartment on Cottage Grove Avenue. However, she has difficulty finding more than seasonal employment and Boone loses one factory job after another, in part because of his alcoholism. Jean finally decides to leave and return to her hometown, the village of Des Graces, Iowa to live with her half-sister. Although her Chicago experience ends, her travails do not since she is mistreated in her relative's household for being "uppity" and while hitch-hiking to California is abducted and nearly raped. After a young white man rescues her from a violent encounter in Indiana, she begins to regain her optimism and by the end of the novel is living in happier circumstances in San Francisco. The novel's portrayal of 1960s Chicago shows a harsh place and not the place of opportunity depicted in many coming-of-age novels.

963. Roe, Edward Payson. *Barriers Burned Away*. New York: Dodd and Mead, 1872. 488pp.

Chicago in this novel is a city whose inhabitants have become so materialistic and devoid of spirituality that the fire of 1871 can be regarded as a necessary cleansing. After Dennis Fleet's father dies leaving nothing but debt and seven young children for his mother to care for, Dennis leaves for Chicago to earn the money his family needs. He eventually finds work as a handyman in an elegant household furnishings store. The owner, Mr. Ludolph, is the youngest son in an aristocratic German family and he is wholly dedicated to building a fortune so he may return with his daughter to Germany and claim the social status to which his lineage entitles them. To Dennis' alarm, he is attracted to Mr. Ludolph's materialistic daughter, Christine, whose secularism conflicts with Dennis' spirituality. When Dennis is asked to help Christine transport art for stage props at a musical evening, he performs a musical solo when one of the performers does not show up and begins to establish himself in society, changing the way Mr. Ludolph thinks of him. The contact with Christine makes Dennis think that she is interested in him and open to his religious faith. After Dennis learns to paint by working with an impoverished artist, Christine asks him to assist her in redecorating her rooms, mostly by modeling for her murals. Without his realization, she is leading him on so that she can paint his expression when he finally asks her to marry him and she rejects him. After the exchange comes to pass, Dennis is emotionally crushed and, physically broken; collapsing at the store he nearly dies. Mr. Ludolph is thrilled by his daughter's strong-willed behavior and evinces no concern for Dennis. In fact, when Dennis is later absent from work to nurse his dying mother and attend her funeral, Ludolph replaces him. Unemployed, Dennis devotes himself to his art, begins to sell pictures, and wins an important award with a prize of $2,000. When the 1871 fire begins, Dennis must choose between saving his money, paintings, and belongings and searching for and saving Christine. He rescues the young woman and, as the city burns, his theological discussion with Christine leads her to Christianity. After the fire, Dennis works as a day laborer, and Christine stays with him to help rebuild Chicago. In addition to the contrasts presented between the spiritually awakened and materialistic in Chicago, the novel contrasts the stereotypes of good Germans, and drunken, superstitious Irish.

964. Roe, Edward Reynolds. *Dr. Caldwell; or, The Trail of the Serpent*. The Pastime Series, vol. 33. Chicago: Laird and Lee, 1889. 251pp.

This temperance novel communicates late-nineteenth-century understandings of alcoholism by presenting the story of Chicagoan Dr. Charles Caldwell. Caldwell has published a well-researched essay on the psychology of alcoholism, however he falls prey to the disease himself. Even though he knows there are alcoholics in his family, when Maria Torrence rejects him, he turns to brandy to ease his broken heart. His continued contact with the Torrence family takes on a scientific cast as he realizes the genetic predetermination of alcoholism their lives demonstrate. Nat Torrence was an alcoholic and of his five children: Edgar dies from alcoholism in a mental institution, Elizabeth becomes a morphine addict, James a compulsive social drinker, and Thomas an abstainer who suffers bi-polar disorder. Only clear-headed Maria lives a healthy life and Caldwell realizes why she rejected him as a suitor. Caldwell's insights cannot save him, however, and he dies an alcoholic.

965. Roeburt, John, Malvin Wald, Henry F. Greenberg, and Al Capone. *Al Capone*. New York: Pyramid Books, 1959. 144pp.

This fictionalized biography of Al Capone is a novelization of a movie with the same title (Allied Artists Pictures, 1959). The book begins with Capone's 1919 arrival in Chicago and his employment as a bouncer at Johnny Torrio's Four Deuces Cafe and concludes with his 1947 death. In addition to chronicling the major events in Capone's life, the book covers the passage and effects of the Volstead Act, the murder of Big Jim Colosimo, the establishment of organized crime in Chicago, the syndicates move to Cicero, Illinois, and the St. Valentine's Day massacre. The importance of Chicago as the headquarters for bootlegging and organized crime is emphasized through much of the book.

966. Rogers, Thomas. *At the Shores*. New York: Simon and Schuster, 1980. 284pp.

This young adult novel about adolescence is set in 1940s Chicago and in the Indiana Dunes thirty miles from the city. Protagonist Jerry Engles progresses from a freshman to a junior at the

University of Chicago Laboratory School. His father, an engineer with a doctorate, works for the Standard Oil Company and Engles' life is solidly middle-class. Even though he realizes that he needs to work hard in school to match his father's success, Engles is constantly distracted by girls. His romances proceed from innocent crushes to a scandalously sexual relationship. When the girl's parents take her to New York and enroll her at the Chapin School, Engles receives a breakup letter and overcome with emotion he tries to commit suicide by drowning. The novel details school and social life in 1940s Hyde Park.

967. Rogers, Thomas. *The Pursuit of Happiness*. New York: New American Library, 1968. 237pp.

Rogers presents some of the social issues of the 1960s in his novel about the love affair of William Popper and Jane Kauffman, each twenty-one-years-old, who live in Hyde Park and are finishing their senior years at the University of Chicago. Both of them are from affluent families and have family members who are concerned about the propriety of their living together without being married. William and Jane differ with each other over the institution of marriage; William thinks they should wed and Jane does not. They also differ over their obligation to get involved in political and social issues, with Jane siding for involvement. Every aspect of their lives becomes newly consequential when William's automobile skids on an icy street and he accidentally kills a pedestrian. William's treatment at the hands of policemen and representatives of the judicial system come to epitomize larger problems with American society to William and Jane. After being imprisoned and witnessing an act of violence about which he is being forced to testify, William escapes, and he and Jane leave the country for Mexico, where they believe they will find happiness. Chicago is undergoing rapid physical changes in the novel as the Hyde Park neighborhood and other areas are experiencing "urban renewal." William's grandmother, with whom the bulk of the family fortune remains, lives on in the Prairie Avenue mansion she moved into as a bride in 1897, but by the end of the novel she has been served notice that she will have to relocate.

968. Rosaire, Forrest. *Uneasy Years*. New York: Alfred A. Knopf, 1950.

This novel set in 1930s Chicago presents the plight of a lower-middle-class family, all of whose members are crippled by economic constraints, even though they have survived the Depression. Laura Conmee believes she is close to her goal of having all three of her children get educations that will give them economic security and social status. Her oldest son, Peter, is completing his master's degree and will be entering a doctoral program. Eighteen-year-old Jean has just entered the University of Chicago and her younger brother, fifteen-year-old Hugh is earning a good record in high school. Only her husband Dave continues to be a worry as he repeatedly brings the family to the brink of eviction from their rented West Side bungalow near North Avenue and Race Street. Dave earns a modest wage in a mail order fulfillment house. His artistic and emotional temperament makes it difficult for him to function in society and he is constantly borrowing against his modest salary to buy art supplies for paintings that have no market. After Laura receives word of an inheritance that includes a house in California and monthly trust fund payments, she plots her divorce and a life free of financial worries. The novel touches on issues of social status, gender roles, and mental health. The fact that the Conmees struggle to obtain the necessities of life and the goods to establish middle-class social status means that the novel describes clothing, food, and furniture in great detail.

969. Rose, Alvin Emanuel [Alan Pruitt, pseud.]. *The Restless Corpse*. Chicago: Ziff-Davis, 1947. 247pp.

The *Chicago Globe's* top crime reporter, Don Carson, is assigned by his newspaper's publisher, "Old Man" Holiday, to find his daughter April and get her to return to the family home in New York City. After eluding Carson twice with aggressive ruses (including pushing him off the Navy Pier at the Chicago Flower Show), April finally gives in during a party at her apartment. However, as the guests are leaving, a murdered man is found in one of the bedrooms and Carson must try to prevent April from getting charged with the crime and exposed in nation-wide newspaper coverage. Unfortunately, Carson has a long list of suspicious characters to investigate, including a known con man, several Germans looking for a white jade Buddha, and a contemporary painter with a bohemian lifestyle. The police arrest April before Carson can solve the case, but in the end he finds the murderers and writes a news story casting April as a heroine, that redeems him in "Old Man" Holiday's eyes and wins April over to becoming his bride. Most of the novel is set inside the affluent apartment building where April lives, along with several murder suspects.

970. Rose, Richard M. *The Satyr Candidate: A Novel by Richard M. Rose*. Hicksville, N.Y.: Exposition Press, 1979. 196pp.

This suspense novel focuses on political corruption in Chicago. During his re-election campaign, Jim Bannister, an Illinois state legislator from Chicago, the candidate is accused of accepting a significant campaign contribution that he did not declare. Even though Bannister could easily prove his innocence against this falsehood, he takes no public action and is subsequently murdered. His friend Steve Redman, a lawyer and former policeman, devotes himself to redeeming Bannister's reputation and uncovers a web of corruption underlying public life.

971. Rosenfeld, Isaac. *Passage from Home*. New York: Dial Press, 1946. 280pp.

The main character in this coming of age novel is fourteen-year-old Bernie Miller. The son of Orthodox Jews, from the time he is a boy, he is fascinated by his Aunt Minna Goodman's heterodoxy. While the rest of the Miller clan lives on the West Side, Minna lives on the North Side. She reads novels, listens to jazz, and lives with her lover. Bernie is also fascinated by Willy Harpsmith, the man who had married his cousin Martha Vogel and then left the city after her death several years before. Willy, born in Tennessee, had traveled the world as a newspaper man and sailor. When Willy reappears at a family gathering, Bernie's father drives him away. So, Bernie seeks Willy out at the YMCA where he is staying and devises a plan to bring Willy and Minna together. Although they eventually move in together and Bernie joins them briefly after a fight with his father, Minna has another suitor, Fred Mason, the owner of a North Side saloon. A rivalry between Mason and Harpsmith ends with Minna's marriage to Mason. Most of the settings in the novel are domestic, although one scene is in a soda shop and another at a baseball stadium. The novel conveys one perspective on working-class Jewish life in Chicago in the 1940s.

972. Ross, Sam. *He Ran all the Way*. New York: Farrar, Straus, 1947. 293pp.

Set in 1940s Chicago, this suspenseful crime novel provides intimate details of domestic and social life in the context of holdup man Nick Robey's story. Robey, in his early twenties, is jobless and lives with his mother, who supported the two of them as a prostitute after Robey's father, a sewer line worker, left them after he began suffering from a lung ailment. With no prospects, Robey falls in with his childhood buddy Al Molin's plan to hold up a ship's payroll officer on the Navy Pier. A policeman breaks in as Molin and Robey are committing their crime and in the confusion, Molin is wounded and the policeman is killed. Robey escapes with a briefcase containing ten thousand dollars, but he was not the mastermind and can think of nothing except to blend in with the crowds on Oak Street Beach. He meets Peg Dobbs and at the end of the afternoon the two head back to her parents' house on Ogden Avenue near Douglas Park. Robey turns the Dobbs house into his hideout and holds the family hostage. To avoid suspicion, he allows the family members, father Casey, mother Ella, and son Mitchell, to pursue daily activities and the novel provides a good deal of detail concerning lower-middle-class domestic life. To her confusion, Peg is still attracted to Robey, despite his criminality, and for a while she helps with an escape plan, and envisions life on the run. However, a dramatic, violent conclusion is inevitable. The novel is unusual for providing so much detail about daily life in the 1940s.

973. Ross, Sam. *The Sidewalks Are Free*. New York: Farrar, Straus, 1950. 308pp.

This novel about the Chicago Jewish immigrant experience is set in the years 1918 and 1919 and told from the viewpoint of eleven-year-old Herschel Melov. Herschel's parents emigrated from Russia, where his mother, Sonya, grew up in a desperately poor household and his father David was the eldest son of a *sofer*, a copier of religious texts and held in high social regard. David rejects his father's profession to become a carpenter and shortly afterwards his father dies of pneumonia and many other family members are killed in a pogrom. He impractically marries dowerless Sonya and they manage to immigrate to the United States. In 1918 David returns from World War I military service, entirely spent in the United States working on construction projects. On his carpenter's earnings, he is able to maintain his wife, son, and niece in a rented apartment near Humboldt Park on Thomas Street on. Then, David receives a ten thousand dollar life insurance payment after his brother's battlefield death and his life fills with turmoil over what to do with the money. Sonya finally insists that he invest the money in a laundry operation. Despite David's hard labor, the business is destined to fail as laundries are consolidating to afford new, time-saving equipment. A crisis comes when David is on the point of collapse with pneumonia. He forces Herschel to help him and the boy accidentally destroys a central component of the laundry's operating equipment. The novel thoroughly explores the meaning of money and social advancement for the characters, as well as the psychological and emotional costs of employment as a wage laborer. Assimilation is another major theme as David gains American citizenship and Herschel is subjected to his teacher's prolonged attempts to get her students to adopt American values and forms of social conduct.

974. Ross, Sam. *Someday, Boy*. New York: Farrar, Straus, 1948. 340pp.

In this novel set in 1920s Chicago, nineteen-year-old Benny Gordon spends the summer after graduating from high school working for a textile company. The son of a dress company worker, Benny grew up on the West Side near Douglas Park. All of his friends are headed to college in the autumn; Benny's only chance at higher education is through winning the Chicago River swimming competition, which he narrowly loses. Convinced that he will never earn enough money in the textile industry, Benny finds work in a real estate office and is soon the envy of his college friends, earning enough money to move his family to a North Side apartment on Wilson Avenue one block from the lake and pay cash for a new Ford automobile. Convinced of his prospects, he throws over his high school girlfriend for Laura Shapiro of Albany Park, whose father, a former bootlegger, now has a legitimate financial services business. When the stock market crashes in 1929, Benny is initially unfazed, even though most of his savings are in his employer's investment accounts. Just as he is about to withdraw his money, he is hospitalized for appendicitis and by the time he recovers, the firm's owner has committed suicide, leaving debts and empty account portfolios behind him. The novel describes daily life for middle-class families and the pastimes of 1920s young people, including swimming in a Jewish settlement house pool and in the lake from various public beaches, and Municipal Pier; going to dances at the Edgewater Beach Hotel; and making weekend trips to the Wisconsin Dells. Before he has an automobile, Benny walks a good deal and describes many neighborhoods, as well as the odors from the stockyards, and the pollution in the Chicago River. In one notable scene, Benny attends a stag party paid for by his firm that includes boxing, live sex acts, poker, and paid-in-advance prostitutes made freely available to attendees.

975. Roth, Philip. *Letting Go*. New York: Random House, 1962. 630pp.

Through the relationships among three educated young people during the 1950s, this novel presents urban academics just as 1960s youth culture is about to transform life in the United States. Gabe Wallach meets the married couple, Paul and Libby Herz, when they are all graduate students together at the University of Iowa and they move to Chicago for faculty positions. The Herzes fell in love at Cornell University and their family origins are a continuing issue since Paul's family in Brooklyn is Jewish and Libby was born Roman Catholic. Gabe, who is from New York City, is the son of Jewish dentist and in the aftermath of his mother's death, has an ever more limited relationship with his father. Both Gabe and Paul reject Jewish religion and culture, alienating their families. The trio confronts implications of women's liberation when Gabe and Libby have an affair, and the degree to which marriage bonds should control sexual expression becomes an issue. Finally, Paul and Libby must explore the degree of control she has over her own body as a liberated woman when she becomes unexpectedly pregnant. They decide to abort the fetus, but the novel illustrates the continuing impact of this choice, long after the pregnancy has been terminated. This coming of age novel is tightly focused on the characters' personal lives and is less concerned with physical descriptions of Chicago.

976. Russell, Charlotte Murray. *The Case of the Topaz Flower*. New York: Crime Club / Doubleday, Doran, 1939. 278pp.

This murder mystery features amateur detective Wally Kent who is in love with the suspect in the case. The murder victim, Harrison Sloane is killed in his locked library, just as guests are gathering to celebrate his fiftieth year in business, with a swing orchestra already playing in the background. The death that appears at first to be a suicide is revealed to be a murder when the Sloane family realizes that a piece of jewelry, the topaz flower, named for their gold mine, is missing. The family mansion is in Lakeside and is well-supplied with servants. Unlike some murder mysteries set almost exclusively in mansions, principal characters here meet in locales around the city to discuss the case, including the Victorian Room at the Palmer House, the Metropolitan Club, the Morrison cocktail lounge, and several cinema palaces, including the Olympus. The 1930s, upper-class milieu makes much of radio, motion pictures, cocktails, bridge, typewriters, mechanical pencils, and horse racing. Multiple wills and several more murders keep the police and Kent confused until the very end.

977. Russell, Charlotte Murray. *Dreadful Reckoning*. New York: Crime Club / Doubleday, Doran, 1941. 276pp.

Seventy-eight-year-old Henry James Bedford, the founder of the Bedford Company, enjoys using his wealth to control his family. He continues to live in the twenty-two room mansion on

Rush Street that he built when his fortune was new and on his birthday insists that all of his children live with him. Because he is also crippling his children's finances by reducing their holdings of his company so that they will have modest incomes, they have little choice. When he is murdered, suspicion is cast in many directions within the family and its social circle. Most of the settings for this novel are inside Bedford's mansion and in other luxurious interiors, like an apartment suite in the Drake Hotel. Descriptions give some indication of the lives of upper-class Chicagoans in the 1930s.

978. Russell, Charlotte Murray. *The Tiny Diamond: A Jane Amanda Edwards Story*. Garden City, N.Y.: Crime Club / Doubleday, Doran, 1937. 277pp.

Forty-something Jane Amanda Edwards has already helped her friend, Police Lieutenant George Hammond, solve murders in her native Rockport, Illinois. Despairing of spending a dull summer in Rockport, she moves her household—that includes her sister, brother, and cook—to Chicago so that she can study criminal psychology at the University of Chicago. On their way to the city, they spend a night in a tourist camp and meet Chicagoan Christopher Ferris. He owns a small apartment building in Chicago, just across the Midway from the University on Sixtieth Street and offers to rent them an apartment. The transaction no longer seems like good luck when Jane is punched in the stomach in a dark hallway on their first night in the apartment and Ferris is murdered. Jane quickly becomes the prime suspect and must deal with the ignorance of the Chicago police while she works on solving the crime. During the course of her investigation Jane learns a great deal about apartment buildings, as well as local businesses, their owners, and neighborhood residents. The seemingly tranquil environs in proximity to the University turn out to house secrets including illicit affairs and illegal drug trafficking

979. Russell, Ruth. *Lakefront*. Chicago: Thomas S. Rockwell, 1931. 291pp.

This book about the moral decay of Chicago from 1835 to the 1920s illustrates the theme using four generations of the O'Maras, an Irish immigrant family. Protagonist Jane O'Mara arrives in Chicago with her extended family in 1835 and finds the frontier settlement's ideal of social equality inspirational. However, her widowed mother thinks life too unrefined in early Chicago and marries boarding house owner Mr. Lannon, whose wealth can insulate her from unpleasantness. Jane resents her mother's selfish motivations and finds Lannon's Whig politics distasteful. Mary Ellen, her older sister, soon elopes with a man traveling with a westward bound wagon train and Jane is left to look after her younger brother, James. When James begins to demonstrate his intelligence, Lannon sees an opportunity to further his social status in an Irish Catholic milieu and pledges to educate the boy if he will become a priest. Freed of her responsibility for James, Jane falls in love and marries sailor Michael Moran. Unfortunately, James discovers he has no calling for the priesthood and is driven out of the Lannon household around the time that Moran dies in a shipwreck. Jane is left to support herself and find money for James' schooling, taking in sewing and renting out a room of her log cabin. James obtains his law degree, fights for social justice, marries, and has a son, before fighting and dying for his political convictions in the Civil War. His son, James O'Mara, II avoids all ethical considerations in his greed, becoming an industrial tyrant and fighting any assertion of laborers' rights with violence. Jane lives to see James O'Mara, III living the life of a common gangster in the 1920s. The novel covers social and political history over a long period of time, rehearsing political arguments over the Civil War and the philosophy behind the rights of labor in the 1880s. Although Jane is periodically inspired by the growth of Chicago and hopes for the city's future, her own family's experience is one of gradual decline.

980. Rutledge, Nancy [Leigh Bryson, pseud.]. *The Gloved Hand: A New Mystery Novel*. Kingston, N.Y.: Quinn, 1947. 127pp.

This work of pulp fiction about police detectives is by an English writer and the detectives and Chicago are presented in stereotypical fashion.

981. St. Johns, Adela Rogers. *Tell No Man*. Garden City, N.Y.: Doubleday, 1966. 444pp.

This religious novel is partly set in 1960s Chicago. The narrator is a writer and journalist who wrote for Chicago newspapers for many years and is connected to upper-class society. So, when Hank Gavin, decides to give up his life as a wealthy Chicago investment counselor, the narrator is able to give the background stories of all of Hank's family members and acquaintances. Although the narrator lives in California during the novel's present and Hank Gavin and his wife move there, all of them visit Chicago frequently. It is also in Chicago that Hank had his conversion experience after the suicide of his friend Colin Rowe. The narrator's visits are devoted to social and charity events and the novel includes many references to actual clubs, restaurants, hotels, and other venues.

982. Sandburg, Helga. *The Wheel of Earth*. New York: McDowell Obolensky, 1958. 396pp.

In 1920s rural Kentucky, Ellen Gaddy loves the farm life of her childhood, despite the harshness of her Christian fundamentalist father. As a young girl, she falls in love with Christian Ay, a temporary hand on a neighboring farm. The son of a Louisville store owner, Christian is in the country as a respite from city life. He forces himself on Ellen and leaves before she realizes she is pregnant. When her bachelor uncle, Garland, comes to the farm for a Christmas visit, Ellen sees her chance to escape her father's censure before her pregnancy becomes obvious and gets herself invited to Chicago. Garland had sold his share of the farm to his brother and used the money to buy a Chicago burlesque house. Building on the endeavor's success, he bought a vaudeville theater and later purchased restaurants. Ellen stays for a time in Garland's large, but poorly kept house, but saves the allowance he gives her to visit her school friend Penny. As a twelve-year-old Penny married a thirty-two-year-old man and already has several children. During her long, summer visit to Penny's farm, Ellen has her baby boy. Leaving him with Penny, she returns to her father's farm, but five years later brings her son into the household. When her father refuses to accept the child, unthinkingly applying his Bible "truths," Ellen travels once again to Chicago. Garland's household now includes Violet, his common-law wife who helps Ellen find work as a housekeeper. Once again, however, Chicago is a place of only temporary escape. Ellen must return home when her mother becomes ill and after she dies, Ellen begins working as a housekeeper on a farm near Penny. Although Ellen's life is hard, she has escaped her father and is confident in her decision to remain in the country, rather than move permanently to Chicago, a place of opportunity and escape for people from rural areas, but not one that can offer the fulfillment Ellen finds in the country.

983. Sanders, Ed. *Shards of God*. New York: Grove Press, 1970. 179pp.

A portion of this novel written from within the Yippie movement is set in Chicago. A good deal of the work describes historical figures, such as Jerry Rubin, Abbie Hoffman, Keith Lampe, and Alan Ginsberg in fantastical terms and makes satirical attacks on American political and cultural figures of the 1960s. Set during 1967 and 1968 the work climaxes with the demonstrations at the 1968 Democratic National Convention in Chicago. Although a number of historical novels deal with the convention, this may be the only one to be written from the perspective of the Yippie movement. The role that sexuality played in the movement is reflected in the work's focus on genitalia and sexual intercourse.

984. Sattley, Helen R. *Shadow Across the Campus*. New York: Dodd, Mead, 1957. 245pp.

Set in the 1950s on the campus of Northwestern University, this young adult novel illustrates campus life for women during the time period, paying particular attention to the effects of sororities. The story is told by contrasting the experiences of three childhood friends: Marjorie Howard, Cecile Engle, and Kate Stewart. Kate and Marjorie are rushed by Zeta Nu Sorority, but Cecile is openly rejected because of her Jewish background. Such blatant prejudice sickens Kate who breaks with the sorority to establish a campus life for herself and Cecile that is satisfying without sorority-based socializing. Marjorie, however, decides to become an agent of change and joins Zeta Nu. She is presented with many opportunities for growth that Cecile and Kate never experience. In this way the story presents the positive aspects of sororities, as well as the negative aspects. The narrative provides many details about daily life in the 1950s.

985. Saxton, Alexander. *Grand Crossing*. N.Y.: Harper and Brothers, 1943. 410pp.

Just as he is about to travel from his summer job in Portland, Oregon back east to begin his senior year at Harvard University, Michael Reed's suitcase and train ticket are stolen. Fortunately, he meets Benjamin Baum, a University of Chicago student who helps him travel by inviting him along to hop freight trains and work odd jobs for food money. Their conversations often focus on social issues and get Reed thinking about his life as an affluent Harvard student. After another semester in Cambridge, he transfers to the University of Chicago. As a newcomer, Reed learns about the city and participates in discussions about unions, Communism, and the situation in Europe. He also makes working-class friends and finds a new girlfriend, a woman who used to go to Bennington, but like him, has begun to find the socially elite vacuous. In a post-Depression era, with a world war approaching, Chicago is contrasted with eastern cities and their archaic pretensions, as a place of greater authenticity in which social stratification has not prevented exchange between the working, middle, and upper classes.

986. Saxton, Alexander. *The Great Midland*. New York: Appleton-Century-Crofts, 1948. 352pp.

This labor novel is set in Chicago's working-class neighborhoods and slums between the nineteen-teens and nineteen-forties, presenting the experiences of members of the Spaas family as they work for the Great Midland Railroad. The novel teaches the reader about labor issues, but also about the major tenets of the Communist Party in America in the 1940s as it agitated for a higher minimum wage, better living conditions for workers, and the end of racism within the labor movement. The role of academics in both the union movement and in Communism is here presented in the love affair and marriage between Dave Spaas, a railroad brakeman, and Stephanie Koviak, who grew up in a Polish immigrant family and now teaches at the University of Chicago. In addition to presenting social and political ideology the novel describes life for working people in Chicago in the 1920s through 1940s and touches on the issues of racism and factionalism within the labor movement and the Communist Party.

987. Schaeffer, Susan Fromberg. *Falling*. New York: Macmillan, 1973. 307pp.

As a thirty-year-old graduate student at the University of Chicago, Elizabeth Kamen attempts suicide. As she undergoes psychoanalysis, flashbacks tell the story of her life and outline the origins of her psychic unease. Not all of the novel is set in Chicago, Elizabeth grew up in New York

City and returns there as an adult. Her grandparents immigrated to the United States from Russia and part of the story touches on the emotional issues faced by immigrants, as well as on aspects of Jewish identity. Much of the Chicago section of the book is focused on the academic community in and around the University of Chicago.

988. Schauffler, Robert Haven. *Where Speech Ends: A Music Maker's Romance*. New York: Moffat, Yard, 1906. 291pp.

This story of Peter Morris' experiences as a classical musician reveals a good deal about the music community in Chicago in the early twentieth century. A Cleveland, Ohio native with a natural musical talent, Morris drops out of Princeton when he is accepted as violinist in Heinrich Wolfgang's Chicago-based orchestra. The musicians are almost all European, and mostly German, and the book exposes "humorous" personality traits of the orchestra members that border on ethnic slurs. Peter Morris quickly falls in love with Gretchen Auber, a harpist who is the concertmaster's daughter, and is horrified to realize that his great friend, prodigy violinist and composer, Franz Hartmann, is also in love with her. For a time the three are friends, but that dynamic is too difficult to maintain and the young men become rivals for Gretchen's hand. In Chicago, the musicians participate in larger ethnic and artistic communities. One of the social events in which Peter engages is a meeting of the Denizens, bohemians involved in various artistic endeavors, who have an Italian feast. After a season at Ravinia, the orchestra begins an eastern tour and when Wolfgang falls ill Hartmann's superior musicianship earns him the conductor's position and Gretchen's heart. Among the "European" tendencies of the musicians are violent passions and jealousies and the use of hypnotism.

989. Schiller, Cicely. *Maybe Next Year*. New York: Prentice-Hall, 1947. 299pp.

Covering the decades between 1910 and 1950, this novel explores the plight of single women in a sexist society. The book uses changing tastes in clothing, music, and novels, as well as historical events to indicate the passage of time as Rose Weber ages from a teenager to a fifty-year-old. Among the major events and eras Rose experiences in Chicago are the influenza epidemic of 1917, armistice celebrations, Prohibition, the Depression, and World War II. As a person of Jewish heritage, Rose faces prejudice when she looks for jobs. In the feverish nightlife fueled by returning World War I veterans she provides company to young men, supporting herself on dinner dates and gifts of "cab fare" money. Eventually she gets engaged to Bernie Cassel, only for him to marry another woman while on a drunken bender. When her mother remarries, Rose is thrown on her own resources. She eventually gets an office job and substitutes sexual affairs for romantic attachments. Through these more straightforward relationships she secures apartments and jobs. By the time she is fifty Rose is exhausted and about to commit suicide. Then, her stepfather dies and she is pulled back into life by the need to care for her mother. This bleak novel makes painfully clear the limited options open to single women from the 1920s to the 1950s and catalogs the office jobs, coffee shops, restaurants, and furnished apartments in which they were forced to spend their days.

990. Schultz, Alan Brener. *The Rise of Elsa Potter*. New York: Simon and Schuster, 1932. 270pp.

This novel set in 1930s Chicago deals with issues faced by women in the workplace. Initially, Elsa Potter is determined to be a writer. However, her interaction with an editor, who repeatedly approaches her with sexual propositions, soon discourages her. She decides to find a way to take advantage of her attractiveness, but remain in control. She enters the business world as "Madame

Elsa," the operator of a fashionable dress shop and eventually develops her own line of cosmetics that make her a wealthy woman. The book is interesting from the standpoint of social history for presenting a fiction in which a woman can be successful in the workplace without directly competing with men.

991. Schwimmer, Walter. *It Happened on Rush Street: A Group of Short Stories and Vignettes.* New York: Frederick Fell, 1971. 235pp.

Divided into two sections, "Short Stories" and "The Rush Street Philosopher," this book consists of fiction and first-person narration that evoke a neighborhood centered on Rush Street that consists of bars, nightclubs, and restaurants. The author was clearly fascinated by the social interactions amongst the diverse people brought together in this area (retirees, gamblers, businessmen, prostitutes, African-Americans, whites, and Roman Catholic nuns and priests). Many of the stories focus on heterosexual relationships, in marriage or outside of it in which apparently jaded people experience romantic love. In other stories, hardened gamblers or petty criminals behave generously towards others and people with seemingly narrow lives are shown to have lived more widely and to be much more interesting than appearances would indicate.

992. Scofield, Charles J. *Altar Stairs.* Illustrated by E. Bert Smith. Chicago: Christian Century, 1903. 320pp.

This melodramatic religious tract is mostly set in an imaginary town named Stonington that is downstate from Chicago. However, the novel's main characters often visit the city for business and pleasure and protagonist Winifred Masters moves to the city with her husband Mr. Southey. Masters grew up the daughter of agnostic Reuben Masters, and is not drawn to religion until she is on the verge of adulthood. Her love for Protestant minister Frederick Sterling, is a major factor in her conversion. Sterling is destined to remain celibate, but Masters finds a suitable husband in Mr. Southey, whom she is able to convert to Christianity. Over the course of the book, Masters is also able to convert her brother, mother, and husband, with only her father remaining a reprobate. The author's concern with spiritual debate means that there is little physical description of Chicago in the book. The book's description of a woman's spiritual influence on others in a sexist society may be of some interest.

993. Scott, Henry E. *The Girl from Macoupin.* Chicago: Laird, Lee, 1894. Republished as *Beauty's Peril; or, The Girl from Macoupin.* Chicago: Laird, Lee, 1895.

In this novel, a girl from the countryside experiences city life while supporting herself with a department store job. No additional information is available.

994. Seely, Herman Gastrell. *A Son of the City: A Story of Boy Life.* Illustrated by Fred J. Arting. Chicago: McClurg, 1917. 341pp.

A school year in the life of ten-year-old John Fletcher, who lives in a neighborhood of Chicago in the first decade of the twentieth century, focuses on seasons and holidays. His neighborhood compatriots form themselves into the Tigers, who function as a sports team and play group, competing in football and baseball games on vacant lots and defending their improvised fort by throwing wild cucumbers. For most of the year Fletcher is determined to win the hand of classmate Louise Martin. When he asks his father how old one must be to marry (twenty-one) and how much money one needs to set up a household (two hundred dollars), he takes his father's joking responses to heart. Through a long list of odd jobs, including raking leaves, shoveling snow, and delivering newspapers he slowly accumulates money. However, he has a rival for Louise's affections in Sidney Dupree. Eventually, Fletcher tires of Louise playing the two off each other; he drops out of the competition and uses his money to purchase a bicycle. Fletcher's neighborhood and school is relatively homogenous, with families living in free-standing houses with yards. However, one of his classmates is African-American and when spring time comes and the lakefront becomes a focus of leisure activity, Fletcher takes note of the Germans, Danes, and Jews.

995. Seifert, Shirley Louise. *Look to the Rose*. Philadelphia: Lippincott, 1960. 382pp.

This work of historical fiction includes well-researched descriptions of Chicago in the 1850s and 1860s. The subject of the biographical novel is Eleanor Lytle Kinzie, granddaughter of the founder of Chicago. At the outset of the work Kinzie is engaged to a Savannah cotton merchant, William Washington Gordon. Three years must pass, however, before the couple can marry, since Gordon must develop his business successfully enough to support a wife in style. Only a short time after Kinzie weds and moves to Savannah, Georgia secedes from the Union and Gordon becomes a colonel in the Confederate Army. For much of the war, Kinzie lives in Savannah and Richmond, until Union General William T. Sherman helps her get back to Chicago to avoid the occupation of Savannah. Gordon survives the war and its immediate aftermath to be reunited with Kinzie and the couple returns to the South where Juliet Gordon Low, their daughter and founder of the Girl Scouts of America is born.

996. Shane, Margaret Woodward Smith [Woodward Boyd, pseud.]. *Lazy Laughter*. New York: Charles Scribner's Sons, 1923. 295pp.

Set in St. Paul, Minnesota and Chicago during the 1920s, this book presents the author's perspective on upper-class women in a somewhat satirical vein. Dagmar Hollowell's mother, Margaret, is the daughter of Charles Montgomery, who, with little effort, accumulated a railroad fortune in the 1850s. Margaret married Paul Hallowell, who speculated with Margaret's money and committed suicide after losing it all. Unable to sustain herself without wealth or a husband, Margaret married John Patlock, a wealthy man for whom she felt little affection, less than six months after Hallowell's suicide. After Dagmar's society debut at nineteen, she weighs her marriage options with calculation. She is in love with Palomon Bennett, who has little money, and knows that Willard Freeman, a newspaper heir, would be the best financial match. Dagmar postpones a commitment by going to Chicago and working for the School Lover's League, a public school reform association. The experience horrifies Dagmar who is appalled by the earnest young women she meets, the physical conditions in her boarding house, and the places to which her work takes her. After she makes friends with the Plunkitt siblings, Martin and Marthena, she shares a flat with Marthena and accompanies her to middle-class entertainments: restaurants, parties, and social functions. However, she takes little pleasure from them. By the end of the novel she has rejected Bennett and another suitor, Alec Jones, the son of the director of the School Lover's League, to return to St. Paul and marry Willard Freeman. The novel is unusual in presenting a young woman who rejects meaningful work and the bohemian freedom of 1920s Chicago to live the ornamental life of a wealthy man's wife.

997. Shane, Margaret Woodward Smith [Woodward Boyd, pseud.]. *The Love Legend*. New York: Charles Scribner's Sons, 1922. 329pp.

Mrs. Harris and her four daughters live in a household without men, since Mr. Harris, formerly the Reverend Tyndall Harris of Hyde Park, left the church, embraced socialism, and became an English professor at the University of Chicago. Mrs. Harris established a separate household in the lakeshore house she inherited from her father, living on the income from a trust also established by her father. Despite her disappointment in love, she remains a romantic and has assured her girls that each will be carried off by a prince and live happily ever after. As the girls grow older they are less enthralled by the love legend and its limited view of female social roles, particularly as Sari wants to become a professional dancer and Nita a commercial artist. The novel shows how the Harris girls, Mrs. Harris' friends, and the daughters of Mrs. Harris' friends deal with the social expectations of romantic love. Chicago of the 1920s with its jazz clubs and nightlife plays a role in the lives of many of the characters and domestic material culture and clothing are prominently detailed.

998. Shane, Margaret Woodward Smith [Woodward Boyd, pseud.]. *The Unpaid Piper*. New York: Charles Scribner's Sons, 1927. 330pp.

This romance novel focuses on the Shaw family of Lakeshore and includes many of the same characters introduced in *The Love Legend*. Mrs. Shaw embraces all modern reforms in dress and diet and expects her family to sleep with the heat off wearing the nightclothes she has created for them. Laura graduates from Rockford College and returns to Lakeshore to socialize at the local country club and date, but postpones marriage. She is introduced to bohemian life in Chicago artistic circles and meets rich Wilton Kildare, a married man who lives in Lakeshore. The two begin an affair that Kildare's wife eventually reveals to Laura's parents, showing them letters written in hotel rooms around the city. The public disgrace ends the affair. Because the story begins before World War I and continues through the early 1920s, there is much discussion of changing fashion and morality. The Chicago real estate boom and the march of high rise buildings up the lakefront have a significant impact on Lakeshore as houses close to the lake get torn down or relocated.

999. Sheldon, Charles M. *The Reformer*. Chicago: Advance; London, U.K.: Ward, Lock, 1902. 299pp.

In this social reform novel, John Gordon returns from a European tour to disappoint his father by announcing his intention to live among the urban poor, rather than enter his father's business. Gordon moves into a settlement house and begins advocating for the enforcement of current housing codes and the passage of stricter legislation to improve housing conditions. His advocacy meets with little success until a fire that brings needless loss of life awakens the public.

1000. Shenton, Edward. *Lean Twilight*. New York: Charles Scribner's Sons, 1928. 291pp.

In this novel about romance, marriage and the social roles available to women, Camar O'Neil grows up the independent daughter of an affluent lawyer in a village on the New Jersey shore. She meets scholarly, New York architect Martin Grove when he comes to the beach to recover from typhoid. In her inexperience, she falls in love before determining that Martin is married. The unsettling experience drives her to make a life for herself away from her family and after passing through Philadelphia, Cleveland, and Detroit, she ends up in Chicago as a twenty-five-year-old and works as a secretary to Richard Jeffrey in an architectural office. After a period of sedate socializing (looking at his antique bottle collection, having dinner at the Palmer House), Jeffrey proposes. O'Neil cannot bring herself to wed a man for whom she does not feel the passion she did for Grove and leaves for Europe. Other affairs follow, and eventually she enters into a white marriage to an affluent man. Her life is turned upside down when she meets Martin again in wartime New York. Although the novel is vague on this point, the marriage of O'Neil's parents was troubled and seems to have entailed violence, adding to O'Neil's ambivalence about marriage and love affairs. The Chicago section of the novel presents the city at a time of growth; O'Neil likes the place because it has the seaside quality of her hometown.

1001. Sherburne, James. *Rivers Run Together*. Boston: Houghton Mifflin, 1974. 208pp.

Sherburne blends journalistic accounts of historical events and people with fictional characters to record the impact of the Democratic National Convention of 1968 on Chicago. To illustrate the local impact, Sherburne employs five characters: Ted Bakersfield and Sari Schram, young idealists; Fred Moler, a Chicago police officer; Mike Rogoff, a world-weary ex-Communist; and Evanston-dwelling Malcolm Tolliver, an aging advertising executive. In addition to peace marches and bloody confrontations, Sherburne helps the reader understand the political process underlying events.

1002. Shuman, Andrew. *The Loves of a Lawyer, His Quandary, and How it Came Out*. Chicago: Keen, Cooke, 1875. 214pp.

Although the city in this romance novel is named Westerly, the setting is clearly Chicago. Protagonist Samuel Traverse describes his life as a boarder with the Wilkins family when he was just starting his legal career as a thirty-year-old. The widowed Jane Wilkins has Frances, her twenty-two-year-old daughter living with her, as well as her orphaned niece, twenty-year-old Laura Ferris. At first they are all on a pleasant social footing, but as time passes and social expectations for marriage become pressing, the women begin to devise ways of encouraging Traverse to choose between them and propose. Even though he continues to love both young women equally, he does eventually marry Ferris, only for her to die early in the marriage. On her deathbed she encourages him to marry Frances and later he does, living out his years in professional and domestic content.

1003. Siegel, Sam. *Hey, Jewboy*. Chicago: S and G Releasing, 1967. 329pp.

Mostly set in the Jewish-American community around Maxwell Street in the 1920s and 1930s, this coming-of-age story begins when the protagonist, Sam, is orphaned at the age of eleven. Although he initially supports himself selling newspapers, Sam is soon involved in organized crime, becoming a messenger for a prostitution ring at fourteen and running alcohol for bootleggers when he is sixteen. By the time he is twenty he participates in armed robbery and by the end of the novel is incarcerated. The book has much of the flavor of a first-hand account of life on the street prior to World War II.

1004. Simmons, Geoffrey S. *The Z-Papers*. New York: Arbor House, 1976. 240pp.

Written by a physician, this novel is primarily set inside the large Presbyterian-St. Luke's Hospital where physicians are trying to save the life of Secretary of Defense Kramer. The secretary, a vice-presidential hopeful, is in Chicago campaigning when he is knifed on a crowded street. At first it seems as though he has narrowly escaped an assassination attempt that has left him with an arm wound. Then, a threatening note arrives indicating that the knife blade was coated with poison that will kill the secretary within twenty-four hours unless the perpetrators provide the antidote in exchange for the freedom of six life-term convicts. The social unrest and issues of the 1970s come through in this story that captures the procedures, administration, and routine of a major, urban hospital of the time period. The culprit in the case is a mad scientist referencing cultural attitudes toward the scientific-military-industrial complex.

1005. Simon, Philip J. *Cleft Roots*. Chicago: Priam Press, 1975. 280pp.

This book about religious identity and intermarriage is partly set in Chicago. Born in 1900, Murray Prescott Stern is the son of a Russian Jew and a woman from Waterville, Maine whose family is Protestant. Growing up in Brooklyn Stern has contact with Jews, but when both his parents die around the time he finishes elementary school, he goes to Waterville to live with his grandparents, eventually becoming a member of the Congregational Church. In college at the University of Illinois-Champaign, his interest in his heritage reawakens and he begins to understand religious prejudice when one woman he dates, Noreen O'Flaherty, the daughter of a Chicago alderman, tries to convert him to Catholicism. In the final section of the book, covering the years 1923 to 1945, Stern lives in Chicago. He opens a law office, marries Noreen, and has two children with her. The children, particularly his son Gabriel, reawaken conflicts over religious faith that nearly end the marriage. As a physical presence, Chicago has little impact in the book, although the city's firmly established ethnic communities, laid out along religious lines, are consequential to Stern's thinking; particularly in the 1930s as news stories cover the treatment of Jews in Europe.

1006. Sinclair, Harold Augustus. *Journey Home*. Garden City, New York: Doubleday, Doran, 1936. 290pp.

In this Depression-era novel, James David Hall lost everything the year of the 1929 stock market crash. The twenty-nine-year-old college graduate lost his job with a New York City brokerage firm, his investments, and his wife, who left town with another man. With no connection to the city, he sets off for New Orleans, but only gets as far as Cincinnati before he falls ill with influenza and is taken in by a riverboat family who later employ him on the boat. With enough earnings to get to Chicago, he lives in a Hyde Park hotel, before his life is changed by meeting bookstore clerk Sondra Moore. She is at the center of a circle of young people, mostly men, who are writers, artists, and musicians, and before long he is developing new interests in books and music and exploring bohemian Chicago. He also gets a job with the Association for the Advancement of American Ideals, operated by the Hon. George Spence. At first he does not realize the operation is a scam that collects membership dues and publishes a monthly magazine for no other purpose than to support Spence. By March of 1931 after losing his job and Sondra, Hall is once again on his way to New Orleans. The eighty pages of the novel set in Chicago capture the spirit of the city among young intellectuals and artists in the midst of the Depression.

1007. Sinclair, Upton. *The Jungle*. New York: Grosset and Dunlap, 1906. 413pp.

Best-known as an exposé of the meat packing industry that led to public outcry and reform, Sinclair's novel is a broader indictment of a society that preyed on immigrant labor. The story is told through the experiences of Lithuanian immigrant Jurgis Rudkus, who arrives in Chicago in the early 1900s with his fiancée, Ona, and her family. Initially, all of them are filled with hope and are emotionally supported by the Lithuanian community in which they marry. However, the near impossibility of securing and holding onto a job leads Rudkus and his family from suffering to despair. When Ona and then their only child die, Rudkus abandons Chicago for the life of a hobo, returning to the city only with the approach of winter to become a beggar. His desperation propels him into crime, which becomes his entrée into the world of political bossism. He can only hold onto this life a short time however before he is once again near starvation. Only when he discovers socialism does he have the interpretive framework for understanding society that may help him overcome his condition. The novel provides extensive material for understanding the life of laborers and immigrants in Chicago at the beginning of the twentieth century.

1008. Sklovsky, Max. *Dynasty: a Novel of Chicago's Industrial Evolution*. Chicago: Americana House 1958. 202pp.

This book deals with issues of social status, capitalism, and gender in the final years of the nineteenth century. Robert Chase, the founder of a successful bank, has only his son Carroll to carry the firm into the future. When he meets the sister of Frank Dodds, his most loyal assistant, he develops the idea that her spiritedness might be the perfect complement to his son's lackluster personality. Myra Dodds agrees to meet Carroll, only out of a concern with not offending her brother's employer. She is a socially aware young woman, involved in the settlement house movement and skeptical of capitalism. She quickly realizes that Carroll Chase is seriously flawed by a lack of ambition and social commitment. As Robert Chase tries to sway her, he is drawn into her world at Hull House, and begins to reassess the working conditions in the foundries he owns. Through Dodds, Chase meets Aaron Bishoff, a recent Ukrainian immigrant with compelling energy and skill in advocating for worker rights. Dodds' attraction to Bishoff deepens into romance. With his Judaism treated as only a slight complication, the two soon marry. Although Dodds does not become a part of Chase's family, she and Aaron continue to influence Chase as he begins to practice a more enlightened management style. Carroll eventually marries and satisfies Chase's wish for an heir, but the 1908 financial crisis shows the effects of corporate capitalism's growth and Carroll's mismanagement on the Chase family firm, and it collapses. Through lengthy exposition, the novel presents a good deal of information about Chicago neighborhoods, the settlement house movement, and late-nineteenth-century business culture.

1009. Smalley, Dave E. *Stumbling*. Newark, N.J.: Barse, 1929. 308pp.

This suspenseful work of science fiction is mostly set in the state prison at Joliet, Illinois. The book explores what would happen if a surgeon was able to alter a convicted murderer's brain so that he no longer remembered his crime or the personal experiences that drove him to murder. In this case, a Chicago doctor successfully performs the surgery, but is not able to win a pardon for his surgically reformed patient, who dies in the hangman's noose anyway. Most of the Chicago content consists of references to locales and scenes in the physician's office.

1010. Smith, Charles Merrill. *Reverend Randollph and the Avenging Angel*. New York: Putnam's Sons, 1977. 245pp.

As an interim pastor at the wealthy Chicago Church of the Good Shepherd near the Loop, Reverend Cesare Paul Randollph has a very comfortable life residing in the church's penthouse apartment. As one of his first official tasks, he performs a wedding ceremony for West Coast actress Lisa Julian. She is killed soon afterwards and after conducting the funeral he investigates the murder. The novel touches on aspects of urban life, particularly the exodus of middle-class and affluent people to the suburbs, and the tendency to see religious observance as an outdated social phenomenon. The nature of social rank in twentieth-century American culture is a major implicit theme. Rev. Randollph, who would formerly have been respected as a minister, is only considered important as a retired professional football player. The murder victim, as a Hollywood actress, has another kind of social eminence, and her father, stepbrother, and fiancé, are considered socially prominent for being physicians. Aspects of gender equality are also an issue. Lisa's family had disapproved of her independence and was pleased that she was becoming a housewife. Contemporary attitudes toward sexuality are crucial to the plot and the murder stems from incidents of childhood rape and incest. Much of the physical description in the novel focuses on the signifiers of wealth and social status (clothing, automobiles, residences, household staff, and club memberships). The Chicago locales mentioned tend to be apartment buildings and houses on Lake Shore Drive and expensive hotels and restaurants.

1011. Smith, Charles Merrill. *Reverend Randollph and the Fall from Grace, Inc.* New York: Putnam's Sons, 1978. 223pp.

This novel takes on the relationship between evangelism and politics. Chicago evangelist, Prince Hartman, has built his independent church, Grace, Inc., from the ground up (including a seminary and field house, in addition to a church). When he approaches the Episcopal Diocese of Chicago asking for ordination, the Reverend Dr. C. P. Randollph is invited to serve on an investigative committee. Before deliberations can begin, Hartman's assistant, Charlie Klemm is poisoned. Later, Martha Bannister is also poisoned. Randollph solves the case when he realizes the political rivalries among Hartman's assistants and traces the killings to Arthur Pendleton, number three in Hartman's chain of command, who gets sexual pleasure from transvestitism. As in other mystery novels featuring Randollph, the clergyman's worldliness and the wealth of his parishioners takes him to expensive apartments, restaurants, shops, and clubs in 1970s Chicago. His romantic friendship with Samantha Stack, who has her own television program, takes him into the world of broadcast media as well.

1012. Smith, Charles Merrill. *Reverend Randollph and the Holy Terror.* New York: Putnam's Sons, 1980. 236pp.

In this mystery novel that touches on the role of organized religion in twentieth-century Chicago, Reverend C. P. Randollph, a character featured in a series of mysteries, marries television reporter Samantha Stack. Around the same time, he receives a nasty poem in the mail, questioning his purity of spirit, since he will be living as a lusty married man in the parsonage of the Church of the Good Shepherd. He learns from the police that a series of ministers and priests in the Chicago area have received similar missives questioning their spirituality and been murdered shortly afterwards. When Randollph decides to go ahead with his public installation as pastor of the Church of the Good Shepherd, the ordaining bishop is gunned down, probably in his stead, and Randollph must find the murderer to save his own life. The novel touches on the politicized campaigns for moral purity launched by fundamentalist Christians during the time period. As in other novels in the series, upper-class lifestyles are a major focus.

1013. Smith, Charles Merrill. *Reverend Randollph and the Wages of Sin.* New York: Putnam's Sons, 1974. 254pp.

Although the Episcopal Church of the Good Shepherd is a Chicago institution that predates the city, when the Rev. Randollph arrives to take over the pastorate, he finds that the church is housed in a modern office tower that includes a hotel. The income from the building is large enough to lavishly fund the church's activities and the penthouse apartment in which Randollph is to reside. Operating as a sort of social club run by very wealthy members of the board of trustees, the church is shaken when the naked corpse of thirty-eight-year-old Mrs. Warlow Reedman, the wife of a trustee and a member of the church choir, is found in the choir practice room. Randollph and a detective from the Chicago police department visit a number of households as they investigate and the detailed descriptions uncover many details of 1970s upper-class life. They discover that the church housekeeper, Mrs. Creedy, killed Reedman for committing adultery on church property.

1014. Smith, Eunice Young. *Jennifer Dances*. Indianapolis: Bobbs-Merrill, 1954. 250pp.

In this novel for children, eleven-year-old Jennifer Hill leaves her family's farm in Aurora, Illinois in October 1909 to live in Chicago with her Aunt Lobelia Ashwood and attend ballet school. Ashwood lives in a freestanding house near the intersection of Ohio and Rush Streets and has a live-in, African-American cook and maid named Dorcas and an African-American houseman. The middle-class Ashwood, teaches Jennifer not to be prejudiced against servants or immigrants, who during this time period are mostly Italian, and Jennifer befriends a paperboy named Tono Morelli, whose father is a composer. Jennifer's dancing school is operated by a Polish woman, Madame Lubescheski, who studied in Paris and Vienna. Through her teacher and aunt, Jennifer is introduced to art and culture in Chicago, fields dominated by European immigrants. Although this school girl novel is focused on Jennifer's experiences with classmates and teachers, as a newcomer to Chicago she is given information about the city and the reader gets a sense of Chicago landmarks and neighborhood life in the early twentieth century.

1015. Smith, Fredrika Shumway. *The Fire Dragon: A Story of the Great Chicago Fire*. Illustrated by Ray Naylor. Chicago: Rand, McNally, 1956. 174pp.

This children's book presents facts about the 1871 fire, as well as lessons about overcoming prejudice and behaving modestly. As the novel opens, twelve-year-old Andy Winthrop rescues a new classmate from the school bully and befriends him. The boy, Terry Shawn, is newly arrived from Ireland, and lives with his father near the gasworks (his mother is dead). Andy's father, Mark, is an affluent real estate investor and Terry's, Tim, works in a planing mill and as a fireman; each is afraid that his son will be negatively influenced by friendship across the socio-economic divide. As an aid to the newcomer, Andy visits downtown Chicago with Terry and they learn about city history from one of Mark's friends. As fires begin in the lumberyards, Tim goes missing, and Terry seeks shelter with the Winthrop family. As fire spreads, Andy and Terry accompany Mark to save documents from his office safe. When Mark disappears in the smoke, they make their way back to the Winthrop family house and help the household servants evacuate Andy's sister and his mother to the lakefront. Their house is destroyed, but they are able to go to the original Winthrop mansion, a stone structure in Peck Court, inhabited by their Aunt Charlotte. The structure is soon designated a relief station by General Sheridan and, after much anxiety, Mark and Tim eventually turn up separately. Mark had been suffering amnesia since a robber struck him and it turns out that Tim was the one who moved him to safety. In a postscript to the story, forty years have passed and Andy and Terry stand at a window and look out over the city that they helped rebuild through their architectural firm. The book presents a number of historical details about daily life, as well as the basic facts about the fire.

1016. Smith, Fredrika Shumway. *Rose and the Ogre*. Boston: Christopher Publishing House, 1948. 184pp.

This work of historical fiction for young adults is set in 1892 and 1893 and presents social history as well as references to historical events such as the Pullman strike and the Columbian Exposition. Sixteen-year-old protagonist Rose Whitney is on the verge of adulthood, part of which means handling difficult people. In her case, Rose must deal with the bullying and complaints of her stepgrandfather, the ogre of the title. He does not, however, prevent Rose from enjoying social events, falling in love, and experiencing the freedom afforded by volunteering at a settlement house. Rose accepts that she cannot change her stepgrandfather and when he dies suddenly, she does not indulge in false sentimentality, even after his will is read and she is his principal heir. Instead, she very practically lays plans for how best to utilize the money.

1017. Smith, George Harmon. [Frank Scarpetta, pseud.]. *Mafia Wipe-Out*. New York: Belmont Tower Books, 1973. 171pp.

This is one of a series of books featuring Philip Magellan, "The Marksman," who is on a vendetta against organized crime, waging his battles in one corrupt 1970s American city after another. The novel's focus on automobile chases, harrowing escapes, and violence leaves little room for more generalized description. Chicago remains a cardboard backdrop for the action.

1018. Smith, Henry Justin. *Deadlines: Being the Quaint, the Amusing, the Tragic Memoirs of a News-Room*. Chicago: Covici-McGee, 1922. 249pp.

Although set in the newsroom of the imaginary *Chicago Press*, the book has more to do with the life of reporters in the nineteen-twenties than the city of Chicago. Several newsroom personalities are presented, including the wise older editor, the newsman who is really a poet, the cub reporter, the star reporter and the author's own superego, named Josslyn. As the book closes, and night deepens, Josslyn is awaiting word of the governor's anticipated death so that he can provide the final details for the front page story.

1019. Smith, Henry Justin. *The Other Side of the Wall*. Illustrated by Clinton Pettee. Garden City, N.Y.: Doubleday, Page, 1919. 342pp.

In this novel about the breaking down of social barriers, the setting is clearly Chicago, although "the city of Deadly Ambitions" is never named directly. Twenty-one-year-old Anne Stone leaves the discomforts of rural Texas to get a job in the city. She has a letter of introduction to the head of an advertising firm from her college president and a friend with whom she can live temporarily, Sally, who had married Dick Crowe of Chicago. The Crowes live in an apartment building named the Annex in Lakeside that, because it faces inland and has no views, is a very middle-class affair. However, the building is attached to the Fannington, with magnificent views of the lake that is occupied by upper-class people. Once Sally secures her advertising job, she is introduced to one of the most important people in the firm, Lance Happerth. Not only does Lance live in the Fannington, but his father-in-law, Barton Fanning, a business mogul, owns the complex. Before long, Sally realizes that the Crowes are unhappy, in part because unsuccessful Dick cannot seem to hold down a job; and that the Happerths are also unhappy. With these examples before her, married life seems problematic. As the First World War begins, Lakeside begins to change and the social divisions represented by the Fannington and the Annex soften. Barton Fanning is revealed to have diverted money from his bank into his private investments, bringing disgrace to his daughter. Through Lance and Pauline, Anne, a nobody from Texas, meets and marries Pauline's brother Tom. Wartime service dramatically changes the lives of Lance Happerth and Dick Crowe. Having confronted life and death realities, Lance can no longer work in advertising and turns to the truth-telling of investigative journalism. Dick Crowe dies a hero's death. As a newcomer to Chicago Sally is given a thorough introduction by various characters and also describes her own explorations, giving the reader a full description of the city in the nineteen-teens. In order to establish social differences, the novel also details leisure activities, domestic furnishings, and social attitudes.

1020. Smith, Henry Justin. *Poor Devil*. New York: Covici Friede, 1929. 281pp.

In this novel, Chicago is a place of unhealthy excitement and false dreams, and its potential for harm is demonstrated in the experiences of Bruce Warren, who leaves the position of small town newspaper editor to work for a large publishing company. In his small town, he is one of the leading citizens, but he has larger ambitions and after marrying Maud Fairlie the whole town turns out to see the couple off to Chicago, where Warren will work for the Faith Publishing Company. As soon as they arrive in the city, they experience financial constraints. Even though they live in a tiny apartment, at the end of the Duluth Avenue Street car line, surrounded by vacant lots, Warren barely makes enough money to pay their expenses. However, he is caught up in the excitement of the architecture, new construction, and ever increasing population of Chicago. Even though he spends his days writing advertising copy, he is gratified to have the assistant editor title with a nationally known publishing house. However, his friend Roger Champion dismisses Faith Publishing for printing condensed materials to cater to lowbrow people who want to appear intellectually and spiritually informed, but do not like to read. Even Warren's immediate supervisor, a man with a doctorate in philosophy, urges Warren to return to newspaper work and take a job offer to manage a syndicate of small town papers. When he turns down the job, his wife is furious and she vents her experience of loneliness and alienation in Chicago. Soon afterwards, though, Warren's supervisor dies at his desk and within an hour Warren is promoted to his position. However, when he realizes that Faith Publishing plagiarizes and that one of the firm's most famous authors only exists as a marketing ploy, he quits his job. Out of work in a market over-supplied with journalists and editors, he becomes desperate and follows the directions of a fellow who says he can get him a theater job. When he shows up, he realizes too late that he is being used to stage a box office hold up. At the end of the novel, Warren is delirious in a hospital bed from his wounds and it seems certain that he will have to leave Chicago. Despite the central message that Chicago offers nothing but unhealthy excitement, many passages provide evocative descriptions of the streetscape and skyline that capture the beauty and romance of the city. The author is also skilled at presenting physical descriptions of office environments, commuting by streetcar, street scenes, and lunch counters. The only specific neighborhoods described are the one in which the Warrens live and the Loop.

1021. Smith. Henry Justin. *The Story of an Incorrigible Dreamer*. Chicago: Covici-McGee, 1924. 252pp.

The hero of this novel, Arthur Josslyn, is a newspaper man who can remember Chicago as far back as the 1890s and tries not to become discouraged as the city fills with apartment buildings, automobiles, and immigrants. The son of a literature professor who went from poverty to penury before his death, Josslyn needs to support his sister Fanny and at twenty-four gets a job as a reporter. He develops a following writing about crimes, gangsters, and politicians, and taking on public causes like gambling and shop lifting. Years pass and eventually Josslyn is made city editor. His sister convinces him that they can afford to move to the suburb of Elmwood and by the time he is forty Josslyn is nearly defeated by the advance of "civilization" with its injustices, cruelties, and subversion of nature; he can only live because of the semi-rural retreat he creates for himself in Elmwood. After he collapses at the office, the newspaper editor sends him on a trip to Europe and he experiences a civilization based on art and culture and not success and ambition. He grudgingly returns to the United States after being called back by the editor to cover a teamster strike. Chicago is viewed with love and hatred in equilibrium in this novel, a balance maintained from the distance of fascinated observation.

1022. Smith, Henry Justin. *Young Phillips, Reporter*. New York: Harcourt, Brace, 1933. 269pp.

Burgess Phillips is at the very beginning of his journalism career at *The Press*. Hired because his father was a respected, but poor (i.e., honest), politician, Phillips has not yet had a chance to prove himself. Phillips' big break comes through his friendship with Roger Firkin who plays in a jazz band. Firkin gives him a chance to sit in as a drummer to eavesdrop on a meeting between Chicago Mayor Gilson and a mobster named Carmeno. In seeking Carmeno's support for a senate race, Gilson pledges kickbacks. *The Press* runs Phillips story and the mayor rides out of town rather than face the clamoring reporters' questions. In the meantime, Phillips is kidnapped and one of *The Press's* rivals prints a retraction that Phillips did not write. After Phillips is released he tries to prove the truth of his original story, but the very room from which he eavesdropped seems to have disappeared. His persistence increases the animosity of the gangsters and despite the protection of hired detectives he is almost blown up by a bomb. He accumulates enough collaborating evidence for his original story that when he presents it at a secret grand jury hearing the mayor resigns. Phillips' life returns to normal, he gets a raise at the newspaper, and is able to propose to the girl he has been dating. Although there is not a great deal of physical description of the city, daily life in a city newsroom and nightclubs and restaurants frequented by gangsters are convincingly described. Disrespect for uniformly corrupt policemen is a running gag throughout the book.

1023. Smith, Mark. *The Death of the Detective*. New York: Alfred A. Knopf, 1974. 596pp.

Arnold Magnuson, a retired police detective, who started his own financially successful security firm, feels old. He lives in a lake side tower in a luxury building his wife chose just before she died. For him street after street of the city brings back memories developed over decades. When a psychopathic murderer begins a serial killing spree, Magnuson is drawn back to detective work. Memories constantly intrude upon his investigation and the result is a multilayered evocation of Chicago over three decades, filled with social detail. Organized crime plays a prominent role in this 1970s novel that also touches on issues of race and ethnicity.

1024. Smith, Terrence Lore. *Murder Behind Closed Doors*, [Phillips Lore, pseud.]. New York: Playboy Press Paperbacks, 1980. 182pp.

This murder mystery is the second by the author to feature a wealthy Evanston lawyer, Leo Roi, who is occasionally drawn into solving crimes. When three gay men are murdered, an advertising executive and two of his friends, Roi explores gay bars and other locales in Chicago and Evanston to solve the case. The novel gives some sense of gay life in the Chicago metropolitan area in the 1970s.

1025. Smith, Terrence Lore. *The Thief Who Came to Dinner*. Garden City, N.Y.: Doubleday, 1971. 176pp.

On the last day of 1966, thirty-one-year-old Webster Daniels quits his mid-level, managerial, white-collar job to begin transforming his life. Previously, he had chosen the well-trod path of college, marriage, and upward mobility. Then his wife Lina deserted him, claiming she could no longer deal with the boredom. With this as his spur, Daniels becomes a very successful jewel thief who uses the contents of one safe to blackmail his victims into introducing him into upper-class life in Winnetka society. With the substantial bankroll he garners form his thefts, Daniels is soon living in a mansion and entertaining the most prominent members of suburban Chicago society. By the end of the novel, in 1968, he has married a beautiful, wealthy woman and looks forward to living on the French Riviera. At the outset of the book Daniels lives in Evanston and spends time in dive bars on Rush Street. He describes the incipient counter culture appearing in the city as well as the jet-set life style of the Kenilworth-Winnetka-Lake Forest area.

1026. Smith, Terrence Lore [Phillips Lore, pseud.]. *Who Killed the Pie Man?: A Mystery*. New York: Saturday Review Press, 1975. 178pp.

This murder mystery presents aspects of cultural life in 1970s Evanston and Chicago, especially openly expressed racism. Soon after Leo Roi, a wealthy amateur detective, discovers the murdered corpse of Dr. Albert Wren, he is hired by an Evanston activist organization campaigning against racial hatred to aid the legal case of the murder defendant, William Frazier "Billie" Blue, an African-American activist. Wren, a retired Northwestern University professor had owned the rare coin shop in which he was shot and operated it with the assistance of Jane Koenig, a Northwestern student and daughter of a Lake Forest multimillionaire. Both Wren and Koenig lived in apartments above the coin shop; Koenig sharing her residence with Billie Blue. Although superstitions concerning a set of missing coins dating back to Roman antiquity keep surfacing, Roi has many less occult leads to follow and eventually identifies a shady stockbroker and a corrupt policeman as the culprits. Roi visits a number of upper-class households and the author catalogs a wide variety of possessions, from cars to neckwear, as signifiers of affluence in the 1970s.

1027. Smith, Wallace. *Are You Decent?* New York: Putnam's Sons, Knickerbocker Press, 1927. 314pp.

All of these ten short stories, originally appearing in *Cosmopolitan Magazine*, are interconnected, since the characters are residents of Mrs. Emily Fisher's boarding house. Mrs. Fisher was a bareback rider in her earlier days as a performer and she caters to circus and vaudeville folk. Although there are descriptions of boarding house life and time spent in restaurants and saloons, most of the action transpires in greenrooms and on stages. The number of acts and performers illustrate the types of public entertainments in Chicago in the 1920s. Not all of the action of the stories takes place in Chicago, since a large aspect of the performer's lives is traveling on the circuit, but all of the performers pass through Chicago and stay at Mrs. Fisher's.

1028. Smith, Wallace. *Bessie Cotter*. New York: Covici-Friede, 1934. 309pp.

This account of Chicago's red-light district in the 1890s takes the position that the area has been there as long as the city, is patronized by the city's most prominent citizens, who often own property there, and is allowed to exist because of the willingness of policemen and city officials to accept bribes. The prostitutes are mostly loveable and honorable and the madams shrewd business women with no other options. In addition to introducing a long list of prostitutes and sketching their personalities and stories, the book includes descriptions of numerous nightclubs and brothels with accounts of the entertainment that typifies each of them. Bessie Colter is the outgoing woman who ties many of the other characters together.

1029. Smucker, Barbara Claasen. *Wigwam in the City*. Illustrated by Gil Miret. New York: Dutton, 1966. 154pp.

In this book for children, a Chippewa Indian family is forced by food shortages and poverty to move from their home on Lac du Flambeau reservation in Wisconsin to a Chicago tenement. The story is told from the perspective of twelve-year-old Susan Bearskin whose seventeen-year-old brother Jim runs away rather than join his parents and sister in a move to the city. The book explains the mixed race origins of the family (a French fur trapper is an ancestor), the government relocation program, and the history of Indians being moved off their land onto reservations. The family is placed in an apartment near the intersection of Clark and Elm Streets. Susan is enrolled in school and her father gets a job in a grocery store. When Susan hears a story about a boy fishing in Lincoln Park she goes there, correct in thinking that it is her brother Jim. When he realizes the police are looking for him he runs from Susan. Later, the Bearskin family learns that he has moved to Minneapolis and has decided to abandon his Chippewa heritage and live as Jim White; however, he pledges to help the family with any money he earns. Although Susan's teacher finds ways to make her feel welcome, the Bearskin family experiences prejudice and have their window broken out by a rock.

1030. Solberg Gunard. *Shelia*. Boston: Houghton Mifflin, 1969. 243pp.

In this novel about racism and the 1960s youth culture, two high school students fall in love in an imaginary suburb of Chicago and suffer the effects of living in a racist society. Wayne Divine, a Caucasian, falls in love with his classmate Sheila Smith, who is both African-American and from a wealthier family than Divine's. Rebelling against the social constraints of their suburb, they travel to Chicago's Near North Side spending time in gay bars, where marginalized people of all sorts gather. In the city, they meet counter culture figures who convince them that only on the West Coast has a society developed that offers the acceptance they seek. Their plan to run away is thwarted before they even get out of Illinois as they become victims of a violent racist attack. Although only one section of the novel is set in Chicago, the youth and bar culture of the Near North Side is vividly presented. The city's role as a place for social experimentation by suburban youth is also clearly outlined. Throughout the novel themes of racism, internalized racism, and gender roles are important.

1031. Sommers, Lillian [Litere, pseud.]. *For Her Daily Bread*. Preface by Col. Robert G. Ingersoll. Globe Library, No. 34. Chicago: Rand, McNally, 1887. 228pp.

Sommers directly addresses the barriers of gender in this novel about women from Memphis, Tennessee, determined to find work other than domestic service in Chicago. Twenty-three-year-old Norma Southstone, her sixteen-year-old sister Florence, and their thirteen-year-old brother Harry are in straitened circumstances since their father drowned (their mother had died previously). The sisters relocate to Chicago with little more than their clothes and have to leave Harry behind to fend for himself, since they do not have enough money for his train ticket. As attractive newcomers to the city they immediately encounter prostitutes who try to lure them into brothels. Only one of their letters of introduction—to the Christian Milk and Water Association—is useful. The organization operates a boarding house and helps women get jobs. The book details the women's struggle to find employment, the inappropriate advances of men in the workplace, and their efforts to learn stenography and telegraphy in a business college with dubious teaching methods. Their life begins to change only when men come to their aid. Judge Westmacott helps them develop new business skills so they can earn more and bring their brother to Chicago. Their lives change again when Norma thwarts a robbery and comes to the attention of the Causey family, part owners of the firm that employs her. The Causeys invite Norma and Florence to social events (a New Year's Eve Ball and theater parties), expanding their acquaintance. When a man in Norma's workplace treats her with over-familiarity, giving the appearance of impropriety, and later co-workers witness prostitutes who accosted her in her first days in Chicago greeting her with familiarity, Norma knows her reputation has been compromised and she quits her job. Fortunately, a man comes to her rescue; James Causey investigates, finds her innocent, and seeks her out and proposes. The novel presents a detailed account that appears to be semi-autobiographical and provides a great deal of information about the plight of women in nineteenth-century society. Although Norma and Florence find jobs to support themselves, their real salvation comes through men who look out for them and offer marriage.

1032. Sommers, Lillian [Litere, pseud.]. *Jerome Leaster of Roderick, Leaster & Co.* Illustrated by Jules Guerin. Chicago: Charles H. Sergel, 1890. 376pp.

In this anti-Catholic work, the hero, Jerome Leaster, rescues the beautiful young Loreau from a burning building. Loreau had inherited a fortune when her mother died in childhood, but she became the ward of a devout Roman Catholic aunt who pushed her into a convent to prepare to become a nun. After Leaster saves her, Loreau can think only of him. The two elope prompting the curses of her aunt and excommunication from her church. Leaster builds a comfortable life for himself and Loreau and they have a child together, Pauline. All is well until Loreau decides to travel back to New York State to introduce Pauline to her aunt. The aunt's behavior so upsets Loreau that when she returns to Chicago, she falls into a period of madness, trying to ritually sacrifice Pauline; when she fails, she tries to kill herself. After recovering in an asylum, Loreau returns to Leaster to find that Pauline has matured into a society favorite and is engaged to a nationally known actor. However, one of Leaster's business partners wants to share in Leaster's fortune by marrying Pauline. He recruits Loreau to forward his suit by playing on her religious beliefs through an alliance with a priest named Father Felix. Falling under the thrall of Felix, Loreau gives him large amounts of money and under the pressure of her mother and the priest, Pauline goes from being carefree to melancholic. Then, when Leaster is on a business trip, Loreau and Felix lock her in a room, without food and water, to break her will. When Leaster returns, he finds Pauline ill with a fever that eventually kills her and can do nothing but rail against his wife and her religion. This anti-Roman Catholic tract is mostly focused on presenting a distorted view of Catholic religious life, although in describing Pauline's secular pastimes it gives some sense of social life in Chicago in the 1880s.

1033. Sommers, Lillian [Litere, pseud.]. *The Unpopular Public.* Chicago: Rand, McNally, 1889. 179pp.

In 1870s Chicago fifteen-year-old Louise Mirden is betrothed by her father, a Chicago innkeeper, to one of his friends. Louise becomes distraught at the prospect of having such an old husband. Her resistance only increases her father's resolve and he begins isolating her socially; forbidding contact with her schoolmates. With no other options available to her, she runs away from home. The novel has little physical description and focuses on the social inequities experienced by women in the time period.

1034. Sontup, Daniel [David Saunders, pseud.]. *M Squad: The Case of the Chicago Cop-Killer.* New York: Belmont Books, 1962. 141pp.

No further information available.

1035. Sparks, Alice Wilkinson. *My Wife's Husband: A Touch of Nature.* Chicago: Laird and Lee, 1897. 303pp.

The first-person narrator of this humorous, anecdotal novel is Elias Chatterton, who owns a farm near Lynxville, New York. He dictates stories about his experiences and observations to a "type writer," a young woman who has set up an office in Lynxville. Part of the humor comes from his rural dialect and colloquialisms, the rest stems from his view of the world. Amongst chapters on religion, the bicycle craze, and inventions are three chapters concerning the Chicago World's Fair ("The Tower of Babel," "Street Car Etiquette," and "The Chicago Relief Committee"). Elias' impressions of Chicago focus on skyscrapers and the nature of their construction, modes of transportation in Chicago, Chicago manners, and the aftermath of the World's Fair. Extensive details are provided about hucksters, boosters, and the suffering working-class people experienced after the fair (when prices were inflated and jobs had ended and many had difficulty affording housing, food, and clothing). When Elias has finished writing his book, he does not know what to do with it, until an acquaintance suggests sending the manuscript to Chicago, with the comment that they publish anything in the city, a reference to the many printing houses in the metropolis.

1036. Spearman, Frank H. *The Close of the Day*. New York: Appleton, 1904. 224pp.

This romance novel set in 1890s Chicago depicts both the world of culture and business, explicitly presenting the city as a place as civilized as eastern cities. Twenty-year-old, Smith College student, Katharine Sims, and forty-year-old millionaire, George Durant, meet while Durant is under the treatment of Sims' physician father, Randolph, for angina pectoris. Although Durant learns that there is no cure for his condition, Dr. Sims dies first. After some months Katharine approaches him for advice about earning a living with her singing. He discourages her from the vaudeville stage and helps her get into the chorus in an opera company. She rises to soloist just as Durant's wholesale coffee business is collapsing. He has decided to marry Sims, and is determined to recover his fortune before proposing. Unfortunately, he dies before achieving his goal. In describing social life in Chicago, the novel makes clear the impact of college boys and girls returning from the east at the end of the social season and particularly their impact on theatrical performances. The Chicago places mentioned tend to be the Athletic Club and Auditorium. The novel refers to the rise of the North Side as the best residential neighborhood and the popularity of yachting parties.

1037. Spearman, Frank H. *Doctor Bryson*. New York: Charles Scribner's Sons, 1902. 308pp.

This novel of 1890s Chicago illuminates two worlds, that of medical practice and that of the boarding house. Henry Elwood Bryson, M.D. built the clinic at Laflin College for the Eye and Ear through skill and hard work. Bryson's life centers on his career, and the novel closely details the operation of the clinic, describing patients and clinic workers. The other world of the novel is the boarding house operated by three unmarried sisters, Anna, June, and Mary Borderly. Their quirky personalities are presented, as well as those of their boarders. The major dramatic conflict of the novel centers on Ruth Eliot, whose need for an eye operation changes Bryson's highly structured life when he becomes romantically interested in her mother Helen Eliot, who is estranged from her husband, but still married. A dramatic accident that leaves Bryson near death during a holiday on Mackinac Island brings the couple closer together and Helen's husband dies at around the same time. Although the Chicago physical setting is not fully developed, the novel provides a good deal of detail about daily life.

1038. Spencer, Ross H. *The Abu Wahab Caper*. New York: Avon Books, 1980. 144pp.

When Chance Purdue is hired to protect members of the Dugan family, he is told that they are being threatened by attempts to steal the sword of Abu Wahab—owned by the Dugans, but originally the property of the Prince of Ishaq. Fortunately for the tough, but slow-witted, Purdue, he is aided by the beautiful Brandy Alexander. She discovers that it is not a sword thieves are trying to steal, but an internal combustion engine one of the Dugans invented that is powerful, compact, and runs on urine. Due to the gambling habits of "Bet-a-Bunch" Dugan, the book includes visits to race tracks.

1039. Spencer, Ross H. *The DADA Caper*. New York: Avon Books, 1978. 189pp.
      Soon after Chicago detective Chance Purdue is hired to protect Candi Yakozi, a mysterious man named Clem Dawson approaches Purdue claiming to represent the United States government. He hires Purdue on a retainer of three hundred dollars per week to track down Ysteb Nivlek, the local head of an organization with the acronym DADA (Destroy America Destroy America) that also appears in other Spencer novels as an arm of the KGB. The inept Purdue never really solves the case. His secretary Betsy finally reveals that out of jealousy she hired an actor to pretend to be federal agent Dawson to keep Purdue distracted from thinking about Candi Yakozi. The person Dawson hired Purdue to search for is actually Betsy (the name he had been given—Ysteb Nivlek—was Betsy's name spelled backwards). Betsy's ploy gets Purdue's attention and they begin to share her apartment. By the end of the novel, he has promised to marry Betsy. Although Chicago places are mentioned, physical setting is not of great importance in the novel.

1040. Spencer, Ross H. *The Reggis Arms Caper*. New York: Avon Books, 1979. 158pp.
      By this, the second in a series of novels featuring Chicago private detective Chance Purdue, Purdue and his new bride, Betsy, a former prostitute, have purchased their favorite bar, Wallace's, at the intersection of Kimball and Belmont. Although both have decided to focus all their attention on the tavern business, Purdue is called back into detective service to protect Princess Sonia of Kaleski during the reunion of his army battalion, a member of which the princess has wed. Not until the end of the novel when his newfound detective colleague Brandy Alexander clues him in, does Purdue realize that Communist agents were mostly concerned with a compound, ibiothane, that Kaleski controls and is used to make purple jelly beans. As with other Spencer novels, Chicago places are mentioned, but physical setting is not crucial to the story.

1041. Spencer, Ross H. *The Stranger City Caper*. New York: Avon Books, 1980. 159pp.
      In most of this novel Chance Purdue is on assignment in a southern Illinois town named Stranger City, sent there by Cool Lips Chericola, a Chicago gangster, to investigate a minor league baseball team. By the time Bobby Cracker's Blitzkrieg for Christ religious crusade turns up in town, Purdue is eager for the help of his detective colleague Brandy Alexander. Alexander clears up any mysteries and identifies Bobby Cracker as Boboi Krakezoff, a KGB agent who has used evangelism to accumulate American currency and to deploy Russian spies throughout the country.

1042. Spencer, Scott. *Endless Love*. New York: Alfred A. Knopf, 1979. 418pp.
      David Axelrod's teenage crush on Jade Butterfield leads to a psychotic obsession that fuels Axelrod's pursuit of Jade and members of her family around the continent over more than a decade. Initially, the Axelrods and Butterfields are Hyde Park residents and participants in the 1960s counter culture. When Axelrod decides to set fire to the Butterfield's house, from which he has been banished for a month, it happens to be on a night when each Butterfield, even the pre-teen children, have taken LSD. When Axelrod returns to the burning house to rescue the family as he had planned and redeem himself, the role is overwhelmingly difficult, given the Butterfields'

drug-addled state, and one of the sons perishes in the blaze. After institutionalization in a mental hospital, Axelrod returns to Chicago and attends Roosevelt University and the novel includes accounts of the youth culture in the city during this time period. Although more than half of the novel is physically set in New York City and Vermont, Chicago remains important throughout as the center of Axelrod's psychic life.

1043. Stahl, John M. *Just Stories*. Chicago: Donohue, 1916. 156pp.

The short stories in this volume blend to create a sense of office life for males in early-twentieth-century Chicago. The first-person narrator, a traveling salesman based in the Loop who takes the Illinois Central commuter train each day to Thirty-sixth Street Station, relates anecdotes about people he has met through work in the voice of a white collar male. Many of the stories focus on couples who are courting or married and deal with the changes women bring into the lives of men through religion, character reform, or behavioral adjustments. Other stories demonstrate the degree to which the narrator and most of his acquaintances are part of a group of city residents who are only recently urbanized and remember with fondness aspects of farm and small town life. In a few stories the narrator is a witness to urban poverty or tragedy.

1044. Stanger, Wesley Allen. *Rescued from Fiery Death: A Powerful Narrative of the Iroquois Theater Disaster: Mighty Flames Graphically Portrayed*. Chicago: Laird and Lee, 1904. 317pp.

This novel is a fictionalized account of the Iroquois Theater fire of December 30, 1903, in which 571 people died. Protagonist Neal Bennington is the son of wealthy Curtis Bennington, an investor. Neal's parents are both cold and remote and Neal's later failures are ascribed to the emotional emptiness of his childhood. As a youth he was preoccupied with glimpsing a beautiful little girl in his neighborhood, Alice Fanning, and day-dreaming about getting to know her. After failing out of college and being unable to find a job, the disgusted Bennington sends Neal to South America; however, his health is broken by the climate before he even reaches Rio de Janeiro and he immediately journeys back to the United States. During his recovery, his mother becomes more affectionate and when he is well, he begins working successfully in his father's office and gets to meet Alice Fanning, now a young woman. Then his father tries to corner the wheat market, is ruined, and dies. Alice will no longer receive the impoverished Neal socially. By coincidence, however, they are both in the Iroquois Theater when the fire begins. Neal saves the unconscious Alice as well as many other people before collapsing with burns himself. Alice, who had been in a box with family members, does not know who saved her, but all of her family was killed. When she sees the news accounts that documents Neal's heroism, she tracks him down, nurses him, and eventually marries him. Wanting Neal and his mother to forget the sorrows they had experienced in Chicago, she decides to move everyone to Baltimore. In a strange coincidence, they visit the city just before a great fire breaks out there that they witness and survive. In the aftermath, Alice stands by her original plan and the investment of her wealth in Baltimore helps revitalize the city.

1045. Starrett, Vincent. *The Blue Door: Murder-Mystery-Detection in Ten Thrill Packed Novelettes*. Garden City, N.Y.: Crime Club / Doubleday, Doran, 1930. 345pp.

The novellas in this collection reference earlier works of detective fiction written by Sir Arthur Conan Doyle and Edgar Allen Poe. Chicago is paralleled with London for being as picturesque and colorful for detective fiction, particularly the Near North Side in the neighborhood around Elm and Dearborn Streets whose bohemian households attract prolonged descriptions. Other settings include Lincoln Park, antiques shops and bookshops on Halsted Street, the Loop, pawnbrokers, Armenian restaurants, the Greek neighborhood, and large apartment buildings. Even though the stories are set in the 1920s, horse-drawn vehicles still ply the city streets and the domestic settings usually include servants. Perhaps, referencing English detective fiction, characters are given to phrases such as, "By Jove!" Several of the stories feature Jimmie Lavender, a character who appears in Starrett's longer works. Many of the stories were previously published in *Pictorial Review*, *Short Stories*, *Real Detective Tales*, *Midweek*, and *The Chicago Daily News*.

1046. Starrett, Vincent. *The Case Book of Jimmie Lavender*. New York: Gold Label Books, 1944. 350pp.

This collection of short stories features a fictional Chicago character created by Starrett for whom he borrowed, with permission, the name of Jimmy Lavender, a pitcher for the Chicago Cubs. The stories were first published in *Mystery Magazine*, *Real Detective Tales*, and *Short Stories*. Lavender has the presence of a stage actor or high-ranking army officer and is literate and cultured. Although most of his cases in this volume focus on solving Chicago crimes, several stories are set abroad or on board ship. Lavender lives on Portland Street with a male assistant, in a dwelling filled with museum-quality curios and books. Many of the mysteries Lavender must solve take him into elegantly furnished apartments (one styled like an Italian palazzo, complete with a Renaissance-style garden), however, gangland figures and nightclub denizens are never far away. The author is pointed about including characters that he considers exotic, including a Russian ballerina, "Negro" dancers, and "China boys." At the center of the crimes in Lavender's cases are antiquities, blackmail, and beautiful women.

1047. Starrett, Vincent. *Coffins for Two*. Chicago: Covici-McGee, 1924. 242pp.

A number of the short stories in this collection are set in Chicago. In "Four Friends of Mavis," a young woman named Mavis Onsrud gets rid of all her suitors but one, through an elaborate plot that gets them institutionalized in an insane asylum. In "The Truth About Delbridge," famous golfer Francis Delbridge becomes obsessed with Chicagoan Sue Graydon. When he challenges Graydon's husband to a game of golf with Mrs. Graydon as the prize, he becomes irate that Mr. Graydon will not take up his challenge, leaves Chicago, and kills his own wife in Philadelphia. Reappearing in Chicago, he comes close to killing Mr. Graydon in his library, and then flees to his country house where he is found dead dressed in a wedding dress and looking at himself in a mirror. Morgan Richardson, the protagonist in "The End of the Story," is a short story writer who usually chooses the same seat each day on the Oak Park Elevated Line. When he gives the same young woman his seat two nights in a row, he decides to pursue other means of becoming acquainted with her, not out of genuine interest, but in order to act out in real life the sort of story that he writes, in which men pursue romances with young women they meet casually in public places. In "The Episode of the Plugged Dime," an impoverished young man tries to pay his street car fare with his last dime, only to discover that it had a whole drilled into it for use as a watch chain ornament and is now plugged, making it worthless. He meets several interesting characters as he tries to exchange the dime for nickels. Scarlett, the attractive young man in "The Man Who Loved Leopards" is successful at picking up Miss Archer while she is waiting for the Oak Park train because he strikes up a conversation based on the fake leopard skin she is wearing. Almost all of this book's Chicago stories explore how strangers make connections in the city, either for romantic or practical reasons.

1048. Starrett, Vincent. *Dead Man Inside*. Garden City, N.Y.: Crime Club / Doubleday, Doran, 1931. 310pp.

A series of Chicago murders attract worldwide attention because the murderer leaves signage with—"Dead Man Inside"—on the doors of rooms concealing the corpses. Initially none of the victims seem to have anything in common: Amos Bluefield was the proprietor of a haberdashery store, Hubert Gaunt a professional gambler, Patrick Lear a renowned actor, and Ellis Greene a bond salesman. Well-known surgeon Dr. John Rainfall and Howard Saxon, a sports journalist, discover Lear's body and decide to investigate. Walter Ghost, a visiting scholar using the Newberry Library, also joins the investigation as a diversion out of the boredom with recovering from appendicitis. The lives of all three men quickly get much more exciting as they become the focus of threats and actual attacks and the number of murder victims grows. The list of suspects includes a bootlegger and a nightclub owner. As with many of Starrett's novel's the Chicago setting is mostly conveyed through stereotypical Chicago characters (sportsmen, gamblers, bootleggers, and showgirls).

1049. Starrett, Vincent. *The End of Mr. Garment*. Garden City, N.Y.: Crime Club / Doubleday, Doran, 1931. 310pp.

One of England's greatest novelists, Stephen Garment, is found stabbed to death in a taxicab outside the house of Chicago society figure Howland Kimbark. Garment had been invited to a party by Kimbark and arrived four hours late. Mysteriously, Garment was alive when he got into the cab and no one else got in during the course of the trip. Local detective Bernard Cicotte makes little headway with the case since there seem to be no clues. However, on a trip to New York, Cicotte's colleague, Dunstan Mollock, meets his friend, scholar and amateur detective, Walter Ghost, who is able to solve the mystery. As in so many novels, Chicago is presented as a place where society figures live opulently in the midst of a gritty urban setting filled with violence and criminality.

1050. Starrett, Vincent. *The Great Hotel Murder*. Garden City, N.Y.: Crime Club / Doubleday, Doran, 1935. 299pp.

Attractive young Blaine Oliver is puzzled when she is kept waiting for Dr. Horace Trample in the hotel lobby where they are to eat breakfast. When knocks and telephone calls do not rouse Trample, the skeptical hotel manager reluctantly opens the door to discover the corpse of Horace Chambers. Trample is found in the room Chambers had checked into. After many drinks the night before, some with Chambers, Chambers had presented Trample with an implausible excuse to exchange rooms. Hotel owner Tony Widdowson, anxious to protect his establishment's reputation, calls upon his friend, Riley Blackwood, a well-known drama critic and successful amateur detective. Concerned that Trample may have been the intended victim, Blaine Oliver, who is also a friend of Blackwood, joins the investigation. As a wealthy, bachelor playboy, Blackwood encourages the detectives to go yachting, nightclubbing, and dancing, even after the case becomes more serious when the real identity of the murdered man revealed to be Jeffrey Cottingham, an important New York City banker. Cottingham was secretly married to Kitty Mock, an actress performing in Chicago who happens to use morphine, the drug that killed her husband. As in most of Starrett's mysteries, a wide number of suspects emerge, including a private detective, an English explorer, Trample (who turns out to be a famous toxicologist), and an architect (who keeps showing up in places connected to the crime). The novel presents scenes from upper-class life in Chicago, as well as presenting the socially marginal, such as hotel employees, cab drivers, denizens of the theater district, and figures involved in the illegal drug trade.

1051. Starrett, Vincent. *Midnight and Percy Jones.* New York: Covici, Friede, 1936. 256pp.

In this murder mystery the victim is a concert singer killed in her fashionable Lake Shore Drive apartment. Amateur detective, theater critic Riley Blackwood, investigates and his prime suspect is radio announcer Percy Jones. Radio broadcasting culture and newsroom culture is prominent in the novel, but 1930s nightlife is also important as characters go to nightclubs to drink and dance to orchestras, some of which are being broadcast over radio. Cultural fascination with the Far East is conveyed through the many references to Chinese people and Confucius. A Hindu stage entertainer, mind reader Raja Singh, is crucial to the plot. Gangsters involved in counterfeiting also play a role. Chicago physical settings are somewhat vague, but the novel does seem to present the social life of affluent people connected to the entertainment industry in Chicago in the 1930s.

1052. Stein, Max. *William Bright, Captain of Commerce: A Story of Commercial Progress.* Chicago: United States Publishing House, 1912. 195pp.

This novel conveys the author's ideas about the consolidation and nationalization of industry and includes appendices that spell out a platform of renewal for the Progressive political party. The plot concerns Helen Stewart and the manufacturing company she inherits upon the death of her father. She has been trained in all aspects of the vaguely described business and can also rely upon twenty-six-year-old William Bright as her manager. Bright worked his way up from the shop floor to a management position under her father's guidance. Almost immediately the pair is challenged by a competitor, which, as a corporation, has significantly greater resources. Struggling together to save the company, Helen and William fall in love and marry. The first half of the novel records the parrying between the company and the corporation, which uses legitimate business techniques and illegal schemes, including a fire, and infiltration of company ranks to incite unrest. When the company fails, William and Helen are left nearly destitute. However, William rejects the job offered by the corporation, finds a way to restructure the company, rebuilds the factory, and sees the business prosper due to customer loyalty. By the end of the novel, a Grand Union League of Progress is taking over the country, drawing all citizens into decision-making bodies that meet on a regular basis to discuss land use and industry. These groups mesh with regional, state, national, and international bodies. Although physical setting is of little importance in the novel, much of the work seems to be set in Chicago, where industrialists and academics join forces.

1053. Stern, Karl. *Through Dooms of Love.* New York: Farrar, Straus, and Cudahy, 1960. 433pp.

Chicago is a place of refuge for families dislocated by World War II in this novel set in 1949. The owner of an important glassworks, Leonhart Radbert had been an important man in Czechoslovakia. Forced to leave the country with few resources other than his family (wife, adult son Franz, and sixteen-year-old daughter Marianne), Radbert went first to Amsterdam, then England (where Franz stayed) and finally to New York City (where Marianne thought she might break into the New York theater world). However, the work she finds is as a fashion model. Following opportunities in Chicago's expanding fashion industry, she settles there with her father after her mother's death. Father and daughter share an appreciation for art, music, and literature and Marianne helps establish him as a lecturer on these topics, mostly to Czech immigrant groups, book clubs, and church associations. Extended emotional trauma begins when Leonhart has a stroke and begins a long decline, during which he becomes mentally ill. Once Leonhart dies, Marianne undergoes a mental collapse and recovers through her friendship with couturier Mrs. Surin, who introduces her to the satisfactions of helping others and to the Roman Catholic Church. Although most concerned with psychological issues experienced by refugees and in father/daughter relationships, the novel also depicts the Chicago fashion industry, medical organizations, social welfare organizations, immigrant associations, and churches. The Radberts live on the North Shore, but settings are also drawn from the greater Chicago metropolitan area.

1054. Stern, Lucille. *The Midas Touch*. New York: Citadel Press, 1957. 286pp.

Baruch (Barry) Selman, the son of early-twentieth-century Orthodox Jewish immigrants to Chicago, resents the demands and social connotations of the religion into which he was born and early in life decides that only wealth will get him the respect and satisfaction he desires. He soon establishes himself and meets Sigrid Ericson through John Clarke, an inventor. Sigrid is studying nursing and Barry loves her blonde beauty and the fact that with her he forgets his Jewish identity. He ignores the importance his father places on tradition and marries Sigrid. Although Sigrid is content with home life, her baby Barbara, and modest possessions, Barry is filled with ambition. In every context, he thinks only of building his business: getting a friend to sell a patent so that he will benefit; establishing a dress shop for his sister so that he can take part of her earnings as a skilled designer; ignoring his home life, and using every social events to make business contacts; and even using Barbara's playmates to build his business network. As the stock market crash approaches, Barry uncannily takes his profits at the market peak and begins purchasing real estate at historically low prices. While everyone else is suffering, he buys and renovates a Winnetka mansion and has a grand housewarming party. By the late 1930s he has become wealthy and obsessed with making more money. His father takes no pleasure in his son's achievements and Sigrid feels unloved. Barry refuses to help distressed acquaintances and family members and when his parents ask him to help organize rescue efforts for European Jews, including family members, he rejects them out of a concern with being publicly identified as a Jew. When his daughter marries a man of whom he disapproves, he changes his will. He does not join Sigrid when her mother is dying, or for the funeral due to business. Eventually, Barry realizes that he has no friends and has been alone in his Gold Coast mansion each night for weeks. On the eve of his most dramatic business deal ever, he learns that Sigrid has been in town nursing his dangerously ill father. In a dramatic sickroom ending, Barry asks forgiveness and pledges to change. The novel includes little physical description of settings, but does detail upper-class social events and mentions names of businesses and neighborhoods. The one-dimensional portrayal of Barry smacks of anti-Semitism.

1055. Steuber, William F., Jr. *The Landlooker*. Indianapolis: Bobbs-Merrill, 1957. 367pp.

Most of this work set in 1871 takes place in Wisconsin where Emil Rohland and his brother Rudolph work selling harnesses made by their Chicago-based family firm. The Rohland family is large and all of the men work in the factory which their father runs cooperatively. The Rohland house on Michigan Avenue is described, as well as Rohland's meetings with politicians and government agents to get federal contracts, and with railway officers to get a preferential rate for shipping his harnesses. The young Emil must learn aspects of his father's business before setting out to be a company agent. So, for a period of time, Emil must spend the day on South Water Street in the market, selling harnesses to learn salesmanship. The most successful vendors are a Jewish man and an African-American and Emil tries to adopt their techniques. Near the end of the novel, after a series of adventures in Wisconsin, Emil and his brother learn of the Chicago fire and make preparations to return to the city, uncertain how deeply the Rohland family has been affected by the disaster. The novel presents information about a large, family manufacturing firm in the early days of the development of nationwide markets that railroad transportation made possible.

1056. Stevens, C. M. (Charles McClellan) [Quondam, pseud.]. *The Adventures of Uncle Jeremiah and Family at the Great Fair: Their Observations and Triumphs.* Illustrated by Henry Mayer. Chicago: Laird and Lee, 1893. 237pp.

In addition to describing the fair, this work has a didactic intent. Jeremiah Jones, a livestock farmer from Park County, Indiana, brings his wife and two of his grandchildren to the Chicago fair. The only time Jones had traveled from home in the past was to fight in the Civil War. Throughout the book Jeremiah references newspaper coverage of the fair and responds. One controversial issue at the time was whether the fair should be open on Sunday. Jeremiah points out that his family visited the Lincoln statue on a Sunday and seeing such art work can have a moral and spiritual benefit. He also finds the fair educational since from the exhibits one can learn about many countries of the world, their achievements, and the planet's diversity. The observations of Jeremiah and his family are not value-free, however. Throughout their visit they make ethnic and racial distinctions, particularly during visits to the African villages, and while attending the beauty pageant. This heavily illustrated work has a number of plot devices to take the book beyond the merely descriptive. Jeremiah is huckstered on several occasions and is later falsely arrested and his grandchildren must find a Chicagoan to aid in his release. Their father has been missing for some years and in a strange coincidence the man who aids them turns out to be their parent. Readers will be interested in the way the book reveals contemporaneous attitudes toward the fair.

1057. Stevens, C. M. (Charles McClellan) [Quondam, pseud.]. *Egyptian Harp Girl.* Chicago: Laird and Lee, 1894. 272pp.

The first part of this mystery novel is set in Egypt and the remainder at the 1893 World's Fair, near the end of the exposition. The plot focuses on the young woman who plays the harp in the Temple of Luxor in the Midway Plaisance and revolves around a secret society of occult practitioners.

1058. Stevens, Grant Eugene. *Wicked City.* Chicago: The Author, 1906. 340pp.

In part, this novel concerns English brothers Robert and Gordon Long. One is the heir to a fortune; the other an illegitimate son and at the outset it is not clear which is which. Since their mother's deathbed confession years before, they have known of the illegitimacy. Later, when their father was on his deathbed, he revealed that a family clock incorporates a secret mechanism that will reveal the identity of the illegitimate son at the end of three years. The illegitimate son will inherit nothing but the clock and the true heir will inherit the entire estate. Robert came to believe that he was the illegitimate son and gave into every evil impulse, including gambling. After imprisonment in London, he escaped to Chicago, the wicked city. It is there that his brother eventually finds him. After much skullduggery on the part of Robert, who employs hoodlums to steal the clock, and engage in other criminal activity he is revealed to be the legitimate son. However, disguises and concealed identities leave the reader in doubt until a dramatic conclusion. Interspersed within the plot of the novel are testimonials that prove that Chicago is no longer the wicked city of the years in which the novel's action transpires. In addition, presumably as a way of promoting sales of the book, there are advertisements for prizes (including a vacation home) that will be awarded to the reader who finds certain hidden words in the text.

1059. Stewart, Charles D. *Buck; Being Some Account of His Rise in the Great City of Chicago.* Illustrated by R. M. Brinkerhoff. Boston: Houghton Mifflin, Riverside Press, 1919. 298pp.

At the beginning of this humorous novel, James Buckingham Summers, the eponymous Buck, is studying at a public university where he majors in classical languages (which he considers the easiest course since he studied Greek and Latin in high school). His father, Zachary, considers anything he studies useless to a small-town businessman. He just wants his son to get a college degree and return to Marysville, Illinois to enter the family business. Then, Zachary hears that Buck has been keeping company with an actress and travels to the university to admonish his offspring. To Zachary's later distress, Buck is too receptive to the observation that at Buck's age Zachary had been making a success of himself. After his father's visit Buck drops out of school. The rest of the novel relates, mostly in epistolary form, Buck's amusing adventures in Chicago, as he begins work as a drayman, then drives a funeral car for an undertaker, and later joins a circus and helps stage a charity musical. Fortunately, he eventually invents a cookie cutter with which he begins to make a fortune and marries an heiress. In several extended passages, the author characterizes Chicago, and physical descriptions, including one of a graveyard, establish the city's identity.

1060. Stone, Irving. *Adversary in the House.* Garden City, N.Y.: Doubleday, 1947. 432pp.

Like other of his works, Stone's biographical novel of Eugene V. Debs is thoroughly researched and presented in great detail. The Chicago aspect of the book is Debs connection to the strike against the Pullman Palace Car Company in 1894 which is covered over roughly fifty pages. However, Chicago is prominently mentioned throughout the novel as a cultural center for Debs' family and other Terre Haute residents, as well as the scene of important lectures and labor actions.

1061. Strande, Wilhelm vom. *Chicago in Tears and Smiles.* Cleveland, Ohio: Press of Lauer and Mattill, 1893. 214pp.

Published at the same time that many books were celebrating the achievements of Chicago, this novel focuses on the 1871 fire as a punishment for sin and a sign of the redemptive power of Christian charity. Before the fire, Dr. Adolphus, a Protestant minister, struggles to establish a German-language school in the city's German immigrant community with the help of his wife. They are joined by William a schoolteacher from New Jersey who comes to the city as a missionary to the city's sinners. As a newcomer, William (and the reader) benefit from many descriptions of the evil city, rife with gambling, alcohol abuse, and poverty (considered a moral failure). William, the good newcomer, is contrasted with Mr. and Mrs. Orlin. Mr. Orlin had grown up the son of wealthy southern plantation owners and has established himself as an affluent lawyer in Chicago; however he is in thrall to alcohol and gambling. Although the 1871 fire is only briefly described, the book includes a long account of the destruction and suffering of the people after the fire, presumably to present images of divine punishment.

1062. Straus, Ralph. *Pengard Awake.* New York: David Appleton, 1920. 299pp.

When Sir Robert Graeme, a bibliophile and connoisseur, takes a trip to the United States with his sister Rosamund, they travel to Chicago to purchase a rare object. As people from England they are introduced to an unusually popular man, John Pengard, who has soon fascinated Rosamund. Curious about the man's origins, Graeme discovers that prior to Pengard's arrival in the city twelve years before, little can be learned about him. He then realizes that some of the character traits and biographical details of Pengard's life approximate those of a fictional character found in a novel in which the protagonist leaves Dover, England to find fortune in Chicago. After time-consuming investigative work he discovers Pengard is Captain Matthieson, a Boer War veteran who received a head injury while escaping captivity and adopted the facts of the fictional character's life as his own. The Chicago of the novel is a place of Anglophilic private clubs and upper-class socializing.

1063. Street, Ada and Julian Street. *Tides*. Garden City, N.Y.: Doubleday, Page, 1926. 412pp.

The present of this family saga is approximately 1880 to 1921 and focuses on Alan Wheelock, a third generation Chicagoan, although through the stories of his grandfather, Zenas Wheelock, the novel covers much of Chicago's history back to the first decade of the nineteenth century. An adventurous young man, Zenas compares the westward movement of settlers across America to ocean tides. Arriving from New Hampshire as a seventeen-year-old with a French trapper, Zenas traded with the Indians during the era when John Kinzie's house was the only permanent structure in the area. Ahead of the tide of western settlement, Zenas was unsuccessful in holding his ground against the rapid transformation of Chicago into a city. He was too honorable to take advantage of others' misfortune after the Chicago fire and later sold off much of his land to pay debts he had no legal obligation no pay. By the 1880s he owned only his original homestead on Napier Place, an area that had become disreputable and filled with houses of prostitution. He is forced to move in with his son, Harris, a refined collector of rare first editions. As a resident of Harris' house in Oakland he watches his grandson Alan grow up and marry the girl from next door. Alan's generation experiences the Columbian Exposition, the Pullman strike, and the city's growth, but by the 1920s Alan, along with many of the city's affluent young people have moved to New York City to participate in a Eurocentric culture and Alan's daughter marries an Italian count. The novel evokes a turn-of-the-century Chicago through neighborhood history and family anecdote in which the major events in the city's history are much more transformative than the personal story of any family member.

1064. Strobel, Marion. *Fellow Mortals*. New York: Farrar and Rinehart, 1935. 300pp.

This tale of affluent family life from 1916 to 1931 relates the stories of Isobel, Newt, Polly, and Ridge the children of Newton and Lettie Ambler, affluent Near North Side residents, and covers the time period, 1916-1931. World War I involves all the Amblers: Newt joins the navy, Ridge the medical corps in Paris, and Newton gets a government job in Washington. The women are engaged in volunteer work and letter writing. After the war, the Ambler children are focused on college life and dating. Newt marries a brewing fortune heiress; Ridge marries a Dutch girl he met while abroad; and Isobel seems destined to marry Thurber Lamb, the son of a University of Chicago professor. Lamb surprises everyone by marrying a German war widow and Isobel begins a long engagement to Dr. Joe Eliot, only wedding him years after Lamb dies in an automobile accident and she finally puts her first, true love in the past. Polly begins a career as a school teacher and seems destined to go unwed, but later surprises everyone by marrying a millionaire banker, Oliver Cromwell Beasley. In the Depression many of the Ambler children move back to the family house. Beasley's bank fails, Newt's wife divorces him after his stock market investments crash, Joe Eliot's hospital fails and Ridge and Eliot return to get positions in Chicago's Presbyterian Hospital. The novel describes family entertainments that encapsulate passing fashions (ukulele clubs, mandolin playing, amateur theatricals) and shows the impact of national and international events on the Chicago family. Surprisingly little is made of Chicago historical events, except for brief references. The Ambler family is clearly affluent enough to be insulated from much that goes on locally beyond the grounds of their house and even in the Depression can find refuge in the family house.

1065. Strobel Marion. *Ice Before Killing*. New York: Charles Scribner's Sons, 1943. 213pp.

In this murder mystery, the prime suspect is Liz Soames, a teenager about to graduate from high school who is the major contender for the United States Figure Skating Championship of 1942. Soames lives in the affluent household of her father Archie Soames, along with her distracted mother, Serena, younger sister Mollie, widowed aunt, Rosalie Soames Plummer, a French maid, and an Irish cook. Serena is so distracted because Archie is a philanderer. His current affair is with Gwen Ellis, the second wife of Vardis Hunter, the senior professional at the private skating club of which the Soames are members, and where Liz has taken lessons for years. When Ellis is murdered, even Liz doubts her own innocence since she resented Gwen so much and cannot quite remember her whereabouts around the time the murder occurred. The novel references Chicago landmarks such as the Wrigley Building, but is focused on family dynamics within the Soames household.

1066. Strobel, Marion. *Saturday Afternoon*. New York: Farrar and Rinehart, 1930. 279pp.

This satire of Chicago cultural life in the 1920s tells the story of Susannah Pease, who has been spending the fortune she inherited from her father to operate a not-for-profit publishing house to foster the careers of Chicago writers. However, decades have passed and the writers have published nothing of significance. In the hope of jolting her writers into productivity, she announces a ten thousand dollar prize for a quality Chicago novel. Knowing that people say she uses her patronage to surround herself with young men, when she realizes she is actually in love with Stephen Canby, she decides to send him abroad with another of her older writers, Amory Junkins, as his guide. She arranges a lakeside picnic to make her announcement to Canby and through a misperception on Canby's part; he goes to alert the authorities that she has drowned. Not able to find him, she goes back to her office. The rest of the novel describes what happens that Saturday afternoon in April of 1927, as Canby, Junkins, and members of Susannah's salon are invigorated at the prospect of works to memorialize Susannah. After being locked in her office all day, Susannah sees the newspapers, understands that the announcement of her death has ignited the renaissance she had hoped to inspire, and decides that only one course of action makes sense. The book includes beautifully rendered descriptions of the reclaimed land along the lake above Lincoln Park, downtown streets near Marshall Fields, and stretches of Wells, Madison and Ohio streets. Clothing, domestic interiors, and food are also described in painterly detail.

1067. Strobel, Marion. *Silvia's In Town*. New York: Farrar and Rinehart, 1933. 309pp.

In this social satire, gossip about Silvia Simpson Fox, a twenty-seven-year-old widow with a young daughter, preoccupies upper-class Chicago. The men are attracted by her beauty and vivaciousness and the women are fascinated by her violation of social norms. Her openness about her affairs, sometimes with married men, has titillated and vexed society for years. Is her casualness in such matters genuine? Why did she marry Tom Fox, instead of Dr. Littlejohn, with whom she was having an affair? Was she really ignorant of Eliza Hickson's love for Fox? After the death of Fox, Silvia spent time in New York City. In the time period the novel covers, October 1930 to May 1931 Silvia returns to Chicago and lives part of the time with writer Stanley Quinn, in a series of rooftop, picturesque cottages on top of a Loop building. Although Silvia claims the affair is casual, Stanley announces plans to spend extended periods with her in Chicago, in between his absences in New York and Bermuda. After Silvia discovers that Eliza Hickson is in love with Stanley, she is with Eliza while Eliza prepares for a trip to Bermuda that coincides with Stanley's. A tragedy occurs when the lid of Eliza's trunk falls unexpectedly on her, crushing her spinal cord. The coroner rules it an accidental death after Silvia demonstrates what happened. Society is delighted at the excitement and the opportunity to gossip even more about Silvia. The amount of detail in the novel about domestic interiors, food, and clothing is almost suffocating. Perhaps, this is due to the longing for 1920s affluence that people had in the depths of the Depression. Although a satire, the novel deals obliquely with the role of women in society, the idleness of the upper class and its constant need for titillating gossip, and the difficulties women have living independently in such a social setting.

1068. Strobel, Marion. *A Woman of Fashion*. New York: Farrar and Rinehart, 1931. 331pp.

In this novel about changing social mores, twenty-seven-year-old Della Nash surprises everyone by re-marrying. After her husband died in World War I, Della inherited his fortune and a Lake Forest house with a pool and stables. When she impulsively marries architect Eric Wesley, in September 1929, soon after meeting him, she forfeits her inheritance to her sister-in-law Ruby Nash. Her father-in-law, a surgeon, acts expeditiously to carry out the provisions of his son's will, in part because of his own financial reverses after the stock market crash of October 1929. The newlyweds move to Eric's studio building near the intersection of Cass and Ohio Streets. When Eric loses his job, the burden of supporting the household falls on Della, who finds work as a model in a fashionable clothing store. When she discovers she is pregnant, she decides to get an abortion based on the financial implications of having a child. Della nearly dies from the operation and must cope with Eric's reaction when he separates from her for a time. Readers will be alarmed by the flippantly callous humor in the book. Christopher Nash has his personal library books bound with the skins of African-Americans he gets from the county morgue and several people make alarming remarks about Jewish people.

1069. Strong, Edmund C. *Manacle and Bracelet; or, the Dead Man's Secret, A Thrilling Detective Story*. Chicago: Ogilvie, 1886. 105pp.

In the first few pages of this book detectives Joseph Kipley and John Shea solve a series of crimes, including murder. They do not realize the crimes are all linked and connected to the household of General Clifton, a wealthy Chicagoan. After Clifton is murdered, however, another detective, Langdon, realizes the larger plot in which Harvey Talcott intends to pass of his accomplice Viola Dale as General Clifton's heiress. Misrepresented identities are at the heart of this melodrama and paintings, not photographs, are the only evidence of identity. Counterfeit currency is also involved in the plot. The novel gives some sense of police procedure and the freedom newsmen had at crime scenes and in police departments, as well as briefly describing suburban Chicago.

1070. Stubbins, Thomas Alva. *Not in Utter Nakedness: A Novel Depicting a Spiritual Pilgrimage*. Boston: Meador, 1936. 360pp.

In this coming-of-age novel, Rex Stanmore, the son of an Indiana newspaper editor, matures from a twelve-year-old boy with unusual gifts, to a thirty-two-year-old man committed to a spiritual crusade to reform humanity. When Stanmore's father decides to sell his newspaper and move west after the death of his wife, twenty-four-year-old Mildred Morford, a wealthy widow, takes

Stanmore into her household. Attracted by Stanmore's gift for premonitions, she teaches him about philosophy and religion. Mildred's affections deepen for him and when he enters adolescence she initiates him to sexual intercourse. Stanmore leaves Mildred to discover the world when he is sixteen and goes on to fight in World War I, write a book on prison reform (after he his wrongful incarceration), and befriend crusading Christian evangelist Frank Foster. By the time Stanmore is thirty-two, he has settled in Chicago, agreeing with Foster's indictment of the city as the epitome of the evils of capitalism. Stanmore becomes part of a circle working on social transformation. His counterparts have disguised identities and use increasingly allegorical language. By the end of the book, Stanmore is headed to Europe to join the "Popular Front." Although the novel contains little physical description of Chicago, from a cultural perspective it is interesting that the novelist regarded the city as the seedbed for dramatic social change.

1071. Sturm, Justin. *The Bad Samaritan*. New York: Harper and Brothers, 1926. 222pp.

In this romance novel Dick Farr leaves small-town, Nashotah, Nebraska, to escape tedium. He relocates to Chicago at twenty-one, but finds no satisfaction in work, even though he gets promoted from the factory floor to a desk job. Then, the experience that could transform his life, falling in love, comes to him in an inconvenient way. He discovers his beloved, Barbara Stewart, on her wedding day. She marries wealthy Robert Weaver, heir to a food canning fortune, and leaves on an extended honeymoon. Three years pass during which Farr's passion deepens. Then, an invitation intended for Barbara's childhood friend Dick Stevens across the hall gets slipped under Farr's apartment hotel door by mistake and Farr goes to a weekend house party at the Weavers' Forest Bluffs estate. He makes little impression on Barbara, but decides her childhood friend Stevens may be the key to winning her over. Over the course of a year, Farr establishes a friendship with Stevens, and increases his contact with Barbara, who has begun to find living with Weaver a tedious and loveless affair. Just as she is about to leave Weaver, he loses his fortune in stock speculation and she feels obligated to stand by him. He turns into a whiny, helpless cad supported by Barbara. Then, Farr carries out an elaborate scheme to let Weaver think he has earned money through a stock tip (that is actually cash supplied by Farr). Feeling successful and independent Weaver separates from Barbara and Farr marries her. Although the novel may be unreliable in presenting an account of upper-class suburban life, social attitudes and perspectives on news topics of the day (such as sales psychology) are revealed in the book's dialogues.

1072. Sublette, Walter [S. W. Edwards, pseud.]. *Go Now in Darkness*. Chicago: Baker Press, 1964. 255pp.

In this novel about race and interracial love in 1960s Chicago, Jake Hardmore reverses his parents' migration from the city to the suburbs. The Hardmores experienced all of the conflict and emotional hardship of moving to a predominantly white neighborhood, but Jake had the benefit of good schools and a comfortable life. However, when it comes time to go to college, Jake is drawn back to the city. He settles in Old Town, a neighborhood filled with young people from a wide range of cultural backgrounds. There he meets Bonnie Field, a Caucasian. The two begin a romance that is not long lasting, but from which each of them learn about themselves and the human condition. The description of Old Town is particularly strong.

1073. Surbridge, Agnes [pseud.]. *The Confessions of a Club Woman*. Illustrated by A. J. Keller. New York: Doubleday, Page, 1904. 241pp.

This mildly fictionalized account of a Chicago woman's experiences as a member of women's clubs is told in the first-person. Johnaphene ("Johnnie") escaped small-town Kansas by marrying Chicago grocer Joseph Henning. At first, Johnnie believes she has entered a world of affluence and social status, only to realize that she barely clings to the lowest rung on the social ladder. Through newspaper accounts, she learns she might distinguish herself through women's clubs. Henning is opposed to Johnnie's activities outside the household, but when she befriends the wife of a Chicago packing-house millionaire, he is forced into leniency. In arranging for speakers, Johnnie directly interacts with men. In this way, she becomes reacquainted with an adolescent crush, Philip Haven, now a prominent clergyman. She also befriends a French count who rapidly starts a romance. After a poison pen letter informs Henning of the flirtation, an insurmountable rift is diverted when Johnnie rushes to her husband's side after a train wreck. Awakened to the dangers of her behavior, Johnnie resigns from club life for two years and when she returns on a limited basis. The novel raises issues of women's role in society, although the dangers of women's involvement outside the home are presented in such extreme fashion (Johnnie neglects the health of her children, seems willing to separate from her husband, and is wooed by a French count), as to strain credulity.

1074. Synon, Mary. *The Good Red Bricks*. Boston: Little, Brown, 1929. 287pp.

This romance novel begins in the 1890s when Violet Caine, Joe Gates, and Sally Burt live near each other on Harrison Street near Union Park. Joe and Sally fall in love and suffer remarkable trials over the next several decades. Although Sally is fascinated by the stage, her singing career is thwarted by political misdealing and Joe's ambition to become a physician gets waylaid by his boxing prowess. His skill leads him into unfortunate alliances with gangsters and gambling syndicates. Although primarily a romance story, the author is also concerned with presenting a nostalgic view of Chicago and the book evokes lower-class neighborhood life during the time period of which she writes.

1075. Tanner, Edward Everett, III [Virginia Rowans, pseud.]. *Love and Mrs. Sargent*. New York: Farrar, Straus, and Cudahy, 1961. 277pp.

From all appearances Sheila Sargent, a widow, is an admirable woman who balances a successful career as a syndicated newspaper columnist with managing a substantial Lake Forest home for her son and daughter. Even though she has a job, Sargent is also a person of note in society circles. However, when working-class reporter Peter Johnson arrives to interview Sargent for a feature news story, Sargent's world crumbles and by the end of the book her twenty-year-old-son decides to join the Army and her daughter moves to New York City, refusing her debutante year. Even Johnson, who had begun an affair with Sargent, also decamps for New York. At the end of the novel Sargent decides to maintain her public image and accept a prestigious "Mother of the Year" award. Patrick's social satire attacks female independence and some aspects of upper-class society life.

1076. Tanous, Peter Joseph and Paul Arthur Rubinstein. *The Wheat Killing*. Garden City, N.Y.: Doubleday, 1979. 273pp.

Set in the near future, this novel about commodities market manipulation is partly set in Chicago, although the action partly transpires in: New York City, Washington, D.C., Calcutta, and

Winfield, Kansas. Chicago commodities broker Jack Donaldson is assigned to the Native American Investment Company (NAICO) account. He develops a relationship with a NAICO investment committee member named Mountain Breeze. The two of them implement a corner in the wheat market that panics Wall Street and spurs a worldwide financial crisis. The novel emphasizes the importance of the Chicago Board of Trade and touches on Native American issues.

1077. Targ, William and Lewis Helmar Herman. *The Case of Mr. Cassidy.* Cleveland: World, 1944. 255pp.

When a serial killer strikes Chicago in the heat of summer, Hugh Morris, refined book collector and amateur criminologist, commits himself to discovering the killer through pure deduction, since the Homicide Bureau, run by his friend Sergeant Daly, has no clues on which to employ their scientific crime-solving methods. When one of the victims is a fellow book collector, wealthy James Cassidy, Morris begins to take discovering the murderer very personally. Despite the refinement of his profession and hobby, Cassidy was separated from his wife and had a chorus girl live-in girlfriend. Through the girlfriend, who is friends with a bookie, the case involves figures from the underworld, so in addition to antiquarian bookstores and the Newberry Library, "Bughouse Square" and various lowly bars play a role in the investigation. The novel is unusual in picking up on the role of Chicago as a center for publishing, the rare book trade, and important book collections.

1078. Taylor, Bert Leston. *The Charlatans.* Illustrated by George Brehm. New York: Grosset and Dunlap, 1906. 390pp.

This satire of Chicago's early-twentieth-century cultural scene eviscerates sham intellectuals and second-rate artists—the charlatans of the title. Adored by her parents, Hope "Princess" Winston grows up on a farm near the imaginary Swiftwater, but her musical talent obligates her to train at a city conservatory. As a student she is quickly drawn into Chicago's classical music scene and soon becomes a toasted concert performer, in part due to the reviews of a newspaper music critic, the elegant and affluent Churchill Gray. By the end of the novel, however, she dismays at being the prey of charlatans and has refocused her energies on the worthier goals of love and marriage. The novel ends with Churchill Gray pursuing Hope to Swiftwater. In addition to rendering a perspective on Chicago cultural life, the novel deals with issues of women's role in society. Most of the *culturati* in the novel are Europeans and many are German.

1079. Taylor, Ellen DuPois. *One Crystal and a Mother.* New York: Harper and Brothers, 1927. 325pp.

In this social satire set in 1920s Chicago, a thirty-year-old woman, her head filled with French romances, moves from the Dakota Territory to Chicago to become a reporter. Her first assignment is to interview Madame Crystal Clemente, a wealthy society woman who lives in a mansion on Lake Shore Drive, about her husband Cyril's suicide. Shortly after the interview Madame Clemente is charged with her husband's murder on the evidence of a household servant. Even though the charge is quickly dismissed, the first-person narrator of the novel, "Madame Reporter," is fascinated by the Clementes. Throughout the novel she interviews some of Crystal's many jilted lovers, presenting a humorous take on upper-class flapper culture, while skewering the idea of sexual and social independence for women. Although Chicago locales are referenced, the inclement weather is the most convincing physical setting in this society novel that catalogs upper-class domestic interiors, clothing, and ways of speaking.

1080. Taylor, Marie E. *Just Boys and Girls of Dear Old Chicago*. Boston: Christopher Pub. House, 1930. 143pp.

Helen Rhodes, who had been a principal in Chicago's public school system for many years, was forced to live on the West Coast for three years as a cure for her tuberculosis. When she recovered her health she returned to her mother's house in Chicago and this book recounts the many visits she receives from teachers and former students. As memories of the past are recounted, not just student life, but the experiences of children and young adults in the early twentieth century get recorded. The stories often center on matters of proper behavior, politeness, and the emergence of pre-romantic friendships between boys and girls.

1081. Teller, Charlotte. *The Cage*. New York: David Appleton, 1907. 340pp.

This novel about social justice is set on the West Side in an area occupied by lumberyards and immigrant laborer housing during the period before the Haymarket Riot; the violent bombing and its aftermath bring the novel to a climactic end. Years before the action of the book, Dr. Hartwell gave up his affluent church to open a mission to the laborers there. His wife could not accept the decision and soon died. However, his daughter Fredericka embraced his cause. As the novel begins, Fredericka is a twenty-year-old; she meets an immigrant socialist, Eugene Harden, and during the course of the book the two fall in love and marry. Life in several of the households neighboring the Hartwell's, including the Irish-American Flanagans, headed by a policeman, and the German-American Schneiders is fully described. The book articulates the social justice issues of the era without easy solutions, except for the redemptive power of love and manual domestic labor. As a whole, the book presents a realistic depiction of life in a working-class Chicago slum at the beginning of the twentieth century.

1082. Thayer, James Stewart. *The Hess Cross*. New York: Putnam's Sons, 1977. 331pp.

This suspenseful novel focuses on international espionage during World War II. Recent German defector, Rudolf Hess is to be interviewed by Enrico Fermi on the University of Chicago campus where Fermi heads the research team conducting nuclear experiments. United States government agent John Crown is in charge of security with no awareness of Nazi intentions to kidnap Fermi. Although focused on espionage plots and counterplots, the novel provides strong descriptions of the University of Chicago and Hyde Park during World War II.

1083. Thayer, Tiffany. *One Woman*. New York: William Morrow, 1933. 435pp.

Journalist, Abe Adams, cannot get the beautiful, dead twenty-nine-year-old Rosita Jean d'Ur out of his mind. He uses her address book to research who she was and why she died. The novel touches on racism (Rosita was part Mexican) and the status of women in society. Rosita had been the kept woman of two different men before she was married and had an illegitimate daughter. Gangsters and the attempted assassination of a Mafia boss all play a part in the story, which is set in the 1930s and incorporates copious amounts of slang from the time period.

1084. Thomas, Ross. *The Porkchoppers*. New York: William Morrow, 1972. 246pp.

By detailing the behind-the-scenes maneuvering in a labor union officer election, the political corruption of early 1970s Chicago is displayed. Incumbent president Donald Cubbin has been in office for almost twenty years. His challenger is his protégé Sammy Hanks, the organization's secretary-treasury, who makes only slightly less money than Cubbin, but wants his prestige. Both men have deep-seated personal problems: Cubbin is an alcoholic and Hanks a manic-depressive.

However, their immediate followers selfishly overlook any weaknesses to share in their candidates' power and benefits. Although the nation-wide union has almost one-million members, the election will be decided by Chicago votes, manipulated by the opposing factions. Cubbin relies on his existing networks and Hanks' followers hire Indigo Boone, an African-American who has earned a reputation for successfully stealing political elections in the city. Many of the Chicago physical settings are hotel rooms. The novel depicts social and political systems and the methods by which they can be manipulated.

1085. Thorne, Paul. *Murder in the Fog*. Philadelphia: Penn, 1929. 307pp.

In this novel of international intrigue, a mysterious murder aboard a Great Lakes freighter, abandoned and adrift in Chicago's harbor, is connected to an opium smuggling operation and missing drugs with a market value of over two hundred thousand dollars. The Chicagoans in charge of the investigation, police detectives Conroy and McCarthy, have tense interactions with secret agents from both the United States and Great Britain. A great deal of the novel is set on the abandoned lake steamer and information is provided about the layout and operations of such vessels. In addition, a lake shore mansion and Chinatown figure prominently. Attitudes toward Chinese-Americans, drug use, and international smuggling operations are all touched upon.

1086. Thorne, Paul. *Spiderweb Clues*. Philadelphia: Penn, 1928. 304pp.

This novel of international intrigue is set in 1920s Chicago. Unscrupulous financier, Clayton Rutherford, is trying to get control of Andrew Lowell's railway car manufacturing company. The threat is serious enough to bring Lowell's young daughter Edith back from studying abroad. The financial battle also brings John Craig West, a wealthy American expatriate, back to the United States, under an assumed identity, as a British secret agent. When Edith Lowell is kidnapped and Clayton Rutherford murdered, attention turns to finding the culprits. The novel's physical descriptions of Chicago tend to be general, but the city is treated as internationally important as a center for the railway industry and financial operation.

1087. Thorne, Paul and Mabel Thorne. *The Secret Toll*. New York: Dodd, Mead, 1922. 268pp.

In this suspense novel, thirty-year-old veteran Robert Forrester has just returned from Europe. Although he inherited a fortune, he became a civil engineer and constructed railroads before the war. He is astonished to receive a threatening letter from the "Friends of the Poor," demanding that he leave ten thousand dollars in an oak tree on Sheridan Lane or suffer death. He soon discovers that over the past year other affluent men have received similar missives; those who ignored the demands were mysteriously killed. Realizing that the police have been ineffective, Forrester hires a private detective agency to help him bring the extortionists to justice, although they prove inept. Soon, he is working with Keith Marten, the detective hired by Midland Banker's Association. Marten identifies the culprits and absolves Mary Sturtevant, a romantic interest of Forrester's, of any involvement in the criminal plot. The book references areas of Chicago without providing much physical description of the city.

1088. Thorne, Paul and Mabel Thorne. *The Sheridan Road Mystery*. New York: Dodd, Mead, 1921. 291pp.

The focus for the police investigation in this murder mystery is an apartment building near the intersection of Sheridan Road and Lawrence Avenue. At two o'clock in the morning, a policeman on patrol hears shots and assists an apartment building tenant who claims he heard a struggle in the apartment above him. The police discover physical evidence that someone was shot, but can find no body. However, Detective David Morgan's interviews with residents help him solve the case. The details Morgan uncovers create a record of life in a large Chicago apartment building in the first decades of the twentieth century. Drug addiction plays a role in the book.

1089. Thorson, Russell Delos and Sarah Winfree Thorson [Kit Christian, joint pseud.]. *Death and Bitters*. New York: Dutton, 1943. 240pp.

This murder mystery is primarily set in the world of radio. In addition to several Near North Side apartment buildings, physical settings include a radio broadcasting building, and a bar, the Loud Speaker, patronized by radio industry employees. Except for the police detective on the case, Lieutenant Jack Reardon, everyone involved in the plot is an actor, aspiring actor, or scriptwriter. Murder victim Morton Ferguson, a one-time actor and skilled blackmailer, has many enemies, a number of whom were in the Loud Speaker, where he was found stabbed to death in a back booth by bartender Pete "Cowboy" Peterson, who was flirting with Ginny Donovan at the time. The two become Reardon's inside informants. Through the investigation, the reader learns about the old vaudeville circuit, radio drama broadcasts, and bar culture (the kinds and quantity of alcohol consumed by various characters is cataloged). The living quarters described include apartment hotels of vastly differing qualities on North Clark and near the intersection of North Dearborn and Division Streets, as well as a converted mansion boarding house on the Near North Side.

1090. Thurber, Alwyn M. *The Hidden Faith: An Occult Story of the Period*. Chicago: Harley, 1895. 294pp.

This reform novel comes out of the spiritualist tradition and deals with a man's discovery of a secret organization working to bring about a new society through spiritual exercises. In the midst of the 1890s economic depression, Edward Thorpe loses his job, leading him to reexamine his life. The South Side resident lives in a cottage with his wife and daughter, but they provide no consolation and even inspire doubts that he should have married. In this mood of self-reflection, Thorpe meets Dr. Emmet Wade, who, due to a near death experience, has developed mystical insight. After Wade cures Thorpe's daughter of a fever, Thorpe is even more open to Wade's influence. Wade takes Thorpe to the offices of the Royal Legion of Justice in the Rookery Building and gets him a job. Under Wade's direction, the Legion's members are dedicated to creating a new social order based on the common good rather than self-interest. In the new order, it is wrong for a man to satisfy his sexual desire with a woman because the act subjugates the woman to base instincts of self-interest. Afterward, Wade guides Thorpe and his wife into a spiritual marriage in which their only intercourse is on the astral plain. Except for cursory mentions of Chicago and public unrest by the unemployed, the city plays little role in the novel, except, symbolically, as the headquarters of the new social order. This symbolism fits the commonly held image of Chicago as a place of social ferment.

1091. Thurber, Alwyn M. *Quaint Crippen, Commercial Traveler*. Chicago: McClurg, 1896. 253pp.

Although the plot of this novel records Quaint Crippen's adventures as a traveling salesman, the real intent is to present a life philosophy with roots in transcendentalism and secular humanism. Crippen gets large orders for the Boston firm he represents, but, to his employer's frustration, never seems to be working. Instead, he uses his travels to develop his life philosophy and spirituality, while engaging acquaintances as a sort of missionary for humanism. Crippen sets out from

Boston and has several adventures before arriving in Chicago, where approximately seventy pages of the book are set. Crippen regards Chicago as the epitome of the United States. During his visit he explores a newspaper office and comments on the profession of journalism, communes with nature in Lincoln Park, and attends church services in opera houses and theaters. He considers this an unusual phenomenon and is critical of the services' vagueness and non-denominational approach. Crippen's stay in Chicago culminates with an Independence Day celebration spent observing and cataloging the ways in which Chicagoans celebrate the holiday. He meets a German anarchist, whom he converts to his philosophical outlook, and, later, meets a reformer trying to improve conditions for household servants through architectural reform to make dwellings more efficient. Crippen's initial amusement gives way to admiration after visiting the reformer's innovative house. Although the novel does not contain much physical description of the city, its treatment as a center of social and philosophical innovation is revealing.

1092. Thurber, Alwyn M. *Zelma, the Mystic; or, White Magic, Versus Black*. Illustrated by W. L. Wells and L. Braunhold. Chicago: Authors, 1897. 380pp.

On the evening that Donald Treat, a once prosperous member of society who is now indigent, is about to freeze to death, he is taken to the residence of Zelma, the Mystic who was assigned by a higher power to renew Treat's life. Without judging him, Zelma states that Treat's plight was brought on by alcohol abuse and that Treat had been under the control of malign spirits. As soon as Treat entered Zelma's dwelling these spirits were driven off. Under Zelma's tutelage Treat develops an understanding of the spiritual realm and begins a new life. Zelma also instructs Adolphus Gilbert, a man of great wealth, to help him understand the responsibilities of affluence and the true nature of charity. Finally, Zelma aids Mrs. Fessenden in opening a women's center to help females appreciate their special skills and teach girls the ethics of motherhood. The novel concludes with Zelma's vision of Chicago as a perfected city that reveals what was wrong with 1890s Chicago.

1093. Thurston, Louise Millicent. *Charley and Eva Roberts' Home in the West*. Boston: Lee and Shepard Publishers; New York: Charles T. Dillingham, 1869. 285pp.

This didactic work of juvenile fiction is set in 1860s Chicago, although the setting is kept fairly generic. After the death of their mother, Christina "Kiss" and Leland Fern moved with their father from Buffalo, New York to Chicago, where he got a factory job. Soon after the move their father is killed, leaving twelve-year-old Leland to look after his seven-year-old sister. A social network soon forms around Leland and Kiss, aiding them and lending advice. This wide circle of young people, somewhat older than the Ferns, work as architects, clerks, teachers, and writers and illustrate the virtues of cleanliness, diligence, domesticity, frugality, good manners, patriotism, sobriety, and religious faith. Before long, Charley and Eva Roberts, a brother and sister who are characters in the author's earlier books, take primary responsibility for Leland and Kiss, helping Leland get a clerk's job and Kiss adopted by a family. The novel describes some office and work settings, as well as the numerous beer gardens frequented by some characters for their meals. In the course of the book, romances lead to marriages. One subplot involves Charley's successful efforts to capture a counterfeiting ring. The novel illustrates aspects of street life in 1860s Chicago and the large number of orphaned or abandoned children fending for themselves.

1094. Tigay, Betty S. *Rich People, and Other Stories*. Chicago: Stein, 1942. 273pp.

Most of the stories in this volume are set in the 1930s in the Chicago Jewish community of recent immigrants. The political situation in Europe forced most of the characters to Chicago with varying degrees of suffering. While many of them try to take pleasure in their new freedom, their happiness is tempered by the memory of relatives who were left behind and of the prejudice they are experiencing in the United States. The stories also deal with the issue of assimilation and the difficulty of maintaining religious faith in a secular country. Although there is some description of clothing and food (mostly connected to religious holidays), there is little focus on physical setting in the stories

1095. Tobenkin, Elias. *God of Might*. New York: Minton, Balch, 1925. 272pp.

This novel conveys aspects of the immigrant experience of Russian Jews in the first decades of the twentieth century. As pogroms begin in Russia, Samuel Wasserstein's Uncle Jacob immigrates to the United States. His peddler's route expands and he is able to buy Samuel passage to the United States in 1899. Jacob arranges for Samuel to work as an apprentice with a storekeeper in North Lincoln, Nebraska. When Samuel visits his uncle briefly in Chicago, he finds life there much different from Nebraska. The Chicago neighborhood is Jewish and Jacob's family mostly socializes with other Russian Jews, maintaining caste-based social identifications from their past lives in Russia. Samuel is introduced to neighborhoods and entertainments by friends his age, but does not find a job, and returns to Lincoln. He is disturbed by the isolation of the Jewish ghetto and thinks small town life might suit him better, since he will be closer to the land and able to garden. His uncle is concerned that Samuel will forget his Jewish heritage by living among Gentiles and when Samuel returns to Chicago ten years later, he announces the final step in a pattern of dramatic assimilation—his engagement to a Christian girl. Now a successful Lincoln businessman, he has anglicized his name and overcome his accent. When Jacob's wife bans Samuel from the Gold household, Samuel sees the action as further evidence that prejudice is much more open in the city. Even though his visits to Chicago are not frequent, the contrasts Samuel makes between his uncle's life and his own are sharply drawn. Clearly the author believes that assimilation and living outside urban ethnic neighborhoods is the best choice for immigrants.

1096. Tobenkin, Elias. *In the Dark*. Garden City, N.Y.: Doubleday, Doran, 1931. 311pp.

Tobenkin tells the story of how a young man gets drawn into Chicago's underworld of organized crime. Wally Brook grows up in a Nevada mining town and after a mine accident kills his father and other family members, his mother becomes ill and dies. Brook relocates to Chicago, thinking such a large city will afford opportunities. He is relieved to get work driving a delivery truck and only slowly realizes that he is delivering bootleg liquor. After a brief period living with a girlfriend, from whom he is separated when she is discovered to be breaking her parole, he lives in the all-male world of a gangster hang-out on the West Side: a combination restaurant and billiard parlor named Harmanns. He loses his innocence, no longer associates sex with love, and engages in casual relationships with a series of women. He also plays minor roles in crimes like the theft of tens of thousands of dollars of furs, earning enough money to support a modest life. Anytime Wally's conscience prompts him to change his life, a payout prevents him from making any changes. Just as he is about to pay off his debts and go back west, he kills a man. The gangsters hold this crime over his head to force him into ever more violent and risky criminal undertakings. The novel details daily life for young men involved in organized crime during the era of Prohibition.

1097. Tobenkin, Elias. *The Road*. New York: Harcourt, Brace, 1922. 316pp.

This social reform novel dealing with women's rights, labor reform, and socialism is partly set in Chicago. During an unhappy childhood in small-town Wisconsin, Raymond Evert's friendship is the best aspect of Hilda Thorsen's life. When Hilda is sixteen, the Everts move to Chicago and soon become wealthy through concrete contracts with the city. As a seventeen-year-old Hilda relocates to Chicago and gets work in a knitting factory, but realizes she will never earn enough money for college. In a chance meeting, Hilda encounters Raymond, now a University of Chicago student, and he volunteers to pay for Hilda's education and eventually make her his wife. However, after he has sex with her, Raymond begins to fear his father's reaction to Hilda and breaks off contact. Pregnant and abandoned, Hilda flees to New York City, has a baby boy, and gets a job in a knitting factory. When the factory burns, killing hundreds, the labor union hires her and she makes a career of advocating for safe working conditions. While working with a Colorado miners' union, she meets a reformed Raymond. He is the husband of a leader in the settlement house movement and works as an advocate for political reform and workers' rights. Despite Raymond's personal growth, when he offers to divorce his wife and marry Hilda, she can no longer imagine losing her independence to wedded life. The novel's Chicago content includes descriptions of the settlement house movement, the lack of opportunities for women, and the reverse discrimination experienced by "native-born" Americans in workplaces dominated by recent immigrants who only hire their countrymen.

1098. Tobenkin, Elias. *Witte Arrives*. New York: Frederick A. Stokes, 1916. 304pp.

Tobenkin's account of immigrant experience focuses on the negative impact of assimilation and the economic desperation of unskilled laborers in the early twentieth century. By the time ten-year-old Emil Witkowski's father summons his wife and children to join him in the United States, he has already begun to assimilate to life in America and given up some aspects of Jewish religious observance. His wife, however, cannot accept the need to assimilate and the issue becomes a continuing source of conflict as Emil grows up. Recognized early on for his intellectual interests, Emil becomes the great hope of his father, who makes certain Emil can attend university. To everyone's surprise, Emil does not prepare for a profession, but takes a liberal arts program, choosing courses out of devotion to learning and truth-seeking. He becomes a journalist, primarily writing about the "Back of the Yards" neighborhood from an implicitly Socialist perspective. One of the women he interviews, Helen Brod, is also from Russia and has intellectual convictions similar to his own. The two quickly fall in love and marry. They can barely support themselves and Emil begins writing magazine articles, putting in extremely long days. When Helen gets pregnant, she secretly has an abortion out of economic necessity. When the editorial policy of Emil's newspaper changes, he decides to move to New York City. Life there in a "model" Lower East Side tenement is somewhat better. However, Helen dies in childbirth, and suffering from debilitating depression, Emil returns to live with his father in Chicago. He eventually writes the labor novel he had planned and is taken up by intellectual society when he returns to New York. By the end of the book it is clear that he will marry a wealthy Christian woman, sympathetic to social reform. The Chicago section of the novel describes some of the despair of the wage laborer's life, but gives few details specific to the city. Emil's socializing takes him to bars and restaurants frequented by German immigrants.

1099. Totheroh, William W. *Why Not?; or, Lawyer Truman's Story*. Chicago: Ward, 1894. 303pp.

After the Chicago fire, Lawyer Truman moves his family out of the city. His experiences over the next twenty years illustrate suburbanization and touch on some of the major social movements in the Chicago area during the time period, especially Progressivism. The village in which Truman settles quickly becomes a suburb and, in a decade, a part of the city from which most residents commute to work. When Truman first arrives, churches are the primary form of social affiliation. By the end of the book the church Truman attends has become so liberal that it is no longer exclusively Christian and tries to espouse the truths underlying all world religions. Clubs and associations proliferate and Truman discusses the social leaders, several of them university professors, who awaken the community to the settlement house movement, and philosophical and intellectual issues. When the Columbian Exposition begins, Truman believes the event will be a chance for visitors to see the social institutions Chicagoans have founded that place them in the first rank of the progressive movement.

1100. Train, M. *Ray Burton: A Chicago Tale*. Chicago: The Author, 1895. 128pp.

The first-person narrator of this book, Ray Burton, recounts his long-suffering life of honesty and hard work from childhood to young manhood. Burton was born around 1870 and relates some of his family's hardship after the Chicago fire. Although their house was undamaged, Burton's father lost his business. After several years of hard manual labor on reclamation efforts, he was able to assemble enough cash to start a commission business with partner James Wentworth. The firm was successful, but Burton missed the farm life of his youth and decided to acquire property near Champaign, Illinois, selling most of his assets to make the purchase. On the day he was to buy the farm, his body is recovered from the Chicago River. Presumably he was robbed and killed for the four thousand dollars he was going to pay for the farm. The thirteen-year-old Ray is forced to leave school and find work. Employed initially as a Western Union messenger, later he is a telegraph operator, a wholesale clothing firm employee, and a court reporter. Despite his hard work, Ray's former schoolmates leave him far behind as they go to college, begin careers, and gain fortunes. Each of his girlfriends also eventually marries someone more financially secure. By the end of the novel, he is an office worker at the World's Fair, a job that he considers the high point of his life. He is on the scene when Wentworth is trampled during the Chicago Day disaster. Afterward, he receives an envelope from Wentworth's lawyer containing Wentworth's confession that he had taken Ray's father's four thousand dollars. Burton had left the money in Wentworth's safe, and Wentworth knew Burton's assailants would be accused of the theft. Ray takes no action on the letter out of respect for Mrs. Wentworth and her daughter Grace, who had married one of Rays' friends. In addition to some very atmospheric descriptions of the Chicago River and the walkways along it, as well as some downtown residential areas, the novel describes Ray's workplaces.

1101. Treat, Roger L. *Endless Road*. New York: Barnes, 1960. 301pp.

The present of this novel is Chicago in the 1950s, however the main characters are journalists who have known each other since preparatory school and numerous flashbacks take the reader to New Haven, Connecticut, Italy during World War II, and, more briefly, to various locations in and out of the United States where newspaper assignments took them. Most of the novel consists of an extended hunt for Peter Fletcher; he is on a bender and his wife Mary gets his friend Jon Baker, a recovering alcoholic, to aid her search. Most of the locales are on the Near North Side and consist of dive bars and flop-house hotels. The interior monologues of characters illustrate the emotional perspective of alcoholics and the conversations between Baker and his non-alcoholic acquaintances present the methods and theories of Alcoholics Anonymous.

1102. Trotti, Lamar, Sonya Levien, and Niven Busch. *In Old Chicago*. Beverley Hills, Calif.: Twentieth Century Fox, 1937. 263pp.

This film script adaptation of Niven Busch's story "We the O'Leary's," imagines the lives of members of the Irish immigrant O'Learys, made infamous by their role in the Chicago fire. After a cross-country wagon train journey with his family, forty-year-old Patrick O' Leary is killed when his horses are spooked just as the O'Learys are entering Chicago. Arriving as a widow with no resources, Mrs. Molly O'Leary opens a laundry to support herself and her sons, Jack and Patrick, in South Chicago. Through hard work, Jack becomes a lawyer, but his brother Patrick is a ne'er-do-well in constant pursuit of chorus girls. One of them aids him in getting political patronage for a saloon and gambling parlor and he pledges to deliver the votes of South Chicagoans as his political boss directs. When Jack is appointed district attorney, he campaigns against voter fraud. Animosity builds between the brothers and Molly is distracted by one such altercation, leaving her untended cow near a kerosene lantern that the beast kicks over, starting the 1871 fire. In the midst of the conflagration the O'Learys hear of Jack's death and Patrick pledges to help build the city of Jack's dreams, rationally organized and free of political corruption, with a government that truly serves its people.

1103. Tucker, Wilson. *The Stalking Man*. A Murray Hill Mystery. New York: Rinehart, 1949. 212pp.

In this murder mystery, insurance investigator Charles Horne is initially the only person to suspect that the death of railroad agent Harley Silvers, while searching for bums riding freight cars, is anything other than an accident. Although Horne currently lives in Boone, Illinois, he used to reside in South Chicago and much of his investigation is set there. In Chicago, Horne consults a large newspaper morgue, and visits a theater, a saloon, and modest houses and apartments. The novel evokes the culture of the 1940s newsroom and touches on cultural attitudes toward mental illness.

1104. Tucker, Wilson. *Time Bomb*. New York: Rinehart, 1955. 246pp.

This suspense novel combines the plot of a detective mystery with elements of science fiction and 1950s conspiracy hysteria. A new political party, the Sons of America, is becoming an influential force in American government. However, a series of bombings calculated to kill party leaders could destroy their movement. Lieutenant Danforth of the Illinois Security Police is charged with finding the murderers. Television, radioactivity, time travel, and implosion devices all appear in the novel in which heroes are working to prevent America from being taken over by a repressive and violent political regime. Although substantially set in Chicago, the novel's futurist perspective makes the physical setting unimportant.

1105. Tucker, Wilson. *The Year of the Quiet Sun*. New York: Ace, 1970. 252pp.

In this futurist novel concerned with environmental stewardship, when the United States Bureau of Standards, decides to conduct a top secret survey they choose Brian Chaney, a demographics expert and controversial best-selling author to implement it. Using a newly developed time machine, Chaney and two other researchers are transported into the year 2000. They discover that the Chicago and Joliet areas have become an environmental disaster and then realize that their time traveling may have triggered it.

1106. Tully, Jim. *Biddy Brogan's Boy*. New York: Charles Scribner's Sons, 1942. 300pp.

In this autobiographical novel, the protagonist, nicknamed "Biddy" Brogan, after his mother, tells of his life growing up in St. Mary's Ohio and later living as a vagabond. The most important women in his life are his mother and his sister Virginia. When he is in his early twenties, Virginia moves to Chicago. She works as a waitress and devotes herself to befriending stray people and stray cats. Marginally employed people of all sorts stay with her for extended periods of time and Biddy alternates time on the road with extended stays with Virginia, where he spends his days in the Chicago Public Library reading. He begins writing and eventually produces a play and a novel, as well as articles for newspapers and magazines. Some of the Chicago characters include a Jewish pawnbroker and an African-American prizefighter.

1107. Tully, Jim. *Blood on the Moon*. New York: Coward-McCann, 1931. 350pp.

Approximately seventy-five pages of this autobiographical novel are set in Chicago. The main character is the grandson of poor Irish immigrants and lived in an orphanage after the death of his mother, before being indentured to a brutal, semi-insane farmer. After failing in his attempt to join the Navy because he was too young, he began the life of a hobo, getting money through petty theft and grifting. After hearing about a beautiful Chicago prostitute named Chlorine, he becomes obsessed by her and decides to leave the warmth of California to spend Christmas in the city. In Chicago, he gets to know Chlorine and comes to admire her strength and philosophical outlook. He also befriends an African-American prize fighter and a vaudeville magician, as well as factory workers and other hobos like himself. In addition to describing the neighborhoods around South State Street and Custom House Place, many anecdotes and song lyrics having to do with the Alaskan gold rush and the Civil War are included and numerous Civil War veterans populate the novel.

1108. Tully, Jim. *Ladies in the Parlor*. New York: Greenberg, 1935. 245pp.

A section of this novel is set in 1930s Chicago and presents life in a house of prostitution whose clients are wealthy and politically influential. The oldest child in a southern Ohio family of nine children, Leora Blair and her siblings had been terrorized by their father. For the first time in her life she experiences affection when as a sixteen-year-old she begins an affair with a local young physician. Soon, she is also having sex with an older wealthy physician and learning from her aunt the ways of manipulating men to her advantage. When her mother dies of a miscarriage, she manipulates her lovers into giving her large sums of money so that she can move to Chicago. She works in the house of Mother Rosenbloom, the most powerful madam in the city, with clients that include mob bosses, a judge, lawyers, doctors, and a professor. These men teach Leora about the workings of society and after Mother Rosenbloom dies, Leora, now twenty-one decides to return to her hometown and marry her first lover, the young physician (who was recently widowed). Although the novel includes little physical description of the city, the author describes ethnic and racial dynamics, particularly in the world of politics.

1109. Tupper, Edith Sessions. *By a Hair's Breadth*. New York: Willard Fracker, 1889. 135pp.

In this murder mystery Jack Morton is found in the room with the victim, millionaire Paul Raymond, but protests his innocence, even though he admits he has no memory of what happened.

Morton had asked to marry Raymond's daughter Kate and been refused because of an abiding enmity between Raymond and Morton's father, initiated by a petty argument years before. After Raymond's refusal, Morton was overcome by emotion and comes to himself handling a knife and standing over Raymond's throat-slashed corpse. Morton is arrested immediately; however, reporter Bob Fleming, lawyer Richard Starr, and Kate Raymond all stand by him. The true culprits turn out to be butler John Sampson and housekeeper Jane Morrison. Morrison had been Paul Raymond's lover in her youth and was abandoned by him when she was pregnant with his child. She plotted revenge for decades, working on a steamship, living in England, and most recently in India, where she was the wife of an English soldier. Upon the soldier's death she returned to the United States with a knife, a powerful narcotic, and her new husband, John Sampson. By lighting the narcotic she was able to drug Raymond and Morton long enough for Sampson to stab Raymond and place the knife in Morton's hands. Soon after his acquittal, Morton and Kate Raymond wed. Although set in Chicago, the novel includes almost no physical description of the city, focusing instead on the insular, upper-class Raymond household.

1110. Turpin, Walter Edward. *O Canaan!* New York: Doubleday, Doran, 1939. 311pp.

Turpin presents the story of the great migration of African-Americans from the Deep South to Chicago beginning in World War I when war industries presented employment opportunities for people who had been politically suppressed as impoverished agricultural laborers in the South. Protagonist Joe Benson moves from Mississippi to settle on Chicago's South Side in 1916. He is fortunate enough to have modest savings that enable him to open a store. He observes the struggles of other members of his community who are unfairly harassed by policemen, fall into alcoholism as jobs disappear after World War I, and whose naïveté make them easy prey for cunning Chicagoans who are pimps and confidence men. Benson invests his profits in real estate and during Prohibition makes a fortune selling alcohol. Just as he is about to convert his profits to a respectable business by investing in a bank, the 1929 stock market takes his savings. He resigns himself to the steady work of a Pullman porter, but lives to see his daughter Essie achieve financial success. The story is presented from the perspective of a member of the African-American community and reveals a great deal about living conditions and social life in this segment of Chicago's population over a period of decades.

1111. Tuthill, Jack. *Sideshows of a Big City Tales of Yesterday and Today*. Chicago: Kenfield-Leach, 1932. 275pp.

Tuthill's view of Chicago is quite bleak. Each of his short stories encompasses some tragedy, usually involving death from murder or suicide. Among the locales he describes are: the ghetto on Maxwell Street, Chinatown, the Chicago River, the Newsboys' Home, the Actors' Home, the "Black Belt," Little Italy, the Rialto, and "Bug-House Square." His characterizations of these areas are vivid, but the behavior of the people who live there border on stereotypical (a black man is carried away by his emotions into committing an assault and an Italian is gunned down gangster-style). Several of his stories are about scams worked on newcomers to the city. He also deals with alcohol addiction (describing a "beer flat" and a "barrel house"), opium dens, a prize fighters' gym, and the deaths (natural or otherwise) of people who have become exhausted from age, addiction, or guilt. In general, his attitude toward women verges on the openly hostile and one of his longest stories is about a divorce case brought by an unscrupulous woman.

1112. Ullman, James Michael. *Lady on Fire*. An Inner Sanctum Mystery. New York: Simon and Schuster, 1968. 214pp.

This 1960s detective novel is mostly set on the Near North Side in furnished apartment hotels, nightclubs, and restaurants and includes casual use of illegal drugs. Chicago private investigator Julian Forbes has been hired by an innocent old man to find Iris Dean, a missing young waitress he had befriended. At first Forbes believes the case has little merit, until he realizes that other people are looking for Dean as well. By the end of the novel he has uncovered an international criminal syndicate with a chain of stores selling hijacked merchandise. As a work of 1960s fiction, the plot centers on large-scale corruption that extends to all levels of government and the police. The politicians fighting organized crime are behaving in their own self-interest, to advance their careers.

1113. Ullman, James Michael. *The Venus Trap*. An Inner Sanctum Mystery. New York: Simon and Schuster, 1966. 223pp.

As a little boy Jon Chakorian does not understand much of what he witnesses in his father Rudy's brownstone in Chicago. Rudy and his business partner Felix Schatzmann use stock manipulation to build the Venus Corporation. Just as their financial improprieties are to come to light, Rudy disappears along with a fortune in diamonds. Although it takes sixteen years, Jon eventually tracks down the man who murdered Rudy and stole the diamonds. A good deal of this novel describes illegitimate business practices and the physical setting in Chicago is not crucial to the plot, however Jon does have allies and enemies linked to organized crime in the city.

1114. Upton, George P. *Letters of Peregrine Pickle*. Chicago: Western News, 1869. 340pp.

Originally appearing as letters in the *Chicago Tribune*, this compilation describes the activities of the fictional characters of Old Blobbs, Mrs. Blobbs, Mignon, Celeste, Aurelia, Blanche, Boosey, and Fitz-Herbert, from the viewpoint of first-person narrator, Peregrine Pickle. The letters record the activities and concerns of upper-middle-class Chicagoans in the late 1860s. Much of the book describes seasonal celebrations including national holidays (Thanksgiving, Christmas, and New Year's Day) and local social occasions (a masquerade ball and a wedding). Character sketches are also included (an organ grinder, a girl from Boston, and a Mrs. Grundy). Pickle, a sociable gossip, is a member of the community about which he writes and assumes his readers are as well. Despite the infra-dig nature of the epistolary work, the collection implicitly reveals aspects of Chicago society (particularly in respect to gender roles and social class).

1115. Van Deventer, Emma Murdoch [Lawrence L. Lynch, pseud.]. *Against Odds: A Romance of the Midway Plaisance*. Chicago: Rand, McNally, 1894. 274pp.

Carl Masters and Dave Brainerd "of the secret service" travel to the World's Fair to thwart a suspected French counterfeiter. Once they are in Chicago, the duo are also asked to capture thieves who stole hundreds of jewels from an exhibit and to locate some young American millionaires who have gone missing at the fair. The detectives also uncover a number of petty crimes. In one case, Masters returns a purse that had been jostled out of a young woman's hands, only to strike up a romance with her. The detectives also find a criminal suspect when they realize that a beautiful woman is actually a man in disguise. Through Masters and Brainerd's investigations, the author provides a detailed account of the fair and the crowds of fair-goers. In addition to all the physical description of the fair and details about fairground criminal activities, the author points out the many opportunities for romantic liaisons in the quiet corners and recesses of the grounds.

1116. Van Deventer, Emma Murdoch [Lawrence L. Lynch, pseud.]. *Shadowed by Three*. Chicago: Donnelly, Gassette and Lloyd, 1879, 738pp.

Although the plot of this mystery involves the search for Madam Elise Schwartz, a young wife who murdered her elderly husband and sister-in-law in Europe and absconded with a fortune, the book really seems an excuse to present a series of Chicago crimes and provide a tour of the city less than a decade after the fire. Although the detectives, Robert Jocelyn, Neil Bathurst, and Clarence Arteveldt, are in their early twenties, they have worked together before in New York City and Europe. The Chicago settings, ranging from upper-class households to tenements, are remarkable for their variety and descriptions of people, buildings, and interiors, providing many revealing social details.

1117. Van Deventer, Emma Murdoch [Lawrence L. Lynch, pseud.]. *A Slender Clue; or, The Mystery of Mardi-Graz*. Chicago: Laird and Lee, 1891. 650pp.

Although some of this novel is set in Chicago and the main character is Chicago detective Rufus Carnes, much of the book is also set in suburbs and towns some distance from the city and the lack of physical description makes it difficult to distinguish where much of the action takes place. Carnes has been hired to trail a forger and confidence man who was imprisoned for ten years and has recently been released. The criminal has so many aliases that his only certain name is Prisoner 46. Immediately upon gaining his freedom, 46 undertakes an elaborate plot that involves gaining the confidence of society figures in an Illinois town named Roseville, where he cleverly gets the townspeople to believe he is an English aristocrat. His scheme involves defrauding several young women of inheritances and the novel traces Carnes' elaborate steps to thwart 46. The reader will be bewildered by Carnes' many disguises, 46's aliases, and sorting out the true location and identities of several missing women, who may be dead, kidnapped, or using assumed names. Much of the latter part of the novel is set in New Orleans.

1118. Van Peebles, Melvin. *A Bear for the FBI*. New York: Trident Press, 1968. 157pp.

In this fictionalized memoir, the protagonist, Edward, grows up as an African-American in the 1940s and 1950s, mostly in suburban Chicago. During Edward's early childhood he lived in an apartment on South Park Boulevard near Fifty-fifth Avenue. During that time period Edward and his family rarely left the apartment, since the neighborhood was filled with negative influences, including nightclubs. However, his father's success in his tailor shop enabled Edward's family to move to the suburbs, broadening Edward's world. Much of Edward's account focuses on social organizations, from Boy Scouts, to summer camp, to High Schools for Christ, and finally to being a college student. The novel touches on the impact of racial prejudice mostly indirectly, and mentions few Chicago landmarks directly except for Riverview Amusement Park.

1119. Van Peebles, Melvin. *The True American: A Folk Fable*. Garden City, N.Y.: Doubleday, 1976. 208pp.

Although this book is a work of social satire dealing with racial prejudice in the United States, social conditions in Chicago in the 1940s through 1960s are depicted. Two men, one black and one white, meet in Hell, then return to life in the hope of changing society. The men appear in Chicago, but neither man really has that much impact because they encounter so much resistance to their message of racial harmony. George Abraham Carver has experiences typical of African-American men of his generation, only being able to get jobs as a manual laborer and having to fight in a segregated Army in World War II. Dave Stock is able to earn a master's degree and a get a lucrative job in advertising. By the end of the book the civil rights movement has begun to meet with some success in the 1960s, but Carver and Stock realize that no significant impact is being made on the essence of racial prejudice.

1120. Van Vorst, Bessie and Marie Van Vorst. *Bagsby's Daughter*. New York: Harper and Brothers, 1901. 338pp.

This romance novel tells the story of the courtship of thirty-year-old Robert Halifax and twenty-three-year-old Violet Bagsby, their honeymoon, and their early married life. An early impediment to the relationship is Violet's father Camden Bagsby, who is marginally acceptable socially—although a millionaire, his money comes from manufacturing Bagsby's Bronchial Capsules. The Bagsbys live at 18 Michigan Avenue, only recently arrived, however, from Grand Rapids and a house near their factory. Halifax is a lawyer with an international practice and impeccable social credentials. The two fall in love at first sight and marry within a few weeks of meeting. Trouble begins on their trip to New York City at the beginning of their honeymoon trip when Patterfield West, a very recent fiancé of Violet's, appears on the train. Through a series of accidents, Halifax misses the boat on which he is to spend his honeymoon with Violet and the ship sails with West on board with Violet, instead. Soon afterwards, Halifax loses his fortune in a stock market debacle. The newspapers make a great deal of Violet and West and Halifax's losses and Bagsby sails to England to redeem his daughter's reputation by severing her ties to Halifax. The lovers are reunited at the very end of the novel, most of which is set in England. The Chicago sections of the novel portray upper-class Chicagoans as equally at home in New York and London as in their hometown and social events include musical evenings, teas, and at-homes.

1121. Vynne, Harold Richard. *Love Letters: A Romance in Correspondence*. New York: Zimmerman's Pocket Library 1898. 170pp.

This epistolary romance novel reveals some aspects of gender relations and courtship in late-nineteenth-century America and very little about Chicago, specifically. When thirty-year-old New York lawyer Frederick Morton travels to Chicago, he is smitten on sight by Chicagoan Helen Merrick. After one date in which they attend a concert of classical music, they are forced to learn about each other through correspondence and a few more brief trips. Morton stays at the Auditorium Hotel and socializes at the Chicago Athletic Club. He lives at the Calumet Club in New York and employs a valet whom he calls to Chicago when he decides to prolong a Chicago trip, getting the valet to bring more clothes and bicycles. Morton and Merrick subsequently bicycle in the grounds of the Columbian Exposition. Other Chicago places mentioned include Field's Department Store and the Field Museum.

1122. Vynne, Harold Richard. *The Woman That's Good: A Story of the Undoing of a Dreamer*. Chicago: Rand, McNally, 1900. 473pp.

Much of this novel is set in Chicago at the time of the World's Fair. Although thirty-year-old Eustace Gaunt is married, he falls in love at first sight upon his introduction to Imogen Leal in Old Vienna at the fair. Gaunt is a journalist who lampoons Chicago society figures in best-selling newspapers and magazines and he is introduced to Imogen by her sister, journalist Hattie Leal. Hattie is disdained from her first appearance in the novel as the sort who writes society columns and drinks cocktails. She has even published a romance novel, *A Flirtation with Fate*, under the pseudonym Mrs. St. Judas (the name by which she introduces Imogen). Eustace, a dreamer, given to wine, dining out, and attending classical concerts, pursues his romance with Imogen because he believes it will be fleeting—she tells him she will soon die of a heart condition. Reality breaks in when his wife sues him for divorce over Imogen and he discovers Imogen is in perfect health. Even though his life has been destroyed by Imogen, Gaunt tries to keep her from being named in the suit and exposed in the press. Much of the novel recounts Eustace's experiences in the Chicago divorce courts to retain visitation rights for his four-year-old son Billy. Since, he must continue to write articles to make a living, Eustace attends various social events, many of which are connected to the Columbian Exposition. Eustace also follows society figures to Washington, D.C., New York, Charleston, and Havana. In addition to showing how unfair divorce proceedings are for men, the book presents society life as dominated by European culture and kept afloat on a steady flow of alcohol.

1123. Wager, Walter H. *Death Hits the Jackpot*. New York: Avon Books, 1954. 189pp.

In 1944, the Office of Strategic Services sent a fortune in American currency for delivery to agents in France and Germany who were gathering information in preparation for the Allied landing at Normandy. The money never reached its destination and efforts to trace it were ineffective. Finally, in 1954, bills with the serial numbers of some of the missing notes began showing up in Chicago. A team of CIA agents is sent to Chicago to find out who is passing the money and recover as much of it as possible. Not surprisingly, gangsters and a beautiful woman are involved, as well as someone on the inside of the original operation. Not all of the novel is set in Chicago and the parts that are tend to adhere closely to stereotypes of the city.

1124. Wagner, Constance Cassady [Constance Cassady, pseud.] and Ruth Cardwell. *Even in Laughter*. Indianapolis: Bobbs-Merrill, 1935. 359pp.

Presenting the suffering of the Depression in quirky, humorous fashion, this novel contrasts affluent society figures' imagined difficulties with the dire circumstances of an Italian immigrant family. Professor and Martha Grayce live in Hyde Park and are skeptical about their daughter-in-law Elinor's fashionable devotion to social work. Their son Stanley is the partner in a law firm with his eye on one of his secretaries and Elinor's attention is focused on Peter Dodd, the brother of Herbert Dodd, her thirty-four-year-old sister Alix's husband. Herbert is a publisher, confronting financial challenges, who keeps his mistress Stella Schuler in a furnished apartment. Much of Elinor's social work is devoted to helping the Bonelli family, whose seventeen-year-old son, Tony, is on his way to becoming a gangster and whose daughter Rose she forces Alix to hire as a maid. The novel gives full descriptions of food and social events in elegant apartments and private clubs.

1125. Wagoner, David. *The Man in the Middle*. New York: Harcourt, Brace, 1954. 248pp.

In this suspense novel, Charlie Bell, a veteran railroad employee, becomes the object of a manhunt after he helps a woman pushed from a train at the crossing where he is on duty. When he realizes that the woman has been killed and men in dark suits have been looking for him, Bell goes undercover in Chicago. His main clues as to who the woman was and why she was killed are a voice recording record concerning a U.S. Senator and photographs of checks made out for large amounts of cash that seem to be evidence of bribery. Spending time in cheap hotels and saloons, Bell tries to stay alive long enough to get out of Chicago without leaving a trail and the reader is left to piece together a blackmail scheme from overheard conversations among police, political operatives, and blackmailers.

1126. Wagoner, David. *Money, Money, Money*. New York: Harcourt, Brace, 1955. 241pp.

In this novel set in 1950s Chicago, the protagonist, Willy Grier, is developmentally disabled. However, because he inherited a fortune from his aunt, he lives independently with an attorney for a guardian. The family house in which he lives, once considered a mansion, is located on Gostlin Street, an area that has changed dramatically and is now occupied by poor and working-class people, many of them immigrants. Because Grier is charitable toward them and spends his days taking care of Piludsky Park, he is a favorite of his neighbors, who treat him respectfully. Grier's life changes when he finds a gangland murder victim in the lake. Soon he is interacting with the police, gangsters, and a beautiful woman; he experiences social stigmas hitherto unknown to him, as well as discovering skills he didn't know he had. Grier's innocence serves as a foil to highlight the ruthlessness of the world beyond Gostlin Street. The social status of developmentally disabled people is a major theme. Many of Chicago's parks form the physical backdrop for the novel.

1127. Wagoner, David. *Rock*. New York: Viking Press, 1958. 253pp.

As a twenty-eight-year-old, Max Fallon returns to his parents' house just outside Chicago. He has completed college, been in the Navy, been married, worked as a salesman, and is recently divorce. His breakup with his wife, with whom he had no children, has left him questioning who he is and where he is headed. His father, a political operative who works as a go-between for contractors seeking city jobs, uses his contacts to get Max a job as a summer lifeguard. Max's life begins to center on summer beach culture and he begins dating a young woman his age, but runs afoul of a gang of hoodlums with which his younger brother Timmy is involved. Wagoner's theme is the disaffected youth culture of the late 1950s and he captures their slang and music.

1128. Walker, Mildred. *Light from Arcturus*. New York: Harcourt, Brace, 1935. 343pp.

From the time she is married, Julia Hauser longs to experience the world beyond the small Nebraska town in which she was born and is destined to spend her life. Wife of a local businessman, she fulfills her social role, caring for her husband and his household and raising four children. Her only experience of the larger world is through displays at the world's fairs she visits with her husband in Philadelphia in 1876, in Chicago in 1893, and once again in Chicago in 1933. The novel shows the importance of these trips for Hauser and speaks to the role world's fairs had on American culture. Little of Chicago beyond the fairgrounds is described; however, the city takes on an important symbolic role for Hauser as the place where she wishes she could live.

1129. Walker, Mildred. *Medical Meeting*. New York: Harcourt, Brace, 1949. 280pp.

Chicago serves as the venue for an international medical convention in this novel. Rural physician Dr. Henry Baker has worked for twelve years in upstate New York developing a treatment for tuberculosis that utilizes a mold culture he has isolated, with his wife Liz serving as his lab assistant. Even though he had not run enough trials, when his daughter became gravely ill with tuberculosis, Baker saved her life with his cure but inadvertently deafened her. When Baker is invited to present his research in Chicago, he believes the convention will afford him far-reaching professional recognition. However, on the morning before he speaks, Baker hears a team of doctors announce a more successful treatment based on similar research. Baker presents his paper anyway and for the first time his wife realizes he treated their daughter with an experimental procedure. Reconciliation is achieved only after the couple returns to their rural home and Liz concedes that Baker's action had saved their daughter's life. Although Chicago is presented as an exciting, opportunity-filled place, the Bakers realize that what the city can offer in terms of recognition and opportunities are not as important to them as their rural, family life.

1130. Walker, Robert W. *Sub-Zero!* New York: Belmont Tower Books, 1979. 189pp.

Although the novel presents some idea of the author's vision of Chicago in 2020, the action is contained within a huge office tower, the Fieldcrest building. Employees of the international Fieldcrest communication group are trapped by an April snow storm that has immobilized the city. As the storm's intensity mounts, scientists announce that a new ice age has begun. Anxieties over the storm begin to take second place, however, to the threat of violent death when two murder victims are discovered, and television weatherman Mark Wertman realizes that he is being stalked.

1131. Wallace, Edgar. *On the Spot.* Garden City, N.Y.: Crime Club / Doubleday, Doran, 1931. 313pp.

This novel, written by an English author whose other works are set in London, is a novelization of his popular play of the same title. Main character Tony Perelli is a mobster kingpin in Chicago and this work illustrates the means by which he maintains his power. He puts enemies "on the spot," manipulates the city's corrupt legal system, and maintains absolute control over his foot soldiers, who operate his empire of bootlegging, slot machines, and prostitution. Not surprisingly, the novel includes little physical description of the city and is of most interest for reflecting the city's image in popular culture as a corrupt gangland.

1132. Wallis, J. H. (James Harold). *The Woman He Chose.* New York: Dutton, 1934. 314pp.

Twenty-nine-year-old attorney Will Drake falls in love with twenty-four-year-old Florabelle Muellich when he successfully defends her on the charge of murdering her husband in this tale that is part murder mystery and part psychological thriller. Will and Florabelle live in Marinique [*sic*], Iowa (a renamed Dubuque) and travel to Chicago for their honeymoon. The couple stays at the Hotel Stevens, the largest in the world, and shop on Michigan Boulevard. Both honeymooners refer to earlier trips to Chicago and memorable activities. As they shop for dresses, the system in which women model the clothes for buyers is described. Over the course of twenty-five pages various Chicago activities are detailed including attending plays, motion pictures, dining out, visiting tourist sites, using beaches, and taking drives. The trip clearly represents such visits by other honeymooners for whom Chicago becomes an annual destination. During the trip Florabelle reveals she will never be able to have children. However, it is not until they return to Marinique that she confesses to murdering her husband and subsequently commits suicide. The novel spends a good deal of time contrasting Drake's family background in colonial New England and the recent immigrant origins of Florabelle.

1133. Walsh, William Thomas. *The Mirage of the Many.* New York: Henry Holt, 1910. 326pp.

In this futurist novel, Chicago is the scene of dramatic social transformation in the 1950s when a self-denominated Socialist Party (that actually espouses Communism) achieves political control and implements broad reforms. The key figure in the movement, Alfred Seebar, is the fiancé of Dorothy Markham, the daughter of Faverell Markham, a wealthy steel manufacturer. As Seebar's party mounts attacks on capitalists like Markham's father and introduces legislation injurious to his business, Dorothy and Alfred become estranged. In a redistribution of wealth, Faverell and Dorothy are forced out of their mansion and Faverell must work in the steel mill he once owned until he is blinded in an industrial accident. After the Socialist Party's rapid success in implementing its full political agenda, the populace rebels against the new social structure. The Individualist Party gains a broad mandate and begins using bombs to destroy all government institutions. Concerned for Dorothy's safety, Seebar finds her and his sincere expressions of remorse win her back. In addition to portraying Chicago as the center of political and social ferment, the city is presented as the dominant industrial center of the United States.

1134. Walz, Audrey Boyers [Francis Bonnamy, pseud.]. *Death by Appointment*. Front Page Mysteries, Fourth Series. New York: Collier and Son, 1931. 317pp.

Although it is usually the gangsters who are responsible for murder in Prohibition-era Chicago, in this mystery novel the city's most influential bootleggers (mostly Italian Mafia figures) are the victims. Dr. Peter Shane, of the University of Chicago's Department of Criminology, and his assistant Francis Bonnamy, solve the crime through employing scientific technique. However, it turns out that the killer (a German archeologist and friend of Shane's) was actually the victim of the gangsters and so Shane does not turn him over to the police. Physical settings in the novel are often private clubs where liquor is illegally served, and the offices of gangsters.

1135. Ward, Florence Jeannette Baier. *The Flame of Happiness*. Philadelphia: George W. Jacobs, 1924. 357pp.

Parts of this romance novel are set in Chicago in the 1910s and early 1920s. Orphaned Barbara Fallows grows up under the guardianship of the stern Dr. Anne Linton on the campus of an all-girls school. In the final years of high school she is sent to a coeducational academy fifty miles outside Chicago and meets Dirck "Ruddy" Harrington Gannet. Although he is five years her senior, she is smitten with him. Dr. Linton disapproves, and is alarmed when she hears from Ruddy's own father that he is a philanderer. Ruddy and Barbara attend the same college and she barely resists marrying him when he enlists during World War I. While he is away she joins a Chicago little theater troupe, and by the time he returns she is twenty-one, old enough to accept his marriage proposal. When Dr. Linton informs Barbara that Ruddy is being unfaithful, she confronts him and breaks off their engagement when he confesses. By the 1920s, Barbara is a confirmed Chicago bohemian, living with a college friend who is having an affair with an architect. She only lives in the city for a little over a year before marrying a college acquaintance, Geoffrey Hale, whose prominent Illinois family lives in Elgin. She does not really love Hale and has one more bout of passion over Ruddy, before deciding to dedicate her life to Hale and to making a success of married life. The novel reveals 1920s cultural attitudes toward marriage and a women's place in society.

1136. Ward, Florence Jeannette Baier. *Phyllis Anne*. New York: James A. McCann, 1921. 245pp.

In this romance novel, Richard Sherrill, a well-known actor, is no longer able to keep his daughter Phyllis Anne away from the stage. After he was widowed, Sherrill sent Phyllis to a boarding school run by nuns. In her late adolescence, she starts impersonating her older sister and escaping to Chicago to see her father on stage. On one of these trips she meets Randy Fosdick, who works in a used bookstore while writing the play that will make his career as a dramatist. On another adventure in the city, Phyllis successfully auditions for a part in one of her father's plays without his knowledge. As soon as she appears before the footlights her acting career is launched and her lengthy on-again-off-again romance with Fosdick can proceed to its inevitable conclusion. Part of the back and forth centers on whether or not a woman can have a career and be a good wife, or whether she should subject her professional interests to her husband's career. Some of the novel is set in New York City, as the center of the theater world, but Chicago is presented as important as well.

1137. Ward, Florence Jeannette. *The Singing Heart*. New York: James A. McCann, 1919. 308pp.
This novel of carefree family life has a very traditional romance story at its center. The Macallisters maintain their connection to Fairfield, Illinois, a suburb of Chicago, even though family members live far-flung lives of achievement and travel all over the world. The most notable Macallister, Alicia, is an internationally known painter, although one is an opera singer, and another a syndicated Chicago columnist. Janey Macallister has stayed at home to take care of her widowed father and the eleven bedroom family house, while teaching school ten months a year. All of the Macallisters return the summer of Janey's twenty-fifth birthday and an eligible young man, thirty-five-year-old Alan Campbell, is invited for her birthday weekend. After a week or so he reappears, having purchased the house next door. For most of the novel Campbell's intentions are unclear, but he is forced to declare himself after the exhibition of Janey's portrait painted by her sister prompts several marriage proposals. Campbell is much more famous than any of the Macallisters and they are surprised he chose Janey, whose worth they had overlooked. Chicago in the novel functions as a place to visit for a break from rural life, but the Macallisters consider their suburb as their hometown, not the city.

1138. Ward, Florence Jeannette Baier. *Wild Wine*. Philadelphia: Macrae-Smith, 1932. 318pp.
In this romance novel powerful businessmen can be intimidated by beautiful women. At least this is the case with Shard McLean. A self-made man, the son of a marginally successful Protestant clergyman, McLean taught himself the construction business, forming his own contracting company when he was twenty-six and taking over the financial support of his widowed mother, sister, and younger brother Mel. A successful man, Shard is still unmarried at thirty-two because he is frightened by the depth of his love for Sabra Nason. Kevin Ferraby is also in love with Sabra and unlike Shard is open in his feelings and will do almost anything to get her, including ruining Shard's business. Chicago in the novel is a place of great opportunity for young businessmen who can take advantage of the 1920s building boom.

1139. Ward, Florence Jeannette Baier. *Women May Learn*. Philadelphia: Macrae-Smith, 1933. 312pp.
In this romance novel of the 1930s set in a fictional suburb of Chicago named Fairfield, three men vie for the hand of twenty-year-old Jill Talcott. Talcott's widowed mother had moved Jill and her brother Stan from Charleston when she inherited a house in Fairfield twelve years before. She scrimped to send Jill away to school and Jill has just returned to begin her adult life. When Jill begins appearing at the local tennis court, golf course, and swim club she is soon attracting attention from Malcolm Coburn who is wealthy, but selfish. He provides social entrée for Jill, from which she immediately benefits by befriending girls who may otherwise have snobbishly dismissed her. Soon Jill is engaged to Malcolm, but when she refuses to elope with him, he breaks the engagement. On the rebound, she nearly marries Stephen Whitney, who is divorced and thirty-five, until she realizes her mother's love for him. Finally, twenty-six-year-old Rufus Harwood, an adventurous bachelor, arrives to marry her and take her back to Charleston. In the suburban setting of the novel, Chicago is a place where many of the men in town work and where the women shop.

1140. Ward, Mary Jane. *Counterclockwise*. Chicago: Henry Regnery, 1969. 250pp.

Although set in the Chicago area, the action of this book mostly transpires in a mental hospital. Successful author Susan Wood was committed after a nervous breakdown several years ago. She recovered and wrote about her experiences in the bestselling book *Hideaway* that was later made into a popular film. Just as she is finishing a speaking tour, and feeling unsettled by the realization that experimentation may be going on in a hospital she toured, she learns that a woman she appointed to the board of her charitable foundation has stolen most of the foundation's assets. A nervous breakdown follows and the book describes her treatment and recovery at Lawton, a mental hospital in the Chicago area.

1141. Ward, Mary Jane. *It's Different for a Woman*. New York: Random House, 1952. 246pp.

With little plot to interfere, Ward captures the inner life and outward trappings of a suburban Chicago upper-middle-class woman—forty-five-year-old Sally Cutter. The setting is an imaginary suburb named Brentwood located twenty miles north of the Loop. Sally is mostly preoccupied by her friendships with other women in her social circle, many of them former schoolmates. Her days are filled with organized social events, including teas, luncheons, meetings, and fund-raising dinners. She has a sixteen-year-old-son, Bradford, and a daughter Tess, who is engaged to marry an internee physician. Her husband George, who is a decade older than she is, works for a publishing firm as an editor and also writes books of his own. On some level, Sally is concerned with his close working relationship with his secretary and their business trips. The family physician is a major presence in the life of Sally, her family, and her friends, and as she enters menopause she contemplates a hysterectomy with anxiety. The culminating event of the novel is Tess's wedding. This major life event causes Sally and other characters to reflect on their lives, including past romances and decisions. Brentwood is a fairly self-contained world for the women in the novel, even though Chicago is so nearby.

1142. Ward, Mary Jane. *The Other Caroline*. New York: Crown, 1970. 216pp.

In telling the story of Caroline Kincaid, a patient at Illinois' Applewood State Hospital for the Insane, Ward alternates between accounts of life in the hospital and of Kincaid's life as a college student and as a young woman in suburban Chicago. Kincaid is married to Jock Dunlop, an electrical engineer. Early in their marriage, the young couple lived in an impoverished area of Chicago, but soon fled back to the affluent suburb in which they grew up. After the move, when Kincaid goes into the city it is usually for a special outing with friends, such as shopping, lunch, or tea. Her descriptions make very clear the disconnect between life in the city and in the suburbs. Aspects of this disconnect are part of the psychic discomfort she experiences as a young mother that finally leads to her breakdown. Although the novel is set in the 1960s the youth culture of the time period does not impact the narrative, nor does the feminist movement. Most of Kincaid's psychic conflicts stem from status anxiety and the relative success of her husband.

1143. Ward, Mary Jane. *The Wax Apple*. New York: Dutton, 1938. 312pp.

The Lundmark and Scherer families have lived in the same duplex in a lower-middle-class area on Diversey Street for twenty years. Now that the young people in each family are in their twenties, romance begins to complicate their lives, particularly when Dozie Scherer falls in love with Aggie Lundmark. The novel is almost exclusively set in the duplex the Scherers own and illustrates the unnatural, claustrophobic atmosphere of too many people living in too small a space. Although Mrs. Scherer and Mrs. Lundmark have dreams for their children, when characters in the novel go beyond the duplex their dreams are crushed by an uncaring world. Mr. Scherer is the character with most contact with the larger world and his work as a foreman in a box factory illustrates the emptiness of assembly line labor.

1144. Ware, Harlan. *Come, Fill the Cup*. New York: Random House, 1952. 246pp.

The hard drinking treated casually in other Chicago novels is problematized as alcoholism in this book. When reporter Lew Marsh is fired, the women's page editor, Paula, tries to help, only to watch helplessly as Lew continually drinks himself into a stupor. Only Lew's friend Charley Dolan, a recovering alcoholic, is able to assist Lew and, after a period of sobriety, help him get his job back. Years pass and Lew gets promoted to city editor. A crisis comes when Lew is forced by the newspaper owner to get involved in the life of the owner's nephew, Boyd Copeland, an alcoholic. Even if Boyd's problem was something other than alcohol, the situation would be complicated for Lew. If not for his alcoholism, Lew, instead of Boyd, would have married Paula and he is still is in love with her. Matters become even more complicated when Lew discovers that Boyd is involved in organized crime. The Chicago setting of the novel is fairly dependent on popular images of the city as mob-controlled.

1145. Warren, Maude Radford. *The Land of the Living*. New York: Harper and Brothers, 1908. 314pp.

This political novel set in early-twentieth-century Chicago tells the story of assimilated Irish immigrants. When Hugh MacDermott's father is killed in an industrial accident, Hugh is unofficially adopted by his ward's political boss, Jim Callahan. Callahan sends him to military school and college, and Hugh returns to Chicago to begin law school. Now a young man, developing his own ideas, Hugh's allegiance to Callahan is tested by an acquaintance with reform politician Henry Furlong. Hugh eventually betrays Callahan by joining Furlong's law firm and working on his political campaigns. Callahan still has designs on Hugh and gets him the position of juvenile court judge that Hugh had coveted. By the end of the novel, an even larger political plum comes Hugh's way—the governorship. Two women are also rivals for Hugh, brassy stenographer Mayme Broomer and recent immigrant Moira Carew. The confused allegiances and misconceived ideals that complicate Hugh's relationship to Callahan and Furlong complicate his relations with Mayme and Moira, as well, although the true lovers, Moira and Hugh, are finally reconciled. Although, like many novels of the time period, this one focuses on political corruption funded by powerful utility and transportation companies, the book's real interest is in descriptions of everyday life. Many of the characters live in boarding houses, and the social interactions and physical settings of such places is detailed. The novel also includes descriptions of office life and makes fine distinctions about social status and behavior, revealing a complex system very much alive at the time the novel was written.

1146. Warren, Maude Radford. *The Main Road*. New York: Harper and Brothers, 1913. 390pp.

Through the life challenges of Janet Bellamy as she matures from a college student to a young woman, this novel deals with many of the issues faced by women in the early 1900s. Bellamy grew up on a Wisconsin farm and understands little of the world when she arrives to study at the University of Chicago. Through her campus social life she meets girls and young men from affluent backgrounds and is introduced to Chicago society. When Janet falls deeply in love for the first time, she assumes that she will marry her young man and live the rest of her life in wedded bliss. However, her beau falls out of love with her not long before she graduates and she learns an important lesson about the nature of romance. Janet lives with her wealthy aunt but is exposed to the lives of the poor through a fellow university student in whom she takes an interest. She later works as a labor movement activist, as a coordinator in a settlement house, and, finally, a suffragette, before finding true love and marrying. In addition to dealing with women's issues, the novel explores the inequalities of social class. Although there are descriptions of domestic interiors and clothing, the novel focuses for the most part on dialogue that presents viewpoints on the social issues with which it is concerned.

1147. Warren, Maude Radford. *Never Give All*. Indianapolis: Bobbs-Merrill, 1927. 322pp.
    Covering the years 1902 to the 1920s, this novel about the role of women in married life and in society is mostly set in Chicago, although in the section covering World War I, two characters go abroad to aid the war effort. Teresa Santley decides to accept Archibald Lane's marriage proposal, even though they have just learned that he received no inheritance from his father and they will have to live on his modest income as a college professor. Teresa's mother opposes the match, thinking Teresa foolish to base her decision solely on love. She would have Teresa choose another suitor, Bertram Carruthers, who combines intellect with ambition and worldliness. The rest of the novel illustrates the sacrifices Teresa makes for romantic love. Even though Teresa enters the marriage as a published novelist, she gives up any thought of continuing her writing career, focusing instead on getting clerical positions to earn household expense money. Over the decades she continues to sacrifice her personal life to the needs of her children and to Lane, helping him with poetry manuscripts that can only be published through subventions. She finally re-evaluates her early decision to place romantic love above all else near the end of the novel as her own daughter begins to consider her suitors. Chicago in the novel is mostly that of upper-middle-class literary society and many of the characters are academics or students.

1148. Warren, Robert Penn. *A Place to Come To*. New York: Random House, 1977. 401pp.
    Most of the Chicago content of this novel is set in the 1940s and 1950s when protagonist, and first-person narrator, Jediah Tewkesbury is in graduate school. The semi-autobiographical work tells of Tewkesbury's rise from obscurity and social disgrace (stemming from the accidental death of his father, killed while urinating or masturbating and drunkenly driving a mule wagon) to international renown as a medievalist. A high school football hero with strength and good looks, Tewkesbury realizes that he will never find honor in his birthplace of Claxford County, Alabama. After college in Tennessee, he begins graduate study at the University of Chicago, where he becomes an acolyte to the internationally known Professor Stahlman. As the first city in which Tewkesbury has ever lived, Chicago receives his thorough description. In addition to a mentor in Stahlman, the city provides him with his first, intense sexual experience in the arms of Dauphine Finkel, a wealthy and famous photographer. However, Tewkesbury also has his first brush with death in the city when he is mugged at knife point. Tewkesbury's studies are interrupted by service in World War II and when he returns he marries the most beautiful coed at the University of Chicago, Agnes Andresen. When Andresen dies tragically young, Tewkesbury moves to Nashville to teach at Vanderbilt University. The novel's Chicago sections skillfully evoke middle and upper-middle-class life in the city in the 1940s and 1950s.

1149. Warrick, LaMar Sheridan. *Yesterday's Children*. New York: Thomas Y. Crowell, 1943. 202pp.

Most of this novel is set in a close-in suburb of Chicago named Elmwood here, but seems based on Evanston. Transpiring during 1940 and 1941 the story of the Weaver family is told through the eyes of Doris Weaver, the mother of the household and focuses on her son Randall, who finishes his senior year of high school and begins college before enlisting in the U.S. Air Force near the end of the book. The public high school, whose student body of three thousand six hundred is composed of children from the most privileged as well as the poorest areas of the suburb, is held up as the epitome of the democratic way of life. It is the way of life Elmwood also presents and that Randall enlists to protect. The degree of social involvement by Elmwood residents is high, as parents and children are involved in a wide variety of organizations, including garden clubs, churches, P.T.A., Hi-Y, the University Club, and various charitable committees. Doris' observations encapsulate the middle-class culture of Midwestern Americans around the beginning of World War II. Urban Chicago mostly serves as the place where Elmwood fathers have their offices.

1150. Washburne, Marion Foster. *The House on the North Shore*. Illustrated by Walter J. Enright and Maginel Wright Barney. Chicago: McClurg, 1909. 287pp.

The teenage children in a family uncover a mysterious connection between their parents and a couple residing in a "haunted house." No additional information is available.

1151. Waterloo, Stanley. *Armageddon*. Chicago: Rand, McNally, 1898. 259pp.

This futurist novel imagines a time in the early years of the twentieth century in which a dreadnought prevents any thought of war and Anglo-Saxons assert their superiority over other races. This future is made possible by Chicago inventor David Appleton who builds an innovative dirigible on the plains just outside the suburbs of Chicago. Appleton obtains financing for his invention from a group of Chicago millionaires and when the Anglo-Saxon alliance must defend itself in a world war, Appleton offers the use of his dirigible to the United States government for use in the aerial bombing of ships. After only one battle, in which Appleton proves the effectiveness of his invention, a treaty is signed in which Austria, France, Italy, Portugal, South America, and Spain concede the superiority of the Anglo-Saxon alliance (Denmark, Germany, Great Britain, Japan, the Netherlands, Norway, Sweden, and the United States) as the "most adapted population to settle new lands." The Anglo-Saxon alliance pledges immediate reform to U.S. immigration laws to admit only certain populations. Use of the Chicago setting is minimal, but the city is presented as the source of invention, skilled industrial labor, and capital. The outspoken and exhaustively presented racism of the novel may be of interest to scholars of the era.

1152. Waterloo, Stanley. *The Launching of a Man*. Chicago: Rand, McNally, 1899. 285pp.

This coming-of-age novel relates events in Robert Sargent's life from the time he is a six-year-old in a frontier house in Michigan until he is engaged to marry. When Sargent finishes his college degree in engineering, he proposes to his childhood sweetheart, Barbara Sloan, who lives with her widowed father, a retired judge and major land owner. Not wanting to abandon her father, and thinking Sargent should be established in his career before marrying, Barbara rejects Sargent. Sargent relocates to Chicago for his first job, but his romantic life soon dominates his attention. He lives in a Wabash Avenue boarding house operated by Mrs. Graves, whose attractive young ward, Elsie Romaine, fascinates Sargent. Romaine is the illegitimate daughter of deceased British music hall performer Kitty Romaine and Graves believes that Elsie might also become a burlesque star, even though Elsie does not want to be an actress. When a romance develops between Elsie and Sargent, Graves is quick to banish Sargent, preventing him from interfering with her designs for Elsie. Sargent pines for the girl and when she suddenly succumbs to pneumonia her death prompts his departure from Chicago. He accepts surveying work for the transcontinental railroad and works in the west for several years before completing his task, Sargent returns to Barbara, who is receptive to the mature young man, and it is clear the two will marry and develop her father's Michigan land. Chicago is clearly found wanting in a contrast between the city and rural Michigan. The city is a place of impersonal business and feverishly unhealthy passions, while Barbara and her family epitomize healthy relationships to nature, to each other, and to their community.

1153. Waterloo, Stanley. *A Man and a Woman*. Chicago: Schulte, 1892. 250pp.

In hagiographical style, the narrator, a friend of Grant Harlson since childhood, relates Harlson's biography from a frontier boyhood, through a political career that includes terms in Congress and is brought to an end by Harlson's death from pneumonia when he is in his sixties. Given the title, it is not surprising that the author focuses on Harlson's romantic life and not on his political convictions. Harlson's first introduction to love is from the wife of a wayfaring lake captain and is soon followed by marriage at a young age that did not work out. When Harlson eventually finds true love, it is with Jean Cornish, a woman twenty years his junior. The narrator celebrates the couple as distinctively American, combining physical vigor, frontier skills, personal integrity independent from the dictates of institutionalized religion, and political skills. These qualities translate into power and respect in an urban environment. Most of the Chicago content deals with Harlson's political campaigns that get him elected a Congressman from the Ninth Ward. Harlson does not kowtow to any political bosses and his final election campaign is so physically demanding that he contracts a fatal case of pneumonia. Implicit to the novel is an 1890s perspective on gender and married life.

1154. Waterloo, Stanley. *The Seekers*. Chicago: Herbert S. Stone, 1900. 257pp.

In this novel about the relationship between physical and spiritual health, young people seek faith cures, explore the teachings of Christian Science, and test the value of patent medicines. Katherine Vaughn, a teacher of modern languages, brings her ill sister Narcissa to the city hoping to find a means of restoring her health. Vaughn lives in the Lake House, a residence hotel on Michigan Avenue operated by Serena Dodge and consisting of several former mansions connected together. Her acquaintance, engineer John Yule, becomes her main support in her search for a cure. Yule, who worked for several years constructing railroads in Siberia, has returned to Chicago to manage a sizable estate, recently inherited from an uncle. The bulk of his relative's wealth stems from a patent medicine business based in Chicago. When Yule realizes that opium is the active ingredient in the company's elixir, he closes the enterprise, giving up a significant income. Christian Science is proven to be the genuine answer to Vaughn and Yule's search. The novel details housing, clothing, and medical treatment, conveying a sense of late-nineteenth-century Chicago.

1155. Watt, Marion Frances. *Maurice: And Other Stories*. Seattle: Ivy Press, 1902. 313pp.

Two of the four short stories in this volume are set in Chicago. Although parts of "Miss Williams: A Story of the Garden City," are set in Paris, winning acceptance in Chicago and not in

New York or Paris, is the longed for goal of sculptress Alice Williams. She grows up in her mother's Chicago boarding house. The story describes the interactions of the guests, the endless games of pinochle, and the politeness everyone must exercise in tight quarters. Plain Alice is interested only in her sculptures and everyone assumes she will remain a spinster. Then, boarder John Searles sees her beauty and she is transformed by his love. Changing her clothing and hairstyle, she becomes beautiful to others and throws away her sculptures. A misunderstanding separates the lovers and the rift becomes insurmountable after Alice receives an income-producing bequest from one of the boarders. She wants John to live with her in a cottage outside the city, but he is concerned about the social implications of her supporting him. He sets out to win his own fortune, but when he discovers that Alice is dying in Paris rushes to her side. She recovers, the two are reconciled, and they take up residence in a South Dakota cottage. She eventually becomes a well-known sculptress, and her career culminates with a recognition ceremony in Chicago's Central Music Hall. In "'Lisabeth: Story of A Chicago Tenement," 'Lisabeth has a crippling orthopedic condition that keeps her in pain and forces her to use crutches. She maintains the household of her brother Tom, who works in a printing plant on Dearborn Street. The two occupy the poorest, least expensive alley rooms they can find, in a fifth floor walk-up. Confined to home and awake at all hours sewing to help support the household, 'Lisabeth accepts her surroundings and is fascinated by her neighbors, finding good things about all of them (except for the man who beats his wife). She helps them as best she can, and when she falls ill with anxiety after Tom loses his job, the neighbors band together and create a wonderful party in her honor. The next day fire breaks out and Tom saves himself, leaving 'Lisabeth behind. Firemen rescue her but she dies clutching her pet canary, in the end, the only creature to remain faithful to her. The story conveys the camaraderie of Chicago tenement life.

1156. Watters, Barbara Hunt [Barbara Hunt, pseud.]. *A Little Night Music*. New York: Rinehart, 1947. 244p.

In post-World War II Chicago, Gavin Macdowell spends his final day alive reflecting on his life. Born in Scotland, Macdowell immigrated to Chicago with his mother after the death of his father. She supported them as a cleaning woman at Marshall Field's until the lung disease she contracted from the Scottish textile mills killed her. Raised by their upstairs neighbor, a widowed Polish woman, Macdowell eventually found work in a secondhand bookstore and married a Polish immigrant. They were briefly happy until she died in childbirth and Macdowell was left to raise his daughter, Hester on his own. Deafened by scarlet fever, her gluttonous appetite and shallow understanding are a burden for Macdowell. Yet, he devotes his life to her and builds a collection of rare books, purchased for less than a dollar each, to provide for Hester's future. The day he learns that he has only two weeks to live, he arranges the sale of his collection to a book dealer for five hundred thousand dollars, only to return home and discover that Hester has burned every volume, in a bizarre outburst of misguided religiosity. Macdowell's only consolation on his final day of life is his conversation with Henry Stubbs, a brilliant mathematician. Macdowell, who has always been alienated from American consumer culture, as epitomized by Chicago, is comforted by Stubbs' shared alienation. Like Macdowell, Stubbs has dropped out of the system, rejecting a doctoral fellowship because his mathematical work would be used for military purposes. In addition to reflections on Chicago as a cultural symbol, the novel includes descriptions of a 1940s automat, the neighborhood around State and Van Buren Streets, and the immigrant neighborhood in which the Macdowells live.

1157. Wayde, Bernard. *The Black Mask; or, the Misterious* [sic] *Marriage: A Romance of Chicago.* Fifteen Cent Romances, No. 8. New York: Ornum, 1872. 97pp.

No additional information available.

1158. Weaver, John Van Alstyne. *Margey Wins the Game.* New York: Alfred A. Knopf, 1922. 110pp.

In this social satire, a debutante transforms herself from the wall flower a society columnist advises to drop out of the social season, to the most popular of the debutantes. Margey Ranson's earliest supporter and the novel's first-person narrator is Larry Baker, inebriate heir to the Baker soap fortune and perennial Yale undergraduate. Margey is a serious girl, devoted to art and literature. Even though she has distinguished New England ancestors and a wealthy father, she has no distinctive style and no light conversation. When she decides to take her debutante year seriously, she drops out of society for three weeks. She returns with a wardrobe based on earlier styles that gives her a distinctive appearance and has read several years' worth of magazines and newspapers on which to base small talk. As the season progresses she becomes the focus of attention at every social event, is selected to lead the cotillion at the biggest event of the social season, and has three marriage proposals. Having proven to herself that she can be a social success, she gives up her achievements to elope with an instructor at the state university. Although the novel is clearly set in Chicago (there are references to the South Side and North Side, as well as the Art Institute and the stockyards), the narrator refers to the city as Dearborn. The book is written in an upper-class patois that is probably a good record of the way in which such people spoke, and is filled with social detail, particularly about typical upper-class activities.

1159. Webster, Henry Kitchell. *An American Family: A Novel of Today.* Indianapolis: Bobbs-Merrill, 1918. 452pp.

This romance novel incorporates union activism, anarchists, and extra-marital affairs to season the plot, which emphasizes the importance of finding one's true love. Visiting her grandmother in Lake Forest, Jean Gilbert meets Hugh Corbett, to whom she is immediately attracted. Hugh's family owns a factory and Hugh has been awakened to the plight of workingmen. When he meets Helena Galicz, the daughter of a famous anarchist, he falls in love with her, and to the horror of his family, marries her. After a time spent in New York City to escape family censure, Helena and Hugh return to Chicago. The two find a niche for themselves in society—Helena as a writer and salon hostess for political liberals and Hugh as an experimental metallurgist. When Jean returns to Chicago from abroad, her grandmother is determined to launch her in society, but her sympathies make Jean more comfortable in Helena's salon where she becomes reacquainted with Hugh. In the knowledge that Helena is having an affair, the two acknowledge their love to each other. When Helena's lover shoots and kills her in a fit of anger over a business proposition, the matter is hushed up and Jean and Hugh can eventually marry. The novel includes physical descriptions of a range of domestic interiors and of Chicago neighborhoods and street scenes. Social class plays a large role in the novel, in which a sympathetic portrayal is given of artistic intellectuals and factory workers.

1160. Webster, Henry Kitchell. *The Banker and the Bear: The Story of a Corner in Lard.* New York: Macmillan, 1900. 351pp.

John Bagsbury comes from a line of bankers and his father devoted his entire life to the family bank, Bagsbury and Company. However, his father's emotional coldness made working with him less attractive for John than having Melville Sponley as a mentor. John does not realize that Sponley is a notorious speculator who is pursuing a friendship only in the hope of eventually benefiting financially. Sponley gets John to join the bank of one of his cronies and John eventually marries Sponley's niece. John's father does not bequeath control of Bagsbury and Company to his son because of John's friendship with Sponley. However, John eventually wins the presidency, after which Sponley plants a spy in John's bank and employs a whole range of devious means to take control, culminating in a run on Bagsbury and Company. Although John at first has difficulty believing the extent of Sponley's betrayal and regrets the actions needed to defeat him, he remains unemotional, focuses on his responsibility to his account holders, to the exclusion of any other consideration, and eventually bankrupts Sponley. In a subplot, the author presents the relationship between John's orphaned niece, Martha ("Dick") Hasselridge and John's college friend Jack Dorlin, who is a writer with a private income. In the end, Jack and "Dick" play key roles in the defeat of Sponley. By contrast with John and his father, "Dick" and Jack are entirely open to their emotions; they hate Sponley's spy and discuss their anxiety over how matters will turn out. In addition to the central role of commodities futures in the plot, a well-known feature of Chicago business life, the theme of emotional coldness has a definite Midwestern aspect, as males from the region continue to be portrayed in popular culture as characteristically reticent and unemotional.

1161. Webster, Henry Kitchell. *The Beginners.* Indianapolis: Bobbs-Merrill, 1927. 308pp.

In this novel about midlife crisis, a wife acts out when she falsely suspects her husband of an affair and the husband leaves a safe job to become an entrepreneur, before deciding a settled life is not so bad. When Julia marries Edward Patterson she assumes he will be a great success because he has had all of the advantages of an East Coast, upper-middle-class background. However, he gets a job with an insurance agency and spends decades with the same firm, eventually getting promoted to the company's Chicago office. The Pattersons settle in Lakeside and years pass during which the couple have two children, Edith and Ed, Jr. Julia vents her frustration with Ed and her distaste for Chicago devoting herself to women's club activities and charity work. After the death of the husband of their next door neighbor, Ruth Ingraham, Julia encourages Ed to help Ruth out. However, when rumors start, she believes them, and leaves with the children to summer on Lake Michigan, leaving behind a confrontational letter. In response, Ed takes a vacation on his own to California, knowing that Ruth will have moved to New York City by the time the Pattersons return at the end of the summer. Julia and Ed's rapprochement is a cool one and Ed's possessions are moved into the spare room. Shortly afterwards an inventor comes into Ed's office to cash out his life insurance policy so that he can start manufacturing his innovative carburetor. Within twenty-four hours Ed has invested in the company and within a few months has given up his job. Despite the fact that Julia and the children have little faith Ed's chances for success, they pull together and begin to make financial sacrifices. Edith leaves high school and takes a business college course; Ed, Jr. begins working to pay his own college expenses; and Julia lets the family cook go. As the firm begins to fail, Ed undergoes a crisis that ends with the epiphany that he is fortunate in his family and life. He severs his connections to the new business and begins working again for an insurance company, reconciled to his wife and certain of his children's affection. In this novel, Chicago is a surprisingly one-dimensional place of business, in which even the young people rarely engage in purely social activities.

1162. Webster, Henry Kitchell. *The Duke of Cameron Avenue*. New York: Macmillan, 1904. 133pp.

Only a vague reference to Chicago establishes the setting of this novel about political corruption and social reform. Albert Gollans is the alderman for a Chicago ward mainly composed of tenements and brothels, but has found many ways of using his position to enrich himself. Douglas Ramsay, the warden of a settlement house in Gollans' district, fights the alderman by proposing city council legislation to improve sanitation, and when Gollans is instrumental in defeating the proposal, mounts an election campaign to get Gollans voted out of office. The campaign fails, but makes Gollans much more cooperative. The novel focuses on political maneuvering and descriptions of corruption to the exclusion of physical description.

1163. Webster, Henry Kitchell. *The Innocents*. Indianapolis: Bobbs-Merrill, 1924. 345pp.

With the same characters as *The Beginners* (entry 1161), this novel covers some of the same action from a slightly different perspective, dealing with the relationship between Ed Patterson and his son Ed, Jr. Ed, Jr. is obsessed with radio technology and the book provides an introduction to the state of radio broadcasting in the early 1920s. He is also on the verge of adulthood, beginning to establish relationships with women and create an identity for himself in the workplace. His experiences with romance and work give him a better understanding of his father and prepare him for his departure to study at the University of Michigan. Suburban Lakeside in the novel is somewhat empty in this summertime account with many families away at lake cabins and husbands in temporary lodging in the city, close to their offices.

1164. Webster, Henry Kitchell. *Joseph Greer and His Daughter*. Indianapolis: Bobbs-Merrill, 1922. 489pp.

Webster contrasts the Chicago "buccaneers" of the 1880s, who established businesses and won huge fortunes, with their cultured descendants, who are coming of age in the 1920s. Fifty-year-old Joe Greer recalls the buccaneers and, in some ways, is one himself. An engineer who lived in South America for many years, he has discovered a manufacturing process utilizing a microbe that can turn cheap American flax straw into linen. To establish his company, he needs investors, and strong distinctions are drawn between capitalists, often utilizing inherited money, and innovators and inventors like Greer who risk their futures on their ideas and own capabilities. At the same time Greer is setting up his factory, he is becoming acquainted with his daughter Beatrice, whom he has not seen since she was an infant, having been estranged from his wife for twenty years. Beatrice moves between high society social circles and her father's with ease, maintaining an independence of character that echoes her father. By the end of the novel she is getting bit parts in films and is performing in stunt-flying airplane exhibitions. Greer disagreed with Beatrice's choice of a husband and her desire to become an entertainer. However, he loses control of her, just as he loses control over his factory. After suffering a skull fracture he begins drinking to ease the pain. By the time he is sober again, financiers control his company, having gained their advantage through stock and futures manipulation. At the end of the novel, he is pursuing a new invention, and setting up a new company. The issues of companionate marriage, social status, the role of women in society and business, and the dangers of capitalism are all major themes in the novel. A number of the characters who appeared in *Mary Wollaston* (entry 1165) also appear as minor characters in this novel.

1165. Webster, Henry Kitchell. *Mary Wollaston*. New York: Burt, 1920. 372pp.

In this coming of age novel, two young people must readjust to upper-middle-class civilian life and having a stepmother not much older than they are. Gynecologist Dr. John Wollaston remarried a glamorous, young opera singer after his first wife's death. His seventeen-year-old daughter Mary was outraged by her father's remarriage and without even trying to get to know her stepmother moved to New York City, eventually dedicating herself to war work. Her brother Rush enlisted in the army and served in France. After Rush returns to the United States in 1919 the siblings journey together to Chicago, newly purposeless. Rush feels too old to go back to school or start some junior position in business and Mary, who has lived on her own and had a responsible position, finds the idea of submitting to a traditional marriage distasteful. To their surprise, they are immediately won over by their thirty-one-year-old stepmother, Paula, although they have difficulty interpreting her friendship with young, bohemian composer, Anthony March. Rush is the first to move out of his father's house, going into a partnership with a fellow veteran to establish a gentleman's farm near the city. Continuing to reside in her father's household Mary observes Paula's unwitting sway over every man with whom she comes into contact. She also realizes her own love for March, but still balks at the idea of traditional marriage. After Dr. Wollaston falls ill, his children and wife realize his financial support may soon end. By the end of the novel Paula has accepted a lucrative singing contract, Rush has begun treating his farm in a business-like way, and Mary is engaged to marry March. She and the composer have devised a contract for a companionate marriage in which Mary will feel like an equal. Issues of social class, particularly as they apply to behavior, are taken very seriously in the novel, even by Mary and Rush, who pay attention to the presence of appropriate chaperones for women. The book includes some general description of Chicago, but provides the most detail about the Ravinia festival, at which Paula performs in the 1920 season.

1166. Webster, Henry Kitchell. *The Painted Scene*. Indianapolis: Bobbs-Merrill, 1916. 400pp.

Many of these ten short stories are set in Chicago's Globe Theatre. Physical settings are usually tightly constrained to the theater and focus mostly on personality types (the ingénue, the wealthy playboy, the hardened older woman). However, at times there are descriptions of living arrangements and socializing outside the theater. Some behaviors of the theater people would have been scandalous at the time (extramarital affairs, and abuse of cocaine and alcohol). Many details about theater operations (support positions, physical layout, costume maintenance, set building, rehearsals, musical composition) are included.

1167. Webster, Henry Kitchell. *Philopena*. Indianapolis: Bobbs-Merrill, 1927. 319pp.

This combination romance and mystery set in the 1920s touches on a number of social and political issues that divided people of the upper classes during the time period. When the young parents of identical twin sisters Celia and Cynthia Howard drown on a camping trip in 1915, the families of their mother and father cannot agree on who should raise them and each twin is raised separately. The Wainwrights are politically conservative and the Howards are liberals, including a suffragette, education reformer, and literary novelist in their number. After a childhood in which the twins found many opportunities to socialize, and even trade places, Celia marries Philip Rowland and moves with him to Chicago. In the first year of Celia's marriage, she is concerned by her husband's mysterious behavior and the twenty-two-year-old twins decide to exchange places while Rowland is away on a business trip so that Celia can investigate. Celia is involved in an accident and cannot return to Chicago before Rowland. Cynthia's awkward situation worsens when, as Celia, she is accused of bigamy by blackmailing lawyer James Beale. When she confesses her true identity to Fred Carpenter, a man Celia said she could trust, he turns out to have married Celia in college, in what she had thought was a false marriage. After marrying Rowland, Celia realized that she was still in love with Carpenter and then she was threatened with disclosure by Carpenter. Cynthia is able to resolve the situation. She had met Rowland before in Italy and fell in love. She lets Celia take over her life as Cynthia and remarry Carpenter as Cynthia. Continuing to live as Celia, Cynthia gradually reveals her true identity to Rowland and they both realize that he had married the wrong woman. Although there are references to Chicago places, most of the Chicago settings are in a hospital and expensive apartments

1168. Webster, Henry Kitchell. *The Real Adventure: A Novel.* Illustrated by R. M. Crosby. Indianapolis: Bobbs-Merrill, 1916. 574pp.

At the beginning of this novel about the role of women in society, Rosalind Stanton is a University of Chicago student. Her mother is a prominent suffragist and hopes that Rosalind will become a lawyer. However, soon after Rosalind meets Rodney Aldrich, a lawyer from a wealthy pre-fire family (a term used to distinguish families prominent before and after the 1871 fire), the two realize they are in love. After they marry, Rodney transforms his bachelor life, and creates an upper-class household and social life, hosting and attending dinners and balls. Rosalind is quickly accepted in society and all would seem to be set for decades of conventional, upper-class marital bliss. However, Rosalind soon realizes that Rodney would have lived modestly on his income and taken pro bono legal work, instead of living as a society figure. When she insists that he do what he wishes, he is adamant that she deserves a luxurious social setting. Rosalind decides that she wants Rodney to be her friend and partner and that she does not want to be merely supported by him. When she realizes she is pregnant, she believes motherhood will provide her with the work that will equalize their relationship, but after her twins are born, Rodney hires a nursemaid and nanny. Realizing she is destined to live inside the gilded cage Rodney's money has created, she decides to move out, telling everyone she is going on an extended trip to visit her ill mother. She actually moves to a boarding house only blocks away physically from her husband, but a world away socially. With no marketable skills, she gets work as an actress based on her appearance and upper-class speaking voice. After a number of challenges and setbacks, and a fearful confrontation with Rodney when he realizes what she is doing, Rosalind moves to New York City and begins to make a name for herself as a costume designer. Rosalind and Rodney finally reconcile when Rodney assures her that he wants her as his friend and equal. Although Rosalind offers to give up her profession to live as his wife in Chicago, they devise a suitable compromise. The novel describes many Chicago social events and, at the other extreme of the social scale, the humble lives of actors and single working women in Chicago. Specific streets, neighborhoods, and businesses are named. However, the book is primarily about social attitudes and much of the text consists of conversation and interior monologues that elucidate issues surrounding companionate marriage and economic equality between husbands and wives.

1169. Webster, Henry Kitchell. *The Sealed Trunk.* Indianapolis: Bobbs-Merrill, 1929. 319pp.

In this mystery novel, Rhoda White, an eighteen-year-old typist in a newspaper office, has happy friendships with her new apartment mates and is excited by the prospect of getting to know reporter Martin Forbes. Then three strangers appear looking for Rhoda McFarland, her real name, and her life becomes frightening. She believes the quest of C. F. Forster, Max Lewis, and Claire Cleveland has something to do with papers with which her father entrusted her, but which she has been too frightened to read since she thinks they concern a scandal in which he was involved at the university where he was a professor. After a series of frightening, and potentially life threatening experiences, through which her flat mate Babe and Martin assist her, she discovers that her father had been set up by C. F. Forster, a wealthy man who forced Professor McFarland to work for him by destroying McFarland's academic career. He also stole McFarland's innovative refining technique, and made his second fortune. By the end of the novel, Rhoda has married Martin (who turns out to be independently wealthy), received a large settlement from Forster, and set in motion a plan to redeem the reputation of her father. The Chicago interest of the novel is in its descriptions of newspaper office life, dancing and socializing at lakefront hotels, and the apartment life of young women sharing skyscraper residences.

1170. Webster, Henry Kitchell. *The Thoroughbred*. Indianapolis: Bobbs-Merrill, 1917. 257pp.

This novel about the shallowness of upper-class life follows the experiences of a young couple, Claire French and Alfred Blair, who have been married for a little more than a year. Blair grew up poor, worked his way through a trade school to learn architecture, and owns a company that builds grain elevators. Claire grew up in a family which seemed affluent, but was accustomed to her father always trying to make ends meet. The first year of married life for Claire has been frustrating because Alfred is constantly distracted by his business and she has little to occupy herself but social events, since the household, in the hands of competent servants, runs itself. When Alfred's company goes bankrupt Claire is incensed. However, when she begins strategizing for living on a reduced income in an apartment on the West Side near Humboldt Park, she is gratified to discover her resourcefulness. Their lower-middle-class home life means they spend much more time with each other and they realize how much they enjoy each other's company. The couple's financial distress is short-lived; even as an employee, Alfred finds opportunities to exercise his entrepreneurial skills. Claire also seizes an opportunity to invest in an invention after selling her jewels. When the invention begins to pay off and Alfred has raised some capital to reestablish his business, the couple decides not to return to fashionable life. Instead, they will live modestly in the country and raise a family, adhering to the middle-class mores that got them through their crisis. Chicago in the novel operates on false social values that Alfred and Claire reject.

1171. Webster, Henry Kitchell. *Who Is the Next?* Indianapolis: Bobbs-Merrill, 1931. 310pp.

In this murder mystery set on a family estate in suburban Chicago, altered wills and family scandals are at the center of the plot. Corporate lawyer Prentiss Murray has been connected to the Lindstrom family for more than a decade, most recently as the legal guardian of Camilla Lindstrom, whose father killed her mother during an attack of insanity and died years later the inmate of an insane asylum. Camilla is the grand-daughter of Oscar Lindstrom and Murray was his lawyer long before Camilla was born. Lindstrom came to Chicago just as the great fire was burning itself out in 1871 and through wise land investments accumulated a fortune. On the night Lindstrom calls Murray to come to his house for a revision of his will the old man is murdered. Two more murders in the household follow before Murray catches the murderer. Most of the novel takes place on the Lindstrom estate and the culprit turns out to be a man impersonating Camilla's brother, who has been traveling in the Far East for several years. Camilla's wealth and derring-do is expressed in the fact that she has just purchased an airplane that she is learning to fly. The novel touches on issues of gender roles.

1172. Weir, Hugh C. *The Young Wheat Scout; Being the Story of the Growth, Harvesting, and Distribution of the Great Wheat Crop of the United States.* Illustrated by Frank T. Merrill. Chicago: Wilde, 1915. 288pp.

This book for young adults is documentary in intent, explaining the wheat industry from growing and harvesting to selling. A cloak of fiction is provided by the plight of Ronald North. North, the son of a Chicago wheat dealer, is trying to learn his father's business. However, when he is entrusted with a package intended for a company researcher in Iowa, he loses it. As he attempts to recover the package he encounters authorities on wheat who discourse on the industry and relate biographical details about important figures such as Cyrus McCormick and the Marsh Brothers. Although Chicago serves as a significant setting, so does Sheffield, Illinois, and Grand Forks, Iowa.

1173. Wellard, James. *The Affair in Arcady.* New York: Reynal, 1959. 312pp.

Through his efforts to write the history of the Tyler family of Arcady, Illinois, Clive Marshall uncovers numerous surprising family secrets, some involving extramarital affairs, but others concerning ties to murder and organized crime. Chicago serves as a setting for some of the investigation and the secrets, but only as a shallow backdrop.

1174. Wellington, A. A. Mrs. *By A Way that They Knew Not.* Chicago: Rand, McNally, 1885. 288pp.

Written with the intent of Christian evangelism, this book contrasts the society life of Edna Byford and her family with the sober devoutness of Edna's school-friend Susie Keith and her family. When Susie invites Edna to spend the summer with the Keiths, in a town outside Chicago, Edna quickly tires of the Keiths' sobriety. She soon returns to her family and the excitement of Chicago's social whirl. Her enjoyment is short lived, however, for her father goes bankrupt and commits suicide. Then, Edna contracts scarlet fever. The physical comforts she had known are gone and the social set she considered her friends treat her with indifference. Over time she has a chance to return to the Keiths and she now embraces their convictions and way of living. The novel includes descriptions of many aspects of 1880 Chicago social life.

1175. Welton, Arthur D. *The Line Between.* New York: Sears, 1933. 317pp.

The action of this novel focuses on a single block on Division Street in Depression-era Chicago. The newest establishment is an elegant gambling parlor, known as the Club, created by Millicent O'Doyle and her partners Pharigo Trent and Pat Marcy. The Club stands out from its competition for being safe from police raids and by offering afternoon tea, cocktails, and a substantial midnight buffet. Also on the block is a hospital operated by the non-traditional Dr. Gibbes. Gibbes rejected a career as a surgeon to practice preventive medicine and healing regimens that involve non-surgical treatments. His head nurse Phyllis Carlotta is the daughter of Inez Carlotta, who operates another business on the block, a fortune-telling parlor. A crisis disrupts the block, when gangster Harrison "Squeegee" Kemp employs thugs to take over the Club. The rest of the novel describes the changing relationships and shifting allegiances among the tenants of the block and the proprietors and patrons of the businesses. Taken as a whole, the book presents a complex description of a seedy neighborhood in the midst of the Depression.

1176. Welton, Arthur D. *Mr. Weld Retires*. New York: Sears, 1933. 293pp.

In this Depression-era novel, a wealthy man's life becomes focused on the people who frequent one of Chicago's parks. John Weld's son forces him to retire from his company by getting him to accept the honorific title of chairman of the board. Only sixty-three-years-old and in good health, Weld is uncertain how to use his leisure until he begins to frequent a public park. Left unnamed in the novel, the park is clearly Chicago's Washington Square and as Weld begins to spend every day there, he decides to aid a number of other park regulars through gifts of money. The desperately poor and hopelessly alcoholic are among the people Weld benefits, but so too are a soapbox orator, a Salvation Army captain, and a fourteen-year-old girl. While presenting his emotion-laden tale, the author constructs an almost sociological record of park visitors from many socio-economic levels.

1177. Welton, Arthur D. *The Twenty-Seventh Ride*. New York: Sears, 1932. 307pp.

In this mystery set during the Depression, officers of a large Chicago bank task assistant cashier John Jenks with quietly finding out what happened to bank president John Mason since they fear calling in the police will endanger the bank's public reputation. A captain during World War I, Jenks has worked as a collection agent and demonstrated his investigative capabilities. Although it quickly becomes apparent that gangster Giuseppe Falcone and the manipulation of a stock offering are relevant to Mason's disappearance, kidnappings, bombings, secret love affairs, and the theft of hundreds of gallons of bootleg whiskey intervene before Jenks solves the case. Chicago in the novel is under the control not only of gangsters, but large corporate firms like the bank.

1178. Wendt, Lloyd and Herman Kogan. *Lords of the Levee; the Story of Bathhouse John and Hinky Dink*. Indianapolis: Bobbs-Merrill, 1943. 384pp.

In this account of late-nineteenth-century Chicago, aldermen and political bosses control the city. The main characters are John J. Coughlin, who established his political career through working in and later owning bathhouses, and gambling parlor and saloon owner Michael "Hinky Dink" Kenna. The book focuses not only on how Coughlin and Kenna established their influence, but also on the paternalistic role they played within their communities, looking out for the poor and keeping neighborhoods safe. The tone of the book is both celebratory and elegiac and probably echoes stories told in the Democratic clubs in which Coughlin and Kenna were powerful men. As Al Capone and other organized crime figures gain control, Coughlin, Kenna, and other political bosses lose power and influence and political life becomes corrupt in new ways.

1179. Wentworth, Edward Chichester. *The Education of Ernest Wilmerding; A Story of Opening Flowers*. Chicago: Covici-McGee, 1924. 268pp.

At the advice of physicians, the wealthy family of young Ernest Wilmerding sends him to San Antonio, Texas to spend the winter of 1879. While resting there, he falls into the company of two men who inculcate in him a fervent conviction to Socialism. When his grandfather dies, Wilmerding returns to Chicago and uses his sizable inheritance to create a settlement house known as the Walt Whitman Brotherhood. Although the book gives some aspects of the settlement house movement in Chicago, it is primarily a Socialist tract, thinly disguised as fiction.

1180. Weverka, Robert and David S. Ward. *The Sting*. New York: Bantam Books, 1974. 154pp.

This novelization of the movie of the same name (Universal Pictures, 1973; screenplay by David S. Ward) closely follows the plot of the film. Johnny Hooker travels to Chicago in 1937 to get the help of renowned confidence man Henry Gondorff to avenge the murder of Luther Coleman. Hooker and Coleman had robbed gangster Doyle Lonnegan and in return Lonnegan killed Coleman. The elaborate scheme Gondorff devises appeals to Lonnegan's enthusiasm for gambling and so cleverly cheats him out of one million dollars that he does not realize he has been taken. The novel's cartoonish version of Chicago is filled with gangsters, speakeasies, and gambling parlors.

1181. Wheaton, Emily. *The Russells in Chicago*. Illustrated by Fletcher C. Ransom. Boston: Page, 1902. 257pp.

When Edward Russell, a Boston lawyer who had interned with a Chicago law firm, is offered a job in the city after graduating from Harvard Law School he eagerly accepts because he found the city's freer, more open society refreshing. His wife Alice is less enthusiastic. Her exposure to the city has been limited to a visit to the World's Fair and contact with the overdressed, nouveaux riches Chicago girls who had attended her boarding school. As they settle into city life, Alice, who is considered haughty and pretentious, is ignored, finding her only real niche as a volunteer with a hospital women's society. Edward, on the other hand, is immediately well-liked and invited everywhere. Tensions emerge and relations between Alice and her husband deteriorate until Alice hears her husband tell Lily Naylor, a woman that Alice admires for her independence and regal bearing, how much he loves Lily. Though Lily rejects Edward, Alice is awakened to the threat of losing her husband and when Lily reaches out to her and helps her concoct a scheme to make Edward jealous, she acquiesces. The scheme brings the couple back together, and through the friendship Alice develops with Lily, she comes to see that Chicago is a desirable place to live. The novel presents a comprehensive listing of early twentieth-century clubs and cultural institutions in the city and includes firsthand accounts of meetings of clubs and charitable boards, as well as social events that include teas, dinners, and balls.

1182. Wheeler, Keith. *The Reef*. New York: Dutton, 1951. 320pp.

Dealing with the difficulties faced by returning World War II veterans, this novel is partly set in Chicago and Wilmette. In 1946, Nickerson Cotton returns to Chicago as a war hero with a Purple Heart and Navy Cross. His transition to civilian life goes very badly, even though he has a midlevel executive job at Owens Soap Corporation waiting for him, through the influence of an army buddy and his own grandfather. Cotton begins drinking heavily and behaving truculently in domestic and workplace settings. Soon, he is estranged from his wife and when he causes a near fatal automobile accident while his eight-year-old son is his passenger talk of divorce begins. Cotton exacerbates his marital difficulties by having several affairs. After he is fired from his job, he gets a chance to redeem himself by taking over a company project in the West Indies. While on his way to this assignment, he makes a detour to Tarawa Atoll in the Gilbert Islands, where he played a crucial role as a commander and believes he caused the deaths of too many of his comrades. The visit is the start of his redemption and renewed control of his life. Chicago in the novel is mostly epitomized by the orderly environments of corporate offices and affluent households from which Cotton is exiled for his behavior.

1183. White, Betty. *I Lived This Story*. Garden City, N.Y.: Doubleday, Doran, 1930. 308pp.

The college life of a 1920s coed at Northwestern University forms the basis for this coming of age novel. Dorinda Clark is thrilled during her freshman year to successfully pledge Gamma Theta sorority and begin dating fraternity men. Not until her junior year does she begin to question whether college can offer more. She broadens her social network to include students who do not belong to fraternities or sororities and begins to disavow the shallowness of her first years of higher education to take more interest in her classes. The book includes references to Chicago and descriptions of lakeside activities and scenes, but maintains a fairly close focus on campus life.

1184. White, Hervey. *Differences*. Boston: Small, Maynard, 1899. 311pp.

This novel about the plight of the working class in Chicago also explores the social constraints on women. Genevieve Radcliffe, a recent graduate of Wellesley College, is engaged to Maynard Neville, a young businessman and aesthete of her social class. While waiting out the socially mandated engagement period, Radcliffe grows frustrated with accompanying her mother to social events. She decides to live and work at Mrs. Purcell's settlement house, in the factory district not far from Goose Island, arousing the fierce opposition of her family and fiancé. At the settlement house she meets young men and women of her own class who engage in social work out of personal commitment or simply to leave their small towns and experience urban life. However, she becomes most intimate with one of her clients, John Ward, a young English immigrant widower, who is an out of work machinist with two young children. His situation teaches her about the brutal consequences of social inequality. She decides to stop accepting her family's allowance and spend only money she earns. After the tragic death of Ward's young daughter, partly brought on by environmental pollution, Radcliffe acknowledges that she has fallen in love with Ward. Not only her family members, but also Mrs. Purcell and her fellow settlement house workers are outspoken about the inappropriateness of someone from Radcliffe's social class marrying a worker. As Radcliffe makes clear her determination, she is disinherited of a fortune by her uncle and loses the friendship of Mrs. Purcell. The novel ends after Ward and Radcliffe wed. He is still unemployed and she is working as a schoolteacher, trying to support their household on a hardship wage. The novel presents living conditions for working families, and describes Chicago's water and air pollution, from which the poor cannot escape.

1185. Whitlock, Brand. *The Gold Brick*. New York: Hurst, 1910. 342pp.

Each of the short stories in this collection deals in some way with elected office. Most stories are set in Chicago but even when Springfield, Illinois serves as a setting, the stories still often have a Chicago aspect. The stories deal with a political cartoonist who can only draw images that express his political conviction, an Irish-American political boss near the end of his career as he decides whether or not to retire to Ireland, and an upper-class man running for a state senate seat who is defeated by the party machine. Although corruption, particularly as it relates to public utility contracts, is a major presence in the stories, several characters are in political life due to personal convictions and emotional connections to Chicago and its people.

1186. Whitlock, Brand. *The Happy Average*. Indianapolis: Bobbs-Merrill, 1904. 347pp.

Although much of this novel about twenty-two-year-old Glenn Marley's efforts to establish himself in life and win the hand of twenty-year-old Lavinia Blair is set in Macochee, Ohio, more than one hundred pages are set in Chicago, to which Marley eventually relocates. Marley, the son of a Methodist preacher, returns to Macochee after finishing college and begins reading law. When he falls in love with Lavinia, her father, Judge Blair, opposes the courtship based on Marley's poor financial prospects. After exploring opportunities in Macochee, Marley realizes that he must move to Chicago. He settles in an Ohio Street boarding house and soon discovers that the city already has approximately four thousand lawyers. As his resources dwindle, he gets work as a manual laborer handling railroad freight. Eventually, he progresses to railroad billing clerk. In daily correspondence with Lavinia, his letters describe many aspects of Chicago life in the early 1900s. Marley's life changes dramatically when James Weston, an aspiring writer, befriends him. Eventually, they share an apartment and Weston helps Marley get a journalist's position. On the strength of a white collar job, the prestige of his name in print, and the friendship of a published novelist, the Judge finally consents to his daughter's marriage. In addition to presenting the experiences of a Chicago newcomer in the early twentieth-century, the novel illustrates the importance of Chicago as a cultural symbol to the small-town residents of Macochee who are titillated by Marley's relocation in a time period of dramatic population shifts from farms and towns to cities. Although they tend to suspect Marley will fail, when he does find suitable employment they are ready to celebrate his success as a native son.

1187. Whitlock, Brand. *Her Infinite Variety*. Illustrated by Howard Chandler Christy. New York: Burt, 1904. 167pp.

Very little of this novel is physically set in Chicago, however much of the content has to do with the attitudes of Chicagoans who look down on their state capitol, Springfield. Morley Vernon, a state senator, must deal with his fiancée Amelia Ansley's conviction that the state government is run by farmers. Amelia is secure in her social superiority as she presides from her parents' Michigan Boulevard drawing room and wishes that Vernon, a Chicago lawyer, would give up politics and devote himself to what really matters: conquering drawing rooms with his charm. To her horror, he is, from Amelia's perspective, duped by a female lawyer, Chicagoan Maria Burley Green, into supporting a bill extending the right to vote in state and local elections to women. Amelia and a cadre of Chicago society women under the command of Mrs. Overman Hodge-Lathrop descend on the state legislature to lobby for the defeat of the legislation and express their outrage with Vernon who could think that women should descend from their exalted domestic sphere to elbow their way to polling places and sully themselves by consorting with politicians. Although the Chicago society women are victorious in the novel, the author makes their concerns seem trivial compared to those of the suffragettes.

1188. Whitmore, Stanford. *Solo*. New York: Harcourt, Brace, 1955. 382pp.

In this account of Chicago's jazz music scene in the 1940s and 1950s, the plot focuses on the success of jazz pianist Virgil Jones and his complex, self-destructive personality. When Jones arrives in the city, unknown and friendless, he lives on the South Side. Desperate for a piano, he goes into Seymour Schwab's music store and plays jazz on the demonstration piano. He is heard by Ross Jaeger, a Julliard trained musician who has abandoned classics to form his own jazz ensemble, for which he composes. Before long, the mysterious Jones is following Jaeger's advice and building a career as a jazz soloist. The main characters in the novel are mostly Caucasians and the jazz promoters, like critic Roger Henneberry, tend to be Jewish. A number of Chicago jazz clubs provide settings: the Leopard Lounge on Sixty-third Street and the Nob Hill on Lake Park Avenue, as well as Near North Side nightclubs. The characters expostulate on the role of jazz in the larger culture and on dangerous effects of the music on its best practitioners

1189. Whitney, Phyllis A. *Red Is for Murder*. A Fingerprint Mystery. Chicago: Ziff-Davis, 1943. 221pp.

Set in the world of Cunningham's, a 1940s Chicago department store, this book displays a detailed knowledge of such institutions. Most of the characters are identified with a very specific skill they use in their store jobs. The main character is Linell Wynn, a copywriter for the store's advertising posters; other characters paint backdrops for displays, model clothing, and work as floorwalkers, sales clerks, and buyers. Many of the workers are young people and romantic intrigue is rife and suspected to be at the root of two murders of store employees. Although the Chicago police are called in, it is the store detective, Sylvester Hering, with his intimate knowledge of the store, who solves the crimes. Most of the descriptions are of the store, however some scenes in apartments and local dining establishments give a sense of the way working-class people of the time lived.

1190. Whitney, Phyllis A. *The Silver Inkwell*. Illustrated by Hilda Frommholz. Boston: Houghton Mifflin, Riverside Press, 1945. 272pp.

This World War II era coming-of-age novel is set on the Near North Side. Patty and Lynn Sheridan enter the workforce without parents to support them; their mother is dead and their father is in Washington engaged in war-related work. Their neighborhood is a marginal one in which gang violence can occur. However, just across Michigan Avenue from them, in an area that is officially the Near North Side, more affluent people live, many of whom are artists and writers. Both Lynn and Patty work in the lower echelons of book culture. Lynn works as a library clerk in a nearby branch of Chicago Public Library and Patty works for a publishing company. Lynn aspires to be a writer and Patty eventually helps her get a job in her firm's children's' department. Through new friends, that include the owner of a bookshop and a published author, Lynn learns about life and writing and by the end of the novel is on her way to fulfilling her writing ambition. The novel provides a sense of what World War II Chicago was like for young people and touches on the issues of social acculturation for immigrants and gang violence.

1191. Whitney, Phyllis A. *Willow Hill*. New York: David McKay, 1947. 243pp.

The imaginary Chicago suburb of the title is set into turmoil when African-Americans begin moving into a federally subsidized housing project on the edge of town. The story is told from the perspective of students at Willow Hill High School, where school newspaper editor Valerie Coleman and her friends play a key role in the successful integration of the school. They support the efforts of their forward-thinking principal and a popular coach and the book's message that racial prejudice is wrong is voiced through authority figures and students. Although this book for young adults is set in a suburb, many of the examples of racial hatred transpire in Chicago, a place from which the new residents of Willow Hill are trying to escape.

1192. Wickware, Francis Sill. *Tuesday to Bed*. Indianapolis: Bobbs-Merrill, 1948. 275pp.

Chicago in this novel is a conference town that epitomizes all that is wrong with postwar American culture to architect Stanton Wylie. Wylie's dark view of Chicago and the United States is deeply affected by a recent revelation. A Harvard University graduate, who worked on the Manhattan Project during the war and is to receive one of the highest awards an architect can earn at the Chicago banquet of the American Association of Architects and Industrial Designers, had seemed to be living the perfect, affluent, suburban life in Westport, Connecticut, married to the attractive Betsy. Just before boarding the famous Century train to Chicago, Wylie learns Betsy is named in the divorce suit being brought by the wife of famous actor Billy Paige. On the long train ride he must suppress his emotions over his wife's affair while submitting to lengthy interviews by Nancy Mainwaring, who is writing an extensive article about him for *Life* magazine. As he reviews for her the main details of his life and reflects on their meaning, he falls in love with the reporter. When the disaffected Wylie makes his acceptance speech at the banquet, he declares that architecture reflects a society's morality, using Chicago as an example. He claims the city expresses the greedy, pig-like morality of Chicagoans and that the only rational course would be an evacuation and leveling of Chicago's buildings in an atomic explosion. Wylie flies back to New York, determined to give up his life in Westport and move to Bermuda. Although he invites Mainwaring to go with him, she rejects his assessment of the United States and finds she has renewed faith in her profession. The slight physical description of Chicago in the novel is related from Wylie's viewpoint.

1193. Wight, Natalie. *Death in the Inner Office*. New York: Phoenix Press 1938. 246pp.

In this novel about 1930s office life, thirty-year-old Lee Farron works in the corporate office of a large soap manufacturing firm, Loring, Jobi, and Epstein in a building on Michigan Avenue close to the Art Institute. The office operation employs many typists, all women and mostly young, separated into pools (i.e., the Correspondence Department, the Reports Department, etc.). A full-time typewriter repairman Mr. Grosbeak keeps the machines in order. The regional salesmen, like Tony Dean, are the glamorous objects of fascination for the typists and secretaries. The typists are supervised by older women who report to the frightening and demanding Mrs. Liz Root, a devotee of efficiency experts. When Root is murdered after discovering that two thousand dollars is missing from office accounts, Lieutenant Clancy of Chicago's Homicide Bureau investigates. Farron quickly becomes Clancy's guide to the close-knit office environment at the soap company. The novel is set almost exclusively inside offices and portrays the forced intimacy of the work environment. Alcohol consumption is a major leisure activity and the inescapable of heat of a Chicago summer gets many references.

1194. Wilcox, Wendell. *Everything Is Quite All Right*. New York: Bernard Ackerman, 1945. 184pp.

Extended sections of this novel are set in Chicago, but the work's focus on emotions and interpersonal relations make the physical setting almost inconsequential. Protagonist Elsie Singer, as the oldest daughter in an impoverished Michigan family, is forced to leave her parents' farm and live with her widowed Aunt Norah in Chicago, while earning money as a housekeeper to send home. Tensions with her aunt and the woman for whom she works drives her to seek companionship and she is soon involved in a romance. However, once she is no longer compelled by financial conditions to be in the city she returns to Michigan and eventually marries. Unlike many Chicago novels, here the city is not considered a place of opportunity and the protagonist never considers making her life there.

1195. Wilder, Thornton. *The Eighth Day*. New York: Harper and Row, 1967. 435pp.

Only a little over seventy pages of this novel is set in Chicago, however Wilder produces a rich portrait of the city as it existed in the early 1900s. After Roger Ashley's father John Ashley is falsely accused of murder, the seventeen-year-old Roger leaves the southern Illinois town in which he grew up (Wilder's imaginary Coaltown). In his hometown he passively benefited from being the well-loved, oldest son in the town's most prominent family. Like many Midwesterners seeking to establish themselves, he moves to Chicago. Psychologically and physically strong, and possessed of a strong work ethic, Roger performs menial jobs (dish washing, hotel night desk clerk, haberdashery salesman, and hospital orderly) with a care that draws people to him. In every experience he looks for his vocation and when he begins working in a newspaper office he finds his life's calling. Soon, he is famous for non-investigative columns that describe people and places that his readers might otherwise ignore. Because he often writes about workers, immigrants, and other disenfranchised Chicagoans, reformers build on his column's popularity to improve the city. When his younger sister Lily arrives to study voice, Roger's attention broadens to include members of Chicago's large music community. Roger's Chicago is diverse, with many struggling, working-class people; the city also has a significant percentage of civic-minded people working to make life better for everyone.

1196. Wilkie, Franc Bangs. *The Gambler, a Story of Chicago Life*. Chicago: Denison, 1888. 328pp.

The author uses the story of Paul Caulkins' downfall to condemn Chicago vice in this morality tale. Dissatisfied with farm life, Paul is inspired by traveling salesman John Lafarge to relocate to Chicago. He arrives in the city with a forty thousand dollar inheritance and confers with Lafarge who advises him to safely invest most of his money and establish a modest bank account to supply his daily needs while preparing to enter Chicago society by engaging in athletics, dancing lessons, and having a good tailor make his wardrobe. In the respectable boarding house where he resides, he meets Eleanor Wright, a young woman from a formerly affluent family, who, in a great coincidence, works as a typist in Lafarge's office. The two are soon dating and, in a relatively short time, marry. Paul invests in a publishing house, Eleanor stops working, and all would seem in place for a satisfying middle-class life. However, Lafarge had been infatuated with Eleanor and once Paul marries her, Lafarge becomes his sworn enemy. The author attributes Lafarge's exaggerated emotions to the fact that he is a Jew, and a "fetich" [*sic*] worshipper. Lafarge's priestess is an African voodoo witch named Natalie. She and Lafarge make a pact to destroy Paul and offer his blood as a sacrifice to their fetishes. Through respectable private club membership, Lafarge gets Paul addicted to drinking and gambling and he loses his money, his investments, and money entrusted to him by his mother. Nothing slows his descent, not even his daughter's birth or the departure of Eleanor. Paul starts an affair with "the Panther", a woman who resides with Natalie. Reduced to penury, it seems as though Lafarge's final revenge on Paul is imminent when the two get into a fight during a card game. However, Paul wrests a pistol from Lafarge's hand and kills him. Paul eludes arrest, but contracts pneumonia. As he lies on his deathbed, he summons Eleanor and pleads for and receives her forgiveness. In a preface, the author had warned readers of the evils of gambling. He claims that speculation, as practiced on the Chicago Board of Trade makes gambling seem legitimate. He also blames influential men in a more direct way when he points out that wealthy men often own gambling houses and the banks that lend money to gamblers. Although he does not catalog other forms of vice, he does describe some of the common tricks of con artists on Chicago streets.

1197. Williams, Brock. *The Earl of Chicago*. New York: Grosset and Dunlap, 1937. 305pp.

Only a brief section of this novel is physically set in Chicago, in a gangland hangout controlled by "the Kid," a young gangster who has been very successful in creating a lucrative underworld business. The Kid has just been released from prison and discovers that another gangster has been siphoning off his business. He travels to New York City to find his enemy and after getting his revenge, accidentally meets an English lawyer in a bar. The lawyer has been sent to the United States to follow up on a rumor that the legitimate heir to the recently deceased Earl of Gorley is living in America. When he notices the Kid's signet ring and discovers his name is Stephen Arthur Kilmount, he realizes he has found the heir to the estate. The rest of the novel deals with the incongruence of a Chicago gangster in the upper reaches of British society. So, although Chicago does not play a physical role, the novel puts forward a Chicago stereotype, the Chicago gangster, complete with slang and garish clothing.

1198. Williams, Wilbur Herschel. *The Merrymakers in Chicago and Their Adventures in That Great City.* Illustrated by Frank Thayer Merrill. Boston: Page, 1920. 321pp.

In this book for children, twenty-three-year-old Ned Merrymaker, on assignment for his New York newspaper to cover the 1920 Republican National Convention in Chicago, is so enthusiastic after he sees the city that he sends for the rest of the orphaned Merrymakers (Carl, fifteen; Marje, fourteen; Jean, ten; and Rex, eight). The young Merrymakers stay with their deceased mother's sister, Esther Fortune, a widow who lives alone in a luxurious apartment on Grand Avenue. They soon meet Gath [*sic*] Singleton, a sixteen-year-old Chicago native, who befriends them and acts as their guide. In between excursions, the children try to help Esther, the victim of sick headaches. On the day the Merrymakers arrive, Esther's newly hired cook quits and the children help manage the household, teaching their aunt by example to be more self-sufficient and spend less time in her parlor and more in her kitchen. Despite their housework, the children have time to visit famous local sites including the Columbian Exposition grounds, the Field Museum, Lincoln Park, and the Marshall Field Store. Although sections of the book convey facts about Chicago, the novel gives little sense of the city and is mostly concerned with instructing readers in the importance of hard work, maintaining physical vigor, and family ties.

1199. Williams, Wilbur Herschel. *Uncle Bob and Aunt Becky's Strange Adventures at the World's Great Exposition.* Chicago: Laird and Lee, 1904. 358pp.

In this humorous work, the Springer family (Bob, Becky, and their daughter Ruth) travel from their rural farm near Skowhegan, Maine to visit the 1904 St. Louis World's Fair. They make a number of stops, including New York City, Philadelphia, Cleveland, Detroit, and Chicago. In Chicago, Bob, who is presented as a rube, is cheated several times by grifters. The family visit and comment on Chicago sites, including the Chicago Board of Trade, stockyards, and the University of Chicago. Approximately sixty pages of the book are set in Chicago, although the descriptions tend toward the style of a travel guide.

1200. Williams, Kirby. *The C. V. C. Murders.* Garden City, N.Y.: Crime Club / Doubleday, Doran, 1929. 323pp.

Set in Chicago in 1926 and 1927, this mystery focuses on murders of members of the Citizens Vigilance Committee (C. V. C.), a secret society. Founded to battle gangsterism, the select membership of the C. V. C. includes a banker, a lawyer, a physician, and a capitalist who use their civic influence on politicians and the police force. Although the novel references bootlegging and organized crime in Chicago, not all of the book is set in the city, but also in Lake Forest and Lake Geneva on private estates. Much of the text is dominated by police procedures and scientific methods for criminal detection employed by Dr. Thackeray Place, a former professor of sociology at the University of Chicago and an established criminologist who appears in other of Williams' books.

1201. Williams, Kirby. *The Opera Murders*. New York: Charles Scribner's Sons, 1933. 259pp.

When middle-aged opera singer Terzazima is found disemboweled with a samurai blade and a recording of Puccini's *Madama Butterfly* on the turntable, her murder is investigated by Dr. Thackeray Place, who aids Merrill Galveston, the assistant to the State's Attorney of Cook County. Soon, the pair is investigating two more opera-related murders. Several Chicagoans in the book are independently wealthy and free to pursue hobbies full time, including opera and archaeology.

1202. Willingham, Calder. *Geraldine Bradshaw*. New York: Vanguard Press, 1950. 415pp.

This novel, set in a large Chicago hotel during World War II, is about a bellhop's seduction of a temporary elevator operator and the aftermath. The staffing of the hotel is highly articulated. In addition to the expected cleaning staff, luggage handlers, and elevator operators, there are tailors, beauticians, launderers, and nurses. Each type of staff has their own uniform and most are associated with specific areas in the hotel. The staff makes sharp social distinctions among themselves, mostly based on regional origin, ethnicity, and race. Working conditions are generally poor and the hotel has made a great effort to prevent unionization. Interactions and conversations are dominated by sex, with the men bragging about their conquests and attempting secret affairs with female staff members. Most of the plot concerns Dick Davenport's pursuit of Geraldine Bradshaw. The two socialize by eating at lunch counters, going to the zoo, and frequenting other public places that cost little or nothing. Eventually, Davenport finds out that Geraldine is pregnant with the baby of her fiancé who is fighting on the Pacific front in the war. By this time Davenport has fallen in love with her and Geraldine is no longer certain that she loves her fiancé. The novel touches on issues of gender roles and attitudes toward sexual expression, and presents examples of bar culture.

1203. Wilson, Margaret. *The Able McLaughlins*. New York: Harper and Brothers 1923. 262pp.

This novel tells the saga of the immigrant Scottish McLaughlin family over several generations. The early part of the novel is set during the Civil War on prairie farms along the Waupsipinnikon River in Iowa and primarily deals with the troubled romance of Wally McLaughlin and his cousin Christie McNair, who has become pregnant against her will by another cousin. When Wally discovers her predicament, he immediately marries Christie and forces the cousin to move west. Much discussion of the neighbors' reaction to Christie's pregnancy is included. Wally's younger brother John goes to law school in Chicago and he introduces a new perspective on the way the McLaughlins live, symbolized by his contempt for their Scottish words and accents. Through him, Chicago standards are introduced into their lives and become an Americanizing influence.

1204. Windsor, William. *Loma: A Citizen of Venus*. St. Paul, Minn.: Windsor and Lewis Publishing, 1897. 429pp.

Scorned by her friends and family for her unwed pregnancy, Myrtle Burnham fixes on suicide as her only option. When she throws herself into Lake Michigan, though, she is rescued by a mysterious creature named Loma. Loma has been sent from her native Venus to find a human child to instruct as an apostle to espouse the philosophy and social order of Venus to earthlings and inculcates Myrtle to aid in the instruction of her baby, which turns out to be a boy. Except for the fact that Chicago is the author's choice as the setting for an incipient revolution in the way humans think about their lives and each other, the book has little to do with the city, consisting mostly of an extended espousal of the authors vision of a Venusian utopia that features a nude populace (clothes are considered unsanitary), whose members have developed all of their faculties and keep them in balance. For them, social status is determined not by wealth or genealogy, but by their human relationships with everyone from strangers to family members and lovers. Apparently dissatisfied with relying solely on his fiction as a device for introducing his ideas, the author appended a treatise on phrenology.

1205. Winslow, Thyra Samter. *Show Business*. New York: Alfred A. Knopf, 1926. 321pp.

When Helen Taylor decides at eighteen to leave her hometown of Medina, Missouri and become a Chicago showgirl she is naïve about where her decision will take her, but she knows that in Medina she does not fit in with the wealthy children in her neighborhood or the poorer girls across town. In Chicago she gets hired for a road show and later appears in a vaudeville production and a carnival. These experiences prepare her well enough so that when she finally gets her chance to appear on a Chicago stage she is a success and sets off to New York City for bigger conquests. The book gives some sense of life among actors in the 1920s and the well-developed theater community in the city.

1206. Wise, Winifred Esther. *Frances a la Mode*. Philadelphia: Macrae Smith, 1956. 224pp.

Set in 1950s Chicago, this young adult book tells the story of Frances Cochrane's transition from high-school student to employee. Frances is hired to work in a department store as an assistant in the fashion coordinator's office. As she matures by developing her creativity and interpersonal skills, she also begins her first romance. The novel presents the world of a 1950s department store in some detail.

1207. Wise, Winifred Esther. *Frances by Starlight*. Philadelphia: Macrae Smith, 1958. 201pp.

Only a small section of this young adult novel is set in Chicago in the 1950s. The book continues the story of Frances Cochrane told in *Frances a la Mode* (entry 1206). Cochrane leaves Chicago where she was studying at the Art Institute for the adventure of living in Los Angeles and gets a job in a Hollywood movie studio, working in the costume department. Even though she finds excitement, she decides to return to her life in Chicago.

1208. Woolfolk, Josiah Pitts [Jack Woodford, pseud.]. *Find the Motive*. New York: Ray Long and Richard R. Smith, 1932. 280pp.

This book is primarily a courtroom drama in which a grandson is tried for murdering his grandfather, Attorney Leonard Buchanan (who is modeled after Clarence Darrow). Buchanan had announced his own death at a dinner party held the night he was murdered each of the dinner guests is a material witness in the trial. The book is more devoted to clever plotting and character analysis than description of Chicago or any aspect of social life in the city.

1209. Woolfolk, Josiah Pitts [Gordon Sayre, pseud.]. *Mirage of Marriage*. New York: Godwin, 1935. 286pp.

In this novel about lower-middle-class domestic life in 1930s Chicago, Elmer and Marie Thayer live with their young daughter Naomi near the Grand Avenue "El" station in a three story apartment building. Now thirty-six-years-old, Elmer, who married seventeen years before, when Marie was sixteen, is bored with his life. He works in the credit department of a bank and during the course of the novel has a brief affair with a stenographer who works for a nearby Loop firm.

However, the novel is not really concerned with plot, but with presenting Elmer's life in great detail, from his personal toilet, to what he eats, to how he feels about his wife and child. Flashbacks present the story of how Elmer and Marie met, as well as major events in their lives together. Restaurants, plays, movies, and parties are described and 1930s material culture, including the Thayers' apartment furnishings, are detailed.

1210. Woolfolk, Josiah Pitts [Jack Woodford, pseud.]. *Sin and Such*. New York: Panurge Press, 1930. 281pp.

Up until the time Arnold Godchaus encounters Alice Marvin on the street and picks her up, he has enjoyed the freedom from responsibility that his wealth and youth affords. From his first meeting with Alice, however, his life and behavior starts to change. Feeling emotions for Alice that he has not previously experienced, he stops behaving toward her in his usual flirtatious manner and begins thinking of engagement and marriage. At the same time, he begins to employ stratagems to push her away, fearful of actually committing himself. Even these actions, however, inadvertently bring the two closer together and his carefree man-about-town life comes to an end. The novel depicts attitudes toward human sexuality and gender relations typical of 1930s Chicago.

1211. Worthington, Elizabeth Strong [Nicholas A. Griffith, pseud.]. *The Biddy Club: and How Its Members, Wise and Otherwise, Some Toughened and Some Tenderfooted in the Rugged Ways of Housekeeping, Grappled with the Troublous Servant Question, to the Great Advantage of Themselves, and as They Hope, of Many Others*. Chicago: McClurg, 1888. 308pp.

The first-person narrator of this work recounts the experiences of his wife Dolly in organizing a club to serve as a forum for women to share their challenges in managing their households and servants. Some members of the club, such as the "Imaginary Millionaire" and the "Frivolous Young Woman" exhibit patterns of thought and behavior that are held up to ridicule and although the behavior of servants is critiqued, the club serves as a school for lady members who learn to treat their servants respectfully and learn some of the sciences of household management, such as human nature, food chemistry, and time efficiency. Although many sections are expository, a number of anecdotes are included to illustrate a variety of points. Even though the Chicago setting is not illustrative, the book includes a great deal of information about the internal workings of upper-middle-class Chicago households. The assessments of social behavior and implicit criteria for making social distinctions may also interest some researchers.

1212. Wren, Percival Christopher. *Mysterious Waye: The Story of "The Unsetting Sun."* New York: Frederick A. Stokes, 1930. 351pp.

This convoluted novel that includes a number of characters with disguised identities focuses on a wealthy man, John Dacre Waye Vanderleur St. Clair's attempts to avenge himself on the men who kidnapped and killed his daughter in order to obtain a famous cursed diamond, the enormous jewel known as "the Setting Sun." The novel is primarily set in England, although it is briefly set in other places, including Chicago. The inclusion here is based on the portrayal of the city as a place through which criminals from all over the world pass. The protagonist bases himself there several times to gather information under an assumed identity.

1213. Wright, Richard. *Eight Men*. New York: Pyramid Books, 1961. 204pp.

The geographic setting of many of these stories dealing with African-American masculinity is unclear and at least one of the works is set abroad. However, one story, "The Man Who Went to

Chicago," is a painful account of a man's attempts to find work in 1950s Chicago and his experience selling insurance to other African-Americans door to door.

1214. Wright, Richard. *Lawd Today*. New York: Walker, 1963. 189pp.
Wright's exploration of the consciousness of African-American postal worker Joe Jackson traces Jackson's experiences over one day: Lincoln's birthday, February 12, 1936. Jackson had earlier forced his wife Lil to have an abortion and now she has a life-threatening tumor about which Jackson rages over having to find money for medical expenses. The free part of Jackson's day is spent around Forty-seventh Street and Forestville Avenue as he meets with friends, stops by a sideshow, lunches at a drugstore counter, and watches a parade. Eventually, at noon, he commences work in the main building of the Chicago Post Office on Dearborn Street and fills the tedium of mail sorting by chatting with the other African-American clerks. After office hours he goes out drinking in a nightclub in his neighborhood that features live jazz music. Throughout the novel, Wright uses advertising materials (posters, fliers, radio broadcasts), newspaper headlines, and dialogue to create a context for Jackson's South Side life.

1215. Wright, Richard. *Native Son*. New York: Harper and Brothers, 1940. 359pp.
Through his character Bigger Thomas, Wright shows the continuing effects of centuries of slavery and racism in American culture. Although Wright is mostly concerned with depicting Thomas' conscious and the effects of internalized racism, he does present highly evocative physical descriptions of Depression-era Chicago. Thomas' family, which lives near Thirty-seventh Street and Indiana Avenue, consists of his mother, brother, and sister. They all live in one small room that occasionally houses rats, as well, in a South Side neighborhood which is racially segregated and ringed by burned out buildings that their owners torched rather than permit African-Americans to occupy. When Thomas gets a job through a charitable organization as the driver for the Daltons, a wealthy Caucasian family, it is the first time that he interacts with white people for any extended period of time and his reaction to the comforts of the Dalton household further contrast living conditions in the segregated city. Other settings include a poolroom and a movie theater.

1216. Wright, Richard. *The Outsider*. New York: Harper and Row 1953. 440pp.
Only the first section of this 1950s novel is set in Chicago. The city represents the trouble-filled life that main character, postal worker Cross Damon, escapes. Estranged from his wife, paying support for three children, threatened by his girlfriend with a statutory rape charge, and deeply in debt, Cross gets a surprising opportunity. He is in a subway accident and escapes the overturned car, but accidentally leaves his coat and all of his identification papers behind. The authorities mistakenly use the papers to identify an accident fatality. Cross decides not to rectify the situation, but to go to New York City and establish a new identity for himself there. Approximately one hundred pages of the novel are set in South Side 1950s Chicago, much of it in apartments and bars.

1217. Wyatt, Edith Franklin. *Every One His Own Way*. Illustrated by William James. New York: McClure, Phillips, 1901. 291pp.
This short story collection presents some of Chicago's turn-of-the-century citizens. In addition to descriptions of places and people, researchers may be interested in the cultural types represented (an office boy, a traveling salesman, a saloon keeper's daughter) and the underlying

theme of all of the stories that people are most fully themselves as they behave without self-consciousness.

1218. Wyatt, Edith Franklin. *The Invisible Gods*. New York: Harper and Brothers, 1923. 433pp.

This account of an entire extended family, the fictional Marshfields, stretches from 1882 to 1921 and summarizes cultural trends in art, literature, and medicine during the time period. At the beginning of the novel, the Marshfields gather to honor their forbear, General Malcolm Marshfield, at the dedication of a statue erected in his honor in Lincoln Park. The general's record of public service has established a precedent that his youngest son, Judge Elijah Marshfield, has followed. Married to Crissie Winthrop, of an old Chicago family, he lives with his wife and children, Joseph and Maisie, in the extensive Winthrop family mansion on the West Side. Because Elijah's brothers have left Chicago and never settled down, Elijah's house has become the venue for Marshfield family gatherings. Elijah's eldest brother, Enos, is a famous explorer of the American west, known for archeological, ornithological, geological, and geographical discoveries. Enos' passion for scientific exploration is so intense as to exclude most ordinary concerns, including enriching himself. Elijah's next oldest brother, Heatherington, has enriched himself as a New York City stockbroker and lives only for his own pleasure. Forced to marry a woman of undistinguished origins after getting her pregnant, Heatherington is now a widower forced to raise his young son, Hancock, and is currently having an open affair with the boy's governess. Heatherington is persuaded to let Enos become Hancock's guardian and allow him to be raised along with Elijah's children. The novel focuses on this generation of Marshfields, exploring the ways that the very different personalities of Joseph, Maisie, and Hancock affect their lives and the rest of the Marshfields. Inquisitive, reflective Joseph becomes a physician and medical researcher and founds a municipal hospital in Chicago. Maisie falls in love with an artist who treats her badly and Hancock devotes himself to literature. The novel touches on issues of race and gender, women's suffrage, civil service reform, and the arts and crafts movement. The Chicago setting is most specific on the domestic level in descriptions of residences and neighborhoods. The tone is often elegiac, particularly as the grounds around Elijah's residence, that had initially included areas relatively unchanged from a time before Chicago was established, get sold off piecemeal to pay debts until nothing is left but the house, which is finally sold to be torn down and replaced with a warehouse.

1219. Wyatt, Edith Franklin. *True Love, a Comedy of the Affections*. New York: McClure, Phillips, 1903. 288pp.

This romance novel is partly set in the imaginary town of Centreville, Illinois and partly set in Chicago. The overt plot concerns the choices two women make in whom to marry. However, the novel also conveys information about gender roles in early-twentieth-century Chicago. The women in the story, Emily and Inez, are cousins with contrasting personalities. Whereas Emily is shy and unaffected, Inez is focused on her own appearance and that of any man she might marry. When they choose mates, Emily picks Dick Colton, a modest man who has earned the respect of his community for his character strengths. Inez chooses Norman Hubbard for his appearance and polished demeanor only to discover that he has no substance and is incapable of standing by her when she needs him.

1220. Yaffe, James. *What's the Big Hurry?* Boston: Atlantic Monthly Press / Little, Brown, 1954. 331pp.

In this fictional memoir, the narrator is a nephew retelling the story of his irascible, but well-intentioned uncle, Dan Waxman. Waxman arrives in Chicago an impoverished seventeen-year-old orphan. Through hard work, he earns the respect of his colleagues in the Jewish business community. The 1929 stock market crash destroys his reputation and his friendships since the men who followed his advice suffered heavy losses. Unable to cope with the open hostility, Waxman moves his family, which includes a wife and daughter, to New York and later to Europe. When he finally returns to Chicago he finds a changed city, but also one in which he can take his place as a respected citizen. The novel's strength lies in its depiction of Chicago's Jewish community and the close personal ties that bound its members to each other.

1221. Yandell, Enid, Laura Hayes, and Jean Loughbrough. *Three Girls in a Flat.* Chicago: Press of Knight, Leonard, 1892. 154pp.

This novel presents the lives of three young women (Virginia "Gene" Fairfax, Marjorie, and "Duke" Wendell) involved in planning the Women's Building for the Columbian Exposition as they host social events and attend dances and teas. Their adventures begin when they move out of the boarding house room they shared and into a seven-room, furnished apartment owned by Marjorie's mother. The flat and its furnishings are detailed, as are the girls' neighbors, especially the incredibly forward Mrs. Brown, a widow with six children who lives downstairs. Aspects of living in a small, nineteenth-century, apartment building are conveyed through the narrative, and readers may be interested by the lack of privacy. This quality is especially evident in the bathrooms, where children can lower items down the "shaft" to the bathroom below and gossips can eavesdrop. The girls' social life includes visits from a wide variety of men and women during "at homes," attending concerts, the opera, lectures, and charity balls. At one point, the girls are invited to Mrs. Palmer's house to view the dedication of the Grant Statue in Lincoln Park and are introduced to Mrs. Grant. Mrs. Palmer's furnishings and art work are described in some detail. The novel has no real plot and includes lengthy exposition concerning planning for the Woman's Building. In addition to capturing what it may have been like to be involved in organizing the Exposition, this book celebrates the new social freedoms women were experiencing in the 1890s in Chicago.

1222. Yates, Katherine M. *Chet.* Illustrated by H. S. DeLay. Chicago: McClurg, 1909. 345pp.

This religious tract for children is mostly set in an Ohio town. However, the protagonist, Chet (a thirteen-year-old), travels to Chicago twice. His trips emphasize the wonder that people like him may have experienced when they traveled to rapidly urbanizing Chicago and experienced such phenomena as public transportation and automobiles. The novel also deals with gender roles (Chet's best friend is thirteen-year-old Bess from next door) and Christian Science. Bess is a Christian Science practitioner and coaches him in its precepts.

1223. York, Carol Beach. *Until We Fall in Love Again.* New York: Franklin Watts, 1967. 141pp.

In this romance novel for young adults, the world is seen through the eyes of sixteen-year-old Dolly Bennett and the result is rich documentation of the material culture, restaurants, stores, and theaters of 1941 Chicago. Dolly's friend from high school, nineteen-year-old Harry Brant, has just started university. Dolly and Harry attend the same church and still see each other regularly in the church youth group. Most of their social activities focus on the neighborhood near the intersection of Halsted and Sixty-third where they both live. The lower-middle-class Bennetts occupy the ground floor of a frame, two-flat building and Mrs. Bennett gives piano lessons from the living room. The novel is devoted to recounting Dolly's anxiety over whether she will become Harry's girlfriend and whether she will get a part in the school play. In addition to going to movies, much of Dolly's socializing focus on visiting the affluent houses of school friends, the furnishings of which are described. By the end of the novel, Dolly has slowly gotten over her crush on Harry and begun to realize her interest in Skip, who is her own age.

1224. Zara Louis. *Blessed is the Man*. Indianapolis: Bobbs-Merrill, 1935. 474pp.

This exhaustive account of the immigrant experience of Jacob Krakauer illustrates the support provided by family ties and Jewish religious and social structures in aiding the establishment of immigrant families in Chicago in the 1880s and 1890s. Krakauer arrives in Chicago as an unmarried man who does not speak English. His earliest job is peddling vegetables from a cart. He supplements his income with coal deliveries. Through his synagogue he finds a woman to marry and begins a family that eventually includes five children. As time goes on he is able to open a store; and then a chain of markets, mostly on the West Side. His religious ties eventually provide him with an entrée to wealthy Jewish merchants who settled in the city decades before him. As his business grows, he creates a large wholesale fruit and vegetable business and builds an office building with the Krakauer name. By the end of the novel he has begun focusing on philanthropic activities (endowing a hospital wing and creating a fund for cancer research—the disease from which his wife dies). The one blemish on his career comes when he invests heavily in the stock market before a dramatic correction and loses a fortune in cash. However, he holds onto businesses and properties by opening a large market on State Street which reinvigorates his company. Although this novel is incredibly detailed, it makes few references to dates, relying on cultural references to clue the reader to the changing decades. The wealth of detail about domestic and social life creates a rich narrative history of the Jewish immigrant experience in Chicago over the last decades of the nineteenth century and the early decades of the twentieth.

1225. Zara, Louis. *Give Us This Day*. Indianapolis: Bobbs-Merrill, 1936. 422pp.

This novel about immigrant life focuses on the Breton community in Chicago and shows the barriers that could still prevent individuals from experiencing the opportunities for which the United States is celebrated. As his father's oldest son, Charles Alexander Brabant is apprenticed in his father's bakery, even though he is absorbed in reading and wants to be apprenticed in his uncle's print shop. Charles may still have managed a freer life had he not fallen in love at an early age with Cecilia MacDonald, the daughter of a successful barber who is a tenant of the Brabant family. Cecilia and Charles date for only a few months, before she tells him she is pregnant. After their hurried marriage, Charles finds out that she was either lying or mistaken. Little happiness comes to their marriage as they eventually have four children, none of whom survive childhood except first-born Maxim, who is congenitally blind. Charles' bakery is successful through the early twentieth century, but as corporations begin to dominate the industry he cannot keep up and loses the bakery. Charles and Cecilia are struggling for food even before the Depression. When he gets a supervisory position in a corporate bakery, he dislikes the work and then discovers he was brought in as a strikebreaker and quits. Working as a house cleaner Cecilia soon dies of exposure. Witness to the suffering of other bakers, Charles convinces a city relief agency to give them supplies so that they can feed themselves and other families in need. The successful operation is closed down after baking corporations complain. Charles falls into despair, catches pneumonia from wandering the streets, and dies. The novel provides rich cultural history about the social re-lationships between apprentice and apprentice, apprentice and master, tenant and landlord, poli-tician and voter, father and son, brother and brother, and husband and wife. While the extended Brabant family includes many professions (dentist, printer, politician, baker, doctor), they have a surprising commitment to individualism that prevents Charles from getting much support from his family, including his son, who is an East Coast mathematics professor. Gender relationships and the attitudes toward sexual relations are candidly presented during Charles and Cecilia's courtship and throughout the novel descriptions of domestic interiors, foodways, clothing, and fashion are presented.

1226. Zara, Louis. *Ruth Middleton*. New York: Creative Age Press, 1946. 435pp.

This novel illustrates in exhaustive detail aspects of what life was like for a lower-class girl in the first decade of the twentieth century in Chicago. The story of Ruth Middleton's life begins with conception; opening with the moment Ruth's mother's ovum is fertilized by her father's sperm and continues up through the time fourteen-year-old Ruth is on the verge of adolescence. Her developing awareness first focuses on physical details of her life in a late-nineteenth-century, lower-class household in Chicago's Marlborough Terrace. As her social awareness develops she comes to understand the dynamics of her family. Her father Mark, the son of a railroad engineer, sacrificed his adventuresome spirit (expressed in time spent in the Alaskan gold fields) to marry Phoebe Hughes, the daughter of a wealthy merchant. In Chicago, he works on a house building crew, his wife's family looks him down upon, and he is filled with misgivings about his skills as a provider. Nonetheless, Ruth has a happy childhood, although she experiences family grief over her mother's miscarriages. She also experiences joy over the birth of two brothers before breast cancer kills her mother when Ruth is thirteen. In Ruth Middleton's world, events outside her neighbor-hood rarely intrude, and the only national events with impacts are President William McKinley's election and reelection and the Spanish American War. The novel's focus is useful for under-standing daily life during the time period. Ruth's lower-class household is described, but so is that of her wealthy Grandmother Hughes and her working-class Grandmother Middleton. Outside the domestic sphere, school, playground activities, and trips to the public library and shops are de-picted. By the end of the novel, boys have begun taking an interest in fourteen-year-old Ruth and there is some discussion of issues surrounding relationships between the sexes. Although family members and friends dismiss Ruth's dream of becoming a physician, her contact with Dr. Fred-erica Winifred, M.D. near the end of the novel at least raises the possibility that her horizons as a woman will not be as limited as her mother's.

1227. Zara, Louis. *Some for the Glory*. Indianapolis: Bobbs-Merrill, 1937. 569pp.

This fictional biography of Michael Hawks, who begins life in the Franklin Street Orphanage and ends the book a viable presidential candidate in the Illinois governor's office, mostly focuses on the political machinations that propel Hawks' career. However, in the course of the novel, the reader learns a good deal about daily life in Chicago neighborhoods. Hawks gets his start as a printing house apprentice where he makes a positive impression on the local political boss. At a young age, he marries a seamstress who urges him to use her savings to buy a share in the print shop where he apprenticed. By working in the local political club, printing political literature, and going out of his way to become acquainted with everyone, Michael rises quickly. He pays attention to the immigrant vote, forms his own political club, and after a few years runs for alderman against the boss-sponsored candidate, winning to represent the Fifth Ward. In office, he builds a stronger political base through his ability to award some political appointments. Although Hawks' career motivations stem from his desire for wealth and power, he is empathetic and gets involved in the plights of his constituents. Through detailed accounts of grade schools, orphanages, tenements, and the plight of white slaves, the book creates a powerful image of Chicago in the early twentieth century, especially after Hawks is elected mayor and has a purview beyond his ward. Zara is surprisingly frank about sexual matters, particularly in relation to prostitution and, in general, provides a good deal of information about the relative social status of men and women.

1228. Ziegler, Elsie Reif. *The Face in the Stone*. Illustrated by Ray Abel. New York: Longmans, Green, 1959. 184pp.

In this novel set in 1894 Chicago, Dushan Lukovich travels from his home country of Serbia with the goal of avenging his father's death. To support himself as he investigates his father's demise, he is employed as a stonecutter on the construction of one of Chicago's early skyscrapers. On the job site he gets involved in another cause—fighting for the rights of his fellow workers who are underpaid and laboring in hazardous conditions. Then he falls in love and his passion for revenge is further diminished so that by the time the truth of his father's death is revealed he accepts the account without violent passion. The novel provides a great deal of information about Chicago's early labor movement as it relates to the building trades (rather than the typical story that focuses on the meat packing industry). The book also touches on the experience of immigrants who must find a balance between their previous lives and the realities of their life in America.

1229. Ziegler, Elsie Reif. *Light a Little Lamp*. New York: John Day, 1961. 191pp.

The subject of this biographical novel, Mary McDowell, was important for founding a settlement house near the University of Chicago and devoting her life to reform work, including advocating for unionization of meat packers, improvements in public sanitation, protective labor legislation for women and children, and improved race relations. Her father, an abolitionist, moved from Cincinnati to Chicago after the Civil War and owned a steel rolling plant. Her mother wanted Mary to find her place in high society and marry a wealthy man. This novel mostly deals with the early 1870s just before and during the Chicago fire, a period of time when Mary had compromised with her mother and agreed to have her debutante year, but refused to give up her social activism. The novel is written in such a way that Mary's experiences during the fire and its aftermath confirm her commitment to working for the good of others and set her on a life course of achievements that made her one of the most respected women in the history of Chicago. In addition to presenting the conditions in which laborers worked and lived in Chicago, the novel portrays the suffering brought about by the fire.

Biographies

Abson, Ben J.
No information available.

Adams, Frederick Upham (December 10, 1859–August 30, 1921)
Known as an inventor, as well as an author, Adams was born in Boston and educated as a mechanical engineer. His best known invention was an electric lamppost patented under his name that was used in municipalities across the United States at the beginning of the era of electrification. An experimental train he created for the Baltimore & Ohio Railroad broke speed records. Later in life he wrote a well-regarded series of articles on American aviation published in the *New York Times* during 1918. Adams' books and novels proposed reform and received national attention. He focused on trust-breaking and advocated a new political party, the American Party. He lived in Chicago for a time and was a city inspector from 1894 to 1897. At the end of his life he was living in Larchmont, New York.
(*New York Times*, 30 August 1921, 11).

Acre, Stephen, *see* Gruber, Frank

Ade, George (February 9, 1866–May 16, 1944)
Born on a farm near Kentland, Indiana, Ade won fame as a humorist. Acclaimed by critics, he was admired by other humorists of his time, such as Samuel Clemens and William Dean Howells. After a liberal arts education at Purdue University Ade worked as a journalist in West Lafayette, Indiana before moving to Chicago in 1893 to begin producing an anonymous daily column, "*Stories of the Streets and of the Town*" for the *Chicago Record*. Written in the new American vernacular Ade discovered on his walks through the city, most of his characters were newcomers to urban life, emigrating to Chicago from rural areas in the United States or from other countries. The perspectives and dilemmas of these characters found an immediate audience in a rapidly urbanizing and industrializing America. Ade developed a "fable in slang" format and his first gathering of fables published as a book appeared in 1900 with additional volumes appearing over several decades, adding to the substantial income from his syndicated weekly column. He wrote several plays and reached his goal of Broadway production with *The College Widow* in 1904. Other stage successes, *The County Chairman* and *The Sultan of Sulu*, entered the American repertory theater earning Ade millions of dollars. He retired to an Indiana estate, named Hazenden, that he had assembled through purchasing large tracts of land. Although his popularity waned in the 1920s, he continued to publish and entertain lavishly, fund-raising for political parties and Purdue University.
(*Dictionary of Literary Biography*, vol. 11, s.v. "Ade, George.").

Adler, Katherine Keith (April 17, 1892–May 25, 1930)

Born into the Keith family of Chicago whose prominent members had lived in the city for several generations, Adler shocked society by publishing a magazine story in her senior year at the University of Chicago that openly recounted her childhood. The work was later expanded and published as *The Girl* (included here). Adler married architect David Adler in 1916. (*New York Times*, 26 May 1930, 15).

Albert, Marvin H. (1924–March 24, 1996)

The author of a large number of paperback originals, mostly mysteries, westerns, and suspense novels, Albert was born in Philadelphia and worked in journalism and publishing, including at *Look* magazine, as well as being a television and motion picture scriptwriter. Albert wrote under a number of pseudonyms, including Al Conroy, Albert Conroy, Ian MacAlister, Nick Quarry, and Anthony Rome. His books featuring detective Tony Rome were adapted for the screen as vehicles for Frank Sinatra. Albert lived in Hollywood for many years, but moved to Menton, France in 1976 where he was inspired to create a new mystery series featuring an American detective, Peter Sawyer, living in France. These books received the most critical attention he garnered in his lifetime. (*Contemporary Authors Online*, New York: Gale Group, 2003, accessed 7 July 2009).

Alcock, Gudrun (April 18, 1908–January 16, 2000)

A graduate of Northwestern University, Alcock was born in Stockholm, Sweden and emigrated as an adult. She worked in advertising and as the first woman's editor of the *Chicago Sun (Times)*, as well as writing books for children. (*Something About the Author*, vol. 56, s.v. "Alcock, Gudrun").

Aldis, Dorothy (March 13, 1896–July 4, 1966)

Best known today for her poetry for very young children and several of her novels for children, Aldis lived in the Chicago area her entire life, except for the time she spent at Miss Porter's School (Farmington, Conn.) and at Smith College (Northampton, Mass.). After two years of college, her parents asked that she return home to Chicago, as was typical at the time for an upper-class woman. Her father, James Keeley, was a managing editor of the *Chicago Tribune* and after securing a job at the paper, for which she applied anonymously; Aldis wrote several of the women's columns on romance, pets, and home decoration. She began writing children's literature after her marriage in 1922 to Graham Aldis, a Chicago real estate executive and the subsequent full-time career of raising their four children. By the time of her death in 1966 Aldis had published twenty-seven books, including the few for adult readers, all written in the 1930s, that are included in this bibliography. [*Dictionary of Literary Biography*, vol. 22, s.v. "Aldis, Dorothy (Keeley)"].

Alger, Horatio, Jr. (January 13, 1832–July 18, 1899)

Born in a Boston suburb (which is now part of Revere) to Horatio Alger, Sr., a Unitarian minister, and Olive Augusta Fenno, the daughter of a prosperous businessman, Alger had a very successful career at Harvard College, graduating in 1852, the winner of several awards and the presenter of the English Oration at commencement. He entered Harvard Divinity School in 1853, but took leaves of absence to work as an editor, schoolmaster and tutor, finally graduating in 1860. His first juvenile novel was published in 1864, the same year he accepted an appointment as minister of the First Unitarian Church in Brewster, Massachusetts. Fifteen months after his installa-

tion, he was forced to resign after being accused of sexual improprieties with boys. He lived the rest of his life in New York City, supporting himself with his writings and, since these never produced an adequate income, tutoring. His "Ragged Dick" and "Luck and Pluck" series are the ones for which he remains best known today, however he also wrote some popular biographies for adults. Flagging sales in the 1870s prompted a trip west to discover new fictional settings, and his visit to Chicago yielded material for books included here. A nervous breakdown in 1896 forced him to retire and live with his sister, Olive Augusta Cheney, and her husband in South Natick, Massachusetts. It was during this period that he contacted Edward Stratemeyer to contract with him to complete several books that, as it turned out, he could no longer write. Stratemeyer continued to publish works under Alger's name after the author's death in 1899.
(*Dictionary of Literary Biography*, vol. 42, s.v. "Alger, Horatio, Jr.").

Algren, Nelson (March 28, 1909–May 9, 1981)
   Algren is one of the writers most closely identified with Chicago for his works of fiction and non-fiction dealing with the city. Born in Detroit, the only son of a machinist, Algren grew up in a working-class neighborhood of Chicago. He graduated from the University of Illinois at Chicago with a journalism degree in 1931. In the Depression-era economy he found no work in Chicago and traveled to New Orleans where he worked as a door-to-door salesman and to Texas where he worked as a gas station attendant. These experiences informed his later work, as did time in prison for vagrancy and later for stealing a typewriter. After hitchhiking back to Chicago, he finished and published his first novel in 1935, based on his time in Texas. His following books, published between 1942 and 1949, including novels and volumes of short stories, established Algren as a Chicago writer. He served as a medical corpsman in the U.S. Army from 1942 to 1945 and began traveling in Europe and South and Central America in 1947, sometimes in the company of Simone de Beauvoir, the French novelist. His book about drug addiction, set in Chicago's slums, *The Man with a Golden Arm*, published in 1949, won the national Book Award and brought him international celebrity. He moved to the East Coast in 1974 when he got an assignment from *Esquire* magazine to cover the retrial of boxer Rubin "Hurricane" Carter. Algren continued to publish, mostly short stories and works of non-fiction (including travel writing) until his 1981 death in Sag Harbor, New York.
(*Contemporary Authors Online*, New York: Gale Group, 2004, accessed, 14 July 2009).

Allee, Marjorie Hill (June 2, 1890–April 30, 1945)
   An award-winning children's author, Allee (née Marjorie Hill), published thirteen books. Born in Carthage, Indiana, Allee graduated from the University of Chicago with a bachelor of philosophy degree in 1911 and was married to a zoology professor at the University with whom she had two daughters.
(*New York Times*, 1 May 1945, 23).

Allen, Geneva
   No information available.

Allen, James
   No information available.

Allen, Steve (Stephen Valentine Patrick William) (December 26, 1921–October 30, 2000)

A son of two vaudevillians, Allen is best known as the comedian who pioneered *The Tonight Show* for NBC television, although he was also an accomplished pianist and composer. The author of more than fifty books, and a social activist, Allen was born in New York City but grew up in Chicago. The work for which he is included here is a semi-autobiographical account of a Depression-era Chicago funeral.
(*New York Times*, 1 November 2000, B13).

Altrocchi, Julia Cooley (July 4, 1893–November 23, 1972)

A 1914 graduate of Vassar (Poughkeepsie, N.Y.), Altrocchi (née Cooley) had published her first book, *Poems of a Child* (Harper), ten years before. Known as an author of poetry and historical fiction for children, in addition to the novel for which she is included here, Altrocchi also wrote the poem "Chicago: Narrative of a City" (n.p., Berkeley, Calif., 1968), for which she won the Stephen Vincent Benet Narrative Poetry Award in 1969. She was the wife of college professor Rudolph Altrocchi.
(*Contemporary Authors Online*, Detroit: Gale, 2002, accessed 3 March 2010).

Anderson, Sherwood (September 11, 1876–March 8, 1941)

Anderson is best known as an important short story stylist, although he expended much of his energy as a writer on producing novels, most of which are considered less than successful. Born in Camden, Ohio, Anderson grew up in Clyde, Ohio, the son of a harness maker and house painter who was more interested in telling stories than his business ventures. Forced to leave high school to help support his family, Anderson first lived in Chicago as a manual laborer in 1895. He left for military service in the Spanish-American War during which he served in Cuba. In 1899 he returned to Ohio and studied for a year at Springfield's Wittenberg Academy before returning to Chicago to work as an advertising copywriter. After his 1904 marriage to the daughter of a Toledo businessman, Anderson started his own mail order business in Elyria, Ohio, where he began writing novels in 1910. After a 1912 nervous breakdown he returned to his advertising job in Chicago in 1913. His novels set in Chicago have many autobiographical elements and the short story collection, for which he is best known, *Winesburg, Ohio*, although an evocation of Clyde, Ohio, includes fictional versions of people Anderson met in Chicago boarding houses in which he was living. In addition to the settings and people he drew upon for his fiction, Chicago was important to Anderson for the group of Chicago Renaissance writers (Floyd Dell, Ben Hecht, Carl Sandburg and others) from whom he received encouragement. Anderson left Chicago in 1917 and lived in New York City, New Orleans and abroad, never spending significant amounts of time in Chicago after 1922.
(*Contemporary Authors Online*, New York: Gale, 2003, accessed 6 June 2009).

Andrews, (Charles) Robert Douglas (Hardy) (October 19, 1908–1999)

The son of Charles R. (a physician) and Mary (Hedding) Andrews in Effingham, Kansas, Andrews attended the University of Minnesota, Northwestern University, and the University of Chicago. A journalist and writer for television and film, as well as a novelist, Andrews began his career as a reporter and then city editor for the *Minneapolis Journal*. He was a reporter for the *Chicago Daily News* and then editor of *Midweek* for that newspaper from 1923 to 1940. He became a radio writer and producer from 1930 to 1947 and a writer and producer for films, beginning in 1936 and for television, commencing in 1950. From 1953, Andrews worked abroad; first in Egypt and India as a film production executive and later as a consultant to U.S. film companies working

on overseas productions in the Far East. Andrews published eleven books and authored or co-authored more than forty screenplays.
(*Contemporary Authors Online*, New York: Gale, 2002; accessed 6 June 2009).

Andrews, Robert Hardy [Shang Andrews, pseud.].
A journalist for the *Chicago Times*, Andrews also published his own single-sheet newspaper that covered news of the red-light district in Chicago and defended prostitution.

Andrews, Shang, *see* Andrews, Robert Hardy

Andrus, Louise (1892–?)
No information available.

Archer, Jeffrey (April 15, 1940–?)
Archer, an English author, has earned a large international audience for works of popular fiction. A graduate of Oxford University (1963-1966), Archer made his fortune a few years after Oxford with his own company, Arrow Enterprises. At age twenty-nine, in 1969, he successfully ran for a seat in the House of Commons as a Conservative candidate and served for five years before an unwise investment cost him much of his wealth. He began writing to repay his debts and his second novel *Shall We Tell the President?* (Viking, 1977) about a plot to assassinate President Edward Kennedy substantially aided him in doing so due to the sensation it created. His two books concerning a feud between a Polish Chicago immigrant hotelier and a New York banker, *Kane and Abel* (Simon and Schuster, 1980) and *The Prodigal Daughter* (Linden Press, 1982), have the Chicago settings for which he is included here. Archer, as a favorite of Margaret Thatcher, returned to political life in 1985, but a series of scandals, including a libel conviction, for which he served two years in prison, disrupted his life until 2000, although he continued to publish best selling fiction and non-fiction (about his prison experiences). He was created a life peer in 1992.
(*Contemporary Authors Online*, Detroit: Gale, 2008, accessed 7 June 2009).

Ardizzone, Tony (August 18, 1949–?)
Ardizzone grew up in Chicago and graduated with honors from the University of Illinois in 1971. He went on to receive an MFA. in 1975 from Bowling Green (Ohio) State University and has had a long career as an academic, teaching as an English instructor at St. Mary Center for Learning in Chicago (1971–73), Bowling Green State University (1975–1978), and at Old Dominion (Norfolk, Va.) University since 1978. He has published short stories and poetry in addition to the novels for which he is included here.
(*Contemporary Authors Online*, Detroit: Gale, 2002, accessed 7 June 2009).

Armstrong, Dwight LeRoy (May 13, 1854–March 29, 1927)
Armstrong was born in Plymouth, Indiana. He was orphaned as a teenager, and worked in a printing office to support himself. After attending Indiana University briefly, he began work as a journalist with the *Chicago Herald*. He later edited newspapers in Indiana and Salt Lake City, Utah. He was the author of several novels.

Aschmann, Helen Tann (?)
Born in Kansas City, Missouri, the daughter of a tinsmith, Aschmann attended the Illinois Institute of Technology (two years) and Northwestern University (one year). She married whole-

sale lumber dealer Charles Aschmann with whom she had two children and worked as a secretary and a staff member for trade journals and newspapers. For seven years, 1946–53, she was a creative writing teacher at Northwestern University, Medill School of Journalism. She is known for her articles, light verse, and short stories, as well as her speaking engagements at writers' conferences, and a wide variety of clubs and organizations. Her only published book is the one for which she is included here.
(*Contemporary Authors Online*, Detroit: Gale, 2002, accessed 7 June 2009).

Ashenhurst, John
    A journalist who worked in Chicago, Ashenhurst was briefly married to Ann Hummert, an advertising executive and radio producer known for establishing the radio serial genre.

Athens, Christopher
    No information available.

Atkinson, Eleanor (January 7, 1863–November 4, 1942)
    Atkinson was the daughter of Isaac M. Stackhouse of Rensselaer, New York. She was married in 1891 to Francis Blake Atkinson who worked as the telegraph editor of the *Chicago Evening Post*. Atkinson wrote a number of books for children, including several works of historical fiction about Abraham Lincoln, although she was best known for her book about Johnny Appleseed and her novel about a dog, *Greyfriars Bobby* (New York: Harper and Brothers, 1912), which remains in print and was made into a movie (Walt Disney Productions, 1961).
(*New York Times*, 11 November 1942, 25).

Babcock, Bernie (1868–June 14, 1962)
    Although she was born in Unionville, Ohio, Bernie Smade moved with her family to Little Rock, Arkansas when she was a girl. She lived there for the rest of her life, marrying William F. Babcock and raising three children. A staff writer for the *Arkansas Democrat*, she later owned and edited the *Arkansas Sketch Book*. She was greatly interested in history and wrote historical novels, several about Lincoln. She also founded the Arkansas Museum of Natural History and Antiquities.
(*New York Times*, 15 June 1962, 27).

Bailey, Bernardine (November 12, 1901–October 21, 1995)
    The daughter of Thomas Oscar and Nellie (Voigt) Freeman, Bailey was married to John Hays Bailey, and later divorced. Educated at Wellesley College (BA), the University of Chicago (MA), and the Sorbonne, University of Paris (certificate), Bailey worked as assistant editor at the Chicago firm Laidlaw Brothers and as directing staff editor of *Childcraft* (now part of Field Enterprises). She wrote more than thirty books for young people and was a contributor of more than two hundred articles to newspapers and magazines. She published more than fifty books of travel photographs for children and her travel picture files formed the basis of a business, 'Round the World Photos, Chicago'.
(*Contemporary Authors Online*, Detroit: Gale, 2002, accessed 8 June 2009).

Bailey, Charles W(aldo), II (April 28, 1929–?)
    Born in Boston and educated at Harvard University (AB, magna cum laude, 1950), Bailey worked as a journalist in Minneapolis and Washington, D.C. He co-authored several works of political fiction with Fletcher Knebel.

Baird, Edwin (1886–1957)

The first editor of pulp magazine *Weird Tales*, and a pioneer in the publication of horror fiction, Baird was the magazine's editor from 1923 until 1924. He had a much longer tenure as editor of another magazine, *Detective Tales*.

Baker, Elizabeth Gillette (November 14, 1923–?)

Born in Rochester, New York, the daughter of Charles L. and Ruth (Otis) Gillette, Baker wed Morton H. Baker in 1947. She was educated at the University of Rochester and worked at the Houghton Mifflin Company in Boston as writer in the advertising department from 1945 to 1948. The author of eight books for middle-grade readers, her work includes light mysteries and a series of books in which her character, Tammy, has outdoor adventures.

(*Contemporary Authors Online*, Detroit: Gale, 2002, accessed 9 June 2009).

Baker, Frederick Sherman (September 15, 1902–April 8, 1976)

The author of three novels, Baker lived most of his life in and around New York City and worked as an editor for E. P. Dutton and Company and St. Martin's Press, as well as other publishing firms.

(*New York Times*, 10 April 1976, 26).

Baker, North (1912–1991)

No information available.

Ball, Jane Mary Eklund (October 4, 1921–?)

The daughter of mining engineer Emil Julius Eklund, Ball was born in Los Angeles, California and educated at the University of California, Los Angeles (BA, 1943) and Stanford University (MA, 1950). She married artist Everett Loran Ball, Jr. in 1951 and taught for more than thirty years at William Howard Taft High School in Woodland Hills, Calif.

(*Contemporary Authors Online*, Detroit: Gale, 2002, accessed 11 May 2009).

Ballinger, Bill Sanborn. (March 13, 1912–March 23, 1980)

Born in Oskaloosa, Illinois and educated at the University of Wisconsin (BA, 1934), between 1935 and 1950 Ballinger held jobs in advertising and journalism (magazines, newspapers, radio) before beginning a career as a screenwriter and dramatist that included producing well-known televisions shows, including *The Dinah Shore Show* and *The Breakfast Club*, and writing more than two hundred scripts for popular suspense and detective television shows. Under several names (Bill Ballinger, Frederic Freyer, B. X. Sanborn) Ballinger also published more than twenty-five mystery novels.

(*Contemporary Authors Online*, New York: Gale, 2003, accessed 11 May 2009).

Balmer, Edwin (July 26, 1883–March 21, 1959)

Balmer was born in Chicago and wrote eighteen books, as well as authoring additional novels with Philip Wylie and William MacHarg. His novel *That Royle Girl* was released as a motion picture in 1925, directed by D. W. Griffiths for Paramount. Another work released on film that received a great deal of attention was the book *When Worlds Collide* (Philadelphia: Lippincott, 1933) that he co-wrote with Philip Wylie. Balmer was also the editor of *Redbook* and served as publisher for the magazine from 1949 until 1953.

(*Contemporary Authors Online*, New York: Gale, 2003, accessed 9 June 2009).

Banks, Charles Eugene (1852–1932)
    No information available.

Banning, Margaret Culkin (March 18, 1891–January 4, 1982)
    Educated at Vassar College (Poughkeepsie, N.Y., BA, 1912), Banning completed further study at Russell Sage College (Troy, N.Y.) and the Chicago School of Philanthropy before marrying lawyer Archibald T. Banning in 1914. The couple had two children before divorcing in 1934. Banning married again in 1944 to LeRoy Salsich, the president of an iron mining company. A longtime advocate for women's rights, she was also an avid club woman, active in the Junior League, the League of American Penwomen, and the Cosmopolitan Club, as well as many others in Duluth, Chicago, and Fort Tyron (N.C.). The author of forty books and more than four hundred short stories, who added to her audience by her frequent contributions to *The Reader's Digest*, Banning frequently chose themes of concern to women, and controversial topics such as mixed religious marriages and birth control. She published a novel in 1979 and was working on another at the time of her death at age ninety.
(*Contemporary Authors Online*, New York: Gale, 2003, accessed 10 May 2009).

Barnes, Margaret Ayer (April 8, 1886–October 26, 1967)
    Born in Chicago into the sort of upper-middle-class household that her novels depict, Barnes attended Bryn Mawr College (Bryn Mawr, Pa.). She was inspired by the feminism of the college's president, M. Carey Thomas, but found no outlet for her incipient activism once she returned to Chicago and, in 1910, married a lawyer, Cecil Barnes, with whom she had three sons between 1912 and 1919. Her life was transformed by an automobile accident in France in 1925. Expected to be bedridden for the rest of her life, she overcame her invalidism through physical effort and, encouraged by childhood friend Edward Sheldon, began writing short stories, some of which were accepted for *Pictorial Review*. Following a suggestion of Sheldon's, she dramatized Edith Wharton's *Age of Innocence*, and her work was eventually produced in a long New York run. She then collaborated with Sheldon on stage and screen adaptations. During the 1930s she wrote and published five novels, including the Pulitzer Prize winner *Years of Grace*.
(*Dictionary of Literary Biography*, vol. 9, s.v., "Barnes, Margaret Ayer").

Barr, Robert (September 16, 1850–October 22, 1912)
    Barr's family emigrated to Wallacetown, Ontario from Glasgow, Scotland when Barr was four. He began learning his father's carpentry trade when still a youngster and only had intermittent opportunities for formal education. His native intelligence led to teaching assignments in country schools and he advanced through certificate examinations, finally receiving an appointment as principal in 1875. However, his anecdotal account of a Lake Erie boat trip, when published in the *Detroit Free Press* in 1875, was so successful that the newspaper's editor offered him a permanent position in 1876. Within five years, Barr was offered the editorship of the newly created London edition of the *Detroit Free Press* (the first overseas edition of an American newspaper). In London, Barr paired his successful editorship with an active social life in the city's literary establishment. In 1891 he created the *Idler Magazine*, in partnership with Jerome K. Jerome; contributors included Arthur Conan Doyle, James Barrie, G. K. Chesterton, and Robert Louis Stevenson. From 1895 to 1902 he took a leave from the successful magazine and devoted himself to his own writing, but returned as editor from 1902 to 1911 when the final issue was published.
(*Dictionary of Literary Biography*, vol. 70, s.v., "Barr, Robert")

Barrett, Mary Ellin (November 25, 1926–?)

Daughter of American composer Irving Berlin, Barrett, whose maiden name was MacKay, grew up in New York City. She attended Bryn Mawr College (1945–1947) and graduated from Barnard College in 1949, Phi Beta Kappa. The author of three novels and a memoir, Barrett, the wife of Marvin Barrett, was book critic at *Cosmopolitan* for many years and a contributor to several magazines, including *Good Housekeeping*, *Glamour*, and *Ladies Home Journal*.

Barton, William Eleazar (June 28, 1861–December 7, 1930)

Born in Sublette, Illinois, Barton had a forty-year career as a Congregational theologian and minister, as well as earning a reputation as a Lincoln scholar for a series of books and articles on the Illinois president. Barton was educated at Berea College (Berea, Ky.) and Oberlin Theological Seminary (Oberlin, Ohio) and began his career as a circuit rider in Tennessee. He later held pastorates in Boston and Oak Park, Illinois (for twenty-five years). After his retirement and a trip around the world, he became Professor of Practical Theology at Vanderbilt University (Nashville, Tenn.) and founded the Collegeside Church there. His son, Bruce Barton, was a well-known public relations expert and author.
(*New York Times*, 8 December 1930, 21).

Barry, Joe, *see* Lake, Joe Barry

Barry, Mike, *see* Malzberg, Barry N.

Bates, Elizabeth (October 5, 1921–?)

Daughter of Alexander (a civil engineer) and Elizabeth Bragdon Willett (a teacher), Bates was born in Evanston, Illinois. She completed coursework at National Park College (Forest Glen, Md.), Beloit College (Beloit, Wis.), and Katherine Gibbs School and worked as a secretary from 1942–1948. She married Edwin R. Bates, a lawyer, in 1947 and they had four children. As Betty Bates, she authored fifteen novels for young readers, mostly dealing humorously with contemporary problems faced by young people.
(*Contemporary Authors Online*, Gale, 2002, accessed 10 May 2009).

Baynes, Jack, *see* Fowler, Bertram B.

Beach, Edgar Rice (1843–May 31, 1930)

Beach was born on an Illinois farm and fought in the Civil War. A journalist on the staff of the *St. Louis Globe Democrat* for more than twenty-five years, he served for sixteen years as the editor of that newspaper's Sunday edition. Before working at the *Globe Democrat*, he taught country school and edited two small-town newspapers.
(*New York Times*, 1 June 1930, 20).

Bech-Myer, Nico, Mrs.
No information available.

Beck, Robert (aka, Iceberg Slim), *see* Maupin, Robert Lee

Bein, Albert [Charles Walt, pseud.] (May 18, 1902–January 4, 1990)

The author of two novels and four plays that ran on Broadway in the 1930s and 1940s, Bein became an author after a dramatic accident. He had been living as a hobo and after an arrest for vagrancy he hopped a freight train, but ran into a hostile brakeman, and lost his leg jumping from the train.

Bellow, Saul (June 10, 1915–April 5, 2005)

Winner of the 1976 Nobel Prize for Literature, Bellow is closely associated with Chicago for his long residence in the city, as well as for his use of Chicago as a setting in some of his books. Although he was born in Lachine, Quebec, his Russian immigrant parents moved the family to the Humboldt Park section of Chicago when he was nine years old. He attended the University of Chicago and graduated from Northwestern University after financial difficulties forced him to transfer. He began studying anthropology at the University of Wisconsin, but returned to Chicago to become a novelist and for long periods of his adult life he lived and worked in the city, teaching for several semesters at the University of Chicago.
(*Dictionary of Literary Biography*, vol. 329, s.v., "Bellow, Saul").

Benchly, Alexandra Jane
No information available.

Bialk, Elisa, *see* Krautter, Elisa Bialk

Bigot, Marie Healey [Marie Healey, Jeanne Mairet, pseuds.] (1843–?)

The daughter of American painter George P. A. Healey, Bigot was the wife of French critic Charles Jules Bigot (1840–1893). Bigot wrote a memoir concerning her father as well as several novels.
(*Encyclopedia Americana*, s.v. "Bigot, Marie Healey").

Bisno, Beatrice
No information available.

Blake, Eleanor (1899–?)
No information available.

Blake, Emily Calvin (1882?–?)
No information available.

Bland, Alden (1911–?)
No information available.

Blank, Clair, *see* Moyer, Clarissa Mabel Blank
No information available.

Bloch, Robert (April 5, 1917–September 23, 1994)

A Chicago native, Bloch sold his first story at age seventeen. His career was influenced by pulp magazines of the 1930s and 1940s. Although he published more than twenty novels and

wrote dozens of scripts for television and film, he is best known for writing the book on which the Alfred Hitchcock film *Psycho* (Paramount, 1960) was based.
(*New York Times*, 25 September 1994, 48).

Blossom, Henry Martyn Jr. (May 6, 1866–March 23, 1919)
   The son of a wealthy insurance executive, Martyn was born in St. Louis, Missouri and began his career working for his father. After publishing several novels, however, he moved to New York City and began writing for the theater. He achieved great success as a librettist and lyricist and repeatedly collaborated with conductor and composer Victor Herbert.
(*American National Biography*, s.v. "Blossom, Henry Martyn Jr.").

Bodenheim, Maxwell (May 26, 1892–February 7, 1954)
   Born to a Jewish mercantile family in Hermanville, Mississippi, with the family name Boden-heimer, Bodenheim is best known as a poet, although he published thirteen novels. He moved with his family to Chicago at the age of nine and became lifelong friends with Ben Hecht. With little formal education, he enlisted in the Army in 1908, but after deserting, served most of his enlist-ment in jail. He returned to Chicago in 1912 and became a part of the *Poetry* magazine circle. In 1916 he moved to Greenwich Village where he spent most of the remainder of his life. His reputa-tion was built on the work he published in the 1920s and he is closely identified with the bohe-mianism of that era. An alcoholic who was indigent at the end of his life, he was shot to death along with his wife by a deranged man in a slum rooming house on the Bowery.
(*Dictionary of Literary Biography*, vol. 45, s.v. "Bodenheim, Maxwell").

Bolton, William
   No information available.

Bonnamy, Francis, *see* Walz, Audrey Boyers

Booth, Christopher Belvard (1889–1950)
   An author of detective stories and Westerns, Booth, who also published under the pseudonym John Jay Chichester, mostly saw his work printed in pulp magazines.

Booth, Emma (Scarr) Mrs. (April 25, 1835–?)
   Born in England, in addition to the novel for which she is included here, Booth wrote poems and composed music.
(*Herringshaw's Encyclopedia of American Biography of the Nineteenth Century*, s.v. "Booth, Emma Scarr, Mrs.").

Borden, Mary (May 15, 1886–December 2, 1968)
   A Chicago native, Borden, the daughter of a businessman, was raised in an evangelical reli-gious household against which she rebelled. Educated at Vassar College (Poughkeepsie, N.Y., BA, 1908), she was married immediately after college to George Douglas Turner, but the marriage ended in divorce after which she took a world tour that brought her to France at the outbreak of World War I. She equipped a frontline mobile hospital unit and managed it, for which services she was awarded the *Croix de Guerre*. The experience inspired her earliest published writing. Borden married Brigadier Edward Louis Spears in 1918 and much of her later writing concerned the wealthy (he became a baronet, diplomat, and Member of Parliament). She achieved notoriety with

a novel about Mary of Nazareth that focused on her humanity, inspiring attacks from publications connected to the Roman Catholic Church. During World War II she once again directed mobile hospital units in France, Cairo, Syria, and Tobruk.
(*World Authors, 1900–1950.* New York: Wilson, 1996, s.v. "Borden, Mary").

Borland, Kathryn Kilby (August 14, 1916–?)

Borland has written a number of books for children, many of them with co-author Helen Ross Speicher. A native of Pullman, Michigan and the daughter of a diamond broker, she was educated at Butler University (Indianapolis, Ind., BS, 1937).
(*Contemporary Authors Online*, Detroit: Gale, 2003, accessed 3 March 2008).

Bowman, Heath (1910–?)

A 1931 graduate of Princeton University (where his papers are housed in the Department of Rare Books and Special Collections), Bowman was a public affairs officer for the U.S. State Department, serving in Chile, France, Italy, and Yugoslavia.

Boyce, Neith (1872–1951)

The daughter of a California newspaper publisher, Boyce was the wife of independently wealthy radical journalist Hutchins Hapgood. The couple lived in locales at the center of modernism in the 1890s through 1920s, including Greenwich Village, Paris, Florence, and Provincetown, where along with friends Susan Glaspell and George Cram Cook they founded the Provincetown Play-house. The author of four well-received novels, Boyce was also the author of plays and memoirs. Her papers and those of her husband are at the Beinecke Rare Book and Manuscript Library.

Boylan, Malcolm Stuart (April 13, 1897–April 3, 1967)

Born in Chicago, the son of novelist Grace Duffie, Boylan worked as a journalist and actor before becoming director of publicity at Universal Studios in the 1920s. He went on to become a highly successful screenwriter with credits for ninety films between 1921 and 1963.
(*Internet Movie Database*, www.imdb.com/name/nm0102167, accessed 11 November 2008).

Bradley, Mary Hastings (April 19, 1882–1976)

Born in Chicago, Bradley graduated from Smith College in 1905 and shortly afterward toured Egypt with a classmate, later publishing stories inspired by the experience. While further researching Egypt in Oxford she met and married Herbert Bradley, a lawyer whose avocations were big game hunting and exploration. With him and her daughter Alice (who would become the well-known science fiction writer known as James Tiptree, Jr.), she went on an American Museum of Natural History expedition to Africa and the Belgian Congo in 1921 and 1922, upon which she based several of her books. She was a war correspondent in World War II for *Collier's Magazine*. Among her honors were an O'Henry Prize, election to membership in the Society of Women Geographers, and presidency of the Society of Midland Authors. Her papers are in the Special Collections of the University of Illinois at Chicago.

Brande, Dorothea (January 12, 1893–December 17, 1948)

A native Chicagoan and daughter of businessman Frederic Shepard Thompson and Alice Prescott Thompson, Brande achieved national attention as the author of self-help books. After attending the University of Chicago and University of Michigan, Brande returned to Chicago to

work as an editor and reporter at the *Journal of the American Medical Association*, *Record-Herald*, and *Tribune*. She moved to the East Coast in 1923 where she held managerial positions at *American Mercury*, *Bookman*, and the *American Review*. After authoring a how-to book on writing that emphasized personal development, she traveled the lecture circuit talking to crowds about writing and self-improvement. Her next book, *Wake Up and Live!* (New York: Simon Schuster, 1936), sold hundreds of thousands of copies. She wrote very little afterwards, but continued to lecture widely.
(*World Authors, 1900–1950*. New York: Wilson, 1996, s.v. "Brande, Dorothea").

Brashler, William (August 11, 1947–?)
    The author of non-fiction, as well as fiction, Brashler has published several books concerning Negro League baseball history. His novel on this topic (*The Bingo Long Traveling All Stars and Motor Kings*. New York: Harper & Row, 1973) was made into a motion picture starring Billy Dee Williams and James Earl Jones (Universal, 1976). Born in Grand Rapids, Mich., Brashler earned degrees at the University of Michigan (BA, 1969) and University of Iowa (MFA, 1971). He worked as a reporter for Lerner Newspapers (Chicago) from 1971 to 1973 and has lived in the city since then as a freelance writer.
(*Contemporary Authors Online*, Detroit: Gale, 2002, accessed 8 August 2009).

Bright, John (1908–September 14, 1989)
    Bright, along with Kubec Glasmon, was the author of successful screenplays for gangster movies featuring such stars as Humphrey Bogart and James Cagney. Bright worked with Glasmon as a reporter in Chicago before moving to Hollywood. He also wrote a biography of Chicago Mayor William Hale Thompson, published in 1930 (New York: Cape & Smith, 1930). One of the ten founders of the Screen Writers Guild, Bright was blacklisted by the House Un-American Activities Committee on and lived in Mexico for several years in the 1950s, before being able to return to the United States in 1958.
(*New York Times*, 16 September 1989, 12).

Brinig, Myron (December 22, 1900–May 13, 1991)
    The author of books considered vulgarly commercial by critics, Brinig's common themes are Jewish assimilation and life on the Western frontier. The son of Romanian immigrants, his family lived in Minneapolis before settling in Butte, Montana where a number of his works are set. He spent much of his adult live as a resident of Manhattan.
(*World Authors 1900–1950*. New York: Wilson, 1996, s.v. "Brinig, Myron").

Brooks, Gwendolyn (June 7, 1917–December 3, 2000)
    Known for her writing set in "Bronzeville," Chicago's African-American South Side, Brooks' poetry won her a Pulitzer Prize (1950) and she was honored by being named poet laureate of Illinois (1968) and having a chair in black literature and creative writing named for her at Chicago's Columbia College. In addition to her poetry, she published books for young adults and two volumes of autobiography. She taught at Columbia College and was a consultant in poetry to the Library of Congress (1985–1986). A lifelong resident of Chicago, Brooks conducted poetry and creative writing workshops in the city for many years.
(*Dictionary of Literary Biography*, vol. 5, s.v. "Brooks, Gwendolyn").

Brooks, Jerome (July 17, 1931–?)

A life-long Chicagoan, Brooks has been a professor of English at various Chicago colleges since 1958. He is a graduate of Roosevelt University (BA, 1953) and George Washington University (MA 1957) and served in the U.S. Army from 1953 to 1955. He has published a number of novels for young adults.

Brower, James Hattan (1867–?)

No information available.

Brown, Frank London (October 7, 1927–March 12, 1962)

Although he was born in Kansas City, Missouri, Brown moved with his family to Chicago's South Side at the age of twelve where he graduated from DuSable High School. He served in the U.S. Army from 1947 and earned his bachelor's degree on the G.I. Bill from Roosevelt University (Chicago) in 1951. He spent several years studying at Kent College of Law (Chicago), at the same time as writing liner notes for jazz recordings and doing freelance writing for the *Chicago Sun-Times*, *Chicago Tribune*, and the *Chicago Defender*. He was a program coordinator for the AFL-CIO in the late 1950s and published *Trumbull Park* (included here), the novel that brought him to national attention in 1959. Brown received a master's degree from the University of Chicago in 1960 and was a doctoral candidate at the University, as well as director of the Union Research Center and fellow of the Committee on Social Thought there when he died of leukemia at the age of thirty-three. He is known for the psychological insights he brought to his portrayals of racism. (*Dictionary of Literary Biography*, vol. 76, s.v. "Brown, Frank London").

Brown, Fred H.

No information available.

Brown, Fredric (October 29, 1906–March 11, 1972)

Known as a prolific and innovative writer of works of science fiction, Brown's first success was his detective novel, *The Fabulous Clipjoint* (included here). He published hundreds of short stories and five novels. Born in Cincinnati, Ohio, he studied at Hanover College (Hanover, Ind.) and the University of Cincinnati, before marrying Helen Ruth in 1929. He worked as an office assistant before working as a newspaper proofreader for the *Milwaukee Journal*. He produced his first works of science fiction in 1941 and became a full-time writer in 1947.

Brown, Helen Dawes (1847–1941)

No information available.

Browne, Howard (April 15, 1908–October 28, 1999)

A writer of hard-boiled detective fiction and creator of the character Paul Pine, Browne was born in Omaha, Nebraska, but fell in love with Chicago as a seventeen-year-old and lived there for twenty-four years. He had a series of jobs as a young man, but the most influential on his writing was his work as a credit manager for a furniture store chain, a job he started in 1929 and continued through the Great Depression. His Pine character was based on a skip tracer he knew from this work. He published his first short stories in the 1930s and got a job with Ziff-Davis publishing company (then located in Chicago), the publisher of a number of pulp magazines that Browne eventually edited between 1941 and 1956. He wrote his first television script in 1956 and afterwards made his career as a writer of scripts and movie screenplays. Most of his novels were pub-

lished in the 1940s and 1950s. He won the Life Achievement Award from the Private Eye Writers of America in 1985.
(*Dictionary of Literary Biography*, vol. 226, s.v. "Browne, Howard").

Brunner, Bernard (1923–?)
    Born in St. Paul, Minnesota, Brunner received his doctorate from the University of Chicago and worked as an English professor at De Paul University.

Bryant, James McKinley (1905–?)
    No information available.

Bryson, Leigh, *see* Rutledge, Nancy

Buck, Pearl S. (June 26, 1892–March 6, 1973)
    A prolific author known for descriptions of Chinese peasant life that humanized Chinese people for Americans, Buck was the winner of the 1938 Nobel Prize for Literature. The daughter of Presbyterian missionary parents, she spent much of her childhood and youth in China. She graduated in 1914 from Randolph-Macon Women's College (Lynchburg, Va.) and earned a master's degree from Cornell University in 1925. Several of her books were made into motion pictures, including her best-known work, *The Good Earth* (New York: John Day, 1931; MGM, 1937). Her books and movie deals earned her financial independence that enabled her to get out of unsatisfactory marriages, care for her daughter, who suffered from phenylketonuria, and set up a foundation to aid mixed race and/or illegitimate children in need of adoption. The winner of the William Dean Howells Medal from the American Academy of Arts and Letters, she was also elected a member of the National Institute of Arts and Letters.
(*Dictionary of Literary Biography*, vol. 329, s.v. "Buck, Pearl S.").

Budd, Lillian (July 21, 1897–April 6, 1989)
    Known for her trilogy of novels that document early twentieth-century Sweden and the Swedish immigrant experience in Chicago, Budd was born in the city and attended Chicago public schools. In addition to her novels for adults, she wrote several books of historical fiction for children.
(*Contemporary Authors Online*, Detroit: Gale, 2003, accessed 3 March 2009).

Burgoyne, Leon E. (1916–?)
    No information available.

Burnett, Frances (Eliza) Hodgson (November 24, 1849–October 29, 1924)
    An English immigrant, Burnett, began publishing stories in popular magazines when she was sixteen. She married Dr. Swan Moses Burnett in 1873, and the couple settled in Washington, where he became a widely known specialist in ophthalmic and aural surgery. Her writings soon achieved popularity, and, after the publication of *Little Lord Fauntleroy* (Scribner's, 1886), she had a significant income that enabled her to live apart from Dr. Burnett. Scandal magazine stories about these domestic arrangements led to a formal divorce from Burnett in 1898. Public criticism of her way of living continued but had no impact on her literary output; she eventually saw more than forty titles into print and authored essays and short stories for a wide range of publications.
(*Dictionary of Literary Biography*, vol. 42, s.v. "Burnett, Frances Eliza Hodgson").

Burnett, W. R. (William Riley) (November 25, 1899–April 25, 1982)

Born in Springfield, Ohio and educated in private schools in that state, Burnett began studying journalism at Ohio State University and eventually found a job in the Ohio Bureau of Labor Statistics that gave him time to write. He had little success until he moved to Chicago and, working as a desk clerk at the Northmere Hotel, became acquainted with people of a sort he had never before met, including a gangster. He soon wrote *Little Caesar* (included here), which sold hundreds of thousands of copies and was made into a movie starring Edward G. Robinson. From then on he experienced great success in writing books that were later turned into films, and published thirty-six novels. Perhaps his best known work adapted for film is *High Sierra* (Warner Bros. Pictures, 1941). He also wrote screenplays and television scripts. In 1980 he received the Grand Masters Award from the Mystery Writers of America in part for originating the gangster novel.
(*World Authors 1900–1950*, New York: Wilson, 1996, s.v. "Burnett, William Riley").

Burnham, Clara Louise (May 26, 1854–June 20, 1927)

Burnham moved with her parents to Chicago from Newton, Massachusetts when she was nine years old and continued to live in the city after her marriage to lawyer Walter Burnham, although she summered in Casco Bay, Maine. The daughter of George F. Root, the composer of "The Battle Cry of Freedom," a Civil War marching song, and other music, Burnham studied music, but began writing novels of romance and domestic life after her marriage. She became a Christian Scientist in 1902, and her novels had the dual intent of telling a story and presenting church teachings. During her long career from 1881 onwards she tended to publish a novel each year, as well as short stories and poems.
(*World Authors 1900–1950*. New York: Wilson, 1996, s.v. "Burnham, Clara Louise").

Burnham, David (1907–?)

Son of a vice president for Chicago, Burlington & Quincy Railroad, Burnham grew up in Kenilworth, Illinois and graduated from Princeton University in 1929.

Burroughs, Edgar Rice (September 1, 1875–March 19, 1950)

Burroughs grew up in the affluent household of his Chicago businessman father. Educated in private schools, including Philips Andover Academy (Andover, Mass.) and Michigan Military Academy (Orchard Lake Village, Mich.), he also spent time on a ranch in Idaho during his youth. After failing the West Point entrance examination, he enlisted in the U.S. Calvary and, following his discharge for health reasons, held a series of minor jobs until publishing a science fiction novel set on Mars. Through his writings that included seventy novels and the highly commercial Tarzan series, he was able to support a lavish lifestyle. The town around his southern California ranch was named Tarzana to honor him and a crater on Mars is named "Burroughs." A good deal of scholarship has been devoted to his writings and the commercialization of his works.

Butterworth, Hezekiah (December 22, 1839–September 5, 1905)

Born in Warren, Rhode Island, Butterworth wrote for *Youth's Companion* between 1870 and 1894 and is credited with doubling the magazine's circulation through the popularity of his writings. He also published seventeen books in his Zig Zag Journeys series, travelogues of trips in Europe, South America, and the United States. Known for his expressions of Christian faith, he lectured on religion and published *The Story of the Hymns* (New York: American Tract Society, 1871).
(*American Authors 1600–1900*. New York: Wilson, 1938, s.v. "Butterworth, Hezekiah").

Butterworth, W. E. (William Edmund) (November 10, 1929–?)

The author of more than one hundred books, about forty percent of them for young adults, Butterworth was honored by the American Library Association for his book *Leroy and the Old Man* (included here) which was designated the Best Book for young Adults in 1980. Born in New Jersey and raised in East Coast cities, he was drafted during the Korean War and continued to work for the U.S. Army in Alabama at the end of his enlistment, until he became a full-time author. He writes under the pseudonyms "Webb Beach," "Walker E. Blake," "James McM. Douglas," "Eden Hughes," "Edmund Sholefield," and "Patrick J. Williams."

Cahill, Holger (January 13, 1887–July, 1960)

Born in Iceland near the Arctic Circle, as Sveinn Kristjan Bjarnarson, Cahill immigrated as a child to the United States with his parents. After his father deserted the family in 1904, Cahill was forced to work on a North Dakota farm. He ran away and worked a number of odd jobs until entering a Canadian orphanage and finishing some formal schooling. After a series of adventurous jobs, including working on a freighter and traveling to the Far East, he settled in New York City as a newspaper reporter and studied at New York University. He changed his name to Edgar Cahill Holger sometime around 1919. Through his friendship with John Sloan, he was introduced in artistic circles and began exhibition work under John Cotton Dana at the Newark Museum (1922–1931). Subsequently he was director of exhibitions at the Museum of Modern Art (1932–1935), the director of the Works Progress Administration's Federal Art Project (1936–1943), and organizer of a countrywide exhibition in 1938, "American Art Today," for the New York World's Fair. He wrote several monographs, a biography, and three novels. His papers are at the Smithsonian Institution's Archives of American Art.

Caldwell, Lewis A. H. (October 12, 1905–1994)

A Chicago native, Caldwell graduated from Englewood High School and received bachelor's and master's degrees from Northwestern University. A probation officer for Cook County for seven years, he later operated a public relations firm and became general manager of Baldwin Ice Company in 1951 and field representative of Hawthorn Melody Farms Dairy in 1961. Elected to the Illinois House of Representatives in 1966, he served to 1979, playing an important role in the Black Caucus. For more than forty years he wrote a weekly column for the *Chicago Crusader* and founded the Cosmopolitan Chamber of Commerce, an interracial trade organization.
(*Daily Transcript*, 88th General Assembly, House of Representatives, State of Illinois, March 23, 1994).

Calmer, Ned (1918–March 9, 1986)

Born in Chicago, Calmer wrote more than twelve books, both fiction and non-fiction, most of which had something to do with his profession, television journalism. A graduate of the University of Virginia, he spent seven years in Paris working as a journalist and a correspondent for the *Chicago Tribune* and the *New York Herald*. As a CBS news analyst, he worked closely with Edward R. Murrow and was a radio correspondent during World War II, mostly abroad.
(*New York Times*, 11 March 1986, D31).

Capone, Al (Alphonse) (January 17, 1899–January 25, 1947)

The gangster at the center of waves of crime and violence in Chicago during the 1920s, when he was at the head of a powerful bootlegging ring, Capone was born in Naples, Italy and grew up in New York's Mulberry Bend slum. He followed a boyhood friend, gangster John Torrio, to Chicago in 1920, to work in his bootlegging operation. Imprisoned in federal prison on a tax conviction, first in Atlanta and then on Alcatraz, Capone was released from confinement with several major illnesses, but lived for another eight years before dying in Miami, Florida of a stroke. (*New York Times*, 26 January 1947, 7).

Capwell, Irene Stoddard
   No information available.

Cardwell, Ruth
   No information available.

Carroll, Charles
   No information available.

Carroll, Loren (March 5, 1904–October 21, 1978)
   A journalist who worked as a foreign correspondent from 1933 to 1951 in Paris and London, Carroll ended his career working for the U.S. State Department as consul general in Quebec (1956–1960) and later Palermo, Italy (1960–1964). Born in Scanlon, Minnesota, his first significant newspaper assignment was in Chicago where he covered the Leopold and Loeb trial and became friends with Clarence Darrow.
(*Contemporary Authors Online*, New York: Thomson Gale, 2007, accessed 12 August 2009).

Carruth, Hayden (August 3, 1921–?)
   Born in Waterbury, Connecticut, the son of journalist, newspaper editor, and lover of poetry, Gorton Veeder Carruth, Hayden Carruth is recognized as one of the most significant and productive of the late-twentieth-century poets of the United States. A 1943 graduate of the University of North Carolina (Chapel Hill), he served in World War II as a member of the U.S. Army Air Corps in Italy. He earned a master's degree from the University of Chicago in 1948 and was the editor of Chicago-based *Poetry* magazine from 1949 to 1950. He then worked as an associate editor at the University of Chicago Press, moving to New York in 1953 for another editorial position with Intercultural Publications. However, he was soon forced to seek treatment for alcoholism and a nervous breakdown. After a series of shock treatments, he moved to rural Vermont, and later lived in Syracuse, New York, teaching at Syracuse University. His poetry has earned him many prizes, including the Ruth Lilly Poetry Prize (1990) and fellowships.
(*Dictionary of Literary Biography*, vol. 5, s.v. "Carruth, Hayden").

Carter, John Stewart (1911–October 21, 1965)
   A graduate of Northwestern University, Carter earned his doctorate at the University of Chicago and taught English at Chicago Teachers' College for more than twenty years. He served in the U.S. Navy during World War II as a lieutenant.
(*New York Times*, 23 October 1965, 31).
Carter, Nicholas, *see* Coryell, John Russell

Cary, Lucian (January 1, 1889–September 9, 1971)
   Born in Hamlin, Kansas, Cary began his newspaper career as a reporter for the *Chicago Tribune* in 1910. He moved to New York City to work for *Collier's* in 1916 and contributed stories to

the publication and later to the *Saturday Evening Post* for many years. He also published several novels and wrote screenplays.
(*New York Times*, 9 September 1971, 46).

Casey, John (January 18, 1939–?)
    The son of Joseph Edward Casey, a lawyer and four-term member of Congress from Massachusetts, and Constance (Dudley) Casey, a political activist, Casey grew up in affluence in Worcester, Massachusetts, receiving his education at St. Albans School (Washington, D.C.) and Le Rosey (Switzerland). He began college at Harvard, but was expelled for bringing a girl into his dormitory room. After six months in the U.S. Army, he returned to Harvard and graduated in 1962, earning a law degree from the Harvard Law School in 1965 and, after passing the District of Columbia bar exam, practiced in his father's firm briefly before leaving to study at the Iowa Writers' Workshop, where he received an MFA in 1968. He has taught creative writing at the University of Virginia since 1972. Casey is the author of several novels, one of which, *Spartina* (New York: Knopf, 1989) won the National Book Award.
(*World Authors 1985–1990*, New York: Wilson, 1995, s.v. "Casey, John").

Casey, Robert J. (Robert Joseph) (March 14, 1890–December 4, 1962)
    Born in Beresford, South Dakota, Casey was a journalist with the *Chicago Daily News* for over twenty-five years. He had important overseas assignments during World War II, covering the defeat of the French Army, the battle of London, and the invasion of Normandy. Casey authored more than thirty books of fiction and non-fiction, a number of them mysteries with Chicago settings.

Cashman, John, *see* Davis, Timothy Francis Tothill

Caspary, Vera (November 13, 1899–June 13, 1987)
    Born into a middle-class Jewish family in Chicago (her father was a millinery buyer for a department store), Caspary yearned for a larger role in the world than that of housewife. She could not afford to go to college and got a job in an advertising firm. She moved to New York City in 1925 to work as editor of *Dance* magazine. She published her first novel in 1929 and brought out two more novels by 1932, by which time she was also writing screenplays. Her 1942 novel *Laura* (Boston: Houghton Mifflin, 1943) was turned into a motion picture produced by Otto Preminger and starring Gene Tierney (Twentieth Century-Fox, 1944). She married film producer I. G. Goldsmith in 1949. She continued to be concerned about the role of women in society and many of her books, including the mystery novels for which she is known, dealt with women's issues.
(*Contemporary Authors Online*, Detroit: Gale, 2003, accessed 20 July 2009).

Cassady, Constance, *see* Wagner, Constance

Cather, Willa (December 7, 1873–April 24, 1947)
    Forced to move with her family from rural Virginia, where she had enjoyed extended family and social networks, to the Nebraska prairie, a major theme of Cather's literary work centered on escaping small-town life to find a place in larger social and cultural contexts. After graduating from the University of Nebraska (Lincoln), she secured a series of editorial jobs that aided her in moving east, first to Pittsburgh and finally to New York City where she worked for *McClure's*

magazine, eventually managing the publication. Her sixteen novels achieved critical and popular success, giving her the financial means to live an increasingly independent life.
(*Contemporary Author's Online*, Detroit: Gale, 2007, accessed 21 July 2009).

Catherwood, Mary Hartwell (December 16, 1847–December 26, 1902)
    Born Mary Hartwell to Marcus (a physician) and Phoebe Thompson Hartwell, Catherwood was raised by her maternal grandparents in Hebron, Ohio after her parents died in Illinois. She graduated from Granville (Ohio) Female College and, after the success of short stories she published in *Wood's Household Magazine*, moved, in 1874, to Newburgh, New York, where the magazine was located. She supported herself as a freelance writer, publishing her first novel in 1875. That same year she moved to Cincinnati, following friends involved with a magazine there. She wed merchant James Steele Catherwood of Hoopeston, Illinois in 1877. Through short stories and novels she became known for depicting farm life in Illinois, Indiana, and Ohio. After residing for several years in Indianapolis, where she was drama critic for the *Saturday Review,* she divided her time between residences in Chicago and Hoopeston. An intimate of James Whitcomb Riley and a friend of other Midwestern writers, she joined with several of them to form the Western Association of Writers. Toward the end of her career, Catherwood wrote about early French explorers and settlers in the West and Canada.
(*Notable American Women, 1607–1950: A Biographical Dictionary*, Cambridge, Mass.: Harvard College, 1971, s.v. "Catherwood, Mary Hartwell").

Chamales, Tom T. (1924–1960)
    Chamales was a World War II veteran who fought in Burma, commanding a battalion by the end of the war. In addition to his war experiences, his writing drew upon his identity as a Greek-American.

Chance, Frank Leroy (September 19, 1877–September 15, 1924)
    Best known as a baseball player and manager, Chance was born in Fresno, California and played on the University of California baseball team in 1894 and 1895. He joined the Chicago Cubs in 1898 and established a reputation as a first baseman before becoming the team's general manager, leading the Cubs to pennants in 1906, 1907, 1908, and 1910. He was later a manager with the New York Yankees, the Boston Red Sox, and the Chicago White Sox. He was inducted into the Baseball Hall of Fame in 1946.
(*New York Times*, 16 September 1924, 18).

Chandler, Peter
    No information available.

Chandler, St. Lawrence
    Chandler was a Chicago businessman committed to various philanthropies. His kindness to the impoverished Duke of Livingstone prompted the elderly man to adopt him. Upon the Duke's death, Chandler acquired the title Marquis of Eckersley.

Channon, Henry (March 7, 1897–October 8, 1958)
    Channon was born in Chicago and his grandfather was an immigrant from England. However, he became a naturalized British citizen shortly before his marriage to Lady Honor Guinness in 1933 and served as a Conservative Member of Parliament from 1935 until his death in 1958. He

was divorced from Lady Guinness in 1945 and was knighted in 1957. He published two successful novels (both included here) and a work of non-fiction on the kings of Bavaria. He kept meticulous diaries, fifty volumes of which he donated to the British Museum during his lifetime with the stipulation that they not be made accessible until 2008.

Chapman, George [Vernon Warren, pseud.] (June 30, 1925–?)
    Born in London, England, Chapman spent his life as an insurance executive in Edmonton, Alberta. He wrote a series of thrillers in the 1950s and 1960s, several of them involving a Chicago detective.
(*Contemporary Authors Online*, Detroit: Gale, 2002, accessed 15 May 2009).

Chappell, Fred A.
    No information available.

Charteris, Leslie (May 12, 1907–April 16, 1993)
    Creator of the detective character Simon Templar, better known as the Saint, Charteris wrote more than forty books featuring the debonair protagonist. Born in Singapore, the son of an Englishwoman and a Chinese surgeon, Charteris began writing at an early age and sold his first novel when he was eighteen. Attending Cambridge University at the time, but disaffected with higher education, he left school without the support of his parents and pursued various exotic occupations (rubber plantation ownership, pearl fishing, gold prospecting, tin mining) to supplement his earnings from his writings. The advent of the Saint in print for the first time relieved Charteris financially and when movies featuring the Saint began to be produced, he became genuinely affluent. Although he primarily lived in England, he made extended visits to the United States to work as a writer in the movie industry in Hollywood and the magazine industry in New York City.
(*World Authors 1900–1950*, New York: Wilson, 1996, s.v. "Charteris, Leslie").

Chatfield-Taylor, Hobart C. (Hobart Chatfield) (March 24, 1865–January 16, 1945).
    In addition to novels, Chatfield-Taylor wrote biographies of Molière and Goldoni. He was born in Chicago.
(*American Authors and Their Books, 1640 to the Present*, New York: Crown, 1962, s.v. "Chatfield-Taylor, Hobart C[hatfield]").

Chinn, Laurene (1902–March 17, 1978)
    Born Laurene Chambers in Alburnet, Iowa, Chinn earned a bachelor's degree from Hastings (Nebraska) College in 1933 and a master's degree later in life from West Texas State College in 1958. After teaching for a time in Kansas public schools during the 1920s, Chinn worked in the personnel office of Western Electric Company in Chicago from 1929–1932. She married Harry Wing Chinn in 1934 and the couple moved to Borger, Texas in 1943, where Chinn was a teacher and from 1947–1978 operated a mail order business for teaching aids in reading. The author of numerous short stories, many for religious magazines, Chinn published five novels.
(*Contemporary Authors Online*, Detroit: Gale, 2003, accessed 5 January 2009).

Christian, Kit, *see* Thorson, Sarah Winfree and Thorson, Delos Russell

Churchill, William Arnold [Arthur Walcott, pseud.] (1877–?)
    No information available.

Clark, Christopher (1911–?)
    No information available.

Clark, Edward C. (1835–1917)
    No information available.

Clark, Herma Naomi (1871?–November 26, 1959)
    The author for more than thirty years of the *Chicago Tribune* column "When Chicago Was Young," Clark was born in Princeton, Illinois, the daughter of Major and Mrs. Atherton Clark. After completing her bachelor's degree at Oberlin College (Oberlin, Ohio), Clark moved to Chicago to become secretary to retired hardware entrepreneur, William Blair. After his death, she continued as personal secretary to his widow, a well-known society figure. She was a member of the Chicago Press Club and one of its historians.
    (*New York Times*, 27 November 1959, 26).

Claro, Joe
    No information available.

Clason, Clyde Burt (1903–1987)
    An advertising copywriter and trade paper editor in Chicago, Clason is known for creating the detective Theocritus Lucius Westborough who was featured in his series of ten crime novels published from 1936 to 1941.

Claudia, Susan [pseud.], *see* Johnston, William

Cleaver, Vera (January 6, 1919–August 11, 1993)
    Vera and her husband, Bill Cleaver, met and married during World War II. After publishing more than 300 pieces of magazine fiction, the Cleavers began writing novels for young adults. After the death of her husband, Vera completed a novel the two of them were working on and went on to write and publish three more books before her own death.
    (*Dictionary of Literary Biography*, vol. 52, s.v., "Cleaver, Vera").

Cleaver, Bill (William Joseph) (March 24, 1920–August 20, 1981)
    Born in Seattle, Washington, Cleaver enlisted in the U.S. Air Corps in 1942 before finishing high school and marrying Vera Allen in 1945. After leaving military service, he worked for a time as a jeweler, but re-enlisted in the U.S. Air Force in 1954 and served in Japan (1954–1955) and France (1956–1958). He and his wife began writing and publishing in pulp magazines and, with increasing reputations, placed work in *Woman's Day* and *McCall's*. They turned their focus on young adult fiction in 1967, and it is for their books in this genre that they are known. Several of their publications won major awards and their novel *Where the Lilies Bloom* (Philadelphia: Lippincott, 1969) was adapted as a motion picture in 1971 (United Artists).
    (*Contemporary Authors Online*, Detroit: Gale, 2003, accessed 6 June 2009).

Cobb, Weldon J.
   No information available.

Cohen, Lester (August 17, 1901–July 17, 1963)
   The success of his first novel, *Sweepings*, included here, led to a career writing screenplays. The best known is his adaptation of Somerset Maugham's *Of Human Bondage* (RKO Radio Pictures, 1934). He published several novels and works of nonfiction.

Collins, Charles (November 19, 1880–March 3, 1964)
   Newspaperman Charles Collins was born in Madison, Indiana and is mainly known for his work as the drama critic of the *Chicago Evening Post* for more than twenty-five years. He also wrote for the *Chicago Tribune*, including a daily feature, "100 Years Ago."
   (*American Authors and Books: 1640 to the Present Day*, third revised edition, Crown, 1972, s.v. "Collins, Charles").

Colter, Cyrus (1910–2002)
   Known as a writer of African-American fiction, Colter grew up in Indiana and Ohio, the son of a man who worked as an actor, insurance salesman, musician, and regional director of the National Association for the Advancement of Colored People. Colter attended Youngstown College (Youngstown, Ohio) and Ohio State University (Columbus, Ohio) and moved to Chicago to attend Chicago-Kent College of Law, from which he graduated in 1940. He entered the military in 1942 and served as a field artillery captain in the European Theatre of Operations. Upon returning to Chicago in 1946, he practiced law until he was appointed Commerce Commissioner for the State of Illinois, a position he held until 1973. He began writing in 1960 as an avocation and with the success of the volume of short stories he published in 1970 entitled *The Beach Umbrella* (included here), he began transitioning to writing full-time. In 1973 he was appointed the Chester D. Tripp Professor of Humanities and chairman of the Department of African-American Studies, continuing in this job until 1978. He published four novels and another volume of short stories before his death.
   (*Dictionary of Literary Biography*, vol. 33, s.v. "Colter, Cyrus").

Converse, Jane
   No information available.

Cook, Bruce (April 7, 1932–November 9, 2003)
   A native of Chicago and graduate of Loyola (Chicago) University (BS, 1955), Cook worked in that city from 1958 to 1965 in editorial and public relations positions, taking time off from 1965 to 1967 to work as a freelance writer. He began working for the *National Observer* (Silver Spring, Md.) as book review editor in 1967 and, starting in 1971 as movie critic. He later worked as a book review editor for the *Detroit News* and *USA Today*, and an entertainment feature writer for the *Los Angeles Daily News*. After 1990, he wrote full-time. The author of five works of nonfiction and twelve novels, Cook wrote mystery and detective fiction under the pen name Bruce Alexander, as well as his own name. He created two series; one featuring detective Antonio "Chico" Cervantes and another featuring Sir John Fielding.
   (*Contemporary Authors Online*, Detroit: Gale, 2004, accessed 25 May 2009).

Cook, William Wallace (April 11, 1867–July 20, 1933)
   The author of hundreds of stories for pulp magazines, Cook worked as a court reporter and journalist. In addition to several novels, he wrote two volumes of advice to writers on earning a living from writing and creating successful plots. He was born and died in Marshall, Michigan.
(*Contemporary Authors Online*, Gale, 2003, accessed, 2 August 2007)

Cooke, Marjorie Benton (1876?–1920)
   Best-known as the author of *Bambi* (Garden City, N.Y.: Doubleday, 1914), Cooke was a lecturer on the woman's suffragist circuit. She lived in New York City.
(*New York Times*, 27 April 1920, 9).

Coons, Maurice [Armitage Trail, pseud.] (1902–1930)
   Son of a theatrical impresario who managed the New Orleans Opera Company, Coons began selling short fiction to magazines as a teenager and by his early twenties was writing entire issues of detective magazines. Fascinated with gangsters, he moved to Chicago in 1925 to do research and lived in Oak Park for several years. He died at the age of twenty-eight from a heart attack brought on by obesity (he weighed three hundred fifteen pounds).
(*Mystery File*, www.mysteryfile.com/blog/?p=303, accessed 24 March 2009).

Corbett, Elizabeth Frances (September 30, 1887–January 24, 1981)
   Born in Aurora, Illinois, Corbett graduated from the University of Wisconsin in 1910 and had a long career as a novelist. Best-known for works of historical fiction, she published more than fifty-nine book-length works between 1916 and 1971.
(*Contemporary Authors Online*, Detroit: Gale, 2003, accessed 6 January 20009).

Corey, Paul Frederick (July 8, 1903–?)
   Born on a farm in Shelby County, Iowa, youngest in a family of seven, Corey's father died when he was two years old. Financial struggle characterized his youth as his mother tried to support the family on the mortgaged farm. When one of her sons took over the farm in 1918, she and Corey moved to Atlantic, Iowa, where he completed high school. He graduated from the University of Iowa in 1925 and lived in Chicago and later New York City, working in various jobs, including as picture researcher for the *Encyclopaedia Britannica* and *National Encyclopedia*. In the early 1930s he purchased a farm in Putnam County, New York and began living a subsistence life with his wife Ruth Lechlitner. He is known for his trilogy of novels dealing with an Iowa farm family between 1910 and 1930, although he also published a number of how-to magazine articles, self-help books, young adult novels, and a science fiction novel.
(*World Authors, 1900–1950*, New York: H. W. Wilson, 1996, s.v. "Corey, Paul Frederick").

Corne, Molly E.
   No information available.

Correll, Charles J. (February 2, 1890–September 27, 1972)
   Radio entertainer Correll was the voice of Andy in the "Amos 'n' Andy" show. A white Southerner, Correll was working for a Chicago firm organizing amateur theatricals for businessmen's luncheons, cocktail parties and other gatherings when Freeman F. Gosden was hired by the same firm in 1920. The two men created a black-face situation comedy act in African-American dialect. By 1931, they had a nationally syndicated radio show that made them wealthy

and was so popular that motion pictures would be stopped mid-reel so the audience could hear the broadcast. The popularity of the show began to wane in the 1940s and a televised version, without Correll and Gosden, was short-lived and criticized as racially insensitive.
(*New York Times*, 27 September 1972, 1).

Corrigan, Mark, *see* Lee, Norman

Corrington, John William (October 28, 1932–November 24, 1988)
    Born in Cleveland, Ohio, Corrington grew up in Shreveport, Louisiana and spent the majority of his life in the South. Not surprisingly, his novels, poetry, and short stories typically deal with Southern themes. A graduate of Centenary (Shreveport, La.) College and Rice University (from which he received an MA in Renaissance Literature), Corrington was a college teacher from 1960 to 1972. He took a leave of absence from Louisiana State University in 1963 to study at the University of Sussex (England) which awarded him a doctorate in 1965. Film producer and director Roger Corman, an admirer of Corrington's writing, offered the author work writing screenplays and when Loyola University (New Orleans) denied Corrington tenure, the earnings from his scripts enabled him to go to law school at Tulane University. He practiced law from 1975 to 1978 and then formed Corrington Productions and began writing for television, establishing a highly lucrative business that enabled him to purchase a twenty-six-acre estate in Malibu, California. In the course of his career he published four novels, a series of detective fiction with his wife, several novellas, and award-winning collections of poetry.
(*American National Biography*, s.v. "Corrington, John William").

Corrothers, James David (July 2, 1869–February 12, 1917)
    Born in Cass County, Michigan, in an area settled by fugitive slaves, Corrothers had a multiracial parentage and was adopted by his Cherokee, Scotch-Irish, paternal grandfather when his mother died in giving birth to him. Raised in poverty in trapping and lumber settlements on the eastern shore of Lake Michigan, Corrothers educated himself while working at a variety of menial jobs, including bootblack in Chicago. He settled in Chicago in the early 1890s and through his friendship with journalist Henry D. Lloyd and temperance crusader Frances E. Willard got the financial support to receive a few years of college education at Northwestern University and Bennett College (Greensboro, N.C.). Although he tried to establish a freelance writing career, racial prejudice stymied him and he began working as a minister for the African Methodist Episcopal church in 1898. He changed denominations several times (Baptist and Presbyterian) and needed to relocate repeatedly (Bath, N.Y.; several towns in New Jersey; New York City; Virginia; Michigan; Washington, D.C.; Massachusetts), however the ministry provided him with an income and the time to write. He is best known for his dialect poetry and prose sketches.
(*American National Biography*, s.v. "Corrothers, James David").

Coryell, John Russell [pseud., Nick Carter] (1851–July 15, 1924)
    Creator of Nick Carter, the detective featured in more than one thousand short stories and novels, Coryell was born in New York City and studied law at the College of the City of New York before joining his ship-building father in China, where he served as consular clerk and vice-consul in Canton and Shanghai. When he returned to the United States, he worked as a newspaper reporter in San Francisco, Sacramento, and Santa Barbara, before returning in 1878 to New York City, where he began writing juvenile stories for magazines. He introduced his Nick Carter cha-

racter in 1886. By 1900 he had stopped writing fiction and began writing social satire and later, general articles for *True Story Magazine*.
(*Mystery and Suspense Writers: The Literature of Crime, Detection and Espionage*, New York: Charles Scribner's Sons, 1998, s.v. "Coryell, John Russell").

Courtney, James [Frank Robinson, pseud.].
No information available.

Cowdrey, Robert H.
No information available.

Craig, M. S. (Mary Shura) (February 27, 1923–January 14, 1991)
An author of children's books and mystery stories for young adults, Craig was born Mary Francis in Pratt, Kansas and grew up in Portland, Oregon and Spokane, Washington. After her 1943 marriage to Daniel Shura she had three children and was inspired to begin writing (Shura died in 1959 and Craig subsequently married Raymond Craig in 1961). During her life she resided in Omaha, Atlanta, Chicago, Boston, and San Francisco and each city inspired works of fiction. She won the Carl Sandburg Literary Arts Award in 1985 and was a president of the Mystery Writers of America.
(*Contemporary Authors Online*, Detroit: Gale, 2003, accessed 7 April 2009)

Crane, Laura Dent
No information available.

Creasey, John [Anthony Morton, pseud.]. (September 17, 1908–June 9, 1973)
British author Creasey was one of the most prolific writers of adventure and detective novels of all time. He wrote more than 560 books, many of them widely translated, that sold 60,000,000 copies. He used twenty-eight pen names.
(*New York Times*, 10 June 1973, 65).

Cromie, Alice Hamilton (May 29, 1914–August 11, 2000)
A book reviewer and newspaper columnist, Cromie (the wife of television host Robert Allen Cromie), was born in Chariton, Iowa and received her bachelor's degree from the University of Texas in 1937. Primarily the author of magazine fiction, she lived in Grayslake, Illinois and published one novel (as well as some volumes of non-fiction). She also worked in promotional advertising and wrote greeting card verse.

Crowley, Mary Catherine
No information available.

Crump, Paul (Orville) (c.1930–2002)
A native of Chicago, Crump grew up in the African-American ghetto. He was jailed for armed robbery when he was sixteen and was convicted of murder when he was twenty-three. Imprisoned on death row, he converted to Christianity and with the support of many people, including journalists and evangelist Billy Graham, made the case that he was reformed and his sentence was

commuted to life in prison. After serving forty years he was released in 1993. His novel *Burn, Killer, Burn!* (included here) was written to discourage others from crime.
(*Contemporary Authors Online*, Detroit: Gale, 2003, accessed 4 March 2010).

Crunden, Allan B. (1878–?)
A graduate of Yale University and a physical geographer, Crunden published one work of fiction, a mystery, with his grandson.

Crunden, Robert Morse. (December 22, 1940–March 23, 1999)
Crunden was a native of Jersey City, New Jersey, the son of an obstetrician and gynecologist. He was educated at Yale and Harvard and his dissertation on Brand Whitlock was published as a prize-winning book. For more than thirty years he taught at the University of Texas as a professor of history and American studies. His only foray into fiction was the work for which he is included here, a mystery novel he wrote with his grandfather.
(Yale University Alumni Office)

Cunningham, Jere (1943–?)
Author of more than five novels, Cunningham is also known as an author of screenplays for film and television.

Cuppy, Will (August 23, 1884–September 19, 1949)
A humorist and book reviewer, Cuppy was born into affluent circumstances in Aurora, Indiana and was educated at the University of Chicago. After finishing his bachelor's degree in philosophy, he continued to take courses at the university for seven years, while living in the Phi Gamma Delta fraternity house. During the same period he covered college news for the *Chicago Daily News*, *Chicago Record-Herald* and other newspapers. The book for which he is included here, *Maroon Tales*, was commissioned by the university to bolster the newly-created fraternity system. He finally submitted a master's thesis in English in 1914 and moved to New York City to work as a journalist for the rest of his life, with the exception of his World War I service as a second lieutenant in the Motor Transport Corps. He published comic pieces in magazines and wrote six books of comic essays.
(*Dictionary of Literary Biography*, vol. 11, s.v. "Cuppy, Will").

Curtis, Wardon Allan (1867–1940)
No information available.

Dailey, Janet (May 21, 1944–?)
Born on a farm in Iowa, Dailey did not begin writing until she was thirty. For the previous ten years she had worked as her husband's secretary. When he sold the company, the couple began traveling the United States in a travel trailer and Dailey was inspired to write a romance novel for each of the fifty states. She typically publishes a dozen books a year with Harlequin and has earned a large reader base, so far selling one hundred million copies of her books.
(*Contemporary Authors Online*, Detroit: Thomson Gale, 2008, accessed 28 February 2010).

Dale, Virginia
No information available.

D'Amato, Barbara (April 10, 1938–)

Creator of a series of mysteries featuring Cat Marsala, a Chicagoan who is a freelance journalist, D'Amato was born in Grand Rapids, Michigan, but has lived in Chicago for many years. Educated at Northwestern University (BA, 1971; MA, 1972), D'Amato has been active in mystery writer organizations, including Sisters in Crime. She has first-hand knowledge of criminal cases; her husband is a law professor and she has worked as a researcher for trial attorneys.
(*Contemporary Authors Online*, Detroit: Gale, 2002, accessed 28 February 2010).

Darrow, Clarence (April 18, 1857–March 13, 1938)

Famed orator and trial attorney Darrow was born in Ohio and received his legal education at the University of Michigan. He began a legal practice in Ohio after his admission to the bar at the age of twenty-one, but moved to Chicago in 1887. An admirer of Judge John P. Altgeld he sought him out and befriended him upon his arrival in the city and first came to public attention as an orator on reform topics. After a few years as a corporate lawyer for railroads, he began to take cases in support of labor; the first notable one involved defending Eugene V. Debs. Other high profile cases followed, including defending William D. Haywood (1906), the McNamara brothers (1911), Leopold and Loeb (1924), and John Thomas Scopes (1925). His view that crime was usually determined by immediate circumstances shaped his two novels and much of his non-fiction writing.
(*Dictionary of Literary Biography*, vol. 303, s.v., "Darrow, Clarence").

Davieson, Sarah
No information available.

Davis, Clyde Brion (May 22, 1894–July 19, 1962)

Author of nineteen novels and magazine fiction, Davis had lived a very full life by the time he started publishing fiction at the age of forty. Born in a small town in Nebraska, Davis' parents ran general stores and made several moves before settling in Kansas City, Missouri, where Davis completed middle school. He left school to become a printer's apprentice, but held many jobs before enlisting during World War I. As a soldier he worked on an Army newspaper and when he returned to civilian life he found work as a reporter and editor, primarily on newspapers in the West, and several of his novels feature journalists. However, as soon as he could begin supporting himself as a novelist in 1937 he stopped being a newspaperman and worked exclusively on his writing for the rest of his life.
(*Dictionary of Literary Biography*, vol. 9, s.v. "Davis, Clyde Brion").

Davis, Dorothy Salisbury (April 26, 1916–?)

Best known for her suspense and mystery novels, Davis, the author of fourteen works of fiction, grew up on Illinois farms near Chicago and attended Barat College of the Sacred Heart in Lake Forest, Illinois. In early adulthood she worked for Swift and Company for a time in the research library and later had jobs in industrial relations and advertising. She moved to New York City with her husband, Harry Davis, an actor, in 1946.
(*World Authors, 1950–1970*, New York: H. W. Wilson, 1975, s.v. Davis, Dorothy Salisbury").

Davis, George (February 4, 1906–1957)

Although he was born in Chicago, Davis moved with his family as a child to Clinton, Michigan and later to Detroit. He began studying at the College of the City of Detroit, but dropped out

to hold jobs, alternately in Detroit and Chicago, at steel plants, and later at the bookshop at Marshall Field's. In 1927 he settled in Paris, France and began the life of a writer, befriending Jean Cocteau and Norman Douglas. In 1931, when he was twenty-five, he won the $10,000 Harper Prize for his first novel. Davis went on to become fiction editor at *Harper's Bazaar* from 1936–1941 and later worked as editor of *Mademoiselle* for eight years. He was a resident of 7 Middagh Street in Brooklyn Heights in the 1940s, along with Gypsy Rose Lee. Such figures as W. H. Auden, Benjamin Britten, and Carson McCullers also lived in the household for extended periods of time.
(*Authors Today and Yesterday*, New York: H. W. Wilson, 1933, s.v. "Davis, George")

Davis, Timothy Francis Tothill [John Cashman, pseud.] (January 14, 1941–?)
Davis is a barrister-at-law in London, England and has written several mysteries under the pseudonym John Cashman.

Dawson, George H. [Michael Storme, pseud.] (c.1914–?)
An English author of pulp fiction in the 1950s, Dawson was a co-founder of Tempest Publishing Company. He created the character Nick Cranley, a Chicago detective whose vividly described encounters with women brought obscenity charges for Dawson.

De Jourlet, Marie [pseud.], *see* Little, Paul Hugo

Dean, S. Ella Wood
No information available.

Dell, Floyd (June 28, 1887–July 23, 1969)
Born in Barry, Illinois, a small town in which his father was the butcher, Dell experienced poverty and embraced socialism as the solution. Although he left school at sixteen, he had a photographic memory and read widely. After working as a reporter for the *Davenport (Iowa) Times* from 1905 to 1908, Dell moved to Chicago where he lived for five years before moving to New York City in 1913. His freelance writing and skilled book reviews for the *Chicago Evening Post* and the *Friday Literary Review* garnered him respect and he began socializing with the Chicago intellectuals and artists that were part of the Chicago Renaissance. Dell is also identified with this movement. After his move to New York, he lived in Greenwich Village and worked as a writer until his retirement in 1947.
(*Contemporary Authors Online*, Gale, 2002, accessed 8 June 2009).

Denison, Thomas Stewart (February 20, 1848–April 7, 1911)
Born in Marshall County, West Virginia, Denison worked as a miner and school teacher. He is best known as a Chicago publisher and as the author of five books.

Derleth, August William (February 24, 1909–July 4, 1971)
The author of more than fifty novels, as well as short stories, poetry, and biographies, Derleth eschewed urban literary culture for small-town life in his native Sauk City, Wisconsin. After graduating from the University of Wisconsin in 1930, Derleth worked as an editorial assistant in Minneapolis, but soon returned to Sauk City and began writing fiction for pulp magazines, as well as working on autobiographical fiction. He was able to focus exclusively on his writing from the

late 1930s and continued working daily until his death, averaging from 750,000 to 1,000,000 published words per year.
(*Dictionary of Literary Biography*, vol. 9, s.v., "Derleth, August").

DeRosa, Tina
    No information available.

Dever, Joseph (1919–December 12, 1970)
    Dever, who owned a public relations firm and worked as an author's agent, was a graduate of Boston College. He served in World War II in the Army Signal Corps and Air Force and lived most of his adult life in the Boston area. He was the author of three novels and a biography of Cardinal Cushing.
(*New York Times*, 14 December 1970, 46).

De Voto, Bernard Augustine (January 11, 1897–November 13, 1955)
    Born in Provo, Utah, De Voto attended the University of Utah and graduated from Harvard University in 1920 after World War I military service. He taught at Northwestern University from 1922 to 1927. He is best known for his editorship of the *Saturday Review of Literature* (1936–1938) and his long-running editorship of *Harper's* "Easy Chair" department (1935–1955), as well as his popular historical works for which he won the Pulitzer Prize, Bancroft Prize, and National Book Award. He was also the author of more than nine novels.
[*Dictionary of Literary Biography*, vol. 256, s.v. "De Voto, Bernard (Augustine)"].

De Vries, Peter (February 27, 1910–September 28, 1993)
    A native Chicagoan, the son of Dutch immigrants who were members of the strict Calvinistic Dutch Reformed Church, De Vries graduated from Calvin College in Grand Rapids, Michigan in 1931, but did not enter the ministry as he had planned. Between 1931 and 1938 he held a variety of jobs before starting work as editor of Chicago-based *Poetry* magazine, a position he held until moving to New York City in 1944 where, with the encouragement of James Thurber, he became a contributor of cartoons to the *New Yorker* magazine with the encouragement of James Thurber. His humorous, frankly sexual novels have found a broad popular audience.
(*Dictionary of Literary Biography*, vol. 6, s.v. "De Vries, Peter").

Dewey, Thomas B. (March 6, 1915–April 22, 1981)
    A highly productive mystery writer who created several series featuring vividly drawn detectives, Dewey is best known for creating the Chicago detective, Mac, who appeared in seventeen novels published between 1953 and 1970, and was notable for being a hard-boiled detective with feelings. Born in Elkhart, Indiana, the son of a college English professor, Dewey graduated from Kansas State Teachers College in 1936 and did postgraduate work at the University of Iowa. He lived in Los Angeles and, during World War II, in Washington, D.C., where he worked in the U.S. State Department. He became a full-time writer in 1952.
(*Dictionary of Literary Biography*, vol. 226, s.v. "Dewey, Thomas B.").

Dobler, Bruce (June 30, 1939–?)
    A native Chicagoan and son of a bookkeeper, Dobler's first job was as a flagman and ticket collector for the Illinois Central Railroad. He held the job while a student at the University of Illinois, Chicago, which he attended from 1957 to 1960. He earned his bachelor's degree from Roose-

velt University (Chicago, Illinois) in 1963 and a master's degree in fine arts from the University of Iowa (Iowa City, Iowa) in 1968. The author of three novels, Dobler has worked as an English professor from 1976 and since 1979 has been employed by the University of Pittsburgh. (*Contemporary Authors Online*, Detroit: Gale, 2002, accessed 28 February 2010).

Dockarty, A. J.
   No information available.

Donelson, Katherine
   No information available.

Donohue, H. E. F.
   No information available.

Donovan, Cornelius Francis (Rev.) (1876–?)
   No information available.

Dooley, Mr., *see* Dunne, Finley Peter

Dos Passos, John (January 14, 1896–September 28, 1970)
   Although he first wrote poetry in response to his war experiences, his novel *Three Soldiers* (Doran, 1921), an attack on war in general, received wide attention and critical acclaim, launching his career. In the 1920s, he lived the life of one of America's prominent men of letters, a friend of Hemingway, Fitzgerald, Edmund Wilson, and Malcolm Cowley. His books earned him a reputation for his insightful criticism of the American capitalist system. After the late 1930s, however, he became increasingly conservative socially and politically, alienating his earlier advocates. (*Dictionary of Literary Biography*, vol. 9, s.v. "Dos Passos, John").

Douglas, Amanda Minnie (July 14, 1831–July 18, 1916)
   Douglas was born in New York City and received her education at the City Institute; however, her family moved to Newark, New Jersey in 1853, and she spent the rest of her life there. Prior to the appearance of her first book in 1866, she published a number of short stories in the *Saturday Evening Post*, *New York Ledger*, and the *Lady's Friend*. From *In Trust* (Lee & Shepard, 1866), her first book, until *Red House Children Growing Up* (Lothrop, Lee, & Shepard, 1916), she published one or two books annually. *Larry* (Lee & Shepard, 1893) received the *Youth's Companion* prize for best young people's fiction. Most of her works were for young adults. She published three extensive series: the Kathie Series, the Little Girl Series, and the Helen Grant Series. Even though her characters sometimes travel, Douglas's works celebrate the virtue of family life and all the traditional virtues with which it is associated. (*American Authors, 1600–1900*, New York: H. W. Wilson, 1938, s.v. "Douglas, Amanda Minnie").

Douglas, Lloyd C. (August 27, 1877–February 13, 1951)
   Douglas was a Protestant minister best known for his novel *The Robe* (Houghton Mifflin, 1943) about the Roman soldier in charge of Jesus of Nazareth's crucifixion who becomes a convert and martyr to Christianity after the events he witnesses. The son of a Lutheran clergyman, Douglas was educated at Wittenberg College and Seminary (Springfield, Ohio) and had a number

of pastorates, first as a Lutheran, and later, as a Congregationalist minister. He lived in Chicago while he was director of religious work at the University of Illinois from 1911–1915. After the publication of several inspirational works, he published a novel, *Magnificent Obsession* (Chicago: Willett & Clark, 1933), that achieved a reputation by word of mouth, eventually selling three million copies, and was made into a motion picture (Universal Pictures, 1935). Like all of his more than eleven novels, the work conveyed a spiritual message and was dismissed by critics for the poor quality of the writing.
(*World Authors, 1900–1950*, New York: H. W. Wilson, 1996, s.v. "Douglas, Lloyd C.").

Drago, Harry Sinclair (March 20, 1888–October 25, 1979)
     A prolific writer of Westerns and other pulp fiction, Drago was born in Toledo, Ohio and worked for a time as a columnist for the *Toledo Bee*. He later moved to New York City to work for a publishing firm and was then inspired to write his first novel, after which he averaged three books per year. He also worked as a scriptwriter in Hollywood from 1928 to 1933, but then he turned his full attention to writing books and resided in White Plains, New York for the rest of his life.
(*Contemporary Authors Online*, Detroit: Gale, 2003, accessed 6 August 2009).

Draper, John Smith
     No information available.

Dreiser, Theodore (August 27, 1871–December 28, 1945)
     Born in Terre Haute, Indiana, the son of German immigrants, Dreiser was one of ten children in an impoverished household. His family lived in various small towns in Indiana during his youth. In 1887 Dreiser moved to Chicago, working menial jobs at first, however after one year of study at Indiana University, he was able to get a job as a newspaper reporter. After several years in Chicago, he moved to St. Louis and Pittsburgh for newspaper jobs and later to New York City to work as a magazine editor. His first novel, *Sister Carrie* (New York: Doubleday, Page, 1900), established his reputation for literary realism. He went on to publish more than thirty books, several of which are set in Chicago.
(*Dictionary of Literary Biography*, vol. 9, s.v. "Dreiser, Theodore").

Driver, John Merritte (1858–1915)
     No information available.

Drought, James (William) (November 4, 1931–June 2, 1983)
     Known as one of the early figures in the small press movement in the United States, Drought was born in Aurora, Illinois and, after service in the Korean War from 1952 to 1954, graduated from Knox College (Galesburg, Illinois, BA, 1956). He was an editor for several Illinois newspapers in the 1950s, but moved to New York City to work as a magazine editor. The rejection of his first novel, *The Secret* (Skylight Press, 1963), by twenty-six publishers inspired him and his wife to establish a publishing firm, intended initially to publish Drought's books. The press went on to become the first small press whose books were reviewed in mass media journals such as the *New York Times Book Review*.

Dubkin, Leonard (1904–1972)

Author of a nature column for the *Chicago Tribune*, Dubkin has been recognized for his early warnings on the importance of conserving natural resources.

Du Bois, Shirley Graham (November 11, 1896–March 27, 1977)

The daughter of African-American minister Reverend David A. Graham, Du Bois' second marriage was to W. E. B. Du Bois (1951). A graduate of Oberlin College (Oberlin, Ohio, AB, 1934; MA, 1935), Du Bois had an active career as a civil rights activist, composer, director of music, and playwright. In addition, she wrote several biographies about African-Americans for young adults.

(*Contemporary Authors Online*, Detroit: Gale, 2003, accessed 14 June 2009).

Duff, Paul James

No information available.

Du Jardin, Rosamund Neal (July 22, 1902–March 1963)

Although she was born in Fairland, Illinois, du Jardin (née Neal) grew up in Chicago and graduated from Morgan Park High School. She later moved with her husband Victor du Jardin to Glen Ellyn, Illinois where she lived most of her life. Du Jardin wrote magazine fiction for women's magazines and published several novels for adults and eighteen for young adults, on which her reputation is based.

Dunne, Finley Peter (July 10, 1867–April 24, 1936)

The creator of the nationally celebrated character Mr. Dooley, about whom songs were composed and a Broadway play staged, Dunne was born in Chicago's Irish-American Sixth Ward and began working as a newspaper office boy after graduating from high school. By the time he was twenty-one he was city editor of the *Chicago Times*. He began publishing Irish dialect pieces in 1892 and developed the character of Mr. Dooley, an Irish-American, Chicago saloonkeeper in 1893. The character achieved his widest popularity during the Spanish-American War; however, he remained an enduring figure in American popular culture. Dunne's earnings from the sales of his first two Mr. Dooley books (compilations of his columns), enabled him to take a leave from the *Chicago Journal* (he was then editor) and travel to England. He afterwards lived in New York City and was editorialist and editor for various widely-distributed magazines; he continued to write Mr. Dooley pieces until 1916.

(*Dictionary of Literary Biography*, vol. 11, s.v. "Dunne, Finlay Peter").

Durkin, James Aloysius

No information available.

Dybek, Stuart (April 10, 1942–?)

Native Chicagoan Dybek has published poetry and short stories and has had a long career as a professor of English. Since 1974 he has taught at Western Michigan University, Kalamazoo. Dybek is known for evoking Chicago immigrant neighborhoods like the one in which he spent his youth. He was educated at Loyola University (Chicago) where he received a bachelor's degree (1964) and a master's degree (1967). He received an MFA from the University of Iowa in 1973.

Eagle, John
    No information available.

Ebel, Camille Layer
    No information available.

Eberhart, Mignon Good (July 6, 1899–1996)
    Born and educated in Nebraska, Eberhart married Alanson C. Eberhart in 1923 and his career as a civil engineer proved influential in two ways. First, she traveled a great deal to keep her husband company on business trips and she wrote as a distraction. Second, many of her romantic, male protagonists are civil engineers. Although she authored several novels and a number of short stories, Eberhart is best known for her mysteries that provide all of the clues needed for the reader to uncover the solution. She wrote more than sixty books during her fifty-year career.
    (*Mystery and Suspense Writers: The Literature of Crime, Detection, and Espionage*, New York: Charles Scribner's Sons, 1998, s.v. "Eberhart, Mignon Good").

Eckert, Allan W. (January 30, 1931–?)
    Although Eckert was born in Buffalo, New York, he was raised in the Chicago area and went to school in the city. Eckert served in the U.S. Air Force from 1948 to 1952 and held a number of jobs as a laborer before starting work as a reporter for the *Dayton (Ohio) Journal-Herald* in 1957 while studying at the University of Dayton (Dayton, Ohio) and Ohio State University (Columbus, Ohio). By 1960 he was a freelance writer for magazines, eventually publishing in most of the country's major publications. Eckert is best known for works of historical fiction and natural history.
    (*Contemporary Authors Online*, Detroit: Gale, 20007, accessed 12 June 20009).

Eddy, Arthur Jerome (1859–1920)
    Chicago lawyer Eddy was born in Flint, Michigan. A member of the firm Wetten, Matthews and Pegler, he was known as an expert on corporate law and organized major firms such as American Linseed Oil Company, American Steel Foundry Corporation, and the National Turbine Company. An art connoisseur who appreciated and wrote about modern art, he championed the Cubists and other avant-garde painters of the early twentieth century.
    (*New York Times*, 22 July 1920, 10).

Edgley, Leslie (1912–2002)
    Crime novelist and screenwriter Edgley wrote under his own name and under the pseudonym Robert Bloomfield, and with his wife Mary Edgley under the shared pseudonym Brook Hastings.

Edwards, James G., *see* MacQueen, James William

Edwards, S. W., *see* Sublette, Walter

Ellis, Edward Sylvester [H. R. Gordon, pseud.] (April 11, 1840–June 20, 1916)
    The author of more than 450 books under numerous pseudonyms, Ellis wrote many books for boys set in the American West and has been credited with contributing significantly to the romantic myths attached to that region. Born in Geneva, Ohio, Ellis' family moved to New Jersey in 1846 and he resided there almost continuously for the rest of his life. A graduate of the State Nor-

mal School at Trenton, New Jersey, Ellis became a teacher. However, during his first year in that employment his book *Seth Jones* was published by Irwin P. Beadle and Company and overnight he became a well-known novelist (the book sold 60,000 copies in its first week of release). His works up until 1883 were of the paperbound, dime-novel genre. Afterwards, he published mostly clothbound work with the firms of Porter and Coates (Philadelphia) and Cassell and Company (London) and in the 1880s he also began writing school books. He had continued to teach in the public schools in the 1860s and 1870s and eventually became superintendent of schools for Trenton, New Jersey. The number and popularity of his novels earned him an honorary master of arts from Princeton College in 1887.
(*Dictionary of Literary Biography*, vol. 42, s.v., "Ellis, Edward Sylvester").

Ellison, Jerome (October 29, 1907–June 9, 1981)
    Born in Maywood, Illinois and a graduate of the University of Michigan (Ann Arbor, Mich., BA, 1930), Ellison had a long career as an editor and contributor to magazines, including *Life* and *Readers Digest*. He was editor-in-chief of *Liberty* magazine (New York) from 1942 to 1943 and managing director of *Collier's* (New York) from 1943 to 1944. Along with such prominent writers as Pearl S. Buck, John Steinbeck, and John Dos Passos, he was a founder and owner-contributor of Associated Magazine Contributors. During World War II he worked for the U.S. Office of War Information, and beginning in 1948 he started teaching journalism at the college level. He was the author of twelve books and many short stories.
(*Contemporary Authors Online*, New York: Thomson Gale, 2007, accessed 8 May 2009).

Emery, Anne McGuigan (September 1, 1907–?)
    Although Emery was born in Fargo, North Dakota, her family moved to Evanston, Illinois when she was nine, and she attended the public schools there and graduated from Northwestern University. Her father was a faculty member at the University of Illinois. She taught public school in Evanston and married John Douglas Emery in 1933, and they eventually had five children. She lived in Evanston almost continuously and her more than twenty-five books for young adults have usually been set in that city.
(*Contemporary Authors Online*, Detroit: Gale, 2008, accessed 8 March 2010).

Eng, Rita
    No information available.

Ernst, Paul (Frederick) [Ernest Jason Fredericks, pseud.]. (c. 1899–1902 – c.1983–1985)

Essipoff, Marie Armstrong (1892–?)
    After her marriage to Ben Hecht, which lasted from 1915–1925, ended, Essipoff, under the name Marie Armstrong Hecht, edited the *Chicagoan*, published in Chicago from June 1926–April 1935 a magazine modeled after the New Yorker. She also published several volumes of poetry in the 1920s and in the 1920s and 1930s created or adapted Broadway plays. Beginning in the 1950s, under her name of Essipoff from a later marriage, she authored books and pamphlets on cooking techniques.

Everett, Henry L.
    No information available.

Ewing, Annmarie (1892–1956)
    No information available.

Fair, Ronald L. (October 27, 1932–?)
    Fair, an African-American author, was born in Chicago and lived there up until 1969, except for a stint in the U.S. Navy from 1950 to 1953. He attended a business school in Chicago and was a court reporter from 1955 to 1966, during which time he published two novels. He taught at Columbia College in Chicago from 1967 to 1968 and subsequently taught one semester at Northwestern University. Since his appointment in 1969 as a visiting fellow at Wesleyan University in Connecticut, he has spent most of his time in Europe. He is the author of poetry, short stories, and six novels.
    (*Dictionary of Literary Biography*, vol. 33, s. v. "Fair, Ronald L.").

Fairbank, Janet Ayer (1878–December 28, 1951)
    Born in Chicago, Fairbank attended the University of Chicago and, in 1900, married Kellogg Fairbank, an attorney and leader in city politics, who was president of the Chicago Shipbuilding Company during World War I. Most of Fairbank's writings are set in Illinois, particularly Chicago. She was a very active clubwoman (with memberships in more than seven clubs) and involved in several philanthropic and civic organizations. A supporter of women's suffrage, she was active in politics, serving as a member of the executive committee of the Democratic National Committee in 1900 and a member of the Woman's Division of the Illinois Democratic National Committee from 1924 to 1928. Her sister was the novelist Margaret Ayer Barnes.
    (*New York Times*, 29 December 1951, 11).

Farrell, James Thomas (February 27, 1904–August 22, 1979)
    One of the best known Chicago writers in the literary tradition of "naturalism," Farrell was born in the city in an impoverished Irish-American family of fifteen (only six children survived to adulthood). His father was a teamster and his mother a domestic servant. Unable to keep him in their crowded household, his parents sent him to live with his maternal grandparents in a better area of Chicago on the southwest Side. He attended Catholic schools and studied at De Paul University and the University of Chicago. After marrying a fellow student, Dorothy Butler, in 1928, Farrell mostly lived in New York, with extended stays in Paris. Although he published more than fifty books before his death in New York in 1979, his reputation is based on the novels and short stories he published in the 1930s.
    (*Dictionary of Literary Biography*, vol. 86, s.v. "Farrell, James T(homas)").

Farson, James Scott Negley (May 14, 1890–December 13, 1960)
    A journalist, Farson was foreign correspondent for the *Chicago Daily News* from 1924–1935. He wrote a series of books about sailing his own yawl in Europe, Egypt, India, and Russia, as well as several novels.
    (*New York Times*, 26 December 1960, 35).

Fast, Howard (November 11, 1914–March 12, 2003)
    Known for historical fiction, Fast published his first novel when he was only eighteen years old, and during his career produced over eighty books and more than seven plays. Born in New York City, Fast was the grandson of Jewish immigrants from the Ukraine. His father was a low-paid skilled laborer employed alternately as an ironworker, cable gripper, and dress factory cutter.

Due to his family's economic situation, Fast dropped out of school and worked odd jobs, including as a page at the New York Public Library. After the publication of his first novel, he wrote full-time. During World War II, he served on the overseas staff of the Office of War Information and later became a war correspondent in the China-Burma-India theater in 1944–1945. Fast's political convictions often determined his choice of topics. His fame and popularity were at their height when he was thirty years old; shortly thereafter, in 1943, he converted to Communism and for the next thirteen years his writing was dominated by political views and doctrinaire style that many readers found objectionable. He was jailed by the House on Un-American Activities Committee as an uncooperative witness. He wrote a series of protest novels in the 1940s presenting the plight of African-Americans and later wrote biographies and historical fiction that presented the liberal and free-thinking aspects of the American tradition, as well as works that displayed aspects of his Jewish identity.
[*Dictionary of Literary Biography*, vol. 9, s.v. "Fast, (Melvin) Howard"].

Fearing, Blanche (1863–August 14, 1900)
    Best known for her poetry, Fearing was born in rural Iowa and was blinded in early childhood. In addition to her poetry, that was favorably reviewed by some of the most respected critics of her day (Oliver Wendell Holmes, Edmund Clarence Stedman, and John Greenleaf Whittier), and several novels, Fearing was notable for being a practicing lawyer. She lived most of her adult life in Chicago.
(*New York Times*, 15 August 1900, 7).

Ferber, Edna (August 15, 1885–April 17, 1968)
    The daughter of unsuccessful small-town merchant Jacob Charles Ferber, a Hungarian immigrant, Ferber spent most of her childhood and young adulthood in Appleton, Wisconsin after a number of moves. However, the Ferbers frequently visited relatives in Chicago. Unable to attend college due to family finances, Ferber held several jobs as a reporter before she began to sell short stories. She published her first novel in 1911 and for more than fifty years published novels, volumes of short stories, and plays that were well received by the public and rejected by critics for their low literary value. Ferber lived in Chicago for a few years after her father's death in 1909, but primarily resided in New York City after 1912.
(*New York Times*, 17 April 1968, 1).

Field, Eugene (September 2, 1850–November 4, 1895)
    Children's poet and newspaper columnist, Field was born in St. Louis, Missouri, the son of Roswell M. Field, a distinguished lawyer remembered for being legal counsel to Dred Scott. At the death of his mother, when Field was six, he was sent with his brother to live with relatives in Amherst, Massachusetts and attend private schools. Between 1868 and 1872 he studied at Williams College (Williamstown, Mass.), Knox College (Galesburg, Ill.) and the University of Missouri (Columbia). Although he never earned a degree he did distinguish himself with his satirical verse and oratory. After a European tour in 1872 and a marriage to the sister of his best friend in 1873, he began working as a reporter. His career took him to St. Joseph, Missouri and Denver before he moved to Chicago in 1883 where he worked for the *Chicago Morning News* and remained for the rest of his life, with the exception of extended travels in California and Europe. The column he developed, "Sharps and Flats," published six days a week, was nationally syndicated and the first of its kind, including verse as well as commentary, Field's work was admired for its humor and gentle satire, often directed at politicians. During his lifetime, Field published more

than thirty-five books, mostly volumes of children's verse that included poems that have entered into the national cultural heritage.
(*Dictionary of Literary Biography*, vol. 23, s.v. "Field, Eugene").

Field, Roswell Martin (September 1, 1851–January 10, 1900)
   A brother of Eugene Field who, like his sibling, had a career as a journalist and author, Field was born in St. Louis, Missouri and educated at Phillips Exeter Academy (Exeter, N.H.) and the University of Missouri (Columbia). Unlike his brother, Field was serious-minded and studied law. Once he inherited an income from his father in 1869, he worked for newspapers in Chicago, Kansas City, New York, San Francisco, and St. Louis. He ended his career writing for the *New York Post* where he had a column for fourteen years. He published several books, many of them sketches of Kansas and Missouri.
(*American Authors, 1600–1900: A Biographical Dictionary of American Literature*, New York: H. W. Wilson Company, 1938, s.v. "Field, Roswell Martin").

Finley, Martha (April 26, 1828–January 30, 1909)
   The author of more than one hundred books for children and a few novels for adults, Finley was born in Chillicothe, Ohio and grew up in Philadelphia and South Bend, Indiana. As an adult, she lived in Philadelphia and Elkton, Maryland. Her life was filled by her writing, including a long-running series of books featuring Elsie Dinsmore. Her work is known for a focus on the importance of the father/daughter relationship and concerns with morality and religion.
(*Dictionary of Literary Biography*, vol. 42, s.v., "Finley Martha").

Fisher, Vardis (March 31, 1895–July 9, 1968)
   Known for the harrowing honesty of his semi-autobiographical fiction and for his fiction and non-fiction about the American West, Fisher was the son of Mormon pioneers who settled first in Annis, Idaho (where he was born) and later on a remote ranch in the Antelope Hills of Idaho. Home-schooled, Fisher's mother moved with him to live in a primitive structure outside Rigby, Idaho so that he could attend high school. Fisher's studies at the University of Idaho were interrupted by military service near the end of World War I, but he finished his bachelor's degree there in 1920 and received his master's degree (1922) and doctorate (1925) from the University of Chicago. While living as a graduate student with his wife and two children, his spouse committed suicide. After a brief try at an academic career, Fisher moved back to Idaho, where he lived in a house he built himself and devoted himself to writing. He was the director of the Idaho Writers' Project of the Works Progress Administration, through which position he established a high standard for the rest of the country's publications by the example of his Idaho guide. Through his work, he also met his third wife, Opal Laurel Holmes, to whom he was married for twenty-eight years.
(*Dictionary of Literary Biography*, vol. 9, s.v. "Fisher, Vardis").

Flavin, Martin (November 2, 1883–December 27, 1967)
   A playwright, screenwriter, and Pulitzer Prize winning novelist, Flavin was born to a successful San Francisco merchant. The family relocated to Chicago while Flavin was still a child and he grew up in that city. Although he started selling short stories in 1905, he gave up writing for twelve years to work in a Chicago wallpaper company. He worked his way up from office boy to vice president. In 1918 he began writing plays part-time and had several Broadway productions (in one of which Bette Davis debuted), eventually retiring to Carmel, California to write full-time in

1926. After some frustration with Broadway, he turned to screenplays and also published his first novel in 1940. His book, *Journey in the Dark* (included here) won him the Pulitzer Prize and the $10,000 Harper Prize.
(*New York Times*, 28 December 1967, 32).

Flinn, John J. (1851–1929)
    No information available.

Flower, Elliott (1863–1920)
    No information available.

Foran, Martin Ambrose (November 11, 1844–June 28, 1921)
    Democratic politician Foran practiced law in Cleveland, Ohio and served three terms in Congress beginning in 1883. He was elected judge of the court of common pleas in 1910 and continued to serve until his death. Born in Choconut Township, Pennsylvania, he attended St. Joseph's College (Philadelphia, Pa.) for two years before fighting as a private in the Civil War.
(*U.S. Congress, Biographical Directory of the United States Congress, 1774 to the Present*, http://bioguide.congress.gov, accessed, 10 July 2009).

Forbes, DeLoris (Florine) Stanton (July 10, 1923–?)
    Mystery writer Forbes was born in Kansas City, Missouri and attended public schools there. She was the assistant editor of the *Wellesley Townsman* from 1958 to 1973 and moved to St. Martin, French West Indies in 1973. She is the author of more than forty books under five pseudonyms, though most commonly she publishes as Stanton Forbes and Tobias Wells.

Forbes, Murray M. (July 20, 1906–January 27, 1987)
    Forbes was a radio actor who portrayed Willie Fitz on the "Ma Perkins" show for twenty-seven years starting in 1933. He also acted on radio soap operas "Guiding Light" and "Today's Children," and such popular series and "Joe Palooka," and "Foxes of Flatbush." His mystery novel *Hollow Triumph* (included here) was a best seller and was adapted to film as *The Scar* (Eagle-Lion Films, 1948).
(*Contemporary Authors Online*, Detroit: Gale, 2002, accessed 29 February 2010).

Forbes, Stanton, *see* Forbes, DeLoris (Florine) Stanton

Forrest, Leon (January 3, 1937–?)
    A native of Chicago's South Side, Forrest attended Hyde Park High School from 1951 to 1955 at a time when there were very few African-American students. He went on to study at Wilson Junior College, Roosevelt University, and the University of Chicago, interrupting his higher education for military service in 1959. While writing for Chicago community weekly newspapers in the 1960s he began his first novel. From 1969 to 1973 he worked with the Black Muslim publication *Muhammed Speaks*. After the success of *There Is a Tree More Ancient Than Eden* (included here) Forrest was appointed associate professor of African-American Studies at Northwestern University where he continues to teach. The author of four novels, Forrest is known for exploring the African-American experience and developing an innovative narrative technique based in oral tradition.
(*Dictionary of Literary Biography*, vol. 33, s.v., "Forrest, Leon").

Fowler, Bertram B. [Jack Baynes, pseud.] (1893–?)
    No information available.

Fox, Fannie Ferber
    No information available.

Fox, Mary Virginia "Ginger" (November 17, 1919–?)
    Born in Richmond, Virginia, the daughter of merchant George Henry Foster, she married manufacturer Richard Earl Fox. A 1940 graduate of Northwestern University (Evanston, Illinois), Fox has written extensively for young adults, mostly works of non-fiction including a series of biographies of women.
    (*Contemporary Authors Online*, Detroit: Gale, 2005, accessed 10 July 2009).

Fraser, John Arthur [Hawkshaw, pseud.].
    No information available.

Fredericks, Ernest Jason, *see* Ernst, Paul Frederick

Freeman, Martin J. (1899–?)
    No information available.

French, Alice [Octave Thanet, pseud.] (March 19, 1850–January 9, 1934)
    The author of eighteen books and many short stories under the pen name Octave Thanet, French claimed to be more concerned with the money she earned from publishing, rather than achieving enduring artistic merit in her writing. Daughter of a prosperous Davenport, Iowa manufacturer, French's family was proud of their New England heritage and she was sent east to be educated, although she did not respond positively to the experience. After a brief European tour, she moved in with her friend Jane Allen Crawford, near Crawford's home in Arkansas and each of them began focusing on their writing while living as a couple. Her works fall into the local color movement; however, her feminist focus makes them distinctive.
    (*Contemporary Authors Online*, Detroit: Gale, 2003, accessed, 21 July 2009).

Friedman, I. K. (Isaac Kahn) (November 3, 1869–September 22, 1931)
    A native of Chicago, the son of a German immigrant, Friedman graduated with a bachelor of law degree from the University of Michigan (Ann Arbor, Mich.) in 1891 and pursued graduate study in political science at the University of Chicago. He began writing for newspapers and magazines in 1894 and published a volume of short stories in 1896. Friedman went on to publish three novels. As a special correspondent to the *Chicago Daily News* he wrote articles touching on economics and sociology and traveled to Japan and China for the newspaper in 1908.
    [*American Naturalistic and Realistic Novelists: A Biographical Dictionary*, Westport, Conn.: Greenwood, 2002, s.v. "Friedman, I. K. (Isaac Kahn)"].

Friend, Oscar J. [Owen Fox Jerome, pseud] (1897–1963)
    Pulp fiction writer Friend wrote in a number of genres including detective fiction, horror, science fiction, and Westerns.

Friermood, Elisabeth Hamilton (December 30, 1903–March 25, 1992)

Author of novels for young people, Friermood was born in Marion, Indiana, the daughter of the local fire chief. She was educated at Northwestern University (Evanston, Ill., 1923–1925) and the University of Wisconsin (Madison, 1934–1939) and worked as a children's librarian in public libraries in Marion, Indiana and Dayton, Ohio for seventeen years. She married her high school sweetheart, Dr. Harold T. Friermood, M.D., who was National Director for Health and Physical Education for the YMCA.

(*Contemporary Authors Online*, Detroit: Gale, 2001, accessed 24 July 2009).

Fuessle, Newton Augustus (1883–1924)

No information available.

Fuller, Henry Blake (January 9, 1857–July 28, 1929)

Native Chicagoan Fuller is known as one of the earliest American realist authors. The grandson of a successful New England judge who moved his family to Chicago in 1848 and made wise investments in railroads, Fuller's youth was comfortable. However, his father was not clever with money and Fuller worked in commercial establishments as a youth to save enough money for a year-long trip to Europe that commenced in 1879. Preferring the emphasis of European culture on artistic and intellectual achievement to Chicago's commercial values, Fuller returned to Europe as soon as he could and stayed in Boston when he got back to the United States. However, his father's death in 1885 forced him back to Chicago to manage the rental properties to which his father's mismanagement had reduced his grandfather's legacy. Fuller's first novel, *The Chevalier of Pensieri-Vani* (Boston: J. G. Cupples, 1890), that he was forced to self-publish, was soon acclaimed and republished in increasingly important editions. Set in Italy, the novel introduces a Chicago traveler to Italian culture to expose the shallowness of American values. Although he continued to travel, Fuller's primary residence remained Chicago for the rest of his life where he became friends in the 1890s with a large number of artists, including Hobart Chatfield-Taylor, Hamlin Garland, Bessie Potter, and Lorado Taft, all members of a circle that came to be called the Little Room for their Friday afternoon salons. The author of fifteen books that frequently laid bare what Fuller considered to be the false values of Chicago, he continues to be regarded as one of the most important portrayers of the city.

(*Dictionary of Literary Biography*, vol. 12, s.v., "Fuller, Henry Blake").

Gaines, Diana (July 28, 1912–February 8, 2002)

A native of Chicago, Gaines was working as an advertising copywriter there when she published her first novel in 1950. She was educated at Smith College (Northampton, Mass., 1929-1931) and the University of Chicago (Ph.B., 1933) and was the wife of a physician. Gaines published most of her work between 1950 and 1962.

(*Contemporary Authors Online*, Detroit: Gale 2002, accessed 3 June 2009).

Gale, Zona (August 26, 1874–December 27, 1938)

Known as one of several American Midwestern writers who addressed themes of the rapid urbanization of rural society, Gale was born in Portage, Wisconsin. She graduated from the University of Wisconsin (Madison) with a master's degree in 1899 and after working for newspapers in Milwaukee, she moved to New York City to work for the *New York Evening World*. After the success of her magazine fiction, she became a full-time freelance writer after little more than a year. She moved back to Portage in 1904 and continued to live there for the rest of her life, mar-

rying local banker William Llewellyn Breese in 1928. In addition to her writing, Gale is known for her commitment to women's suffrage and to the La Follette progressive movement in Wisconsin. She won the Pulitzer Prize in 1921 for her play *Miss Lulu Bett*.
(*Dictionary of Literary Biography*, vol. 78, s.v. "Gale, Zona").

Galloway, Paul [Mike Holiday, joint pseud. with Bob Greene]
    No information available.

Garfield, Brian (Wynne). (January 26, 1939–?)
    Born in New York City, Garfield, the son of a lawyer and architect, grew up in Arizona and was educated at the University of Arizona (Tucson, Ariz., BA, 1959; MA, 1963). Garfield is the author of more than seventy Westerns and mysteries published under his own name and several pseudonyms.
(*Contemporary Authors Online*, Detroit: Gale, 2001, accessed 13 January 2009).

Garland, Hamlin (September 14, 1860–March 4, 1940)
    Raised on farms in Wisconsin, Iowa, and South Dakota, Garland embraced the economic theory of Henry George and tried to improve the lot of farmers, frontier dwellers, and American Indians through more than fifty works of fiction and non-fiction. Although his idealistic portrayals were intended to evoke admiration and support for his subjects, his subjects themselves often resented his works.
(*Dictionary of Literary Biography*, vol. 186, s.v. "Garland, Hamlin").

Gatchell, Charles (1853–1910)
    A physician and medical school professor, Gatchell was born in Cincinnati, Ohio and graduated from Pulte Medical College (Cincinnati, Ohio) in 1874 (M.D.). He was a professor at the University of Michigan (Ann Arbor) from 1877–1880 and 1889–1893. He began teaching at the Hahneman Medical College (Chicago, Illinois) in 1902. In addition to publishing medical books, Gatchell published three novels.
(Hinsdale, Burke A. *History of the University of Michigan*, Ann Arbor: University of Michigan, 1906).

Gault, William Campbell (March 9, 1910–December 27, 1995)
    Author of a number of novels set in the world of Chicago professional football, Gault is best known for his detective fiction of the 1950s. Born in Milwaukee, Gault attended the University of Wisconsin (Madison) for one year and after serving in the U. S. Army in World War II moved to Southern California in 1945, where he lived for the rest of his life. In the course of his career he published more than three hundred short stories and over fifty books.
(*Dictionary of Literary Biography*, vol. 226, s.v. "Gault, William Campbell").

Gerson, Noel Bertram [Leon Phillips, pseud.] (November 6, 1914–November 20, 1988)
    The author of more than three hundred books, Bertram was a Chicago native, the son of newspaperman Samuel Philip Gerson, who would later manage the Shubert theaters in Chicago. A graduate of the University of Chicago (BA, 1934; MA, 1935), he worked as a reporter and in World War II was a captain in military intelligence. He returned to civilian life to work as a script writer for radio and television, publishing his first novel in 1950. Many of Gerson's novels were

fictionalized biographies or works of historical fiction. He lived most of his adult life in New York City and Connecticut.
(*American National Biography*, s.v. "Gerson, Noel Bertram").

Gerstenberg, Alice (1885–1972)

Born in Chicago to wealthy parents (Erich and Julia Weischendorff Gerstenberg), Gerstenberg graduated from Bryn Mawr College (Bryn Mawr, Pa.) in 1907, and began writing plays. From 1908–1943 she was active in the theater, writing more than forty plays. Considered a pioneer in the "little theater" movement, she was one of the original members of the Chicago Little Theatre (founded by Maurice Brown in 1912). She was founder, producer, and president of the Playwrights' Theatre of Chicago and active with the group from 1922–1945. In the 1950s she ran the Alice Gerstenberg Experimental Theatre Workshop and in the 1960s the Alice Gerstenberg Theatre. Her play *Overtones* is still performed. Gerstenberg's papers are at The Newberry Library in Chicago.

Gillian, Michael

No information available.

Givins, Robert Cartwright, [Snivig Trebor, pseud.]

No information available.

Gizycka, Eleanor, *see* Patterson, Eleanor Medill

Glasmon, Kubec (1889–March 13, 1938)

One of the most successful and well-known screenwriters from the early days of the talking film industry, Glasmon was born in Rocioz, Poland and emigrated with his family to the United States as a young adult. He studied dentistry and pharmacy, establishing a business in Hollywood, California. He began writing crime stories with John Bright, a younger man Glasmon had hired to operate his soda fountain. The two had their first major success with a script that became *The Public Enemy* (Warner Brothers) starring James Cagney. The film earned them a Best Original Story Oscar nomination. Bright and Glasmon were writing partners until 1932, and helped found the Screenwriters Guild. During Glasmon's career he worked with Warner Bros., Paramount, Columbia, Fox, Universal, and MGM.
(*New York Times* Online, http://movies.nytimes.com/person/91711/Kubec-Glasmon/biography, accessed 15 August 2009).

Glaspell, Susan (July 1, 1876–July 27, 1948)

Born in Davenport, Iowa and a graduate of Drake University in Des Moines, soon after graduation Glaspell began working for Des Moines newspapers, but then turned her attention to writing short stories, instead. She married writer George Cram Cook in 1913 and moved with him to Provincetown, Massachusetts, where he helped found the Provincetown Players in 1915. Much of Glaspell's writing is concerned with the Midwest and a common theme is the difficulty a female character has in ameliorating the dissonance between her modern outlook and the conventions of her home community.
(*World Authors 1900–1950*, New York: H. W. Wilson, 1996, s.v. "Glaspell, Susan").

Glazer, Mitchell [Miami Mitch, pseud.] (1953–?)
An author of screenplays and a film producer, Glazer was born in Key Biscayne, Florida and raised in Miami. He attended Clark University (Worcester, Mass.) and graduated from New York University. During the late 1970s he was a reporter for *Crawdaddy!* music magazine before entering the film industry.

Gleeson, William (1843–?)
No information available.

Godley, Robert [Franklin James, pseud.] (1908–1957)
No information available.

Goetzinger, Clara Palmer
No information available.

Gooch, Fani Pusey
No information available.

Gordon, Gordon (March 12, 1906–March 14, 2002)
Gordon co-authored many crime fiction novels, several of which have been adapted for film, with his first wife, Mildred (Nixon) Gordon, and second wife, Mary (Dorr) Gordon. He was born in Anderson, Indiana and educated at the University of Arizona (Tucson) where he met his first wife. After working as editor of the *Tucson Citizen* newspaper, Gordon was a publicist for 20th Century Fox (1935–1942), and during World War II was an FBI counter-intelligence agent.

Gordon, H. R., *see* Ellis, Edward Sylvester

Gordon, Mildred (July 24, 1912–February 3, 1979)
Born Mildred Nixon in Eureka, Kansas, Gordon co-authored many crime fiction novels with her husband Gordon Gordon. The Gordons met while both were students at the University of Arizona (Tucson). A journalist and writer who briefly edited a newspaper and magazine in the 1930s, Gordon was a freelance magazine writer from 1938–1942 and wrote novels full time with her husband from 1950 until her death in 1972. Although their novels often had exotic locales, to which the Gordons traveled to gather information, their most successful books were quite domestic and focused on a household cat. One of these books was made into the motion picture, *That Darn Cat* (Walt Disney Productions, 1963).
(*Contemporary Authors Online*, Gale, 2002, accessed 20 January 2009).

Gordons, The, *see* Gordon, Gordon and Gordon, Mildred

Gosden, Freeman F. (May 5, 1899–December 10, 1982)
Co-creator of the radio comedy *Amos 'n' Andy* with Charles J. Correll, Gosden was born in Richmond, Virginia. His interest in radio was inspired by his World War I experience as a wireless operator in the U.S. Navy. The first shows he did with Correll were in Chicago. In 1925 they aired on WEBH (Chicago) in *Correll and Gosden, the Life of the Party*, a variety show. They

initiated the situation comedy, *Sam & Henry* on WGN (Chicago) in 1926. The *Amos 'n' Andy* show began airing in 1928 and continued until 1960.
(*New York Times*, 11 December 1982, 29).

Graham, Marie
 Daughter of a Chicago judge, Marie married John Snitzler. A staff member of the *Chicago Evening Post*, Graham wrote poetry, as well as light fiction, and was an avid clubwoman; belonging to a number of ancestry-based organizations.

Granger, Bill (June 1, 1941–?)
 A Chicago native, Granger, the son of carpenter William Cecil, was educated at DePaul University in Chicago (1959–1963) and served in the U.S. Army from 1963–1965. The author of more than twenty books of fiction and non-fiction, Granger also had a long career as a journalist, working as a reporter and columnist for the *Chicago Tribune* and *Chicago Sun-Times*. Granger is best known for mystery and espionage novels, particularly those written as part of the "November Man" series that focus on a disillusioned international spy who is unable to leave the employ of the U.S. government.
(*Twentieth-Century Crime and Mystery Writers*, 3rd ed., New York: St. James Press, 1991, s.v. "Granger, Bill").

Granville, Austyn
 No information available.

Greeley, Andrew M. (Andrew Moran) (1928–?)
 Born in Oak Park, Illinois, Greeley was ordained as a priest in the Roman Catholic Church in 1954 and earned a doctorate in sociology from the University of Chicago in 1962, while involved in parish work. A common theme of his writing is how out of touch the Catholic hierarchy is with the true needs of church members and he has used his many popular novels to share his views on the church and morality. Most of his works are set in the Chicago metropolitan area.
(*Contemporary Popular Writers*, Detroit: St. James Press, 1997, s.v. "Greeley, Andrew M.").

Greene, "Bob" Robert Bernard, Jr. [Mike Holiday, joint pseud. with Paul Galloway] (March 10, 1947–?)
 Widely syndicated columnist for the *Chicago Tribune*, Greene was born in Columbus, Ohio. He received his journalism degree in 1969 from Northwestern University and began working for the *Chicago Sun-Times* and within two years had his own column. He began writing books, mostly collections of articles, at around the same time.
(*Dictionary of Literary Biography*, vol. 185, s.v. Greene, Robert Bernard, Jr.").

Greenlee, Sam (July 13, 1930–?)
 A native of Chicago, Greenlee was educated at the University of Wisconsin (Madison, BS, 1952) and did graduate coursework at the University of Chicago (1954–1957). After service in the U.S. Army (1952–1954), he worked as a Foreign Service officer for the United States Information Service (1957–1969). The novel for which he is included here, *The Spook Who Sat by the Door*, was a co-winner of the *London Sunday Times* book of the year award in 1969.
(*Contemporary Authors Online*, Detroit: Gale, 2001, accessed 3 November 2009).

Grimm, George (1859–1945)
    No information available.

Gruber, Frank [Stephen Acre, John Vedder, pseuds.] (February 2, 1904–December 9, 1969)
    The author of more than fifty-eight mystery novels and westerns, Gruber also wrote motion picture and television scripts and was the creator of popular television series, such as *The Texan*. His most popular character from his mystery novels was Johnny Fletcher whose financial scrapes were often considered as entertaining as the mysteries he was trying to solve. Born in Elmer, Minnesota, he had a high school education, and after various jobs freelance writing and editing trade journals, he was able to become a full-time writer in 1934.
(*Contemporary Authors Online*, Detroit: Gale, 2003, accessed 3 November 2009).

Guest, Judith (Judith Ann) (1936–?)
    Born in Detroit, Michigan and educated at the University of Michigan (Ann Arbor, BA, 1958), Guest sent her first novel, *Ordinary People*, as an unsolicited manuscript to Viking Press in 1975. The work was the first unsolicited manuscript the publisher accepted in twenty-six years and it became a best seller that was the selection of four book clubs and garnered a large sum for paperback rights. Adapted as a screenplay, the movie *Ordinary People* was released by Paramount in 1980, directed by Robert Redford and starring Mary Tyler Moore and Donald Sutherland. Guest has continued to publish books that explore modern family life.
(*Contemporary Authors Online*, Detroit: Gale, 2005, accessed 3 March 2010).

Gunther, John (August 30, 1901–May 29, 1970)
    Known for his war journalism and travel writing, Gunther was born in Chicago and grew up there, graduating from the University of Chicago in 1922. He began working for the *Chicago Daily News* in 1922 and later was a foreign correspondent for the newspaper (1924–1936). Subsequently, he held similar positions with the North American Newspaper Alliance and the National Broadcasting Company, for whom he was a World War II war correspondent. He was later a European correspondent for *Look* and a special writer for the *New York Herald Tribune*. After 1960, he worked as an author, lecturer, and network radio commentator. Although he continued to write and publish until the end of his life, a book published in 1949 about the death of his seventeen-year-old son, *Death Be Not Proud* (Harper-Collins) remains his most read work.
(*Contemporary Authors Online*, 2000; accessed 11 March 2008).

Haas, Joseph L. (1929–1971)
    No information available.

Hailey, Arthur (April 5, 1920–November 24, 2004)
    Canadian writer Hailey is known for creating meticulously researched suspense novels that sold millions of copies and were usually adapted for television or film. Born in Luton, England, Hailey enlisted in the Royal Air Force during World War II and began publishing short fiction during his military service. He immigrated to Canada after the war, settling in Toronto where he worked in editorial positions for a trade publication until he sold a screenplay to Canadian Broadcasting Corp., which led to jobs writing for television networks. After 1959 he began writing novels full-time.
(*New York Times*, 26 November 2004, C6).

Hale, Arlene (June 16, 1924–1982)

A prolific author of romance and mystery novels for young adults under her own name and five pseudonyms, Hale was born in New London, Iowa and lived her whole life there, although she also traveled widely. From 1941 until 1954, when she became a full-time freelance writer, Hale worked in various clerical positions in Burlington, Iowa.
(*Contemporary Authors Online*, Detroit: Gale, 2001, accessed 3 November 2009).

Hale, Edward Everett (April 3, 1822–June 10, 1909)

The author of hundreds of literary works, including biographies, essays, novels, sermons, and travel books, Hale was a scion of one of Boston's most prominent families, a graduate of Harvard University (AB, 1839; AM, 1842; STD, 1879) and an ordained Unitarian minister.
(*Dictionary of Literary Biography*, vol. 74, s.v. "Hale, Edward Everett").

Hale, Helen

No information available.

Hall, Grace Darling (1905–?)

No information available.

Halper, Albert (August 3, 1904–January 19, 1984)

Many of Chicago native Halper's works are set in the city, although he lived in New York City after 1928. The son of Lithuanian-Jewish immigrants, his first job was in his father's West Side grocery store. He later worked in a clothing store, a mail-order house, a foundry, and in Chicago's main post office. In 1924 and 1925 he took courses in Northwestern University's evening program. His Chicago novels capture working-class life and its challenges, and several of his mid-career novels are works of social protest, although they advocate no particular reform or political solution.
(*Dictionary of Literary Biography*, vol. 9, s.v., "Halper, Albert").

Ham, Roswell, Jr. (1919–?)

Ham's father was a scholar of Elizabethan drama and the president of Mount Holyoke College for twenty years, commencing in 1937. Ham was educated at Hotchkiss School and Yale University and served during World War II in the U.S. Air Force. In addition to three novels, Ham wrote for television.
(*New York Times*, April 5, 1958, 23).

Hansen, Harry (December 26, 1884–January 2, 1977)

Hansen was born in Davenport, Iowa, and after graduating from high school worked for the *Davenport Republican* before attending the University of Chicago, from which he graduated in 1909. After working for several university publications, he became a reporter for the *Chicago Daily News*, for which he was a World War I war correspondent. When he returned to Chicago in 1919, he worked as the newspaper's literary editor, a position he held until 1926, covering one of Chicago's great literary periods. He later held editorial positions in New York City with *Harper's*, *Redbook*, the *New York World-Telegram*, *World Almanac*, and *Hastings House Publishers*.
(*World Authors, 1900–1950*, New York: H. W. Wilson, 1996, s.v. "Hansen, Harry").

Hanson, Harvey (August 25, 1941–?)
    A Chicago native, Hanson's father was a laborer and his mother a dietician. He worked in Chicago at the post office, Bee Bindery, and several banks between 1962 and 1970, before moving to New York City in 1970 to become a shoe designer. He later worked as a photographer's representative in Manhattan.
(*Contemporary Authors Online*, Detroit: Gale, 2001, accessed 11 March 2009).

Hapgood, Hutchins (May 21, 1869–November 18, 1944)
    Although he lived most of his life on the East Coast, Hapgood was born in Chicago and grew up there. He was educated at Harvard University, from which he received his bachelor's and master's degrees. After conducting post-graduate studies in German universities, he taught at Harvard and the University of Chicago, before joining the staff of the *New York Commercial Advertiser* in 1897. He married fellow staff member and novelist Neith Boyce in 1899. He went on to write for a number of New York newspapers and magazines and was known for human interest stories that portrayed those at the margins of society, like new immigrants and the poor. He socialized with Bernard Berenson, Clarence Darrow, Emma Goldman, Ernest Hemingway, and Gertrude Stein, living part of the year in Provincetown, Massachusetts where he and his wife were active with the Provincetown Players.
(*World Authors, 1900–1950*, New York: H. W. Wilson, 1996, s.v. "Hapgood, Hutchins").

Harding, Kenneth [pseud.], *see* Little, Paul H. (Paul Hugo)

Harris, Frank (February 14, 1856–August 26, 1931)
    Born in Galway, Ireland and educated in England and Wales, Harris ran away from school at fifteen and traveled to the United States in steerage. He worked in New York City, Chicago, and Denver in 1871 and 1872 before joining his two older brothers in Lawrence, Kansas where he became a lawyer in 1875. He studied at the Sorbonne in Paris in 1876 and after 1878 studied literature, philosophy, and philology in German universities. He was appointed editor of the *Fortnightly Review* in 1886 and after his dismissal in 1894 purchased the *Saturday Review* with money from his wealthy wife, transforming the publication into a noted literary journal. After an extended period of research in New York City and Chicago, he published his first novel, *The Bomb*, in 1909 (included here). In 1916, he purchased *Pearson's Magazine*, which he owned until 1922 when he moved to Nice with his Irish lover, a woman twenty years his junior. He published his four-volume *Life and Loves* between 1922 and 1927.
(*Dictionary of Literary Biography*, vol. 197, s.v., "Harris, Frank").

Harris, Larry M., *see* Janifer, Laurence M. (Laurence Mark)

Harrison, William (October 29, 1933–?)
    Best known for novels set in Africa, Harrison was born in Texas and attended Texas Christian University (Fort Worth, Tex.). He later studied at Vanderbilt University (Nashville, Tenn.) and the University of Iowa (Iowa City). He began teaching at the University of Arkansas (Fayetteville, Ark.) in 1964 and subsequently co-founded the creative writing program there.
(*World Authors, 1995–2000*, New York: H. W. Wilson, 2000, s.v. "Harrison, William").

Hart, Frank
    No information available.

Hart, John, *see* Potter, Jack

Hawkins, Odie (July 6, 1937–?)
   Born in Chicago, Hawkins attended Wilson Junior College (Chicago, Ill.) from 1956–1957 and then worked for the U.S. Postal Service in Chicago as a mail clerk, starting in 1958, before serving for two years in the U.S. Army (1962–1964). He moved to Los Angeles in 1966 and has lived in California ever since. His novels reflect his African-American experience. In addition to writing he has taught in Watts Writers' Workshops and written television scripts, especially for the *Sanford and Sons* television series.
   (*Contemporary Authors Online*, Detroit: Gale, 2001, accessed 11 March 2009).

Hawkshaw, *see* Fraser, John Arthur

Hawthorne, Julian (June 22, 1846–July 21, 1934)
   The son of novelist Nathaniel Hawthorne, Julian was born in Peabody, Massachusetts, but lived abroad with his family during much of his childhood. He attended Harvard College (1863–1865) and then studied engineering at the Lawrence (Mass.) Scientific School and in Dresden, Germany. After working several years in the New York City Department of Docks he lost his job. Hawthorne began writing to support his family and published short stories and several novels a year, mostly romances and tales of the supernatural. By the turn of the century he was mostly writing syndicated newspaper articles. After his incarceration in Atlanta for mail fraud involving a mining prospectus, he published a book about his prison experiences and then lived quietly from 1914 onwards in California, writing newspaper articles and editing the collected works of his father.
   (*World Authors, 1900–1950*, New York: H. W. Wilson, 1996, s.v. "Hawthorne, Julian").

Hayes, Laura
   No information available.

Healey, Mary, *see* Bigot, Marie Healey

Hecht, Ben (February 28, 1894–April 18, 1964)
   Known as one of the major figures in the Chicago Renaissance, Hecht was born on New York City's Lower East Side, spent his youth in Racine, Wisconsin, and did not move to Chicago until he was a young man. He was hired by the *Chicago Journal* in 1910 and later worked for the *Chicago Daily News*. He published his first novel, *Erik Dorn*, in 1921 (included here) and three more by the end of 1924, when he moved to New York City to become a playwright. After his Broadway success with *The Front Page* (co-authored with Charles MacArthur), Hecht went on to a career as a highly paid screenwriter, producing scripts for more than seventy movies.
   (*Dictionary of Literary Biography*, vol. 9, s.v. "Hecht, Ben").

Heed, Rufus
   No information available.

Heeler, Ward [pseud.]
   No information available.

Herber, William
    No information available.

Herbst, Josephine (1897–1969)
    A novelist who addressed the changing social issues of her day, Herbst was most active in the 1920s and 1930s. She was born in Sioux City, Iowa and lived in Weimar Germany and Paris in the 1920s, befriending Nathan Asch, Ernest Hemingway, and John Herrmann, whom she married in 1926. Several of her novels deal with the plight of rural people in an urbanizing America, and in a trilogy of novels covering the period from the Civil War through the 1930s she traces the experiences of a single family defeated by capitalism.
    (*Dictionary of Literary Biography*, vol. 9, s.v. "Herbst, Josephine (Frey)").

Herrick, Robert (April 26, 1868–December 23, 1938)
    Author of twenty-five novels and numerous short stories, Herrick was born in Cambridge, Massachusetts into a prominent New England family and he graduated from Harvard College. In 1893, after teaching for several years at the Massachusetts Institute of Technology, he was hired, along with his friend Robert Morss Lovett, to create a composition and rhetoric program at the University of Chicago. In 1914 he was a European correspondent for the *Chicago Tribune* and, after publishing a series of essays expressing his disenchantment with contemporary America, resigned his academic position in 1923 to write polemical novels. He was appointed government secretary of the Virgin Islands in 1935 and lived there for the few remaining years of his life.
    (*Dictionary of Literary Biography*, vol. 78, s.v. "Herrick, Robert").

Herter, Lori
    No information available.

Hill, Agnes Leonard (Scanland) (1842–1917)
    Born in Louisville, Kentucky, the daughter of Dr. Oliver Langdon and Agnes Leonard Langdon, Hill wrote for newspapers and published poetry and evangelical writings. She was the assistant pastor of St. Paul's Universalist Church in Chicago (1896–1905). Beginning in 1905, she served as the pastor of the Congregational Church in Wollaston, England. In the 1880s she lived in Denver, Colorado and edited the *Chaffee County (Buena Vista, Colo.) Times*. She married Leonard Hill of Chicago soon after the 1871 fire and wrote for the *Chicago Times*, supporting herself through her writings after the death of her husband.
    (*Herringshaw's American Blue-Book of Biography*, New York: American Publishers' Association, 1914, "Hill, Mrs. Agnes Leonard").

Hinrichsen, William H. (1850–1907)
    No information available.

Hix, J. Emile
    No information available.

Hjerstedt, Gunard [Day Keene, pseud.] (c.1904–1969)
    A prolific author of radio scripts, pulp fiction, and paperback originals, Hjerstedt was born on Chicago's South Side and acted in repertory theater in the 1920s. A principal writer for the *Little*

Orphan Annie radio show in the 1930s, Hjerstedt began writing for pulp magazines in the 1940s and went on to publish several works of book-length fiction each year in the 1950s and 1960s.

Holley, Marietta (1836–c.1926)

Author of dialect sketches and creator of an immensely popular character, Samantha, Holley was a humorist who consistently used her writing to attack the liquor trade and advocate for the rights of women. Born on a farm in Jefferson County, New York, with the exception of trips to New York City, she lived her whole life in or near the house where she was born. A retiring person, she consistently refused even the most attractively paid offers to speak in public or travel. Although her books are set all over the United States and Europe, they are the result of her careful research, rather than firsthand knowledge. Samantha and her acquaintances, which make up the characters of Holley's books, live in the fictional Jonesville. First introduced in a book published in 1873, they appeared in her fiction through 1914.
(*Dictionary of Literary Biography*, vol. 11, s.v. "Holley, Marietta").

Holmes, Mrs. M. E.

No information available.

Holt, Alfred Hubbard (1897–?)

Holt, the grandson of pioneer and early Chicago businessman Gurdon S. Hubbard (1802–1886) was an etymologist who published books on the origins of American words and usages, as well as American place-names.

Holt, Isabella (September 2, 1892–March 12, 1962)

Holt was the author of children's books and nine novels for adults.
(*New York Times*, 13 March 1962, 32).

Homewood, Charles Harry (1914–May 18, 1984)

A World War II veteran, Homewood was a journalist and broadcaster as well as the author of seven novels. His career as journalist lasted from 1957 to 1973 and included the position of Midwest bureau chief for *Newsweek* and editorialist for the *Chicago Sun-Times*. He was also the moderator of *Fact of the Matter*, a discussion program on WTTW-TV that was syndicated to thirty-two Public Broadcasting Service stations. He wrote novels after retiring from journalism in 1973.
(*Chicago Tribune*, 22 May 1984).

Homewood, Harry, *see* Homewood, Charles Harry

Horan, Kenneth (1890–?)

No information available.

Horton, George (October 11, 1859–June 5, 1942)

Born in Fairville, New York and educated at the University of Michigan (Ann Arbor, BA, 1878) and the George Washington University (Washington, D.C., LittD, 1903), Horton was a classicist, diplomat, and journalist. His skills as a student of Greek led to his appointment as consul in Athens (1893–1898). He was the literary editor of several Chicago newspapers (the *Chicago Times-Herald*, 1899–1901 and the *Chicago American*, 1901–1903). He returned to Athens in 1906 as consul general and was later consul general to Salonika and Smyrna. During World War I he

was involved in relief work and retired from the United States consular service in 1924 after his last assignment to Budapest. In addition to his other writings, Horton's poetry was critically acclaimed.
(*New York Times*, 10 June 1942, 21).

Hough, Emerson (June 28, 1857–April 30, 1923)
    Hough grew up on the Iowa frontier and graduated from the University of Iowa (Iowa City). Although he practiced law briefly (1881–1883) in White Oaks, New Mexico, he began working as a journalist in Iowa and Ohio, before moving to Chicago to become the manger of a local office of *Field and Stream*, for which he wrote articles informed by his outdoor experiences in the United States and Canada. He also began publishing Western fiction full of romance and adventure. His articles on the wildlife of Yellowstone were considered an important impetus in congressional legislation to protect the park's bison. He wrote several non-fiction books about the West, but his most popular works were stereotypical Western novels. In addition, he penned adventure novels for young adults, and works of historical fiction.
(*World Authors 1900–1950*, New York: H. W. Wilson, s.v. "Hough, Emerson").

Howard, Fred Steven (1910–?)
    No information available.

Howland, Bette (January 28, 1937–?)
    A Chicago native and graduate of the University of Chicago (BA, 1955), Howland is known for short stories that explore social settings she has experienced. Her first published book was a novel that presented life in a psychiatric ward, a work that grew out of her institutionalization after an attempted suicide.
(*Contemporary Authors Online*, Detroit: Gale, 2002, accessed 13 March 2009).

Hudson, Jay William (March 12, 1874–May 11, 1958)
    A son of an affluent Cleveland, Ohio couple, Hudson attended Hiram (Ohio) College and Oberlin (Ohio) College before earning his bachelor's and master's degrees at the University of California. He went on to complete another masters at Harvard College and a doctorate in philosophy there in 1908. He accepted a teaching position at the University of Missouri in 1908 and remained on the faculty for the rest of his life, serving as John Hiram Lathrop chair from 1930 to 1944 and becoming an emeritus professor in 1944. In 1922, he published his first novel, set in France. The novel's sequel was a best seller. He wrote a total of five works of fiction and published an additional five books of non-fiction, mostly on philosophy.
(*World Authors 1900–1950*, New York: H. W. Wilson, 1996, s.v. "Hudson, Jay William").

Hufford, Susan (December 15, 1940–?)
    Although she was born in Cincinnati, Hufford earned her bachelor's degree at DePauw (Ind.) University in 1960. She went on to earn a master's degree from Temple (Pa.) University the following year. In addition to her writing, Hufford is a professional actress and singer who has appeared in Broadway productions (*Fiddler on the Roof* and *Billy*). Most of her books are gothic romances.
(*Contemporary Authors Online*, Detroit: Gale, 2001, accessed 3 March 2009).

Hughes, Langston (February 1, 1902–1967)

One of the most accomplished African-American writers the United States has produced, Hughes was born in Joplin, Missouri. His parents separated while he was an infant and he was raised by his mother and maternal grandmother, mostly in Lawrence, Kansas. Hughes graduated from Central High School in Cleveland, Ohio in 1920 and traveled in the South and Mexico before enrolling at Columbia University in 1921. He spent much of his time in New York City over the next two years exploring Harlem. Restless for travel, he worked on freighters in 1923 and spent time in Europe before returning to the United States in 1924. He studied at Lincoln (Pa.) University (1926–1929) and subsequently became a major figure in American cultural life, producing poetry, plays, novels, short stories, and autobiographical works.
(*Dictionary of Literary Biography*, vol. 86, 1989, s.v. "Hughes, Langston").

Hunt, Barbara, *see* Watters, Barbara (Hunt)

Hutchens, Paul (April 7, 1902–1977)

A Baptist minister, Hutchens mostly wrote inspirational books published by Eerdmans, and books for young people that taught Christian virtues. He created a series, featuring the "Sugar Creek Gang," mostly set in a small town in Indiana, which resembled Thorntown, Indiana where he had grown up. The boys in the gang, that includes several sets of brothers and their friends, are all pre-adolescent, except for Big Jim. In addition to the thirty-six books he wrote for this series, Hutchens wrote several other books for children and twenty-one books for adults.
(*Contemporary Authors Online*, 2001, Detroit: Gale, accessed 13 March 2009),

Hutcheson, Frank
No information available.

Jackson, Charles Tenney (October 15, 1874–?)
No information available.

Jackson, Margaret Weymouth (February 11, 1895–April 5, 1974)

Jackson, who published more than three hundred stories in magazines such as *Ladies Home Journal*, *McCall's*, and *Saturday Evening Post*, began contributing to *Farm Life* when she was twenty years old. She was eventually employed as woman's editor and assistant editor of *Farm Life* and, later, as associate editor of *Better Farming*. Jackson won the O. Henry Prize twice and was a lecturer for many years at Indiana University. She was born in Eureka Springs, Arkansas.
(*Contemporary Authors Online*, Detroit: Gale, 1998, accessed 12 March 2009).

Jakes, John (March 31, 1932–?)

Although he was born in Chicago, Jakes moved frequently during his childhood since his father was an executive with the Railway Express agency. He sent stories to pulp magazines when he was still a child, but started writing in earnest after enrolling in the creative writing program at DePauw (Ind.) University. He went on to earn a master's degree in American literature from Ohio State University and began a doctoral program at that school, but left academia for the more lucrative business of advertising. His first job was in Chicago, where he lived from 1954 to 1961. Jakes continued to work in advertising until 1971, when he began writing full-time. Known for mass-market, historical fiction, he has produced works in many genres, including Westerns,

science fiction, and books for children. His two family sagas have found tens of millions of readers and been made into television mini-series.
(*Dictionary of Literary Biography*, vol. 278, s.v. "Jakes, John").

James, Alice
    No information available.

James, Franklin [pseud.], *see* Godley, Robert

Janifer, Laurence M. (Laurence Mark). [Larry M. Harris, pseud.]. (March 17, 1933–July 10, 2002)
    In addition to being a prolific author of works of science fiction, Janifer was an entertainer, both as a musician from 1950–1959 and as a comedian from 1957–1970. He was born in Brooklyn, and attended The City College of the City University of New York. Janifer published more than thirty-five books under several pseudonyms.
(*Contemporary Authors Online*, Detroit: Gale, 2002, accessed 14 March 2009).

Jauchius, Dean
    No information available.

Jaynes, Clare, *see* Mayer, Jane Rothschild and Spiegel, Clara

Jelley, Symmes M. [pseud.], *see* Mooney, James

Jerome, Owen Fox [pseud.], *see* Friend, Oscar J.

Johnson, Charles Richard (1948–?)
    Born in Evanston, Illinois, Johnson was educated at Southern Illinois University (BA, 1971; MA, 1973) and worked as a cartoonist and reporter at the *Chicago Tribune* and *St. Louis Proud*, before becoming a teacher and full-time writer. He has been a faculty member at the University of Washington since 1976 and has held the Pollock Professor for Excellence in English Chair since 1982. Johnson won the National Book Award in 1990 and was named a MacArthur Foundation Fellow in 1998.
(*Dictionary of Literary Biography*, vol. 33, s.v. "Johnson, Charles Richard").

Johnson, Curtis Lee (May 26, 1928–?)
    Born in Minneapolis, Minnesota, Johnson was educated at the University of Iowa (BA, 1951; MA, 1952). He worked as an editor from 1954 onwards for presses located in Chicago, where he also lived. Some of the publishers for which he worked were: Aldine; Britannica Schools; Davis; Scott; Foresman; and St. Clair Press. In addition to publishing five works of fiction, he has edited many volumes, and published more than two hundred articles, columns, reviews, and short stories in various periodicals.
(*Contemporary Authors Online*, Detroit: Gale, 2007, accessed 14 March 2009).

Johnston, William [Susan Claudia, pseud.] (January 11, 1924–?)
    The author of paperback original fiction and novelizations of screenplays and television series, Johnston was born in Lincoln, Illinois, and served in the U.S. Navy Air Corps during World

War II. After working for several years as a radio news reporter in Joliet, Illinois (1947–1950), and as a press agent for ten years at a public relations agency (Tex McCrary Public Relations Agency, 1950–60), Johnston began working full-time as a freelance writer in 1960.
(*Contemporary Authors Online*, Detroit: Gale, 2002, accessed 24 February 2009).

Jones, Ira L.
No information available.

Jones, Jack (June 14, 1924–?)
A journalist, Jones was born in El Paso, Texas and educated at the University of Southern California (BA, 1949). He has worked as a reporter with the *Los Angeles (Calif.) Daily News* (1949–1954); *Los Angeles (Calif.) Times* (1954–1978) and the San Diego edition of that newspaper since 1978. Jones is the author of three novels and more than fifteen short stories for men's magazines.
(*Contemporary Authors Online*, Detroit: Gale, 2008, accessed 5 May 2009).

Judson, Clara Ingram (May 4, 1879–May 24, 1960)
The author of more than seventy-nine books for children, Judson began her writing career when she realized the need for newspaper content for children. After a foray in her hometown newspaper in Richmond, Indiana, within six weeks she was publishing a nationally syndicated column, "Bedtime Tales." Soon afterwards, in 1915, she published her first book. Born in Logansport, Indiana, Judson grew up Indianapolis and was a school teacher. After marrying James M. Judson, she lived in Richmond, Indiana, Chicago, and Evanston, Illinois. Beginning in World War I, Judson began a public speaking career addressing domestic topics. In addition to her lectures, for many years she broadcast a weekly radio program in the Chicago area.
(*Chicago Tribune*, 11 November 1956, 44).

Kaminsky, Stuart M. (September 29, 1934–?)
Known as a mystery writer, Kaminsky had a long career in academia, first as a writer and editor, and then as a professor. Born in Chicago, Kaminsky graduated from the University of Illinois (BS, 1957; MA, 1959) and Northwestern University (PhD, 1972). He has worked at, or taught at, the University of Illinois, Urbana-Champaign; University of Illinois, Chicago; University of Chicago; Northwestern University; and Florida State University. The author of numerous novels, short stories, and screenplays, Kaminsky has also written mystery series featuring colorful detectives. One of these series, begun in 1991, records the adventures of Chicago policeman Abe Lieberman.
(*Contemporary Authors Online*, Gale, 2007, accessed 14 March 2008).

Kantor, MacKinlay (February 4, 1904–October 11, 1977)
Born in Webster City, Iowa, after leaving high school, Kantor began working on the town newspaper, where his mother also worked. After a few years, he left for Chicago in 1925, hoping to get a newspaper job. He barely supported himself working on a city surveying crew and freelance writing short stories and articles while working on his first novel. The book, published in 1928 as *Diversey* (included here) launched his career and he went on to publish another eight novels in the next six years. Only the first two of Kantor's novels are set in Chicago; he is best known for his works of historical fiction, mostly dealing with the Civil War.
(*Dictionary of Literary Biography*, vol. 9, s.v. "Kantor, MacKinlay").

Karlins, Marvin (October 4, 1941–?)

An academic who has for the most part published work related to his research interests, Karlins was born in Minneapolis and graduated from the University of Minnesota (BA, 1963) and Princeton University (MA, 1965; PhD, 1966). He has taught at Princeton University, the University of Pittsburgh, and the University of South Florida, initially in the field of psychology and later in business administration.
(*Contemporary Authors Online*, Detroit: Gale, 2002, accessed 14 March 2008).

Keeler, Harry Stephen (November 3, 1890–January 22, 1967)

The author of over seventy novels, Keeler was born and grew up in Chicago in his widowed mother's boarding house for thespians. A graduate of Armour Institute (now Illinois Institute of Technology) with a degree in electrical engineering, he began publishing serialized novels in magazines in 1914 and published his first book in 1924. Almost all of Keeler's works are mysteries and he is known for inventing the form known as the "webwork novel," in which hundreds of seemingly unrelated events prove to be interlinked. Perhaps because of his use of this literary form Keeler wrote some of the longest mystery novels ever published, including one with over seven hundred pages. Starting in the 1930s and throughout the 1940s and 1950s, Keeler published novels in series. The length of his novels and their challenging narrative formats left Keeler with few readers by the 1950s, although he continued to write until his death.
(*Contemporary Authors Online*, Detroit: Thomson Gale, 2005, accessed 14 August 2009).

Keenan, Henry Francis (1850–1928)

Born in Rochester, New York, Keenan fought for the Union Army in the Civil War and was wounded in the battle of Drury's Bluff, Virginia. He returned to Rochester and starting in 1868 worked as a reporter. He later worked on newspapers in Indianapolis and New York City, and as a correspondent in Washington, D.C. and Paris. He began writing novels full-time after 1883. He is best known for *The Money-Makers*, the novel for which he is included here.
(*Reader's Encyclopedia of American Literature*, New York: Harper-Collins, 1991, s.v. "Keenan, Henry Francis").

Keene, Day, *see* Hjerstedt, Gunard

Kelly, Regina Zimmerman (January 4, 1898–April 9, 1986)

Although she was born and raised in New Orleans, Kelly graduated from the University of Chicago (PhB, 1920) with a degree in education and took courses in journalism at Northwestern University. She began teaching high school history at Chicago's Austin High School immediately after graduating from college in 1920 and has lived on Chicago's North Side and worked her entire career there. Kelly is known for her well-researched works of historical fiction for young adults and she has had a particular interest in Midwestern history.
(*Contemporary Authors Online*, Detroit: Gale, 2001, accessed 12 March 2009).

Kencarden, Stuart

No information available.

Kennedy, Adam (c.1920–October 16, 1997)

A noted painter and actor as well as the author of fifteen novels, Kennedy was born in Lafayette, Indiana and graduated from De Pauw (Ind.) University and also studied at Chicago Profes-

sional School of Art. He worked as an account executive at Grant Advertising in Chicago, as well as an art director and illustrator for *Esquire* and *Coronet*. As an actor, Kennedy performed on Broadway and in Europe and appeared in over three hundred television programs.
(*Contemporary Authors Online*, Detroit: Gale: 2003, accessed 14 March 2009).

Kennedy, Mark
   No information available.

Kent, Mona (1909–1990)
   Kent is known as a scriptwriter for radio and television who was most active between 1940 and 1951. She is most closely identified with *Portia Faces Life*, a radio soap opera she created and for which she wrote every episode. However, she created several other soap operas and contributed to pioneering science fiction television program *Captain Video and His Video Rangers*. Her only novel was the one for which she is included here.
(Library of American Broadcasting, University of Maryland, www.lib.umd.edu/LAB, accessed 14 May 2009).

King, Charles (October 12, 1844–1933)
   A soldier for seventy years who rose to the rank of general, King wrote sixty novels (most are set on the Western frontier) that had the sentimentalized plots of other popular, nineteenth-century fiction. King's novels were informed by his own experiences and featured accurate details about life on the frontier. King studied at Columbia College (now University) where his grandfather was president, interrupting his class work to enlist in the Union Army during the Civil War. He attended West Point from 1862 to 1865. He was posted to the West during the 1874 Apache campaign in Arizona and against the Sioux in 1876. Although an arm wound forced his retirement to Milwaukee in 1879, at which time he began his writing career, King was commissioned as a general at the time of the Spanish-American War in 1898 and was posted to the Philippines. His writing found a broad audience. King's books tell us a great deal about frontier conditions and military service in the 1870s through 1890s and begin reflecting the realist movement that was becoming popular in literature near the end of his career.
(*Dictionary of Literary Biography*, vol. 186, s.v. "King, Charles").

Kinzie, Mrs. John H. (Juliette Augusta McGill) (September 11, 1806–September 15, 1870)
   Born in Middletown, Connecticut and educated at boarding school, including at the famous Emma Willard's school in Troy, New York, in 1830 Kinzie married John H. Kinzie, son of the fur trader of the same name who was one of the founders of Chicago. She moved with her husband to Fort Winnebago, Wisconsin, after their marriage, where he was an Indian agent. However, in 1834, the couple moved to Chicago where they became prominent in the city's civic life and social development as active members of the Episcopal Church and founders of the Chicago Historical Society.

Kirk, Hyland (1846–1917)
   Kirk was a reformer and activist in the nineteenth-century vegetarian movement with a particular interest in the rights of animals.

Kirkland, Joseph (January 7, 1830–April 28, 1893)

Born in Geneva, New York, Kirkland experienced frontier life with his family in Michigan from 1835 to 1843. The Kirklands moved back East to New York City in 1843 and, in 1846, after his father's death, the seventeen-year-old Kirkland found work on sailing ships as a way of financing travel in England, Germany, and France. After his return, and a stint at *Putnam's Monthly Magazine* as a clerk and reader, Kirkland moved to Chicago and worked as an auditor for the Illinois Central Railroad from 1855 to 1858. He later managed a coal company in Tilton, Illinois, before enlisting in the Twelfth Illinois Volunteer Infantry in 1861. He returned to managing the Tilton-based coal company that later opened offices in Chicago where Kirkland moved in 1867. The 1871 Chicago fire, followed by the financial panic of 1873, destroyed his business and he studied law and was admitted to the bar in 1880, at the age of fifty. One of the founders of the Chicago Literary Club, he began writing in earnest in 1877, and published his first novel, *Zury: The Meanest Man in Spring County* (Boston: Houghton, Mifflin), in 1887 to wide acclaim from critics and other writers. His writing blended the local colorist approach with realism and influenced other Midwestern authors like Sherwood Anderson. He went on to publish two more less successful novels and a volume on Chicago history.
(*Dictionary of Literary Biography*, vol. 12, s.v. "Kirkland, Joseph").

Klamm, Allis McKay, *see* McKay, Allis

Klasne, William (1933–?)

Klasne worked as a Chicago policeman and began writing after his retirement.

Knebel, Fletcher (1912–1993)

Knebel had a long and successful career as a journalist before writing his first novel. He grew up in middle-class comfort in suburban, Cleveland, Chicago, and New York City. Educated at Miami University of Ohio, he worked for newspapers in Pennsylvania, Tennessee, and Ohio before moving to Washington, D.C. in 1936 as a correspondent to the *Cleveland (Ohio) Plain Dealer*. He served in the U.S. Navy during World War II, returning to journalism after the war. The daily column "Potomac Fever" that he began in 1951 for Cowles Communications was nationally syndicated and appeared for the next thirteen years. In 1962, a book he co-authored with Charles W. Bailey, II, *Seven Days in May*, was published by Harper and Row. A great success, the novel was released as a movie in 1964 (Warner Bros.), starring Kirk Douglas, Burt Lancaster, and Fredric March. He afterward wrote thirteen more books and had lifetime sales figures of over six million copies. An advocate of the legalization of marijuana, he was also a member of the Hemlock Society. Suffering from a heart condition and lung cancer, he took his own life in 1993.
(*New York Times*, 28 February 1993, 44).

Knott, William Wilson

No information available.

Kogan, Herman (November 6, 1914–March 8, 1989)

A Chicago native and graduate of the University of Chicago (BA, 1936), Kogan was a journalist and later worked in broadcasting. He worked for all of the major Chicago newspapers before starting his own publication, *Panorama* magazine in 1962. In 1965 he became an assistant general manager at Field Enterprises, a Chicago television station. He later hosted a radio program about

writers and writing. He wrote extensively about Chicago in works of fiction and non-fiction.
(*Contemporary Authors Online*, Detroit: Thomson Gale, 2007, accessed 23 March 2009).

Komroff, Manuel (September 7, 1890–December 10, 1974)
　　An author of historical fiction, Komroff was born in Kingston, New York and studied at Yale
University. A socialist prior to 1920, he traveled to Petrograd in 1917 at the time of the Russian
Revolution and after the Bolsheviks took power, he fled, and traveled in Siberia, Japan, and
Shanghai, before returning to the United States in 1918. In New York City he worked in low-level,
editorial positions and wrote in his spare time. After the success of *Coronet* in 1930 (included
here), he was able to devote himself to writing fiction and nonfiction full-time, although his other
works never matched his earlier success.
(*World Authors*, 1900–1950, New York: H. W. Wilson, 1996, s.v. "Komroff, Manuel").

Krautter, Elisa (Bialk) (October 4, 1912–February 28, 1990)
　　Chicago native, Krautter, grew up in Lincoln Park and studied at Northwestern University
School of Journalism. She worked for neighborhood newspapers in Chicago and wrote for pulp
magazines until she began placing work with *Good Housekeeping* in 1932. She married a Chicago
advertising executive, L. Martin Krautter, in 1934 and as her children grew up she began writing
for children, eventually publishing twenty-eight books, mostly in the 1950s and 1960s.
(*Contemporary Authors Online*, Detroit: Gale, 2003, accessed 31 July 2007).

Kurtz, Ann
　　No information available.

Lait, Jack (March 13, 1883–April 1, 1954)
　　During a fifty-year career as a journalist, Lait, who was born in New York City, was editor of
the *New York Daily Mirror* and the *Sunday Mirror*. He wrote a syndicated column, "All in the
Family," for twenty years and with Lee Mortimer co-wrote the books *New York Confidential*,
Chicago Confidential, and *Washington Confidential*. In addition to several novels, Lait wrote five
plays that appeared on Broadway.
(*New York Times*, 2 April 1954, 27).

Lake, Joe Barry [Joe Barry, pseud.]
　　No information available.

Lally, John Patrick
　　No information available.

Lamb, Martha Joanna (1829–January 2, 1893)
　　Born in Plainfield, Massachusetts, she married Charles A. Lamb in 1852 and moved with him
to Chicago where she was a founder of the Half Orphan Asylum (to aid children with only one
parent who could not provide for them) and the Home for the Friendless. She was also the secretary of Chicago's first sanitary fair in 1863. After 1866 she lived in New York City and published
books on the history of Manhattan, as well as works for children. She became the editor of the
Magazine of American History in 1883.
(*New York Times*, 3 January 1893, 5).

Lamensdorf, Leonard (June 22, 1930–?)

Lamensdorf was born in Chicago and graduated from the University of Chicago (BA, 1948). After receiving his law degree from Harvard University in 1952 and completing additional graduate study in 1953, he was an attorney and real estate developer for more than thirty years, developing shopping malls. He founded SeaScape Press to publish his novels, many of which are for children.

(*Contemporary Authors Online*, Detroit: Gale, 2008, accessed 21 March 2009).

Lardner, Ring (March 6, 1885–September 25, 1933)

Born in Niles, Michigan, not far from South Bend, Indiana, Lardner was the son of a wealthy man who provided tutors for his education on the family estate, until he entered a local public high school. By the time Lardner graduated, his father had lost his fortune. Lardner lived for a time in Chicago as a menial laborer, and then returned to Niles where, after several false starts, he began writing for the *South Bend Times*. His coverage of baseball games earned him a job on the *Chicago Inter-Ocean* newspaper. He later was a sportswriter on the *Chicago Examiner* and the *Chicago Tribune*. For the *Tribune*, he began writing a column in Midwestern dialect. Not long after working as a World War I correspondent based in France, Lardner moved to New York City. From there he contributed to magazines and wrote a nationally syndicated column. From 1928 on, he lived in East Hampton, New York and contributed to *The New Yorker* and *Collier's*, as well as other magazines and a number of newspapers, mostly writing boxing and baseball stories. During his lifetime he earned a reputation as an important writer of short stories and accomplished humorist that remains undiminished.

(*Dictionary of Literary Biography*, vol. 171, s.v. "Lardner, Ring").

Larsen, Nella (April 13, 1891–March 30, 1964)

The illegitimate daughter of an African-American cook and an immigrant Danish mother, Larsen's early life and later writing were shaped by the struggle to live as a multiracial person in a racist society. When her mother married a Danish man in 1894, Larsen was sent to Nashville, Tennessee to finish high school and her existence was covered up by her mother. In 1912, Larsen moved to New York City and completed a nursing education program in 1915. After working awhile as a nurse, she completed a library training program and worked at the New York Public Library from 1922 to 1926. She began publishing her work during this period and won a reputation as a member of the Harlem Renaissance and in 1929 became the first African-American woman to receive a Guggenheim Foundation Fellowship. In 1930 after being falsely accused of plagiarizing one of her short stories and discovering the infidelity of her husband, a prominent black physicist, Larsen stopped writing and later returned to nursing from 1944 to 1964. Her writings have long been out of print, but as they have been republished in recent years, her two novels have received new and very favorable attention.

(*American National Biography*, "Larsen, Nella").

Latimer, Jonathan Wyatt (October 23, 1906–June 23, 1983)

A Chicago native and graduate of Knox College, Latimer began his career at the *Chicago Herald-Examiner* in 1929 as a police reporter, a position that provided him with material for the mystery novels he wrote beginning in 1935, while working as a ghostwriter for Secretary of the Interior Harold Ickes. He was later a successful Hollywood screenwriter and ended his career as a writer for television series, including *Perry Mason* in the 1960s.

(*Contemporary Authors Online*, Gale, 2006, accessed, 21 March 2009).

Laughlin, Clara Elizabeth (August 3, 1873–March 3, 1941

Although she was born in New York City, Laughlin moved with her family to Chicago while a child and graduated from North Division High School in 1890. She lived the remainder of her life in the city. Her first job was as the editor of a religious weekly, but by 1902 she was publishing romance stories and novels. After World War I she devoted herself to writing travel books in the "So You're Going to..." series that she created, along with Clara Laughlin Travel Services, both of which took advantage of post-war interest in traveling to Europe and the new ease with which people could travel by automobile and train in the United States.
(*New York Times* 4 March 1941, 23).

Lawrence, Catherine Ann (1921–?)

No information available

Lawson, Don (May 20, 1917–January 27, 1990)

Born in Chicago, Lawson grew up in Downers Grove, Illinois, graduated from Cornell (Mt. Vernon, Iowa) College (BA, 1939), and attended the University of Iowa Writers' Workshop (1939 and 1940). He served in the U.S. Air Force from 1944 through 1945 and worked for *Compton's Encyclopedia* from 1946 to 1973. He is the author of more than forty books for children, most of which deal with American history.
(*Contemporary Authors Online*, Detroit: Gale, 2003, accessed 10 March 2009).

Lawson, Robert (October 4, 1892–1957)

An award-winning author and illustrator of children's books, Lawson grew up in New York City and attended the new York School of Fine and Applied Arts (1911–1914). He worked as a commercial artist for magazines and in World War I worked on the French front, designing camouflage. After difficult years during the Depression, he began getting work from Doubleday for children's book illustrations in 1930 and had his first international success with the *Story of Ferdinand*. The first book he wrote for children was published in 1939. He went on to write sixteen more and published his last book, about the Chicago World's Fair, in 1957, the year of his death).
(*Dictionary of Literary Biography*, vol. 22, s.v. "Lawson, Robert").

Lee, Ella Dolbear

No information available.

Lee, Jennette (Perry) (November 10, 1860–1951)

No information available.

Lee, Norman [Mark Corrigan, pseud.] (1905–1962)

A British writer, who also used the pseudonyms Raymond Armstrong and Roberton Hobart, wrote several detective series, one featuring Mark Corrigan an American private investigator and another featuring Laura Scudamore, who was known as the "Sinister Widow."

Leiber, Fritz Reuter (December 24, 1910–September 5, 1992)

Known for his science fiction and fantasy novels, Leiber was born and educated in Chicago, earning his bachelor of philosophy in biological sciences from the University of Chicago. His father was a well-known Shakespearean actor who toured with his own company and later acted in

motion pictures; Leiber also acted in his youth. Leiber authored numerous books and short stories from the 1940s to the 1970s.
(*World Authors 1975–1980*, New York: H. W. Wilson, 1985, s.v. "Leiber, Fritz Reuter").

Le Jemlys, *see* Mooney, James

Lengel, William Charles (1888–1965)
    No information available.

Levin, Meyer (October 8, 1905–July 9, 1981)
    A native Chicagoan, Levin was born in the ghetto, but worked his way through the University of Chicago, graduating in 1924. Employed as a reporter for the *Chicago Daily News* until 1925, he then traveled to Paris to study painting at the Academie Moderne. He returned to reporting at the *Chicago Daily News*, although he was also writing fiction and published his first novel in 1929. In the same year, he went to Palestine to live on a kibbutz and most of his writing from this time dealt with Jews and Zionism. The author of twenty-six novels, he often used Chicago as a setting.
(*New York Times*, 11 July 1981, 16).

Lewin, Michael Z. (July 21, 1942–?)
    A prolific author of detective fiction and radio plays, Lewin was born in Springfield, Massachusetts, grew up in Indianapolis, Indiana and was educated at Harvard University (AB, 1964) and Cambridge University (1964–1965). After a few years as a secondary school science teacher, Lewin has since been a full-time writer. Many of his books feature detective Albert Samson of Indianapolis, Indiana.
(*St. James Guide to Mystery and Detective Fiction*, 4th edition, St. James Press, Detroit, 1996, s.v. "Lewin Michael Z.").

Lewis, Edwin Herbert (1866–1938)
    No information available.

Linn, James Weber (May 11, 1876–July 16, 1939)
    Born in Winnebago, Illinois, Linn's aunt was Jane Addams, the founder of Hull House. When his mother died, Addams lent the eighteen-year-old Linn the money to attend the recently founded University of Chicago. He graduated in 1897 and after working for less than a year at the *Chicago Record*, he returned to complete graduate work at the University. He was appointed to a teaching position in English composition and was a faculty member until his death, for twelve years serving as dean of men in the junior college. A columnist for Chicago newspapers, and magazine contributor, he also published three novels, five textbooks, and a biography. Near the end of his life he became actively involved in politics and was elected as a representative to the Illinois legislature. He lived his entire adult life in Chicago and resided at 1357 East Fifty-Sixth Street at the time of his death.
(*New York Times*, 17 July 1939, 23).

Linton, Adelin Sumner Briggs [Aldin Vinton, pseud.] (1899–?)
    No information available.

Litere, *see* Sommers, Lillian

Little, Paul H. (Paul Hugo) [Kenneth Harding, Marie de Jourlet, pseuds.]. (February 5, 1915–June 22, 1987)

Little was born in Chicago and resided there for most of his life. He attended the University of Chicago and graduated from Northwestern University in 1937. Little had a twenty-year career (1944–1964) in advertising, working for several Chicago firms, including Armour. He subsequently worked as a full-time, freelance writer (1964–1987), writing under his own name and ten pseudonyms. He was the author of more than seven hundred novels, many of them "pulps," and some of them pornographic.

(*Contemporary Authors Online*, Detroit: Gale, 2003, accessed 24 March 2009)

Lobell, William

No information available.

London, Jack (January 12, 1876–November 22, 1919)

Best known as a practitioner of literary naturalism and identified for setting his fiction in wilderness areas, London was born and raised in San Francisco and he had adventures like serving as a hand on a sealing schooner and marching on Washington, D.C. as part of Coxey's Army even before he finished high school. He later participated in the Klondike gold rush, and joined the socialist party before he began publishing his writing in 1899. His connection with Chicago is primarily through his interest in socialism and labor reform and his identification of that city with these social movements. London died at the age of forty, a probable suicide, unable to make a satisfying life for himself despite his critical and financial success as a writer.

(*Dictionary of Literary Biography*, vol. 8, s.v. "London, Jack").

Loose, Harry J.

No information available.

Lorenz, Tom

No information available.

Lorimer, George Horace (October 6, 1867–October 22, 1937)

Son of George Claude Lorimer, an evangelical Baptist minister who became nationally famous and served for many years at Tremont Temple in Boston, Lorimer was born in Louisville, Kentucky, but moved with his family a number of times during childhood. In 1899, while Lorimer was attending Yale, one of his Chicago parishioners, meat-packing magnate Philip D. Armour, offered him a job through which Lorimer thought he would become wealthy. He did achieve early success as the manager of Armour's canning department and he married Alma Viola Ennis, whose father was a prominent Chicago judge. However, true wealth seemed too far away to Lorimer, so he struck out on his own business venture that failed. For solace he turned to writing, secured a reporter's job at the *Boston Post*, and became literary editor of the *Saturday Evening Post* in 1898. Lorimer became managing editor in 1899 and helped owner Cyrus Curtis transform the *Post*, creating one of the nation's most influential publications, read by most middle-class Americans. He was editor for more than forty years and made the fortune he had craved as a young man.

(*Dictionary of Literary Biography*, vol. 91, s.v. "Lorimer, George Horace").

Lory, Robert (Edward) [V. J. Santiago, pseud.] (December 29, 1936–?)

An author of science fiction and horror books under several pen names, Lory was born in Troy, New York and served in the U.S. Army (1954–1957). He graduated from what is now the State University of New York at Binghamton (BA, 1961) and from the Washington School of Art (Chicago) (Dipl., 1973). He is best known for his Dracula and Horrorscope series of novels.
(*Contemporary Authors Online*, Detroit: Gale, 2009, accessed 11 March 2009).

Loux, DuBois Henry (1867–?)
    No information available.

Lovett, Robert Morss (December 25, 1870–February 8, 1956)

Lovett was a literary critic and author who taught at the University of Chicago (1893–1936). He was on the editorial board of the *New Republic* (1921–1940), and was government secretary of the Virgin Islands (1939–1943).
(*New York Times*, 9 February 1956, 31).

Lucas, Cleo
    No information available.

Lund, Roslyn Rosen
    No information available.

Lynch, Lawrence L., *see* Van Deventer, Emma Murdoch

Lytle, H. M.
    No information available.

MacDonald, John D. (July 24, 1916–December 28, 1986)

The creator of the Travis McGee detective mystery series, MacDonald wrote books in several genres other than mystery-detection, including adventure-suspense, science fiction, and manners and morals. Born in Sharon, Pennsylvania, he grew up in Utica, New York and attended the Utica Free Academy. He graduated with business degrees from Syracuse University (1938) and Harvard Business School (MBA, 1939). He began work in the insurance industry, but after serving in the U.S. Army in World War II devoted himself to writing for pulp magazines, eventually publishing more than sixty novels while mostly living in Sarasota, Florida and traveling widely, especially by cruise ship.
(*Mystery and Suspense Writers: The Literature of Crime, Detection, and Espionage*, New York: Scribners, 1998, s.v. "MacDonald, John W.").

MacHarg, William Briggs (1872–February 21, 1951)

The author of numerous short stories for *Collier's* and *The Saturday Evening Post*, as well as two novels, MacHarg also co-authored five books of fiction with Edwin Balmer. MacHarg's father was a consulting engineer to the city of Chicago and although he attended the University of Michigan, MacHarg dropped out to become a reporter with *The Chicago Tribune* and became its Sunday editor in 1899. He based wrote many popular stories for magazines that featured police

man "O'Malley," a character based on a Prohibition-era policeman MacHarg had gotten to know in New York City.
(*New York Times*, 22 February 1951, 29).

MacQueen, James [James G. Edwards, Jay McHugh, pseuds.] (1900–1954)
No information available.

Mairet, Jeanne, *see* Bigot, Marie Healey

Maitland, James
No information available.

Maling, Arthur (Gordon) (June 11, 1923–?)
Son of a Chicago businessman and the owner of Maling Brothers, a retail shoe-store chain, based in Chicago from 1946–1972, Maling graduated from Harvard University in 1944. He has lived most of his life in Chicago and is the author fifteen mystery novels, some of them award winners.
(*Contemporary Authors Online*, Detroit: Gale, 2001, accessed 12 March 2009).

Maloff, Saul (September 6, 1922–?)
The author of two novels, as well as an editor and literary critic, Maloff was born in New York City and spent most of his life there as an academic. He was educated at City College (BA, 1943) and the University of Iowa (MA, 1947; PhD, 1952). Maloff served in the U.S. Army during World War II (1943–1946). His fiction explores family life and values.
(*Contemporary Authors Online*, Detroit: Gale, 2001, accessed 15 May 2009).

Malzberg, Barry N. (Barry Nathaniel) [Mike Barry, pseud.] (1939–?)
Science fiction writer Malzberg was born in New York City and lived most of his adult life there. He earned his bachelor's degree at Syracuse University in 1960 and returned for graduate study in 1964 after working at the New York City Departments of Heal and Mental Hygiene. He began writing for pulp magazines in 1967 and has published more than forty-three novels.
(*Dictionary of Literary Biography*, vol. 8, s.v. "Malzberg, Barry N(athaniel)").

Marion, Frances (November 18, 1886–May 12, 1973)
Born Frances Marion Owens and named for her Revolutionary War hero ancestor Frances Marion, the author had an affluent childhood in San Francisco and was about to attend Bryn Mawr College when the San Francisco fire wrecked her father's finances and she was forced to attend the University of California, Berkeley, instead. She left school to marry one of her art instructors (the first of four marriages, most of which lasted for only a few years). After her second marriage, she moved to Hollywood and began working for the film industry, soon finding her niche as a screenwriter. During her twenty-five year career she wrote in their entirety or could be credited on more than three hundred scripts, the most famous being *The Big House*, *The Champ* (for both of which she won Academy Awards for best writing), and *Dinner at Eight*.
(*Dictionary of Literary Biography*, vol. 44, s.v. "Marion, Frances").

Marlowe, Derek (May 21, 1938–November 14, 1996)
Known for his crime and espionage fiction, Marlowe was born in London, England and attended the University of London (1957–1960). He wrote plays and screenplays in addition to novels and lived the last decade of his life in Hollywood, California.
(*Contemporary Authors Online*, Gale, 2000, accessed 24 March 2009).

Marshall, James (May 12, 1896–August 11, 1986)
A lawyer for more than sixty years, Marshall started the firm Marshall, Bratter, Seligson & Klein in 1937 and continued with it until 1982 (the firm became Marshall, Bratter, Greene, Allison & Tucker). He was the author of one novel and four works of non-fiction. Active in his native New York City, Marshall served on the New York City Board of Education for seventeen years, and as president from 1938–1942. On the national and international stage, Marshall founded the National Resources Defense Council, was on several U.S. delegations to UNESCO, and served as vice-president of the American Jewish Committee. For twelve years, from 1953–1965, he taught public administration at New York University.
(*New York Times*, 11 August 1986, D20).

Marshall, Sidney
No information available.

Mason, Edith Huntington
No information available.

Masselink, Ben (November 13, 1919–January 12, 2000)
Born in Grand Rapids, Michigan, Masselink attended DePauw (Ind.) University (1937–1940). He was enlisted in the U.S. Marine Corps and from 1941–1945 posted to the Marshall Islands and Okinawa, attaining the rank of sergeant and combat correspondent. He worked as a laborer and tile setter's assistant after demobilization before writing full-time. The author of seven books, he was also a television writer, creating scripts for programs such as *Dr. Kildare* and *The Wonderful World of Disney*. He was also a creative writing instructor at the University of Southern California for twenty years.
(*Contemporary Authors Online*, Detroit: Gale, 2005, accessed 24 March 2009).

Masters, Edgar Lee (August 23, 1868–March 5, 1950)
The son of an attorney, Masters was born in Garnett, Kansas, but grew up in Petersburg and Lewistown, Illinois. He studied briefly at Knox College in Galesburg, Illinois, then read law with his father, eventually passing the bar examination in 1891 and entering his father's law practice. He moved to Chicago and to open his own law practice, representing poor clients against corporations and other commercial interests. From 1903 until 1911, he was a legal partner of Clarence Darrow. While working as an attorney, he wrote poems and stories for newspapers and magazines and had published four books of poetry before 1915. In 1915 he published *Spoon River Anthology* (New York: MacMillan), the book of poetry that remained his greatest success, even though he wrote and published poetry and novels for another thirty-five years. He moved to New York City in 1923 and lived there for most of the rest of his life in the Chelsea Hotel.
(*World Authors, 1900–1950*, New York: H. W. Wilson, 1996, s.v. "Masters, Edgar Lee").

Maupin, Robert Lee [Robert Beck, Robert Maupin Beck, Iceberg Slim, pseuds.] (August 14, 1918–April 28, 1992)

Maupin was born and grew up in the African-American ghetto of Chicago. He attended the Tuskegee Institute, but from roughly 1937–1962 he worked as a pimp. Incarcerated several times, Maupin decided he was too old for a life of crime and moved to Los Angeles where he gave up heroin and became an insecticide salesman. His first book, published in 1967, was a memoir entitled *Pimp: The Story of My Life* (Los Angeles.: Holloway House). A paperback best seller, the book inspired Maupin to write novels that achieved a huge readership, particularly in the African-American community. By the time of his death, it was estimated that Maupin's works had sold over six million copies.
(*Contemporary Authors Online*, Detroit: Thomson Gale, 2008, accessed 12 March 2009).

Maxwell, William (August 16, 1908–July 31, 2000)

A fiction editor at *The New Yorker* over forty years (1936–1976), Maxwell was a native of Lincoln, Illinois. He moved to Chicago with his father and brothers when he was ten years old after his mother died from influenza. He published six novels, several of them semi-autobiographical and dealing with small-town life, as well as several books for children, and some short story collections. An editor for some of the most prominent twentieth-century American writers, he also published a volume of his correspondence with Frank O'Connor. He lived most of his adult life in Manhattan.
(*New York Times*, 1 August 2000, 9).

Mayer, Jane Rothschild (December 30, 1903–September 3, 2001)

Born into an affluent family in Kansas City, Missouri and a graduate of Vassar College (AB, 1925), Mayer was interested in writing from an early age, but her father discouraged her from anticipating any sort of career as a middle-class endeavor. When she made friends with Clara Spiegel at Vassar, who was also interested in writing, the two of them decided to collaborate under joint pseudonym, Clare Jaynes. The two co-authored four novels. Mayer went on to use other pseudonyms for her own work and decades later published a novel under her own name. For most of her adult life she lived in Chicago, the wife of David Mayer Jr. When he died in 1960, after thirty-three years of marriage, Mayer stopped writing and devoted herself to charitable and cultural organizations.
(*Chicago Tribune*, 6 September 2001, 2-9).

Mazzaro, Ed
No information available.

McAlpine, Dale K. (1893–?)
No information available.

McConaughy, J. W.
No information available.

McCord, Joseph (1881–January 27, 1943)

The author of numerous novels and short stories for pulp magazines, McCord was born in Moline, Illinois and graduated from the University of Iowa. He worked as a reporter for the *Balti-*

more Sun and the *Brooklyn Eagle*. During World War I he worked in a steel plant and he died while working in a defense plant on the West Coast during World War II.
(*New York Times*, 30 January 1943, 15).

McCutcheon, George Barr (July 26, 1866–October 23, 1928)
Brother of John T. McCutcheon, a prominent cartoonist, McCutcheon began writing when he was a child and had a story accepted by *Waverley Magazine* when he was nineteen. Born near Lafayette, Indiana, where he grew up, he graduated from Purdue University where he was friends with Booth Tarkington and George Ade. After college, he worked as a reporter on the *Lafayette (Ind.) Journal* and was later city editor for the *Lafayette (Ind.) Courier* from 1893 to 1901. He published his first novel *Graustark* (Chicago: H. S. Stone and Company) in 1901; the romance set in a fictitious Balkan kingdom would remain his most popular work and was later adapted into a successful stage play. During his career McCutcheon wrote a total of forty-four novels; several were adapted into long-running plays.
(*New York Times*, 24 October 1928, 1).

McCutcheon, John T. (May 6, 1870–June 10, 1949)
The brother of novelist George Barr McCutcheon was famous as a cartoonist for the *Chicago Tribune*. Born in Lafayette, Indiana, McCutcheon graduated from Purdue University and moved to Chicago soon afterwards, working initially for the *Chicago Morning News* (later called the *Chicago Record*). His best remembered cartoons are related to presidential campaigns, the Spanish-American War, and World War I. In 1932 he won the Pulitzer Prize for Editorial Cartooning.
(*New York Times*, 11 June 1949, 17).

McDougall, Ella L. Randall [Preserved Wheeler, pseud.]
No information available.

McEvoy, Joseph Patrick (1895–August 8, 1958)
A humorist who worked as a journalist and editor, McEvoy also published plays and poetry. During the 1920s and 1930s he published short stories in the popular magazines of the day and several of his works were made into movies. He later authored a hit play and wrote several novels that were adapted for the screen. He was also the originator of the *Dixie Dugan* syndicated comic strip that ran from 1929 to 1966 with illustrations by John H. Streibel. In the 1940s and 1950s he was a regular contributor to *Reader's Digest* and was on the magazine's editorial board at the time of his death.
(*New York Times*, 10 August 1958, 92).

McGivern, William P[eter] [Bill Peters, pseud.] (December 6, 1922–November 18, 1982)
Born in Chicago, McGivern is best known as a writer of twenty-three "tough-guy" mysteries. His childhood and young adulthood was divided between Chicago (where his mother operated a dress-design shop on South Michigan Boulevard) and Mobile, Alabama. He worked as a laborer for the Pullman Company in Chicago (1937–1939) and began selling stories to pulp magazines in 1940. He served in the U.S. Army during World War II (1943–1946). Except for working as a reporter and book reviewer for the *Philadelphia Evening Bulletin* (1949–1951), he worked full-time as a writer. In addition to his novels, he also wrote eight screenplays and thirty television

scripts. Nine of his novels were adapted as motion pictures. The most popular character he created was David Bannion, who is street savvy, but also engages in intellectual pursuits. (*New York Times*, 21 November 1982, 44).

McGovern, John (1850–1917)
   No information available.

McGrath, Tom, Lieutenant
   No information available.

McHugh, Jay [pseud.], *see* MacQueen, James William.

McInerny, Ralph (February 24, 1929–?)
   Creator of several fictional detectives, including Andrew Broom, Sister Mary Dempsey, and best-known, Father Roger Dowling, McInerny was born in Minneapolis, the son of an engineer. A 1952 graduate of the University of Minnesota (MA, philosophy and classics) and of Laval University (PhD, philosophy, 1954), he has been a professor at the University of Notre Dame since 1955. An author of works in his academic discipline, he did not begin publishing fiction until 1960 when he started submitting popular writing to women's magazines under pseudonyms. Since the 1970s, he has since published more than sixty fiction books, as well as continuing to publish works for an academic audience.
   (*Dictionary of Literary Biography*, vol. 306, s.v. "McInerny, Ralph").

McKay, Allis [aka Allis McKay Klamm]
   No information available.

Meadowcroft, Enid La Monte (March 31, 1898–November 23, 1966)
   For many decades a school teacher in New Jersey and in New York City at the Browning School for Boys (1928–1941), Meadowcroft began writing stories for her students and later found authorship to be a way to express her interest in historical research. She went on to publish a number of works of historical fiction for children, some of which are set in the Midwest.
   (*Contemporary Authors Online*, Detroit: Gale, 2001, accessed 10 March 2010).

Means, Mary
   Co-authored books with Theodore Saunders under the joint pseudonym Denis Scott.

Meeker, Arthur (1902–October 22, 1971)
   The son of Arthur Meeker, an Armour executive, and Grace Murray Meeker, a socialite, Meeker grew up in great privilege in Chicago living first at 1815 Prairie Avenue and later at 3030 Lake Shore Drive. The family also owned Arcady Farm near Lake Forest. Meeker studied at Princeton and Harvard without graduating and for a time in his youth wrote travel and society pieces for the *Chicago American*, the *Chicagoan*, the *Chicago Herald*, and the *Chicago Daily News*, before finding success with his historical novels. He traveled in Europe for extended periods of time and mostly resided in New York City when he was in the United States.
   (*Electronic Encyclopedia of Chicago*, Chicago: Chicago Historical Society, 2005, accessed 12 March 2010).

Merlanti, Ernesto Giuseppe (1895–?)
   No information available.

Merriman, Charles Eustace [joint pseud.], *see* Richardson, George

Merwin, Bannister (1873–February 22, 1922)
   An important figure in the early days of motion pictures, Merwin was brother to Samuel Merwin. Their father Orlando Hastings Merwin was an important insurance agent based in Chicago and a partner in the American Real Estate Company, and their mother Ellen Merwin née Bannister was the daughter of the Rev. Dr. Henry Bannister, a professor at Northwestern University. Merwin was a writer and editor employed by *Munsey Magazine*, before working in the film industry beginning in the early 1900s. He had writer credits for over one hundred and forty motion pictures produced between 1909 and 1921 and also directed sixty-two motion pictures between 1910 and 1921.
   (*Internet Movie Database*, www.imdb.com/name/nm0102167, accessed 13 March 2010).

Merwin, Samuel (October 6, 1874–October 17, 1936)
   Born in Evanston, Illinois, and a graduate of Northwestern University, Merwin edited magazines, operated a playhouse, and wrote plays before he began attracting attention for his short stories and serialized fiction just before World War I. Initially, he used his work to advocate social upheaval to overturn the conservatism of Americans. He also was an outspoken proponent of women's suffrage, influenced, perhaps, by his aunt, Frances E. Willard. In the 1920s he reversed his earlier stance and was openly critical of an American society that had abandoned traditions and used the suffering of World War I as an excuse for embracing licentiousness. He railed, in particular, against flappers, whom he identified as the trivial product of the promising women's rights movement.
   (*New York Times*, 18 October 1935, N8).

Meyer, Lucy Rider (1849–1922)
   Meyer was a deaconess in the United Methodist Church and published inspirational works.

Miller, Francesca Falk (1888–1969)
   No information available.

Millspaugh, Clarence Arthur (1908–?)
   No information available.

Milman, Harry Dubois
   No information available.

Mitch, Miami [pseud.], *see* Glazer, Mitchell

Mizner, Elizabeth Howard (August 24, 1907–January 8, 1992)
   An author of historical fiction for children, Mizner was born in Detroit, Michigan and educated at the University of Michigan (BA, 1930; MA, 1935) and Wayne State University (graduate study, 1930–1932). After teaching for one year at Shorter College in Rome, Georgia (1935–1936),

Mizner became a freelance writer, authoring more than nineteen books, most of which are set in her favorite time period, the mid-1800s.
(*Contemporary Authors Online*, Detroit: Gale, 2001, accessed 26 March 2010).

Molloy, Paul (July 4, 1924–?)

Born in Winnipeg, and educated at the University of Manitoba (BA, 1941), Molloy worked in Canadian gold and copper mines before getting a newspaper job in Montreal. After working with United Press International as bureau manager in Quebec City, Molloy immigrated to the United States in 1950 (he was naturalized in 1956) and worked in Tulsa, Oklahoma; New York City; and Memphis, Tennessee before working as a television and radio critic for the *Chicago Sun-Times* (1957–1970). He was later a features-writer and during much of his career produced radio and television programs.
(*Biographical Dictionary of American Newspaper Columnists*, Westport, Conn.: Greenwood, 1995, s.v. "Molloy, Paul George").

Monteleone, Thomas F. (April 14, 1946–?)

An author of science fiction for children and adults, Monteleone was born in Baltimore, Maryland, and educated at the University of Maryland, College Park, earning a bachelor's of science (1968) and a master's degree (1973). After working as a psychotherapist (1969–1978), Monteleone began working full-time as a writer, and later a publisher, through Borderlands Press. He is the author of over one hundred short stories, more than twenty books, and several screenplays.
(*Contemporary Authors Online*, Detroit: Thomson Gale, 2005, accessed, 16 November 2009).

Montgomery, Louise (1864–?)

No information available.

Montross, Lois Seyster (1897–September 12, 1961)

Born Lois Seyster in Kempton, Illinois, Montross was a 1919 graduate of the University of Illinois. Her first books, fictional portrayals of university life, were collaborations with her husband Lynn Montross, who had also attended the University of Illinois. The author of ten novels in the 1930s, Montross also published short stories and essays in popular magazines in the 1930s and 1940s. She was divorced from Lynn Montross in 1933 and later married John Ford.
(*New York Times*, 18 September 1961, 29).

Montross, Lynn (1895–January 28, 1961)

Known as a military historian, Montross wrote widely about the United States armed services, although he specialized in the American Revolution. He was also an author of short stories and articles for popular magazines in the 1930s and 1940s. Born in Nebraska, Montross attended the University of Nebraska and the University of Illinois. He served as a military scout in World War I with the American Expeditionary Force. From 1950 until the end of his life he was the official historian of the U.S. Marine Corps.
(*New York Times*, 30 January 1961, 23).

Moody, Minnie Hite (June 23, 1900–October 25, 1993)

Known as a writer of newspaper and magazine columns, book reviews, poetry, and historical fiction, Moody was the wife of Wilkie "Coach" Osgood Moody, director of athletics for the Atlanta public school system, the city in which the couple resided for thirty-three years. However, Moody was born in Granville, Ohio and retained the 1850s family house in which she had been born, and the couple returned there after Coach retired. She was the author of five novels. Moody's papers are at Emory University.

Mooney, James [Symmes Jelley, Le Jemlys, pseuds.]
    No information available.

Moore, Ward (1903–1978)
    Best known as a writer of science fiction stories for popular magazines, Moore also published five novels. Born in Madison, New Jersey, Moore's family moved several times during his childhood, to Montreal and later to New York City where he spent most of his childhood. He moved around the country in the 1920s, taking what work he could find, and frequently living in Milwaukee or Chicago. His preference was always for the post of bookstore clerk, although he also worked in foundries and as a sheet-metal worker. He settled in California in 1929 and remained there for the rest of his life, working full-time as a writer after the success of his first novel in 1942, *Breathe the Air Again* (included here).
    (*Dictionary of Literary Biography*, vol. 8, s.v. "Moore, Ward").

Morgan, Al (Albert Edward) (January 16, 1920–?)
    A broadcast media writer and producer, Morgan was born in New York City and served in World War II, earning the Bronze Star, Purple Heart, Silver Star, and *Croix de Guerre* with palms (France). He had a long career with major television networks in New York City, including Columbia Broadcasting System (1941–1953) and National Broadcasting Corporation for which he was senior editor of *Home Show* (1954–1956) and producer of the *Today Show* (1961–1969). He began writing novels and plays in 1969 and has authored more than eleven books and had two plays produced on Broadway.
    (*Contemporary Authors Online*, Detroit: Gale, 2002, accessed 20 January 2010).

Morris, Henry O.
    No information available.

Morris, Ira (Victor) (November 11, 1903–1972)
    Morris had a brief career in newspaper offices and with book publishers before becoming a full-time writer in 1934. He was born in Chicago and attended Milton Academy, graduating from Harvard University in 1925. He subsequently completed graduate work at Heidelberg University. The author of more than ten novels, he has contributed short stories widely to popular magazines.
    (*Contemporary Authors Online*, Detroit: Gale, 2002, accessed 10 November 2009).

Morton, Anthony, *see* Creasey, John.

Motley, Willard (July 14, 1909–March 4, 1965)
    The author grew up in a middle-class, African-American family in Chicago and graduated from Englewood High School in 1930. Born out of wedlock, he was encouraged to believe that his mother was his sister and that his grandparents were actually his parents. After high school Motley worked in a variety of jobs, including cook, migrant laborer, shipping clerk, and radio scriptwriter. At the same time he was writing short stories that he was unable to place until a series of accounts

about his mid-1930s journeys to California were published in *Commonweal* and other magazines. He returned to Chicago in 1939, but chose to abandon the comfortable neighborhood in which he grew up to live in a slum. His experiences there were the inspiration for his novel *Knock on Any Door* (included here). This work of literary realism was praised by critics and was also a best seller that was made into a motion picture of the same name in 1949 starring Humphrey Bogart (Santana Productions distributed by Columbia Pictures). A sequel, *Let No Man Write My Epitaph* (included here), followed that was less well received but also made into a motion picture (Columbia Pictures, 1960). From 1951 until the end of his life Motley lived in Mexico, first in Mexico City and then near Cuernavaca.
(*New York Times*, 5 March 1965, 30).

Moyer, Clarissa Mabel Blank (August 5, 1915–August 15, 1965)
    Born in Allentown, Pennsylvania as Clarissa Mabel Blank, young adult novelist Moyer began publishing under the name Clair Blank soon after she graduated from high school in 1933. Within one year she published the first four novels in the Beverly Gray series, having written all the books while still in high school. Although a college graduate, Moyer worked as a secretary and typist before her marriage to George Moyer in 1943, after which she devoted herself to domestic life (including raising two sons) and writing Beverly Gray books.
(http://www.series-books.com, accessed 12 December 2009).

Mundis, Jerrold (March 3, 1941–?)
    Born in Chicago, the son of business executive James M. Mundis, the author attended Beloit (Wis.) College from 1959–1961 and graduated from New York University in 1963. He has been a full-time author since 1966, publishing more than fifteen books under his own name and the pseudonyms Robert Calder and Eric Corder.
(*Contemporary Authors Online*, Detroit: Gale, 2001, accessed 3 April 2009).

Nablo, James Benson (1910–?)
    No information available.

Nathan, Robert Louis
    No information available.

Nearing, Scott (August 6, 1883–August 24, 1983)
    The offspring of an affluent Pennsylvania family that owned a productive coal mine, Nearing developed a leftist socialist perspective in the early twentieth century that continued to evolve throughout his life, but was rooted in the concept that capitalism is evil. He earned his doctorate in economics from the University of Pennsylvania in 1909. After beginning a career as an academic, but finding his views too controversial for staid academe, he focused his attention on writing as the form of teaching for which he was best suited. He simplified his life dramatically and began researching and writing, producing at least one major work each year until his death. His political views received a great deal of attention and he was in demand as a speaker through many periods of his life. His books on living simply and returning to the land were also extremely popular in the 1960s.
(*Dictionary of Literary Biography*, vol. 303, s.v. "Nearing, Scott").

Nelson, Shirley (1949–?)

Nelson's parents were members of a Freewill Baptist utopian community, The Shiloh Society, located near Durham, Maine where she was raised. She is the author of works concerned with religion and is a book reviewer for periodicals, among them *Christian Century*.
(*Contemporary Authors Online*, Detroit: Thomson Gale, 2004, accessed 14 November 2009).

Neville, Edith
No information available.

Newman, Charles (May 27, 1938–March 15, 2006)

Newman had a long career as an academic. A graduate of Yale University (BA, summa cum laude, 1960) and Balliol College, Oxford University (1961), he has taught at Northwestern University (1963–1975), Johns Hopkins University (1975–1978) and Washington University (St. Louis, Missouri) (1985–2006). The recipient of numerous grants and fellowships for creative writing, his work tends to focus on threatened humankind in a technological age.
(*Contemporary Authors Online*, Detroit: Gale, 2006, accessed 12 March 2009).

Nicholas, Griffith A. [pseud.], *see* Worthington, Elizabeth Strong

Nichols, Edward Jay (November 2, 1900–February 24, 1986)

Born in Whiting, Indiana and a graduate of the University of Chicago (PhB, 1925), Columbia University (MA, 1928), and Pennsylvania State University (PhD, 1939), Nichols had a long career as an English professor at Pennsylvania State University (1928–1965). In addition to writing two novels, Nichols has published articles and books on topics in American history.
(*Contemporary Authors Online*, Detroit: Gale, 2002, accessed 12 March 2009).

Nielsen, Helen (1918–2002)

Mystery writer Nielsen was born in Roseville, Illinois and studied at the Chicago Art Institute. In addition to nineteen books, she published short stories and wrote television scripts. Her first job was as a costumer at Old Globe Theatre Productions in Chicago (1934–1935). After working for a time as a freelance commercial artist, she moved to California and worked in aeronautical drafting during World War II, before becoming an apartment house owner and manager.
(*Contemporary Authors Online*, Detroit: Gale, 2003, accessed 3 December 2009).

Norris, Frank (March 5, 1870–October 25, 1902)

Considered a key figure in the development of American naturalism, Norris was born in Chicago, the son of a wholesale jeweler and real estate investor. His family moved to San Francisco when he was fourteen years old. He studied painting at the Atelier Julien and English and French off and on between 1887 and 1895 at the University of California, Berkeley, as well as Harvard University. He began working in 1895 for the *San Francisco Chronicle* as a foreign correspondent. He later worked for the S. S. McClure Syndicate in New York City before becoming a novelist and freelance writer.
[*Dictionary of Literary Biography*, vol. 186, s.v. "Norris, (Benjamin) Frank(lin), (Jr,)"].

Norris, Hoke (October 8, 1913–1977)

A journalist, Norris published two novels. She was born in Holly Springs, North Carolina and educated at Wake Forest College (BA, 1934), and the University of North Carolina (graduate

study, 1946). After working for North Carolina newspapers (1934–1955), she worked for the *Chicago Sun-Times* and the *Chicago Daily News*. She later worked as publicity director for the Chicago Public Library (1971–1977).
(*Contemporary Authors Online*, Detroit: Gale, 2001, accessed 2 April 2009).

North, Sterling (November 4, 1906–December 22, 1974)
    Born in Edgerton, Wisconsin, North was a graduate of the University of Chicago (BA, 1929). A literary editor and critic, he built a reputation as a children's author, and his book *Rascal: A Memoir of a Better Era* (Dutton, 1963) won numerous awards and was released as a movie (Walt Disney Pictures, 1969). He lived in Chicago from 1925 to 1943 and worked for the *Chicago Daily News*.
(*New York Times*, 23 December 1974, 30).

Noyes, Henry (1910–June 22, 2005)
    The son of missionaries to China, Noyes was born in that country and did not leave until age nine, when he moved to Canada with his parents. Educated at the University of Toronto, Noyes went on to earn a doctorate in English literature from the University of London in 1938. He became head of the creative writing department at the University of Missouri in 1939. In 1945 he moved to Chicago where he was an outspoken advocate of normalizing relations with China and the Soviet Union. His political views blacklisted him out of even manual labor jobs and he founded his own business, China Books and Periodicals, in 1960, to provide printed materials to scholars, organizations, and leftist bookstores. He moved the firm to San Francisco in 1963 and for twenty-five years it was the sole distributor in the United States of books, magazines, and newspapers from China.
(*San Francisco Chronicle*, 8 July 2005, B-6).

Oates, Joyce Carol (June 16, 1938–?)
    Author of more than four hundred fifty published short stories and novels, Oates was born in Lockport, New York, and was educated at Syracuse University (BA, 1960) and the University of Wisconsin (MA, 1961). She has held posts at several universities, including at Princeton, where she has been a professor for several decades.
(*Dictionary of Literary Biography*, vol. 130, s.v. "Oates, Joyce Carol").

O'Brien, Howard Vincent [Clyde Perrin, pseud.] (1888–September 30, 1947)
    Born in Chicago and a 1910 graduate of Yale University, O'Brien held editorial positions on literary and art magazines and later entered the advertising industry before serving in World War I as a first lieutenant in the field artillery. Later, he was literary editor for the *Chicago Daily News* (1928–1932); however, he was best known for his topical column "All Things Considered," which he wrote for that newspaper from 1932 until his death. He was the author of six books including novels and memoirs.
(*New York Times*, 1 October 1947, 29).

O'Connor, Richard [Patrick Wayland, pseud.] (March 10, 1915–February 15, 1975)
    Born in LaPorte, Indiana, O'Connor grew up in Milwaukee, Wisconsin and attended public schools there. For a time he was an actor before working as a journalist on newspapers in Boston, Chicago, Detroit, Los Angeles, New Orleans, New York, and Washington, D.C. From 1957 until his death he worked full-time as a biographer and novelist. An author of biographies, histories,

mysteries, and Westerns, he published under his own name and the pseudonyms Frank Archer, John Burke, and Patrick Wayland.
(*Contemporary Authors Online*, Detroit: Gale, 2000, accessed 9 March 2009).

O'Donnell, Simon
   No information available.

O'Hara, Boris
   No information available.

O'Hara, John (1905–April 11, 1970)
   For thirty-six years a financially successful writer, O'Hara was born into the family of an affluent doctor in Pottsville, Pennsylvania, but just as he was to enter Yale University in 1925, his father died and O'Hara's financial security ended. He began writing for Pennsylvania newspapers before moving to New York City in 1927. In 1928 he started publishing stories in the *New Yorker* and by 1934, the fame he earned with the publication of *Appointment at Samarra* took him to Hollywood where he worked as a well-paid film writer and reviser until the mid-1940s. The author of more than thirty novels and books of short stories, O'Hara mostly wrote about eastern Pennsylvania, Hollywood, and the New York City-Philadelphia-Washington, D.C. corridor. His only work set in Chicago, *Pal Joey,* became a great success when it was adapted for Broadway as a musical by Rodgers and Hart in 1940.
[*Dictionary of Literary Biography*, vol. 86, s.v. "O'Hara, John (Henry)"].

Okun, Lawrence Eugene (August 14, 1929–?)
   A physician with a specialty in obstetrics and gynecology who has worked most of his career in California, Okun was born in Kalamazoo, Michigan and was educated at Western Michigan University (BS, 1951) and the University of Michigan (MD, 1958). He served in the U.S. Air Force (1951–1954) and has authored only the book for which he is included here.

Olesker, J. Bradford (1949–?)
   No information available.

Olsen, Tillie (January 14, c1912–2007)
   Known for her fiction articulating working class, feminist, and Jewish perspectives, Olsen was born Tillie Lerner into a large family of Russian Jewish immigrants and grew up in Omaha, Nebraska. Her parents were laborers and political activists and members of the Nebraska Socialist Party. Forced to drop out of high school during the Depression, Olsen's own political activism emerged and she was jailed for trying to organize packing house workers in Kansas City, Missouri. With incipient tuberculosis, she moved to California in 1933, eventually settling in San Francisco, where she spent the rest of her life. She married a union printer, Jack Olsen, in 1937, got involved in local political activities and raised four daughters before starting to write in 1955, inspired by taking a creative writing class at San Francisco State University. She won a fellowship to Stanford University the following year and, in 1959, a Ford Foundation grant to finish the stories that would be published as *Tell Me a Riddle* (Dell, 1961). She was immediately recognized as a major talent and she became absorbed in writing and teaching.
(*Dictionary of Literary Biography*, vol. 206, s.v. "Olsen, Tillie").

Osborn, Catherine B. (June 16, 1914–?)

A teacher in private schools and colleges, Osborn ended her career as the dean of Flora Stone Mather College (Case Western Reserve University) (1959–1969). The daughter of Clarence Powers, a college professor, and Sarah (Babbitt) Bill, Osborn was educated at Bryn Mawr College (BA, 1935; MA 1939). She married physician James W. Osborn in 1939. Osborn co-authored a book with Margaret Waterman.

(*Contemporary Authors Online*, Detroit: Gale, 2003, accessed 25 April 2009).

Ozaki, Milton K. [Robert O. Saber, pseud.] (June 14, 1913–1989)

The son of a Japanese man, Frank Jingoro Ozaki, and a Caucasian woman, Augusta Rathbum, Ozaki was born in Racine, Wisconsin. He attended Ripon College for two years where he majored in English and learned to play bridge. In 1935 he moved to Chicago, where he worked as a hairdresser, eventually opening his own salon on the Gold Coast. However, most of his income derived from playing bridge for money. In 1941 he became a National Master, but lost interest in bridge during World War II. He published his first mystery in 1946 and went on to write twenty-five hard-boiled mysteries published under his own name and the pseudonym Robert O. Saber. After the decline in the market for pulp fiction, Ozaki changed his focus and began writing about bridge, eventually moving to Colorado and later Nevada where he was prosecuted for operating a business to sell doctoral degrees. He is noted for the detective characters he created and for being the first mystery writer of Japanese ancestry.

(*San Francisco Nichi Bei Times Weekly,* 15 May 2008, 1).

Paine, Lauran Bosworth [Mark Carrel, pseud.] (February 25, 1916–1995)

Born in Duluth, Minnesota and educated in private schools in Illinois and California, Lauran was a rancher in northern California before turning to writing full-time. The author of over nine hundred works of genre fiction under dozens of pseudonyms, he is best known for his seven hundred Westerns, although he also wrote romance novels (under female pseudonyms) and mysteries. Several of his books were adapted for film, including *The Open Range Men*, released as *Open Range*, directed and starring Kevin Costner (Touchstone, 2003).

(*Contemporary Authors Online*, Detroit: Gale, 2006, accessed 3 April 2009).

Palumbo, Dennis James (November 18, 1929–?)

A native of Chicago and graduate of the University of Chicago (MA, 1958; PhD 1960), Palumbo has had a long career as an academic with a focus on public policy, criminal justice, and public administration. Most of his books are in these disciplines.

(*Contemporary Authors Online*, Detroit: Gale, 2007, accessed 14 March 2009).

Paradise, Viola

No information available.

Parker, Mary Moncure (1862–1941)

No information available.

Parrish, Randall (1858–1923)

Born George Randall Parrish in Kewanee, Illinois, Parrish studied at Griswold College (Davenport, Iowa), Union College of Law (Chicago), and graduated from Iowa State University with a law degree. He was active in Kansas politics in the 1880s before an adventurous period on

the frontier, working on the railroad as a cowboy, and prospecting for gold in New Mexico and Arizona. He became a reporter in 1885, working for a number of newspapers including the *Chicago Times*. In 1902 he worked for the Associated Press in Chicago and published his first work of fiction in 1903, after which he devoted himself full-time to writing fiction. He moved back to his hometown in 1904.
(Henry L. Kiner. *History of Henry County Illinois*, vol. II., Chicago: Pioneer, 1910, s.v. "Parrish, Randall").

Parrish, Robert (1918–?)
    No information available.

Patchin, Frank (1861–1925)
    No information available.

Patterson, Eleanor Medill [aka Eleanor Gizycka] (November 7, 1881–July 24, 1948)
    A native of Chicago, the granddaughter of Joseph Medill (owner of the *Chicago Tribune*), her father was the managing editor of the newspaper and her mother was an ambitious society woman focused on becoming the official hostess of Washington from the family mansion on Dupont Circle. Briefly the wife of Polish Count Gizycki, she devoted her twenties and thirties to romantic affairs and travel around the country in her private railroad car. She did not begin writing until after her marriage to a New York lawyer, Elmer Schlesinger, in 1925. She became best known in the 1930s for creating the *Washington Times-Herald*, the first all-day daily paper, with six daily editions. She owned the paper from 1939 until her death in 1948.
(*Dictionary of Literary Biography*, vol. 29, s.v. "Patterson, Eleanor Medill").

Patterson, Joseph Medill (January 6, 1879–May 26, 1946)
    Patterson created the *New York Daily News* in 1919, a newspaper known for its innovative format and having the highest Sunday circulation in the country. A native Chicagoan, Patterson was the grandson of Joseph Medill, editor of the *Chicago Tribune* and a major figure in nineteenth-century American journalism. As a young man, after graduating from Yale University in 1901, Patterson became involved in Chicago politics. After the death of his father he took an active role in managing the *Chicago Tribune* with great success before founding his own newspaper.
(*Dictionary of Literary Biography*, vol. 29, s.v. "Patterson, Joseph Medill").

Paulsen, Gary (May 17, 1939–?)
    Although he was born in Minneapolis, Minnesota, Paulsen moved to Chicago with his mother at the age of three, when his father, a career military officer, was ordered to Europe to serve under General Patton in World War II. At the end of the war, the family was reunited in Manila where Paulsen's father had been posted. After two quarters in college and military service, Paulsen worked a variety of jobs including at a satellite tracking firm in California. An outdoorsman and dogsledder, Paulsen has written a number of successful books for young adults, many of them survival or coming of age stories.
(*Contemporary Authors Online*, Detroit: Gale, 2008, accessed 5 March 2009).

Payne, Philip (1867–?)
    No information available.

Payne, Will (1865–1954)
    No information available.

Pearce, John Irving
    No information available.

Peattie, Elia Wilkinson (January 15, 1862–July 12, 1935)
    Although she was born in Kalamazoo, Michigan, Peattie grew up in Chicago. She married Chicago journalist Robert Burns Peattie in 1883 and became a reporter with the *Chicago Tribune*, and later the *Chicago Daily News*. After working on newspapers in Omaha, Nebraska (1888–1896), Peattie returned to Chicago to work as the literary editor of the *Chicago Tribune*. She published pieces of short fiction widely in popular magazines of the day and wrote several books, mostly for children and young adults.
    (*Herringshaw's National Library of American Biography*, s.v. "Peattie, Elia Wilkinson").

Peattie, Louise Redfield (June 14, 1900–1965)
    The daughter of prominent Chicago corporate lawyer Robert Redfield, Peattie was privately educated in the city and married Donald Culross Peattie in 1923. The couple lived in Washington, D.C., Provence, and the French Riviera before settling in Santa Barbara, California in 1934. Donald Peattie was a novelist and well-known naturalist. Louise Peattie was primarily active in the 1920s and 1930s as a romance novelist.
    (*World Authors, 1900–1950*, New York: H. W. Wilson, 1996, s.v. "Peattie, Louise Redfield").

Peck, Richard (April 5, 1934–?)
    An author of poetry and award-winning fiction for young adults, Peck was born in Decatur, Illinois and educated at DePauw (Ind.) University (BA, 1956) and Southern Illinois University (MA, 1959). He has taught English in high school and college. His work is known for realistic dialog and dealing with contemporary social issues).
    (*Contemporary Authors Online*, Detroit: Gale, 2008, accessed 2 February 2009).

Pendleton, Don (1928–1995)
    Pendleton had no formal education, but he wrote more than eighty books and is credited with introducing the action-adventure genre. Born in Little Rock, Arkansas, in 1941 as a fourteen-year-old he lied about his age to enlist in the U.S. Navy. In 1957, he enrolled in a mail order writing course and published a book before he completed the program. Although he began writing full-time when he was forty, producing a few mysteries and science fiction books each year, his breakthrough came when he wrote the first book featuring Mack Boland, "The Executioner," who battled the Mafia.
    (*New York Times,* 28 October 1995, 50).

Peters, Bill [pseud.], *see* McGivern, William

Petrakis, Harry Mark (June 5, 1923–?)
    Born in St. Louis, Missouri, the son of an Eastern Orthodox priest, Petrakis grew up in Chicago. He attended the University of Illinois and worked various jobs including as a laborer and steelworker before becoming a free-lance writer and lecturer in 1960. Much of his work is drawn

from his knowledge of the Chicago Greek community and deals with the American immigrant experience. In addition to novels, he has published many short stories.
(*Contemporary Authors Online*, Detroit: Thomson Gale, 2007, accessed 14 March 2009).

Pflaum, Melanie (April 12, 1909–March 2004)
The daughter of Edward and Judith Loewenthal, Pflaum was educated at the University of Wisconsin (1927–1928) and the University of Chicago (PhB, 1929). In 1930, she married Latin American studies professor Irving Peter Pflaum. She worked in various editorial positions and as a freelance writer until 1955, after which she devoted herself to writing novels and teaching creative writing. She and her husband lived in a number of countries in Europe, South America, Latin America, and for an extended period of time in Chicago (1942–1959).
(*Contemporary Authors Online*, Detroit: Gale, 2001, accessed 14 March 2009).

Phelon, William A.
No information available.

Phillip, Quentin Morrow (1904–?)
No information available.

Phillips, David Graham (October 31, 1867–1911)
An 1887 graduate of Princeton University, Phillips began his career as a newspaperman in Cincinnati and, in 1890, while quite young, was hired by Charles A. Dana to work on the staff of the *New York Sun*. Through his work at the *Sun*, opinion pieces for magazines, and his later work for the *New York World* he exposed corruption of all kinds and crusaded against poverty and disease. After the 1901 success of his pseudonymous novel *The Great God Success* (published under the name John Graham by Stokes), he resigned from the *World* in 1902 to devote himself to fiction as a more effective way of advocating his reform agenda. His exposé *The Treason of the Senate,* published as a series in *Cosmopolitan* in 1906, earned him Theodore Roosevelt's epithet "Man with the Muck-Rake." Eventually publishing more than twenty-five novels with average sales of one hundred thousand copies each, Phillips assailed the evils of great wealth and the political influence it bought, as well as calling for the enfranchisement of women. Phillips was mortally wounded when he was shot by Fitzhugh Coyle Goldsmith, a Washingtonian who was obsessed with the idea that the Goldsmith family had been maligned in Phillips' novels.
(*Dictionary of Literary Biography*, vol. 303, s.v. "Phillips, David Graham").

Phillips, Leon, [pseud.], *see* Gerson, Noel B. (Noel Bertram)

Pickard, William John
No information available.

Piercy, Marge (March 31, 1936–?)
Poet and novelist, Piercy was born in Detroit, Michigan in a working class household. She earned her bachelor's degree from the University of Michigan in 1957 and a master's degree from Northwestern University in 1958. Initially supporting herself with the sort of menial jobs she could find on Chicago's South Side, she left for New York City in the late 1960s to work as an organizer for Students for a Democratic Society (SDS). She published her first book in 1968 and

has built a career as a widely respected author. Since 1971 she has lived in Wellfleet, Massachusetts.
(*Dictionary of Literary Biography*, vol. 120, s.v. "Piercy, Marge").

Pinkerton, Allan (1819–1884)
Scottish immigrant Pinkerton was born in Glasgow and arrived in the United States in 1842. He settled in Dundee, Illinois, but in 1850, after working as a detective and sheriff, founded the Pinkerton National Detective Agency in Chicago. During the Civil War, he was the head of the federal intelligence network and his private firm subsequently functioned in official capacities for the government. The agency was repeatedly used by capitalists to suppress the labor movement, often through the use of force.
(*Chambers Biographical Dictionary*, New York: Chambers, sixth edition, 1997, s.v. "Pinkerton, Allan").

Pinkerton, Myron
No information available.

Plagemann, Bentz (July 27, 1913–February 8, 1991)
Born in Springfield, Ohio, Plagemann worked in bookstores in Cleveland, Chicago, Detroit, and New York City (1932–1942). He served in the U.S. Navy (1942–1945) as a pharmacist's mate. After 1947 he devoted himself full-time to writing, having published novels in 1941 and 1946. He went on to write and publish fourteen more books and contributed to many periodicals.
(*Contemporary Authors Online*, Detroit: Gale, 2003, accessed 3 April 2009).

Plum, Mary (1892–1962)
No information available.

Pollard, Percival (January 29, 1869–December 17, 1911)
A Prussian immigrant who arrived in the United States in 1885, initially Pollard worked for a railroad and later as a reporter in St. Joseph, Missouri. He moved to Chicago in 1891 where he worked for magazines. The success of his articles and literary criticism attracted national interest and he moved to New York City in 1896 where he published in *Criterion*. He is best remembered for his criticism, in which he called for American writers to look for inspiration in *fin de siecle* European culture.
(*Contemporary Authors Online*, Detroit: Thomson Gale, 2007, accessed, 15 May 2009).

Postgate, John William (1851–May 4, 1921)
A journalist and editor, Postgate was born in Hartlepool, England, but lived most of his life in New York City. His first editor position was with the *New York Herald*. He was later mining editor for the *New York Sun* and went on to be editor and publisher of the *American Mining News*. In his final years, he was an editor for the *Globe and Literary Digest*.
(*New York Times*, 4 May 1921, 9).

Potter, Jack [John Hart, pseud.]
No information available.

Potter, Margaret Horton Black (May 20, 1881–December 22, 1911)

The daughter of steel manufacturer Orrin W. Potter and sister of Edwin C. Potter, an executive with Illinois Brick Company, Potter's first novel, written while she was still in her teens, was suppressed because the Chicago socialites it portrayed were too thinly veiled. She was married in 1902 to John Donald Black, a son of General John C. Black, president of the United States Civil Service Commission. Although she published nine novels, her addiction to morphine increasingly affected her life. She was committed to an insane asylum by court order in 1910, the same year her husband divorced her. At the time of her death from a morphine overdose she was a resident of the Chicago Beach Hotel.
(*New York Times*, 23 December 1911, 5).

Powers, J. F. (James Farl) (July 8, 1917–June 12, 1999)

The author of many short stories and two novels, Powers won the National Book Award in 1963 for *Morte d'Urban* (included here). Born in Jacksonville, Illinois, he attended Northwestern University and worked as a creative writing teacher at several colleges and universities before working at St. John's University (Collegeville, Minnesota) from 1976 to 1993. He won a Guggenheim fellowship and three Rockefeller fellowships.
(*Contemporary Authors Online*, Detroit: Gale, 2004, accessed 3 April 2009).

Powers, John R. (November 30, 1945–?)

Author of several works dealing with his youth in Chicago and as a student in Roman Catholic schools that he identifies as fictionalized memoirs, Powers was born in Chicago. He attended parochial schools and received all of his higher education at Chicago colleges and universities (Loyola University, BS, 1967; Northwestern University, MA, 1969, PhD, 1975). He has been a professor of speech at Northeastern Illinois University (Chicago) since 1972. A weekly columnist for the *Chicago Daily News* since 1977, he is also a contributor to Chicago-based magazines.
(*Contemporary Authors Online*, Detroit: Thomson Gale, 2007, accessed 9 November 2009).

Pratt, Mrs. Eleanor Blake Atkinson [aka Eleanor Blake]

No information available.

Pruitt, Alan, *see* Rose, Alvin Emanuel

Pugh, Charles (February 28, 1948–?)

A Chicago native, Pugh received an associate's degree from Wright College (1968) and a bachelor's degree from the University of Illinois at Chicago Circle (1970). He places himself within the "griot" tradition of the African-American community and sees his written work as keeping with that role.
(*Contemporary Authors Online*, Detroit: Gale, 2006, accessed 18 July 2009).

Purdy, James (July 17, 1923–March 13, 2009)

Playwright, poet, and novelist, Purdy was born in Fremont, Ohio, a small town near Lake Erie. The poverty and provincialism he experienced as the middle child in a family of five boys shaped his earliest works, and throughout his career most of his stories have been set in the Midwest. He escaped Ohio by attending the University of Chicago, however during his undergraduate career he transferred to the University of Puebla in Mexico. After graduation he taught in a private boys' school in Havana, Cuba. He returned to Chicago to take graduate courses at the University

of Chicago and later took additional courses at the University of Madrid in Spain. He has published more than thirty books and lived most of his adult life in Brooklyn, New York.
(*New York Times*, 14 March 2009, A19).

Quammen, David (February 24, 1948–?)

Quammen is the author of eight books and numerous magazine pieces, most concerning the natural world. He was born near Cincinnati, Ohio and studied at Yale University with Robert Penn Warren. After living in Chicago, working in an African-American ghetto, he wrote his first novel about race relations. He completed a two-year fellowship at Oxford University studying William Faulkner. Upon his return to the United States he moved to Montana, supporting himself as a bartender and guide. In 1979 he became a full-time writer and in 1981 began a fifteen-year stint as a columnist with *Outside* magazine. His nature writing has won awards and his occasional scientific thrillers have sold well.
(*World Authors, 1990–1995*, New York: H. W. Wilson, 1999, s.v. "Quammen, David").

Quick, Herbert (October 31, 1861–May 10, 1925)

Quick wrote fiction, much of it set in his native Iowa, and non-fiction concerned with commerce, rural issues, and transportation. He was born in Grundy County, Iowa, the son of a farmer and lumberman. Educated in poorly funded country schools and at a teacher's institute in Grundy Center, he began his professional life as a teacher, eventually being appointed principal. He studied law under a practicing lawyer and passed the Iowa bar exam in 1889. He established a practice in Sioux City and became involved in city politics, holding the office of mayor from 1898 to 1900. He was the associate editor for several Midwestern magazines before his appointment by President Woodrow Wilson to the Federal Farm Loan Bureau in 1916. He began publishing books in 1901, starting with volumes of folklore and fantasy. He was best known in his lifetime for producing works of historical fiction set in Iowa and contributing to American regionalism.
(*World Authors, 1900–1950*, New York: H. W. Wilson, 1996, s.v. "Quick, Herbert").

Quinlan, Sterling (October 23, 1916–March 11, 2007)

Quinlan, a journalist, radio actor, and television executive, had a career in broadcasting that extended over thirty-five years. Born in Maquoketa, Iowa, he began writing for Chicago community newspapers in 1930, but soon was acting in radio broadcasting. Involved in this work in Chicago; Cleveland; Hollywood; and Gary, Indiana, Quinlan started working in broadcasting management positions in 1947 and worked for Chicago radio station WBKB for twenty years, later holding positions with other Chicago broadcasting organizations. He has published eight volumes of fiction and non-fiction.
(*Contemporary Authors Online*, Detroit: Gale, 2002 accessed 4 March 2009).

Quint, Wilder Dwight (November 15, 1863–January 4, 1936)

A journalist, Quint graduated from Dartmouth College in 1887 and began writing for Boston newspapers that year. He worked as a reporter and editor at the *Boston Advertiser*, *Boston News*, *Boston Traveler*, and *Boston Post*. He co-authored several books with George Tilton Richardson under the shared pseudonym of Charles Eustace Merriman.
(*Who's Who in New England*, Chicago: Marquis, 1916, second edition, s.v. "Quint, Wilder Dwight").

Quondam, *see* Stevens, C. M.

Randolph, Georgiana Ann [Craig Rice, pseud.] (June 5, 1908–1957)
    Chicago native Randolph worked as a crime reporter, freelance writer, publicity manager, and radio and motion picture script writer. Randolph's mystery books were very popular and several of her works were adapted as motion pictures. Her detectives often fortify themselves with alcohol and Randolph was an alcoholic who died of a barbiturate and alcohol overdose at a relatively young age. She was married four times and had three children during her fourth marriage to Lawrence Lipton. In addition to her more than twenty-four mysteries, she ghost-wrote two mysteries with performer Gypsy Rose Lee.
    (*Contemporary Authors Online*, Detroit: Gale, 2004, accessed 15 March 2009).

Rapp, William Jourdan (June 17, 1895–August 12, 1942)
    Playwright and media executive Rapp was born in New York City and lived most of his life there. He graduated from Cornell University (BS, 1917) and was in the U.S. Medical Corps during World War I, assigned to a unit testing water potability. After the war he studied bacteriology at the Sorbonne (1919–1920) and went on to work as a public health consultant in the Near East for four years. He became involved in publishing and broadcasting through his work with the religious publications firm Cook Publishing in Elgin, Illinois, for whom, over time, he edited thirty publications. Later (1926–1942) he was the editor of *True Story*, a magazine with two million readers. In 1937 he co-founded C. D. Morris Associates, radio producers. During his career he authored hundreds of scripts for radio soap operas, and several plays.
    (*New York Times*, 13 August 1942, 19).

Raskin, Ellen (March 13, 1928–August 8, 1984)
    Not until she had illustrated hundreds of articles and created more than one thousand book jackets did Raskin begin writing her own books. These were initially picture books for children, but over time she began writing mysteries for older children. Her books won awards for their illustrations. Born in working-class poverty in Milwaukee, Wisconsin, Raskin attended the University of Wisconsin (1945–1949), however she lived most of her adult life in New York City.
    (*Dictionary of Literary Biography*, vol. 52, "Raskin, Ellen").

Rathborne, St. George Henry (December 26, 1854–December 16, 1938)
    Known as one of the most prolific dime novelists, Rathborne wrote under more than twenty pseudonyms for the most prominent publishers of the genre, including Beadle and Adams, A. L. Burt and Hurst and Lee. Although he was born in Covington, Kentucky, he grew up in Cincinnati and graduated from the public schools there. He lived in Chicago for periods of time as an editor, but also worked in New York for publishing firms. He wrote seventy novels and over 250 dime novels for boys, many of them in his "Doctor Jack" series.
    (*New York Times*, 17 December 1938, 48).

Raymond, Clifford (1875–1950)
    No information available.

Raymond, Evelyn (1843–1910)
    No information available.

Rayne, Martha Louise
    No information available.

Rayner, William (January 1, 1929–?)

English writer Rayner graduated from Wadham College, Oxford University, in 1952 and taught English in England and Africa before becoming a full-time freelance writer in 1970. Several of his books are for children or young adults. His best-known work is historical fiction set in the American West. He has published more than eighteen books.
(*Contemporary Authors Online*, Detroit: Gale, 2001, accessed 4 April 2009).

Rea, M. P. (Margaret Paine)

No information available.

Read, Opie (December 22, 1852–November 2, 1939)

Read was a pioneering newspaperman, popular Chautauqua lecturer, and the author of over fifty books. He is best known for his contributions to American regionalism in literature and most of his works were set in the South. He was born in Nashville, Tennessee and grew up in Gallatin, Tennessee. He began publishing humorous sketches about people he had met or stories he had heard in African-American or Southern working-class dialect. After learning to set type, he worked on newspapers in Tennessee, Kentucky, and Arkansas. In 1882 he began publishing his own newspaper, the *Arkansas Traveler*, that was filled with sketches, rather than news stories. The success of the publication prompted a move of the operation to Chicago in 1887. Read began including serialized portions of his work, later published as novels, and between 1891 and 1914 mostly spent his time writing novels. His days on the Chautauqua circuit between 1912 and the 1920s made him a national celebrity as the Arkansas Traveler or Kentucky Colonel; however, he never returned to live in the rural South, but continued to live in Chicago from 1928 until his death at 5000 Harper Avenue.
(*Dictionary of Literary Biography*, vol. 23, s.v. "Read, Opie").

Reed, Myrtle (September 27, 1874–August 17, 1911)

A native Chicagoan who lived all her life in the city, Reed was the daughter of two literary, religious people. Her father, Hiram Von Reed, was a Campbellite preacher and editor of religious magazines who created Chicago's first literary magazine, the *Lakeside Monthly*. Her mother was a self-taught student of comparative religion whose books on Eastern religions and the Bible were acclaimed by scholarly associations in England. Encouraged to write from a young age, Reed edited the school newspaper at West Division High School. Shortly after graduating in 1893, she began submitting romance stories to national magazines and published her first romance novel with George H. Putnam in 1899. Her life and writing changed after the young Canadian man with whom she had carried on a long correspondence moved to Chicago; after an epistolary courtship of fifteen years they were married. Her work began to portray homemaking as a woman's highest form of fulfillment and she started publishing cookbooks. Her writings presented her own marriage as the epitome of marital bliss. The daunting role of perfect husband drove her husband to drink. Reed mitigated the dissonance between her ideal and real life with the sedative drug veronal and finally overdosed on the preparation. The ideal she had presented in thirteen romance books and many short stories had been widely appealing as her large estate and significant annual royalty income demonstrated.
(*Notable American Women, 1607–1950: A Biographical Dictionary*, Cambridge, Mass.: Harvard University Press, Belknap Press, 1971, s.v. "Reed, Myrtle").

Reilly, Patricia [Anna Bell Ward, pseud.] (?–?)
    No information available.

Renken, Aleda (June 21, 1907–?)
    The author of books for children was born in Jefferson City, Missouri and attended Warrens-
burg Teachers College, the University of Missouri, and Lincoln University (Jefferson City, Mo.).
In addition to freelance writing, she worked for the Jefferson City Department of Conservation as
the circulation manager of *Conservationist*, a position she held for almost fifty years.
(*Contemporary Authors Online*, Detroit: Gale, 2002, accessed 13 November 2009).

Rhodes, James A. (September 13, 1909–March 4, 2001)
    A four-term Republican governor of Ohio, Rhodes is best known for ordering troops onto the
campus Kent State University to put down Vietnam war protests—an action that led to the shooting deaths of four students. Born in Coalton, Ohio, near Huntington, West Virginia, Rhodes was
the son of a coal miner. He attended, but did not graduate from, Ohio State University. In 1934, he
entered politics in Columbus, Ohio, eventually serving as mayor of that city (1942–1953). He later
served four terms as governor of Ohio (1963–1970, 1974–1982). In addition to several books of
historical fiction co-authored with Jauchius Dean, Rhodes published works on social and educational policy.
(*New York Times*, 6 March 2001, A19).

Rice, Craig [pseud.], *see* Randolph, Georgiana Ann

Richardson, George Tilton (1863–September 11, 1938)
    Richardson was a journalist who worked on Boston newspapers for much of his career before
becoming editor of the *Worcester (Mass.) Evening Post*. He wrote successful plays and co-
authored fiction with Wilder Dwight Quint under the joint pseudonym Charles Eustace Merriman.
(*New York Times*, 12 September 1938, 17

Richardson, John (October 4, 1796–May 12, 1852)
    The son of a military surgeon, at age fifteen Richardson enlisted with a Canadian regiment as
a soldier in the War of 1812 and fought in battles near Lake Erie before his capture and imprisonment in the battle of Moraviantown (Kentucky) in 1813 (released July 1814). He received a commission and went to Europe to fight against Napoleon, then served in Barbados and Grenada. Ma-
laria forced him to leave active duty and in the 1820s and 1830s he lived in London and Paris
where he began writing. His fictionalized accounts of the frontier and of historical events reflected
his admiration for Indian warriors and fed popular interest in America (his maternal grandmother
was an Ottawa). He returned to active service in 1835 and campaigned in Spain. In 1837 he traveled to Canada where he became involved in politics and journalism. In 1849 he moved to New
York City and published serialized novels in *Sartain's Union Magazine of Literature and Art*
(Philadelphia) and short stories in other magazines. Straitened finances led to his death from mal-
nourishment.
(*Dictionary of Canadian Biography, 1851–1860*, vol. 8, Toronto: University of Toronto Press,
2000, s.v. "Richardson, John").

Richardson, Merrick Abner (1841–?)
    No information available.

Richberg, Donald Randall (July 10, 1881–November 27, 1960)

An author in several genres—poetry, journalism, political studies, and fiction—Richberg was a prominent Chicago lawyer, serving as attorney for the city and for Illinois, and becoming a specialist on railroad labor relations. He was a figure in national politics during the New Deal and helped to draft important pieces of legislation, such as the Taft-Hartley Act and the act that established the National Recovery Administration (NRA). He served as chief administrator of the NRA until 1935, when the act that established the agency was deemed unconstitutional. He returned to private law practice, but in 1949 accepted a faculty position at the University of Virginia School of Law teaching constitutional law.
(*A Dictionary of American History*, Indianapolis: Wiley-Blackwell, 1997, s.v. "Richberg, Donald Randall").

Richberg, Eloise O. Randall (c.1926–?)

The only daughter of Donald Randall Richberg, the author was the offspring of her father's third marriage to Florence Weed (to whom he was married from 1924 until his death in 1960). She graduated from the National Cathedral School in 1944, which was also her debutante year. She graduated from Wellesley College in 1948. Richberg married Archibald A. Campbell, a lawyer and gentleman farmer in Wytheville, Virginia February 19, 1950.

Richert, William (c.1942–?)

Best known for his career in the film industry as an actor, director, producer, and screenwriter, Richert left his native state of Florida as a seventeen-year-old for Hollywood. He began his film career with a documentary and went on to be a screenwriter for six motion pictures and director of four. He was writer and director for his most successful movie, *A Night in the Life of Jimmy Reardon* (Island Pictures, 1988) starring River Phoenix. The film was an adaptation of his novel *Aren't You Even Gonna Kiss Me Good-by?* (included here). Richert acted in a number of television shows and movies, but is best known for his performance as Bob in the Gus van Sant film *My Own Private Idaho* (Fine Line Features, 1991).

Rickett, Frances (February 16, 1921–?)

Born in Covington, Kentucky, Rickett was educated at DePauw (Ind.) University (BA, 1943). During World War II she was a civilian cryptanalyst for the U.S. Army Signal Corps (1943–1945). She completed graduate study in fine arts at the Catholic University of America (MA, 1947) and worked as a radio staff writer and later a staff writer for the National Broadcasting Corporation in New York City, contributing to soap opera scripts. She was on the staff of *Woman's Day* (1956–1957) and has subsequently worked as a freelance writer, publishing more than nine novels and continuing to write for television and radio.
(*Contemporary Authors Online*, Detroit: Gale, 2001, accessed, 4 April 2009).

Riesenberg, Felix (April 9, 1879–November 19, 1939)

Born in Milwaukee, Wisconsin, the son of a sea captain, Riesenberg went to sea at the age of sixteen and was a sailor for twelve years. During this time, he was part of the Wellman Polar Expedition (1906–1907) and was navigator of the dirigible *America*, the first such craft to fly over North Polar Regions. Riesenberg was educated at Columbia University, receiving a degree in civil engineering (1911). He was commander of the *U.S.S. Newport* during World War I and again from

1923–1924. As a writer he was known for autobiographical accounts of life at sea, maritime histories, and novels. He also wrote technical books and movie and radio scripts.
(*New York Times*, 19 November 1939, 38).

River, W. L. (Walter Leslie) (December 15, 1903–November 1, 1981)
    River lived most of his life in California and was best known as the author of screenplays produced in the 1930s and 1940s.
(*Internet Movie Database*, www.imdb.com/name/nmo2729179, accessed 11 March 2009).

Roberts, Edith (1902–?)
    Born Edith Elizabeth Kneipple, Roberts used her married name from her first marriage on books included here. She later became Edith Kneipple Van Dusen. Several of her novels were adapted as motion pictures, including *That Hagen Girl* (Doubleday, 1946) which starred a teenage Shirley Temple and Ronald Reagan (Warner Bros., 1947).

Roberts, John Hawley (c.1897–December 8, 1949)
    Born in Peoria, Illinois, Roberts was a graduate of the University of Chicago in English (PhD, 1919). He began his academic career there as a fellow (1922–1923), going on to serve as an instructor (1923–1926) before moving to Williams College where he was still teaching at the time of his death.
(*New York Times*, 9 December 1949, 31).

Robinson, Frank M. [James Courtney, pseud.]. (1926-)
    Born in Chicago, Robinson was an office boy at science fiction publisher Ziff-Davis before he was drafted into the Navy for World War II. After his term was up he went to college, majoring in physics, but returned to the Navy during the Korean War. He went to graduate school in journalism and worked for Chicago-based publications, eventually taking over the "Playboy Advisor column" in 1969, a position he left in 1973 to move to San Francisco and begin writing full-time. Openly gay, Robinson was a speechwriter for gay politician Harvey Milk. The author of more than sixteen books, three of his novels have been made into movies. The most popular of these was *Towering Inferno* (Twentieth Century-Fox, 1974) that was also partially based on another author's book.
(*Twentieth Century Science Fiction Writers*, New York, N.Y.: St. Martin's, 1981, s.v. "Robinson, Frank M.")

Robinson, Herbert B.
    No information available.

Robinson, Rose (1932–?)
    A Chicago native, Robinson received her bachelor's degree from the School of the Art Institute of Chicago and later took courses at the University of Chicago, DePaul University, and Western Reserve University (now Case Western Reserve University). She is the author of one novel.
(*Contemporary Authors Online*, Detroit: Gale, 2002, accessed 7 April 2009).

Roe, Edward Payson (March 7, 1838–July 19, 1888)
    Roe grew up on his family's farm near Modena, New York. After a conversion experience as a young adult, he decided to train for the Presbyterian ministry. He studied at Williams College,

entered Auburn Seminary in 1861, and was ordained in 1862. During the Civil War he served as a chaplain and later attended Union Theological Seminary in New York City before accepting a pastorate in Highland Falls, New York. He traveled to Chicago not long after the 1871 fire and was inspired to write *Barriers Burned Away*. From then until the end of his life he wrote popular novels with Christian themes that achieved large readerships in the 1870s and 1880s, selling more than five million copies.
(*Dictionary of Literary Biography*, vol. 202, s.v. "Roe, Edward Payson").

Roe, Edward Reynolds (?–?)
    No information available.

Roeburt, John (c.1909–May 24, 1972)
    The author of detective novels and radio and television scripts, Roeburt was born in New York City and lived there his entire life. After graduating with a law degree from New York University, Roeburt worked for a time as a crime reporter on the staff of the *Brooklyn Eagle*.
(*New York Times*, 24 May 1972, 50).

Rogers, Thomas (1927–2007)
    The author of four novels, Rogers was born in Chicago and educated at Harvard University (BA, 1950) and the University of Iowa (MA, 1952; PhD, 1960). He became a college teacher in 1955 and, after working for six years at the University of Chicago, became a professor at Pennsylvania State University, where he remained for the rest of his career.
(*Contemporary Authors Online*, Detroit: Gale, 2007, accessed 20 August 2009).

Rosaire, Forrest (1902–1977)
    Rosaire was the author of magazine fiction in the 1930s and 1940s, using the pseudonym J. J. des Ormeaux. He published additional stories and three novels under his own name.

Rose, Alvin Emanuel [Alan Pruitt, pseud.] (December 13, 1903–May 28, 1983)
    Born in Chicago, Rose began his career in 1927 as a *Chicago Tribune* reporter and filed one of the first stories on the 1929 St. Valentine's Day Massacre. He served as city editor of the *Chicago Times* (1935–1938), but resigned to become an official in the Chicago Relief Administration (later known as the Chicago Welfare Administration). Rose continued with that agency until 1957 when he was appointed executive director of the Chicago Housing Authority, a job from which he retired in 1967.
(*Contemporary Authors Online*, Detroit: Gale, 1998, accessed 11 March 2009).

Rose, Richard M.
    No information available.

Rosenfeld, Isaac (March 10, 1918–July 15, 1956)
    A native of Chicago and childhood friend of Saul Bellow, Rosenfeld grew up in a lower-middle class Jewish family and was early interested in intellectual matters, particularly philosophy. Educated at the University of Chicago (MA, 1941), he began a doctoral program in logic at New York University. Living in New York City's Greenwich Village in the 1940s, he established a reputation as a public intellectual through essays in *New Republic*, *Partisan Review*, and *The Nation* as a local sage, and a respected book reviewer. The author of one novel, respected short

stories, and some award winning poetry, he was suffering writer's block by the end of the 1940s and took up university teaching, first at the University of Minnesota in the early 1950s and later at the University of Chicago where his papers were deposited.

Ross, Sam (March 10, 1912–March 30, 1998)
 A childhood immigrant with his family from Kiev, Russia, in 1913, Ross was raised in Chicago and attended Northwestern University. Before he began writing novels, the first of which was published in 1947, Ross worked as a publicity agent, reporter, and radio scriptwriter and with the Federal Writers' Project. He was in the U.S. Merchant Marine during World War II and worked as a sportswriter when he returned to civilian life. In addition to publishing books, Ross wrote for television shows, including *Ben Casey*, *Mannix*, and *The Fugitive*. He also taught at the University of California, Irvine and the University of California, Los Angeles.
(*Los Angeles Times*, 25 April 1998, A22).

Roth, Philip (1933–?)
 Born and raised in Newark, New Jersey, Roth received degrees from Bucknell (Pa.) University (BA, 1954) and the University of Chicago (MA, 1955) before serving in the U.S. Army. After sustaining a back injury during basic training, he began a doctoral program at the University of Chicago. He ended his formal education in 1957 to begin writing full-time and published his first novel, *Goodbye Columbus* (Houghton Mifflin), in 1959. The book established him as a writer and he began teaching at the University of Iowa and Princeton University. The financial success of *Portnoy's Complaint* (Random House, 1969) made it possible for him to stop teaching. He has gone on to publish books and short stories that have made him one of the best-known authors in the United States and he has won a PEN/Faulkner Award, a Pulitzer Prize and several National Book Circle Awards.
(*Dictionary of Literary Biography*, vol. 173, s.v. "Roth, Philip (Milton)").

Rowans, Virginia [pseud.], *see* Tanner, Edward Everett, III

Rubinstein, Paul Arthur (January 29, 1935–?)
 Born in Warsaw, Poland, the son of concert pianist Arthur Rubinstein, the author became a naturalized U.S. citizen and was educated at Yale University (1951–1953), the University of Pennsylvania (BS, 1956) and Fordham University (1961–1962). After one year of active service in the U.S. Army (1958–1959), Rubinstein served in the U.S. Army Reserve (1959–1966). A businessman, he worked for RCA Red Seal Records as an advertising manager (1959–1968) before becoming a stockbroker with Becker Securities (1968–1976) and later with L. F. Rothschild and Towbin Unterberg. Except for novels written with Peter Tanous, Rubinstein has mostly written and contributed to cookbooks. (*Contemporary Authors Online*, Detroit: Gale, 2001, accessed 11 March 2010).

Russell, Charlotte Murray (May 22, 1899–May 22, 1992)
 Born in Rock Island, Illinois, where she lived most of her life, Russell was a Phi Beta Kappa graduate of the University of Chicago. After further study at McGill University, she taught French and Latin at Rock Island High School before marrying Marcus J. Russell in 1925. Depression-era economic difficulties prompted Russell to begin publishing book-length fiction. She is known a practitioner of the "cozy school" of mystery writing typical of Agatha Christie, one of the first in the United States. A number of her books feature Jane Amanda Edwards, a self-satisfied, full-

figured spinster. From 1935–1955 Russell published twenty mysteries before giving up writing to become a book cataloger at the Rock Island Public Library.
(Tom Schantz and Enid Schantz, www.ruemorguepress.com, accessed 11 March 2009).

Russell, Ruth
    No information available.

Rutledge, Nancy [Leigh Bryson, pseud.] (1901–1976)
    A popular writer of crime fiction in the period 1944–1960, Rutledge published ten novels and had eight mysteries serialized in magazines, including the *Saturday Evening Post* and *Redbook*.

Saber, Robert O. [pseud.], *see* Ozaki, Milton K.

St. Johns, Adela Rogers (May 20, 1894–August 10, 1988)
    A first-hand witness to the early days of the motion picture industry, working as an entertainment journalist and screenwriter, St. Johns lived long enough to be a favorite commentator on a period that became history. Born in Los Angeles, the daughter of well-known criminal lawyer Earl Rogers, at nineteen St. Johns became a reporter with the *San Francisco Examiner*, owned by her father's friend, William Randolph Hearst. After on-the-job training she left the newspaper in the early 1920s to specialize in interviewing motion picture actors for *Photoplay* magazine, earning her the sobriquet "Mother Confessor of Hollywood." She also wrote short stories for *Cosmopolitan* and the *Saturday Evening Post*, as well as screenplays. When she returned to writing for Hearst newspapers she covered national events that roused the country's emotions (e.g., the Lindbergh trial, the assassination of Huey Long, the abdication of King Edward VIII). One of the best recognized journalists of her time, in 1948 "the girl reporter" left journalism for college teaching and the writing of books, including a biography of her father. As early as the 1960s when she was a frequent guest of Jack Parr's on the *Tonight Show* she was regarded as a valued link to legends of the film industry. She continued to fulfill this role, particularly in regards to silent film stars. She was awarded the United States Medal of Freedom in 1970 for her contributions to journalism.
(*New York Times*, 11 August 1988, D20).

Sandburg, Helga (November 24, 1918–?)
    The daughter of poet Carl Sandburg, the author was born in Maywood, Illinois. She attended Michigan State University and the University of Chicago. Her father's personal secretary until his death, she was for several years a manuscript curator of her father's papers at the Library of Congress, and then an administrative assistant of the papers of Woodrow Wilson at the Woodrow Wilson Foundation in New York City, before starting a career as a lecturer in 1961. She wrote books about her father, several novels, and a number of stories for children.
(*Contemporary Authors Online*, Detroit: Gale, 2002, accessed 15 August 2009).

Sanders, Ed (August 17, 1939–?)
    A member of the 1960s counter culture, friend of many of the movement's major figures, and participant in its most important events, Sanders is known for his poetry and his book on the Manson family. Born in Kansas City, Missouri, Sanders read Allen Ginsberg's *Howl* and Jack Kerouac's *On the Road* as a college freshman at the University of Missouri, Columbia and moved to New York City to participate in the Beat movement. He took classes in Greek at New York University while working as a night clerk in a Times Square cigar store. He completed his

bachelor's degree in 1963 and spent the next several decades participating in acts of civil disobedience and publishing poetry.
[*Dictionary of Literary Biography*, vol. 244, s.v. "Sanders, (James) Ed(ward)"].

Santiago, V. J. [pseud.], *see* Lory, Edward

Sattley, Helen R. (January 8, 1909–February 8, 1999)
A professional librarian, Sattley was born in St. Paul, Minnesota and educated at Northwestern University (BA, 1933; MA, 1934) and Western Reserve University (now Case Western Reserve University) (BS in library science, 1936). She worked as a public school librarian, a library school professor (Columbia University, Western Reserve University) and from 1953 onwards as the director of school libraries for the New York City Board of Education. She published three novels.
(*Contemporary Authors Online*, Detroit: Gale, 2002, accessed 7 April 2009).

Saunders, David [pseud.], *see* Sontup, Daniel

Saunders, Theodore
Co-authored books with Mary Means under the joint pseudonym Denis Scott; no additional information available.

Saxton, Alexander (July 16, 1919–?)
A historian, Saxton was born in Great Barrington, Massachusetts, the son of Eugene Francis Saxton, editor-in-chief of Harper and Brothers, and grew up in New York City. He was educated at Phillips Exeter Academy and began studying at Harvard College, but was dissatisfied and transferred in his junior year to the University of Chicago (AB, 1940). After employment for a time on *Common Ground* magazine in New York City, he worked as a laborer and later as a switchman for the railroad in Chicago. In 1943 he enlisted in the U.S. Maritime Training School and was stationed in the New York City area during World War II. He later returned to graduate school at the University of California, Berkeley (MA, 1962; PhD, 1967) and has taught American history at the University of California, Berkeley; Wayne State University; and the University of California, Los Angeles. He is known for his historical fiction and non-fiction books.
(*Contemporary Authors Online*, Detroit: Gale 2003, accessed 7 November 2009).

Sayre, Gordon, [pseud.], *see* Woolfolk, Josiah Pitts

Scanland, Agnes Leonard, *see* Hill, Agnes Leonard (Scanland)

Scarpetta, Frank [pseud.], *see* Smith, George Harmon

Schaeffer, Susan Fromberg (March 25, 1941–?)
Born Susan Fromberg in Brooklyn, New York, she grew up there and on Long Island. She was educated at the University of Chicago (BA, 1961; MA, 1963; PhD, 1966) in English literature. She began her teaching career in the city, teaching at Wright Teachers College and later at the Illinois Institute of Technology, before moving to New York City to teach at Brooklyn College. She has published poetry, short stories, and critically acclaimed novels.
(*World Authors 1980–1985*, New York: H. W. Wilson, 1991, s.v. "Schaeffer, Susan Fromberg").

Schauffler, Robert Haven (April 8, 1879–November 24, 1964)
     Schauffler was a prolific essayist, as well as a poet and biographer. A trained cellist who con-
certized, he frequently wrote about music and musicians. He was born in Bruenn, Austria, the son
of American missionaries who returned to the United States in 1881. Schauffler attended Northwestern University and graduated from Princeton (BA, 1902). He later studied for two years at the
University of Berlin and was a student of noted cellists in the city. Schauffler also played tennis
and competed in the Olympics. He lived most of his life in New York City's Greenwich Village
and earned a living by contributing to magazines.
(*World Authors, 1900–1950*, New York: H. W. Wilson, 1996, s.v. "Schauffler, Robert").

Schiller, Cicely
     No information available.

Schultz, Alan Brener
     No information available.

Schwimmer, Walter (May 25, 1903–September 1, 1989)
     A Chicago native, Schwimmer lived his entire life in the city. Initially a real estate agent and
columnist, he began working in radio advertising in the 1930s and established a reputation with
his radio commercials and with the quiz program he created, *Tello Test* that began broadcasting in
1936 and ran for twenty years. He began work in television in the 1940s, eventually owning the
firm Television Business. For two decades he produced television programs and specials, including the 1964 Nobel Prize ceremony broadcast.
(*Contemporary Authors Online*, Detroit: Gale, 2002, accessed 7 November 2009).

Scofield, Charles J. (December 25, 1853–?)
     A native of Carthage, Illinois, Scofield lived in the town all of his life, except for the college
years he spent at Christian University in Canton, Missouri. The son of a lawyer, he studied law
with his brother and was admitted to the Illinois bar in 1875. Between 1885 and 1897 he served as
a circuit, appellate, and a state supreme court judge, while participating in a legal practice he
founded and serving as an unpaid pastor in churches of the Disciples of Christ.
(*Biographical Review of Hancock County, Illinois*, Chicago: Hobart, 1907, s.v. "Scofield, Charles
J.").

Scott, Denis [joint pseud.], *see* Means, Mary and Saunders, Theodore

Scott, Henry E.
     No information available.

Seely, Herman Gastrell (1891–?)
     No information available.

Seifert, Shirley Louise (1888–1971)
     Known for the careful research on which her historical fiction was based, Seifert often chose
to dramatize important figures, such as Ulysses S. Grant, Jefferson Davis, and George Rogers
Clark. However, she also told the stories of now-forgotten Americans, focusing in all of her work
on Kentucky and Missouri. She was born in St. Peters, Missouri, and graduated from Washington

University in St. Louis with majors in classical and modern languages. After working for a time as a teacher, she took courses in journalism and began writing. She published her first short story in 1919.

(*New York Times*, 4 September 1971, 24).

Seltzer, Charles Alden (August 15, 1875–February 9, 1942)
    No information available.

Shane, Margaret Woodward Smith (1896–September 4, 1965)
    An author of novels and plays, Shane was most active in the 1920s and 1930s. In the 1920s she wrote novels using the pseudonym Woodward Boyd. She was the wife of Thomas A. Boyd, also a novelist, as well as a biographer. In the 1930s she wrote plays using the name Peggy Shane. One play, "Mr. Big," that she co-authored with Arthur Sheekman was produced on Broadway in 1941 by George S. Kaufman. After the death of her first husband, she later married Theodore Shane, also a writer.

(*New York Times*, 5 September 1965, 57).

Sheldon, Charles M. (February 26, 1857–February 24, 1946)
    Although he was born in Wellsville, New York, Sheldon was the son of a Congregationalist minister who was a circuit preacher in South Dakota, where Sheldon was raised in a log cabin. He graduated from Brown University (AB, 1883) and Andover Seminary (BD, 1886). He began his career as a minister in Vermont, but then moved to Topeka, Kansas in 1889 where he was minister of the Central Congregational Church for twenty years before becoming editor-in-chief of the *New York Christian Herald* (1920–1925) and, afterwards, contributing editor (1925–1946). He began publishing religious fiction in a Chicago magazine, *Advance*, in which he applied Gospel teachings to urban settings. The success of these stories prompted a series of books, beginning in 1897, with the same themes. For a time the books sold more copies than the Bible, although Shane's failure to properly apply for copyright protection meant that other publishers' sales formed a high percentage of the more than six million copies in print. In addition to publishing more than thirty social gospel novels, Sheldon had a long career as a social commentator in magazines and newspapers.

(Henry Warner Bowden, *Dictionary of Religious Biography*, Westport, Conn.: Greenwood, 1993, s.v. "Sheldon, Charles M.").

Shenton, Edward (1895–1977)
    No information available.

Sherburne, James May 22, 1925)
    Born in East Lansing, Michigan, Sherburne attended Berea College, graduated from the University of Kentucky (BA, 1947), and served on active duty with the U.S. Naval Reserve (1943–1946). In 1947, he began working in advertising in Chicago, and was employed as a copywriter in six firms in the city between then and 1968. He subsequently taught English and advertising at Columbia (Chicago) College, Berea (Ky.) College, Eastern Kentucky University, Bellarmine (Ky.) College and in the Louisville (Ky.) Public Schools. He published eight novels between 1971 and 1984.

(*Contemporary Authors Online*, Detroit: Gale, 2002, accessed, 7 April 2009).

Shuman, Andrew (November 8, 1830–May 5, 1890)

Born in Lancaster County, Pennsylvania, Shuman was orphaned early in life and held jobs in a drugstore, printing office, and with a newspaper before attending Hamilton (N.Y.) College (1851–1853), leaving in his junior year to become editor of the *Syracuse Daily Journal*. In 1856 he became an editor of the *Chicago Evening Journal* and took up residence in Evanston, Illinois, where he lived for the remainder of his life. In addition to long service as president of the *Chicago Evening Journal* Company (1878–1890), he was a commissioner of the state penitentiary (1868–1874) and lieutenant governor of Illinois (Republican, 1877–1881).
(Jeriah Bonham, *Fifty Years' Recollections*, Peoria, Ill.: Franks, 1896, 481-483).

Shura, Mary Francis, *see* Craig, Mary Francis Shura

Siegel, Sam
No information available.

Simmons, Geoffrey (July 28, 1943–?)

Born in Camp Gordon, Georgia, Simmons is a physician with a practice in internal medicine in Eugene, Oregon. The author of more than six novels, Simmons writes fiction inspired by medical quandaries such as determining a treatment for a national figure poisoned with an unknown toxin, or a course of action when an antibiotic bacteria is discovered.
(*Contemporary Authors Online*, Detroit: Gale, 2002, accessed 17 April 2009).

Simon, Philip J. (1901–?)
No information available.

Sinclair, Harold Augustus (May 8, 1907–May 24, 1966)

A native of Chicago, Sinclair was the son of a railroad fireman who abandoned the family when Sinclair was still a youngster. He was sent to live with an aunt and uncle in Bloomington, Illinois. He also lived in Florida, Texas, and Chicago in the 1920s, working at menial jobs and as a trumpeter in a dance band. He captured his Depression-era experiences in his first book, *Journey Home* (included here). He later wrote historical fiction chronicling small-town, Illinois life and recounting the early biography of George Rogers Clark. He also authored a history of New Orleans.
(*Contemporary Authors Online*, Detroit: Gale, 2002, accessed, 11 November 2009).

Sinclair, Upton (1878–1968)

Known as the most prominent muckraker in the early twentieth-century, using works of fiction to advocate for social reform, Sinclair was the scion of two wealthy Virginia families who suddenly lost their money. He grew up in Baltimore and New York City. To support his undergraduate education at The City College of New York, he wrote jokes, juvenile novels, and short stories. He turned to adult fiction in 1904 and in 1906 published the work that transformed his career, *The Jungle* (included here). He went on to publish more than sixty books. In the 1930s he became directly involved in politics and ran for governor of California in a campaign that was attacked by Metro-Goldwyn-Mayer because Sinclair proposed higher taxes on the movie industry to alleviate poverty in the state. Near the end of his life he was honored by President Lyndon Johnson at the signing ceremony for the Wholesome Meat Act.
(*Dictionary of Literary Biography*, vol. 9, s.v. "Sinclair, (Beall) Upton").

Sklovsky, Max (1877–December 16, 1967)

Born in Lithuania and immigrating with his parents in the first year of his life to the United States, Sklovsky was a graduate of the Illinois Institute of Technology and the first college educated engineer to be hired by John Deere and Company. He joined the firm in 1902 as a technical engineer and at the time of his retirement in 1945 was chief engineer. During World War I and II Sklovsky received special commission from the U.S. Army to improve munitions manufacturing. (Ralph W. Sanders, *Ultimate John Deere*, Stillwater, Minn.: Voyageur Press, 2001, 50).

Smalley, Dave E.

No information available.

Smith, Charles Merrill (1919–February 23, 1985)

A minister in the United Methodist Church, Smith wrote satire and mysteries, as well as inspirational works. His book-length satire, *How to Become a Bishop Without Being Religious* (Doubleday, 1965), was a best seller. In the 1970s, Smith's most popular books were a series of mystery novels featuring Rev. C. P. Randollph, a clergyman who had been a football player for the Chicago Rams and as the minister at Chicago's Episcopal Church of the Good Shepherd, he has many opportunities to solve murders and other mysteries.

Smith, Eunice Young (June 10, 1902–November ?, 1993)

An author of works for children and young adults, Smith often illustrated her own work. She was born in Mishawaka, Indiana and attended Rosary College (1921) and Lakeview Commercial Art School (1921). She also studied at the Chicago Academy of Fine Arts in 1945 and began a career as a book illustrator that year working from 1945 through 1962 for a series of Chicago firms, including David Cook, Follette, Albert Whitman, and Society of Visual Education (a producer of filmstrips).
(*Contemporary Authors Online*, Detroit: Gale, 2002, accessed 12 December 2009).

Smith, Fredrika Shumway (July 30, 1877–March 7, 1968)

A children's author, Smith's interest in history led her to write a number of biographies for young people. She spent most of her life in the Chicago area and was involved in local chapters of ancestry organizations including the Colonial Dames Society and the Illinois Society of Mayflower Descendants. She was also active in the Antiquarian Society of the Art Institute of Chicago.
(*Contemporary Authors Online*, Detroit: Gale, 2002, accessed 12 November 2009).

Smith, George Harmon [Frank Scarpetta, pseud.] (January 12, 1920–?)

Born in Spearsville, Louisiana, Smith had a long career in the public school system and is best known for his books for children, especially *Bayou Boy* (Follett, 1965) that was adapted as a motion picture of the same name (Walt Disney, 1971). During World War II Smith served in the U.S. Navy (1942–1943) and later earned two master's degrees (University of Arkansas, MS, 1954; University of Mississippi, MA, 1962). His career of more than thirty years in public education included positions as head coach, principal, and director of federal programs. In addition to his books for children, Smith wrote more than fifty adventure and suspense novels, many under the pseudonyms Peter McCurtin and Frank Scarpetta.
(*Contemporary Authors Online*, Detroit: Gale, 2001, accessed 12 March 2010).

Smith, Henry Justin (1875–February 9, 1936)

A Chicago native who attended the University of Chicago, Smith was a journalist, as well as historian and novelist. Except for 1924–1926 when he was director of public relations for the University of Chicago, Smith worked for the *Chicago Daily News* from 1899 until his death in the positions of reporter, city editor, assistant managing editor, news editor, and managing editor (1926–1936).
(*New York Times*, 10 February 1936, 17).

Smith, Mark (November 19, 1935–?)

In addition to a career of several decades as an English professor, Smith published seven novels. Born in Charlevoix, Michigan, he graduated from Northwestern University (BA, 1960). As a young man he lived for five years as a merchant marine, European traveler, poet, and bohemian artist in Boston, before publishing his first novel and subsequently getting teaching jobs. Smith is known for the literary quality of his mystery novels that are usually existentialist in nature. He taught at the University of New Hampshire, Durham with numerous visiting professorships and advisory appointments to other institutions.
[*Dictionary of Literary Biography Yearbook: 1982*, Detroit: Gale, 1983, s.v. "Smith, Mark (Richard)"].

Smith, Terrence Lore [Phillips Lore, pseud.] (October 27, 1942–December 7, 1988)

The author of eight mystery novels, Smith was born in Freeport, Illinois and worked as a drug and alcohol counselor. His first novel, *The Thief Who Came to Dinner* (Doubleday, 1971), was a best seller and adapted for a film by the same title (Warner Bros., 1973) starring Ryan O'Neal. At the time of his death, he was a courier for the Pikes Peak (Colo.) Library District and lost control of a library van in poor road conditions.
(*New York Times*, 8 December 1988, D18).

Smith, Wallace (1888–January 31, 1937)

A native of Chicago, Smith's career included work as a journalist (in Mexico covering Pancho Villa), an illustrator, and a Hollywood screenwriter, as well as an author of novels and short stories. Smith's illustrations for a privately printed work by his friend Ben Hecht were found to be obscene by authorities and Smith spent a brief time in jail. From 1929 on he worked in Hollywood, writing screenplays for early talking motion pictures.
(*New York Times*, 1 February 1937, 19).

Smucker, Barbara Claassen (September 1, 1915–July 29, 2003)

A children's book author whose fiction raises issues of social justice, Smucker was born in Newton, Kansas and educated at Kansas State University (BS, 1936). She worked as a school teacher and reporter before marrying Mennonite minister Donovan E. Smucker. The couple lived in Chicago for a number of years while Pastor Donovan taught at Mennonite Biblical Seminary. They later lived in West Point, Mississippi; Ontario, Canada; and Bluffton, Ohio. In addition to writing children's books, Smucker was a librarian for many years.
(*Global Anabaptist Mennonite Encyclopedia Online*, accessed 8 April 2009).

Solberg, Gunard (August 15, 1932–?)

A secondary school teacher and the author of books for young adults, Solberg was born in Chicago and educated at the University of Wisconsin (BS, 1955) and the University of California, Berkeley (graduate study, 1957–1959).
(*Contemporary Authors Online*, Detroit: Gale, 2002, accessed 8 April 2008).

Sommers, Lillian, [Litere, pseud.]

No information available.

Sontup, Daniel [pseud. David Saunders] (November 3, 1922–2003)

Born in New York City, Saunders served in the U.S. Air Force during World War II and was educated at New York University (BA, 1950). From 1951 to 1961 he worked in New York City as an editor and technical writer for various firms. He is known for pulp fiction published under the pseudonyms David Saunders and John Clarke.
(*Contemporary Authors Online*, Detroit: Gale, 2002, accessed 7 April 2009).

Sparks, Alice Wilkinson

No information available.

Spearman, Frank H. (September 6, 1859–December 29, 1937)

Known for his short stories and novels about railroads and the American West, Spearman was born in Buffalo, New York, and educated at Lawrence College (Appleton, Wis.). After several years on the road as a traveling salesman, Spearman settled into the banking industry, becoming the president of a small bank in Wisconsin by the time he was twenty-nine. His stories were all based on his acquaintance with trainmen, rather than from direct experience of working on the railroad, however his writings inspired a great deal of interest and he achieved several best sellers that were adapted for the screen. In the 1930s he also had a successful career in Hollywood as a screenwriter.
(*New York Times*, 31 December 1937, 16).

Speicher, Helen Ross (September 14, 1915–?)

Born Helen Ross Smith, the daughter of a physician, Speicher grew up in Indianapolis and graduated from Butler University (BS, journalism, 1937). She married Kenneth E. Speicher, an attorney. A writer of books for children, most have been collaborations with college friend Kathryn Kilby Borland. Speicher also wrote children's Bible stories telecast on WLW-TV, Indianapolis and published by United Methodist Publishing.
(*Contemporary Authors Online*, Detroit: Gale, 2003 accessed, 3 March 2009).

Spencer, Ross (August 21, 1921–July 25, 1998)

Born in Hughart, West Virginia, Spencer served in the U.S. Army field artillery during World War II and in the U.S. Air Force during the Korean War. As a civilian he worked as a laborer in the aircraft, railroad, steel, and trucking industries before starting his own landscaping and chain link fence business. He did not publish his first novel until he was fifty-seven years old, but went on to publish thirteen mystery novels, many of them set in the Chicago metropolitan area.
(*Contemporary Authors Online*, Detroit: Gale, 2003, accessed 7 November 2009).

Spencer, Scott (September 1, 1945–?)

Although he was born in Washington, D.C., the son of a steelworker and union organizer, Spencer grew up in Chicago. He graduated from the University of Wisconsin, Madison (BA 1969) and published his first novel in 1973. His second novel, published in 1979, *Endless Love* (included here), was the basis for a popular film (*Endless Love*, Polygram Film Entertainment, 1981) directed by Franco Zeffirelli and starring Brooke Shields. Several of his subsequent novels have also been adapted for film.

(*Dictionary of Literary Biography Yearbook: 1986*, Detroit: Gale, 1987, s.v. "Spencer, Scott").

Spiegel, Clara (December 6, 1904–1997)

Born in Chicago, Spiegel had a long writing collaboration with Jane Mayer using the shared pseudonym of Clare Jaynes. The two met while attending Vassar College. Spiegel (née Gatzert) traveled widely, particularly after divorcing Frederick Spiegel in the late 1940s. She enjoyed big game hunting and went on safaris, engaged in active outdoor sports, rode horses, and skied. She was a well-known hostess in the 1950s, particularly in the sporting communities of Ketchum and Sun Valley, Idaho. Most of her papers are at Boise State University; letters written to her by Ernest Hemingway and members of his family are at the Newberry Library.

Stahl, John M. (1860–1944)

No information available.

Stanger, Wesley Allen (1880–July 7, 1961)

Stanger lived in Chicago while working as a reporter for the Hearst newspapers. He was later an editor and publisher and worked for trade organizations. For many decades he was a resident of Cranford, New Jersey and served as the first chief inspector of the New Jersey Department of Alcoholic Beverage Control. In New Jersey he was involved in Republican politics and made an unsuccessful run for U.S. Congress.

(*New York Times*, 8 July 1961, 19).

Starrett, Vincent (October 26, 1886–January 5, 1974)

Although he was born in Toronto, Canada, Starrett moved with his family to Chicago when he was four years old. His father was an accountant for the Carson, Pirie, Scott Department Store. After dropping out of high school in 1904, Starrett got a job with the *Chicago Inter-Ocean* and later worked for the *Chicago Daily News* and the *Chicago Tribune*. Starrett sold his first short story to *Collier's Weekly* in 1916 and began submitting material to pulp magazines, as well. A bibliophile and skilled bibliographer, in the 1920s he began publishing essays about book collecting and later published several books about his adventures as a collector. Although he collected literary first editions and built collections of specific titles, he is best-known today as a collector of Sherlockiana. He began writing mystery stories for pulp magazines in 1925 to supplement his income. His first full-length detective novel was published in 1929. He continued to publish detective fiction until 1964 and created three memorable fictional characters, Jimmie Lavender, and the detective team of Walter Ghost and Dunstan Mollock, modeled on Sherlock Holmes and Dr. Watson. With the exception of a three-year trip around the world, Starrett lived most of his adult life in Chicago.

(*Dictionary of Literary Biography*, vol. 187, s.v. "Starrett, Vincent").

Stein, Max

No information available.

Stern, Karl (April 8, 1906–November 7, 1975)

Psychiatrist Karl Stern was a naturalized citizen of Canada who wrote a memoir about his religious conversion from Judaism to Catholicism, as well as several works of fiction. Born in Cham, Bavaria, Germany he was educated at the Universities of Munich, Berlin, and Frankfurt, from which he received his MD in 1930. He was trained in psychiatry at the German Institute for Psychiatry (1932–1936). After research in London, he immigrated to Canada in 1940 where he taught at McGill University, the University of Ottawa, and, for the longest period, at the University of Montreal (1955–1975). He also worked as psychiatrist-in-chief at St. Mary's Hospital in Montreal from 1958–1968.

(*Contemporary Authors Online*, Detroit: Gale, 2002, accessed 19 March 2009).

Stern, Lucille
No information available.

Steuber, William F. (1904–October 2005)

Born in Prairie du Sac, Wisconsin, Steuber was a surveyor and highway engineer as well as an author of historical fiction. A graduate of the University of Wisconsin-Madison College of Engineering in 1930, Steuber joined the Wisconsin Highway Safety Promotion Department in 1937, combining his avocational interest in motion picture photography with his training in engineering to produce highway safety films and supporting materials. From 1939–1969 he worked as an engineer with the Wisconsin Division of Highways rising from to the second highest position within the agency. He wrote three novels and one work of non-fiction.

(University of Wisconsin-Madison, Steuber Prize homepage, http://tc.engr.wisc.edu/Steuber, accessed 19 March 2009).

Stevens, Charles McClellan [Quondam, pseud.] (1861–?)
No information available.

Stevens, Grant Eugene
No information available.

Stewart, Charles D. (1868–1960)
No information available.

Stone, Irving (July 14, 1903–August 26, 1989)

Stone was born Irving Tennenbaum in San Francisco, California and lived most of his life in that state. He was educated at the University of California, working his way through school with odd jobs; he graduated in 1923 and began teaching economics at the University of Southern California while working on a master's degree that he never finished. Working on becoming a writer, he moved first to New York City and, later, Paris. His first published work was a lengthy biography of Vincent Van Gogh. After it became a best seller, Stone's career was made and he went on to publish many biographical novels that were hailed for the documentary research behind them, even if historians sometimes disagreed with his interpretation of the lives about which he wrote.

(*New York Times*, 28 August 1989, B6).

Strande, Wilhelm vom
    No information available.

Straus, Ralph (September 5, 1882–June 5, 1950)
    An English writer, Straus was a Dickens scholar and literary critic as well as a novelist. Born in Manchester, England, he was educated at Harrow and Pembroke College, Cambridge University.
(*New York Times*, 7 June 1950, 29).

Street, Ada Hilt (?–1926)
    Ada Hilt was born in La Porte, Indiana and married Julian Street in 1900. The couple co-authored several books.

Street, Julian Leonard (April 18, 1879–February 19, 1947)
    Although Street was born in Chicago, he was educated at Ridley College Preparatory School in St. Catharines, Ontario and lived most of his life in New York City and abroad. A friend of George Ade, Booth Tarkington, and Theodore Roosevelt, Street wrote about art and theater for newspapers around the beginning of the twentieth century. He co-authored several travel books about the United States with the artist Wallace Morgan in the 1910s. He wrote several novels, but he is best known as a travel essayist and writer on gastronomy. His contributions to the knowledge of gastronomy and his efforts to popularize French wines and cooking were acknowledged by the government of France with the Chevalier's Cross of the Legion of Honor. In the 1920s and 1930s several of his novels and stories were adapted as motion pictures.
(*New York Times*, 20 February 1947).

Storme, Michael [pseud.], *see* Dawson, George H.

Strobel, Marion (1895–1966)
    Strobel was associate editor of *Poetry* (1919–1924) and co-editor (1943–1949). She is the author of several volumes of poetry, as well as novels, and is also known for her literary criticism. She was the mother of American Abstract Expressionist painter Joan Mitchell (1926–1992).

Strong, Edmund C.
    No information available.

Stubbins, Thomas Alva (1870–?)
    No information available.

Sturm, Justin (1899–August 6, 1967)
    The author of two novels, Sturm was also a playwright and sculptor. Educated at Phillips Exeter Academy and Yale University where he was a fullback on the football team (AB, 1922), several of Sturm's plays had Broadway runs. In his portrait sculpture he captured José Ferrer, Ernest Hemingway, Westbrook Pegler, and Gene Tunney. His wife was Katherine McCormack, a Broadway producer and restaurateur. Sturm lived much of his adult life in Westport, Connecticut.
(*New York Times*, 8 August 1967, 39).

Sublette, Walter [S. W. Edwards, pseud.] (September 6, 1940–?)
     Sublette, a Chicago native, is a published poet and has long been affiliated with *Playboy* magazine as an editor. He attended the University of Chicago at Chicago Circle.
(*Contemporary Authors Online*, Detroit: Gale, 2002, accessed 12 November 2009)

Sullivan, James William (1848–September 28, 1938)
     No information available.

Surbridge, Agnes [pseud.].
     During the year after this author published her scathing account of Chicago clubwomen, literary columnists speculated over the author's identity, but the mystery remained unsolved.

Swanson, Harold N. [Anna Bell Ward, pseud.]. (?–?)
     No information available.

Synon, Mary
     A reform Chicago journalist, Synon was active in the Catholic Civics Clubs organization of the Roman Catholic Church in the United States. Through these organizations she helped young people apply Church social teaching that opposed discrimination based on race and social class. In 1943, she was awarded an honorary doctor of laws degree by Rosary College (River Forest, Ill.) for her work as consultant on American citizenship to Catholic University.
(*New York Times*, 28 May 1943, 16).

Tanner, Edward Everett, III [Virginia Rowans, pseud.] (May 18, 1921–November 6, 1976)
     An author of satires who wrote under the pseudonyms Patrick Dennis and Virginia Rowans, Tanner was born in Evanston, Illinois, the son of a stockbroker, and attended Evanston High School and studied at the Art Institute of Chicago. After serving as a volunteer ambulance driver in World War II in the American Field Service, he settled in New York City, working as an advertising manager for *Foreign Affairs* magazine. After the success of his work *Auntie Mame* (Vanguard, 1955), which was adapted as a Broadway play and film, Tanner became a millionaire and wrote additional books for an appreciative audience and his own amusement.
(*New York Times*, 7 November 1976, 39).

Tanous, Peter Joseph (May 21, 1938–?)
     Born in New York City, Tanous was a graduate of Georgetown University (BA, 1960) and served in the U.S. Army (1961–1963). He began working with Smith, Barney Harris, and Upham as an investment advisor in 1963 and worked in the securities industry in New York City, Paris, and Washington, D.C.
(Ellis Island Medal of Honor, www.neco.org/awards/recipients, accessed 23 April 2008).

Targ, William (March 4, 1907–July 22, 1999)
     A Chicago native, Targ lived most of his adult life in Cleveland, Ohio and New York City. He was born William Targownik, legally changing his name in 1946. He is best known for his coups as a book publisher, identifying manuscripts that would be great financial successes (including Mario Puzo's *The Godfather*) and working with authors such as Simone de Beauvoir and Art Buchwald. Most of his own books were anthologies and works on book collecting. He got his first job as an eighteen-year-old with Macmillan in Chicago, and later worked for Black Archer Press

in Chicago, before becoming editor-in-chief and vice-president of World Publishing Company (Cleveland), 1942–1964; and editor-in-chief and vice-president of G. P. Putnam's Sons (New York), 1964–1999.
(*Contemporary Authors Online*, Detroit: Gale, 2002, accessed 20 August 2007).

Taylor, Bert Leston (November 13, 1866–March 19, 1921)
A reporter and columnist who spent most of his professional life in Chicago, Taylor was born in New York City and attended City (New York) College (1881–1882). After working for several New England newspapers, he moved to Chicago in 1899 and soon had his own column for the *Chicago Journal* that alternated between humor and features. In 1901 he was hired by the *Chicago Tribune* and worked for that newspaper until 1921 except for a one year hiatus (1903–1904), working for the *New York Telegraph*. He is remembered for his light verse and for the column "A Line o' Type or Two" that he began in 1901. Although perhaps not the first newspaper column, as is sometimes claimed, his work helped develop this journalistic format.
(*Dictionary of Literary Biography*, vol. 25, s.v. "Taylor, Bert Leston").

Taylor, Ellen Du Pois (1889–?)
No information available.

Taylor, Marie E.
No information available.

Teller, Charlotte (March 3, 1876–December 30, 1953)
Daughter of Colorado attorney James Harvey Teller, the author's uncle was U.S. Senator Henry Moore Teller, who served as Secretary of the Interior under President Chester Arthur. A graduate of the University of Chicago (BA, 1899), Teller soon began publishing short stories and news features in magazines and newspapers. She was married to Frank Minitree Johnson in 1902, but the couple was soon estranged and later divorced. During the estrangement, Teller lived with her grandmother at 3 Fifth Avenue in New York City, a near neighbor of Samuel Clemens residing at 51 Fifth Avenue. On the pretense of getting assistance with a play about Joan of Arc, Teller began an acquaintanceship with the author that lasted several years and may have included romantic intentions on the part of Clemens.
(*New York Times*, 12 March 1922, 39).

Thanet, Octave, *see* French, Alice

Thayer, James Stewart (May 28, 1949–?)
Novelist and attorney, Thayer was born in Eugene, Oregon and graduated from Washington State University (BA, 1971) and the University of Chicago (JD, 1974). He lived most of his adult life in Seattle, Washington. The author of more than eleven books, Thayer's works tend to be thrillers.
(*Contemporary Authors Online*, Detroit: Gale, 2002, accessed 14 April 2009).

Thayer, Tiffany Ellsworth (March 1, 1902–August 23, 1959)
Born in Freeport, Illinois, Thayer's youth was spent there (1902–1910) and later in Rockford, Illinois (1910–1916). He quit high school as a sophomore and moved to Chicago where he lived until 1922 working for newspapers and seasonally with touring theatrical companies (his parents

were both actors). He moved to New York City in 1926 to become a full-time actor, but when this plan was thwarted began work as an advertising copywriter. He published his first novel in 1930, the best seller *Thirteen Men* (Grosset, Dunlap). After a period of Hollywood script-writing (1932–1936), he returned to New York City where he divided his time between working in advertising six months a year and writing on Nantucket six months a year. He eventually published nineteen novels under his own name and many others under pseudonyms.
(*World Authors, 1900–1950*, New York: H. W. Wilson, 1996, s.v. "Thayer, Tiffany Ellsworth").

Thomas, Ross (February 19, 1926–December 18, 1995)
A native of Oklahoma, Thomas served in the Philippines during World War II and later graduated from the University of Oklahoma. He worked for a number of years in public relations, eventually founding his own firm. In addition, he was a federal political consultant (1964–1966) before becoming a full-time freelance writer. Known for critically acclaimed works of political espionage, he wrote twenty-five novels and several screenplays.
(*New York Times*, 19 December 1995, B14).

Thorne, Paul
The author of several mysteries, some of which he co-authored with his wife Mabel, Thorne's books were published in the years 1921–1931.

Thorne, Mabel
Wife of author Paul Thorne, Mabel Thorne co-authored two mysteries with him in the early 1920s.

Thorson, Russell [Kit Christian, joint pseud. with Sarah Winfree Thorson] (October 14, 1906–July 6, 1982)
Known as a radio performer, Thorson was at one point in two soap operas, one of which was *I Love a Mystery*. He went on to appear as a character actor in hundreds of episodes of popular television shows in the 1950s through 1970s.
(*Internet Movie Data Base*, www.imdb.com, accessed 12 July 2009).

Thorson, Sarah Winfree [Kit Christian, shared pseud. with Russell Thorson]
Thorson was a 1925 graduate of Hollins University in Roanoke, Virginia.

Thurber, Alwyn M.
No information available.

Thurston, Louise Millicent (September 19, 1842–?)
Born in Lancaster, Massachusetts and a school teacher in Lynn, Massachusetts in the 1850s and 1860s. Thurston began publishing stories for children through the Sunday School Society in the late 1860s and published a series of books featuring the character "Charley Roberts" with Lee & Shepard in the 1870s. Several of Thurston's married sisters had relocated to Chicago, although she appears to have remained on the East Coast.
(*19th-Century Girls' Series*, www.readseries.com, accessed 24 March 2010).

Tigay, Betty S.
No information available.

Tobenkin, Elias (February 11, 1882–October 19, 1963)

An author of novels dealing with the immigrant experience, Tobenkin was also a journalist and author on international affairs. An immigrant with his family from Belorussia, Tobenkin attended high school in Madison, Wisconsin and graduated from the University of Wisconsin (BA, 1902; MA, 1906). He began his career as a journalist in Milwaukee, Wisconsin, but joined the staff of the *Chicago Tribune* in 1907. He became a freelance journalist in New York City in 1910. He published four novels between 1916 and 1925; however, during his own life time he was best known as an expert on Eastern Europe, writing extensive commentary and analysis from 1917 to 1937.
(*American National Biography*, "Tobenkin, Elias").

Totheroh, William W.
No information available.

Trail, Armitage [pseud.], *see* Coons, Maurice

Train, M.
No information available.

Treat, Roger L. (1906–October 6, 1969)

A sportswriter and critic of segregation politics on teams and in leagues, Treat wrote for several newspapers during his career, including the *Baltimore News American*, *Chicago Herald American*, *Danbury (Conn.) News Times*, *Washington (D.C.) Daily News*, and the *Washington (D.C.) Post*. The author of several books for children and a pulp novel, Treat was best known for his book about the racehorse Man o' War and an encyclopedia of the National Football League. He documented his struggles with alcoholism in the book for which he is included here.

Trebor, Snivig C. [pseud.], *see* Givins, Robert Cartwright

Trotti, Lamar (October 18, 1898–August 28, 1952)

For twenty years a Hollywood screenwriter, Trotti was born in Atlanta, Georgia and graduated from the University of Georgia with a degree in journalism in 1921. After working for the *Atlanta Georgian*, he worked as a publicist in New York for what is now known as the Motion Picture Association of America (1924–1930). He moved to Hollywood and in 1932 began work as a screenwriter for Fox Pictures on such successful ventures as *The Ox-Bow Incident* (1943), and *Cheaper by the Dozen* (1950), and with a number of biographical pictures.
(*Dictionary of Literary Biography*, vol. 44, s.v. "Trotti, Lamar").

Tucker, Wilson (November 23, 1914–October 6, 2006)

Author of more than twenty-four mystery and science fiction novels, Tucker was born in Deer Creek, Illinois and grew up in Normal, Illinois, where he graduated from high school. For more than thirty years he was a motion picture projectionist at theaters in Bloomington and Normal, Illinois. In addition to writing books, he published short stories in magazines, many under the pseudonym Bob Tucker.
(*Contemporary Authors Online*, Detroit: Gale, 2006, accessed 25 March 2009).

Tully, Jim (June 3, 1888–1947)

Tully's harsh childhood and adolescence became the basis for autobiographical fiction that launched his writing career. The impoverished household into which Tully was born in St. Mary's, Ohio was broken up after the death of his mother when he was seven years old. After spending four years in a Cincinnati orphanage, Tully was sent to work on a farm when he was eleven. He ran away when he was fourteen, and lived within the hobo community for seven years. As a twenty-one-year-old he tried to become a boxer, but after a number of successful fights, gave up boxing after a dramatic loss. He had various jobs in sales and as a newspaperman in Ohio, before publishing an autobiographical novel in 1922 with the help of author Rupert Hughes. He published a series of similar works between then and 1932. In the early 1930s he began interviewing movie stars and earned a reputation for his frank interviews that soon made him the highest paid journalist in Hollywood.
(Stanley Kunitz, *Authors Yesterday and Today*, New York: H. W. Wilson, 1933, s.v. "Tully, Jim").

Tupper, Edith Sessions (1862–August 3, 1927)

Born in Panama, New York, Tupper was the wife of Horace E. Tupper and is primarily known for magazine fiction. She adapted a number of stories and novels for film in the period 1917 to 1920.
(*New York Times*, 4 August 1927, 21).

Turpin, Walter Edward (April 9, 1910–November 19, 1968)

Although he was born in Oxford, Maryland, Turpin moved with his family to New Jersey when he was twelve. His mother was a domestic, however she sent him to Morgan Academy, a private high school in Baltimore, Maryland. She also introduced him to her employer, Edna Ferber. The author advised Turpin, encouraged his literary ambitions, and introduced him to editors, publishers, and writers. He moved to New York City in 1931, the year he graduated from Morgan College (later Morgan State College and now Morgan State University), and commenced graduate work at Columbia University (MA, 1934). He published his first book in 1937, a multi-generational novel dealing with the African-American experience. For the rest of his life he taught college English, mostly at Morgan State College, where he was employed from 1949 until his death, and wrote novels that presented his African-American perspective.
(*Dictionary of Literary Biography*, vol. 51, "Turpin, Walter Edward").

Tuthill, Jack [aka James M. Tuthill] (?–October 31, 1952)

Tuthill was an actor who was for many years the head of a touring company known as the Jack Milton players. He retired from the circuit in approximately 1932 and was living in New Jersey at the time of his death.
(*New York Times*, 2 November 1952, 88).

Ullman, James Michael (1925–1997)

A journalist for the *Chicago Tribune*, Ullman also wrote mysteries, including short stories and four novels.

Upton, George P. (October 25, 1834–May 19, 1919)

A music critic who wrote for the *Chicago Tribune* for more than fifty years, Upton was born in Roxbury, Massachusetts. The year after his graduation from Brown University in 1854, he

moved to Chicago. He was city editor of the *Chicago Evening Journal* from 1856 to 1862 and began writing music reviews during that time. He was hired as city editor of the *Chicago Tribune* in 1862, later becoming news editor, then from 1868 to 1871 literary, dramatic, and art critic, working as a reporter for the newspaper after 1871. He organized Chicago's Apollo Club in 1872 and wrote books on musicology and about the history of musical performance in Chicago, as well as one book of humorous sketches (included here).
(E. Douglas Bomberger, *Brainard's Biographies of American Musicians*, Greenwood, 1999, s.v. "Upton, George Putnam").

Van Deventer, Emma Murdoch [Lawrence L. Lynch, pseud.]
    The author of more than twenty detective novels from the 1870s to 1890s, Van Deventer used the male pseudonym Lawrence L. Lynch.

Van Peebles, Melvin (August 21, 1932–?)
    Van Peebles was born in Chicago and raised in Phoenix, Illinois. He graduated from Ohio Wesleyan University (BA, 1953) and served in the U.S. Air Force for more than three years. After marrying a German woman and living for a time in San Francisco working as a postal clerk, Van Peebles, an African-American, became frustrated with the lack of opportunity for a person of color to break into the Hollywood movie industry as a writer and moved to Europe, first to Holland to study astronomy, and then to France, where he published several novels in French. In 1967, he directed a full-length, feature film based on one of his novels. The movie, dealing with a romance between an African-American soldier and a white French woman, was acclaimed in France and won the critic's choice award at the San Francisco Film Festival. Van Peebles used the success to break into the American film industry; he made number of films dealing with African-American themes. The best-known is *Sweet Sweetback's Baadasssss Song* (Independent, 1971) that became the top grossing independent film of 1972. Van Peebles continued as a filmmaker, but over time also published fiction and became an established songwriter and recording artist. His son, actor Mario Van Peebles, has appeared in several of Van Peebles' films. After his childhood, Van Peebles spent little time in Illinois and through much of his adult life divided his time among New York, Los Angeles, and various locations in Europe.
(*Current Biography*, New York: H. W. Wilson, 1999, s.v."Van Peebles, Melvin").

Van Vorst, Bessie (nee McGinnis) (1873–May 18, 1928)
    The wife of John Van Vorst, and, some years after his death, Hughes Le Roux [editor of *The Matin* (Paris, France)], Van Vorst was the author of several reform works with her sister-in-law Marie Louise Van Vorst. The two women, both with privileged backgrounds, actually worked in factories for brief periods of time in the early twentieth-century to gather information for their reform writings.
(*New York Times*, 27 November 1914, 11).

Van Vorst, Marie Louise (November 23, 1867–December 16, 1936)
    The daughter of a lawyer and jurist, Van Vorst dedicated herself to reform, decrying conditions for women working in factories in her books and articles. She wrote her first novel in 1901 with her widowed sister-in-law, Bessie (McGinnis) Van Vorst. She was also a vocal proponent of American entrance into World War I. Her knowledge of conditions in Europe helped her make a compelling case in essays and a novel. She was appointed to a war relief position in Italy after

World War I, and became a painter in the last decades of her life, after marrying an Italian nobleman, Count Gaetano Cagiati, in 1916.
(Alden Whitman, *American Reformers*, New York: H. W. Wilson, 1985, s.v. "Van Vorst, Marie Louise").

Vedder, John [pseud.], *see* Gruber, Frank

Vynne, Harold Richard (c.1863–September 14, 1903)
    An English immigrant, Vynne spent about ten years in Chicago. His first employment in the city was as personal secretary to Melville E. Stone, founder of the *Chicago Daily News*. Vynne later met the proprietor of the paper, Col. Ed Mann, on a trip to New York City and subsequently became the editor of *Town Topics* after marrying Mann's daughter. Vynne's first marriage to the daughter of a Chicago real estate developer had ended in divorce after a short time and his second marriage ended similarly. Vynne returned to Chicago and drank himself to death, a tenant of the Poorhouse Hospital of Cook County in his final weeks.
(*New York Times*, 15 September 1903, 9).

Wager, Walter H. (September 4, 1924–July 11, 2004)
    Thriller and science fiction writer Wager began his career as an aviation lawyer. He was born in New York City and educated at Columbia University (BA, 1943), Harvard University (LLB, 1946), and Northwestern University (LLM, 1949). In 1952 he became a senior editor at the United Nations Secretariat. He would later work as a writer, producer, or editor for Columbia Broadcasting, National Broadcasting Company, *Playbill*, and *Show*. From the 1960s through 1980s he worked in public relations for the American Society of Composers, Authors, and Publishers, The Juilliard School, Mann Music Center, and Eugene O'Neill Theater Center. He published his first novel in 1954 and published two dozen more by the end of his career. Several of his novels were adapted as major motion pictures.
(*Contemporary Authors Online*, Detroit: Gale, 2006, accessed, 17 April 2009).

Wagner, Constance Cassady [Constance Cassady, pseud.] (February 12, 1903–June 21, 1984)
    No information available.

Wagoner, David (June 5, 1926–?)
    Wagoner was born in Massillon, Ohio and grew up in Whiting, Indiana. A graduate of Pennsylvania State University (BA, 1947) and Indiana University (MA, 1949), he taught at DePauw, Indiana, and Pennsylvania State universities before beginning a faculty appointment at the University of Washington in 1954. Wagoner published several volumes of poetry in addition to novels.
[*Dictionary of Literary Biography*, vol. 5, s.v. "Wagoner, David (Russell)"].

Walcott, Arthur [pseud.], *see* Churchill, William

Wald, Malvin (August 8, 1917–March 6, 2008)
    Born in New York City and a graduate of Brooklyn College (BA, 1936), after serving in World War II, Wald began working in the film industry as a screenwriter and had a long career that spanned 1941 to 1979.
(*Contemporary Authors Online*, Detroit: Gale, 2008, 7 April 2009).

Walker, Mildred (May 2, 1905–May 27, 1998)

Walker, the daughter of a Baptist minister, grew up in Vermont and Pennsylvania and attended Wells College (Aurora, N.Y.). The wife of Ferdinand Ripley Schemm, a cardiologist, much of her work is set in rural areas in the Midwest and West, representative of the localities where her husband had practices.
(*New York Times*, 1 June 1998, 11).

Walker, Robert W. (November 17, 1948–?)

An author of mystery and suspense novels, Walker was born in Corinth, Mississippi. A graduate of Northwestern University (BS, 1971; MS, 1972), he worked in records administration (1972–1981) in the Chicago area after which he taught English and writing at Bethune-Cookman College (Daytona Beach, Florida) (1987–1994) and later at Daytona Beach Community College beginning in 1994.
(*Contemporary Authors Online*, Detroit: Gale, 2001, accessed 25 March 2009).

Wallace, Edgar (1875–1932)

An English author, Wallace was the illegitimate son of stage actors. His mother placed him with a fisherman in Greenwich, England and paid a modest sum for his care. As a young man Wallace ran away from home to become a fisherman, but suffered seasickness. Later he joined the Army and was eventually posted to South Africa where he became acquainted with a minister's family, who furthered his education (he had been forced to quit school at twelve years old) and encouraged his interest in writing. He eventually married one of the minister's daughters, became a journalist, and soon afterwards moved back to England. A self-published novel that was an overnight success established his literary career and he went on to write 173 novels, 24 plays, 61 sketches, and more than 2,000 short stories. Wallace wrote mostly mysteries and crime fiction and was famous for the quantities of writing he produced.
(Robin Winks, ed. *Mystery and Suspense Writers*, Scribner's 1998, s.v. "Wallace, Edgar").

Wallis, J. H. (James Harold) (January 23, 1885–January 13, 1958)

A journalist and politician, Wallis was born in Dubuque, Iowa. He was publisher and editor of the *Dubuque Daily News* and, until 1919, was managing editor of the *Dubuque Times Journal*. A Dubuque alderman for six years, Wallis spearheaded a campaign promoting a city manager form of government for the city. He was the author of eleven novels and six detective mysteries. One of his books, *Once Off Guard* (Dutton, 1942) was adapted into the film *The Woman in the Window* (International Pictures, 1944) directed by Fritz Lang.
(www.encyclopediadubuque.org, accessed 25 March 2009).

Walsh, William Thomas (September 11, 1891–January 22, 1949)

Walsh was a historian of fifteenth and sixteenth century Europe. He was born in Waterbury, Connecticut and educated Yale University. Early in his career he worked as a newspaper reporter on Connecticut and Philadelphia newspapers, but became an educator starting in 1918 at the Roxbury School, where he went on to head the English Department. From 1933 until his retirement in 1947, he was an English professor at Manhattanville College in New York City.
(Matthew Hoehn, ed., *Catholic Authors, Contemporary Biographical Sketches, 1930–1947*, Newark, N.J.: St. Mary's Abbey, 1948, s.v. "Walsh, William Thomas").

Walt, Charles [pseud.], *see* Bein, Albert

Walz, Audrey Boyers [Francis Bonnamy, pseud.] (1907–February 14, 1983)
A native of Mobile, Alabama, Walz received her bachelor's degree Phi Beta Kappa from the University of Chicago. She wrote twelve mysteries under the name Francis Bonnamy. She also wrote several historical novels with her husband, former *New York Times* correspondent Jay Walz. (*New York Times*, 17 February 1983, D23).

Ward, Anna Bell [pseud.], *see* Patricia Reilly and Harold N. Swanson

Ward, Florence Jeannette Baier (1886–1959)
No information available.

Ward, Mary Jane (August 27, 1905–1981)
Although she was born in Fairmount, Indiana, Ward grew up in Evanston, Illinois and spent most of her life there. She graduated from Evanston High School and attended Northwestern University (1915–1917). The wife of Edward Quayle, a statistician, prior to 1946 Ward published articles, short stories, and book reviews, as well as two novels that received some critical notice, but did not sell well. In 1946 her book, *The Snake Pit* appeared, became a best seller, and was later made into a movie (Twentieth Century-Fox, 1948). Ward continued to write and published four more novels.
(*World Authors, 1900–1950*, New York: H. W. Wilson, 1996, s.v. "Ward, Mary Jane").

Ware, Harlan (July 14, 1902–May 7, 1967)
In addition to publishing fiction, Ware wrote for film and television. He was living in Evanston, Illinois at the time of his death.

Warren, Maude Radford (January 2, 1875–July 6, 1934)
The novelist and writer of news features Maude Radford was born at Wolfe Island, Ontario, Canada, and educated at the University of Chicago, receiving a bachelor's and a master's degree from the institution before teaching literature and composition there. She married Prof. Joseph Parker Warren, also of the university. In 1907, she published her first novel and went on to write more than fifteen books. During World War I she was a war correspondent (1916–1919), while volunteering in canteen work, and with army organizations and the YMCA. She served at Argonne, Chateau-Thierry, St. Mihiel, and Verdun. Afterwards, she traveled in Russia, Rumania, the Near East, and the Arctic, writing stories for magazines and newspapers.
(*New York Times*, 6 July 1934, 11).

Warren, Robert Penn (1905–September 15, 1989)
Considered one of America's most notable twentieth-century authors, Warren was born in the small town of Guthrie, Kentucky, near the Tennessee border. A precocious student, he graduated high school at fifteen and earned degrees at Vanderbilt University, Yale, and Oxford (on a Rhodes Scholarship) by the time he was twenty-three years old. He then began the career of a writer and English professor that he was to pursue for the rest of his life.
(*Dictionary of Literary Biography*, vol. 152, s.v. "Warren, Robert Penn").

Warren, Vernon [pseud.], *see* Chapman, George

Warrick, LaMar Sheridan (November 10, 1894–February 24, 1992)
A book reviewer, journalist, and college professor, Warrick was born LaMar Sheridan in Detroit, Michigan. She was educated at Northwestern University (BA, 1915; additional study in journalism) and worked as general secretary for the national office of the Epworth League. She married Walter D. Warrick and lived most of her married life in Evanston, eventually teaching on an adjunct basis in the Northwestern University School of Journalism. Her one novel, *Yesterday's Children*, for which she is included here, won the 1944 prize for fiction by the Chicago Foundation for Literature.
(*Ludington (Mich.) Daily News*, 28 February 1992, 2).

Washburne, Marion Foster (1863–?)
No information available.

Waterloo, Stanley (1846–October 11, 1913)
A newspaperman who published a number of novels, Waterloo was an owner and founder of newspapers in St. Louis, Missouri and St. Paul, Minnesota, before a long career as an editorial writer on the *Chicago Tribune*. He resided for many years in Chicago and was an active member and past president of the Chicago Press Club. He was born in St. Clair, Michigan and was an 1869 graduate of the University of Michigan.
(*New York Times*, 11 October 1913, 11).

Waterman, Margaret (October 6, 1909–Febraruy 1, 2001)
A graduate of Mount Holyoke College (AB, 1931) and the University of Wisconsin (MA, 1933, PhD, 1942), Waterman had a long career as an English instructor (1939–1973), teaching at the University of Colorado, Boulder; Hiram (Ohio) College, Lake Forest (Ill.) College, and Case Western Reserve University (Ohio) before becoming the editor of the *Dictionary of American Regional English*, a position she held for several decades.
(*Contemporary Authors Online*, Detroit: Gale, 2001).

Watt, Marion Frances
No information available.

Watters, Barbara (Hunt) (October 17, 1907–January 2, 1984)
A native of Chicago, Watters was best known as an astrologer. She attended the University of Chicago (1923–1925), Art Institute of Chicago (1925–1927), and, later, Brown University (1954–1957). In addition to publishing short stories and four novels, Watters wrote on astrology and was the founder of the National Academy of Astrologists.
(*Contemporary Authors Online*, 2002, accessed 3/13/2008).

Wayde, Bernard
No information available.

Wayland, Patrick [pseud.], *see* O'Connor, Richard

Weaver, John Van Alstyne (July 17, 1893–June 14, 1938)
Born in Charlotte, North Carolina, and a graduate of Hamilton (N. Y.) College, (BA, 1914), Weaver was an assistant book editor at the *Chicago Daily News* (1915–1920), with a break during

which he served in the U.S. Army (1917–1919). He was then literary editor at the *Brooklyn Daily Eagle* until 1924, before becoming a freelance writer, publishing poetry and fiction. After 1928 he was a screenwriter in Hollywood.
(*World Authors 1900–1950*, New York: H. W. Wilson, 1996, s.v. "Weaver, John Van Alstyne").

Webster, Henry Kitchell (September 7, 1875–December 9, 1932)
    A prolific author, Webster wrote best-selling mysteries, novels, and hundreds of pieces for pulp magazines under five pen names and anonymously. Except for his years studying at Hamilton College, Webster spent his entire life in the Chicago suburb of Evanston, Illinois. It was there that he set up a business–like office to write and manage the publication of fiction as efficiently as possible, complete with a stenographer to take his dictation.
(*World Authors 1900-1950*, New York: H. W. Wilson, 1996, s.v. "Webster, Henry Kitchell").

Weir, Hugh C. (May 1 1884–March 15, 1934)
    Born in Vergennes, Illinois, Weir began working as a reporter at sixteen on the *Springfield (Ohio) Sun*. He is best known as a screenwriter credited with more than three hundred screenplays, the first of which he sold when he was twenty. Eventually, he returned to journalism, but his success had changed his status dramatically in the field and he mostly interviewed and wrote about the most prominent people of his time. A founder of Tower Magazines, which published six magazines, including *American Spectator*, and had a combined circulation of over 1.6 million, he made headlines by suing Rev. Billy Sunday over authorship of stories based on the Bible.
(*New York Times*, 18 March 1934, 35).

Wellard, James [Howard] (January 12, 1909–1987)
    A British author who was born and died in London, England, Wellard traveled widely from 1939 to 1961. During World War II he was a foreign correspondent for the *Chicago Times* and traveled throughout Europe and North Africa. From 1946 to 1954 he was a foreign correspondent based in Italy, after which he taught in the United States at the University of Illinois and Longwood (Va.,) College. In addition to respected non-fiction works, particularly those concerning the history and archaeology of North Africa, Wellard wrote detective thrillers, historical novels, and romances.
(*Contemporary Authors Online*, Detroit: Gale, 2002, accessed 17 April 2009).

Wellington, A. A.
    No information available.

Welton, Arthur D. (1867–1940)
    No information available.

Wendt, Lloyd (May 16, 1908–October 21, 2007)
    A native of Spencer, South Dakota, Wendt attended Sioux Falls (S. Dak.) College (1928–1929) and completed his education at Northwestern University (SB, 1931; SM 1934). He worked as a journalist for fifty years (1927–1977), initially on Sioux Falls newspapers, but from 1929 onwards for Chicago newspapers, including the *Chicago American*, *Chicago Today*, and, for the bulk of his career, at the *Chicago Tribune* where he ended his career as associate Sunday editor

and associate editor (1975–1977). Most of the books he published were works of non-fiction, including a pictorial history of Chicago.
(*Contemporary Authors Online*, Detroit: Gale, 2007, 17 April 2009).

Wentworth, Edward Chichester
    No information available.

Weverka, Robert (November 17, 1926–?)
    Born in Los Angeles and educated at the University of Southern California (BA, 1950), Weverka worked as a salesman and later an advertising director, before founding his own advertising agency, Weverka & Associates, in Beverley Hills, of which he was the president (1957–1968). Afterwards, he became a freelance writer of movie novelizations, publishing sixteen such works between 1972 and 1980.
(*Contemporary Authors Online*, Detroit: Gale, 2002, accessed 17 April 2009).

Wheaton, Emily
    No information available.

Wheeler, Keith (April 17, 1911–?)
    A journalist, Wheeler was born in Carrington, North Dakota and attended Huron (S.Dak.) College for one year (1934–1935). He later worked as a columnist, foreign correspondent, and war correspondent for the *Chicago Times* (1937–1951). In 1951 he began working for *Life* and *Time* in New York City and eventually wrote nine non-fiction works for Time-Life Books between 1973 and 1983. His six earlier works of fiction and non-fiction were published between 1945 and 1971.
(*Contemporary Authors Online*, Detroit: Gale, 2002, accessed 18 April 2009).

Wheeler, Preserved [pseud.], *see* McDougall, Ella L. Randall

White, Betty
    No information available.

White, Hervey (1866–October 19, 1944)
    Although White published several novels when he was in his thirties, he is best known as the founder of the Maverick Colony near Woodstock, New York. Born in New London, Iowa, White studied at the University of Kansas and graduated from Harvard University (AB, 1894). He then lived in Chicago and worked with Jane Addams at Hull House, until, in 1900, along with Bolton Brown and Ralph Whitehead, he founded the Byrdcliffe Colony. In 1902, he founded the Maverick Colony on his own land, intending it to be a place where young people could practice art. He later began operating a summer theater there where plays bound for Broadway were given their first performances and actors such as Helen Hayes and Edward G. Robinson worked early in their careers. White also established a concert series and the Maverick Press.
(*New York Times*, 21 October 1944, 17).

Whitlock, Brand (4 March 1869–24 May 1934)
    Born in Ohio, Whitlock worked as journalist before his admission to the bar of the state of Ohio. After working as a lawyer in Toledo, Ohio (1897–1905), he served as a reform mayor of that town (1904–1913). From 1913–1919 he served as U.S. minister to Belgium (1913–1919) and

as ambassador to Belgium (1919–1922). His efforts to relieve wartime suffering and its aftermath earned him numerous honors from Belgium and other countries. He wrote more than seventeen books of fiction and non-fiction.
(*New York Times*, 25 May 1934, 21).

Whitmore, Stanford (July 23, 1925–?)
    Born in Sioux City, Iowa, Whitmore was raised on Chicago's South Side. He served in the U.S. Marine Corps in World War II and was subsequently educated at Stanford University (AB, 1950; MA, 1954).

Whitney, Phyllis A. (September 9, 1903–February 8, 2008)
    The daughter of an American shipping line representative, Whitney's youth was spent in China, Japan, and the Philippines. After the death of her father, she moved back to the United States in 1918 with her mother, who was terminally ill with cancer. Following her mother's death two years later, Whitney lived with an aunt in Chicago and graduated from McKinley High School there in 1924. Although she wanted to attend college, she was not able to afford the costs and worked at the Chicago Public Library and in bookstores. After publishing her first book for children, she worked as a children's book editor at the *Chicago Sun* (1942–1946) and subsequently at the *Philadelphia Inquirer*. Starting in 1947 she was a freelance writer, publishing more than seventy-five books of juvenile fiction, adult romantic suspense, and mysteries. She traveled frequently throughout her life and was known for the care with which she established the physical settings of her novels based on direct observations.
(*World Authors, 1900–1950*, New York: H. W. Wilson, 1996, s.v. "Whitney, Phyllis A[yame]").

Wickware, Francis Sill (January 31, 1883–October 12, 1940)
    Born in Eastons Corners, Ontario, Wickware began a career as a mining engineer, but went on to become a writer and editor. He was educated at McGill University (AB, 1904; BS, 1906, mining engineering) and during college worked summers as a mine surveyor. Upon his graduation he was named a Dawson Research Fellow at McGill and taught courses in mining engineering and English. He became associate editor of *The Engineering Magazine of New York and London* (1907–1911), and moved to New York City. In 1911, he became editor of *The American Yearbook* (1911–1920), later joining the firm of D. Appleton and Company as editor and continuing in his position after a merger with the Century Company in 1933 at the Appleton-Century Company.
(*New York Times*, 13 October 1940, 50).

Wight, Natalie
    No information available.

Wilcox, Wendell (1906–1981)
    Wilcox was a prolific novelist and short-story writer who published in *The New Yorker* and *Harper's Bazaar*. Wilcox resided in Chicago. The author's papers are at Princeton University.

Wilder, Thornton (April 17, 1897–December 7, 1975)
    The son of Amos Parker Wilder, a newspaper editor and U.S. Consul to China, Wilder was born in Madison, Wisconsin, but spent part of his youth in China. He was a graduate of Yale University (AB, 1920) and Princeton University (AM, 1926) and began his work life as a teacher at the Lawrenceville (N.J.) School (1921–1929). He was a lecturer in comparative literature at the

University of Chicago (1930–1936) and wrote for motion picture studios at the same time. Best known as a playwright, he wrote novels throughout his career, winning the Pulitzer Prize (*The Bridge of San Luis Rey*, Boni, 1927); and the National Book Award (*Eighth Day*, Harper, 1967). His plays *Our Town* and *The Skin of Our Teeth* also won Pulitzer Prizes in 1938 and 1943, respectively.
[*Dictionary Literary Biography*, vol. 4, s.v. "Wilder, Thornton (Niven)"].

Wilkie, Franc B. (1830–1892)
    Born in Saratoga County, New York, Wilkie was a runaway for part of his youth, living on his own in New York City for two years. When he returned home, he worked as a carpenter and stone mason, while preparing himself for college. He worked as a reporter for the *Schenectady (N.Y.) Star* while studying at Union College. In 1857 he moved to Davenport, Iowa and worked on the *Evening News* in that city. During the Civil War, he was a correspondent for the *New York Times*, traveling with the Union Army in the West. After the war, he worked for the *Chicago Times* and was living in the city at the time of the 1871 fire, afterwards working on the behalf of the owner of the newspaper, W. F. Storey, he supervised the construction of the *Times* Building, for many years a Chicago landmark. He was also the organizer of the Chicago Press Club and that organization's first president.
(*National Cyclopedia of American Biography*, vol. I, s.v. "Wilkie, Franc Bangs").

Williams, Brock (1894–February 19, 1964)
    Williams was a British screenwriter who wrote hundreds of screenplays and adaptations for the English film industry between 1932 and 1955.

Williams, Kirby
    No information available.

Williams, Robert Dolly [pseud.], *see* Potter, Margaret Horton Black

Williams, Wilbur Herschel (1874–1935)
    No information available.

Willingham, Calder (December 23, 1922–February 19, 1995)
    Willingham commenced his writing career in his early twenties with a novel that became notorious for depicting corruption, sadism, and sodomy at the Citadel. The author was born in Atlanta and privately educated at the Darlington School in Rome, Georgia, as well as at the Citadel. He attended the University of Virginia and for a number of years lived as a freelance writer, continuing to publish works in the 1950s and 1960s that were considered scandalous for their portrayal of sexual acts. He was also a screenwriter with credits for several major motion pictures in the 1970s. He wrote the screenplay for his own novel *Rambling Rose* (Delacorte Press, 1972), and the 1991 production starred Laura Dern and Robert Duvall (Carolco Pictures).
(*World Authors, 1900–1950*, New York: H. W. Wilson, 1996, s.v. "Willingham, Calder").

Wilson, Margaret (January 16, 1882–October 6, 1973)
    A native of Traer, Iowa, Wilson graduated from the University of Chicago with her bachelor's degree in 1904. A lifelong Presbyterian, concerned with religious and moral issues, after college Wilson was a missionary in India for twelve years. She began writing when she returned to the

United States in 1916, publishing several of her short stories. Her breakthrough came with the publication of her first novel, *The Able McLaughlins* (included here), which won the Pulitzer Prize. She went on to publish ten more books, some of which were non-fiction works of sociology. (*Dictionary of Literary Biography*, vol. 9, s.v. "Wilson, Margaret").

Windsor, William (1857–?)

The author won national attention as the leader of a seventy-five-member sect in St. Louis, Missouri who practiced dirt eating as an aid to health. Windsor was described as a sometime lawyer and student of natural science. In addition to lecturing to his membership on a nightly basis in the Merchants' League Building at Eighteenth and Olive Streets, he gathered river bottom sand, sterilized it, and sold it to his adherents in small bags for twenty-five cents each.
(*New York Times*, 16 December 1901, 1).

Winslow, Thyra Samter (March 15, 1893–December 2, 1961)

An author of short stories, novels, and screenplays, much of Winslow's work is set in her native state of Arkansas, where she was born in Fort Smith. She lived in New York City as an adult, working as the drama critic for the *Gotham Guide*. Her short stories were published in *Cosmopolitan*, *Good Housekeeping*, the *New Yorker*, the *Saturday Evening Post*, and *Town and Country*. (*Contemporary Authors Online*, Detroit: Gale, 2002, accessed 18 April 2009).

Wise, Winifred Esther (1906–?)

Born in Fond du Lac, Wisconsin, Wise graduated from the University of Wisconsin (BA, 1930). She worked in Chicago as an editor for *Compton's Picture Encyclopedia* (1930–1933) and as a copywriter and later an advertising executive for Marshall Field's (1939–1952), before becoming a full-time freelance writer. She has published widely in magazines, but most of her books are for children.

Woodford, Jack [pseud.], *see* Woolfolk, Josiah Pitts

Woolfolk, Josiah Pitts [Gordon Sayre, Jack Woodford, pseuds.] (March 25, 1894–May 16, 1971)

An author of pulp fiction and how-to books on writing and publishing under several pseudonyms, Woolfolk also wrote for the motion picture industry. He grew up in Chicago, living with an affluent grandmother while his father worked as a physician in private practice in Sioux City, Iowa (his mother died when he was quite young). Although his father returned to Chicago to teach at Rush Medical College, he died at the age of forty-nine. The author of more than one hundred books, Woolfolk began writing and publishing in the 1920s. He later founded his own publishing house, the Jack Wood Press, in the 1930s. Woolfolk's books on writing are still highly regarded and have been credited by Piers Anthony, Ray Bradbury, and Robert Heinlein.
(*Washington Post*, 19 May 1971, p. B6).

Worthington, Elizabeth Strong [Griffith A. Nicholas, pseud.] (1888–1908)

No information available.

Wren, Percival Christopher (1885–November 23, 1941)

Englishman Wren was a collateral descendant of architect Sir Christopher Wren and was one of the best-known soldier authors after the publication of his book *Beau Geste* in 1924. An avid sportsman at Oxford University who engaged in boxing, cricket, football, and golf, he traveled to exotic places after his graduation, eventually settling in Bombay, India, where he worked in government administration for ten years in Bombay as the assistant director of education. He served in the Indian Army in World War I, serving in East Africa until 1917 when an injury forced his retirement from active service. He then began writing a series of books on the Foreign Legion. (*New York Times*, 24 November 1941, 17).

Wright, Richard (September 4, 1908–November 28, 1960)
One of the first African-American writers to achieve a major reputation in American literature, Wright was born in Roxie, Mississippi and moved to Chicago in 1927 where he found work in the U.S. Post Office. He later had a job with the Works Progress Administration Federal Writer's Project (1935–1937). Primarily self-educated and concerned with the sociological aspects of racism, Wright joined the Communist party in Chicago in 1932 (although his concerns about the party's ideological policing led him to resign from the party in 1944). Most of his early writing was for left-wing publications. However, in 1938 he won a contest sponsored by *Story* magazine that enabled him to publish his first book, *Uncle Tom's Children* (Harper, 1938). The critical acclaim the book received launched his career. He wrote about his life in Chicago in several autobiographical works, although from 1946 until his death he lived primarily in Paris, France. (*Contemporary Authors Online*, Detroit: Gale, 2009, accessed 12 December 2009).

Wyatt, Edith Franklin (September 14, 1873–October 1958)
Daughter of a railroad and mining engineer, Wyatt grew up in Chicago. She attended Bryn Mawr College (1892–1894) and taught at a private school for five years before teaching at Hull House and participating in the Chicago salon known as the Little Room. She published much of her fiction between 1900 and 1910, later devoting herself full-time to working as a social commentator and Progressive activist, vaunting the rights of workers, children and working-class women. She lived in Chicago all her life, although her activism involved travel and she was a friend of many of the prominent authors and activists of her day. Her writing was championed by William Dean Howells, and she was a friend of Jane Ayer Fairbank, Dorothy Canfield Fisher, Henry B. Fuller, John T. McCutcheon, Booth Tarkington, as well as Jane Addams, Theodore Roosevelt, and Ida Tarbell. Wyatt's papers are at the Newberry Library.

Wylie, Philip (1902–1971)
Wylie wrote more than one hundred books and hundreds of essays and short stories. An author of serious fiction, sometimes acclaimed by critics, he also wrote a large number of popular fiction works to add to his income. Disillusioned early in life through his relationship with his mother, the educational system (he was expelled from Princeton for poor grades and a bad attitude), the institution of marriage (he was forced to write pulp fiction to support his first wife who constantly demanded money and openly had affairs), the judicial system (he lost a paternity case and was forced to pay child support), his work was often calculated to expose hypocrisy and deride institutions, attitudes, and values that he despised. During World War II he attacked Americans for a perceived lack of patriotism. Later, he presented gloomy scenarios of nuclear warfare and environmental disaster. He co-authored several books with Edwin Balmer.

Yaffe, James (March 31, 1927–?)
A Chicago native, Yaffe was the son of immigrants. His father arrived in the United States a poor man, but established himself as a successful businessman by the time his son was growing. Yaffe was educated at the Fieldston School in New York City and at Yale University (BA, 1948).

After a year of service in the U.S. Army, stationed in Shanghai, China, he began writing full-time, publishing short stories in major literary periodicals. His novels have been noted for their convincing depictions of Jewish-American families in Chicago and New York City. Yaffe wrote eleven novels, two short story collections, short stories and plays. He began teaching in the English Department at Colorado (Colorado Springs) College in 1968.
(*Contemporary Authors Online*, Detroit: Gale, 2002, accessed 25 October 2009).

Yandell, Enid (1870–1934)
A sculptor who was born in Louisville, Kentucky, Yandell studied at the Cincinnati (Ohio) Art Academy and was later an assistant to Karl Bittner in New York City and studied with Frederick MacMonnies in Paris, France. She created the caryatids that supported the roof garden of the Women's Building at the World's Columbian Exhibition in Chicago in 1893.
(Jules Heller and Nancy Heller, *North American Women Artists of the Twentieth Century: A Biographical Dictionary*, New York: Garland, 1995, s.v. "Yandell, Enid").

Yates, Katherine M. (1865–October 25, 1951)
Yates was the author of seventeen books, most of them published from 1903–1919.

York, Carol Beach (January 21, 1928–?)
A Chicago native, York has written more than forty books for young adults, as well as publishing short stories and non-fiction in magazines for children and women. Born Carol Beach, she attended Thornton Junior College (Harvey, Ill.) and married Richard Marten York with whom she had a daughter, Diana Carol.
(*Contemporary Authors Online*, Detroit: Gale, 2001, accessed 22 August 2009).

Zara, Louis (August 2, 1910–October 5, 2001)
Born in New York City, Zara studied at the University of Chicago and began a long career in publishing in Chicago, working for Ziff-Davis, where he was vice-president (1946–1953) and later general manager of the book division (1959–1961). Zara was later editor-in-chief of the General Trade Division of Follett in New York City (1962–1965). In addition to writing novels, historical fiction, and short stories, Zara wrote for radio and television. He also wrote non-fiction books on rocks and gems, of which he was a collector.
(*New York Times*, 23 October 2001, A20).

Ziegler, Elise Reif (1910–?)
A Chicago native, Ziegler attended Crane Junior College, the University of Illinois, and Northwestern University. She worked as a copywriter for Sears and Roebuck until her marriage to Norman A. Ziegler in 1933. Afterwards, she was a homemaker and freelance writer.

Appendix A
Works First Published after 1980

Abraytis, Ron. *Are You Clumping Trubs?* North Augusta, S.C.: Writers Block, 1995. 191pp.

Acker, Rick. *Dead Man's Rule.* Grand Rapids, Mich.: Kregel, 2005. 316pp.

Adams, Melodie. *In the Family Way.* New York: Harlequin, Silhouette Books, 1990. 187pp.

Albert, Marvin. *The Untouchables.* New York: Ballantine, 1987. 218pp.

Alexander, Carly. *The Secret Life of Mrs. Claus.* New York: Strapless / Kensington Books, 2005. 382pp.

Alexander, Carrie. *The Madcap Heiress.* Love and Laughter, no. 8. New York: Harlequin Books, 1996. 186pp.

Amberg, Jay. *Blackbird Singing.* New York: Forge, 1998. 302pp.

Anshaw, Carol. *Seven Moves.* Boston: Houghton Mifflin, 1996. 220pp.

Archer, Jeffrey. *The Prodigal Daughter.* New York: Simon and Schuster, Linden Press.1982. 464pp.

Ardizzone, Tony. *Taking It Home: Stories from the Neighborhood.* Urbana: University of Illinois Press, 1996. 155pp.

———. *Heart of the Order.* New York: Henry Holt and Company, 1986. 314pp.

Aswani, 'Ala. *Chicago.* Translated by Farouk Abdel Wahab. New York: Harper, 2007. 342pp.

Atkins, Ace. *Leavin' Trunk Blues: A Nick Travers Mystery.* New York: Thomas Dunne Books, 2000. 322pp.

Atlas, James Robert. *The Great Pretender.* New York: Atheneum, 1986. 277pp.

Austin, Lynn N. *A Proper Pursuit*. Minneapolis, Minn.: Bethany House, 2007. 432pp.

Axelrood, Larry. *The Advocate*. Nashville, Tenn.: Cumberland House, 2000. 254pp.

Axelrood, Larry. *Death Eligible: A Darcy Cole Novel*. Nashville, Tenn.: Cumberland House, 2004. 287pp.

———. *Plea Bargain*. Nashville, Tenn.: Cumberland House, 2002. 286pp.

Bailey, Barbara. *When I Get Older I'll Understand*. Pittsburgh: Sterling House, 2000. 184pp.

Bailey, George. *West Side Stories*. Chicago: City Stoop Press, 1992. 181pp.

Baisden, Michael. *God's Gift to Women: How Much Is One Night of Passion Really Worth?* New York: Touchstone, 2002. 292pp.

Baker, Nikki. *In the Game: A Virginia Kelly Mystery*. Tallahassee, Fla.: Naiad Press, 1991. 171pp.

———. *The Ultimate Exit Strategy: A Virginia Kelly Mystery*. Tallahassee, Fla.: Naiad Press, 1995. 229pp.

Balliett, Blue. *The Wright 3*. Illustrated by Brett Helquist. Waterville, Maine: Thorndike Press, 2006. 318pp.

Ballis, Stacey. *Inappropriate Men*. Don Mills, Ont.: Harlequin, Red Dress Ink Books, 2004. 346pp.

———. *Room for Improvement*. New York: Penguin, Berkley Books, 2006. 294pp.

———. *Sleeping Over*. Don Mills, Ont.: Harlequin, Red Dress Ink Books, 2005. 345pp.

Barrett, Neal. *Pink Vodka Blues*. New York: Kensington, 1997. 276pp.

Barrow, Adam. *Blind Spot*. New York: Dutton, 1997. 291pp.

Barton, Frederick Preston. *The El Cholo Feeling Passes*. Atlanta: Peachtree, 1985. 461pp.

Bates, Andrew. *Heralds of the Storm*. Year of the Scarab Trilogy, bk. 1. Clarkson, Ga.: White Wolf, 2001. 285pp.

———. *Lay Down with Lions*. Year of the Scarab Trilogy, bk. 2. Clarkson, Ga.: White Wolf, 2001. 288pp.

Bauer, Joan. *Rules of the Road*. New York: G. P. Putnam's Sons, 1998. 201pp.

Bausch, Richard Carl. *Violence.* Boston: Houghton Mifflin / Seymour Lawrence, 1992. 293pp.

Baxter, Holly. *Tears of the Dragon.* Scottsdale, Ariz.: Poisoned Pen Press, 2005. 300pp.

Becker, John Leonard. *Jaime: An Autobiographical Novel in Short Stories.* Boston: David R. Godine, 1981. 165pp.

Bell, Christine. *The Seven-Year Atomic Make-Over Guide: And Other Stories.* New York: Norton, 1996. 186pp.

Bellow, Saul. *The Actual.* New York: Viking, 1997. 103pp.

———. *The Dean's December.* New York: Harper and Row, 1982. 312pp.

———. *Him with His Foot in His Mouth, and Other Stories.* New York: Harper and Row, 1984. 294pp.

———. *Something to Remember Me By.* New York: Viking, 1991. 222pp.

Belton, Sandra. *Store Bought Baby.* New York: Greenwillow Books, 2006. 246pp.

Benson, O. G. *Cain's Wife.* New York: Harper and Row, Perennial Library, 1985. 200pp.

Benson, Raymond. *Sweetie's Diamonds.* Waterville, Maine: Five Star, 2006. 359pp.

Beres, Michael. *Final Stroke.* Palm Beach, Fla.: Medallion Press, 2007. 502pp.

Berg, Elizabeth. *Say When.* New York: Atria Books, 2003. 262pp.

Bernard, Hannah. *Their Accidental Baby.* Romance, no. 3774. New York: Harlequin, 2003. 184pp.

Bernhardt, William. *Capitol Murder.* New York: Random House, 2006. 368pp.

———. *Hate Crime.* New York: Random House, 2004. 366pp.

Berriault, Gina. *The Lights of Earth.* San Francisco: North Point Press, 1984. 157pp.

Berry, Venise T. *All of Me: A Voluptuous Tale.* New York: Dutton, 2000. 274pp.

Bertrand, Yolande. *Dark Road Home.* Los Angeles: Holloway House, 1984. 177pp.

Bethancourt, T. Ernesto. *Doris Fein: Legacy of Terror.* New York: Holiday House, 1983. 133pp.

Bielski, Ursula. *Chicago Haunts: Ghostly Lore of the Windy City*. Chicago: Lake Claremont Press, 1997. 274pp.

———. *Chicago Haunts: Ghostlore of the Windy City*. Chicago: Lake Claremont Press, 1998. 277pp.

———. *More Chicago Haunts: Scenes from Myth and Memory*. Chicago: Lake Claremont Press, 2000.

Birmingham, Stephen. *The Auerbach Will*. Boston: Little, Brown, 1983. 430pp.

Bishop, Carly. *Heart Throb*. Intrigue, no. 323. New York: Harlequin, 1995. 248pp.

———. *Hot Blooded*. Intrigue, no. 314. New York: Harlequin, 1995. 248pp.

Black, Jeff. *Planting Eli*. New York: Southern Tier Editions / Harrington Park, 2006. 173pp.

Black, Kole. *The Chance She Took*. Woodbury, Conn.: Spaulden, 2007. 262pp.

Black, Michael A. *A Final Judgment: A Ron Shade Novel*. Waterville, Maine: Five Star, 2006. 344pp.

———. *The Heist*. Waterville, Maine: Five Star, 2005. 292pp.

———. *A Killing Frost*. Waterville, Maine: Five Star, 2002. 271pp.

———. *Windy City Knights: A Ron Shade Novel*. Waterville, Maine: Five Star, 2004. 328pp.

Blair, Alaric. *The End of Innocence: A Journey into the Life*. South Bend, Ind.: Mirage, 1998. 249pp.

Bland, Eleanor Taylor. *A Cold and Silent Dying*. New York: St. Martin's, Minotaur, 2004. 261pp.

———. *Dead Time*. New York: St. Martin's, 1992. 211pp.

———. *A Dark and Deadly Deception*. New York: St. Martin's, Minotaur, 2005. 262pp.

———. *Done Wrong*. New York: St. Martin's, 1995. 216pp.

———. *Fatal Remains*. New York: St. Martin's, Minotaur, 2003. 272pp.

———. *Scream in Silence*. New York: St. Martin's, Minotaur, 2000. 290pp.

———. *Whispers in the Dark*. New York: St. Martin's, Minotaur, 2001. 244pp.

———. *Windy City Dying*. New York: St. Martin's, Minotaur, 2002. 324pp.

Blank, Martin. *Shadowchase: A Novel of Murder*. New York: St. Martin's, 1989. 168pp.

Block, Lawrence. *No Score: A Chip Harrison Novel*. New York: Signet, 1996. 269pp.

Bloomquist, Tim. *Which Way from Here*. Traverse City, Mich.: Noslo, 2000. 343pp.

Blum, Carol O'Brien. *Anne's Head*. New York: Dial, 1982. 275pp.

Boeshaar, Andrea. *Broken Things*. Faded Photographs, ser. 1. Uhrichsville, Ohio: Barbour, 2003. 346pp.

Bolks, Shane. *Reality TV Bites*. New York: Avon Books, 2006. 279pp.

Bonansinga, Jay R. *Bloodhound*. New York: Onyx, 1999. 328pp.

————. *The Killer's Game*. New York: Simon and Schuster, 1997. 300pp.

Bond, Stephanie. *Two Sexy!* Blaze, no. 3. New York: Harlequin, 2001. 248pp.

Boone, Mark Allen. *The Demise of Luleta Jones*. Lisle, Ill.: Blacksmith Books, 2006. 261pp.

Booth, Coleen E. *Getting Connected*. New York: Harlequin, Silhouette Books, 1995. 185pp.

Borges, Luz. *Debt of Love*. Translated by Asa Zatz. New York: Kensington, 2000. 191pp.

Borisch, Sarah Allan. *The Protocol*. New York: Simon and Schuster, 1981. 448pp.

Bosak, Steven. *South Side Stories*. Oak Park, Ill.: City Stoop Press, 1993. 171pp.

Bowen, Fred, and Ann Barrow. *Playoff Dreams*. Atlanta: Peachtree, 1997. 95pp.

Boyd, Brendan C. *Blue Ruin: A Novel of the 1919 World Series*. New York: Norton, 1991. 339pp.

Boyle, Thomas. *The Cold Stove League*. Chicago: Academy Chicago, 1983. 228pp.

Bradford, Barbara Taylor. *Love in Another Town*. New York: HarperCollins, 1995. 181pp.

Bradley, Laurel. *Crème Brûlée Upset*. Adams Basin, N.Y.: Wild Rose Press, 2007. 261pp.

Brant, Kylie. *Hard to Handle*. Intimate Moments, no. 1108. New York: Harlequin, Silhouette Books, 2001. 250pp.

Branton, Matthew. *The House of Whacks*. New York: Bloomsbury, 1999. 250pp.

Brashler, William. *Traders*. New York: Atheneum, 1989. 306pp.

Brashler, William, and Reindeer Van Til [Crabbe Evers, joint pseud.]. *Murder in Wrigley Field*. New York: Bantam Books, 1991.

Braun, Jackie. *Found: Her Long-Lost Husband*. Secrets We Keep, no. 3982. New York: Harlequin, 2007. 187pp.

Brichoux, Karen. *Separation Anxiety*. New York: New American Library, 2004. 233pp.

Brightfield, Richard. *The Roaring Twenties: Chicago, 1920*. The Young Indiana Jones Chronicles, bk. 7. New York: Bantam Books, 1993. 119pp.

Brindel, June Rachuy. *Nobody is Ever Missing: Stories*. Chicago: Story Press, 1984. 158pp. 273pp.

Brod, D. C. *Brothers in Blood*. New York: Walker, 1993. 273pp.

———. *Heartstone*. Waterville, Maine: Five Star, 2005. 483pp.

———. *Masquerade in Blue*. New York: Walker, 1991. 215pp.

———. *Murder in Store*. New York: Walker, 1989. 241pp.

———. *Paid in Full: A Quint Mccauley Mystery*. Unity, Maine: Five Star, 2000. 280pp.

Brooks, Jerome. *Knee Holes*. New York: Orchard Books, 1992. 128pp.

———. *Naked in Winter*. New York: Orchard Books, 1990. 182pp.

Brown, Carrie. *The Hatbox Baby*. Rockland, Mass.: Compass Press, 2000. 333pp.

Brown, Dee. *Conspiracy of Knaves*. New York: Henry Holt, 1986. 392pp.

Brown, Fern G. *Our Love*. New York: Ballantine, Fawcett Juniper Books, 1986. 119pp.

Browne, Howard. *Pork City*. New York: St. Martin's / Joan Kahn, 1988. 264pp.

Buckman, Daniel. *Because the Rain*. New York: St. Martin's, 2007. 212pp.

———. *Water in Darkness*. New York: Akashic Books, 2001. 193pp.

Buehler, L. *The Lion Tamer: A Caged Death*. Hurst, Tex.: Echelon Press, 2004. 276pp.

Buehler, L. *The Rosary Bride: A Cloistered Death: A Grace Marsden Mystery.* Crowley, Tex.: Echelon Press, 2003. 219pp.

Burbridge, Edward Kenith. *Chicago Boy: The Life and Crimes of a Southside Street Fighter.* West Covina, Calif.: LA and Chicago River Underground Press, 1991. 295pp.

Burke, Patrick. *Stringer.* Rockville, Md.: James A. Rock / Yellowback, 2007. 343pp.

Burks, Cris. *Neecey's Lullaby.* New York: Broadway Books, 2005. 211pp.

Burnett, W. R. *Good-bye, Chicago: 1928: End of an Era.* New York: St. Martin's, 1981. 175pp.

Buss, Fran Leeper. *Journey of the Sparrows.* New York: Lodestar Books, 1991. 155pp.

Butcher, Jim. *Blood Rites: The Dresden Files.* New York: Roc, 2004. 372pp.

———. *Dead Beat: A Novel of the Dresden Files.* New York: Roc, 2006. 396pp.

———. *Death Masks: Book Five of the Dresden Files.* New York: Roc, 2003. 378pp.

———. *Fool Moon: The Dresden Files, Book 2.* New York: Roc, 2001. 342pp.

———. *Grave Peril: Book Three of the Dresden Files.* New York: Roc, 2001. 378pp.

———. *Proven Guilty: A Novel of the Dresden Files.* New York: Roc, 2006. 404pp.

———. *Storm Front: A Novel of the Dresden Files.* New York: Roc, 2007. 311pp.

———. *Summer Knight: Book Four of the Dresden Files.* New York: Roc, 2002. 371pp.

———. *White Night: A Novel of the Dresden Files.* New York: Roc, 2007. 407pp.

Byrne, John. *Whipping Boy.* New York: Dell, 1992. 498pp.

Byrnes, Thomas. *My Angel's Name is Fred: Tales of Growing Up Catholic.* New York: Harper and Row, 1987. 257pp.

Caldwell, Laura. *A Clean Slate.* Don Mills, Ont.: Harlequin, Red Dress Ink Books, 2003. 312pp.

———. *The Night I Got Lucky.* Don Mills, Ont.: Harlequin, Red Dress Ink Books, 2005. 249pp.

Cameron, Julia. *The Dark Room.* New York: Carroll and Graf, 1998. 436pp.

Campbell, Bebe Moore. *Your Blues Ain't Like Mine.* New York: Putnam, 1992. 332pp.

Campbell, Will D. *The Convention: A Parable.* Atlanta: Peachtree, 1988. 406pp.

Campbell, R. Wright. *The 600-Pound Gorilla.* New York: New American Library, 1987. 236pp.

————. *Boneyards.* New York: Pocket Books, 1992. 298pp.

————. *The Cat's Meow: A Jimmy Flannery Mystery.* New York: New American Library, 1988. 199pp.

————. *The Gift Horse's Mouth: A Jimmy Flannery Mystery.* New York: Pocket Books, 1990. 198pp.

————. *Hip-Deep in Alligators: A Jimmy Flannery Mystery.* New York: New American Library, 1987. 206pp.

————. *In a Pig's Eye: A Jimmy Flannery Mystery.* New York: Pocket Books, 1991. 217pp.

————. *The Junkyard Dog.* New York: Signet, 1986. 190pp.

————. *The Lion's Share.* New York: Mysterious Press, 1996. 246pp.

————. *Nibbled to Death by Ducks.* New York: Pocket Books, 1989. 220pp.

————. *Pigeon Pie.* New York: Mysterious Press, 1998. 229pp.

————. *Sauce for the Goose.* New York: Warner Books, 1994. 229pp.

————. *Thinning the Turkey Herd: A Jimmy Flannery Mystery.* New York: New American Library, 1988. 185pp.

Carmichael, Emily. *Becoming Georgia.* New York: Penguin, Berkley Sensation, 2003. 327pp.

Carrillo, H. G. *Loosing My Espanish.* New York: Pantheon, 2004. 325pp.

Carroll, James. *Memorial Bridge.* Boston: Houghton Mifflin, 1991. 495pp.

Carroll, Lenore. *Annie Chambers.* Wichita, Kans.: Watermark, 1989. 195pp.

Carroll, William A. *Tales from the Windy City.* New York: Vantage, 2004. 179pp.

Carson, Paul. *Final Duty.* London: Heinemann, 2000. 321pp.

Carter, Cassandra. *Fast Life*. New York: Harlequin, Kimani, 2007. 296pp.

Carter, Charlotte. *Jackson Park*. New York: Ballantine, One World, 2003.

———. *Trip Wire: A Cook County Mystery*. New York: Ballantine, One World, 2005. 175pp.

Case, Dave. *Out of Cabrini: A Macbeth Novel*. Waterville, Maine: Five Star, 2006. 341pp.

Casserly, Jack. *The Dancing Angel*. New York: Donald I. Fine, 1994. 272pp.

Castillo, Ana. *Peel My Love Like an Onion*. New York: Doubleday, 1999. 213pp.

Castillo, Linda. *The Shadow Side*. New York: Penguin, Berkley Sensation, 2003. 375pp.

Chadwick, Elizabeth. *Elusive Lovers*. New York: Leisure Books, 1994. 444pp.

Charles, Robert J. *Broken Vows: A Novel of Betrayal*. New York: Dembner Books, 1981. 224pp.

Chercover, Sean. *Big City, Bad Blood*. New York: William Morrow, 2007. 294pp.

Chernoff, Maxine. *American Heaven*. Minneapolis, Minn.: Coffee House, 1996. 218pp.

———. *Bop: Stories by Maxine Chernoff*. New York: Random House, Vintage Contemporaries, 1987. 126pp.

———. *A Boy in Winter*. New York: Crown, 1999. 241 pp.

———. *Plain Grief*. New York: Summit Books, 1991. 222pp.

———. *Signs of Devotion*. New York: Simon and Schuster, 1993. 222pp.

Chicago Works: A New Collection of Chicago Authors' Best Stories. Chicago: Morton, 2003. 200pp.

Child, Lee. *Die Trying*. New York: Putnam, 1998. 374pp.

Christenberry, Judy. *When the Lights Went Out*. New York: Harlequin, Silhouette, 2001. 184pp.

Christman, Elizabeth. *Ruined for Life*. Mahwah, N.J.: Paulist Press, 1987. 136pp.

Churchill, Jill. *The Accidental Florist: A Jane Jeffry Mystery*. New York: William Morrow, 2007. 209pp.

———. *Bell, Book, and Scandal: A Jane Jeffry Mystery*. New York: William Morrow, 2003. 213pp.

Churchill, Jill. *The Class Menagerie*. New York: Avon Books, 1994. 217pp.

————. *A Farewell to Yarns*. New York: Avon Books, 1991. 214pp.

————. *Fear of Frying*. New York: Avon Books, 1997. 216pp.

————. *Grime and Punishment*. New York: Bantam, 1989. 185pp.

————. *A Groom with a View: A Jane Jeffry Mystery*. New York: Avon Books, Twilight, 1999. 218pp.

————. *The House of Seven Mabels: A Jane Jeffry Mystery*. New York: William Morrow, 2002. 234pp.

————. *A Knife to Remember: A Jane Jeffry Mystery*. New York: Avon Books, 1994. 216pp.

————. *The Merchant of Menace: A Jane Jeffry Mystery*. New York: Avon Books, Twilight, 1998. 214pp.

————. *A Midsummer Night's Scream: A Jane Jeffry Mystery*. New York: William Morrow, 2004. 227pp.

————. *Mulch Ado About Nothing: A Jane Jeffry Mystery*. New York: William Morrow, 2000. 216pp.

————. *A Quiche before Dying: A Jane Jeffry Mystery*. New York: Avon Books, 1993. 187pp.

————. *Silence of the Hams: A Jane Jeffry Mystery*. New York: Avon Books, 1996. 280pp.

————. *War and Peas*. New York: Avon Books, 1996. 216pp.

Cisneros, Sandra. *Caramelo*. New York: Knopf, 2002. 443pp.

———— .*House on Mango Street*. Houston: Arte Publico Press, 1983. 103pp.

Citron, Lana. *Spilt Milk*. New York: Scribner, 2001. 234pp.

Clark, Jack. *Westerfield's Chain*. New York: St. Martin's, Minotaur, 2002. 308pp.

Clarke, Gerald P. *The Drone Virus*. San Jose, Calif.: Writer's Digest, Writer's Showcase, 2000. 275pp.

Cobb, James H. *West on 66*. New York: Thomas Dunne Books, 1999. 364pp.

Cochran, Molly, and Warren Murphy. *The Broken Sword*. New York: Tor Books, 1997. 381pp.

Codell, Esmé Raji. *Sahara Special*. New York: Hyperion Books for Children, 2003. 175pp.

———. *Vive La Paris*. New York: Hyperion Books for Children, 2006. 210pp.

Cohen, Charles. *Silver Linings*. New York: Dell, 1989. 279pp.

———. *Those Lake View Wives*. New York: Donald I. Fine, 1989. 253pp.

Cohen, Florence Chanock. *The Sea of Stones: A Novel in Three Parts*. New York: Pushcart, 1993. 322pp.

Cohn, Robby, and Deborah Kearns. *The Other Side of the Table*. Chicago: Chandler / White, 1996. 133pp.

Cole, Stephen. *Resurrection*. The Wereling, no. 3. New York: Razorbill, 2003. 264pp.

Collier, James Lincoln. *The Jazz Kid*. New York: Holt, 1994. 216pp.

———. *The Worst of Times: A Story of the Great Depression*. Columbus, Ohio: Waterbird Books, 2004. 142pp.

Collins, Max Allan. *Bones. Buried Deep*. New York: Pocket Star Books, 2006. 300pp.

———. *Chicago Confidential: A Nathan Heller Novel*. Waterville, Maine: Wheeler, 2002. 292pp.

———. *Damned in Paradise: A Nathan Heller Novel*. New York: Dutton, 1996. 308pp.

———. *Dying in the Post-War World: A Nathan Heller Casebook*. Woodstock, Vt.: Foul Play Press, 1991. 251pp.

———. *Kill Your Darlings*. New York: Walker, 1984. 212pp.

———. *Kisses of Death: A Nathan Heller Casebook*. Norfolk, Va.: Crippen and Landru, 2001. 206pp.

———. *The Million-Dollar Wound*. New York: St. Martin's, 1986. 335pp.

———. *Mourn the Living: A Nolan Novel*. Unity, Maine: Five Star, 1999. 182pp.

———. *Neon Mirage*. New York: St. Martin's, Thomas Dunne, 1988. 275pp.

———. *Road to Paradise*. New York: William Morrow, 2005. 289pp.

———. *Road to Purgatory*. New York: William Morrow, 2004. 288pp.

Collins, Max Allan. *True Crime*. New York: St. Martin's, 1984. 357pp.

———. *True Detective*. New York: St. Martin's, 1983. 358pp.

Collins, Max Allan, José Luis Garcia Lopez, Robert Lappan and Josef Rubenstein. *On the Road to Perdition. Book 1. Oasis*. New York: Paradox Press, 2003. 93pp.

Collins, Max Allan, José Luis Garcia Lopez, and Steve Lieber. *On the Road to Perdition. Book 2. Sanctuary*. New York: Paradox, 2003. 96pp

Collins, Max Allan, Richard Rayner, and Robert Lappan. *Road to Perdition*. New York: Paradox Press, 1998. 294pp.

Colter, Cyrus. *The Amoralists & Other Tales: Collected Stories*. New York: Thunder's Mouth Press, 1988. 283pp.

———. *The Hippodrome*. Chicago: Northwestern University, TriQuarterly Books, 1994. 213pp.

Connolly, William Anthony. *The Obituaries*. Lake Forest, Calif.: Behler, 2004. 220pp.

Conrad, James. *Making Love to the Minor Poets of Chicago*. New York: St. Martin's, 2000. 436pp

Cook, Elsa E. *Satin Dolls*. New York: Pocket Books, 1987. 442pp.

Coon, Helen C., and James Converse. *The House at the Back of the Lot*. Newton, Kans.: Faith and Life Press, 1982. 147pp.

Cooper, Susan Rogers. *Funny as a Dead Comic: A Kimmey Kruse Mystery*. New York: St. Martin's, 1993. 214pp.

Coover, Robert. *Whatever Happened to Gloomy Gus of the Chicago Bears?* New York: Simon and Schuster, Linden Press, 1987. 120pp.

Copeland, Patty. *Always Annie*. Bensalem, Pa.: Meteor, 1992. 220pp.

Corbett, David. *Blood of Paradise*. New York: Ballantine Books, 2007. 426pp.

Cormany, Michael. *Lost Daughter*. Secaucus, N.J.: Irma Heldman Book, Lyle Stuart, 1988. 210pp.

———. *Polaroid Man*. New York: Irma Heldman / Birch Lane Press Book / Carol Communications, 1991. 228pp.

Cormany, Michael. *Red Winter*. New York: An Irma Heldman / Lyle Stewart Book / Carol Communications, 1989. 202pp.

———. *Rich or Dead*. New York: An Irma Heldman / Birch Lane Press Book / Carol Group, 1990. 190pp.

———. *Skin Deep is Fatal*. New York: Carol Group, 1992. 194pp.

Cote, Lyn. *Whispers of Love*. Blessed Assurance Series. Nashville, Tenn.: Broadman and Holman, 1999. 280pp.

Coulter, Brenda. *A Season of Forgiveness*. New York: Steeple Hill, 2007. 249pp.

Coulter, Catherine. *The Target*. Rockland, Mass.: Wheeler, 1998. 372pp.

Cousins, Amy Jo. *At Your Service*. New York: Harlequin, Silhouette Books, 2004. 185pp.

Covington, Michael. *Chances*. Columbus, Ohio: Triple Crown, 2007. 240pp.

Cox, Carol. *Fair Game: A Romance Mystery*. Uhrichsville, Ohio: Barbour, 2007. 315pp.

———. *Ticket to Tomorrow: A Romance Mystery*. Uhrichsville, Ohio: Barbour, 2006. 317pp.

Craft, Michael. *Eye Contact, The Mark Manning Series*. New York: Kensington Books, 1998. 342pp.

———. *Flight Dreams, A Mark Manning Mystery*. New York: Kensington Books, 1997. 230pp.

Craig, Mary Francis Shura. *The Third Blonde*. New York: Dodd, Mead, 1985. 204pp.

———. *The Chicagoans: Dust to Diamonds*. New York: A Jove Book, 1981. 308pp.

Crane, Elizabeth. *All This Heavenly Glory: Stories*. New York: Little, Brown, 2005. 230pp.

Creed, Frank. *Flashpoint*. Lafayette, Ind.: Writers' Cafe Press, 2007. 190pp.

Creevy, Patrick. *Lake Shore Drive*. New York: Tor Books, 1992. 383pp.

Cresswell, Jasmine. *No Sin Too Great*. Don Mills, Ont.: Harlequin, MIRA Books, 1996. 403pp.

Crill, Doug. *Ghost of Sijan*. Illustrated by Daniel J. Frey. Toledo, Ohio: Dark Dance Productions, 2004. 80pp.

Crimmins, Jerry. *Fort Dearborn*. Evanston, Ill.: Northwestern University Press, 2006. 431pp.

Croft, Barbara. *Moon's Crossing*. Boston: Houghton Mifflin, 2003. 198pp.

Cross, Gilbert B. *Terror Train!* New York: Atheneum, 1987. 111pp.

Cullars, Sharon. *Again*. New York: Brava / Kensington Books, 2006. 297pp.

Cuneo, Mary Louise. *Anne Is Elegant*. New York: HarperCollins, 1993. 167pp.

Cunningham, Alvin Robert. *United We Stand*. Huntington, W.Va.: University Editions, 1990. 126pp.

Curtis, Jack. *No Mercy*. New York: Walker, 1995. 151pp.

D'Amato, Barbara. *Authorized Personnel Only*. New York: Forge, 2000. 334pp.

———. *Good Cop, Bad Cop*. New York: Forge, 1998. 301pp.

———. *Hardball*. New York: Scribner, 1990. 210pp.

———. *Hard Bargain: A Cat Marsala Mystery*. New York: Scribner, 1997. 281pp.

———. *Hard Case: A Cat Marsala Mystery*. New York: C. Scribner's Sons, 1994. 258pp.

———. *Hard Christmas: A Cat Marsala Mystery*. New York: Scribner, 1995. 282pp.

———. *Hard Evidence: A Cat Marsala Mystery*. New York: Scribner, 1999. 255pp.

———. *Hard Luck: A Cat Marsala Mystery*. New York: Scribner's, 1992. 242pp.

———. *Hard Tack: A Cat Marsala Mystery*. New York: Scribner's, 1991. 229pp.

———. *Hard Women: A Cat Marsala Mystery*. New York: Charles Scribner's, 1993. 249pp.

———. *Help Me Please*. New York: Forge, 1999. 336pp.

———. *Killer.App*. New York: Forge, 1996. 350pp.

D'Amato, Barbara, and Brian D'Amato. 2001. *Hard Road: A Cat Marsala Mystery*. New York: Scribner, 2001. 286pp.

Dams, Jeanne M. *Holy Terror in the Hebrides: A Dorothy Martin Mystery*. New York: Walker, 1997. 184pp.

Davies, Frances. *Love Thy Neighbor*. New York: Penguin, Berkley, 1984. 181pp.

Davis, Jay, and Don Davis. *Bring on the Night*. New York: Tor Books, 1993. 403pp.

Davis, Marc. *Dirty Money*. New York: Dell, 1992. 211pp.

De Grazia, Don. *American Skin*. New York: Scribner Paperback Fiction, 2000. 295pp.

De Rosa, Tina. *Paper Fish*. New York: City University of New York, Feminist Press, 1996. 157pp.

Devine, Eleanore. *You're Standing In My Light; and Other Stories*. Boston: Beacon Press, 1990. 126pp.

De Vita, Sharon. *Child of Midnight*. New York: Harlequin, Silhouette Books, 1996. 248pp.

Deaver, Julie Reece. *Chicago Blues*. New York: HarperCollins, 1995. 170pp.

———. *The Night I Disappeared*. New York: Simon Pulse, 2002. 242pp.

———. *Say Goodnight, Gracie*. New York: Harper and Row, 1988. 214pp.

———. *You Bet Your Life*. New York: HarperCollins, 1993. 209pp.

DeYoung, Suzanne, and Dennis DeYoung. *A Love Foretold*. Chicago: High Road, 2003. 220pp.

Dickinson, Charles. *Rumor Has It*. New York: William Morrow, 1991. 232pp.

———. *The Widows' Adventures*. New York: William Morrow, 1989. 381pp.

Diehl, William. *Primal Fear*. Heinemann, 1992. 508pp.

———. *Reign in Hell*. New York: Ballantine Books, 1997. 400pp.

———. *Show of Evil*. New York: Ballantine Books, 1995. 483pp.

Dillard, J. M. *The Fugitive*. New York: Dell, 1993. 259pp.

DiPego, Gerald. *Keeper of the City*. Garden City, N.Y.: Doubleday, 1987. 275pp.

Dixon, Mark. *Crime Wave*. New York: Penguin, Berkley Books, 1988. 202pp.

Dixon, Stephen. *Fall and Rise*. San Francisco: North Point Press, 1985. 245pp.

Dokey, Cameron. *Carrie: Heart of Courage*. New York: Avon Books, 1998. 185pp.

Dowd, Tom. *Burning Bright*. New York: Roc, 1994. 280pp.

Doyle, Roddy. *Oh, Play That Thing*. New York: Viking, 2004. 378pp.

Drought, James. *An Exercise in Nostalgia: So Long Chicago (*also *So Long Chicago: An Exercise in Nostalgia)*. Westport, Conn.: Skylight Press, 1982. 144pp.

Drue, Floreta. *Trees That Listen*. New York: Spenchan Press, 2005.

Dryden, Diane. *The Accidental King of Clark Street*. Waterford, Va.: Capstone Fiction, 2007. 215pp.

Duberman, Martin B. *Haymarket*. New York: Seven Stories Press, 2003. 330pp.

Dubowski, Cathy East, and Tom J. Astle. *Family Reunion*. New York: Disney Press, 2000. 141pp.

Duey, Kathleen, and Karen A. Bale. *Fire, Chicago, 1871*. New York: Aladdin Paperbacks, 1998. 171pp.

Dulaney, Kim L. *The Beautiful Ones*. Chicago: Unique Expressions, 2002. 263pp.

Duncan, Alice. *A Bicycle Built for Two*. New York: Kensington, 2002. 347pp.

———. *Coming up Roses*. New York: Kensington, 2002. 314pp.

———. *Just North of Bliss*. New York: Kensington, 2002. 315pp.

Dunn, Robert. *Cutting Time: A Novel of the Blues*. New York: Coral Press, 2003. 302pp.

Dybek, Stuart. *Coast of Chicago*. New York: Knopf, 1990. 173pp.

———. *I Sailed with Magellan*. New York: Farrar, Straus and Giroux, 2003. 307pp.

Dymmoch, Michael Allen. *The Death of Blue Mountain Cat*. New York: St. Martin's, 1996. 328pp.

———. *The Fall: A Thriller*. New York: Thomas Dunne Books, 2004. 246pp.

———. *The Feline Friendship*. New York: Thomas Dunne Books, 2003. 310pp.

———. *Incendiary Designs*. New York: Thomas Dunne Books, 1998. 296pp.

———. *The Man Who Understood Cats*. New York: St. Martin's, 1993. 244pp.

———. *White Tiger*. New York: Thomas Dunne Books / St. Martin's, Minotaur, 2005. 311pp.

Eckert, Allan W. *Gateway to Empire*. Boston: Little, Brown, 1983. 688pp.

———. *The Scarlet Mansion*. Boston: Little, Brown, 1985. 500pp.

Edwards, Andrea. *Make Room for Daddy*. New York: Harlequin, Silhouette, 1993. 250pp.

———. *On Mother's Day*. New York: Harlequin, Silhouette Books, 1996. 250pp.

———. *Power Play*. New York: Avon Books, 1984. 342pp.

Elkeles, Simone. *How to Ruin My Teenage Life*. Woodbury, Minn.: Flux, 2007. 281pp.

Elliott, Stephen. *Happy Baby*. New York: Picador, 2005. 191pp.

———. *A Life without Consequences*. San Francisco: MacAdam / Cage, 2001. 186pp.

———. *What It Means to Love You*. San Francisco: MacAdam / Cage, 2002. 195pp.

Ellis, Chauncey. *Rage of a People*. Libertyville, Ill.: Soaring Eagle, 1995. 316pp.

Ellis, David. *Jury of One*. New York: G. P. Putnam's Sons, 2004. 374pp.

Ellis, Wesley. *Lone Star and the Chicago Showdown*. New York: Jove Books, 1993. 182pp.

Elrod, P. N. *A Chill in the Blood*. New York: Ace Books, 1998. 327pp.

———. *Cold Streets: A Novel of the Vampire Files*. New York: Ace Books, 2004. 327pp.

———. *The Dark Sleep*. New York: Ace Books, 1999. 359pp.

———. *Song in the Dark*. New York: Ace Books, 2005. 377pp.

———. *The Vampire Files*. New York: Ace Books, 2003. 464pp.

Elward, James Joseph. *Ask for Nothing More*. New York: Harper and Row, 1984. 250pp.

Engleman, Paul. *Catch a Fallen Angel*. New York: Mysterious Press, 1986. 199pp.

———. *Left for Dead: A Mark Renzler Novel*. New York: St. Martin's, 1996. 232pp.

———. *The Man with My Cat*. New York: St. Martin's Minotaur, 2000. 228pp.

———. *The Man with My Name*. New York: St. Martin's, 1994. 214pp.

Enright, Michael. *Daisies in the Junkyard*. New York: Tom Doherty Associates, 2002. 237pp.

Evers, Crabbe. *Murder in Wrigley Field*. New York: Bantam Books, 1991. 247pp.

Everson, David H. *Suicide Squeeze*. New York: St. Martin's / A Thomas Dunne Book, 1991. 248pp.

Fairbanks, Lauren. *Sister Carrie*. Normal, Ill.: Dalkey Archive Press, 1993. 208pp.

Faust, Ron. *Split Image*. New York: Forge, 1997. 218pp.

Ferguson, Maggie. *Fever Rising*. Intrigue, no. 408. New York: Harlequin, 1997. 248pp.

Ferguson, Marvin P. *Boys on the Gold Coast*. Crystal Lake, Ill.: Parker, 1993. 247pp.

Ferris, Joshua. *Then We Came to the End*. New York: Little, Brown, 2007. 387pp.

Fielding, Joy. *Tell Me No Secrets*. New York: William Morrow, 1993. 377pp.

Fiffer, Sharon Sloan. *Buried Stuff*. New York: St. Martin's, 2005. 278pp.

———. *Dead Guy's Stuff*. New York: St. Martin's Minotaur, 2002. 307pp.

———. *Killer Stuff*. New York: St. Martin's Minotaur, 2001. 306pp.

———. *The Wrong Stuff*. New York: St. Martin's Minotaur, 2003. 275pp.

Fink, John. *Painted Leaves*. New York: St. Martin's, 1995. 266pp.

Finley, Patrick. *Diamond in the Rough*. Chicago: Bari Press, 1986. 229pp.

Fitzgerald, Kathleen Whalen. *The Good Sisters*. Chicago: Contemporary Books, 1981. 251pp.

Fitzgerald, William Edward. *Arenas of Greed*. Elk Grove Village, Ill.: DeVin, 1990. 535pp.

Ford, Darnella. *Naked Love*. New York: Kensington, 2007. 290pp.

Ford, John M. *The Last Hot Time*. New York: Tor Books, 2000. 205pp.

Forrest, Leon. *Divine Days*. Chicago: Another Chicago Press, 1992. 1138pp.

Foti, Silvia. *The Diva's Fool*. Laurel, Md.: Echelon, 2007. 286pp.

Franco, Marjorie. *Genevieve and Alexander*. New York: Atheneum, 1982. 242pp.

Frangello, Gina. *My Sister's Continent*. Portland, Ore.: Chiasmus Press, 2005. 319pp.

Frank, Morry. *Southside Rudy Yid*. Chicago: Silverback Books II, 1994. 222pp.

Franklin, Stella Maria Sarah Miles. *On Dearborn Street*. Brisbane: University of Queensland Press, 1981. 219pp.

Frasier, Anne. *Hush*. New York: Onyx, 2002. 378pp.

Fredrickson, Jack. *A Safe Place for Dying*. New York: St. Martin's, Minotaur / Thomas Dunne Books, 2006. 296pp.

Freeman, Steve. *Aw, Here It Goes!* New York: Pocket Books, 1998. 144pp.

Freer, Dave, and Eric Flint. *Pyramid Scheme*. Riverdale, N.Y.: Baen Books, 2001. 418pp.

Freund, Edith. *Chicago Girls*. New York: Poseidon Press, 1985. 427pp.

———. *Dare to Dream*. London, U.K.: W. H. Allen, 1987. 509pp.

———. *Women of the World*. London, U.K.: W. H. Allen, 1986. 512pp.

Fritscher, Jack. *What They Did to the Kid: Confessions of an Altar Boy*. San Francisco: Palm Drive, 2000. 373pp.

Fuller, Jack *The Best of Jackson Payne*. New York: Knopf, 2000. 321pp.

———. *Our Fathers' Shadows*. New York: William Morrow, 1987. 224pp.

Gerson, Noel Bertram [Dana Fuller Ross, pseud.]. *Illinois!* New York: Bantam Books, 1986. 304pp.

Gage, Elizabeth. *Intimate*. New York: Pocket Books, 1995. 498pp.

Gardaphe, Fred L. *New Chicago Stories*. Chicago: City Stoop Press, 1990. 192pp.

Garland, Ardella. *Details at Ten*. New York: Simon and Schuster, 2000. 207pp.

———. *Hit Time*. Waterville, Maine: Thorndike Press, 2002. 222pp.

Garwood, Julie. *Murder List*. New York: Ballantine Books, 2004. 403pp.

Gaynor, M. *Chicago Joe and the Showgirl*. London: New English Library, 1990. 160pp.

Geary, Rick. *The Beast of Chicago: An Account of the Life and Crimes of Herman W. Mudgett*. A Treasury of Victorian Murder, vol. 6. New York: NBM, 2003. 80pp.

Genandt, Judy. *Half-Life*. San Jose, Calif.: ToExcel, 1999. 273pp.

Gerard, Cindy. *The Secret Baby Bond*. New York: Harlequin, Silhouette Books, 2002. 187pp.

Gerson, Corinne. *Oh, Brother*. New York: Atheneum, 1982. 125pp.

Gettel, Ronald. *Twice Burned*. New York: Walker, 1983. 196pp.

Giancana, Sam, and Bettina Giancana. *30 Seconds*. New York: Warner Books, 1998. 421pp.

Gifford, Barry. *A Good Man to Know: A Semi-Documentary Fictional Memoir*. Livingston, Mont.: Clark City Press, 1992. 164pp.

Gifford, Barry Colby. *An Unfortunate Woman*. San Francisco: Donald S. Ellis / Creative Arts, 1984. 171pp.

Glass, Joseph. *Blood: A Susan Shader Novel*. New York: Simon and Schuster, 2000. 399pp.

———. *Eyes*. London: Pan, 1999. 344pp.

Glass, Suzanne. *The Sculptors*. London: Century, 2002. 423pp.

Gleiter, Jan. *Lie Down with Dogs*. New York: St. Martin's, 1996. 225pp.

Gold, Kristi. *His E-Mail Order Wife*. New York: Harlequin, Silhouette Books, 2002. 185pp.

Goldsborough, Robert. *Death in Pilsen*. Laurel, Md.: Echelon Press, 2007. 264pp.

———. *Shadow of the Bomb: A Snap Malek Mystery*. Laurel, Md.: Echelon Press, 2006. 232pp.

———. *Three Strikes You're Dead*. Memphis, Tenn.: Echelon Press, 2005. 270pp.

Gonzales, Laurence. *The Last Deal*. New York: Atheneum, 1981. 283pp.

Gordon, Jeffie Ross. *Jacquelyn*. New York: Scholastic, 1985. 343pp.

Gordon, Laura. *Dominoes*. Intrigue, no. 282. New York: Harlequin, 1994. 250pp.

Gorman, Edward. *Cold Blue Midnight*. New York: St. Martin's, 1996. 282pp.

Gorman, Edward. *Daughter of Darkness*. New York: Daw Books, 1998. 333pp.

———. *Murder in the Wings*. New York: St. Martin's, 1986. 163pp.

Gosling, Paula. *Tears of the Dragon*. London: Allison and Busby, 2004. 288pp.

Gould, Philip. *Kitty Collins*. Chapel Hill, N.C.: Algonquin Books, 1986. 346pp.

Granger, Bill. *Drover and the Zebras: The New Drover Novel*. New York: William Morrow, 1992. 252pp.

———. *The El Murders*. New York: Henry Holt, 1987. 246pp.

———. *The Infant of Prague: A November Man Novel*. New York: Warner Books, 1987. 257pp.

Granger, Bill [Joe Gash, pseud.]. *Newspaper Murders, A Chicago Police Mystery*. New York: Holt, Rinehart and Winston, 1985. 164pp.

———. *Priestly Murders: A Chicago Police Mystery*. New York: Holt, Rinehart and Winston, 1984. 163pp.

Granger, Bill [Bill Griffith, pseud.]. *Time for Frankie Coolin*. New York: Random House, 1982. 269pp.

Greeley, Andrew M. *All About Women*. New York: Tor Books / Tom Doherty, 1990. 372pp.

———. *Angel Fire*. New York: Warner Books, 1988. 304pp.

———. *Angels of September*. New York: Warner Books, 1986. 451pp.

———. *Ascent into Hell*. New York: Warner Books, 1983. 371pp.

———. *The Bishop and the Missing L Train: A Blackie Ryan Story*. New York: Forge, 2000. 285pp.

———. *The Bishop and the Three Kings: A Father Blackie Ryan Mystery*. New York: Penguin, Berkley Books, 1998. 298pp.

———. *The Bishop at Sea: A Father Blackie Ryan Mystery*. New York: Penguin, Berkley Books, 1997. 287pp.

———. *The Bishop at the Lake: A Bishop Blackie Ryan Novel*. New York: Forge, 2007. 268pp.

———. *The Bishop Goes to the University: A Blackie Ryan Story*. New York: Forge, 2003. 250pp.

Greeley, Andrew M. *The Bishop in the Old Neighborhood: A Blackie Ryan Story*. New York: Forge, 2005. 300pp.

———. *The Cardinal Sins*. New York: Warner Books / Bernard Geis Associates, 1981. 350pp.

———. *The Cardinal Virtues*. New York: Warner Books, 1990. 449pp.

———. *A Christmas Wedding*. New York: Forge, 2000. 349pp.

———. *Fall from Grace*. New York: Putnam, 1993. 367pp.

———. *Golden Years, The O'Malleys in the Twentieth Century*. New York: Forge: Godalming, 2005. 291pp.

———. *Happy Are the Clean of Heart: A Father Blackie Ryan Mystery*. New York: Warner Books, 1986. 268pp.

———. *Happy Are the Meek: A Blackie Ryan Story*. New York: Warner Books, 1985. 264pp.

———. *Happy Are the Merciful: A Blackie Ryan Mystery*. New York: Jove Books, 1992. 240pp.

———. *Happy Are the Oppressed: A Father Blackie Ryan Mystery*. New York: Jove Books, 1996. 307pp.

———. *Happy Are the Peace Makers: A Blackie Ryan Novel*. New York: Jove Books, 1993. 300pp.

———. *Happy Are the Poor in Spirit: A Blackie Ryan Novel*. New York: Jove Books, 1994. 295pp.

———. *Happy Are Those Who Mourn: A Blackie Ryan Novel*. New York: Jove Books, 1995. 288pp.

———. *Happy Are Those Who Thirst for Justice: A Father Blackie Ryan Mystery*. New York: Mysterious Press, 1987. 302pp.

———. *Irish Cream: A Nuala Anne Mcgrail Novel*. New York: Forge, 2005. 319pp.

———. *Irish Crystal: A Nuala Anne Mcgrail Novel*. New York: Forge, 2006. 301pp.

———. *Irish Eyes: A Nuala Anne Mcgrail Novel*. New York: Forge, 2000. 320pp.

———. *Irish Lace: A Nuala Anne Mcgrail Novel*. New York: Forge, 1996. 303pp.

———. *Irish Linen: A Nuala Anne Mcgrail Novel*. Detroit: Thorndike Press, 2007. 351pp.

Greeley, Andrew M. *Irish Mist: A Nuala Anne Mcgrail Novel.* New York: Forge, 1999. 319pp.

———. *Irish Stew! A Nuala Anne Mcgrail Novel.* New York: Tom Doherty Associates, 2002. 303pp.

———. *Irish Whiskey: A Nuala Anne Mcgrail Novel.* New York: Forge, 1998. 369pp.

———. *Lord of the Dance.* New York: Warner Books / Bernard Geis Associates, 1984. 401pp.

———. *A Midwinter's Tale.* New York: Forge, 1999. 383pp.

———. *Patience of a Saint.* New York: Warner Books / Bernard Geis Associates, 1987. 446pp.

———. *Rite of Spring.* New York: Warner Books / Bernard Geis Associates, 1987. 436pp.

———. *Second Spring: A Love Story, The O'Malleys in the Twentieth Century.* New York: Forge, 2004. 347pp.

———. *Star Bright! A Christmas Story.* New York: Forge, 1998. 127pp.

———. *St. Valentine's Night.* New York: Warner Books, 1989. 435pp.

———. *Summer at the Lake.* New York: Forge, 1997. 412pp.

———. *Thy Brother's Wife.* New York: Warner Books / Bernard Geis Associates, 1982. 350pp.

———. *Virgin and Martyr.* New York: Warner Books / Barnard Geis Associates, 1985. 438pp.

———. *Wages of Sin.* New York: Putnam's Sons, 1992. 349pp.

———. *White Smoke: A Novel About the Next Papal Conclave.* New York: Forge, 1996. 384pp.

———. *Younger Than Springtime.* New York: Forge, 1999. 348pp.

Greenberg, Marilyn S. *The Rabbi's Life Contract.* Garden City, New York: Doubleday, 1983. 231pp.

Gross, Leonard. *Mirror.* New York: Harper and Row, 1981. 331pp.

Grote, JoAnn A. *Emily Makes a Difference: A Time of Progress and Problems (1893).* Sisters in Time, no.16. Uhrichsville, Ohio: Barbour, 2004. 143pp.

Grote, JoAnn A., and Wallenta Adam. *Chicago World's Fair.* American Adventure, no. 29. Uhrichsville, Ohio: Barbour, 1998. 144pp.

Guilfoile, Kevin. *Cast of Shadows*. New York: Knopf, 2005. 319pp.

Gutman, Dan. *Shoeless Joe & Me: A Baseball Card Adventure*. New York: HarperCollins, 2002. 163pp.

Haddad, C. A. *Caught in the Shadows*. New York: St. Martin's, 1992. 229pp.

Hamada, Sachiko. *Forest in F Minor*. Boulder, Colo.: Suisei International, 2007. 233pp.

Hamilton, Jane July. *Disobedience*. New York: Anchor Books, 2001. 272pp.

Hanlon, Sean. *Jump Cuts*. New York: Pocket Books, 1994. 323pp.

Harler, Anne. *New Girl in Town*. Worthington, Ohio: Willowisp, 1987. 110pp.

Harris, E. Lynn. *And This Too Shall Pass*. New York: Anchor Books, 1996. 347pp.

————. *If This World Were Mine*. New York: Doubleday, 1997. 318pp.

Harris, Jennifer. *Pink*. New York: Harrington Park Press, Alice Street Editions, 2007. 161pp.

Hartzmark, Gini. *Bitter Business*. New York: Fawcett, Columbine, 1995. 307pp.

————. *Fatal Reaction*. New York: Ivy Books, 1998. 352pp.

————. *Final Option*. New York: Ivy Books, 1994. 306pp.

————. *Rough Trade*. New York: Ivy Books, 1999. 293pp.

Harvey, Michael T. *The Chicago Way*. New York: Alfred A. Knopf, 2007. 303pp.

Hatcher, Robin Lee. *Another Chance to Love You*. New York: Steeple Hill, 2006. 251pp.

Hayes, Sally Tyler. *Second Father*. New York: Harlequin, Silhouette, 1997.62pp. 251pp.

————. *Temporary Family*. New York: Harlequin, Silhouette Books, 1996. 249pp.

————. *Wife, Mother - Lover?* New York: Harlequin, Silhouette, 1998. 249pp.

Heinemann, Larry. *Cooler by the Lake*. New York: Farrar, Straus and Giroux, 1992. 241pp.

Hellmann, Libby Fischer. *Chicago Blues*. Madison, Wis.: Bleak House Books, 2007. 456pp.

Hellmann, Libby Fischer. *An Eye for Murder*. Scottsdale, Ariz.: Poisoned Pen Press, 2002. 316pp.

———. *An Image of Death*. New York: Penguin, Berkley, 2003. 285pp.

———. *A Shot to Die For*. Scottsdale, Ariz.: Poisoned Pen Press, 2005. 301pp.

Hemon, Aleksandar. *Nowhere Man: The Pronek Fantasies*. New York: Nan A. Talese, 2002. 242pp.

———. *The Question of Bruno*. London: Picador, 2000. 230pp.

Henderson, Dee. *Danger in the Shadows, The O'Malley Series*. Sisters, Ore.: Multnomah, 2002. 373pp.

———. *God's Gift*. New York: Steeple Hill Books, 1998. 232pp.

———. *The Negotiator, The Omalley Series*. Carol Stream, Ill.: Tyndale House, 2005. 312pp.

Herman, Charlotte. *Millie Cooper, Take a Chance*. Illustrated by Helen Cogancherry. New York: Dutton, 1988. 100pp.

———. *A Summer on Thirteenth Street*. New York: Dutton Children's Books, 1991. 181pp.

Herriges, Greg. *Secondary Attachments*. New York: William Morrow, 1986. 251pp.

———. *Someplace Safe*. New York: St. Martin's, 1984. 216pp.

Higgs, Liz Curtis. *Unveiling Mary Magdalene*. Colorado Springs, Colo.: Waterbrook Press, 2001. 306pp.

Hingle, Metsy. *And the Winner Gets—Married!* New York: Harlequin, Silhouette Books, 2002. 186pp.

Hobbs, Sterling. *The Black Angels*. Los Angeles: Holloway House, 1993. 227pp.

Hoffman, Eva. *The Secret*. New York: Ballantine Books, 2002. 265pp.

Hoffmann, Kate. *Always a Hero (Temptation)*. Richmond, Surrey: Harlequin, Mills and Boon, 2000. 217pp.

———. *Wanted: Wife*. New York: Harlequin, 1994. 216pp.

Holland, Steve. *Kenan & Kel: He Said, He Said*. New York: Simon Pulse, 2000. 96pp.

Holmes, B. L. *Mega*. Racine, Wis.: Mother Courage Press, 1991. 197pp.

Holton, Hugh. *Chicago Blues.* New York: Forge, 1996. 384pp.

———. *Criminal Element.* New York: Forge, 2002. 511pp.

———. *The Devil's Shadow.* New York: Forge, 2001. 382pp.

———. *The Left Hand of God.* New York: Forge, 1999. 384pp.

———. *Presumed Dead.* New York: Forge, 1994. 317pp.

———. *Red Lightning.* New York: Forge, 1998. 319pp.

———. *Time of the Assassins.* New York: Forge, 2001. 383pp.

———. *Violent Crimes.* New York: Forge, 1997. 383pp.

———. *Windy City.* New York: Forge, 1995. 319pp.

Hoobler, Dorothy, and Thomas Hoobler. *The 1920s: Luck, The Century Kids.* Brookfield, Conn.: Millbrook Press, 2000. 160pp.

———. *The 1930s: Directions, The Century Kids.* Brookfield, Conn.: Millbrook Press, 2000. 159pp.

Hoobler, Dorothy, Thomas Hoobler, and Rob Sauber. *Florence Robinson: The Story of a Jazz Age Girl, Her Story.* Parsippany, N.J.: Silver Burdett Press, 1997. 123pp.

Hoover, Paul. *Saigon, Illinois.* New York: Random House, Vintage Books, 1988. 229pp.

Horan, Nancy. *Loving Frank.* New York: Ballantine, 2007. 362pp.

Horan, Richard. *Life in the Rainbow.* South Royalton, Vt.: Steerforth Press, 1996. 164pp.

Horwood, William, and Helen Rappaport. *Dark Hearts of Chicago.* London: Hutchinson, 2007. 633pp.

Hotze, Sollace. *Summer Endings.* New York: Clarion Books, 1991. 165pp.

House, Richard. *Bruiser.* New York: Serpent's Tail, 1997. 218pp.

Howard, Clark. *City Blood: A Novel of Revenge.* New York: Penzler Books, 1994. 330pp.

———. *Hard City.* New York: Dutton, 1990. 513pp.

Howland, Bette. *Things to Come and Go; Three Stories.* New York: Alfred A. Knopf, 1983. 165pp.

Hribal, C. J. *The Company Car*. New York: Random House, 2005. 402pp.

Hunt, James Patrick. *Maitland*. Waterville, Maine: Five Star, 2005. 247pp.

———. *Maitland under Siege*. Waterville, Maine: Five Star, 2006. 247pp.

Hunter, Fred. *The Chicken Asylum*. New York: St. Martin's, Minotaur, 2002. 245pp.

———. *Government Gay*. New York: St. Martin's, 1997. 215pp.

———. *The Mummy's Ransom*. New York: St. Martin's, Minotaur, 2002. 265pp.

———. *National Nancys*. New York: St. Martin's, 2000. 232pp.

———. *Presence of Mind*. New York: Walker, 1994. 212pp.

———. *Ransom at Sea*. New York: St. Martin's, Minotaur, 2003. 278pp.

———. *Ransom at the Opera*. New York: St. Martin's, Minotaur, 2000. 244pp.

———. *Ransom for a Holiday*. New York: St. Martin's, 1997. 229pp.

———. *Ransom for a Killing*. New York: St. Martin's, 1998. 228pp.

———. *Ransom for an Angel: A Jeremy Ransom/Emily Charters Mystery*. New York: Walker, 1995. 237pp.

———. *Ransom for Our Sins: A Jeremy Ransom/Emily Charters Mystery*. New York: Walker, 1996. 257pp.

———. *Ransom Unpaid*. New York: St. Martin's Minotaur, 1999. 216pp.

Hurley, Ann. *Year of the Poet*. New York: Harlequin, Silhouette, 1985. 186pp.

Hutchens, Paul. *The Chicago Adventure*. Chicago: Moody Press, 1997. 109pp.

Hyer, Richard. *Riceburner*. New York: Charles Scribner's Sons, 1986. 242pp.

Hyland, M. J. *How the Light Gets In*. Camberwell, Australia: Penguin. 317pp.

Hyzy, Julie A. *Deadly Blessings*. Waterville, Maine: Five Star, 2006. 347pp.

———. *Deadly Interest: An Alex St. James Mystery*. Waterville, Maine: Five Star, 2006. 390pp.

Izzi, Eugene. *Bad Guys*. New York: St. Martin's, 1988. 245pp.

———. *The Booster*. New York: St. Martin's, 1989. 244pp.

———. *The Criminalist*. New York: Avon Books, 1998. 341pp.

———. *Invasions*. New York, 1990. 311pp.

———. *King of the Hustlers*. New York: Bantam Books, 1989. 277pp.

———. *A Matter of Honor*. New York: Avon Books, 1997. 424pp.

———. *Prowlers*. New York: Bantam Books, 1991. 341pp.

———. *Safe Harbor*. New York: Avon Books, 2000. 342pp.

———. *The Take*. New York: St. Martin's, 1987. 246pp.

———. *Tony's Justice*. New York: Bantam Books, 1993. 388pp.

———. *Tribal Secrets*. New York: Bantam Books, 1992. 376pp.

———. *Mr. X*. New York: Simon and Schuster, 1995. 272pp.

Izzi, Eugene [Nick Gaitano, pseud.]. *Jaded*. New York: Simon and Schuster, 1996. 256pp.

———. *Special Victims*. New York: Simon and Schuster, 1994. 234pp.

———. *Spent Force*. London: Headline Feature, 1996. 249pp.

Jackson, Brenda. *True Love*. Washington, D.C.: BET, 2000. 317pp.

Jackson, Dave. *Forty to Life*. Minneapolis, Minn.: Bethany House, 2007. 331pp.

Jackson, Edwardo. *Ever After*. New York: Villard Books, 1999. 334pp.

Jackson, Joshilyn. *Gods in Alabama*. New York: Warner Books, 2005. 275pp.

Jackson, Neta. *The Yada Yada Prayer Group*. Nashville, Tenn.: Integrity, 2003. 388pp.

———. *The Yada Yada Prayer Group Gets Caught*. Nashville, Tenn.: Integrity, 2006. 406pp.

———. *The Yada Yada Prayer Group Gets Down*. Nashville, Tenn.: Integrity, 2004. 403pp.

Jackson, Neta. *The Yada Yada Prayer Group Gets Real.* Nashville, Tenn.: Integrity, 2005. 406pp.

———. *The Yada Yada Prayer Group Gets Rolling.* Nashville, Tenn.: Thomas Nelson, 2007. 403pp.

———. *The Yada Yada Prayer Group Gets Tough.* Nashville, Tenn.:Integrity, 2005. 373pp.

Jacob, John. *Long Ride Back.* New York: Thunder's Mouth Press, 1988. 320pp.

Jaffee, Annette Williams. *Recent History.* New York: G. P. Putnam's Sons, 1988. 268pp.

Jakes, John. *American Dreams.* New York: Dutton, 1998. 495pp.

———. *Homeland.* New York: Doubleday, 1993. 785pp.

James-Enger, Kelly. *Did You Get the Vibe?* New York: Strapless / Kensington, 2003. 297pp.

———. *White Bikini Panties.* New York: Strapless / Kensington Books, 2004. 279pp.

Jenkins, Jerry B. *Rookie.* Brentwood, Tenn.: Wogemuth and Hyatt, 1991, 447pp.

———. *The Youngest Hero.* New York: Warner Books, 2002. 376pp.

Jenkins, John and Chris Fabry. *Windy City Danger, Red Rock Mysteries.* Carol Stream, Ill.: Tyndale House, 2006. 234pp.

Jenkins, John, and Mark Weaver. *City of Lies: The Century War Chronicle.* Freedom Series, bk. 2. Manassas, Va.: Reconciliation Press, 1998. 153pp.

Jens, Tina L. *The Blues Ain't Nothin': Tales of the Lonesome Blues Pub.* Darien, Ill.: Design Image, 2002. 208pp.

Jensen, Kathryn. *Getting Real: Christopher, The Loop.* New York: Harlequin, Silhouette Books, 1994. 186pp.

Joe, Yolanda. *Bebe's by Golly Wow.* New York: Dell, 1998. 339pp.

———. *This Just In.* New York: Doubleday, 2000. 281pp.

———. *Video Cowboys: A Georgia Barnett Mystery.* New York: Simon and Schuster, 2005. 245pp.

John, Sally. *Flash Point.* In a Heartbeat, bk. 2. Eugene, Ore.: Harvest House, 2004. 348pp.

———. *In a Heartbeat.* In a Heartbeat, bk. 1. Eugene, Ore.: Harvest House, 2004. 376pp.

John, Sally. *Moment of Truth*. In a Heartbeat, bk. 3. Eugene, Ore.: Harvest House, 2005. 390pp.

Johns, Rebecca. *Icebergs*. New York: Bloomsbury, 2005. 297pp.

Johnson, Charles Richard. *Dreamer*. New York: Scribner, 1998. 236pp.

Johnson, Denis. *Angels*. New York: Knopf, 1983. 209pp.

Johnson, Margaret. *After the Storm*. Grand Rapids, Mich.: Serenade / Serenata Books, 1987. 224pp.

Johnson, R. M. *The Harris Men*. New York: Simon and Schuster, 1999. 335pp.

———. *Love Frustration*. New York: Simon and Schuster, 2002. 338pp.

Jones, D. J. H. *Murder at the MLA*. Athens: University of Georgia Press, 1993. 217pp.

Jones, Dylan. *Unnatural Acts*. New York: St. Martin's, 1996. 279pp.

Jones, Traci L. *Standing against the Wind*. New York: Farrar, Straus and Giroux, 2006. 184pp.

Joseph, Frank S. *To Love Mercy*. Huntingdon, W.Va.: Mid-Atlantic Highlands, 2006. 291pp.

Just, Ward Swift. *Jack Gance*. Boston: Houghton Mifflin / Richard Todd, 1989. 279pp.

———. *Twenty-One Selected Stories*. New York: Houghton Mifflin / Richard Todd, 1990. 389pp.

———. *An Unfinished Season*. Boston, New York: Houghton Mifflin, 2004. 251pp.

Kaempfer, Rick. *Severance*. Hoboken, N.J.: ENC Press, 2007. 243pp.

Kahn, Michael A. *Grave Designs: A Rachel Gold Mystery*. New York: Signet, 1992. 351pp.

Kallmaker, Karin. *Wild Things*. Tallahassee, Fla.: Naiad Press, 1996. 228pp.

Kaminsky, Stuart M. *Always Say Goodbye: A Lew Fonesca Mystery*. Detroit: Wheeler, 2006. 272pp.

———. *The Big Silence: An Abe Lieberman Mystery*. New York: Forge, 2000. 268pp.

——— .*The Dead Don't Lie: An Abe Lieberman Mystery*. New York: Forge, 2007. 301pp.

———. *Exercise in Terror*. New York: St. Martin's, 1985. 278pp.

———. *The Last Dark Place: An Abe Lieberman Mystery*. New York: Forge, 2004. 254pp.

Kaminsky, Stuart M. *Lieberman's Choice*. New York: St. Martin's, 1993. 216pp.

———. *Lieberman's Day*. New York: Henry Holt, 1994. 260pp.

———. *Lieberman's Folly*. New York: St. Martin's, 1991. 216pp.

———. *Lieberman's Law*. New York: Henry Holt, 1996. 309pp.

———. *Lieberman's Thief*. New York: Henry Holt, 1995. 238pp.

———. *Not Quite Kosher: An Abe Lieberman Mystery*. New York: Forge, 2002. 254pp.

———. *Terror Town: An Abe Lieberman Mystery*. New York: Forge, 2006. 256pp.

Kantner, Seth. *Ordinary Wolves*. Minneapolis: Milkweed Editions, 2005. 324pp.

Kantra, Virginia. *Guilty Secrets*. New York: Harlequin, Silhouette Books, 2004. 249pp.

Kathleen, Susan. *Nomad's Land*. Chicago: Deus Ex Machina, 2007. 236pp.

Katz, Michael J. *Last Dance in Redondo Beach*. New York: G. P. Putnam's Sons, 1989. 255pp.

———. *Murder Off the Glass*. New York: Walker, 1987. 218pp.

Kchodl, Joseph J., Wendy Caszatt-Allen, and Jim DeWildt. *The Disappearance of Dinosaur Sue*. Traverse City, Mich.: Mackinac Island Press, 2006. 144pp.

Keene, Carolyn [pseud.]. *The Case of the Rising Stars*. New York: Pocket Books, 1989. 152pp.

———. *The Joker's Revenge*. New York: Pocket Books, 1988. 149pp.

———. *Mystery Train*. New York: Pocket Books, 1990. 220pp.

———. *The Teen Model Mystery, Nancy Drew Mystery Stories*. New York: Pocket Books, 1995. 154pp.

Keevers, Thomas J. *The Chainsaw Ballet*. Waterville, Maine: Five Star, 2007. 239pp.

———. *Music across the Wall*. Waterville, Maine: Five Star, 2003. 221pp.

———. *What the Hyena Knows*. Waterville, Maine: Five Star, 2006.

Kelly, Cathy. *Letter from Chicago*. Dublin: New Island Books, 2002. 80pp.

Kelly, Leslie. *Overexposed*. Blaze, 347. New York: Harlequin, 2007. 249pp.

Kelly, Mary Pat. *Special Intentions*. Dublin: New Island Books, 1997. 380pp.

Kennedy, Eugene Cullen. *Father's Day*. Garden City, N.Y.: Doubleday, 1981. 488pp.

———. *Queen Bee*. Garden City, N.Y.: Doubleday, 1982. 330pp.

Kilian, Michael. *The Big Score*. New York: St. Martin's, 1993. 393pp.

Killingsworth, Renee Prewitt. *Morning Drive to Midnight*. Ann Arbor, Mich.: Proctor, 1999. 286pp.

Kimball, K. M. *The Secret of the Red Flame*. New York: Aladdin Paperbacks, 2002. 222pp.

King-Bey, Deatri. *Beauty and the Beast*. Brooklyn, N.Y.: Parker, 2006. 226pp.

———. *Whisper Something Sweet*. Mira Loma, Calif.: Parker, 2007. 213pp.

King, Katina. *Ride Wit' Me*. Fort Lee, N.J.: Young Diamond Books, 2006. 144pp.

Kirby, Susan E. *Ike and Porker*. Boston: Houghton Mifflin, 1983. 145pp.

Kirchner, Bharti. *Sharmila's Book*. New York: Plume, 2000. 296pp.

Kirk, Cindy. *When She Was Bad*. New York: Avon Books, 2007. 340pp.

Kirkwood, Valerie. *Trace of a Woman*. New York: Kensington, 1998. 379pp.

Kistler, Julie. *Scandal*. Blaze, no. 268. New York: Harlequin, 2006. 250pp.

Klass, Sheila Solomon. *Kool Ada*. New York: Scholastic, 1991. 167pp.

Klawans, Harold Leo. *Sins of Commission*. Chicago: Contemporary Books, 1982. 340pp.

Knister, Raymond. *Hackman's Night; and Taxi Driver*. Windsor, Ont.: Black Moss Press, 2007. 168pp.

Koertge, Noretta. *Who Was That Masked Woman?* New York: St. Martin's, 1981. 244pp.

Komie, Lowell B. *The Humpback of Lodz*. Chicago: Swordfish Chicago, 2004. 377pp.

———. *The Judge's Chambers and Other Stories*. Chicago: Academy Chicago, 1987. 83pp.

Komie, Lowell B. *The Last Jewish Shortstop in America*. Chicago: Swordfish Chicago, 1997. 210pp.

Konrath, Joe. *Bloody Mary: A Jacqueline "Jack" Daniels Mystery*. New York: Hyperion, 2005. 307pp.

———. *Dirty Martini*. New York: Hyperion, 2007. 292pp.

———. *Rusty Nail: A Jacqueline "Jack" Daniels Thriller*. New York: Hyperion, 2006. 292pp.

———. *Whiskey Sour: A Jack Daniels Mystery*. New York: Hyperion, 2004. 270pp.

Koontz, Dean R. [Leigh Nichols, pseud.] *The Key to Midnight*. New York: Penguin, Berkley Books, 1995. 439pp.

Kopp, Nancy. *Absent Witness*. New York: Onyx, 1999. 370pp.

———. *Acts and Omissions*. New York: Signet, 1994. 431pp.

———. *Blind Trust*. New York: Onyx, 2003. 340pp.

———. *Final Justice*. New York: Onyx, 2002. 341pp.

Korbel, Kathleen. *Simple Gifts*. New York: Harlequin, Silhouette Books, 1994. 248pp.

Korbel, Kathleen, Carla Bracale Cassidy, and Lori Herter. *Shadows '93: A Romantic Collection from the Dark Side of Love*. New York: Harlequin, Silhouette Books, 1993. 375pp.

Korman, Gordon, and Victor Vaccaro. *Nose Pickers from Outer Space*. New York: Scholastic, 1999. 137pp.

Kreisman, Bruce. *Off the Bench*. Bend, Ore.: Salvo Press, 2001. 200pp.

Kraus, Jim, and Terri Kraus. *The Unfolding*. Uhrichsville, Ohio: Barbour, 2003. 302pp.

Krueger, William Kent. *Mercy Falls*. New York: Atria Books, 2005. 344pp.

Kuper, Daniela. *Hunger and Thirst*. New York: St. Martin's, 2004. 275pp.

LaFaye, A. *Edith Shay*. New York: Viking, 1998. 183pp.

———. *Nissa's Place*. New York: Simon and Schuster Books for Young Readers, 1999. 244pp.

Lafferty, R. A. *Tales of Chicago*. Weston, Ont.: United Mythologies Press, 1992. 109pp.

Laird, Thomas. *Black Dog*. Waterville, Maine: Chivers / Thorndike, 2004. 243pp.

———. *Cutter*. New York: Carroll and Graf, 2001. 250pp.

———. *Season of the Assassin*. New York: Carroll and Graf, 2003. 234pp.

Lamstein, Sarah. *Hunger Moon*. Asheville, N.C.: Front Street Books, 2003. 109pp.

Langer, Adam. *Crossing California*. New York: Riverhead Books, 2004. 432pp.

———. *The Washington Story: A Novel in Five Spheres*. New York: Riverhead Books, 2005. 400pp.

Lanigan, Catherine. *Dangerous Love*. Don Mills, Ont.: Harlequin, MIRA Books, 1996. 411pp.

———. *In Love's Shadow*. Don Mills, Ont.: Harlequin, MIRA Books, 1998. 378pp.

———. *The Way of the Wicked*. New York: Avon Books, 1993. 437pp.

LaPietra, Mary. *The Disguise of Love*. Grand Rapids, Mich.: Zondervan, 1985. 192pp.

Larsen, Eric. *I Am Zoe Handke*. Chapel Hill: Algonquin Books, 1992. 216pp.

Lawlor, Laurie. *Exploring the Chicago World's Fair, 1893*. New York: Pocket Books, 2001. 212pp.

Lawrence, Terry. *Before I Wake*. New York: Bantam Books, 1995. 401pp.

Lee, Adrianne. *Prince under Cover*. Toronto: Harlequin Books, 2002. 248pp.

Lenhard, Elizabeth. *Chicks with Sticks: (Knit Two Together)*. New York: Dutton, 2006. 262pp.

———. *Chicks with Sticks: It's a Purl Thing*. New York: Speak, 2006. 261pp.

———. *Chicks with Sticks: Knitwise*. New York: Dutton Children's Books, 2007. 260pp.

Levin, Meyer. *The Architect*. New York: Simon and Schuster, 1981. 413pp.

Levitsky, Ronald. *The Innocence That Kills*. New York: Scribner's, 1994. 254pp.

Lieberman, Syd. *Streets and Alleys: Stories with a Chicago Accent*. Little Rock, Ark.: August House, 1995. 189pp.

Lindell, Arthur G. *School Section Sixteen*. New York: Vantage Press, 1983. 257pp.

Lindsay, Tony. *Chasin' It*. Amityville, N.Y.: Urban, 2004. 248pp.

———. One Dead Lawyer. Jamaica, Queens, N.Y.: Q-Boro Books, 2007. 223pp.

———. *One Dead Preacher*. Alexandria, Va.: BlackWords, 2000. 208pp.

———. *Prayer of Prey: A Supernatural Tale of Suspense*. Alexandria, Va.: BlackWords Press, 2002. 252pp.

———. *Street Possession*. New York: Urban Books, 2004. 256pp.

Linz, Cathie. *Private Account*. New York: Dell, 1984. 242pp.

———. *Too Smart for Marriage*. New York: Harlequin, Silhouette, 1998. 187pp.

Little, Eddie. *Another Day in Paradise*. New York: Viking, 1998. 263pp.

Lockwood, Cara. *Dixieland Sushi*. New York: Downtown Press, 2005. 283pp.

Lombardo, Billy and Gladys Swan. *The Logic of a Rose: Chicago Stories*. Kansas City, Mo.: University of Missouri-Kansas City, BkMk Press, 2005. 146pp.

Lorenz, Tom. *Serious Living*. New York: Viking. 1988. 213pp.

Lowery, Darrin. *Still Crazy*. Atlanta, Ga.: Black Pearl Books, 2005. 313pp.

Lowndes, Natalya. *Chekago*. London: Hodder and Stoughton, 1988. 384pp.

Lucas, Leanne. *Addie Mccormick and the Chicago Surprise*. Eugene, Ore.: Harvest House, 1993. 136pp.

Luke, Christopher. *Unfinished Business*. Boca Raton, Fla.: Cool Hand Communications, 1993. 358pp.

Lyons, Tom Wallace. *The Pelican and After: A Novel About Emotional Disturbance*. Richmond, Va.: Prescott, Durrell, 1983. 268pp.

MacBride, Kate. *Love's Tormented Flame*. New York: Pinnacle Books, 1982. 343pp.

Machin, Meredith. *Outrageous Fortune*. New York: St. Martin's / Marek, 1985. 295pp.

Mackenzie, Myrna. *The Baby Wish*. New York: Harlequin, Silhouette Books, 1994. 186pp.

———. *Morning Beauty, Midnight Beast*. New York: Harlequin, Silhouette Books, 2004. 298pp.

MacLean, Julianne. *Sleeping with the Playboy*. New York: Harlequin, Silhouette Books, 2003. 187pp.

MacNeill, Alastair. *Counterplot*. London: Victor Gollancz, 1999. 250pp.

Madlock, Felicia. *Sins of the Father*. Amityville, N.Y.: Urban, 2004. 288pp.

Maher, Mary. *The Devil's Card*. New York: St. Martin's, 1992. 243pp.

Major, Clarence. *Dirty Bird Blues*. San Francisco: Mercury House, 1996. 279pp.

Malcolm, John. *Mortal Ruin: A Tim Simpson Mystery*. New York: Charles Scribner's Sons, 1988. 190pp.

Maling, Arthur. *Lover and Thief*. New York: Harper and Row, 1988. 230pp.

Manderino, John. *The Man Who Once Played Catch with Nellie Fox*. Chicago: Academy Chicago, 1998. 262pp.

———. *Sam and His Brother Len*. Chicago: Academy Chicago, 1994. 234pp.

Margolis, Elaine. *Pulse*. San Jose, N.Mex.: Writer's Showcase, 2000. 253pp.

Mark, Grace. *The Dream Seekers*. New York: William Morrow, 1992. 412pp.

Markels, Bobby. *Popper*. Mendocino, Calif.: Stone Press, 1986. 80pp.

Markey, Judy. *The Daddy Clock*. New York: Bantam Books, 1998. 261pp.

———. *Just Trust Me*. Don Mills, Ont.: Harlequin, MIRA Books, 2004. 313pp.

Marks, Kathy. *The Littlest Detective*. Richmond, Surrey: Mills and Boon, 1997. 219pp.

Marsh, Carole. *The Mystery of the Chicago Dinosaurs*. Carole Marsh Mysteries, no. 6. Peachtree City, Ga.: Gallopade International / Carole Marsh Books, 2003. 145pp.

Martin, Ann M. and Susan Tang. *Karen's Big Move*. New York: Scholastic, 1998. 105pp.

———. *Karen's Big City Mystery*. New York: Scholastic, 1998. 106pp.

Martínez-Serros, Hugo. *The Last Laugh and Other Stories*. Houston, Tex.: Arte Publico Press, 1988. 198pp.

Martino, Carmela. *Rosa, Sola*. Cambridge, Mass.: Candlewick Press, 2005. 236pp.

Martins, Richard. *The Cinch*. New York: Villard Books, 1986. 269pp.

Massatt, Brian. *Knights of the Red Cross*. San Jose, N.Mex.: Writer's Showcase, 2000. 238pp.

Massic, Elizabeth. *The Great Chicago Fire, 1871*. New York: Pocket Books, 1999. 212pp.

Masterton, Graham. *Headlines*. New York: St. Martin's, 1986. 468pp.

Matas, Carol. *Rosie in Chicago: Play Ball!* New York: Aladdin Paperbacks, 2003. 125pp.

Matthews, Alex. *Cat's Claw*. Philadelphia: Intrigue Press, 2000. 272pp.

———. *Death's Domain, The Sixth Cassidy Mccabe Mystery*. Philadelphia: Intrigue Press, 2001. 315pp.

———. *Murder's Madness*. Oak Park, Ill.: Veiled Intent Press, 2007. 339pp.

———. *Satan's Silence, the Second Cassidy Mccabe Mystery*. Angel Fire, N.Mex.: Intrigue Press, 1997. 296pp.

———. *Secret's Shadow*. Angel Fire, N.Mex.: Intrigue Press, 1996. 291pp.

———. *Vendetta's Victim, the Third Cassidy Mccabe Mystery*. Angel Fire, N.Mex.: Intrigue Press, 1998. 222pp.

———. *Wanton's Web, the Fourth Cassidy Mccabe Mystery*. Angel Fire, N.Mex.: Intrigue Press, 1999. 254pp.

Mayr, Ilsa. *Summer Flames*. New York: Avalon Books, 2007. 217pp.

McAlpine, Gordon. *Joy in Mudville*. New York: Dutton, 1989. 212pp.

McBride, Mary. *Ms. Simon Says*. London: Warner Forever, 2004. 331pp.

McCall, Thomas. *Beyond Ice, Beyond Death*. New York: Hyperion, 1995. 294pp.

———. *Payment in Kind*. New York: Hyperion, 1993. 259pp.

———. *A Wide and Capable Revenge*. New York: Hyperion, 1993. 259pp.

McCarthy, Erin. *Smart Mouth*. New York: Brava, 2004. 282pp.

McConnell, Christopher. *A Nation of Amor*. Sag Harbor, N.Y.: Permanent Press, 1993. 187pp.

McConnell, Frank D. *Blood Lake*. New York: Walker, 1987. 237pp.

———. *Liar's Poker*. New York: Walker, 1993. 214pp.

———. *Murder Among Friends*. New York: Walker, 1983. 186pp.

McDonald, Bill. *Dakota Incarnate: A Collection of Short Stories*. Minneapolis: New Rivers Press, 1999. 112pp.

McElroy, Paul. *Tracon*. Newcastle, Wash.: Japphire, 2000. 493pp.

McEvoy, John. *Blind Switch*. Scottsdale, Ariz.: Poisoned Pen Press, 2004. 278pp.

———. *Riders Down*. Scottsdale, Ariz.: Poisoned Pen Press, 2006. 254pp.

McGivern, William Peter. *A Matter of Honor*. New York: Arbor House, 1984. 334pp.

McGlothin, Victor. *Ms. Etta's Fast House*. New York: Kensington, 2007. 321pp.

McGuire, Molly. *My Prince Charming*. American Romance, no. 484. New York: Harlequin, 1993. 250pp.

McInerny, Ralph. *Slattery: A Soft-Boiled Detective*. Waterville, Maine: Five Star, 2004. 208pp.

McInerny, Ralph [Monica Quill, pseud.]. *And Then There Was Nun: A Sister Mary Teresa Mystery*. New York: Vanguard Press, 1984. 172pp.

———. *Half Past Nun: A Sister Mary Teresa Mystery*. New York: St. Martin's, 1997. 198pp.

———. *Leave of Absence*. New York: Atheneum, 1986. 210pp.

———. *Let Us Prey: A Sister Mary Teresa Mystery*. New York: Vanguard Press, 1982. 208pp.

———. *Not a Blessed Thing! A Sister Mary Teresa Mystery*. New York: Vanguard Press, 1981. 192pp.

———. *Nun of the Above: A Sister Mary Teresa Mystery*. New York: Vanguard Press, 1985. 186pp.

———. *Nun Plussed: A Sister Mary Teresa Mystery*. New York: St. Martin's, 1993. 216pp.

———. *Sine Qua Nun: A Sister Mary Teresa Mystery*. New York: Vanguard Press, 1986. 182pp.

———. *Sister Hood: A Sister Mary Teresa Mystery*. New York: St. Martin's, 1991. 218pp.

McInerny, Ralph [Monica Quill, pseud.]. *The Veil of Ignorance*. New York: St. Martin's, 1988. 200pp.

McKade, Maureen. *Convictions*. New York: Penguin, Berkley Sensation, 2005. 313pp.

McKelvy, Charles. *Billy, and other Stories*. Harbert, Mich.: Dunery Press, 1992. 417pp.

———. *Chicagoland*. Harbert, Mich.: Dunery Press, 1988. 347pp.

McKelvy, Natalie. *Where's Ours?* Chicago: Academy Chicago, 1987. 274pp.

McKinney, David E., and David D. McKinney. *Bloodlines*. New York: Vantage Press, 2000. 260pp.

McKissack, Pat. *Color Me Dark: The Diary of Nellie Lee Love*. New York: Scholastic, 2000. 218pp.

McManus, James. *Chin Music*. New York: Crown, 1985. 199pp.

———. *Curtains*. Chicago: Another Chicago Press, 1985. 128pp.

———. *Ghost Waves*. New York: Grove Press, 1988. 331pp.

———. *Out of the Blue*. New York: Crown, 1984. 246pp.

McMillan, Terry. *A Day Late and a Dollar Short*. New York: Viking, 2001. 431pp.

McNally, John. *The Book of Ralph*. New York: Simon and Schuster, 2005. 304pp.

McNaught, Judith. *Every Breath You Take*. New York: Ballantine Books, 2005. 334pp.

Meluch, R. M. *Chicago Red*. New York: New American Library, 1990. 319pp.

Meno, Joe. *Hairstyles of the Damned*. Chicago: Punk Planet Books, 2004. 270pp.

Merritt, Jackie Myles Lori. *Her Best Defense*. New York: Harlequin, Silhouette Books, 2005. 298pp.

Mertz, Barbara Gross [Barbara Michaels, pseud.]. *Search the Shadows*. New York: Atheneum, 1987. 358pp.

Mesmer, Sharon. *In Ordinary Time*. Brooklyn, N.Y.: Hanging Loose Press, 2005. 128pp.

Metz, Melinda. *Lucy*. New York: HarperCollins World, 2000. 240pp.

Meyer, Nicholas. *Confessions of a Homing Pigeon*. New York: Dial Press, 1981. 378pp.

Meyers, Nancy, and Charles Shyer. *I Love Trouble*. New York: Signet, 1994. 240pp.

Michael, Judith. *The Real Mother*. New York: Morrow, 2005. 421pp.

Michaels, Barbara. *Search the Shadows*. New York: Atheneum, 1987. 358pp.

Michod, Alec. *The White City*. New York: St. Martin's, 2004. 232pp.

Miles, Cassie. *Full Steam*. Bensalem, Pa.: Meteor, 1990. 221pp.

———. *Not on His Watch*. New York: Harlequin, 2002. 249pp.

Miles, Keith. *Saint's Rest: A Merlin Richards Mystery*. New York: Walker, 1999. 224pp.

Miller, Judith. *Whispers Along the Rails*. Postcards from Pullman, no. 2. Minneapolis: Bethany House, 2007. 377pp.

Miller, Richard. *Tanglefoot: An (Almost) True Story of Civil Wars and Cities*. Monterey, Calif.: DFI Books, 2005. 365pp.

Miller, Sue. *Family Pictures*. New York: Harper and Row, 1990. 389pp.

Miller, Susan B. *Indigo Rose*. New York: Bantam Books, 2005. 291pp.

Mills, Charles. *The Truth Trackers*. Hagerstown, Md.: Review and Herald, 2001. 144pp.

Mills, Jenna. *A Verdict of Love, Family Secrets*. New York: Harlequin, Silhouette Books, 2003. 248pp.

Mills, Jon. *When God Wept*. Island Park, N.Y.: Whittier, 2003. 155pp.

Minger, Elda. *Another Chance at Heaven*. New York: Harlequin Books, 1999. 219pp.

Mitchard, Jacquelyn. *The Deep End of the Ocean*. New York: Viking, 1996. 434pp.

Monroe, Steve. *'46, Chicago*. New York: Hyperion, Talk Miramax Books, 2002. 256pp.

———. *'57, Chicago*. New York: Hyperion, Talk Miramax Books , 2000. 226pp.

Moore, Y. Blake. *Slipping*. New York: Ballantine, One World Books, 2005. 273pp.

Moore, Yanier. *Triple Take*. New York: Villard, 2003. 272pp.

Moquist, Richard. *Eye of the Agency: A Sadie Greenstreet Mystery*. New York: St. Martin's, 1997. 207pp.

Murphy, Jim. *The Great Fire*. New York: Scholastic, 1995. 144pp.

Murphy, Patrick T. *Drowning in Hot Water*. Poughkeepsie, N.Y.: Vivisphere, 2000. 174pp.

Myers, Walter Dean. *The Journal of Biddy Owens, the Negro Leagues*. New York: Scholastic, 2001. 141pp.

Nash, Jay Robert. *A Crime Story*. New York: Delacorte Press, 1981. 294pp.

———. *The Mafia Diaries*. New York: Delacorte Press, 1984. 253pp.

Navarro, Yvonne. *Mirror Me*. Hiram, Ga.: Overlook Connection Press, 2004. 295pp.

———. *Deadrush*. New York: Bantam Books, 1995. 351pp.

Naylor, Phyllis Reynolds, and Marcy Dunn Ramsey. *Cuckoo Feathers*. Tarrytown, N.Y.: Marshall Cavendish, 2006. 88pp.

Nelscott, Kris. *Days of Rage*. New York: St. Martin's, Minotaur, 2006. 336pp.

———. *Smoke-Filled Rooms*. New York: St. Martin's, Minotaur, 2001. 308pp.

———. *Stone Cribs*. New York: St. Martin's, Minotaur, 2004. 323pp.

———. *Thin Walls*. New York: St. Martin's, Minotaur, 2002. 387pp.

Nelson, Antonya. *Talking in Bed*. Boston: Houghton Mifflin, 1996. 275pp.

Nickles, Elizabeth. *Hype*. New York: New American Library Books, 1989. 293pp.

Nielsen, Wayne F. *Semblance of Balance*. Pittsburgh, Pa.: Sterling House, 2002. 223pp.

Nixon, Cornelia. *Angels Go Naked*. Washington, D.C.: Counterpoint, 2000. 286pp.

Nixon, Joan Lowery. *Land of Promise*. New York: Bantam, 1993. 170pp.

Novak, Jan. *The Grand Life*. New York: Poseidon Press, 1987. 250pp.

Oates, Joyce Carol. *Marya: A Life*. New York: Dutton, 1986. 310pp.

O'Brien, Patricia. *Good Intentions*. New York: Simon and Schuster, 1997. 367pp.

O'Connell, Catherine. *Well Bred and Dead: A High Society Mystery*. New York: Harper, 2007. 335pp.

Odom, Bettye. *Colored Grits*. Lansing, Ill.: Macro Group, 2004. 177pp.

Odom, Mel. *F.R.E.E. Lancers*. Lake Geneva, Wis.: TSR, 1995. 311pp.

Ojikutu, Bayo. *47th Street Black*. New York: Three Rivers Press, 2003. 413pp.

———. *Free Burning*. New York: Three Rivers Press, 2006. 383pp.

Olcott, Anthony. *Murder at the Red October*. Chicago: Academy Chicago, 1981. 226pp.

Olds, Bruce. *The Moments Lost: A Midwest Pilgrim's Progress*. New York: Farrar, Straus and Giroux, 2007. 468pp.

O'Neal, Denise I. *On the Line*. Chicago: Banbury, 2002. 343pp.

O'Rourke, Michael. *O'Banion's Gift*. Edina, Minn.: St. John's, 2003. 346pp.

Osa, Nancy. *Cuba 15*. New York: Delacorte Press, 2003. 277pp.

Osborne, Karen Lee. *Hawkwings*. Chicago: Third Side Press, 1991. 217pp.

Pacotti, Pamela. *Winds of Desire*. New York: Pageant Books, 1988. 402pp.

Page, Carole Gift. *Storms over Willowbrook*. Nashville, Tenn.: Thomas Nelson, 1998. 275pp.

Page, Jake. *Apacheria*. New York: Ballantine, 1998. 342pp.

Palmer, Diana [Susan Spaeth, pseud.]. *Love by Proxy*. New York: Harlequin, Silhouette, 1985. 188pp.

———. *The Savage Heart*. Rockland, Mass.: Wheeler, 1997. 311pp.

Palmer, Michael. *The Fifth Vial*. New York: St. Martin's, 2007. 372pp.

Paretsky, Sara. *Bitter Medicine*. New York: William Morrow, 1987. 321pp.

———. *Blacklist: A V. I. Warshawski Novel*. New York: G. P. Putnam's Sons, 2003. 415pp.

———. *Blood Shot*. New York: Delacorte Press, 1988. 328pp.

Paretsky, Sara. *Burn Marks*. New York: Dell, 1990. 340pp.

———. *Deadlock: A V. I. Warshawski Mystery*. Garden City, N.Y.: Dial Press, 1984. 252pp.

———. *Fire Sale*. New York: G. P. Putnam's Sons, 2005. 402pp.

———. *Ghost Country*. New York: Delacorte Press, 1998. 386pp.

———. *Guardian Angel*. New York: Delacorte Press, 1992. 370pp.

———. *Hard Time: A V. I. Warshawski Novel*. New York: Delacorte Press, 1999. 385pp.

———. *Indemnity Only*. New York: Dell, 1982. 244pp.

———. *Killing Orders*. New York: William Morrow, 1985. 288pp.

———. *Total Recall: A V. I. Warshawski Novel*. New York: Delacorte Press, 2001. 414pp.

———. *Tunnel Vision*. New York: Delacorte Press, 1994. 432pp.

———. *Windy City Blues: A. V. I. Warshawski Stories*. New York: Delacorte Press, 1995. 258pp.

Parshall, Craig. *Trial by Ordeal*. Eugene, Ore.: Harvest House, 2006. 330pp.

Pastore, Clare. *Journey to America: Aniela Kaminski's Story: A Voyage from Poland During World War II*. New York: Penguin, Berkley Jam Books, 2002. 182pp.

Patterson, James. *Sam's Letters to Jennifer*. Boston: Little, Brown, 2004. 263pp.

Pearson, Ryne Douglas. *Simple Simon: A Thriller*. New York: William Morrow, 1996. 256pp.

Peck, Richard. *Fair Weather*. New York: Dial Books, 2001. 139pp.

———. *New York Time*. New York: Delacorte Press, 1981. 212pp.

Peeples, Wendell. *Deadly Oath*. New York: Vantage Press, 1996. 140pp.

Pendleton, Don. *Don Pendleton's Mack Bolan: Save the Children*. The Executioner, no. 94. New York: Worldwide, 1986. 253pp.

Perkin, Norah-Jean. *Crazy in Chicago*. Corvalis, Ore.: Fiction Works, 2001. 230pp.

Perrin, Kayla. *Sweet Honesty*. Washington, D.C.: BET, 1999. 251pp.

Peterson, Ann Voss. *Laying Down the Law.* Intrigue, no. 674. New York: Harlequin, 2002. 251pp.

Petrakis, Harry Mark. *Collected Stories.* Chicago: Lake View Press, 1987. 359pp.

———. *Days of Vengeance.* Garden City, N.Y.: Doubleday, 1983. 279pp.

———. *Ghost of the Sun.* New York: St. Martin's, 1990. 262pp.

———. *The Orchards of Ithaca.* Carbondale: Southern Illinois University Press, 2004. 270pp.

———. *Twilight of the Ice.* Carbondale: Southern Illinois University Press, 2003. 173pp.

Pevsner, Stella. *Jon, Flora, and the Odd-Eyed Cat.* New York: Pocket Books, 1997. 188pp.

———. *Sister of the Quints.* New York: Clarion Books, 1987. 177pp.

———. *Would My Fortune Cookie Lie?* New York: Clarion Books, 1996. 186pp.

Philbin, Tom, and Dana Stevens. *Blink.* New York: Jove Books, 1994. 183pp.

Philipson, Morris H. *Somebody Else's Life.* Chicago: University of Chicago Press, 1987. 298pp.

Phillips, Susan Elizabeth. *It Had to Be You.* New York: Avon Books, 1994. 376pp.

———. *Match Me If You Can.* New York: William Morrow, 2005. 386pp.

———. *Nobody's Baby but Mine.* New York: Avon Books, 1994. 376pp.

———. *This Heart of Mine.* New York: Avon Books, 2001. 370pp.

Pinkwater, Daniel Manus. *The Education of Robert Nifkin.* New York: Farrar, Straus and Giroux, 1998. 167pp.

Podojil, E. William. *The Tenth Man.* New York: Southern Tier Editions, 2004. 410pp.

Pollack, Neal. *Chicago Noir.* New York: Akashic Books, 2005. 252pp.

Pomeranz, Gary. *Out at Home.* Boston: Houghton Mifflin, 1985. 231pp.

Power, Susan. *Roofwalker.* Minneapolis: Milkweed Editions, 2002. 199pp.

Powers, John R. *The Junk-Drawer Corner-Store Front-Porch Blues.* New York: Dutton, 1992. 209pp.

Prate, Kit. *A Woman of Chicago*. Wayne, Pa.: Banbury Books, 1983. 378pp.

Preston, John. *Lethal Silence*. New York: Alyson, 1987. 118pp.

Proctor, George W. *V: The Chicago Conversion*. Sevenoaks: New English Library, 1985. 184pp.

Purdy, James. *Gertrude of Stony Island Avenue*. New York: William Morrow, 1997. 182pp.

———. *In the Hollow of His Hand*. New York: Weidenfeld and Nicolson, 1986. 254pp.

Pynchon, Thomas. *Against the Day*. New York: Penguin Press, 2006, 1085pp.

Quinn, Patrick. *Thick as Thieves*. New York: Crown, 1995. 242pp.

Raleigh, Michael. *A Body in Belmont Harbor*. New York: St. Martin's, 1993. 277pp.

———. *Death in Uptown*. New York: St. Martin's, 1991. 247pp.

———. *In the Castle of the Flynns*. Naperville, Ill.: Sourcebooks Landmark, 2002. 347pp.

———. *Killer on Argyle Street*. New York: St. Martin's, 1995. 248pp.

———. *The Maxwell Street Blues: A Chicago Mystery Featuring Paul Whelan*. New York: St. Martin's, 1994. 280pp.

———. *The Riverview Murders: A Paul Whelan Mystery*. New York: St. Martin's, 1997. 213pp.

Randisi, Robert J. *Arch Angels*. New York: Thomas Dunne Books, 2004. 355pp.

———. *Blood of Angels*. New York: Leisure Books, 2004. 355pp.

Raney, Deborah. *Over the Waters*. New York: Harlequin, Steeple Hill, 2005. 336pp.

Ransom, Candice F. *Magician in the Trunk*. Time Spies, bk. 4. Renton, Wash.: Mirrorstone, 2007. 112pp.

Rautbord, Sugar. *The Chameleon*. New York: Warner Books, 1999. 516pp.

Rautbord, Sugar, and Elizabeth Nickles. *Girls in High Places*. New York: New American Library, 1986. 437pp.

Ray, B. K. *South Side Dreams*. New York: Urban Books, 2005. 245pp.

Ray, Brian. *Next Stop Past Nowhere*. London: X Press, 2003. 240pp.

Reasoner, James. *Battle Lines: The Last Good War*. New York: Forge, 2001. 423pp.

Reaves, Sam. *Bury It Deep*. New York: G. P. Putnam, 1993. 272pp.

————. *Dooley's Back*. New York: Carroll and Graf, 2002. 274pp.

————. *Fear Will Do It*. New York: G. P. Putnam's Sons, 1992. 269pp.

————. *Get What's Coming*. New York: G. P. Putnam's Sons, 1995. 252pp.

————. *Homicide 69*. New York: Carroll and Graf Publishers, 2007. 569pp.

————. *A Long Cold Fall*. New York: Putnam, 1991. 255pp.

Reed, Mary Hutchings. *Courting Kathleen Hannigan*. Chicago: Amp&rsand, 2007. 255pp.

Reed, Rick R. *Penance*. New York: Dell, 1993. 371pp.

Rees, Geoffrey. *Sex with Strangers*. New York: Farrar, Straus and Giroux, 1993. 245pp.

Resnick, Mike. *The Branch*. New York: New American Library, Signet, 1984. 191pp.

Rettenmund, Matthew. *Boy Culture*. New York: St. Martin's, 1995. 181pp.

Reynolds, Sean. *Dying for a Change*. San Francisco, Calif.: Suspect Thoughts, 2007. 256pp.

Riley, Jocelyn. *Crazy Quilt*. New York: William Morrow, 1984. 215pp.

Robbins, David. *Chicago Run*. New York: Dorchester, 1991. 192pp.

Roberts, Nora. *Private Scandals*. New York: Jove Books, 1994. 384pp.

Robin, Robert. *Something in Common*. New York: Simon and Schuster, 1985. 252pp.

Robinet, Harriette. *Children of the Fire*. New York: Atheneum, 1991. 134pp.

————. *Missing from Haymarket Square*. New York: Atheneum Books for Young Readers, 2001. 143pp.

Robinson, C. Kelly. *No More Mr. Nice Guy*. New York: Villard / Strivers Row, 2002. 276pp.

Robinson, C. Kelly. *The One That Got Away*. New York: New American Library, 2005. 272pp.

Roby, Kimberla Lawson. *It's a Thin Line*. New York: Kensington, 2002. 275pp.

Rodi, Robert. *Closet Case*. New York: Dutton, 1993. 330pp.

———. *Drag Queen*. New York: Dutton, 1995. 259pp.

———. *Fag Hag*. New York: Dutton, 1992. 296pp.

———. *Kept Boy*. New York: Dutton, 1996. 323pp.

———. *What They Did to Princess Paragon*. New York: Dutton, 1994. 281pp.

———. *When You Were Me*. New York: Kensington, 2007. 426pp.

Roemer, William F. *Mob Power Plays: The Mob Attempts Control of Congress, Casinos, and Baseball*. New York: S.P.I. Books, 1994. 278pp.

Romano, Tony. *When the World Was Young*. New York: HarperCollins, 2007. 309pp.

Rosales, Melodye. *Minnie Saves the Day*. Boston: Little, Brown, 2000. 84pp.

Rose, Jeanne. *Good Night, My Love*. New York: Harlequin, Silhouette Books, 1996. 248pp.

Rose, Karen. *Count to Ten*. New York: Warner Vision Books, 2007. 564pp.

———. *Nothing to Fear*. New York: Warner Books, 2005. 515pp.

———. *You Can't Hide*. New York: Warner Books, 2006. 518pp.

Rosemoor, Patricia. *Fake I. D. Wife*. Intrigue, no. 703. New York: Harlequin, 2003. 249pp.

———. *Hot Case*. Bombshell, no. 24. New York: Harlequin, Silhouette Books, 2004. 295pp.

———. *Hot Zone*. Blaze, no. 95. New York: Harlequin, 2003. 250pp.

———. *Improper Conduct*. Blaze, 55. New York: Harlequin, 2002. 248pp.

———. *On the List*. Intrigue, no. 791. New York: Harlequin, 2004. 249pp.

———. *Sheer Pleasure*. Blaze, no. 35. New York: Harlequin, 2002. 248pp.

Rosemoor, Patricia. *Torch Job*. Intrigue, no. 219. New York: Harlequin, 1993. 253pp.

———. *VIP Protector*. Intrigue, no. 707. New York: Harlequin, 2003. 250pp.

Rosenberger, Joseph. *Ninja Nightmare*. Shadow Warrior, no. 3. New York: Dell, 1988. 184pp.

Rosnau, Wendy. *Last Man Standing*. New York: Harlequin, Silhouette Books, 2003. 248pp.

Ross, Sam. *Melov's Legacy*. Sag Harbor, N.Y.: Second Chance Press, 1984. 308pp.

Roth, Philip. *The Anatomy Lesson*. New York: Farrar, Straus and Giroux, 1983. 291pp.

Rue, Nancy N. *The Caper*, Christian Heritage Series: The Chicago Years, no. 5. Minneapolis: Bethany House, 2000. 177pp.

———. *The Capture*, Christian Heritage Series: The Chicago Years, no. 4. Minneapolis: Bethany House, 1999. 177pp.

———. *The Chase*, Christian Heritage Series: The Chicago Years, no. 2. Minneapolis: Bethany House, 1999. 180pp.

———. *The Pursuit*, Christian Heritage Series: The Chicago Years, no. 6. Minneapolis: Bethany House, 2000. 174pp.

———. *The Stunt*, Christian Heritage Series: The Chicago Years, no. 3. Minneapolis: Bethany House, 1999. 192pp.

———. *The Trick*, Christian Heritage Series: The Chicago Years, no. 1. Minneapolis: Bethany House, 1999. 195pp.

Rutkoff, Peter M. *Shadow Ball: A Novel of Baseball and Chicago*. Jefferson, N.C.: McFarland, 2001. 228pp.

Saberhagen, Frederick Thomas. *A Century of Progress*. New York: Tom Doherty Associates, 1983. 315pp.

Sackett, Susan. *A Taste of Passion*. New York: Zebra Books, 1992. 448pp.

Sáenz, Benjamin Alire. *The House of Forgetting*. New York: HarperCollins, 1997. 341pp.

Sa`id, Mahmud. *Two Lost Souls*. Schaumburg, Ill.: Joshua Tree, 2006. 158pp.

Sakey, Marcus. *The Blade Itself*. Detroit: Thorndike Press, 2007. 307pp.

Sallee, Wayne Allen. *The Holy Terror*. Shingletown, Calif.: Mark V. Ziesing, 1992. 300pp.

Schaub, Christine. *Finding Anna, Music of the Heart*. Minneapolis: Bethany House, 2005. 316pp.

Schellie, Don. *Shadow and the Gunner*. New York: Four Winds Press, 1982. 136pp.

Schott, Penelope Scambly. *A Little Ignorance*. New York: Clarkson N. Potter, 1986. 232pp.

Schrader, E. G. *For the Defendant*. New York: Dorchester, 2004. 356pp.

Schreiber, Mark. *Star Crossed*. Woodbury, Minn.: Flux, 2007. 305pp.

Schwegel, Theresa. *Officer Down*. New York: St. Martin's, Minotaur, 2005. 274pp.

———. *Person of Interest*. New York: St. Martin's, Minotaur, 2007. 372pp.

———. *Probable Cause*. New York: St. Martin's, Minotaur, 2007. 292pp.

Scott, Robert. *The Finding of David*. New York: Gay Presses of New York, 1984. 193pp.

Sennett, Frank. *Nash, Metropolitan*. Waterville, Maine: Five Star, 2004. 248pp.

Shafer, Charles. *Chicago Stretch*. Frederick, Md.: Hilliard Harris, 2003. 252pp.

Shapiro-Rieser, Rhonda. *A Place of Light*. New York: Poseidon Press, 1983. 286pp.

Sharpe, Jon. *Canyon O'Grady 24: Chicago Six-Guns*. New York: Signet, 1993. 172pp.

Shaw, Janet Beeler. *Taking Leave*. New York: Viking, 1987. 294pp.

Sheldon, Jean. *Identity Murder*. Albuquerque: Bast Press, 2007. 252pp.

Sherburne, James Robert. *Death's White City: A Paddy Moretti Novel*. New York: Fawcett, Gold Medal, 1988. 244pp.

Sherer, Michael W. *Death Came Dressed in White*. New York: HarperPaperbacks, 1992. 309pp.

———. *Death Is No Bargain: An Emerson Ward Mystery*. Waterville, Maine: Five Star, 2006. 368pp.

———. *A Forever Death*. Unity, Maine: Five Star, 2001. 279pp.

———. *An Option on Death*. New York: Dodd, Mead, 1988. 244pp.

Shields, Carol. *A Fairly Conventional Woman*. Toronto: MacMillan, 1982. 216pp.

Shields, Trish. *Inferno*. Monroe, Mich.: One-in-Ten, 2003. 276pp.

Sibley, Linda, and Dea Marks. *David's Adventures at the Chicago World's Fair*. Logan, Iowa: Perfection Learning, 2002. 84pp.

Simmons, John. *Lamplighter*. New York: Fawcett, Gold Medal, 1984. 217pp.

Sinclair, April. *Coffee Will Make You Black*. New York: Hyperion, 1994. 239pp.

———. *I Left My Back Door Open*. New York: Hyperion, 1999. 290pp.

Singer, Norma. *Not Old, Not Full of Days*. Long Branch, N.J.: Vista, 1996. 381pp.

Skom, Edith. *The Charles Dickens Murders*. New York: Delacorte Press, 1998. 295pp.

———. *The Mark Twain Murders*. Tulsa, Okla.: Council Oak Books, 1989. 277pp.

Small, Lass. *Balanced*. Desire, no. 800. New York: Harlequin, Silhouette Books, 1993. 184pp.

Smartypants, Mimi. *The World According to Mimi Smartypants*. New York: Avon Books, 2006. 240pp.

Smith, Charles Merrill. *Reverend Randollph and the Splendid Samaritan*. New York: G. P. Putnam's Sons, 1986. 223pp.

———. *Reverend Randollph and the Unholy Bible*. New York: G. P. Putnam's Sons, 1983. 221pp.

Smith, Deborah. *When Venus Fell*. New York: Bantam Books, 1998. 353pp.

Smith, Greg Leitich. *Ninjas, Piranhas, and Galileo*. Boston: Little, Brown, 2003. 179pp.

———. *Tofu and T. Rex*. Boston: Little, Brown, 2005. 162pp.

Smith, Joseph C. *The Day the Music Died*. New York: Grove Press / Kent Carroll, 1981. 446pp.

Smith, Sarah Jane. *No Thanks, and Other Stories*. Kalamazoo, Mich.: New Issues, Western Michigan University, 2001. 201pp.

Snelling, Lauraine. *The Brushstroke Legacy*. Colorado Springs: WaterBrook Press, 2006. 392pp.

Solwitz, Sharon. *Bloody Mary*. Louisville, Ky.: Sarabande Books, 2003. 290pp.

Sonoda, Kenichi. *Gunsmith Cats Burst.* Milwaukie, Ore.: Dark Horse, 2007. 188pp.

Soos, Troy. *Murder at Wrigley Field.* New York: Kensington Books, 1996. 296pp.

Soule, Maris. *Thrill of the Chase.* Loveswept, no. 768. New York: Bantam Books, 1995. 230pp.

Spallone, Jennie. *Deadly Choices.* Sierra Vista, Ariz.: WhoooDoo Mysteries, 2005. 205pp.

Spencer, Ross Harrison. *The Devereaux File.* New York: Donald I. Fine, 1990. 310pp.

———. *Echoes of Zero.* New York: St. Martin's, 1981. 175pp.

———. *The Fifth Script.* New York: Donald I. Fine, 1989. 244pp.

———. *Kirby's Last Circus.* New York: Donald I. Fine, 1987. 253pp.

———. *The Missing Bishop.* New York: Mysterious Press, 1985. 268pp

———. *Monastery Nightmare.* New York: Mysterious Press, 1986. 225pp.

Spencer, Scott. *Waking the Dead.* New York: Alfred A. Knopf, 1986. 395pp.

Sprinkle, Patricia Houck. *Murder at Markham.* New York: St. Martin's, 1988. 218pp.

Staub, Wendy Corsi. *Getting It Together, The Loop.* New York: Harlequin, Silhouette Books, 1994. 184pp.

Steel, Danielle. *Wings.* New York: Delacorte Press, 1994. 400pp.

Steele, Irene J. *Some Glad Morning.* Lisle, Ill.: Blacksmith Books, 2007. 218pp.

Stein, Harry. *Hoopla.* New York: Dell, 1983. 316pp.

Stella, Leslie. *The Easy Hour.* New York: Three Rivers Press, 2003. 265pp.

Stern, Richard G. *Almonds to Zhoof: Collected Stories.* Evanston, Ill: Northwestern University Press, TriQuarterly Books, 2005. 610pp.

———. *A Father's Words.* New York: Arbor House, 1986. 189pp.

———. *Noble Rot; Stories 1949-1988.* New York: Grove Press, 1989. 367pp.

Stein, R. Conrad. *Me and Dirty Arnie.* New York: Harcourt, Brace, Jovanovich, 1982. 132pp.

Stevens, Amanda. *The Littlest Witness*. Intrigue, no. 549. New York: Harelquin, 2000. 248pp.

———. *Secret Admirer*. Intrigue, 553. New York: Harlequin, 2000. 256pp.

Steward, Samuel Morris [Phil Andros, pseud.]. *Below the Belt & Other Stories*. San Francisco: Perineum Press, 1982. 128pp.

Stewardson, Dawn. *The Mummy Beads*. Harlequin Intrigue, no. 261. New York: Harlequin, 1994. 251pp.

Stockanes, Anthony Edward. *Ladies Who Knit for a Living*. Urbana: University of Illinois Press, 1981. 131pp.

Stokes, Jordan, and Matt Belinkie. *Gilded Delirium*. New York: Spark, 2007. 202pp.

Stone, Katherine. *The Cinderella Hour*. Don Mills, Ont.: Harlequin, MIRA Books, 2005. 345pp.

———. *A Midnight Clear*. New York: Warner Books, 1999. 328pp.

Strasser, Todd, and Sam Harper. *Rookie of the Year*. New York: Trump Club, 1993. 84pp.

———. *Ferris Bueller's Day Off*. New York: New American Library, 1986. 196pp.

Strong, Jonathan. *Offspring*. Cambridge, Mass.: Zoland Books, 1995. 225pp.

Strother, Pat Wallace [Vivian Lord, pseud.]. *Once More the Sun*. New York: Fawcett, Gold Medal, 1982. 350pp

Stuart, Anne. *One More Valentine*. American Romance, no. 473. New York: Harlequin, 1993. 253pp.

Summer Rain, Mary. *Ruby*. Charlottesville, Va.: Hampton Roads 2005. 392pp.

Sussman, Susan. *Time Off from Good Behavior*. New York: Pocket Books, 1991. 274pp.

Sussman, Susan, and Sarajane Avidon. *Audition for Murder*. New York: St. Martin's, 1999. 279pp.

Sutton, Remar. *Long Lines*. New York: Weidenfeld and Nicolson, 1988. 259pp.

Swartz, Mark. *H2O*. Berkeley, Calif.: Soft Skull Press, 2006. 166pp.

———. *Instant Karma*. San Francisco: City Lights Books, 2002. 112pp.

Taylor, Valerie. *The Girls in 3-B*. New York: City University of New York, Feminist Press, 2003. 206pp.

Theroux, Paul. *Chicago Loop*. New York: Random House, 1990. 196pp.

Thompson, Jean. *City Boy*. New York: Simon and Schuster, 2004. 306pp.

Thornburg, Newton Kendall. *Beautiful Kate*. Boston: Little, Brown, 1982. 230pp.

Tooley, S. D. *Nothing Else Matters: A Sam Casey Mystery*. Schererville, Ind.: Full Moon, 2000. 288pp.

———. *When the Dead Speak*. Schererville, Ind.: Full Moon, 1999. 303pp.

Toombs, Jane. *Out of the Blue*. Goose Creek, S.C.: Vintage Romance, 2005. 220pp.

Trautvetter, Janet, Sarah Roark, and Myranda Sarro. *Three Shades of Night*. Stone Mountain, Ga.: White Wolf, 2006. 286pp.

Travis, Tristan, Jr. [pseud.]. *Lamia*. New York: Dutton, 1982. 434pp.

Trice, Dawn Turner. *Only Twice I've Wished for Heaven*. New York: Crown, 1996. 304pp.

Turow, Scott. *Pleading Guilty*. New York: Farrar, Straus and Giroux, 1993. 386pp.

Tyree, Omar. *Cold Blooded: A Hardcore Novel*. New York: Simon and Schuster Paperbacks, 2004. 181pp.

Vachss, Andrew H. *Everybody Pays: Stories*. New York: Vintage Books, 1999. 368pp.

Villines, Melanie. *Tales of the Sacred Heart*. Libertyville, Ill.: BogFire, 1999. 224pp.

Walker, Charlotte. *Yesterday's Bride*. Intimate Moment, no. 768. New York: Harlequin, Silhouette Books, 1997. 248pp.

Walker, David J. *All the Dead Fathers*. New York: St. Martin's, Minotaur, 2005. 320pp.

———. *Applaud the Hollow Ghost*. New York: St. Martin's, 1998. 273pp.

———. *A Beer at a Bawdy House*. New York: St. Martin's, Minotaur, 2000. 307pp.

———. *The End of Emerald Woods*. New York: St. Martin's, Minotaur, 2000. 310pp.

Walker, David J. *Fixed in His Folly*. New York: St. Martin's, 1995. 262pp.

————. *Half the Truth*. New York: St. Martin's, 1996. 275pp.

————. *No Show of Remorse*. New York: St. Martin's, Minotaur, 2002. 292pp.

————. *A Ticket to Die For*. New York: St. Martin's, 1998. 260pp.

Walker, Robert W. *City for Ransom*. Alastair Ransom Series, bk. 1. New York: Avon Books, 2006. 324pp.

————. *City of the Absent*. Alastair Ransom Series, bk. 2. New York: Avon Books, 2007. 310pp.

————. *Shadows in the White City*. Alastair Ransom Series, bk. 3. New York: Avon Books, 2007. 339pp.

Walsh, Caroline E., and Dan Hatala. *Sosa's Homers*. Logan, Iowa: Perfection Learning, 2001. 80pp.

Walton, Darwin McBeth. *Dance, Kayla!* Morton Grove, Ill.: Albert Whitman, 1998. 155pp.

Ward, Darwin S. *Becoming Alec*. Madison, Wis.: MBM Press, 2007. 240pp.

Wargin, Kathy-jo, and Karen Busch Holman. *Mitt & Minn's Illinois Adventure*. Ann Arbor, Mich.: Mitten Press, 2007. 162pp.

Warner, Gertrude Chandler, and Charles Tang. *The Windy City Mystery*. Morton Grove, Ill.: A. Whitman, 1998. 120pp.

Washington, AlTonya. *A Lover's Mask*. Romance, no. 35. New York: Harlequin, Kimani Press, 2007. 297pp.

Watanna, Onoto, Linda Trinh Moser, and Elizabeth Rooney. *"A Half Caste" and Other Writings*. Urbana: University of Illinois Press, 2003. 180pp.

Watson, Margaret. *The Dark Side of the Moon*. Intimate Moments, no. 779. New York: Harlequin, Silhouette Books, 1997. 248pp.

Watson, Mark. *Bullet Points*. London: Chatto and Windus, 2004. 275pp.

Waugh, Carol-Lynn Rössel, Frank D. McSherry, and Martin Harry Greenberg. *Murder and Mystery in Chicago*. New York: Dembner Books, 1987. 258pp.

Weaver, Ingrid. *Loving the Lone Wolf.* Intimate Moments, no. 1369. New York: Harlequin, Silhouette Books, 2005. 251pp.

Webb, Debra. *Colby Rebuilt.* Intrigue, no. 1023. New York: Harlequin, 2007. 250pp.

———. *Keeping Baby Safe.* Intrigue, no.732. New York: Harlequin, 2003. 248pp.

———. *Striking Distance.* New York: Harlequin, 2004. 297pp.

Weinberg, Robert E. *The Black Lodge.* New York: Pocket Books, 1991. 275pp.

———. *A Logical Magician.* New York: Ace Books, 1994. 232pp.

Weiner, Jody. *Prisoners of Truth.* San Francisco: Council Oak Books, 2006. 256pp.

Weir, Theresa. *Long Night Moon.* New York: Bantam Books, 1995. 343pp.

Weis, Margaret, and David. Baldwin. *Dark Heart.* New York: HarperPrism, 1998. 341pp.

Wells, Q. B. *Blackface.* Baltimore, Md.: Art Official Media, 2006. 128pp.

Wessel, John. *Kiss It Goodbye.* London, U.K.: Methuen, 2002. 334pp.

———. *Pretty Ballerina.* New York: Simon and Schuster, 1998. 240pp.

———. *This Far, No Further.* New York: Simon and Schuster, 1996. 333pp.

Whack, Rita Coburn. *Meant to Be.* New York: Strivers' Row, 2002. 307pp.

Wheeler, Susan. *Record Palace.* Saint Paul, Minn.: Graywolf Press, 2005. 278pp.

White, Pat. *The American Temp and the British Inspector.* Intrigue, no. 968. New York: Harlequin, 2007. 249pp.

———. *Practice Makes Mr. Perfect.* Romance, no. 1677. New York: Harlequin, Silhouette Books, 2003. 186pp.

White, Tiffany. *Male for Sale.* Yours Truly, no. 3. New York: Harlequin, Silhouette, 1995. 186pp.

Whitefeather, Sheri. *Cherokee Marriage Dare.* Desire, no. 1478. New York: Harlequin, Silhouette Books, 2002. 186pp.

Whittingham, Richard. *State Street.* New York: Donald I. Fine, 1991. 291pp.

Whittingham, Richard. *Their Kind of Town*. New York: Donald I. Fine, 1994. 374pp.

Wicker, Amberlina. *Made in Heaven*. New York: Pinnacle Books, Windsor, 1995. 253pp.

———. *Private Matters*. New York: Kensington, 1996. 316pp.

Wiggs, Susan. *The Firebrand*. Don Mills, Ont.: Harlequin, MIRA Books, 2001. 400pp.

———. *The Hostage*. Don Mills, Ont.: Harlequin, MIRA Books, 2000. 402pp.

———. *The Mistress*. Don Mills, Ont.: Harlequin, MIRA Books, 2000. 400pp.

Wiley, Michael. *The Last Striptease*. New York: Thomas Dunne Books / St. Martin's, Minotaur, 2007. 247pp.

Wilks, Eileen. *Expecting—and in Danger*. Desire, no. 1472. New York: Harlequin, Silhouette Books, 2002. 185pp.

Winston, Andrew. *Looped*. Chicago: Agate, 2005. 409pp.

Winters, Angela. *Sudden Love*. Washington, D.C.: BET, 1999. 288pp.

———. *Sweet Surrender*. New York: Kensington, 1998. 282pp.

Wise, Robert L. *Tagged, The Tribulation Survival Series*. New York: Warner Books, 2004. 296pp.

Wolfe, Bronwyn. *Longer Than Forever: An Angel's Touch*. New York: Dorchester, Love Spell, 1995. 392pp.

Wolfe, Gene. *Free Live Free*. New York: Orb, 1999. 403pp.

Wolfert, Adrienne, and Justin Bell. *Making Tracks*. New York: Silver Moon Press, 2000. 90pp.

Woods, Sherryl. *Twilight*. New York: Kensington, 1997. 319pp.

Woodson, J. L. *Superwoman's Child: Son of a Single Mother*. Chicago: Macro, 2005. 204pp.

Wright, T. M. *The Ascending*. New York: Tor Books, 1994. 222pp.

Wubbels, Lance. *In the Shadow of a Secret, The Gentle Hills*. Minneapolis: Bethany House, 1999. 286pp.

Zabytko, Irene. *When Luba Leaves Home: Stories*. Chapel Hill, N.C.: Algonquin Books, 2003. 230pp.

Zagel, James. *Money to Burn*. New York: Penguin, Berkley Books, 2003. 273pp.

Zimmerman, Jack. *Gods of the Andes*. Villa Park, Ill.: Wig Wam, 2006. 248pp.

Zimmerman, Robert Dingwall. *Dead Fall in Berlin*. Boston: Hall, 1990. 279pp.

Zubro, Mark Richard. *Another Dead Teenager*. New York: St. Martin's, 1995. 194pp.

———. *Are You Nuts?* New York: St. Martin's, 1998. 243pp.

———. *Dead Egotistical Morons*. New York: St. Martin's, Minotaur, 2003. 280pp.

———. *Drop Dead: A Paul Turner Mystery*. New York: St. Martin's, 1999. 245pp.

———. *An Echo of Death*. New York: St. Martin's, 1994. 194pp.

———. *File under Dead*. New York: St. Martin's, Minotaur, 2004. 264pp.

———. *Here Comes the Corpse*. New York: St. Martin's, Minotaur, 2002. 273pp.

———. *Nerds Who Kill*. New York: St. Martin's, Minotaur, 2005. 261pp.

———. *One Dead Drag Queen*. New York: St. Martin's, Minotaur, 2000. 246pp.

———. *The Only Good Priest*. New York: St. Martin's, 1991.

———. *Political Poison*. New York: St. Martin's, 1993. 194pp.

———. *The Principal Cause of Death*. New York: St. Martin's, 1992. 182pp.

———. *Rust on the Razor*. New York: St. Martin's, 1996. 212pp.

———. *Sex and Murder.Com*. New York: St. Martin's, Minotaur, 2001. 294pp.

———. *Sorry Now?* New York: St. Martin's, 1991. 179pp.

———. *The Truth Can Get You Killed*. New York: St. Martin's, 1997. 211pp.

Appendix B
Annotated Works Listed
Chronologically

1852–1890

946. Richardson, Major. *Wau-nan-ge; or, The Massacre at Chicago: A Romance of the American Revolution.* New York: Long and Brother, 1852. 126pp. Republished as *Hardscrabble; or, The Fall of Chicago a Tale of In dian Warfare.* New York.: de Witt, 1856. 99pp.

632. Kinzie, John H. Mrs. *Wau-Bun, the "Early Day" in the North-West.* New York: Derby and Jackson, 1856. 498pp.

53. Anonymous. *The Walder Family: A Story for Families and Sabbath Schools, Written in Chicago.* Chicago: Griggs, 1864. 211pp.

51. ———. *Luke Darrell, the Chicago Newsboy.* Chicago: Tomlinson Brothers, 1865. 377pp.

52. ———. *Mabel Ross, the Sewing-Girl.* Illustrated by J. Hyde. Chicago: Tomlinson Brothers, 1866. 432pp.

48. ———. *The Broken Pitcher; or, The Ways of Providence.* Chicago: Tomlinson, 1866. 282pp.

1093. Thurston, Louise Millicent. *Charley and Eva Roberts' Home in the West.* Boston: Lee and Shepard Publishers; New York: Charles T. Dillingham, 1869. 285pp.

1114. Upton, George P. *Letters of Peregrine Pickle.* Chicago: Western News, 1869. 340pp.

549. Hill, Agnes Leonard (Scanland). *Heights and Depths.* Chicago: Sumner, 1871. 271pp.

963. Roe, Edward Payson. *Barriers Burned Away.* New York: Dodd and Mead, 1872. 488pp.

1157. Wayde, Bernard. *The Black Mask; or, the Misterious (sic) Marriage: A Romance of Chicago.* Fifteen Cent Romances, No. 8. New York: Ornum, 1872. 97pp.

507.   Hale, Edward Everett, ed. *Six of One by Half a Dozen of the Other; An Every Day Novel by Harriet Beecher Stowe, Adeline D. T. Whitney, Lucretia P. Hale, Frederic W. Loring, Frederic B. Perkins, and Edward E. Hale.* Boston: Roberts Brothers, 1872. 245pp.

106.   Bigot, Marie Healy. *Lakeville; or, Substance and Shadow.* New York: David Appleton, 1873. 238pp.

651.   Lamb, Martha Joanna. *Spicy.* New York: Appleton, 1873. 178pp.

883.   Pinkerton, Frank (Allan Frank). *Claude Melnotte as a Detective, and Other Stories.* Chicago: Keen, Cooke, 1875. 282pp.

884.   ———. Frank (Allan Frank). *The Detective and the Somnambulist and The Murderer and the Fortune Teller.* Chicago: Keen, Cooke, 1875. 241pp.

1002.   Shuman, Andrew. *The Loves of a Lawyer, His Quandary, And How it Came Out.* Chicago: Keen, Cooke, 1875. 214pp.

929.   Rayne, Martha Louise. *Against Fate. A True Story.* Chicago: Keen, Cooke, 1876. 251pp.

37.   Andrews, Robert Hardy [Shang Andrews, pseud.]. *Cranky Ann, the Street-Walker: A Story of Chicago in Chunks.* Chicago, 1878. 80pp.

45.   ———. *Wicked Nell, a Gay Girl of the Town.* Chicago: Comet, 1878. 73pp.

195.   Catherwood, Mary Hartwell. *The Dogberry Bunch.* Boston: Lothrop, 1879. 86pp.

706.   Maitland, James. *Suppressed Sensations, or Leaves from the Note Book of a Chicago Reporter.* Chicago: Rand, McNally, 1879. 254pp.

1116.   Van Deventer, Emma Murdoch [Lawrence L. Lynch, pseud.]. *Shadowed by Three.* Chicago: Donnelly, Gassette and Lloyd, 1879, 738pp.

195.   Catherwood, Mary Hartwell. *The Dogberry Bunch.* Boston: Lothrop, 1879. 86pp.

38.   Andrews, Robert Hardy [Shang Andrews, pseud.]. *Irish Mollie, Or a Gambler's Fate, a True Story of a Famous Chicago Tragedy.* Chicago: Garden City Books, 1882. 98pp.

23.   Alger, Horatio. *The Train Boy.* New York: Carleton, 1883. 298pp.

477.   Givins, Robert Cartwright [Snivig C. Trebor, pseud.]. *Land Poor: A Chicago Parable.* Chicago: Franklin, 1884. 117pp.

622.   Keenan, Henry Francis. *The Money-Makers: A Social Parable.* New York: David Appleton, 1885. 337pp.

781. Mooney, James [Le Jemlys; Jelley, Symmes M., pseud.]. *Shadowed to Europe: A Chicago Detective on Two Continents*. Illustrated by True Williams. Chicago: Belford, Clarke, 1885. 357pp.

1174. Wellington, A. A. Mrs. *By A Way that They Knew Not*. Chicago: Rand, McNally, 1885. 288pp.

247. Cowdrey, Robert H. *Foiled. By a Lawyer. A Story of Chicago*. Chicago: Clark and Longley Printers, 1885. 337pp.

276. Denison, Thomas S. *An Iron Crown: A Tale of the Great Republic*. Chicago: The Author, 1885. 560pp.

885. Pinkerton, Frank (Allan Frank). *Dyke Darrel, The Railroad Detective; or, The Crime of the Midnight Express*. Chicago: Fred C. Laird, 1886. 121pp.

1069. Strong, Edmund C. *Manacle and Bracelet; or, the Dead Man's Secret, A Thrilling Detective Story*. Chicago: Ogilvie, 1886. 105pp.

144. Brown, Helen Dawes. *Two College Girls*. Boston: Houghton Mifflin, 1886. 325pp.

435. Foran, Marlin Ambrose. *The Other Side, A Social Study Based on Fact*. Cleveland, Ohio: Ingham, Clarke, Booksellers / Washington, D. C.: Gray and Clarkson, Printers and 1886. 461pp.

478. Givins, Robert C. [Snivig C. Trebor, pseud.]. *The Millionaire Tramp*. Chicago: Cook County Review, 1886. 181pp.

479. Givens, Robert C. [Snivig C. Trebor, pseud.]. *The Unwritten Will: A Romance*. Chicago: Rhodes and McClure, 1886. 214pp.

555. Holmes, M. E. Mrs. *A Desperate Woman*. Chicago: Laird and Lee 1886. 174pp.

886. Pinkerton, Frank (Allan Frank). *Jim Cummings; or, the Great Adams Express Robbery*. Chicago: Laird and Lee, 1887. 152pp.

887. Pinkerton, Myron. *The Stolen Will; or The Rokewood Tragedy*. Chicago: Laird and Lee 1887. 138pp.

894. Postgate John William. *A Woman's Devotion; or, The Mixed Marriage*. Chicago: Rand, McNally, 1887. 270pp.

1031. Sommers, Lillian [Litere, pseud.]. *For Her Daily Bread*. Preface by Col. Robert G. Ingersoll. Globe Library, No. 34. Chicago: Rand, McNally, 1887. 228pp.

311. Draper, John Smith. *Shams; or, Uncle Ben's Experience with Hypocrites: A Story of Simple Country Life, Giving a Humorous and Entertaining Picture of Every Day Life and Incidents in the Rural Districts, with Uncle Ben's Trip to the City of Chicago and to California, and His Experience with the Shams and Sharpers of the Metropolitan World.* Chicago: Thompson and Thomas, 1887. 412pp.

780. Mooney, James. [Le Jemlys, pseud.]. *Lawyer Manton of Chicago: A Detective Story of Thrilling Interest.* Chicago: Eagle, 1888. 201pp.

1196. Wilkie, Franc Bangs. *The Gambler, a Story of Chicago Life.* Chicago: Denison, 1888. 328pp.

1211. Worthington, Elizabeth Strong [Nicholas A. Griffith pseud.]. *The Biddy Club: and How Its Members, Wise and Otherwise, Some Toughened and Some Tenderfooted in the Rugged Ways of Housekeeping, Grappled with the Troublous Servant Question, to the Great Advantage of Themselves, and as They Hope, of Many Others.* Chicago: McClurg, 1888. 308pp.

814. O'Donnell, Simon. *The Runaway Wife; or, Love and Vengeance.* Chicago: Laird and Lee, 1889. 172pp.

892. Postgate John T. *The Stolen Laces: An Episode in the History of Chicago Crime; From the Diary of Ex-Chief Denis Simmons, of the Chicago Police.* The Pinkerton Detective Series, Vol. 28. Chicago: Laird and Lee, Publishers. 1889. 175pp.

964. Roe, Edward Reynolds. *Dr. Caldwell; or, The Trail of the Serpent.* The Pastime Series, vol. 33. Chicago: Laird and Lee, 1889. 251pp.

1033. Sommers, Lillian [Litere, pseud.]. *The Unpopular Public.* Chicago: Rand, McNally, 1889. 179pp.

1109. Tupper, Edith Sessions. *By a Hair's Breadth.* New York: Willard Fracker, 1889. 135pp.

22. Alger, Horatio. *Luke Walton; or, the Chicago Newsboy, Way to Success Series.* Philadelphia: Coates, 1889. 346pp.

49. Anonymous. *The Great Cronin Mystery; or, the Irish Patriot's Fate.* Chicago: Laird and Lee, 1889. 199pp.

264. Davieson, Sarah. *The Seldens in Chicago.* New York: Brentano's, 1889. 189pp.

476. Givins, Robert Cartwright [Snivig C. Trebor, pseud.]. *Jerry Bleeker; or, Is Marriage a Failure?* The Pastime Series, Vol. 30. Chicago: Laird and Lee, 1889. 206pp.

748. McGovern, John. *Daniel Trentworthy: A Tale of the Great Fire of Chicago.* Chicago: Rand, McNally, 1889. 281pp.

749.   McGovern, John. *David Lockwin: The People's Idol.* Chicago: Donohue, Henneberry, 1889. 297pp.

1032.   Sommers, Lillian [Litere, pseud.]. *Jerome Leaster of Roderick, Leaster & Co.* Illustrated by Jules Guerin. Chicago: Charles H. Scrgcl, 1890. 376pp.

98.   Beach, Edgar Rice. *Stranded, a Story of the Garden City.* Chicago: Donohue, Henneberry, 1890. 348pp.

443.   Fraser, John Arthur [Hawkshaw, pseud.]. *A Wayward Girl's Fate.* Chicago: Eagle, 1890. 243pp.

487.   Gooch, Fani Pusey. *Miss Mordeck's Father.* New York: Dodd, Mead, 1890. 288pp.

1891–1920

1117.   Van Deventer, Emma Murdoch [Lawrence L. Lynch, pseud.]. *A Slender Clue; or, The Mystery of Mardi-Graz.* Chicago: Laird and Lee, 1891. 650pp.

210.   Chatfield-Taylor, Hobart Chatfield. *With Edge Tools.* Chicago: McClurg, 1891. 315pp.

248.   Cowdrey, Robert H. *A Tramp in Society.* Chicago: Schulte, 1891. 289pp.

302.   Donelson, Katharine. *Rodger Latimer's Mistake.* Chicago: Laird and Lee, 1891. 378pp.

634.   Kirkland, Joseph. *The Captain of Company K.* Chicago: Dibble, 1891. 351pp.

637.   Knott, William Wilson and Austyn Granville. *Stolen Sweets, or W. W. W. & W: A Romance with a Moral, the Acme of Realistic Fiction.* Chicago: Bow Knot, 1891. 368pp.

861.   Peattie, Elia Wilkinson. *The Judge.* Chicago: Rand, McNally, 1891.

1153.   Waterloo, Stanley. *A Man and a Woman.* Chicago: Schulte,1892. 250pp.

1221.   Yandell, Enid, Laura Hayes, and Jean Loughbrough. *Three Girls in a Flat.* Chicago: Press of Knight, Leonard, 1892. 154pp.

118.   Booth, Emma Scarr. *A Willful Heiress.* Buffalo, N.Y.: Charles Wells Moulton, 1892. 230pp.

169.   Butterworth, Hezekiah. *In the Boyhood of Lincoln.* New York: David Appleton, 1892. 266pp.

171.   ———. *Zigzag Journeys on the Mississippi from Chicago to the Islands of the Discovery.* Boston: Estes and Lauriat, 1892. 319pp.

205.   Chappell, Fred A. *Bill and Brocky, a Story of Boy Life in Chicago Especially Adapted to the Understanding of Old Boys.* Chicago: Harrison, Chappell and Davis, 1892. 99pp.

223.   Cobb, Weldon J. *A World's Fair Mystery.* Chicago: Melbourne, 1892. 369pp.

322.   Duff, Paul James. *Woman's Duplicity: A Story of High Life in Chicago.* Chicago: Stein, 1892. 226pp.

367.   Everett, Henry L. *The People's Program; The Twentieth Century is Theirs, A Romance of the Expectations of the Present Generation.* New York: Workmen's Publishing, 1892. 213pp.

47.   Anonymous. *The Beginning; A Romance of Chicago As It Might Be. With Introductory Letters by Hon. Hempstead Washburne, Dr. H. W. Thomas, Judge Tuthill, Judge Tuley, Judge Kohlsaat, and Professor Swing.* Chicago: Charles H. Kerr, 1893. 126pp.

138.   Brown, Fred H. *For One Dollar's Worth.* Chicago, 1893. 177pp.

222.   Cobb, Weldon J. *The Victim of a Crime.* Chicago: Weeks, 1893. 369pp.
        This book is a later publication of the entry that follows.

223.   ———. *A World's Fair Mystery.* Chicago: Melbourne, 1892. 369pp.

413.   Fearing, Blanche [Raymond Russell, pseud.]. *Asleep and Awake.* Chicago: Charles H. Kerr, 1893. 199pp.

457.   Fuller, Henry Blake. *The Cliff-Dwellers.* Illustrated by Thure de Thulstrup. New York: Harper and Brothers, 1893. 324pp.

525.   Hawthorne, Julian. *Humors of the Fair.* Illustrated by Will E. Chapin. Chicago: Weeks, 1893. 205pp.

554.   Holley, Marietta. *Samantha at the World's Fair, by Josiah Allen's Wife.* Illustrated by Baron C. de Grimm. New York: Funk and Wagnalls, 1893. 694pp.

630.   King, Charles. *Foes in Ambush.* Philadelphia: Lippincott, 1893. 263pp.

633.   Kirk, Hyland C. *The Revolt of the Brutes; A Fantasy of the Chicago Fair.* New York: Dillingham, 1893. 123pp.

741.   McDougall, Ella L. Randall. *From Side Streets and Boulevards: A Collection of Chicago Stories.* Chicago: Donnelley and Sons, 1893. 352pp.

771.   Milman, Harry Dubois. *Mr. Lake of Chicago.* The Criterion Series. New York: Street and Smith, 1893. 219pp.

795.   Neville, Edith. *Alice Ashland: A Romance of the World's Fair.* New York: Peter Fenelon Collier, 1893. 216pp.

936.   Read, Opie. *The Colossus.* Chicago: Laird and Lee 1893. 254pp.

951.   Richberg, Eloise O. Randall. *Bunker Hill to Chicago.* Chicago: Dibble, 1893. 151pp.

1056.   Stevens, C. M. (Charles McClellan) [Quondam, pseud.]. *The Adventures of Uncle Jeremiah and Family at the Great Fair: Their Observations and Triumphs.* Illustrated by Henry Mayer. Chicago: Laird and Lee, 1893. 237pp.

1061.   Strande, Wilhelm vom. *Chicago in Tears and Smiles.* Cleveland, Ohio: Press of Lauer and Mattill, 1893. 214pp.

924.   Rathborne, St. George Henry. *The Bachelor of the Midway.* New York: Mascot, 1894. 314pp.

993.   Scott, Henry E. *The Girl from Macoupin.* Chicago: Laird, Lee, 1894. Republished as *Beauty's Peril; or, The Girl From Macoupin.* Chicago: Laird, Lee, 1895.

1057.   Stevens, C. M. (Charles McClellan) [Quondam, pseud.]. *Egyptian Harp Girl.* Chicago: Laird and Lee, 1894. 272pp.

1099.   Totheroh, William W. *Why Not?; or, Lawyer Truman's Story.* Chicago: Ward, 1894. 303pp.

1115.   Van Deventer, Emma Murdoch [Lawrence, L. Lynch, pseud.]. *Against Odds: A Romance of the Midway Plaisance.* Chicago: Rand, McNally, 1894. 274pp.

56.   Armstrong, Dwight Leroy. *Byrd Flam in Town, Being a Collection of that Rising Young Author's Letters, Written at Chicago, and Published in The Trumpet, A Paper of General Circulation, at True's Mills, Indiana—Being Furthermore Shrewdly Construed as a Gentle Roast of Certain Business, Social, Political, Religious and Military Flams of a Great City.* Shadows Library, Vol. 1, No. 1. Chicago: John Bearhope, 1894. 139pp.

99.   Bech-Meyer, Nico, Mrs. *A Story from Pullmantown.* Chicago: Charles H. Kerr, 1894. 110pp.

165.   Burnham, Clara Louise. *Sweet Clover: A Romance of the White City.* Boston: Houghton Mifflin, 1894. 411pp.

170.   Butterworth, Hezekiah. *Zigzag Journeys in the White City; With Visits to the Neighboring Metropolis.* Boston: Estes and Lauriat, 1894. 320pp.

207.   Chatfield-Taylor, Hobart Chatfield. *An American Peeress.* Chicago: McClurg, 1894. 293pp.

253.   Crowley, Mary Catherine. *The City of Wonders: A Souvenir of the Worlds Fair*. Detroit, Mich.: William Graham, 1894. 162pp.

301.   Dockarty, A. J. *Midway Plaisance, the Experience of an Innocent Boy from Vermont in the Famous Midway*. Chicago: Chicago World Book, 1894. 259pp.

427.   Finley, Martha. *Elsie at the World's Fair*. New York: Dodd, Mead, 1894. 259pp.

491.   Granville, Austyn, and William Wilson Knott. *If the Devil Came to Chicago: A Plea for the Misrepresented by One Who Knows What It Is to Be Misrepresented Himself*. Illustrated by F. Holme. Chicago: Bow-Knot, 1894. 352pp.

924.   Rathborne, St. George Henry. *The Bachelor of the Midway*. New York: Mascot, 1894. 314pp.

21.   Alger, Horatio. *Adrift in the City; or, Oliver Conrad's Plucky Fight*. Philadelphia: John C. Winston, 1895. 325pp.

158.   Burnett, Frances Hodgson. *Two Little Pilgrims' Progress: A Story of the City Beautiful*. New York: Charles Scribner's Sons, 1895. 191pp.

208.   Chatfield-Taylor, Hobart Chatfield. *Two Women & a Fool*. Illustrated by Charles Dana Gibson. Chicago: Stone and Kimball, 1895. 232pp.

321.   Duff, Paul James. *Crimson Love; A Realistic Romance of Guilty Passion*. Chicago, 1895. 169pp.

414.   Fearing, Blanche. *Roberta*. Chicago: Charles H. Kerr, 1895. 424pp.

430.   Flinn, John J. *The Mysterious Disappearance of Helen St. Vincent; A Story of the Vanished City*. Chicago: George K. Hazlitt, 1895. 304pp.

461.   Fuller, Henry Blake. *With the Procession*. New York: Harper and Brothers, 1895. 336pp.

468.   Garland, Hamlin. *Rose of Dutcher's Coolly*. Chicago: Stone and Kimball, 1895. 403pp.

742.   McDougall, Ella L. Randall [Preserved Wheeler, pseud.]. *One Schoolma'am Less*. Chicago: Donnelley and Sons, 1895. 217pp.

891.   Pollard, Percival. *Cape of Storms, a Novel*. Chicago: Echo, 1895. 216pp.

1090. Thurber, Alwyn M.. *The Hidden Faith: An Occult Story of the Period*. Chicago: Harley, 1895. 294pp.

1100. Train, M. *Ray Burton: A Chicago Tale*. Chicago: The Author, 1895. 128pp.

3.   Ade, George. *Artie. A Story of the Streets and Town*. Chicago: Herbert S. Stone, 1896. 192pp.

112.   Blossom, Henry Martyn, Jr. *Checkers; A Hard-Luck Story*. Chicago: Herbert S. Stone, 1896. 239pp.

424.   Field, Eugene. *The House: An Episode in the Lives of Reuben Baker, Astronomer, and of His Wife Alice*. New York: Charles Scribner's Sons, 1896. 268pp.

448.   Friedman, I. K. (Isaac Kahn). *The Lucky Number*. Chicago: Way and Williams, 1896. 217pp.

572.   Hutcheson, Frank. *Barkeep Stories*. The Melbourne Series; no. 48. Chicago: Weeks, 1896. 212pp.

631.   King, Charles. *A Tame Surrender: A Story of the Chicago Strike*. Philadelphia: Lippincott, 1896, 277pp.

852.   Payne, Will. *Jerry the Dreamer*. New York: Harper and Brothers, 1896. 299pp.

876.   Phelon, William A. *Chimmie Fadden Out West: A Sequel to Chimmie Fadden*. Chicago: Weeks, 1896. 171pp.

893.   Postgate, John William. *The Mystery of Paul Chadwick: A Bachelor's Story*. Chicago: Laird and Lee, 1896. 248pp.

935.   Read, Opie. *The Captain's Romance, or Tales of the Backwoods*. Chicago: Tennyson Neely, 1896. 319pp.

1091.   Thurber, Alwyn M. *Quaint Crippen, Commercial Traveler*. Chicago: McClurg, 1896. 253pp.

2.   Adams, Frederick Upham. *President John Smith: The Story of a Peaceful Revolution*. Chicago: Charles H. Kerr, 1897. 290pp.

11.   Ade, George. *Pink Marsh: A Story of the Streets and Town*. Chicago: Herbert S. Stone, 1897. 197pp.

209.   Chatfield-Taylor, Hobart Chatfield. *The Vice of Fools*. Illustrated by Raymond M. Crosby. Chicago: Herbert S. Stone, 1897. 310pp.

1035.   Sparks, Alice Wilkinson. *My Wife's Husband: A Touch of Nature*. Chicago: Laird and Lee, 1897. 303pp.

1092.   Thurber, Alwyn M. *Zelma, the Mystic; or, White Magic, Versus Black*. Illustrated by W. L. Wells and L. Braunhold. Chicago: Authors, 1897. 380pp.

1204.   Windsor, William. *Loma: A Citizen of Venus*. St. Paul, Minn.: Windsor and Lewis Publishing, 1897. 429pp.

57.   Armstrong, Dwight Leroy. *Dan Gunn; The Man From Mauston; A Countryman Who Did Up the Town*. Chicago: Rand, McNally, 1898. 235pp.

245.   Coryell, John Russell [Nicholas Carter, pseud.]. *The Twelve Tin Boxes; or, Bob Ferret's Chicago Tangle*. New York: Street and Smith, 1898. 219pp.

324.   Dunne, Finley Peter. *Mr. Dooley in Peace and in War*. Boston: Small, Maynard, 1898. 260pp.

541.   Herrick, Robert. *The Gospel of Freedom*. New York: Macmillan, 1898. 287pp.

543.   ———. *Love's Dilemmas*. Chicago: Stone, 1898. 193pp.

551.   Hix, J. Emile. *Can a Man Live Forever?* Chicago: Western News, 1898. 143pp.

855.   Payne, Will. *The Money Captain*. Chicago: Herbert S. Stone, 1898. 323p.

947.   Richardson, Merrick Abner. *Chicago's Black Sheep and Bonny McClear's Friends*. Chicago: Giles E. Miller, 1898. 306pp.

961.   Robinson, Herbert B. *Chester*. Chicago: Conkey, 1898. 145pp.

1121.   Vynne, Harold Richard. *Love Letters: A Romance in Correspondence*. New York: Zimmerman's Pocket Library 1898. 170pp.

1151.   Waterloo, Stanley. *Armageddon*. Chicago: Rand, McNally, 1898. 259pp.

7.   Ade, George. *Doc' Horne: A Story of the Streets and Town*. Illustrated by John T. McCutcheon. Chicago: Herbert S. Stone, 1899. 292pp.

244.   Coryell, John Russell [Nicholas Carter, pseud.]. *The Crescent Brotherhood; or, Nick Carter's Chicago Double*. New York: Street and Smith, 1899. 205pp.

325.   Dunne, Finley Peter. *Mr. Dooley in the Hearts of His Countrymen*. Boston: Small, Maynard, 1899. 285pp.

331.   ———. *What Dooley Says*. Chicago: Kazmar, 1899. 235pp.

766.   Merwin, Samuel and Henry Kitchell Webster. *The Short Line War*. New York: Macmillan, 1899. 334pp.

898.   Potter, Margaret Horton Black. [Robert Dolly Williams, pseud.]. *A Social Lion*. Chicago: Donnelley and Sons, 1899. 432pp.

938.   Read, Opie. *Judge Elbridge*. Chicago: Rand, McNally, 1899. 295pp.

1152.   Waterloo, Stanley. *The Launching of a Man*. Chicago: Rand, McNally, 1899. 285pp.

1184.   White, Hervey. *Differences*. Boston: Small, Maynard, 1899. 311pp.

9.   Ade, George. *More Fables*. Illustrated by Clyde J. Newman. Chicago: Herbert S. Stone, 1900. 218pp.

24.   Alger, Horatio and A. M. Winfield. *Out for Business; or, Robert Frost's Strange Career*. Philadelphia: John Wanamaker, 1900. 287pp.

62.   Babcock, Bernie. *The Daughter of a Republican*. Chicago: New Voice Press, 1900. 15pp.

95.   Barton, William Eleazar. *The Prairie Schooner; A Story of the Black Hawk War*. Illustrated by H. Burgess. Boston and Chicago: Wilde, 1900. 382pp.

314.   Dreiser, Theodore. *Sister Carrie*. New York: Doubleday, Page, 1900. 557pp.

329.   Dunne, Finley Peter. *Mr. Dooley's Philosophy*. Illustrated by William Nicholson, E. W. Kemble, and F. Opper. New York: Russell, 1900. 263pp.

449.   Friedman, I. K. (Isaac Kahn). *Poor People*. Boston: Houghton Mifflin, 1900. 244pp.

469.   Gatchell, Charles. *What a Woman Did*. Chicago: Era, 1900. 337pp.

489.   Graham, Marie. *A Devout Bluebeard*. New York: Abbey Press, 1900. 300pp.

547.   Herrick, Robert. *The Web of Life*. New York: Macmillan, 1900. 356pp.

767.   Meyer, Lucy Rider. *Deaconess Stories*. Introduction by Dwight L. Moody. Chicago: Hope Publishing, 1900. 253pp.

928.   Raymond, Evelyn. *The Sun Maid: A Story of Fort Dearborn*. New York: Dutton, 1900. 326pp.

1122.   Vynne, Harold Richard. *The Woman That's Good: A Story of the Undoing of a Dreamer*. Chicago: Rand, McNally, 1900. 473pp.

1154.   Waterloo, Stanley. *The Seekers*. Chicago: Herbert S. Stone, 1900. 257pp.

1160.   Webster, Henry Kitchell. *The Banker and the Bear: The Story of a Corner in Lard*. New York: Macmillan, 1900. 351pp.

328.   Dunne, Peter Finley. *Mr. Dooley's Opinions*. New York: Russell, 1901. 212pp.

447.   Friedman, I. K. (Isaac Kahn). *By Bread Alone*. New York: McClure, Phillips and Co, 1901. 481pp.

460.   Fuller, Henry Blake. *Under the Skylights*. New York: Appleton, 1901. 382pp.

690.   Lorimer, George Horace. *Letters from a Self-Made Merchant to His Son*. Boston: Small, Maynard, 1901. 312pp.

765.   Merwin, Samuel and Henry Kitchell Webster. *Calumet "K."* Illustrated by H. C. Edwards. New York: Macmillan, 1901. 345pp.

840.   Parker, Mary Moncure. *A Girl of Chicago*. New York: Tennyson Neely, 1901. 140pp.

859.   Payne, Will. *The Story of Eva*. Boston: Houghton Mifflin, Riverside Press, 1901. 340pp.

1120.   Van Vorst, Bessie and Marie Van Vorst. *Bagsby's Daughter*. New York: Harper and Brothers, 1901. 338pp.

1217.   Wyatt, Edith Franklin. *Every One His Own Way*. Illustrated by William James. New York: McClure, Phillips, 1901. 291pp.

243.   Corrothers, James David. *The Black Cat Club: Negro Humor & Folklore*. Illustrated by J. K. Bryans. New York: Funk and Wagnalls, 1902. 264pp.

330.   Dunne, Finley Peter. *Observations by Mr. Dooley*. New York: Russell, 1902. 279pp.

432.   Flower, Elliott. *Policeman Flynn*. Illustrated by Frederic Dorr Steele. New York: Century, 1902. 294pp.

550.   Hinrichsen, William H. *Plots and Penalties*. Chicago: Rhodes and McClure, 1902. 458pp.

562.   Horton, George. *The Long Straight Road*. Illustrated by Troy and Margaret West Kinney. Indianapolis: Bowen-Merrill, 1902. 401pp.

583.   Jones, Ira. L. *The Richer—The Poorer*. Illustrated by Thomas B. Thompson. Chicago: Fiction, 1902. 321pp.

680.   Linn, James Weber. *The Second Generation*. New York: Macmillan, 1902. 305pp.

693.   Loux, DuBois. Henry. *Ongon: A Tale of Early Chicago*. New York: C. Francis Press, 1902. 182pp.

857.   Payne, Will. *On Fortune's Road: Stories of Business*. Chicago: McClurg, 1902. 290pp.

999. Sheldon, Charles M. *The Reformer*. Chicago: Advance; London, U.K.: Ward, Lock, 1902. 299pp.

1037. Spearman, Frank H. *Doctor Bryson*. New York: Charles Scribner's Sons, 1902. 308pp.

1155. Watt, Marion Frances. *Maurice: And Other Stories*. Seattle: Ivy Press, 1902. 313pp.

1181. Wheaton, Emily. *The Russells in Chicago*. Illustrated by Fletcher C. Ransom. Boston: Page, 1902. 257pp.

8. Ade, George. *In Babel; Stories of Chicago*. New York: McClure, Phillips, 1903. 357pp.

10. ———. *People You Know*. Illustrated by John T. McCutcheon and Others. New York: Russell, 1903. 224pp.

259. Curtis, Wardon Allan. *The Strange Adventures of Mr. Middleton*. Chicago: Herbert S. Stone, 1903. 311pp.

425. Field, Roswell Martin. *The Bondage of Ballinger*. Chicago: Revell, 1903. 214pp

434. Flower, Elliott. *The Spoilsmen*. Boston: Page, 1903. 324pp.

446. Friedman, I. K. (Isaac Kahn). *The Autobiography of a Beggar: Prefaced by Some of the Humorous Adventures & Incidents related in The Beggar's Club*. Boston: Small, Maynard, 1903. 350pp.

738. McCutcheon, George Barr. *The Sherrods*. Illustrated by C. D. Williams. New York: Dodd, Mead, 1903. 343pp.

764. Merwin, Samuel. *The Whip Hand: A Tale of the Pine Country*. Illustrated by Frederic Rodrigo Gruger. New York: Doubleday, Page, 1903. 299pp.

768. Meyer, Lucy Rider. *Mary North*. New York: Fleming H. Revell, 1903. 330pp.

800. Norris, Frank. *The Pit: A Story of Chicago*. New York: Doubleday, Page, 1903. 421pp.

854. Payne, Philip. *The Mills of Man*. Chicago: Rand, McNally and Co, 1903. 476pp.

856. Payne, Will. *Mr. Salt*. Illustrated by Charles H. White. Boston: Houghton Mifflin, 1903. 330pp.

878. Phillips, David Graham. *Golden Fleece: The American Adventures of a Fortune Hunting Earl*. Illustrated by Harrison Fisher. New York: McClure, Phillips, 1903. 326pp.

937. Read, Opie. *Confessions of a Marguerite*. Chicago: Rand, McNally, 1903. 164pp.

940.   Reed, Myrtle. *The Shadow of Victory: A Romance of Fort Dearborn*. New York: Grosset and Dunlap, 1903. 413pp.

944.   Richardson, George Tilton and Dwight Quint Wilder [Charles Eustace, joint pseud.]. *Letters from a Son to His Self-Made Father: Being the Replies to Letters from a Self-Made Merchant to his Son*. Illustrated by Fred Kulz. Boston: New Hampshire Publishing Corporation, 1903. 289pp.

992.   Scofield, Charles J. *Altar Stairs*. Illustrated by E. Bert Smith. Chicago: Christian Century, 1903. 320pp.

1219.   Wyatt, Edith Franklin. *True Love, A Comedy of the Affections*. New York: McClure, Phillips, 1903. 288pp.

5.   Ade, George. *Breaking into Society*. New York: Harper and Brothers, 1904. 208pp.

97.   Beach, Edgar Rice. *Hands of Clay: A Great City's Half—And the Other Half*. St. Louis: Edward R. Eddins, 1904. 348pp. Originally published in 1890 as *Stranded* (*see* entry 98).

232.   Cook, William Wallace. *Wilby's Dan*. Illustrated by C. B. Falls. New York: Dodd, Mead, 1904. 325pp.

306.   Douglas, Amanda Minnie. *A Little Girl in Old Chicago*. New York: Dodd, Mead, 1904. 324pp.

426.   Field, Roswell Martin. *Little Miss Dee*. Chicago: Revell, 1904. 241pp.

495.   Grimm, George. *Pluck*. Milwaukee, Wis.: Germania, 1904, 284pp.

540.   Herrick, Robert. *The Common Lot*. New York: Macmillan, 1904. 426pp.

691.   Lorimer, George Horace. *Old Gorgon Graham; More Letters from a Self-Made Merchant to His Son*. New York: Doubleday, Page, 1904. 308pp.

844.   Parrish, Randall. *When Wilderness Was King: A Tale of the Illinois Country*. Chicago: McClurg, 1904.

850.   Payne, Philip. *Duchess of Few Clothes: A Comedy*. Chicago: Rand, McNally, 1904. 341pp.

908.   Quick, Herbert. *Aladdin & Co.: A Romance of Yankee Magic*. New York: Grosset, 1904. 337pp.

1036.   Spearman, Frank H. *The Close of the Day*. New York: Appleton, 1904. 224pp.

1044. Stanger, Wesley Allen. *Rescued from Fiery Death: A Powerful Narrative of the Iroquois Theater Disaster: Mighty Flames Graphically Portrayed.* Chicago: Laird and Lee, 1904. 317pp.

1073. Surbridge, Agnes [pseud.]. *The Confessions of a Club Woman.* Illustrated by A. J. Keller. New York: Doubleday, Page, 1904. 241pp.

1162. Webster, Henry Kitchell. *The Duke of Cameron Avenue.* New York: Macmillan, 1904. 133pp.

1186. Whitlock, Brand. *The Happy Average.* Indianapolis: Bobbs-Merrill, 1904. 347pp.

1187. ———. *Her Infinite Variety.* Illustrated by Howard Chandler Christy. New York: Burt, 1904. 167pp.

1199. Williams, Wilbur Herschel. *Uncle Bob and Aunt Becky's Strange Adventures at the World's Great Exposition.* Chicago: Laird and Lee, 1904. 358pp.

93.   Barr, Robert. *The Speculations of John Steele.* New York: Frederick A. Stokes, 1905. 308pp.

176.   Capwell, Irene Stoddard. *Mrs. Alderman Casey.* New York: Fenno, 1905. 175pp.

263.   Darrow, Clarence. *An Eye for an Eye.* New York: Fox, Duffield, 1905. 213pp.

317.   Driver, John Merritte. *Purple Peaks Remote, A Romance of Italy and America.* Chicago: Laird and Lee, 1905. 418pp.

431.   Flower, Elliott. *The Best Policy.* Illustrated by George Brehm. Indianapolis: Bobbs-Merrill, 1905. 268pp. short stories

433.   ———. *Slaves of Success.* Illustrated by Jay Hambidge. Boston: Page; Colonial Press, 1905. 304pp.

445.   French, Alice [Octave Thanet, pseud.]. *The Man of the Hour.* Illustrated by Lucius Wolcott Hitchcock. New York: Grosset and Dunlap, 1905. 477pp.

544.   Herrick, Robert. *The Memoirs of an American Citizen.* Illustrated by F. B. Masters. New York: Macmillan, 1905. 351pp.

879.   Phillips, David Graham. *The Plum Tree.* Illustrated by E. M. Ashe. Indianapolis: Bobbs-Merrill, 1905. 389pp.

896.   Potter, Margaret Horton Black. *The Fire of Spring.* Illustrated by Sydney Adamson. New York: David Appleton, 1905. 357pp.

945.   Richardson, George Tilton and Dwight Quint Wilder [Charles Eustace Merriman, joint pseud.]. *A Self-Made Man's Wife, Her Letters to Her Son: Being the Woman's View of Certain Famous Correspondence*. Illustrated by F. T. Richards. New York: Putnam's Sons, Knickerbocker Press, 1905. 249pp.

86.   Banks, Charles Eugene. *John Dorn, Promoter*. Chicago: Monarch Books, 1906. 361pp.

347.   Ellis, Edward Sylvester [H. R. Gordon, pseud.]. *Black Partridge, or The Fall of Fort Dearborn*. New York: Dutton, 1906. 302pp.

508.   Hale, Helen. *Where Life Is Real*. Cincinnati, Ohio: Jennings, Graham, 1906.

737.   McCutcheon, George Barr. *Jane Cable*. New York: Dodd, Mead, 1906. 336pp.

988.   Schauffler, Robert Haven. *Where Speech Ends: A Music Maker's Romance*. New York: Moffat, Yard, 1906. 291pp.

1007.   Sinclair, Upton. *The Jungle*. New York: Grosset and Dunlap, 1906. 413pp.

1058.   Stevens, Grant Eugene. *Wicked City*. Chicago: The Author, 1906. 340pp.

1078.   Taylor, Bert Leston. *The Charlatans*. Illustrated by George Brehm. New York: Grosset and Dunlap, 1906. 390pp.

450.   Friedman, I. K. (Isaac Kahn). *The Radical*. New York: Appleton, 1907. 362pp.

467.   Garland, Hamlin. *Mart Haney's Mate; or, Money Magic*. New York: Harper and Brothers, 1907. 280pp.

661.   Laughlin, Clara Elizabeth. *Felicity: The Making of a Comedienne*. Illustrated by Alice Barber Stevens. New York: Charles Scribner's Sons, 1907. 426pp.

687.   London, Jack. *The Iron Heel*. New York: Grosset and Dunlap, 1907. 354pp.

694.   Lovett, Robert Morss. *A Wingéd Victory*. New York: Duffield, 1907. 431pp.

880.   Phillips, David Graham. *The Second Generation*. New York: Appleton, 1907.

909.   Quick, Herbert. *The Broken Lance*. Illustrated by C. D. Williams. Indianapolis: Bobbs-Merrill, 1907. 546pp.

934.   Read, Opie. *The Bandit's Sweetheart*. Chicago: Thompson and Thomas, 1907. 225pp.

1081.   Teller, Charlotte. *The Cage*. New York: David Appleton, 1907. 340pp.

199.   Chandler, St. Lawrence, Marquis of Eckersley. *A Human Note*. Illustrated by Jay LaBrun Jenkins. Kansas City, Mo.: Hudson Press, 1908. 208pp.

345.   Eddy, Arthur Jerome. *Ganton & Co.; A Story of Chicago Commercial and Social Life*. Chicago: McClurg, 1908. 415pp.

847.   Patterson, Joseph Medill. *Little Brother of the Rich*. Chicago: Reilly, Britton, 1908. 361pp.

897.   Potter, Margaret Horton Black. *The Golden Ladder*. New York: Harper and Brothers, 1908. 434pp.

1145.   Warren, Maude Radford. *The Land of the Living*. New York: Harper and Brothers, 1908. 314pp.

135.   Brower, James Hattan. *The Mills of Mammon*. Illustrated by F. L. Weitzel and Henderson Howk. Joliet, Ill.: Murray, 1909. 491pp.

481.   Glaspell, Susan. *The Glory of the Conquered: The Story of a Great Love*. New York: Frederick A. Stokes, 1909. 376pp.

520.   Hapgood, Hutchins. *An Anarchist Woman*. New York: Duffield, 1909. 308pp.

521.   Harris, Frank. *The Bomb*. New York: Mitchell Kennerley, 1909. 312pp.

759.   Merwin, Bannister. *The Girl and the Bill*. Illustrated by Troy Kinney, Margaret West Kinney, and Harrison Fisher. New York: Dodd, Mead, 1909. 371pp.

851.   Payne, Will. *The Automatic Capitalists*. Illustrated by Leslie L. Benson. Boston: Richard G. Badger, Gorham Press, 1909. 150pp.

1150.   Washburne, Marion Foster. *The House on the North Shore*. Illustrated by Walter J. Enright and Maginel Wright Barney. Chicago: McClurg, 1909. 287pp.

1222.   Yates, Katherine M. *Chet*. Illustrated by H. S. DeLay. Chicago: McClurg, 1909. 345pp.

84.   Balmer, Edwin and William Briggs MacHarg. *The Achievements of Luther Trant*. Illustrated by William Oberhardt. Boston: Small, Maynard, 1910. 365pp.

197.   Chance, Frank L. *The Bride and the Pennant; The Greatest Story in the History of America's National Game, True to Life—Intensely Interesting*. Preface by Charles A. Comiskey. Chicago: Laird and Lee, Publishers, 1910. 182pp.

233.   Cooke, Marjorie Benton. *The Girl Who Lived in the Woods*. Illustrated by Margaret West Kinney and Troy Kinney. Chicago: McClurg, 1910. 430pp.

258.   Cuppy, Will. *Maroon Tales: University of Chicago Stories*. Chicago: Forbes, 1910. 337pp.

327.   Dunne, Peter Finley. *Mr. Dooley Says*. New York: Charles Scribner's Sons, 1910. 239pp.

372.   Fairbank, Janet Ayer. *In Town, & Other Conversations*. Illustrated by Rebecca Kruttschnitt. Cover Design by J. O. Smith. Chicago: McClurg, 1910. 222pp.

574.   Jackson, Charles Tenney. *My Brother's Keeper*. Illustrated by Arthur William Brown. Indianapolis: Bobbs-Merrill, 1910. 324pp.

662.   Laughlin, Clara Elizabeth. *Just Folks*. New York: Macmillan, 1910. 377pp.

697.   Lytle, H. M. *The Tragedies of the White Slaves: True Stories of the White Slavery Taken from Actual Life; Each One Dealing with a Different Method by Which White Slaves Have Become Innocent Victims to Destruction*. Chicago: Charles C. Thompson, 1910. 193pp.

719.   Mason, Edith Huntington. *The Politician*. Illustrated by The Kinneys. Chicago: McClurg, 1910. 409pp.

853.   Payne, Will. *The Losing Game*. Illustrated by F. R. Gruger. New York: Dillingham, 1910. 352pp.

1133.   Walsh, William Thomas. *The Mirage of the Many*. New York: Henry Holt, 1910. 326pp.

1185.   Whitlock, Brand. *The Gold Brick*. New York: Hurst, 1910. 342pp.

63.   Babcock, Bernie. *With Claw and Fang; A Fact Story in a Chicago Setting*. Indianapolis: Clean Politics, 1911. 112pp.

271.   Dean, S. Ella Wood. *Love's Purple Dream*. Chicago: John Forbes, 1911. 343pp.

313.   Dreiser, Theodore. *Jennie Gerhardt*. New York: Harper and Brothers, 1911. 430pp.

735.   McConaughy, J. W. and Edward Sheldon. *The Boss*. New York: Fly, 1911. 316pp.

848.   Patterson, Joseph Medill. *Rebellion*. Illustrated by Walter Dean Goldbeck. Chicago: Reilly and Britton, 1911. 355pp.

950.   Richberg, Donald Randall. *The Shadow Men*. Chicago: Forbes, 1911. 312pp.

250.   Crane, Laura Dent. *The Automobile Girls at Chicago; or, Winning Against Heavy Odds*. Philadelphia: Henry Altemus, 1912. 254pp.

415.   Ferber, Edna. *Buttered Side Down*. New York: Frederick A. Stokes, 1912. 230pp.

474.   Gerstenberg, Alice. *Unquenched Fire*. Boston: Small, Maynard, 1912. 417pp.

563.   Hough, Emerson. *John Rawn: Prominent Citizen*. Illustrated by M. Leone Bracker. Indianapolis: Bobbs-Merrill, 1912. 385pp.

573.   Jackson, Charles Tenney. *The Midlanders*. Illustrated by Arthur William Brown. Indianapolis: Bobbs-Merrill, 1912. 386pp.

625.   Kencarden, Stuart. *A Mother of Unborn Generations*. New York: Broadway, 1912. 214pp.

663.   Laughlin, Clara Elizabeth. *The Penny Philanthropist: A Story That Could Be True*. Illustrated by Victor Semon Pérard. New York: Fleming H. Revell, 1912. 217pp.

668.   Lee, Jennette (Perry). *Mr. Achilles*. New York: Dodd, Mead, 1912. 261pp.

739.   McCutcheon, John T. *Dawson '11, Fortune Hunter*. New York: Dodd, Mead, 1912. 159pp.

775.   Montgomery, Louise. *Mrs. Mahoney of the Tenement*. Illustrated by Florence Scovel Shinn. Boston: Pilgrim Press, 1912. 168pp.

842.   Parrish, Randall. *Gordon Craig; Soldier of Fortune*. Illustrated by Alonzo Kimball. Chicago: McClurg, 1912. 366p.

948.   Richberg, Donald Randall. *In the Dark*. Chicago: Forbes, 1912. 308pp.

1052. Stein, Max. *William Bright, Captain of Commerce: A Story of Commercial Progress*. Chicago: United States Publishing House, 1912. 195pp.

66.   Baird, Edwin. *The City of Purple Dreams*. Illustrated by Craig M. Wilson. Chicago: Browne, 1913. 411pp.

332.   Durkin, James Aloysius. *The Auto Bandits of Chicago: A Correct Account of the Greatest Detective Work in the History of Chicago's Police Force*. Chicago: Charles C. Thompson, 1913. 190pp.

484.   Gleeson, William. *Vice and Virtue a Story of Our Times*. Illustrated by F. A. Gibson. Chicago: Mecklenberg, 1913. 603pp.

545.   Herrick, Robert. *One Woman's Life*. New York: Macmillan, 1913. 405pp.

702.   MacHarg, William Briggs and Edwin Balmer. *The Surakarta*. Illustrated by Lester Ralph. Boston: Small, Maynard, 1913. 369pp.

845.   Patchin, Frank. *The Range and Grange Hustlers at Chicago; or, The Conspiracy of the Wheat Pit*. Philadelphia: Altemus, 1913. 249pp.

860.   Pearce, John Irving. *The Strange Case of Eric Marotté: A Modern Historical Problem-Romance of Chicago*. Illustrated by Carle J. Blenner and Norman Tolson. Chicago: Pettibone, 1913. 366pp.

1146.   Warren, Maude Radford. *The Main Road*. New York: Harper and Brothers, 1913. 390pp.

316.   Dreiser, Theodore. *The Titan*. New York: Boni and Liveright, 1914. 551pp.

808.   O'Brien, Howard Vincent. *New Men for Old*. New York: Mitchell Kennerley, 1914. 320pp.

863.   Peattie, Elia Wilkinson. *The Precipice*. Illustrated by Howard E. Smith. Boston: Houghton Mifflin, 1914. 417pp.

194.   Cather, Willa. *The Song of the Lark*. Boston: Houghton Mifflin, Riverside Press, 1915. 490pp.

312.   Dreiser, Theodore. *The Genius*. New York: John Lane, 1915.

483.   Gleeson, William. *Can Such Things Be: A Story of a White Slave*. Chicago: The Author, 1915. 325pp.

862.   Peattie, Elia Wilkinson. *Lotta Embury's Career*. Boston: Houghton Mifflin, Riverside Press, 1915. 214pp.

1172.   Weir, Hugh C. *The Young Wheat Scout; Being the Story of the Growth, Harvesting, and Distribution of the Great Wheat Crop of the United States*. Illustrated by Frank T. Merrill. Chicago: Wilde, 1915. 288pp.

36.   Anderson, Sherwood. *Windy McPherson's Son*. New York: John Lane, 1916. 347pp.

164.   Burnham, Clara Louise. *Instead of the Thorn*. Boston: Houghton Mifflin, Riverside Press Cambridge, 1916. 390pp.

168.   Burroughs, Edgar Rice. *The Girl from Farris's*. Originally published in *All-Story Magazine* (Frank A. Munsey, 1916). Kansas City, Mo.: House of Greystoke, 1965. 160pp.

235.   Corbett, Elizabeth. *Cecily and the Wide World: A Novel of American Life Today*. New York: Henry Holt, 1916. 344pp.

643.   Lait, Jack. *Beef Iron and Wine*. Garden City, New York: Doubleday, Page, 1916. 316pp.

679.   Lewis, Edwin Herbert. *Those About Trench*. New York: Macmillan, 1916. 326pp.

700.   MacHarg, William Briggs and Edwin Balmer. *The Blind Man's Eyes*. Illustrated by Wilson C. Dexter. New York: Burt, 1916. 367pp.

1043.   Stahl, John M. *Just Stories*. Chicago: Donohue, 1916. 156pp.

1098.   Tobenkin, Elias. *Witte Arrives*. New York: Frederick A. Stokes, 1916. 304pp.

1166.   Webster, Henry Kitchell. *The Painted Scene*. Indianapolis: Bobbs-Merrill, 1916. 400pp.

1168.   ———. *The Real Adventure: A Novel*. Illustrated by R. M. Crosby. Indianapolis: Bobbs-Merrill, 1916. 574pp.

14.   Adler, Katherine Keith. *The Girl*. New York: Henry Holt, 1917. 251pp.

35.   Anderson, Sherwood. *Marching Men*. New York: John Lane, 1917. 314pp.

61.   Atkinson, Eleanor. *Hearts Undaunted: A Romance of Four Frontiers*. New York: Harper, 1917. 354pp.

417.   Ferber, Edna. *Fanny Herself*. Illustrated by J. Henry. New York: Frederick A. Stokes, 1917. 323pp.

564.   Hough, Emerson. *The Man Next Door*. New York: David Appleton, 1917. 309pp.

644.   Lait, Jack. *Gus the Bus and Evelyn, the Exquisite Checker*. Garden City, N.Y.: Doubleday, Page, 1917. 342pp.

653.   Lardner, Ring. *Gullible's Travels*. Illustrated by May Wilson Preston. Indianapolis: Bobbs-Merrill, 1917. 255pp.

701.   MacHarg, William Briggs and Edwin Balmer. *The Indian Drum*. New York: Grosset and Dunlap, 1917. 367pp.

763.   Merwin, Samuel. *Temperamental Henry: An Episodic History of the Early Life and the Young Loves of Henry Calverly, 3rd*. Illustrated by Stockton Mulford. Indianapolis: Bobbs-Merrill, 1917. 382pp.

994.   Seely, Herman Gastrell. *A Son of the City: A Story of Boy Life*. Illustrated by Fred J. Arting. Chicago: McClurg, 1917. 341pp.

1170.   Webster, Henry Kitchell. *The Thoroughbred*. Indianapolis: Bobbs-Merrill, 1917. 257pp.

416.   Ferber, Edna. *Cheerful, by Request*. Garden City, N.Y.: Doubleday, Page, 1918. 366pp.

459.   Fuller, Henry Blake. *On the Stairs*. Boston: Houghton Mifflin, Riverside Press, 1918. 265pp.

465.   Gale, Zona. *Birth*. New York: Macmillan, 1918. 402pp.

761.   Merwin, Samuel. *Henry Is Twenty: A Further Episodic History of Henry Calverly 3rd*. Illustrated by Stockton Mulford. Indianapolis: Bobbs-Merrill, 1918. 385pp.

1159.   Webster, Henry Kitchell. *An American Family: A Novel of Today*. Indianapolis: Bobbs-Merrill, 1918. 452pp.

81.   Balmer, Edwin. *Ruth of the U. S. A.* Illustrated by Harold H. Betts. Chicago: McClurg, 1919. 361pp.

127.   Bradley, Mary Hastings. *The Wine of Astonishment*. New York: David Appleton, 1919. 312pp.

326.   Dunne, Finley Peter. *Mr. Dooley on Making a Will and Other Necessary Evils*. New York: Charles Scribner's Sons, 1919. 221pp.

454.   Fuessle, Newton A. (Newton Augustus). *The Flail*. New York: Moffat, Yard, 1919. 328pp.

456.   Fuller, Henry Blake. *Bertram Cope's Year*. Chicago: Aldenbrink Press, 1919. 314pp.

655.   Lardner, Ring. *Own Your Own Home*. Illustrated by Fontaine Fox. Indianapolis: Bobbs-Merrill, 1919. 123pp.

762.   Merwin, Samuel. *The Passionate Pilgrim, Being the Narrative of an Oddly Dramatic Year in the Life of Henry Calverly, 3rd*. Indianapolis: Bobbs-Merrill, 1919. 403pp.

1019.   Smith, Henry Justin. *The Other Side of the Wall*. Illustrated by Clinton Pettee. Garden City, N.Y.: Doubleday, Page, 1919. 342pp.

1059.   Stewart, Charles D. *Buck; Being Some Account of His Rise in the Great City of Chicago*. Illustrated by R. M. Brinkerhoff. Boston: Houghton Mifflin, Riverside Press, 1919. 298pp.

1137.   Ward, Florence Jeannette. *The Singing Heart*. New York: James A. McCann, 1919. 308pp.

80.   Balmer, Edwin. *Resurrection Rock*. New York: Grosset and Dunlap, 1920. 383pp.

119.   Borden, Mary. *The Romantic Woman*. New York: Alfred A. Knopf, 1920. 347pp.

274.   Dell, Floyd. *Moon-Calf*. New York: Alfred A. Knopf, 1920. 394pp.

420. Ferber, Edna. *Half Portions*. Garden City, N.Y.: Doubleday, Page, 1920. 315pp.

688. Loose, Harry J. *The Shamus: A True Tale of Thiefdom and an Exposé of the Real System in Crime*. Boston: Christopher Publishing House, 1920. 296pp.

858. Payne, Will. *The Scarred Chin*. New York: Dodd, Mead, 1920. 310pp.

1062. Straus, Ralph. *Pengard Awake*. New York: David Appleton, 1920. 299pp.

1165. Webster, Henry Kitchell. *Mary Wollaston*. New York: Burt, 1920. 372pp.

1198. Williams, Wilbur Herschel. *The Merrymakers in Chicago and Their Adventures in That Great City*. Illustrated by Frank Thayer Merrill. Boston: Page, 1920. 321pp.

1921–1950

167. Burroughs, Edgar Rice. *The Efficiency Expert*. Originally published in *Argosy All-Story Weekly*, October 8 through October 29, 1921. Kansas City, Mo.: House of Greystoke, 1966. 84pp.

272. Dell, Floyd. *The Briary-Bush*. New York: Alfred A. Knopf, 1921. 425pp.

419. Ferber, Edna. *The Girls*. New York: Grosset and Dunlap, 1921. 374pp.

455. Fuessle, Newton A. (Newton Augustus). *Gold Shod*. New York: Boni and Liveright, 1921. 243pp.

528. Hecht, Ben. *Erik Dorn*. New York: Putnam's Sons, 1921. 409pp.

558. Holt, Isabella. *The Marriotts and the Powells: A Tribal Chronicle*. New York: Macmillan, 1921. 328pp.

740. McCutcheon, John T. *The Restless Age*. Illustrated by the Author. Indianapolis: Bobbs-Merrill, 1921. 218pp.

1088. Thorne, Paul and Mabel Thorne. *The Sheridan Road Mystery*. New York: Dodd, Mead, 1921. 291pp.

1136. Ward, Florence Jeannette Baier. *Phyllis Anne*. New York: James A. McCann, 1921. 245pp.

82. Balmer, Edwin. *That Breath of Scandal*. Boston: Little, Brown. 1922. 360pp.

418. Ferber, Edna. *Gigolo*. Garden City, N.Y.: Doubleday, Page, 1922. 291pp.

529. Hecht, Ben. *Gargoyles*. New York: Boni and Liveright, 1922. 346pp.

531.   Hecht, Ben. *A Thousand and One Afternoons in Chicago.* Design and illustrated by Herman Rosse. Chicago: Covici-McGee, 1922. 289pp.

699.   MacHarg, William Briggs. *Peewee.* Chicago: Reilly and Lee, 1922. 276pp

721.   Masters, Edgar Lee. *Children of the Market Place.* New York: Macmillan, 1922. 469pp.

760.   Merwin, Samuel. *Goldie Green.* Indianapolis: Bobbs-Merrill, 1922. 341pp.

841.   Parrish, Randall. *The Case and the Girl.* New York: Alfred A. Knopf, 1922. 343pp.

949.   Richberg, Donald Randall. *A Man of Purpose.* New York: Thomas Y. Crowell, 1922. 329pp.

997.   Shane, Margaret Woodward Smith [Woodward Boyd, pseud.]. *The Love Legend.* New York: Charles Scribner's Sons, 1922. 329pp.

1018.   Smith, Henry Justin. *Deadlines: Being the Quaint, the Amusing, the Tragic Memoirs of a News-Room.* Chicago: Covici-McGee, 1922. 249pp.

1087.   Thorne, Paul and Mabel Thorne. *The Secret Toll.* New York: Dodd, Mead, 1922. 268pp.

1097.   Tobenkin, Elias. *The Road.* New York: Harcourt, Brace, 1922. 316pp.

1158.   Weaver, John Van Alstyne. *Margey Wins the Game.* New York: Alfred A. Knopf, 1922. 110pp.

1164.   Webster, Henry Kitchell. *Joseph Greer and His Daughter.* Indianapolis: Bobbs-Merrill, 1922. 489pp.

50.   Anonymous. *Grey Towers, A Campus Novel.* Chicago: Covici-McGee, 1923. 287pp.

79.   Balmer, Edwin. *Keeban.* Boston: Little, Brown, 1923. 295pp.

113.   Bodenheim, Maxwell. *Blackguard.* Chicago: Covici-McGee, 1923. 215pp.

122.   Boyce, Neith. *Proud Lady.* New York: Alfred A. Knopf, 1923. 316pp.

542.   Herrick, Robert. *Homely Lilla.* New York: Harcourt, Brace, 1923. 293pp.

567.   Hudson, Jay William. *Nowhere Else in the World.* New York: David Appleton, 1923. 383pp.

723.   Masters, Edgar Lee. *Nuptial Flight.* New York: Boni and Liveright, 1923. 376pp.

724.   ———. *Skeeters Kirby.* New York: Macmillan, 1923. 394pp.

778.   Montross, Lynn and Lois Montross. *Town and Gown*. New York: George H. Doran, 1923. 283pp.

809.   O'Brien, Howard Vincent. *The Terms of Conquest*. Boston: Little, Brown, 1923. 357pp.

810.   O'Brien, Howard Vincent [Clyde Perrin, pseud.]. *The Thunderbolt*. Chicago: McClurg, 1923. 283pp.

996.   Shane, Margaret Woodward Smith [Woodward Boyd, pseud.]. *Lazy Laughter*. New York: Charles Scribner's Sons, 1923. 295pp.

1203. Wilson, Margaret. *The Able McLaughlins*. New York: Harper and Brothers 1923. 262pp.

1218. Wyatt, Edith Franklin. *The Invisible Gods*. New York: Harper and Brothers, 1923. 433pp.

77.   Balmer, Edwin. *Fidelia*. New York: Dodd, Mead, 1924. 368pp.

423.   Ferber, Edna. *So Big*. Garden City, N.Y.: Doubleday, Page, 1924. 360pp.

530.   Hecht, Ben. *Humpty Dumpty*. New York: Boni and Liveright, 1924. 383pp.

546.   Herrick, Robert. *Waste*. New York: Harcourt, Brace, 1924. 449pp.

722.   Masters, Edgar Lee. *Mirage*. New York: Boni and Liveright, 1924. 427pp.

807.   O'Brien, Howard Vincent [Clyde Perrin, pseud.]. *The Green Scarf: A Business Romance Having to Do with a Man Who Is Determined to Win Success without the Help of Wealth or Family Prestige*. Chicago: McClurg, Donohue, 1924. 323pp.

881.   Pickard, William John. *A Spider Phaeton and Other Stories*. Chicago: Will Ransom, 1924. 163pp.

1021. Smith. Henry Justin. *The Story of an Incorrigible Dreamer*. Chicago: Covici-McGee, 1924. 252pp.

1047. Starrett, Vincent. *Coffins for Two*. Chicago: Covici-McGee, 1924. 242pp.

1135. Ward, Florence Jeannette Baier. *The Flame of Happiness*. Philadelphia: George W. Jacobs, 1924. 357pp.

1163. Webster, Henry Kitchell. *The Innocents*. Indianapolis: Bobbs-Merrill, 1924. 345pp.

1179. Wentworth, Edward Chichester. *The Education of Ernest Wilmerding; A Story of Opening Flowers*. Chicago: Covici-McGee, 1924. 268pp.

83.   Balmer, Edwin. *That Royle Girl*. New York: Dodd, Mead, 1925. 358pp.

226.   Collins, Charles. *The Sins of Saint Anthony; Tales of the Theatre.* Introduction by Henry Kitchell Webster. Chicago: Covici, 1925. 265pp.

304.   Donovan, Cornelius Francis (Rev.). *The Left Hander.* Chicago: Meier, 1925. 301pp.

373.   Fairbank, Janet Ayer. *The Smiths.* Indianapolis: Bobbs-Merrill, 1925. 433pp.

654.   Lardner, Ring. *You Know Me Al: A Busher's Letters.* New York: Scribner, 1925. 247pp.

777.   Montross, Lynn. *East of Eden.* New York: Harper and Brothers, 1925. 299pp.

811.   O'Brien, Howard Vincent. *What a Man Wants.* Garden City, N.Y.: Doubleday, Page, 1925. 344pp.

954.   Riesenberg, Felix. *P.A.L.: A Novel of the American Scene.* New York: Robert M. McBride, 1925. 340pp

1095. Tobenkin, Elias. *God of Might.* New York: Minton, Balch, 1925. 272pp.

117.   Booth, Christopher B. *Mr. Clackworthy.* New York: Chelsea House, 1926. 255pp.

225.   Cohen, Lester. *Sweepings.* New York: Boni and Liveright, 1926. 447pp.

241.   Correll, Charles J. and Freeman F. Gosden. *Sam 'N' Henry.* Illustrated by Samuel Jay Smith. Chicago: Shrewesbury, 1926. 189pp.

422.   Ferber, Edna. *Show Boat.* Garden City, N.Y.: Doubleday, Page, 1926. 303pp.

503.   Gunther, John. *The Red Pavilion.* New York: Harper and Brothers 1926. 269pp.

526.   Hecht, Ben. *Broken Necks, Containing More "1001 Afternoons."* Chicago: Pascal Covici, Publisher, 1926. 344pp.

527.   ———. *Count Bruga.* New York: Boni and Liveright, 1926. 319pp.

539.   Herrick, Robert. *Chimes.* New York: Macmillan, 1926. 310pp.

1063. Street, Ada and Julian Street. *Tides.* Garden City, N.Y.: Doubleday, Page, 1926. 412pp.

1071. Sturm, Justin. *The Bad Samaritan.* New York: Harper and Brothers, 1926. 222pp.

1205. Winslow, Thyra Samter. *Show Business.* New York: Alfred A. Knopf, 1926. 321pp.

75.   Balmer, Edwin. *Dangerous Business.* New York: Burt, 1927. 279pp.

78.   ———. *Flying Death.* New York: Dodd, Mead, 1927. 198pp.

173.   Cahill, Holger. *Profane Earth*. New York: Macaulay, 1927. 383pp.

224.   Cohen, Lester. *The Great Bear*. New York: Boni and Liveright, 1927. 357pp.

275.   Dell, Floyd. *An Unmarried Father*. New York: George H. Doran, 1927. 301pp.

410.   Farson, Negley. *Daphne's In Love*. New York: Century, 1927. 309pp.

601.   Keeler, Henry Stephen. *Find the Clock: A Detective Mystery of Newspaper Life*. New York: Dutton, 1927. 338pp.

717.   Marshall, James. *Ordeal by Glory*. New York: Robert M. McBride, 1927. 288pp.

839.   Paradise, Viola. *The Pacer*. New York: Dutton, 1927. 278pp.

956.   River, W. L. (Walter, Leslie). *Death of a Young Man*. New York: Simon and Schuster, 1927. 206pp.

998.   Shane, Margaret Woodward Smith [Woodward Boyd, pseud.]. *The Unpaid Piper*. New York: Charles Scribner's Sons, 1927. 330pp.

1027.   Smith, Wallace. *Are You Decent?* New York: Putnam's Sons, Knickerbocker Press, 1927. 314pp.

1079.   Taylor, Ellen DuPois. *One Crystal and a Mother*. New York: Harper and Brothers, 1927. 325pp.

1147.   Warren, Maude Radford. *Never Give All*. Indianapolis: Bobbs-Merrill, 1927. 322pp.

1161.   Webster, Henry Kitchell. *The Beginners*. Indianapolis: Bobbs-Merrill, 1927. 308pp.

1167.   ————. *Philopena*. Indianapolis: Bobbs-Merrill, 1927. 319pp.

4.   Ade, George. *Bang! Bang!* New York: Sears, 1928. 147pp.

89.   Barnes, Margaret Ayer. *Prevailing Winds*. Boston: Houghton Mifflin, Riverside Press, 1928. 298pp.

452.   Friend, Oscar J. [Owen Fox Jerome, pseud.]. *The Red Kite Clue*. New York: Edward J. Clode, 1928. 303pp.

486.   Goetzinger, Clara Palmer. *Smoldering Flames; Adventures and Emotions of a Flapper*. Chicago: Zuriel, 1928. 314pp.

575.   Jackson, Margaret Weymouth. *Beggars Can Choose*. Indianapolis: Bobbs-Merrill, 1928. 319pp.

585.   Judson, Clara Ingram. *Alice Ann*. Illustrated by John M. Foster. Newark, N.J.: Barse, 1928. 300pp.

589.   Kantor, MacKinlay. *Diversey*. New York: Coward-McCann, 1928. 345pp.

614.   Keeler, Harry Stephen. *Sing Sing Nights*. New York: Dutton, 1928. 397pp.

618.   ———. *The Voice of the Seven Sparrows*. New York: Dutton, 1928. 304pp.

657.   Larsen, Nella. *Quicksand*. New York: Alfred A. Knopf, 1928. 301pp.

846.   Patterson, Eleanor Medill [aka Eleanor Gizycka]. *Fall Flight*. New York: Minton, Balch, 1928. 277pp.

955.   Riesenberg, Felix. *Red Horses*. New York: Robert M. McBride, 1928. 336pp.

1000.   Shenton, Edward. *Lean Twilight*. New York: Charles Scribner's Sons, 1928. 291pp.

1086.   Thorne, Paul. *Spiderweb Clues*. Philadelphia: Penn, 1928. 304pp.

100.   Bein, Albert [Charles Walt, pseud.]. *Love in Chicago*. New York: Harcourt, Brace, 1929. 254pp.

108.   Blake, Emily Calvin. *The Third Weaver*. Chicago: Willett, Clark and Colby, 1929. 252pp.

115.   Bodenheim, Maxwell. *Sixty Seconds*. New York: Horace Liveright, 1929. 280pp.

161.   Burnett, W. R. (William Riley). *Little Caesar*. New York: Dial Press, 1929. 308pp.

181.   Cary, Lucian. *The Duke Steps Out*. Garden City, N.Y.: Doubleday, Doran, 1929. 288pp.

185.   Casey, Robert J. (Robert Joseph). *The Secret of 37 Hardy Street*. Indianapolis: Bobbs-Merrill, 1929. 322pp.

192.   Caspary, Vera. *The White Girl*. New York: Sears, 1929. 305pp.

200.   Channon, Henry. *Joan Kennedy*. New York: Dutton, 1929. 255pp.

309.   Drago, Harry Sinclair and Edmund Goulding. *The Trespasser*. Photographic illustrations. New York: Burt, 1929. 268pp.

395.   Farrell, James T. (James Thomas). *New Year's Eve, 1929*. New York: Smith, 1967. 144pp.

411.   Farson, Negley. *Fugitive Love*. New York: Century, 1929. 267pp.

502.   Gunther, John. *The Golden Fleece*. New York: Harper and Brothers, 1929. 421pp.

616.   Keeler, Harry Stephen. *The Spectacles of Mr. Cagliostro*. London, U.K.: Hutchinson, 1929. 384pp.

617.   ———. *Thieves' Nights, the Chronicles of De Lancey, King of Thieves*. New York: Dutton, 1929. 321pp.

638.   Komroff, Manuel. *Coronet*. 2 vols. New York: Coward McCann, 1929. 677pp.

656.   Larsen, Nella. *Passing*. New York: Alfred A. Knopf, 1929. 215pp.

677.   Levin, Meyer. *Reporter*. New York: John Day, 1929. 409pp.

1009.   Smalley, Dave E. *Stumbling*. Newark, N.J.: Barse, 1929. 308pp.

1020.   Smith, Henry Justin. *Poor Devil*. New York: Covici Friede, 1929. 281pp.

1074.   Synon, Mary. *The Good Red Bricks*. Boston: Little, Brown, 1929. 287pp.

1085.   Thorne, Paul. *Murder in the Fog*. Philadelphia: Penn, 1929. 307pp.

1169.   Webster, Henry Kitchell. *The Sealed Trunk*. Indianapolis: Bobbs-Merrill, 1929. 319pp.

1200.   Williams, Kirby. *The C. V. C. Murders*. Garden City, N.Y.: Crime Club / Doubleday, Doran, 1929. 323pp.

13.   Adler, Katherine Keith. *The Crystal Icicle*. New York: Harcourt Brace, 1930. 287pp.

40.   Andrews, Robert Hardy. *One Girl Found: A Sequel to "Three Girls Lost."* New York: Grosset and Dunlap, 1930. 246pp.

43.   Andrews, Robert Hardy. *Three Girls Lost*. New York: Grosset and Dunlap, 1930. 284pp.

92.   Barnes, Margaret Ayer. *Years of Grace*. Boston: Houghton Mifflin, 1930. 581pp.

116.   Bodenheim, Maxwell. *A Virtuous Girl*. New York: Horace Liveright, 1930. 260pp.

160.   Burnett, W. R. (William Riley). *Iron Man*. New York: Lincoln MacVeagh, Dial Press, 1930. 312pp.

178.   Carroll, Loren. *Wild Onion*. New York: Grosset and Dunlap, 1930. 312pp.

184.   Casey, Robert J. (Robert Joseph). *The Secret of the Bungalow*. Indianapolis: Bobbs-Merrill, 1930. 304pp.

186.   Casey, Robert J. (Robert Joseph). *The Voice of the Lobster*. Indianapolis: Bobbs-Merrill, 1930. 306pp.

189.   Caspary, Vera. *Music in the Street*. New York: Grosset and Dunlap, 1930. 306pp.

234.   Coons, Maurice [Armitage Trail, pseud.]. *Scarface*. New York: Clode, 1930. 286pp.

458.   Fuller, Henry Blake. *Not on the Screen*. New York: Alfred A. Knopf, 1930. 276pp.

569.   Hughes, Langston. *Not Without Laughter*. New York: Alfred A. Knopf, 1930. 324pp.

590.   Kantor, MacKinlay. *El Goes South*. New York: Coward-McCann, 1930. 297pp.

593.   Keeler, Harry Stephen. *The Amazing Web*. New York: Dutton, 1930. 320pp.

604.   ———. *The Fourth King*. New York: Dutton, 1930. 317pp.

605.   ———. *The Green Jade Hand: In Which a New and Quite Different Type of Detective Unravels a Mystery Staged in Chicago, Bagdad on the Lakes, London of the West*. New York: Dutton, 1930. 327pp.

612.   ———. *The Riddle of the Yellow Zuri, A Mystery Novel*. A Dutton Clue Mystery. New York: Dutton, 1930. 294pp.

645.   Lait, Jack. *Put on the Spot*. New York: Grosset and Dunlap, 1930. 212pp.

674.   Levin, Meyer. *Frankie and Johnnie*. New York: John Day, 1930. 212pp.

806.   O'Brien, Howard Vincent. *An Abandoned Woman*. Garden City, N.Y.: Doubleday, Doran, 1930. 310pp.

889.   Plum, Mary. *The Killing of Judge MacFarlane*. New York: Harper and Brothers 1930. 292pp.

926.   Raymond, Clifford. *The Men on the Dead Man's Chest*. Indianapolis: Bobbs-Merrill, 1930. 255pp.

941.   Reilly, Patricia and Harold N. Swanson [Anna Bell Ward, pseud.]. *Big Business Girl: By One of Them*. Chicago: Burt, 1930. 278pp.

960.   Roberts, John Hawley. *Narcissus*. New York: Sears, 1930. 301pp.

1045.   Starrett, Vincent. *The Blue Door: Murder-Mystery-Detection in Ten Thrill Packed Novelettes*. Garden City, N.Y.: Crime Club / Doubleday, Doran, 1930. 345pp.

1066.   Strobel, Marion. *Saturday Afternoon*. New York: Farrar and Rinehart, 1930. 279pp.

1080.   Taylor, Marie E. *Just Boys and Girls of Dear Old Chicago.* Boston: Christopher Pub. House, 1930. 143pp.

1183.   White, Betty. *I Lived This Story.* Garden City, N.Y.: Doubleday, Doran, 1930. 308pp.

1210.   Woolfolk, Josiah Pitts [Jack Woodford, pseud.]. *Sin and Such.* New York: Panurge Press, 1930. 281pp.

1212.   Wren, Percival Christopher. *Mysterious Waye: The Story of "The Unsetting Sun."* New York: Frederick A. Stokes, 1930. 351pp.

1.   Abson, Ben J. *On to the White House.* Chicago: True Truth, 1931. 188pp.

42.   Andrews, Robert Hardy. *The Stolen Husband, a Chicago Novel.* New York: Grosset and Dunlap, 1931. 238pp.

44.   ———. *Windfall: A Novel About Ten Million Dollars.* New York: John Day, 1931. 280pp.

114.   Bodenheim, Maxwell. *Duke Herring.* New York: Horace Liveright, 1931. 242pp.

153.   Bryant, James McKinley. *Sporting Youth.* New York: Alfred H. King, 1931. 287pp.

163.   Burnett, W. R. (William Riley). *The Silver Eagle.* New York: Lincoln MacVeagh, Dial Press, 1931. 310pp.

166.   Burnham, David. *This Our Exile.* New York: Charles Scribner's Sons, 1931. 423pp.

201.   Channon, Henry *Paradise City.* New York: Dutton, 1931. 246pp.

268.   Davis, George. *The Opening of a Door.* New York: Harper and Brothers, 1931. 265pp.

273.   Dell, Floyd. *Love Without Money.* New York: Farrar and Rinehart, 1931. 365pp.

310.   Drago, Harry Sinclair. *Women to Love: A Romance of the Underworld.* New York: Amour Press, 1931. 251pp.

451.   Friend, Oscar J. [Owen Fox Jerome, pseud.]. *The Murder at Avalon Arms.* New York: Edward J. Clode, 1931. 309pp.

480.   Glasmon, Kubec and John Bright. *The Public Enemy.* New York: Grosset and Dunlap, 1931. 280pp.

608.   Keeler, Harry Stephen. *The Matilda Hunter Murder.* New York: Dutton, 1931. 741pp.

695. Lucas, Cleo. *I Jerry Take Thee Joan*. Garden City, N.Y.: Doubleday, Doran, 1931. 297pp.

715. Marion, Frances. *The Secret Six*. New York: Grosset, 1931. 129pp.

743. McEvoy, Joseph Patrick. *Mister Noodle: An Extravaganza*. New York: Simon and Schuster, 1931. 186pp.

903. Pratt, Mrs. Eleanor Blake Atkinson [aka Eleanor Blake]. *The Jade Green Cats*. New York: Robert M. McBride, 1931. 244pp.

927. Raymond, Clifford. *Our Very Best People*. Indianapolis: Bobbs-Merrill, 1931. 313pp.

979. Russell, Ruth. *Lake Front*. Chicago: Thomas S. Rockwell, 1931. 291pp.

1048. Starrett, Vincent. *Dead Man Inside*. Garden City, N.Y.: Crime Club / Doubleday, Doran, 1931. 310pp.

1049. ———. *The End of Mr. Garment*. Garden City, N.Y.: Crime Club / Doubleday, Doran, 1931. 310pp.

1068. Strobel, Marion. *A Woman of Fashion*. New York: Farrar and Rinehart, 1931. 331pp.

1096. Tobenkin, Elias. *In the Dark*. Garden City, N.Y.: Doubleday, Doran, 1931. 311pp.

1107. Tully, Jim. *Blood on the Moon*. New York: Coward-McCann, 1931. 350pp.

1131. Wallace, Edgar. *On the Spot*. Garden City, N.Y.: Crime Club / Doubleday, Doran, 1931. 313pp.

1134. Walz, Audrey Boyers [Francis Bonnamy, pseud.]. *Death by Appointment*. Front Page Mysteries, Fourth Series. New York: Collier and Son, 1931. 317pp.

1171. Webster, Henry Kitchell. *Who Is the Next?* Indianapolis: Bobbs-Merrill, 1931. 310pp.

191. Caspary, Vera. *Thicker Than Water*. New York: Grosset and Dunlap, 1932. 426pp.

366. Essipoff, Marie Armstrong. *My First Husband*. New York: Greenberg, 1932. 308pp.

408. Farrell, James T. (James Thomas). *Young Lonigan: A Boyhood in Chicago Streets*. New York: Vanguard Press, 1932. 308pp.

595. Keeler, Harry Stephen. *The Box from Japan*. New York: Dutton, 1932. 765pp.

642. Lait, Jack. *The Beast of the City*. New York: Grosset and Dunlap, 1932. 218pp.

793.   Nearing, Scott. *Free Born, An Unpublishable Novel*. New York: Urquhart Press, 1932. 237pp.

990.   Schultz, Alan Brener. *The Rise of Elsa Potter*. New York: Simon and Schuster, 1932. 270pp.

1111.   Tuthill, Jack. *Sideshows of a Big City Tales of Yesterday and Today*. Chicago: Kenfield-Leach, 1932. 275pp.

1138.   Ward, Florence Jeannette Baier. *Wild Wine*. Philadelphia: Macrae-Smith, 1932. 318pp.

1177.   Welton, Arthur D. *The Twenty-Seventh Ride*. New York: Sears, 1932. 307pp.

1208.   Woolfolk, Josiah Pitts [Jack Woodford, pseud.]. *Find the Motive*. New York: Ray Long and Richard R. Smith, 1932. 280pp.

18.   Aldis, Dorothy. *The Magic City: John & Jane at the World's Fair*. New York: Minton, Balch & Company, 1933. 95pp.

59.   Ashenhurst, John M. *The World's Fair Murders*. Boston: Houghton Mifflin, 1933. 256pp.

91.   Barnes, Margaret Ayer. *Within This Present*. Boston: Houghton Mifflin, 1933. 611pp.

125.   Bradley, Mary Hastings. *Old Chicago*. Illustrated by Edward C. Caswell. 4 vols. New York: David Appleton, 1933.

159.   Burnett, W. R. (William Riley). *Dark Hazard*. New York: Harper and Brothers, 1933. 295pp.

183.   Casey, Robert J. (Robert Joseph). *Hot Ice*. Indianapolis: Bobbs-Merrill, 1933. 309pp.

336.   Eberhart, Mignon Good. *The Dark Garden*. Garden City, N.Y.: Crime Club / Doubleday, Doran, 1933. 312pp.

387.   Farrell, James T. (James Thomas). *Gas-House McGinty*. New York: Vanguard Press, 1933. 364pp.

576.   Jackson, Margaret Weymouth. *Sarah Thornton*. Indianapolis: Bobbs-Merrill, 1933. 310pp.

600.   Keeler, Harry Stephen. *The Face of the Man from Saturn*. New York: Dutton, 1933. 254pp.

619.   ———. *The Washington Square Enigma, A Mystery Novel*. New York: Dutton, 1933. 247pp.

667.   Lee, Ella Dolbear. *Jean Mary Solves the Mystery*. New York: Burt, 1933. 256pp.

779.   Moody, Minnie Hite. *Once Again in Chicago*. New York: King, 1933. 268pp.

803.   North, Sterling. *Tiger*. Chicago: Reilly and Lee, 1933. 314pp.

890.   Plum, Mary. *Murder at the World's Fair*. New York: Harper and Brothers, 1933. 255pp.

1022.   Smith, Henry Justin. *Young Phillips, Reporter*. New York: Harcourt, Brace, 1933. 269pp.

1067.   Strobel, Marion. *Silvia's In Town*. New York: Farrar and Rinehart, 1933. 309pp.

1083.   Thayer, Tiffany. *One Woman*. New York: William Morrow, 1933. 435pp.

1139.   Ward, Florence Jeannette Baier. *Women May Learn*. Philadelphia: Macrae-Smith, 1933. 312pp.

1175.   Welton, Arthur D. *The Line Between*. New York: Sears, 1933. 317pp.

1176.   ———. *Mr. Weld Retires*. New York: Sears, 1933. 293pp.

1201.   Williams, Kirby. *The Opera Murders*. New York: Charles Scribner's Sons, 1933. 259pp.

76.   Balmer, Edwin. *Dragons Drive You*. New York: Dodd, Mead, 1934. 289pp.

214.   Clark, Edward C. *The Fatal Element*. New York: Empire, 1934. 304pp.

236.   Corbett, Elizabeth. *The House Across the River*. New York: Reynal and Hitchcock, 1934. 274pp.

281.   De Voto, Bernard. *We Accept with Pleasure*. Boston: Little, Brown, 1934. 471pp.

377.   Farrell, James T. (James Thomas). *Calico Shoes*. New York: Vanguard Press, 1934. 303pp.

399.   ———. *The Short Stories of James T. Farrell*. New York: Vanguard Press, 1934. 534pp.

409.   ———. *The Young Manhood of Studs Lonigan*. New York: Vanguard Press, 1934. 412pp.

511.   Halper, Albert. *The Foundry*. New York: Viking Press, 1934. 499pp.

514.   ———. *On the Shore; A Young Writer Remembering Chicago*. New York: Viking Press, 1934. 257pp.

570.   Hutchens, Paul. *Romance of Fire*. Wheaton, Ill.: Van Kampen Press, 1934. 197pp.

610.   Keeler, Harry Stephen. *The Mystery of the Fiddling Cracksman*. A Dutton Clue Mystery. New York: Dutton, 1934. 317pp.

611.   ———. *Riddle of the Traveling Skull*. New York: Dutton, 1934. 288pp.

650.   Lally, John Patrick. *Anne Herrick*. Chicago: Burt, 1934. 251pp.

1028.   Smith, Wallace. *Bessie Cotter*. New York: Covici-Friede, 1934. 309pp.

1132.   Wallis, J. H. (James Harold). *The Woman He Chose*. New York: Dutton, 1934. 314pp.

19.   Aldis, Dorothy. *Their Own Apartment*. New York: G.P. Putnam's Sons, 1935. 240pp.

29.   Algren, Nelson. *Somebody in Boots*. New York: Vanguard Press, 1935. 326pp.

88.   Barnes, Margaret Ayer. *Edna, His Wife: An American Idyll*. Boston: Houghton Mifflin, Riverside Press, 1935. 628pp.

193.   Cather, Willa. *Lucy Gayheart*. New York: Alfred A. Knopf, 1935. 231pp.

307.   Douglas, Lloyd C. *Green Light*. Boston: Houghton Mifflin, Riverside Press, 1935. 326pp.

342.   Eberhart, Good Mignon. *The House on the Roof*. Garden City, N.Y.: Doubleday, Doran, 1935. 302pp.

388.   Farrell, James T. (James Thomas). *Guillotine Party and Other Stories*. New York: Vanguard Press, 1935. 305pp.

389.   ———. *Judgment Day*. New York: Vanguard Press, 1935. 465pp.

403.   ———. *Studs Lonigan: A Trilogy*. New York: Vanguard Press, 1935. 465pp.

428.   Fisher, Vardis. *We Are Betrayed*. Garden City, N.Y.: Doubleday, Doran / Caldwell, Idaho: Caxton Printers, 1935. 369pp.

441.   Fox, Fannie Ferber. *Chocolate or Vanilla*. New York: Alfred A. Knopf, 1935. 274pp.

444.   Freeman, Martin J. *The Case of the Blind Mouse*. A Dutton Clue Mystery. New York: Dutton, 1935. 256pp.

509.   Hall, Grace Darling, and Ernesto Giuseppe Merlanti. *Honor Divided*. New York: Fleming H. Revell, 1935. 224pp.

518.   Hansen, Harry. *Your Life Lies Before You*. New York: Harcourt, Brace, 1935. 305pp.

603.   Keeler, Harry Stephen. *The Five Silver Buddhas: A Mystery Novel.* New York: Dutton, 1935. 281pp.

615.   ———. *The Skull of the Waltzing Clown.* A Dutton Clue Mystery. New York: Dutton, 1935. 247pp.

639.   Krautter, Elisa Bialk [Elisa Bialk, pseud.]. *On What Strange Stuff.* Garden City, N.Y.: Doubleday, Doran, 1935. 301pp.

658.   Latimer, Jonathan. *Headed for a Hearse.* Garden City, N.Y.: Crime Club / Doubleday, Doran, 1935. 306pp.

789.   Moyer, Clarissa Mabel Blank [Clair Blank, pseud.]. *Beverly Gray at the World's Fair.* New York: Blue Ribbon Books, 1935. 250pp.

864.   Peattie, Louise Redfield. *Fugitive.* Indianapolis: Bobbs-Merrill, 1935. 295pp.

1050.   Starrett, Vincent. *The Great Hotel Murder.* Garden City, N.Y.: Crime Club / Doubleday, Doran, 1935. 299pp.

1064.   Strobel, Marion. *Fellow Mortals.* New York: Farrar and Rinehart, 1935. 300pp.

1108.   Tully, Jim. *Ladies in the Parlor.* New York: Greenberg, 1935. 245pp.

1124.   Wagner, Constance Cassady [Constance Cassady, pseud.] and Ruth Cardwell. *Even in Laughter.* Indianapolis: Bobbs-Merrill, 1935. 359pp.

1128.   Walker, Mildred. *Light from Arcturus.* New York: Harcourt, Brace, 1935. 343pp.

1209.   Woolfolk, Josiah Pitts [Gordon Sayre, pseud.]. *Mirage of Marriage.* New York: Godwin, 1935. 286pp.

1224.   Zara Louis. *Blessed is the Man.* Indianapolis: Bobbs-Merrill, 1935. 474pp.

85.   Balmer, Edwin and Philip Wylie. *The Shield of Silence.* New York: Frederick A. Stokes, 1936. 310pp.

212.   Churchill, William Arnold [Arthur Walcott, pseud.] and William Arnold Kirschberger. *Uncertain Voyage.* New York: Atwood and Knight, 1936. 384pp.

218.   Clason, Clyde B. *The Fifth Tumbler.* Garden City, N.Y.: Crime Club / Doubleday, Doran, 1936. 303pp.

338.   Eberhart, Mignon Good. *Fair Warning.* Garden City, N.Y.: Doubleday, Doran, 1936. 304pp.

374. Fairbank, Janet Ayer. *Rich Man, Poor Man*. Boston: Houghton Mifflin, 1936. 626pp.

406. Farrell, James T. (James Thomas). *A World I Never Made*. New York: Vanguard Press, 1936. 508pp.

620. Keeler, Harry Stephen. *The Wonderful Scheme of Mr. Christopher Thorne*. New York: Dutton, 1936. 503pp.

621. ———. *X. Jones of Scotland Yard*. New York: Dutton, 1936. 448pp.

659. Latimer, Jonathan. *The Lady in the Morgue*. Garden City, N.Y.: Crime Club / Doubleday, Doran, 1936. 296pp.

681. Linn, James Weber. *This Was Life*. Indianapolis: Bobbs-Merrill, 1936. 304pp.

682. ———. *Winds Over the Campus*. Indianapolis: Bobbs-Merrill, 1936. 344pp.

704. MacQueen, James [James G. Edwards, pseud.]. *F Corridor: A New Hospital Mystery*. Garden City, N.Y.: Crime Club / Doubleday, Doran, 1936. 275pp.

1006. Sinclair, Harold. *Journey Home*. Garden City, New York: Doubleday, Doran, 1936. 290pp.

1051. Starrett, Vincent. *Midnight and Percy Jones*. New York: Covici, Friede, 1936. 256pp.

1070. Stubbins, Thomas Alva. *Not in Utter Nakedness: A Novel Depicting a Spiritual Pilgrimage*. Boston: Meador, 1936. 360pp.

1225. Zara, Louis. *Give Us This Day*. Indianapolis: Bobbs-Merrill, 1936. 422pp.

20. Aldis, Dorothy. *Time at Her Heels*. Boston: Houghton Mifflin, 1937. 236pp.

30. Allee, Marjorie Hill. *The Great Tradition*. Boston: Houghton Mifflin, 1937. 205pp.

46. Andrus, Louise. *Though Time Be Fleet*. Boston: Lothrop, Lee and Shepard, 1937. 328pp.

65. Bailey, Bernadine. *Puckered Moccasins; a Tale of Old Fort Dearborn*. Chicago: Whitman, 1937. 293pp.

126. Bradley, Mary Hastings. *Pattern of Three*. New York: David Appleton-Century, 1937. 305pp.

220. Clason, Clyde B. *The Purple Parro; A Theocritus Lucius Westborough Story*. Garden City, N.Y.: Crime Club / Doubleday, Doran, 1937. 319pp.

379.   Farrell, James T. (James Thomas). *Can all this Grandeur Perish?* New York: Vanguard Press, 1937. 308pp.

386.   ———. *Fellow Countrymen; Collected Stories.* London, U.K.: Constable, 1937. 439pp.

510.   Halper, Albert. *The Chute.* New York: Viking Press, 1937. 558pp.

609.   Keeler, Harry Stephen. *The Mysterious Mr. I.* London, U.K.: Ward, Lock, 1937. 308pp.

671.   Lengel, William Charles. *Candles in the Wind.* New York: Ives Washburn, 1937. 296pp.

676.   Levin, Meyer. *The Old Bunch.* New York: Viking Press, 1937. 964pp.

683.   Linton, Adelin Sumner Briggs [Aldin Vinton, pseud.]. *Mystery in Green.* New York: Phoenix Press, 1937. 284pp.

705.   MacQueen, James [Jay McHugh, pseud.]. *Sex Is Such Fun.* New York: Godwin, 1937. 284pp.

776.   Montross, Lois. *No Stranger to My Heart.* New York: Appleton-Century, 1937. 281pp.

978.   Russell, Charlotte Murray. *The Tiny Diamond: A Jane Amanda Edwards Story.* Garden City, N.Y.: Crime Club / Doubleday, Doran, 1937. 277pp.

1102. Trotti, Lamar, Sonya Levien, and Niven Busch. *In Old Chicago.* Beverley Hills, Calif.: Twentieth Century Fox, 1937. 263pp.

1197. Williams, Brock. *The Earl of Chicago.* New York: Grosset and Dunlap, 1937. 305pp.

1227. Zara, Louis. *Some for the Glory.* Indianapolis: Bobbs-Merrill, 1937. 569pp.

17.   Aldis, Dorothy. *All the Year Round.* Boston: Houghton Mifflin Company, Riverside Press, 1938. 245pp.

90.   Barnes, Margaret Ayer. *Wisdom's Gate.* Boston: Houghton Mifflin, 1938. 370pp.

107.   Bisno, Beatrice. *Tomorrow's Bread.* Philadelphia: Jewish Publication Society of America, 1938. 328pp.

128.   Brande, Dorothea Thompson. *My Invincible Aunt.* New York: Farrar and Rinehart, 1938. 376pp.

130.   Brinig, Myron. *May Flavin.* New York Farrar and Rinehart, 1938. 406pp.

219.   Clason, Clyde B. *The Man from Tibet.* Garden City, N.Y.: Crime Club / Doubleday, Doran, 1938. 302pp.

239. Corne, Molly E. *Death at a Masquerade*. New York: Mill, 1938. 256pp.

277. Derleth, August William. *Any Day Now*. Illustrated by Mathias Noheimer. Chicago: Normandie House, 1938. 134pp.

339. Eberhart, Mignon Good. *The Glass Slipper*. Garden City, N.Y.: Doubleday, Doran, 1938. 275pp.

341. ———. *Hasty Wedding*. Garden City, N.Y.: Doubleday, Doran, 1938. 301pp.

396. Farrell, James T. (James Thomas). *No Star Is Lost*. New York: Vanguard Press, 1938. 637pp.

523. Hart, Frank J. *The Speed Boy: A Story of the Big League*. Illustrated by Charles Copeland. Chicago: Lakewood House, 1938. 226pp.

561. Horan, Kenneth. *It's Not My Problem*. New York: Doubleday Doran, 1938. 266pp.

594. Keeler, Harry Stephen. *Behind That Mask: A Detective Novel*. New York: Dutton, 1938. 287pp.

602. ———. *Finger, Finger: A Mystery Novel*. New York: Dutton, 1938. 536pp.

736. McCord, Joseph. *The Piper's Tune*. Philadelphia: Macrae Smith, 1938. 304pp.

754. McKay, Allis (aka Allis McKay Klamm). *Woman About Town*. New York: Macmillan, 1938. 278pp.

770. Millspaugh, Clarence Arthur. *Men Are Not Stars*. New York: Doubleday, Doran, 1938. 365pp.

904. Pratt, Mrs. Eleanor Blake Atkinson [Eleanor Blake, pseud.]. *Wherever I Choose*. New York: Putnam's Sons, 1938. 271pp.

922. Rapp, William Jourdan. *Poolroom*. New York: Lee Furman, 1938. 312pp.

1143. Ward, Mary Jane. *The Wax Apple*. New York: Dutton, 1938. 312pp.

1193. Wight, Natalie. *Death in the Inner Office*. New York: Phoenix Press 1938. 246pp.

121. Bowman, Heath. *All Your Born Days*. Indianapolis: Bobbs-Merrill, 1939. 348pp.

217. Clason, Clyde B. *Dragon's Cave: A Theocritus Lucius Westborough Story*. Garden City, N.Y.: Crime Club / Doubleday, Doran, 1939. 269pp.

240.   Corne, Molly E. *A Magnet for Murder*. New York: Mill, 1939. 254pp.

349.   Ellison, Jerome. *The Prisoner Ate a Hearty Breakfast*. New York: Random House, 1939. 218pp.

559.   Holt, Isabella. *A Visit to Pay*. Indianapolis: Bobbs-Merrill, 1939. 329pp.

599.   Keeler, Harry Stephen. *The Chameleon: A Mystery-Adventure Novel*. New York: Dutton, 1939. 299pp.

802.   North, Sterling. *Seven Against the Years*. New York: Macmillan, 1939. 326pp.

815.   O'Hara, John. *Pal Joey*. New York: Grosset and Dunlap, 1939. 195pp.

914.   Randolph, Georgiana Ann [Craig Rice, pseud.]. *8 Faces at 3*. An Inner Sanctum Mystery. New York: Simon and Schuster, 1939. 308pp.

976.   Russell, Charlotte Murray. *The Case of the Topaz Flower*. New York: Crime Club / Doubleday, Doran, 1939. 278pp.

1110.   Turpin, Walter Edward. *O Canaan!* New York: Doubleday, Doran, 1939. 311pp.

34.   Altrocchi, Julia Cooley. *Wolves Against the Moon*. New York: Macmillan, 1940. 572pp.

266.   Davis, Clyde Brion. *Sullivan*. New York: Farrar and Rinehart, 1940. 279pp.

284.   De Vries, Peter. *But Who Wakes the Bugler?* Illustrated by Charles Addams. Boston: Houghton Mifflin, Riverside Press, 1940. 297pp.

308.   Douglas, Lloyd C. *Invitation to Live*. Boston: Houghton Mifflin, Riverside Press, 1940. 303pp.

340.   Eberhart, Mignon Good. *The Hangman's Whip*. Garden City, N.Y.: Doubleday, Doran, 1940. 275pp.

385.   Farrell, James T. (James Thomas). *Father and Son*. New York: Vanguard Press, 1940. 616pp.

515.   Halper, Albert. *Sons of the Fathers*. New York: Harper and Brothers, 1940. 431pp.

606.   Keeler, Harry Stephen. *Man with the Crimson Box*. New York: Dutton, 1940. 317pp.

672.   Levin, Meyer. *Citizens*. New York: Viking Press, 1940. 650pp.

913.   Randolph, Georgiana Ann [Craig Rice, pseud.]. *The Corpse Steps Out*. An Inner Sanctum Mystery. New York: Simon and Schuster, 1940. 305pp.

921.   Randolph, Georgiana Ann [Craig Rice, pseud.]. *The Wrong Murder*. An Inner Sanctum Mystery. New York: Simon and Schuster, 1940. 311pp.

1215.   Wright, Richard. *Native Son*. New York: Harper and Brothers, 1940. 359pp.

12.   Ade, George. *Stories of the Streets and of the Town: From "The Chicago Record" 1893-1900*. Illustrated by John T. McCutcheon. Chicago: Caxton Club, 1941. 274pp.

215.   Clark, Herma. *The Elegant Eighties: When Chicago Was Young*. Forward by John T. McCutcheon. Chicago: McClurg, 1941. 258pp.

238.   Corey, Paul Frederick. *County Seat*. Indianapolis: Bobbs-Merrill, 1941. 418pp.

348.   Ellison, Jerome. *The Dam*. New York: Random House, 1941. 176pp.

383.   Farrell, James T. (James Thomas). *Ellen Rogers*. New York: Vanguard Press, 1941. 429pp.

496.   Gruber, Frank [Vedder, John K., pseud.]. *The Last Doorbell*. New York: Henry Holt, 1941. 294pp.

498.   ———. *The Navy Colt*. A Johnny Fletcher Mystery. New York: Farrar and Rinehart, 1941. 278pp.

571.   Hutchens, Paul. *The Sugar Creek Gang in Chicago*. Grand Rapids, Mich.: Eerdmans, 1941. 88pp.

607.   Keeler, Harry Stephen. *The Man with the Wooden Spectacles*. New York: Dutton, 1941. 378pp.

613.   ———. *The Sharkskin Book, A Mystery Novel*. New York: Dutton, 1941. 286pp.

718.   Marshall, Sidney. *Some Like It Hot*. New York: William Morrow, 1941. 278pp.

750.   McGrath, Tom, Lieutenant. *Copper*. Boston: Bruce Humphries, 1941. 317pp.

877.   Phillip, Quentin Morrow. *We Who Died Last Night*. St. Meinrad, Ind.: Grail, 1941. 299pp.

920.   Randolph, Georgiana Ann [Craig Rice, pseud.]. *The Right Murder*. An Inner Sanctum Mystery. New York: Simon and Schuster, 1941. 311pp.

931.   Rea, M. P. (Margaret Paine). *Compare These Dead!* Garden City, N.Y.: Crime Club / Doubleday, Doran, 1941. 271pp.

932.   Rea, M. P. (Margaret Paine). *A Curtain for Crime*. New York: Crime Club / Doubleday, Doran, 1941. 269pp.

959.   Roberts, Edith. *This Marriage*. Indianapolis: Bobbs-Merrill, 1941. 306pp.

977.   Russell, Charlotte Murray. *Dreadful Reckoning*. New York: Crime Club / Doubleday, Doran, 1941. 276pp.

28.   Algren, Nelson. *Never Come Morning*. New York: Avon Publications, 1942. 191pp.

397.   Farrell, James T. (James Thomas). *$1000 A Week and Other Stories*. New York: Vanguard Press, 1942. 226pp.

500.   Gruber, Frank [Stephen Acre, pseud.]. *The Yellow Overcoat*. New York: Dodd, Mead, 1942. 232pp.

513.   Halper, Albert. *The Little People*. New York: Harper and Brothers, 1942. 402pp.

557.   Holt, Isabella. *Aunt Jessie*. Indianapolis: Bobbs-Merrill, 1942. 292pp.

730.   Mayer, Jane Rothschild and Clara Spiegel [Clare Jaynes, joint pseud.]. *Instruct My Sorrows*. New York: Random House, 1942. 383pp.

782.   Moore, Ward. *Breathe the Air Again*. New York: Harper Brothers 1942. 445pp.

911.   Randolph, Georgiana Ann [Craig Rice, pseud.]. *The Big Midget Murders*. An Inner Sanctum Mystery. New York: Simon and Schuster, 1942. 365pp.

958.   Roberts, Edith. *Little Hell—Big Heaven: a City Arabesque*. Indianapolis: Bobbs-Merrill, 1942. 327pp.

1094.   Tigay, Betty S. *Rich People, and Other Stories*. Chicago: Stein, 1942. 273pp.

1106.   Tully, Jim. *Biddy Brogan's Boy*. New York: Charles Scribner's Sons, 1942. 300pp.

394.   Farrell, James T. (James Thomas). *My Days of Anger*. New York: Vanguard Press, 1943. 403pp.

429.   Flavin, Martin. *Journey in the Dark*. New York: Harper and Brothers, 1943. 432pp.

647.   Lake, Joe Barry [Joe Barry, pseud.]. *The Third Degree*. New York: Mystery House, 1943. 256pp.

933.   Rea M. P. (Margaret Paine). *Death of an Angel*. Garden City, N.Y.: Crime Club / Doubleday, Doran, 1943. 266pp.

985.   Saxton, Alexander. *Grand Crossing.* New York: Harper and Brothers, 1943. 410pp.

1065.   Strobel Marion. *Ice Before Killing.* New York: Charles Scribner's Sons, 1943. 213pp.

1089.   Thorson, Russell Delos and Sarah Winfree Thorson [Kit Christian, joint pseud.]. *Death and Bitters.* New York: Dutton, 1943. 240pp.

1149.   Warrick, LaMar Sheridan. *Yesterday's Children.* New York: Thomas Y. Crowell, 1943. 202pp.

1178.   Wendt, Lloyd and Herman Kogan. *Lords of the Levee; the Story of Bathhouse John and Hinky Dink.* Indianapolis: Bobbs-Merrill, 1943. 384pp.

1189.   Whitney, Phyllis A. *Red Is for Murder.* A Fingerprint Mystery. Chicago: Ziff-Davis, 1943. 221pp.

31.   Allee, Marjorie Hill. *The House.* Illustrated by Helen Blair. Boston: Houghton Mifflin, Riverside Press, 1944. 181pp.

70.   Baker, North and William Bolton. *Dead to the World.* Garden City, N.Y.: Crime Club / Doubleday, Doran, 1944. 246pp.

102.   Bellow, Saul. *Dangling Man.* New York: Vanguard Press, 1944. 191pp.

261.   Dale, Virginia. *Nan Thursday.* New York: Coward-McCann, 1944. 174pp.

282.   De Vries, Peter. *Angels Can't Do Better.* New York: Coward-McCann, 1944. 181pp.

405.   Farrell, James T. (James Thomas). *To Whom It May Concern.* New York: Vanguard Press, 1944. 204pp.

598.   Keeler, Harry Stephen. *The Case of the Lavender Gripsack.* New York: Phoenix, 1944. 256pp.

664.   Lawrence, Catherine Ann. *The Narrowing Wind.* New York: Dodd, Mead, 1944. 214pp.

731.   Mayer, Jane Rothschild and Clara Spiegel [Claire Jaynes, joint pseud.]. *My Reputation.* Cleveland, Ohio: World, 1944. 288pp. This title is a reissue of the authors' earlier work, *Instruct My Sorrows.*

732.   ———. *These Are the Times.* New York: Random House, 1944. 273pp.

772.   Mizner, Elizabeth Howard. *Dorinda.* New York: Lothrop, Lee and Shepard, 1944. 303pp.

1046.   Starrett, Vincent. *The Case Book of Jimmie Lavender.* New York: Gold Label Books, 1944. 350pp.

1077.   Targ, William and Lewis Helmar Herman. *The Case of Mr. Cassidy.* Cleveland: World, 1944. 255pp.

174.   Caldwell, Lewis A. H. *The Policy King.* Illustrated by Frederick S. Banks. Chicago: New Vistas Publishing House, 1945. 303pp.

646.   Lake, Joe Barry [Joe Barry, pseud.]. *The Fall Guy.* New York: Mystery House, 1945. 256pp.

728.   Maxwell, William. *The Folded Leaf.* New York: Book Find Club, 1945. 310pp.

757.   Meeker, Arthur. *The Far Away Music.* Boston: Houghton Mifflin, 1945. 308pp.

798.   Nichols, Edward J. *Hunky Johnny.* Boston: Houghton Mifflin, Riverside Press Cambridge, 1945. 246pp.

917.   Randolph, Georgiana Ann [Craig Rice, pseud.]. *The Lucky Stiff.* An Inner Sanctum Mystery. New York: Simon and Schuster, 1945. 251pp.

1190.   Whitney, Phyllis A. *The Silver Inkwell.* Illustrated by Hilda Frommholz. Boston: Houghton Mifflin, Riverside Press, 1945. 272pp.

1194.   Wilcox, Wendell. *Everything Is Quite All Right.* New York: Bernard Ackerman, 1945. 184pp.

145.   Browne, Howard. [John Evans, pseud.]. *Halo in Blood.* Indianapolis: Bobbs-Merrill, 1946. 245pp.

393.   Farrell, James T. (James Thomas). *More Fellow-Countrymen.* London, U.K.: Routledge, 1946. 223pp.

412.   Fast, Howard. *The American, A Middle Western Legend.* New York: Duell, Sloane, Pierce, 1946. 337pp.

436.   Forbes, Murray. *Hollow Triumph.* Chicago: Ziff-Davis, 1946. 339pp.

649.   Lake, Joe Barry. *The Triple Cross; a Rush Henry Mystery.* New York: Mystery House, 1946. 256pp.

756.   Means, Mary and Theodore Saunders [Denis Scott, joint pseud.]. *The Beckoning Shadow.* Indianapolis: Bobbs-Merrill, 1946. 288pp.

791.   Nablo James Benson. *The Long November.* New York: Dutton, 1946. 223pp.

824.   Ozaki, Milton K. *The Cuckoo Clock.* Chicago: Ziff-Davis, 1946. 261pp.

971.   Rosenfeld, Isaac. *Passage from Home*. New York: Dial Press, 1946. 280pp.

1226.   Zara, Louis. *Ruth Middleton*. New York: Creative Age Press, 1946. 435pp.

27.   Algren, Nelson. *The Neon Wilderness*. Garden City, N.Y.: Doubleday, 1947. 286pp.

109.   Bland, Alden. *Behold a Cry*. New York: Charles Scribner, 1947. 229pp.

111.   Bloch, Robert. *The Scarf*. New York: Dial Press, 1947. 247pp.

141.   Brown, Fredric. *The Fabulous Clipjoint*. New York: Dutton, 1947. 224pp.

265.   Davis, Clyde Brion. *Jeremy Bell*. New York: Rinehart, 1947. 313pp.

291.   Dewey, Thomas B. *Draw the Curtain Close*. New York: Jefferson House, 1947. 212pp.

315.   Dreiser, Theodore. *The Stoic*. Garden City, N.Y.: Doubleday, 1947. 310pp.

368.   Ewing, Annemarie. *Little Gate*. New York: Rinehart, 1947. 278pp.

391.   Farrell, James T. (James Thomas). *The Life Adventurous and Other Stories*. New York: Vanguard Press, 1947. 313pp.

421.   Ferber, Edna. *One Basket; Thirty-One Short Stories*. Chicago: Peoples Book Club, 1947. 581pp.

485.   Godley, Robert [Franklin James, pseud.]. *Killer in the Kitchen*. New York: Lantern Press, 1947. 281pp.

538.   Herbst, Josephine. *Somewhere the Tempest Fell*. New York: Charles Scribner's Sons, 1947. 344pp.

587.   Judson, Clara Ingram. *The Lost Violin; They Came from Bohemia*. Illustrated by Margaret Bradfield. Boston: Houghton Mifflin, Riverside Press, 1947. 204pp.

596.   Keeler, Harry Stephen. *The Case of the Barking Clock*. New York: Phoenix Press, 1947. 255pp.

786.   Motley, Willard. *Knock on Any Door*. New York: David Appleton-Century, 1947. 504pp.

830.   Ozaki, Milton K. *A Fiend in Need*. Chicago: Ziff-Davis, 1947. 232pp.

969.   Rose, Alvin Emanuel [Alan Pruitt, pseud.]. *The Restless Corpse*. Chicago: Ziff-Davis, 1947. 247pp.

972.   Ross, Sam. *He Ran all the Way*. New York: Farrar, Straus, 1947. 293pp.

980.   Rutledge, Nancy [Leigh Bryson, pseud.]. *The Gloved Hand: A New Mystery Novel.* Kingston, N.Y.: Quinn, 1947. 127pp.

989.   Schiller, Cicely. *Maybe Next Year.* New York: Prentice-Hall, 1947. 299pp.

1060.   Stone, Irving. *Adversary in the House.* Garden City, N.Y.: Doubleday, 1947. 432pp.

1156.   Watters, Barbara Hunt [Barbara Hunt, pseud.]. *A Little Night Music.* New York: Rinehart, 1947. 244pp.

1191.   Whitney, Phyllis A. *Willow Hill.* New York: David McKay, 1947. 243pp.

73.   Ballinger, Bill Sanborn. *The Body in the Bed.* New York: Harper and Brothers, 1948. 242pp.

147.   Browne, Howard [John Evans, pseud.]. *Halo for Satan.* Indianapolis: Bobbs-Merrill, 1948. 214pp.

206.   Charteris, Leslie. *Call for the Saint.* Garden City, N.Y.: Crime Club / Doubleday, 1948. 190pp.

499.   Gruber, Frank. *The Scarlet Feather.* A Johnny Fletcher Mystery. New York: Rinehart, 1948. 249pp.

597.   Keeler, Harry Stephen. *The Case of the Jeweled Ragpicker.* New York: Phoenix Press, 1948. 256pp.

703.   MacQueen, James. [James G. Edwards, pseud.]. *But the Patient Died.* Garden City, N.Y.: Crime Club / Doubleday, 1948. 189pp.

745.   McGivern, William P. *But Death Runs Faster.* Red Badge Detective Series. New York: Dodd, Mead, 1948. 231pp.

755.   Meadowcroft, Enid La Monte. *By Secret Railway.* New York: Thomas Y. Crowell, 1948. 275pp.

769.   Miller, Francesca Falk. *The Sands: The Story of Chicago's Front Yard.* Chicago: Valentine-Newman, 1948. 215pp.

843.   Parrish, Robert. *My Uncle and Miss Elizabeth.* New York: Beechhurst Press, 1948. 221pp.

915.   Randolph, Georgiana Ann [Craig Rice, pseud.]. *The Fourth Postman.* An Inner Sanctum Mystery. New York: Simon and Schuster, 1948. 243pp.

957. Roberts, Edith. *The Divorce of Marcia Moore*. Garden City, N.Y.: Doubleday, 1948. 249pp.

974. Ross, Sam. *Someday, Boy*. New York: Farrar, Straus,1948. 340pp.

986. Saxton, Alexander. *The Great Midland*. New York: Appleton-Century-Crofts, 1948. 352pp.

1016. Smith, Fredrika Shumway. *Rose and the Ogre*. Boston: Christopher Publishing House, 1948. 184pp.

1192. Wickware, Francis Sill. *Tuesday to Bed*. Indianapolis: Bobbs-Merrill, 1948. 275pp.

26. Algren, Nelson. *The Man with the Golden Arm*. Garden City, N.Y.: Doubleday, 1949. 343pp.

39. Andrews, Robert Hardy. *Legend of a Lady: The Story of Rita Martin*. New York: Coward-McCann, 1949. 342pp.

68. Baker, Frederick Sherman. *Bradford Masters*. New York: Dutton, 1949. 254pp.

71. Ball, Jane Mary Eklund. *The Only Gift*. Boston: Houghton Mifflin, Riverside Press, 1949. 278pp.

72. Ballinger, Bill Sanborn. *The Body Beautiful*. New York: Harper and Brothers, 1949. 244pp.

146. Browne, Howard [John Evans, pseud.]. *Halo in Brass, A Paul Pine Mystery*. Indianapolis: Bobbs-Merrill, 1949. 222pp.

361. Emery, Anne McGuigan. *Senior Year*. Illustrated by Beth Krush. Philadelphia: Westminster Press, 1949. 208pp.

398. Farrell, James T. (James Thomas). *The Road Between*. New York: Vanguard Press, 1949. 463pp.

497. Gruber, Frank. *The Leather Duke*. A Murray Hill Mystery. New York: Rinehart, 1949. 247pp.

586. Judson, Clara Ingram. *The Green Ginger Jar: A Chinatown Mystery*. Illustrated by Paul Brown. Boston: Houghton Mifflin, Riverside Press, 1949. 210pp.

629. Kent, Mona. *Mirror, Mirror, on the Wall*. New York: Rinehart, 1949. 307pp.

640. Krautter, Elisa Bialk. *Taffy's Foal*. Illustrated by William Moyers. Boston: Houghton Mifflin, 1949. 179pp.

686.   Lobell, William. *The Steed Success*. New York: Reader Press, 1949. 758pp.

746.   McGivern, William P. *Heaven Ran Last*. A Red Badge Mystery. New York: Dodd, Mead, 1949. 247pp.

758.   Meeker, Arthur. *Prairie Avenue*. New York: Alfred A. Knopf, 1949. 318pp.

821.   Ozaki, Milton K. [Robert O. Saber, pseud.]. *The Black Dark Murders*. Kingston, N.Y.: Handi-Book Editions, 1949. 158pp.

1103.   Tucker, Wilson. *The Stalking Man*. A Murray Hill Mystery. New York: Rinehart, 1949. 212pp.

1129.   Walker, Mildred. *Medical Meeting*. New York: Harcourt, Brace, 1949. 280pp.

74.   Ballinger, Bill Sanborn. *Portrait in Smoke*. New York: Harper and Brothers, 1950. 213pp.

87.   Banning, Margaret Culkin. *Give Us Our Years*. New York: Harper and Brothers, 1950. 274pp.

123.   Boylan, Malcolm Stuart. *Tin Sword*. Boston: Little, Brown, 1950. 312pp.

139.   Brown, Fredric. *Compliments of a Fiend*. A Guilt Edged Mystery. New York: Dutton, 1950. 256pp.

213.   Clark, Christopher. *Good Is for Angels*. New York: Harper and Brothers, 1950. 237pp.

357.   Emery, Anne McGuigan. *Going Steady*. Philadelphia: Westminster Press, 1950. 189pp.

375.   Farrell, James T. (James Thomas). *An American Dream Girl*. New York: Vanguard Press, 1950. 302pp.

464.   Gaines, Diana. *Tasker Martin*. New York: Random House, 1950. 342pp.

648.   Lake, Joe Barry. *Three for the Money*. Kingston, N.Y.: Handi-Book Editions / Quinn, 1950. 123pp.

670.   Leiber, Fritz Reuter. *The Sinful Ones*. New York: Universal, 1950. 319pp.

747.   McGivern, William P. *Very Cold for May*. A Red Badge Mystery. New York: Dodd, Mead, 1950. 246pp.

820.   Ozaki, Milton K. [Robert O. Saber, pseud.]. *The Affair of the Frigid Blonde*. A Handi-Book Mystery. Kingston, N.Y.: Quinn, 1950. 127pp.

968. Rosaire, Forrest. *Uneasy Years*. New York: Alfred A. Knopf, 1950.

973. Ross, Sam. *The Sidewalks Are Free*. New York: Farrar, Straus, 1950. 308pp.

1202. Willingham, Calder. *Geraldine Bradshaw*. New York: Vanguard Press, 1950. 415pp.

1951–1980

140. Brown, Fredric. *Death Has Many Doors*. New York: Dutton, 1951. 215pp.

162. Burnett, W. R. (William Riley). *Little Men, Big World*. New York: Alfred A. Knopf, 1951. 308pp.

293. Dewey, Thomas B. *Handle with Fear; A Singer Batts Mystery*. New York: Mill / William Morrow, 1951. 218pp.

305. Dos Passos, John. *Chosen Country*. Boston: Houghton Mifflin, Riverside Press, 1951. 485pp.

404. Farrell, James T. (James Thomas). *This Man and This Woman*. New York: Vanguard Press, 1951. 205pp.

553. Hjerstedt, Gunard [Day Keene, pseud.]. *To Kiss or Kill*. New York: Fawcett, 1951. 169pp.

788. Motley, Willard. *We Fished All Night*. New York: Appleton-Century-Crofts, 1951. 560pp.

799. Nielsen, Helen. *Gold Coast Nocturne*. New York: Ives Washburn, 1951. 203pp.

826. Ozaki, Milton K. [Robert O. Saber, pseud.]. *The Dove*. Kingston, N.Y.: Quinn, 1951. 150pp.

829. Ozaki, Milton K. *The Dummy Murder Case*. Hasbrouck Heights, N.J.: Graphic, 1951. 190pp.

833. Ozaki, Milton K. [Robert O. Saber, pseud.]. *The Scented Flesh*. Kingston, N.Y.: Quinn, 1951. 127pp.

1182. Wheeler, Keith. *The Reef*. New York: Dutton, 1951. 320pp.

124. Bradley, Mary Hastings. *Nice People Poison*. New York, London [and] Toronto: Longmans, Green, 1952. 216pp.

190. Caspary, Vera. *Thelma*. Boston: Little, Brown, 1952. 342pp.

270.   Dawson, George H. [Michael Storme, pseud.]. *Hot Dames on Cold Slabs*. New York: Leisure Library, 1952. 128pp.

337.   Eberhart, Mignon Good. *Dead Men's Plans*. New York: Random House, 1952. 246pp.

362.   Emery, Anne McGuigan. *Sorority Girl*. Illustrated by Richard Horwitz. Philadelphia: Westminster Press, 1952. 191pp.

407.   Farrell, James T. (James Thomas). *Yet Other Waters*. New York: Vanguard Press, 1952. 414pp.

475.   Gillian, Michael. *Warrant for a Wanton*. New York: Mill, 1952. 246pp.

517.   Ham, Roswell. *The Gifted*. New York: Avon, 1952. 191pp.

556.   Holt, Alfred Hubbard. *Hubbard's Trail*. Chicago: Erle Press, 1952. 319pp.

744.   McGivern, William P. [Bill Peters, pseud.]. *Blondes Die Young*. Red Badge Detective Series. New York: Dodd, Mead, 1952. 240pp.

785.   Morris, Ira Victor. *The Chicago Story*. Garden City, N.Y.: Doubleday, 1952. 347pp.

1141.   Ward, Mary Jane. *It's Different for a Woman*. New York: Random House, 1952. 246pp.

1144.   Ware, Harlan. *Come, Fill the Cup*. New York: Random House, 1952. 246pp.

101.   Bellow, Saul. *The Adventures of Augie March*. New York: Viking Press, 1953. 536pp.

131.   Brooks, Gwendolyn. *Maud Martha*. New York: Harper, 1953. 180pp.

156.   Budd, Lillian. *Land of Strangers*. Philadelphia: Lippincott, 1953. 369pp.

204.   Chapman, George Warren [Vernon Warren, pseud.]. *Brandon Takes Over*. London: John Gifford, 1953. 192pp.

319.   Dubkin, Leonard. *Wolf Point, an Adventure in History*. New York: Putnam, 1953. 184pp.

320.   Du Bois, Shirley Graham. *Jean Baptiste Pointe De Sable, Founder of Chicago*. New York: Messner, 1953. 180pp.

334.   Eagle, John. *The Hoodlums*. New York: Avon Publications, 1953. 139pp.

346.   Edgley, Leslie. *The Runaway Pigeon*. Garden City, N.Y.: Crime Club / Doubleday, 1953. 188pp.

384.   Farrell, James T. (James Thomas). *The Face of Time*. New York: Vanguard Press, 1953. 366pp.

488.   Gordon, Mildred and Gordon Gordon [The Gordons, pseud.]. *Case File: FBI*. Garden City, N.Y.: Crime Club / Doubleday, 1953. 189pp.

512.   Halper, Albert. *The Golden Watch*. Illustrated by Aaron Bohrod. New York: Holt, 1953. 246pp.

516.   Ham, Roswell G. *Account Overdue*. London, U.K.: Neville Spearman, 1953. 215pp.

628.   Kennedy, Mark. *The Pecking Order*. New York: Appleton-Century-Crofts, 1953. 278pp.

823.   Ozaki, Milton K. [Robert O. Saber, pseud.]. *Chicago Woman (The Dove)*. New York: Pyramid Books, 1953. 158pp.

895.   Potter, Jack. [John Hart, pseud.]. *The Heavy Day*. Springfield, Ill.: The Author, 1953. 127pp.

1216.   Wright, Richard. *The Outsider*. New York: Harper and Row 1953. 440pp.

202.   Chapman, George [Vernon Warren, pseud.]. *The Blue Mauritius*. London: John Gifford, 1954. 189pp.

203.   Chapman, George [Vernon Warren, pseud.]. *Brandon Returns*. London: John Gifford, 1954. 191pp.

297.   Dewey, Thomas B. *Prey for Me*. An Inner Sanctum Mystery. New York: Simon and Schuster, 1954. 210pp.

532.   Heed, Rufus. *Ghosts Never Die*. New York: Vantage Press, 1954. 180pp.

536.   Herber, William. *King-Sized Murder*. A Main Line Mystery. Philadelphia: Lippincott, 1954. 222pp.

734.   McAlpine, Dale K. *Marie Naimska: A Saga of Chicago*. Philadelphia: Dorrance, 1954. 242pp.

827.   Ozaki, Milton K. *Dressed to Kill*. Cover Illustrated by Walter Popp. Hasbrouck Heights, N.J.: Graphic Books, 1954. 189pp.

836.   Ozaki, Milton K. [Robert O. Saber, pseud.]. *Too Young to Die*. Hasbrouck Heights, N.J.: Graphic Books, 1954. 190pp.

1014.   Smith, Eunice Young. *Jennifer Dances*. Indianapolis: Bobbs-Merrill, 1954. 250pp.

1123.   Wager, Walter H. *Death Hits the Jackpot*. New York: Avon, 1954. 189pp.

1125.   Wagoner, David. *The Man in the Middle*. New York: Harcourt, Brace, 1954. 248pp.

1220.   Yaffe, James. *What's the Big Hurry?* Boston: Atlantic Monthly Press / Little, Brown, 1954. 331pp.

69.   Baker, Frederick Sherman. *Hidden Fire*. Boston: Little, Brown, 1955. 308pp.

157.   Burgoyne, Leon E. *Ensign Ronan, a Story of Fort Dearborn*. Philadelphia: Winston, 1955. 184pp.

537.   Herber, William. *Live Bait for Murder*. A Main Line Mystery. Philadelphia: Lippincott, 1955. 221pp.

623.   Kelly, Regina Zimmerman. *Beaver Trail*. New York: Lothrop, Lee and Shepard, 1955. 237pp.

660.   Latimer, Jonathan. *Sinners and Shrouds*. An Inner Sanctum Mystery. New York: Simon and Schuster, 1955. 250pp.

812.   O'Connor, Richard. *Guns of Chickamauga*. Garden City, N.Y.: Doubleday, 1955. 288pp.

825.   Ozaki, Milton K. [Robert O. Saber, pseud.]. *A Dame Called Murder*. Hasbrouck Heights, N.J.: Graphic, 1955. 190pp.

831.   Ozaki, Milton K. *Maid for Murder*. Bound with Chase, James Hadley, *Dead Ringer*. New York: Ace Double Novel Books, 1955. 141pp.

834.   Ozaki, Milton K. [Robert O. Saber, pseud.]. *Sucker Bait*. Hasbrouck Heights, N.J.: Graphic, 1955. 190pp.

1104.   Tucker, Wilson. *Time Bomb*. New York: Rinehart, 1955. 246pp.

1126.   Wagoner, David. *Money, Money, Money*. New York: Harcourt, Brace, 1955. 241pp.

1188.   Whitmore, Stanford. *Solo*. New York: Harcourt, Brace, 1955. 382pp.

246.   Courtney, James [Frank M. Robinson, pseud.]. *The Power*. Philadelphia: Lippincott, 1956. 219pp.

288.   Dewey, Thomas B. *The Brave, Bad Girls*. An Inner Sanctum Mystery. New York: Simon and Schuster, 1956. 244pp.

343.   Eberhart, Mignon Good. *Postmark Murder*. New York: Random House, 1956. 305pp.

354.   Emery, Anne McGuigan. *First Love, True Love*. Philadelphia: Westminster Press, 1956. 189pp.

473.   Gerson, Noel B. (Noel Bertram) [Leon Phillips, pseud.]. *When the Wind Blows*. New York: Farrar, Straus and Cudahy, 1956. 311pp.

673.   Levin, Meyer. *Compulsion*. New York: Simon and Schuster, 1956. 495pp.

832.   Ozaki, Milton K. *Never Say Die*. New York: Wyn, Ace Books, 1956. 138pp.

835.   Ozaki, Milton K. [Robert O. Saber, pseud.]. *A Time for Murder*. Hasbrouck Heights, N.J.: Graphic Books, 1956. 189pp.

1015.   Smith, Fredrika Shumway. *The Fire Dragon: A Story of the Great Chicago Fire*. Illustrated by Ray Naylor. Chicago: Rand, McNally, 1956. 174pp.

1206.   Wise, Winifred Esther. *Frances a la Mode*. Philadelphia: Macrae Smith, 1956. 224pp.

148.   Browne, Howard. *The Taste of Ashes*. New York: Simon, 1957. 282pp.

256.   Crunden, Allan B. and Robert Morse Crunden. *Roses and Forget-Me-Nots: A Study of Intrigue in Chicago*. New York: Vantage Press, 1957. 129pp.

355.   Emery, Anne McGuigan. *First Orchid for Pat*. Philadelphia: Westminster Press, 1957. 185pp.

359.   ———. *Married on Wednesday; A Junior Novel*. Philadelphia: Macrae Smith, 1957. 224pp.

381.   Farrell, James T. (James Thomas). *Dangerous Woman and Other Stories*. New York: Vanguard Press, 1957. 160pp.

440.   Fowler, Bertram B. [Jack Baynes, pseud.]. *Meet Morocco Jones; In the Case of the Syndicate Hoods*. Greenwich, Conn.: Crest Original / Fawcett Publications, 1957. 144pp.

534.   Herber, William. *The Almost Dead*. A Main Line Mystery. Philadelphia: Lippincott, 1957. 222pp.

666.   Lawson, Robert. *The Great Wheel*. New York: Viking Press, 1957. 188pp.

669.   Lee, Norman [Mark Corrigan, pseud.]. *Dumb as They Come*. London, U.K.: Angus and Robertson, 1957. 224pp.

916.   Randolph, Georgiana Ann [Craig Rice, pseud.]. *Knocked for a Loop*. An Inner Sanctum Mystery. New York: Simon and Schuster, 1957. 219pp.

918.   Randolph, Georgiana Ann [Craig Rice, pseud.]. *My Kingdom for a Hearse*. An Inner Sanctum Mystery. New York: Simon and Schuster, 1957. 249pp.

984.   Sattley, Helen R. *Shadow Across the Campus*. New York: Dodd, Mead, 1957. 245pp.

1054.   Stern, Lucille. *The Midas Touch*. New York: Citadel Press, 1957. 286pp.

1055.   Steuber. William F., Jr. *The Landlooker*. Indianapolis: Bobbs-Merrill, 1957. 367pp.

15.   Albert, Marvin. *Party Girl*. Greenwich, Conn.: Gold Medal Books / Fawcett Publications, 1958. 128pp.

280.   Dever, Joseph. *Three Priests*. Garden City, N.Y.: Doubleday, 1958. 453pp.

299.   Dewey, Thomas B. *You've Got Him Cold*. An Inner Sanctum Mystery. New York: Simon and Schuster, 1958. 184pp.

353.   Emery, Anne McGuigan. *A Dream to Touch*. Philadelphia: Macrae Smith, 1958. 190pp.

356.   ———. *First Love Farewell*. Philadelphia: Westminster Press, 1958. 171pp.

463.   Gaines, Diana. *Marry in Anger*. Garden City, N.Y.: Doubleday, 1958. 309pp.

535.   Herber, William. *Death Paints a Portrait*. A Main Line Mystery. Philadelphia: Lippincott, 1958. 223pp.

577.   Jakes, John [Jay Scotland, pseud.]. *The Seventh Man*. New York: Mystery House, 1958. 221pp.

729.   Mayer, Jane Rothschild. *The Year of the White Trees*. New York: Random House, 1958. 282pp.

787.   Motley, Willard. *Let No Man Write My Epitaph*. New York: Random House, 1958. 467pp.

822.   Ozaki, Milton K. *Case of the Cop's Wife*. New York: Fawcett Publications, Gold Medal Books, 1958. 141pp.

910.   Quinlan, Sterling. *The Merger*. Garden City, N.Y.: Doubleday, 1958. 331pp.

919.   Randolph, Georgiana Ann [Craig Rice, pseud.]. *The Name is Malone: Ten Stories Complete and Unabridged*. New York: Pyramid Books, 1958. 192pp.

982.   Sandburg, Helga. *The Wheel of Earth*. New York: McDowell Obolensky, 1958. 396pp.

1008.   Sklovsky, Max. *Dynasty: a Novel of Chicago's Industrial Evolution.* Chicago: Americana House, 1958. 202pp.

1127.   Wagoner, David. *Rock.* New York: Viking Press, 1958. 253pp.

1207.   Wise, Winifred Esther. *Frances by Starlight.* Philadelphia: Macrae Smith, 1958. 201pp.

137.   Brown, Frank London. *Trumbull Park; a Novel.* Chicago: Henry Regnery, 1959. 432pp.

142.   Brown, Fredric. *The Late Lamented.* New York: Dutton, 1959. 192pp.

154.   Buck, Pearl S. *Command the Morning.* New York: John Day, 1959. 317pp.

155.   Budd, Lillian. *April Harvest.* New York: Duell, Sloan and Pearce, 1959. 309pp.

196.   Chamales, Tom T. *Go Naked in the World.* New York: Scribner, 1959. 461pp.

350.   Emery, Anne McGuigan. *Dinny Gordon, Freshman.* Philadelphia: Macrae Smith, 1959. 190pp.

363.   ———. *That Archer Girl.* Philadelphia: Westminster Press, 1959. 175pp.

365.   Ernst, Paul Frederick [Ernest Jason Fredericks, pseud.]. *Lost Friday.* London, U.K.: Robert Hale, 1959. 189pp.

720.   Masselink, Ben. *The Crackerjack Marines.* Boston: Little, Brown, 1959. 275pp.

869.   Petrakis, Harry Mark. *Lion at My Heart.* Boston: Little, Brown, 1959. 238pp.

943.   Rhodes, James A. and Dean Jauchius. *The Trial of Mary Todd Lincoln.* Indianapolis: Bobbs-Merrill, 1959. 187pp.

965.   Roeburt, John, Malvin Wald, Henry F. Greenberg, and Al Capone. *Al Capone.* New York: Pyramid Books, 1959. 144pp.

1173.   Wellard, James. *The Affair in Arcady.* New York: Reynal, 1959. 312pp.

1228.   Ziegler, Elsie Reif. *The Face in the Stone.* Illustrated by Ray Abel. New York: Longmans, Green, 1959. 184pp.

67.   Baker, Elizabeth Gillette. *Fire in the Wind.* Boston: Houghton Mifflin, 1961. 244pp.

267.   Davis, Dorothy Salisbury. *The Evening of the Good Samaritan.* New York: Charles Scribner's Sons, 1961. 430pp.

283.   De Vries, Peter. *The Blood of the Lamb.* Boston: Little, Brown, 1961. 246pp.

352.   Emery, Anne McGuigan. *Dinny Gordon, Sophomore*. Philadelphia: Macrae Smith, 1961. 185pp.

360.   ———. *The Popular Crowd*. Philadelphia: Westminster Press, 1961. 170pp.

376.   Farrell, James T. (James Thomas). *Boarding House Blues*. New York: Paperback Library, 1961. 220pp.

400.   ———. *Side Street, And Other Stories*. New York: Paperback Library, 1961. 224pp.

665.   Lawson, Don. *A Brand for the Burning*. London, U.K.: Abelard-Schuman, 1961. 254pp.

1075.   Tanner, Edward Everett, III [Virginia Rowans, pseud.]. *Love and Mrs. Sargent*. New York: Farrar, Straus, and Cudahy, 1961. 277pp.

1213.   Wright, Richard. *Eight Men*. New York: Pyramid Books, 1961. 204pp.

1229.   Ziegler, Elsie Reif. *Light a Little Lamp*. New York: John Day, 1961. l91pp.

60.   Athens, Christopher. *The Big Squeeze*. Chicago: Chicago Paperback House, 1962. 190pp.

211.   Chinn, Laurene. *Believe My Love*. New York: Crown, 1962. 221pp.

230.   Converse, Jane. *Alias Miss Saunders, R.N.* Thorndike, Maine: Thorndike Press, 1962. 266pp.

254.   Crump, Paul. *Burn, Killer, Burn!* Chicago: Johnson, 1962. 391pp.

294.   Dewey, Thomas B. *How Hard to Kill*. New York: Simon and Schuster, 1962. 221pp.

402.   Farrell, James T. (James Thomas). *Sound of a City*. New York: Paperback Library, 1962. 176pp.

442.   Fox, May Virginia. *Ambush at Fort Dearborn*. New York: St. Martin's Press, 1962. 173pp.

462.   Gaines Diana. *The Knife and the Needle*. Garden City, N.Y.: Doubleday, 1962. 336pp.

624.   Kelly, Regina Zimmerman. *Chicago: Big-Shouldered City*. Chicago: Reilly and Lee, 1962. 158pp.

899.   Powers, J. F. (James Farl). *Morte D'Urban*. Garden City, N.Y.: Doubleday, 1962. 336pp.

975.   Roth, Philip. *Letting Go*. New York: Random House, 1962. 630pp.

1034.   Sontup, Daniel [David Saunders, pseud]. *M Squad: The Case of the Chicago Cop-Killer.* New York: Belmont Books, 1962. 141pp.

6.   Ade, George. *Chicago Stories.* Illustrated by John T. McCutcheon. Chicago: Henry Regnery, 1963. 278pp. This is a republication of *Stories of the Streets and of the Town.*

58.   Aschmann, Helen Tann. *Connie Bell, M. D.* New York: Dodd, Mead, 1963. 301pp.

143.   Brown, Fredric. *Mrs. Murphy's Underpants.* New York: Dutton, 1963. 185pp.

179.   Carruth, Hayden. *Appendix A.* New York: Macmillan, 1963. 302pp.

298.   Dewey, Thomas B. *A Sad Song Singing.* An Inner Sanctum Mystery. New York: Simon and Schuster, 1963. 192pp.

318.   Drought, James. *The Secret.* Norwalk, Conn.: Skylight Press, 1963. 173pp.

323.   Du Jardin, Rosamond. *Young & Fair.* Philadelphia: Lippincott, 1963. 187pp.

401.   Farrell, James T. (James Thomas). *The Silence of History.* Garden City, N.Y.: Doubleday, 1963. 372pp.

871.   Petrakis, Harry Mark. *The Odyssey of Kostas Volakis.* New York: David McKay, 1963. 271pp.

1214.   Wright, Richard. *Lawd Today.* New York: Walker, 1963. 189pp.

103.   Bellow, Saul. *Herzog.* New York: Viking Press, 1964. 341pp.

290.   Dewey, Thomas B. *Don't Cry for Long.* An Inner Sanctum Mystery. New York: Simon and Schuster, 1964. 189pp.

351.   Emery, Anne McGuigan. *Dinny Gordon, Junior.* Philadelphia: Macrae Smith, 1964. 169pp.

636.   Knebel, Fletcher and Charles W. Bailey II. *Convention.* New York: Harper and Row, 1964. 343pp.

773.   Molloy, Paul. *A Pennant for the Kremlin.* Garden City, N.Y.: Doubleday, 1964. 185pp.

1072.   Sublette, Walter [S. W. Edwards, pseud.]. *Go Now in Darkness.* Chicago: Baker Press, 1964. 255pp.

168.   Burroughs, Edgar Rice. *The Girl from Farris's.* Originally published in *All-Story Magazine* (Frank A. Munsey, 1916). Kansas City, Mo.: House of Greystoke, 1965. 160pp.

180.   Carter, John Stewart. *Full Fathom Five*. Boston: Houghton Mifflin, Riverside Press, 1965. 246pp.

296.   Dewey, Thomas B. *Portrait of a Dead Heiress*. An Inner Sanctum Mystery. New York: Simon and Schuster, 1965. 187pp.

303.   Donohue, H. E. F. *The Higher Animals: A Romance*. New York: Viking Press, 1965. 273pp.

358.   Emery, Anne McGuigan. *The Losing Game*. Philadelphia: Westminster Press, 1965. 140pp.

506.   Hale, Arlene. *Chicago Nurse*. New York: Ace, 1965. 127pp.

813.   O'Connor, Richard [Patrick Wayland, pseud.] *The Waiting Game*. Garden City, N.Y.: Crime Club / Doubleday, 1965. 188pp.

872.   Petrakis, Harry Mark. *Pericles on 31st Street*. Chicago: Quadrangle Books, 1965. 213pp.

167.   Burroughs, Edgar Rice. *The Efficiency Expert*. Originally published in *Argosy All-Story Weekly*, October 8 through October 29, 1921. Kansas City, Mo.: House of Greystoke, 1966. 84pp.

237.   Corbett, Elizabeth. *The Old Callahan Place*. New York: Appleton-Century, 1966. 311pp.

369.   Fair, Ronald L. *Hog Butcher*. New York: Harcourt, Brace and World, 1966. 182pp.

392.   Farrell, James T. (James Thomas). *Lonely for the Future*. Garden City, N.Y.: Doubleday, 1966. 263pp.

552.   Hjerstedt, Gunard [Day Keene, pseud.]. *Chicago 11*. New York: Dell, 1966. 220pp.

698.   MacDonald, John D. *One Fearful Yellow Eye*. A Fawcett Gold Medal Book. Greenwich, Conn.: Fawcett Publications, 1966. 224pp.

796.   Newman, Charles. *New Axis; or, The "Little Ed" Stories, An Exhibition*. Boston: Houghton Mifflin, Riverside Press, 1966. 175pp.

867.   Petrakis, Harry Mark. *A Dream of Kings*. New York: David McKay, 1966. 180pp.

952.   Richert, William. *Aren't You Even Gonna Kiss Me Good-by?* New York: David McKay, 1966. 247pp.

981.   St. Johns, Adela Rogers. *Tell No Man*. Garden City, N.Y.: Doubleday, 1966. 444pp.

1029. Smucker, Barbara Claasen. *Wigwam in the City*. Illustrated by Gil Miret. New York: Dutton, 1966. 154pp.

1113. Ullman, James Michael. *The Venus Trap*. An Inner Sanctum Mystery. New York: Simon and Schuster, 1966. 223p.

149. Browne, Howard and Boris O'Hara. *The St. Valentine's Day Massacre*. New York: Dell, 1967. 158pp.

150. Brunner, Bernard. *The Face of Night*. New York: Frederick Fell, 1967. 235pp.

251. Creasey, John [Anthony Morton, pseud.]. *Affair for the Baron*. New York: Walker, 1967. 191pp.

287. De Vries, Peter. *The Vale of Laughter*. Boston: Little, Brown, 1967. 352pp.

289. Dewey, Thomas B. *Death and Taxes*. A Red Mask Mystery. New York: Putnam's Sons, 1967. 190pp.

395. Farrell, James T. (James Thomas). *New Year's Eve, 1929*. New York: Smith, 1967. 144pp.

727. Maupin, Robert Lee [Iceberg Slim, pseud.]. *Trick Baby: The Story of a White Negro*. Los Angeles: Holloway House, 1967. 312pp.

837. Paine, Lauran Bosworth [Mark Carrel, pseud.]. *A Sword of Silk*. London, U.K.: Robert Hale, 1967. 191pp.

888. Plagemann, Bentz. *The Heart of Silence*. New York: William Morrow, 1967. 159pp.

906. Purdy, James. *Ace Chisholm and the Works*. New York: Farrar, Straus, 1967. 241pp.

912. Randolph, Georgiana Ann [Craig Rice, pseud.]. *But the Doctor Died*. New York: Lancer Books, 1967. 158pp.

1003. Siegel, Sam. *Hey, Jewboy*. Chicago: S and G Releasing, 1967. 329pp.

1195. Wilder, Thornton. *The Eighth Day*. New York: Harper and Row, 1967. 435pp.

1223. York, Carol Beach. *Until We Fall in Love Again*. New York: Franklin Watts, 1967. 141pp.

278. Derleth, August William. *The Prince Goes West*. New York: Meredith Press, 1968. 158pp.

295.   Dewey, Thomas B. *The King Killers*. A Red Mask Mystery. New York: Putnam's Sons, 1968. 184pp.

378.   Farrell, James T. (James Thomas). *A Brand New Life*. Garden City, N.Y.: Doubleday, 1968. 371pp.

505.   Hailey, Arthur. *Airport*. Garden City, N.Y: Doubleday, 1968. 440pp.

652.   Lamensdorf, Leonard. *Kane's World*. New York: Simon and Schuster, 1968. 378pp.

684.   Little, Paul H. (Paula Hugo Little) [Kenneth Harding, pseud.]. *Pushers*. Atlanta, Ga.: Pendulum Books, 1968.

713.   Maloff, Saul. *Happy Families*. New York: Charles Scribner's Sons, 1968. 375pp.

967.   Rogers, Thomas. *The Pursuit of Happiness*. New York: New American Library, 1968. 237pp.

1112.   Ullman, James Michael. *Lady on Fire*. An Inner Sanctum Mystery. New York: Simon and Schuster, 1968. 214pp.

1118.   Van Peebles, Melvin. *A Bear for the FBI*. New York: Trident Press, 1968. 157pp.

16.   Alcock, Gudrun. *Turn the Next Corner*. New York: Lothrop, Lee, and Shepard, 1969. 160pp.

64.   Bailey, Bernadine. *José*. Boston: Houghton Mifflin, 1969. 141pp.

105.   Benchly, Alexandra Jane. *If the Heart Be Hasty*. Berwyn, Ill.: Chekhov Publications, 1969. 280pp.

136.   Brown, Frank London. *The Myth Maker*. Chicago: Path Press, 1969. 179pp.

380.   Farrell, James T. (James Thomas). *Childhood Is Not Forever*. Garden City, N.Y.: Doubleday, 1969. 300pp.

390.   ———. *Judith*. Athens, Ohio: Duane Schneider, 1969. 363pp.

453.   Friermood, Elisabeth Hamilton. *Peppers' Paradise*. Garden City, N.Y.: Doubleday, 1969. 259pp.

494.   Greenlee, Sam. *The Spook Who Sat by the Door*. New York: Richard W. Baron, 1969. 248pp.

522.   Harrison William. *In a Wild Sanctuary*. New York: William Morrow, 1969. 320pp.

592.   Karlins, Marvin. *The Last Man Is Out*. Englewood Cliffs, N.J.: Prentice-Hall, 1969. 217pp.

708.   Maling, Arthur. *Decoy*. New York: Harper and Row, 1969. 199pp.

726.   Maupin, Robert Lee [Robert Beck, pseud.]. *Mama Black Widow*. Los Angeles: Holloway House, 1969. 312pp.

801.   Norris, Hoke. *It's Not Far, But I Don't Know the Way*. Chicago: Swallow Press, 1969. 155pp.

819.   Osborn, Catherine B. and Margaret Waterman. *Papa Gorski*. New York: Harcourt, Brace and World, 1969. 273pp.

874.   Petrakis, Harry Mark. *The Waves of Night, and Other Stories*. New York: David McKay, 1969. 230pp.

875.   Pflaum, Melanie. *The Gentle Tyrants*. New York: Carlton Press, 1969. 274pp.

882.   Piercy Marge. *Going Down Fast*. New York: Trident Press, 1969. 349pp.

962.   Robinson, Rose. *Exile in the Air*. New York: Crown Publishers, 1969. 159pp.

1030. Solberg Gunard. *Shelia*. Boston: Houghton Mifflin, 1969. 243pp.

1140. Ward, Mary Jane. *Counterclockwise*. Chicago: Henry Regnery, 1969. 250pp.

151.   Brunner, Bernard. *The Golden Children*. New York: Frederick Fell, 1970. 350pp.

221.   Cleaver, Vera and Bill Cleaver. *The Mimosa Tree*. Philadelphia: Lippincott, 1970. 125pp.

227.   Colter, Cyrus. *The Beach Umbrella*. Iowa City: University of Iowa Press, 1970. 225pp.

242.   Corrington, John William. *The Bombardier*. New York: Putnam's Sons, 1970. 255pp.

371.   Fair, Ronald. *World of Nothing: Two Novellas*. New York: Harper and Row, 1970. 133pp.

470.   Gault, William Campbell. *Quarterback Gamble*. New York: Dutton, 1970. 137pp.

710.   Maling, Arthur. *Go-Between*. New York: Harper and Row, 1970. 204pp.

907.   Quammen, David. *To Walk the Line*. New York: Alfred A. Knopf, 1970. 236pp.

983.   Sanders, Ed. *Shards of God*. New York: Grove Press, 1970. 179pp.

1105.   Tucker, Wilson. *The Year of the Quiet Sun*. New York: Ace, 1970. 252pp.

1142.   Ward, Mary Jane. *The Other Caroline*. New York: Crown, 1970. 216pp.

286.   De Vries, Peter. *Into Your Tent I'll Creep*. Boston: Little, Brown, 1971. 244pp.

437.   Forbes, DeLoris (Florine) Stanton [Stanton Forbes, pseud.]. *The Sad, Sudden Death of My Fair Lady*. Garden City, N.Y.: Crime Club / Doubleday, 1971. 161pp.

626.   Kennedy, Adam. *The Scaffold*. New York: Trident Press, 1971. 346pp.

797.   Newman Charles. *The Promise Keeper, A Tephramancy: Divers Narratives on the Economics of Current Morals in Lieu of a Psychology, Here Embodied in an Approved Text Working Often in Spite of Itself; Certain Profane Stoical Paradoxes Explained, Literary Amusements Liberally Interspersed, Partitioned with Documents & Conditioned by Imagoes, Hearty Family-Type Fare, Modern Decor, Free Parking*. New York: Simon and Schuster, 1971. 249pp.

805.   Oates, Joyce Carol. *Wonderland*. New York: Vanguard Press, 1971, 512pp.

866.   Pendleton, Don. *The Executioner: Chicago Wipe-Out*. New York: Pinnacle Books, 1971. 187pp.

991.   Schwimmer, Walter. *It Happened on Rush Street: A Group of Short Stories and Vignettes*. New York: Frederick Fell, 1971. 235pp.

1025.   Smith, Terrence Lore. *The Thief Who Came to Dinner*. Garden City, N.Y.: Doubleday, 1971. 176pp.

33.   Allen, Steve. *The Wake*. Garden City, N.Y.: Doubleday, 1972. 177pp.

229.   Colter, Cyrus. *The Rivers of Eros*. Chicago: Swallow Press, 1972. 219pp.

249.   Craig, M.S. (Mary Shura). *The Shop on Threnody Street*. New York: Coronet Book / Grosset and Dunlap, 1972. 160pp.

370.   Fair, Ronald. *We Can't Breathe*. New York: Harper and Row, 1972. 216pp.

472.   Gerson, Noel B. (Noel Bertram). *The Sunday Heroes*. New York: William Morrow, 1972. 288pp.

565.   Howard, Fred (Fred Steven). *Charlie Flowers & the Melody Gardens*. New York: Liveright, 1972. 218pp.

578.   James, Alice. *Decision to Love*. New York: Dell, 1972. 154pp.

591.   Kantor, MacKinlay. *I Love You, Irene*. Garden City, N.Y.: Doubleday, 1972. 347pp.

783.   Morgan, Al (Albert Edward). *The Whole World Is Watching*. New York: Stein and Day, 1972. 252pp.

865.   Peck, Richard. *Don't Look and It Won't Hurt*. New York: Holt, Rinehart and Winston, 1972. 173pp.

930.   Rayner, William. *Seth & Belle & Mr. Quarles and Me: The Bloody Affray at Lakeside Drive*. New York: Simon and Schuster, 1972. 157pp.

1084.   Thomas, Ross. *The Porkchoppers*. New York: William Morrow, 1972. 246pp.

25.   Algren, Nelson. *The Last Carousel*. New York: Putnam's Sons, 1973. 435pp.

269.   Davis, Timothy Francis Tothill [John Cashman, pseud.]. *The Gentleman from Chicago; Being an Account of the Doings of Thomas Neill Cream, M.D. (M'Gill), 1850-1892*. New York: Harper and Row, 1973. 310pp.

439.   Forrest, Leon. *There Is a Tree More Ancient Than Eden*. New York: Random House, 1973. 163pp.

868.   Petrakis, Harry Mark. *In the Land of Morning*. New York: David McKay, 1973. 290pp.

901.   Powers, John R. *The Last Catholic in America: A Fictionalized Memoir*. New York: Saturday Review Press, 1973. 228pp.

987.   Schaeffer, Susan Fromberg. *Falling*. New York: Macmillan, 1973. 307pp.

1017.   Smith, George Harmon. [Frank Scarpetta, pseud.]. *Mafia Wipe-Out*. New York: Belmont Tower Books, 1973. 171pp.

110.   Bloch, Robert. *American Gothic*. New York: Simon and Schuster, 1974. 222pp.

120.   Borland, Kathryn Kilby and Helen Ross Speicher. *Good-by to Stony Crick*. Illustrated by Deanne Hollinger. New York: McGraw-Hill, 1974. 138pp.

175.   Calmer, Ned. *Late Show*. Garden City, N.Y.: Doubleday, 1974. 335pp.

285.   De Vries, Peter. *The Glory of the Hummingbird*. Boston: Little, Brown, 1974. 276pp.

300.   Dobler, Bruce. *Icepick, A Novel about Life and Death in a Maximum Security Prison*. Boston: Little, Brown, 1974. 460pp.

471.   Gault, William Campbell. *Wild Willie, Wide Receiver*. New York: Dutton, 1974. 147pp.

580.   Johnson, Charles Richard. *Faith and the Good Thing*. New York: Viking Press, 1974. 196pp.

581.   Johnson, Curt (Curtis Lee). *Nobody's Perfect*. Illustrated by David Dynes. Pomeroy, Ohio: Carpenter Press, 1974. 236pp.

627.   Kennedy, Adam. *Somebody Else's Wife*. New York: Simon and Schuster, 1974. 349pp.

678.   Lewin, Michael Z. *The Enemies Within*. New York: Alfred A. Knopf, 1974. 225pp.

709.   Maling, Arthur. *Dingdong*. New York: Harper and Row, 1974. 245pp.

714.   Malzberg, Barry N. (Nathaniel) [Mike Barry, pseud.]. *Chicago Slaughter*. Lone Wolf Series, no. 6. New York: Berkeley Medallion, 1974. 192pp.

818.   Olsen, Tillie. *Yonnondio: From the Thirties*. New York: Delacorte Press / Seymour Lawrence, 1974. 196pp.

942.   Renken, Aleda. *The Two Christmases*. St. Louis, Mo.: Concordia, 1974. 96pp.

1001.   Sherburne, James. *Rivers Run Together*. Boston: Houghton Mifflin, 1974. 208pp.

1013.   Smith, Charles Merrill. *Reverend Randollph and the Wages of Sin*. New York: Putnam's Sons, 1974. 254pp.

1023.   Smith, Mark. *The Death of the Detective*. New York: Alfred A. Knopf, 1974. 596pp.

1180.   Weverka, Robert and David S. Ward. *The Sting*. New York: Bantam Books, 1974. 154pp.

32.   Allen, James and Geneva Allen. *God Bless This Child, A Novel*. Hicksville, N.Y.: Exposition Press, 1975. 180pp.

104.   Bellow, Saul. *Humboldt's Gift*. New York: Viking Press, 1975. 487pp.

152.   Brunner, Bernard. *Six Days to Sunday*. New York: McGraw-Hill, 1975. 307pp.

187.   Caspary, Vera. *The Dreamers*. New York: Pocket Books, 1975. 361pp.

466.   Garfield, Brian. *Death Sentence*. New York: Evans, 1975. 209pp.

504.   Haas, Joseph. *Vendetta*. Chicago: Henry Regnery, 1975. 219pp.

519.   Hanson, Harvey. *Game Time*. New York: Watts, 1975. 87pp.

560.   Homewood, Charles [Harry Homewood, pseud.]. *A Matter of Size*. Chicago: O'Hara, 1975. 154pp.

584. Jones, Jack. *The Animal*. New York: William Morrow, 1975. 220pp.

707. Maling, Arthur. *Bent Man*. New York: Harper and Row, 1975. 227pp.

900. Powers, John R. *Do Black Patent-Leather Shoes Really Reflect Up?: A Fictionalized Memoir*. Chicago: Henry Regnery, 1975. 227pp.

953. Rickett, Frances. *An Affair of Doctors*. New York: Arbor House, 1975. 316pp.

1005. Simon, Philip J. *Cleft Roots*. Chicago: Priam Press, 1975. 280pp.

1026. Smith, Terrence Lore [Phillips Lore, pseud.]. *Who Killed the Pie Man?: A Mystery*. New York: Saturday Review Press, 1975. 178pp.

129. Brashler, William. *City Dogs*. New York: Harper and Row, 1976. 277pp.

177. Carroll, Charles. *Chicago*. New York: Pocket Books, 1976. 265pp.

344. Eckert, Allan W. *The HAB Theory*. Boston: Little, Brown, 1976. 566p.

382. Farrell, James T. (James Thomas). *The Dunne Family*. Garden City, N.Y.: Doubleday, 1976. 326pp.

501. Guest, Judith. *Ordinary People*. New York: Viking, 1976. 263pp.

582. Johnston, William [Susan Claudia, pseud.]. *Mrs. Barthelme's Madness*. New York: Putnam's Sons, 1976. 281pp.

692. Lory, Robert Edward [V. J. Santiago, pseud.]. *Chicago, Knock, Knock, You're Dead*. Vigilante, no. 4. New York: Pinnacle Books, 1976. 184pp.

712. Maling, Arthur. *Ripoff*. New York: Harper and Row, 1976. 248pp.

790. Mundis, Jerrold. *Gerhardt's Children*. New York: Atheneum, 1976. 305pp.

817. Olesker, J. Bradford. *No Place Like Home*. New York: Putnam's Sons, 1976. 185pp.

1004. Simmons, Geoffrey S. *The Z-Papers*. New York: Arbor House, 1976. 240pp.

1119. Van Peebles, Melvin. *The True American: A Folk Fable*. Garden City, N.Y.: Doubleday, 1976. 208pp.

134. Brooks, Jerome. *The Testing of Charlie Hammelman*. New York: Dutton, 1977. 129pp.

182. Casey, John. *An American Romance*. New York: Atheneum, 1977. 321pp.

260.   Dailey, Janet. *A Lyon's Share*. Janet Dailey Americana Series. New York: Harlequin, 1977. 186pp.

438.   Forrest, Leon. *The Bloodworth Orphans*. New York: Random House, 1977. 383pp.

493.   Greene, Bob and Paul Galloway [Mike Holiday, pseud.]. *Bagtime*. New York: Popular Library, 1977. 283pp.

524.   Hawkins, Odie. *Chicago Hustle*. Los Angeles: Holloway House, 1977. 224pp.

533.   Heeler, Ward [pseud.]. *The Election: Chicago-Style*. Chicago: Feature, 1977. 166pp.

753.   McInerny, Ralph M. *The Seventh Station: A Father Dowling Mystery*. New York: Vanguard Press, 1977. 212pp.

774.   Monteleone, Thomas F. *The Time-Swept City*. New York: Popular Library, 1977. 287pp.

902.   Powers, John R. *The Unoriginal Sinner and the Ice-Cream God*. Chicago: Contemporary Books, 1977. 330pp.

1010.   Smith, Charles Merrill. *Reverend Randollph and the Avenging Angel*. New York: Putnam's Sons, 1977. 245pp.

1082.   Thayer, James Stewart. *The Hess Cross*. New York: Putnam's Sons, 1977. 331pp.

1148.   Warren, Robert Penn. *A Place to Come To*. New York: Random House, 1977. 401pp.

55.   Ardizzone, Tony. *In the Name of the Father*. Garden City, N.Y.: Doubleday, 1978. 208pp.

231.   Cook, Bruce. *Sex Life*. New York: Evans, 1978. 288pp.

252.   Cromie, Alice Hamilton. *Lucky to be Alive?* New York: Simon and Schuster, 1978. 317pp.

257.   Cunningham, Jere. *The Visitor*. New York: St. Martin's, 1978. 282pp.

566.   Howland, Bette. *Blue in Chicago*. New York: Harper and Row, 1978. 183pp.

588.   Kaminsky, Stuart M. *You Bet Your Life*. New York: St. Martin's Press, 1978. 215pp.

675.   Levin, Meyer. *The Harvest*. New York: Simon and Schuster, 1978. 670pp.

696.   Lund, Roslyn Rosen. *The Sharing*. New York: William Morrow, 1978. 216pp.

733.   Mazzaro, Ed. *Chicago Deadline*. London, U.K.: New English Library, 1978. 176pp.

751.   McInerny, Ralph M. *Bishop As Pawn: A Father Dowling Mystery*. New York: Vanguard Press, 1978. 219pp.

794.   Nelson, Shirley. *The Last Year of the War*. New York: Harper and Row, 1978. 255pp.

873.   Petrakis, Harry Mark. *A Petrakis Reader*. Garden City, N.Y.: Doubleday, 1978. 384pp.

905.   Pugh, Charles. *The Hospital Plot*. Port Washington, N.Y.: Ashley Books, 1978. 269pp.

923.   Raskin, Ellen. *The Westing Game*. New York: Dutton, 1978. 185pp.

1011.   Smith, Charles Merrill. *Reverend Randollph and the Fall from Grace, Inc.* New York: Putnam's Sons, 1978. 223pp.

1039.   Spencer, Ross H. *The DADA Caper*. New York: Avon, 1978. 189pp.

132.   Brooks, Jerome. *The Big Dipper Marathon*. New York: Dutton, 1979. 134pp.

228.   Colter, Cyrus. *Night Studies*. Chicago: Swallow Press, 1979. 774pp.

711.   Maling, Arthur. *The Koberg Link*. New York: Harper and Row, 1979. 244pp.

716.   Marlowe, Derek. *The Rich Boy from Chicago*. New York: St. Martin's Press, 1979. 440pp.

725.   Maupin, Robert Lee [Iceberg Slim, pseud.]. *Airtight Willie & Me*. Los Angeles: Holloway House, 1979. 245pp.

752.   McInerny, Ralph. *Lying Three: A Father Dowling Mystery*. New York: Vanguard Press, 1979. 250pp.

838.   Palumbo, Dennis James. *City Wars*. New York: Bantam Books, 1979. 152pp.

849.   Paulsen, Gary. *Meteorite Track 291*. New York: Dell Books / G/M Publishing, 1979. 221pp.

870.   Petrakis, Harry Mark. *Nick the Greek*. Garden City, N.Y.: Doubleday, 1979. 302pp.

970.   Rose, Richard M. *The Satyr Candidate: A Novel by Richard M. Rose*. Hicksville, N.Y.: Exposition Press, 1979. 196pp.

1040.   Spencer, Ross H. *The Reggis Arms Caper*. New York: Avon, 1979. 158pp.

1042.   Spencer, Scott. *Endless Love*. New York: Alfred A. Knopf, 1979. 418pp.

1076. Tanous, Peter Joseph and Paul Arthur Rubinstein. *The Wheat Killing*. Garden City, N.Y.: Doubleday, 1979. 273pp.

1130. Walker, Robert W. *Sub-Zero!* New York: Belmont Tower Books, 1979. 189pp.

54. Archer, Jeffrey. *Kane & Abel*. New York: Simon and Schuster, 1980. 540pp.

94. Barrett, Mary Ellin. *American Beauty*. New York: Dutton, 1980. 310pp.

96. Bates, Elizabeth *Love is Like Peanuts*. New York: Holiday House, 1980. 125pp.

133. Brooks, Jerome. *Make Me a Hero*. New York: Dutton, 1980. 152pp.

172. Butterworth, W. E. (William Edmund). *Leroy and the Old Man*. New York: Four Winds Press, 1980. 154pp.

198. Chandler, Peter. *Bucks*. New York: Avon, 1980. 262pp.

216. Claro, Joe. *My Bodyguard*. New York: Scholastic Book Services, 1980. 94pp.

262. D'Amato, Barbara. *The Hands of Healing Murder*. New York: Charter Communications / Grosset and Dunlap, 1980. 248pp.

279. DeRosa, Tina. *Paper Fish*. Chicago: Wine Press, 1980. 137pp.

333. Dybek, Stuart. *Childhood and Other Neighborhoods*. New York: Viking Press, 1980. 201pp.

482. Glazer, Mitchell [Miami Mitch, pseud.], Dan Ackroyd, John Landis. *The Blues Brothers*. New York: A Jove Book, 1980. 245pp.

490. Granger, Bill. *Public Murders*. New York: Jove, 1980. 275pp.

492. Greeley, Andrew Moran. *Death in April*. New York: McGraw-Hill, 1980. 246pp.

548. Herter, Lori. *No Time for Love*. Candlelight Romance, 574. New York: Dell, 1980. 187pp.

568. Hufford, Susan. *Going All the Way*. New York: New American Library; A Signet Book / Times Mirror, 1980. 359pp.

635. Klasne, William. *Street Cops*. Englewood Cliffs, N.J.: Prentice-Hall, 1980. 234pp.

685. Little, Paul H. (Paula Hugo Little) [Marie De Jourlet, pseud.]. *Trials of Windhaven*. Los Angeles: Pinnacle Books, 1980. 421pp.

689.   Lorenz, Tom. *Guys Like Us*. New York: Viking Press, 1980. 255pp.

792.   Nathan, Robert Louis. *Coal Mine No. 7*. New York: St. Martin's Press, 1980. 279pp.

804.   Noyes, Henry. *Hand Over Fist*. Boston: South End Press, 1980. 322pp.

816.   Okun, Lawrence Eugene. *On the 8th Day*. Millbrae, Calif.: Celestial Arts, 1980. 217pp.

966.   Rogers, Thomas. *At the Shores*. New York: Simon and Schuster, 1980. 284pp.

1012.   Smith, Charles Merrill. *Reverend Randollph and the Holy Terror*. New York: Putnam's Sons, 1980. 236pp.

1024.   Smith, Terrence Lore. *Murder Behind Closed Doors*, [Phillips Lore, pseud.]. New York: Playboy Press Paperbacks, 1980. 182pp.

1038.   Spencer, Ross II. *The Abu Wahab Caper*. New York: Avon, 1980. 144pp.

1041.   ———. *The Stranger City Caper*. New York: Avon, 1980. 159pp.

Index

The numbers refer to entries, not page numbers.

About the Author

James A. Kaser, professor and archivist at the College of Staten Island/CUNY, has worked as an archivist and special collections librarian for twenty years. He is also the author of *The Washington, D.C. of Fiction: A Research Guide* (Lanham, Md.: The Scarecrow Press, 2006) and *At the Bivouac of Memory: History, Politics, and the Battle of Chickamauga*. New York: Peter Lang, 1996. Kaser is a magna cum laude, Phi Beta Kappa, graduate of Kenyon College and earned a master's degree in library science from Kent State University and a master's degree and doctorate from Bowling Green State University in American culture studies.

Breinigsville, PA USA
16 January 2011
253347BV00006B/1-44/P